The **Rough Guide**

Turkey

written and researched by

Rosie Ayliffe, Marc Dubin,

John Gawthrop and Terry Richardson

with additional research and contributions by

Joe Fullman, Sarah Gear, Jon Gorvett, Francesco Martinelli,

Paul Sentobe and Martin Stokes

ROUGH
GUIDES

NEW YORK • LONDON • DELHI

www.roughguides.com

Contents

Outdoor adventure travel colour section following p.312

Food and drink colour section following p.568

Turkey's religious architectural heritage colour section following p.824

3

◁◁ Athena temple, Side ◁ Süleymaniye Camii, İstanbul

Introduction to

Turkey

Turkey is a country with a multiple identity, poised uneasily between East and West – though, despite the tourist-brochure cliché, it is less a bridge between the two than a battleground, a buffer zone whose various parts have been invaded and settled from every direction since the beginning of recorded history. The country is now keen to be accepted on equal terms by the West: long the only NATO member in the Middle East region and a major recipient of US military aid, it has, since late 2005, officially been a candidate for EU membership, potential culmination of a modernization process begun late in the nineteenth century. But despite Turkish involvement with

Europe dating back to the twelfth century, it is by no stretch of the imagination a thoroughly Western nation, and the contradictions – and fascinations – persist.

Turkey is a **vast country** – France would fit within its boundaries with plenty of room to spare – incorporating characteristics of Middle Eastern and Aegean, as well as Balkan and trans-Caucasian, countries. Mosques coexist with Orthodox churches; Roman theatres and temples crumble alongside ancient Hittite cities; and dervish ceremonies or gypsy festivals are as much a part of the social landscape as classical music concerts or delirious sports fans. The one constant in all this – and one of the things that makes Turkey such a rewarding place to travel – is the **Turkish people**, whose reputation for friendliness and hospitality is richly deserved; indeed you risk causing offence by refusing to partake of it, and any transaction can be the springboard for further acquaintance. Close to the bigger resorts or tourist attractions, much of this is undoubtedly merce-

△ Pistachios and other produce on sale at market, İstanbul

nary, but in most of the country the warmth and generosity is genuine – all the more amazing when recent Turkish history has demonstrated that outsiders usually only bring trouble in their wake.

Politically, modern Turkey was a bold experiment, founded on the remaining Anatolian kernel of the **Ottoman Empire**, once among the world's largest, and longest-lasting, imperial states. The country arose from defeat after World War I, almost entirely the creation of a single man of demonic energy and vision – **Kemal Atatürk**. The Turkish war of independence, fought against those victorious Allies intending to pursue imperialistic designs on Ottoman territory, has (with slightly stretched analogy – Turkey was never a colony) often been seen as the prototype for all Third-World "wars of lib-

Fact file

• Besides Russia, Turkey is the only nation incorporating both Asian and – albeit just three percent of a **total area** of 814,578 sq km – European territory. A 8333-kilometre **coastline** is lapped by four seas – the Black Sea, the Sea of Marmara, the Aegean and the Mediterranean. Numerous **peaks** exceed 3000m, the highest 5165-metre Ararat (Ağrı Dağı) near the Armenian border. The largest **lake** is Lake Van (3713 sq km) in the far southeast.

• The **population** of about 70 million is 98 percent Muslim (Sunni or Alevî sect), with dwindling **religious minorities** of the Armenian Apostolic, Greek Orthodox, Syrian Orthodox, Jewish and Catholic faiths. Besides standard Turkish, two dialects of Kurdish are widely spoken, while other **languages** heard include Arabic, Laz, Circassian, Albanian, Macedonian, Bulgarian, Romany and Greek. Well over half the inhabitants live in **urban areas**; the largest cities, İstanbul, Ankara (the capital), İzmir and Adana, account for about 24 million people.

• Since 1922, when the last sultan was deposed, Turkey has been a **republic**. The single-chamber *Büyük Meclis* or **Grand National Assembly** in Ankara has 550 seats, and the head of state (elected by this parliament) is the **president**. Both are answerable to a **National Security Council** dominated by elements of the armed forces.

• Since 1950 the Turkish **economy** has often been in crisis, with inflation devaluing the currency and unemployment approaching 25 percent. Recovery following the 2000–01 crash has yielded recent annual growth rates of about five percent. The most important **foreign-exchange earners** are tourism, clothing and food, with automobiles and household appliances set to follow.

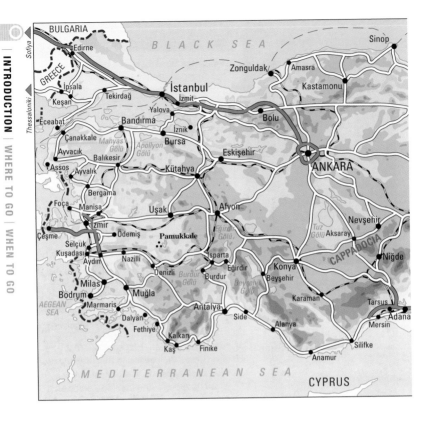

△ Nargile pipe by firelight

eration". It led to an explicitly **secular republic**, though one in which almost all of the inhabitants are at least nominally **Muslim** (predominantly Sunni but also Alevî, a variant of Shi'ism). Turkey's heritage as home to the caliphate and numerous dervish orders, plus contemporary Islamist movements, still often deflects its moral compass south and east rather than northwest.

Turks, except for a small minority in the southeast, are not Arabs, and loathe being mistaken for them; despite a heavy lacing of Persian and Arabic words, the **Turkish language** alone, unrelated to any neighbouring one except Azeri, is

6

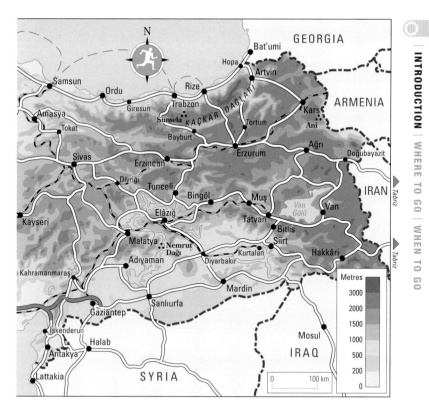

sufficient to set its speakers apart. The **population** is, however, in spite of official efforts to enforce uniformity, remarkably heterogeneous ethnically. When the Ottoman Empire imploded from the 1870s to the 1920s, large numbers of Muslim Slavs, Kurds, Greeks, Albanians, Crimean Tatars, Azeris, Daghestanlis, Abkhazians and Circassians – to name only the most numerous non-Turkic groups – streamed into Anatolia, the safest refuge in an age of anti-Ottoman nationalism. This process has continued in recent years from formerly Soviet or Eastern Bloc territories (including even a few Christian Turks or Gaugaz from Moldavia), so that the **diversity** of the people endures, constituting one of the surprises of travel in Turkey.

There are equally large disparities in levels of **development and income**. İstanbul boasts clubs as expensive and exclusive as any in New York or London, while town-centre shops are full of imported luxury goods, yet in the chronically backward eastern interior you'll encounter standards and modes of living scarcely changed from a century ago. Following a severe crash in 2000–01, the Turkish economy has significantly recovered, though its debt

Camels

Despite stereotypes overseas, camels play a diminished role in modern Turkey. Most are now just tourist attractions, used for pleasure-riding or as photographic props in places like Pamukkale and Side. The last (just barely) working herd is resident on the Turquoise Coast, moving materials into and out of a roadless area near Kekova. It wasn't always so, however; camel caravans hauling freight still crisscrossed most of Anatolia until the 1960s, though in their last years the cargo tended to be salt, figs, cotton or light flints instead of the gemstones, spices and woven finery of yore. Before the Balkan Wars of 1912–13, camel caravans extended northwest as far as Bosnia; beyond this point the beasts contracted fatal respiratory conditions brought on by the damp central European climate. In Muslim folklore the perceived haughty demeanour of camels is attributed to their knowledge of the hundredth, mystical epithet of Allah – humans only know the conventional ninety-nine.

burden remains staggering. This uneven profile is one of several factors which concern its potential EU partners: has Westernization struck deep roots in the culture, or does it extend no further than a mobile-phone- and credit-card-equipped urban elite?

Turkey has been continuously inhabited and fought over for close on ten millennia, as the layer-cake arrangement of many **archeological sites** and the numerous fortified heights testify. The juxtaposed ancient monuments mirror the bewildering **succession of states** – Hittite, Urartian, Phrygian, Hellenistic, Roman, Byzantine, Armeno-Georgian – that held sway here before the twelfth century. There is also, of course, an overwhelming number of graceful **Islamic monuments** dating from the eleventh century onwards, as well as magnificent city **bazaars**, still holding their own despite the encroachments of chain stores and shopping malls. The country's modern architecture is less pleasing, the consequence both of government policy since 1950 and of returned overseas workers eager

▽ Turkish flag

8

to invest their earnings in real estate – an ugliness manifest at most **coastal resorts**, where the beaches are rarely as good as the tourist-board hype. Indeed it's **inland** Turkey – Asiatic expanses of mountain, steppe, lake, even cloud forest – that may leave a more vivid memory, especially when accented by some crumbling *kervansaray*, mosque or castle.

Where to go

▽ Village women, Barla, near Eğirdir

Western Turkey is not only the more economically developed but also by far the more visited half of the country. İstanbul, straddling the straits linking the Black and Marmara seas, is touted as Turkish mystique par excellence, and understandably so: it would take weeks to even scratch the surface of the old imperial capital, still the cultural and commercial centre of the country. Flanking it on opposite sides of the Sea of Marmara are the two prior seats of the Ottoman Empire, Bursa and Edirne, each with their complement of attractions and regal atmosphere. The sea itself is flecked with tranquil, frequently overlooked islands, ideal havens when the cities get too much – and just beyond the Dardanelles and its World War I battlefields lie two larger Aegean islands, only opened to outsiders during the late 1980s.

As you move south, the Classical character of the **Northeast Aegean** comes to the fore in the olive-swathed country around Bergama and Ayvalık, perhaps the two most compelling points in the region. Just outside İzmir, the old Ottoman princely training ground of Manisa and the originally Lydian city of Sardis, lost in vineyards, make a fine pair, while İzmir itself is the functional introduction to the **Central and Southern Aegean**, a magnet for travellers since the eighteenth century. The archeological complex at Ephesus overshadows in visitors' imaginations the equally deserving ancient Ionian sites of Priene and Didyma, or the ruins of Aphrodisias and Labranda in old Caria. Also inland are the tranquil expanse of Bafa Gölü, and the architectural

9

Turkey's youth

About 55 percent of Turkey's estimated population of 70 million is under 30 years old, a far younger profile than any of its potential stablemates in the EU. This distribution may, however, age in coming decades, as the birth rate has declined from a high of 4.7 percent during the 1950s to just 1.5 percent in 1999. The country's youth are not, however, especially well educated: though literacy approaches ninety percent for both genders, only ten percent of adolescents complete secondary education, and perhaps five percent receive some sort of higher education. Despite this, there are far too many qualified graduates at present for the shrunken job market, with underemployment as common as unemployment. So a very likely consequence of EU membership and full freedom of movement within Europe would be substantial emigration from Turkey, either permanent or temporary.

showcase town of Muğla. Be warned that the coast itself is heavily developed, though the star resorts – of which Çeşme is perhaps the quietest and Bodrum the most characterful – make comfortable bases from which to tour the interior. Don't overlook such evocative hill-towns as Şirince, Birgi or Tire, which still exist in something of an Ottoman time-warp.

Beyond the huge natural harbour at Marmaris, the Aegean becomes the Mediterranean; tourism levels drop slightly and the shore becomes more convoluted and pine-forested. Yacht and schooner cruises are popular and easily arranged in brazen Marmaris or the more pleasant town of Fethiye, principal centre of the **Turquoise Coast**. Two of the finest and largest beaches in the country sprawl at Dalyan and Patara, close to the eerie tombs of the Lycians, the fiercely independent locals of old. Further east, Kaş and Kalkan are small but busy resorts, good places to rest up between explorations into the mountainous hinterland. Beyond the relatively untouched beaches around ancient Olympos, Antalya is Turkey's fastest-growing city, a sprawling place located at the beginning of the **Mediterranean coast** proper. This lengthy shore, reaching as far as the Syrian border, boasts extensive sands and archeological sites – most notably at Perge, Side and Aspendos – though its western parts get swamped in high season. Once past castle-topped Alanya, however, tourist numbers diminish, and the stretch

△ Mount Ararat

between Silifke and Adana offers innumerable minor points of interest, particularly the Roman city of Uzuncaburç and the romantic offshore fortress at Kızkalesi. Further east, Arab-flavoured Antakya is the heart of the **Hatay**, culturally part of Syria.

There are spectacular attractions inland in **South Central Anatolia**, where you're confronted with the famous rock churches, subterranean cities and tuff-pinnacle landscapes of Cappadocia. The dry, bracing climate, excellent local wine, the artistic and architectural interest of the area, plus the chance to go horse-riding or hot-air ballooning, could occupy you for as much as ten days, taking in the largest town in the area, Kayseri – with its bazaar and tombs – on the way north. You might also pause at Eğirdir or Beyşehir – historic towns fronting two of the numerous lakes that spangle the region – or in Konya, which, for both its Selçuk architecture and associations with the Mevlevî dervishes, makes for an appealing stopover on the way to or from the coast.

Ankara, hub of **North Central Anatolia**, is Turkey's capital, a planned city whose contrived Western feel gives some concrete (in all senses) indication of the priorities of the Turkish Republic; it also has the outstanding Museum of Anatolian Civilizations. Highlights of the region include the bizarre, isolated temple of Aezani, near Kutahya to the west; the Ottoman museum-town of

11

Safranbolu; the exquisitely decorated early Turkish monuments at Divriği; and the remarkable Hittite sites of Hattuşaş and Alacahöyük. If you're travelling north to the Black Sea, you should also look in on the Yeşilırmak valley towns of Sivas, Tokat and Amasya, each with its quota of early Turkish monuments. The **Black Sea** shore itself is surprisingly devoid of architectural interest other than a chain of Byzantine-Genoese castles, but the beauty of the landscape goes some way to compensate. The oldest and most interesting towns between utilitarian Samsun and industrial Zonguldak are Sinop, the northernmost point of Anatolia, and Amasra, also easily reached from Safranbolu. East of Samsun, a four-lane highway brings you to fabled Trabzon, once a seat of a Byzantine sub-empire and today a base for visits to the marvellous monasteries of Aya Sofya and Sumela.

The Ankara–Sivas route also poises you for the trip along the Euphrates River and into the hitherto invisible "back half" of Turkey – the East. Your first stop in **Northeastern Anatolia** is likely to be Erzurum, highest and bleakest major city of Turkey, from where you can head on to visit the temperate and church-studded valleys of southern medieval Georgia or go trekking in the Kaçkar mountains – Turkey's most popular hiking area – walling off the area from the Black Sea. Rapidly improving Kars is worth visiting, with nearby Ani, the ruined medieval Armenian capital, and various other

Armenian monuments in the area – though many of these require some ingenuity and resourcefulness to seek out.

South of here, the **Euphrates and Tigris Basin** represents Turkey at its most Middle Eastern. Gaziantep, approached from points west, is the functional gateway to some centres of genuine interest, and has a wonderful mosaic museum. Further east, Urfa and nearby Harran are biblical in both appearance and history; Mardin, with its surrounding monasteries, is the homeland of Turkey's Syrian Orthodox minority. The colossal heads of Nemrut Dağı, however, reproduced endlessly on brochures and travel posters, are the real attraction here, and mightily impressive despite heavy commercialization. Diyarbakır, a swarming, vivid metropolis on the Tigris, is the last real urban centre before the largely Kurdish-populated areas around **Lake Van**, an unearthly blue, alkaline expanse just beyond the canyon-flank town of Bitlis. After some years as a no-go area, it is again possible – with a judicious ear to the ground for current conditions – to travel the main routes through this rewarding region. Urartian, Selçuk and Armenian monuments abound within sight of the water, most notably at Çavuştepe, Ahlat and Akdamar, though you almost certainly will have to stay in Van town, an oasis sprawling on the eastern shore behind its ancient, rock-hewn citadel. East of Van looms the fairy-tale Kurdish castle of Hoşap, though excursions into the spectacular Cilo-Sat mountains beyond have long been limited by the prevailing political situation. A day's journey north of Van, just outside of Doğubeyazıt, you'll find the isolated folly of İşak Paşa Sarayı, staring across to Mount Ararat – the very end of Turkey.

Storks

Between May and September, storks in their nests balanced atop domes, utility poles or dead trees are a common sight across western Turkey, which is near the northern end of a migratory flyway connecting winter quarters in Africa with a summer habitat in the Balkans. The clattering of

the birds' beaks is an equally common sound. Storks mate for life, and the breeding pair often returns to the same nest year after year to raise new chicks, preferably near a lake or swamp which provides an ample food supply of frogs and small fish. They are considered lucky in both Christian and Islamic belief, and rarely harmed (especially once local hunters are informed that their meat is unappetizing); some municipalities even go so far as to build special platforms to augment favourite stork-nesting perches.

When to go

Turkey has a wide variety of climates, and there's a good chance that no matter when you want to go, somewhere in the country will be at least tolerable, if not ideal – although you should also pay attention to the basic seasonal patterns of tourist traffic.

△ Grand Bazaar, Istanbul

Of the coastal areas, **İstanbul** and the area around the **Sea of Marmara** have a relatively damp, Balkan climate, with muggy summers and cool, rainy (though seldom snowy) winters. Bear in mind that competition for facilities between June and August can be stiff. Things are similarly busy during summer on the popular **Aegean and Mediterranean coasts**; climatic conditions, too, can be difficult during July and August, especially between İzmir and Antakya, where the heat is tempered only slightly by offshore breezes. Perhaps the best time to visit these coastal regions is in spring or autumn, when the weather is gentler and the holiday crowds rather thinner. Late October and early November sees the **pastırma yazı**, or "Indian summer", an idyllic time with the scarcity of charter flights and open facilities as the only drawbacks. Indeed, even during winter, the **Turquoise** and Mediterranean coasts are – except for brief rainy periods in January and February – still fairly pleasant, and beyond Alanya up to the Hatay, winters can be positively balmy, though you may still not be able to brave the water. The **Black Sea** is something of an anomaly, with temperate summers and exceptionally mild winters for so far north, and rain likely during the nine coolest months of the year, lingering as mist and subtropical humidity during summer – but it does have the advantage of being less crowded than the Mediterranean or Aegean during the summer.

Anatolia forms a natural fortress, its entire coast backed by mountains or hills, cutting off the interior from any moderating maritime influences. **Central**

Anatolia is mostly semi-arid steppe, with a healthy, bracing climate – warm but not unpleasant in summer, cool and dry in the relatively short winters, which last approximately from late November to late March. Cappadocia in particular makes a colourful, quiet treat throughout spring and autumn – indeed well into December, when its rock formations dusted with snow are especially beautiful. As you travel east, into **Northeast Anatolia** and around **Lake Van**, the altitude increases and conditions are deeply snowy between October and April, making late spring and summer by far the best (in some cases the only) time to visit, when you'll also find it more comfortable and less populated than on the teeming coast. As you move into the lower **Euphrates and Tigris Basin**, a more pronounced Middle Eastern influence exerts itself, with winters that are no worse than in central Anatolia but torrid summers – and without the compensation of a nearby beach.

Average midday temperatures in °C &°F

	Jan	Feb	Mar	Apr	May	Jun	Jul	Aug	Sep	Oct	Nov	Dec
İstanbul												
°C	6	6	7	12	17	21	24	24	20	16	12	8
°F	43	43	45	54	63	70	75	75	68	61	54	47
İzmir												
°C	9	10	12	16	21	25	28	28	24	19	15	11
°F	48	50	54	61	70	77	82	82	75	66	59	52
Antalya												
°C	11	12	13	17	21	23	29	29	25	21	16	12
°F	52	54	56	63	70	77	84	84	77	70	61	54
Ankara												
°C	1	1	5	12	17	20	24	24	19	13	8	3
°F	34	34	41	54	63	68	75	75	66	56	47	37
Trabzon												
°C	8	8	9	12	16	20	23	24	20	17	14	10
°F	47	47	48	54	61	68	73	75	68	63	57	50
Diyarbakır												
°C	2	4	9	14	20	26	31	31	25	18	10	5
°F	35	39	48	57	68	79	88	88	77	65	50	41

36

things not to miss

It's not possible to see everything Turkey has to offer in one trip – and we don't suggest you try. What follows is a selective and subjective taste of the country's highlights: outstanding buildings and historic sites, natural wonders and exciting activities. They're all arranged in five colour-coded categories to help you find the very best things to see, do and experience. All entries have a page reference to take you straight into the Guide, where you can find out more.

01 Ihlara Valley, Cappadocia Page **658** • Take a streamside walk along the lushly vegetated valley floor, pausing to visit painted cave-churches up the slopes.

02 White-water rafting on the Köprülü Çayı Page 545 & Outdoor adventure travel colour section

• This scenic river, tumbling down from the Toros mountains to the Mediterranean, is perfect for novice rafters.

03 Cruising the southwest coast Page 514

• The deeply indented coastline between Bodrum and Olympos is the venue for multi-day cruises on a *gület*, or traditional wooden motor-schooner.

04 Nemrut Dağı Page 864

• Monumental mountain-top temple-tomb complex, built by Antiochus I (64–38 BC), a little-known but vain and arrogant ruler of the kingdom of Commagene, in a remote area of southeastern Turkey.

05 Camel wrestling Page 277

• These seasonal bouts between two male camels in rut draw vast crowds across the Aegean region.

06 Oil wrestling Page **231** • Though a popular sport across Turkey, the best time to see olive-oil-coated contestants get to grips with each other is during Edirne's Kırkpınar Festival.

07 Museum of Anatolian Civilizations, Ankara Page **685** • Housing finds of all native cultures from the Stone Age to about 700 BC, this superb museum is the one must-see in the capital.

08 Gözleme Page **64** • The Turkish-village version of crêpes have enjoyed a comeback since the 1980s; watching their concoction is part of the fun.

09 Acropolis of ancient Pergamon Page **304** • Pergamon was one of the chief Roman cities of Anatolia, and extensive ruins remain; shown here is the restored Trajan temple.

10 Byzantine frescoes, Cappadocia Page **624** • About 150 of Cappadocia's rock-hewn churches contain fine examples of early Christian frescoes; shown is an example from the most-visited Göreme complex.

11 Roman theatre at Aspendos

Page **543** • The best way to appreciate the largest and best-preserved theatre in Anatolia is by attending the summertime opera and ballet festival.

12 Outdoor restaurants

Page **64** • The Ottomans introduced the concept of dining al fresco to Europe, and outdoor seafood restaurants especially do a roaring trade in warmer weather.

13 Hittite capital of Hattuşa

Page **715** • The second-millennium-BC capital of the Hittites still impresses, with perimeter walls extending to six kilometres.

14 Lycian Way long-distance path

Page **458** & *Outdoor adventure travel* colour section •This marked path passes through some of the most scenic portions of the Turquoise Coast; shown is the medieval cobbled section between Ovacık and Kozağaçı.

19

15
Underground city, Kaymaklı
Page **630** •
Burrowed out of soft volcanic tuff, this subterranean labyrinth provided refuge for Cappadocians from the Hittite through to the Byzantine eras.

16 Acropolis of ancient
Assos Page **294** • At the summit, with views of Greek Lésvos, stands this restored Doric Athena temple; the architecturally preserved medieval village occupies the slopes below.

17 "Beehive" houses,
Harran Page •
858 These timeless, mud-built dwellings at Harran, close to the Syrian border between the Euphrates and Tigris rivers, are inhabited by ethnic Arabs.

18
Hot-air ballooning over Cappadocia Page
524 & *Outdoor adventure travel* colour section •
A lighter-than-air float gives you an unrivalled perspective on the "fairy chimneys" and other aspects of the landscape.

19 Ancient Ephesus Page **365** •
This major Aegean city was inextricably
linked with the history of early Christianity; St
Paul addressed one of his epistles to its citizens.

21 Koza Hanı, Bursa Page **259** •
The silk-cocoon auction which takes place
in this fifteenth-century *han* during early summer
is the basis for one of Turkey's distinctive natural
crafts.

23 Kapalı Çarşı, İstanbul Page
151 • The hard sell reaches its apotheosis
in what's claimed to be the largest covered
bazaar in the world. Touristy but still compelling.

20 North Aegean coast
Page • **313** Peppered with
lovely, low-key resorts in former fishing
villages, like Foça, this stretch of coast
offers a refreshing respite from the more
developed resorts in the south.

**22 Aya Sofya museum,
İstanbul** Page **127** & *Turkey's
religious architectural heritage* **colour
section** • The seemingly unsupported
dome of Aya Sofya, built during the sixth
century as a Byzantine church, is one of
the architectural marvels of the world.

24 Flowers at Lake Van
Page **893** • Early summer sees
the highland meadows around Van
carpeted with gorgeous wild flowers
like these.

25 Whirling dervishes

Page **618** • Members of a sect founded by the Konya-based Sufi mystic Mevlâna conduct "turning" ceremonies to effect union with God.

26 İztuzu beach

Page **467** • This long beach, at the edge of extensive, bird-haunted wetlands, is just one among dozens of little-developed strands along Turkey's coast between Marmaris and Mersin.

27 Orthodox monastery of Sumela

Page **772** • Built into the side of a palisade high up in the Pontic mountains, this Byzantine foundation harbours excellent if damaged frescoes.

28 Fairy chimneys

Page **625** • Cones of volcanic tuff, often with basalt slabs teetering on top, make a bizarre spectacle in the geological fantasy landscape of Cappadocia.

29

Football Page **93** • Football in Turkey is a national obsession, and victories by the national team or any of the major İstanbul clubs (Beşiktaş, Galatasaray or Fenerbahçe) are accompanied by frenzied celebrations in cities across the country.

ACTIVITIES | CONSUME | EVENTS | NATURE | SIGHTS |

30

Kaçkar Dağları Page **830** • Lying just inland from the Black Sea, this glacially sculpted granite mountain-range, spangled with dozens of lakes, is Turkey's premier trekking venue.

32 **Antakya Archeological Museum** Page **583** • A unique collection of mosaics unearthed from the villas of Roman and Byzantine Antioch are well displayed in one of Turkey's finest provincial museums.

31 **Churches of the Georgian valleys** Page **820** • Numerous medieval churches northeast of Erzurum are among the most striking monuments in northeastern Anatolia; shown is İşhan, one of the largest and oldest.

33
Visiting a hamam Page **62** • Bathers relaxing on the central heated stone of a hamam are enjoying one of the traditional sensual comforts of Turkey.

34
İşak Paşa Sarayı Page **922** • Strategically situated on the Silk Route, this architecturally eclectic seventeenth-century palace is one of eastern Turkey's most emblematic sites.

35
Drinking tea Page **68 & *Food and drink* colour section** • Tea from the Black Sea has been the Turkish national drink since the 1930s, and it's available everywhere, at almost any hour.

36
Riverbank culture at Amasya Page **722** • The tombs of the ancient Pontic kings are juxtaposed with graceful Ottoman mansions along the Yeşilırmak in Amasya.

Basics

Basics

Getting there

Flights from the UK or Ireland to Turkey take between three and a half to five hours depending on your starting/ending point. There are several gateway airports at each end, though London and İstanbul are still the busiest year-round. Just two carriers fly direct to Turkey from North America (down to one in winter), so most North Americans reach Turkey via a European gateway airport. Many travellers from Australia and New Zealand use a Round-the-World (RTW) ticket that includes İstanbul, but there are direct flights from Sydney. The long trans-Europe train journey to Turkey is not straightforward and always much more expensive than flying. Driving overland through Europe can also be expensive and time-consuming, but once inside the country the effort can prove worthwhile. Using any overland means, you'll save bother and time by taking ferries between Italy and Turkey, or between outlying Greek islands and the Turkish coast, thus avoiding long detours through Eastern Europe.

Airfares to Turkey from Europe and North America always depend on the **season**, with the highest during Easter week and from June to early September; fares drop during the "shoulder" seasons – April/May and late September/October – and you'll get the best prices during the low season, November to March (excluding Christmas and New Year weeks, when seats are at a premium). Note also that flying on weekends from North America can add $50 or so to the round-trip fare; prices quoted below assume midweek travel. Australian and New Zealand fares have their low season from mid-January to the end of February and October/November; high season is mid-May to August, plus December to mid-January; and shoulder season the rest of the year.

Booking flights online

Booking online can save both money and time. Even if you don't like buying online, it's worth visiting the airlines' websites to size up current fares (although the sites often don't have the really inexpensive deals).

Online booking agents and general travel sites

Ⓦ **www.cheapflights.co.uk** (UK & Ireland), Ⓦ **www.cheapflights.com** (US), Ⓦ www **.cheapflights.ca** (Canada) or Ⓦ www **.cheapflights.com.au** (Australia & New Zealand) Not a booking site itself, but maintains links to the travel agents offering the deals.

Ⓦ **www.cheaptickets.com** Discount flight specialist. US only.

Ⓦ **www.etn.nl/discount.htm** A hub of consolidator and discount agent Web links, maintained by the nonprofit European Travel Network.

Ⓦ **www.expedia.co.uk** (UK & Ireland), Ⓦ **www .expedia.com** (US) or Ⓦ **www.expedia.ca** (Canada) Discount airfares, all-airline search engine and daily deals.

Ⓦ **www.geocities.com/thavery2000** An extensive list of airline websites and US toll-free numbers.

Ⓦ **www.kelkoo.co.uk** Useful UK-only price-comparison site, checking several sources of low-cost flights (and other goods and services) according to specific criteria.

Ⓦ **www.lastminute.com** (UK & Ireland), Ⓦ **www.lastminute.com.au** (Australia) or Ⓦ **www.lastminute.co.nz** (New Zealand) Good holiday-package and flight-only deals available at very short notice.

Ⓦ **www.opodo.co.uk** Popular and reliable source of cheap UK airfares. Owned by, and run in conjunction with, nine major European airlines.

Ⓦ **www.orbitz.com** Comprehensive Web travel source, with the usual flight, car rental and hotel deals but also great follow-up customer service. US only.

Ⓦ **www.priceline.co.uk** or Ⓦ **www.priceline .com** Name-your-own-price auction website that can knock around forty percent off standard website fares. You can't choose the airline or flight

Fly less – stay longer! Travel and climate change

Climate change is a serious threat to the ecosystems that humans rely upon, and air travel is among the fastest-growing contributors to the problem. Rough Guides regard travel, overall, as a global benefit, and feel strongly that the advantages to developing economies are important, as is the opportunity of greater contact and awareness among peoples. But we all have a responsibility to limit our personal impact on global warming, and that means giving thought to how often we fly, and what we can do to redress the harm that our trips create.

Flying and climate change

Pretty much every form of motorized travel generates CO_2 – the main cause of human-induced climate change – but planes also generate climate-warming contrails and cirrus clouds and emit oxides of nitrogen, which create ozone (another greenhouse gas) at flight levels. Furthermore, flying simply allows us to travel much further than we otherwise would do. The figures are frightening: one person taking a return flight between Europe and California produces the equivalent impact of 2.5 tonnes of CO_2 – similar to the yearly output of the average UK car.

Fuel-cell and other less harmful types of plane may emerge eventually. But until then, there are really just two options for concerned travellers: to reduce the amount we travel by air (take fewer trips – stay for longer!), and to make the trips we do take "climate neutral" via a carbon offset scheme.

Carbon offset schemes

Offset schemes run by climatecare.org, carbonneutral.com and others allow you to make up for some or all of the greenhouse gases that you are responsible for releasing. To do this, they provide "carbon calculators" for working out the global-warming contribution of a specific flight (or even your entire existence), and then let you contribute an appropriate amount of money to fund offsetting measures. These include rainforest reforestation and initiatives to reduce future energy demand – often run in conjunction with sustainable development schemes.

Rough Guides, together with Lonely Planet and other concerned partners in the travel industry, are supporting a **carbon offset scheme** run by climatecare.org. Please take the time to view our website and see how you can help to make your trip climate neutral.

ⓦ**www.roughguides.com/climatechange**

times (although you do specify dates) and the tickets are nonrefundable, nontransferable and nonchangeable. Bookings from the UK/US only.
ⓦ**www.skyauction.com** Auctions tickets and travel packages using a "second bid" scheme. The best strategy is to bid the maximum you're willing to pay, since if you win you'll pay just enough to beat the runner-up regardless of your maximum bid. Bookings from the US only.
ⓦ**www.travelocity.co.uk** (UK & Ireland), ⓦ**www.travelocity.com** (US) or ⓦwww .travelocity.ca (Canada) Destination guides, hot Web fares and deals for car rental, accommodation and lodging as well as fares.
ⓦ**www.travelselect.com** A subsidiary of lastminute.com (see overleaf) that is useful and fairly easy to use, but without most of the guff and banner adverts of the better-known sites.
ⓦ**www.travelshop.com.au** Australian website

offering discounted flights, packages, insurance and online bookings.
ⓦ**www.travel.co.nz** Comprehensive online travel company, with discounted fares. New Zealand only.
ⓦ**www.zuji.com.au** Destination guides, hot fares and great deals for car rental, accommodation and lodging.

Flights and tours from the UK and Ireland

Most of the cheaper flights from Britain and Ireland to Turkey are charters, which are sold either with a package holiday or (increasingly commonly) as a flight-only option. For longer stays or more flexibility, or if you're travelling out of season (when few charters are available), you'll need a scheduled flight. You can fly direct from the UK to İstanbul, İzmir, Bodrum, Dalaman and Antalya. Reaching any other destination in Turkey involves a change of flights in İstanbul, though if you're flying with Turkish Airlines you can get a heavily discounted **domestic connecting flight** to most of the internal airports which they serve. It's also worth considering **indirect (ie one-stop) flights** with other European airlines. These may well be cheaper than direct flights, and on the likes of Swiss, Air France or Lufthansa (which serves several Turkish airports direct from Germany), in-flight service may be superior. You can also use **Frequent Flyer** miles to reach İstanbul from the UK: usually between 20,000 and 30,000 miles are required.

Charter and "no frills" budget flights

The three largest and most reliable companies offering **charter flights** to Turkey are the charter arms of Thomas Cook, First Choice and Thomsons. Thomas Cook in particular offers a great deal of flexibility (you can choose different departure and return airports, flexible dates and even book one-ways – though you pay a supplement for this). You can book tickets on these through their designated agents (see list on p.30), or, generally a cheaper option, online.

Departures are most commonly from London Gatwick, Birmingham and Manchester. In summer, additional regional airports, such as Belfast, Edinburgh, Norwich, Bristol, Cardiff, Leeds-Bradford, East Midlands, Glasgow or Newcastle, are served. There are now year-round charters to Antalya, while those serving İzmir, Dalaman, and Bodrum usually operate from late April/early May to late October. Late-night or dawn departures are the norm, though more civilized hours are available in off-peak times.

In peak season these flights are often scarcely cheaper than scheduled services, but you do avoid having to change planes in İstanbul. As an example for the most common route, budget between £120–200 for a Gatwick–Dalaman ticket in spring or autumn, £250–300 in peak season.

The budget airline easyJet offers return flights to İstanbul for around £150, between March and October. From here it is possible to fly on to many other Turkish destinations, including the resort towns, using a cheap internal flight (see p.56).

An alternative way to reach Turkey from the UK is to fly to a German airport with Ryanair or easyJet, and connect with a German or Turkish charter to your Turkish destination. The most reliable of these operators are German Wings and Condor (German), and Sunexpress (Turkish). Fares vary massively according to departure date, but can be as low as €20 one way.

Note that if you are travelling with children under 12, scheduled airlines usually give a generous discount, charters and budget carriers none.

Scheduled flights

Scheduled flights have longer ticket validities (30, 60, 90 or even 180 days), involve fewer or (occasionally) none of the typical restrictions applicable to charters, and often leave at more sociable hours. However, many of the cheaper, shorter-duration fares do have advance-purchase and/or minimum-stay requirements, and severe restrictions on date changes or refunds. The widest choice of scheduled flights from the UK is with the Turkish national carrier, **Turkish Airways** (THY), and with **Cyprus Turkish Airways** (KTHY).

THY links London Heathrow with İstanbul three times daily year-round, and there are once-daily flights from Manchester to İstanbul. Thirty-day fares don't vary much across the year: London to İstanbul costs £200–215, Manchester £232–235, taxes included, though if you're willing to use the less popular dawn departures at both ends you can fly out of season for less than £200. Discounted Turkish domestic add-ons with THY are more convenient, but with the proliferation of private domestic carriers (see "By plane", p.56) they are not necessarily the best value. Fares from İstanbul to a Mediterranean resort start at 55YTL (€33) with the private carriers, from 80YTL (€48) with Turkish Airlines.

KTHY offers direct flights to the southwest coast, with useful services out of several UK airports. Typical winter patterns are twice-weekly London Stansted–Antalya, once-weekly Stansted–İzmir, once-weekly Stansted–Dalaman and twice-weekly London Heathrow–İzmir. During summer, schedules are more comprehensive; daily Stansted–Antalya; four-weekly Stansted–Dalaman and Stansted–İzmir; three-weekly Heathrow–İzmir and four-weekly Manchester–Dalaman; and two-weekly Gatwick–Dalaman, Gatwick–Antalya and Heathrow–Antalya. Depending on the season, thirty-day return fares run £200–290 for Stansted–Dalaman, £220–350 for Heathrow–İzmir. One-way tickets cost about seventy percent of these prices, while tickets valid for six weeks cost slightly more. Note that KTHY is not easy to deal with: the airline doesn't show up on most travel-website searches (airline code KY), so you must usually book with the airline or its agents direct, and if you are paying by credit card you must fax a photocopy of both your passport and credit card. Even worse, summer schedules do not appear until sometime in April, making early booking very difficult. It is also likely that the number of planes touching down in Turkish airports (all flights are actually en-route to Ercan in Northern Cyprus) will decrease as the ban on direct flights to Turkish Cyprus looks set to be lifted.

British Airways has thrice-daily services from London Heathrow to İstanbul. Fares considerably undercut those of THY, at around £200 most of the year, rising to £215 in July and August (though you'll pay more for more convenient flight times). Flights from Manchester are usually £275, rising to £300 in July and August, but entail a flight to Gatwick, followed by a coach transfer to Heathrow.

From Belfast, there are year-round daily scheduled services on British Airways, involving a stop in London or Manchester, but prices are ridiculously high (in excess of £550 in July and August). **From Dublin**, you'll do better on one-stop itineraries with Air France or KLM, but these are also expensive at around €600 in July and August. A cheaper option is to take a budget Ryanair or similar flight to the UK (Stansted is the principal hub of KTHY), and then on to İstanbul. There are also two weekly flights from Belfast to Antalya with KTHY.

Airlines

Air France UK ☏0845/0845 111, Republic of Ireland ☏01/605 0383, ⓦwww.airfrance.co.uk.

British Airways UK ☏0845/773 3377, Republic of Ireland ☏0141/222 2345, ⓦwww.britishairways.com.
Cyprus Turkish Airlines (KTHY) UK ☏020/7930 4851, ⓦwww.kthy.net.
easyJet UK☏0871/750 0100, ⓦwww.easyjet.com.
Germanwings UK☏0870/252 1250, ⓦwww.germanwings.com.
KLM UK ☏08705/074 074, ⓦwww.klmuk.com.
Lufthansa UK ☏0845/773 7747, Republic of Ireland ☏01/844 5544, ⓦwww.lufthansa.com.
Ryanair UK ☏0870/156 9569, Republic of Ireland ☏01/609 7800, ⓦwww.ryanair.com.
Sunexpress Germany ☏0180/5959 590, ⓦwww.sunexpress.com.tr.
Swiss UK ☏0845/601 0956, Republic of Ireland ☏01890/200515, ⓦwww.swiss.com.
Turkish Airlines (THY) UK ☏020/7766 9300 or 0161/489 5289, ⓦwww.thy.com.

Flight and travel agents

Alternative Travel UK ☏020/7923 3230, ⓦwww.alternativeturkey.com. Specialist Turkish travel agency, good for flight-only deals.
Avro UK ☏0870/036 0111, ⓦwww.avro.co.uk. Seat-only sales of charter flights to Antalya (from Gatwick and Dalaman) and Dalaman from Gatwick only.
CTA Holidays UK ☏020/7930 4851. Agents for KTHY and specialists for holidays in Turkish Cyprus.
First Choice UK ☏0870/850 3999. Cheap flights to Antalya, Bodrum and Dalaman from May to October.
Gemstone Travel UK ☏01344/353807, ⓦwww.gemstonetravel.co.uk. Cheap flights to coastal Turkey, especially Bodrum and Dalaman.
Lee Travel Cork ☏021/427 7111, ⓦwww.leetravel.ie. Flights and holidays worldwide.
The London Flight Centre UK ☏020/7244 6411, ⓦwww.topdecktravel.co.uk. Long-established agent dealing in discount flights.
North South Travel UK ☏01245/608291, ⓦwww.nstravel.demon.uk. Flight agency offering discounted fares – profits are used to support projects in the developing world, especially the promotion of sustainable tourism.
Rosetta Travel Belfast ☏028/9064 4996, ⓦwww.rosettatravel.com. Flight and holiday agent.
STA Travel UK ☏0870/160 6070, ⓦwww.statravel.co.uk. Worldwide specialists in low-cost flights and tours for students and under-26s, though other customers welcome. A dozen branches across England, especially on or near university campuses.
Student & Group Travel Dublin ☏01/677 7834. Student and group specialists, mostly to Europe.
Thomas Cook UK ☏0750 0512,

@www.flythomascook.com. Best source for charters to Turkey, and the clearest website.

Thomson Holidays UK ☎0870/190 0737, @www.thomsonfly.com. Flight-only deals to Dalaman and Bodrum.

Trailfinders UK ☎020/7628 7628, Republic of Ireland ☎01/677 7888, @www.trailfinders.com. One of the best-informed and most efficient agents for independent travellers, for scheduled flights only; branches in all the UK's largest cities, plus Dublin.

Package tours and special-interest holidays

Over seventy companies in the UK offer some sort of Turkish beach, city or sailing holiday. The bulk of these target İstanbul and the coast between Çeşme and Alanya, but you needn't feel tied to a rigid programme since most outfits also feature fly-drive plans. As southern Turkey has such short, balmy winters, coastal yachting (*gület*) and accommodation packages are available from April to November (though you may have to use scheduled airlines rather than charters for the months cited). A few companies handle inland holidays, particularly to Cappadocia, while special-interest programmes include trekking, bird-spotting, scuba diving, white-water rafting and battlefield tours.

A three- or four-night **city break** to İstanbul starts at around £200 for three-star bed-and-breakfast accommodation (including flights and transfers), rising to around £550 for the same break in one of the city's classic hotels. The determining price for city breaks is the departure airport, the cheapest taking advantage of easyJet's Luton–İstanbul run.

Prices for a cheap and cheerful, two-week **beach package**, staying in a resort pension or two-star hotel (with breakfast), start at around £300 per person (double occupancy) in low season, including flights; a four-star hotel will set you back about £650–750. Quality self-catering villas tend to cost over £700 per person for the same low-season period (flight included), increasing to almost £850 at peak periods. **Fly-drive**-only deals weigh in at around £450 per person for four adults travelling for two weeks in high season, around £550 if there are only two of you.

A week's **yachting or cruising** holiday (plus two days on land) will cost £450–600

per person (double occupancy basis) depending on season, booked in the UK through an agent, but only £300–450 if arranged in Turkey directly with skippers. **Overland/hiking** trips range from £250–300 for a week along the Lycian Coast arranged locally, to £700–750 for a higher-quality land/sea adventure booked in the UK. **Specialist holidays**, relying on the services of expert natural history/archeological guides, tend to be priciest of all, from £1250–1800 for two weeks. All these figures exclude the cost of the flight to Turkey.

General tour operators

Anatolian Sky ☎0121/325 5500, @www.anatolian-sky.co.uk. Middle-of-the-road-to-upmarket hotels and apartments on the southwest coast (particularly Kalkan, Dalyan, Akyaka, İçmeler, Orhaniye, Selimiye, Fethiye and Ölüdeniz), classic hotels in İstanbul, and tailor-made and fly-drive programmes.

Cachet Travel ☎020/8847 3846, @www.cachet-travel.co.uk. Small selection of classy (but very reasonably priced) premises, including exclusive representation of idyllic Turquoise Coast properties in remote locales such as Karaağaç, the Montenegro Ranch near Antalya, and Taşbükü; also somewhat more usual properties at Dalyan, Göcek, Ovacık Üzümlü and Cappadocia, plus guided special-interest tours, fly-drives and select İstanbul hotels.

Exclusive Escapes ☎020/8065 3500, @www.hiddenturkey.com. Offers a range of private villas, yacht cruises, city-breaks and special-interest tours.

IAH ☎0870/027 2921, @www.iah-holidays.co.uk. All kinds of special-interest/tailor-made tours in Turkey and Turkish Cyprus, from walking to golf, diving to Grand Prix watching.

Mark Warner ☎0870/770 4222, @www.markwarner.co.uk. Two all-inclusive clubs on the Bodrum peninsula; sports and childcare laid on, thus excellent venues for families with kids.

Simply Turkey ☎020/8541 2204, @www.simply-travel.com. Quality self-catering villas or restored cottages in exclusive coastal locations such as Gümüşlük, Karakaya and Yalıkavak on the Bodrum peninsula, and Akyaka, Dalyan, Ölüdeniz and Kalkan, as well as gourmet hotels in İstanbul and Cappadocia (with hot-air ballooning an option there). Guided walking and botanical tours, plus painting and birdwatching courses; also a tailor-made and fly-drive department.

Sunquest ☎0870/366 1553, @www.sunquestholidays.co.uk. Long-established beachhols outfit, with a budget-to-mid-range presence in most coastal resorts between Çeşme and Patara. Now owned by First Choice.

Tapestry Holidays ☎020/8235 7777, ⓦwww .tapestryholidays.com. Currently the best-quality Turkey operator, with a state-of-the-art website that permits virtual 3D tours of prospective accommodation. Selection of smallish but top-drawer *pansiyons* and hotels along the Turquoise Coast, with emphasis on the Bozburun peninsula, Kalkan, Kaş, Göcek, the Ölüdeniz area (including exclusive representation of Ocakköy), Akyaka and Turunç Bay. Also *gület* cruises, watersports, special-interest (hiking, drawing-and-painting) holidays plus a tailor-made department and fly-drives. Inland, well-selected accommodation in İstanbul and Cappadocia (where troglodytic hotels and ballooning are featured).

Turkish Collection (Ilios Travel) ☎01403/259788, ⓦwww.iliostravel.com. Very high-quality (and thus pricey) villas-with-pool on the Bodrum and Datça peninsulas, plus somewhat more conventional accommodation at Akyaka.

Trekking and adventure operators

Adrift ☎01488/684509, ⓦwww.adrift.co.uk. Whitewater rafting on the Çoruh River from late May to late July; ten-day programme.

Exodus Travel ☎020/8675 5550, ⓦwww.exodus .co.uk. Strong on mountain biking, hiking and *gület* cruises along the Lycian Coast, Cappadocia and the St Paul Trail. Well priced at under £700 for nine to twelve days, including flights, with accommodation in small hotels and village houses.

Explore Worldwide ☎01252/760 000, ⓦwww .explore.co.uk. Camping treks in Lycia, the Toros ranges and Cappadocia, plus a range of less strenuous, overland minibus tours (one-, two- or three-week) across the country, which can be combined with one- or two-week *gület* cruises.

The Imaginative Traveller ☎020/8742 8612, ⓦwww.imaginative-traveller.com. Nine- to 17-day explorations of the best of Turkey, travelling by bus, *gület* or even bicycle, camping out or staying at *pansiyons*. Some unusual stops, opportunities for light walking and keen pricing, make this about the best overland group-tour operator for Turkey. Tie-in programmes around ANZAC Day, for London-based Antipodeans.

Travelbag Adventures ☎01420/541 007, ⓦwww.travelbag-adventures.com. Stands out for its "Family Adventures" programme pitched at veteran overland travellers, now with children, who want to introduce their offspring to the delights of expeditions. An eight-day Lycian Coast adventure includes Kekova and Tahtalı Dağ; 20 percent off for kids over 5.

Sailing and cruising operators

Day Dreams ☎020/7637 8921, ⓦwww.day-dreams-travel.com. Twenty-strong fleet of *gülets* and schooners, which host "house parties" for singles and couples; ten days aboard in June or September cost a bit under £900, flights exclusive.

Nautilus Yachting ☎01732/867445, ⓦwww .nautilus-yachting.co.uk. Bare-boat charters out of Marmaris, Bodrum and Göcek, plus set one- or two-week flotilla itineraries between Selimiye, Göcek and Kalkan.

Setsail ☎01737/764443, ⓦwww.setsail.co.uk. Flotilla holidays between Göcek, Fethiye and Orhaniye; also bare-boat charter.

Sunsail ☎023/9222 2222, ⓦwww.sunsail.com. Flotilla holidays out of Göcek, Marmaris and Bodrum, taking in the Turquoise Coast and the peninsulas between Bodrum and Marmaris.

Tussock Cruising ☎020/8510 9292, ⓦwww. tussockcruising.com. Has a fleet of nine wooden *gülets* specially adapted so that you actually travel under sail power rather than (as with most such craft) with merely decorative rigging. Vessels accommodate parties of six to eighteen.

Special-interest holidays

Andante Travels ☎01722/715 800, ⓦwww .andantetravels.co.uk. Offers upmarket tours covering most of Turkey's major (and many minor) archeological and historical sites, led by distinguished professors or other experts in their fields.

British Museum Traveller ☎020/7436 7575, ⓦwww.britishmuseumtraveller.co.uk. Most years offers a pair of ten- to fifteen-day archeological tours in spring and autumn, led by experts. Past outings have focused on lesser-known Ottoman or Selçuk sites, the standard Aegean classical ruins, or very early settlements of inner Anatolia by way of Byzantine or Armenian monuments.

Cox & Kings ☎020/7873 5018, ⓦwww.coxandk-ings.co.uk. Botanical tour operators which have at least one trip annually to Turkey, usually in early July to the Kaçkar mountains.

Gölköy Centre ⓦwww.yogaturkey.co.uk, marketed through Neal's Yard Agency ☎0870/444 2702, ⓦwww.nealsyardagency.com. Yoga "farm" on Bodrum peninsula, which offers week-long courses, also encompassing painting, walking, shiatsu and assorted "personal growth" themes, from May to October; budget £365–400 per person per week, including full board and activities but not flights.

Greentours ☎01298/83563, ⓦwww.greentours
.co.uk. Offers up to three annual, two-week natural-
history holidays (emphasis on birds, orchids and
butterflies), typically to Lakeland, the Kaçkar foothills
and the Van basin. Enthusiastic English guides know
their subjects in incredible depth.

Gullivers Natural History Holidays
☎01525/270100. Birdwatching, botany and general
springtime natural-history tours; past (and annually
changing) bases/areas have included Antalya with the
lakes and river deltas nearby, and Kuşadası with its
surrounding mountains, lakes and deltas.

Holt's Tours ☎01304/612248, ⓦwww.holts
.co.uk. Battlefields specialist with a one-week tour of
western Turkey, focused on Gallipoli and the Dardanelles, in autumn (thus avoiding ANZAC Day mayhem).

Huzur Vadisi ⓦwww.huzurvadisi.com, marketed
through Neal's Yard Agency ☎0870/444 2702,
ⓦwww.nealsyardagency.com. One- and two-week
programmes of light walks (May & Oct only) and
yoga at a secluded, three-acre complex consisting
of felt yurts or nomad dwellings around a renovated
farmhouse and stone-clad pool, 10km inland of
Göcek. Around £400 a week, including full board and
activities but not flights; cheaper for nonparticipants.

Flights and tours from North America

No matter where you're flying from, İstanbul
is by far the cheapest gateway airport. For
the best value, try to pick up a bargain trans-
atlantic fare to Europe, then arrange the final
Turkey-bound leg of the journey yourself;
onward flights from the UK are detailed on
p.30.

Turkish Airways (THY) is the only carrier
flying direct year-round from North America,
with daily flights from New York (JFK) to
İstanbul, and four weekly out of Chicago.
There are half a dozen code-share feeder
flights to these hubs on its partner, American
Airlines, from several major cities, including
San Francisco and Miami. **Delta Airlines** is
the only other airline offering a direct service
(April–Oct), from New York to İstanbul, while
United Airlines generally has the cheapest
stopping fares via Frankfurt. All other flights
route through **European hubs**, such as
London, Paris, Frankfurt, Milan and Zürich.
The best choice is Lufthansa via Frankfurt,
while other reasonable options include Brit-
ish Airways, Air France, KLM, Alitalia and
Swiss.

THY has the most comprehensive selection
of **connecting flights** within Turkey, a major
incentive to booking with them at least part of
the way. THY normally charges about US$80
extra for these cities when the domestic leg is
purchased as part of an international itinerary,
but specialists, such as Turkish Tursan Tours
(see "Flight and travel agents" below), can
often book you straight through for no extra
charge, or book you through with a stop in
İstanbul for an extra US$40 or so.

Tax-inclusive one-month fares out of **New
York** vary from $640–850 in winter, up to
$1060–1350 in peak season; it's usually
worth paying the paltry difference for the nonstop service with Delta or THY. For **Chicago**,
the corresponding ranges are $700–850 win-
ter, but $1100–1380 in summer (with THY's
nonstop flight at the higher end of the band).
From **San Francisco**, the seasonal bands
are $700–1000/$1200–1600. From **Miami**,
expect to pay $750–850/$1100–1500, with
British Airways undercutting at $750.

There are no direct flights from Canada to
Turkey, but several airlines do fly to İstanbul
via major European hubs. From **Montréal**
to İstanbul winter fares start at C$2000 on
British Airways via London and C$1100 on
United via Washington, DC, and Frankfurt,
climbing to C$1550–2500 in summer with
the same airlines.

Specialist tour operators can take you
off the beaten track in Turkey, or simply offer
some companionship on your travels, but
the best of the cultural or adventure tours
do not come cheap. You can expect to pay
a minimum of US$2500 for a 14-day land-
and-sea combo (inevitably with a couple of
days in İstanbul at the start and end). Flights
are never included in the tour price, but most
tours include all meals (excluding drinks),
guides and ground transport.

Airlines

Air Canada ☎1-888/247-2262, ⓦwww
.aircanada.ca.
Air France ☎1-800/237-2747, Canada ☎1-
800/667-2747, ⓦwww.airfrance.com.
Alitalia ☎1-800/223-5730, Canada ☎1-800/361-
8336, ⓦwww.alitalia.com.
American Airlines ☎1-800/433-7300, ⓦwww
.aa.com.

British Airways ☎1-800/AIRWAYS, ⓦwww
.british-airways.com.
Delta Air Lines ☎1-800/241-4141, ⓦwww
.delta.com.
KLM/Northwest ☎1-800/447-4747, Canada
☎514/397-0775, ⓦwww.klm.com.
Lufthansa ☎1-800/645-3880, Canada ☎1-
800/563-5954, ⓦwww.lufthansa.ca.com.
Turkish Airlines (THY) ☎1-800/874-8875,
ⓦwww.thy.com.
United Airlines ☎1-800/538-2929, ⓦwww
.united.com.

Flight and travel agents

Air Brokers International ☎1-800/883-3273
or 415/397-1383, ⓦwww.airbrokers.com.
Consolidator and specialist in RTW and Circle-Pacific
tickets.
Airtech ☎212/219-7000, ⓦwww.airtech.com.
Standby seat broker; also deals in consolidator fares
and courier flights.
Educational Travel Center ☎1-800/747-5551 or
608/256 5551, ⓦwww.edtrav.com. Student/youth
discount agent.
High Adventure Travel ☎1-800/350-0612 or
415/912-5600, ⓦwww.airtreks.com. Round-the-
world and Circle-Pacific tickets. The website features
an interactive database that lets you build and price
your own RTW itinerary.
New Frontiers/Nouvelles Frontières ☎1-
800/677-0720 or New York 212/986-6006, ⓦwww
.NewFrontiers.com. French discount-travel firm.
Other branches in LA, San Francisco and Québec City.
STA Travel ☎1-800/777-0112 or 1-800/781-
4040, ⓦwww.sta-travel.com. Worldwide specialist
in independent travel; also student IDs, travel
insurance, car rental, rail passes etc.
Student Flights ☎1-800/255-8000 or 480/951-
1177, ⓦwww.isecard.com. Student/youth fares,
student IDs.
TFI Tours International ☎1-800/745-8000 or
212/736-1140. Consolidator.
Travel Avenue ☎1-800/333-3335, ⓦwww
.travelavenue.com. Full-service travel agent that
offers discounts in the form of rebates.
Travel Cuts Canada ☎1-800/667-2887, US
☎416/979-2406, ⓦwww.travelcuts.com. Canadian
student-travel organization.
Turkish Tursan Travel ☎212/888-1180. Turkish
specialist consolidator, based in New York.
Worldtek Travel ☎1/800-243-1723, ⓦwww
.worldtek.com. Discount travel agency for worldwide
travel.

Specialist tour operators

Adventures Abroad ☎1-800/665-3998 or
604/303-1099, ⓦwww.adventures-abroad.com.
Offers moderately active seven- to ten-day jaunts
in western Turkey, 13–20-dayers in the east of the
country.
Cultural Folk Tours ☎1-800/935-TURK or
858/566-5951, ⓦwww.boraozkok.com. Up to
nine annual departures by this 1978-established
San Diego–based company, led (and musically
accompanied) by Bora Özkök himself. A cut above
the usual bus-tour dross, it offers some real insight
into seldom-visited regions of the country (and
central Asia as an add-on, if numbers permit).
Geographic Expeditions ☎1-800/777-8183
or 415/922-0448, ⓦwww.geoex.com. Spring and
autumn departures for its 17- and 21-day trek-plus-
gület-cruises (10 days afloat off the Turquoise Coast),
five-day Cappadocia add-on available.
M/S Cavurali ☎0090/242 4192 441, ⓦwww.
cavurali.com. Quality cruises on the Finike (Turquoise
Coast) based on the 20-mètre Cavurali gület led by
the genial Turkish-American Enver Lucas.
Mythic Travel ☎1-800/228-0593 pin 12 or
831/438-3031, ⓦwww.mythic-travel.com.
Distinctly New Age "Magic Carpets" (as opposed to
tours) with themed tags like "Mary and the Divine
Feminine", "Jewish Life" and "Sufi Solstice".
Wilderness Travel ☎1-800/368-2794 or
510/558-2488, ⓦwww.wildernesstravel.
com. Offers two trips: 17 days encompassing
İstanbul, Cappadocia and the far southeast, plus
a 16-dayer incorporating a ten-day cruise using
the same personnel and itinerary as Geographic
Expeditions.

Flights and tours from Australia and New Zealand

There are no direct flights from Australia or
New Zealand to Turkey. However, several
weekly scheduled flights will get you there
after either a plane change or short layover
in the airline's hub – typically Bahrain, Bang-
kok, Singapore or Milan – before the final
leg of the journey. A marginally less expensive, but far more time-consuming strategy
would involve taking a flight to London and
then proceeding from there with the benefit
of the well-developed package industry (see
p.31).

Flights booked directly through the airlines tend to be more expensive than those

bought from discount agents, who will have the latest information on limited specials offered throughout the year. **Round-the-world tickets** including Turkey use combinations of airlines, and could be worth considering for a long trip taking in many destinations; generally some free stopovers are allowed, with fares starting at A$2000/NZ$2500.

Two-stop itineraries from Sydney are around A$1900 in low season to A$2600 high season, with Gulf Air. **From New Zealand**, Lufthansa flies to İstanbul for NZ$2100 year-round.

Airlines

Air New Zealand Australia ☎ 13 24 76, New Zealand ☎ 0800/737 000 or 09/357 3000, ⓦ www.airnz.com.
British Airways Australia ☎ 02/8904 8800, New Zealand ☎ 09/356 8690, ⓦ www.britishairways.com.
Emirates Australia ☎ 02/9290 9700 or 1300/303 777, New Zealand ☎ 09/377 6004, ⓦ www.emirates.com.
Gulf Air Australia ☎ 02/9244 2199, New Zealand ☎ 09/308 3366, ⓦ www.gulfairco.com.
KLM Australia ☎ 1300/303 747, New Zealand ☎ 09/309 1782, ⓦ www.klm.com.
Lufthansa Australia ☎ 1300/655 727 or 02/9367 3887, New Zealand ☎ 09/303 1529 or 008/945 220, ⓦ www.lufthansa.com.
Malaysia Airlines Australia ☎ 13 26 27, New Zealand ☎ 0800/657 472, ⓦ www.mas.com.my.
Qantas Australia ☎ 13 13 13, New Zealand ☎ 0800/808 767 or 09/357 8900, ⓦ www.qantas.com.au.
Singapore Airlines Australia ☎ 13 10 11 or 02/9350 0262, New Zealand ☎ 0800/808 909 or 09/303 2129, ⓦ www.singaporeair.com.
Thai Airways Australia ☎ 1300/651 960, New Zealand ☎ 09/377 3886; ⓦ www.thaiair.com.
Turkish Airlines Australia ☎ 02/9299 8400, ⓦ www.thy.com.

Flight and travel agents

Anywhere Travel Australia ☎ 02/9663 0411 or 018/401 014, ⓔ anywhere@ozemail.com.au.
Destinations Unlimited New Zealand ☎ 09/373 4033.
Flight Centres Australia ☎ 02/9235 3522 or 13 16 00, New Zealand ☎ 09/358 4310, ⓦ www.flightcentre.com.au.

STA Travel Australia ☎ 1300/360 960, ⓦ www.statravel.com.au; New Zealand ☎ 0508/782 872, ⓦ www.statravel.co.nz.
Thomas Cook Australia ☎ 13 17 71 or 1800/801 002, ⓦ www.thomascook.com.au; New Zealand ☎ 09/379 3920, ⓦ www.thomascook.co.nz.
Trailfinders Australia ☎ 1300/780 212, ⓦ www.trailfinders.com.au.

Specialist tour operators

Adventures Abroad New Zealand ☎ 0800/800434, ⓦ www.adventures-abroad.com. Offers seven- to ten-day jaunts in western Turkey, 13–20-dayers in the east of the country.
Adventure World Sydney ☎ 02/8913 0755, Perth ☎ 08/9226 4524, ⓦ www.adventureworld.com.au; New Zealand ☎ 09/524 5118, ⓦ www.adventureworld.co.nz. Not, in fact, very adventurous eight-day road trips of western Turkey, or 14 days including Cappadocia; three-day add-on for the ANZAC sites available.
Sun Island Tours Australia ☎ 02/9283 3840, ⓦ www.sunislandtours.com.au. Offers three-to five-day land tours in the west and, more compellingly, a week-long *gület* cruise from Bodrum to the Marmaris peninsula and back.
World Expeditions Australia ☎ 1300/720 000 for closest of five branches; New Zealand ☎ 0800/350354, ⓦ www.worldexpeditions.com.au. Probably the most interesting Antipodean adventure operator for Turkey: does a 22-day "Turkey Panorama", including five days' trekking and three days' cruising, plus a 16-day botany tour in the Toros mountains.

By rail from Europe

Travelling to Turkey **by rail** is both slow and expensive, and only makes sense if you want to visit several other countries en route. The most direct route **from the UK** begins with the Eurostar service from London Waterloo to Brussels, then an overnight sleeper to Vienna, followed by a daytime Euro-City departure to Budapest, and finally two more nights aboard a sleeper to İstanbul (including a change of engine in Bucharest), making a total journey of three nights, four days. The return trip is likely to set you back between £350–500, depending on whether you use a couchette or treat yourself to a sleeper compartment, and assuming you have a rail pass (see overleaf).

An alternative strategy, potentially cheaper if slower, is to get to Italy by train and then proceed by ferry to Greece or even all the way to Turkey (see below).

Rail passes

The best train deal is provided by an **Inter-Rail pass**, which offers unlimited travel (except for express-train supplements and reservation fees) on a zonal basis within 28 European rail networks. These passes are only available to European residents, and you must provide proof of residency before being allowed to purchase one. To reach Turkey via the route described above, you really need an all-zone pass. For under-26s, you're looking at £285 for an all-zone pass valid for one month's second-class travel, £405 if you're over 26.

InterRail passes do not allow free travel between Britain and the continent, although InterRail Pass holders are eligible for discounts on rail travel in Britain and Northern Ireland, the cross-Channel ferries, and the London–Paris Eurostar service.

However, for North Americans, Australians and New Zealanders, a standard **Eurail Pass** (available from many discount and youth/student travel operators) is unlikely to pay for itself, whether going to, or travelling in, Turkey. This is among the many reasons for the popularity of the Fez Bus pass scheme (see "Getting around", p.49).

Rail contacts

Euro Railways ☏1-800/533-3341, ⓦwww .eurorailways.com. Really good all-in-one outlet for all sorts of passes and tickets (though you can't get a simple fare to İstanbul).

InterRail ⓦwww.inter-rail.co.uk. You may save some money by booking your pass via the InterRail website.

The Man in Seat 61 ⓦwww.seat61.com. Named after British rail-buff Mark Smith's favourite seat on the Eurostar, this noncommercial site is full of practical advice and planning on any train journey from the UK to just about anywhere in Eurasia (including Turkey). You can't buy tickets here, but all the necessary contacts are provided.

By car and ferry from Europe

In theory you can **drive from the UK** to Turkey in three to four days. However, this allows little time for stopping and sleeping, and it makes sense to slow down and take in a few places en route. For the full story on customs formalities and car insurance cover once in Turkey, see "Getting around", p.55.

Given Serbia's still war-damaged infrastructure, and the poor (and painfully slow) road links from Hungary to Bulgaria via Romania, the safest, if not exactly most direct, route is **through France, Italy and Greece**. You can cut the driving time by planning to take a ferry from Italy, direct to Turkey; and there are also short-hop ferry or hydrofoil services from five Greek islands to the southwestern Turkish coast.

The fastest way to start your journey is by using the **Eurotunnel** service (☏0870/535 3535, ⓦwww.eurotunnel.com) via the Channel Tunnel, though some may prefer the traditional **cross-Channel ferry/hovercraft** links between England or Ireland and France. For full route and fare details, it's best to contact your local travel agent.

Ferries from Italy

Ferries run from both Ancona and Brindisi in Italy to Çeşme, near İzmir. **Marmara Lines** (ⓦwww.marmaralines.com) has boats running from late March to the end of October, departing Ancona on a Saturday. A Pullman seat (o/w) in high season is €140 and an average-sized car €160. Boats from Brindisi depart on a Wednesday and cost €80 for a Pullman seat (o/w) and €120 for a car. **MedEuropeanSeaways (Mesline)** operates a service between mid-June and mid-September from Brindisi to Çeşme (departs Brindisi Sat and Wed); high-season charges are €148 for a Pullman seat, €158 for a car. For information on Mesline check out ⓦwww.ferries.gr.

Ferries and catamarans from Greece

Many travellers take the short-hop ferries or catamarans over from the **Greek islands** of Lésvos, Híos, Sámos, Kálymnos, Kastellorizo/Meis, Kós and Rhodes to the respective Turkish ports of Ayvalık, Çeşme, Kuşadası, Bodrum, Kaş, Marmaris and Fethiye. Services are daily in season (early May to early Oct) and, except for the Kálymnos- and Fethiye-based services, they still run after a fashion in winter, but you may have to wait a week between departures. One-way prices of €20–40 make them vastly overpriced for the distances involved; full details of every service are given at the end of the North Aegean and the Central and Southern Aegean chapters.

Note that at the time of writing the only reliable **car-shuttle services** are from Lésvos to Ayvalık and from Híos to Çeşme, with passenger fares around €40 and cars €70 and up.

The best source of information on the above services is ⓦwww.ferries.gr.

Red tape and visas

To enter Turkey you'll need a full passport, and a number of countries require visas, available only at the port of entry – do not pester Turkish embassies or consulates in your home country. Visas for citizens of the UK and Ireland cost £10/€15; US citizens are charged US$20; and Australians and New Zealanders pay US$5 for their visa. Citizens of Israel, Italy, Portugal and Spain currently also require visas to enter Turkey.

Note that while cashiers at much-frequented ports of entry, such as İstanbul's Atatürk airport, nonchalantly convert between different currencies (usually to your disadvantage) and give change for large notes, officials at less-used land or sea border crossings can be highly inflexible. For example, UK nationals may be required to pay in sterling only, and change for £20 notes will not be given.

Tourist visas are multiple entry and valid for three months from the date of issue – if you leave on a day-trip, for example to Greece, you should not have to pay for a new visa on re-entry. Most visitors are allowed to remain in Turkey for three months (South Africans, however, are given only one month); during this time it is forbidden to take up employment.

Once inside the country, you can **extend your visa** once only, for a further three months, by applying to the Foreigners' Department (Yabancı Bürosu) of the Security Division (Emniyet Müdürlüğü) in any provincial capital. Do this well before your time expires; it may take several weeks to process. If you know in advance that you want to stay longer, you should apply to the consulate in your own country for a **long-stay visa**. On arrival in Turkey, the Yabancı Bürosu will convert it to a residence permit (ikamet tezkeresi), valid initially for one year (two with a work permit). Further renewals will be for three or five years. In either case, you will be required to show means of support (savings, a regular income from abroad or legal work in Turkey) and relinquish your passport until the permit is issued. Many people still nip across to a Greek island, Bulgaria or Northern Cyprus every three months and re-enter Turkey to obtain a new three-month stamp, rather than go through the trouble of applying for a residence permit. Depending on the ports of entry/exit you may need to stay out of the country for at least 24 hours (Kaş–Meis is traditionally one of the more lenient, same-day-return crossings). Also, if the police have received a complaint that you are working, they may not readmit you.

Turkish embassies and consulates abroad

Australia 60 Mugga Way, Red Hill, Canberra ACT 2603 ☏ 02/6295 0227.
Canada 197 Wurtemburg St, Ottawa, ON K1N 8L9 ☏ 613/789-4044.
Ireland 11 Clyde Rd, Ballsbridge, Dublin 4 ☏ 01/668 5240.
New Zealand 15–17 Murphy St, Level 8, Wellington ☏ 04/472 1290.
South Africa 1067 Church St, Hatfield 0181, Pretoria ☏ 012/342 5063.
UK 43 Belgrave Square, London SW1X 8PA ☏ 020/7393 0202.
USA 2525 Massachusetts Ave NW, Washington, DC 20008 ☏ 202/612 6700.

Customs and border inspections

Since Turkey's customs union with the EU in the year 2000, most European travellers are free to bring in valuable electronic gadgets without having them written into their passport. But since Turkey is not yet actually an EU member, **duty-free limits** – and sales – for alcohol and tobacco are still prevalent. Limits are posted clearly at İstanbul's Atatürk airport, and apply for all frontiers. If you haven't exploited your allowance at your departure airport, it's as well to know that you can usually buy duty-free goods at your Turkish port of arrival, at prices considerably cheaper than northern European airports.

Checks on the way out may be more thorough; customs at seaports like Kuşadası and Marmaris are apt to be more inquisitive than their laxer brethren at the airports. Only an idiot would try and take **drugs** through Turkish customs, although it's more likely that the guards will be on the lookout for **antiquities** and **fossils** – there is a ready market in Turkey and abroad for rare specimens. Penalties for trying to smuggle these out include long jail sentences, plus a large fine. For a discussion on what constitutes an antiquity, see "Bazaars and shopping", p.87.

Health

No special inoculations are required for visiting Turkey, although if you don't want to take any chances, jabs against typhoid and tetanus are suggested, particularly if you're travelling to eastern Anatolia. Some visitors also take the precaution of getting injections against hepatitis A. For a summer visit it's probably worth the discomfort – the risk is possibly greater in İstanbul than in remote rural areas. Malaria is generally a seasonal (April–July) problem in the regions between Adana and Mardin (mainly the area covered in Chapter 11), and incidence has skyrocketed recently around Şanlıurfa in areas newly irrigated by the Southeastern Anatolian Project (see box on p.845). However, for brief visits you shouldn't need prophylactic drugs. For up-to-date advice consult a travel clinic with experience in exotic diseases.

Health problems

You're unlikely to encounter many health problems in Turkey. **Tap water** is heavily chlorinated and probably safe to drink, though not exactly delectable (except in restaurants, which serve it chilled and minimally filtered). In İstanbul, where it comes out of the tap an off-putting orange colour, it is absolutely to be avoided in favour of bottled water. **Rural springs** are labelled *içilir*, *içilbelir* or *içme suyu* (all meaning "potable"), or *içilmez* (not drinkable). Many people experience bouts of mild **diarrhoea**, and the chances of this happening increase the longer you stay in the country. As a precaution take anti-diarrhoea tablets with you (you'll be able to buy a locally produced variant if you forget). Lomotil or Imodium, trade names for the antiparastaltic diphenoxylate, are easily available in Turkey and will allow you to travel without constantly running to the bathroom, but do not kill the bug that ails you. Buscopan, also on sale locally, is particularly good for stomach cramps resulting from food poisoning and sunstroke. For electrolyte replacement resulting from dehydrating diarrhoea, Ge-Oral powder dissolved in pure water is a good local remedy. Particularly during the hot summer months, more serious **food poisoning** is a possibility – even in the biggest cities and resorts, and especially in southeastern Turkey. In restaurants, avoid dishes that look as if they have been standing around and make sure meat and fish are well grilled. Don't, whatever you do, eat stuffed mussels in summer. If you're struck down, the best thing is to let the bug run its course and drink lots of fluids; eating plain white rice and yoghurt also helps. Stubborn cases will need a course of antibiotics – pharmacists (see opposite) are trained to recognize symptoms and you don't need a prescription for the antibiotics. In theory, a state clinic (*Develet Polikliniği*) will treat foreigners for a very small fee.

Animal hazards

Snakes and **scorpions** can lurk among the rocks and stones at archeological sites, and in the nooks and crannies of ground-floor accommodation. There are two kinds of vipers (*engerek* in Turkish): the very deadly, metre-long Ottoman viper, fortunately quite rare, and the smaller, more common and less dangerous asp viper. Neither is particularly aggressive unless disturbed; both are most commonly seen during long, but not too hot, spring days. **Mosquitoes** are a problem in some places, and since no good topical repellents are available locally, you should bring your own. At night mozzies are most easily dispatched with locally sold incense coils (*spiral tütsü*) or an *Esem Mat*, a small, electrified tray that slowly vapourizes an odourless disc during the course of a night. The word for mosquito netting is *çibindirik*,

provision of which by hotels and *pansiyons* in areas of heavy infestation is becoming almost standard.

Rabies is perhaps the greatest potential danger, and the giant Sivas-Kangal sheepdogs are the most obvious possible source, though they are rarely aggressive unless their flock is closely approached. Be wary of any animal that bites, scratches or licks you, particularly if it's behaving erratically. First aid involves flushing a wound with soap and water after encouraging limited bleeding. Apply antiseptic and bandage if necessary, but do not suture, and seek medical attention immediately. A six-injection course of human diploid cell vaccine (HDCV) – given in the arm – needs to be started within 72 hours, followed by a single jab of human rabies immunoglobulin (HRIG).

Medical treatment

For minor complaints, head for the nearest **pharmacy** (*eczane*). Even the smallest town will have at least one, where you'll be able to obtain remedies for ailments such as diarrhoea, sunburn and flu. In larger towns, *eczane* staff may know some English or German. Pharmacists in Turkey are able to dispense medicines, invariably locally produced, that would ordinarily require a prescription abroad. Medication prices are low, but you may find it difficult to find exact equivalents to your home prescription, so bring it, and a good supply of the actual medication you may need, along. **Night-duty pharmacies**, often found near main hospitals, are known as *nöbet(ci)*; a list of the current rota is posted in Turkish in every chemist's front window, as "Nöbetçi Eczaneleri". For more serious ailments you'll find well-trained **doctors** in larger towns and cities. Most of these are specialists, advertising themselves by means of signs outside their premises. A *diş tabibi* or *hekimi* is a dentist, a *tıbbî doktor* will treat ailments of all kinds, while an *operatör* is a qualified surgeon. If you're not sure what's wrong with you, it's best to go instead to one of the free state clinics (*sağlık ocağı*), which can give diagnoses and prescriptions, or a **hospital** (*hastane*), indicated by a blue street sign with a large white "H" on it. Hospitals are either public (*Devlet Hastane* or *SSK Hastanesi*) or private (*Özel Hastane*); the latter are vastly preferable in terms of cleanliness and standard of care, and since all foreigners must pay for any attention anyway, you may as well get the best available. Fees are lower than in northern Europe and North America but still substantial enough to make insurance cover essential. The medical faculties of major universities – eg İstanbul, İzmir, Edirne and Bursa – also have affiliated teaching hospitals that are infinitely better than the state hospitals, but less expensive than the private ones. Admission desks of private hospitals can also recommend their affiliated doctors if you don't want or need to be an in-patient, and your consulate or the tourist office may also be able to provide you with the address of an **English-speaking doctor**. If you're too ill to move, but must summon a doctor, hotel-room visits will cost about €50, with perhaps another €25 for medication delivered from a local pharmacy. If you're on an all-inclusive **package tour**, the better companies will have arrangements with competent, English-

speaking doctors in or near the resort. In a medical **emergency** summon an ambulance by dialing ☏112.

Contraception and feminine hygiene

About a dozen international brands of **birth control** pills (*doğum kontrol hapı*) are sold over the counter at pharmacies. **Condoms** are also sold in most pharmacies and supermarket chains such as Gima and the larger branches of Migros, which stock a good range of imported brands; don't buy off street-carts, where stock may be tampered with or expired. The "proper" word is *preservatif*, the slang term *kılıf* ("hood"). AIDS and other sexually transmitted diseases are now prevalent in Turkey.

Tampons are available from pharmacies and supermarkets for the same price as in the UK; Orkid is the adequate domestic brand of "sanitary towel".

Insurance

There are not yet any reciprocal health-care privileges between Turkey and the European Union, so it's essential to take out an insurance policy before travelling to cover against theft, loss, illness or injury. Before paying for a new policy, however, check whether you are already covered: some all-risks homeowners' or renters' insurance policies may cover your possessions when overseas, and many private medical schemes (such as BUPA and WPA) offer coverage extensions for abroad.

A specialist travel insurance company can sell you a suitable policy, or consider the travel insurance deal we offer (see box below). A typical travel insurance policy usually provides cover for the loss of baggage, tickets and – up to a certain limit – cash, cards or travellers' cheques, as well as cancellation or curtailment of your journey.

Most policies exclude so-called **dangerous sports** unless an extra premium is paid: in Turkey this can mean scuba diving, whitewater rafting, paragliding, windsurfing and trekking, though probably not kayak-

ing or jeep safaris. Many policies can be chopped and changed to eliminate coverage you don't need – for example, sickness and accident benefits can often be excluded or included at will. If you do take **medical coverage**, ascertain whether benefits will be paid as treatment proceeds or only after return home, and whether there is a 24-hour medical emergency number. When securing **baggage cover**, make sure that the per-article limit – typically under £500/€750 – will cover your most valuable possession, otherwise see about

B

Rough Guide travel insurance

Rough Guides has teamed up with Columbus Direct to offer you travel insurance that can be tailored to suit your needs.

Readers can choose from many different travel insurance products, including a low-cost backpacker option for long stays, a short break option for city getaways, a typical holiday package option, and many others. There are also annual multi-trip policies for those who travel regularly, with variable levels of cover available. Different sports and activities (trekking, skiing, etc) can be covered if required on most policies.

Rough Guides travel insurance is available to the residents of 36 different countries with different language options to choose from via our website – ⓦwww.roughguidesinsurance.com – where you can also purchase the insurance. Alternatively, UK residents should call ☏0800/083 9507; US citizens should call ☏1-800/749-4922; Australians should call ☏1 300/669 999. All other nationalities should call ☏+44 870/890 2843.

getting it covered under a homeowner policy. Travel agents and tour operators are likely to require travel insurance when you book a package holiday – you're not obliged to take theirs, though you may be required to sign a declaration saying that you already have a policy with a particular company.

If you need to make a medical **claim**, you should keep receipts for medicines and treatment, and in the event you have anything **stolen or lost**, you must obtain an official statement from the police (or the airline that lost your bags). In the wake of growing numbers of fraudulent claims, most insurers won't even entertain a claim unless you have a police report.

Information, maps and websites

Before you set off on your trip it's worth a visit to a Turkish tourist office (officially known as the Information Office of the Embassy), where you'll be able to pick up a few very basic maps and glossy brochures. Don't overload your luggage with these, however, as much the same choice is available within Turkey itself. What you should take with you are decent regional maps, since those on sale locally are generally inadequate. Turkey-related sites on the Internet are not wildly exciting; many are in Turkish only and/or have a very short life span.

Tourist offices

Most Turkish towns of any size will have a *Turizm Danışma Bürosu* or **tourist office** of some sort, often lodged inside the public library or *Belediye* (city hall) in the smaller places. However, outside the larger cities and obvious tourist destinations there's often very little actual information to be had, and the staff may well try to dismiss you with a selection of useless brochures. Lists of accommodation for all budgets are sometimes a useful feature of the more heavily patronized offices; the staff, however, will generally not make bookings. In the more frequented spots – with some sterling exceptions – staff made world-weary by the steady stream of visitors can be perfunctory at best in the discharge of their duties. On the other hand, staff in out-of-the-way places can be embarrassingly helpful.

The best plan is to have a specific question – about bus schedules, festival ticket availability or museum opening hours – although in remote regions there is no guarantee that there will be anyone who can speak English.

Tourist office **opening hours** generally adhere to a standard schedule of 8.30am to 12.30pm and 1.30pm to 5.30pm, Monday to Friday. Between May and September in big-name resorts and large cities, these hours extend well into the evening and through much of the weekend. In winter, by contrast, many tourist offices in out-of-the-way spots will be shut most of the time.

Turkish information offices abroad

ⓦ **www.tourismturkey.org**
Australia Room 17, Level 3, 428 George St, Sydney, NSW 2000 ☏ 02/9223 3055, ✉ turkish@ozemail.co.au.
Canada Constitution Square, 360 Albert St, Suite 801, Ottawa, ON K1R 7X7 ☏ 613/230-8654.
Ireland Refer to the embassy (see p.38).
New Zealand Refer to the embassy (see p.38).
UK First Floor, 170–173 Piccadilly, London W1V 9DD ☏ 020/7766 9300.
USA 821 United Nations Plaza, New York, NY 10017 ☏ 212/687-2194; 2525 Massachusetts Ave NW, Washington, DC 20008 ☏ 202/612-6800.

Turkey on the Internet

We've indicated relevant hotel and tour-company websites throughout the Guide, but the websites listed below provide general background for Turkey. Many of the following are also travel-related, though there are also a few good general, current events and news sites. Most local resort-based sites are poor, with scanty or obsolete information.

Useful websites

General

ⓦ **www.biletix.com** An online booking service for arts, cultural, music and sports events (mainly in İstanbul and Ankara), in both English and Turkish.
ⓦ **www.hitit.co.uk** An excellent "alternative" online guide, readable and generally sound, though weak on anything east of Cappadocia since the authors are based on the Turquoise Coast.
ⓦ **www.mymerhaba.com** Intended for expats/long-term residents, and strongest on İstanbul, but

nonetheless an authoritative and wide-ranging site with lots of goodies (including arcana about the likes of *sahlep*, *boza* and *nargiles*, plus news of upcoming events and ticket-booking functions).
ⓦ **www.tapu.co.uk** Been to Turkey on holiday a dozen times, can't tear yourself away? This site flogs real estate, though most properties are along the Turquoise Coast.
ⓦ **www.trekkinginturkey.com** Valuable information on major trekking areas and long-distance routes, with links to relevant outdoor-activity-type sites.
ⓦ **www.turkeycentral.com** Essentially a portal to a claimed figure of nearly 5000 other sites; most of the links are useful – "diving" gets you a list of dive operators and venues, "skiing" gets an assortment of winter resorts – but some (eg, "maps") promise far more than they deliver.
ⓦ **www.turkeygaytravel.com** Fill in the online form with your criteria and this site will help you find gay-friendly accommodation, particularly in İstanbul. Also a few useful reviews of clubs and discos in the capital.
ⓦ **www.twarp.com** İstanbul-based site that offers regional thumbnail sketches and a very limited accommodation-booking facility.

Antiquities and architecture

ⓦ **www.exploreturkey.com** Excellent background on the country's historical monuments, written by an archeologist, though coverage is strongly biased towards İstanbul, Cappadocia and the southwest coast, and last updated in 2004.
ⓦ **www.patriarchate.org/ecumenical_patriarchate/chapter_4** Literate coverage of İstanbul's numerous Byzantine monuments, though you need broadband speeds to load the lavish illustrations quickly.

Specific destinations

ⓦ **www.chez.com/galata/e_index.html** Covers the Galata and Beyoğlu districts of İstanbul – lots of interesting maps, photos and video clips, with English text.
ⓦ **www.kackarmountains.com** Despite the name, also offers well-written, lavishly photographed coverage of the Lycian Way, St Paul Trail, Aladağlar, Mt Ararat and volcanos of the central plateau, as well as the Pontic Kaçkar range. Maintained by recommended domestic trekking agency Middle Earth, but offers plenty of sensible advice for those who want to set off on their own.
ⓦ **www.kalkan.org.tr** Probably the best resort-specific site, with features on the village and surrounds and a good selection of profiled lodging.

News and views

ⓦ **www.ntv.com.tr/news/ENGLISH_Front .asp** One of the very few domestic websites offering good news coverage in passable English; updated almost daily.

ⓦ **www.turkishembassy.org** The official party line, maintained by the Turkish Embassy in the US; also good for customs and visa rules, etc.

ⓦ **www.turkishdailynews.com** Updated daily, this gives abridged versions of all this English-language paper's print-version stories, both current and archived.

ⓦ **www.turkishnews.com** A site nominally run by Turkish alumni of American universities, but hitting the "Turkish News" links takes you to the utterances of the government's press and information office.

Touring and city maps

Stock up on maps *before* you leave, as Turkish-produced ones are neither detailed nor accurate. That said, very few of those available outside – or inside – the country are remotely reliable, since ordnance-survey-based cartography and/or large-scale coverage is completely absent.

The least bad **touring maps**, more or less accurately showing many smaller villages, are the series of seven folding maps put out by Kartographischer Verlag Reinhard Ryborsch (Frankfurt, Germany), which cover the entire country at a scale of 1:500,000. They are sporadically available in the UK – usually some sheets are "between" printings" – but both original and pirated versions can be found at better bookshops in İstanbul, Ankara and the larger resorts like Bodrum or Kuşadası; the Turkish distributor is Koreks (☏0212/236 4893 or 0312/256 5523). Reasonable second choices, also periodically difficult to obtain, include the Insight *Turkey West* at 1:800,000, which is easy to read and has up-to-date motorway tracings, and Reise Know-How's 1:700 000 *Mediterranean Coast and Cyprus*, which despite the title covers the entire southern and western third of the country with passable accuracy. A third option is Geo-Center/Euromap's *West Turkey* at 1:750,000; its regional offerings at 1:600,000, if they can still be found, are also worth considering. Reasonably reliable 1:250,000 maps of Lycia, Pamphylia and Pisidia (there are four different language versions), produced by Sabri Aydal, are available from decent Turkish bookshops

and local museums. The reverse of each has some useful information about the sites in the area covered by the map.

Tourist offices in İstanbul, Ankara, Antalya, Bursa and İzmir (as well as overseas offices) stock reasonable, free **city street plans**, although the İstanbul one is restricted to the centre and lacks detail. The quality of local sketch plans available at provincial tourist offices varies widely.

There are very few maps of Turkish cities **on sale**, and when available they are rarely good value. Notable exceptions are GeoCenter's easy-to-read 1:7500 EuroCity plan of central İstanbul, plus its exhaustive, ring-bound A–Z atlas (harder to find), including pages at scales of 1:15,000 and 1:7500. The latter is available only in good İstanbul bookshops, alongside the slightly less accurate, locally published Asya A–Z atlas. One or the other is a worthwhile investment if you plan to spend a lot of time in the city. Otherwise, the Canadian-produced ITMB map (1:11,000) has the best street-grid depiction and shows both banks of the Bosphorus, although it's one of the flimsiest products; Hallwag's 1:10,500 offering is the better-jacketed runner-up. Failing these, you're stuck with the Cartographia offering, or the laminated Insight Fleximap (both 1:12,500). Note that only the Asya atlas shows the Asian side of the city in any detail.

Trekking maps

It is virtually impossible to obtain large-scale topographical maps of specific areas for **trekking** (except for the Lycian Way and St Paul Trail; see pp.458 & 608). The only (medium-scale) maps available are 1:250,000 topographic sheets from the Harita Genel Müdürlügü (General Mapping Ministry ☏0312/595 2072) in the Dikmen district of Ankara. You will need to speak reasonable Turkish to get in the door – it's best to have a local get them on your behalf.

Overseas, it is possible to obtain photocopies of a 1:200,000 series prepared with German assistance in 1944, but again with some difficulty: the Turks have security or copyright protocols with other NATO countries, and permission must be obtained from relevant military authorities before copying commences. In Britain you should consult the Map Room at the Royal Geographical Society (1 Kensington

Gore, London SW7 2AR (☎020/7591 3050), which will then refer you to the Directorate of Geographic Information in Surrey for a permit. This may not be granted automatically – you will need to present yourself as a serious researcher or someone organizing an expedition. If you're part of a decently funded expedition, contact Omni Resources in the US (☎910/227-8300, ⓦwww.omnimap.com.); it has copies of large-scale Soviet topographic/geological maps for most areas of the country, but the cost – several thousand dollars for

a full set – is prohibitive for most punters.

Usable enough maps for the most popular trekking areas can be found in *Trekking in Turkey* (Lonely Planet, o/p). The Turkish Tourist Office has discontinued its out-of-date and inaccurate "Mountaineering" brochure. More worryingly, it implied that climbers were free to head off into the Cilo-Sat and other restricted ranges in Turkey's still-tense Kurdish southeast. *The Mountains of Turkey* (Cicerone/Hunter) reproduces this brochure's sketches without correction or elaboration.

Costs, money and banks

Turkey is no longer as cheap as it was, and in the coastal resorts prices now match or even exceed those in Greece, Spain or Portugal. Much of the less visited interior, however, remains very good value for foreign travellers. Domestic inflation, which until recently ran at seventy percent annually, had dropped to single figures by summer 2005. Despite this, given Turkey's historically volatile currency, we've only quoted museum admissions (which must be paid in local currency), domestic transportation costs, hamam entries and meals (usually payable in local currency) in Turkish lira, while all accommodation and special activity prices in the Guide are given in euro (occasionally £ sterling in some British-dominated resort areas). This should give a fairly reliable idea of what you'll be paying on the spot, even if inflation rages once again in the country.

Average costs

In terms of a **daily budget**, a frugal existence relying exclusively on bus travel, food from simple eateries and the cheapest grades of accommodation won't set you back more than £17/€25 a day per person. Incidentally, you won't save much by assembling picnic materials at a grocer's – even the poorest Turks eat out frequently, and you may as well too. If you're entitled to one, a student identity card – FIYTO being more influential than ISIC – will shave a healthy chunk off the cost of selected museum or entertainment tickets, and trains. For any degree of comfort, including rooms with en-suite bath and the occasional splurge on a boat outing or at the bazaar, allow an average daily expenditure of £30/€45. And for £55/€82 a day you

could be staying in four- and five-star hotels – especially east of Ankara – renting a car (as one of a couple) and splurging in fashionable restaurants. As for specifics, **accommodation** costs range from about £4/€6 per person in the most basic dosshouses to £65/€97.50 a head for five-star resort hotels with every mod con; mid-range hotels with decent amenities weigh in somewhere around £12/€18.50 per person in large provincial towns and coastal centres. **Food** also varies widely in price: it's difficult to spend more than £5/€7.50 apiece for a two-course meal with a beer once off the tourist circuit, but easy to get through three times that amount in a resort town. **Transport** is more consistent – bus fares vary between £3/€4.50 and £3.50/€5 per 100km travelled, more local routes with shorter distances are proportionately

44

Tipping

A service charge of ten to fifteen percent is levied at the fancier restaurants, but as this goes directly to the management, the waiters and busboys should be left five percent again if they deserve it. In some places a mandatory tip (*garsoniye*) accompanies the service charge. Round odd taxi fares upwards (you may not have a choice, as the driver may genuinely not have small change); hotel and train-sleeper porters should be tipped appropriately, the latter often presenting you with a chit stating the required amount.

more expensive. The better long-distance trains charge about the same as a good bus company, with small suppléments for sleeping facilities, but still represent excellent value for the extra comfort gained. Domestic air ticket prices are on a par with those in northern Europe.

Currency, cash and travellers' cheques

As a result of hyperinflation, Turkish currency had, until recently, acquired a baffling number of zeroes (a 100,000-lira coin was worth less than five pence, a million-lira note equalled about forty pence). In January 2005, with inflation curbed, the government introduced the **Yeni Türk Lira** (New Turkish Lira), abbreviated as YTL. The zeroes have now gone, but it may take some time before Turks stop talking in millions. **Coins** are in denominations of 5, 10, 25 and 50 kuruş, as well as 1 lira, whilst **notes** come in denominations of 1, 5, 10, 20, 50 and 100 lira.

Rates for foreign currency are always better inside Turkey, so don't bother buying YTL at home before you leave. Conversely, don't leave Turkey with unspent YTL, as you won't get a decent exchange rate for them anywhere outside the country. It's wise to take a fair wad of **hard currency** with you to Turkey (euros are the most widely accepted in the Mediterranean coastal areas, sterling is fine for the UK-dominated resorts, while conservative eastern Turkey still likes the dollar), as you can often use it to pay directly for souvenirs or accommodation (prices for both are frequently quoted in hard currency). Although theft and pickpocketing are on the increase in tourist areas, leaving a money belt in hotel lockers is safe enough under normal circumstances. **Travellers' cheques** are, frankly, not worth the bother: most exchange offices (see below) and banks refuse them, while the post office absolutely no longer accepts them.

All institutions charge a hefty commission on travellers' cheque transactions.

Banks and other exchange services

Unless things change dramatically, the lira's newfound stability means that you can change large amounts of cash at a time without worrying that inflation will erode its value. You should, though, keep all foreign exchange slips with you until departure, if only to prove the value of purchases made in case of queries by customs.

Most state **banks** (the best of these are the Ziraat Bankası and Halk Bankası) are open Monday to Friday, 8.30am to noon and 1.30 to 5pm. Private banks such as Garanti Bankası and Köç operate throughout the day; larger branches of Garanti open on Saturdays from 11am to 3pm. Foreign exchange transactions won't, however, be undertaken after 4.45pm. State banks give a better exchange rate than private banks, though neither charge commission for cash. Queues, especially in state banks, can be long. Most now have an automated queuing system; take a ticket from the machine and wait for your number to appear on the digital display. **Döviz**, or exchange houses, are found all over western Turkey (especially in resorts) and along the Black Sea. They buy and sell foreign currency of most sorts instantly, and have the convenience of long opening hours and short or nonexistent queues. Some, however, charge commission, and the rate given is not as high as in the banks.

Outside normal banking hours, you can also use the special exchange booths run by banks in coastal resorts, airports and ferry docks. The local **post and telephone office** (PTT), particularly in a sizable town, is often able to change foreign currency without commission.

Value added tax

The Turkish variety *(Katma Değer Vergisi* or *KDV),* ranging from eight to 23 percent depending on the commodity, is included in the price of virtually all goods and services (except car rental, where the fifteen-percent figure is usually quoted separately). Look for the notice *Fiyatlarımız KDV Dahildir* (VAT included in our prices) if you think someone's trying to do you for it twice. There is a VAT refund scheme for large souvenir purchases made by those living outside Turkey, but it's such a rigmarole to get that it's probably not worth pursuing; if you insist, ask the shop to provide a *KDV İade Özel Fatura* (Special VAT Refund Invoice), assuming that it participates – very few do, and they tend to be the most expensive shops.

Credit/debit cards and ATMs

A major **credit card** is invaluable for domestic ferry and plane tickets, and also for waiver of a huge cash deposit when renting a car. Credit cards are now widely used in hotels, shops, restaurants and filling stations with no commission (though some hotels offer discounts for cash rather than credit card payments). Swipe readers plus **chip-and-PIN** protocol are now the norm in most of Turkey – if you do not know the PIN for your card, whether debit or credit, you probably won't be able to use it.

The simplest way to get hold of money in Turkey is to use the widespread **ATM** (cashpoint) network, now found even in the smaller towns of the east. Bank ATMs – most reliably those of Garanti Bankası, Yapı Kredi Bankası, İşbank, Akbank, Pamukbank, Halk Bank, Ziraat Bankası, Koçbank, Vakıf Bank, Oyak Bank and HSBC – will accept any debit cards that are part of the Cirrus, Maestro or Plus systems. Screen prompts are given in English on request. The daily ATM withdrawal limit for most cards is about £250/€375 equivalent (or £80–200/€120–300 per transaction), depending on the bank or even individual ATM. You can also normally get cash advances (in YTL only) at any bank displaying the appropriate sign. You can also use Visa or MasterCard to get cash from ATMs, though American Express holders are currently restricted to those of Akbank. All use of a credit card to obtain cash results in a 2.75 percent commission, plus "transaction fee", being levied by your home bank. However, don't rely entirely on plastic, as Turkish ATM networks are prone to crashing (though the "down" periods are seldom long). Avoid "stand-alone" booths found on resort quays, as these may only be serviced once weekly, so if it eats your card (not unknown), too bad. It's safest to use ATMs during normal working hours so help can be summoned if needed. Also, spurious "transaction declined" messages are common; try another bank or try again during off-peak phone hours.

Getting around

Public transport is fairly comprehensive in Turkey, and only on major routes and during public holidays do you need to book tickets in advance. Although the train network is rather skeletal, there's an all-embracing network of buses that spans the country, offering reasonably priced, comfortable and efficient long-distance travel. Shorter distances within towns and cities or between rural villages are covered by the Turkish institution of the dolmuş (shared transport). A domestic ferry and sea-bus network covers İstanbul and the Sea of Marmara. State airline

THY's domestic monopoly has now been broken, and four private companies offer competitively priced domestic flights. All internal flights are routed through either İstanbul or Ankara. Car rental is also an option; rates can be very high, but there are bargains to be had, particularly out of season. Driving yourself is often the only way to reach remote spots, and will enable you to see more of the country during a brief visit. "Travel details" at the end of each chapter rounds up all the relevant routes and schedules.

By train

Turkey's train network is run by **Turkish State Railways** (TCDD; ⓦwww.tcdd.gov.tr/tcddwebenglish/index.html). This English-language website provides full timetable and ticket information.

Turkish trains are best used to span the distances between the three main cities (İstanbul, Ankara and İzmir) and the provincial centres. Turkey's first rail lines were built by the British in the mid-nineteenth century, in part to get the fig harvest to İzmir; later, German companies built the line to Europe used by the Orient Express, as well as the Turkish section of the Berlin-to-Baghdad railway. Limited construction budgets meant that lines were forced to follow tortuous routes around Turkey's many mountain ranges (rather than tunnel through them) and this, coupled with chronic subsequent under-investment, means that Turkish trains may take up to twice as long as buses on the same route. However, they do have the considerable advantage of additional comfort at comparable or lower prices. Short-hop journeys in the Aegean region may be downright frustrating, though longer, inter-city express journeys can be delightful and wonderfully scenic.

Takeaway **timetables** are only sporadically issued – apparently, to make life more difficult for terrorists intent on derailing or attacking locomotives. Sometimes a small printed timetable is available, detailing İstanbul commuter trains and local services, as well as intercity and some international departures, but it does not cover other major routes. Neither is the internationally published Thomas Cook handbook reliable, so in fact the only way to get accurate **information** is to go to the station in person, scan the placards and then confirm departures with staff.

The better **services** west of Ankara, denoted *mavı tren* or *ekspresi*, are reason-ably quick, though still much slower than buses. In the east, however, punctuality and service standards begin to slip. Avoid any departure labelled *yolcu* (local) – they're excruciatingly slow.

On long-haul journeys you may still have a choice between a first- and second-class seat, though this distinction is being slowly phased out in favour of a single standard of service. **First class** features Pullman-style seats and air conditioning/heating according to season; **second-class** wagons have Pullman seating or (in the east) continental-style, six-person compartments with narrow corridors on one side. In second-class carriages, single **women travelling alone** will be looked after by the conductor, which generally means delivery into a family or mixed-gender compartment. **Nonsmoking cars** are always available; ask for an *içmeyen vagon* when booking.

There's almost always a **dining car** on trains west of Ankara – the limited menus aren't so bad or expensive as to require bringing your own food. All long-distance services are supposed to have a licensed *büfe* wagon. In the east check on the availability of food and drink, and bring your own if necessary (though most wayside stations will have snacks of some sort on offer). On major train routes it's essential to make a **reservation** in advance. This can be done anytime between one month and three hours before departure, but the most popular services sell out long in advance, as does just about everything at public holidays. Though the TCDD booking system is theoretically computerized, in practice it may be difficult to book an Ankara–İstanbul journey from İzmir, for example, and almost impossible to arrange sleeper facilities from a station that's not your start-point. **Credit cards** are not yet accepted as payment for train fares.

Fares and passes

Regular **fares** on the better trains cost about the same per kilometre as the buses. Typical prices are 22YTL first-class on the Ankara–İstanbul route, 33YTL for a Pullman seat on the İstanbul–Tatvan route. Buying a return ticket brings the fare down by twenty percent, while foreign **students** with appropriate identification are entitled to a thirty-percent discount on train tickets. InterRail, Eurail and Eurodomino **passes** are valid all over Turkey, though you're unlikely to get full value from any of these trans-European passes. The one-month **TrenTur** card, purchased from major stations in Turkey, is potentially better value at around 100YTL a month for unlimited second-class travel, 400YTL for a sleeping car. There are three different kinds of **sleeping facilities** on Turkish trains. *Küşetli* is a couchette in a six-seat, second-class compartment, where bunks pull down from the wall at night and you share with strangers; you'll pay a supplement of about fifteen percent on the basic ticket price for pillow only, thirty percent for full bedding. *Örtülü küşetli* is a better category with usually only four bunks per compartment, with bedding provided. *Yataklı* first-class suites have one or two (sometimes three) beds with full linen supplied; reckon on paying around 80YTL İstanbul–Denizli (for Pamukkale), for a single bed in such a compartment, 50YTL each for two sharing. From İstanbul to Van, at least double the distance, a one-bed compartment is 69YTL, 58YTL each for two sharing. This discrepancy reflects the fact that some lines have been fitted with new carriages. Given that this will barely amount to three times the supplement for *küşetli*, you may as well coddle yourself.

By long-distance bus

An immensely popular form of transport, the Turkish **long-distance bus** is a crucial part of the country's modern culture. There is no single, national bus company in Turkey and most routes are covered by several firms, which usually have ticket booths both at the **otogars** (bus terminals) and in the city centre. If you buy your ticket at a sales office (*yazıhane*) in the centre you should ask about free service buses to the *otogar*, especially

if (as most now are) it's located a few miles out. Most companies provide small minibuses even for a single passenger; the question to ask is *servis araba var mı?* These buses will often also take passengers from *otogars* into town centres, but this is a more erratic system – the transfer cannot be guaranteed within the long-distance ticket price and may be charged extra.

There's no such thing as a comprehensive national bus **timetable**, although individual companies often provide their own. **Prices** vary considerably between top- and bottom-drawer companies, though convenience of departure and onboard service are equally important criteria. If in doubt, inspect the vehicle out in the loading bay (*peron* in Turkish) and ask at the ticket office how long the trip will take. It's worth bearing in mind that long-haul journeys (over 10hr) generally take place at night, and that because of rest stops buses never cover more than 60km an hour on average, no matter what you're told. As a broad example of fares, İstanbul–Antalya costs around 40YTL with a standard bus company, 70YTL with a premium company like Ulusoy (see below). Antalya–Göreme is around 40YTL, İzmir–Antalya 25YTL. *Otogars*, especially in touristed areas, are full of **touts** waiting to escort you to their company's window once you state your destination – though it may not have the most convenient departure, nor the best service and seats.

When buying tickets, ask to see the **seating plan**: if you crave fresh air, request front-row seats behind the driver, whose window may be the only open ventilation on the coach. **Nonsmoking** is now the rule on long-haul coaches, though this can't be implicitly assumed on the dilapidated coaches running to remote rural areas; most Turks hate open windows or vents, with the latter often welded shut on the more down-at-heel Turkish buses. Seats over the wheels (usually numbers 5–8 and 33–36 on the standard Mercedes O302 model) have cramped legroom and take the worst of the road bumps. Unacquainted women and men are not allowed to sit next to each other, and you may be asked to switch your assigned seat to accommodate this convention. To avoid the disadvantages of Turkish bus travel, make use of the country's two **premium coach companies**: Ulusoy and Varan. Their seats are more comfortable than most, with nonsmoking strictly enforced, and they don't segregate single passengers by sex. Kamil Koç and Pamukkale, while not quite as enlightened, are two of the best standard outfits, in that order of preference. There have been some horrific accidents on buses – directly related to the practice of paying drivers a low base salary, plus a top-up fee for every trip done. Thus the temptation is to drive beyond the fatigue barrier, and it's of course the better companies who are likely to pay more for relief drivers. Be warned that most buses play music – either electronic Turkish pop or a Western equivalent – until the lights go out. Some buses also show films (strictly in Turkish), an additional nuisance/diversion depending on your mood. Partial compensation for this is the attention of the **muavin**, or driver's assistant, who can supply drinking water on demand, and will appear several times in a journey with aromatic cologne for freshening up. Every ninety minutes there will be a fifteen-minute **rest stop** (*mola*) for tea and toilet visits, and there are less frequent half-hour pauses for meals at purpose-built roadside cafeterias. Many of the better companies supply free coffee/tea/ soft drinks as well as cling-wrapped cakes.

By backpacker bus

An alternative to the standard long-distance bus is the backpacker-oriented **Fez Bus**, which operates a seasonal pass scheme connecting the most popular spots in the western half of the country: the Turquoise Coast, Antalya, Side, Cappadocia, Pamukkale, Ephesus, Bergama and Gallipoli. The passes are valid for an entire tourist season (departures every two days; late April to early November) and are used on a hop-on, hop-off basis, though you must re-book onward seats 48 hours in advance to guarantee a seat. Further advantages are door-to-door service to designated budget accommodation, nonsmoking vehicles, and the services of an English-speaking steward/tour guide. The obvious disadvantage is that this is a guaranteed way of getting stuck in assorted overlanders' ghettos, and being kept pretty insulated from the host country.

There are four passes/routes available. The most extensive (€189) begins and ends in İstanbul (though you can start or finish anywhere on the circuit), taking in Gallipoli, Troy, Ephesus, Pamukkale, Marmaris, Fethiye, Kaş, Olympos, Antalya and Cappadocia. The other three passes are shorter, cheaper adaptations of the same circuit. There's a small discount for students plus assorted possible add-ons (eg, a *gület* cruise or Gallipoli battlefield tour). It's a moderately stiff price tag for what's usually a three-to-four-week itinerary, but the issuers claim the passes are transferable in the presence of a Fez rep, so you could sell unused months on.

Fez Bus agents

Fez Travel Akbıyık Cad 15, Sultanahmet, İstanbul ☎212 /516 9024, ⊛www.fezbus.com.
Interest and Activities Holidays Hartfield House, 173 Hartfield Rd, London SW19 3TH ☎020/8251 0208. Sole UK agent for Fez Bus.

By dolmuş

The Turkish institution of the **dolmuş** or shared transport, could profitably be imitated in the West: it's practical, economical and ecologically sound. The idea is that a vehicle – a car or small van (*minibüs* in Turkish) – runs along set routes, picking passengers up and dropping them off along the way. You will be expected to switch seats so that women do not sit next to strange males, though in the bigger cities and tourist areas this convention is rapidly dying out. To stop a dolmuş, give a hand signal as for a normal taxi and if there's any room at all (the word *dolmuş* means "stuffed"), they'll stop and let you on. To get out, say *inecek var* (literally, "there's a getting out") or *müsait bir yerde* ("at a convenient place"). Eight-seater diesel transit vans with windows serve as dolmuşes in most cities, particularly İzmir, but in Trabzon the dolmuşes are ordinary-taxi lookalikes. In İstanbul, the classic American 1950s cars, which long had the monopoly on most routes, have now been banned except for use as "special tourist taxis" and wedding limos.

On busy **urban routes** it's better to take the dolmuş from the start of its run, at a stand marked by a blue sign with a black-on-white-field "D", sometimes with the destination indicated – though usually you'll have to ask to learn the eventual destination, or look at the dolmuş' windscreen placard. On less popular routes the driver will often depart before the vehicle is full, making it easier to hail in mid-route. The **fare** is invariably a flat rate (usually 1YTL) making it very good value for cross-city journeys, not so great for a one-stop hop.

Intertown and village services are always provided by twelve- to fifteen-seater minibuses, and in these instances the term "dolmuş" is seldom used. For the remotest villages there will only be two services a day: to the nearest large town in the morning and back to the village in mid-afternoon. Generally, though, minibuses run constantly between 7 or 8am and 7pm in summer, stopping at sunset in winter or extending until 10 or 11pm (or even later) near popular resorts. **Fares** are low, hardly more than urban bus prices and about the same as coaches between towns, but it's always difficult to know how much to pay if you're only going part of the way. However, everybody else on board will know; just state your destination and hand over a roughly appropriate stack of coins or notes (not too large in denomination), and you'll invariably get the right change. If you sit near the front, you'll have to relay other people's fares and repeat their destinations to the driver – no mean feat if you don't speak the language.

By city bus and taxi

In larger towns the main means of transport are the two-tone **city buses**, which take pre-purchased tickets available from kiosks near the main terminals, newsagents, or from kerbside touts (at slightly inflated prices). The only exceptions are **private buses** in İstanbul, which look the same as those run by the *Belediye* (city hall) and whose drivers issue tickets in exchange for cash. Yellow city **taxis** are everywhere, with ranks at appropriate places, though in rush hour finding a free cab can be difficult. Hailing one in the street is the best way to get a cab, but in suburban areas there are useful street-corner telephones from which you can call (if you can make yourself understood). Urban vehicles all have working, digital-dis-

play meters and **fares** are among the lowest in the Mediterranean. Each town sets its own taxi rates, which includes the minimum charge and a unit charge for the distance covered. İstanbul, Ankara and most provincial cities are considerably cheaper than taxis operating in coastal resort areas. Between midnight and 6am the tariff is raised by fifty percent. In cities, it's illegal to ask for a flat fare, though attempted rip-offs of foreigners aren't unheard of. Out in the country, you'll have to bargain.

Hitchhiking

As in most other countries these days, **we do not recommend hitching in Turkey** as a safe method of getting around. However, you may be forced to exercise this option where public transport is scarce or nonexistent, and lifts tend to be frequent and friendly – you may be expected to share tea with the driver on reaching your destination. Rural Turks hitch too – if you see a group at the roadside waving you down in your own car, it's a good bet that no bus or dolmuş is forthcoming anytime soon, and you'd be performing a useful service by giving them a lift.

On routes that are well served by buses or minibuses, the general consensus among Turks is that there's little point in hitching since public transport is so cheap, and they will be less inclined to view hitchhikers favourably. You do sometimes see Turkish women – older, conservatively dressed villagers – hitching near the Aegean coast. However, you also see prostitutes soliciting truck drivers along the main highways, and on balance it's not a good idea for foreign women to hitch alone, especially in the east of the country. With male company, it need be fraught with no more peril, and possibly less, than elsewhere around the Mediterranean.

By car

Given the excellent bus services, you don't need to drive in Turkey to get between the major centres, but having a car does add some flexibility to your travels. However, you really need to be an experienced, level-headed driver in order to tackle the challenging highway conditions. You could bring your own car, though this creates administrative hurdles; many people choose to rent instead, though you'll find rates on a par with most of Europe.

Road regulations

You **drive on the right**, and yield to those approaching from the right, even on the numerous roundabouts. **Speed limits**, seldom observed, are 50km/hr within towns and 40km/hr if towing a trailer or caravan; while on the open road, limits are 90km/hr for saloon cars, 80km/hr for vans, 70km/hr if you're towing something; and on motorways (*otoyol* in Turkish), 120km/hr for saloon cars, 100km/hr for vans and small trucks. Turkey has the second highest European **accident rate** (after Portugal), and it's easy to see why: Turkish drivers are in the main an impatient bunch who lean on the horn and tailgate brazenly if they feel the traffic isn't moving fast enough. **Drink-driving laws** are in line with those of the European Union – 50mg of alcohol per 100ml of blood (roughly equal to one hard drink or two glasses of wine) is the upper limit for private drivers.

Traffic control points at the approaches to major cities are frequent, and although the police manning them are mostly interested in overweight trucks and expired insurance/registration certificates, they may halt foreigners. They can be rude and unnerving, and if things get sticky you should pretend total ignorance of Turkish, whatever your linguistic abilities. However, you might well be waved through simply upon showing your foreign ID. If it's your own vehicle, it may be inspected for real or imagined equipment defects (especially lights), though you'll probably be sent to the nearest repair shop rather than cited. If you've rented a car, make sure the rental company provides the insurance certificate, the pollution compliance certificate (*eksoz muayene tasdiknamesi*) and the vehicle registration, or certified copies thereof.

Despite the deficiencies of many Turkish drivers, don't expect to get away with blatant **driving offences** without being noticed. Radar stake-outs are predictably located, usually at the edge of busy resorts or towns. Major violations, such as jumping red lights, speeding or turning illegally,

carry fines of up to 90YTL; you'll be given a ticket, which you then take to a designated bank to pay, or fined on the spot. Do heed the signposted **no-parking zones**, especially in resorts. Local police are very industrious with tow trucks, though you usually get advance warning in the form of slowly cruising patrol cars yelling out the plate numbers of offenders over their loudspeakers. Fines of about 30YTL (50YTL if you've been towed) are not outrageous by European standards, but you will waste considerable time hunting down the pound where your vehicle has been taken, not to mention overcoming the language barrier with staff. Generally, it's wisest to patronize the covered (*katlı*) or open *otoparks*. In open parking lots you may well be required to leave your keys so the attendant can move your car. Charges vary considerably according to the city and situation of the *otopark*. If you park on the street, you may return to find a chit on your windscreen (typically 3–4YTL for up to half a day in coastal resorts) and a roving attendant will nail you for the amount before you drive off.

Road conditions

Ordinary **main roads** are usually adequately paved, but often dangerously narrow. This is not so much of a problem in the relatively uncrowded east, but it makes driving quite hair-raising in the west. The most popular archeological sites and other points of interest are admirably marked by large **white-print-on-brown-field signs**; however, side roads to minor sites or villages are often poorly signposted and inaccurately shown on maps. Moreover, roads optimistically shown on maps may be unfinished or submerged under one of the many new reservoirs.

Toll highways, marked with white-on-green signs, are springing up and, especially for novice foreign drivers, are well worth the modest tolls (2–5YTL) to use. Main ones finished at the moment include İstanbul–Ankara, bypassing the hilly, curvy nightmare between Gerede and Adapazarı and missing only one section of tunnel; İstanbul–Edirne; Adana–Gaziantep; Adana–Pozantı through the Cilician Gates; İzmir–Çeşme; and İzmir–Denizli, cutting through the mountains

Road signs

Dur	Stop
Tek yön	One way
Çıkmaz sokak	Dead end/cul-de-sac
Yol kapalı	Road closed
Yol boyunca	Road narrows
Tırmanma şeridi	Overtaking lane
Araç çıkabilir	Vehicles exiting
Yaya geçidi	Pedestrian crossing
Yol yapımı	Roadworks
Bozuk satıh	Rough surface
Düşük banket	Abrupt verge/shoulder
Şehir merkezi	City centre
Park yapılmaz/edilmez	No parking
Araç giremez	No entry
Aracınız çekilir	Your car will be towed
Giremez	No entry
Askeri bölge	Military zone
Heyelan bölgesi, heyelanlı bölge	Landslide zone

to skirt the horrific E-24 between Selçuk and Denizli. Typical **hazards** include the local flair for overtaking right, left and centre, preferably on a curve; failure to signal turns; and huge trucks (the ubiquitous TIRs) either ambling along at walking pace or whizzing past at kamikaze speeds. Additionally, small-town driving features all the following: trotting horsecarts, pedal bicyclists in the fast lane (with no lights), blithely reversing tractors, pedestrians or livestock strolling heedlessly out in front of you, and buses and minibuses halting without warning to take on passengers invisible to you. The commonest **minor mishaps** involve smashed windscreens, for which passing lorries churning up barrages of gravel are the main culprit, and shredded tyres. If you rip a tyre (not difficult to do on the many rocky tracks), go to a *lastıkçı* (tyre workshop). In many cases the damage can be skilfully repaired; otherwise a new tyre for a compact A- or B-group car runs to about 65YTL, a slightly used but acceptably treaded specimen around half that amount. Always check that the spare tyre and tool kit are sound and complete before leaving the rental agency. Turks wrestle ordinary saloon cars up and down some appalling **dirt roads**, and so do most foreigners, especially with rental cars (one reason the price of car rental is fairly steep). Do not assume that because a minibus gets through that your 2WD model

automatically can as well – Turkish minibuses typically have twice the ground clearance and twice the engine displacement that you do.

Night driving is best not attempted by beginners – be prepared for unlit vehicles (especially, in rural areas, tractors), flocks of sheep or goats (distinguished by massed green-eye shine) and an extra quota of lumbering trucks, not to mention intercity coaches. If you're forced to drive after dark in isolated areas, it's not a bad idea to open windows enough to smell invisible goat flocks and tractor exhaust wafted from in front of you! Oncoming cars will typically flash their lights at you whether or not your high beams are on – contrary to British or North American convention, this actually means "Don't even think of overtaking, *I'm* coming through". **Safety equipment**, such as flares or warning triangles, are little used (though triangles are obligatory and rental cars should have them), and usually the first hint you'll have of a breakdown or wreck ahead, night or day, are either piles or lines of stones on the asphalt.

Fuel and repairs

Filling stations are ubiquitous throughout most of the country and open long hours, so it's pretty difficult to run out of fuel. Fuel costs are very high because of government taxes and even diesel (*mazot or dizel*) is 2YTL per litre. Petrol (*benzin*), available in four-star (*süper*) and lead-free (*kurşunsuz*) grades, goes for around 2.7YTL per litre. Car rental firms generally prefer you to use unleaded, but in some remote eastern areas it may be difficult to find. LPG (*gaz*) is the cheapest fuel, at 1.4YTL per litre, but only the odd rental outfit has cars with this option.

In western Turkey, roadside **rest-stop culture** conforming to Italian or French notions has arrived in a big way. You can eat, pray, patch a tyre, phone home, shop at mini-marts and, sometimes, even sleep at what amount to small hamlets (essentially the descendants of the medieval *kervansarays*) in the middle of nowhere. In the east, except around Gaziantep and Urfa, you'll find more basic amenities.

Credit and debit cards (Visa Electron, Visa and MasterCard but also American Express) are widely honoured for fuel purchases in much of Turkey, but you'll find this facility less often southeast of a line connecting Gaziantep, Elazığ and Rize, especially in cases where the phone link to the bank (to get transaction approval) fails – in which case you're out of luck. Signs prominently advertise *Kredi Kart Komisyonu Sıfır* or *0%* (no commission on credit cards), since the amount is charged virtually immediately to your account via the same sort of online apparatus prevalent in Europe and North America. If the filling station doesn't have such a notice, it's best to take your business elsewhere if you have a choice. As with most card transactions in Turkey, chip-and-PIN protocol is the norm. Car **repair workshops** and spare-part dealers are located in industrial zones called *sanayis* at town outskirts. Fiat, Renault, Ford, Skoda, Mercedes and Fargo are the most common brands catered for, usually instantly, though Turkish mechanics will attempt to fix anything and are getting progressively more used to repairing exotic foreign models, especially Peugeot, Hyundai and Toyota, all manufactured in Turkey. It's easy and cheap to get parts for most big-name brands, though you may have problems outside the largest towns for less-common models, such as Citroen or Rover. If possible, seek out a factory-authorized workshop in a large town; if

not in stock, parts can be ordered on a day's notice, while labour charges are very cheap by foreign standards – a third to a half of the cost in northern Europe or North America.

Car rental

To rent a car you need to be at least 21 (27 for Groups E and above), with a **driving licence** held for at least one year. An **International Driving Permit**, from the RAC or AA in Britain/Australasia or the AAA/CAA in North America, is not essential – your own home licence will do at a pinch – but is very helpful, especially at traffic-control points (show the cops your IDP, not your main home licence, in case they decide to keep it for any reason). **Rental rates** can be exorbitant, usually at least as much as in the UK. The minimum over-the-counter rates of the largest international chains start at 105YTL/€63 a day in summer, all-inclusive; Turkish chains may charge fifteen to twenty percent less, and often you'll find a one-off outlet that's willing to let a Group A car go for as little as 40YTL/€24 per day outside of peak season. Weekly rates can bring considerable savings, and it is well worth hunting around for a good deal if you want a car for three days or longer. There is some **regional variation**: south-coast locations (Antalya, Fethiye) are noticeably cheaper than west-coast resorts (Kuşadası, İzmir), and either is far less expensive than relatively untouristed towns such as Erzurum or Van, where monopoly situations prevail, or İstanbul, where overheads are high. Especially if you rent from Hertz, Avis, Budget, Sixt, Europcar or Thrifty (branded as Decar in Turkey), you'll have to exploit every discount scheme available to bring the price down: Frequent Flyer membership programme partner-codes, THY boarding passes presented at airport agency desks and discount vouchers obtained at home before departure are all effective bargaining chips. You'll also need to flash a **credit card** to cover the estimated rental total.

Rental companies will usually allow you to rent in one town and drop off in another, provided they have an office in your destination, though you may have to pay a hefty **drop-off charge** – which will also be levied if you are renting from an airport or town where the company concerned does not maintain a permanent office. **Unlimited kilometrage** is invariably a better deal than any time-plus-distance rate. Basic **insurance** is usually included, but CDW (Collision Damage Waiver) is not, and given typical driving conditions taking this out is virtually mandatory. Along with KDV (Value Added Tax), all these extras can push up the final total considerably. If you intend renting a vehicle for a longish period, or rent cars abroad regularly, it is well worth taking out an **annual CDW excess policy** (around £50/US$80 per annum) through UK-based Insurance 4 Car Hire (℡0044 207 012 6300, ⓦwww.insurance4carhire.com) – should you smash a rental car, this will pay the deductible for you (typically €400–600). If you can commit to a rental period of one to four weeks, you should **pre-book**, either as part of a fly-drive scheme with a tour operator, or with a major **car rental agency** (see below). Promotional deals come and go, so call as many agencies as possible and ask for a complete itemization of charges. Reserving from North America, count on a minimum of US$280 per week, all-inclusive; the most advantageous UK rates (£175–200 weekly, all-inclusive, according to season) are available through Transhire/Skycars. Otherwise, you're best off dealing in person with small Turkish companies, especially off-season. Beware of the booking request functions on the websites of the major chains such as Avis or Hertz, which do exactly that – make requests only. All too often in peak season, the booking, although initially accepted, will come back after several days marked "denied, car category unavailable". Particularly if you have an esoteric rental need, get cracking on it weeks, if not months, in advance. Have companies fax or email you a formal confirmation form, with a reference code, to make it more difficult for staff to deny all knowledge of your booking upon arrival. Very few outlets rent out Group A cars any more. If you manage to find one, you'll most likely be furnished with a Toros Renault 12. Although uncomfortable for long distances, this is the workhorse of rural Turkey and is excellent for unsurfaced village and mountain roads – plus it is well known by every mechanic in the nation, and spares are ubiquitous. If you've

pre-booked from overseas with a chain, you may be given the Şahin (equivalent to a Fiat 131) or (better) a Ford Fiesta or Fiat Palio, the latter with a useful fifty-litre fuel tank. Slightly more expensive Group C cars include the reliable Renault Clio and spacious Fiat Abea. The domestically produced Toyota Corolla four-door or the Hyundai Accent four-door are also well worth the extra outlay as Group B/C cars, when available. The more powerful Ford Focus (G group) stocked by many outlets provides greater comfort and overtaking power. If you want a **4WD** to bash along the rough roads of eastern Anatolia, the only model usually offered is the Suzuki Vitara jeep (typically Group E), and these go quickly in season.

When checking a car out, agency staff should make a thorough diagrammatic notation of any **blemishes** on the vehicle – it's in your interest to make sure they do this. If you have an accident serious enough to immobilize you and/or cause major damage to other people's property, the traffic police will appear and administer alcohol tests to all drivers, results of which must also be submitted along with an official **accident report** (*kaza raporu*) in order to claim insurance cover. It's an offence to move a vehicle involved in a car crash before the police give the all-clear – leave it where it is, even if you're blocking traffic, otherwise all drivers involved risk a 50YTL spot fine for "leaving the scene of an accident". For **minor scratches or dents** – especially if you're at fault – it's far less of a palaver to go to the nearest *sanayi* and have them repaired for a few lira. Rental insurance never covers smashed windscreens or ripped tyres; it's up to you to fix these as cheaply as possible.

Car rental agencies

Avis Australia ℡13 63 33, Canada ℡1-800/272-5871, Republic of Ireland ℡01/605 7500, New Zealand ℡09/526 2847 or 0800 655 111, UK ℡0870/606 0100, US ℡1-800/331-1084; ⓦwww.avis.com.
Budget Australia ℡1300/362 848, Republic of Ireland ℡01/9032 7711, New Zealand ℡0800/652 227 or 09/976 2222, UK ℡0800/181 181, US ℡1-800/527-0700; ⓦwww.drivebudget.com.
Cosmo Thrifty Northern Ireland ℡028/9445 2565, ⓦwww.thrifty.co.uk.
Dollar Australia ℡02/9223 1444 or 1800/358

008, US ☎1-800/800-6000; ⓦwww.dollar.com.
Europcar Republic of Ireland ☎01/614 2800, UK
☎0845/722 2525; ⓦwww.europcar.com.
Hertz Australia ☎13 30 39, Canada ☎1-800/263-
0600, Republic of Ireland ☎01/813 3416, New
Zealand ☎0800/654 321, UK ☎08708/44 88 44,
US ☎1-800/654-3001; ⓦwww.hertz.com.
National Australia ☎13 10 45, New Zealand
☎0800/800 115 or 03/366 5574, UK ☎08705/365
365, US ☎1-800/227-7368; ⓦwww.nationalcar
.com.
Sixt Republic of Ireland ☎1850/206 088, UK no
general phone number, consult website; ⓦwww
.e-sixt.com.
Thrifty Australia ☎1300/367 227, New Zealand
☎09/309 0111, UK ☎01494/751 600, US ☎1-
800/367-2277; ⓦwww.thrifty.com.
Transhire/Sycars UK ☎0870/789 8000,
ⓦwww.transhire.com

Bringing your own car

Arriving at the frontier in your own car, you'll
be asked for the following **documentation**:
an International Driving Permit or home
licence, registration papers or logbook (originals or certified copy), and a Green Card or
other proof of internationally valid third-party
insurance. You'll be issued with a Turkish
temporary registration (*araba tezkeresi*), separate from the passport stamp, valid for six
months and to be mandatorily surrendered
at your point of exit.

Your car will be **registered in your passport** for a maximum stay of 180 days, and
must leave the country when you do. (If you
have to return home by plane for an emergency, the vehicle can be stored in a customs lock-up for a daily charge. This is best
avoided, as the bureaucracy is nightmarish
and corruption endemic.) Since tourist visas
are typically only for three months, border
officials may only grant ninety days unless
you can offer a convincing reason why you're
staying longer, and explain that you intend
to get your visa renewed with the Security
Division (*Emniyet Müdürlüğlü*). If you leave
Turkey briefly and then return in the vehicle,
you'll get a shorter allowance the second
time around – only six months of tourist use
in any twelve-month period is permitted. A
vehicle can only be used on foreign plates
for six months; after this time they must be
changed to Turkish plates. This procedure

is only available to those legally employed in
Turkey and involves a police inspection, an
expensive bank guarantee and a fat sheaf of
forms. In general, if you plan to spend more
than six months in the country, leave your
car at home and lease or buy one in Turkey.
Similarly, you should also apply for a Turkish
driving licence after six months; the police
don't seem to care, but if you have a crash
you'll find that your insurance is invalid.

If your car is written off while in Turkey,
the remains must be transported to a customs compound, and the full-page stamp
in your passport cancelled. Similarly, if it's
stolen, you'll have to get a report from the
Vilayet (Provincial Authority) to get rid of the
passport endorsement. Bring a fluent Turk-
ish-speaker along, as none of the officialdom
concerned are likely to speak English.

The British Green Card **insurance** system is
still required in Turkey until or unless it becomes
a full member of the EU. With either the AA or
RAC, a thirty-day Green Card is provided free
to members, but for longer stays there is an
additional charge. You must keep the receipt
of such payments for display to Turkish officials; it may be requested at the frontier, and
your Green Card will not be considered valid
beyond the initial month without it.

British motoring associations provide comprehensive cover, including breakdown and
recovery service, legal aid and car replacement. In Turkey they occasionally work in
conjunction with the **Turkish Touring and
Automobile Association** (TTOK; Büyükdere
Cad, Oto Sanayi Sitesi Yanı, Seyrantepe,
Dördüncü Levent, İstanbul ☎0212/282
8140), which can advise on Turkish insurance and related matters. You will always
have to pay to be towed, and you'll also
pay for its breakdown service unless you've
equipped yourself with an insurance policy
prior to arrival. North Americans will have to
pay on the spot in any case since the AAA
has no reciprocal agreement with the TTOK.
The 24-hour TTOK nationwide **emergency
breakdown number** is ☎0212/280 4449;
there are unfortunately no toll-free services
or numbers for each province. If an English
speaker is unavailable, you'll have to find
someone to translate for you, or contact
the main İstanbul headquarters during office
hours.

By bicycle and motorbike

Touring Turkey by **bicycle** is perfectly possible for experienced cyclists, so long as you avoid the hottest months and the busiest roads. Flying in with a bike in your luggage is no more complicated than it is to any other destination, and sometimes it's not even charged as excess baggage.

You do, however, have to be prepared for the lack of maintenance facilities, and your own novelty value. The only pushbikes rural Turks are used to seeing are old clunkers used strictly for sedate pedalling around town. A homegrown mountain-bike industry has emerged in most of the major cities, but you should bring **spares** of everything small or light and not count on the admittedly ingenious local mechanics to improvise parts. Because you'll probably opt for back roads, where few foreigners pass by, you'll draw crowds at any rest stop. Accept the inevitable and reckon that bike and bags are usually more, rather than less, secure guarded in this manner while you go to have a tea.

The main **dangers** to you and your bike will be potholed pavements and the elements – and bicycle theft is rife in the western cities of Turkey. Most back-road drivers are surprisingly courteous, perhaps because they're so stunned at the sight of you, though be prepared for some gratuitous horn-honking. You can skirt many potential trouble-spots or skip boring stretches by judicious use of the ferry and train network, on which you can usually transport your machine for free. With a bit of forethought and common sense, it's even possible and enjoyable to pedal through İstanbul (though you're not allowed to cycle across the Bosphorus bridges). Choose routes so as to avoid traffic; after 10am on a normal workday you should be fine, though avoid going up the Bosphorus coast roads in rush hour or at weekends. **Rental facilities** are as yet few and far between in Turkey; the few outlets we know about are mentioned in the text.

Much the same advice applies to riding around Turkey on a **motorbike**, though these are not transported free on the ferries, but charged at their own special rates. In larger resorts and big cities there will be at least one motorbike **rental agency**, or a car

rental company which also rents out motor-scooters and mopeds (*mobilet*). You'll need an appropriate driving licence, and most companies insist that it has been held for at least a year. Before renting any kind of bike, make sure it's physically capable of coping with the terrain you want to use it for.

By ferry

With the effective demise of the state-owned Turkish Maritime Lines, Turkey's internal ferry network is now more or less confined to İstanbul and the Sea of Marmara. İstanbul Deniz Ötobüsleri (🌐www.ido.com.tr) operates both ferries and (the faster and more expensive) sea buses along the Bosphorus, between European and Asian sides of the same strait, and to the Princess Islands. Longer runs across the Sea of Marmara to Yalova, Bandırma, Mudanya and the Marmara islands (Chapter 2) are the preserve of sea buses. Any of the trans-Marmara car-ferry links, specifically to Armutlu or the islands, saves time compared to the dreary, circuitous road journey, but are relatively expensive with a vehicle.

Private companies offer services from Taşucu, Mersin and Alanya to Girne in **Northern Cyprus**, and a state-owned ferry still plies between Mersin and Famagusta. Details of these are given in the relevant town accounts.

By plane

Türk Hava Yolları (THY; ☎0212/225 0566, 🌐www.thy.com), the state-run airline that's now semi-privatized, still offers the most comprehensive domestic flight network. However, it now faces stiff competition from private airlines. Most reliable of these are Onur Air (☎0212/663 2300, 🌐www.onurair.com.tr) and Atlasjet (☎0216/444 0387, 🌐www.atlasjet.com), with Pegasus (🌐www.pgsfly.com) and Fly Air (☎0212/424 3737) newer additions to the internal flight scene. There are regular services between İstanbul, Ankara and İzmir, and from İstanbul to most other major Turkish centres (and quite a few minor ones). Most journeys to the east (except to Adana, and certain Diyarbakır, Gaziantep, Van and Malatya flights) involve a connection in Ankara, with frequently long layovers there – try to avoid stopping flights when booking. Onur Air offers direct flights from İstanbul to Adana, Antalya, Diyarbakır, Erzerum, Gaziantep, İzmir, Kayseri, Kars, Malatya, Samsun and Trabzon. Atlasjet covers the same destinations plus Nevşehir, Sivas and Van. Fly Air operates between İstanbul and Adana, Antalya, İzmir and Trabzon, whilst Pegasus covers Adana, Ankara, Antalya, Trabzon and Van. Fares with THY can be reasonable – for example, the one-way fare from Sabiha Gökçen, İstanbul to Antalya (tax inclusive) starts at 80YTL, but İstanbul–Dalaman is a less reasonable 149YTL, though THY does offer variable student, youth and family discounts.

Fares with Atlas, Onur, Pegasus and Fly Air start, in general, from 55YTL one way and are very good value if you are flying to

or from İstanbul. If you are flying from other start points, you will find that THY flights through the hub airports of İstanbul or Ankara are better coordinated, reducing stopover times. Regardless of what you may be told, appearing at the airport an hour before your scheduled flight departure is adequate leeway for completing the strict security procedures. You may be required to identify your luggage from amongst a pile of bags on the runway before getting on; this is a measure to prevent terrorists from checking in a bomb and then not boarding, so if you don't point out your bag it won't be loaded on, and may be destroyed. All flights, domestic and international, as well as most of Atatürk airport in İstanbul, are **nonsmoking**.

Accommodation

Finding a bed for the night is generally no problem in Turkey, except in high season at the busier coastal resorts and larger towns. Lists of category-rated hotels, motels and the better *pansiyons* (pensions) are published by local tourist offices, and we've listed the best options throughout the Guide. Prices, while cheap by most Western European standards, are no longer rock-bottom, and can be downright exorbitant in İstanbul. To some extent facilities have improved correspondingly, though not surprisingly you often get less for your money in the big tourist resorts, and little choice between fleapits or four-star luxury in relatively untouristed towns of the interior. However, with the Turkish economy as it is, backpackers can often afford to go mid-range, and those on mid-range budgets can sometimes secure rooms at the best hotels available east of Cappadocia, so there's absolutely no reason to slum it in the mistaken belief that you're seeing the "authentic" Turkey.

If you take your chances with a **tout** rather than our recommendations, note that certain outfits, particularly in İstanbul, Kuşadası, Selçuk, Antalya, Kaş and Cappadocia, have generated serious complaints from ex-clients, ranging from dangerous plumbing to extortion and false imprisonment. If, on the other hand, you like where you have stayed, you may very well find that your accommodation proprietor keeps business cards on hand for similar establishments in other

towns; often they have visited each other, or have some idea of what's on offer. This informal network can work very well indeed, with proprietors making a simple phone call to arrange both a stay and a transfer from the *otogar* for you.

Rooms are, almost without exception, on the small side by European standards, with rarely enough power points, or places to sit down other than the bed itself, and dim lighting (or occasionally dazzling fluorescent

Accommodation price codes

In this book, hotels, motels and *pansiyons* have been categorized according to the price codes outlined below. The short description appended to each code should give a rough idea of what you'll get for your money.

Category price ranges are given in euros and YTL, though you'll usually be quoted in the former, particularly with places in categories ⑥ and up. These price ranges represent the minimum you can expect to pay for a **double room in high season**. For backpackers' hostels, trekkers' lodges and coastal "treehouses", where guests are charged per person, euro rates, rather than a numerical code, are given in the Guide. By law, prices for rooms at any establishment must be displayed at the reception desk. Most places in band ❷ and above will have **en-suite bathroom facilities** of some kind. For band ❸ and up **breakfast** (see p.63) will be automatically included, while below that taking it is negotiable. At slack times, it's worth **bargaining**. Lone travellers, for example, may be able to upgrade to a double room for the price of a single. The walk-in price of establishments in bands ⑤–⑥ is invariably much higher than if the room is booked as part of a package. If you want to stay in this level of accommodation for a week or more it is worth making your reservation through an agency before arriving in Turkey. Some hotels offer discounts for cash and Internet bookings.

❶ **up to €13/21.5YTL** Budget hotels in untouristed areas without en-suite facilities; also, so-called "treehouse" accommodation along the southwestern coast, and trekkers' lodges in the Kaçkar mountains.

❷ **€14–24/23–40YTL** The few surviving 1970s-vintage *pansiyons* – some with sink or shower cubicles added at a later date – plus more recent purpose-built *pansiyons*. The latter often have balconies, bedside furniture and sometimes other individual touches, as well as en-suite baths, toilets, linen and towels.

Slightly more salubrious hotels in the interior, though these may not have full attached bathrooms.

❸ **€25–31/41–51YTL** Establishments in touristed areas that straddle the border between a *pansiyon* and a one-star hotel, often with roof terraces for breakfast, and perhaps a bar and small swimming pool; occasionally handled by package-tour operators. Relatively hygienic hotels in the interior, with fully equipped bathrooms, room phones and TV. Hot water more reliable than in lower categories, but still not guaranteed.

strips) even in the newer, three- to five-star establishments. **Single rooms** generally go for just over half the price of a double, since proprietors are well used to lone (male) business travellers. Rooms with **en-suite bath** are generally about 25 percent more than unplumbed ones; triples are also usually available, costing about thirty percent more than a double.

To avoid **noise**, pick a room away from main thoroughfares or mosque minarets (not easy), or one with double-glazing. You'll never cause offence by asking to see another room, and you should never agree on a price for a room without seeing it first. Though break-ins aren't the norm in Turkey, **security** should be at least a token consid-

eration; paradoxically, some rooms in fancier hotels cannot be locked with a latch or button from the inside, only by key from outside – a particular hazard for women travelling alone. Prostitution is another likely source of noise or at least comings and goings (so to speak) at all hours. It's a potential issue during the off-season, when hotels have to find ways of paying the bills, and can affect any grade of accommodation. That said, the phenomenon seems to have abated considerably since the boom years immediately after the opening of the ex-Communist-bloc borders.

Water should be tested to verify claims of *devamlı/24 saat sıcak su* (constant/24-hour hot water) – always to be treated sceptically. If provided by a solar heater, it will be exhaust-

④ €32–49/53–81YTL Good-value two-star hotels and *pansiyons* in resorts, sometimes in restored old buildings; invariably with some package-tour presence. Often with extra touches such as attached restaurant and rural-antique decor. Air conditioning/heating makes an appearance.

⑤ €50–62/82.5–102YTL Comfortable, if sometimes small-roomed, three-star hotels and *pansiyons*; this category includes many (often overpriced) places in İstanbul's Sultanahmet district, top-end establishments in the Anatolian interior and restored *kervansarays*, which may appear to be underpriced but often suffer from creeping damp or on-site nightclub noise. Attached bar/restaurant is more or less mandatory, as are room phones and winter heating. Ottoman antiques in common areas, kilims in rooms etc, more or less de rigueur.

⑥ €63–93/104–153YTL Four-star hotels and the smaller holiday villages, plus *özel* (special) architectural revival projects. Full-sized bathtubs usually present, as well as extra facilities such as a pool, private beachfront, watersports gear and tennis courts.

⑦ €94–123/155–203YTL More exclusive four-star hotels and bunga-low complexes. All of the preceding amenities will be provided, prob-ably duplicated (ie two pools, two restaurants, two snack cafés, two drinks-bars) and more grandly laid out – rooms may resemble small suites. Additional touches such as telecom services, hairdresser, organ-ized excursions etc. Standard of breakfast starts to be higher than usual; there should be no excuse for lack of hot water.

⑧ over €123/203YTL Restored classics, such as the *Pera Palas* or *Çırağan Palace* in İstanbul, plus five-star de luxe behemoths often affiliated to an international chain. At coastal resorts, luxury digs are often rather remote, necessitating use of the hotel's shuttle or a local taxi to get into the nearest town (the idea being to encourage you to spend more money on-site). Breakfasts, ideally, will be generous and varied. All other creature comforts and distractions to hand. Prices in this range can run as high as €300/495YTL a night or more per room; the Guide notes the actual price of anything higher than €150/248YTL.

---

ed with astonishing reliability after 5pm or so even in multi-starred hotels; in the absence of an electric back-up system, there is little you can do short of moving. Before giving up completely, however, try the right-hand tap; the nominal "hot" and "cold" convention is sometimes reversed in Turkey. Bathtubs and sinks almost never have plugs, so a universal plug is worth bringing from home. Especially on the south and southwest coast, **air con-ditioning** is almost always found in most establishments of category **⑥** and above. It's invariably of the "split-level" variety, doubling as heating during the cooler months. **Dou-ble beds** for couples are becoming more popular; the magic words are *Fransız yatak* ("French" bed), not *çift yatak* ("double" bed),

which actually refers to the number of beds in the room. Incidentally, in many conserva-tive (read Islamist-dominated) rural areas, hotel management may refuse to let a het-erosexual couple share a room, let alone a bed, unless there is documentary evidence that they are married (just a ring may not work, especially if passport names remain different). The police may make trouble for them if proprietors are lenient on this point, as a law exists to this effect, so there's little you can do in this situation short of finding other lodgings that will accept you as you are.

Button and light coding in **lifts/elevators** is a potential source of mystification. "Ç" stands for *çağır* or "call"; a lit-up "K" means *katta*, that is, the car is already on your floor; illuminated "M" is *meşgül* or "in use"; "Z" stands for *zemin kat*, the ground floor, while "A" means *asma kat* or mezzanine.

Hotels

Turkish hotels are graded on a scale of one to five stars by the Ministry of Tourism; there is also a lower tier of unstarred establishments rated by municipalities. At the **four- and five-star** level you're talking international-standard mod cons and prices, and breakfasts which are actually (in contrast to most of those offered at lower-ranked establishments) worth turning up for. **Two- or three-star** outfits are less expensive and may have slightly more character; some of these are historic buildings restored as accommodation, often with mixed results. While turning a disused *kervansaray* into a hotel may seem laudable, the presence of a noisy nightclub in the central courtyard rather negates their function as accommodation. Restored-mansion inns in the Anatolian interior such as Amasya, Gaziantep, Urfa, Sinasos and Safranbolu, or village-house inns found along the Aegean coast, are generally more successful, though preservation considerations may mean that not every room is en suite. Many of the best **boutique hotels**, which blur "star" definitions, are described in *The Little Hotel Book* by Sevan and Müjde Nişanyan, published by the Boyut Press and readily available in Turkey. The book is also available in the UK, more expensively, as *Alistair Sawday's Special Places to Stay in Turkey*.

The **unrated hotels** licensed by municipalities can be virtually as good as the lower end of the one-star class, sometimes with wall-to-wall carpeting (not always clean), en-suite baths and phones. On average, though, expect spartan rooms with possibly a washbasin and certainly a shower (never a tub), with a squat toilet down the hall. Count on €4–6 per person for such comforts, with showers sometimes carrying an additional €1–2 charge. Some places, especially in the east or interior, are jail-like dosshouses where the bedding, winter or summer, tends to be yellowed sheets topped by a thick quilt wrapped in a seldom-laundered slipcover anchored by safety pins. These establishments are listed only when a town has nothing better.

At the roughest end of the spectrum – not recommended in this guide – you may pay by the bed (5–7YTL apiece) rather than the room, so potentially you'd be sharing quarters with strangers unless you buy up all the beds. There will often be no shower in the building, certainly not a hot one. Such places tend to be patronized by villagers in town on business and thus attract an exclusively male clientele.

Pansiyons and apartments

Often the most pleasant places to stay are **pansiyons** (pensions), small guesthouses that proliferate anywhere large numbers of holidaymakers do. If there are vacancies in season, touts in the coastal resorts and other tourist targets descend on every incoming bus, dolmuş or boat. Or look for little signs with the legend *Boş oda var* ("Empty rooms free"). *Pansiyons* almost universally have en-suite facilities, and many feature common gardens or terraces where breakfast (about €1.50–5.50 a head when not included in the room price) is served. Rooms tend to be spartan but clean, furnished in one-star hotel mode and always with two sheets (*çarşafs*) on the bed. Hot water is generally solar-heated at seaside locations, or supplied out of wood- or coal-fired boilers elsewhere. Laundry facilities – even if just a drying line and a plastic bucket – are almost always present, and washing will often be done for you cheaply, a big advantage over most low-grade hotels. In addition, the proprietors are apt to be younger and friendlier than hotel staff – though this may be manifested in an unduly attentive attitude to lone female guests. Prices are often rigidly controlled by the local tourist authorities, set according to the establishment's rating. **Self-catering apartments** are becoming widespread in coastal resorts, and are mostly pitched at vacationing Turks or foreigners arriving on pre-arranged packages. Some are available to walk-in trade – local tourist offices maintain lists – and apart from the weekly price the major (negotiable) outlay will be for the large gas bottle feeding the stove. Ensure, too, that kitchens are equipped well enough to make them truly self-catering.

Hostels, lodges and treehouses

With the abundance of budget *pansiyons* and downmarket working-men's hotels, there are relatively few **hostels** outside İstanbul. Sometimes a *pansiyon* in a major resort will have roof space or a "group room" set aside. Most other supposed "hostels" – called *yurts* – are rather poky dormitories aimed at local students on summer holiday and are unlikely to cater for you; this, and the fact that there is only one *bona fide* IYHF-affiliated hostel in the country, makes the purchase of an IYHF card before you leave a total waste of money.

The lack of official, foreigner-pitched youth hostels has been amply filled by **backpackers' hostels**, found most notably in İstanbul, Çanakkale, Selçuk, Köyceğiz and Fethiye. Basically 1970s *pansiyons* which have been adapted to feature multi-bedded rooms, laundry and Internet facilities, self-catering kitchen, tours and lively bars, they can be fair value – costs vary from €8–12 a head in a dorm – but also do a pretty good job of insulating clients from the host country.

In recent years a large number of **trekkers' lodges** have sprung up in the foothills of the Kaçkar mountains, especially on the south slope, and along the Lycian Way. These generally offer a choice between communal sleeping on mattresses arrayed on a wooden terrace, or more enclosed double-to-quadruple, non-en-suite rooms – strangely, cooking facilities may often be absent. Costs are comparable to the backpackers' hostels.

Found principally on the southwestern coast between Antalya and Fethiye are the so-called **"treehouses"**, often ramshackle collections of elevated shacks or even just open platforms made of rough timber. These may have bedding inside, but equally often just provide sleeping-bag space for up to twenty people, at hostel/trekking-lodge prices. Some of the more luxurious models provide proper, pricier rooms for two, with doors, windows and electric current (but never en-suite plumbing) provided.

Campsites and chalets

Wherever *pansiyons* are found, there will probably also be **campsites** – often run by the same people, who in the absence of a proper site may simply allow you to crash out in the *pansiyon*'s garden. Charges per head run from a couple of euros for such an arrangement to €5 in a well-appointed site at a major resort, plus fees of around €1–4 per tent. You may also be charged for your vehicle – anything from €2 to €7, depending on the site and season. Campsites often **rent out tents** for a euro or two to those showing up without canvas. They also sometimes provide A-frame **chalet accommodation**, which can be anything from a stuffy garden shed with a bed inside to a fairly luxurious affair with bathroom. Prices vary (from €9 to €19 per night), as does construction quality; most sleep a maximum of two.

The most appealing campsites are well-amenitied ones managed by the **Ministry of Forestry**; look for brown wooden signs with yellow lettering. There are 25 of them in shady groves at strategic locations (mostly coastal) across the west of the country, and they make an ideal choice if you have your own transport, especially a combi-van or car and caravan. Most are open April to October inclusive, with maximum charges of €5 per tent, €6 per van and €1 per person; inland sites are much cheaper, and fifty-percent discounts apply to holders of IYHF or FIYTO cards.

Various makeshift roadside **"kampings"**, essentially nothing more than some clumps of trees with parking and picnic space for Turkish weekenders, are unlikely to appeal to most foreigners. **Camping rough** is not illegal, but hardly anybody does it except when trekking in the mountains, and, since you can expect a visit from curious police or even nosier villagers, it's not really a choice for those who like privacy.

Hamams (Turkish baths)

As the standard of living has increased in Turkey, and all but the very poorest families inhabit houses or apartments with showers, the hamam's once-pivotal role in both hygiene and social discourse has declined. A visit, however, is still well worth it, especially to warm up during the cooler months. İstanbul in particular boasts many historic hamams worth experiencing for their architecture alone. Many tourists never partake because they anticipate sexual hassles or intense culture shock. In fact, after a day at the ruins or in the bazaar, a corner of a bath-house is likely to be an oasis of tranquillity in comparison. Bear in mind that in tourist areas the price of hamams has rocketed, and some are very efficient at parting you from your money (a massage can add massively to the cost, for example).

Virtually all Turkish towns have at least one hamam per neighbourhood. The only exceptions to this are some of the coastal resorts, which were formerly populated by Orthodox Christians, who didn't build such structures. Baths are usually signposted, but if in doubt look for the distinctive external profile of the roof domes, visible from the street. Baths are either permanently designated for men or women, or sexually **segregated** on a schedule – look for the words *erkekler* (men) and *kadınlar* (women), followed by a time or day range written on a placard by the door. Women, alas, tend to be allotted far more restricted hours, usually midweek during the day.

On entering, you leave your **valuables** in a small locking drawer, the key of which (often on a wrist/ankle-thong) you keep with you for the duration of your wash. Bring soap, shampoo and a shaving mirror, which are either not supplied or are expensive to buy on the spot. The basic **admission charge** varies depending on the level of luxury. Ordinary hamams should charge around 5–8YTL, and the price is normally clearly indicated by the front desk; hamams in coastal tourist resorts and İstanbul can be much more expensive (12–15YTL). Men will be supplied with a *peştamal*, a thin, wraparound sarong; women usually have to specifically request one but, in fancier spas, more often wear bathing costumes. Both sexes get *takunya*, awkward wooden clogs, and later a *havlu*

or proper drying towel. Changing cubicles (*camekân* in Turkish), equipped with a reclining couch, are sometimes shared and rarely lock except in the better hamams – thus the safe-drawer.

The *hararet* or **main bath chamber** varies from plain to ornate, though any hamam worth its salt will be dressed in marble at least up to chest height. Two or more *halvets*, semi-private corner rooms with two or three *kurnas* (basins) each, lead off from the main chamber. The internal temperature varies from tryingly hot to barely lukewarm, depending on how well run the baths are. Unless with a friend, it's one customer to a set of taps and basin; refrain from making a big soapy mess in the basin, which is meant for mixing pure water to ideal temperature. Use the scoop-dishes provided to sluice yourself, being careful not to splash your neighbours; on Fridays especially they may have just completed their *abdest* (ritual ablution), and would have to start all over again if touched by an "infidel's" water. It's also considered good etiquette to clean your marble slab with a few scoopfuls of water before leaving.

It's not done for men to drop their *peştamal*: **modesty** is the order of the day, and washing your lower half through or under the cloth is an important acquired technique. Women are less scrupulous about covering up, though they too keep their knickers on. Communal bathing in Turkey is essentially a chaste business, though unsolicited male-to-male advances are a potential – if rare – hazard, especially in unsophisticated rural areas.

More than one foreign female visitor has been brought up short by the sight of a matronly figure advancing on them, beckoning with a straight razor: religious Turkish women **shave** all over, though usually not at the baths. Alternatively, the locals stalk about swathed to waist height in green depilatory paste, like New Guinea mud-women. Men, incidentally, are expected to shave their faces in the *tıraşlık*, a section of the *soğukluk* cooling-down room located between the foyer and the main chamber.

At the heart of the hamam is the *göbek taşı* or "navel stone", a raised platform positioned directly over the wood- or coal-fired furnaces that heat the premises. In a good bath the *göbek taşı* will be piping hot, and covered with prostrate figures using their scoop-dishes or special pillows as headrests. It's also the venue for vigorous (to say the least) **massages** from the *tellâk* or masseur/masseuse, whose technique is inspired more by medieval rack-and-wheel practices than by New Age touchy-feely methods – be warned. A *kese* (abrasive mitt) session from the same person, in which untold layers of dead skin and grime are whisked away, will probably be more to most people's tastes. Agree terms in advance with the *tellâk*, which should be about equal to the basic bath charge. If you prefer, you can buy a *kese* at any chemist's and rub yourself down. Traditionally, only male *tellâks* massaged men, and female masseuses women, but since the 1990s there has been increased incidence of men massaging women in the more touristy baths. If this is not to your liking, decline offers or even request a same-sex masseur from the management.

Upon return to your cubicle you'll be offered tea, soft drinks or mineral water, any of which is a good idea since the baths dehydrate you. These, like a massage, are charged as extra; if in doubt, consult the price placard over the reception desk. Except in the heavily touristed establishments, **tips** above and beyond the listed fees are not required or expected.

Food and drink

At its finest, Turkish food is among the best in the world. Indeed, gourmets often rank it as one of the three classic cuisines (along with French and Chinese), with many venerable dishes descended from Byzantine or Ottoman palace cuisine. There are enough climate zones in the country to grow or raise most ingredients locally; and the quality of the raw materials has not yet been compromised by mass-marketing standards and regulations.

Prices, except for the fancier cuts of meat and for seafood, aren't going to break your budget either, with three-course meals starting at around 12YTL (€7.25/£5). However, you'll pay more (often a lot more!) at the major resorts, where standards have sadly declined as tourism has taken hold. Unadventurous travellers are prone to get stuck in a kebab rut and come away moaning about the monotony of the cuisine; in fact, all but the strictest vegetarians should find enough variety to satisfy them.

A summary of eating places and specialities follows, but for a full **menu reader**, turn to p.1052.

Breakfast

The so-called "Turkish" **breakfast** (*kahvaltı*) served at modest hotels and *pansiyons* is almost invariably a pile of spongy white bread slices with a pat of margarine, a slice of processed cheese, a dab of pre-packed jam and a couple of olives. Only tea is likely to be available in quantity; seconds are likely to be charged for, as are extras such as *sahanda yumurtalar* (fried eggs). In the better hotels and top-end *pansiyons* you can anticipate iced butter, preserves that actually contain fruit chunks, a variety of breads and pastries, fresh fruit slices, a choice of olive and cheese types, and an array of cold and hot meats, plus eggs in various styles.

You can breakfast better on a budget by simply using street stands or snack joints, which serve some of Turkey's best food. Many workers start the morning with a **börek**, a rich, flaky, layered pastry containing bits of mince or cheese; these can be found either at a tiny *büfe* (stall-café) or from a street cart. Others content themselves with a simple **simit** (bread rings speckled with sesame seeds) or a bowl of **çorba** (soup) with lemon.

Street snacks

With breakfast over, vendors hawk **lahmacun**, small, round Arab-style pizzas with a thin meat-based topping. Visitors from Britain may find to their surprise that **kebabs** (*kebap* in Turkish) per se are not generally considered takeaway food unless wrapped in a section of *dürüm*, an increasingly popular type of paratha-like bread; more often you'll find *döner* or *köfte* in takeaway stalls, served on a baguette or hamburger bun. Alternatively, try a **sandwich** (*sandviç*), a baguette chunk with various fillings (often *kokoreç* – offal – or fish), though it is extremely unwise to eat street fish in İstanbul; most of it comes from the pollutant-laced waters of the Sea of Marmara. In coastal cities deep-fried **mussels** (*midye tava*) are often available, as are *midye dolması* (mussels stuffed with rice, pine nuts and allspice) – though these are best avoided in summer months, especially if offered unrefrigerated by street vendors.

Not to be confused with *lahmacun* is **pide**, Turkish pizza – flat bread with various toppings, served to a sit-down clientele in a *pideci* or *pide salonu*. The big advantage of this dish is that it's always made to order: typical styles are *kaşarlı* or *peynirli* (with cheese), *yumurtalı* (with egg), *kıymalı* (with mince), and *sucuklu* (with sausage). Most *pidecis* don't light their ovens until 11am or so, thus making it an obvious lunchtime treat.

Other specialities worth seeking out are **mantı** – the traditional Central Asian, meat-filled ravioli, served drenched in yoghurt and spice-reddened oil – or **gözleme**, a crêpe-like delicacy for which there is now a veritable craze in tourist resorts and Turkish towns alike. In any sizable town you'll also find at least one **kuru yemiş** stall, also known as a *leblebeci*, where nuts and dried fruit are sold by weight – typically in 100g shots. Aside from the usual offerings, keep an eye out for *cezeriye*, a bar made of carrot juice, honey and nuts; the east-Anatolian winter/spring snack of **peştil** (dried fruit), most commonly apricot and peach, pressed into sheets; and **tatlı sucuk**, a fruit, nut and molasses roll (not to be confused with meat *sucuk* or sausage).

Restaurants

Various types of eatery fill the need for more substantial sit-down food. A **lokanta** is a restaurant emphasizing *hazır yemek*, pre-cooked dishes kept warm in a steamtray. Here also can be found *sulu yemek*, "watery food" – which is just that, hearty chunks swimming in broth or sauce. Despite their often clinical appearance, food at the best *lokantas* (especially in İstanbul) may well prove your most delicious and memorable taste of Turkish cooking.

A "**restoran**", a self-bestowed title for anything from a motorway bus pit-stop to a white-tablecloth affair, will provide *ızgara yemek* or meat dishes grilled to order. A **çorbacı** is a soup kitchen; **kebapçıs** and **köftecıs** specialize in the preparation of kebab and *köfte* respectively, with a limited number of side dishes – usually just an array of salad, yoghurt and desserts. **İskembe salonus** are a Turkish institution, aimed at revellers as they emerge from clubs or taverns in the early hours, and open until 5 or 6am. Their main dish is tripe soup laced liberally with garlic oil, vinegar and red pepper flakes, an effective hangover antidote/preventative. They also sell *piliç* (small chickens), which can usually be seen spit-roasting in the window.

At an **ocakbaşı**, the grill and its hood is placed centre-stage, so that the diners can watch their meat being prepared. Even more interactive is the **kendin pişir kendin ye** (cook-it-and-eat-it-yourself) establishment, where a *mangal* (barbecue with coals), a specified quantity of raw meat, and condiments such as *kekik* (oregano) and *kimyon* (cumin) are brought to your outdoor/indoor table. Such places are excellent value, and you get to inspect the state of the meat; they also occasionally offer *tandır kebap*, a side of lamb or goat roasted in an oven.

Most budget-priced restaurants are **alcohol-free** (*içkisiz*); any **licensed** place (marked *içkili*) is likely to be more expensive. A useful exception is a **meyhane** (tavern), in its truest incarnation a smoky dive where eating is considered secondary to tippling. In the fancier ones, though, the food – mostly unusual delicacies – can be very good and not always drastically marked up in price; the best of these sort are found in İstanbul. No self-respecting Turkish woman, however, would be caught dead in most of them, and unfortunately very few *meyhanes* are the sort of spot where an unaccompanied foreign woman can go without comment, and some will seem dodgy to Western men too. That said, any foreign men or couples bold enough to visit the more decorous *meyhanes* will be treated with the utmost courtesy. In restaurants, unaccompanied women may be ushered into the *aile salonu* (family parlour), usually upstairs or discreetly behind a curtain.

Prices per platter vary widely according to the type of establishment: from a couple of lira a head at a simple boozeless soup kitchen up to 10–15YTL at the flashier resort restaurants and İstanbul establishments. The fancier places will inevitably levy a ten-percent extra *servis* (service) charge and, to compound the pain, add on a separate *garsoniye* (waiter's tip).

Portions, especially in *meyhanes*, tend to be tiny, so if you're a big eater you may need to order two main courses. Many places don't have **menus**: you'll need to ascertain the prices beforehand and review bills carefully when finished. Tallying up items you never ate, or presenting diners with dishes they didn't order, are fairly common gambits;

so is having your plate whisked away before you're done with it. This last habit is not so much a ploy to hurry you along, but derives from the Turkish custom of never leaving a guest with an "empty" or "dirty" plate before them. *Kalsın* ("may it remain") is the term to stop this practice in mid-air.

Dishes and specialities

In a *çorbacı*, soup (*çorba*) and salad (*salata*) predominate. The most frequently encountered **soups** are *mercimek* (lentil), *ezo gelin* (rice and vegetable broth – thick enough to be an appetizing breakfast), *paça* (trotters) or *işkembe* (tripe). *Çoban* (shepherd's) *salatası* is the generic term for the widespread cucumber, tomato, onion, pepper and parsley **salad** (approach the peppers with caution); *yeşil* (green) salad, usually just some *marul* (lettuce), is only seasonally available. A range of soups and salads can also be found in *lokantas* and high-class restaurants; here the so-called *mevsim salatası* or seasonal salad – perhaps tomato slices, watercress, red cabbage and lettuce hearts, sprinkled with cheese and drenched in dressing – resembles a Western salad and makes a welcome change from "shepherd's" salad. In any *içkili restoran* or *meyhane*, you'll find more of the **mezes** (appetizers) for which Turkey is justly famous – usually a bewildering array of rich purees, vinaigrettes and fried-then-chilled dishes kept (sometimes for too long) in refrigerated display cases. These are the best dishes for vegetarians to concentrate on, since many are free of meat, while the variety of vegetables and pulses used, combined with vitamin-retentive cooking methods, will sustain your dietary needs. During the Muslim fasting month of Ramadan, a poor-to-nonexistent selection of *mezes* is available – as they won't be eaten at midday, few chefs reckon it worth the bother to prepare them just for after-dark consumption.

Along with dessert (see overleaf), *mezes* are really the core of Turkish cuisine. The best and most common include *patlıcan salatası* (aubergine mash), *piyaz* (white haricot vinaigrette), *semizotu* (purslane weed, usually in yoghurt), *mücver* (courgette croquettes), *sigara böreği* (tightly rolled cheese pastries), *beyin salatası* (whole lamb's/sheep's brain), turşu (pickled vegetables), *imam bayıldı* (cold baked aubergine with onion and tomato) and *dolma* (any stuffed vegetable, but typically peppers or tomatoes).

Bread is good if an hour or two old, but otherwise is spongy and stale, best for scooping up *mezes* and the like. Flat unadorned *pide* is served with soup, during Ramadan and at *kebapcıs*; while loaves of *kepekli* (wholemeal) or *çavdar* (rye bread; only from a *fırın* or bakery) afford relief in the largest cities. In villages, cooked *yufka* – the basis of *börek* pastry – makes a welcome respite, as does *bazlama* (similar to an Indian paratha).

Most people return from Turkey having sampled only the standard *beyaz peynir* (like Greek feta) at breakfast but other Turkish **cheeses** deserve mention, especially as picnic or snack fare. *Dil peynir* ("tongue" cheese), a hard, salty cheese that breaks up into mozzarella-like filaments, and the plaited *oğru peynir*, can both be grilled or fried like Cypriot halloúmi. *Tulum peynir* is a strong, salty, almost granular goat's cheese cured in a goatskin; it is used as a *börek* stuffing, although together with walnuts, it makes a very popular *meze*. *Otlu peynir* from the Van area is cured with herbs and eaten at breakfast; cow's-milk *kaşar*, especially *eski* (aged) *kaşar* from the Kars region, is also highly esteemed.

Main courses are nutritious if often plainly presented. In *hazır yemek* restaurants, *kuru fasulye* (bean soup – rather like baked beans in tomato sauce), *taze fasulye* (French beans), *sebze turlu* (vegetable stew) and *nohut* (chickpeas) are the principal **vegetable** dishes. Vegetarians should, however, be aware that even though no meat may be visible in these dishes, they're almost always made with lamb- or chicken-based broth; even bulgur and rice may be cooked in meat stock. You might ask *İçinde et suyu var mı?* (Does it contain meat stock?), but it's best to confine yourself to *mezes* and salads, when available.

Dishes containing meat include *mussaka* (not as good as the Greek rendition), *karnıyarık* (a much better Turkish variation), *güveç* (clay-pot fricassee), *tas kebap* (a meat and vegetable combo), *hunkar beğendi* (beef stew on a bed of pureed eggplant and cheese), *saray kebap* (beef stew topped

with bechamel sauce and oven-browned), *macar* (Hungarian) *kebap* (stewed meat and vegetables topped with mashed potato and cheese, then baked) and *saç kavurma*, an inland Anatolian speciality made from meat, vegetables, spices and oil, fried up in a *saç* (the Turkish wok).

Grilled meat dishes from the *ızgara* (grill) include several variations on the stereotypical kebab. *Adana kebap* is spicy, with a sprinkling of purple sumac herb betraying Arab influence; *İskender kebap*, best sampled in Bursa, is heavy on the flatbread and yoghurt. *Köfte* (meatballs), *şiş* (stewed meat chunks, usually mutton or beef) and *çöp* (bits of lamb or offal) are other options. When ordering, if you've any appetite, specify *bir buçuk* (a portion and a half – adequate) or *çift* (double portion – generous). Grilled dishes normally come with a slice or two of *pide* and raw vegetable garnish – never inside pitta bread as in Britain. Potentially more exciting titbits such as *pirzola* (lamp chop), *böbrek* (kidney), *yürek* (heart), *ciğer* (liver), *koç yumurtası* (ram's egg) or *billur* (crystal) – the last two euphemisms for testicle, less commonly found of late. A *karışık ızgara* (mixed grill) is always good value. Chicken (*piliç* or *tavuk*) is widely available, though not as cheap as you'd think.

Fish and seafood is good, if usually pricey, and sold by weight more often than by item (35–40YTL per kilo is the rule – anything cheaper is a good deal). Buy with an eye to what's in season (as opposed to farmed or frozen and imported), and don't turn your nose up at humbler items, which in all likelihood will be fresher because they turn over faster. Budget mainstays include *sardalya* (sardines – grilled fresh), *palamut* (autumn tuna), *akya* (amberjack), *kefal* (grey mullet, a south-Aegean speciality) and *sangöz* (black bream). *Çipura* (gilt-head bream) and *levrek* (sea bass), when suspiciously cheap, are almost invariably farmed.

Desserts and sweets

After the occasionally functional presentation of main dishes, Turkish chefs pander shamelessly and elegantly to the sweet tooth. Sticky-cake addicts and pudding freaks will find every imaginable concoction at the closest **pastane** (sweet shop).

Aşure

Aşure is the Turkish variant of a food with deep religious symbolism, found in Muslim, Christian and Jewish communities throughout Anatolia and the Balkans. The word is derived from the Arabic word for "ten", referring to *aşure günü*, or the tenth of the month of Muharrem, when Hasan and Hussein, sons of the fourth caliph Ali and grandsons of Mohammed, were slain at the Battle of Karbala, becoming martyrs for the Shiites and their allied sects in Turkey, the Alevîs and the Bektaşis. The latter have incorporated *aşure* fully into their ritual: after fasting for the first ten days of Muharrem, Bektaşi elders invite initiates to a private ceremony where the fast is broken over a communal meal of *aşure*. It is supposed to be made from forty different ingredients, courtesy of a legend which claims that after the Ark's forty-day sail on the Flood, and the first sighting of dry land, Noah commanded that a stew be made of the remaining supplies on board – which turned out to number forty sorts of food. An alternative name for the dish is thus "Noah's pudding", but today you'll be fortunate to find half that number of ingredients, even in a devotional recipe. You can also buy bags of prepackaged *aşure* mix in Turkish markets, and many kebab joints or *pastanes* serve it much of the year.

The syrup-soaked **baklava**-type items are pretty self-explanatory on a glance into the glass display cabinet – all permutations of a sugar, flour, nut and butter mix. The best is reckoned to be *antep fistikli sarması* (pistachio-filled baklava) – pricey at 2.5–3.5YTL per serving; other baklavas tend to be *cevizli* (walnut-filled), and cheaper. In recent years, *künefe* – the "shredded wheat" filaments of *kadayif* perched atop white cheese, baked in a shallow tray and soaked in syrup – has become ubiquitous as a dessert offered in kebab and *lahmacun* places; both *baklava* and *künefe* are often served, luxuriously if not exactly healthily, with large dollops of ice cream.

More mysterious, less sweet and healthier are the **milk-based** dishes, which are popular all over the country. *Süpangile* ("süp" for short, a corruption of *soupe d'Anglais*) is an incredibly dense, rich chocolate pudding with sponge or a biscuit embedded inside. More modest dishes are *keşkül* (a vanilla and nut-crumble custard), and *sütlaç* (rice pudding) – one dessert that's consistently available in ordinary restaurants. The most complicated dish is *tavukgöğsü*, a cinnamon-topped morsel made from hyper-boiled and strained chicken breast, semolina starch and milk. *Kazandibi* (literally "bottom of the pot") is *tavukgöğsü* residue with a dark crust on the bottom – not to be confused with *fırın sütlaç*, which looks the same but is actually *sütlaç* pudding with a scorched top baked in a clay dish.

Grain-based sweets are some of the best that the country has to offer. Especially if you coincide with the appropriate holiday, you'll get to sample *aşure* (see box above), a sort of rosewater jelly laced with pulses, wheat berries, raisins and nuts. The best-known Turkish sweet, *lokum* or "**Turkish Delight**", is pretty much ubiquitous, available from *pastanes* and the more touristy shops. It's basically solidified sugar and pectin, flavoured (most commonly) with rosewater, sometimes pistachios, and sprinkled with powdered sugar.

There are also nearly a dozen recognized sorts of **helva**, including the *tahini*-paste chew synonymous with the concoction in the West, although in Turkey the term usually means any variation on the basic theme of baked flour or starch, butter, sugar and flavoured water.

Ice cream is an excellent summer treat, provided it's genuine *Maraşlı döşme dondurma* (whipped in the Kahraman Maraş tradition – a bit like Italian gelato), not factory-produced rubbish. Consistent warm weather prompts the stationing outside of restaurants of outlandishly costumed young men with swords selling the stuff. Being served is half the fun: you may be threatened or cajoled at (blunted) sword point into buying, after which the cone is presented to you on the point of the sword after a twirl or three, and a bell rung loudly to celebrate the transaction. These, however, have been overtaken by upmarket parlours selling every conceivable flavour of ice cream from ginger to mulberry; the best chain of these is Mado, with high prices (5YTL for a three-scoop portion) but equally high quality.

Final choices include *kabak tatlısı* (candied squash usually served in autumn with walnut chunks and *kaymak*, or clotted cream); *ayva tatlısı* (stewed quince served with nuts or dried fruit, topped with *kaymak* and dusted with grated pistachio); or **summer fruit** (*meyve*), which generally means *kavun* (Persian melon, honeydew) or *karpuz* (watermelon).

Tea, coffee and soft drinks

Tea, grown along the Black Sea since the 1930s, is the national drink and an essential social lubricant – you'll inevitably be offered some within twenty minutes of your arrival in Turkey. Tea is properly prepared in the *çaydanlık*, a double-boiler apparatus, with a larger water chamber underneath the smaller water receptacle containing dry leaves, to which a small quantity of hot water is added. After a suitable wait the tea is decanted into tiny tulip-shaped glasses, then diluted with more water to taste: *açık* is weak, *demli* or *koyu* steeped. Sugar comes as cubes on the side; milk is never added. If you're frustrated by the usual tiny glass at breakfast, ask for a *düble çay* (a "double tea", served in a juice glass).

Herbal **teas** are also popular in Turkey, particularly *ıhlamur* (linden flower), *kuşburnu* (rose hip), *papatya* (camomile) and *ada çay* ("island" tea), an infusion of a type of sage common in all coastal areas. Most of the much-touted **apple tea** (*elma çay*) in fact contains chemicals and not a trace of apple essence, though it is becoming possible to find natural (*doğal*) formulas as opposed to artificial (*sintetik*).

Coffee is not as commonly drunk in Turkey, despite the fact that the Ottomans first introduced the drink to Europe from Yemen. Instant is increasingly popular, now available in several brands besides the inevitable Nescafé. It's much stronger, however, than Anglo-Saxon formulas, brewed more in line to German tastes. The traditional, fine-ground Turkish coffee is preferable, brewed

up *sade* (without sugar), *orta şekerli* (medium sweet) or *çok şekerli* (cloying). Only in the very largest cities and most cosmopolitan resorts will you find Western notions (and Western pricings) of coffee, such as filtered or cappuccino, though the EU customs union has made the raw materials easier – if not cheaper – to find in the appropriate aisles of major supermarkets. For an extended session of drinking either tea or coffee, you retire to a **çay bahçesi** (tea garden), which often will also serve ice cream and soft drinks.

Certain traditional beverages tend to accompany particular kinds of food or appear at set seasons. *Sıcak süt* (hot milk) is the perennial complement to *börek*, though in winter it's fortified with *salep*, the ground-up tuber of *Orchis mascula*, a phenomenally expensive wild orchid gathered in coastal areas between Antalya and İzmir. **Sahlep** is a good safeguard against colds (and also reputedly an aphrodisiac), though because of its cost most prepackaged varieties are heavily adulterated with powdered milk, starch and sugar – only in the İzmir bazaar will you find the real thing at full strength. **Ayran** (watered-down yoghurt), is always on offer at *pidecis* and *kebapçıs*, and is good cold but not so appetizing if – as it sometimes is – lukewarm and lumpy. In autumn and winter, you'll find stalls selling **boza**, a delicious, mildly fermented millet drink flavoured with grape juice. Similarly tangy **şıra**, a lightly alcoholic grape juice acceptable to religious Muslims and available in late summer and autumn.

Fruit juice (*meyva suyu*) can be excellent if it comes as pulp in a bottle, available in such flavours as *kayısı* (apricot), *şeftali* (peach) and *vişne* (sour cherry). The recent wave of thin, preservative-spiked cardboard-packaged juice drinks is distinctly less thrilling, though there are a few, more pricey, locally produced pure fruit juices in packets. The good stuff is so thick you might want to cut it with **spring water** (*memba suyu*), or fizzy **mineral water** (*maden suyu*). A PVC bottle of water costs no more than 1YTL in a restaurant; in many establishments chilled, potable tap water in a glass bottle or a jug is routinely provided at each table, for which there should be no extra charge. You can request lemon wedges to squeeze into this for improved taste. *Meşrubat* is the generic term for all types of carbonated **soft drinks**.

Alcoholic drinks

Since the accession of the nominally Islamist AK Parti at most governmental levels since 2002, there's good news and bad news concerning **alcoholic drinks** (*içkiler*) in Turkey. They are still available theoretically without restriction in resorts – even being sold within 200m of a mosque, normally a no-no – though booze has vanished from all municipally owned concessions in any AK-run town (of which there are quite a few), and you will have some thirsty moments at all establishments in conservative interior towns such as Afyon, Konya, Erzerum or Diyarbakır. Worse for drinkers, the ruling party has conveniently found a convergence between Islamic morality and fiscal opportunity by slapping a twenty-percent excise tax on all alcohol, bringing prices to well over that prevailing in any European country. The only bright spot was the 2004 sale and break-up of the *Tekel*, or state alcohol-producing monopoly, which resulted in increased competition and product quality amongst distilled spirits.

Beer (*bira*) is sold principally in returnable bottles but also in cans (expensive) and on draught (*fıcı bira* in Turkish), which is cheaper. There are two principal domestic brands, both at about five-percent alcohol content. **Efes Pilsen**, the most popular beer in Turkey, can be over-yeasty; it's normally sold as a half-litre bottle, though in resort areas comes as 33cl bottles or cans of "Lite" (low alcohol), "Dark" (6.1 percent), and "Extra" (7 percent). Efes has an alternate label (Marmara 34, available in 70cl bottles or 50cl cans) and is also the local licensee-brewer of Becks (33cl bottles, 50cl cans) and Miller (same sizes). **Tuborg** also generates varying opinions, though since foreign backer Carlsberg began brewing Carlsberg per se locally (33/50cl bottles, 50cl cans, also draught) its market share has improved. Tuborg's sub-label Venus is a bit lighter both in price and taste. Tekel's Asırlık Türk Bırası, available in Migros markets, is a pale brew akin to wheat beer, which is cheaper than other domestic labels and makes a nice change. **Imported** bottled beers (such as Corona, Bud or Heineken) are now available

in the largest cities, at a price. Prices for beer vary widely, from 2YTL per bottle in a shop to 5YTL in a middle-of-the-road bar, with even higher prices prevailing in trendier clubs. There are, as yet, very few relatively civilized beer **pubs** (*birerme*) as opposed to the ubiquitous **beer hall** (*birahane*), imitation-German-style establishments, which often have a distinctly aggressive atmosphere – best avoided.

Wine (*şarap*), from vineyards scattered across western Anatolia between Cappadocia, the Euphrates Valley, Thrace and the Aegean, is often better than average. There has lately been a huge upswing of interest in fine wine, with expensive imported labels available in most upmarket town-centre or hotel restaurants and the better-stocked supermarkets. Local wines are also now better distributed, resulting in a huge variety in the bigger cities, though quality remains variable. Red wine is *kırmızı*, white *beyaz*, rose *roze*. In shops, count on paying 7–17YTL (€4–10+) for a bottle of low-to-mid-range wine, or as much as 25YTL (€15+) for a bottle from some obscure, self-styled boutique winery that may be scarcely better than the major players.

The market is currently dominated by two large vintners: Doluca (try their Antik premium labels, or Moskado Sek) and Kavaklıdere (whose Çankaya white, Angora red and Lâl rose are especially commendable). Kavaklıdere also produces a sparkling white, İnci Damalası, the closest local thing to champagne. Other smaller, regional brands to watch for include Turasan (red is excellent, though their white's a bit too sweet), Narbağ, Peribacası (Cappadocia) and Kavalleros (Sea of Marmara), though Merih Rosé is disgusting and eminently avoidable. Feyzi Kutman red in particular is superb, though alas rarely found outside the largest centres. Similarly confined to their areas of production are cheap-and-cheerful whites from Bozcaada and Şirince, plus Majestik red, available only around İzmir. Another affordable producer worth seeking out is Sevilen, which makes organic reds – Merlot and Cabernet – at premium prices, as well as a palatable, MOR label, Tellibağ.

The Turkish national aperitif is **rakı**, not unlike Greek ouzo but rougher and stronger, usually drunk over ice and topped up with bottled water. Since the end of the Tekel monopoly, private distilleries of varying quality have proliferated. The privatized Tekel is still a major player, however, with a range of labels: Yeni (45 percent), the cheap but not so nasty Külüb (48 percent), Altınbaş (50 percent) and Tekirdağ (45 percent), distilled in that town using recycled sherry casks. "Cheap" is only a relative concept lately, with a 70cl bottle of *rakı* costing about 20YTL (€12) in a shop, and a double *rakı* in a *meyhane* running to 5YTL (€3). The *meyhane* routine of an evening is for a group of men to order a big bottle of *rakı*, a bucket of ice and

a few bottles of water, and then slowly drink themselves under the table between bites of seafood *meze* or nibbles of *çerez* – the generic term for pumpkin seeds, chickpeas, almonds etc, served on tiny plates.

Stronger **spirits** – *cin* (gin), *votka* (vodka) and *kanyak* (cognac) – are available as the usual imported labels or cheaper but often nastier *yerli* (locally produced) variants, including Tekel. Domestically produced **liqueurs** are often given on the house at the end of a meal. For the most part they are quite cloying, but bearable exceptions include Mocca and Acıbadem (almond liqueur).

Communications

Most fixed-line telecommunication services are provided by TT (Türk Telekom), distinguished by its blue-on-turquoise call boxes. In the largest towns and tourist resorts, the phone division of the main PTT (Posta Telefon ve Telegraf) building is open until midnight (7pm on Sundays), with mail accepted daily from 8am until 5pm; separate TT buildings, where present, tend to keep roughly the same hours. Elsewhere, the PTT adheres to standard civil-service hours, with complete closure on Saturday afternoon and Sundays.

Postal services

Stamps are only available from the PTT, whose website (⦿www.ptt.gov.tr) has a (not necessarily up-to-date) English-language listing of services and prices. **Overseas letter** rates are rapidly approaching uniformity with those in EU countries; airmail (*Uçakla*) rates to Europe are about 0.8YTL for up to 20g, 17.5YTL for 2kg, the maximum weight for letters. Delivery to Europe or North America can take seven to ten days, but *acele* (express) service is available for a surcharge assessed in 50-gramme increments from 33YTL for the first 500gm, cutting delivery time for the EU to about three days. Registered (*taahuklu*) service costs about 2YTL extra and by itself is enough to guarantee somewhat faster as well as secure delivery, but you'll need to fill in two forms, one in Turkish, one in French! It's more expensive but less hassle to send letters and pack-

ages via a private cargo company; they exist in all sizable cities, and most of them handle overseas parcels. The best known are Yurtiçi Kargo and Aras Kargo, plus the more expensive international companies DHL and UPS. You will have to complete a declaration of the contents; it will cost about 26YTL for three-working-day delivery of a 500-gramme A4-size letter-style package to the UK, 40YTL for a 500–1000-gramme parcel. If you opt instead for the PTT, which is cheaper, do it in a medium-sized town with an airport and enlist the help of a sympathetic supervisor who understands the rules. For non-EU destinations, boxes should be presented unsealed for potential inspection; at main branches folded cardboard packing kits are usually sold. Though most of these may be supplied, it's best to come prepared with tape, twine, indelible marker, scissors, supporting invoices and certificates – and plenty of patience. There is no *acele* parcel service and rates vary for each country, but as an example, a surface parcel to the UK costs 34YTL for the first kilo, plus 6.2YTL for each additional kilo, while an air parcel is 39YTL for the first kilo, 8YTL for each additional one.

Posting slots are clearly labelled – *yurtdışı* for overseas, *yurtiçi* for inland, *şehiriçi* for local. Street-corner post boxes are just about non-existent these days. To receive mail **poste restante** (general delivery), articles should be addressed to you, c/o "Postrestant, Merkez Postanesi, [city name], Turkey".

Telephones

PTT or TT premises are the best place to make phone calls. The **Türk Telekom** website (ⓦ www.turktelekom.com.tr) has an English-language page listing all services and tariffs. Inside the PTT/TT, or just adjacent, there is usually a row of card (*telekart*) phones and/or a *kontürlü* (metered, clerk-attended) phone, the latter sometimes in a closed booth. **Public phones** elsewhere are fairly common, typically found on resort quays, in public parks and at filling stations or street corners. The standard Turkish phone replies are the Frenchified *Allo* or the more local *Buyurun* (literally, "Avail yourself/ at your service"). Connection standards in rural areas are far worse than in the big cities, and you will typically have to dial two or three times to reach your party, even within the same area code.

Two breeds of **phonecards** (*telekarts*) are available: ordinary *telekarts* in denominations of 30, 60 and 100 units and so-called "smart" *telekarts* in the same denominations. *Telekarts* are used in exactly the same manner as British or North American ones, though you have little warning before being cut off; wait for the number of units remaining to appear on the screen before dialling. A steadily increasing number of phones have also been adapted to accept foreign **credit cards**. **Metered booths** inside PTTs or TTs, or at street kiosks (look for signs reading *kontürlü telefon bulunur*) work out more expensive than cards, but are certainly far cheaper than hotels, and also tend to be quieter (plus you won't be cut off). Their disadvantage is that you can't see the meter

ticking over, and instances of overcharging are not unknown. Turkey uses a system of eleven-digit **phone numbers** nationwide, consisting of four-digit area or mobile-provider codes (all starting with "0") plus a seven-digit subscriber number. To call a number in Turkey **from overseas**, dial your country's international access code, then 90 for Turkey, next the area or mobile code minus the initial zero, and finally the subscriber number. To call home **from Turkey**, dial ☎00 followed by the relevant international dialling code (see list below), then the area code (without the intitial zero if there is one), then the number.

Overseas call rates are better value than they were, at 0.25YTL/min to Europe or North America. Try not to make anything other than local calls from a hotel room – there's usually a minimum 100-percent surcharge on phonecard rates.

Most hotels in our categories ❸ and above have **faxes** and it is usually simpler to send and receive one there than to use the PTT's fax service. At about a minute per transmitted page, this is a far cheaper way of staying in touch transcontinentally than chatting – as well as being a reliable way of making reservations.

Useful telephone numbers

Directory assistance ☎118
International operator (reverse charges) ☎115
Postal code assistance ☎119
Intercity operator ☎131

International dialling codes

Australia ☎61
Ireland ☎353
Netherlands ☎31
New Zealand ☎64
UK ☎44
US & Canada ☎1

Mobile phones

Given the Turkish penchant for chatting and last-minute arrangements, **mobile phones** have become an essential accessory in Turkey – **mobile numbers** are prefixed ☎0542, ☎0543, ☎0532, ☎0535 and ☎0555. There are now three networks, the best being Turkcell, which has the widest network coverage and the largest subscriber base. If you are in the country longer than a week, and/or intend to phone home frequently, you will definitely save loads of money by purchasing a local SIM card and pay-as-you-go package. These are available from the (seemingly countless) mobile-phone outlets in town and city centres advertising *kontürlü* SIM cards. With Turkcell, it costs about 22YTL for the number (which can take up to 24 hours to activate) and the first 100 units, with additional 100 units or 250 units costing 11YTL and 23.5YTL respectively; often specials apply, such as a SIM plus 250 units for 33YTL. Typically calls cost 0.9YTL/min to Europe and North America, while an SMS message to the UK costs around 0.3TL. To purchase a SIM card, you'll need to present your passport for photocopying. Just take your phone along to one of the mobile outlets and they'll fit the new card, "unblock" your phone if necessary (this is not illegal and will not void your existing home-based contract), and even enter the scratchcard unit number and get the units credited to your phone for you.

Alternatively, any GSM mobile based in northern Europe, Australia or New Zealand should work fine in Turkey; North American users will only be able to use tri-band rigs. You will definitely be charged extra for incoming calls when abroad, though discount plans are available to reduce the cost by as much as seventy percent. In terms of Turkish networks, there's little to distinguish between them as roaming partners or the eventual (often horrendous) bill to be paid back home after using any of them, which will brusquely convince you to buy a Turkish SIM next time. Not being subject to EU rules means that Turkish mobile providers seem to charge guest users what they like, to the tune of £1.10 per minute for calls to Britain (including voicemail retrieval), 33p per minute for incoming calls, even with a discount plan (over double that without one). Ringing either a Turkish landline or mobile with an overseas SIM card will cost about 45–50p per minute.

Email and Internet

Email and Internet use has caught on in a big way in Turkey, especially in the bigger towns where Türk Telekom has invested in infrastructure; elsewhere low-capacity phone lines can mean chronic frustration in maintaining ISP connections. For your own email needs, you can use the various **Internet cafés** that have sprung up in virtually every Turkish town and city. Rates tend to be 2YTL per hour maximum, with shorter periods often available; cafés with ADSL connections are a bit pricier. Be warned that many Internet cafés are excessively smoky havens for bored teenagers playing endless "shoot-em-up" computer games. More seriously, the Turkish-character keyboard you'll probably be faced with may cause some frustration. Beware in particular of the dotless 'ı' (confusingly enough found right where you'll be expecting the conventional 'i') which, if entered by mistake, will make an email address invalid – the dotted western "eye" is located second key from right, middle row. You can sign up in advance for a free Web-based email address that can be accessed from anywhere, for example Yahoo (ⓦwww.yahoo.com) or Hotmail (ⓦwww.hotmail.com). Once you've set up an account, you can use these sites to pick up and send mail from any Internet café or hotel with Internet access. One big disadvantage of Hotmail is that your mailbox storage quota is very small, so it must be collected regularly or you will lose messages.

Some Internet cafés (and posher hotels) also have wireless connection, generally for incoming mail only; however if you have a POP3 account (generally most ISPs other than Yahoo and Hotmail), you can reply and compose outgoing mail on your own laptop using ⓦwww.mail2web. You will need a North American–standard cable (UK ones will *not* work), lightweight and easily purchasable in Turkey, with RJ-11 male terminals at each end. Many newer hotel rooms have RJ-11 sockets, but older ones still have phones hard-wired into the wall, in which case you should come prepared with an RJ-11 female-female adaptor – which weigh and cost next to nothing – for making a splice between your cable and the RJ-11 end of the cable between the wall and phone (which you simply unplug). No international ISPs maintain points of presence in Turkey, so in the absence of a wireless service you're looking at an international call to retrieve your mail.

The media

Newspapers and magazines weren't even allowed in the country until the middle of the nineteenth century; since then, however, lost time has been made up for with a vengeance. Over forty mastheads, representing the full gamut of public tastes from elevated to gutter, compete for readers' attention. The airwaves were controlled exclusively by the government until the late 1980s, but with satellite dishes and overseas transmitters widely available, a vast quantity of private, cable and digital stations – mostly of poor quality – flourishes across Turkey.

Turkish-language publications

An independent press didn't exist in Turkey until the middle of the nineteenth century, when an Englishman, William Churchill, started the first nonofficial publication, the *Cerde-I-Havadis* (Journal of News). Today, it's estimated that out of a population of over 63 million, fewer than ten percent actually read newspapers, with circulation figures – at best a few hundred thousand daily – boosted by those collecting special promotional coupons for consumer goods.

Around seventy percent of the **newspapers** sold are produced by two giant media conglomerates, the Doğan group and the Sabah group. Three titles – **Sabah**, **Hürriyet** and **Milliyet** – dominate the middle market, mixing gossip, sleaze and plenty of football with serious political and economic news. All three include weekly TV guides with their Saturday editions. Slightly to the left of these stands **Radikal**, the best paper to pick up in the big cities for listings of cinema, exhibitions and concerts (often with discount coupons for the latter).

The only surviving high-end newspaper is venerable **Cumhuriyet**, founded as the mouthpiece of the Turkish republic in 1924. Nowadays, it mixes conservative nationalism with old-style socialism and struggles to survive. Distinctly downmarket are heavily illustrated **Posta**, **Star**, **Akşam** and **Vatan**, which offer rather dubious news coverage – and principally something for corner shops to wrap vegetables in, thus the idiom "asparagus news" for these rags.

Of more interest are Turkey's Islamist papers, which give surprisingly intelligent coverage. Of the biggest sellers, **Yeni Şafak** and **Zaman**, the former is a strong supporter of the Justice and Development (AK) Party elected to power in 2002, while the latter takes a more independent line.

On the far right, **Türkiye** usually sticks to a predictable ultra-nationalist line. On the far left, two titles – **Evrensel** and the "pro-Kurdish" **Özgür Politika** – stand out. Both have had their problems with the authorities; *Özgür Politika* in particular is the direct descendant of four successive publications that were closed down between 1994 and 1999.

The principal weekly **magazines** are the picture-driven **Tempo** and **Aktüel** which serve up a diet of showbiz gossip, news and features, including politics. Usually good for a laugh are two pages of pics from celebrity bashes featuring the famous, the nearly famous and the wannabes, shrink-wrapped into atrocious "designer" garb. A vast range of other weekly and monthly glossies includes Turkish versions of most major women's magazines, and even the lads' mag *FHM*.

Turkey also has an insatiable market for weekly **satirical comics** whose content invariably revolves around sex and other foibles of the human condition, often delivering a subtle, or not-so-subtle, political message. Turkey's caricature artists are among the cruellest and most graphic in the world, but seem miraculously immune from legal proceedings. However, title turnover is

(Self-)censorship and Turkish writers

The forcible closure of publications, confiscation of assets and prosecutions of journalists or editors, at the behest of the **State Security Tribunal** (*Devlet Güvenlik Mahkemesi*), were depressingly common in Turkey during the 1980s and 1990s. Most "infractions" were related to alleged insults or impertinence to government officials, accounts of official misdeeds and financial scandals, "denigrating Turkish identity" (especially highlighting the history or current status of Kurds or Armenians) and anything resembling advocacy of communism (banned in Turkey). Judicious self-censorship in the Turkish press was encouraged by even more direct threats to journalists' well-being. Throughout the 1990s the staff of pro-Kurdish publications were physically attacked, often fatally, by shadowy groups alleged to have links with security forces; most egregious was the assassination of *Cumhuriyet* columnist and national pundit Uğur Mumcu in 1993. In late 1999 a watershed of sorts was finally crossed when, after more than forty "unsolved" killings of journalists since 1990, six police officers were sentenced to short jail terms for the beating to death in 1995 of *Evrensel* photographer Metin Göktepe.

The more open political climate that has prevailed since the millennium has periodically made it safer for journalists to criticize the establishment without consequences. Turkey's campaign to enter the EU prompted changes to various laws restricting press and political freedom, including a redraft (though not a repeal) of the infamous Article 8 of the so-called Anti-Terror Law, often dubbed Turkey's "thought crime" statute, and the abolition of the State Security Tribunals in 2004. Early in 2002, American professor Noam Chomsky appeared as a witness and co-defendant in the trial of a pro-Kurdish publisher charged with "disseminating separatist propaganda", and all charges were gratifyingly dropped.

However, like the traditional march of the janissaries, free speech in Turkey has been broadly a case of two steps forward, one step back; 2005 was a particularly bad year for court cases, with activist local prosecutors stepping into the breach left by the demise of the higher security tribunals. Sixteen journalists were put on trial (with twelve guilty verdicts), whilst during 2004–05 over forty authors were also prosecuted, most famously novelist Orhan Pamuk, who was threatened with up to three years in prison for remarks made the previous year to a Swiss newspaper in which he stated openly that 30,000 Kurds and one million Armenians had been killed in Anatolia during the twentieth century. After several months of preliminary hearings, the case – in which the EU had been taking a strong interest – was dropped in January 2006, but similar cases against other, less high-profile journalists such as Hrant Dink, editor of the bilingual Armenian-Turkish paper *Agos*, are continuing. Although conditions can't compare to previous decades when jailings, woundings and killings were the preferred methods of intimidating troublesome writers, the effect of the mischievous-and-worse court cases – often instigated privately by aggrieved nationalists complaining to prosecutors – has been to re-create a climate of fear and insecurity, and once again prompt self-censorship.

fairly rapid, with artist-management disputes resulting in frequent walkouts and the establishment of spin-offs. During the late 1980s, pioneer **Gırgır** was the third biggest-selling adult comic in the world after America's *Mad* and the Soviet Union's *Krokodil*, until the cartoonists responsible decamped to other titles – though *Gırgır* still exists. More recent big-sellers included *Limon*, which spawned *Leman*, which in turn gave birth to current

favourite **Le Manyak**, whose star character is a politically incorrect tom-cat, Şerafettin. The latest entrant is the far more political – and arguably less funny – **Penguen**, which lampoons the ruling elite.

English-language publications

The longest-running English-language newspaper, sold wherever foreigners congregate, is the **Turkish Daily News**, now majority-owned by the Doğan group, and with useful cinema listings for İstanbul, İzmir and Ankara. If you're interested in Turkish politics, the *TDN* serves as a good resource, though its failure to contextualize can be frustrating for those unfamiliar with the country. The Sunday edition has less up-to-date news than the daily, but includes a summary of the week's events tucked in between tedious "analysis" articles penned by "experts" in fractured English. **The New Anatolian**, set up by a rump faction from the *TDN*, displays even ropier English but is often available when its rival isn't.

Glossy magazines include the bimonthly **Istanbul: The Guide**, sold at newsstands or available free in many of the city's larger hotels – features are weak but listings are OK. The same is true for **Time Out Istanbul**, the local imprint of the London listings mag, which has a 64-page English edition (3.5YTL) of what's-on listings and useful coverage of new bars, clubs and restaurants. The monthly travel and culture mag **Atlas** boasts good Turkish-language travel features on Turkey and overseas, plus excellent photography; its excellent twice-yearly supplement, *Arkeo*, has English summaries of all pieces. The surprisingly good Turkish Airlines bilingual in-flight magazine **Skylife** (free on the plane, otherwise on sale at larger newsagents) has a wide variety of features on little-known Turkish destinations, crafts and historical episodes. Any of these is cheaper and more down-to-earth than bimonthly **Cornucopia**, which dwells in its own bubble-world of property restoration, decadent food and auction-house interiors, plus sound-bite features by writers commissioned more for their name or connections than anything else.

British and American newspapers are easily available in Anglophone resorts and the three largest cities, generally arriving late in the evening of publication day. Easiest to find are usually *The Guardian* (European edition), the *International Herald Tribune* and *USA Today*.

Television

Turkish TV has come a long way since the early 1980s, when it was restricted to a single, closely controlled, state-run channel. The advent of satellite dishes essentially broke the public-broadcasting monopoly, as Turkish-language (and, sporadically, Kurdish-language) programmes were beamed in from European transmitters. Private terrestrial channels were not slow to proliferate and have now overtaken public stations in terms of viewer numbers. According to the national broadcasting authority, RTUK, there are about 260 licensed channels, public and private, throughout the country, though the overwhelming majority are local services restricted to one town and not noted for adventurous programming.

Quality in the private sector is fairly low, and the political/religious affiliation of the proprietors – often newspaper moguls or banks – is seldom in doubt. Politically biased reporting, as well as a multitude of other RTUK-defined misdemeanours, are treated severely, with the normal punishment being to take the channel off the air for a couple of days, replacing programmes with a screen explaining which law has been infringed. Legal reforms in 2002 specifically allowed for broadcasting in "non-Turkish" languages, specifically Kurdish, though as yet this hasn't amounted to more than a couple of (geographically restricted) hours per week.

Up to four television channels of the **state-owned TRT** (Turkish Radio and Television) are available, depending on where you are and what time it is. Public programming veers between foreign historical drama series dubbed in Turkish, American films (also dubbed) and talking-heads panel discussions, punctuated by classical Turkish musical interludes, variety shows, soaps and chirpy, US-style advertisements. TRT-1 has a fairly balanced output not dissimilar to British channels, while TRT-2 is the arts and cultural channel; TRT-3 offers live coverage of parliament, and TRT-4 is nominally educational. Another state channel, GAP (*Güney Anadolu Programı* or "South Anatolian Programme"), is reserved for reruns and easy-watching pap aimed at those whose first language is Kurdish or Arabic.

Among **private channels** offering light entertainment, film reruns and current affairs, Show, Star, ATV, Kanal D and Kanal Altı are generally the easiest to pick up. NR 1 and Kral devote their time mainly to Turkish pop videos and short "youth"-related features;

Power Turk serves up Turkish pop; while Dream is probably the best of the lot, with a mix of pop, rock, hip-hop and alternative/indie sounds. Best (Turkish-only) **news coverage** is generally reckoned to be that of NTV and CNN Türk. CNN Türk's output is a mix of news, reviews and interviews similar to its international namesake. NTV's sister channel CNBC-e, a joint venture with America's NBC, devotes evenings and weekends to a bizarre mix of B-movies and US TV shows such as *Seinfeld, South Park, The Simpsons and My Name is Earl*, all in English with Turkish subtitles.

Ideological bias is most apparent on the **religious and far-right-wing channels**. Generally reckoned to be the most Islamic is **Samanyolu** ("Milky Way"), also known as STV, while Kanal Yedi and Flash also maintain a religious stance. TGRT offers a mixed diet of programmes with a right-wing slant, although its current-affairs coverage is very professionally put together.

Satellite TV is common in homes, bars and restaurants, particularly in the Aegean and Mediterranean resorts where live English Premier League soccer is a big attraction, particularly on TV8 which shows games live each Sunday (6pm Turkish time), usually the 5pm kick-off Saturday games as well, plus highlights from the rest of European football. Otherwise you'll find BBC World, BBC Prime, Cinebeş (all-films), CNN and other usual suspects on hotel-room TVs.

Live Turkish Premier League **football** is now exclusive to Turkey's only **digital TV** platform, Digiturk, which you'll find in many bars and cheaper restaurants, predictably packed on match nights. Occasionally terrestrial channels buy the rights to show a big-league game live, but they mostly make do with a highlights package. National team games and second division matches still appear live on TRT, while European club matches go out live on certain private channels such as Star or Show.

Radio

Frequency-crowding on the effectively unregulated airwaves means that even popular channels are almost impossible to pick up without interference. The cacophony seems set to continue as a long-promised

frequency auction has been postponed by successive governments.

Up to four **public radio stations** broadcast between 7am and 1am, though certain channels start earlier or end later. Radyo Üç (The Third Programme or TRT-3), most commonly found at 88.2, 94 and 99MHz, broadcasts the highest proportion of Western music. It also airs **news bulletins in English** at 9am, noon, 2pm, 5pm, 7pm and 10pm, though these tend to be heavily edited propaganda snippets focusing on the movements and utterances of government ministers.

As with television, mediocre **private radio** stations have multiplied almost unbearably, but by playing dial roulette on your personal stereo or car radio, you can often snare some decent jazz, rock, blues or classical programmes. In İstanbul, Açık Radyo (FM 94.9) provides a mixed diet of Western rock, jazz and soul, while Radio Blue (FM 94.5) offers Latin and jazz. Other big names offering Western music and production values include Capitol FM (99.5), Kiss FM (90.3) and Metro FM (97.2), the latter received across much of the country. Many resorts have their own local station on which you may find some programming in English. **English-language foreign services** – including Voice of America and the BBC World Service – can be picked up on short wave, although you'll need to be fairly adept at tuning. The BBC World Service can also theoretically be received on medium wave along the south coast closest to the BBC transmitter on Cyprus.

Cinema

The arrival of TV in Turkey cut the number of cinema screens in the country from around three thousand at the start of the 1970s to just a few dozen by the early 1990s. Thanks to new multi-screen complexes appearing in big shopping centres, the number has since rebounded to several hundred, mostly in İstanbul, Ankara, İzmir, Adana and Antalya, but also in such previously unlikely spots as Antakya, Kayseri, Gaziantep, İskenderun, Diyarbakır and even Van.

Western first-run releases and quality Turkish films supplement the old diet of shoot-em-ups and kung-fu flicks. **Foreign films** are shown in the original language with Turkish subtitles, apart from kid-orientated films which are dubbed into Turkish; screenings (a *seans* in Turkish), up to five daily, generally start at 11.30am or noon, following at around 3pm, 6pm, 9pm and usually midnight. **Tickets** usually cost 5–8YTL, with reduced general admission one night weekly (usually Mondays) and concessions for students and teachers. Most films have a fifteen-minute break mid-action, to allow cigarette-smokers to satisfy their habit in the stairways and cafés. For a detailed overview of the homegrown Turkish film industry, see Contexts, p.1023.

Admission to museums, sites and mosques

Museums are generally open from 8.30 or 9am until 5.30 or 6pm, and closed on Monday, though in the case of some smaller museums you may have to find the *bekçi* (caretaker or warden) and ask him to open up. All sites and museums are closed on the mornings of public holidays (see p.79), while Istanbul's palaces are generally closed on Mondays and Thursdays. Some of Istanbul's most fascinating smaller Byzantine monuments are only accessible by permission from the Directorate of Aya Sofya, located in the grounds of Aya Sofya. Certain isolated monuments beside the Armenian border also require permission to visit, which can be granted only by the military authorities in Ankara.

Admission prices

Admission prices for foreigners to sites in major tourist areas have rocketed in recent years. Current charges are 2YTL for minor sites, 4–5YTL at sites of middling interest and 10–15YTL for major attractions such as Ephesus, Cappadocian cave-churches and İstanbul's Aya Sofya. FIYTO student cards should ensure **free admission** to museums and sites; ISIC cards will usually – though not always – net you a fifty- to sixty-percent **reduction**. Teachers theoretically should be granted the same discount as students – but proving this status at the entrance might not be so easy. Those over 65 are also supposed to gain free entrance to museums and sites; bring your passport as proof of age. A few minor sites not administered by the Ministry of Culture, such as private museums or ones managed by Islamist municipalities, may charge foreigners much more than locals and not recognize any discount schemes.

Archeological sites

Major archeological sites are generally open daily from just after sunrise until just before sunset; owing to budgetary constraints, current schedules feature later opening and earlier closing than in previous years. Some smaller archeological sites are only guarded during the day and left unfenced, permitting (in theory) a free wander around in the evening. Others are staffed until dark by a solitary warden, who may have enough English to give you a guided tour, for which he will probably expect a tip. However, in recent years surveillance at sites both fenced and unenclosed has been improved in the wake of antiquities theft and furtive visits after posted closing hours can result in your being picked up by the *jandarma*.

Never pay **entrance fees** unless the wardens can produce a ticket, whatever other documentation they may have. If you don't take a ticket, crooked sellers can resell the same ticket over and over again, pocketing the proceeds. Keep tickets with you for the duration of your visit and even afterwards, as sites often straddle the route to a good beach – in theory the ticket is valid for the entire day sparing you repayment if you re-cross the area.

Mosques

There's no admission fee for entry to mosques, but you may be asked by the caretaker or *imam* to make a small donation. If so, put it into the collection box rather than someone's hand. Larger mosques frequented by tourists are open all the time – others only for *namaz*, or Muslim prayer, five times a day. **Prayer times**, which last around twenty minutes, vary according to the time of year, but generally occur at dawn, late morning, midday, late afternoon and sundown; often a chalkboard will be posted outside the door with exact hours for that day. Outside prayer times it's sometimes possible to find the *imam* and ask him to open up; just ask passers-by where his house is. Whether or not you're required to, it's a courtesy for women to cover their heads before entering a mosque, and for both men and women to cover their legs (shorts are considered particularly offensive) and upper arms – in some mosques pieces of material are distributed at the door. In some of the larger mosques women will be encouraged to view the premises from the women's galleries upstairs. Shoes should always be removed: unless there's an attendant outside, pick your shoes up, carry them inside and place them on the racks near the door. It's better to wait until prayer is finished and then go in, rather than enter while it's in progress, although at any time you will find a few individuals at prayer. As long as you keep a distance and speak quietly you won't disturb anyone unduly.

Opening hours and public holidays

White-collar workers keep conventional Monday to Friday 9am to 6pm schedules, with a full lunch hour; civil servants (including tourist offices and museum staff) in theory work 8.30am to 5.30pm, but in practice hours can be much more erratic, including two-hour lunches – don't expect to get important official business attended to the same day after 2.30pm. Ordinary shops, including those in malls and large department stores, are open continuously from 8.30 or 9am until 7 or 8pm (and even later in many major cities and resorts), depending on the owner. Craftsmen and bazaar stallholders keep marathon hours, often working from 9am to 8 or 9pm, Monday to Saturday, with only the hastiest of breaks for meals, tea or prayers. Even on Sunday the tradesmen's area may not be completely shut down – though don't count on this.

National secular public holidays are generally marked by processions of schoolchildren or the military, or else by some demonstration of national strength and dignity, such as a sports display. Banks and government offices will normally be closed on these days; where they are not, we say so in the list opposite. Many shops, and all banks and offices, also close during the main religious festivals (see "Festivals", opposite).

Turkish public holidays

January 1 *Yılbaşı* – New Year's Day.
April 23 *Ulusal Egemenlik ve Çocuk Bayramı* – Independence Day, celebrating the first meeting of the new Republican parliament in Ankara, and Children's Day.
May 19 *Gençlik ve Spor Günü* – Youth and Sports Day, also Atatürk's birthday. **May 29** Festival to commemorate İstanbul's capture by Mehmet the Conqueror in 1453 (İstanbul only).
July 1 *Denizcilik Günü* – Navy Day (banks and offices open).
August 26 *Silahlı Kuvvetler Günü* – Armed Forces Day (banks and offices open).
August 30 *Zafer Bayramı* – Celebration of the Turkish victory over the Greek forces at Dumlupınar in 1922.
September 9 *Kurtuluş Günü* – Liberation Day, with parades and speeches marking the end of the Independence War (İzmir only).
October 29 *Cumhuriyet Bayramı* – commemorates the proclamation of the Republic by Atatürk in 1923.
November 10 The anniversary of Atatürk's death in 1938. Observed at 9.05am (the time of his death), when the whole country stops whatever it's doing and maintains a respectful silence for a minute. It's worth being on a Bosphorus ferry this morning, when all the engines are turned off, and the boats drift and blow their foghorns mournfully.

Festivals

There are two kinds of celebration in Turkey: religious festivals, observed all over the Islamic world on dates determined by the Muslim Hijra calendar; and annual cultural or harvest extravaganzas held in various cities and resorts across the country.

Religious festivals

As the Islamic calendar is lunar, the dates of the four important religious festivals drift backwards eleven days each year (twelve in a leap year) relative to the Gregorian calendar. However, future dates of festivals as given on Islamic websites are provisional, owing to factors such as when the moon is sighted and the international dateline, so you should expect variance of a day or so in the ranges given in the lists overleaf.

Perhaps the most important religious festival is **Ramadan** (*Ramazan* in Turkish), the Muslim month of daylight abstention from food, water, tobacco and sexual relations, occurring during late autumn during the first decade of the new millennium. Ramadan is not a public holiday: life carries on as normal despite the fact that half the population is fasting from sunrise to sunset (with a huge incidence of traffic accidents during the last hour or so of fasting – drivers beware). Some restaurants close for the duration or severely curtail their menus, others discreetly hide their salons behind curtains, but at most establishments you will be served with surprisingly good grace. Koranic injunction allows pregnant and nursing mothers, the infirm and travellers to be excused from obligatory fasting; immediately after dark there's an orgy of eating by the famished in places public and private, and you may well find restaurants sold out of everything within an hour of sunset.

Kadir Gecesi (The Eve of Power) takes place between the 27th and 28th days of the month of Ramadan, the time when Mohammed is supposed to have received the Koran from Allah. The mosques – even more brilliantly illuminated than usual for the whole month – are full all night, as it's believed that prayers at this time have special efficacy; those who can't make it out tend to stay home reading the Koran and praying. On **Arife**, the last day of Ramadan, it is customary to go to the cemeteries and pay respects to departed ancestors; many rural restaurants are shut that evening. The three-day **Şeker Bayramı** (Sugar Holiday) is held at the end of Ramadan, celebrated by family get-togethers and the giving of presents and sweets to children, and restrained general partying in the streets and restaurants; on the first night after *Arife* you will have to book well in advance for tables at better restaurants. The four-day **Kurban Bayramı** (Festival of the Sacrifice), in which the sacrificial offering of a sheep represents Abraham's son Ishmael (a Koranic version of the Old Testament story) is marked by the slaughter of over 2.5 million sheep. Only the wealthiest families can afford to buy a whole animal, so part of the meat is distributed to the poor of the neighbourhood. Sheep are brought from all over Anatolia to the big cities (as depicted in the Yılmaz Güney film *The Herd*), and sold on street corners in the weeks leading up to the festival. They are killed by the traditional Islamic method of a slit gullet, in any open space available – now legally restricted, with use of apartment-building gardens now forbidden. During *Şeker* and *Kurban Bayram*s, which are also public holidays (see list on p.79 for dates), travel becomes almost impossible: from the afternoon leading up to the first evening of the holiday (a Muslim festival is reckoned from sunset) – and on the first and last days themselves – public transport is completely booked up, and unless you plan in advance you won't get a seat on any long-distance coach, train, plane or ferry. Note that the already high accident rate on Turkey's roads soars

in these national holidays, with 95 killed and many more injured during the 2005 *Şeker Bayramı* period. Many shops and all banks, museums and government offices close during the holiday periods (although corner grocery stores and most shops in resorts stay open). When these festivals occur close to a national holiday, the whole country effectively grinds to a halt for up to a week, with resorts packed for the duration.

Şeker Bayramı dates

Oct 23–25, 2006
Oct 12–14, 2007
Oct 1–3, 2008
Sept 20–22, 2009

Kurban Bayramı dates

Dec 30, 2006–Jan 2, 2007
Dec 19–22, 2007
Dec 7–10, 2008
Nov 27–30, 2009

Cultural festivals

Cultural festivals are most interesting in the cities and resorts with the resources to attract international-name acts. Just about every sizable town will have some sort of yearly bash, though many are of limited interest to outsiders. We've highlighted the best below, most of which are described in fuller detail in the Guide. Be aware that some of the relatively minor events do not take place in slack years.

İstanbul's most important festivals are organized by the **İstanbul Foundation for Culture and Arts** (see p.196), which promotes a heavyweight annual programme. There's a full festival calendar for İstanbul on p.196, but – as a taster – the season kicks off in mid-April with the **İstanbul International Film Festival**, followed by the **International İstanbul Theatre Festival** (May) and the **International İstanbul Music Festival** (June). The city also sees two major jazz festivals, separate pop, rock and blues events, and the **İstanbul Biennial**, an autumn art exhibition held every two years, usually revolving around a set theme.

The **International İzmir Festival** (June & July) also manages to attract name acts, with many performances at Ephesus theatre and Çeşme castle. The **Aspendos Opera and Ballet Festival** (usually 10 performances from mid-June to early July) is the Mediterranean Coast's big highbrow event.

Less spectacular, but still meriting a look if you happen to be in the area, are: the **Ephesus Festival** (second or third week of May); the **Pamukkale Song Festival** (late June); the **Bursa Festival** (last three weeks of July); the **Bodrum Festival** (early Sept); and the **Antalya Altın Portakal** ("Golden Orange") **Film Festival** (late Sept to early Oct).

A number of more unusual events are also worth coinciding a visit with, not least the **camel wrestling** at Selçuk in mid-January, though bouts (between two male camels in rut) occur throughout Aydın province during December and January, as well as at Kumluca on the Turquoise Coast towards the end of January. You might also try and see the **oil wrestling** (*yağlı güreş*) in Kırkpınar near Edirne in early summer (usually mid-June; and see p.231), and the **bullfighting** – again between randy beasts – which forms the climax of the Kafkasör festival at Artvin in late June. One of the few public performances of a religious nature – with emphasis on the word "performance" – is the **Mevlâna (Dervish) Festival** at Konya on December 10–17 (p.618), though the importance of this festival has lessened now that there are at least thrice-weekly performances in the city's Cultural Centre. İstanbul hosts more genuine performances, and Dervish ceremonies – featuring the so-called "Whirling Dervishes" – have sprung up elsewhere in the country, largely where there are tourist dollars to be made. The only other public devotional observance is the **Hacı Bektaş Veli** commemoration at Hacıbektaş village in Cappadocia, during the latter half of August, when Bektaşis and their affiliates, the Alevîs, meet for a weekend of ritual singing and dancing. This is preceded by a similar festival in early June, honouring the second most important Alevî saint, **Pir Abdal Musa**, in Tekke village near Elmalı in Antalya province. **Folk-dance** festivals are always worth a detour, providing an opportunity to see some of the country's best dance groups performing a sample of the varied repertoire of Turkish dances in traditional costumes. There are folk festivals in Silifke in May, in Foça in June and in Samsun in July. More spontaneous, and therefore more difficult to track down, are the music-and-dance gatherings of the Gypsies in Thrace during spring and early summer, though Edirne's Spring Festival and Kırklareli's Takava Festival are both permanent fixtures.

Agricultural festivals play an important part in Turkish rural life. The Diyarbakır Watermelon Festival in mid- or late September is basically a competition for the most outsized of the region's fruit. Ürgüp's Grape Harvest Festival in mid-September culminates a season of celebrations in the Cappadocia region, including a Handicrafts and Pottery Festival at Avanos during August. The trodden grape is honoured by drinking some of Turkey's finest white wines from the local thimble-sized, earthenware vessels. Other agricultural products are ingested at Bolu's Mengen Chefs' Contest in August – the region is purportedly home to the country's best cooks.

Bazaars and shopping

Consuming interests are high on the agenda of most visitors to Turkey. Even those who arrive determined not to buy will be shortly persuaded otherwise by the myriad street merchants, store owners and affiliated touts who cannot resist the hard sell – as intrinsic to Turkish culture as tea and hospitality – and by the occasionally respectable quality of goods available.

Bazaars, shops, department stores and malls

There are several types of traditional bazaar in Turkey, which continue to coexist with the modern American/European-style shopping malls that dominate the wealthier districts of every large city.

First are the **covered bazaars**, found in larger towns such as İstanbul, Bursa and Kayseri. These are essentially medieval Ottoman shopping malls, comprising several *bedestens*, or domed buildings, at which particular types of goods were sold, linked by various covered arcades, which in turn were also originally assigned to a particular trade – though strict segregation has long since broken down.

Surrounding these covered bazaars are large areas of **small shops**, basically open-air extensions of the covered areas and governed by the same rules: each shop is a separate unit with an owner and apprentices, and successful businesses are not allowed to expand or merge. Prices on the street are often a bit lower than in the *bedestens* owing to lower rents.

In addition there are weekly or twice-weekly **street markets** in most towns or in different areas of cities, arranged on the same lines as those in northern Europe and selling roughly similar everyday household products. More exotic are the semi-permanent **flea markets** (*bit pazarı*, literally "louse markets"), ranging in quality from street stalls where old clothes are sold and resold among the homeless, to lanes of shops where you can buy secondhand clothes, furniture or occasionally an antique of real aesthetic or monetary value.

In many cities, particularly in İstanbul, shopping for everyday household goods, clothes, furniture and accessories is increasingly done in Western-style department stores and shopping malls. They're often situated some way from the centre, but we've picked out the most useful in the Guide. The main homegrown **department store** chain is Yeni Karamürsel, with outlets in İstanbul, İzmir and Ankara, plus several other spots; however, branches of European superstores like Praktiker and Carrefour are now found in İstanbul and Ankara.

Best buys

The best selection of good-quality wares is to be found in the major tourist centres: İstanbul, Cappadocia, Bursa and the coastal resorts. Don't think that you'll find bargains or a better selection in the production centres for a particular craft in the interior: wholesalers and collectors have been there long before you.

Apart from the variety and visual impact of goods on sale in Turkish bazaars, and the tantalizing prospect of picking up something worthwhile, the main reason to visit is for the challenge of **bargaining**. As a guideline, begin at a figure rather lower than whatever you are prepared to pay, perhaps around half of your shopkeeper's starting price. Once a price has been agreed on, you are ethically committed to buy, so don't commence haggling unless you are reasonably sure you want the item. There are other psychological tactics to engage in, such as enquiring about several articles in a shop before you even look at the thing you really want, or proposing to go elsewhere for some comparison shopping. "Assistance" from touts will automatically bump up the price thirty to fifty percent, as they will be getting a commission. Also, be prepared to hand over between three and seven percent extra if paying by credit card; your bargaining position is strongest with crisp, bunched notes, either foreign or YTL.

Carpets and kilims

Turkish **carpets and kilims** are world famous, though they are no longer necessarily cheaper in Turkey than overseas. The selection is best in İstanbul, whose shopkeepers scour the countryside; thus there are relatively few rugs on sale near their source. A kilim, or pile-less rug, is flat-woven and double-sided (that is, the pattern should look much the same top or bottom); a *cicim* is a kilim with additional designs stitched onto it; while *sumak* technique, confined in Turkey to saddlebags, involves wrapping extra threads around the warp.

Vigilance is the rule when shopping for any kind of floor covering; it's easy to pay over the odds for inferior quality. One useful test, ensuring that the colours aren't going to run the first time you try to clean off a coffee stain, is to wet a white rag and rub the carpet, then check to see if any colour has come off. If it has, it doesn't bode well for the future, and the dyes certainly aren't natural. Since older, handmade, natural-dyed rugs are getting rarer all the time, genuine collector's items are often salvaged from deteriorated larger works, and more or less skilfully repaired; saddle or cradle bags may be opened to become small rugs. A handwoven rug will usually show its pattern clearly on the reverse, unlike a machine-made one. Hand-spun yarn can be identified by the fringe, which is unevenly twisted, tight and ravelled to the ends.

You can buy a new, artificially dyed *çeyrek* ("quarter", 1m by 1.5m) kilim for around €50–83, and **prices** go up according to quality, age and design. A small woollen rug made with natural dyes would be $66–166 bought new, a larger one around $208–291. Silk carpets start in the hundreds of dollars for a tiny one, and go up to hundreds of thousands.

Natural dyes, especially in earth tones, are now being used in manufacturing again, and they tend not to fade as quickly as chemical ones. This renaissance was pioneered by DOBAG, a co-operative with headquarters in Ayvacık (see box on p.294), dedicated both to ethical treatment of the weavers and to traditional methods, pigments and designs. All of their carpets bear a distinctive leather certification tag.

Chemical dyes first appeared during the 1870s, and their use up until the 1980s is easy to spot because the colours are either garish (especially the oranges) or fade mud-dily except at the roots. Overly bright rugs are often left out for sun-fading or are bleached in lye or chlorine. The latter two processes are particularly undesirable as they weaken the fabric; bleach-faded rugs will smell of chlorine when you rub a wet finger on the pile.

It's now difficult to find a carpet vendor who will admit that his stock is anything other than natural-dyed. However, such claims are usually spurious, since most carpets are still made using artificial dyes, albeit the so-called "natural-identical" ones with more subtle, light-fast, gradually fading pigments.

The test for pure **wool** is setting light

to a fine strand. If the charred remains are crumbly, it's wool; if they're sticky, it's synthetic fibre. A strand of **silk** will not flame, but makes an ash and smells organic when it burns; synthetic silk glows and smells of chemicals. The price of a silk carpet depends on the number of knots per square centimetre – this is usually 64 or 81, but very fine ones are made with 144 or 196 per square centimetre. There should be no flaws visible on the back of a silk rug.

It's worth finding out as much as you can about the origins of the carpet, the symbolic meanings of its motifs and the production methods. This will increase the nostalgic value of the product, and during such dis-cussions you should be able to decide if your dealer is trustworthy, and whether his final price will be fair or not. If you're very seri-ous about carpet-buying, preliminary visits to carpet shops in your home country, to an ethnological museum or two and a perusal of some of the recommended titles on the subject (listed under "Books" in Contexts) will be worthwhile.

Jewellery

Jewellery should also be bought with care, since imitations abound. Fake amber melts on exposure to an open flame, but a test isn't advisable without the permission of the pro-prietor. Gold, silver and semi-precious stones, of which amber and turquoise are the most common, are sold by weight, with almost total disregard for the disparate level of craftsman-ship involved. One particularly intricate method is *telkâri* or wire filigree, most of which comes from eastern Turkey, particularly Diyarbakır and Trabzon. Bear in mind that the price per gramme of silver or gold can be bargained down, making a substantial difference to the eventual total. Gold in particular can be very good value – many people still use it as a form of savings account – and is almost pure (and soft) at 22 carat, such that gold *telkâri* bangles bend easily. Also remember that sterling silver items should bear a hallmark – anything else could well be a nickel or pewter alloy.

Copperware

Copperwork is not as common as in the days when it was an essential part of a newly-wed couple's household furnishings, and very little of it is still hammered out from scratch, or of really heavy gauge. Still, the articles are very handsome and if you want to buy at source, keep an eye out in the bazaars of eastern Anatolia. Since copper is mildly toxic, vessels intended for use in the kitchen must be tinned inside – one layer for use as a tea kettle, three for use with food. If the layer is absent or deteriorated, have it (re)done at the nearest *kalaycı* or tinsmith for a nominal fee. If you live in a hard-water area, the vessel is from such a place in Turkey, a layer of mineral deposits will quickly build up, serving the same protective function.

Antique copperware is a cult in itself, though not quite as exalted as that of the carpet. Pieces from the Republican (post–World War I) era are sold roughly by weight at about €5 per kilo; for Ottoman trays and vessels, you'll be asked whatever the dealer thinks he can get away with, based loosely on age, weight and provenance. Cheap, newer, thin-gauge ware with machine-pressed designs comes from Kayseri, Gaziantep or Kahramanmaraş and won't be older than 1960 or cost more than €29. At the opposite end of the price/quality scale is embossed work from Bosnia, such as a late nineteenth-century *sefer tası* (lunchbox set, tiffin) for about €58–70; older Greek- or Armenian-produced trays or vessels, identifiable by their distinctive lettering, for €100–200; and incredibly heavy, early nineteenth-century Persian or Anatolian trays or vessels with a sultan's monogram, for which asking prices of €1000 and up are not unheard of. Best deals have historically been in Ankara's Bakırcılar Çarşısı, though staff from embassies and multinational corporations living locally have had a predictable effect on prices. Antique shops in Kaş, Cappadocia and Bergama are well presented but usually vastly overpriced, while İstanbul's old copper market, near the Nuruosmariye Camii, has for years been completely gentrified.

Clothing

Turkey's **clothing** industry has raised its profile somewhat since Rifat Özbek and half-Turkish Nicole Farhi appeared on the scene with their lines of orientally influenced designer togs, and Turkish designs are beginning to match the quality of local fabrics such as Bursa silk and Angora wool. Nowadays you will pay near-Western prices for **genuine** locally designed items at reputable shops, which rarely sell fakes – local brands are aggressively protected, if necessary by police raids at the behest of corporate lawyers.

Foreign designer-clothing can also be found, at European prices – except during the end-of-season/end-of-line sales which are worth catching. Non-exported Turkish designer labels such as Collezione, Rodi and Mavi are also worth a look. In general the best bargains are to be had from **street markets** and oddments stores where you can fetch seconds, samples or overstock of Western brands (including British high-street chains) produced for export but not generally marketed locally.

Only street vendors peddle **imitation** Lacoste, Polo, Ralph Lauren, Quiksilver, Tommy Hillfiger, Adidas, Nike, Levi Strauss and Benetton items of decidedly varying quality, some made in Turkey under licence but much of it merchandise bootlegged in the best pirating tradition of Asia. Occasionally this is done with panache and humour (eg, a sign in Bodrum reading "Genuine Fake Rolexes"), but most of the time the marketing and results are furtive and shabby: real Italian- or English-language labels slapped onto local products that shrink two sizes or fade at the first washing. Prices too good to be true are the dead giveaway; neither should you be taken in by "near" brand-names like Benelton or Adidos with copycat logos. Some fake soccer shirts (mostly Turkish, English, German and Dutch clubs) do make good buys, as their material is fairly robust.

Bear in mind that T-shirts or other articles of clothing prominently featuring the **Turkish flag** are, bizarrely, illegal. A long-forgotten law banning the use of the national flag in clothing was "rediscovered" in 2001 and used to prosecute sellers of red tees bearing the Turkish star and crescent. Their disappearance from shops prior to the 2002 World Cup, coupled with the appearance of vast numbers of cheap vintage football shirts for export, led many Turks to support their national team decked out in red "CCCP" and

"England 1966" shirts. The law is due for repeal, though it's unclear when.

Leather goods

There are always a number of well-stocked **leather** outlets in any important tourist centre, though the industry was originally based in western Anatolia where alum deposits and acorn-derived tannin aided the tanning process. Today, İzmir and İstanbul still have the largest workshops, though the retail business also booms on the Mediterranean coast, particularly in Antalya and Alanya. Jackets are the most obvious purchase, the prices of which vary from a paltry €66 to over €250, with a minimum of about €125 for anything half-decent. If you're not interested in big outlays, men's or women's wallets are excellent and durable; Maraş brand may be the best in quality, but the Marchila, Guard or Pikaldi lines are very nearly as good for half the price. The variety of designs is staggering, so allow for plenty of browsing time. Women's **shoes** come in a wide range of colours, but curiously only up to about European size 40.

Nargiles

The **nargile**, or hookah, is doubtless one of those Ottoman hangovers, like fezzes and dervishes, that Atatürk might have wished to consign to the dust heap of history. However, it has endured in republican Turkey, indulged in for hours along the central and north Aegean coasts by cafés-full of contentedly puffing gentlemen. Since the millennium, nargile smoking has become particularly trendy amongst educated youth, who patronize pseudo-Ottoman cafés in just about any town with a university.

A functional *nargile* is not a plastic toy nor *objet d'art* as sold in so many trinket shops, but should have a lamb's-leather, wire-reinforced tube, all-brass or lathed-hardwood plumbing and a clear glass or crystal chamber. If you find an older, crystal item, it will be an antique and worth upwards of €83. Expect to pay €29 for an 18-inch model with a blown glass bowl; cast ones with visible mould marks aren't so valuable. A wood superstructure looks better, but brass ones last longer. The tubes (*marpuçlar*) wear out after a few years but are sold separately in speciality shops, most notably in İstanbul's Mısır Çarşısı.

If you intend to use the *nargile* when you get home, remember to buy *tömbeki*, or compressed tobacco (again most easily in the Mısır Çarşısı in İstanbul), as you won't find it easily outside Turkey – most of it is in fact now produced in Egypt. You'll also have to convince customs authorities that your *nargile* isn't narcotics paraphernalia and you'll need a source of live coals to drop into the brazier end – matches don't work well. Also, the brazier tends to be fitted with meltable plastic mesh inside, so for practical use you'll need to install a small copper mesh, easily available for a few pennies in North European and American head shops or hippy boutiques.

Music and musical instruments

Traditional Turkish **musical instruments** are sold cheaply all over Turkey. The most easily portable are the *ney*, the Mevlevî flute made from a length of calamus reed, the *davul* or drum, and the *saz*, the long-necked Turkish lute. In İstanbul the main sales points are along Atatürk Bulvarı below the Valens Aqueduct, especially the IMC centre in Unkapanı, and along the upper reaches of Yüksek Kaldırım and its continuation Galipdede Caddesi, across from the Mevlevi *semahane*, near the top station of the Tünel in Beyoğlu. You are less likely to get a "toy" version if you buy instruments at specialist shops like these, or from the craftsmen themselves. A *kaval* (end-blown flute) is compact and inexpensive at about €8, and a *saz* is good value for around €166, though you can pay five times that for a top-notch model. Rock and jazz musicians might like to score, a bit cheaper than abroad, a set of cymbals from one of two world-famous brands – Istanbul and Zildjian – both made by İstanbul-based or İstanbul-origin Armenian companies.

Since Turkey joined the EU customs union in 2000, the available selection of imported **cassettes** and, especially, **CDs** has grown dramatically, with specialist shops catering for jazz, world and dance music springing up in bigger cities. The rapid spread of CD copiers has spurred a boom in the sale of secondhand genuine CDs, as collectors buy, duplicate and then sell on their original. Currently, imported or under-licence new CDs cost the equivalent of €12.50–16, new Turkish-music CDs €6–10, secondhand foreign CDs €6.60–8 and cassettes around €5–6.60. The burgeoning interest in world music has led to a simultaneous rediscovery of Turkey's native music traditions. A steady stream of new CD issues and reissues of long-forgotten ethnic music has followed; see p.1014 for a discography of recommended items.

If your conscience doesn't nag you, Turkey has a flourishing **pirating industry** for every sort of CD – computer games, DVDs and Playstation as well as music – for about €0.80 each. Not only street traders, but supposedly reputable shops keep lists of titles available for pirating under the counter – all of which keeps the police busy.

Games, mementoes and accessories

A **tavla** or backgammon set makes another good souvenir of Turkish popular culture, since it's played in coffeehouses and gaming halls all over the country. The cheapest wooden sets cost around €5; a medium-size apparatus of inlaid, painted cedar-wood (*şedir*) runs to about €25, and you can easily pay over €83 for inlaid mother-of-pearl and ivory. Most boards come from Damascus, as any reputable dealer will admit; if you're not confident that the inlay material is genuine and not just stencilled on, it's better to settle for the painted-wood kind, which is more difficult to fake. Dice and pieces should be included, and many boards have a chess/checkers grid on the exterior; an olive-wood set of chessmen will set you back another €6.

Mavi boncuk (blue bead) key rings, lintel ornaments and animal collars are sold all over the place to ward off *nazar* (the evil eye). Bath **loofahs** (in Turkish, *lifi*) are common at İstanbul's Mısır Çarşısı and in the coastal resorts; even at tourist prices, they cost one-third to one-half of what they would at home, and weigh next to nothing in your luggage.

Other possible memorabilia, easily found in the shops of any covered bazaar, are probably best obtained from the towns in which they originate. These include **meerschaum pipes** carved from *lületaşı* stone quarried near Eskişehir; **Karagöz puppets**, representing the popular folk characters Karagöz and Hacıvat, preferably made from camel skin in Bursa; **towelling and silk goods**, again in Bursa – although the all-cotton bedding and towels at dedicated retail outlets nationwide are excellent value; **onyx**, available all over Cappadocia, but especially Hacıbektaş; and **Kütahya ceramics**, which may not be the finest ever produced in Turkey, but since the kilns of İznik closed down are the best available. Middle-grade enamelled tiles suitable for fireplace surrounds won't cost more than €2.50 apiece at either of the two Kütahya factories making them – in tourist resorts, boutiques will demand up to €6 for the same, so it's worth loading up a car with some if you're passing through Kütahya. Tiles, as opposed to kitsch objects, may not be found easily in the town itself – you have to ask to be taken to the factories outside of town. In another league entirely are the products of the **İznik Foundation**, whose patterns are subtly altered to prevent counterfeiting by others; they can cost upwards of €125 each and are startlingly different from anything else on offer.

Spices and foodstuffs

Acknowledging the slight risk of having certain goods confiscated on return to the European Union or North America, locally produced **spices, condiments and foodstuffs** can be recommended as a compact, lightweight souvenir purchase. Low-grade saffron (*zafran*), the stamen of a particular kind of crocus, is still gathered in northern Anatolia. Sumac (*sumak*) is a ground-up purple leaf for sprinkling on barbecued meats and salad onions, much encountered in districts with an Arab heritage. Vanilla (*vanilya*) pods are bigger and cheaper in Turkey than elsewhere, and pure *sahlep* powder (ground-up orchid root; see p.68), while not cheap by any standard, can be found nowhere else (easiest in İzmir). *Pekmez* (molasses of grape, mulberry or carob pods) is phenomenally nutritious and, though a potential mess in your baggage, makes a splendid ice-cream topping or baking ingredient;

rural people typically mix grape *pekmez* with *tahini* (sesame paste) to make an appetizing, high-calorie snack. Olive oil, most famously from Gemlik, is a worthwhile purchase, as is Defne Sabunı (laurel-scented olive-oil soap from Antakya, excellent for getting grease stains off clothes). Both hot and sweet peppers are made into concentrated pastes (*salçalar*), while dried aubergine/eggplant shells are convenient for stuffing. Pomegranate seeds are the basis of *nar eksisi*, sour grenadine syrup, which can either flavour drinks, garnish aubergine slices or liven up stews (Migros supermarkets stock it). Many visitors acquire a taste for Black Sea tea; the best blends change from year to year, with little quality control within a single brand, but go for the best available and it still won't break the bank.

Antiques and smuggling: a warning

Some of the more popular archeological sites, particularly Ephesus and Pamukkale, are periodically the haunt of characters peddling "**antiks**" of doubtful authenticity. These freelance salesmen are remarkably tenacious, but in the majority of cases you would simply be throwing money away; in the unlikely event you were sold something genuine, you would be liable for prosecution.

Under Turkish law it is an offence to buy, sell, attempt to export or even possess museum-calibre antiquities (which includes fossils). Exact age limits are not specified in lawbooks, suggesting that decisions by customs officials are arbitrary and subjective, though a principal measure of antiquity is rarity.

In the case of **carpets** handled by established dealers, you run a very slight risk of investing a lot of money in a supposed "collector's item" that turns out to be collectable only by the Turkish Republic. If you're apprehensive about a proposed purchase, ask the dealer to prepare both a *fatura* (invoice) recording the exact purchase price – also necessary to satisfy customs – and a declaration stating that the item is not an antiquity. If you're still not reassured, you may want to consult staff at the nearest museum, who will issue a certificate if necessary.

Should you be caught **smuggling** out anything restricted, the Turkish authorities will be unimpressed by any excuses or connections and will very likely make an example of you – as they did an American woman in 1986, who unsuccessfully claimed ignorance of a purchase's vintage and served six months of a much longer prison sentence before escaping with the assistance of her legal counsel.

Crime, personal safety and etiquette

Despite popular, *Midnight Express*–type stereotypes, you're unlikely to encounter any trouble in Turkey. Having said this, pickpocketing and purse snatching are becoming common in İstanbul (see p.120) and other major cities, as is burglary and theft. Violent street crime is fortunately rare. Keep your wits about you and an eye on your belongings just as you would anywhere else, and make sure your passport is secure at all times, and you shouldn't have any problems. Indeed, most people are still scrupulously honest: it is far more likely that someone draws your attention to money fallen from your wallet onto the pavement, rather than pocket it themselves. Except for well-known "red-light" districts, and some eastern towns, women are probably safer on their own than in other European countries.

The police, army and gendarmerie

Civilian police come in a variety of sub-divisions, and are treated with a healthy respect by the locals. Once low-paid and ill-trained, recent years have seen their pay rise substantially (reducing corruption), and graduate intake programmes have raised the overall level of education of the police force. The "glass-walls" policy (designed to make the police more accountable for their actions) was introduced, at least partially, to satisfy the Europeans as Turkey strives for full EU membership, and as a result, attitudes towards suspects have improved considerably. Having said this, for most foreigners, uniformed men with guns and the language barrier can still make a visit to a police station uncomfortable. **If you are arrested** for any reason, the best general rule is to stay polite and patient – getting irate tends to be counterproductive. While waiting for the commanding officer to arrive, smile a lot and try to communicate by word or gesture with your captor; you'll find that matters get much more relaxed. You have **the right to make a phone call** to a friend, hotelier or consul.

The blue-uniformed **Polis** are the everyday security force in cities and towns with populations over 2000; the most you'll probably have to do with them is a request for help in finding a street. The **Trafik Polis**, recognized by their white caps and two-toned vehicles (usually Renault Clios or Fords), are a branch of this service and their main responsibility seems to be controlling intersections and doing spot checks on vehicles at approaches to towns. İstanbul and several other large towns have a rapid-response squad of red-and-black-uniformed motorbike police known as the *yunus* (dolphin) *polis*; they are generally courteous and helpful to tourists and may speak some English. The *Trafik Polis* in İstanbul also have a black-and-yellow-liveried motorbike branch, not particularly known for their courtesy towards anyone. In the towns you're also likely to see the **Belediye Zabıtası**, the navy-clad market police, who patrol the markets and bazaars to ensure that tradesmen aren't ripping off customers – approach them directly if you have reason for complaint.

Turkey's huge armed forces play a fairly high-profile role in maintaining law and order. In most rural areas, law enforcement is in the hands of the **jandarma** or gendarmerie, a division of the regular army charged with law enforcement duties. Gendarmes, despite their military affiliation, are often kitted out not in fatigues but well-tailored gear, modelled on the French uniform, to make them appear less threatening; most of them are conscripts who will be courteous and helpful if approached. However, their officer corps may be in the hip pockets of powerful local interests – so complaining to them about illegal buildings, desecration of archeological sites or rip-off roadside restaurants is often a futile exercise. Another branch of the army is the **military police** or *Askeri İnzibat*, with white helmets bearing the letters *As İz*, white holsters and lanyards. They keep order among the large numbers of conscripts you'll see on the streets of some Turkish towns.

Restricted areas

There is a large and visible army and gendarmerie presence in the Kurdish-dominated southeast of the country, where checkpoints control travel on a few major, and some rural, roads. In the mountains around the towns of Hâkkari and Siirt, all around Mardin, Doğubeyazit, Bitlis, Diyarbakır, Muş and Bingöl, and between Kemah and Tunceli, there was – until the 1999 arrest of PKK leader Abdullah Öcalan – a full-scale insurrection under way. Although the situation has improved considerably, the instability in neighbouring Iraq and the calling off of a (unilateral) ceasefire by the much-depleted PKK in 2005, not to mention the serious economic woes of this war-ravaged region, mean it will be some time before matters return completely to normal in the affected regions. You can find more details about the situation on p.895.

In **remote areas of the east** you're likely to attract the attention of the *jandarma* (and quite possibly the plain-clothes secret police, who generally stand out a mile from the locals) who'll want to know what you're doing and where you're going. This may involve, at most, a rather tedious, though polite, interrogation. Lone males especially may find themselves suspected of being journalists with Kurdish sympathies. As a rule, keep calm, smile a lot, and emphasize wherever possible that you are a *turist* (tourist). The only areas where you absolutely need a **permit** are within a few hundred metres of the eastern border, especially the ever-tense frontier with Armenia; we've detailed specific instances in the Guide. The **Kurdish-populated areas** along the border with Iraq and Syria fall into a sort of grey zone: while it's not forbidden for outsiders to visit them – tourism authorities are often loath to admit that there's any lingering problem – local authorities may try to prevent you from going and will take no responsibility for your safety.

Avoiding trouble

As well as the usual warnings on drugs and exporting antiquities, you are advised to avoid **insulting Atatürk or Turkey**, and never to deface, degrade, or tear up currency or the flag; drunkenness will likely be considered an aggravating, not a mitigating factor. Try not to be drawn into **serious disputes**, since while things rarely turn violent in Turkey, when they do they can turn *very* violent – if anybody seems to be insulting or provoking you, walk away. **Don't take photographs** near the numerous, well-marked military zones. Don't "raid" **archeological sites** after posted closing hours (see p.77). And last but not least, don't engage in any **missionary or proselytization activities** among the locals, or attempt to import evangelical literature. Touring the Christian sites with the Bible or a scholarly work is certainly OK, but distributing tracts isn't. At the very least you will seriously offend the object of your proselytizing.

Despite the courtesy and honesty of most Turks, certain crimes aimed specifically at tourists should be guarded against: there have been an increasing number of **gas-and-rob** operations in train compartments, and of **knockout drugs** being introduced into food and drink. Especially if travelling alone, be suspicious of young men working in pairs or trios who befriend you and then ply you with comestibles procured out of sight. You're quite likely to wake up hours later with a splitting headache, minus your bags and valuables. More seriously, there is a thriving black market in **stolen EU passports** in Turkey, furnished to refugees from further east in Asia; a direct consequence of this was that in İstanbul some solo male Britons with Latin or Asian surnames and appearance were murdered during the late 1990s, for their passports. If you fit this description, we advise you to use better quality hotels or *pansiyons*, and to be especially vigilant against both drug-and-rob and gas-and-rob scams.

Touts

Local authorities have in general realized that touts give their resorts a bad name, and clamped down. So if you are pestered, it's usually only necessary to turn to someone in authority. The exceptions to this are at the bus stations at Nevşehir, Eğirdir, Pamukkale, Selçuk and Kuşadası, and maybe one or two other places. Ninety-five percent of the time they will be collecting commissions on the accommodation or services they lead you to. Most are good-natured, but will take advantage of your gullibility, tiredness and disorientation, particularly if you arrive late at night or in the early morning and are at your most vulnerable. Occasionally they can be stubbornly persistent or even abusive if spurned; see the survival techniques mentioned opposite. Carpet touts are a more widespread problem in major cities.

Sexual harassment

Successful relationships/marriages between Turkish men and foreign women are still comparatively rare, despite Turkey's rapid Westernization, and are generally confined to mature individuals, with similar backgrounds and education, who have had some experience of each other's countries. The average female traveller is most likely to come across poorer, less well-educated young (and not so young!) men working in the tourist sector as waiters, bartenders or shop assistants. Often working far away from their home towns, and without the restraining influence of their conservative families, they tend to look upon foreign women as both rich and an easy lay.

Turkish society remains deliberately gender-segregated in many public areas (except in major tourist spots and the most cosmopolitan parts of the major cities) as well as in private life, so if a **woman travelling alone** wants to avoid the company of men, it's not too difficult. Simply seek the company of Turkish women at every opportunity and you will generally be protected by them. Places where you will *not* find unaccompanied Turkish women include the streets, bars and restaurants at night, so this policy does actually limit your options of independent enjoyment. If you do want to head out for an evening, try to go as part of a group – mixed-sex ideally, though even in an all-female group, when you'll undoubtedly get some unwelcome attention (just as you would in most Western cities), at least you will be protected. If you do go out alone at night, be warned that you may well be mistaken for a prostitute (see p.92).

Turkish women have over the years adopted successful tactics to protect themselves from **harassment**. To imitate them, avoid eye contact with men and try and look as confident and purposeful as possible. When all else fails, the best way of neutralizing harassment is to make a public scene. You won't elicit any sympathy by swearing in Turkish, but the words *Ayıp* ("Shame!") or *Beni rahatsız ediyorsun* ("You're disturbing me"), spoken very loudly, generally have the desired effect – passers-by or fellow passengers will deal with the situation for you. *Defol* ("Piss off!") and *Bırak beni* ("Leave me alone") are stronger retorts. In general, Turkish men will back down when confronted and cases of violence against strangers are very rare; the back streets of most Turkish towns are a lot safer at night than those of (say) London. This is partly due to excessive police presence; do not hesitate to ask them for help.

Etiquette and body language

Hospitality, *misafirperverlik* in Turkish, remains one of the pillars of rural Turkish culture away from tourist areas and dealing gracefully with invitations is crucial to avoid causing offence. Such offers usually have no ulterior motives, with nothing expected in return except your company and possible entertainment value. If you really can't spare the time, you can mime "thanks" by placing one hand on your chest and point-

ing with the other to your watch and then in the direction you're headed. Even **a tea-break** will take a while, because you should stop for at least two, or none at all; drinking only one glass may be interpreted as casting aspersions on their tea. The first offer of **food** or a full meal should be declined on your part – if it's sincere it will be repeated at least twice and convention demands that you accept the third offer. Don't attempt to reciprocate; later you can send a postcard from your hometown or a print of a snapshot you take of your new friends.

If you're **invited into a home**, remove your shoes at the door and if a meal is served at a low table with seating on the floor, hide your stockinged feet under the table or a dropcloth provided for the purpose. You should in fact **never point your feet**, shod or otherwise, at anyone, as they're considered unclean in every sense. When scooping food with bread sections from a communal bowl, **use your right hand** – the left is reserved for intimate toilet operations. Do not openly pick your teeth or blow your nose at table or on the street; if you use toothpicks provided at restaurants, cover your mouth while doing so, like a harmonica-player. In some public areas, particularly when it comes to travel and entertainment, the sexes are **segregated** as far as is practicable. In a bus, dolmuş, cinema or theatre, for example, if given a choice of seats, women should always sit next to another woman, and men should not sit next to a woman without her permission. Couples should refrain from making excessive **gestures of affection** in public. **Nudism** at the beach is not on, though at resorts such as Assos frequented by Turkish "*entels*" (trendies) or any Mediterranean beach resort with a large foreign presence you can get away with some discreet topless sunning. **Beachwear** (as in bikini tops and bottoms, briefs etc) should be confined to the beach and wearing halter tops or ultra-tight or short shorts on the street is considered bad taste, even if your hosts are too polite to say so.

If you venture much off the tourist track, you will have to accept that being **stared at** is part of the experience and not considered rude, as is possibly being mobbed by small children who may or may not wish to guide you to the local ruins, beg for pens and candy or even pelt your car with stones. In remoter areas, **people of colour** may find themselves ogled, as well as receiving unsolicited comments – ranging from *Arap!* (a Black!) to the notionally more appreciative *çok güzel* (very pretty!). Turkey is in fact one of the least racist countries around the Mediterranean; read the box about "The Sudanese of Turkey" on p.337 to get an idea of what place blacks occupy in the Turkish psyche. The situation has improved greatly since the arrival of numerous African and South American footballers, with most teams boasting at least a couple of black players in their squad.

Turks employ a variety of **body language** not immediately obvious to most outsiders. Clicking the tongue against the roof of the mouth and simultaneously raising the eyebrows and chin means "no" or "there isn't any"; those economical of movement will rely on their eyebrows alone. By contrast, wagging the head rapidly from side to side means "Explain, I don't understand", while a single, obliquely inclined nod means "yes". Rubbing bunched fingers and thumb together means "loadsamoney", usually when referring to nefarious dealings or local corruption. Clicking fingers sharply indicates "good, top quality (merchandise, football player etc)".

Women in Turkey

There is a wide divergence of views on acceptable behaviour and roles for women, both according to social class and region of the country. Countrywide, most freedom exists in İstanbul and the west and south coasts, which are almost on a par with European mores; in more devout, traditional areas women and girls behave more conservatively. However, even in the most modern cities, dress is more modest than that of visiting hordes. Headscarves are becoming more popular in the religious enclaves of western towns, and the difference with the east is less marked. The headscarf is forbidden in government offices and universities, a restriction dating from Atatürkist attempts to impose Western values, which the present government would like to lift.

Middle-class women have long worked as public-sector employees (including the police and civil services) and in private white/blue-collar jobs including hotels and airlines, but are almost totally absent from the bazaars, restaurants and bars, except in tourist hotels. The spread of fast-food chains and supermarkets is opening up more job opportunities in resorts and cities. In the rural areas, many women work outside the home harvesting cotton, carnations or tea and bring their own produce alone to local markets or wholesalers.

Family issues

While in country areas parents still reserve the right to choose wives for their sons, in cities a Western attitude prevails and couples are even beginning to live together outside marriage. Abortion is available on demand, with or without the father's consent, contraceptives are readily available over the counter, and a baby can now be registered to unmarried parents. The **birth rate** is declining rapidly – though there's still a huge disparity between the east and west of the country – and is currently estimated at 2.8 children per married couple. The law awards men considerable say over the welfare of their children, including preventing them from going abroad with the mother without the father's permission. In mixed-nationality marriages this has sometimes led to the kidnapping of offspring, but foreign-court custody judgements can be enforced in Turkey. Once a separation has taken place, **divorce** law is fairly even-handed, providing divorce in a minimum time as long as a settlement can be made for the children, property acquired during the marriage divided equitably, and maintenance payments made for the wife while the case is ongoing. **Girls' education**, especially in the east, is often neglected by poor families, but the EU and UN are helping local authorities conduct back-to-school campaigns.

Prostitution

Nowhere is Turkish women's subordinate status more apparent, however, than in Turkey's numerous municipal **brothels**. Strange as it may seem in a nominally Muslim culture, prostitution is legal and highly organized by every large municipality – the idea being that some women protect the virtue of others by acting as foils for male lust. Organized prostitution tends to be a feature of certain obvious hotels in a town's bazaar area, or more commonly is concentrated in purpose-built compounds, complete with gate and police guard, known as the *genelev* (general or public house). İstanbul's notorious İkibuçuk *genelev*, just below the Galata Tower, is the largest such (and so named for the long-ago days when you could indulge for two and a half – *ikibuçuk* – liras), managed until her death in 2001 by the Armenian Mathilde Hanım, for many years the nation's biggest taxpayer.

The **prostitutes** themselves are licensed, and supposedly examined regularly for STDs, but are effectively the chattel of the mobsters who run most of the business across Turkey. If they attempt to flee the brothels to which they are tied by a system of debt bondage, the police are likely to work them over before returning them to their workplace. Many of the women (estimated at 100,000 nationwide) have literally been sold by their family or ex-spouse for real or imagined transgressions of the rural moral code; others, if suspected of "immoral acts", are committed – like lunatics to an asylum – to the *genelev*s by shadowy tribunals, which operate in each province "for the maintenance of public morality". A high proportion use amphetamines or other drugs much of the time, some attempt suicide, and few are able to save much money by the time they're forcibly retired between age 35 and 40. Perhaps the greatest obstacle to full civil rights for prostitutes is official policy; the Constitutional (Supreme) Court, for example, ruled in 1989 that the rape of a prostitute should carry a prison term only one-third as long as that for other rapes, though this was subsequently changed owing to outcry over the definition of a prostitute.

One advantage of legalized prostitution was that at least it was confined to one part of any town and men in search of paid sex largely confined to that area. With the collapse of the Soviet Union and Eastern Bloc in 1990, all that changed, and Turkey was soon invaded by legions of "professional" Russian, Ukrainian, Romanian and Moldavian women or "**natashas**", as they are familiarly known. These women are not confined to the municipal brothels and often frequent city bars, some hotels and certain streets. The knock-on effect of this for female travellers is that they can sometimes be mistaken for prostitutes by local men assuming that any foreign woman out at night and not accompanied by a man must be on the game. If you wander through **red-light districts** such as Laleli/Aksaray in İstanbul, or stumble across known pick-up points on major highways, you can expect to be followed by kerb crawlers; it's usually enough to explain that you're not a *natasha*.

Clearly it's best for female travellers to avoid staying in hotels that are used by prostitutes. Of course none of these hotels are recommended in this guide, but hotel managers and clientele change, so keep an eye out.

Further information

If you have the interest and time to become involved in women's issues, you could visit the Women's Library and Information Centre Foundation, Fener Mahallesi, Fener Vapur Iskelesi Karşısı, Fener-Haliç, 34220 İstanbul ⊤0212/534 9550, ℗523 7408 (Mon–Sat 9am–5.30pm). It's a women's library and information centre, mainly used by women's organizations and activists and the media, and includes foreign-language books and periodicals.

Gay life

It would be an understatement to say that Turkish society is deeply ambivalent about male homosexuality; it has been so since Ottoman times, when the imperial culture was rampantly bisexual, and transvestite dancers and entertainers were the norm. Atatürk tried to stamp out such decadent holdovers, but in recent years transvestite – or transsexual – entertainers such as Bülent Ersoy and the late Zeki Müren have become national heroes. That has not, however, stopped macho males from verbally or physically abusing such personalities in public – and getting away with it.

Homosexual acts between adults over 18 are legal, but existing laws against "spreading homosexual information" in print – ie advocating the lifestyle – is no longer enforced, otherwise *Time Out İstanbul* would have been banned from its first issue. However, in recent years a "Gay Pride" festival in İstanbul was cancelled under pressure from the authorities, and the few gay bars in İstanbul have been raided in the past by the police, who forced customers to submit to STD testing; they still routinely beat drag queens on the streets. Aside from the adulated entertainers cited above, public attitudes are generally intolerant – or closeted – except in resorts such as Side or Alanya and, surprisingly enough, in the otherwise religious stronghold of Bursa, considered the gay capital of Turkey. *İbne* (catamite, passive male partner) is a deadly Turkish insult, while there is no specific word for the active role.

Despite all the foregoing, there are currently two activist groups locally: a chapter of the gay-rights group **Lambda** (Ⓦ www.lambdaistanbul.org/; Turkish only), and an "alternative" gay/lesbian group, **Kaos** (Ⓦ www.geocities.com/kaosgl), which published an eponymous "research" magazine from 1994 to 2000 (still well archived).

Sports and outdoor activities

The Turks have been sports fanatics since the inception of the Republic, but success in the international arena was long confined to Naim Süleymanoğlu's spectacular Olympic weightlifting coup in 1988, when everyone in the country was treated to infinite television replays of his winning clean-and-jerk. He repeated this feat in the 1992 and 1996 Olympiads for a hat trick. In 2002, the Turkish national football team made it all the way to the World Cup semi-finals, but have flagged recently and failed to reach the 2006 World Cup Finals – much to the chagrin of their ultra-patriotic fans. More prosaically, some of the ski-resort hotels are used by Turkish and foreign football teams for summer high-altitude training.

Football

To the casual observer, it may appear that **football** (soccer) is more popular than Islam in Turkey, and the game certainly excites passions that discussing politics can't. Although the history of organized clubs in İstanbul extends back to the first decade of the twentieth century, it wasn't until the 1960s that things really got going. As in other countries, the British were mostly responsible for introducing the sport and many of the early teams were either largely expat or filled by the Greek or Armenian minorities. Galatasaray, however, was formed by Muslim students of the French-run Galatasary Lycée. Although there are well-supported **teams** in every town and village, most people profess allegiance to one of the "Big Four" first-division teams: the three İstanbul sides Galatasaray, Beşiktaş or Fenerbahçe (see p.177) – all established early in the 1900s – or the relative newcomer Trabzonspor, formed only in the 1960s.

The larger stadiums hold up to 30,000 fans (all seated) and **matches** are usually on weekend evenings (to ensure maximum advertising revenue for the pay-channel they are invariably broadcast on) between September and May. Not surprisingly, matches shown on the pay channel always involve one (or more – derby matches generate maximum interest) of the "Big Four". Many bars now have big screens, and can be very atmospheric, especially for derby games. Money is actually the biggest problem in Turkish football – not a lack of it, but the fact that top clubs have far too much and can buy up any emerging talent (especially African and South American). Of late, however, this traffic has become reciprocal, with many Turkish players playing for teams across Europe. Local teams have been more conspicuously successful in European competition, most notably when Galatasaray won the UEFA Cup in 2000 (the first Turkish side ever to do so), beating Arsenal 4–1 on penalties.

Sadly, Turkish football usually hits the headlines thanks to the less savoury aspects of the game. Charges of bribery and corruption are common and violence sporadically occurs. Unusually, this isn't a Western import; in a famous incident of 1967, a match between Kayserispor and Sivas resulted in forty dead and three hundred injured during running street-battles after the match. More recently in 2000, two English supporters of Leeds United were stabbed to death in Taksim Square, allegedly for insulting the Turkish flag, during running street-fighting with Galatasaray fans.

If you're (un)lucky enough to be caught in the aftermath of one of the bigger games, you're not likely to forget it. While a losing team occasionally gets attacked by its own supporters, more likely you'll witness delirious celebrations, with flag-waving fans leaning on the horns of cruising cars embroiled in massive traffic jams. An estimated 200,000 fans crammed İstanbul's Taksim Square to celebrate the Turkish national team reaching the finals of the 1995 European Championships, but this was nothing compared to the delirium that broke out in mid-2002 when Turkey reached the semifinals of the World Cup for the first time since 1954; against all the odds the national team finished third, beating South Korea in the consolation match after being eliminated by eventual cup-winners Brazil. When the team returned to Turkey, an estimated three million people turned out to greet the players.

Skiing

Turkey is normally thought of as a summertime holiday destination, but there are a number of serviceable **ski resorts**, though as yet only a couple are up to European standards. The oldest, most famous and perhaps most overrated resort is **Uludağ**, above Bursa, with easy and intermediate runs, but maximum altitude is 2232m, slopes are prone to mist and snow turns slushy after February. The **Saklıkent** complex in the Beydarlağı near Antalya would seem potentially ideal for an early spring sea-cum-ski holiday, but snow cover tends to be thin and it's considered something of a joke amongst serious skiers – and omitted from most current tourist literature. Nearby, and opened in 2001, is the **Davraz** centre near İsparta; it's meant primarily as a teachers' club, but is open to all. Snow conditions here are more reliable than Saklıkent, and the single hotel comfortable enough (it's also possible to stay in nearby Eğirdir, where accommodation is plentiful) but prices have risen sharply since 2004. Roughly midway between İstanbul and Ankara, near Bolu, **Kartalkaya** is better than any of the foregoing, despite a modest top altitude of 2223m; facilities, with three chairlifts and seven T-bars, now nearly

See the outdoor adventure travel colour insert for more on Turkey's sporting activities.

match those of Uludağ, plus there are several red and black runs (though again slush is a problem from February on). The longest season and best snow conditions by far are at **Palandöken**, near Erzurum, where the top lift goes over 3000m and the Turkish Olympic team trains; there are three chairlifts, one T-bar and a three-kilometre-long gondola car to service a mix of blue and red runs (there are only two advanced, half-hour runs for the team to sink its teeth into). At **Tekir Yaylası** on Erciyes Dağı near Kayseri, the season is nearly as long, the snow almost as powdery, and the top lift is 2770m (one to 3100m is planned), though thus far runs are only green and red grade, served by two chairlifts and two T-bars. **Sarıkamış**, near Kars, is having a Dedeman chain hotel built, in theory to augment the one existing, but only has two chairlifts and one T-bar to service a handful of runs (mostly red and blue grade); top lift is 2634m.

Your nearest overseas Turkish tourism office (see p.42) can provide you with a brochure listing Turkey's ski resorts and information on the fancy resort hotels for each ski area, but if you're willing to forego doorstep skiing, it's surprisingly easy and cheap to do it based, say, in nearby Erzurum or Bursa rather than on the slopes. The Turkish State Meteorological Service gives information on snow heights at the various resorts (ⓦwww.meteor.gov.tr).

Mountaineering and hiking

Although only Turks who have come through the university-linked walking and outing clubs trek and hike for pleasure, there is plenty of scope for these activities. You'll find details on specific hiking routes through the Kaçkar Dağları and a selection of walks on Bursa's Uludağ and along the Turquoise Coast, in the Guide, but if you're daunted at the prospect of going alone, contact one of the adventure-travel companies listed in the "Getting there" section on p.32.

At present, the **Kaçkar Dağları**, running parallel to the Black Sea, is the most reward-ing area for treks and a number of companies organize expeditions there. The **Cilo and Sat massifs** along the Iraqi border are even more spectacular, but owing to Kurdish troubles are regrettably off-limits to outsiders, as they have been for much of the past three decades. The range opened, at least theoretically, in 2002, and a Turkish nonmilitary expedition climbed Resko peak. Following the US/British invasion of Iraq and renewed PKK attacks, the Cilo–Sat are again effectively closed to outsiders, despite the lifting of emergency rule. Next up in interest are the **Toros (Taurus) ranges**, which form a long chain extending from central Turkey to above the main Turquoise Coast resort areas; again various tour companies can take you to the best places. During the cooler months, the mountains of Lycia in particular offer some interesting peak-bagging ascents, as well as – down in their foothills – Turkey's first official long-distance trail, the **Lycian Way** (see p.458). A second long-distance marked walking trail, the **St Paul Trail**, links the Mediterranean coast east of Antalya with the Turkish Lake District (see p.608), offering spectacular trekking through this remote part of the Toros.

Aside from this, high-altitude **mountaineering** in Turkey consists mostly of climbing the volcanos of the central plateau. Serious trekkers may not find these mountains quite as interesting as the more conventional ranges, but all offer superb views from their summits. Most famous is 5165m **Ağrı Dağ (Ararat)** on the eastern borders of Turkey. Out of bounds for most of the 1990s, it is now "open" again, but requires a special permit (see p.923). By contrast, Erciyes and Hasan Dağı near Cappadocia are excellent for winter ascents, without any of the expense or bureaucracy prevalent at Ararat. **Süphan Dağı** (4434m) is Turkey's second highest peak, and stands in splendid isolation on the northern fringes of Lake Van in the far east of the country.

If you go alone, you'll need to be fully kitted out, since alpine huts are nonexistent; if you've gaps in your equipment, note that only İstanbul and Ankara have European-standard mountaineering shops (as opposed to hunting-and-fishing-gear outlets). **Water** can be a problem in the limestone strata of the Toros and on the volcanos, detailed **maps** are very difficult to obtain (see p.43) and **trails** (when present) are faint. But the unspoilt quality of the countryside and the friendliness of other mountaineers go a long way in compensation.

Rock climbing is in its infancy in Turkey, but there are signs that it could become a climbers' mecca in the mould of Spain, with cheap flights, winter sun and countless rock faces. A good starting place is **Geyikbayırı**, in the mountains some 25km west of Antalya, which has over a hundred bolted climbs on a limestone face graded up to 10-. For information see ⓦ www.geyikbayiri.com.

Rescue services are no match for those in more developed mountain areas in Europe and the US, but things are improving. The local *jandarma* (see p.88) will turn out in an emergency, and AKUT (Search and Rescue Association; ⓦ www.akut.org. tr) have established some eight centres across western, southern and central Turkey (though not, as yet, in the very popular Kaçkar range in the northeast of the country). The growth of AKUT has more to do with technical mountaineers volunteering to help victims of the devastating İstanbul and Bingöl earthquakes (and the feeble response of the Turkish authorities to them) than to the rescue of walkers and climbers. President of the organization is Nasuh Mahruki, Turkey's most famous mountaineer. Unless you are very fortunate, communication in anything other than Turkish with either of these potential rescuers will prove difficult.

Birdwatching

Turkey attracts a tiny fraction of the birdwatchers that (for example) Israel does, but most of the same migrating birds pass over both countries. Because of the variety of Turkish terrain and temperature, and Turkey's role as a halfway house between the birds of the northern palearctic (the temperate zone across Eurasia) and those of the Middle East or Africa, in an active birdwatching holiday you could expect to tick off nearly three hundred different species.

Below is a suggested route for a birdwatching tour; sites marked * are also described in the main text. All of the sites lie within a few hours' drive of each other and form a neat circle based on Adana airport; Birecik is the furthest at five hours' drive from the airport. Spring arrives early here; the **best months** are February to May and, for the southbound migrations, late September to early October.

In the early morning, the steep scree slopes of the jagged **Aladağlar** are good for Caspian snowcock, Radde's and alpine accentor and crimson-winged finch.

The *****Sultansazlığı marshes** occupy a depression between Erciyes and the west flank of the Aladağlar. Because the salty marsh water doesn't freeze, it attracts many overwintering ducks. Migrating waders stop off here, and there are breeding Dalmatian and white pelicans. The **Ereğli marshes**, 80km southwest of Niğde, are similar, with a chance of spotting greater sand plover.

The *****Göksu delta** near Silifke is a huge area of canals, sand dunes and marsh. Rarities demonstrating the tremendous range of habitat include the black francolin, Smyrna kingfisher and Audouin's gull. The **Sertavul pass** 50km to the north is good for passing raptors, including flocks of vultures.

Durnalık, en route to Birecik, has dry valleys with eastern rock nuthatch, red-tailed wheatear, cinereous bunting and Upcher's warbler.

Birecik, on the Euphrates River, offers a variety of dry habitats plus sandbanks; rarities include Bruce's scops owl, yellow-throated and pale rock sparrow, Menetrie's warbler, see-see partridge, black-bellied and pin-tailed sandgrouse, cream-coloured courser and a pair of eagle owls. Except for a few specimens in an aviary, the famous bald ibises that used to breed during the summer here have vanished since the 1950s, victims of pesticide poisoning and other human interference. The **delta of the Tarsus Çayı** near Tarsus is good for any waders you didn't get at Göksu, plus the Smyrna kingfisher. Finally, **Belen**, the pass over the Nur mountains south of İskenderun, offers excellent raptor-watching opportunities, but you have to time it just right. The Turkish Forestry Ministry organizes a bird photography safari hereabouts during the first week of October.

Useful birdwatching contacts

Türkiye Doğal Hayatı Koruma Derneği (DHKD) Büyük Postane Cad43–45. Kat 5–6, Bahçekapı 34420 İstanbul ☎ 0212/528 2030, ℱ 528 2040, Ⓦ www.dhkd.org . The "Society for the Protection of Nature" (the local branch of the World Wildlife Fund) sells a book describing endangered Turkish environments, including many of those cited above, plus bird charts and other publications, all in English.

Greentours See "Special interest holidays", p.33. Ian Green of Greentours has a book listing all Turkey's species, describing the sites above and with helpful sketch maps to get you to the right place.

Kuşbank (Doğa Derneği), Meşrütiyet Cad, Bayındır 2 Sok 48/7, Kızılay, Ankara Ⓦ www.kusbank. org. Operates a database of bird species and distribution in Turkey, as reported by local and foreign birdwatchers.

Watersports, diving and rafting

Opportunities for engaging in various **watersports** abound at the Turkish coastal resorts. You can count on renting windsurfing (and even kite-surfing), kayaking and snorkelling gear just about anywhere, and at the more developed sites water-skiing, sailing and yachting will be on offer – the yachts chartered either bare-boat or (more likely) as part of a guided, skippered three- to fifteen-day coastal cruise. For the possibilities of pre-booking such a cruise, see the "Getting there" sections starting on p.27; for advice on arranging something on the spur of the moment, see the box on p.413.

Because of the presumed number of antiquities still submerged off Turkey, **scuba diving** is strictly regulated and is principally available out of Bodrum, Marmaris, Fethiye, Adrasan, Kalkan and Kaş, with appreciable fish numbers only at the last two spots. Of late, **wreck diving** around the Gallipoli peninsula has also become popular and the nearby Gulf of Saros also supports a couple of dive operators taking advantage of abundant local marine life. Only four rivers – the Köprülü Çayı east of Antalya, the Akköprü (or Dalaman Çayı) behind the Turquoise Coast, the Çoruh in the Kaçkar and the Göksu in the Toros mountains – are suitable for **whitewater rafting**. All bar the Köprülü are chronically under threat from hydroelectric projects. The first three rivers receive regular attention from adventure-travel operators; again, see "Getting there", p.27, for specifics.

Other activities

Kaş is the focus of **canyoning**, with a number of suitable gorges within a few hours' drive. The Kıbrıs Çayı, between Sütleğen and Kemer on the way to Gömbe, makes an excellent one-day beginners' outing after snowmelt is finished; the Kaputaş and Saklıkent gorges are more technical expeditions involving thirty-metre drops. Saklıkent can be traversed in two full days (summer only), Kaputaş in one and a half (best April–June) – though it's also possible to do the lowest five drops only by using a side entrance. Elsewhere, the Köprülü canyon and another unnamed one near Manavgat on the Mediterranean coast are the main venues.

Paragliding is practised at Ölüdeniz and Kaş on the Turquoise Coast; it's marginally cheaper to indulge at Kaş, though either is pricey compared to, say, the Pyrenees, as "tolls" and assorted other backhanders must be paid to the forest service and municipalities involved for crossing their land en route to the launching sites. That said, these are two of the most spectacular venues in the world, with clear, stable conditions most of the year. **Hot-air ballooning** is rather more elitist (but equally popular) and restricted at present to Göreme in Cappadocia.

Work

Turkey has a chronically high unemployment rate even amongst graduates, variable but generally low wages and no special privileges for EU citizens – all factors intensified by the economic crash of 2001. It's hardly a bright picture for potential job-seekers, but many foreigners do work in Turkey for varying periods, even on a tourist visa, though this is strictly illegal.

Teaching is the most obvious employment, though the best-paid jobs involve working for a foreign employer, for example a contractor on a World Bank water project or a management job at a NATO base. You have to be pretty lucky, in the right place at the right time, to get one of these. If you have a skill that is in demand, large Turkish companies may be able to offer you employment, although there are various kinds of jobs, including medical work, which a foreigner is not allowed to do. For qualified **nannies**, work is relatively easy to find, especially in İstanbul; agencies advertise in the *Turkish Daily News*.

The paperwork

If you intend to work from the start, it's far preferable to obtain a job offer and get a work permit before you arrive (though this is far easier said than done and applications now often take even longer than they used to). Contact the Turkish embassy or consulate in your home country (see "Red tape and visas", p.37) or, failing that, in a country bordering Turkey, to obtain a **work permit** (*çalışma tezkeresi*). As well as your written offer of employment from inside Turkey, you'll need proof of your educational qualifications, passport photos and the requisite embassy forms filled out and fees paid. Possession of a **work visa** for a permanent job automatically entitles you to a residence permit for an initial two-year period (though this has to be applied for, and paid for, separately). It also, at least theoretically, entitles you to bring your car into Turkey for more than six months (see p.55).

Teaching

Most of the foreigners working in Turkey are **teaching English** as a foreign language in one of the major cities. Conditions and rates of pay vary according to the required qualifications, local cost of living and the attractiveness of the area; a job in İstanbul will pay more than twice that in a south-coast resort. The best rates are paid at the private universities teaching *hazırlık* (preparatory) classes – ie coaching rich, indolent teenagers through a year of intensive English.

Teaching in a state university or *Anadolu Lisesi* (the equivalent of old-style British grammar schools) is less stressful, but your first pay packet can be delayed until the vetting procedure (checking your credentials and political background) is completed by the appropriate ministry and in practice it's rare for foreigners to be employed. Both the above types of schools require an English degree and preferably a TEFL (Teaching English as a Foreign Language) certificate.

*Dershane*s (private cramming academies) and private high schools may employ people with other degrees or no degree at all; a TEFL qualification is sometimes enough. Some may also provide accommodation, at least for an initial period. Examine contracts carefully (they're usually for one calendar year), checking the hours when you will have to actually be in the school for extra duties, as well as teaching hours. Turkish school terms are quite different from England; two long terms are separated by a fortnight's break and the summer break is for three months; you won't have Christmas or Easter off!

Teaching posts for the bigger outfits are advertised in *The Guardian's* educational section and the *Times Educational Supplement* in Britain, in the *International Herald Tribune* and the *Turkish Daily News* in Turkey, but, especially if you are looking for temporary work, private schools are probably best approached on the spot. Check whether the job will enable you to apply for a work permit.

Tourism-related work

There is always work available at tourist resorts during the summer months, for example at the backpackers' treehouses on the Turquoise Coast. Very little of it is legal and after three months you will have either to leave the country to get a second entry visa or apply for a three-months' extension inside the country (see p.37). In the view of the locals, you are taking a job away from a Turk, so if you cause offence, they are likely to complain to the *jandarma*. If this happens, you will be initially warned not to work; if you persist, you'll definitely be deported. If you have any dispute with an employer (most commonly being underpaid or not paid at all), you obviously have no legal recourse. Foreigners are not allowed to work as certified archeological **tour guides** – one rule that is enforced, as in most Mediterranean countries – though tour companies may employ you to do PR work in their office, or as a

courier to meet groups from the airport and take them to their hotel. **Carpet and leather shops** will often employ English-speakers on a commission basis, in which case you will work long hours trying to pull in your quota of likely tourists. **Yacht and gület** captains may take on foreign staff to cook and clean, or host guests.

Voluntary work

Voluntary work at **rural-aid projects** all over Turkey is organized by Gençtur, the website of which has an English-language version telling you how to apply. Its camps generally involve manual labour in Turkish villages. Basic accommodation is provided, either in guesthouses or dormitories, and food is prepared for you by the villagers. **Conservation** volunteers are organized through the World Wildlife Fund and its Turkish branch the DHKD (see "Birdwatching", p.97); past projects have included bird-habitat surveys and turtle protection.

Voluntary work contacts

Gençtur Yerebatan Cad 15/3 34410 Sultanahmet, İstanbul ☎0212/520 5274, ☞519 0864, ☜www .genctur.com.tr.
International Voluntary Service 162 Upper New Walk, Leicester LE1 7QA ☎01533/549430. Gençtur-affiliate organization.

Directory

Addresses In Turkish addresses, street names precede the number; if the address is on a minor alley, this will usually be included after the main thoroughfare it leads off. If you see a right-hand slash between two numbers, the first is the building number, the second the flat or office number. A letter following a right-hand slash is more ambiguous: it can mean either the shop or unit number, or be part of the general building number. Standard abbreviations, also used in this book, include "Cad" for *Cadde(si)* (avenue

or main street), "Bul" for *Bulvarı* (boulevard), "Meyd" for *Meydan(ı)* (square), "Sok" for *Sokak/Sokağı* (alley) and "PK" for *Posta Kutu* (Post Box). Other useful terms are *kat* (floor), *zemin kat* (ground floor), *asma* (mezzanine), *han(ı)* (office block), *mahalle* (district or neighbourhood) and *çıkmaz(ı)* (blind alley). *Karşısı* means "opposite to", as in *PTT karşısı*. A five-digit postcode system exists, but is sporadically used; it is much more important to include the district when addressing mail. For example: Halil Güner, Kıbrıs Şehitler Cad,

Poyraz Sok, Ulus Apartmanı 36/2, Kat 1, Delikliçınar, 34800 Direkköy, means that Halil Güner lives on Poyraz Sokak no. 36, just off Kıbrıs Şehitler Caddesi, on the first floor, Flat 2, of the Ulus apartments, in the Delikliçınar area of a larger postal district known as Direkköy.

Bargaining You can haggle for souvenir purchases, minor repair services, rural taxis where no rate is posted, car rental, hotels out of season and meals – especially seafood ones – at eateries where a menu is absent. You shouldn't have to bargain for dolmuş or bus tickets, though some of the stewards selling fares on long-distance coaches are less than honest; if in doubt, check to see what others are paying for the same distance.

Beaches All Turkish beaches are free in theory, though the luxury compounds that straddle routes to the sand will control access in various ways. Never pay a fee for a beach-lounger or umbrella, unless the seller can produce a ticket. Periodically there can be quite a lot of tar on south-coast beaches facing the Mediterranean shipping lanes. For tar globs on your feet, olive oil is a far more effective, ubiquitous – and safer – solvent than white spirit or nitro thinner.

Camping gas It's possible to find small 190ml cartridges for camping stoves relatively easily. Likely sales-points include hunting and outdoor-sports shops in İstanbul, Migros supermarkets and many outlets of the Aygas and Milangas chain of gas-bottle storefronts. In the Guide, we give some confirmed addresses for towns near the Kaçkar mountains; for the very few, and constantly changing, stockists along the Lycian Way or St Paul Trail, consult Ⓦwww.trekkinginturkey.com.

Children They're adored in Turkey; childless couples will be asked when they plan to have some and bringing children along guarantees red-carpet treatment almost everywhere. Three- or four-bed hotel rooms are easy to find, and airlines, ships and trains offer substantial discounts. Baby formulas are cheap and readily available, as are disposable nappies.

Departure tax None is currently charged at airports – it's included in air-ticket prices – though İstanbul, Çeşme (long-haul dock),

Kuşadası, Marmaris, Antalya, Taşucu and Mersin seaports, all controlled by Turkish Maritime Lines, do levy varying amounts on departing international passengers.

Disabled travellers Turkey makes poor provision for disabled travellers. Sidewalk corners and archeological sites do not have ramps, hotels below three stars in rating lack lifts and there is no adapted public transport. For advice, current information and specialist tours, contact: UK, Holiday Care ☎01293/774 535, minicom ☎01293/776 943, Ⓦwww.holidaycare.org.uk; Ireland, Irish Wheelchair Association ☎01/833 8241, Ⓔiwa@iol.ie; US, Mobility International ☎541/343-1284, Ⓦwww.miusa.org; Australia, Australian Council for Rehabilitation of the Disabled ☎02/6282 4333; New Zealand, Disabled Persons Assembly ☎04/801 9100.

Electric power 220 volts, 50 cycles, out of double round-pin sockets. British appliances need a 3-to-2 plug adaptor, with a minimum 5-amp fuse (7.5-amp is better) to permit operation of a hair dryer or travel iron; North American ones both a square-to-round-pin adaptor and a transformer (except for dual-voltage shavers, which need only the former).

Emergencies Police ☎155; rural gendarmerie ☎156; traffic police ☎154; fire brigade ☎110; rural forest fires ☎177; ambulance ☎112. These calls cost one card unit.

Essentials On most trips it's worth packing the following: universal bath plug (they're rarely supplied, to prevent you from doing laundry in the washbasin); camera film if you haven't gone digital; contact lens accessories (only a basic range of solutions is available locally); mosquito repellent; sunblock (at least factor 15); brand toiletries; a torch (flashlight); travel alarm clock; personal stereo or MP3 player (invaluable on long bus journeys); and a water container.

Laundry These are slowly appearing in tourist resorts, but there are dry-cleaning (*kuru temizleme*) establishments in most large towns, and *pansiyons* and large hotels will do your washing for a small consideration.

Left luggage An *emanet* (left-luggage) service is available at nearly all bus and train stations and at İstanbul airport; there are no lockers, you pay the attendant upon return of article(s) in exchange for your claim ticket.

Prices, usually for a maximum of 24 hours, vary according to the amount of mandatory insurance – for nice foreign backpacks, suitcases or holdalls, you'll be charged the most expensive rate, about 11YTL per item (9YTL for carry-on size) at İstanbul airport, perhaps 2YTL per day at a provincial *otogar* like Antalya's.

Smoking Tobacco smoke can be a major nuisance, despite an ongoing nationwide anti-smoking campaign. Tangible results thus far include designated no-smoking cars on most trains, and prohibition of smoking on all domestic flights and waiting lounges (the latter systematically ignored), İstanbul ferries and on all long-haul buses. Dolmuşes are also theoretically nonsmoking, though the driver habitually puffs away. So too are cinemas, with intermissions scheduled primarily as a ciggy break.

Time Turkey is two hours ahead of GMT in winter; as in Europe, daylight saving is observed between the last weekend in March and the last one in October – clocks change at 2am of the Sunday concerned.

Toilets Except in the plusher resort hotels and restaurants, most public toilets are of the squat-hole variety, found either in public parks or (more infallibly) next to any mosque. They cost anywhere from about thirty kuruş in isolated areas to 1YTL in İstanbul or touristy resorts. Also keep a supply of toilet paper with you (available 'in Turkey) – Turks wash

themselves off either with the bidet or toilet-rim spout, or the special vessel filled from the handy floor-level tap. You may well become a convert to this method, reserving the paper – which shouldn't be thrown down the hole – for drying yourself off.

Guide

Guide

İstanbul and around

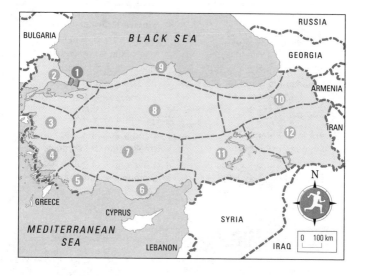

CHAPTER 1 # Highlights

* **Cruise the Bosphorus**
Float past sumptuous vil-
las, imposing fortresses,
timeworn fishing villages
and two intercontinental
bridges. See p.119

* **Afternoon tea at the
Pera Palas Hotel** Pas-
sengers from the Orient
Express used to stay
here, in one of the city's
most atmospheric hotels.
See p.125

* **Aya Sofya** The Church
of the Divine Wisdom
was the largest enclosed
space in the world for a
thousand years.
See p.127

* **Topkapı Palace** Con-
template the majesty of
the Ottoman sultanate in
the fine buildings, gilded
pavilions and immaculate
gardens. See p.129

* **Kariye Museum** Fres-
coes portraying the life
of Christ are among
the most evocative of
all İstanbul's Byzantine
treasures. See p.166

* **İstiklâl Caddesi**
İstanbul's most elegant
street boasts a wealth
of palaces, churches,
shops, restaurants and
bars. See p.172

* **Nevizade Sokak** Soak
up the atmosphere in
one of the numerous tra-
ditional fish restaurants
or bars along İstanbul's
liveliest street. See p.187

* **İstanbul Modern** Bold
attempt to showcase
(mainly Turkish) contem-
porary art in a converted
warehouse with stunning
views over the Bospho-
rus. See p.195

△ Frecoes in the Kariye Museum

İstanbul and around

The two faces of **İstanbul** can come as something of a shock. In many ways, it is very much a European city – with tree-lined boulevards, chic café-bars and modern shopping malls – but step away from the main drag and you enter another age and another culture. Scrap-metal merchants with handcarts, *hamals* (stevedores) carrying burdens of merchandise twice their own size and weight, hapless beggars and shoeshine boys, all frequent the backstreets around the city centre, loudly proclaiming their business until late at night.

Yet İstanbul is the only city in the world to have played capital to consecutive **Christian and Islamic empires**, both of which have left remarkable legacies.

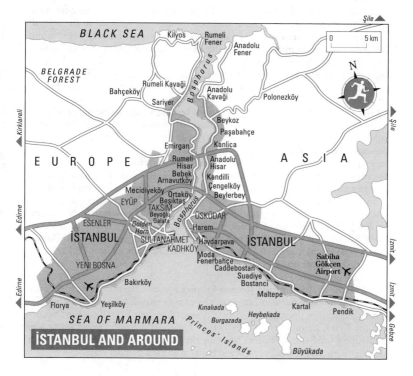

İSTANBUL AND AROUND

Sultanahmet, the cultural centre of the city, is home to the imposing **Aya Sofya**, the former Byzantine church, and the six-minaretted **Sultanahmet Camii** (or Blue Mosque). The juxtaposition of the two cultures would be fascinating enough in itself, but it's made more so by the fact that the transition between them was a process of assimilation and adoption. The city walls of Theodosius II have been preserved because they were refortified by Mehmet the Conqueror, and most of the city's churches were reconsecrated as mosques – not least Aya Sofya itself, which was a constant source of inspiration to Islamic architects.

Monumental architecture aside, there are a wealth of other fascinating sights in and around İstanbul. Ancient **bazaars** still function as they have for centuries, including the largest covered bazaar in the world, the **Kapalı Çarşı**. Sultanahmet's famous **Topkapı Palace** is stuffed with Ottoman treasures, while the opulent **Dolmabahçe** and **Yıldız palaces** have formidable Bosphorus views. The city's diverse neighbourhoods reward a stroll, too, from the conservative, mosque-studded Islamic quarters of **Eyüp** and **Fatih**, to the atmospheric European districts of **Beyoğlu** and modern **Taksim**.

Dividing Europe from Asia, the **Bosphorus** strait offers visitors and residents alike respite from the hurly-burly of the city. Here, you'll find the city's upmarket suburbs and, further to the north, **coastal villages**, many of which offer incredible views, interesting historical sites, parks (even open forestland) and some fine fish restaurants. The **Princes' Islands**, a traditional refuge from political turmoil on the mainland, are worth visiting for their traffic-free natural beauty and nineteenth-century mansions.

Some history

While there is archeological evidence of a Mycenaean settlement dating from the thirteenth century BC, in popular tradition the city was founded in the seventh century BC by **Byzas the Megarian** – hence the original name of Byzantium. The site was chosen in accordance with a Delphic oracle instructing the settlers to found a city "opposite the city of the blind" and they concluded that this must refer to Chalcedon, modern-day Kadıköy, since earlier settlers had built their city in blithe ignorance of the obvious strategic merits of the peninsula, Saray Burnu, in front of their eyes.

Over the next thousand years, Byzantium became an important centre of trade and commerce, though it was not until the early fourth century AD that a decision was taken that would elevate the city to the pinnacles of wealth, power and prestige. For more than 350 years, Byzantium had been part of the Roman province of Asia. On Diocletian's retirement in 305, Licinius and **Constantine** fought for control of the empire. Constantine finally defeated his rival on the hills above Chrysopolis (Üsküdar) and chose Byzantium as the site for the new **capital of the Roman Empire**.

It was a fine choice. The seven hills on which Constantine was to build the new capital (a deliberate echo of Rome – indeed the city was originally to be called New Rome) commanded the Bosphorus and the natural harbour of the Golden Horn. The site was protected by water on two sides and its landward side was easily defensible. It was also well placed for access to the troublesome frontiers of both Europe and the Persian Empire.

In 395, the **division of the Roman Empire** between the two sons of Theodosius I left Constantinople as capital of the eastern part of the empire. It rapidly developed its own distinctive character, dissociating itself from Rome and adopting the Greek language and **Christianity**. Long and successful government was interrupted briefly, in Justinian's reign, by the Nika riots in 532, soon after which the city (particularly Aya Sofya) was rebuilt on an even grander scale.

Half a century later, however, the dissolution of the Byzantine Empire had begun, as waves of Persians, Avars and Slavs attacked from the north and east. The emperor Heraclius stemmed the tide, but in the following centuries decline was constant. The empire was overrun by Arab invaders in the seventh and eighth centuries, and by Bulgars in the ninth and tenth. Only the city walls saved Constantinople, and even these could not keep out the **Crusaders**, who breached the sea walls in 1204 and sacked the city. The Byzantines, led by Michael Palaeologus, finally regained control, but many of the major buildings had fallen into disrepair, and the empire was greatly diminished in size.

As the Byzantine Empire declined, the **Ottoman Empire** expanded. The Ottomans established first Bursa, then Edirne, as their capital, and Ottoman territory effectively surrounded the city long before it was taken. In 1453, **Mehmet II (the Conqueror)** – also known as Fatih Sultan Mehmet – besieged the city. It fell after seven weeks and, after the capture and subsequent pillage, Mehmet II began to rebuild the city, beginning with a new palace and following with the Mosque of the Conqueror (Fatih Camii) and many smaller complexes. Mehmet was tolerant of other religions, and actively encouraged Greeks and Armenians to take up residence in the city. His successor Beyazit II continued this policy, settling Jewish refugees from Spain into the city in an attempt to improve the economy and the skills of the workforce.

In the century following the Conquest, the victory was reinforced by the great military achievements of **Selim the Grim** and by the reign of **Süleyman the Magnificent** (1520–66), "the Lawgiver" and greatest of all Ottoman leaders. His attempted conquest of Europe was only thwarted at the gates of Vienna, and the wealth gained in his military conquests funded the work of **Mimar Sinan**, one of the finest Ottoman architects.

A century after the death of Süleyman, the empire began to show signs of **decay**. Territorial losses abroad combined with corruption at home, which insinuated its way into the very heart of the empire, Topkapı Palace itself. Newly crowned sultans emerged, often insane, from the institution known as the Cage (see p.134), while others spent time in the harem rather than on the battlefield, consorting with women who increasingly became involved in grand-scale political intrigue.

As Ottoman territory was lost to the West, succeeding sultans became interested in Western institutional models. A short-lived parliament of 1876 was dissolved after a year by Abdülhamid II, but the **forces of reform** led to his deposition in 1909. The end of World War I saw İstanbul occupied by Allied, mainly British, troops as the victors procrastinated over how best to manage the rump of the once great empire. After the War of Independence, Atatürk's declaration of the Republic and the creation of a new capital in Ankara effectively solved the problem. İstanbul, meanwhile, retained its importance as a centre of trade and commerce, and remains today the powerhouse of the nation's economy and cultural life.

The **population** of Greater İstanbul is now around fifteen million (almost twenty-five percent of the entire country). With 300,000 migrants arriving annually from elsewhere in Turkey, this growth looks set to continue. Many, however, are housed in overcrowded, low-quality buildings that were directly responsible for the high death toll in the **earthquake** of August 1999, when a large number of buildings collapsed in areas to the west and east of the city.

İstanbul has less **green space** per head of population than almost any other European city, while **traffic congestion** and a crowded public-transport system slow down movement within the city. There are grand plans to improve matters – including twenty-six new roads, eleven flyovers and five more bridges over the Bosphorus – though many İstanbul residents remain sceptical of the projects.

Greater İstanbul's council has overseen clean-up programmes in some outlying neighbourhoods and has beautified other areas around the city, but there's no effective programme to deal with the expansion of **shantytown dwellings**, other than tacitly to allow more construction. Poverty remains endemic in these areas, though, by contrast, the Bosphorus suburbs are developing rapidly into wealthy neighbourhoods for the professional classes.

İstanbul

Although Ankara has replaced **İSTANBUL** as the capital of Turkey, the old imperial capital retains its cultural and economic dominance and the average İstanbul citizen will display nothing but pride in his city to a foreigner. However, beneath the surface lies an undercurrent of ambivalence, suffused by *hüzün* (melancholy), best illustrated in the autobiographical *İstanbul: Memories of a City* (2005) by Orhan Pamuk, Turkey's most famous novelist. Born, raised, and still living in İstanbul, Pamuk says:

I was slowly coming to understand that I loved İstanbul for its ruins, its *hüzün*, for the glories once possessed and later lost.

But while the traditional sights and ancient buildings may always be there, the romantic veneer of the Ottoman city may not. İstanbul has the youngest population of any European city and, as Turkey begins to reform its once rigid conservative society (particularly as it seeks to gain entry into the European Union), the city's youth increasingly demands the same recreational pastimes as their European counterparts. Where they once met over a cup of apple tea and a backgammon board (girls often cloaked and veiled), today's rich and bright young things enjoy the bars and nightclubs which spring up almost daily, where they can drink alcohol freely and dance until 6am. Shopping malls feature international brands catering to young people with piercings and tattoos; *Hard Rock Café* T-shirts and DVDs are sold amongst the trinkets in the covered bazaar; and there are reputedly more branches of *McDonalds* in the city than in New York. In August 2005, a previously unimaginable cover of *Newsweek* sported a dazzling photograph of a couple of young Istanbulites (including a very scantily clad girl) dancing at a city nightclub, under the headline "Cool Istanbul – Europe's Hippest City".

Whether yours is the İstanbul of the Blue Mosque and the Topkapı Palace, or the downtown dance clubs and swish Bosphorus cocktail bars, the city takes time to get to know. Three to four days is enough to see the major historical sights in Sultanahmet and take a ferry trip out for the afternoon on the Bosphorus. But plan on staying a week, or even two, if you want to explore fully the attractions off the usual tourist trail in the outlying suburbs and islands.

Orientation

İstanbul is divided in two by the **Bosphorus**, a narrow 30km strait that links the Black Sea and the Sea of Marmara, separating Europe from Asia. Feeding into the southern end of the strait from the European side is the **Golden Horn**, an inlet of water that starts as two small streams about 7km from the mouth of the Bosphorus. The quarters along the Golden Horn are dominated by light industry, while the majority of İstanbul's residential suburbs are located along the shores of the Sea of Marmara and on the hills above the Bosphorus.

İstanbul effectively has two **city centres**, separated by the Golden Horn but both situated on the European side of the Bosphorus. The Sultanahmet district is the historical core of the city, while Taksim lies at the southern end of an extensive business district. The two can easily be made out from the water, distinguished respectively by the landmarks of the Topkapı Palace and the modern *Marmara Hotel.*

Most visitors spend the majority of their time around **Sultanahmet**, the centre of both the Byzantine and Ottoman empires. The most visited sites are close to each other on or around the main road and tramline of **Divan Yolu** – namely **Topkapı Palace, Aya Sofya, Sultanahmet Camii** (the Blue Mosque), the **Museum of Turkish and Islamic Art**, and the **Kapalı Çarşı** (covered bazaar). Downhill from Sultanahmet is the major transport hub of **Eminönü**, where trams connect with the city's largest ferry terminal and the main train station. This district is handy for the **Mısır Çarşısı** (spice bazaar) and **Galata bridge**, gateway to the Golden Horn.

West of the covered bazaar, the district of **Beyazit** – stretching to the crown of one of the city's seven hills – is home to İstanbul's **university** and the impressive **Süleymaniye Camii**. West of Beyazit lie the commercial district of **Laleli** and the transport hub of **Aksaray**, with the overtly Islamic, mosque-studded, districts of **Fatih** and **Zeyrek** beyond.

Some 6km west of Topkapı Palace, stretching between the Sea of Marmara and the Golden Horn, are the remarkably intact Byzantine **city walls**. It's simple enough to get out here by bus or train for a walk on the fortifications at **Yedikule** and a visit to the spectacular frescoes and mosaics of the **Kariye Museum**. Further out, **Eyüp** is home to one of the most important mosques in the Islamic world.

From Sultanahmet and Eminönü, you're most likely to cross the Golden Horn by the Galata bridge, entering the port area of **Karaköy,** then heading up the steep hill to the ancient **Galata** district. Near the northern end of Galata bridge is the **Tünel**, the French-built underground funicular railway, which chugs up to **Beyoğlu**, the city's elegant nineteenth-century European quarter. From the upper Tünel station, an antique tram runs the length of Beyoğlu's pedestrianized boulevard, **İstiklâl Caddesi**, to **Taksim Square**, the twin focal points of the modern city's best hotels, bars, clubs and restaurants.

North of Taksim, and on the metro line, are the city's newest business districts of Harbiye, Etiler and Nişantaşi, location of many airline offices and embassies. Downhill from Taksim, on the Bosphorus shore, lie **Beşiktaş** and **Ortaköy**, inner-city districts with scenic waterside locations and a number of historic palaces and parks. Across the straits, in Asia, the main centres of **Üsküdar** and **Kadıköy** form part of İstanbul's commuter belt, but also have a few architectural attractions and decent shops, restaurants and clubs.

Arrival and information

İstanbul's main **points of arrival** are Atatürk airport and Esenler bus station – both in the suburbs – and the centrally located Sirkeci train station. There's little accommodation (see p.120) around Esenler and the airport, so from these you'll need to take a taxi or public transport to Sultanahmet or Taksim/Beyoğlu. For all **departure information**, see "Listings", p.203.

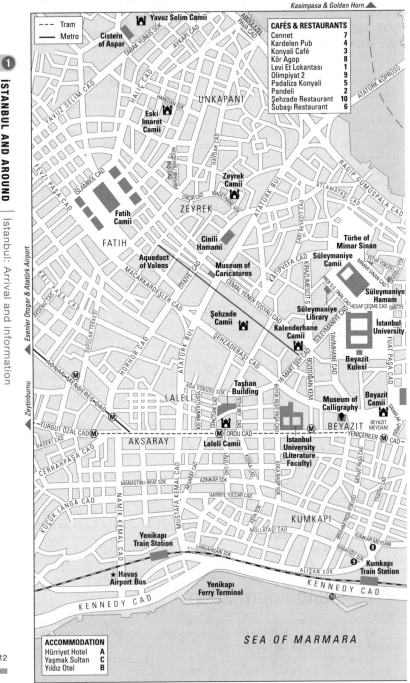

Kasimpasa & Golden Horn ▲

--- Tram
— Metro

Cistern of Aspar

Yavuz Selim Camii 🕌

TABAK YUNUS SOK
HALIÇ CAD
AYKAPI CAD
ABDÜLEZEL PAŞA CAD
ATATÜRK KÖPRÜSÜ

YAVUZ SELIM CAD

HANEDAN SOK
Eski İmaret Camii
ŞEBNEM FERAH İBRAHIM PAŞA SOK
HAYDAR CAD

UNKAPANI

FEVZİ PAŞA CAD
İSLAMBOL CAD
HALİÇ CAD
MACARKARDEŞLER CAD

Zeyrek Camii
CIRCIR CAD
İBADETHANE SOK

ZEYREK

RAGIP GÜMÜŞPALA CAD
ATLAMATAŞI CAD

Fatih Camii

FATİH

Aqueduct of Valens

Cinili Hamami

Türbe of Mimar Sinan

SİTULAR TEKKESİ
ADNAN MENDERES CAD
HORHOR CAD
İTFAIYE CAD
CEMAL YENER TOSYALI CAD
MACARKARDEŞLER CAD

Museum of Caricatures

Süleymaniye Camii

SARI BEYAZIT CAD
KATİPYEFA CAD
KIRAZLI MESCIT SOK
MİMAR SİNAN CAD
FETVA YOKUŞU CAD

Süleymaniye Hamam

Şehzade Camii 🕌
ŞEHZADEBAŞI CAD

Süleymaniye Library

Kalenderhane Camii

PROF S.S. ONAL CAD
HESAP ÇEŞME CAD
İSMETİYE
SÜLEYMANIYE CAD
TAVNHANE CAD

İstanbul University

FUAT PAŞA CAD

Esenler Otogar & Atatürk Airport ▲
Zeytinburnu ▲

16 MART ŞEHİDLERİ CAD
BOZDOĞAN KEM

Beyazit Kulesi

Taşhan Building

AĞA YOKUŞU SOK
BÜYÜK REŞIT PAŞA CAD
FETHİ BEY CAD
GENÇTÜRK CAD
ZEYNEP KAMIL SOK

LALELİ

Museum of Calligraphy

Beyazit Camii 🕌

SAHAFLAR ÇARŞISI

BEYAZIT MEYDANI

TURGUT ÖZAL CAD (M)
ORDU CAD (M)
YENİÇERİLER (M) CAD
BEYAZIT

AKSARAY

Laleli Camii

İstanbul University (Literature Faculty)

HASEKİ CAD
CERRAHPAŞA CAD
MANASTIRLI RIFAT SOK
NAMIK KEMAL CAD
MUSTAFA KEMAL CAD
AKSARAY CAD
AZIMKAR SOK
LALELİ CAD
KOCA RAGIP CAD
KOSKA CAD
MITHAT PAŞA CAD
MİTHAT CAD

HAYRIYE TÜCCAR CAD

KUMKAPI

KÜÇÜK LANGA CAD

Yenikapı Train Station

MOLLATAŞI CAD
İBRAHIM PAŞA CAD
KUMKAPI MEYDANI

LANGAHISARI SOK
BABAHATTİ SOK

★ Havaş Airport Bus

Yenikapı Ferry Terminal

ALİŞAN SOK
Kumkapı Train Station

KENNEDY CAD
KENNEDY CAD
KENNEDY CAD

SEA OF MARMARA

CAFÉS & RESTAURANTS
Cennet	7
Kardelen Pub	4
Konyali Café	3
Kör Agop	8
Levi Et Lokantası	1
Olimpiyat 2	9
Padaliza Konyali	5
Pandeli	2
Şehzade Restaurant	10
Şubaşı Restaurant	6

ACCOMMODATION
Hürriyet Hotel	A
Yaşmak Sultan	C
Yıldız Otel	B

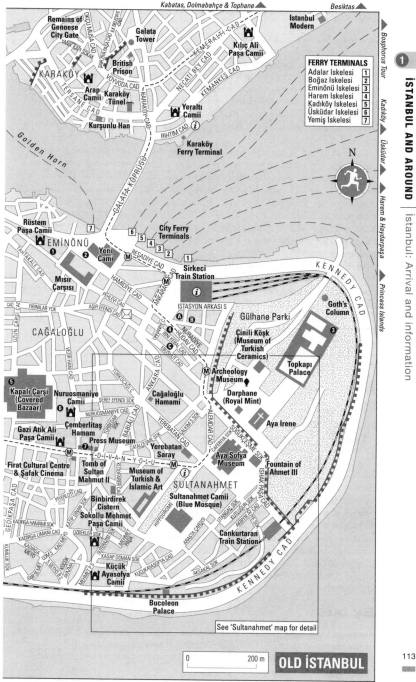

Kabatas, Dolmabahçe & Tophane ▲

Besiktas ▲

Bosphorus Tour ▶
Kadıköy ▶
Üsküdar ▶
Harem & Haydarpaşa ▶
Princess Islands ▶

Remains of Genoese City Gate
Galata Tower
Istanbul Modern
Kılıç Ali Paşa Camii
British Prison
KARAKÖY
Arap Camii
Karaköy Tünel
Yeraltı Camii

FERRY TERMINALS
Adalar Iskelesi 1
Boğaz Iskelesi 2
Eminönü Iskelesi 3
Harem Iskelesi 4
Kadıköy Iskelesi 5
Üsküdar Iskelesi 6
Yemiş Iskelesi 7

Kurşunlu Han
Karaköy Ferry Terminal

Golden Horn

N

Rüstem Paşa Camii
EMINÖNÜ
Yeni Cami
City Ferry Terminals
Misir Çarşısı
Sirkeci Train Station
ISTASYON ARKASI S
Gülhane Parki
Goth's Column
Çinili Köşk (Museum of Turkish Ceramics)
Topkapı Palace
CAĞALOĞLU
Archeology Museum
Kapalı Çarşı (Covered Bazaar)
Nuruosmaniye Camii
Cağaloğlu Hamami
Darphane (Royal Mint)
Aya Irene
Gazi Atik Ali Paşa Camii
Çemberlitaş Hamam
Press Museum
Yerebatan Saray
Aya Sofya Museum
Fountain of Ahmet III
Firat Cultural Centre & Şafak Cinema
Tomb of Sultan Mahmut II
Museum of Turkish & Islamic Art
SULTANAHMET
Binbirdirek Cistern
Sokollu Mehmet Paşa Camii
Sultanahmet Camii (Blue Mosque)
HIPPODROME
Cankurtaran Train Station
Küçük Ayasofya Camii
KENNEDY CAD
Bucoleon Palace

See 'Sultanahmet' map for detail

0   200 m

OLD İSTANBUL

By air

İstanbul's **Atatürk airport** (Atatürk Hava Limanı) is 12km west of the centre at Yeşilköy, near the Sea of Marmara. It has two adjacent terminals, a kilometre apart: international (*dışhatları*) and domestic (*içhatları*). The Havaş **bus service** runs from both the international and the domestic terminals to the THY (Turkish Airlines) office on the north side of Taksim Square (every 30min 5am–11pm; 8YTL); journey time into İstanbul is twenty to forty minutes, depending on the traffic. The only scheduled stop is at Aksaray (outside the *Gar* nightclub), 200m from Yenikapı train station, from where you can take a municipal train to Cankurtan station (for Sultanahmet).

The **metro** (see "City transport", p.118) runs from Atatürk airport to the city centre. The first train is at 6am, the last at 12.40am, with departures every ten minutes at peak times. To reach it follow signs for "Hafif Metro/Rapid Transit". Buy two *jeton*s (1.10YTL each) from the kiosk. Get off at Aksaray and head the short distance to the Yusufpaşa tram stop (this is where you need the second *jeton*). The tram runs to Sultanahmet and across the Golden Horn, via the Galata bridge, to Kabataş. It's possible to change from the metro to the tram at Zeytinburnu, where the respective stations are much closer, but the tram is slower than the metro at peak times.

Alternatively, a **taxi** from the airport to Sultanahmet or Taksim will cost around 18YTL (fifty percent more between midnight and 6am) – consult the tourism sign posted outside the arrivals hall for exact fares. Many hotels can arrange airport taxi collections (on request) for 20YTL.

Returning to the airport, a **shuttle bus** collects passengers from their hotel, pension or hostel in Sultanahmet and takes them to Atatürk airport for 6YTL.

İstanbul has a second airport on the Asian side, **Sabiha Gökçen**, near Pendik. From here shuttle buses coincide with arrivals (usually from Germany) and run to Taksim or Harem *otogar* for 8YTL.

By train

İstanbul has two mainline **train stations**, one in Europe at Sirkeci, the other, at Haydarpaşa, across the Bosphorus in Asia. The two are linked by ferry.

Two daily trains from Western Europe arrive at **Sirkeci train station**, located 250m above Eminönü ferry terminal: from Athens (23hr) via Thessaloniki (16hr) and Üzünköprü (6hr), and from Budapest (33hr) via Sofia (14hr) and Bucharest (18hr). The latter service connects with the rest of the European train network at Budapest. At Sirkeci it's easy to find a taxi, or catch the tram from outside the station directly uphill to Sultanahmet, Laleli and on to Aksaray (where you can change onto the metro to reach the main intercity bus station at Esenler).

Trains from Asian Turkey arrive at **Haydarpaşa train station**, 1km north of Kadıköy. Ferries across the Bosphorus to Eminönü (for Sultanahmet) leave from in front of the station, and arrive directly below Sirkeci station. If you are staying on the Asian shore, buses, dolmuşes and taxis run from Haydarpaşa to Kadıköy and Üsküdar.

By bus

There are two major **otogars** (bus stations) in İstanbul: Esenler is 10km northwest of the centre on the E800 (İstanbul–Edirne toll road); Harem is on the Asian side between Üsküdar and Kadıköy. All national bus services stop at both, regardless of destination, and both are open 24 hours.

Esenler bus station is well organized and some 150 companies have numbered ticket stands here. Most bus companies run free service buses to and from Taksim, or can arrange for you to travel on one run by another company. To get to Sultanahmet from Esenler, take the metro (every 15min 6am–1am) from the station in the centre of the *otogar* to Aksaray and switch to the tram to Sultanahmet. After 1am, your only option is to take a taxi into town (around 10YTL). Travelling from the city centre to Esenler by metro, remember to get off at *Otogar*, not *Esenler* station. There's a (free) shuttle service from Taksim or Sultanahmet to Esenler (usually an hour before departure) for tickets booked through a travel agent or bus company's city offices.

Arriving in İstanbul by bus from Asia, it's worth disembarking at **Harem**, saving a tedious journey to Esenler through terrible traffic snarl-ups. From Harem, regular ferries cross the Bosphorus to Eminönü (every hour, daily 7am–10pm) and there are private boats running to Beşiktaş and Kabataş. Dolmuşes run every few minutes to Kadıköy and to Üsküdar, leaving from the south side of the complex, beyond the ticket offices. From either of these suburbs, ferries cross to Eminönü, or from Üsküdar to Beşiktaş for Taksim. Taxis are available everywhere, but you must pay the (3YTL) bridge toll on top of the fare.

By ferry

Car ferries, operated by Turkish Maritime Lines, cross the Bosphorus from Harem to Eminönü. **Sea bus** car and passenger services from Yalova, Bandırma (on the İzmir–İstanbul route) and the islands of Avşı and Marmara arrive at the **Yenikapı ferry terminal**, off Kennedy Caddesi in Kumkapı, just south of Aksaray. From here, simply catch the train from Yenikapı station across the road from the ferry terminal; it's two stops to Sultanahmet (Cankurtaran station) or three to Sirkeci. Frequent buses depart Yenikapı for Taksim via Aksaray.

Cruise-ship arrivals will go through customs and immigration procedures at **Karaköy International Maritime Passenger Terminal**, across the Galata bridge from Eminönü. From here take the tram to Sultanahmet, or the Tünel up to Beyoğlu and the antique tram to Taksim Square; alternatively, take a taxi.

Information

The most helpful **tourist office** in the city is on Divan Yolu Caddesi, in Sultanahmet, near the Hippodrome (daily 9am–5pm; ☎0212/518 8754). Others can be found in the international arrivals area of **Atatürk airport** (daily 24hr; ☎0212/573 4136); in **Sirkeci train station** (daily 9am–5pm; ☎0212/511 5888); at **Karaköy International Maritime Passenger Terminal** (Mon–Sat 9am–5pm; ☎0212/249 5776); and in the **Hilton Hotel arcade** on Cumhuriyet Caddesi (Mon–Sat 9am–5pm; ☎0212/233 0592). Each hands out an abundance of city maps and leaflets and the staff have an excellent working knowledge of most European languages.

City transport

İstanbul has a wide choice of means of transport, from ferry to high-speed tram. All **public transport** tends to be overcrowded and pickpocketing is becoming more common; if you have any trouble with this, or with sexual harassment, make other passengers aware of the fact – try calling *imdat*, meaning "help". The newly extended tramway links most parts of the city that you're likely to want to visit, while the bus system is daunting, but manageable on certain routes. The municipal trains are ramshackle but efficient, while taxis and dolmuşes (shared taxis) are

Akbils – automatic travel passes

An **akbil** (automatic travel pass) is worth considering if you're staying for a few days or more. After paying an initial, refundable, deposit of 6YTL, these can be "charged" to whatever value you require at kiosks at Eminönü, Sirkeci, Aksaray, Taksim and the Tünel, or at the automatic terminals in main *otogar*s. The passes are accepted on all municipal and some private buses, sea buses, ferries, trains (for local journeys only), the metro and the tram. All either have *akbil* machines or turnstiles; press the *akbil* against the receptor and the appropriate journey cost (including a small discount) is deducted. Weekly and monthly passes are also available, but as you need a photo ID card these are probably only of interest to long-stayers.

very reasonably priced with knowledgeable – if not necessarily good – drivers. However, by far the best way to explore a city that, historically, has put its best face towards the water is by ferry, with the year-round **Bosphorus Tour** a favoured way of seeing the sights.

Traffic jams are unavoidable in İstanbul, though the historic Sultanahmet district is relatively traffic-free and easily explored on foot. Otherwise, expect to spend time in tailbacks as you travel to and from other areas of interest – it can take an hour by road from Sultanahmet to Ortaköy, for example. Where possible, travel by tram, metro, suburban train or ferry, though these can all be jam-packed at peak times.

Buses

İstanbul's **buses** (*otobus* in Turkish) come in a range of colours, with the bulk being the red-and-blue municipality buses. There are also a substantial number of privately run, green-and-white or orange-and-white ones, which are usually older and shabbier looking. Main bus stops boast large route maps and lists of services. Most buses run daily from 6.30am to 11.30pm, though last buses depart from the outlying suburbs much earlier. For all municipal buses, either use an *akbil* or buy a ticket in advance, which you deposit in the metal box next to the driver on boarding. On privately-run buses, the conductor will accept cash, and some companies accept *akbil*s.

Tickets are sold at *otogar* ticket kiosks next to main bus, tram or metro stops (regular ticket 1.30YTL). Touts at most main stops also sell them for a small mark-up. Buy a good supply when you get the chance, since you can walk for miles trying to find a ticket kiosk in suburban areas: better still, use an *akbil*.

On the European side **main bus terminals** are at Eminönü, Taksim Square, Beşikataş and Aksaray, and on the Asian side at Üsküdar and Kadıköy. Few buses pass through Sultanahmet (with the notable exception of the extremely useful #T4 bus, which links Sultanahmet and Taksim), so the easiest thing to do is walk, or catch the tram three stops, down the hill to the bus station at Eminönü (sited in front of the ferry terminal). **From Eminönü** there are buses to Taksim, west-bound services to Aksaray and Topkapı, and services to the Bosphorus shore through Beşiktaş, Ortaköy and Arnavutköy to Bebek where you'll have to change to continue on through the suburbs as far as the village of Rumeli Kavaği. Buses **from Taksim Square** head through Mecidiyeköy to the northern suburbs, down along the Bosphorus through Beşiktaş, Ortaköy and Aranvutköy, and across the horn to Topkapı and Aksaray.

Useful routes include: #12 and #14 (Kadıköy to Üsküdar); #15/A (Üsküdar to Beylerbeyi, Kanlıca and Anadolu Kavaği); #22 and #22/C (Eminönü to Karaköy, Beşikataş, Arnavutköy and Bebek); #25/A (Eminönü to Beşikataş, Levent,

△ The antique tram on İstiklâl Caddesi

Maslak, Sariyer and Rumeli Kavaği); #30 (Sultanahmet to Eminönü, Karaköy and Beşikataş); #84 (Eminönü to Sultanahmet, Aksaray and Topkapı); and #23/B (Taksim to Beşikataş and Ortaköy).

Trains

The **municipal train network** – operated by *Türkiye Cumhuriyeti Devlet Demiryolları* (TCDD) – consists of one line on either side of the Bosphorus. It's hardly comprehensive, but elaborate plans exist to link the two via a tunnel under the Sea of Marmara.

Trains are frequent and cheap, though crowded at morning and evening rush hours; daily hours of operation are 7am to 9.30pm. One line runs **from Haydarpaşa** (enquiries on ☎0212/336 0475) out to Göztepe and Bostancı, and along the Gulf of İzmit to Gebze; the other, **from Sirkeci** (☎0212/527 0051), runs to Halkala, along the shores of the Sea of Marmara, stopping at Kumkapı (known for its fish restaurants), Yenkapı (for the sea-bus ferry terminal), Yedikule fortress and Yeşilköy, not far from the airport. Journeys cost the same flat **fare** (1.10YTL) and *akbil*s are accepted on local lines. At Sirkeci, you buy a *jeton* (metal token) from the kiosk (insert it at the turnstile), but Haydarpaşa still uses tickets, again available from kiosks.

There is also a one-stop underground funicular train line, between Karaköy and İstiklâl Caddesi in Beyoğlu, known as the **Tünel** (every 15min, daily 8am–9pm); use an *akbil* or *jeton* (0.90YTL), available at the kiosks on entry.

Trams

The **main tram** service runs from Zeytinburnu and Merter via Topkapı Gate to Aksaray (where it connects with the metro), Laleli, the University, Beyazit, Cemberlitaş, Sultanahmet, downhill to Eminönü, and across the Galata bridge to Fındıklı, via Karaköy (Galata) and Tophane. Trams are frequent and operate from 7.30am to 9pm. Approaching trams signal their arrival with a bell and passengers must wait on the concrete platforms, placed at regular intervals along the tracks.

Note that the tram stops are marked, confusingly, by the same "M" sign as the metro. *Jeton*s (1.10YTL) can be bought at booths next to the platforms and are deposited in turnstiles on entry, or you can use an *akbil*.

The **antique tram** (with ticket collectors in appropriately antiquated uniforms) runs between the Tünel station, at the Beyoğlu end of İstiklâl Caddesi, for 1.5km to Taksim Square (every 15min, daily 9am–9pm; 1.10YTL). Tickets can be purchased from kiosks at either end of the route or at the one fixed stop halfway at Galatasaray School; *akbil*s are also accepted.

The metro

Once the building of a tunnel underneath the Golden Horn has been completed, the **metro**, or *hızlı tramvay* (high-speed tram), will connect the whole of the European side of İstanbul. At present the service is limited to a line on each side of the horn. The **southern line** runs west from Aksaray via the intercity *otogar* near Esenler, to Atatürk airport. Although it's called a metro, only small sections of this line run underground. On the **northern side** of the Golden Horn, the Taksim to Levent section is truely underground, and runs from Taksim Square via Omsmanbey, Şişli and Gayrettepe to Levent. Metro trains leave every fifteen minutes (daily 6am–11.15pm); **tickets** (1.10YTL) are inserted in turnstiles on entry, or use an *akbil*.

Dolmuşes and minibuses

Dolmuşes are shared taxis running on fixed routes, departing only when full (*dolmuş* means full). Modern yellow taxicabs and converted yellow vans have replaced the 1950s' Fords, Cadillacs, Dodges, Plymouths and Chevrolets that used to ply the streets. These may lack the romance of the past but are infinitely more comfortable and seldom break down. **Minibus** services on longer routes tend to run along main arteries and depart according to a schedule known only to their drivers.

Both dolmuşes and minibuses display their destination in the window. A flat **fare** (fixed by the municipality) is levied: watch what Turkish passengers are paying – usually 1–2YTL – shout your destination to the driver and pay accordingly, passing the money via other passengers. Dolmuş and minibus stands at points of origin are denoted with a signpost "D" and are prevalent all over the city. Services can be hailed at any point along the route; they are most frequent during rush hour and operate later than the regular buses, sometimes until 2am. To get off, politely call *müsait bir yerde* or *inecek* (pronounced "inejek") *var*.

Taxis

Taxis are ubiquitous and invariably painted yellow. **Fares** are reasonable: expect to pay around 8YTL from Taksim to Sultanahmet, with an extra 3YTL toll in addition to the fare when crossing either of the Bosphorus bridges. All taxis are equipped with **meters**, but check that the driver switches it on to avoid arguments later. Be careful that you're not charged either ten times what's shown on it, or the night rate (an extra fifty percent that should only be levied between midnight and 6am). Older meters have two small lights marked *gündüz* (day) and *gece* (night); on newer meters the rate flashes up alternately with the running cost. If there's any trouble, start discussing the *polis*, especially at any suggestion of a flat fare, and if necessary note the registration number and call the Tourist Police (see "Listings").

Ferries, sea buses and sea taxis

The main **ferry** company is the efficient İDO (*İstanbul Deniz Otobüsleri*; enquiries on ℡0212/444 4436), with seasonal timetables available from the ferry terminals and from tourist offices. On the busiest routes – such as Eminönü to Kadıköy or Üsküdar – there are generally three to five ferries an hour between 6am and midnight; all have a flat fare of 1YTL each way. Increasingly, ferry services are being replaced by the faster **sea buses** (*deniz otobüsleri*), though these run less frequently except at peak commuter times. Sea-bus fares are a flat 4YTL for most destinations (making the long hops cheap, short ones dear), but 5YTL for the Princes' Islands and 6YTL to Yalova on the south shore of the Sea of Marmara. For both ferries and sea buses, buy a *jeton* and deposit it at the turnstile on entry, or use your *akbil* (and save over 1YTL per trip).

The busiest routes are also served by several other small, privately-run ferries, many under the umbrella of the co-operative **Turyol**. Most Turyol boats leave from a terminal just west of the Galata bridge in Eminönü, for a wide range of destinations; tickets are sold at kiosks on the quayside.

At the main **City Ferry Terminal** at Eminönü – between Sirkeci train station and the Galata bridge – there is a line of ferry quays or terminals (*iskelesi* in Turkish) clearly marked with the destination points of the ferries (bear in mind that these terminals used to be numbered, and still are on the tourist-office city maps). From right to left, as you look at the Golden Horn from Eminönü, the first is Adalar İskelesi for ferries to the Princes' Islands (regular departures from 7am–11pm). The next three terminals are for destinations on the Asian side: Harem İskelesi (frequent departures from 7.30am–9.10pm for car and passenger ferries); Üsküdar İskelesi (frequent departures from 6.30am–11.30pm); and Kadıköy İskelesi (frequent departures from 7.30am–9.10pm). Ferries from Boğaz İskelesi run up the Bosphorus to Rumeli Kavaği (see Bosphorus Tour, below). The terminal nearest to (the east side of) the Galata bridge is Eminönü İskelesi for sea buses to Beşiktaş, Üsküdar, Kadıköy, Sariyer, Bostancı, and Bakırköy. On the west side of Galata bridge is Yemiş İskelesi, for ferries up the Golden Horn to Eyüp via Kasimpaşa, Fener and Balat (roughly hourly 7am–8pm).

Less frequent İDO ferry routes go from Karaköy (on the other side of the Galata bridge) to Kabataş, Beşiktaş, Ortaköy and Bebek, with a couple of departures during peak commuter hours only; and from Beşiktaş to Kadıköy or Üsküdar (roughly every hour 8am–9pm).

There are numerous other sea-bus routes, including Bakırköy to Bostancı via Kadıköy and Yenikapı (hourly between 7.30am–10pm), and from Kabataş to the Princes' Islands in the Sea of Marmara (6–12 daily). **Timetables** are available from all sea-bus terminals and at ⓦwww.ido.com.tr under *"tarife bilgileri"*. Sea buses also operate further afield, from İstanbul to Bandırma and Yalova on the opposite shore of the Marmara (see p.270 and p.247).

The Bosphorus Tour

From Boğaz İskelesi İDO operates the popular daily **Bosphorus Tour** (*Boğaz Hatti*), a cruise to Rumeli Kavağı and Anadolu Kavağı, the most distant villages up the Bosphorus on the European and Asian sides respectively. Trips depart daily during summer (June–Oct) at 10.35am, noon and 1.35pm, and return from Anadolu Kavağı at 3pm, 4.15pm and 5pm (7pm at weekends), crisscrossing from one side to the other. The rest of the year there is just one departure at 10.35am, returning at 3pm. The return journey costs 7.5YTL and takes about an hour and a half each way, with stops at Beşiktaş, Kanlica, Emirgan, Yeniköy, Sariyer, Rumeli Kavağı and Anadolu Kavağı. You can jump off in any of these places, but you pay again to re-board.

City Crimewatch

İstanbul is undoubtedly far safer than most European or North American cities, and cases of mugging and assault against tourists are rare. Having said this, the crime rate is soaring (thirty percent up according to recent statistics), due in part to the increasing disparity between rich and poor.

For the average visitor, **pickpocketing** is the main cause for concern: be particularly careful around Sirkeci station and the Eminönü waterfront, and around Taksim (especially at night). Be wary of the gangs of street kids hawking packs of tissues and the like – they'll jostle you while an accomplice empties your pockets. A daypack worn on your back is an easy target. Either lock it with a small lock, or carry it on your front. You should also be careful on public transport, particularly when it is crowded.

Lone males heading out for the night should be wary of **confidence tricksters**. The usual scenario is to be approached by a friendly Turkish male, who'll suggest a good club or bar to go to. In the bar there are (surprise, surprise) some attractive females, who your "friend" suggests buying drinks for. When the bill comes (to you), it can run into hundreds of euros. Even if you don't have enough cash on you, you'll be forced to pay with your credit card. In cases like this it is very difficult to prove criminal intent – use your common sense and avoid the situation arising. The **spiking of drinks** is also on the increase: make sure you buy your own drinks if you have any doubts at all about whom you are with.

Accommodation

Finding somewhere to stay in İstanbul is rarely a problem and supply usually exceeds demand, though as the city stages more and more prestigious events, such as the 2005 European Cup Final and the country's first Formula One Grand Prix, this could change. To ensure you get the place you want, phone or email ahead, up to a week in advance in high season.

It's essential to have a look at a room before you check in, as prices are not always a reliable indication of quality. By law, room rates should be displayed in the foyer and, because of the fluctuating Turkish exchange rate, most establishments quote **prices in euros or US dollars** (though paying in Turkish lira is equally acceptable). Advertised prices can be unrealistically high, having been fixed in a busy season or for the benefit of tour companies, and those hotels that ask €70–100 per night may bargain. Many hotels offer discounts for cash or booking through their **website**, though note that even moderately pricey establishments may not always accept credit cards; Ⓦ www.istanbulbudgethotels.com is worth checking before you leave home.

Sultanahmet

Some of the city's best small hotels and *pansiyon*s – and many of its worst hostels – are in **Sultanahmet**, the heart of touristic İstanbul, within a few minutes' walk of the Blue Mosque, Topkapı Palace and Aya Sofya. Those around the **Hippodrome** are particularly well placed to give an on-location sense of history. A high concentration of accommodation is to be found in and around **Akbıyık Caddesi and Cankurtaran**, while the hotels off **Divan Yolu Caddesi** have the advantage of being handy for the Topkapı–Eminönü tram. All the places reviewed below are marked on the Sultanahmet map on p.121.

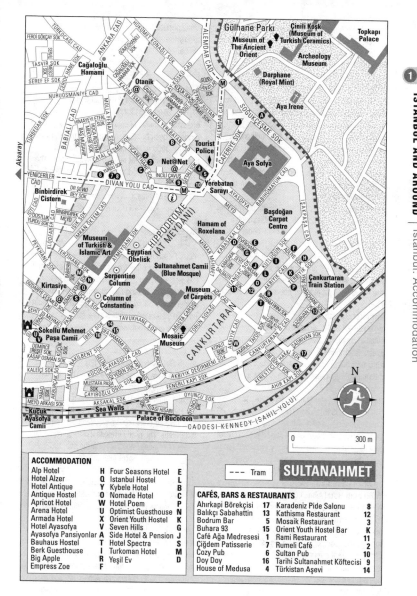

ACCOMMODATION

Alp Hotel	**H**	Four Seasons Hotel	**E**
Hotel Alzer	**Q**	Istanbul Hostel	**L**
Hotel Antique	**Y**	Kybele Hotel	**B**
Antique Hostel	**O**	Nomade Hotel	**C**
Apricot Hotel	**W**	Hotel Poem	**P**
Arena Hotel	**U**	Optimist Guesthouse	**N**
Armada Hotel	**X**	Orient Youth Hostel	**K**
Hotel Ayasofya	**V**	Seven Hills	**G**
Ayasofya Pansiyonlar	**A**	Side Hotel & Pension	**J**
Bauhaus Hostel	**T**	Hotel Spectra	**S**
Berk Guesthouse	**I**	Turkoman Hotel	**M**
Big Apple	**R**	Yeşil Ev	**D**
Empress Zoe	**F**		

CAFÉS, BARS & RESTAURANTS

Ahırkapi Börekçisi	17	Karadeniz Pide Salonu	8
Balıkçı Sabahattin	13	Kathisma Restaurant	12
Bodrum Bar	5	Mosaik Restaurant	3
Buhara 93	15	Orient Youth Hostel Bar	K
Café Ağa Medresesi	1	Rami Restaurant	11
Çiğdem Patisserie	7	Rumeli Café	2
Cozy Pub	6	Sultan Pub	10
Doy Doy	16	Tarihi Sultanahmet Köftecisi	9
House of Medusa	4	Türkistan Aşevi	14

--- Tram   **SULTANAHMET**

0 —— 300 m

Around the Hippodrome

Hotel Alzer At Meydanı 72 ☏0212/516 6262, ⊛www.alzerhotel.com. Not the most characterful of the area's hotels, but the extremely comfortable rooms have cable TV, air conditioning, central heating and safe box; the roof terrace has stunning views over walnut trees to the Blue Mosque and the sea. Rooms at the back overlooking the Hippodrome are €20 dearer. Good value. ❼

Hotel Antique Küçükayasofya Cad, Oğul Sok 17 ☏0212/516 4936, Ⓔhotelantique@superonline. com. Hotel in a quiet neighbourhood with miniscule rooms, but offering excellent value for the level of service. There's a roof terrace where you can have a drink looking directly at the dome of the Blue Mosque. **❹**

🏃 **Arena Hotel** Şehit Mehmet Paşa Yokuşu, Üçler Hamam Sok 13–15 ☎0212/458 0364, ⊛www.arenahotel.com. Extremely well run hotel, converted from an Ottoman mansion, formerly the family house of the owner. Spacious rooms with repro antique furnishings, air conditioning, cable TV and safe box. The large bathrooms are immaculate, some with tubs. A nice touch – white bathrobe, slippers and flowers laid out on the bed. Communal hamam downstairs and a fifteen-per-cent discount for cash. **❻**

Hotel Ayasofya Demirci Reşit Sok 28, off Mehmet Paşa Sok ☎0212/516 9446, ℮info@ayasofya.com. Very good value, in a restored wooden mansion-house just down from the Hippodrome. Despite the mock-wood vinyl flooring and modern furniture, the rooms are very pleasant, and the bathrooms spotless. The roof terrace commands fine views and is a mass of pot plants and shrubs. **❺**

Optimist Guesthouse At Meydanı 68 ☎0212/638 9580, ℮zuboz8@yahoo.com. Funky place in a tall, narrow, yellow-painted building overlooking the Hippodrome. Rooms are sparsely furnished but spacious, as are the bathrooms, and the manager is a real character. It has a street-side café/pub. **❹**

Hotel Spectra Şehit Mehmet Paşa Yokuşu ☎0212/516 3546, ⊛www.hotelspectra.com. Concrete facsimile of an Ottoman house, and a little impersonal (it's part of the *Best Western* chain) with large, comfortable and nicely furnished rooms, good views from the terrace and free Internet access in the lobby for guests. Ten-percent discount for cash. **❻**

Turkoman Hotel Asmalı Çeşme Sok, Adliye Yana 2 ☎0212/516 2956, ⊛www.turkomanhotel.com. Converted house in nineteenth-century Turkish style, right on the Hippodrome and opposite the Egyptian obelisk, with fine views of the Blue Mosque from the roof terrace. Each attractive room is named after one of the old Turkoman tribes, and has a brass bed and wooden floors. Free airport transfers. **❼**

Around Topkapı Palace

Ayasofya Pansiyonlar Soğukçeşme Sok ☎0212/513 3660, ℮ayapans@escourtnet.com. A row of pastel-coloured houses reconstructed in nineteenth-century style, in a peaceful cobbled street tucked away behind the back wall of the Aya Sofya. The setting is fantastic and lit up

atmospherically at night, but the rooms are rather simply furnished, perhaps in an attempt to match the period feel. **❽**

Around Divan Yolu Caddesi

🏃 **Kybele Hotel** Yerebatan Cad 35 ☎0212/511 7766, ⊛www.kybelehotel.com. Atmospheric, unusual, late nineteenth-century rendered brick building, colourfully painted. Inside are over 3000 multi-hued antique-style light fittings and some great original Bakelite radios. The spacious rooms sport marbled wallpaper and old wood flooring. Breakfast is served in a courtyard full of candelabras, cushions, empty bottles and other knick-knacks. Friendly staff. Recommended. **❻**

🏃 **Nomade Hotel** Ticarethane Sok 15 ☎0212/511 1296, ⊛www.hotelnomade.com. Described as "ethnic trendy" by the French designer responsible for its chic interior, this hotel has white-floored rooms finished in bold colours, with rich coordinating fabrics and blonde-wood modernist furniture. The charming and sophisticated twin sisters who run it ensure excellent service. There's a great roof terrace, too. Recommended. **❻**

Cankurtaran

Alp Hotel Akbıyık Cad, Adliye Sok 4 ☎0212/517 9570, ⊛www.alpguesthouse.com. This fine establishment, with a dark wood exterior, is situated down a quiet lane. The smallish rooms are immaculately furnished, some with four-poster beds, and have air conditioning, wooden floors and tidy bathrooms. The pretty breakfast terrace commands views of palaces, mosques and the sea. **❻**

🏃 **Apricot Hotel** Akbiyik Cad 75 ☎0212/638 1658, ⊛www.apricothotel.com. Relaxed but very professionally run, in a restored house at the quiet end of this popular street. Rooms are tastefully furnished, painted in soothing colours, and the bathrooms are immaculate. Air conditioning, double glazing and cable TV are standard. The roof terrace has fine sea views, is liberally studded with pot plants, and the breakfast is high quality. Good value, recommended. **❺**

Antique Hostel Kutlugün Sok 51 ☎0212/638 1637, ⊛www.antiquehostel.com. Friendly place and a good choice if you're after the quiet life (no bar, no alcohol on the premises!). The semi-basement dorm rooms (€8) are well decorated and kitted out and are better value than the doubles, though these are air-conditioned and have TVs. **❸**

Armada Hotel Ahırkapı Sok 24 ☎0212/455 4455, ⊛www.armadahotel.com.tr. Quality hotel featuring Ottoman-style rooms, all with central heating, double glazing and air conditioning. Rooms are tastefully decorated, with Edirne-style painted wood friezes. The rooftop terrace has lovely views over the sea and, at night, the illuminated mosques of Sultanahmet. A lavish breakfast spread includes home-made jams and pastries. ❽

🏃 **Bauhaus Hostel** Bayramfırını Sok 11–13 ☎0212/638 6534, @www.travelinistanbul .com. With a mix of dorm bunks (€9–12 depending on number of bunks per room) and doubles, this is a homely, clean and friendly option. There's a nice roof terrace, a *kilim*-cushioned sitting area and free Internet use, but breakfast is extra. Good value. ❷

🏃 **Berk Guesthouse** Kutlugün Sok 27 ☎0212/517 6561, @www .berkguesthouse.com. Old-fashioned family-run place with eight standard rooms, plus a couple of spacious luxury rooms with minibar, air conditioning and TV. The nineteenth-century mansion has been lovingly restored, and has great views of the former prison – now converted into the *Four Seasons Hotel* – from the rooftop lounge and terrace. Standard rooms ❹, luxury rooms ❻

Big Apple Bayram Fırını Sok 12 ☎0212/517 7931. Good value, cheerful hostel sporting a large lobby with billiard table (free) and well-kitted-out dorms (18YTL) with wooden floors, and bunk beds with new mattresses. Shared, clean, separate toilet and shower on each floor. You can use the kitchen, and there's a nice covered terrace and a small roof terrace, both with decent outlooks.

🏃 **Empress Zoe** Akbıyık Cad, Adliye Sok 10 ☎0212/518 2504, @www.emzoe .com. Owned by American Ann Nevans, who has decorated throughout with her personal touch – the nineteen rooms are in dark wood with richly coloured textiles, accessed by a narrow spiral staircase. Part of the basement walls belong to the remains of the Byzantine Palace and the sun terrace has panoramic views of the Blue Mosque and Aya Sofya. Ten-percent discount for cash. ❼

Four Seasons Hotel Tevfikhane Sok 1 ☎0212/638 8200, @www.fourseasons.com. Until the early 1980s, this formidable building still served as the Sultanahmet Prison before being completely renovated as one of the city's leading hotels. The watchtowers and exercise court are still evident beneath the flowers and vines, but the 54 beautiful high-ceilinged rooms are unrecognizable as former cells. Excellent, attentive service at this five-star luxury establishment, though suite prices reach ridiculous levels. ❽

🏃 **İstanbul Hostel** Kutlugün Sok 35 ☎0212/516 9380, @www.istanbulhostel. net. All round, probably the best of İstanbul's hostels, in the heart of the backpacker quarter,

with 64 dorm beds (€8), two double rooms, and spotless, shared, marble bathrooms. The beds are good quality and comfy. The cosy cellar-bar has big-screen satellite TV, video, a fireplace and Internet access, and there are more bars on the roof terrace, as well as regular entertainment from belly dancers. ❸

Orient Youth Hostel Akbıyık Cad 13 ☎0212/517 9493, @www.orienthostel.com. Friendly, popular hostel with a lively rooftop bar and a good restaurant. It's worth visiting for the Friday-night party even if you are staying elsewhere. Dorms, painted bright blue (€11) are basic but clean; waterless doubles are not really worth the extra. ❹

🏃 **Hotel Poem** Terbıyık Sok 12 ☎0212/638 9744, @www.hotelpoem.com. Very friendly family-run establishment, in two adjoining nineteenth-century wooden mansion-houses. Rooms are named after famous Turkish poets or their poems (you can stay in "Nirvana"!) and have air conditioning and immaculate bathrooms. The downstairs terrace is shaded by walnut and fig trees, while the roof terrace has panoramic views of the Aya Sofya and the sea. Rooms with a sea view cost twenty percent extra. Free Internet access. Recommended. ❻

Seven Hills Tevkifhane Sok 8 ☎0212/516 9497, 516 9498 or 516 9499, @www.hotelsevenhills. com. Deluxe hotel in a newly restored mansion with all the trimmings and the usual stunning views from its sumptuous roof terrace (which doubles as an expensive fish restaurant). All rooms are furnished to the highest standard, with some sporting Jacuzzis and balconies (€70 extra). ❽

🏃 **Side Hotel & Pension** Utangaç Sok 20 ☎0212/517 2282, @www.sidehotel.com. Pricier en-suite rooms on the hotel side, cheaper ones with shared bathroom in the pension, both sharing the extensive breakfast terraces, which have great views of the Princes' Islands. The whole complex, owned by three charismatic brothers, is bright, spacious and friendly. Recommended. Pension ❹, hotel ❺

🏃 **Yeşil Ev** Kabasakal Cad 5 ☎0212 517 6785, @www.turing.org.tr. On a leafy cobbled street between Aya Sofya and the Blue Mosque. Built in the style of the house that originally occupied the site, *Yeşil Ev* ("Green House") is furnished in period (mid-nineteenth-century) style, with wood-panelled ceilings and antique rugs. The rooms are good value for this quality; "Pasha's Room" (€140) has its own Turkish bath and ostentatious Ottoman bedroom suite. There's a fine garden restaurant with a central marble fountain open to nonresidents. ❽

Sirkeci

The area around **Sirkeci station**, famous as the last (east-bound) stop on the Orient Express, has much in its favour: Sultanahmet and the city's most famous sites are a short walk away up the hill; it's a stone's throw to the ferry terminals on the Golden Horn in Eminönü; and the fleshpots of İstiklâl Caddesi lie just across the Galata bridge. It is also on the tramway line, making the short hop up to Sultanahmet or across to Galata easy. Hotels in this working, bustling neighbourhood tend to be much better value than in Sultanahmet or Taksim, which may appeal to budget travellers keen to avoid the backpacker joints around Cankurtan. On the downside, there's a paucity of decent eating places (with a couple of honourable exceptions listed on p.181), and it has the transitional feel common to areas around major stations the world over. The places reviewed below are marked on the "Old İstanbul" map on pp.112–113.

Hürriyet Hotel Nöbethane Cad, Serdar Sok 19 ☎0212/520 3787, ℗520 3788. Excellent value, Kurdish-run hotel tucked away behind the station. New beds, white linen, clean carpets and spacious rooms. The en-suite bathrooms are very clean, and there's 24-hour hot water. ❷

Yaşmak Sultan Ebusuud Cad 18–20 ☎0212/528 1343, ⓦwww.hotelyasmaksultan .com. Well-established, professionally-run place in an old building on a corner plot, in a quiet part of Sirkeci, near Gülhane Parkı. The rooms are old-fashioned in an unfashionable way, but have all mod-cons. There's a roof bar with great views, and a sauna. ❼

Yıldız Otel Nöbethane Cad 36 ☎0212/520 5254. Far better than the grotty exterior suggests, this hotel is about as cheap as they come. The staff are very friendly and the female cleaners keep the place spotless. Rear rooms have views over the station roof to the sea. It's very basic and the showers are often cold, but with doubles cheaper than a couple of dorm beds in Sultanahmet, who's complaining! ❷

Taksim and around

Taksim is the city's major business and shopping district, with a wide range of hotels aimed largely at tour groups and business travellers. Rates here are usually higher than in other areas, but bargains can be found. It's not so convenient for sightseeing in Sultanahmet, but Taksim affords easy access to the Bosphorus and Beyoğlu, and comes into its own at night as the city's cultural, culinary and entertainment centre. At the northwestern end of İstiklâl Caddesi there are several hotels in **Tepebaşı**, centred on Meşrutiyet Caddesi, which you can reach by taking a tram along İstiklâl Caddesi to the halfway stop at Galatasaray School. There are also a couple of options close to the **Galata** tower; to get there, stay on the tram to the end of the line at Tünel. **Cihangir**, on the northern side of Sıraselviler Caddesi, is a bohemian backwater with splendid views of the Bosphorus. All the places reviewed below are marked on the "Taksim and Beyoğlu" map on pp.170–171.

Off Taksim Square

Otel Avrupa Topçu Cad 32, Taksim ☎0212/250 9420, ℮otelavrupa@superonline.com. Small rooms with small beds and shared bathrooms – though some are en-suite with TV – but it's very friendly and there's a pleasant breakfast room. On a quiet street, this is a bargain in an area where most other hotels are in the luxury class. French and German spoken. ❹

Marmara Hotel Taksim Square ☎0212/251 4696, ⓦwww.themarmara.com.tr. Premier five-star hotel right on Taksim Square, one of İstanbul's landmark buildings. The 410 luxurious rooms all have great views over Beyoğlu, and facilities include swimming pool, Turkish bath, spa, and a number of restaurants – the best being the ground-floor *Brassiere* for some serious people-watching over coffee, pastries and Turkish sweets. ❽

Otel Sato İstiklâl Cad, Bekar Sok 5, Beyoğlu ☎0212/245 2579. Basic twin rooms, with tiny bathrooms and no breakfast available. But it's clean and ideally situated for İstanbul's nightlife.

ISIC-card carriers get an exceptional fifty-percent discount. ④

Vardar Palace Hotel Sıraselviler Cad 54, Taksim ⊤0212/252 2888, ⊛www.vardarhotel.com. Renovated, late nineteenth-century apartment building. There are no views at the back and rooms at the front are noisy, but it's a reasonable option for the Taksim area, with period furniture, spacious rooms and a friendly atmosphere. ⑥

Tepebaşı, İstiklâl Caddesi and Galata

Bahar Apart Hotel İstiklâl Cad 61 ⊤0212/245 0702, ⊕244 1708. Right in the heart of the action near the Taksim end of this buzzing street, with dark but comfortable rooms, separate sitting areas and tiny kitchens with tea/coffee-making facilities. Back rooms are much quieter. Good value for the area and size of accommodation. ⑥

Büyük Londra Oteli Meşrutiyet Cad 117, Tepebaşı ⊤0212/249 1025, ⊛www.londrahotel.com. Palatial, mid-nineteenth-century townhouse. Many of the rooms are time-worn and cluttered with battered period furniture, which gives the hotel its retro-bohemian charm. Some rooms have been modernized and inevitably have lost their raffishness, and room prices vary between €65–150. Ernest Hemingway stayed here in 1922 when he was a journalist covering the Turkish War of Independence. ⑥

Hotel Devman Asmalımescit Sok 52 ⊤0212/245 6212, ⊛www.taksim.com/?islem=mekan&g=772. Modern hotel in the arty nineteenth-century backstreets off İstiklâl Caddesi, with spotless blue-tiled bathrooms, coordinating furnishings and a decent open-buffet breakfast. Good value for the location, and handy for the nightlife. ④

🏃 **Galata Residence** Bankalar Cad, Hacı Ali Sok 27, Galata ⊤0212/292 4841, ⊛www.galataresidence.com. Beautifully restored late nineteenth-century building, offering one- and two-bedroom apartments with fully equipped kitchens. There's a roof-terrace restaurant and a café in the vaulted cellar, with cheaper apartments across the road more suited to business travellers. Weekly rates are €650 for a two-bed apartment, daily rates higher, longer stays cheaper still. ⑧

Monopol Hotel Meşrutiyet Cad 223, Tepebaşı ⊤0212/251 7326, ⊕251 7333. Opposite the US Embassy, the comfortable rooms here have one to four beds, air conditioning, satellite TV and a fridge. Excellent value for such a prominent area, but the front rooms can get noisy at night when the Beyoğlu bars turn out. ⑤

Pera Palas Meşrutiyet Cad 98–100, Tepebaşı ⊤0212/251 4560, ⊛www.perapalas.com. A contender for the most atmospheric hotel in İstanbul, the *Pera* deserves a visit if only for a coffee in the chandeliered *American Bar* or the exquisite tearooms and a visit to the "powder room". Built in the nineteenth century to accommodate Orient Express passengers, its rooms are marked with the names of famous occupants such as Agatha Christie and Graham Greene. Rooms start from €170, but package deals booked through tour operators abroad are better value. ⑧

🏃 **Hotel Silviya** Asmalımescit Sok 54 ⊤0212/292 7749, ⊕243 6115. Very clean and friendly hotel, with spacious, carpeted rooms painted a soothing green, and spotless bathrooms with decent-quality fittings. The (very average) breakfast is taken in the small ground-floor TV room. Perfect situation for sampling the vibrant nightlife around, but quiet. Great value – recommended. ③

Cihangir

Cihangir Hotel Arslan Yatağı Sok 33 ⊤0212/251 5317, ⊛www.cihangirhotel.com. Situated in a quiet backstreet in one of the town's more atmospheric quarters. Excellent service, large rooms (those with tremendous Bosphorus views carry a €10 surcharge) with TVs, air conditioning and minibars, and a huge buffet breakfast served on a commanding terrace. ⑥

🏃 **Villa Zurich** Akarsu Yokuşu Cad 44–46 ⊤0212/293 0604, ⊕249 0232. Delightful, good-value hotel offering large, well-equipped doubles with satellite TV, air conditioning and a baby-sitting service. Rooms with a stunning panorama of the Bosphorus are €80, city-view rooms are €55. The rooftop terrace has the best views of all, and serves as the breakfast salon, and in the evening a very well regarded fish restaurant (full meal including drinks €25–40). ⑤

On the Bosphorus

The suburbs along the shores of the Bosphorus make an interesting alternative to staying in the city centre and are fairly easy to reach by bus or ferry. There are cheap hotels on the Asian side, in **Kadıköy** and **Üsküdar**, though they are unused to tourists. There are no budget options on the European side of the Bosphorus – you pay a massive premium for the waterfront locations.

Beşiktaş

Çırağan Palace & Kempinski Hotel Çırağan Cad 84 ☎0212/258 3377, ⓦwww.ciragan-palace.com. Twelve suites in an elaborately restored Ottoman palace right on the Bosphorus, on the European side, with every luxury imaginable for upwards of €750 per night. For mere mortals, there are spacious rooms in the adjacent modern five-star *Kempinski*, though even here rooms cost from €300. Guests at both have use of the several restaurants serving gourmet cuisine, large outdoor pool and health club. ❽

Kadıköy

Hotel Eysan Rıhtım Cad 26 ☎0216/346 2440, ⓕ418 9582. Built in 1928 and originally a military school, this faded four-star hotel is more or less opposite the ferry, overlooking the chaos of traffic on Rıhtım Caddesi. On the plus side, the rooms are extremely large, with plenty of room for armchairs and desks, the bathrooms are clean, and the staff friendly. ❻

Üsküdar

Yeni Saray Oteli Salmani Pak Cad, Çeşme Sok 33 ☎0216/310 9282, ⓕ334 5655. Pleasant family-run hotel with restaurant, bar, café and a terrace overlooking the Bosphorus. Rooms are equipped with modern furniture, have air conditioning and double glazing (essential for front rooms overlooking the bustling street). It's just to the right of and behind the Mihrimah Camii, above a *McDonalds*, more or less opposite the ferry. ❻

Campsites

The city's **campsites** are located towards the airport. Coming out of town by car, follow signs to the airport along the main coast road and the suburbs of Bakırköy and Ataköy are a couple of kilometres before the airport. They are both easily accessible from Sirkeci by train or are a cheap taxi ride (3–5YTL) from the airport. If you have booked an organized overland trip from İstanbul to Cairo or other destinations in the Middle East or Asia, you are quite likely to be joining your overland truck at one of these campsites. Both sites listed below are open year-round and are useful locations for those with their own transport, as parking is almost impossible at central hotels or hostels.

Ataköy Mocamp Rauf Orbay Cad, Ataköy ☎0212/662 8282 or 661 8235, ⓕ661 7322. Well-sited near the shore and handy for transport; facilities include a swimming pool, bar and restaurant. Take the train to Bakırköy train station from Sirkeci (the campsite is conveniently marked on the map on the inside of the train), or bus #72 from Taksim or Aksaray.

Londra Camping Bakırköy, E5 motorway, beyond Ataköy ☎0212/560 4200, ⓕ559 3438. Facilities are fine with some motel-style rooms, but it's a pretty grim location on a motorway, behind a garage and next to one of the largest truck stops in Europe. Take the #72 bus from Taksim or Aksaray, or the fast tramway to Ataköy and walk up the service road on the left-hand side of the motorway.

Sultanahmet

Most short-stay visitors spend all their time in **Sultanahmet**, home of İstanbul's main sightseeing attractions: the Topkapı Palace, heart of the Ottoman Empire; the Sultanahmet Camii (better known as the Blue Mosque); and the greatest legacy of the Byzantine Empire, the church of Aya Sofya. Here also are the ancient Hippodrome, the Museum of Islamic Culture (housed in the former Palace of İbrahim Paşa), the Yerebatan underground cistern and the Kapalı Çarşı, the largest covered bazaar in the world. The monumental architecture, attractive parks and gardens, street-side cafes, and the benefits of a relatively traffic-free main road (courtesy of the tramline) combine to make this area pleasant for both sightseeing and staying.

On the negative side, large numbers of persistent **hustlers** gather around the Hippodrome and Divan Yolu Caddesi, badgering new arrivals to visit their carpet shop or offering to act as a guide. Ignore them in a friendly but firm manner, otherwise you'll end up spending more time (and money) on carpet shopping than you dreamed possible.

Aya Sofya

For almost a thousand years **Aya Sofya**, or Haghia Sophia (daily except Mon 9am–6pm, upper galleries close at 5.30pm; 15YTL), was the largest enclosed space in the world, designed to impress the strength and wealth of the Byzantine emperors upon their own subjects and visiting foreign dignitaries alike. Located between the Topkapı Palace and Sultanahmet Camii on the ancient acropolis, the first hill of İstanbul, the church dominated the city skyline for a millennium, until the domes and minarets of the city's mosques began to challenge its eminence in the sixteenth century.

Considering the vicissitudes undergone by the building over the centuries it's perhaps surprising to find Aya Sofya still standing at all. As it is, after years of work, the restored interior of the dome has finally emerged from its scaffolding, while restorations have also improved its formerly neglected brick-and-stonework exterior.

Some history

Aya Sofya, "the Church of the Divine Wisdom", is the third church of this name to stand on the site; it was commissioned in the sixth century by Emperor Justinian after its predecessor had been razed to the ground in the Nika revolts of 532. The architects, **Anthemius of Tralles** and **Isidore of Miletus**, were to create a building combining elements in a manner and on a scale completely unknown to the Byzantine world, and no imitation or rival would subsequently be attempted until the sixteenth century. It remained an important symbol of Byzantine power long after the empire itself had been destroyed and became the inspiration, not to say obsession, of the greatest of all Ottoman architects, Mimar Sinan, who devoted his lifetime to the attempt to surpass its technical achievements.

For a thirty-metre **dome** to hover over a seemingly empty space, rather than being supported by solid walls, was unprecedented and the sheer dimensions of the projected structure meant that the architects had no sure way of knowing that their plans would succeed. The building was initially constructed in five years, but twenty years and several earthquakes later the central dome collapsed and the task of rebuilding it went to **Isidorus the Younger**, the nephew of one of the original architects. He increased the height of the external buttresses and of the dome itself and, less certainly, removed large windows from the north and south tympanum arches, thus initiating the gradual blockage of windows that has resulted in the dim half-light in which visitors now grope.

The worst desecration was in 1204, when it was ransacked by Catholic soldiers during the **Fourth Crusade**. The altar was broken up and shared among the captors, the hangings were torn, and mules were brought in to help carry off silver and gilt carvings. A prostitute was seated on the throne of the patriarch and she "sang and danced in the church, to ridicule the hymns and processions of the orientals". Two and a half centuries later, in 1452, the Byzantine Church reluctantly accepted union with the Catholics in the hope that Western powers would come to the aid of Constantinople against the Turks, but they were too late. On May 29, 1453, those who had said they would rather see the turban of a Turk than the hat of a cardinal in the streets of Constantinople got their way when the city was captured. **Mehmet the Conqueror** rode to the church of Aya Sofya and stopped the looting that was taking place. He had the building cleared of relics and he said his first prayer there on the following Friday. Later, a wooden minaret was built at the southwest corner of the building, not to be replaced until the late sixteenth century, when Mimar Sinan was called upon to restore the building.

Extensive restorations were carried out on the mosaics in the mid-nineteenth century by the Swiss **Fossati brothers**, but due to Muslim sensitivities the mosaics were later covered over again. The angels that the Fossatis had painted in the west pendentives of the nave were even given medallions to hide their faces. The building continued to function as a **mosque** until 1932, when further renovations were carried out, and in 1934 Aya Sofya was opened as a **museum**.

The building

The main body of the building approximates to a **domed basilica**, with a basic octagonal shape split in two and a domed rectangle inserted. Thus Aya Sofya is both centralized and domed – forms that were gaining in popularity for prestigious monuments of the sixth century – but it retains a longitudinal axis and side aisles. At the diagonals of the octagon are semicircular niches (exedrae). The galleries, which follow the line of these exedrae around the building, are supported by rows of columns and by four piers, which are also the main support of the dome.

Most interesting of the internal decorations are the marbles and the mosaics. Look closely, however, and you'll see that many of the "marble" wall panels are actually trompe-l'oeil, covering areas that would originally have borne frescoes or mosaics. Of the **marbles** that remain, some are purple-coloured Egyptian porphyry, a rare volcanic rock that was not quarried at the time, so must have been pilfered from elsewhere. The columns supporting the galleries and the tympanum walls are verd antique marble, while those in the upper gallery of the exedrae are Thessalian marble. These ranges of columns, above and below the gallery, are not aligned one above the other, an irregularity thought outrageously daring and structurally unsound by contemporaries. Of those in the exedrae, the poet Paul the Silentiary wrote: "One wonders at the power of him, who bravely set six columns over two, and has not trembled to fix their bases over empty air." Upstairs in the western gallery a large circle of green Thessalian marble marks the position of the **throne of the empress**.

Byzantine **mosaics** were designed to be seen by lamp- or candlelight, which shows off the workmanship to its best advantage: flickering light reflected in pieces of glass or gold, which had been carefully embedded at minutely disparate angles, give an appearance of movement and life to the mosaics. What remains of the **abstract mosaics**, and of the large areas of plain gold that covered the underside of the dome and other large expanses of wall and ceiling, dates from the sixth century. Some of the prettiest of this work can be seen under the arches of the south gallery and in the narthex (the entrance porch).

The **figurative mosaics**, all of which date from after the Iconoclastic era (726–843), are located in the narthex, the nave, the upper gallery and the vestibule. Some of the most impressive are in the south gallery where, beyond a pair of false marble doors on the west face of the pier, there's a comparatively well-lit mosaic of a **Deisis**, depicting Christ, the Virgin and St John the Baptist. Although this mosaic is partly damaged, the three faces are all well preserved: that of John the Baptist is especially expressive, betraying great pain and suffering, while the Virgin has downcast eyes and an expression of modesty and humility.

On the east wall of the south gallery, contiguous with the apse, is a **mosaic of Christ flanked by an emperor and empress**. The inscriptions over their heads read "Zoë, the most pious Augusta" and "Constantine in Christ, the Lord Autocrat, faithful Emperor of the Romans, Monomachus". It is believed that the two figures are those of Constantine IX Monomachus and Empress Zoë, who ruled

Byzantium in her own right with her sister Theodora before she married Constantine, her third husband.

The other mosaic in the south gallery, dating from 1118, depicts the **Virgin and Child between Emperor John II Comnenus and Empress Irene**, and their son Prince Alexius, added later. This is a livelier, less conventional work than that of Zoë and Constantine, with faces full of expression: Prince Alexius, who died soon after this portrait was executed, is depicted as a wan and sickly youth, his lined face presaging his premature death.

Other mosaics include a Virgin and Child in the apse and, one of the most beautiful of all the Aya Sofya mosaics, a **Virgin and Child flanked by two emperors**. The latter is located in the Vestibule of Warriors, now serving as an exit, and to see it you have to turn around and look upwards after you have passed through the magnificent **Portal of the Emperor**. Dated to the last quarter of the tenth century, the mosaic shows Emperor Justinian, to the right of the Virgin, offering a model of Aya Sofya, while Emperor Constantine offers a model of the city of Constantinople. This is the only mosaic that has been properly lit and the effect must be near to that intended by the artists.

Also worth noting is the famous brass-clad **weeping column**, located in the northwest corner of the aisle and usually identifiable by the crowd it attracts. A legend dating from at least 1200 tells how St Gregory the Miracle-worker appeared here and subsequently the moisture seeping from the column has been believed to cure a wide range of conditions.

What is left of the structures from Aya Sofya's time as a **mosque** are a *mihrab*, a *mimber*, a sultan's loge, and the enormous wooden plaques that bear sacred Islamic names of God, the Prophet Mohammed and the first four caliphs. These and the inscription on the dome by the calligrapher Azzet Efendi all date from the time of the restoration by the Fossati brothers.

Topkapı Palace

The **Topkapı Palace** (daily except Tues 9am–5pm) was both the symbolic and the political centre of the Ottoman Empire for nearly four centuries, until the removal of the imperial retinue to Dolmabahçe, by Sultan Abdülmecid I in 1853. It is a beautiful setting in which to wander and contemplate the majesty of the Ottoman sultanate, as well as the cruelty exemplified by institutions like the harem and "the Cage".

Originally known as *Sarayı Cedid*, or New Palace, Topkapı was built between 1459 and 1465 as the seat of government of the newly installed Ottoman regime. It was not at first a residence: Mehmet the Conqueror had already built what would become known as the Old Palace on the present site of İstanbul University and even after he himself moved, his harem stayed on at the old site.

In accordance with Islamic tradition, the palace consists of a collection of buildings arranged around a series of courtyards, similar to the Alhambra in Granada or a Moghul palace in India. Although this creates an initial impression of disorder, in fact the arrangement is meticulously logical. The first courtyard was the service area of the palace and open to all, while most of the second court and its attendant buildings were devoted to the Divan, or Council of State, and to those who had business with it. The pavilions of judges were located at the Orta Kapı (the entrance to the palace proper, between the first and second courtyards), in accordance with the tradition that justice should be dispensed at the gate of the palace.

The third courtyard was mainly given over to the palace school, an important imperial institution devoted to the training of civil servants, and it is only in the fourth courtyard that the serious business of state gives way to the more pleasur-

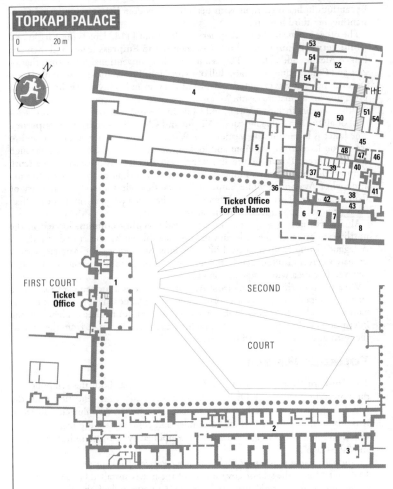

TOPKAPI PALACE

0   20 m

FIRST COURT
Ticket Office

1 Ortakapi or Middle Gate

Ticket Office for the Harem

36

SECOND COURT

2

3

1 Ortakapi or Middle Gate

2 Kitchens and cooks' quarters
(Porcelain & glass collection)

3 Reconstructed kitchen

4 Stables and Harness rooms

5 Barrack of the Halberdiers

6 Hall of the Divan

7 Offices of the Divan

8 Inner Treasury (Arms & armour collection)

9 Gate of Felicity (Bab-üs Saadet)

10 Quarters of the White Eunuchs (Costume collection)

11 Throne room

12 Ahmet III library

13 Mosque of the school, now the library

14 Harem mosque

15 Court of the Room of the Robe

16 Room of the Robe of the Prophet

17 Rooms of the Relics of the Prophet

18 Hall of the Treasury
(Sultans' portraits & miniature collection)

19 Hall of the Pantry (Museum Directorate)

20 Pavilion of Mehmet II, now the Treasury

21 Disrobing chamber of Selim II hamam

22 Site of Selim II hamam

23 Site of Selim II hamam boilers

24 Hall of the Expeditionary Force

25 Circumcision Köşkü

26 Terrace and bower

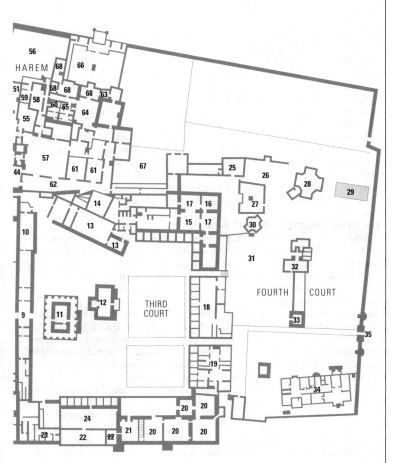

27 Pool	**41** Quarters of the Chief Black Eunuchs	**55** Sultan Ahmet Kiosk
28 Baghdad Köşkü	**42** Quarters of the Treasurer	**56** Harem Garden
29 Pool	**43** Quarters of the Chamberlain	**57** Valide court
30 Revan Köşkü	**44** Aviary Gate (Kuşhane Kapisi)	**58** Valide's dining-room
31 Tulip garden	**45** Courtyard of the Women of the Harem	**59** Valide's bedroom
32 Mustafa Paşa Köşkü	**46** Kitchen of the Women	**60** The Valide's hamam
33 Physician's tower	**47** Hamam of the Women	**61** Kadin's quarters
34 Mecidiye Köşkü-restaurant	**48** Stairs to bedrooms	**62** Golden Road
35 Third Gate	**49** Laundry	**63** Ahmet III dining-room
36 Entry to the Harem (Carriage Gate)	**50** Women's dormitory	**64** The Throne Room Within
37 Mosque of the Black Eunuchs	**51** Apartments of senior women	**65** The Sultan's hamam
38 Court of the Black Eunuchs	**52** Court of women's hospital	**66** Osman III Terrace
39 Barrack of the Black Eunuchs	**53** Hospital hamam	**67** Terrace of Selâmlik Garden
40 Princes' school	**54** Hospital kitchen quarters	**68** Apartment of the Selamlik (Sultan's Rooms)

able aspects of life. Around the attractive gardens here are a number of pavilions erected by successive emperors in celebration of their victories. Here, the glorious views and sunsets could be enjoyed in privileged retreat from their three- to four-thousand-member retinue.

The various adjustments made to the structure and function of the buildings were indicative of the power shifts in the Ottoman Empire over the centuries. During the "Rule of the Harem" in the sixteenth century, for example, a passageway was opened between the Harem and the Divan, while in the eighteenth century, when the power of the sultan had declined, the offices of state were transferred away from the "Eye of the Sultan" (the window in the Divan through which a sultan could monitor proceedings) to the gateway that led to the palaces of the Grand Vezir known as the Sublime Port.

The **entrance** to Topkapı Palace is to the right and behind Aya Sofya, up Babıhümayun Caddesi. There is no fee to enter the first courtyard. The entry fees for the Palace (12YTL) and the Imperial Treasury (10YTL) are paid at a **ticket booth** located to the right of the middle gate that leads through to the second courtyard. Another ticket booth is located at the entrance of the Harem, where you can pay a further 10YTL for a guided tour of the Harem.

The first courtyard and Aya Irene

Entering the first courtyard from the street through Mehmet the Conqueror's **Bab-ı Hümayün**, the great defensive imperial gate opposite the fountain of Ahmet III, it's hard to believe that this is the outer courtyard of a former imperial palace: all is taxi ranks and coaches and their disembarking tour parties. Such a melee, however, is entirely in keeping with the origins of the first courtyard, which, as the palace's service area, was always open to the general public. The **palace bakeries** are behind a wall to the right of the courtyard and the buildings of the **imperial mint and outer treasury** (all currently closed) are behind the wall north of the church of Aya Irene. In front of Aya Irene were located the quarters of the straw-weavers and carriers of silver pitchers, around a central courtyard in which the palace firewood was stored. The church itself was variously employed as an armoury and storage space for archeological treasures.

Today, **Aya Irene**, "the Church of the Divine Peace", is generally closed to visitors, but can be opened for large groups by special request at the Directorate of Aya Sofya, located at the entrance of Aya Sofya. It is also open for occasional exhibitions or concerts, such as those during the summer İstanbul music festival. The original church was one of the oldest in the city, but it was rebuilt along with Aya Sofya after being burnt down in the Nika riots of 532. Around the semicircular apse is the only **synthronon** (seating space for clergy in the apse of a church) in İstanbul to have survived the Byzantine era. It has six tiers of seats with an ambulatory running behind the fourth tier.

Ortakapı, the second courtyard and the Divan

To reach the second courtyard you pass through the Bab-üs Selam, "the Gate of Salutations", otherwise known as the **Ortakapı**, or middle gate (where the entry fee is collected). Entering through Ortakapı, with the gateway to the third courtyard straight ahead of you, the Privy Stables of Mehmet II (closed to the public) are on your immediate left, while beyond them are the buildings of the Divan and the Inner Treasury and the entrance to the Harem. Opposite the Divan, on the right side of the courtyard, is the kitchen area.

The gardens between the paths radiating from the Ortakapı are planted with ancient cypresses and plane trees, rose bushes and lawns. Originally they would also have been resplendent with peacocks, gazelles and, most impor-

△ Tokapı Palace

tantly, fountains. Running water, considered to have almost mystical properties by Muslims, was supplied in great quantity to the palace from the Byzantine cistern of Yerebatan Saray (see p.141). This **second courtyard** would have been the scene of pageantry during state ceremonies, when the sultan would occupy his throne beneath the Bab-üs Saadet, "the Gate of Felicity". At all times, even on one of the three days of the week when the courtyard was filled with petitioners to the Divan, silence reigned here, as people obeyed the rules of conduct imposed in the presence – actual or potential – of the sultan.

As you enter the buildings of the **Divan**, to the left of the courtyard, you'll see the metal grille in the Council Chamber (the first room on the left), called "the Eye of the Sultan". Through this he could observe the proceedings of the Divan, where the eminent imperial councillors sat in session and which took its name from the couch running around the three walls of the room. The building dates essentially from the reign of Mehmet the Conqueror, and the Council Chamber was restored to its sixteenth-century appearance in 1945, with some of the original İznik tiles and arabesque painting. The other two rooms of the Divan have retained the Rococo decorations of Ahmet III.

The **Divan tower** is visible from many vantage points all over the city. Rebuilt in 1825, the classical lines of the octagonal structure, with its tall windows between engaged Corinthian columns and its lead-covered conical spire, look rather out of place here, but it's certainly an impressive landmark and a nice foil for the domes of the Divan. The tower is opened for strictly chaperoned guided tours twice a day: admission to the balconies is not allowed, but the panoramic Bosphorus views through the windows are exceptional. Ask at the main ticket booth at the entrance of the second courtyard for times of tours.

Next to the Divan is another building from Mehmet the Conqueror's original palace, the **Inner Treasury**, a six-domed hall preceded by a double-domed vestibule and supported internally by three piers. The **arms and armour collection** here juxtaposes much exquisite craftsmanship with barbaric-looking exhibits, such as a seventeenth-century executioner's sword and some seven-foot-long double-handed swords of which wearied Europeans were relieved during one Turkish campaign or another. It is also interesting to compare the swords of various

The Cage

The Cage was adopted by Ahmet I as an alternative to fratricide, which had become institutionalized in the Ottoman Empire since the days of Beyazit II. To avoid wars of succession, Beyazit ruled that a sultan should execute his brothers upon his accession to the throne. The Cage was introduced as a way around this practice, but in the event proved a less than satisfactory solution. After the death of their father, the younger princes would be incarcerated along with deaf mutes and a harem of concubines, while their eldest brother acceded to the throne. They remained in the suite of rooms of the Harem known in Turkish as *Kafes* (the Cage) until such time as they were called upon to take power themselves. The concubines never left the Cage unless they became pregnant, and great care was taken to prevent this, either by the removal of their ovaries or by the use of pessaries, since if it did occur they were immediately drowned.

The decline of the Ottoman Empire has in part been attributed to the institution of the Cage. The sultans who spent any length of time there emerged crazed, avaricious and debauched. Osman II, for example, enjoyed archery, but only when using live targets, including prisoners of war and his own pages. He was assassinated by the janissaries, to be replaced by Mustafa I, who had all but died of starvation in the Cage and was even more mad than his predecessor. He too was assassinated. The worst affected of all, however, was İbrahim, better known as Deli İbrahim (İbrahim the Mad). He spent 22 years in the Cage, and when they came to take him out he was so sure he was about to be assassinated that he had to be removed forcibly. His reign was characterized by sexual excess and political misrule (his mother Köşem once complained that there was not enough wood for the Harem fires and he responded by having his grand vizier executed). Eventually, in response to a rumour of harem intrigue, İbrahim had all of his 280 concubines (excluding his favourite, Şeker Para) drowned in the Bosphorus.

Ottoman sultans: that of the Conqueror appears altogether more effective than the finely wrought example attributed to that patron of the arts, Süleyman the Magnificent.

Across the courtyard are the **palace kitchens and cooks' quarters**, with their magnificent rows of chimneys, best seen in profile from a distance (for example from Kennedy Caddesi, which runs around the Marmara shore). Much of this complex was destroyed by fire in 1574, though the chimneys were reconstructed by Mimar Sinan, as were eight of the ten domes behind them (the two southern-most domes date to the reign of Mehmet the Conqueror). The ten kitchens, which had a staff of 1500, all served different purposes. The two at the far end, where sweets and *helva* were made, have been restored complete with a fascinating array of utensils. The other rooms house a collection of some of the finest porcelain in the world, an ever-changing display continually replenished from the vast Topkapı collection.

The third courtyard

As you pass through the **Bab-üs Saadet**, "the Gate of Felicity", the **Throne Room** is immediately in front of you. This building, mainly dating from the reign of Selim I, was where the sultan awaited the outcome of sessions of the Divan in order to give his assent or otherwise to their proposals. The grey marble building at the centre of the third courtyard, the **Ahmet III Library**, is not generally open to the public. It is restrained and sombre compared to his highly decorative fountain outside the gates of the palace.

The room to the right of the gate and throne room and library, southwest of the courtyard, is the **Hall of the Expeditionary Force**, sometimes referred to as the Hall of the Campaign Pages (Seferli Koğuşu), which houses a collection of embroidery and a very small selection from the imperial costume collection. The latter includes a charming little outfit of Selim I's – red with yellow circles – prompting the question of where he could have acquired his epithet "the Grim". Behind the hall is the hamam of Selim II, who fell there in a drunken stupor and died later of his injuries.

The Treasury

The **Imperial Treasury** is housed in the rooms that once functioned as the Pavilion of Mehmet II, which takes up most of the southeast side of the third courtyard, to the right of the entrance. The building is on two floors and a colonnaded terrace leads from the courtyard into the lower rooms, whose interior plasterwork, including shell-shaped niches, stalactite capitals and ogee (slightly pointed) arches over the windows, is typical of the fifteenth century. The first two rooms – the right-hand one of which was used as the *camekan* or disrobing chamber of the hamam of Selim II – are beautifully proportioned and domed. The last two rooms are at right angles, with an attractive loggia at the angle where they meet.

The first room contains a number of highly wrought and extremely beautiful objects, including a delicate silver model of a palace complete with tiny birds in the trees, a present to Abdül Hamid II from Japan. The next two rooms – memorials to the excess and bad taste of the megalomaniacal – are always thronged and there are certainly plenty of thrills to be had if you like your gemstones big and your precious metals abundant.

The big crowd-puller in room two is the **Topkapı Dagger**, which starred alongside Peter Ustinov in the Sunday-matinee classic *Topkapi*. A present from Mahmut I to Nadir Shah that was waylaid and brought back when news of the shah's death reached Topkapı, the dagger is decorated with three enormous emeralds, one of which conceals a watch. In the third room the **Spoonmaker's Diamond**, the fifth largest diamond in the world, is invariably surrounded by a gawping crowd, which perhaps gives some impression of the effect it must have had during its first public appearance, adorning Mehmet IV's turban at his coronation in 1648. The rest of this room is a succession of increasingly grotesque and jewel-studded exhibits and you might well be tempted to make good your escape.

The fourth room boasts a bejewelled throne, and the hand and occipital bone of John the Baptist, but otherwise it's a relative haven of restraint and good taste. Ivory and sandalwood objects predominate, refreshingly simple materials whose comparative worth is determined by craftsmanship rather than quantity.

Across the courtyard from the Treasury, the Pavilion of the Holy Mantle houses the **Rooms of the Relics of the Prophet**, holy relics brought home by Selim the Grim after his conquest of Egypt in 1517. The relics were originally viewed only by the sultan, his family and his immediate entourage on days of special religious significance, but were opened to the public in 1962. They include a footprint, hair and a tooth of the Prophet Mohammed, as well as his mantle and standard, swords of the first four caliphs and a letter from the Prophet to the leader of the Coptic tribe. The most precious of the relics are kept behind glass, attractively arranged and lit.

Next to this, the former **Hall of the Treasury** houses a selection from Topkapı's **collection of paintings and miniatures**, but this is currently closed for restoration, with no clear indication as to when it will reopen. The miniatures date from the reign of Süleyman the Magnificent to that of Ahmet III, the Tulip Age, but above all they come from the reign of Murat III. He commissioned three works, the *Hünername* (the "Book of Accomplishments"), the *Shahanshahname* (the "Book of the King of Kings") and the *Surname* (the "Book of Festivals"), the first two of which glorified the exploits of the sultans, while the last was a depiction of the glorious parade that followed the circumcision ceremony of the sultan's son (nowadays Turks make home videos on the same theme).

The fourth courtyard

The **fourth courtyard** is entered through a passageway running between the Hall of the Treasury and the display of clocks and watches in the Silahdar Treasury. It consists of several gardens, each graced with pavilions, the most attractive of which – from where you get a totally new perspective of the city from Galata to Fatih – are located around a wide marble terrace beyond the tulip gardens of Ahmet III.

The **Baghdad Köşkü**, the cruciform building to the north of the terrace, is the only pavilion presently open to the public. It was built by Murat IV to celebrate the conquest of Baghdad in 1638. The exterior and cool, dark interior are tiled in blue, turquoise and white, and the shutters and cupboard doors are inlaid with tortoiseshell and mother-of-pearl. If you think this is redolent of unseemly excess, take a look at the attractive pool and marble fountain on the terrace, scene of debauched revels among İbrahim I and the women of his harem. Deli İbrahim, or **İbrahim the Mad**, emerged dangerously insane from 22 years in the Cage, his reign culminating in a fit of sexual jealousy when he ordered death by drowning in the Bosphorus for the 280 concubines of his harem – only one of them lived to tell the tale, when she escaped from the sack in which she was bound and was picked up by a passing French ship and taken to Paris.

The **Circumcision Köşkü**, in the Portico of Columns above the terrace, also dates from the reign of İbrahim the Mad. You'll have to peer through the windows to get any idea of the interior, but outside it's covered in İznik tiles of the sixteenth and early seventeenth centuries. There doesn't seem to be much of a design about these – any number of different patterns are represented – but they include some of the most beautiful panels from the very best İznik period. At the other end of the Portico of Columns is the **Revan Köşkü**, built to commemorate the capture of Erivan in the Caucasus by Mehmet IV.

The **Mecidiye Köşkü** – the last building to be erected at Topkapı – commands the best view of any of the Topkapı pavilions. It's been opened as the expensive *Konyali Café* (see p.186) and on a clear day from its garden terrace you can identify most of the buildings on the Asian shore of the Bosphorus.

The Harem

The **tour of the Harem** (daily except Tues 10am–4pm, every 30min from the Harem entrance in the second courtyard; 10YTL) is extremely popular, so arrive early as tickets sell out and queues are massive later in the day. The tour (which lasts 1hr 40min) is conducted at breakneck speed, but can be interesting with a little background knowledge and a few pertinent questions.

The word "harem" means "forbidden" in Arabic; in Turkish it refers to a suite of apartments in a palace or private residence where the head of the household lived with his wives, odalisques (female slaves) and children. The Harem in Topkapı lies between the sultan's private apartments and the quarters of the Chief Black Eunuch. It consisted of over four hundred rooms, centred on the suites of the sultan and his mother, the Valide Sultan. Around these, in descending order of rank, were the apartments of the wives, favourites, sultan's daughters, princes, housekeepers, maids and odalisques. The Harem was connected to the outside world by means of the **Carriage Gate**, so called because the odalisques would have entered

The women of the harem

The women of the harem were so shrouded in mystery that they became a source of great fascination to the world in general. The most renowned among them was probably Haseki Hürrem, or Roxelana as she was known in the West, wife of Süleyman the Magnificent. Prior to their marriage, it was unusual for a sultan to marry at all, let alone to choose a wife from among his concubines. The marriage, and the subsequent installation of the harem women in the palace, established the women of the harem, and especially the **Valide Sultan** (the mother of the reigning sultan), in a position of unprecedented power. This was the beginning of a new age of harem intrigue, in which women began to take more control over affairs of state, often referred to as the "Rule of the Harem".

Roxelana began this new order in characteristic vein: she persuaded Süleyman to murder both his grand vizier, İbrahim Paşa, and his son, the heir apparent, Mustafa – the latter in order to make way for her own son, Selim the Sot. The favourite of Selim the Sot, **Nur Banu**, made a significant change to the layout of the harem when she became Valide Sultan in her turn. She moved her suite of apartments from one end of the Golden Road to the other, so that it was located next to that of her son, Murat III. She was now lodged near to the entrance of the Divan and could easily listen in on affairs of state. Nur Banu encouraged her son in debauchery (he fathered a total of 103 children, 54 of whom survived him) and persuaded him to murder his most able minister, the grand vizier Sokollu Mehmet Paşa.

The number of **odalisques** (female slaves) employed in the harem increased steadily with the decline of the Ottoman Empire and by the reign of Abdülaziz (1861–1876) there were 809 in Topkapı. Many were imported from Georgia and Caucasia for their looks, or were prisoners of war, captured in Hungary, Poland or Venice. Upon entering the harem, they would become the charges of the *haznedar usta*, who would teach them how to behave towards the sultan and the other palace inhabitants. The conditions in which the majority of these women lived were dangerously unhygienic and many of them died from vermin-carried and waterborne diseases, or from the cold of an İstanbul winter. The women who were chosen to enter the bedchamber of the sultan, however, were promoted to the rank of imperial odalisque, given slaves to serve them, and pleasant accommodation. If they bore a child, they would be promoted to the rank of favourite or wife, with their own apartments. If the sultan subsequently lost affection for one of these women, he could give her in marriage to one of his courtiers. The following account of life in the Topkapı harem, given by Hafsa Sultan, a wife of Mustafa II (1695–1703), dispels a couple of popular myths about life there:

The claims that the sultan throws a handkerchief at the girl he prefers are quite untrue. The sultan asks the Chief Black Eunuch to call whichever of the girls he desires and his other women take her to the baths, perfume her body and dress her gracefully in clothes appropriate to the circumstances. The sultan sends the girl a gift and afterwards goes to the room where she is. There is no truth either in the claim that the girl crawls to the sultan's bed.

their carriages here when they went on outings. To the left of the Carriage Gate as you enter the Harem is the Barracks of the Halberdiers of the Long Tresses, who carried logs and other loads into the Harem. The Halberdiers, who also served as imperial guardsmen, were only employed at certain hours and even then they were blinkered. The Carriage Gate and the Aviary Gate were both guarded by black eunuchs, who were responsible for running the harem, but only allowed to enter in daylight hours. At night the female housekeepers took charge and reported any unusual occurrences to the Chief Black Eunuch.

The **Court of the Black Eunuchs**, the first area to be visited on the tour, dates mainly from a rebuilding programme begun after the great fire of July 24, 1665. The fire, started by a malicious servant, damaged most of the Harem as well as the Divan. The tiles in the eunuchs' quarters date from the seventeenth century, suggesting that the originals were destroyed in the fire.

The *Altın Yol* or **Golden Road** ran the entire length of the Harem, from the quarters of the Black Eunuchs to the fourth courtyard. It was down this road in 1808 that the last of the great Valide Sultans, Aimée Dubbucq de Rivery, fled with her son Mahmut to escape the deaf mutes, hired assassins of the janissaries. The life of the prince was saved by a Georgian odalisque called Cevri Khalfa, who flung a brazier of red-hot coals into the faces of the pursuers. The prince escaped to become Mahmut II, later given the title of "Reformer". Strategically located at the beginning of the Golden Road were the **apartments of the Valide Sultan**, also rebuilt after 1665. They include a particularly lovely domed dining room. A passageway leads from her apartments to those of the women she controlled, the senior women of the court. These were well-designed, compact apartments, with an upper gallery in which bedding was stored, windows and a hearth.

Beyond the Valide Sultan's apartments, to the north, are some of the most attractive rooms of the palace. These were the apartments and reception rooms of the *selamlik*, the sultan's own rooms. The largest and grandest of them is the **Hünkar Sofrası**, the Imperial Hall, where the sultan entertained visitors. Another important room in this section is a masterwork of the architect Sinan: the **bedchamber of Murat III**, covered in sixteenth-century İznik tiles and kitted out with a marble fountain and, opposite, a bronze fireplace surrounded by a panel of tiling representing plum blossom.

The northernmost rooms of the Harem are supported by immense piers and vaults, providing capacious basements that were used as dormitories and storerooms. Below the bedchamber is a large indoor **swimming pool**, with taps for hot and cold water, where Murat is supposed to have thrown gold to women who pleased him. Next to the bedchamber is the light and airy **library of Ahmet I**, with windows overlooking both the Bosphorus and the Golden Horn; beyond this is the **dining room of Ahmet III**, whose walls are covered in wood panelling painted with bowls of fruit and flowers, typical of the extravagant tulip-loving sultan. To the southwest of the bedchamber are two rooms originally thought to be the notorious **Cage** (see box on p.134), though this is no longer believed to be the case. The Cage was actually situated in various rooms on the floor above. Other areas often visited on a tour include the **dormitories** of the favourite women, located up stone stairs on a beautiful terrace overlooking the fourth courtyard, and the **boating pool** of Murat III.

It's usual to depart from the Harem by way of the **Aviary Gate**, or Kuşhane Kapısı. One of the most infamous of all the Valide Sultans, Mahpeyker Sultan, also known as *Köşem*, "the leader", was assassinated here. She was the effective ruler of the Ottoman Empire during the reigns of her two sons, Murat IV and İbrahim the Mad, and since she was not banished to the old palace after the death of İbrahim (as was customary), she also ruled during the reign of her grandson Mehmet IV. She was eventually murdered on the orders of a jealous rival, the new Valide Turhan Hatice, by the Chief Black Eunuch. At the age of 80 the toothless old woman was stripped naked and strangled, after allegedly putting up a ferocious struggle.

Gulhane Parkı and around

Gulhane Parkı surrounds Topkapı Palace on all sides and was once the extended gardens of the sultans. It is now a public park with a relaxed atmosphere, particularly at weekends when the crowds of families indulge in cheap traditional Turkish fast-foods and listen to free concerts by *arabesk* musicians or pop performers. The park is also home to a squalid zoo, with caged dogs and threadbare camels. Other nearby attractions are worthier of attention: the **Darphane**, or Royal Mint; the city's **Archeology Museum**; and the ceramics on display in the **Çinili Köşk**, or Tiled Pavilion.

The Darphane

Located next to Gulhane Parkı, though also entered from the first courtyard of Topkapı Palace, the **Darphane** (Royal Mint; Wed–Sun 9.30am–5.30pm; free; Ⓦ www.tarihvakfi.org.tr) was moved to this site in 1715, although there is evidence that coins were struck hereabouts as early as the sixteenth century. Most of the current buildings date from the 1830s and the reign of Mahmut II. The monetary reforms introduced by Abdülmecit between 1839 and 1861 saw the introduction of modern steam-powered machinery to improve the quality of coins produced. The place was largely abandoned in 1967, with the buildings and remaining equipment left undisturbed until the mid-1990s. It's now run by the Turkish Economic and Social History Foundation, which has lovingly restored the complex, opening part as a fascinating museum where smelting equipment, imported European coin presses and assorted artefacts are displayed. There's also exhibition space and a theatre where high-brow Turkish plays are performed in summer.

The Archeology Museum

The Archeology Museum complex, which includes the Museum of the Ancient Orient and Çinili Köşk (see p.140; all daily except Mon 9am–4pm; combined entry 5YTL), can be entered either through Gulhane Parkı or from the first courtyard of the Topkapı Palace.

The **Archeology Museum** itself (Arkeoloji Müzesi) is centred on the excavations at Sidon in 1887 of Hamdi Bey, the Director of Ancient Antiquities. These brought to light a group of sarcophagi, together with other monuments of Phoenician origin but of quite disparate styles – evidence of the variety of influences absorbed into Phoenician culture from neighbouring civilizations.

The sarcophogi are housed in the two rooms to the left of the entrance on the ground floor. The **Lycian Sarcophagus**, in the room immediately on your left, depicts centaurs, sphinxes and griffons, as well as scenes from Greek mythology. It is in the Lycian style, but the carvings show a Peloponnesian influence in the stocky bodies and broad faces of the human figures. In the same room are the anthropoid sarcophagi from Sidon, which illustrate the fifth-century BC fashion for Egyptian models in Greek sculpture. The **Tabnit Sarcophagus**, the oldest Sidon discovery, is in fact Egyptian in origin. A hieroglyphic inscription on the chest of this alabaster mummy-case states that it belonged to an Egyptian commander named Penephtah and a later inscription suggests that Tabnit, himself the father of a pharaoh, was its second occupant.

The **Sidamara Sarcophagus**, again in the first room on the left, dates from the third century AD and is the most important remaining example of its type. This room is full of similar sarcophagi, discovered elsewhere in Anatolia; on many of them a hand-held drill has been used for much of the carving, especially of the foliage, which is roughly executed in comparison with the Sidon sarcophagi.

The **Alexander Sarcophagus** is in the second room to the left of the entrance lobby. It's covered with scenes of what is presumed to be Alexander the Great hunting and in battle, but since Alexander himself is known to have been buried in Alexandria this cannot be his sarcophagus. It is ascribed variously by different sources to a ruler of the Seleucid dynasty or to the Phoenician Prince Abdolo-nyme. It appears that the sarcophagus dates from the end of the fourth century BC. The metal weapons originally held by warriors and huntsmen on the sar-cophagi were stolen prior to the excavations of Hamdi Bey, presumably when the burial chambers were looted.

The Ionic architecture of another of the Sidon sarcophagi, the **Sarcophagus of the Mourning Women**, is repeated in the exterior of the museum itself. This one shows eighteen members of the harem of King Straton (who died in 360 BC) in various poses of distress and mourning. To drive the point home, a funeral cortege is shown proceeding around the lid of the sarcophagus. As with the Alexander Sarcophagus, traces of the original paintwork can still be seen on the surface of the marble.

The museum's **upper rooms** are a joy: beautiful, well-lit displays, thorough explanatory aids, audiovisual back-up and a comfortable environment that encourages visitors to linger, a far cry from Turkey's provincial museums where nervous curators follow you about switching lights on and off. Exhibits worth mentioning range from jewellery discovered at Troy – some beautiful gold work including a head ornament with leaves as fine as paper – and Phrygian finds from near Arslantaş, the lion rock-cut tomb near Afyon Karahisar.

The Museum of the Ancient Orient

The **Museum of the Ancient Orient** (Eskı Şark Eserleri Müzesi) – just to the north of the main entrance to the museum complex – contains a small but dazzling collection of Anatolian, Egyptian and Mesopotamian artefacts. The late Hittite basalt lions flanking the entrance look newly hewn, but they actually date from the ninth century BC, giving a taste of the incredible state of preservation of some of the exhibits inside.

These include the oldest peace treaty known to mankind, the **Treaty of Kadesh** (1280–1269 BC), which was signed when a battle fought on the River Orontes (today's Ası Nehri in Anatolia), between Pharaoh Ramses II and the Hittite king Muvatellish, ended in a stalemate. The treaty includes a ceasefire agreement and pledges of a mutual exchange of political refugees, and was originally engraved onto silver tablets. None of these survive, though the treaty was also inscribed in hieroglyphics on the mortuary temple of Ramses II in Thebes and the copy on display in the museum was uncovered during excavations at the site of the Hittite capital of Hattuşa (see p.715). A copy of the treaty decorates the entrance to the UN building in New York.

The blue-and-yellow **animal relief** in the corridor beyond the first room dates from the reign of Nebuchadnezzar (604–562 BC), the last hero-king of Babylonia, when it would have lined the processional way in Babylon. Other exhibits were taken from the palace-museum of Nebuchadnezzar, located at the Ishtar Gate. Another massive relief, in Room 8, depicts the **Hittite king Urpalla** presenting gifts of grapes and grain to a vegetation god, who is three times his own size and wearing a rather attractive pair of curly-toed boots. This is a plaster copy of a relief found at İvriz Kaya near Konya, dating from the eighth century BC.

Other exhibits include a **Sumerian** love poem and a tablet of Sumerian proverbs dating from the eighteenth century BC. There's also a figure of a duck, with an inscription identifying it as a standard weight belonging to a priest called Musal-lim Marduk: it weighs about 30kg and dates from around 2000 BC, making it the oldest known standard measure.

Çinili Köşk

The graceful **Çinili Köşk** or Tiled Pavilion – a few metres north of the Museum of the Ancient Orient – was built in 1472 as a kind of grandstand, from which the sultan could watch sporting activities such as wrestling or polo. It now houses the **Museum of Turkish Ceramics**, displaying tiles of equal quality to those in Topkapı Palace and İstanbul's older mosques, along with well-written explanations of the different periods in the history of Turkish ceramics. Look particularly for polychrome tiles of the mid-sixteenth to mid-seventeenth centuries, dating from the longest and most successful period of tile production. Interesting exhibits include a mosque lamp from the Sokollu Mehmet Paşa Camii (see p.145), a ceramic coffee-cooler in which beans were placed after roasting and before grinding, and Murat III's attractive little fountain in the wall of the last room of all, after the İznik collection.

Yerebatan Sarayı

From either Topkapı Palace or the Aya Sofya, it's a quick stroll across the tram tracks to the **Yerebatan Sarayı** (daily 9am–6pm; 10YTL), the "Sunken Palace" – also known as the Basilica Cistern. It's one of several underground cisterns, this one buried under the very core of Sultanahmet and is the first to have been extensively excavated. Although generally crowded, it warrants a prolonged exploration: the entrance is on Caferıya Sok, with the exit on Yerebatan Caddesi, above the largest hall of the cistern.

Probably built by the emperor Constantine in the fourth century, and enlarged by Justinian in the sixth, the cistern was supplied by aqueducts with water from the Belgrade Forest. It in turn supplied the Great Palace and later Topkapı Palace. The cistern fell into disuse after the Ottoman conquest and its existence was only brought to public attention in 1545 by the Frenchman **Petrus Gyllius**. He had been led to it by local residents, whose houses were built over the cistern and who had sunk wells into it. They even kept boats on the water from which they could fish its depths – Gyllius' interest was first aroused when he found fresh fish being sold in the streets nearby.

Restorations were undertaken in 1987: 50,000 tons of mud and water were removed, the walls were covered to make them impermeable and eight of the columns were sheathed in concrete to fortify the structure. The construction of raised pathways to replace the rowboats used by early tourists may seem a desecration, but they do facilitate a leisurely examination of interesting bits of masonry, as does the careful spotlighting.

The largest covered cistern in the city, at 140m by 70m, Yerebatan held 80,000 cubic metres of water. The small brick **domes** are supported by 336 columns, many of which have Corinthian capitals. The columns' varied styles probably indicate that they were made from the recycled remnants of earlier structures. The two **Medusa heads** at the southwest corner, brought to light when the cistern was drained, are thought to have been used as construction, rather than decorative, material.

The Hippodrome

The arena of the **Hippodrome**, formerly the cultural focus of the Byzantine Empire, is now the site of a long and narrow municipal park known as **At Meydanı**, or Square of Horses. It is overshadowed by the Palace of İbrahim Paşa on one side and Sultanahmet Camii on the other, but its historical significance predates that of most other major monuments in İstanbul.

A stadium was first constructed by the Roman emperor Septimius Severus in 200 AD and later enlarged by Constantine the Great for the performance of court ceremonies and games. Estimated to have held up to 100,000 people, the original orientation and dimensions of the 480-metre-long arena have been more or less

Crowd trouble in Constantinople

The **Hippodrome factions** originated in ancient Roman trade guilds, which in Byzantine times developed further associations: "the Blues" were generally upper-class, politically conservative and orthodox regarding religion; while "the Greens" were from the lower classes and more radical in their political and religious views.

The factions were a focus for serious rivalry in Constantinople, centred on the circus events in the Hippodrome. In 532 the rivalry was forgotten when members of the Blue faction combined forces with the Greens against the emperor Justinian in protest at heavy taxation and in the resulting **riots** – which derived their name from the battle cry *Nika* (Victory) – much of the city, including the church of Aya Sofya, was destroyed. It was the former courtesan, Empress Theodora, who eventually shamed Justinian to action and, as a result, 30,000 Greens and a few hundred Blues were trapped and massacred by the forces of General Belisarius in the Hippodrome. Chariot racing was banned for some time after this and it was a number of years before the Green faction recovered to the extent that they could compete in either the sporting or the political arena.

preserved by the present-day park, although its amphitheatre was destroyed in the construction of the Sultan Ahmet mosque. Nonetheless, the Hippodrome continued to be a focus of state ceremony for the Ottoman sultans.

The large open space would now be little more than a pleasant respite from the surrounding hubbub if interest were not aroused by the several monuments strewn randomly along its length. At the south end of the park are three survivors of the array of obelisks, columns and statues that originally adorned the *spina*, the raised central axis of the arena, around which chariots raced. Northernmost of these is the **Egyptian Obelisk**, originally 60m tall, though only the upper third survived shipment from Egypt in the fourth century. The obelisk was commissioned to commemorate the campaigns of Thutmos III in Egypt during the sixteenth century BC, but the scenes on its base commemorate its erection in Constantinople under the direction of Theodosius I. Among the figures depicted are dancing maidens with musicians, Theodosius and his family watching a chariot race (south side) and a group of captives kneeling to pay homage to Theodosius (west side).

The **Serpentine Column** comes from the Temple of Apollo at Delphi, where it was dedicated to the god by the 31 Greek cities that defeated the Persians at Plataea in 479 BC. The column was brought to Constantinople by Constantine the Great. The three intertwining bronze serpents originally had heads, which splayed out in three directions from the column itself. The jaw of one of the serpents was lopped off by Mehmet the Conqueror on his arrival in Constantinople as an act of defiance against such symbols of idolatry and the remaining heads were probably removed in an act of vandalism at the beginning of the eighteenth century. However, one of the heads is on display in the "Istanbul through the Ages" exhibit at the Archeology Museum.

The third ancient monument on the *spina* is a huge lump of masonry, a 32-metre-high column of little or no decorative or practical worth. The emperor Constantine Porphyrogenitus was presumably of this opinion in the tenth century, since he restored the pillar and sheathed it in gold-plated bronze. This ornamentation was taken and melted down by the Crusaders during the sacking of Constantinople in 1204. The origins of this so-called **Column of Constantine** are uncertain, but an inscription records that it was already decayed when Constantine restored it.

△ Sultanahmet Camii, the Blue Mosque

Sultanahmet Camii: the Blue Mosque

On the southeastern side of the Hippodrome is the **Sultanahmet Camii**, or Blue Mosque. Its instantly recognizable six minarets, imposing bulk and prominent position on the İstanbul skyline combine to make it one of the most famous and visited monuments in the city. Despite this, many architectural historians are scathing about the Blue Mosque's aesthetic merit.

Before construction began, in 1609, objections were raised to the plan of a six-minareted mosque. It was said to be unholy to rival the six minarets of the mosque at Mecca, and perhaps more pertinently it would be a great drain on state revenues. The true cause of the objections, however, probably had more to do with the need to destroy several palaces belonging to imperial ministers to make way for construction.

From the **outside**, the building is undeniably impressive, particularly on the all-important approach from Topkapı Palace. Above the level of the courtyard the mosque is a mass of shallow domes and domed turrets, hardly broken by a single straight line. The **courtyard**, best approached from the attractive and graceful west portal, is surrounded by a portico of thirty small domes and has the same dimensions as the mosque itself.

You can enter through the courtyard, despite signs in English and German asking visitors to use the side entrance facing Aya Sofya. Lone tourists, as opposed to groups, will not create ill-will by entering here as long as they are suitably covered (limbs for men and women, heads for women) and do not intrude on worshippers. At the side entrance, you will invariably encounter large crowds.

Inside, four **"elephant foot" pillars** (so called because of their size) of five metres in diameter impose their disproportionate dimensions on the interior, appearing squashed against the outer walls and obscuring parts of the building from every angle. But it's the predominantly blue colour of the internal decoration that is the biggest draw, from which the name "Blue Mosque" is derived. The

143

tiles – over twenty thousand of them – constituted such a tall order that the İznik kilns were practically exhausted. Still in evidence are the clear bright colours of the best period of İznik ware, including flower and tree panels as well as more abstract designs.

At the northeast corner of the Sultanahmet complex is the richly decorated and elegant **royal pavilion**, approached by ramp and giving access to the sultan's loge inside the mosque – the ramp meant that the sultan could ride his horse right up to the door of his chambers. The royal pavilion now houses a **Museum of Carpets** (Halı Müzesi; Tues–Sat 9am–4pm; 2YTL), which traces the history of Turkish carpets through the ages and includes some ancient, priceless pieces.

Between May 1 and September 30 there is a free **sound and light show** conducted from the small seating area in the park between the Blue Mosque and Aya Sofya. Images are projected onto the surrounding buildings to a musical and spoken accompaniment – performed in English, French, Turkish and German on alternate evenings from 7.30pm onwards. Unfortunately, the event attracts a large number of hustlers.

The tomb of Sultan Ahmet

Outside the precinct wall to the northwest of the mosque is the *türbe* or **tomb of Sultan Ahmet** (Tues–Sat 9am–4pm; free), decorated, like the mosque, with seventeenth-century İznik tiles. Buried here along with the sultan are his wife and three of his sons, two of whom (Osman II and Murat IV) ruled in their turn. This successive rule of brothers was only possible because Sultan Ahmet had introduced the institution of the Cage (see box on p.134), thus relieving himself and his sons of the burden of fratricide upon accession to the throne. Unfortunately, both Ahmet's own brother Mustafa and his son Osman were completely mad and unfit to rule by the time they left the Cage to take up the reins of office. Murat IV only escaped this fate by succeeding to the throne at the age of 10, before the conditions in the Cage had affected him.

İbrahim Paşa Sarayı: the Museum of Turkish and Islamic Art

The **İbrahim Paşa Sarayı** (Palace of İbrahim Paşa), on the eastern side of the Hippodrome, is now the **Museum of Turkish and Islamic Art** (Türk ve İslam Eserleri Müzesi; daily except Mon 9am–5pm; 4YTL), an attractive, well-planned museum, containing one of the best-exhibited collections of Islamic artefacts in the world. The sixteenth-century setting of cool, darkened rooms around a central garden courtyard obviates the necessity for expensive technology to keep the sun off the remarkable exhibits, which highlight the wealth and complexity of Islamic art and culture. The museum boasts an excellent courtyard **café**.

The palace itself is one of the few private Ottoman residences to have survived – at least in part – the fires that periodically destroyed large areas of the city. Much of the building has, however, disappeared. What remains was rebuilt in stone – to the original plan – in 1843. Originally completed in 1524 for İbrahim Paşa, Süleyman the Magnificent's newly appointed grand vizier, the palace is a fitting memorial to one of the most able statesmen of his time, whose abilities were matched only by his accumulation of wealth and power. His status can be judged from the proportions of the palace's rooms and by its prominent position next to the Hippodrome: later sultans were to use its balconies to watch the festivities below. İbrahim controlled the affairs of war and state of the Ottoman Empire for thirteen years and fell from grace partly as a result of the schemings of Süleyman's wife, Roxelana. Even so, it doesn't seem unreasonable that Süleyman should distrust a servant who could say to a foreign ambassador: "If I command that something should be done, and he [the sultan] has commanded to the contrary, my wishes and not his are obeyed." The strangled body of İbrahim Paşa was found in a room of Topkapı Palace. Süleyman the Magnificent ordered it to be buried in an unmarked grave and İbrahim Paşa's possessions, not least the palace, reverted to the crown.

The museum exhibits

The main concentration of exhibits deals with Selçuk, Mamluk and Ottoman Turkish art, though there are also several important Timurid and Persian works on display.

The **Selçuk Empire**, centred in Konya, preceded that of the Ottomans in Anatolia and it is interesting to trace influences from one to the other. Ceramic techniques, for example, were obviously well developed by the Selçuks, judging from the wall tiles on display in the museum, and the wood carvings from Konya also suggest a high level of craftsmanship and artistry, which may have influenced later Ottoman work.

Other impressive exhibits include sixteenth-century Persian miniatures, which like many Ottoman works defy the Islamic stricture against depicting human or animal forms. Pictures in lacquer and leather-bound Persian manuscripts feature a tiger ripping into an antelope and another of a dancing girl dated 1570. The tiny Sancak Korans were meant for hanging on the standard of the Ottoman imperial army in a jihad (holy war), so that the word of God would precede the troops into battle.

The **Great Hall** of the palace is occasionally devoted to special exhibitions about aspects of Islamic art, but more usually it houses a collection of **Turkish carpets** that is among the finest in the world. These range from tattered remains dating from the thirteenth century to carpets that once adorned İstanbul's palaces, some weighing in at thousands of kilograms. On the basement floor, there is an exhibition of the **folk art** of the *Yörük* tribes of Anatolia, which includes examples of a *kara çadır* (literally "black tent", a domicile woven from goat hair that can still be seen in central and eastern Anatolia) and a *topakev* (a tent constructed around a folding frame, used by nomads in Anatolia and Mongolia for over a thousand years). There is also a fascinating display of what life was like in a late-Ottoman wooden house in Bursa.

The Hamam of Roxelana

The double-domed building between the Sultanahmet Camii and Aya Sofya is the **Hamam of Roxelana** (Haseki Hürrem Sultan Hamamı; daily except Tues 9.30am–5pm; free). Built by Mimar Sinan in 1556, it replaced the Byzantine baths of Zeuxippus on the same site and was named in honour of Süleyman's wife, Roxelana. The 75-metre-long hamam served the worshippers at the mosque of Aya Sofya. The hamam has been restored with stained-glass windows and varnished wooden doors with the original marble fountains in the changing rooms. The building now serves as a showroom for traditional handwoven carpets and kilims, which are for sale (at a price).

Sokollu Mehmet Paşa Camii

A pleasant couple of minutes' walk from the southwest corner of the Hippodrome leads down the steep Mehmet Paşa Yokuşu to **Sokollu Mehmet Paşa Camii** (open at prayer times only, but the *imam* may be around to unlock it during the day).

This, one of Mimar Sinan's later buildings (1571), appears to have been omitted almost entirely from tourist itineraries. Sokollu Mehmet Paşa, who commissioned the mosque, was the last grand vizier of Süleyman the Magnificent and it was his military expertise that later saved the Ottoman Empire from the worst effects of the dissolute rule of Selim the Sot. He was eventually assassinated as a result of the intrigues of Nur Banu, the mother of Murat III, who was jealous of his power.

The large mosque **courtyard** is surrounded on three sides by the rooms of the *medrese*, now occupied by a boys' Koran school (the boys inhabit the dervish lodge at the back of the mosque and can be seen seated in the porch studying the Koran during term time). At the centre of the courtyard is a handsome fountain with a pretty upcurved parapet to its dome.

The **interior** of the mosque is distinguished by the height of its dome and the impressive display of İznik tiles on its east wall. These are from the best period of Turkish ceramics: the white is pure, the green vivid and the red intense. Calligraphic inscriptions are set against a jungle of enormous carnations and tulips, and the designs and colours are echoed all around the mosque and in the conical cap of the *mimber*, the tiling of which is unique in İstanbul. While the stained-glass windows are copies, some of the original, extremely delicate **paintwork** can be seen in the northwest corner below the gallery and over the entrance. Embedded in the wall over the entrance and above the *mihrab* are pieces of the Kaaba from Mecca.

Küçük Ayasofya Camii

Located some 500 metres below the Blue Mosque, downhill on Küçük Ayasofya Caddesi is **Küçük Ayasofya Camii**, the "small mosque of Aya Sofya" (open prayer times only, though currently undergoing major restoration and closed to the public). Like its larger namesake on the opposite side of the Hippodrome, it was built as a church between 527 and 536 to service the palace of Hormisdas, and is thought to precede its namesake. It was originally named after two Roman soldiers, **Sergius** and **Bacchus**, who were martyred for their faith and later became the patron saints of Christians in the Roman army, then was renamed because of its resemblance to Aya Sofya. The church was converted into a mosque comparatively early in the sixteenth century during the reign of Beyazit II.

Like most Byzantine churches of this era, its **exterior** is unprepossessing brick and only inside can the satisfying proportions be properly appreciated. It is basically an octagon with semicircular niches at its diagonals, inscribed in a rectangle, but both these shapes are extremely irregular. This has been variously ascribed to a pragmatic solution to an awkward space at planning stage, or to shoddy workmanship. The original marble facing and gold leaf have vanished, but a frieze honouring Justinian, Theodora and St Sergius runs around the architrave under the gallery.

The sea walls and the Great Palace

At Küçük Ayasofya Camii you're almost down at the Sea of Marmara and close to the best-preserved section of the **sea walls**, built in 439 by Cyrus, prefect of the East. They originally stretched from Saray Burnu to the city walls of Constantine the Great, and were later extended by Theodosius to meet his land walls, with thirteen gates piercing the eight-kilometre course. Theophilus, the last Iconoclast emperor, rebuilt the walls in the ninth century to hold off a possible Arab invasion.

Nowadays the best way to see the walls is by train, since the tracks run along their length and on out of the city; indeed parts were destroyed when the rail lines were built. The best-preserved remains are a stretch of a couple of kilometres between Ahır Kapı, near the Cankurtaran train station, and Kumkapı, with a walkway along Kennedy Caddesi.

The Palace of Bucoleon and the Great Palace

About halfway between Küçük Ayasofya Camii and the Cankurtaran train station the facade of the Palace of Bucoleon, a seaside annexe to the **Great Palace of the Byzantine emperors**, is one of the most melancholy and moving survivors of Constantinople. The Great Palace was an immense structure, covering around five square kilometres from Sultanahmet to the sea walls. At its height it consisted of several separate palaces, including the Palace of Bucoleon and the Magnaura Palace – substantial sections of which also survive. In 1204 the palace was taken over by the Crusaders and a description by one illuminates the splendours they discovered:

Within the palace there were fully 500 halls all connected with one another and all made with gold mosaic. And in it were fully 30 chapels, great and small, and there was one of them that was called the Holy Chapel, which was so rich and noble that there was not a hinge or a band nor any other small part that was not all of silver, and there was no column that was not of jasper or porphyry or some other precious stone.

By the time the Latins left in 1261, the palace was virtually destroyed, and funds were never found to repair it.

It's easy to miss what's left of the **Palace of Bucoleon**, especially if you pass at speed along Kennedy Caddesi. It is draped in beautiful red vine and set back from the road with a little park in front. Three enormous marble-framed windows set high in the wall offer glimpses of the remains of a vaulted room behind. Below the windows, marble corbels give evidence of a balcony that would have projected over a marble quay (the waters of the Marmara once reached almost as far as the palace walls). For the rest of the Great Palace you'll need a lively imagination: you could wander 200m along Kutlugün Sokak to visit the **Başdoğan carpet centre**, where shop owners allow free access to the impressive complex of vaulted basements, or travel further down towards the coast where fragments of wall and ancient palace, on streets or tucked away in back-lots, are all that survive. Further sections of the palace exist under land currently belonging to the *Four Seasons Hotel* (see p.123). Excavated in 1998, these are said to contain a vaulted chapel with some frescoes still intact.

The Mosaic Museum

The other substantial reminders of the Great Palace are the mosaics displayed in the **Mosaic Museum** (Büyüksaray Mozaik Müzesi; daily except Mon 9am–4.30pm; 4YTL), 500m inland from the Palace of Bucoleon, on Torun Sokağı. It can be reached by running the gauntlet of salespeople in the **Arasta Çarşısı** – a renovated street-bazaar selling tourist gifts, whose seventeeth-century shops were originally built to pay for the upkeep of the nearby Sultanahmet Camii.

Many of the mosaics in the museum are presented *in situ*, so that some idea of their original scale and purpose can be imagined. The building has been constructed so that some of the mosaics are viewed from a catwalk above, but can also be examined more closely by descending to their level. These remains were part of a mosaic peristyle, an open courtyard surrounded by a portico. To the south of the portico and down to the Palace of Bucoleon were the private apartments of the emperor, while the public sections of the palace were located to the north. Among the mosaics, probably dating from Justinian's rebuilding programme of the sixth century, are portrayals of both animals in their natural habitats, and domestic scenes. These include a vivid illustration of an elephant locking a lion in a deadly embrace with its trunk and two children being led on the back of a camel.

Eminönü and around

Once the maritime gateway to the city, **Eminönü** remains one of the largest and most convenient transport hubs, where buses, ferries, trams and trains converge. **Sirkeci train station** here is effectively the first and last station of the European rail network (there's a helpful tourist office inside the station). The Eminönü **waterfront** – with its line of ferry terminals and small fishing boats serving up fried-fish sandwiches to passing commuters – is likely to be most people's first introduction to the **Golden Horn** (see box on p.149), the inlet of water that divides the European shore. There are several notable attractions in the area, especially the famous spice bazaar and a couple of worthy mosques, including the landmark Yeni Cami.

Eminönü is within easy reach of Sultanahmet. Catch the tram for three stops, or walk the couple of kilometres down the hill, through the area's commercial backstreets, invariably thronged with *hamal*s (stevedores) bent double under burdens twice their size.

Cağaloğlu

From Sultanahmet, it's a simple matter to follow the tramline past the northern walls of Topkapı Palace down to Eminönü. The alternative route is to continue along Yerebatan Caddesi as it climbs the hill into the district of **Cağaloğlu** and then turn down Ankara Caddesi into Eminönü. Cağaloğlu was traditionally the centre of Turkey's newspaper industry, but with the exception of the old and well-respected *Cumhuriyet*, the press has long since moved into high-tech media centres on the outskirts of town.

The major attraction here is the **Cağaloğlu Hamamı** on Kazım Ismail Gürkan Caddesi (daily: men 7am–10pm, women 8am–8pm; 16YTL for self-service bath, 24–48YTL for assisted baths and massages; Ⓦwww.cagalogluhamami.com.tr); the women's entrance to the hamam is around the corner on Cağaloğlu Hamam Sok. The most popular baths this side of town, they are famous for their beautiful *hararet*s or steam rooms – open cruciform chambers with windowed domes supported on a circle of columns. The baths were built in 1741 by Mahmut I to pay for the upkeep of his library in Aya Sofya, and the arches, basins and taps of the hot room, as well as the entries to the private cubicles, are all magnificently Baroque. Florence Nightingale is said to have bathed here and the hamam has appeared in several movies, including an Indiana Jones adventure.

Yeni Cami

The **Yeni Cami**, or "new mosque", is a familiar city landmark, sited across the busy road from Eminönü's ferry terminal. An imposing building, whose pigeon-covered steps are popular with hawkers and pickpockets, it was the last of İstanbul's imperial mosques to be built, and its history gives an interesting perspective on harem power-struggles. It was erected for the Valide Sultan Safiye ("the light one", a beautiful Venetian woman who some said was a Venetian spy), mother of Mehmet III and one of the most powerful of the Valide Sultans, who effectively ruled the whole empire through the weakness of her son. This was the only imperial mosque to be built during the reign of Mehmet III and the site chosen by Safiye was regarded as wholly inappropriate. It occupied a slum neighbourhood inhabited by a sect of Jews called the Karaites, who were relocated across the Horn to Hasköy. A synagogue and church had to be demolished to make room for it. The site was also dangerously close to the water's edge and the building programme was constantly plagued by seepage from the Horn.

An even greater hindrance to its construction was court politics. The original architect was executed for heresy and the work was interrupted again by the death of Mehmet III and the banishment of his mother to the Old Palace. Construction had reached as far as the lower casements when it was halted, and the Karaites returned to camp out in the rubble. It was another sixty years before the Valide Sultan Turhan Hatice, mother of Sultan Mehmet IV, completed the building.

The lower chambers of the Kasir (royal entrance), at the northeast corner of the mosque, now house the **Ayvalik and Aydin Agricultural Foundation** shops (Mon–Fri & Sun 8am–noon & 1–5pm, Sat 8am–1pm), selling good-quality olives, olive oil and other produce more cheaply than regular shops.

Mısır Carşısı: the spice bazaar

The most atmospheric part of the Yeni Cami mosque complex is the **Mısır Carşısı** (daily 9am–7pm), the "Egyptian Bazaar", better known as the **spice bazaar** because the main bulk of produce on sale has traditionally been spices. Completed a few years before Yeni Cami, the L-shaped bazaar was endowed with customs duties from Cairo (which explains its name); it has 88 vaulted rooms and chambers above the entryways at the ends of the halls. One of these, over the main entrance opposite the ferry ports, now houses the Greek *Pandeli* restaurant (see p.188).

Despite its name, the range and quality of spices in the bazaar is noticeably feeble and prices are not cheap. Of more interest are the varieties of *lokum* (Turkish delight) and the many bizarre concoctions being passed off as aphrodisiacs – also available in cheaper shops in the adjacent backstreets. It's also a good place to pick up towels, bed linen and basketware. Outside is a line of shops stocking coffee, dried fruit, spices, and everything you need to set up your own kebab stall.

The Golden Horn

The derivation of the name **Golden Horn** is obscure (the Turkish name, *Halic*, simply means "estuary"). One fanciful suggestion is that it was coined during the fifteenth-century siege of the city, when all the gold and precious objects the Byzantine citizens could collect were thrown into the inlet to save them being taken by the advancing Ottoman forces. Visitors in Ottoman times wrote about the area's perfumed waters, though by the 1950s the author Yaşar Kemal described it in *The Sea-Crossed Fisherman* as "a filthy sewer filled with empty cans and rubbish and horse carcasses, dead dogs and gulls and wild boars and thousands of cats, stinking . . A viscid, turbid mass, opaque, teeming with maggots." Recent years have seen a huge improvement, though swimming is still not recommended!

Despite the pollution, the Golden Horn is one of the finest natural harbours in the world and its fortunes have been closely linked with those of the city. On two separate occasions, capture of the Horn proved to be the turning point of crucial military campaigns. The first occasion, in 1203–04, was when the Crusaders took the Horn and proceeded to besiege the city for ten months, until they breached the walls separating the inlet from the city. The second was a spectacular *tour de force* by Mehmet the Conqueror, who was prevented from entering the Horn by a chain fastened across it and so carried his ships overland at night and launched them into the inlet from its northern shore. Mehmet then constructed a pontoon across the top of the Horn over which he transported his army and cannons in preparation for the siege of the land walls, which were finally breached in 1453.

For the Ottoman Empire, the Horn was a vital harbour, supplying the Genoese, Venetian and Jewish trading colonies on its northern shore. It was also a site for ship construction, still very much in evidence, though most shipbuilding yards have moved east of İstanbul to Tuzla.

Rüstem Paşa Camii

One of the most attractive of İstanbul's smaller mosques is **Rüstem Paşa Camii**, a short walk west of the spice bazaar. Built for Süleyman the Magnificent's grand vizier Rüstem Paşa (who was responsible along with Roxelana for the murder of the heir apparent Mustafa), the mosque dates from the year he died, 1561, and was probably built in his memory by his widow Mihrimah, Roxelana's daughter.

Designed by Sinan on an awkward site, the mosque is easy to miss as you wander the streets below. At ground level on the Golden Horn side an arcade of shops occupies the vaults, from where a flight of steps leads up to the mosque's terrace. Through an attractive entrance portal is a wide courtyard and a tiled double portico along the west wall. It's almost like entering a theatre, with the tiles of the portico as backdrop and the mosque interior, whose dimensions are not immediately apparent, backstage.

The **tiles**, inside and out, are among the best in any mosque in Turkey. They date from the finest period of İznik tile production, when techniques for producing tomato-red – slightly raised above the other colours – had been perfected. Designs covering the walls, piers and pillars, and decorating the *mihrab* and *mimber*, include famous panels of tulips and carnations and geometric patterns. Inside are galleries supported by pillars and marble columns and about as many windows as the structure of the mosque will allow. Only the inappropriate and ugly nineteenth-century painting detracts from the overall effect.

From Sultanahmet to Beyazit

Beyazit is the district centred on the buildings of İstanbul University and the covered bazaar. Relatively little explored by tourists, it's a quarter that deserves some time, and the university and its surrounding mosques – Nuruosmaniye, Beyazit Camii and Süleymaniye – are all interesting. Then of course there's the bazaar itself, as well as the most famous of İstanbul's secondhand-book markets and a couple of its oldest hamams.

Along and around Divan Yolu

The main approach from Sultanahmet to Beyazit is **Divan Yolu**, a major thoroughfare that gained its name because it was the principal approach to the Divan. Hordes of people would pour along it three times a week to make their petitions to the court. These days it still gets crowded, but its once shabby, run-down demeanour has given way to a more upmarket spruceness.

At 64m by 56m, the **Binbirdirek Cistern** (Cistern of a Thousand and One Columns) is the second largest cistern in the city. It's open to the public in the incongruous guise of a shopping mall, and is accessible via an entrance in its impressively thick retaining wall on Atmeydani Sokak. Originally the hall was over 12m high, as can be seen from the small area of four columns excavated to the original floor. The cistern is thought to have been built under the palace of Philoxenus, one of the Roman senators who accompanied Emperor Constantine to the city. It dried up completely around the fifteenth century and was later used as a spinning mill until the early twentieth century.

Continuing along Divan Yolu, you'll pass the elaborate 1838 **Tomb of Sultan Mahmut II** and the seventeenth-century library building of the Köprülü Külliye. The latter is now home to a handicraft shop and café and a small **Press Museum** (Mon–Sat 10am–6pm; free) containing exhibits on the press and printing dating back to the sixteenth century.

At the next road junction is the **Çemberlitaş** ("the hooped stone"), a burnt column of masonry, also known as the **Column of Constantine.** Erected by Constantine the Great in 330 AD, it commemorated the city's dedication as capital of the Roman Empire. For the next sixteen centuries the city was known as Constantinople. The column consists of seven drums of porphyry surmounted by a statue of the emperor. The iron hoops from which it derives its Turkish name were bound around the joints in the porphyry after an earthquake in 416 damaged the column. The current scorched condition dates from the great fire of 1779, which destroyed much of the surrounding area.

Across Vezirhanı Caddesi from the column is the celebrated four-hundred-year old **Çemberlitaş Hamamı** (daily 6am–midnight; 15YTL, 22YTL with massage; ⓦwww.cemberlitashamami.com.tr), founded in the sixteenth century by Nur Banu, one of the most powerful of the Valide Sultans. Its central location means that the masseurs are well used to foreigners, making it a good place to be initiated into the rites of the Turkish bath.

Turn up Vezirhanı Caddesi to the **Nuruosmaniye Camii** at the back of the covered bazaar. Begun by Mahmut I in 1748 and finished seven years later by Osman III, this mosque was the first and most impressive of the city's Baroque mosques, and set the fashion in Baroque and Rococo architecture for the following century. The architect is unknown, but its radical design suggests foreign influences.

Further along Yeniçeriler Caddesi, the **Gazi Atık Ali Paşa Camii** is one of the oldest mosques in the city. It was built in 1496 by Atık Ali Paşa, a eunuch who rose to the rank of grand vizier under Sultan Beyazit II. Its design, a rectangular room divided unequally by a huge arch, predates that of the larger, more famous mosques. The gardens boast a quiet café that offers *nargile* and is frequented by students from the nearby university and migrant Turks from the Balkans.

Kapalı Çarşı: the covered bazaar

With sixty-six streets and alleys, over four thousand shops, numerous storehouses, moneychangers and banks, a mosque, post office, police station, private security guards and its own health centre, İstanbul's **Kapalı Çarşı** (Mon–Sat 9am–7pm) is said to be the largest **covered bazaar** in the world. In addition to the retail outlets the *han*s or market halls in and around the bazaar are the location of workshops, where craftsmen make some of the goods sold in the bazaar.

Originally, a particular type of shop was found in a certain area, with street names reflecting the nature of the businesses. Many of these distinctions are now blurred because the trade in certain goods has moved on, while that of others has expanded to meet new demands. In Ottoman times the bazaar consisted of both a covered and an open area centred on a *bedesten*, a domed building where foreign trade took place and valuable goods were stored. In İstanbul the commercial centre was based around two *bedesten*s, both inside the covered bazaar. The **İç Bedesten** probably dates from the time of the Conquest, while the **Sandal Bedesten** was added in the sixteenth century to cope with the quantity of trade in fine fabrics that the capital attracted. However, the bazaar extends much further than the limits of the covered area, sprawling into the streets that lead down to the Golden Horn. This whole area was once controlled by strict laws laid down by the trade guilds, thus reducing competition between traders. Each shop could support just one owner and his apprentice, and successful merchants were not allowed to expand their businesses. Similar unwritten laws control market forces among traders in the covered bazaar even today.

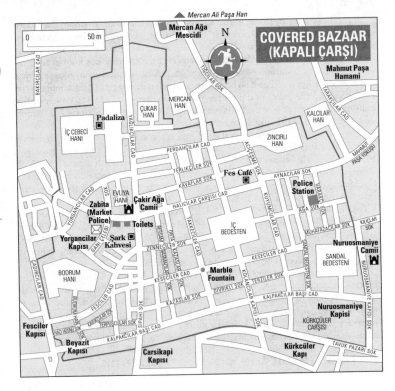

Visiting the bazaar

The best time to visit is during the week as Saturday sees the bazaar and its surroundings crowded with local shoppers. Expect to get lost as most streets are either poorly marked or their signs are hidden beneath goods hung up on display. However, try finding Kavaflar Sok for **shoes**, Terlikçiler Sok for **slippers**, Kalpakçılar Başı and Kuyumcular *caddesi*s for **gold**, and Tavuk Pazarı Sok, Kürkçüler Sok, Perdahçılar Caddesi and Bodrum Han for **leather clothing**. Carpet-sellers are just about everywhere, with more expensive collector's pieces on sale on Halıcılar Çarşısı, Takkeciler and Keseciler *caddesi*s, and cheaper ones in the tiny Rubiye Han or İç Cebeci Han. **Ceramics** and leather and kilim **bags** can be found along Yağlıkçılar Caddesi, just off it in Çukur Han, and also along Keseciler Caddesi. For details of specific shops, see p.198.

The old bazaar (or İç Bedesten), located at the centre of the maze, was traditionally reserved for the most precious wares because it could be locked at night. You'll still find some silver and gold on sale, but these days the emphasis is more on reproduction brass ship-fittings, fake scrimshaw and souvenirs. For a more authentic experience check out Kalcılar Han where you will see **silver** being cast and worked with skills that have been handed down over the generations.

The best of the traditional **cafés** in the bazaar is the *Şark Kahvesi* on Yağlıkçılar Sokak, almost opposite Zennecilar Sokak, while a more contemporary alternative is the *Fes Café* on Halıcılar Çarşısı Caddesi: both offer a welcome respite from the hurly-burly of this shopping mecca. Whether you actually enjoy the experience of wandering around here is very much a matter of temperament and mood; you'll either find the hassle from traders intolerable, or you'll be flattered to be paid more attention in one afternoon than you've received in your entire life. These days the Society of Kapalı Çarşı Traders polices the area, issuing warnings to those deemed too intimidating, so if you find yourself uncomfortably targeted, either keep moving or look around for one of the maroon-uniformed security guards. However, if you have time to spend in idle chat you may discover some of the more interesting characters who work in these parts and at least everyone is friendly and cheerful. If you're determined to avoid the banter, you'll have to look and dress like a Turk, but even then don't always bank on success.

Beyazit Meydanı

Beyazit Meydanı, the main square of Beyazit, marks the principal approach to İstanbul University. Here, entered through a small *bit pazarı*, or flea market, is the famous **Sahaflar Çarşısı**, the secondhand-booksellers' market. A little enclave of wonderful shops, it's run by some of the quarter's best-known and worst-tempered characters. The Ottoman book market dates back to the eighteenth century, but long before that there was a Byzantine book and paper market on the site. After the conquest it lost its original identity to the spoonmakers, though booksellers gradually moved back in once printing and publishing were legalized in the second half of the eighteenth century.

The Ottomans were uneasy with human pictorial representation and used calligraphy for artistic expression. On the west side of the square the tradition is reflected in a small **Museum of Calligraphy** (Mon–Fri 9am–4pm; free), formerly a theological college, now containing some interesting examples of this highly developed Ottoman art form.

To the east of the square, **Beyazit Camii**, completed in 1506, is the oldest surviving imperial mosque in the city. It has a sombre courtyard full of richly coloured marble, including twenty columns of verd antique, red granite and porphyry. Inside, the building is a perfect square of exactly the same proportions as the courtyard (although the aisles make it feel elongated). The sixteenth-century fittings, including the carvings of the balustrade, *mihrab* and *mimber*, are all highly crafted. Walking straight past the mosque from Beyazit Meydanı and on through the Sahaflar Çarşısı, you'll find another entrance to the covered bazaar.

İstanbul University

İstanbul University commands an impressive position at the crown of one of the city's seven hills. The fire tower located in the grounds, Beyazit Kulesi, is a landmark all over the city. The main building and some of its subsidiaries have a certain grandeur, especially when approached through the main gateway (the best time to do this is at 9am in term-time, when the national anthem, the *İstiklâl Marşı*, is played and everyone in the vicinity freezes for the duration).

İstanbul University has been a centre of **political activity** of the Left, the Right and Muslim fundamentalists, with occasional demonstrations, lock-ins and even violence on the campus. Parts of the university have since been relocated to Avcilar on the Edirne highway, and in recent times student unrest has died down, though feelings still run high about wearing religious garb. In 1999 trouble erupted over the ban on headscarf-clad female students attending courses and this remains a controversial issue today.

The location of the university is historically significant. It occupies the site of the Old Palace of Mehmet the Conqueror – imperial residence from 1453 until it burned to the ground in 1541. The palace was rebuilt to serve as a residence for concubines who had been retired after the accession of a new sultan. What's now the main university building was constructed by the French architect Bourgeois, in 1866, to house the Ministry of War. This moved to Ankara in 1923, along with the other departments of state, when the university (which until then had been scattered around the city in various *medrese*s of the imperial mosques) was relocated here.

Apart from the monumental gateway, where you enter the campus, the most impressive building on the site is a small *köşk*, to the right of the entrance. This is part of the original Bourgeois complex and has Baroque interior decoration.

The Süleymaniye complex

Heading north, downhill, through the university grounds, you will emerge in front of a collection of buildings considered to be the finest of all the Ottoman mosque complexes. Built by the renowned architect **Mimar Sinan** (see box opposite) in honour of his most illustrious patron, Süleyman the Magnificent, it is arguably his greatest achievement.

When the imperial entourage moved to Topkapı, the grounds of the Old Palace were given over to the new complex, in what must have been a most attractive location overlooking the Golden Horn and its waterside parks and gardens. Süleymaniye Camii and its satellites, completed in just seven years from 1550, are built along traditional Islamic lines. The mosque is centralized beneath a dome at the very centre of the entire complex, but the whole achieves a perfection of form and a monumentality of appearance that set it apart from other Ottoman architecture.

Approaching from the university side, the first street encountered before entering the mosque precincts is Prof. Sıddık Sami Onal Caddesi, formerly **Tıryakı Çarşısı**, "market of the addicts". The name derives from the fact that the coffee-houses in this street, whose rents augmented the upkeep of the foundation, used also to serve hashish, to be smoked on the premises or taken away. The present line of student cafés here may be seedy but are evidently nothing like as interesting as the establishments they replaced.

Behind the shop fronts in this street is the **Süleymaniye Library** (Mon–Sat 8.30am–5pm), housed in the Evvel and Sani *medrese*s. These buildings, mirror images of each other, are situated around shady garden courtyards. Süleyman established the library in an effort to bring together collections of books scattered throughout the city: works were gathered from eleven palaces and date from the reigns of six different sultans. The library is open to the public, though – to protect the originals – all the works are preserved on microfilm. There is also a book restoration department, where the original bindings are closely imitated.

Other buildings of interest in the vicinity include the **Tomb of Mimar Sinan**, on Mimar Sinan Caddesi. The tomb is in a triangular garden, which was the location of the architect's house during construction work. At the corner of the triangle is an octagonal eaved fountain. Perhaps there is no nicer way of being remembered than by providing the gift of water to passing strangers, but in Sinan's case it nearly caused his downfall. The fountain, as well as Sinan's house and garden, were liberally supplied with water, but when the mosques further down the pipeline began to run short, Sinan was charged with diverting the water supply for his household needs. The garden beyond the fountain now houses his tomb, with its magnificent carved turban, a measure of the architect's high rank. The eulogy written on the south wall of the garden picks out the bridge at Büyükçekmece as Sinan's greatest achievement.

Mimar Sinan, master builder

Many of the finest works of Ottoman civil and religious architecture throughout Turkey can be traced to one man, a genius who had the good luck to come of age in a rich, expanding empire willing to put its considerable resources at his disposal. **Mimar Sinan** (1489–1588) served as court architect to three sultans – Süleyman the Magnificent, Selim II and Murat III – but principally to the first, who owed much of his reputation for "magnificence" to this gifted technician.

Little is known of Sinan's early life except that he was born in a small village near Kayseri, the son of Greek or Armenian Christian parents. Even his birthdate is open to question, since it is established that he was conscripted into the janissaries in 1513, which would have made him a good ten years older than the typical recruit. In any case, prolonged military service in all of the major Ottoman campaigns of the early sixteenth century compelled Sinan to travel the length and breadth of southeastern Europe and the Middle East, giving him the opportunity to become familiar with the best Islamic – and Christian – monumental architecture there. Sinan was immediately able to apply what he had learned in the role of military engineer, building bridges, siegeworks, harbours and even ships, which earned him the admiration of his superiors. These included Sultan Süleyman, who in recognition of his abilities appointed him court architect in April 1536.

During Sinan's first twelve years in the job, he did little out of the ordinary, undertaking only relatively minor public works throughout Anatolia and the Balkans. In 1548 he completed his first major religious commission, İstanbul's Şehzade Camii, and shortly thereafter embarked on a rapid succession of ambitious projects in and around the capital, including the waterworks leading from the Belgrade Forest and the Süleymaniye Camii. After exhausting the potential of the great city Sinan turned his matured attention to the provinces, gracing Edirne with the Selimiye Camii in 1569–75, and a decade later fulfilling a longstanding wish as a devout Muslim by overseeing the restoration of the Harem-i-Zerif mosque in Mecca.

Unusually for his time, Sinan could make an objective assessment of his talents: he regarded most of his pre-1550 works as apprentice pieces and posterity has generally agreed with the self-evaluations in his memoirs, the *Tezkeret-ül-Bünyan*. Despite temptations to luxury he lived and died equally modestly, being buried in a simple tomb he made for himself in his garden in the grounds of the Süleymaniye Camii – the last of more than five hundred constructions by Sinan, large and small, throughout the empire.

Otherwise, the buildings of the Süleymaniye complex served the usual functions. On Şifahane Sokak is the *imaret* (soup kitchen), which despite its ornate design was constructed as a public kitchen supplying food for the local poor (fittingly, it now houses a restaurant) and *kervansaray* (hotel). A *mektep* (primary school) stands on the corner of Saddak Sami Onal Caddesi and Süleymaniye Caddesi, and there are Koran schools and a language school, which taught the proper pronunciation of Arabic for reading the Koran. There's also a triangular wrestling ground (now used as a car park), located to the south of the cemetery.

The **Süleymaniye hamam**, built by Sinan in 1557, is on the corner of Mimar Sinan Caddesi and Dökmeciler Hamamı Sokak (daily 6.30am–midnight; 15YTL, 20YTL with massage; Ⓦ www.suleymaniyehamami.com). Legend has it that the great architect took all his baths here from 1557 to 1588. It is a beautiful building, but in a terrible state of repair.

The mosque itself, **Süleymaniye Camii**, is preceded by a rectangular courtyard, whose portico stands on columns of porphyry, Marmara marble and pink Egyptian granite (which are said to have come from the royal box of the Hippodrome), and by four tapering minarets. Semi-domes supporting the huge central dome to east and west alternate with arches, in front of which is a set of three domes. The east and west flanks of the mosque are distinguished by two-storey loggias, accessible from within the mosque, which support an eave protecting those performing their ablutions at the taps below.

The doorway into the mosque is high and narrow, its wooden doors inlaid with ebony, mother-of-pearl and ivory. Move inside, and the sense of light and space is paramount – a dome 53m high (twice its diameter), surmounting a perfect square of 26.5m. There are no side aisles and the double panes of 200 windows ensure a softly filtered light. The dome collapsed during the earthquake of 1766, while in the nineteenth century further damage was done by the Fossati brothers, whose attempt at Ottoman Baroque redecoration jars with the inherent simplicity of the building. The original crystal lamps have also been replaced by glassware supported on a rather cumbersome iron frame, though the stained glass of İbrahim the Mad remains, above a graceful marble *mimber*.

In the adjacent **cemetery** (daily 5.30am–8pm) are located the tombs of Süleyman the Magnificent and of Haseki Hürrem, or Roxelana, his powerful wife. Süleyman's tomb is particularly impressive: its doors are inlaid with ebony, ivory, silver and jade, and the turban of Süleyman the Magnificent is huge. Above, the spectacular inner dome has been faithfully restored in red, black and gold inlaid with glittering ceramic stars. Both here, and in the neighbouring tomb of Roxelana, original tiles and some fine stained-glass have survived the centuries.

Laleli and Aksaray

Heading west from Beyazit up Ordu Caddesi, you arrive at an appalling tangle of road intersections where Adnan Menderes Caddesi crosses Ordu Caddesi. This is the main focus of the districts of **Aksaray** and **Laleli**, whose atmosphere is distinctly different from anywhere else in İstanbul. In part, it's the dispiriting effect of the constant roar of traffic, but it's also because – in Laleli especially – there's no real sense of community. Many of the inhabitants are Iranian refugees and Arab students, and, more recently, Russians and Eastern Europeans buying everything and anything the Turks might have a mind to sell.

Both districts have sights worth seeing and you should certainly wander away from the main road to explore some of them. Laleli, in particular, is a big import/export area for textiles, cheap clothes and shoes, car parts and leather, attracting coachloads of shoppers from the former eastern bloc. You are more likely to hear Russian spoken here than Turkish. The area has aquired a notorious reputation as a centre of prostitution and thievery, and you would be well advised to keep your wits about you if you visit at night.

Laleli Camii

The **Laleli Camii** complex, on Ordu Caddesi opposite the Laleli tram stop, is in the Ottoman Baroque tradition of Nuruosmaniye and the Ayazma Camii in Üsküdar, but the mosque itself owes more to traditional Ottoman architecture. It was founded by Mustafa III, whose octagonal tomb is located at the southeast gate. Selim III, who was assassinated by his janissaries, is also buried there.

The main Baroque elements in the mosque complex are the use of ramps (including one which the reigning sultan would have used to ride up to his loge), the grand staircases and the detail, for example in the window grilles of the tomb and in the carved eaves of the *sebil* (drinking fountain). Inside, a mass of pillars dominates, especially to the west, where the columns beneath the main dome seem to crowd those supporting the galleries into the walls. Back outside, the foundations of the mosque are used as a covered **market**, selling the cheapest of clothes and acting as an inducement for the local populace to worship at the mosque.

At the back of the Laleli complex, between Fethi Bey and Gençturk *caddesi*s, is another smaller covered bazaar, the **Taşhan**, originally built as an inn in 1793 by Sultan Mustafa III to entertain his guests. The building has been restored as a two-tiered bazaar surrounding two open courtyards, with a couple of restaurants located in the vaults beneath.

The Aqueduct of Valens and Kalenderhane Camii

An alternative route from Beyazit into Laleli takes you up Şehzadebaşi Caddesi towards the Şehzade Camii (another creation of the ubiquitous Mimar Sinan), following the line of the magnificent **Aqueduct of Valens**. Recently renovated, the aqueduct was originally built during the late fourth-century waterworks programme carried out by the emperor Valens, and was part of a distribution network that included reservoirs in the Belgrade Forest and various cisterns located around the city centre. It was in use right up to the end of the nineteenth century, having been kept in good repair by successive rulers, who maintained a constant supply of water to the city in the face of both drought and siege. More than six hundred of its original thousand metres are still standing and the best view is from where the aqueduct crosses Atatürk Bulvarı, where it reaches a height of eighteen and a half metres.

The ninth-century Byzantine Church of Kyriotissa, near where the aqueduct now ends, was renamed **Kalenderhane Camii** after the Kalender dervishes who converted it into a *tekke* (Dervish monastery) after the conquest. It has the cruciform ground-plan typical of Byzantine churches of its time, with much of the marble revetment and sculpture still in place. The apse has been closed off, but the mosque toilet-keeper will usually unlock the crypt, which still boasts extensive frescoes.

Zeyrek

Crossing Atatürk Bulvarı brings you into **Zeyrek**, an attractive area notable for its steep, cobbled streets and ramshackle wooden houses interspersed with small mosques. There are also wonderful views of the Süleymaniye mosque complex. Crossing the road is something of an ordeal (local drivers seem to regard it as a Grand Prix test-track) and the convoluted streets of Zeyrek are confusing. It's worth persevering, however, in order to track down a handful of interesting sights, including two former Byzantine churches in contrasting states of repair.

Museum of Caricatures

The **Museum of Caricatures** (Karikatür ve Mizah Müzesi; Mon–Fri 9am–6pm; free) stands on Atatürk Bulvarı between Cemal Yener Tosyalı Caddesi and the aqueduct, housed in the rooms of Gazanfer Medrese around a pretty garden courtyard with a marble fountain. Cartoons are an important popular art form in Turkey: most papers employ a number of cartoonists and the weekly *Gırgır* was the third best-selling comic in the world before many of its employees left to set up the rival *Avni*. The collection includes pieces dating back to 1870, with many exhibits concentrating on political satire. Temporary exhibitions change every week and feature work by both international and Turkish cartoonists, while the museum also organizes silk-screen and other workshops, including some for children.

Çinili Hamamı

The **Çinili Hamamı** (daily 8.30am–8pm; 12YTL, 15YTL with massage) or "tiled baths", on İtfaiye Caddesi, provide a welcome respite from sightseeing. This double hamam, which was built for the great sixteenth-century pirate-admiral Barbarossa, has been beautifully restored to working order and has a particularly friendly atmosphere. Notice the huge dome and the marble floors and fountain of the *camekan* (changing room), the enormous, octagonal, marble massage-table in the main room of the *hararet* (steam room) and the toilets, which are continually flushed by water draining from the *hararet*. There are still a few of the original tiles on the walls in the men's section, but none are evident through the continual clouds of steam in the women's baths. The blissful bath experience can be nicely rounded off in the *Gül Lokantası*, behind the basketball court on the other side of Atfaiye Caddesi. This little basement kebab-joint has a discreet but friendly atmosphere peculiar to establishments in areas slightly off the tourist agenda and as such is a rarity in İstanbul.

Zeyrek Camii

In the heart of Zeyrek nestles **Zeyrek Camii**, the former Church of the Pantocrator, built in the twelfth century and converted into a mosque at the time of the conquest. To get here, take İtfaiye Caddesi northwards, then turn left on to İbadethane Arkası Sokak.

The building is officially open only at prayer times, though you may be able to persuade the *imam* to open the door for you (his house is up the stone steps behind the wooden door, next to the mosque). It originally consisted of two churches and a connecting chapel, built between 1118 and 1136 by John II Comnenus and Empress Irene. The chapel was built as a mausoleum for the Comnenus dynasty and continued to be used as such by the Paleologus dynasty. Although the tombs have been removed, there is still evidence of the graves beneath the pavement. Empress Irene also founded a monastery nearby, which was to become one of the most renowned religious institutions in the empire and later the official residence of the Byzantine court, after the Great Palace had been reduced to a ruin. No trace remains of the monastery, nor of its hospice, asylum or hospital.

The **mosque**, which occupies the south church, is also in an advanced state of dilapidation and it's difficult to believe that it was once an imperial mausoleum. Among the surviving features are the revetments of the south apse and the original marble doorframes. The floor, naturally, is covered in carpets but the *imam* may pull one of these back to give a glimpse of the coloured marble underneath: an interlacing geometric pattern with figures of animals in its borders.

Eski İmaret Camii

Another attractive Byzantine church can be found within walking distance, albeit by a rather convoluted route. To get there, return to İbadethane Sokak and follow it to Çirçir Caddesi. Take a right off here onto Nevşehirli İbrahim Paşı Caddesi, then a left into Hanedan Sokak, and you'll see the church, now known as the **Eski İmaret Camii**, ahead of you. To get in you'll need to arrive at prayer time or hope to find the *imam* at home (his house is connected to the mosque down a flight of stone steps). Founded at the end of the twelfth century by Empress Anna Delessena, the mother of Alexius I Comnenus, this four-column structure is similar to the south church of the Pantocrator, evidence of a return to traditional Byzantine forms, perhaps in reaction to the encroaching political threat from east and west.

Eski İmaret has one of the most interesting exteriors of all the Byzantine churches in İstanbul. As ever, it's hemmed in by surrounding buildings, but in this case the wooden houses provide an attractive frame as you approach down Küçük Mektep Sokak. The roof and twelve-sided dome retain their original curved tiles, while the eaves are decorated with a zigzag of bricks. Other designs in the brickwork include swastikas and Greek keys. Inside, some of the original fittings remain, notably the red marble doorframes and a floral decoration around the cornice supporting the dome. The two side apses also retain their original windows and marble cornice.

Fatih

The reputation of **Fatih** ("the Conqueror") as a conservative Islamic area is deserved, though it's not associated with intolerance towards visitors of different religious and cultural persuasions. Fatih was one of the first districts to elect an Islamist mayor, and you may notice more covered women about the streets, many of them wearing headscarves or full *chador*, and men sporting long white beards. The majority of people, however, will be dressed as in the rest of İstanbul. It's worth bearing in mind, though, that locals here may be more likely to take exception to naked limbs and (perhaps understandably) to having their picture taken without due warning.

To get to Fatih, simply follow the line of the Valens aqueduct from the north side of Atatürk Bulvarı and keep going in the same direction when you run out of aqueduct. Or from Eminönü or Sultanahmet, take any bus going to Edirnekapı and get off at the Fatih mosque complex.

Fatih Camii

Fatih Camii, the "Mosque of the Conqueror", on İslambol Caddesi, was begun ten years after the conquest of İstanbul, in 1463, and completed in 1470. In 1766, however, it was almost completely destroyed in an earthquake: only the courtyard, the entrance portal of the mosque, the south wall of the graveyard and the bases of the minarets survived; the rest was rebuilt.

The **outer precinct** of the mosque is large enough to accommodate the tents of a caravan. It is enclosed by a wall and, to north and south, by the *medrese* (theological academy) buildings, which accommodated the first Ottoman university. The **inner courtyard** of the mosque is one of the most beautiful in the city. Verd antique and porphyry columns support a domed portico with polychrome edges, while an eighteenth-century fountain is surrounded by four enormous poplar trees. Over the windows outside the courtyard in the west wall the first verse of the Koran is inscribed in white marble on verd antique. At either end of the mosque portico there are inscriptions in the early İznik *cuerda seca* technique, whereby coloured glazes were prevented from running into each other by a dividing line of potassium permanganate, which outlined the design. The inscription over the mosque portal records the date and dedication of the mosque, and the name of the architect, **Atık Sinan**. He was supposedly executed the year after its completion on the orders of Mehmet, because the dome wasn't as large as that of Aya Sofya.

The **interior**, painted in drab colours without a tile in sight, is rarely empty, even outside prayer times. It appears to be a social meeting place as well as a centre of serious Koranic study for both women and men. As in all mosques, the men occupy the main body of the building while the women's section is confined to the anterior regions, where you'll find an unusual old bronze water-pump with silver cups.

The **tombs** of Mehmet II and of one of his wives, Gülbahar (Wed–Sun 9am–4.30pm), are situated to the east of the mosque. The originals were destroyed in the earthquake, and while Gülbahar's tomb is probably a replica of the original, the *türbe* of the Conqueror is sumptuous Baroque. **Çorba Kapısı**, the "Soup Gate", to the southeast of the mosque, is original, inlaid in porphyry and verd antique.

Yavuz Selim Camii

Built on a terrace on the crest of one of İstanbul's seven hills (the fifth, counting from Topkapı's), **Yavuz Selim Camii** – also called the Selimiye – holds a commanding position over the surrounding suburbs. It lies on Yavuz Selim Caddesi and is a twenty-minute walk from Fatih Camii, though a nicer approach is to take a ferry up the Golden Horn from Eminönü to Aykapı ferry terminal and walk up to the mosque, again about twenty minutes.

Viewed on the approach down Yavuz Selim Caddesi, the mosque presents one of the most impressive facades to be seen in the city. This is in part because of its position next to the **Cistern of Aspar**, one of three open cisterns built during the fifth and sixth centuries in Constantinople. For centuries this space housed market gardens and a village, but these were cleared years ago and sections are now in use as an attractive park, as well as basketball and tennis courts.

The mosque of Yavuz Selim, or Selim the Grim, was probably begun in the reign of Selim and completed by Süleyman, but its dates are not certain. Close up, the exterior is rather bleak, a fitting memorial to a man with such a reputation for cruelty. There's no pretty cascade of domes and turrets, just a large dome atop a square room with a walled courtyard in front of it. Once inside the courtyard walls, however, this simple, restrained building emerges as one of the most attractive of all the imperial mosques. A central fountain is surrounded by tall cypress trees, the floor of the portico is paved with a floral design, while its columns are a variety of marbles and granites.

The **domed rooms** to the north and south of the mosque – which served as hostels for travelling dervishes – are characteristic of early Ottoman architecture. In the mosque itself, under the sultan's loge (supported on columns in a variety of rare marbles) is paintwork in designs reminiscent of the delicacy of Turkish carpets or ceramics.

The **tomb of Selim the Grim** (daily except Tues 9.30am–4.30pm), beside the mosque, has lost its original interior decoration, but retains two beautiful tiled panels on either side of the door. Other tombs in the complex include that of four of Süleyman the Magnificent's children, probably the work of Sinan.

Along the city walls

Theodosius II's **city walls** are among the most fascinating Byzantine remains to be found in Turkey. Well-preserved remnants can still be found along the whole of their six-and-a-half-kilometre length, despite the 1999 earthquake, which caused several unrestored portions to collapse. Sadly, the ongoing renovation process gives barely a nod to historical accuracy: some sections have been completely

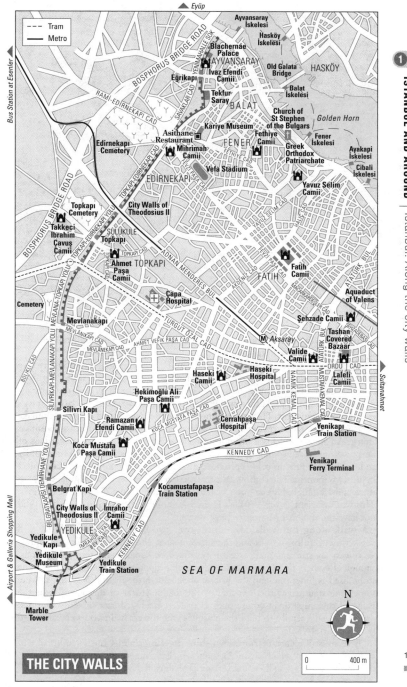

THE CITY WALLS

0   400 m

△ The city walls

rebuilt in newly dressed stone and cement bricks; while certain additional details, such as medieval-style flourishes, quite possibly never existed.

The land walls were named after Theodosius II, even though he was only twelve years old when their construction was started in 413. The walls – stretching from the Marmara to Tekfur Saray, 2km further out than the previous walls of Constantine – were planned by Anthemius, Prefect of the East, to accommodate the city's expanding population. They were almost completely destroyed by an earthquake in 447 and had to be rebuilt in haste, since Attila's forces were on the point of attack. An ancient edict was brought into effect whereby all citizens, regardless of rank, were required to help in the rebuilding. The Hippodrome factions of Blues and Greens (see box on p.142) provided 16,000 labourers and finished the project in just two months. The completed construction consisted of the original wall, 5m thick and 12m high, plus an outer wall of 2m by 8.5m, and a 20-metre-wide moat. This was sufficient to repel Attila's Huns who numbered several thousand but did not have the skill or patience for siege warfare.

A **walk along the walls** takes a little over two hours, though a full day will allow time to fully enjoy it and the adjacent sites. Most of the outer wall and its 96 towers are still standing; access is restricted on some of the restored sections, though elsewhere there's the chance to scramble along the crumbling edifice. The stone used is limestone and the bricks, about 30cm square and 5cm thick, were sometimes stamped with the name of the manufacturer or donor and bear the name of the emperor in whose reign they were made. Mortar mixed with brick dust was used liberally to bind the masonry; the towers had two levels, separated by brick barrel-vaults.

There are still plenty of run-down **slum dwellings** along the Theodosian city walls, the worst of which are in Topkapı, which is dangerous after dark. However, it's highly unlikely you'll encounter any problems in daytime.

If time is limited, the three best **sites** to visit are the Yedikule fortifications and surrounding district; Kariye Museum, a former Byzantine church containing some of the best-preserved mosaics and frescoes in the world; and Mihrimah Camii, a Mimar Sinan mosque. **Buses** from Eminönü or Sultanahmet include the #80 to Yedikule, #84 to Topkapı and #39 or #86 to Edirnekapı, or take the tram to Topkapı. To reach the north end of the walls take the ferry from Eminönü to Ayvansaray İskelesı on the Golden Horn, just before the Haliç bridge. The best way to reach the southern end is to take a local **train** from Sirkeci to Yedikule on the Marmara shore.

Yedikule and around

At the southern end of the walls, **Yedikule** is around 5km from Sultanahmet. It's an attractive quarter, full of churches since it is a centre of Rum Orthodoxy: the dwindling congregations of such churches, scattered throughout İstanbul, are the last remaining descendants of the Byzantine Greeks. When you leave the train station, on Yedikule İstasyon Caddesi, head away from the sea along Halit Efendi Sokak and you reach İmrahor İlyas Bey Caddesi, Yedikule's main street. Here you'll find a concentration of quaint, Greek-influenced houses and some pretty churches.

The name Yedikule ("seven-tower") refers to the fortifications in this area, namely the triumphal arch of the Golden Gate – constructed here by Theodosius I in 390, even before the walls themselves – and the towers and walls later added by Mehmet the Conqueror.

İmrahor Camii

The only ancient building of any note in the vicinity of Yedikule is the ruined **İmrahor Camii**, the former Church of St John of Studius, at İmam Aşır Sokak, off İmrahor İlyas Bey Caddesi. To get there, walk straight up Halit Efendi Sokak from the train station and you'll see the remains on your right. Whatever anyone may suggest to the contrary, there is no entrance fee.

The church, built in 463, was connected to a monastery of the *akoimetai* or "unsleeping", whose inhabitants prayed in relay around the clock. The monks lived according to the strict rules of St Basil: even melancholy was considered a sin and the monks were required to keep before them the spectre of death by repeating the words "We shall die!" over and over. They still found time, however, to transcribe books for mass circulation and monks even came to the monastery from Russia to learn the trade. The monastery gained particular renown under the auspices of **Abbot Theodore**, an outspoken defender of images and critic of the Byzantine court, who established it as the centre of a renaissance in Byzantine scholarship. Although he died in exile on the Princes' Islands, the reputation of the institution survived him and the monastery was home to the University of Constantinople during the first half of the fifteenth century. Its greatest claim to historical fame, though, came in 1042, when the tyrant **Michael V** took refuge here from a popular revolution. He made his way to the church by ship, but was discovered, dragged from the altar and blinded.

As you approach the **church entrance** you'll see four large columns with acanthus capitals, supporting a horizontal carved entablature. This is the entrance to the narthex and the east wall of the atrium, which was square and probably colonnaded. The interior of the church was a simple, almost square basilica. The aisles were partitioned off by rows of columns, six of which have survived; these too are capped with acanthus capitals and support a horizontal entablature. The interlace floor is twelfth-century, but what remains of the original fittings suggests that the church was sumptuously decorated, in contrast to its simple structure.

The Yedikule Museum

The most impressive sections of wall have been designated the **Yedikule Museum** (Yedikule Müzesi; daily except Mon 9am–4pm; 4YTL), situated to the south-west of İmrahor Camii on Yedikule Meydanı Sokak, Yedikule Caddesi. Follow Kuyulu Bakkal Sokak (or, from the station, Yedikule İstasyon Cad) straight to the entrance.

The so-called **Golden Gate**, flanked by two marble towers, stood alone – a tri-umphal arch in the path of important visitors of state and of conquering emperors (generals were never permitted to pass through the gate, even after successful campaigns). Nowadays, the shape of the three arches is still visible on both sides of the wall, but it takes a degree of imagination to invest the structure with the glamour and dignity it must once have possessed. Michael Palaeologus was the last emperor to ride through the gate in triumph, when the city was recaptured from occupying Crusaders. After the empire went into decline, the gold-plated doors were removed and the entrance bricked up.

The other five towers of the Yedikule fortifications were added by Mehmet the Conqueror, and with their twelve-metre-high curtain walls they form the enclave that can be seen today. Despite its design this was never actually used as a castle, but two of the towers served as prisons and others were used as treasuries and offices for the collection of revenue of the *Vakıf* or pious foundation.

The two **prison towers** are those immediately to the left of the entrance: the "tower with inscriptions" and the tower on the north side of the Golden Gate. The inscriptions around the outside of the first of these were carved into the walls by pris-oners. Many of these were foreign ambassadors on some hapless errand. The prison in the second tower doubled as an execution chamber: the wooden gallows and "well of blood", into which heads would roll, are still to be seen, and the odd instrument of torture can be found lying about outside in the courtyard. The most famous victim of the execution chamber was Osman II. He was deposed and murdered in 1622 by his janissaries, thus providing Ottoman history with its first case of regicide.

It's worth spending some time climbing around the battlements with the lizards. You can look across to the Marble Tower, where the sea and land walls meet beyond the railway line on the Marmara coast, and also see a good stretch of the walls to the north.

Yedikule, Belgrat, Silivri and Mevlana gates

North along the walls, the first of the public gateways is the **Yedikule Kapı**. This is still in use: traffic wardens compete to direct traffic through the narrow entry, with its Byzantine eagle cut in the blackened marble overhead.

The land in and around the first section between Yedikule and **Belgrat Kapı** is in use as market gardens, and access is difficult because of fences, deep ditches and so forth. Belgrat Kapı was a military gate, different from a public gateway in that there was no bridge crossing the moat beyond the outer walls. It was named for the captives who were settled in this area by Süleyman the Magnificent after his capture of Belgrade in 1521. The walls here, which are floodlit at night, have been substantially renovated and it's now one of the best places to walk along the parapet. North from Belgrat Kapı to **Silivri Kapı** the walls are largely untouched, though the sections around Silivri Kapı itself have been extensively renovated.

There is more restoration work at the **Mevlanakapı**, and also some interesting inscriptions on the outer wall. The Theodosian walls reached completion at this gate, since it was here that the Greens, building from the Marmara, met the Blues, who were working southwards from the direction of the Golden Horn. A Latin inscription to the left of the gate celebrates this fact: "By the command of Theodosius, Constan-tine erected these strong fortifications in less than two months. Scarcely could Pallas [Athena] herself have built so strong a citadel in so short a time."

Topkapı

A road system dominates the outer side of the one-kilometre Mevlanakapı to Topkapı section of wall and a pleasant pavement has been constructed along the moat, but again it's difficult to walk along the walls themselves. Just south of Topkapı the walls have been destroyed to make way for the enormous thoroughfare of Turgut Özal Caddesi, which you'll have to cross – though it's not easy – with the tramway running in the middle of a busy dual carriageway. Once over it, continue inside the walls, until you reach the area called Kaleiçi and the **Topkapı** (the "Gate of the Cannonball"), named after the most powerful cannon of Mehmet the Conqueror (see below), some of whose enormous stone cannon-balls have been placed around the inside of the gate. To get here by public transport, take a tram from Sirkeci, Sultanahmet or Aksaray.

At Kaleiçi you can get a decent midday meal at any of the *lokanta*s and *pide* or kebab salons on Topkapı Caddesi. At the south eastern end of this street, on the left, is the **Ahmet Paşa Camii**, a Sinan mosque dating from 1554. In the porch there are original tiles made in the *cuerda seca* technique and despite some heavy-handed renovation it's worth having a look inside at the original arabesque painting under the galleries.

Another delightful mosque lies on Topkapı-Davutpaşa Caddesi (south off Davutpaşa Caddesi). The wooden **Takkeci İbrahim Çavuş Camii** (open for prayers only) retains much that is original, including its wooden dome and some fine tile panels from the best İznik period. The mosque was founded in 1592 by the eponymous *takkeci*, a maker of the distinctive felt hats (*takke*) worn by dervishes. The income of an artisan could not have been equal to the cost of building a mosque, however modest, and around this fact no doubt has grown the myth of its origins.

It is said that the hatmaker was told in a dream to go to Baghdad, where he would find a great treasure buried under a vine tree in the garden of an inn. He duly set off on his donkey and, arriving at the place of his dream, he began to dig under said vine. The innkeeper came out and enquired his business, admonished him and advised him to return to the place from which he had started his journey. On arriving back in Topkapı, the *takkeci* found two bags of gold on the present site of the mosque. Burying one in the ground, he used the other to finance the building of his mosque, the idea being that if this mosque were destroyed then another could be built in its place with the buried gold. The *imam* who tells this story to visitors points out a panel of faïence tiles depicting plump red grapes hanging on vines, jokingly suggesting that these are corroborative evidence of his story. And in such a poor parish who can blame him for clinging to the fond hope that sufficient funds are buried beneath the wooden mosque to finance its rebuilding should the need arise?

Edirnekapı

Between Topkapı and Edirnekapı there is a pronounced valley, formerly the route of the Lycus river, now taken by Vatan Caddesi. At this point the walls are at their least defensible, since the higher ground outside gives the advantage to attackers. The famed **Orban cannon** of Mehmet the Conqueror was trained on this part of the walls during the siege of 1453, hence their ruinous state. It was here, too, that Constantine XI rode into the midst of the Turkish army after he realized that all hope of holding out was gone.

Edirnekapı itself is a small-time suburb with a large *otogar* for local buses. The gate of Edirnekapı takes its name from the route to modern Edirne, which passed through even in Byzantine times. Also left over from the Byzantine era is the smallest of the ancient city's open cisterns, located about 50m from the *otogar* on the left of Fevzi Paşa Caddesi (Edirnekapı's main street), below the level of the road. It's now the site of the Vefa football stadium, but the original dimensions of the cistern can still be seen. Buses straight to Edirnekapı from town include the #34 or #39 from Eminönü and #86 from Eminönü and Sultanahmet.

The **Mihrimah Camii** is a little to the left of the *otogar* as you face the walls. Mihrimah, the favourite daughter of Süleyman the Magnificent, had a passion for architecture as great as that of her husband Rüstem Paşa, and the couple commissioned many of Sinan's early works. Mihrimah Camii, situated on the highest of İstanbul's seven hills, dates from somewhere around the middle of the sixteenth century. It's raised on a platform and can be seen from all over the city, with the area beneath occupied by shops.

The mosque and its dependencies have suffered in two earthquakes, the second of which brought the minaret tumbling down onto the mosque itself. During renovation the interior was filled with twentieth-century arabesque stencilling, though other aspects compensate, especially the light flooding in through the windows and the graceful white-marble *mimber*. Note the skilful fake marbling of the arches under the eastern gallery. The mosque's nearby **hamam** has also been poorly restored but at least is still functioning.

The Kariye Museum

The **Kariye Museum** (Kariye Müzesi; daily except Wed 9am–6pm; 10YTL), formerly the church of St Saviour in Chora, is decorated with a superbly preserved series of **frescoes and mosaics** portraying the life and miracles of Christ. It's among the most evocative of all the city's Byzantine treasures, thought to have been built in the early twelfth century on the site of a much older church far from the centre: hence "in Chora", meaning "in the country". Between 1316 and 1321 the statesman and scholar Theodore Metochites rebuilt the central dome and added the narthexes and mortuary chapel.

To reach the museum from Edirnekapı, take Vaiz Sokak off Fevzi Paşa Caddesi and a second right onto Kariye Bostana Sokak, a street with a number of picturesquely renovated wooden houses, painted in pastel colours. There's no direct transport from the city centre.

The narthexes

The mosaics and frescoes date from the same period as the renovations carried out by Metochites and depict the life of Christ in picture-book sequence. The first series to be followed is a set of dedicatory and devotional panels located in the two narthexes. Inside the church, the most prominent of the mosaics is that of **Christ Pantocrator**, bearing the inscription "Jesus Christ, the Land of the Living". Opposite this, above the entrance, is a depiction of the Virgin and angels, with the inscription "Mother of God, the Dwelling Place of the Uncontainable". The third in the series is located in the inner narthex and depicts Metochites offering a model of the building to a seated Christ. The hat he is wearing is called a *skiadon*, or "sunshade". SS Peter and Paul are portrayed on either side of the door leading to the nave, and to the right of the door are Christ with his Mother and two benefactors, Isaac (who built the original church) and a female figure, described in the inscription as "Lady of the Mongols, Melane the Nun".

In the two domes of the inner narthex are medallions of Christ Pantocrator and the Virgin and Child, and in the fluting of the domes, a series of notable figures – starting with Adam – from the **Genealogy of Christ**. The **Cycle of the Blessed Virgin** is located in the first three bays of the inner narthex. These mosaics are based on the apocryphal gospel of St James, which gives an account of the birth and life of the Virgin and was very popular in the Middle Ages. Episodes depicted here include the first seven steps of the Virgin (taken when she was six months old); the Virgin caressed by her parents, with two beautiful peacocks in the background; the Virgin presented as an attendant at the temple (where she remained from the age of 3 to 12); the Virgin receiving a skein of purple wool, as proof of her royal blood; Joseph taking the Virgin to his house, in which is also depicted one of Joseph's sons by his first wife; and Joseph returning from a six-month business trip to find his wife pregnant.

The next cycle, to be found in the lunettes of the outer narthex, is that of the **Infancy of Christ**. The mosaics can be followed clockwise, starting with Joseph dreaming, the Virgin and two companions, and the journey to Bethlehem. Apart from well-known scenes such as the Journey of the Magi and the Nativity, there are depictions in the seventh bay (furthest right from the main entrance) of the Flight into Egypt, which includes the apocryphal Fall of Idols (white and ghostly-looking figures) from the walls of an Egyptian town as the holy family passes by. In the sixth bay is the Slaughter of the Innocents, complete with babies impaled on spikes.

The **Cycle of Christ's Ministry** fills the vaults of the outer narthex and parts of the south bay of the inner narthex. It includes wonderful scenes of the Temptation of Christ, with dramatic dialogue (Matthew 4: 3–10) that could almost be in speech bubbles, beginning:

Devil: If thou be the Son of God, command that these stones be made bread.
Christ: It is written, Man shall not live by bread alone, but by every word that proceedeth out of the mouth of God.

The nave and funerary chapel

In the nave, the main frescoes echo the mosaics, featuring the death of the Virgin, over the door and, to the right of this, another depiction of Christ. The best known of all the works in the church, however, are the frescoes in the **funerary chapel** (known as the pareccelsion) to the south of the nave. These comprise depictions of the Resurrection, the Last Judgement, Heaven and Hell and the Mother of God. Below the cornice are portraits of the saints and martyrs.

The most spectacular of the frescoes is the **Resurrection**, also known as the Harrowing of Hell. This is a dramatic representation of Christ in action, trampling the gates of Hell underfoot and forcibly dragging Adam and Eve from their tombs. A black Satan lies among the broken fetters at his feet, bound at the ankles, wrists and neck, but still writhing around in a vital manner. To the left of the painting, animated onlookers include John the Baptist, David and Solomon, while to the right Abel is standing in his mother's tomb; behind him is another group of the righteous.

Other frescoes in the chapel, in the vault of the east bay, depict the **Second Coming**. In the east half of the domical vault Christ sits in judgement, saying to the souls of the saved, on his right, "Come ye blessed of my Father, inherit the kingdom prepared for you from the foundation of the world." To the condemned souls on the left he says, "Depart from me, ye cursed, into everlasting fire, prepared for the devil and his angels." Below, a river of fire broadens into a lake in which are the souls of the damned. Their torments are illustrated in the lunette of the south wall and comprise the Gnashing of Teeth, the Outer Darkness, the Worm that Sleepeth Not and the Unquenchable Fire.

The tomb in the north wall of the pareccelsion has lost its inscription, but is almost certainly the **tomb of Metochites**, the donor of the church.

Eyüp

Eyüp is one of the holiest places in Islam, its mosque being the site of the tomb of Eyüp Ensari, the Prophet Mohammed's standard-bearer. Muslims come here from all over the Islamic world on pilgrimage – if you're going to come, try not to visit on Fridays, out of respect for conservative worshippers.

The mosque is most easily reached by boat up the Golden Horn from Eminönü – it's the last **ferry** stop before the Horn peters out into two small streams, and the mosque and tomb are about a ten-minute walk from the ferry terminal on Camii Kebir Caddesi. Or catch the #39/A **bus** from Eminönü, which drops you off at the ferry terminal.

Eyüp Camii

One of the small group of companions of the Prophet, **Eyüp Ensari** was killed during the first Arab siege of Constantinople (674–678); a condition of the peace treaty signed following the siege was that his tomb be preserved. Later, the mosque here, **Eyüp Camii**, hosted the investiture ceremonies of the Ottoman sultans: indeed, mosque and tomb face each other across the courtyard that was used for the ceremony. The exact site is marked by a raised platform surrounded by railings, from which two plane trees grow.

The original mosque, built by Mehmet the Conqueror in honour of Eyüp Ensari, was destroyed in the eighteenth century, probably by the same earthquake that put paid to Fatih Camii. The present Baroque replacement, filled with light, gold, pale stone and white marble, was completed in 1800. The **tomb of Eyüp Ensari** (Tues–Sun 9.30am–4.30pm) is far more compelling, however (footwear should be removed and women should cover their heads before entering). Its facade and vestibule are covered in tile panels from many different periods and, although the overall effect is a bit overwhelming, the panels constitute a beautiful and varied display of the art form; you could spend weeks visiting individual buildings to see as many different designs and styles.

Other tombs and Eyüp cemetery

There are a number of other important tombs in the Eyüp district, as it was a popular place of burial for Ottoman dignitaries. Two of these, the **tombs of Sokollu Mehmet Paşa and Siyavus Paşa** (Tues–Sun 9.30am–4.30pm), stand opposite each other on either side of Camii Kebir Caddesi, five minutes' walk from Eyüp Camii towards the Golden Horn. Five years before his assassination, Sokollu Mehmet Paşa commissioned Mimar Sinan to build his tomb. It is an elegantly proportioned octagonal building of around 1574, notable for its stained glass, some of which is original; connected to the tomb by an elegant three-arched colonnade is a former Koran school. Siyavus Paşa's tomb, on the other hand, was probably actually built by Sinan for the children of Siyavus Paşa, who had died young. It's decorated with İznik tiles.

Eyüp is still a popular burial place and the hills above the mosque are covered in plain modern stones interspersed with beautiful Ottoman tombs. To the north of the mosque, off Silahtarağa Caddesi, Karyağdı Sokak leads up into the **Eyüp cemetery**. Following the signs up this lane through the graveyard – most beautiful at sunset with an arresting view of the Golden Horn – it takes about twenty minutes from Eyüp Camii to reach the romantic **Pierre Loti Café** (daily 8am–midnight) overlooking the Horn, where waiters in Ottoman costume serve up Turkish coffee. The café was made famous by the autobiographical novel of Pierre Loti (the pen name of Julien Marie Viaud), a young French naval officer and writer of romantic novels and travel books, who fell in love with the green eyes of a Circassian harem girl called Aziyade in nineteenth-century İstanbul.

Karaköy, Galata and Beyoğlu

Directly across the Golden Horn from Eminönü is the district of **Karaköy**, reached via the Galata bridge. It's been a port area since Byzantine times, when the north shore of the Horn was a separate settlement from Constantinople. In the late nineteenth century, the dockside was home to İstanbul's least salubrious rooming-houses and seediest taverns.

Above Karaköy's docks the settlement at **Galata**, initially known as Sykai, is as old as Constantinople itself. The **Genoese occupation** of Galata began when they gave active support to Byzantine emperor Michael Paleologus in his attempt to drive out the Crusaders. In return, he signed a treaty in March 1261, signing Galata over to them as a semi-independent colony. The Byzantines no doubt lived to regret the privileges granted to the colony when the Genoese repaid them with neutrality during the final siege of Constantinople by Mehmet the Conqueror. The new sultan showed his gratitude by allowing the Genoese to retain their commercial and religious establishments, although arms were to be handed over and the walls torn down. The Genoese subsequently built one of the city's most famous landmarks here, the **Galata Tower**.

During the early centuries of Ottoman rule, many Spanish Jews, Moorish traders, Greeks and Armenians settled in Galata, which became established as the city's **European quarter**. In time, foreign powers set up their embassies in the area, and it became a popular haunt of visiting merchants, traders, seamen and adventurers.

While Galata was used exclusively to define the area within the city walls, the word **Pera** (Greek for "beyond" or "across") was originally used interchangeably with Galata to refer to the area across the Horn from Constantinople. Later it came to denote the district above Galata, present-day **Beyoğlu**, to which the European quarter gradually spread as Galata became too crowded. By the mid-nineteenth century Pera was the area of choice for the main European powers to build their ambassadorial palaces. The declining empire increasingly relied on the skills of the Galata bankers to secure funds from abroad. The fiscal boom led to the construction of new buildings, designed to reflect the power and status of their owners, and it is this imported **architecture** that still dominates Beyoğlu. The completion of the Orient Express Railway in 1889 encouraged an influx of tourists, accommodated by a growing number of large hotels, such as the splendid *Pera Palas Hotel*. Around the same time Pera became a favoured haunt – and subject matter – of a school of **artists** heavily influenced by European "salon" painting of the nineteenth century.

The **nightlife** of the quarter was notoriously riotous even in the seventeenth century, when one Evliya Çelebi wrote "Whoever says Galata says taverns." By the nineteenth and early twentieth centuries, the area had become fashionable for its operettas, music halls, inns, cinemas and restaurants, and it was only after the exodus of the Greek population from İstanbul in the 1920s that Galata and Pera began to lose their cosmopolitan flavour. Other minorities left too, partly as a result of the wealth tax imposed on ethnic communities between 1942 and 1944 and the area declined rapidly.

In recent years Beyoğlu has been transformed. Its main boulevard, **İstiklâl Caddesi**, was pedestrianized in 1990 and its antique tramway reinstalled (see "City

Crossing the Golden Horn

Any number of **buses** cross the Golden Horn via two bridges: **Galata Köprüsü** (from Eminönü) and **Atatürk Köprüsü** (from Aksaray). Most useful is the #T1 from Eminönü, which crosses Galata Köprüsü to Karaköy and follows the coast road around to the ferry terminal at Kabataş before climbing the hill to Taksim Square. From there the route continues in a loop to cross the other Golden Horn bridge, Atatürk Köprüsü, travelling under the Aqueduct of Valens on Atatürk Bulvarı to Aksaray, where it takes a left turn along Ordu Caddesi through to Beyazit before skirting around Sultanahmet back to Eminönü. The #T4 follows exactly the same route but in the opposite direction.

From Eminönü there are regular commuter **ferries** on the short hop across to Karaköy, though there is little need to catch one when the easiest and most interesting way to cross the Horn is to **walk over the Galata Köprüsü** from Eminönü past the fishermen and hawkers.

transport", p.118). Today, the thoroughfare bustles with life virtually twenty-four hours a day, and the side streets off it are host to scores of lively bars, clubs and restaurants, many of which stay open until six in the morning. The sleazier side of Beyoğlu culture has not completely disappeared, but the "adult" cinemas, hostess bars and unofficial brothels that remain have been exiled to a few streets between İstiklâl Caddesi and the parallel Tarlabaşı Bulvarı.

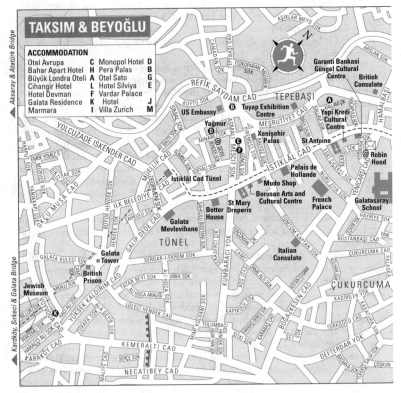

Across Galata bridge to Karaköy

Despite being the vital link between the two sides of European İstanbul, the **Galata Köprüsü** (Galata bridge) is not exactly beautiful. Recent developments have improved things, however, with the shops beneath the surface road now thriving, and the tram rumbling across the bridge. In spite of the traffic fumes, the stroll across is very pleasant – past the throngs of anglers and with great views of both shores. On the northern side, look out for the small market on the left where bucket-loads of live fish and crabs are sold.

Once over the bridge, you will have reached the port area of **Karaköy**, from where you can either walk up to Beyoğlu on the steep Yüksek Kaldırım Caddesi, past the Galata Tower, or take the **Tünel** underground train (daily 9am–9pm; 0.90YTL); the Tünel entrance is on Tersane Caddesi, just to the left of the first road junction beyond the bridge. There is also a useful **tourist office** in Karaköy's main ferry terminal to the right of the bridge.

Karaköy's port and Ottoman shipyard was once enclosed within the walls of the Castle of Galata. In 1446 the Byzantines stretched a great chain across the mouth of the Horn to prevent enemy ships from entering. Originally constructed around 580, the subterranean keep of the castle is thought to be preserved as the **Yeraltı Cami**, or "Underground Mosque", on Kemankeş Caddesi. Inside is a forest of thick columns, supporting a low, vaulted ceiling. Two tombs in one corner

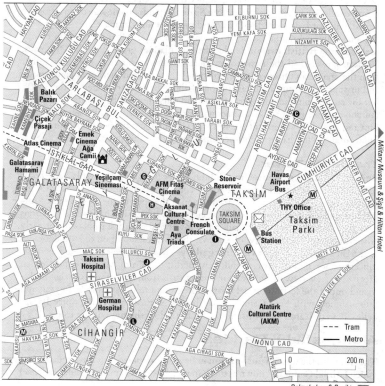

Dolmabahçe & Beşiktaş ▼

purport to be those of Muslim martyrs killed in the first Arab siege of Byzantium (674–678 AD).

At the far end of the port area is another mosque, the **Kiliç Ali Paşa Camii**, constructed in 1580 by Sinan, and essentially a smaller copy of Aya Sofya. Kiliç Ali Paşa was one of the great Ottoman admirals, an Italian by birth who was captured by Algerian pirates and converted to Islam.

Galata and the Galata Tower

The most obvious landmark in the area is the Galata Tower, but there are a few other interesting places to stop and break the steep ascent on the way up from Galata bridge to İstiklâl Caddesi. The Zülfaris Synagogue on Meydanı Perçemli Sokak is home to the **Jewish Museum** (Mon & Thurs 10am–4pm, Fri & Sun 10am–2pm; 1YTL). Its small but fascinating display includes documents and photographs donated by local Jewish families, chronicling Turkish Jews since they first came to the country over seven hundred years ago.

About 400m below the Galata Tower, on Yanık Kapı (or "Burned Gate") Sokak, is the only remaining Genoese **city gate**. Somewhat the worse for wear, it still boasts a marble slab bearing the Cross of St George. Of the many churches that once crowded the narrow streets of Galata, few original structures now remain. One notable exception is the unusual building on Fütühat Sokak, now a mosque known as **Arap Camii**. With its tall square tower and pyramidal roof, it was, under the Genoese, the largest church in Galata. It was converted into a mosque to serve the needs of the Moorish community that settled here in the early sixteenth century following their expulsion from Spain. It stands on one side of an attractive closed courtyard, decorated with assorted pieces of ancient marble.

About 100m below the tower, at Galata Külesi Sokak 61, is an even more unusual relic, the **British prison**. Under the capitulations granted by the Ottomans, Western powers had the right to try their citizens under their own law, rather than the draconian Ottoman code, so consulates possessed their own courthouses and prisons. The court as an institution of the consulate originated in the 1600s, but the current building dates from 1904 and today houses the **Galata House** restaurant-café (see p.186). The owners will happily show you graffiti left by former inmates, including a sketch of the Rock of Gibraltar and the poignant words, "An unfavourable wind has brought the ship of my life to this shore."

The Galata Tower

Built in 1349 by the Genoese, the **Galata Tower** (Galata Kulesi; daily 9am–8pm; 8YTL) sits on the site of a former tower constructed by Justinian in 528. Originally known as the Tower of Christ, it stood at the apex of the several sets of fortifications that surrounded the Genoese city-state. It has had a number of functions over the centuries, including a jail, a fire tower and even a springboard for early adventurers attempting to fly. Nowadays, there's a restaurant on the top floor.

At 61m high, the tower's **viewing gallery** – reached by elevator – offers magnificent panoramas of the city and views across the Sea of Marmara and Golden Horn. The best view of Eminönü in particular is from here: the boats that nudge in and out of the ferry terminal form a foreground to the skyline of Beyazit and Sultanahmet, with Yeni Cami directly below Nuruosmaniye, the Spice Bazaar below Beyazit Camii and Rüstem Paşa Camii below the Beyazit fire tower.

Along İstiklâl Caddesi

The exit from the upper **Tünel station** in Beyoğlu is fronted by a small square from which **İstiklâl Caddesi** (known as the "Grand Rue de Pera" prior to Independence)

In the barber's chair

A trip to the *kuaförü* or *berber* plays an important role in Turkish male grooming and is a part of daily social life, especially as Turkish barbers tend to double up as layman psychiatrists. The ritual starts with a read of the newspaper and a glass of apple tea – or a chat about football if you speak some Turkish – whilst you wait your turn.

Once you are in the chair, much hairwashing and rubbing down with fluffy towels follows until it is time to try to communicate with the barber what you'd like to look like when you leave. Important phrases to remember include the following: *Ucundan azıcık* (don't take too much off); *Sıfıra vur* (take it all off); *Sakalı alalım* (give me a shave, literally "take my beard"); *Sinek kaydı* ("a fly would slide") or *Kaymak gibi* ("like cream") both meaning clean shaven; *Pis sakal* (designer stubble); and *Sıhhatler olsun!* ("good health to you", an expression only used after a haircut or shave). A good tactic is to ask for something short in the first place and be ready to modify your expectations – remember that clippers are an especially valued item in the Turkish barbering world.

After the haircut there may well be a pause for more tea and/or a cigarette, by both the client and the barber, before he lathers you up for a shave with a cut-throat razor. This is followed by a dousing down with jaw-stinging cologne before the grooming stage begins in earnest. Ear hairs are zapped with a lit cotton bud soaked in methylated spirits, wayward cheek hairs are attacked with twisted cotton, and nose hairs are plucked with such dexterity the numbness lasts only a fraction of a second. The whole process is rounded off by a massage of the neck and shoulders, and possibly another hairwash and dabbing of the eardrums to remove any unwanted wax.

The whole experience will last about an hour and cost little more than 10YTL. There are *kuaförü* or *berber*s all over İstanbul; try Cihangir Erkek Kuaförü, Akarsu Cad 49, Cihangir, just below Beyoğlu ℡0212/251 1660 (Mon–Sat 9am–7pm), which is used to foreigners and where some English is spoken.

---

heads 1.5km north towards Taksim Square. Make a brief detour a few metres down to the right, along Galipdede Caddesi, and an unassuming doorway on the left leads to the courtyard of the **Galata Mevlevîhane**, also referred to as the Divan Literature Museum (daily except Tues 9am–4pm; 2YTL). A former monastery and ceremonial hall of the whirling dervishes (see p.616), the building now serves as a museum to the Mevlevî sect, which was banned by Atatürk along with other Sufi organizations because of its political affiliations. Exhibitions include musical instruments and dervish costumes and the building itself has been beautifully restored to late eighteenth-century splendour. The Whirling Dervishes perform *sema* dances to Sufi music at 5pm on the second and last Sunday of every month (May–September at 5pm, October–April at 3pm; 25YTL), with the main ceremony on December 17, the annual Mevlâna holiday.

Further along İstiklâl Caddesi, on your right, is the **Botter House,** a fine Art Nouveau apartment building with a carved stone facade and wrought-iron balcony. Commissioned in 1901 as a showroom, workshop and family house by Dutchman Jan Botter, tailor and couturier to Sultan Abdülhamid II, it is one of a number of structures around İstanbul designed by the Italian architect Raimondo D'Aronco. Further up on the right is the newly restored **Palais de Hollande** at İstiklâl Caddesi 393. Built in 1858 on the site of the home of Cornelis Haga, the first Dutch diplomat in Constantinople during the fifteenth century, it now houses the Consulate to the Netherlands.

Many other buildings lining İstiklâl Caddesi are also typically European, like the **Mudo** shop at no. 401, with a beautifully preserved Art Nouveau interior, and selling very expensive toys and retro or kitsch ornaments. The oldest church in the area is **St Mary Draperis** at no. 429, which dates from 1789, although the

Franciscans built their first church on the site in the early fifteenth century. Better known is the Franciscan **church of St Antoine** at no. 325, a fine example of red-brick neo-Gothic architecture. Originally founded in 1725 it was demolished to make way for a tramway at the beginning of the century and rebuilt in 1913.

Further along İstiklâl Caddesi you can detour down Nuru Ziya Sok to the imposing **French Palace**, with its large central courtyard and formally laid-out gardens, the residence of ambassadors and consuls from 1831 until the present day. Below the Palace, on Tom Tom Kaptan Sok, stands the **Italian Consulate**, originally the Palazzo di Venezia, built in the seventeenth century. Casanova stayed here in 1744, and according to his memoirs he didn't make a single conquest, although one Ismail Efendi claims to have been seduced by him. Turning left off İstiklâl Caddesi, Hamalbaşı Sok, leads in 100m to the **British Consulate**, an impressive Renaissance-style structure, designed by Charles Barry, architect of the British Houses of Parliament.

The northernmost stretch of İstiklâl Caddesi and its offshoots boasts many of the area's bars and restaurants, all within easy walking distance of one another (see p.188 for reviews). The famous **Çiçek Pasaj** (Flower Passage) had its heyday in the 1930s when the music and entertainment was supplied courtesy of anti-Bolshevik Russian emigrés. These days it's home to a collection of attractive but rather over-priced and touristy restaurants – it's far better to head through to the **Balik Pazarı** (fish market), particularly **Nevizade Sokak**, a street dedicated to fish restaurants (all with outside tables), and incredibly lively bars and clubs.

Taksim Square and around

At the northern end of İstiklâl Caddesi is **Taksim Square**, the heart of modern İstanbul. The size of Taksim Square is undeniably impressive, which is just as well since there's little else to be said in its favour. As an imitation of a grand Western plaza, it's not a great success, lacking the essential monumental architecture to balance its broad expanse and robbed of any real atmosphere by its confusing traffic system. It is however, a central pivot of İstanbul's, and indeed Turkey's, main business area and is regarded as a symbol of the secular Turkish republic. Indeed in 1997, when the fleeting Islamist Virtue Party's government unveiled plans to build a mosque in the square, they were soon forced to abandon the idea in the face of public disapproval.

Taksim Square

Taksim in Turkish means "distribution" and the low **stone reservoir** on the south side is the building from which Taksim Square takes its name. Constructed in 1732 to distribute water brought from the Belgrade Forest by aqueduct, the *taksim*'s octagonal annexe, located on the İstiklâl Caddesi side, has stone bird-houses above its door that are carved to look like miniature Ottoman houses.

Steps on the north side of the square above the main bus terminal lead up to the pleasant **Taksim Parkı**, with its bench-lined paths and open-air tea gardens. The rare occurrence of a park here – wholly untypical of traditional Islamic city planning – is a glorious relief after you've been grubbing around in the backstreets of the old quarters.

The **Atatürk Cultural Centre** (Atatürk Kültür Merkezi or AKM; see p.198) is to the east of the square and is one of the leading venues for İstanbul's various international festivals. It is also home to the State Opera and Ballet, the Symphony Orchestra and the State Theatre Company (though tickets for anything worthwhile tend to sell out a long time in advance).

The Military Museum

The **Military Museum** (Askeri Müzesi; Wed–Sun 9am–5pm; 2YTL) is about 1.5km north of Taksim Square, along Cumhuriyet Caddesi. It's well worth visiting, not least to hear the marching band, which plays outside on summer afternoons between 3pm and 4pm when the museum is open. To get there, walk or catch a bus north along Cumhuriyet Caddesi to the İstanbul Radyoevi (radio building). Turn right after the building and follow the road around to the left behind the military barracks, continue along Gümüz Sokak, past the *Lutfi Kırdar Spor Salonu*, and the museum entrance is on the right.

The **Mehter Band** originated in 1289. Its members were janissaries, who would accompany the sultan into battle, and the band became an institution, symbolizing the power and independence of the Ottoman Empire. During public performances, band members sang songs about their hero-ancestors and Ottoman battle victories. They had considerable influence in Europe, helping create new musical styles, such as Spanish *a la turca*, and inspiring numerous composers (examples include Mozart's *Marcia Turca* and Beethoven's *Ruinen von Athens, Opus 113*). The kettledrum, *kös* in Turkish, was also introduced into the West as a result of interest in the Mehter Band. The band was abolished by Mahmut II in 1826, along with the janissary corps, and only re-established in 1914 when new instruments were added. The pieces played nowadays include some dating from the seventeenth and eighteenth centuries and others written by Giuseppi Donizetti for Mahmut II's new army.

Housed in the military academy where Atatürk received some of his education, the museum itself is one of the most impressive in the country, evidence of the Turks' intense pride in their military history. Inside, there is a comprehensive collection of military memorabilia proudly displayed and labelled in English. The most striking exhibits are the cotton- and silk-embroidered tents used by campaigning sultans. You'll also find a rich collection of Ottoman armour and weaponry, including beautifully ornamented *jambiyah* daggers, and a piece of the chain used by the Byzantines to close off the entrance of the Golden Horn in 1453.

Hasköy

Hasköy lies a couple of kilometres further up the Golden Horn from Beyoğlu and Karaköy, north of the Atatürk Köprüsü. For centuries the area was a Jewish village, and it still boasts a number of synagogues, cemeteries and many old Jewish houses, though most of Istanbul's approximately 20,000 Jews have now moved further out of the city. It was also the location of an Ottoman naval shipyard and of a royal park, which was cultivated as a fruit orchard throughout the centuries of Ottoman rule. Today however, it's a largely unremarkable suburb of old dockyards and light industrial buildings, with only the excellent **Rahmi M. Koç Industrial Museum** at Hasköy Cad 27 (Tues–Fri 10am–5pm, Sat & Sun 10am–7pm; 6.5YTL; ⓦwww.rmk-museum.org.tr) making the trek out here worthwhile. Constructed in the eighteenth century as a factory making anchors and their chains, the museum's arching brickwork and spacious halls have been authentically restored. The work was carried out by Rahmi M. Koç, one of Turkey's most famous – and wealthiest – industrialists, to house his private collection of models, machines, vehicles and toys, originating from all over Turkey and Europe but mainly from Britain. The best time to visit is Saturday afternoon when there are special exhibitions based around the collection of slot machines, the old Kadıköy–Moda tram and the history of flight.

Upstairs, the starboard main engine of the Kalender steam ferry, made in New-castle-upon-Tyne in 1911 and decommissioned in the 1980s, is the main exhibit – press a button and you can see its pistons move. Downstairs are a number of old bikes, from penny-farthings to an early Royal Enfield motorbike complete with basket chair for side carriage. The model railway is disappointing in terms of moving parts; far better is the ship's bridge, reconstructed from a number of Turkish and British vessels of the 1920s to 1940s. All the instruments are explained in English, with sound effects and working parts, including an echo sounder, an early dimmer switch and a very loud alarm bell. The museum's ongoing projects include raising the Australian navy's first submarine, sunk off Gallipoli in World War I. For those disinclined to contemplate the marvels of the industrial age, the *Café du Levant* (closed Mon) in the museum grounds is a good French bistro.

The easiest way to get here is to either catch **bus #47/A** from Eminönü, on the opposite side of the Horn, or the **ferry** that runs between Eminönü and Eyüp, getting off at Kasimpaşa ferry terminal, from where it is a short walk to the museum.

Tophane

Tophane is a mixed area of run-down dockland dotted with venerable Ottoman buildings, most notable of which are the **Kiliç Paşa Camii** dating from 1780, and the more recent **Nusretiye Camii** (1822). The district is also home to the city's contemporary art collection, **Istanbul Modern** (Tues–Sun 10am–6pm; 5YTL, free on Thurs 10am–2pm), in a revamped warehouse on the edge of the Bosphorus, just in front of the Nusretiye Camii. The museum's interior is all big, blank white walls and an exposed ventilation system, with picture windows giving views across the Bosphorus to the Topkapı Palace. The collection includes the best of modern Turkish art, as well as some intriguing video installations from foreign artists. There's a reference library, a cinema showing arts and independent movies, and a trendy café with a terrace right on the edge of the Bosphorus. It may not be on the scale of the Guggenheim or Tate Modern, but it is well worth a visit. For it to have to come to fruition under a so-called Islamic government shows just how far Turkey has changed in the last few years.

To reach the museum from Sultanahmet, take the tramway to the stop just west of Nusretiye Camii, from where it's a three-minute walk.

Beşiktaş

Northeast of Taksim Square, along the Bosphorus, the busy suburb of **Beşiktaş** is one of the best-served transport hubs in the city. Most visitors to Beşiktaş are here to see the Dolmabahçe Palace, successor to Topkapı as the residence of the Ottoman sultans. However, it's worth aiming to spend a few more hours in the neighbourhood if you can, to visit the city's excellent Maritime Museum, as well as Yıldız Parkı and palace. It's also home to one of İstanbul's three major football teams (see box opposite).

Concrete shopping centres and a sprawling fruit and vegetable market cluster around the main shore road and **ferry terminal**, in front of which stands the **bus station**. To get here take bus #23/B, #B/2, #40/A or #40 from Taksim, or #25, #25/A or #30 from Eminönü; ferries run to and from Kadıköy and Üsküdar.

Fever pitch

İstanbul has three top football teams, each of which receive fanatical support – match times remain one of the few occasions when the city streets fall silent. Having said this, attendances at matches (as opposed to TV viewing) have fallen, and Galatasaray's move to the massive Atatürk Stadium was short-lived as fans refused to put up with the journey to the suburbs and the atmosphereless, half-empty ground. Beşiktaş, Fenerbahçe and Galatasaray dominate the Turkish league season (Aug–May), during which the other smaller teams from the rest of Turkey routinely line up for a battering from the İstanbul giants. There are two Turkish daily newspapers, *Fotomaç* and *Fanatik*, devoted almost entirely to the three İstanbul heavyweights, and matches are staggered over each weekend in season so television coverage of the three doesn't clash. Virtually every male in Turkey supports one of the **big İstanbul three**, no matter where he lives, with his local team (excepting Trabzonspor fanatics) coming second.

Galatasaray are the only Turkish club side to have achieved European success, beating Arsenal in the 2000 EUEFA cup final. Their stranglehold on the domestic front, however, has been broken in recent years and Atatürk's team, Fenerbahçe, are currently top dogs. They have won a record number of Turkish league championships and managed to inflict Manchester United's first ever European home defeat in 1996. Beşiktaş, İstanbul's third team (though don't mention this statistic to their fans), tends to favour foreign coaches and players to keep them competitive with the other two, but have managed only one league title in recent years. The most exciting matches to watch are the local derbies, after which the streets fill with flag-waving supporters and every taxi driver in town has his hand on his car horn. After Turkey came third in the 2002 World Cup, an estimated million and a half of the city's residents took to the streets to welcome the Turkish team home – almost all the players belonged to one of the three İstanbul clubs.

Beşiktaş (☏0212/236 7202, ⓦwww.besiktasjk.com) play at the most convenient and attractive ground of the three, İnönü Stadium on Kadırgalar Cad, between Taksim and Beşiktaş, opposite the Dolmabahçe Palace; walk down the hill, or take bus #23/B from Taksim Square or #30 from Sultanahmet or Eminönü. The wealthiest club, **Fenerbahçe** (☏0216/369 0784, ⓦwww.fenerbahce.com), play at the Şükrü Saracoğlu Stadyumu on Bağdat Cad in Kızıltoprak on the Asian side of the Bosphorus; take a ferry to Kadıköy, then a dolmuş marked "Cadde Bostan". **Galatasaray** (☏0212/251 5707, ⓦwww.webaslan.com) play at the Ali Sami Yen Stadyumu in Mecidiyeköy; catch any bus marked "Mecidiyeköy" from near the *McDonalds* in Taksim Square. Tickets are sold at the stadiums two days before a match. For regular fixtures tickets range from 22–200YTL, derby matches 44–275YTL. Beşiktaş and Fenerbahçe tickets are also available online from Biletix (ⓦwww.biletix.com) and larger Migros supermarkets as well as branches of the clothing shop Vakkorama, though Galatasaray tickets are only available at the stadium.

Dolmabahçe Palace

Dolmabahçe Palace (daily except Mon & Thurs 9am–4pm; Selâmlik 12YTL, Harem 8YTL) is the largest and most sumptuous of all the palaces on the Bosphorus, with an impressive 600-metre-long waterside frontage. Built in the nineteenth century by various members of the Balian family, it's not so much magnificent as grotesque, an excessive display of ostentatious wealth suggesting that good taste suffered along with the fortunes of the Ottoman Empire. Indeed, critics see the palace's wholesale adoption of Western architectural forms as a last-ditch effort to muster some respect for a crumbling and defeated empire.

The palace lies on the site of the harbour from which Mehmet the Conqueror launched his attack on Constantinople. The harbour was completely filled with

△ Dolmabahçe Palace

stones on the order of Ahmet I at the beginning of the seventeenth century (*dolmabahçe* means "filled garden") and later became a shoreside grove of small palaces and pavilions, set aside for imperial use. These were demolished to make way for Sultan Abdül-Mecid's new enterprise: a palace to replace Topkapı as the imperial residence of the Ottoman sultans. It was built by Armenian architect Karabet Balian and his son Nikoğos between 1843 and 1856 and, as is often pointed out on the guided tour, everything you see coloured yellow is **gold**. The decor is a virtual assault on the senses, but it's worth trying to ignore the worst of the excesses and concentrate on the (slightly) less vulgar palace highlights, such as the inlaid parquet floors, translucent pink-alabaster imperial baths or the famous double staircase with crystal balusters.

The palace is divided into **selâmlik** and **harem** by the 36-metre-high **throne room** (double the height of the rest of the rooms), held up by 56 elaborate columns. The ceremonies conducted here were accompanied by an orchestra playing European marches and watched by women of the harem through the *kafes*, grilles behind which women were kept hidden even in the days of Westernization and reform. The four-tonne chandelier in the throne room, one of the largest ever made, with 750 bulbs, was a present from Queen Victoria. Atatürk, the founder of the Turkish Republic, died here in his private apartment in 1938.

In the east wing of the palace, the former apartments of the heir to the throne house the **Museum of Fine Arts** (Resim ve Heykel Müzesi; Wed–Sun 10am–4pm; free), usually entered from the Kaymakamlık building, which used to house the palace staff, around 300m further along the main road from the Dolmabahçe entrance. The best of the collection dates from the late nineteenth and early twentieth centuries, and gives an intriguing insight into the lifestyle and attitudes of the late Ottoman Turks. Highlights are the works of Osman Hamdi Bey (1842–1910) – the first Ottoman Muslim painter to have his work displayed abroad – including *Woman with Mimosas*, and the wonderful painting of a mosque doorway by Osman Hamdi's pupil, Şevret Dağ.

The Maritime Museum

Back towards the ferry landing in Beşiktaş, the **Maritime Museum** (Deniz Müzesi; daily except Wed & Thurs 9am–12.30pm & 1.30–5pm; 2YTL) on Barbaros Hayrettin Paşa Iskelesı Sok, off Beşiktaş Caddesi, is one of the most entertaining museums in İstanbul. The collection is divided between two buildings, the one facing the water housing sea-going craft while the other, on Cezayir Caddesi, is devoted to the maritime history of the Ottoman Empire and the Turkish Republic. Most of the labels are in Turkish but the best of the exhibits – such as the enormous wooden figureheads depicting tigers and swans, and the display of items from Atatürk's yacht, the *Savarona* – need little explanation. Next door, the exhibition continues with a collection of caïques, which were used to row the sultans to and from their homes along the Bosphorus. The oarsmen – the *Bostanci* – reputedly barked like dogs whilst they rowed so as not to overhear the sultans talking. The largest of these caïques, dating from 1648, needed an incredible 144 oarsmen to power it. The lovely mother-of-pearl inlay of the sultan's kiosk can be viewed from above via a purpose-built walkway.

Çırağan Sarayı

A ten-minute walk from the main square in front of Beşiktaş ferry terminal, in the direction of Ortaköy, brings you to the **Çırağan Sarayı** on Çırağan Caddesi. This sumptuous palace, with 300m of marble facade facing the shore, is now a luxury hotel but was built originally as a palace when Sultan Abdulmecid decided to move his official residence from Dolmabahçe in 1855. It was completed in 1874, during the reign of Abdülaziz, and it was here that Abdülaziz was either murdered or committed suicide – the cause of death was never established. Murat V was later imprisoned here after being deposed by his brother. Following a period of abandonment, Çırağan housed the Turkish parliament for two years in 1908, before a fire reduced it to a blackened shell in 1910. It was restored in 1991 to its present magnificence as İstanbul's foremost luxury hotel, the *Çırağan Palace & Kempinski Hotel* (see p.126).

Like Dolmabahçe, Çırağan was designed along the lines of a European palace, but Arabic touches were added on the orders of Abdülaziz – such as the honeycomb stalactites decorating the windows. Unfortunately, the modern block of the *Kempinski Hotel* slightly mars the view of the palace from the Bosphorus, but the *Gazebo* restaurant provides a magnificent setting for a traditional afternoon tea, while *Tuğra* (see p.190) is the place for a grand Ottoman night out.

A bridge crosses Çırağan Caddesi from the palace to Yıldız Parkı, which allowed the harem women private access to the park – on the odd occasion they were given permission to enter of course.

Yıldız Parkı

Opposite the Çırağan Sarayı on Çırağan Caddesi is the public entrance to **Yıldız Parkı** (daily: summer 9am–6pm; winter 9am–5.30pm; free), a vast wooded area dotted with mansions, pavilions, lakes and gardens, which was the centre of the Ottoman Empire for thirty years during the reign of Abdülhamid II. The buildings in and around the park constitute Yıldız Palace, a collection of structures in the old Ottoman style that are a total contrast to Dolmabahçe. Most of the pavilions date from the reign of Abdülaziz, but it was Abdülhamid – a reforming sultan whose downfall was brought about by his intense paranoia – who transformed Yıldız into a small city and power base.

Its superb hillside location makes Yıldız Parkı one of the most popular places in İstanbul for city-dwellers thirsting for fresh air and open spaces: on public holidays the park is always crowded. To reach the palace buildings it's best to return to the main square in Beşiktaş and take any bus or minibus up Barbaros Bulvarı (it's not far to walk, but it's a steep hill). Get off just after the British Council building, and follow the signs to Yıldız Üniversitesi and Şehir Müzesi off to the right. Of the many buildings in the park, only the Yıldız Palace Museum and the Şale Köşkü are open to the public, though it's easy enough to wander around the outside of the other pavilions, each with marvellous terraces and panoramic views of the Bosphorus.

Şale Köşkü and Yıldız Palace Museum

The most important surviving building in the park is the **Şale Köşkü** (daily except Mon & Thurs 9.30am–5pm; Oct–Feb closes 4pm; guided tours obligatory, 4YTL). The first of the pavilion's three separate sections was modelled on a Swiss chalet, while the second and third sections were built to receive Kaiser Wilhelm II on his first and second state visits, in 1889 and 1898. The most impressive room, the Ceremonial Hall, takes up the greater part of the third section, with a Hereke carpet so big (approximately 400 square metres) that part of a wall was knocked down to install it. In the attractive dining room, at the top of the central stairway in the central section, the dining chairs were carved by the reclusive Abdülhamid himself.

In the same complex, the **Yıldız Palace Museum** (Yıldız Sarayı Müzesi; daily except Mon 9.30pm–6pm; 2YTL) is housed in Abdülhamid's converted carpentry workshop, and exhibits items and furniture from throughout the palace. Whilst not in their original grand settings in the pavilions, there are some exquisite porcelain pieces, giant vases and more of the joinery produced by the sultan himself.

Ortaköy

Ortaköy is 1km from Beşiktaş, past Yıldız Parkı and the Çırağan palace. This former Bosphorus backwater was traditionally an area of tolerance – a mosque, church and synagogue have existed side by side for centuries – though its erstwhile character has been hijacked by flash nightclubs, expensive restaurants and theme bars springing up in even the tiniest of fishermen's cottages.

To get to Ortaköy take a #23/B, #B/2, #40/A or #40 **bus** from Taksim, or a #25, #25/A or #30 from Eminönü; or you can take a bus or **ferry** to Beşiktaş and walk (about 15min). This last way is the best bet on public holidays and weekends as the traffic is dreadful on this road.

When Ortaköy was just a tiny fishing village, university students and teachers used to gather here to sip tea and discuss weighty topics. It's a time remembered in the name of the Sunday *entel*, or "intellectual", **market**, a crowded affair held on the waterfront square, which sells all kinds of arts and crafts. There are also daily market stalls selling trendy silver jewellery and sunglasses on the waterfront, or **Ortaköy boardwalk** as it's rather pretentiously known. This is also the location of the attractive, Baroque **Büyük Mecidiye Camii**, built in 1855, and some of the liveliest teahouses on the Bosphorus. Just to the left of the mosque is a small jetty from where short **cruises** head up the Bosphorus as far as the second (Fatih) bridge, touching on both the European and Asian sides en route for (3YTL). Cruises also head the other direction, down to Kız Kulesi (Maiden's Tower; see p.183) off Üsküdar at 1pm, 3pm and 5pm (7YTL). Finally, the small **Sinan hamam** (daily men 8am–10pm, women 8am–7.30pm) in the centre of the district is much better value than many of the larger baths, at under 12YTL per person, or 16YTL with a massage.

Kadıköy, Moda and Haydarpaşa

Across the Bosphorus, on the Asian side, the suburb of **Kadıköy** may at first seem unpromising, with only views of the European shore to recommend it. However, it's a lively place, with good shops, restaurants, bars and cinemas. Towards the end of the nineteenth century, when the introduction of steam-driven ferries made commuting across to Beyoğlu feasible, Kadıköy became a popular residential area for wealthy Greeks, Armenians and foreign businesspeople. The main road south from Kadıköy is **Bağdat Caddesi**, part of the old silk route from China though it's of little architectural merit, and today is a place to pose, and to shop for the clothes to pose in.

In Kadıköy itself, the best place for clothes is **Gen Azim Gündüz Caddesi** (formerly Bahariye Caddesi), which is a right turn off Söğütlüçeşme Caddesi, the wide, steep street leading uphill from the ferry jetty. There's more fun to be had sorting through the great mounds of junk, old carpets and kilims that can be found for sale in the **bit pazar** (flea market) on Özellik Sokak.

Directly south of Kadıköy is the more upmarket suburb of **Moda**, reached by taking Moda Caddesi off Söğütlüçeşme Caddesi and turning left up any of its side-streets. It's a pleasant area for aimless wandering, particularly popular with courting couples who cruise Moda Caddesi, stopping at *Ali Usta*, at no. 266, a well-known ice-cream parlour that attracts vast queues on summer evenings.

North of Kadıköy, across the bay, is the mainline **Haydarpaşa train station**, jutting out into the Bosphorus. Completed in 1908 by a German architect as part of Germany's grandiose plans for a Berlin to Baghdad railway, the palace-like building was presented to Sultan Abdül Hamit II by Kaiser Wilhelm II. The stained glass is particularly impressive, and it's well worth a look even if you are not heading into Asian Turkey by rail. You can reach it directly by ferry from Eminönü, or it's a ten-minute walk from Kadıköy ferry terminal.

Directly north of the station, between the sea and Tıbbiye Caddesi, is the Marmara University and the **British War Cemetery** (daily 7am–7pm), a beautifully kept spot sheltering the dead of the Crimean War and the two world wars. To find it, turn off Tıbbiye Caddesi into Burhan Felek Caddesi, between the university building and the military hospital. A few minutes' walk northeast of the university, along Kavak Iskele Caddesi, is the imposing **Selimiye Barracks** (closed to the public), whose northwest wing was used as a hospital by the British during the Crimean War (1854–56). **Florence Nightingale** lived and worked in the northern tower, where she reduced the death toll among patients from twenty percent to two percent, and established universally accepted principles of modern nursing.

Opposite the barracks, across Çeşme-i Kebir Sokak on Selimiye Camii Sokak, the **Selimiye Camii** was constructed, along with the nearby hamam, for the use of the barracks' soldiers. The largest Muslim graveyard in İstanbul, the **Karaca Ahmet Mezarlığı**, is a ten-minute walk away on Tıbbiye Caddesi, in the direction of Üsküdar. It's a sprawling place shadowed by ancient cypress trees, thought to have been founded in the mid-fourteenth century and now with an estimated one million graves. Any number of buses, including the useful #12 and #14, head north from Kadıköy, past the train station and slightly inland, to Üsküdar, passing the **Capitol** shopping mall (see p.203) in Altunizade.

Üsküdar

There's plenty of evidence of religious conservatism in **Üsküdar** (a corruption of "Scutari" – the name used for what was a separate town in the late Byzantine era), particularly in the dress of its inhabitants. The area has been characterized by wholesale migration from the more Islamic regions of Anatolia and has long been a centre of Islamic mystical sects.

To get to Üsküdar take a ferry from Eminönü or Beşiktaş, or bus #12 or #14 or a dolmuş from Kadıköy. You'll be dropped in Üsküdar's main square and quayside, which doubles as an enormous bus park. From here buses run up the Bosphorus, as far as Anadolu Kavağı (leaving from in front of İskele Camii on Paşa Liman Caddesi), and to the Black Sea resorts of Ağva and Sıle (see "Around İstanbul, p.217).

Although there are some fine imperial mosques in and around the suburb, modern Üsküdar is primarily renowned as a shopping centre. It has an abundance of street stalls selling fresh produce, particularly fish and vegetables, and innumerable family-run supermarkets that stock obscure varieties of Anatolian cheeses. Secondhand furniture and ornaments are sold at the **Üsküdar bit pazar** (flea market) in Büyük Hamam Sokak and there are also some reasonable jewellery and clothes shops. Along the quayside at **Salacak** are some good pavement cafés and bars, offering fantastic views of Topkapı Palace and İstanbul.

The most obvious mosque is **İskele** or **Mihrimah Camii**, opposite the ferry landing on İskele Meydanı. This sits on a high platform, fronted by an immense covered porch that is the perennial haunt of old men in knitted hats complaining about the changing times while they peruse the square below. Designed by Mimar Sinan and built in 1547–48, this is the only Ottoman mosque with three semi-domes (rather than two or four), a result of the requirements of a difficult site against the hillside behind.

Directly across the main square from the İskele Camii is the **Yeni Valide Camii**. Built between 1708 and 1710 by Ahmet III in honour of his mother, it is most easily identified by the Valide Sultan's green, birdcage-like tomb, whose meshed roof was designed to keep birds out while allowing rain in to water the garden tomb below (now rather untidily overgrown). There is an attractive *şadırvan* (ablutions fountain) in the courtyard; the grilles of its cistern are highly wrought, their pattern echoed in the stone carvings above.

One of the most attractive mosques in Üsküdar is the **Çinili Cami**, or Tiled Mosque, which dates from 1640. To get there on foot, take Hakimiyet-i Milliye Caddesi out of the centre and turn left into Çavuşdere Caddesi; after passing Çavuşdere fruit and veg market, continue to climb the same street and you'll see the mosque on your right. The tiles are mainly blues and turquoise, but there's a rare shade of green to be found in the *mihrab*. Below the mosque, in the same street, is the beautifully restored **Çinili Hamamı** (men 8am–10pm, women 8am–8pm; 12YTL), which retains its original central marble stones for massage and acres of marble revetments. It's an extremely clean hamam and the pride of its workers.

The **Atık Valide Külliyesi** is just a short walk from Çinili Cami: go back down Çavuşdere Caddesi and turn left into Çinili Hamam Sokak and you'll find the mosque on the right. Dating from 1583, the complex is a work of the master architect Mimar Sinan, built for Nur Banu, wife of Selim II and mother of Murat III. The mosque courtyard, meant to be the most beautiful in İstanbul, has been closed for restoration for a number of years and the mosque is entered through a side-door. Worth inspecting are the underside of the wooden galleries on three sides of the interior, which are beautifully painted, and the İznik tiles covering the *mihrab*.

From Üsküdar's main square, İskele Meydanı, minibuses to Ümraniye run past the foot of **Büyük Çamlıca**, the highest hill on the Asian side. If you get off at Kısıklı

Camii you can walk up Kısıklı–Büyük Çamlıca Caddesi, turning right just before the *Büyük Çamlıca Et Lokantası* to reach the park – a walk of fifteen minutes or so. The effort is rewarded by refreshingly cooler temperatures and by spectacular views of the Bosphorus and the European shore. The **café** on the hill (daily 9am–midnight) has been tastefully refurbished.

To the south of Üsküdar on an island in the Bosphorus, is the small white **Kız Kulesi** (Maiden's Tower), also known as Leander's Tower. Many myths are associated with it: in one a princess, who was prophesied to die from a snake bite, came here to escape her fate, only to succumb to it when a serpent was delivered to her retreat in a basket of fruit. The tower also featured in the 1999 James Bond film, *The World Is Not Enough*. It's now a **museum** (daily except Mon noon–7pm; free), doubling as an expensive restaurant in the evening. It can be reached from Salacak (on the main coast road between Üsküdar and Harem) by **boat** (midday–10pm; every twenty minutes) and from Ortaköy (see p.180) and Kabataş.

Eating

İstanbul is home to Turkey's best restaurants, including several that lavish time and skill on old Ottoman cuisine. The city has its fair share of top-class international restaurants, and, thanks to the lengthy coastline, fish is a firm menu favourite. Snacks, too, are ubiquitous, with kebab stands, pastry shops, fast-food outlets and cafés across the city catering to locals, workers and tourists alike. Restaurants around tourist honey-pot Sultanahmet tend to be of poorer quality and are more expensive than elsewhere in the city.

Workers' **cafés** and *lokanta*s open as early as 6am and serve until 4pm; other cafés generally open daily between 9am and 9pm. **Restaurants** open for lunch and dinner, with last orders at 10 or 11pm, with more popular areas (such as Nevizade Sokak) and live-music venues staying open until the early hours. In the more commercial districts, eateries follow the shops and close on a Sunday. **Credit cards** are widely accepted in all but the smallest restaurants. We've included telephone numbers for places where it's wise to **reserve a table**.

Cafés and restaurants are located on the relevant **maps**: Sultanahmet (p.121); Eminönü, Beyazit, Kumkapı and Laleli on the Old İstanbul map (pp.112–113); and Galata, Beyoğlu and Taksim on the map on pp.184–185.

Cafés and budget eating

Until recent times, café society in İstanbul was limited to a glass of tea, a puff on a *nargile* or a shot of *rakı* in a male-dominated teahouse. But today's cafés are as wide ranging as in any other European city, from traditional workers' taverns and student beer-halls, where cafeteria-type fare is dished out, to sophisticated continental cafés serving trendy coffees and imported alcoholic drinks.

Budget options include *lokanta*-style buffets (where what you see is what you get), and *pide* or *kebap salonu* for cheap and filling meat- and bread-based staples. Barrow-boys all over the city offer *simit*s and other bread-type snacks, fishermen in Kadıköy, Karaköy and Eminönü serve dubious fish sandwiches off their boats, while sizzling tangles of sheep innards (*kokoreç*) are sold from booths and pushcarts in the more salubrious areas. **Prices** vary depending on the establishment and location, but range from 0.35YTL for a *börek* (cheese-, spinach- or meat-filled pastry) to 1.5YTL or so for a takeaway kebab, or five times this or more for coffee and cake in an upmarket café.

Sultanahmet

Ahırkapi Börekçisi Ahırkapi Sok 64, Cankurtaran. Tiny *börek* bakery in the backstreets towards Kennedy Cad. Dispenses traditional Turkish meat, cheese or spinach pastries, which make great snacks or cheap lunches.

Buhara 93 Sıfa Hamamı Sok 12. Wide range of traditional fare including competitively priced kebabs (5–8YTL), hence it's consistently full of locals at lunchtime. There's a terrace with potted plants and a nice dark-wood interior.

Café Ağa Medresesi Caferiye Sok, Soğukkuyu Çıkmazı. A peaceful café just northwest of the Aya Sofya, in the courtyard of a former *medrese*. It also doubles as an art school, with classes in calligraphy and marbling. Ideal for a soup or *çay* stop

after exploring the Aya Sofya.

Çiğdem Patisserie Divan Yolu Cad 62. For over forty years it has offered a good selection of both Turkish and non-Turkish pastries and sweets.

Doy Doy Sıfa Hamamı Sok 13. A backpacker's favourite (off Küçükayasofya Cad at the Hippodrome end), with a well-deserved reputation for cheap and well-prepared kebabs, *pide* and *sulu yemek*. Try the unusual *fıstıklı fırın beyti* (oven-cooked kebab with pistachios). Dining is on four floors, including a roof terrace with great views of the harbour and night-time light show over the Blue Mosque. No alcohol.

Karadeniz Pide Salonu Divan Yolu Cad, Bıçkı Yurdu Sok 1. Cheap and unremarkable with plastic tables and plates, but the food – particularly a

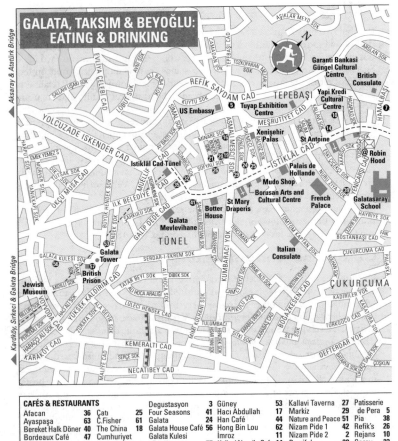

GALATA, TAKSIM & BEYOĞLU: EATING & DRINKING

CAFÉS & RESTAURANTS		Degustasyon	3	Güney	53	Kallavi Taverna	27	Patisserie	
Afacan	36	Çatı	25	Four Seasons	41	Hacı Abdullah	17	Markiz	29	de Pera	5
Ayaspaşa	63	C.Fisher	61	Galata	24	Han Café	44	Nature and Peace	51	Pia	38
Bereket Halk Döner	40	The China	18	Galata House Café	56	Hong Bin Lou	62	Nizam Pide 1	42	Refik's	26
Bordeaux Café	47	Cumhuriyet		Galata Kulesi		İmroz	11	Nizam Pide 2	2	Rejans	10
Canım Ciğerim	16	Meyhanesi	4	Restaurant	57	Kallavi Nargile Cafe	14	Parsifal	30	Saray	23

good *kiremit kebap* (lamb cooked on a clay dish) – is very popular with locals. Expect to pay around 6YTL for a *pide*, a little more for grills.

Konyali Café Mecidiye Pavilion, Topkapı Palace. Open during palace hours for coffee and pastries and set-priced buffet lunches geared towards coach parties. Some compensation for the ridiculous prices – there is little other choice of refreshments inside the palace – is the terrace set amongst the palace gardens, with a great view over the Bosphorus. Closed Tues.

Sultan Pub Divan Yolu Cad 2. Pleasant but touristy café-bar in a prominent position, with tables outside in summer, offering Turkish and international dishes for 13–16YTL a head and plenty of cold beer on tap.

Tarihi Sultanahmet Köftecisi Divan Yolu 4. Longest established of the three *köfte* specialists at this end of Divan Yolu, and well-frequented by Turkish celebrities (check out the framed newspaper clippings and thank-you letters on the tiled walls). A plate of tasty meatballs, pickled peppers, fresh bread and a spicy tomato-sauce dip will set you back a bargain 4YTL.

Eminönü

Kardelen Pub Muradiye Cad 3, Sirkeci. Unpretentious and best of the cluster of *meyhane*s on this street near the station. Worth walking down to from Sultanahmet's tourist traps. Ivy-covered facade, zany tilted roof terrace, hearty *meze*s from 3YTL and grills around 7YTL. Much beer and *rakı* are downed, especially when one of

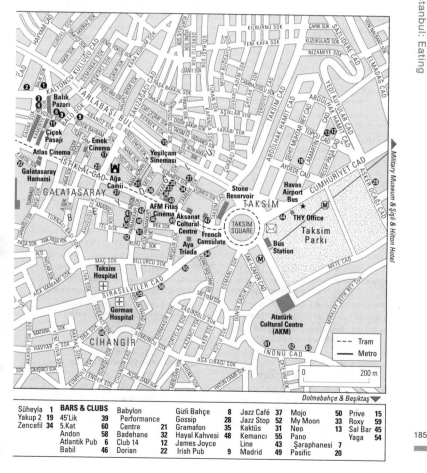

Military Museum & Şişli & Hilton Hotel

Dolmabahçe & Beşiktaş ▼

Süheyla	1	**BARS & CLUBS**		Babylon		Gizli Bahçe	8	Jazz Café	37	Mojo	50	Prive	15
Yakup 2	19	45'Lik	39	Performance		Gossip	28	Jazz Stop	52	My Moon	33	Roxy	59
Zencefil	34	5.Kat	60	Centre	21	Gramafon	35	Kaktüs	31	Neo	13	Sal Bar	45
		Andon	58	Badehane	32	Hayal Kahvesi	48	Kemancı	55	Pano		Yaga	54
		Atlantik Pub	6	Club 14	12	James Joyce		Line	43	Şaraphanesi	7		
		Babil	46	Dorian	22	Irish Pub	9	Madrid	49	Pasific	20		

Istanbul's top three football teams are on the big screen TVs.

Konyali Ankara Cad 233, Sirkeci. Excellent pastry and cake shop opposite the train station, open by 7am and frequented by the quarter's business-people, who eat their breakfast standing at the marble-topped counters. An affordable 4YTL for coffee and pastry. Closed Sun.

Beyazit

Subaşı Restaurant Nuruosmaniye Cad 48, Çarşı Kapı. Behind Nuruosmaniye Camii, just inside the main entrance of the covered bazaar, this spit-and-sawdust place (with real sawdust) serves excellent lunchtime food to the market traders, far better than anything else in the same price range in the area. Go early (noon–1pm) as it gets packed and food may run out.

Galata

Galata House Café Galata Külesi Sok 61 ☎0212/245 1861. A café housed in the former British prison, serving good coffee, home-made *böreks*, cakes and jams. Full meals are available (mains around 13YTL) including both Turkish and Georgian cuisine. Closed Mon.

🏃 **Güney** Opposite Galata Tower. A workers' favourite with *saray kebap* (beef stew topped with bechamel sauce and oven-browned) that has to be tasted to be believed. It's one of the best *lokantas* in town; you'll be lucky to find a seat at lunchtime.

Beyoğlu

Afacan İstiklâl Cad 331. Best of the area's many self-service *lokantas*, with a wide selection of meat and some vegetarian dishes, prepared to a high standard at very reasonable prices (from 3YTL) per plate).

🏃 **Bordeaux Café** French Cultural Centre, İstiklâl Cad 2. Wonderful place to escape the street noise, with tables set out in the green courtyard of the imposing, nineteenth-century French Cultural Centre. French breakfasts (*croissant*, *café au lait* and *pain au chocolat*) served up to 11am, delicious *crêpes* (6YTL) and French-style baguette sandwiches (5–6YTL). Open 9am to 10pm, closed Sundays. You need to show your passport to get in.

Bereket Halk Döner İstiklâl Cad 28. Very popular with local shoppers, this no frills self-service joint serves standard kebabs and grills, plus more unusual dishes like *paşa köftesi*, an individual, cheese-topped shepherd's pie for 5.5YTL. The downstairs eating-area is no-smoking.

Canım Ciğerim Minare Sok 1. Small, trendy but very popular place with set menus of ten chicken, lamb or liver *şiş* skewers served with fresh flat *lavaş* bread and four varieties of salad, plus grilled vegetables (9.5YTL per person).

Kallavi Nargile Café Kavalli Sok 2. Take the elavator to this calming, wood-walled and -floored café for a coffee (4YTL) or a puff on a *nargile*, and enjoy fine views over the Bosphorus.

Markiz İstiklâl Cad 360–2. Restored to its former glory, this wonderful patisserie is worth visiting for its exquisite Art Nouveau faïence-tile murals alone – *L'Automne* and *Le Printemps* by Annoux. The delightful art-deco glasswork is a bonus, though the food, served by smart, nostalgically attired staff, is not cheap at around 11YTL for a coffee and cake.

🏃 **Nizam Pide** İstiklâl Cad, Büyükparmakkapı Sok. Offers the best beans and rice in town, and excellent *pides* (4–5YTL). A second branch on Kalyoncu Kulluğu Cad, behind Nevizade Sok in the fish market, has framed articles from Turkish newspapers proclaiming it to be one of the top ten *pide* outlets in Turkey.

Patisserie de Pera *Pera Palas Hotel*, Meşrutiyet Cad 98–100, Tepebaşı ☎0212/251 4560. It would be worth splashing out for the turn-of-the-century elegance alone, though the delicious cakes and coffee and the excellent service also appeal. Booking advised for the traditional afternoon tea (12YTL for tea and a cake).

Pia İstiklâl Cad, Bekar Sok 7. Pleasant split-level café attracting a trendy clientele. It's a popular pre- and post-cinema hangout, with a good selection of English-language magazines to browse through, and decent pasta, though a *café latte* doesn't come cheap.

🏃 **Saray** İstiklâl Cad 102–104. Best value of İstanbul's upmarket patisseries, serving mouthwatering profiteroles. Established in 1935, the emphasis is on classic Turkish desserts such as *fırın sütlaç* (baked rice pudding), *irmik helvası* (semolina with nuts) and *baklava*-type sweets, including wonderful *fıstık sarma* (pistachios packed in a syrup-drenched pastry roll).

Kadiköy

Divan Pastanesi Bağdat Cad 361, Erenköy. Very classy joint selling the best pastries and cakes, and with a good line in attractively boxed sweets and *lokum* (Turkish delight). Sit outside and watch the Bağdat people as you indulge. Other branches all over the city, including inside the *Divan Hotel* in Taksim.

Restaurants

Restaurants in **Taksim** and **Beyoğlu** cater for theatre- and cinema-goers and young people filling up before a night out, as well as for those who want to spend all evening over a meal and a bottle of *rakı*. The most atmospheric spot is undoubtedly the **Balık Pazarı**, or fish market, especially **Nevizade Sokak**, where restaurants serve *mezes*, kebabs and fish, accompanied by the sound of serenading street musicians: the hubbub is nonstop and the atmosphere wonderful. The restaurant situation in the old city has improved significantly in recent years, though establishments in **Sultanahmet** and elsewhere still don't compare with Beyoğlu for variety or quality. **Kumkapı**, south of Laleli, off the coast road, Kennedy Caddesi, is a charming area of narrow streets where wandering *fasıl* bands – musicians playing traditional Turkish instruments – will serenade you over a *rakı*. There are some fifty fish restaurants here, surrounding the small square, Kumkapı Meydanı, serving up anything that scuttles or swims, from swordfish, sea bass and red mullet to lobster, giant prawns and calamari. It's a popular spot on a balmy summer evening, with candlelit tables spilling out on to the traffic-free streets. Otherwise you can try your luck in the cobbled streets around the ferry terminal in **Ortaköy**, where there are numerous trendy options rubbing shoulders with older, more traditional establishments.

Restaurant **prices** vary considerably depending on what and where you eat. Expect to pay more for extras, such as live music or to dine on a terrace overlooking the Bosphorus, while fish is always pricier than meat. Main courses start from 5YTL at a cheap restaurant frequented by locals, though run up to 40YTL or more at a swish restaurant with all the trimmings. Set meals at 40–60YTL represent the best value, with a wide choice of *mezes* followed by a substantial main course, Turkish desserts and, usually, half a bottle of wine or *rakı*.

Sultanahmet

Balıkçı Sabahattin Cankurtan. Fish restaurant by Cankurtan station, five minutes' walk but a world away from the tourist joints up the hill. It's not cheap (it's the in-place for moneyed locals) but about as atmospheric as you can get, with vine-shaded tables set out in a narrow alley in summer, and a wood-floored dining room in winter in an old wooden house in winter. Starters begin at 5YTL, mains around 30YTL, with every kind of locally caught fish on the menu.

House of Medusa Yerebatan Cad, Muhterem Efendi Sok 19. Indoor and outdoor tables offering a wide selection of Turkish dishes. Main courses are a steep 13–22YTL, but it's not a bad choice for a civilized lunch.

Kathisma Restaurant Yeni Akbıyık Cad 26. Fish and meat dishes, excellent sweets to follow, and a wine menu, all served in a cavernous bare-brick dining room. On Wednesday lunchtimes you'll coincide with the street market outside the front door.

Mosaik Restaurant Divan Yolu Cad, İncili Çavuş Sok 1. Nicely restored, late nineteenth-century house, with tables on the street and an atmospheric, separate downstairs bar (with small beers at 5YTL). Serves a range of less common Turkish

dishes, including Armenian, Greek and Kurdish specialities.

Rami Restaurant Utangaç Sok 6 ⓣ0212/517 6593. Restored Ottoman townhouse full of antiques, with great views from the roof terrace. Offers a mixture of stews, *mezes* and oven-baked dishes – including some fish. Excellent food but at 16–24YTL for a main course alone, it's expensive. It's opposite the Arasta bazaar, near the Mosaic Museum.

Rumeli Café Divan Yolu Cad, Ticarethane Sok 8. Friendly, cosmopolitan atmosphere in nicely restored bare-brick and wood surroundings – there are also a few candlelit tables on the street and a funky roof terrace. Jointly run by the twin sisters from the *Nomade* hotel opposite and a couple of laid-back Kurds, it's not cheap (a rocket, goat's cheese, walnut, tomato and dried fruit salad is 11YTL) but is excellent quality. The *tatlı kaçamaklar* (nearest translation "sweet, illicit flirt") is a deliciously rich chocolate soufflé with vanilla ice-cream, and a nut-topped sauce.

Türkistan Aşevi Tavukhane Sok 36. Popular with tour groups, largely because of its prominent position by the Hippodrome, it has an ethnically styled interior and nightly live music. Check out the unusual Central Asian dishes, such as *Türkistan pilavı* (rice mixed with meat and carrots) for 6YTL or the cold yoghurt soup with chickpeas, barley and mint at 2.5YTL.

Beyazit

Cennet Divan Yolu Cad 90. Specializes in *gözleme* (filled filo-pastry pancakes, akin to the Indian stuffed paratha) for 4YTL. Best avoided in the evening when the faux-Ottoman entertainment begins, with musicians dressed in Osmanlı costume doing their noisy rounds. It's near the Çemberlitaş Hamamı.

Padaliza Kapalı Çarşı, off Yağlıkcılar Cad. Easily the best eating establishment in the covered bazaar (near the main entrance, at the entrance to Cebeci Han) in a beautifully restored, exposed brick, barrel-vaulted *han*. The waiters are white-shirted, black-tied and black-trousered, but are friendly rather than formal, and dish up delicious stuffed vegetables (4YTL), and kebabs at 6YTL. There are some tables in the bustling alley outside. There's no alcohol: not a bad thing as you need to keep your wits about you in the bazaar!

Eminönü

Levi Et Lokantası Tahmis Kalçın Sok, Çavuşbaşı Han 23/6. Small first-floor place, overlooking the square to the west of the Mısır Çarşısı. If you want to sample kosher Sephardic food, prepared mainly for İstanbul's Jewish community, this is the place to come. Unusual dishes (around 10YTL) include *ağristada* (meatballs in béchamel sauce), *patlican reynada* (aubergine and mince fritters) and *armide de domat* (a puree of rice and tomatoes). The (Muslim) owner is very friendly. Wine served. Best at lunchtimes, as it usually closes around 7pm, though closes after lunch on Fri, and all day Sat.

Pandeli Mısır Çarşısı 51, Hamıdıye Cad ℡0212/527 3909. Go through the main entrance of the spice bazaar on the shore side and turn back towards the doorway; on your right is a staircase leading up to the restaurant. Over seventy years old, decorated throughout with blue and white tiling and run by Greek and Turkish owners, it is known particularly for its sea bass. İstanbulites are divided as to the quality of the food, but everyone is unanimous about the truculence of the ageing waiters. Main courses from 16YTL. Lunch only noon–3.30pm, closed Sun.

Kumkapı

Kör Agop Ördekli Bakkal 7–9 ℡0212/517 2334. Third-generation Armenian-owned fish restaurant, one of the oldest in town (since 1938) and hugely popular. Offers a standard selection of seasonal

fish, *mezes* and salads, accompanied by a *fasil* band in the evening. Not cheap, at about 28YTL a head, but a reliable night out.

Olimpiyat 2 Kumkapı Meyd. A favourite among locals for its excellent service, guaranteed high quality and large range of fish, from bluefish to sea bass. Mains around 18YTL.

Şehzade Restaurant Kennedy Cad, Balakçalar Çarşısı 28. Right by the sea, with a waterside terrace, so you can watch the boats go out to the sound of the *fasil* band. The menu specializes in lobster, crab and prawn, with main courses starting at 16YTL.

Edirnekapı

Asithane *Kariye Hotel*, Kariye Camii Sok 18 ℡0212/534 8414. See The City Walls map on p.161. Garden-restaurant next door to the Kariye Museum. It's expensive, but you may feel like splashing out for good service and food in such a peaceful (if distant) location. The menu is described as nouvelle Ottoman cuisine – plenty of meat- and fruit-based stews from 13YTL, or try the *hükar beğendi* (tender lamb with aubergine puree). Meals served on a lovely terrace swamped by roses, accompanied by classical Turkish music.

Galata

Galata Kulesi Restaurant Galata Tower, top floor ℡0212/293 8180. Despite the belly dancing and the spectacular views, at 96YTL per person (fixed menu, dinner at 8pm, show at 9pm) this is an expensive place with little real atmosphere.

Beyoğlu

Çatı İstiklâl Cad, Orhan A. Apaydan Sok 17, Tünel ℡0212/251 0000. Crowded at weekends (when you might want to book), but deserving of its glowing reputation, this restaurant-bar spreads over two floors. Live music and reasonably priced food, including unusual dishes such as desserts made from tomatoes and aubergines. Main courses start at 16YTL but the set meals represent much better value, with all-you-can-eat *mezes*. Closed Sun.

Cumhuriyet Meyhanesi Sahne Sok 47, Balık Pazarı. Excellent selection of *mezes* and fish dishes from 19YTL a head, in a restaurant located at the heart of the fish market. Sit upstairs for a bird's-eye view of the fish stalls in the market below and try to avert your eyes from the offal shop across the alleyway whilst you're eating.

Degustasyon Sahne Sok 41, Balık Pazarı ℡0212/292 0667. Fish-market tavern run by Nazim, Turkish TV's star chef. Dishes mix Turkish and international flavours, such as the chicken soya stir-fry, and set menus are 24YTL (meat) or

32YTL (fish). Lesser-known Turkish wines available, plus a selection of imports from Bulgaria and Georgia. There are cheaper options in the surrounding fish market, but a lot of thought has been put into this menu.

Four Seasons İstiklâl Cad 509, Tünel ☎0212/293 3941. Popular with expats for its classy, English-style,

△ The restaurants along Nevizade Sokak are some of Istanbul's most atmospheric

old-world charm and sweet trolley. Not cheap, but you get what you pay for. Lunchtime set menus are great value at 8YTL. Closed Sun.

Hacı Abdullah İstiklâl Cad, Sakızağacı Cad 17 ☎0212/293 8561. One of the best traditional restaurants in town sports a high-ceilinged atrium salon at the back. Main courses from 9YTL – try the *hunkar beğendili kebap* (beef stew on a bed of aubergine and cheese puree) and the *ayva tatlı* (stewed quince with clotted cream). Strictly no alcohol served.

İmroz Nevizade Sok 24. This Greek-owned İstanbul institution has been dishing up reasonably priced fish dishes (mains 12YTL) since 1942. Spread over three floors, it is perhaps the liveliest of the fish restaurants in the Balık Pazarı area.

Nature and Peace İstiklâl Cad, Büyükparmakkapı Sok 21. Earthy vegetarian restaurant on a lively street, where specialities include green lentil balls, falafels and nettle soup, from around 5.5YTL a dish. Some chicken dishes served, too; the only alcohol available is wine.

Parsifal Kurabiye Sok 13. Sophisticated, inexpensive menu blending Turkish and international styles, with an imaginative menu of non-meat dishes, such as leek and soya burgers.

Refik's Sofyalı Sok 10–12, Tünel. Modest *rakı*-infused Turkish joint, specializing in Black Sea cuisine. *Kara lahana dolmasi* is an unusual stuffed cabbage, popular with the locals. Refik Baba, the good-natured owner, likes to chat in numerous languages, though he doesn't speak much of any. Full dinner with booze, 26YTL. Closed Mon.

Rejans İstiklâl Cad, Emir Nevruz Sok 17 ☎0212/243 3882. This famous establishment was founded by White Russians in the 1930s and

thrives on its nostalgic reputation. It's somewhat shabby and staid, but, considering the quality of the food, not too expensive. Main courses (barbecued salmon, grilled quail) start from 13YTL, accompanied by the excellent lemon vodka. Lunches noon–2pm; dinner 7–10pm.

Zencefil Kurabiye Sok 3. The ever-changing menu includes vegetarian versions of various Turkish dishes from as little as 5YTL plus some chicken and fish specials, great salads, home-made breads, herbal teas and local wines. Closed Sun.

Taksim

Ayaspaşa İnönü Cad 77 ☎0212/143 4892. Famous basement Russian restaurant that's been cooking for over fifty years, with a friendly atmosphere and good service. It offers a selection of Russian favourites, such as *borscht* and *palaçinka*.

C.Fisher İnönü Cad 51. Atmospheric restaurant-bar fronting this very busy street. Good value for fish, with steamed sea bass at 13YTL.

The China Lamartin Cad 17. The first Chinese restaurant in Turkey, still preparing excellent food – their speciality is chicken with vegetables and almonds – and a friendly atmosphere. Closed Sun.

Hong Bin Lou İnönü Cad 53 ☎0212/243 6379. Chinese restaurant, with good-value weekdays-only set-lunch menus (10–15YTL). Popular with the local Chinese community, so booking advised at weekends.

Beşiktaş

Hanedan Balik Babaros Meyd. Large, fairly formal establishment (meat served downstairs – the roast lamb is especially good – and fish and seafood upstairs), popular with locals and tourists alike for its reliable food, served with abundant fresh *pide*. It's on the front next to the ferry jetty, so the window tables afford good views of the Bosphorus. Expect to pay 52YTL upwards a head with drinks.

Tuğra *Çıragan Palace & Kempinski Hotel*, Çaragan Cad 84 ℡0212/258 3377. Ottoman restaurant with one of the most spectacular settings in the city, providing a stunning view over the Bosphorus. Expect to pay Western prices, up to 52YTL for a main course alone – though these include unexpected menu items such as *Çerkez tavuğu* (chicken in walnut sauce) and a laden dessert trolley. Dress to impress. Dinner only; closed Mon.

Ortaköy

Carne Muallim Naci Cad 41 ℡0212/260 8425. Upmarket kosher restaurant, with New York diner–style decor. Vegetarians will enjoy the hummus and *falafel* for 12YTL, but fish dishes are pricy (35YTL). Bookings essential. Closed Fri evening & Sat until 9pm.

Çınar İskele Meydanı. Watch the promenaders on the waterfront and the sunset over the Bosphorus from this simple but lively restaurant, with reasonably priced seafood (fish mains from 12YTL, *meze* 4YTL).

Üsküdar

Huzur (Arabin Yeri) Salacak Iskelesi 20. Run by a group of Arabic-speaking Turks from the Hatay, serving grilled fish or seafood with salad for a reasonable 13YTL. The restaurant has a rather faded charm and an undeniably wonderful view of the European side of the Bosphorus at sunset.

Kanaat Selmanipak Cad 25. One of the city's more famous *lokantas*, established in 1933, featuring copies of İznik-tile panels from the Selimiye Camii in Edirne and a copper chimney-piece. Meals are reasonably cheap at about 11YTL a head; no alcohol served.

Nightlife

Traditionally, İstanbul nightlife meant **meyhanes** (taverns) and **gazinos** (drinking clubs serving *mezes*, with entertainment from singers and oriental dancers). The latter have largely faded away and have been replaced by overpriced and tacky all-singing, all-dancing **cabarets** geared towards coachloads of tourists. Some traditional and atmospheric *meyhanes* still exist, where a *fasil* band might accompany your bottle of *rakı*, but these too are slowly being eclipsed by café-bars and modern nightclubs.

With such a youthful population, a booming economy and relentless westernization, it is not surprising that Istanbul is establishing a major reputation for **clubbing**. The best **bars** and **clubs** are in Beyoğlu, Taksim, Ortaköy and the richer European Bosphorus suburbs (where bright young things turn up for a night out in SUVs or even yachts), and over the water in Kadıköy.

Bars

For a Muslim city, İstanbul is far from dry, and away from conservative Islamic areas (forget Fatih and Eyüp, for example) you'll find bars ranging from the dangerously seedy to the chic and overpriced. **Sultanahmet**'s tourist-orientated bars are dull in comparison to buzzing **Beyoğlu**, where drinking goes on well into the early hours. There's a variety of bars along the lively *soks* leading off **İstiklâl Caddesi**, at the Taksim Square end – from jazz joints to sophisticated cafés, and from basement bars where Turkish youth practice their guitars to a fair number of dubious establishments that should be avoided altogether. (All Beyoğlu bars are marked on the map on pp.184–185.) On the Bosphorus, **Ortaköy** on the European shore and **Kadıköy**, on the Asian side, have both seen a recent blossoming of drinking haunts. For Ortaköy, take a taxi or bus the short distance from Taksim Square; to reach Kadıköy's Kadife Sokak, walk or take a taxi from the Kadıköy ferry terminal south down Moda Caddesi, until it turns into Doktor Esat Işık Caddesi – Kadife Sokak is on the left.

The monthly magazine *Time Out İstanbul* (ensure you buy the English-language version) is available from newsstands all over the city for 3.5YTL. It is the best source of listings and features on what to do and see in the city. Other English-language publications include the bimonthly *İstanbul: The Guide*, available in hotel lobbies or bookshops for 5YTL, and the quarterly *City Plus* (®www.cityplus-turkey.com) from newsstands for 5YTL. Both have a useful listings section plus reviews of expensive restaurants and designer clothes shops. **Cornucopia**, a glossy bimonthly covering the Ottoman arts scene, auctions, galleries and exhibitions, is available from bookshops that stock foreign newspapers and publications.

The line between İstanbul's bars and cafés tends to blur, with most open during the day to serve food and coffee, becoming more alcoholic as the evening progresses. A cover charge is often introduced between 10pm and 2am if there is live music.

Sultanahmet

Bodrum Bar Divan Yolu Cad, Seftali Sok 3. Small, unremarkable basement bar, but one of the few options in the area for a late-night drink.

Cozy Pub Divan Yolu Cad 66. Modern, Western-style pub that appeals to tourists – hence the high prices. Outside tables are not a bad place to watch the world go by on the Divan Yolu Cad.

Orient Youth Hostel Bar Yeni Akbıyık Cad 13. Rooftop bar at the hostel, with a cheap menu and good views of the Bosphorus and Sea of Marmara. It's frequented by travellers from surrounding hostels in the evening; there are belly-dancing shows on Friday nights.

Beyoğlu

45'Lik Yeni Çarşıa Cads 60. New venue concentrating on alternative rock (no live bands) witth a grungy feel and a pleasant garden area out back, and possibly the cheapest beers around.

Atlantik Pub Nevizade Sok 27. Great place to nurse a bigger than pint-sized Efes beer (5YTL for 70cl) and watch the good-time-seeking hordes pour down the alley.

Babil İpek Sok 18. Small bar on a couple of floors of a narrow house, attracting a bohemian set.

Badehane General Yazgan Sok 5. Small winter venue that spills out onto the alley in a big way in the summer. Crowded with students and alternative youth, it serves cheap beer with people-watching and occasional live bands providing the entertainment.

Dorian Turnacıbaşı Kartal Sok 5. Small bar specializing in blues music, with live bands playing in a cramped but atmospheric room at weekends. Beer prices rise from 3YTL to 5YTL when there's live music, but no cover charge.

Gramafon Tünel Meyd 3. At the very end of İstiklâl Cad, right next to Tünel station. Stylish, late-night bar with occasional jazz performances and good people-watching opportunities from the outside tables. Small cover charge if there's a band on.

Hayal Kahvesi İstiklâl Cad, Büyükparmakkapı Sok 19. Attractive brick-and-wood joint with good live jazz and blues every night from 11pm.

James Joyce Irish Pub Irish Centre, Balo Sok 26. Housed in a wonderfully ornate nineteenth-century apartment block, the centre's focal point is the lively pub (with expensive Guinness) but there's also the *U2* music bar in the basement, a game bar with big-screen sports TV, the rooftop *Lemon Tree* café-bar, a library and Internet access.

Kaktüs İstiklâl Cad, Imam Adnan Sok 4. Favoured drinking, meeting and eating haunt of the TV and advertising crowd, and prominent (but not exclusively) gay venue. Good coffee and salads available, plus a selection of imported beers.

Madrid İpek Sok 20. Beyoğlu's only Spanish-themed bar with a Spanish owner. The converted four-storey house, with a tight iron spiral staircase, boasts the cheapest beer in the area, good music and a raucous weekend atmosphere.

My Moon İstiklâl Cad, Bekar Sok 16. Long, low wooden room with a line of bar stools along a well-stocked bar for *Cheers*-style drinking.

Pano Şaraphanesi İstiklâl Cad, Hamalbaşı Cad 26, Galatasaray. Beautifully restored century-old Greek wine bar, on the opposite corner to the British Consulate. Beer, local wine and good-value food available (*meze* 3.5YTL, pasta dishes 9YTL and steaks 16YTL). The owners also run *Cumhuriyet Meyhane*, another historical drinking den, just round the corner in the Fish Market.

Pasific Sofyalı Sok . Small, friendly bar with a good selection of rock/indie music and well-priced

İSTANBUL AND AROUND | İstanbul: Nightlife

beer (4YTL for draught Tuborg). It's a struggle to find a seat on the alleyway tables in summer.

Ortaköy

Rock House Café *Princess Hotel*, Dereboyu Cad. İstanbul's answer to the *Hard Rock Café*. Bar and restaurant (serving ribs, chilli, steaks and burgers), with live bands after 10pm. It's a barn of a place, but gets very busy at weekends.

Kadıköy

Hera Kadife Sok 10, Caferağa Mah. The rock and jazz grooves don't quite gel with the pseudo-Ottoman decoration, but it's a popular spot. Hot food is served, too, including tasty *börek*.

Isis Kadife Sok 26, Caferağa Mah. Three-storey townhouse that's a café by day and bar-disco at night. Cutting-edge music and good food, plus a garden open during the summer months.

Lal Kadife Sok 19, Caferağa Mah. Relaxed café-bar, open all day from breakfast until 2am, with intimate seating and lighting, Latin grooves, and good *börek* and salads.

Clubs and live music

İstanbul's dance **clubs** may surprise Western visitors. The best ones are imaginative in decor with sounds that are bang up to date, while **live music** – jazz, rock, blues, R&B, reggae and salsa – is plentiful around the backstreets of Beyoğlu. Expect to spend no less than you would in London, New York or Sydney on a night out. Most places have entry charges (anything from 10YTL to 50YTL) and tend to be open from around 9pm until 2 or 4am.

Local and visiting foreign bands also play at a welter of annual **festivals** – including two jazz festivals, a rock festival, an international music festival, plus separate dance and techno and blues events. See the festival calendar on p.196 for more details.

Beyoğlu

Babylon Performance Centre Şeybender Sok 3, Asmalımescit, Tünel ☎0212/292 7368, ⓦwww. babylon-ist.com. İstanbul's premier live-music club (one of the "Best 100 Jazz Clubs of the World", according to US magazine *Downbeat*) with a regular programme of local and foreign groups playing jazz, reggae and cutting-edge dance. Drinks are expensive and concert tickets 16–40YTL (booking office across the street, open daily from noon); performances start around 10pm.

Gizli Bahçe İstiklâl Cad, Nevizade Sok 27. In the fish market above the *Atlantik Pub* – enter through an unmarked rusty wrought-iron door and head up (if the doorman likes the look of you) to the second and third floors of an Ottoman townhouse. There are sofas to lounge on, and a balcony to escape the smoke and sweat. The music's loud and the atmosphere deliciously illicit. Daily 9pm–4am.

Jazz Café Hansun Galip Sok 20, off Büyükparmakkapı Sok ☎0212/252 0694, ⓦwww.jazzcafeistanbul.com. More blues than mainstream jazz, despite the name, in an intimate club with high tables overlooking the tiny stage. A real mix of talent from new bands to studio artists. Shows start at 10.30pm. Daily 4pm–2am.

Jazz Stop Tel Sok 2, off Büyükparmakkapı Sok ☎0212/252 9314. Stylish, atmospheric, bare-brick basement club with steep cover charge – one of İstanbul's leading venues for jazz and flamenco. Owned by the band members of the local jazz group Moğollar, who perform regularly. Performances start about 11pm. Mon–Sat 4.30pm–4am.

Line İstiklâl Cad, Büyükparmakkapı Sok 14. Sophisticated dance club, with live music from 11pm, currently attracting İstanbul's top bands. Daily 10pm–2am.

Mojo İstiklâl Cad, Büyükparmakkapı Sok 26. Ultra-modern basement club, recently revamped, with live music most nights – best when the blues bands turn up. Has seen sets by Turkey's leading rock/punksters, Duman. Daily 9pm–4am.

Taksim

5.Kat Sıraselviler Cad, Soğancı Sok 7. In trendy Cihangir, this is a sumptuous dance-club with a great reputation and even better views over the Bosphorus. The beer is expensive, though.

Andon Sıraselviler Cad 89 ☎0212/251 0222. Massively popular with İstanbul's fashionable set, this features five overwhelming floors, each with their own personality: dancing in *Pera* to İstanbul's best DJs; wine and cheese in the second-floor *Wine House*; live Turkish music and belly dancing in *Müdavim Bar*; a fourth-floor *meyhane* with seafood snacks, *fasil* band and *rakı*; and fifth-floor roof-terrace restaurant. A fixed-price menu of

60YTL includes unlimited local alcoholic drinks; booking advised. On Friday and Saturday the 20YTL admission charge includes one drink.

Gossip *Hyatt Regency Hotel*, Taşkışla Cad. Expensive hotel club sporting avant-garde decor. Mainstream bands play from May to Sept, but there's a nicer atmosphere in the relaxing garden area, decorated with trailing ivy and oil lamps. Mon–Sat 8pm–4am.

Kemancı Sıraselviler Cad .The decor is *Alien* meets Marilyn Manson, all gloomy black metal, but the former thrash-metal basement area has now become the *Riddim* hip-hop club. Plays mainly classic rock/grunge music, with live bands from 11.30pm at weekends. There's a terrace out back with wonderful views over the Bosphorus. Beers 6YTL.

Roxy Arslan Yatağı Sok 113, Sıraselviler Cad ☏0212/245 6539, ⓦwww.roxy.com.tr. DJs and live bands play rock, R&B, jazz and dance music in this posy, pricey bar-disco, which attracts a mixed crowd – rich students to 1980s throwbacks. Daily 6pm–3.30am.

Yaga Sıraselviler Cad 67. An unassuming entrance opens up to all sorts of treats inside – several levels of bars, a dance floor, giant TV screen and garden with comfy cushions. Bands play Wed–Sun at 10pm. Café and restaurant open during the day, cover charge levied after 9pm, when things liven up. Daily noon–4am.

Ortaköy

Laila Muallim Nacı Cad 54. Massive outdoor club much frequented on sultry summer nights (open June to September) by the city's *nouveau riche*. You'll need to dress up and even then will probably be made to feel like a grunge aficionado, that's if you get past the bouncers.

Q Jazz Bar *Çıragan Palace Hotel Kempinski*, Çaragan Cad 32 ☏0212/258 3377, ⓦwww.infoqjazz-club.com. With its beautiful Bosphorus views from the terrace, this is a class joint in a sumptuous hotel and you won't get in unless they like the look of you. Past performers have included Whitney Houston and Ray Charles so expect to pay insanely high cover charges and drinks prices. Different sections feature jazz, Latin and salsa sounds, while famous Turkish club DJs appear most nights. Daily 10pm–2.30am.

Reina Muallim Nacı Cad 120. Summer drinking outside until dawn for the bright young things who manage to get through the door. There are dance floors, video screens and bars all directly overlooking the Bosphorus, and overpriced sushi – early birds get 30 percent off drinks between 6 and 8pm. June–Sept only, daily 6pm–4am.

Gay and lesbian İstanbul

Despite the widespread enthusiasm for transvestite and transsexual singers and entertainers in Turkey, homosexuality is still taboo and it is possible to be arrested for cruising (see Basics, p.93). The main centre of the **Turkish gay scene** is in and around Taksim, where most of the places reviewed below can be found.

A rundown of the İstanbul scene can be found at ⓦwww.qrd.org/qrd/world/europe/turkey/guide, the homepage of **Lambda** (Turkey's foremost gay-liberation group). Lambda also issues a bimonthly magazine called *cins*, but it's almost impossible to get hold of – try asking for it at the Pandora bookshop (p.199). Otherwise the weekly *Time Out İstanbul* reviews gay and lesbian venues.

Cafés

Han Café Cumhuriyet Cad 9, Taksim. In a prominent position in Taksim Square (next to *McDonalds*), this huge café-bar is busy all day from breakfast. Gays and lesbians frequent the back bar. Daily 10am–midnight.

Bars and clubs

Barbahçe Sıraselviler Cad, Soğancı Sok 7. In the same building as *5.Kat* (see Taksim clubs, p.192) but on the first floor, this place has an excellent reputation amongst İstanbul's gay sophisticates. Open daily 8am–4am.

Club 14 Abdulhakhamit Cad, Belediye Dükkanları 14, Taksim. Tiny late-night spot with a young crowd, lively atmosphere, good music and friendly staff. Daily except Mon, 11pm–4am.

Love Bar Cumhuriyet Cad 349, Harbiye. Spacious club (free admission) where DJs spin a wide range of sounds from garage to traditional Turkish. It's opposite the Military Museum and near the Osmanbey metro station. Open Wed, Fri

and Sat 1am–4am.
Neo Lamartin Cad 40, Taksim. Popular bar with upmarket professionals, quite yuppyish but one of İstanbul's consistently crowded gay venues. Daily except Mon 10pm–2am.
Prive Tarlabasi Bul 28, Taksim. Gay-only dance

club, with a devoted following due to its reputation as a pick-up place. It's a bit more middle-aged and less trendy than *Club 14*, its sister club, and the ancient Western pop tunes will appeal to people who like words with their music. Admission charge only at weekends. Daily midnight–4am.

Cabaret and Turkish music

Cabaret is probably the most expensive way to develop a feel for the Orient. Even in the more reputable places an exorbitant entrance fee is levied, you are overcharged for anything you eat or drink and belly dancers expect to be given generous amounts of money (stuffed in their bras) by foreign tourists. It's wise to avoid the touts, particularly around the *Hilton* and other five-star hotels on Cumhuriyet Caddesi, who may lead you to less salubrious places – it's better to stick to the more established venues, the best of which are reviewed below. Unless otherwise stated, the cabaret venues have daily **performances**, with dinner served at 7.45pm, with the show running from 8.30pm to around midnight.

A less expensive and more authentic alternative to cabaret is a night of **traditional Turkish music** (see Contexts, p.999) in a friendly bar-restaurant. Most venues offer either *bağlama*, played on the *saz* (a long-necked stringed lute), or *fasil*, heavy on the violin with *ud* (lute), *darabuka* (drum) and maybe a *zurna* (clarinet). In bars featuring livelier music, you'll be expected to dance. As well as the places around Beyoğlu listed below, most of the fish restaurants in Kumkapı on the Sultanahmet side of the Horn have live *fasil* music in the evenings. Expect to pay 40–60YTL per head for *mezes* and a couple of drinks in a restaurant that provides traditional live music.

Cabaret venues

Kervansaray Cumhuriyet Cad 30, Harbiye ☎0212/247 1630, ⓦ www.kervansaraytr.com. Not far from the *Hilton*, it's a huge, pillared, chandeliered hall where you won't feel comfortable unless you dress up a bit. Expensive at 120YTL a head, 80YTL without food, but the club has a good reputation for its floor show, which includes oriental and folk dancers.
Orient House *President Hotel*, Tiyatro Cad 27, Beyazit ☎0212/517 6163, ⓦ www.orienthouseistanbul.com. Traditional Turkish and folk music, plus belly dancing. A four-course meal with wine and show is 120YTL a head; show and wine but no meal costs 80YTL.
Sultana's Cumhuriyet Cad 16, Harbiye ☎0212/219 3904-5, ⓦ www.sultanas-nights.com. Oriental and folklore show, costing 120YTL with dinner, 72YTL without, plus free transport from any hotel (cheaper rates can be negotiated if you just turn up at the door). Members of the audience are expected to participate in the Harem dance.
Turkish Cultural Dance Theatre Firat Culture Centre, Divan Yolu, Sultanahmet ☎0212/517 8692, ⓦ www.dancesofcolours.com. Presents *Dances of Colours* from ten different regions of

Turkey, including belly dancing and Whirling Dervishes, in an air-conditioned auditorium next to the Çemberlitaş tram stop. This is purely theatre, with no dinner or the other trappings of a club. Twice-weekly shows (40YTL) on Tues at 5.15pm and Fri at 7pm.

Fasil and bağlama venues

Galata İstiklâl Cad, Orhan Apaydın Sok 11, Tünel, Beyoğlu ☎0212/293 1139. Old-style *meyhane* with a set menu of a succession of quality *mezes*, including *rakı* or wine, for around 24YTL. Tables surround the *fasil* band; bookings essential. Closed Sun.

Kallavi Taverna Kurabiye Sok 16, Beyoğlu. Small, traditional restaurant, recently moved to this location. Fixed menu of 40YTL includes 10 starters, 4 entrees, a main and fruit, plus unlimited local drinks. Live *fasil* music most nights. It's very popular with the locals; there's another branch at Şefik Bey Sok, Kadıköy. Closed Sun.
Sal Bar İstiklâl Cad, Büyükparmakapı Sok 18, Beyoğlu. A relaxed atmosphere in a low-ceilinged room with coffee tables and couches. The *bağlama*

band starts early, from 5pm, often inspiring *halays*, Turkish line-dancing. There are a number of other similar venues on Hasnun Galip Sok, around the corner.

Süheyla Kalyoncu Kulluk Cad 45, Beyoğlu. Friendly late-night *lokanta* behind the fish market, serving *mezes* accompanied by live band. Closed Sun.

Yakup 2 Asmalı Mescit Sok 35, Tünel, Beyoğlu ☎ 0212/249 2925. Casual and noisy, one of the last of the old brigade of *meyhanes*. It has a faded charm and smoke-stained decor and is still frequented by artists, journalists and intellectuals. The *mezes* (3.5YTL) are particularly recommended, and reasonably priced fish and kebabs are also served, with *rakı* by the bottle. Booking required on a Friday evening.

Arts, entertainment and festivals

İstanbul hosts a decent variety of annual cultural **festivals** and matches other European cities for the breadth of its **arts scene**. State-subsidized theatre, opera and ballet make performances affordable for all and there's something going on almost every night at various venues around the city. Music features heavily over the summer months when international festivals draw musicians from all over the world.

Tickets for many cultural events, as well as sporting events, can be purchased online from **Biletix** (☎ 0216/556 9800, ⊛ www.biletix.com.), whose website is in both Turkish and English. There are also many Biletix outlets around the city, the most useful of which is the Ada bookstore on İstiklâl Caddesi.

Art exhibitions

In addition to the galleries listed below, **Atatürk Cultural Centre** (see "Theatres and concert halls", p.198) hosts temporary exhibitions, as do a number of high-tech galleries sponsored by banks and large corporations. Many of these are found along İstiklâl Caddesi in Beyoğlu, attached to the banks. The most important event for artists is the **International İstanbul Biennial**, established in 1987 and held in October in odd-numbered years. Works of art have traditionally been displayed in some of the oldest and most historic buildings in Sultanahmet, notably in Topkapı Palace, though in 2005 all the venues were in Beyoğlu, within a fifteen-minute walk of each other. The entry fee of 15YTL (7YTL for students) includes a short guide to the artists and their works.

Aksanat Cultural Centre İstiklâl Cad 16–18, Beyoğlu ☎ 0212/252 3500, ⊛ www.akbank.com.tr/sanat. Changing exhibitions of art and sculpture from well-known local artists, and interesting films of jazz and classical concerts shown on a giant screen.

Borusan Arts & Cultural Centre İstiklâl Cad 421, Tünel, Beyoğlu ☎ 0212/292 0655, ⊛ www.borusansanat.com. Also home to the Borusan Philharmonic Orchestra (p.198), with state-of-the-art exhibition space showing established Turkish artists as well as international names.

İstanbul Modern Meclis-I Mebusan Caddesi, Liman İşletmeleri Sahası Antropo 4, Karaköy ☎ 0212/334 7300, ⊛ www.istanbulmodern.org. Turkey's answer to Tate Modern, with regularly changing exhibits by contemporary Turkish and foreign artists.

Pera Müzesi Meşrutiyet Cad 141, Tepebaşı ☎ 0212/334 9900. Top three floors of a grand, wonderfully restored, nineteenth-century building exhibiting regularly changing works by contemporary Turkish artists.

Platform Garanti Contemporary Arts Centre İstiklâl Cad 276 ☎ 0212/233 2238. Changing arts and photography exhibitions in a 1960s building.

Sakıp Sabancı Museum İstenye Cad 22, Emirgan ☎ 0212/277 2200. Housed in a 1920s villa known as the Atlı Köşk, and owned by one of Turkey's wealthiest families, the Sabancıs, this recent addition to the Istanbul arts scene proved that its facilities were world class by holding a major Picasso exhibition in 2005/6 – the first of its kind in Turkey. Entry 10YTL (open Tues, Thurs, Fri & Sun 10am–6pm, Wed & Sat 10am–10pm, closed Mon).

Yapı Kredi Cultural Centre İstiklâl Cad 285, Beyoğlu ☎0212/293 3710, ⓦwww.yapikredi.com .tr. International photography exhibitions in a large space on one floor, next to the Galatasaray School.

Film

There are hundreds of **cinemas** (*sinemasi*) all over İstanbul showing mainly Hollywood releases with Turkish subtitles. Many of the modern complexes are situated in large shopping malls, with the best old-style cinemas in Beyoğlu, once the centre of domestic film production. Most still have a fifteen-minute coffee and cigarette interval. Tickets cost around 8YTL, with discounts before 6pm and for students and teachers. The annual **International Film Festival** (mid-April to May) takes place mainly at cinemas in Beyoğlu.

AFM Akmerkez Akmerkez Shopping Mall, Etiler ☎0212/282 0505. The city's largest multiplex, surrounded by a vast food court and Akmerkez's palatial shops. Sound and screen quality is the best in town.
AFM Fitaş İstiklâl Cad 24–26, Beyoğlu ☎0212/292 1111. A popular ten-screen cinema not far from Taksim Square, showing the newest films, with a trendy pub upstairs and a vast range of CDs and books in the shop out front.

Atlas İstiklâl Cad 209, Beyoğlu ☎0212/252 8576. Newly restored cinema with an arty atmosphere in the adjoining bar. Offbeat Hollywood movies and homespun Turkish farces.
Emek Yeşilçam Sok 5, İstiklâl Cad, Beyoğlu ☎0212/293 8439. This huge atmospheric auditorium (875 seats) built in the 1920s is a popular venue during the International Film Festival.

İstanbul's festivals

The annual festival calendar is pretty full – at least between April and October, when most of the best events take place. The highlights are detailed below; for more information, consult the city tourist offices or the İstanbul Foundation for Culture and Arts (see "Theatres and concert halls", opposite).

April
International Film Festival Turkish, European and Hollywood movies premiere at İstanbul's cinemas, plus the best of the non-English-speaking world's releases from the previous year and new prints of classic films – visiting celebrities add glitz and glamour.

May
Conquest Celebrations Week-long celebration of the Ottoman conquest of old Constantinople (May 29, 1453) – concerts by the Ottoman Mehter military band, fancy dress processions and fireworks.
International Puppet Festival A celebration of Turkish Shadow Theatre, or *karağz* – silent puppets tell their tale behind a two-dimensional screen.
International Theatre Festival The year's best Turkish plays (both local avant-garde and established theatre groups) and performances by visiting foreign theatres – some plays enacted out at open-air venues.

June
International Bosphorus Festival A bizarre range of musical and dance events from rock, pop and ballet, to big-band sounds and disco divas.

June/July
The International Music Festival Concerts, recitals, dance and opera – this hugely successful festival was launched in 1973 to celebrate Turkey's fifty years of independence and brings top-notch orchestras and soloists from all over the world to perform in such atmospheric venues as the church of Aya Irene.

Şafak Yeniçeriler Cad, at the Çemberlitaş tram stop ⓣ0212/516 2660. The closest cinema to Sultanahmet, buried in the bowels of a shopping centre, with seven screens showing the latest Western releases.

Yeşilçam İmam Adnan Sok 10 ⓣ0212/249 8006. This retro, bohemian, single-screen basement cinema is the best place to see Turkish and foreign art-house movies, and is the cheapest in the area, too.

Theatres and concert halls

There are regular **classical music**, **ballet** and **opera** performances in İstanbul, held at Taksim's Atatürk Cultural Centre and at other venues across the city. The main annual event is the **International Music Festival** during June and July, which includes jazz, classical and world music concerts, as well as performances by the İstanbul State Symphony Orchestra. **Theatre** is popular, but it's mostly Turkish plays that are performed on the thirty or so stages in the city. The **State Theatre Company** puts on occasional plays in English at the Atatürk Cultural Centre and foreign theatre groups such as the Royal Shakespeare Company perform in İstanbul during May's **International Theatre Festival**. Information on all music and theatre events, and on the various cultural festivals, is available from the **İstanbul Foundation for Culture and Arts**, İstiklâl Cad 146, Beyoğlu ⓣ0212/334 0700, ⓦwww.istfest.org.

July/August

International Jazz Festival Two weeks of gigs and jamming sessions from world-class performers (with the definition of jazz stretched to include rock artists such as Lou Reed and Marianne Faithful).

Rumeli Hisarı Fortress Concerts Nightly summer concerts within the walls of this Ottoman fortification overlooking the Bosphorus – a varied programme from classical to rock.

Rock N' Coke ⓦwww.rockncoke.com. A weekend of Western and Turkish rock held on an airfield 50km to the west of the city; service buses run from Taksim. Headliners in recent years have included The Cure, Korn and The Offspring.

September

Electronica Music Festival ⓦwww.pepsielectronicafest.com. Held in Belgrade Forest to the northwest of the city, and sponsored by Pepsi and a local radio station, this is the place for nonstop electronic dance action. Top acts have included Mylo, Sasha and Nick Warren.

İstanbul Arts Fair A week-long fair selling the work of some fifty or so İstanbul galleries and visiting foreign artists – paintings, sculptures, pottery and fabrics.

October

Akbank International Jazz Festival Two-week festival concentrating on traditional jazz, with performers such as Dave Holland and Henry Threadgill. Events include film screenings, informal jamming sessions and drum workshops. Varied venues include the Byzantine church of Aya Irene and the Babylon Performance Centre in Beyoğlu.

Efes Pilsen Blues Festival Two-day late-night blues festival – a showcase of new local talent and famous foreign bands.

International İstanbul Biennial A major event held every two years (odd-numbered); artists from over thirty countries exhibit at locations around the city.

Filmeki Week-long film festival brings the pick of the crop from Cannes, Sundance and Berlin to İstanbul, hosted by the Emek Sineması (see "Film" on p.196).

Atatürk Cultural Centre (AKM) Taksim Square; Theatre ☎0212/251 5600; Opera & Ballet ☎0212/243 2011; Symphony Orchestra ☎0212/243 1068. Multi-purpose venue shared by the Symphony Orchestra, State Theatre Company, and State Opera and Ballet. Leading venue during the various international festivals and has regular performances of classical music on Friday evenings and Saturday mornings, plus opera and ballet on Thursday and Friday nights throughout the year. Ticket prices are subsidized by the government, so remain low (8–13YTL). The box office is open daily 10am–6pm; student discounts available, but no credit cards.

Borusan Arts and Cultural Centre İstiklâl Cad 421, Tünel, Beyoğlu ☎0212/292 0655, ⓦwww. borusansanat.com. Home to the Borusan Philharmonic Orchestra, one of Turkey's most successful private orchestras, which performs two monthly concerts (tickets 16–24YTL). Also boasts one of the country's most extensive CD libraries.

Cemal Reşit Rey (CRR) Darülbedai Cad 1, Harbiye ☎0212/231 5497, ⓦwww.crrks.org. Chamber music, classical, jazz and Turkish music, plus regular performances by visiting international orchestras. Venue for the International Music Festival in June and the CRR Piano Festival in December. Daily performances (season Oct–May; 8–16YTL) at 8pm; no credit cards.

Kenter Theatre Halaskargazi Cad 35, Harbiye ☎0212/246 3589. Theatre founded by the famous Turkish actress Yıldız Kenter who appears in most of the plays. Some English-speaking performances such as Shakespeare and Chekhov, and venue for the Turkish Shadow Play performed on most weekend mornings. Box office daily 11am–6pm; tickets 8–16YTL.

Shopping

Shopping in İstanbul is an experience. Whether it is a pleasant one or not depends on your ability to ignore the hustlers when you're not in the mood, and to bargain hard when you are. At times the city seems like one enormous bazaar, so knowing where to look is the trick. Don't miss the Kapalı Çarşı, the **covered bazaar**, a hive of over four thousand little shops selling the contents of a lifetime of shopping lists. But scattered around the city are a number of other shopping districts, which are just as interesting – **Ortaköy**, for arts and crafts; **Nişantaşı** for international fashion; and the Mısır Çarşısı, or **spice bazaar**, for spices and sweets.

İstiklâl Caddesi in Beyoğlu is İstanbul's main shopping street and is traffic-free save for an antique tram. Many major Turkish and international chain stores can be found along here, as well as a few interesting covered markets, bootleg CD stalls, and clothing and secondhand-book markets. For upmarket shopping try **Nuruosmaniye Caddesi**, the modern pedestrianized street that leads to the main entrance of the covered bazaar. Here, every alternate shop seems to sell either top-of-the-range carpets or gold jewellery.

There are **carpet shops** all over İstanbul, particularly in and around the covered bazaar (Takkeciler Caddesi has a good concentration), but also in the flea markets of Kadıköy and Üsküdar, and secondhand shops around Altıpatlar Sokak, off İstiklâl Caddesi. Buying a carpet involves the psychological game of bargaining; play it with the right people, otherwise you will be ripped off (see "Basics", p.82). Out of the centre, **shopping malls** have taken off in a big way, good for homeware and furniture as well as clothes, though in malls prices are clearly marked and there's no room for bargaining.

Opening hours for most shops are Monday to Saturday 10am to 7pm, though the modern shopping malls stay open daily until 10pm. Supermarkets and hypermarkets open 9am to 10pm every day but smaller food shops close much earlier. The covered bazaar opens Monday to Saturday 9am to 7pm and is credit-card friendly, as are all shops except the smallest of grocers (*bakals*) or kiosks.

Books, maps and prints

There are some good stockists of English-language **books** around the city, and it's also rewarding to browse through the secondhand-book markets and shops. The best-known **Sahaflar Çarşısı** (old book market) is the one at Beyazit (see p.153), at the Beyazit side of the covered bazaar, next to Beyazit Camii – though these days it's probably better for finding old prints of İstanbul. Numerous secondhand bookstores cluster in **Beyoğlu**, especially in the backstreets off the east side of İstiklâl Caddesi and down towards the Çukurcuma antique district. The annual **İstanbul Book Fair** in late October is held in the İstanbul Sergi Sarayı on Meşrutiyet Cad, near the *Pera Palas Hotel*.

Ada İstiklâl Cad 20. Good source of glossy coffee-table books; also sells Turkish and foreign CDs and is a Biletix outlet.

Aypa Kitabevi Mimar Mehmet Ağauu Cad 19, Sultanahmet. Broad range of books, cards and maps. Opens at 6.30am.

Beyoğlu Sahaflar Çarşısı İstiklâl Cad, Beyoğlu. Good book-market in the streets surrounding the Balık Pazarı (fish market), where some of the shops specialize in English-language texts.

Denizler Kitabevi İstiklâl Cad 395, Beyoğlu. Specialists in nautical books and charts, plus an extensive range of collectors' books on Turkey and the Ottomans.

Dünya Kitabevi İstiklâl Cad 469, Beyoğlu. Upmarket outlet specializing in coffee-table hardbacks and a broad range of English-language newspapers and magazines. Café on site for leisurely reading.

Eren Sofyala Sok 34, Tünel, Beyoğlu. Art and history books, old maps and miniatures.

Galeri Kayseri Divan Yolu Cad 58, Sultanahmet. The biggest distributor of English-language books

in Turkey, with a vast range of books on Ottoman history and all other imaginable Turkish topics.

Homer Yeni Çarşşı Cad 28, Beyoğlu. A wonderful selection of anything archeological, historical and cultural written on Turkey, and has even been known to stock the odd *Rough Guide*.

Librairie de Pera Galapdede Cad 22, Tünel, Beyoğlu. Excellent selection of antiquarian books, including English-language ones, plus maps of the Ottoman Empire, prints and photographs.

Natural Akbiyik Cad 31, Sultanahmet. Secondhand foreign-book exchange a few doors along from the *Orient Youth Hostel* – buy, sell, or swap two for one.

Pandora İstiklâl Cad, Büyükparmakkapı Sok 3, Beyoğlu. Excellent selection of foreign-language books on three storeys; carries some gay literature and will order books on request.

Robinson Crusoe İstiklâl Cad 389, Tünel, Beyoğlu. Reasonably priced, extensive collection of English-, French-, and German-language books, and a number of guides and maps.

Fashion: clothes, fabrics and leather

Turkish fashion designs are beginning to compete on the catwalks, thanks to Rıfat Özbek, the darling of the European fashion world. Other names to watch out for in Turkish *haute couture* are Bahar Korçan, Gönül Paksoy, Ferruh Karakaşli and Murat Taşin, all of whom are working with the best Turkish fabrics: leather so fine that it is now processed for the Italian market and sold at inflated prices under Italian labels, Bursa silk and the universally famous Angora wool. Paksoy also uses hand-processed vegetable dyes. While Turkish designers often imitate European styles, they do occasionally flirt with Eastern motifs and designs, creating more of a distinctive effect.

Bargain clothing

Many Western high-street stores have their clothes produced in Turkey and a number of stalls and markets across the city specialize in seconds, production overruns and samples at bargain prices (2–4YTL for T-shirts and tops, 8–12YTL for trousers and 8–16YTL for casual jackets). Fakes abound but garments that belong to Western high-street brands not marketed in Turkey are probably genuine. Cheap, locally made clothes can be found in any number of shops, particularly in the wholesale backstreets of Laleli.

Beşiktaş Pazar Beşiktaş. Saturday bazaar held in a warren of streets on either side of Şair Nedim Cad at the back of Beşiktaş (follow Şair Nedim Cad for about ten minutes from the ferry terminal). It's pot-luck what you'll find, as just about any kind of clothing can turn up here.

Beyoz İş Merkezi İstiklâl Cad 331–369. Three floors of bargain end-of-line and seconds clothing, with the odd genuine bargain for the persistent.

Salıpazar Kuşdili Cad, Kadıköy. Held on Tuesdays, Fridays and Sundays, reached by going uphill from the ferry terminal along Söğütlüçeşme Cad until it becomes Kuşdili Cad. Similar to Beşiktaş Pazar, but with a European-style Sunday flea market selling jewellery and antiques.

Sirkeci Pazar Yeni Cami Meydanı, opposite Mısır Çarşısı (spice bazaar). Held on Sundays on the open square opposite the bazaar and in the adjacent backstreets. Cheap Turkish clothes and sportswear, though anything with a Western label is likely to be a fake.

Terkoz Çıkmaz Beyoğlu. A side-street off İstiklâl Cad; next to the Paşabahçe glass store, down towards Tünel. Open daily and crammed with stalls selling overruns bearing British, French and German high-street names.

Ulus Pazar Nispetiye Cad, Etiler. Held on Thursdays on the opposite side of Nispetiye Cad from Akmerkez shopping mall. High-street labels, though more expensive than in the other street markets.

High-street and designer clothes

You'll find all the usual **high-street fashion stores** in İstanbul, including Benetton, Diesel, DKNY, Escada, Lacoste, Levi's and Polo Ralph Lauren, as well as the more upmarket Armani, Versace and Gucci. **Turkish stores** (with multiple branches) to watch out for include: Beymen, Damat Tween, Homestore, Karaca, La Luna, Mudo City, Mudo, OXXO, Silk and Cashmere, and Yargıcı. Vakko is one of the oldest and best-known fashion chains in İstanbul; Vakkorama is its youth-market offshoot. For **shoes**, look for Desa, Hotiç and Vetrina.

Designer clothing outlets in İstanbul are mainly located in the shopping malls (see overleaf) or in the streets around the districts of **Nişantaşı**, **Osmanbey** and **Şişli** (take any bus north from Taksim Square, from outside *McDonalds*). There are more stores on **İstiklâl Caddesi**, and on **Bağdat Caddesi** on the Asian side of the Bosphorus near Kadıköy. Bursa **towelling**, among the best in the world, is available all over town, with many shops grouped in Nişantaşı and Şişli.

Beyman Akmerkez Shopping Mall, Etiler. Quality chain-store for tailored men and women's suits, dress shirts, silk ties and scarves and other accessories for the well-turned-out executive.

Mavi İstiklâl Cad 117, Beyoğlu; and in all shopping malls. Gap-inspired jeans label, good-quality denimwear, T-shirts, sweat tops and funky bags.

Silk & Cashmere Akmerkez Shopping Mall, Etiler; and other branches, including a duty-free shop at Atatürk airport. Scarves, hats, gloves, sweaters and shirts, using imported fabrics from China.

Vakko İstiklâl Cad 123–125, Beyoğlu; Akmerkez Shopping Mall, Etiler, and other branches; ⓦ www .vakko.com.tr. Classy fifty-year-old Turkish fashion

label renowned for its sense of style and use of fine fabrics. The clothes don't come cheap though, and you have to dress up a bit simply to get in the flagship store on İstiklâl Cad where you may come under some scrutiny from the rather snooty assistants. Vakkorama is the younger version aimed at wealthy teenagers. At the **Vakko Sales Store**, at Seylülislam Hayri Cad in Eminönü, items can be picked up for a quarter of the regular price.

Yargıcı Akmerkez Shopping Mall, Etiler, and other branches. Turkey's answer to Marks & Spencers – well-made and reasonably priced clothing from work suits to sportswear and underwear.

Leather

Leather is big business in Turkey, with raw pelts imported for processing from as far away as Australia and New Zealand. Turks wear a lot of leather and, increasingly, designs are matching the quality of the raw material. Prices are reasonable provided you don't get ripped off. The classiest outlets are listed below, but if you are prepared to do the legwork, cheaper shops can be found in Aksaray and Laleli, and in the covered bazaar, particularly in Vezirhan Sokak.

BB Kuyulu Sok 9–12, covered bazaar; and Yağlıkçalar Cad 143, covered bazaar. European designers, competitive prices.

Derishow Akmerkez Shopping Mall, Etiler; Bağdat Cad 381, Suadiye; and Akkavak Sok 18, Nişantaşı. Fine-quality leather goods.

Desa İstiklâl Cad 140, Beyoğlu; and Akmerkez,

Capitol and Galleria shopping malls. Top-quality Turkish designs; representatives of Samsonite.

De-Sa Ortakazlar Cad 8–10, covered bazaar. Good selection of leather and kilim bags.

Taki Nuruosmaniye Cad 96, Sultanahmet. Sophisicated shop with prices to match, near the covered bazaar.

Markets, arts, crafts and antiques

Bit pazarları or **flea markets** (literally "louse markets") make for excellent shopping, whether you're settling in the city and need furniture or simply looking for souvenirs. İstanbul is also a wonderful place for **antique** collectors. The choices run from traditional Turkish pieces to more obscure items from Europe. Remember, though, that while Turkish antiquities may be bought and sold, it's illegal to export them (punishable with five to ten years' imprisonment). An item under a hundred years old will pose few problems, but exporting a seventeenth-century Ottoman sword is another matter. Storeowners are always ready with explanations on the history of specific items. Below is listed an assortment of markets and odd shops selling arts, crafts and antiques.

Sultanahmet

Caferağa Medresesi Caferiye Sok. Next to the *Inter Youth Hostel*, the central courtyard is a pleasant tree-shaded café, while the surrounding shops sell leather, jewellery, calligraphy, carpets and miniatures.

İstanbul Handicrafts Centre Kabasakal Cad 5, next to the *Yeşil Ev Hotel*. Restored *medrese* where artists and craftsmen are keeping alive traditional skills such as *ebru* marbling, calligraphy, lace-making and embroidery.

Food shopping

The best places for food shopping are the weekly street markets in just about every residential area, or the municipality-run **Halk Paşarlar** (people's markets). The latter are permanent markets with small cubicle-like shops (including grocers, butchers and delicatessens), usually open from Monday to Saturday and specializing in fresh, cheap produce.

You can find **imported Western foods** in the major supermarket chains, such as Migros or Macrocenter, which have branches throughout the city, or in many of the delis that crowd the narrow streets behind Kadıköy harbour on the Asian shore.

The **Balak Pazarı**, or fish market off İstiklâl Caddesi in Beyoğlu, is a fascinating daily market selling much more than just fish. There's everything from fresh ducks, quails, regional cheeses, coffee beans and spices to farm-fresh eggs, *crème fraiche* and Beluga caviar scooped from a bucket. Pork, bacon and other hard-to-find ingredients are sold at a shop called Şutte (no. 21); while at Bunsa (no. 26) sun-dried tomatoes, fresh ginger, and a wide selection of health foods are available.

Dried fruit and exotic herbs can be found in the **Mısır Çarşısı** (spice bazaar) in Eminönü; while the **Eminönü Pazarı** (to the right of the spice bazaar) is a crowded market selling olives, olive oil, fresh vegetables, cheeses and pastrami. Also here is Kurukahveci Mehmet (Tahmiş Cad 66), the most famous outlet for **Turkish coffee**.

For a taste of **boza**, the Anatolian drink made from fermented *dari* (a type of wheat) flavoured with grape juice and cinnamon, try the oldest producer in Turkey, Vefa Bozacısı (Vefa Katip Çelebi Cad 102), just down from the Süleymaniye mosque. For traditional **Turkish cheese and meat products** visit one of the many family-owned supermarkets in Üsküdar, where you'll find specialities from all over Turkey.

Beyazit and the covered bazaar

Beyazit Pazar Beyazit Meyd. Held on Sundays in the square and the surrounding streets, with everything from stolen mobile phones to Russian army-surplus gear. Also the odd stall selling kilims, embroidery and other handicrafts from Central Asia.

Emin Çömez Yağlıkçılar Cad 101–103, covered bazaar. Excellent hat stall, well-stocked in winter with Russian and Turkish wool, leather and fur. This street is also good for traditional Anatolian textiles.

İç Bedesten Covered bazaar. The "Old Bazaar" is where the most precious objects have traditionally been kept. It's the place to go for antiques, reproductions and souvenirs of every kind, from Ottoman hamam slippers to pistols and silver jewellery.

Kato Export Halıcılar Cad 55, covered bazaar. Ottoman copper and Byzantine icons from the eighteenth and nineteenth centuries.

May Kolancılar Kapısı Sok 7, covered bazaar. Kilim bags, belts, purses and so forth, as well as ceramics.

Sarnıçlı Han Çadırcılar Cad 5, covered bazaar. A wholesale and handicraft bazaar: lots of copperware.

Sivaslı İstanbul Yazmacısı Yağlıkçılar Cad 57, covered bazaar. Hand-woven and hand-embroidered textiles, both old and new.

Sofa Nuruosmaniye Cad 42, Cağaloğlu. Old prints, maps, calligraphy, contemporary art and quality ceramics.

Yurt Antika Cebeci Han 51, covered bazaar. Central Asian carpets, kilims and textiles, some antique. It supplies to many other shops, so prices tend to be lower, and smaller items, such as cushions, go from 3YTL.

Fatih

Deli Kızın Yeri Halıcılar Cad 42. Opposite the main entrance of Fatih Camii, "Crazy Lady's Place" sells a vast amount of junk and collectibles, including limited-edition clothes, wall-hangings, scarves, Christmas decorations and unusual objects from Turkish artists. Linda is the crazy lady and she plans to open another branch in the covered bazaar. Closed Sun.

Horhor antique market Kırık Tulumba Sok. The famous weekend market behind Fethiye Camii with its rare Ottoman furniture is beyond most pockets, but it's a fascinating place to browse.

Beyoğlu

Atlas Pasaj İstiklâl Cad 209. An arcade behind the Atlas cinema filled with shops selling bric-a-brac, antiques and all sorts of kitsch – model cars, fur-trimmed lamps, ship's lanterns. One useful shop sells international brands of backpacks.

Aznavur Pasaj İstiklâl Cad. Opposite Galatasaray Yapı Kredi bank, two floors of small shops and stalls selling crafts, clothing, music and bric-a-brac.

Nobonb Çukuurlu Çeşme Sok 12. A real treasure-trove, with anything from antiques to secondhand costumes, and with a café on site.

Çukurcuma

Antikarnas Kuloğlu Mah, Faik Paşa Yokuşu 15. Turkish, Ottoman and European antiques – it specializes in religious icons.

Çukurcuma bit pazar In the streets below the Galatasaray Hamam. There are a number of antique shops here selling everything from valuable paintings, prints and carved wooden doors to bric-a-brac and books. To get there walk down Yeniçarsi Cad from İstiklâl Cad and turn left into Çukurcuma Sok.

Ortaköy

Artisan İskele Sok 9. Extensive range of antique silverware.

Entel Ortaköy Boardwalk, waterfront square, next to the ferry terminal. The daily market sells just about everything, from arts and crafts to junk and antiques, and is an enjoyable experience if you don't mind the crowds. The best day to go is Sunday for the Ortaköy "intellectual market" when the best stalls sell obscure music cassettes and dissident literature.

Pegasus İskele Sok 4. Designer jewellery, some inspired by Ottoman motifs, some contemporary.

Kenser Canfener Sok 14. Specializes in Kütahya pottery; it's an easy shop to find because of the beautiful tiles on the outside walls.

Hazal Halı Mecidiye Köprüsü Sok 9. Some colourful, quality carpets and kilims, beautifully displayed.

Kadıköy

Kadıköy bit pazar Özellik Sok, off Soğutluçeş me Cad. Daily street market where there's fun to be had sorting through the great mounds of furniture, household junk and old carpets and kilims, with some clothes on Tuesdays and fresh food on Fridays.

Üsküdar

Üsküdar bit pazar Büyük Hamam Sok, off Hakimiyet-i Milliye Cad. A 10min walk uphill from the ferry terminal – a bargain damaged or secondhand carpet can sometimes be picked up in this warren of antique shops full of junk and collectibles.

Music and musical instruments

Turkish music aside, you'll find a good general selection of world music, classical, pop and jazz in the music shops listed below and in the many outlets on İstiklâl Caddesi and in the shopping malls. Bulgarian-made bootlegs are sold along the backstreets of Taksim Square and Eminönü. Traditional musical instruments are on sale in the covered bazaar, though prices are much better at any one of the myriad of instrument shops on and around Galipdede Caddesi, near the upper Tünel station in Beyoğlu.

Akusta CD and Hi-fi Showroom Abdi İpekçi Cad 40, Nişantaşı. Classical, jazz, rock and world music, and state-of-the-art hi-fi equipment to play it on.

IMÇ Atatürk Bul, Unkapını. This dingy concrete shopping precinct just over the Atatürk bridge on the Golden Horn is the nerve centre of the Turkish music business. CD and tape prices tend to be 25 percent lower here than elsewhere.

Metropol İstiklâl Cad 140, Beyoğlu. A fine selection of Turkish sounds, many released on its own label.

Shopping malls

Akmerkez Nisbetiye Cad, Etiler, 5km north of Taksim. The largest of the new Western-style shopping centres, with restaurants and a cinema, and shops carrying most top Turkish brands, plus quality European and American outlets. Take bus #58/N or #59/N from Eminönü; #59/N or #559/C from Taksim; or a free twice-daily shuttle bus if you are staying in one of the five-star hotels.

Capitol Mahir İz Caddesi, Altunizade, on the Asian side of the Bosphorus. Take the ferry from Eminönü to Üsküdar or Kadıköy, then any dolmuş or bus that runs between these two ferry terminals via Altunizade. More user-friendly than Akmerkez, with a more affordable mix of Turkish chain stores and international brands (including British Home Stores and Mothercare), two cinemas, a giant food-court in the basement, and large Migros hypermarket.

Galleria Sahil Yolu, Ataköy. Five minutes' walk south along the coast road, Rauf Orbay Cad, from the Bakarköy train station and sea-bus terminal. It includes an ice-skating rink surrounded by fast-food cafés, a bowling alley, and the best of Turkish and European shops.

Listings

Airlines Most airlines have their offices around Taksim Square, or Elmadağ and Nişantaşı, the suburbs further north along Cumhuriyet Cad. THY (Turkish Airlines; ℡0212/663 6300, ⓦwww .turkishairlines.com), is the semi-privatized state carrier with the most domestic services, though Atlas Jet (℡0212/663 2000, ⓦwww.atlasjet .com), Fly Air (℡0212/424 3737, ⓦwww.flyair .com.tr) and Onur Air (℡0212/233 3800, ⓦwww .onurair.com.tr) also run domestic flights (see "Travel details", p.56). For international services, contact: Air France ℡0212/256 4356; Alitalia ℡0212/231 3391; Air Portugal ℡0212/240 4575; Austrian Airlines ℡0212/240 5032; Balkan Bulgarian Airlines ℡0212/245 2456; British Airways ℡0212/234 1300; Egypt Air ℡0212/231 1126; El-Al ℡0212/246 5303; Emirates Airlines ℡0212/293 5050; Gulf Air ℡0212/231 3450; KLM ℡0212/230 0311; Kuwait Airlines ℡0212/240 4081; Lufthansa ℡0212/288 1050; Northern Cyprus–Turkish Airlines ℡0212/267 0973; Olympic Airways ℡0212/247 3701; Qantas ℡0212/231 2850; Singapore Airlines ℡0212/232 3706; Swiss ℡0212/219 6419.

Airport Atatürk airport, Yeşilköy; flight enquiries ℡0212/663 0793. Havaş (℡0212/465 4700) runs buses to the airport from Cumhuriyet Cad, Taksim, next to the DHL office, a few doors up from the THY (Turkish Airlines) office; departures every thirty minutes, on the hour (daily 5am–11pm; 8YTL; journey time 20–40min, depending on traffic. Konuş Turizm (℡0212/660 1706, ⓦwww .konusturizm.com), and a number of travel agents on Divan Yolu Cad, as well as most hotels in Sultanahmet and Taksim, can arrange an airport transfer for around 8YTL. Yume (℡0212/522 7347, ⓦwww.yumetours.com) arranges shuttles to Sabiha Gökçen airport.

Banks and exchange Exchange offices (döviz) around Eminönü, Sultanahmet and Taksim, and on most main city thoroughfares, change cash without commission and usually at good rates, are open daily from 9am to 8pm (sometimes later in peak season) and are generally more efficient than banks. Some will change travellers' cheques, but charge a commission for this. There are also exchange offices at the airport (24hr), Esenler *otogar* (daily 8.30am–11pm) and Sirkeci station (daily 9am–5pm, also changes travellers' cheques). Opening hours for banks are Mon–Fri 9am–12.30pm & 1.30–5pm, though the larger branches of Garanti Bankası stay open through lunch and open between 9am–11.30am on Saturday mornings; most major banks have ATMs, some of which also dispense US$ and euros. The PTT (post office) operates an exchange booth outside Sultanahmet Camii in the summer (April–Sept daily 9am–5pm) and there's a 24-hour ATM next to it.

Bus companies All the following are based at Esenler *otogar*: Barış (bay 37 ☎0212/658 4002), for the Black Sea coast; Birçik (bay 154 ☎0212/658 1714), for the Black Sea coast; Kamil Koç (bays 144–146 ☎0212/252 7223, ⓦwww.kamilkoc.com.tr), to Ankara and southern resorts; Mersin (bay 8 ☎0212/658 3527), for the east; Metro (bays 51–52 ☎0212/658 3235), for the Black Sea coast; Nevtur/Göreme (bay 24 ☎0212/658 0771), for Cappadocia; Pamukkale (bays 41–42 ☎0212/249 2791), to the west and southern coasts; Ulusoy (bay 127 ☎0212/471 7100, ⓦwww.ulusoy.com.tr), to major cities and the Black Sea coast; Varan (bays 1–2 ☎0212/251 7474, ⓦwww.varan.com.tr), for western and southern destinations including nonstop luxury services to Ankara, İzmir and south-coast resorts. Also, see "Travel details" at the end of the chapter.

Car rental Avis, Atatürk airport ☎0212/663 0646, and the *Hilton Hotel*, Cumhuriyet Cad, Harbiye ☎0212/241 7896, ⓦwww.avis.com.tr; Beyaz Rent-a-car, Yeşim Sok 20, Akatlar ☎0212/351 2660, ⓦwww.beyazrentacar.com; Budget, Atatürk airport ☎0212/663 0858, and Cumhuriyet Cad 19, Harbiye ☎0212/253 9200; Decar, Atatürk airport ☎0212/465 4524 ⓦwww.decar.com; Europcar, Atatürk airport ☎0212/254 7710, and Topçu Cad 1, Taksim ☎0212/254 7788; Green Rent-a-car, Cumhuriyet Cad 23, Taksim ☎0212/232 6767; Hertz, Atatürk airport ☎0212/663 0807, and Cumhuriyet Cad 295, Harbiye ☎0212/233 1020.

Consulates Australia, Tepecik Yokuşu 58, Etiler ☎0212/257 7050; Canada, Büyükdere Cad 107/3, Gayretepe ☎0212/272 5174; New Zealand, Yesilçimen Sok 75, Ihlamur ☎0212/327 2211; United Kingdom, Meşrutiyet Cad 34, Tepebaşı, Beyoğlu ☎0212/293 7540; United States, Meşrutiyet Cad 104–108, Beyoğlu ☎0212/251 3602.

Cycling Cyclists should make a point of visiting Yeşil Bisiklet (Lalezar Cad 8, Selamiçeşme, Kadıköy ☎0216/363 5836), a cycling club and shop, which offers a maintenance service, rents out bikes and organizes trips.

Dentists Reliable options where English, German or French are spoken include: German Hospital Dental Clinic, Sıraselviler Cad 119, Taksim ☎0212/293 2150; Hakan Kaya, Çamlık Girişi 6, Etiler ☎0212/263 1649; Prodent Can Ergene, Valikonağı Cad 109, Nişantaşı ☎0212/230 4635; Reha Sezgin, Halazkargazi Cad 48, Şeker Apt, 5th floor no. 9, Harbiye ☎0212/240 3332.

Emergencies Ambulance ☎112; Fire ☎110; Police ☎155.

Hamams Most central, and the most frequented by tourists, are the Çemberlitaş Hamam (see p.151) near the covered bazaar and Cağaloğlu Hamam; other good ones include the Çinili Hamamı, off İtfaiye Cad in Zeyrek (p.158), the Çinili Hamamı, opposite the Çinili Cami in Üsküdar (p.182) and the Galatasaray Hamam on Turnacıbaşı Sok, Beyoğlu (daily: men 8am–8pm, women 8am–8pm; bath 24YTL, massage 13YTL extra).

Hospitals The Taksim First Aid Hospital at Sıraselviler Cad 112, Taksim ☎0212/252 4300, is state-run and deals with emergencies only; patients are often referred to one of the hospitals listed below. For emergencies, as well as regular doctor's appointments, private foreign hospitals are better, though more expensive than the state hospitals, which are understaffed and overcrowded. One of the city's best-equipped is the American Hospital, Güzelbahçe Sok 20, Nişantaşı (☎0212/231 4050); while the European Hospital, off Mehmetçik Cad, Mecidiyeky (☎0212/212 8811), is modern and more female-friendly than others. The German Hospital, at Sıraselviler Cad 119, Taksim (☎0212/293 2150), also has a dental and eye clinic.

Internet access Internet cafés have sprung up everywhere, catering predominantly to students, and generally open daily 9am–9pm, sometimes as late as 11pm. Well-located places include: Internet Club, İstiklâl Cad, Bekar Sok 20, Beyoğlu; Kirtasiye Internet, Suterazisi Sok 5, Sultanahmet; Net@Net Internet Café, Divan Yolu Cad, İncili Çavuş Sok 33, Sultanahmet; Otanik Internet Café, Alayköşkü Cad 2, Cağaloğlu; and Robin Hood, off İstiklâl Caddesi on Yeni Çarşı Cad 24.

Language classes Bosphorus University (☎0212/257 5039, ⓦwww.boun.edu.tr) offers an intensive eight-week summer course for around €300, and a regular two-term Turkish course. For a range of courses throughout the year (and class size usually limited to twelve), try Turkish Time, in the same offices as English Time, İstiklâl Cad 251, Beyoğlu (℡0212/293 9723, @www.turkishtime.com), or the Tömer school, Halaskargazi Cad 330, Şişli (℡0212/232 5832, @www.tomer.com.tr).

Laundry You might find a laundry service in your hotel or *pansiyon*, otherwise try: Active Laundry, Divan Yolu Cad, Dr Eminpaşa Sok 14, behind the *Cozy Pub* (daily 8am–8pm); or Star Laundry, Yeni Akbıyık Cad 18, Çankurtaran, opposite the *Orient Hostel* (daily 8am–7pm). Dry cleaners (*kuru temizlemecisi*) include: Morve-Site, Üçler Sok 4/A, at the far end of the Hippodrome (Mon–Sat 9am–6pm); and Safi, İstiklâl Cad, Bekar Sok 24, Beyoğlu (Mon–Fri 10am–7pm). There is an expensive drive-in laundry and dry cleaners at the *Hyatt Regency Hotel*, north of Taksim Square, which has a 3hr express service.

Left luggage Left-luggage offices (*Emanet* in Turkish) can be found at Atatürk airport (open 2hr, 9YTL per item) and in Haydarpaşa train station.

Libraries American Library and Computer Centre, American Embassy, Meşrutiyet Cad 108, Tepebaşı, Beyoğlu (Mon–Fri 10am–3.30pm; ℡0212/251 2675). The British Council Library, *Conrad Hotel*, Barbaros Bul, Beşiktaş (Mon–Thurs 11am–5.30pm, Fri & Sat 11am–4pm, closed Sun, Sat 9.30am–2.30pm ℡0212/327 2705) welcomes browsers, but to borrow books there's an annual membership of 65YTL, students 15YTL. The Süleymaniye Library, Ayşekadın Hamam Sok 35, Beyazıt (Mon–Sat 8.30am–5pm; ℡0212/520 6460), has a rich reference collection on Ottoman history and culture. The Turkish Touring and Automobile Association, Soqukçeşme Sok, Sultanahmet (Mon, Wed & Fri 10am–noon & 1.30–4.30pm; ℡0212/513 3660), has a library of books concerning the history of İstanbul.

Newspapers and magazines The kiosk just off Taksim Square at the top of Sıraselviler Cad sells a broad range of European publications at reasonable prices. For women's, men's, music and lifestyle magazines try: Dünya bookshop, İstiklâl Cad 469, Beyoğlu; the Metropol music shop, İstiklâl Cad 140, Beyoğlu; or Pandora bookshop, İstiklâl Cad, Büyükparmakkapı Sok 3, Beyoğlu.

Pharmacies Pharmacies (*Eczane*) are found everywhere and Turkish pharmacists are qualified to give injections, take blood pressure and treat minor wounds. In each İstanbul neighbourhood they take turns in providing a 24hr service called *Nöbetçi*. At night, the *Nöbetçi* rota is posted on the window of the other pharmacies.

Photography Cheapest place to buy camera film is from bulk dealers in the Altın Han or Kastel İş Merkezi on Hamidiye Caddesi in Sirkeci – it's 25–50 percent cheaper than the competition. The

Refo chain offers quality, normal-priced processing, though most of their outlets are in the northern suburbs; more central is Yalçınlar, which has around twenty branches all over İstanbul, including one opposite the train station in Sirkeci. Or try Gold Colour at Barbaros Bul 66, Beşiktaş.

Police Reports of theft or loss should be made to the Tourist Police, located in a prominent blue wooden building at Yerebatan Cad 6, Sultanahmet (℡0212/527 4503); there are English-speaking officers on the premises 24hr a day. Any commercial misdealings should be reported to the *Zabita* (market police) offices found all over town, including a handy one in Sultanahmet, at the far end of the Hippodrome. For work and resident permits, contact the Emniyet Müdürlüğü (police headquarters), at the Emniyet metro stop on Vatan Caddesi, Aksaray.

Post offices The main post office (PTT) is on Yeni Posthane Cad in Sirkeci, not far from the train station (daily 8am–midnight for telephone and telegrams, 8am–8pm for letters, 9am–5.30pm for full postal services). Other branch offices – including those at Cumhuriyet Cad in Taksim Square, at Kadıköy on İskele Meydanı in front of the ferry terminal, at Beşiktaş shopping arcade and on Hakimiyeti Milliye Cad, Üsküdar – are open daily 8.30am–12.30pm and 1.30–5pm. Smaller branch offices are usually open Mon–Fri 8am–3pm. Address poste restante (general delivery) mail to Büyük PTT, Yeni Posthane Cad, Sirkeci.

Swimming pools For a substantial fee you can use the pools in the major hotels including: the indoor pool at the *Merit Antique Hotel*, Ordu Cad 226, Laleli; and the outdoor pools at the *Hilton*, Cumhuriyet Cad, Harbiye; the *Hyatt Regency*, Taşkışla Cad, Taksim; and the *Marmara Hotel*, Taksim Square. Temporary membership available at gyms with pools include the Plaza Health Club, *Dorint Park Plaza Hotel*, Topçu Cad 23, Taksim, and Planet Health Club, Muallim Naci Cad 170, Kuruçeşme.

Telephones İstanbul has two phone-number prefixes, one for Europe, one for Asia, which must be used when calling the opposite shore; Europe ℡0212, Asia ℡0216. Local and international calls can be made from any public booth or at the PTTs (post offices). Useful clusters of booths can be found in Sultanahmet, Taksim Square and Sirkeci train station. Most accept phonecards, which can be bought at PTT counters, newsagent kiosks and shops.

Travel agents Travel agents are concentrated along Divan Yolu Cad in Sultanahmet and Cumhuriyet Cad in Taksim. Most can book destinations anywhere in Turkey, and arrange hotel stays, car rental and transfers to the airport or bus station: try Imperial, Divan Yolu Cad 30, Sultanahmet (☎ 0212/513 9430, ⓦ www.imperial-turkey.com); and Marco Polo, Divan Yolu Cad 54, Sultanahmet (☎ 0212/519 2804, ⓔ marcopolo@superonline.com). For budget tours, bus tickets and backpacker travel, contact Backpackers Travel, Yeni Akbiyik Cad 22, Sultanah-

met (☎ 0212/638 6343, ⓦ www.backpackerstravel. com), or Yoyça Tours, Yeni Akbiyik Cad 16, Sultanahmet (☎ 0212/518 4773, ⓔ oycatours@super-online.com). Skytur, İstiklâl Cad, Demir Han 344 (☎ 0212/245 9575), on the second floor opposite the Dutch Consulate, is a good outlet for domestic flight tickets.

Around İstanbul

The most obvious day-trip from İstanbul is **along the Bosphorus**, the upper reaches of which present a mixture of ancient fortresses, waterside villages, historic palaces, walks and views. Sadly most of the **Black Sea resorts** within easy reach have fallen prey to the developers, and Şile, Ağva and Kilyos have all lost some of their charm. However, the **Princes' Islands** in the Sea of Marmara seem to have preserved an independent character and wild beauty, despite the hordes of partying teenagers who descend through the summer months.

Along the Bosphorus

One of the world's most eulogized stretches of water, the **Bosphorus** is a source of pride for İstanbul's residents and of admiration for its visitors. The thirty-kilometre strait divides Europe and Asia and connects the Marmara and Black seas, its width varying from 660 to 4500 metres, and its depth from fifty to several hundred metres. Its name derives from the Greek myth of Io, lover of Zeus, whom the god transformed into a cow to conceal her from his jealous wife Hera. She plunged into the straits to escape a gadfly, hence Bosphorus, or "Ford of the Cow".

Around 80,000 cargo ships, oil tankers and ocean liners pass through the strait each year, while for residents and visitors alike the Bosphorus remains İstanbul's most important transport artery. The passenger ferries and sea buses that weave their way up and down from shore to shore provide one of the city's real highlights: along the way are imperial palaces and ancient fortresses interspersed with small fishing villages and wooden *yalis* (waterside manions), many in a state of precarious disrepair. Despite its pollution the Bosphorus is also full of fish – from swordfish to *hamsi* (a small fish belonging to the anchovy family) – served at restaurants in villages all the way along the strait.

To tour the Bosphorus and its shoreside villages you'll need a ferry **timetable** (*vapur tarifesi*, available from ferry terminals or the tourist offices), a handful of ferry *jetonlar* and some bus tickets, or an *akbil* travel pass (see p.116). Ferries are reasonably frequent, but if you get stranded up the Bosphorus, buses and dolmuşes run along the Asian and European shores back to the city.

If you prefer to have your itinerary planned in advance, however, take the **Bosphorus Tour** (see p.119), which leaves throughout the year from the ferry terminal at Eminönü. To ensure a good outside seat in summer, arrive at least half an hour before departure – it's not worth making the trip if you have to sit in the bowels of the boat with screaming children, missing all the views. Alternatively, **Lüfer** (☎0216/308 6770, ⓦwww.luferteknleri.com) runs a daily trip during the summer months (June–Sept) on the company's namesake, a *lüfer*, a small converted fishing boat, from Beylerbeyi on the Asian side and Çamlıbahçe (between Arnavutköy and Bebek) on the European side. The boat runs up to the Black Sea, where it drops anchor for lunch, swimming and sunbathing before coming back in the afternoon. Tickets cost €20 and you can book through Sultanahmet travel agencies.

The European shore

The **European shore** is very built up almost as far as the first Bosphorus bridge. Beyond Ortaköy the scenery mellows and the most charming of the villages, Arnavutköy and Bebek, are popular haunts of the rich, who are responsible for the growing commercialization of once simple waterside retreats. Further north, the fish restaurants in the villages of Sariyer and Rumeli Kavağı make pleasant destinations for lunch or dinner. West of Sariyer is the Belgrade Forest, offering quiet, rural surroundings in İstanbul's nearest tract of woodland. There are several ferry options on the European side or catch the very useful **#25/A bus**, which runs from Eminönü along the coast to Rumeli Kavağı.

Arnavutköy

From Ortaköy the coast road runs north under the first of the two Bosphorus intercontinental bridges – the kilometre-long **Atatürk bridge**, completed in time to celebrate the Turkish Republic's 50th anniversary in 1973. A couple of kilometres beyond the bridge is **ARNAVUTKÖY**, one of the most beautiful of all the Bosphorus villages, especially when seen from the water, famous for its line of *yalıs*, wooden waterfront mansions with their boat moorings carved out beneath them. The inner village, its streets lined with wooden houses, is worth exploring and it's also worth trying out one of the few **tavernas** run by the surviving Greek community, which feature live entertainment. *Bekriya*, on the second floor of 1 Cadde 90 (closed Sun), is a small low-key *meyhane* where a lone *ud* player goes from table to table; *Reis*, further along at 1 Cadde 115, is a more stylish option, a **café-bar** with a lovely waterside setting, the hangout of the local youth. In the other direction, again on the waterside, *Pupa Tropikal*, 1 Cadde 17 (closed Mon), is İstanbul's only African **bar**, frequented by Turks, Western expats and Africans alike.

△ Boats on the Bosphorous

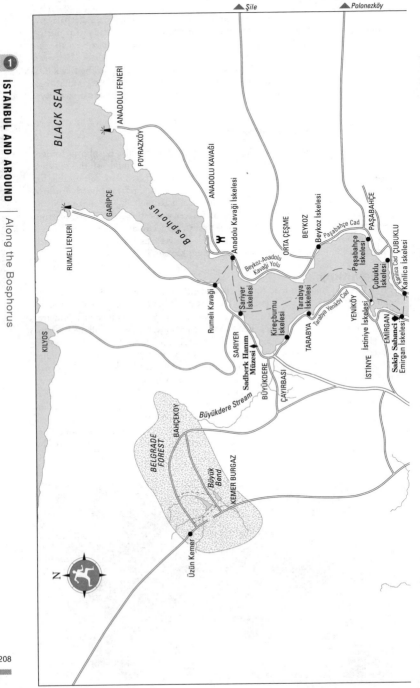

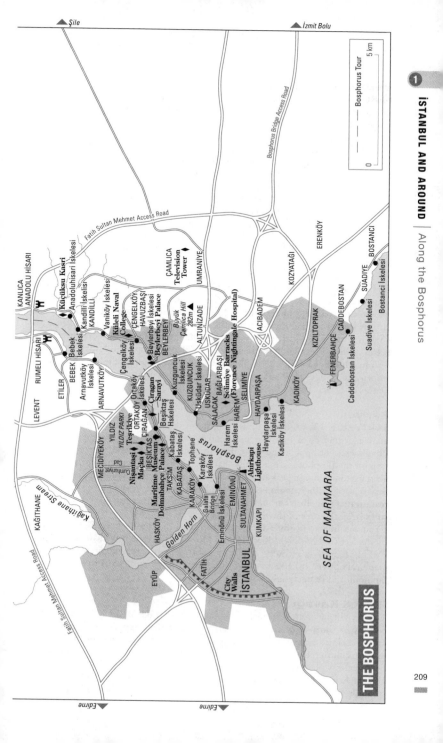

THE BOSPHORUS

ISTANBUL AND AROUND | Along the Bosphorus

209

Şile — İzmit Bolu

Bosphorus Bridge Access Road

Bosphorus Tour

0   5 km

Fatih Sultan Mehmet Access Road

ERENKÖY

KOZYATAĞI

BOSTANCI

SUADİYE

CADDEBOSTAN

Bostancı İskelesi

Suadiye İskelesi

Caddebostan İskelesi

FENERBAHÇE

KIZILTOPRAK

ACIBADEM

KADIKÖY

Kadıköy İskelesi

HAYDARPAŞA

Haydarpaşa İskelesi

SELİMİYE

HAREM

Harem İskelesi

ÜSKÜDAR

SALACAK

BAĞLARBAŞI

Selimiye Barracks (Florence Nightingale Hospital)

Üsküdar İskelesi

KUZGUNCUK

Kuzguncuk İskelesi

ALTUNİZADE

ÜMRANİYE

Büyük Çamlıca Hill 282m

ÇAMLICA Television Tower

BEYLERBEYİ

Beylerbeyi Palace

Beylerbeyi İskelesi

ÇENGELKÖY

HAVUZBAŞI

Çengelköy İskelesi

KANDİLLİ

Vaniköy İskelesi

Küleli Naval College

Kandilli İskelesi

Anadoluhisarı İskelesi

Küçüksu Kasrı

KANLICA ANADOLU HİSARI

SEA OF MARMARA

KUMKAPI

SULTANAHMET

İSTANBUL

FATİH

City Walls

EYÜP

Ahırkapı Lighthouse

EMİNÖNÜ

Eminönü İskelesi

Golden Horn

Galata Bridge

HASKÖY

KAĞITHANE

Kağıthane Stream

MECİDİYEKÖY

LEVENT

ETİLER

BEBEK

Bebek İskelesi

RUMELİ HİSARI

ARNAVUTKÖY

Arnavutköy İskelesi

YILDIZ

YILDIZ PARKI

BEŞİKTAŞ

Beşiktaş İskelesi

ORTAKÖY

Ortaköy İskelesi

Çırağan Sarayı

ÇIRAĞAN

Nişantaşı Teşvikiye Maçka

Cumhuriyet Cad

Maritime Museum Dolmabahçe Palace

TAKSİM

KABATAŞ

Kabataş İskelesi

KARAKÖY

Karaköy İskelesi

Tophane

Edirne

There are a couple of evening **boats** to Arnavutköy and Bebek from Eminönü; to get back, take the #B/2 or #40/A **bus** to Taksim, or the #25/A to Eminönü, which stop running at around 11.30pm.

Bebek and around

BEBEK (Turkish for baby) is the beginning of real wealth on the Bosphorus, and the suburbs from here to Sariyer encompass some of the most beautiful, priceless Bosphorus *yalıs*. The fifteen-minute walk from Arnavutköy follows an attractive park-fringed promenade, popular with swimming children and sunbathing pensioners. City-dwellers drive to Bebek to eat ice cream in the village square, which is also the gathering place for rich-kid bikers. If you arrive by boat, to the left of the jetty is Bebek's most famous building, the waterfront **Hıdıv Sarayı** (Khedive's Palace), an Art Nouveau-style mansion belonging to the Egyptian consulate. North of the ferry terminal, fishermen rent out **rowing boats** by the hour.

Above Bebek, up the extremely steep Küçük Bebek Caddesi, there's a little **park** known as the *balkon* (balcony) with extensive Bosphorus views and a café. Between the mosque and Bebek Park is *Bebek Kahvesi*, Cevdet Paşa Cad 137, a century-old no-frills **café**, always full of people who get together to chat, play backgammon or watch their dogs romp around the park.

A fifteen-minute walk along the promenade north of Bebek, is the impressive **fortress of Rumeli Hisarı** (Tues–Sun 9am–4.30pm; 2YTL). Grander than its counterpart, Andalou Hisarı, across the strait (see p.212), this Ottoman fortress was constructed in four months in 1452, before the Ottoman conquest of the city. It houses a small open-air theatre, providing a summer-evening venue for concerts and plays, particularly during the International Music Festival (see p.196). The fortress lies in the shadow of the second Bosphorus bridge, the **Fatih Sultan Mehmet bridge**. Completed in 1988, it's amongst the world's longest suspension bridges (1090m), and spans the Bosphorus at the point where King Darius of Persia crossed the straits by pontoon bridge in 512 BC.

Sariyer

SARIYER is 12km further up the European shore from Bebek, after the unremarkable suburbs of Emirgan and Yeniköy (stops on the Bosphorus Tour), and Büyükdere, with public transport links to the Belgrade Forest (see p.211). Also a stop on the Bosphorus Tour cruise, Sariyer has a sea-bus terminal for faster connections to the city in peak hours. It's famous for its milk puddings and *böreks*, and between ferries there is ample time for a leisurely lunch in any one of the seafood **restaurants** that cluster around the quayside or in the daily fish market (one of the city's largest), north of the ferry terminal.

You can idle away some time with a visit to the **Sadberk Hanım Museum**, Büyükdere Cad 27–29 (Sadberk Hanım Müzesi; daily except Wed 10.30am–6pm; 2YTL), and its beautifully displayed assortment of archeological and ethnographical objects. It's 300m south of the Sariyer jetty; bus #25/A to Sariyer from Eminönü and Beşiktaş passes by.

Rumeli Kavağı

The last village on the European Bosphorus shore is **RUMELI KAVAĞI**, a 2km dolmuş or short ferry ride from Sariyer. Nicer than Sariyer, with more of a village feel, it's no more than a string of houses, with some delightful **fish restaurants** clustered around its ferry terminal. Particular favourites include *Ayder Balik*, a classy place where you order fish specials off a big tray; the cheaper *Süper Yedigün*, which has an open terrace on the roof; and *Yedi Gün*, whose shrimp casserole is excellent. There's also a small private swimming **beach** here, one of the very few along the Bosphorus, though it is often restricted to women and children only.

The easiest way to get here is on the Bosphorus Tour, when restaurant owners expectantly await the arrival of the ferry. If you're intending to make an evening of it remember that the last bus from Rumeli Kavağı to Eminönü, the #25/A, leaves at 10pm from near the jetty, while the last dolmuş to Sariyer leaves at 11pm, from where there are later buses back to Taksim and Eminönü. There is also a local ferry connecting Rumeli Kavağı with Anadolu Kavağı on the opposite Asian shore, and with Sariyer.

Belgrade Forest

Several kilometres west of Sariyer, off the main road to Kılyos in the Istranca hills, **Belgrade Forest** (Belgrad Ormanları) was originally a hunting preserve of the Ottomans. The pine, oak and beech forest is now a popular retreat from the rigours of the city. It's most easily reached by car though determined non-drivers can take a dolmuş from Sırmacılar Sok in the suburb of Büyükdere, on the Bosphorus, to the village of **BAHÇEKÖY**, on the east side of the forest. From here it is a 1.5km walk to **Büyük Bend reservoir** and the largest picnic ground in the forest, where there's a tea garden, first-aid stand and gymnastic equipment in the trees for joggers and athletes.

A sophisticated system of dams, reservoirs, water towers and aqueducts is still in evidence around the forest, which supplied İstanbul with most of its fresh water during Byzantine and Ottoman times. The most impressive of the aqueducts is the *Uzun* or **Long Aqueduct**, a 1km walk south of Büyük Bend beyond Kemer Burgaz. Its tiers of tall, pointed arches were built by Sinan for Süleyman the Magnificent in 1563. Close to the reservoir are the remains of Belgrade village; the name came about after the capture of Belgrade in 1521, when a community of Serbian well-diggers, prisoners-of-war of Süleyman, were settled here to take over the upkeep of the water-supply system. In the seventeenth century the forests' attractions were discovered by the foreign community of İstanbul, who came to seek refuge from a particularly nasty pestilence that was wiping out half the city, and for the next century or so many wealthy Christians had second homes here. In the 1890s the village was evacuated by Abdül Hamid II, who believed the inhabitants were polluting the city's water supply.

The Asian shore

On the Asian side of the Bosphorus are vast suburbs and small villages, all virtually unknown to tourists. The Bosphorus Tour (see p.119) calls in at some of the villages on the way to its final stop Anadolu Kavağı, the last village on the Asian side. Buses run here (stopping at the villages and suburbs in between) from Üsküdar's main bus station in front of the İskele Camii and ferry terminal, with the **#15/D** running along the entire coast from Üsküdar to Anadolu Kavağı.

Kuzguncuk

Dolmuşes and buses follow the coast road the two or three kilometres from Üsküdar to **KUZGUNCUK**. There are ferries across to Beşikataş from here, as well as a good **fish restaurant** on the shore, İsmet Baba, at Acadiye Cad 96–98 (T0216/333 1232). This is one of those genuine old establishments that it's hard to find on the Bosphorus these days, with a fine view of Ortaköy Camii on the other side and twenty varieties of *meze*, the fish of the day and *rakı* all for around 32–40YTL per person.

A thirty-minute walk from the village up İcadiye Sokak is the **Jewish cemetery**, with its white marble gravestones laying flat on the ground instead of standing upright. İstanbul's Jewish community largely originates from 1492, when Beyazit II gave refuge to Jews escaping the Spanish Inquisition; some still speak "Ladino", a language close to fifteenth-century classical Spanish. The Ottomans benefited from the commercial acumen of the Jewish community, which still plays an important part in the Turkish economy.

Beylerbeyi

The main attraction of **BEYLERBEYI**, the next village, 500m along and on the other side of the first Bosphorus bridge, is the **Beylerbeyi Palace** (daily except Mon & Thurs 9.30am–5pm; guided tours 6YTL), a nineteenth-century white marble summer residence and guesthouse of the Ottoman sultans. Much admired by contemporary visitors from Europe – after her stay in 1869, Empress Eugénie had its windows copied in the Tuileries Palace in Paris – the palace is still popular with Western visitors. The interior decoration was designed by Sultan Abdülaziz himself, while some of the furniture, including the matching dining chairs in the harem and the *selamlık*, was carved by Sultan Abdülhamid II during his six years of imprisonment here up to his death in 1918. The central staircase, with its fanciful twisting shape, is perhaps the highlight, but there are all kinds of details to savour here, from the neo-Islamic patterns on the ceilings down to the beautiful Egyptian *hasır*, the reed matting on the floor.

Çengelköy and around

ÇENGELKÖY is a pretty village, a short walk from Beylerbeyi, around the next bend of the Bosphorus. Its main landmark building, the *kuleli*, once served as a hospital under the direction of Florence Nightingale in the Crimean War, though it's currently closed to the public.

A ten-minute bus ride from Çengelköy is **Küçüksu Kasrı**, sometimes known as Göksu Palace (daily except Mon & Thurs 9.30am–4pm; 2YTL), which takes both its names from the two nearby streams that empty into the Bosphorus. After passing a boatyard to your left you'll cross a bridge over the Küçüksu Deresi (see overleaf); get off at the next stop, walk back to the sign saying "Küçük Saray Aile Bahcesi" and you'll find the palace at the end of a drive. Built by Nikoğos Balian, son of the architect of Dolmabahçe, its exterior is highly ornate – the Rococo carving is best seen from the Bosphorus, the intended approach. The whole of the palace interior is decorated with lace and carpets from Hereke and lit by Bohemian crystal chandeliers. The floors are mahogany, inlaid with rose- and almond-wood and ebony; upstairs is an ebony table on which Sultan Abdülaziz was wont to arm-wrestle with visitors of state.

Anadolu Hisarı and Kanlıca

The **Küçüksu Deresi** and the **Göksu** are the streams formerly known to Europeans as the "Sweet Waters of Asia", their banks graced by picnicking parties of Ottoman nobility. On the north bank of the Göksu stands the Ottoman fortress of **Anadolu Hisarı** (always open; free), beneath the towering Fatih bridge.

Beyond the bridge, bus #15/D continues to **KANLICA**, famed for its yoghurt, which can be eaten at any of the little quayside restaurants. Ferries run back under the bridge and across to Bebek (see p.210) from here and the #15/D continues the 12km or so on to the village of Anadolu Kavağı.

Anadolu Kavağı

The last call on the Bosphorus Tour from Eminönü is **ANADOLU KAVAĞI**, where the boat stops for a couple of hours. The village has a distinct, if dilapidated, charm – balconied houses with boat-mooring stations overlook the Bosphorus, while the main street is lined with excellent **fish restaurants** and food stands, where fishermen sell their wares directly to the restaurant owners.

Sprawling across an overgrown hilltop above the town, is the Byzantine **fortress** (always open; free) from which the village takes its name. It affords excellent views of the Bosphorus and, approaching from above you'll see various Greek inscriptions and even the imperial logo of the Paleologus dynasty (a cross with the letter "b" in each corner, which stands for "King of Kings, who Kings it over Kings"). To get to the fortress, take Mirşah Hamam Sokak from the dock and walk uphill for half an hour.

From the jetty back in the village, bus #15/D runs to Üsküdar, or catch a ferry to Sariyer on the European side, where there's a sea-bus terminal and buses to Taksim.

The Princes' Islands

The **Princes' Islands**, in the Sea of Marmara between 15km and 30km southeast of the city, have always been a favourite retreat from the mainland. Four of the nine islands are easily accessible by ferry from İstanbul and, in the summer public holidays, see a steady stream of visitors that threaten to destroy the peace and tranquillity. On the largest island, Büyükada, the local population of 6500 swells each summer to over 40,000. That said, it's usually easy enough to escape the crowds. Apart from the odd police or utility vehicle, no cars are allowed on the islands, so **transport** is either by foot, *phaeton* (horse-drawn carriage), bike or donkey. The proximity to İstanbul of these romantic retreats make them an easy day-trip, but if you do wish to overnight you'll find accommodation both over-priced and, especially on summer weekends, hard to come by.

Some history

The islands have been inhabited since Classical times, but their first claim to fame derived from the copper mines of Chalkitis – modern **Heybeliada** – long since exhausted (but still visible near Çam Limanı). In the Byzantine era, numerous convents and monasteries were built on the islands and these became favoured – because of their proximity to the capital and ease of surveillance – as luxurious prisons for banished emperors, empresses and princes (often after they had been blinded). After the conquest, the islands were largely neglected by the Ottoman Turks and became a place of refuge for Greek, Armenian and Jewish communities.

In 1846 a ferry service was established and the islands became popular with Pera's wealthy merchants and bankers, but it was only in the early years of the Republic that the islands became İstanbul's favourite summer resort. Mosques began to appear in the villages, and hotels and apartment buildings soon followed. A Turkish naval college was established on Heybeliada and the islands received the rubber stamp of republican respectability when Atatürk's private yacht was moored here as a training ship.

Not all of the islands have romantic connotations. **Sivriada**, which is uninhabited and cannot be visited, gained public notoriety in 1911 when all the stray dogs in İstanbul were rounded up, shipped out there and left to starve; while **Yassıada** is best known as a prison island, used for the detention of political prisoners. It was here that Adnan Menderes and two of his former ministers were hanged on the night of September 16, 1961, after a military coup.

Since Büyükada and Heybeliada were declared centres of tourism, they've been a focal point for further development and legislation restricting the height of new buildings to a 7.5-metre, two-storey limit is widely flouted. The pressure group

Ada Vakfı (the Princes' Islands Foundation) continues its attempts to preserve what's left of the islands' heritage and, despite the changes, the essence of a trip to the islands is still escape from the noise, stress and pollution of the city.

Getting there

The islands are easy to reach, but get to the ferry at least an hour before departure in summer, especially on Sundays as the queues can be massive. The Turkish Maritime Lines **ferry** from Sirkeci pier, Adalar İskelesi, runs to Büyükada, Heybeliada and Burgazada (Mon–Sat 12 daily, Sun 15 daily; 2–3 daily during winter; 1hr 30min–2hr; 4YTL return). There is also a more expensive but much quicker **sea bus** (*deniz otobüs*) service from Kabataş (near Beşiktaş) to Büyükada, Heybeliada and Burgazada (12 daily, much less frequently in winter; 25–45min; 12YTL).

Island hopping among the four larger islands – Büyükada, Heybeliada, Burgazada and Kınalıada – is easy, but check ferry times at the dock and don't rely simply on a timetable; the service is notoriously changeable. An *akbil* or a handful of *jeton*s makes island hopping easier.

Büyükada

Büyükada (the "Great Island", the original *Prinkipo*, or "Prince's Island", in Greek) is the largest of the islands and has long been inhabited by minorities. It has traditionally been a place of retreat or exile, and Leon Trotsky lived here from 1929 to 1933, when he began to write his *History of the Russian Revolution*. He spent most of his time at **İzzet Paşa Köşkü**, an attractive wooden mansion on Çankaya Caddesi, built by a Greek banker and later owned by Abdülhamid's chief of police. It was also the house where, in 1933, Trotsky's daughter committed suicide. On the same road, further back towards the ferry landing, is another fine wooden mansion, the **Con Paşa Köşkü**, with a two-storey colonnaded portico, elaborately carved in honey-coloured wood. These large mansions of Büyükada tend to have beautiful gardens full of magnolia, mimosa and jasmine, and in the surrounding pine forests myrtle, lilac and rock roses grow wild, so the scents of the island on a summer's evening are one of its most memorable aspects.

The island consists of two hills, both surmounted by monasteries. The southernmost, **Yüce Tepe**, is the location of the **Monastery of St George**, probably on the site of a twelfth-century building. Close up, it consists of a series of chapels on three levels, with the oldest – containing a sacred spring – on the lowest level. In Byzantine times the monastery was used as an insane asylum and iron rings set into the floor of the chapels were used for restraining the inmates. To reach the monastery, take a *phaeton* to the small park on the main road that goes over the hill, from where a steep path leads up several hundred metres to the monastery. Alternatively, take a donkey from the stables at the bottom of this path.

The monastery on the northern hill, **İsa Tepe**, is a nineteenth-century building. Three families still inhabit the precincts and there are services in the chapel on Sundays. The adjacent **café** is famous for its wine; at one time this was produced at the monastery itself.

Practicalities

Ferries and **sea buses** dock at two adjacent terminals on Büyük İskele Cad in Büyükada's main town, from where the main square and most of the hotels, restaurants and shops are just a short walk away. With motor vehicles banned, there are **bike rental** shops (13YTL per day) everywhere. **Phaeton** (horse-and-carriage) tours (for up to four people; short tour 16YTL, long tour 21YTL) leave from the *phaeton* park off the main square on Isa Çelebi Sok, 50m above the ferry terminal.

Donkey rides (about 8YTL per ride) up the hills start from a little park found just up Kadayoran Caddesi from the centre of town.

Accommodation is uniformly expensive, though the chance to stay in a grand restored mansion may be appealing. There are lots of good fish restaurants along the shore to the left of the ferry terminal. One street back from the shore road, İskele Caddesi has a selection of cheaper cafés, selling all the usual Turkish dishes.

Accommodation

Büyükada Princess İskele Meyd ☎216/382 1628, ℻382 1949. Offers neatly furnished air-conditioned rooms with TV and minibar in a nine-teenth-century building with pool. Prices may be negotiable, and drop anyway at the beginning and end of the season by up to twenty percent. ❺

Saydam Planet II İskele Meyd ☎0216/382 2670, ℻382 3848. A beautifully renovated wooden man-sion, but the glorious exterior is not matched by the somehow characterless rooms. It also suffers from being virtually on the jetty, with constant streams of people embarking and disembarking a stone's throw away. Suite rooms are fifty percent more expensive. ❼

Hotel Splendid Nisan Cad 23 ☎216/382 6950, ℠www.splendidhotel.com. Dating from 1908, and once host to Edward VIII and Wallis Simpson, it has serious fin de siècle grandeur, with cupolas, balconies, a good restaurant, excellent service and a garden with a swimming pool. The reception sells a lovely replica poster advertising the hotel in its heyday for 10YTL. ❻

Eating and drinking

Alibaba Restaurant Gülistan Cad 20. A good choice out of the several restaurants on the water-front to the left of the jetty, with similar prices and ambience. It's a friendly place with white table-cloths, fish meals from 11–41YTL and the usual selection of meze. Alcohol served.

Heybeliada

Heybeliada, or the "Island of the Saddlebag", has managed to retain much of its village identity, and there is a strong community spirit among its permanent residents. It's a beautiful place, known for the beaches to which İstanbul residents flock in their hundreds at weekends. The family of the famous İstanbul writer, Orhan Pamuk, spent the summer in one of the island's fine wooden Art-Nouveau-style mansions.

Heybeliada's main point of interest is the nineteenth-century Greek Orthodox School of Theology, the Aya Triada Manastiri, majestically situated on the peak of the island's northernmost hill. It's a pleasant fifteen-minute walk through pine forest (or take a phaeton; see "Practicalities", p.216), but getting inside the compound is by appointment only (☎0216/351 8563; Mon–Sat 10am–noon & 2–4pm; free). You'll need to prove scholarship credentials to view the library of 230,000 books, including an important collection of Byzantine manuscripts. The building is set in beautiful grounds, and encloses a pretty, eight-hundred-year-old church, with a stunning gilt iconostasis. Orthodox priests were trained here until the government closed it in 1973 (recent attempts to reopen it have foundered), and you can see the dusty classroom filled with age-blackened desks where the acolytes received instruction.

Other buildings you might come across during a stroll around the island include the Heybeliada Sanatorium, a private home for TB sufferers located off Çam Limanı Yolu on the south side of the island. The Naval High School (Deniz Harp Okulu), on the east side of the island, along the coast road from the main jetty, was originally the Naval War Academy, situated here since 1852. There is also a further orthodox church, that of Aya Nikola, a prominent red-and-cream building with a curious clocktower, just behind the waterfront in the town centre.

There are several beaches around the island, though swimming in the polluted waters is at your own risk.

Practicalities

Ferries and **sea buses** arrive at Heybeliada ferry terminal on the main quayside of Rıhtım Caddesi. Walking and cycling are good ways to enjoy Heybeliada, its pine forests and hills making for scenic rides and rambles; there's **bike rental** near the quayside at İmralı Sok 3. Prices for **phaetons** from Ayyıldız Caddesi (which runs parallel to the front) to various destinations around the island are posted on a board in the street; **tours of the island** are also available (short tours for 16YTL, longer ones 25YTL).

The island is more low-key and **accommodation** is cheaper than neighbouring Büyükada, though booking in advance is recommended, particularly at weekends. The **restaurants** cater to locals all year round and consequently there are plenty to choose from – generally good, simple and cheap, offering standard *lokanta*, kebab and *pide* fare; most are situated on Ayyıldız Caddesi.

Merit Halki Palas Refah Şehitler Cad 88 ℡0216/351 0025, ⊛www.merithotels.com. Nineteenth-century villa, restored in dubious taste by the *Merit Hotel* group as the only five-star hotel on the islands, incorporating gymnasium, Jacuzzi and outdoor pool. In the restaurant you can get a three-course meal, usually featuring fish, for around 32YTL a head, served in a lovely poolside setting. **❼**

Özdemir Pansiyon Ayyıldız Cad 41 ℡0216/351 1866, ⊛www.adalar-ozdemirpansiyon.com. Cheapest option on the island, with tiny chalet-type en-suite rooms with a shower over squat loos, plus larger rooms in the main block. Both are comfortable enough. Note that prices rise by fifty percent on Friday and Saturday nights. No breakfast. **❶**

Prenset Pansiyon Ayyıldız Cad 74 ℡216/351 9388. This converted apartment building with wood-trimmed exterior offers reasonable value, despite most rooms not having views. Friendly management, comfortable rooms with immaculate modern bathrooms, and central heating in winter. Prices rise thirty percent at weekends. **❹**

Burgazada and Kınalıada

The other two islands served by public ferry are Burgazada and Kınalıada, both small and relatively unspoilt, though holiday homes now outnumber those of permanent residents. In winter the villages around their jetties are practically ghost towns.

Burgazada

Burgazada has a fascinating small **museum** (Tues–Fri 10am–noon & 2–5pm, Sat 10am–noon; free) at Burgaz Çayırı Sok 15, on the other side of the square from the church of St John the Baptist (the dome of which is the town's most prominent landmark). The museum is dedicated to the novelist **Sait Faik** (often described as the Turkish Mark Twain), who lived here, and the house has been so carefully preserved that you feel you're trespassing. In the writer's bedroom a pair of pyjamas is neatly folded on the bed, with a towel on the rack beside it. You get an immediate impression of the man, whose exceptional character is evidenced by the simple bohemian style of furnishings in his island home.

A quarter of an hour's walk from the ferry terminal to the western part of the island brings you to the *Sait Faik* **restaurant**, which has terraces looking out over a little headland to the sea.

Kınalıada

Kınalıada, "Henna Island", takes its name from the red colouring of its eastern cliffs; in Greek it was known as *Proti*, since it's the nearest of the islands to the mainland. Like Heybeliada, Kınalıada's history is notable for exiles, including Romanus IV Diogenes, deposed after his disastrous defeat at the Battle of Manzikert by the Selçuk Turks. Today, its population is seventy percent Armenian. The island is rather bare and barren and is probably the least impressive of all as it is covered in houses. However, it's a favourite for swimming and its beaches are less polluted by sewage than those of the other three islands.

Black Sea resorts

The **Black Sea** and a few of its resorts are easily accessible from İstanbul and, if you're staying in the city for any length of time, these seaside villages make good day-trips or weekend breaks. Bear in mind, however, that much of the development along this coast has been uncontrolled, with some resorts appallingly built-up: they can be quite disappointing in high season, particularly, when they tend to fill with disgruntled Russian package tourists.

Kılyos

The nearest resort on the European side of the Bosphorus, **KİLYOS** is fairly easily accessible by regular minibus-dolmuş from Sariyer (see p.210), from where there's a direct road of about 12km. Sadly, the former Greek fishing village has succumbed to a tide of holiday-home development and the beach is dirty. There's little of interest; the area's most imposing monument – a medieval Genoese castle – is occupied by the Turkish army and off-limits. The last dolmuş back to Sariyer from Kılyos leaves at around 8pm.

Şile

A main road from Asian İstanbul to **ŞILE** has led to increased development as it's now feasible to live here and commute into town, or have a weekend summer-house. It's 70km, or about a 1hr 15min drive from Üsküdar, with several buses departing daily from the bus station in Üsküdar on Doğancilar Caddesi (on the hour 9am–4pm).

Out of season it's easy to see Şile's attraction, perched on a clifftop overlooking a large bay and tiny island, with white sandy **beaches** stretching off to the west. There's also the pretty French-built black-and-white-striped lighthouse and the fourteenth-century Genoese castle on a nearby island. However, the town is best avoided during the summer months, when it's far too busy, and the sea has a strong undercurrent, with several people drowning here every year.

Şile's main historical claim to fame is that it was visited by Xenophon and his Ten Thousand, the army that was left leaderless when its officers were all murdered by the Persians. They stayed in Şile, then known as Kalpe, and Xenophon wrote in his memoirs about how well the site suited the establishment of a city. Apart from tourism, the town's only other industry is the production of *Şile bezi*, a kind of cheesecloth that local women embroider by hand and that is sold all over Turkey. There are plenty of unremarkable **hotels** in town, though you are unlikely to want to stay.

Ağva

About 50km further along the coast east from Şile, the village of **AĞVA** is a quieter, marginally less developed spot, more worthy of the journey from İstanbul. To get there, catch one of the Şile buses from Üsküdar, which continue on for another hour to Ağva. The last buses back to Üsküdar via Şile leave at 6pm in summer; in winter they leave at 5pm at the weekend, 3pm on a weekday.

The village is set in a beautiful location between two rivers, the Yezilçay and the Göksü, both of which are fished to provide the livelihood of the local community. Ağva's **beach** has fine golden sand, but the currents here are notoriously strong so it's not recommended that you swim unless there are plenty of people around to help in the event of any trouble. There are a few small **hotels** in Ağva, some with fish restaurants attached. On the banks of the Yeşilçay River, the *Motel Tahir* (☎0216/721 8012; ❹) has simple clean en-suite doubles and serves *kiremit kebap* in the evenings by the river, though it often closes during winter if it's quiet.

Polonezköy

The small Polish village of **POLONEZKÖY** could be visited on your way to the coast if you were driving, but there's no public transport. It is around a 20km drive from Üsküdar, west of the main İstanbul–Şile road.

Polonezköy ("village of the Poles") was established in 1848 by **Prince Czartorisky**, the leader of the Polish nationals, who was granted exile in the Ottoman Empire. His main aim, along with other Eastern European exiles such as the poet Adam Mickiewicz and Hungarian nationalist leader Kossuth, was to establish a union of the Balkan races, including Romanians, Circassians and Turks, to counteract Panslavic expansion. The village has long attracted international interest – among its most famous visitors have been Liszt, Flaubert, Pope John Paul I and Lech Wałesa – and became known to tourists in the 1970s, when it was popular among İstanbulites in search of illicit pig meat, hard to find in the city. Following the building of the new Bosphorus bridge, Polonezköy became the fashionable place for İstanbul residents to own a second home away from the city's deathly pollution.

Of the original Central European-style wooden houses, with their balconies and flower gardens, few now remain. On the plus side, the designation of the village and surrounding area as İstanbul's first national park has slowed the development that threatened to ruin the surrounding countryside. There's a 4.5-kilometre jogging and walking track to the north of the village which wends through the forest of pine, chestnut, oaks and hornbeams, crossing over streams on little wooden bridges.

Hotels here are mostly quite pricey: one of the nicest is the *Polka Country Hotel* (☎0216/432 3220, ℱ432 3042; ❻), at Cumhuriyet Yolu 36, a lovingly restored half-timbered farmhouse dating from 1905, with exposed beams. It has a pool, and pork chops feature on the menu.

Travel details

Buses

The main bus terminals are at **Esenler** (☎0212/658 0505) on the European side, and **Harem** (☎0216/333 3763) on the Asian side. All national bus services stop at both, regardless of where they are going in Turkey (see "Listings", p.204, for company contact details). All international buses use Esenler *otogar* only. The longer trips are overnight. If you book your ticket through one of the company's city offices, of which there are numerous branches, or through a travel agent, a shuttle service is provided from Sultanahmet and Taksim to the bus station.

Black Sea coast (served by Ulusoy, Dağıştanlı, Metro, Birçik, Barış): Artvin (1 daily; 22hr); Hopa (3 daily; 19hr); Rize (4 daily; 19hr); Samsun (4 daily; 9hr); Trabzon (9 daily; 16hr).

Cappadocia (Nevtur/Göreme Seyahat has the most direct service, and is the most comfortable, reliable and fast of the companies serving Cappadocia, and the only one which drops in Göreme village): Avanos (3 daily; 11hr); Göreme (3 daily; 11hr); Nevşehir (3 daily; 11hr); Ürgüp (3 daily; 11hr 30min).

Eastern Turkey (served by Mersin): Adana (2 daily; 19hr); Antakya (2 daily; 18hr); Antep (4 daily; 20hr); Diyarbakır (3 daily; 19hr); Doğubeyazit (1 daily; 24hr); Erzurum (3 daily; 18hr); İskenderun (3 daily; 18hr); Konya (7 daily; 11hr); Mardin (1 daily; 22hr); Tokat (3 daily; 16hr); Urfa (1 daily; 21hr).

Mediterranean and Aegean coasts (served by Varan, Ulusoy, Pamukkale, Kamil Koç): Alanya (12 daily; 14hr); Antalya (several in the evening from 6pm; 12hr); Ayvalık (hourly; 9hr); Bodrum (hourly; 13hr); Datça (1 daily; 17hr); Fethiye (3 daily in the evening; 14hr); İzmir (hourly; 10hr); Kuşadası (5 daily; 11hr); Marmaris (4 daily; 11hr); Side (several in the evening from 6pm; 13hr).

Western Turkey (served by Kamil Koç, Pamukkale, Varan, Uludar Hakiki Koç): Ankara (hourly; 6hr); Balıkesir (hourly; 8hr); Bandırma (hourly; 6hr); Bursa (hourly; 5hr); Çanakkale (hourly; 5hr 30min); Denizli (3 daily; 10hr); Edirne (hourly; 2hr 30min); Kütahya (6 daily; 5hr 30min); Uşak (4 daily; 8hr 30min).

Out of Turkey To Bulgaria (with Avar, Trakya and Alpar): Sofya (daily; 12hr).

To Georgia (with Ortadoğu and Buse): Batum (3 weekly; 22hr); Tiflis (3 weekly; 22hr).

To Greece (with Ulusoy, Derya and Varan): Athens (6 weekly; 23hr 30min); Thessaloniki (6 weekly; 12hr 30min).

To Russia (with Ortadoğu): Moscow (2 weekly; 36hr).

Trains

Most train services to the rest of Turkey depart from **Haydarpaşa** (☎0216/336 4470 or 337 9911) on the Asian side. International trains to Europe, and local trains to Turkey's European peninsula, depart from **Sirkeci** (☎0212/527 0050 or 527 0051) on the European side. The tourist office in Sirkeci station can advise on all international journeys and it's advisable to purchase tickets in advance from station ticket offices, or from travel agents that deal directly with the Turkish Railways. International tickets can be paid for in either Turkish lira, US$ cash or euros.

Haydarpaşa station to: Adana (3 weekly; 29hr); Adapazarı (11 daily; 2hr 45min); Afyon (3 daily; 13hr 30min); Ankara (6 daily; 7hr 30min–9hr); Arifiye (3 daily; 3hr); Denizli (1 daily; 14hr 25min); Erzurum (1 daily; 35hr); Eskişehir (3 daily; 6hr 20min); Gaziantep (3 weekly; 38hr 40min); Gebze (2–3 hourly; 30min); Halep (2 weekly; 40hr); İzmir (2 daily; 11hr); Kars (3 weekly; 42hr); Kayseri (3 weekly; 21hr); Konya (3 weekly; 13hr 35min); Tatvan (3 weekly; 45hr).

Sirkeci station to: Athens (1 daily at 8.35pm; 23hr; pullman 94.5YTL; note that this is not

a direct service. Once over the border with Greece, times depend on making connections in Üzünköprü, 6hr, and Thessaloniki, 16hr); Budapest (1 daily at 11am; 33hr; sleeper 167YTL), via Sofya (14hr; Pullman 34YTL, sleeper 44YTL) and Bucharest (18hr; Pullman 63YTL, sleeper 129YTL) – change at Budapest for onward services to Prague, Venice and Vienna; Edirne (1 daily at 3.50pm; 6hr); Halkalı, at the end of the local line (daily every 30min; 45min).

Sea buses

The main **sea bus services** (☎0212/516 1212, ⊛www.ido.com.tr) are from Yenikapı (off Kennedy Cad in Kumkapı).

Kartal (on the Asian shore) to: Yalova (no cars; at least 5 daily; 35min).

Yenikapı to: Bandırma (car ferry; at least 5 daily; 2hr; many connect with the train to İzmir); Marmara islands (no cars; summer only, daily except Sun; 2hr 45min); Mudanya (no cars; 2 daily; 1hr 45min); Yalova (car ferry; at least 7 daily; 1hr).

Flights

See "Listings", p.203, for airline-company contact details.

THY (Turkish Airlines)

Atatürk airport to: Adana (at least 8 daily; 1hr 35min); Ankara (at least 12 daily; 1hr); Antalya (9 daily; 1hr 15min); Batman via Ankara (5 weekly; 3hr 20min); Bodrum (at least 5 daily; 1hr 10min); Dalaman (at least 3 daily; 1hr 20min); Denizli (6 weekly; 1hr 10min); Diyarbakır (at least 4 daily; 2hr); Elaziğ (1 daily; 1hr 45min); Erzincan via Ankara (3 weekly; 3hr 25min); Erzurum (at least 2 daily; 2hr); Gaziantep (at least 1 daily; 1hr 50min); İzmir (at least 10 daily; 1hr); Kars via Ankara (1 daily; 3hr 25min); Kayseri (3 daily; 1hr 25min); Konya (1 daily; 1hr 10min); Malatya (at least 1 daily; 1hr 35min); Mardin via Ankara (4 weekly; 3hr 45min); Muş (5 weekly; 3hr 30min); Samsun (3 daily; 1hr 20min); Şanlıurfa (6 weekly; 1hr 50min); Trabzon (at least 5 daily; 1hr 45min); Van (2 daily; 2hr).

Onur Air

Atatürk airport to: Adana (3 daily; 1hr 30min); Antalya (3 daily; 1hr); Diyarbakır (2 daily; 1hr 45min); Erzerum (1 daily; 1 hr 50min); Gaziantep (1 daily; 1hr 45min); İzmir (3 daily; 1hr); Kayseri (1 daily; 1hr 15min); Kars (1 daily 1hr 50min); Malatya (1 daily; 1hr 30min); Samsun (1 daily; 1 hr 15min); Trabzon (2 daily; 1hr 50min).

Atlas Jet

Atatürk airport to: Adana (at least 2 daily weekdays, 1 on Sat; 1hr 30min); Ankara (1 daily weekdays; 1hr); Antalya (at least 20 daily; 1hr 10min); Bodrum (at least 12 daily; 1hr 10min); Dalaman (at least 5 daily; 1hr 10min); Erzincan via Ankara (2 weekly; 3hr); Izmir (at least 11 daily; 1hr); Malatya (daily except Sat; 1hr 30min); Siirt via Ankara (3 weekly; 3hr 5min); Sivas (daily except Sat; 1hr); Trabzon (at least 1 daily except Sat; 2hr); Van (daily except Sat; 2hr).

Fly Air

Atatürk airport to: Adana (daily except weekends; 1hr 30min); Izmir (daily except weekends; 1hr); Trabzon (1 daily; 2hr).

Around the Sea of Marmara

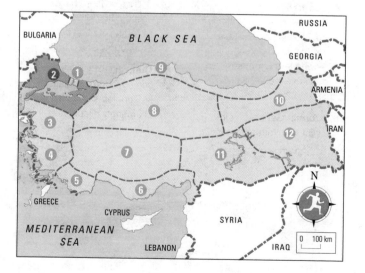

Highlights

✴ **Selimiye Camii** The masterpiece of architect Mimar Sinan, considered to be the finest mosque in Turkey. See p.232

✴ **Kırkpınar festival** Wrestlers slicked down head-to-toe in olive oil battle it out every July in a 600-year-old tournament at Edirne. See p.231

✴ **Battlefield sites and cemeteries** The Gelibolu peninsula pays testament to the Allied defeat during World War I, remembered each year on Anzac Day. See p.239

✴ **Termal** Get steamy in winter at Termal's near-scalding hot springs – ancient baths where people have come to take the cure since Byzantine times. See p.247

✴ **İznik** Sleepy town nestled in an olive-mantled valley, famous for its sixteenth-century tiles. See p.248

✴ **Bursa's Silk-Cocoon Hall** Centrepiece of Bursa's covered bazaar, occupied by silk-breeders at the auction held every June. See p.259

✴ **Cumalikizik** A finely preserved Ottoman village, its cobbled streets full of charmingly dilapidated houses. See p.264

△ Edirne's Selimiye Camii

Around the
Sea of Marmara

D espite their proximity to İstanbul, the shores and hinterland of the **Sea of Marmara** are neglected by most foreign travellers. This is not altogether surprising – here the country is at its most Balkan and, at first glance, least exotic – but there are good reasons to come: above all the exquisite early Ottoman centres of **Edirne** and **Bursa**. If your appetite is whetted for more of the same, the historic towns of **Lüleburgaz** and **İznik** make good postscripts to the former imperial capitals.

For many citizens of the Commonwealth nations and Ireland, a pilgrimage to the extensive and moving World War I battlefields and cemeteries on the **Gelibolu (Gallipoli) peninsula** may involve personal as well as national history. The northern Marmara port of **Gelibolu** is one starting-point for guided excursions of the memorial sites, although it's **Eceabat** (along with Çanakkale, described in the next chapter) that is the better base for either an organized or do-it-yourself tour.

With more time at your disposal you might consider venturing up to northern **Thrace**, which offers a rolling landscape of forests and slow-moving rivers, dotted with prehistoric and Iron Age tombs and the remains of Byzantine frontier towns – most notably the coastal fortress of **Kıyıköy**. The region boasts a large settled Romany population whose annual spring celebration at **Kırklareli** is one of the most memorable festivals held anywhere in Turkey.

The four inhabited **Marmara islands** on the south side of the Sea of Marmara attract local tourism due to their proximity to İstanbul, Edirne and Bursa. Their short summer season and unglamorous image mean that the islands – and indeed much of the Marmara coastline – are relatively unspoilt, and you may enjoy the status of being the only foreigner in town. Meanwhile, for evocative inland scenery, visit **Uluabat Gölü** and **Manyas Gölü** – shallow lakes that support a dwindling fishing community and a bird sanctuary respectively – or **Uludağ**, a mountain resort popular with skiers in winter and hikers in summer.

Before 1923, much of the Marmara region's population was Greek Orthodox. Following the establishment of the Turkish Republic and the exchange of populations, massive immigration – both internal and from abroad – changed the mix. The result is an ethnic stew that includes people of Çerkez (Circassian), Artvinli and Greek Muslim descent, but consists predominantly of **Pomak**, **Bosnian** and **Macedonian Muslims**, and especially **Bulgarian Turks**. All of them had in fact been trickling in for decades, as Austro-Hungarian or Christian nationalist vic-

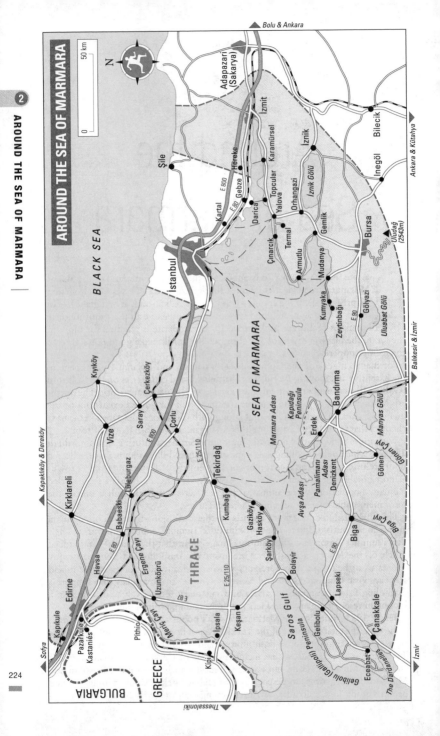

AROUND THE SEA OF MARMARA

0   50 km

N

BLACK SEA

SEA OF MARMARA

THRACE

BULGARIA

GREECE

Saros Gulf

▲ Bolu & Ankara

Adapazarı (Sakarya)

İzmit

Hereke
Karamürsel
Topçular
Yalova
Orhangazi
İznik
İznik Gölü
Bilecik

Gebze
Darıca
Termal
Gemlik
Bursa
İnegöl
Uludağ (2543m)

Kartal
Çınarcık
Armutlu
Mudanya

İstanbul

Şile

Kıyıköy

Çerkezköy
Saray
Çorlu
Vize
Lüleburgaz
Babaeski
Kırklareli

Kumyaka
Zeytinbağı
Gölyazı
Uluabat Gölü
Manyas Gölü

Marmara Adası
Kapıdağı Peninsula
Erdek
Bandırma

Avşa Adası
Paşalimanı Adası
Denizkent

Gönen Çayı

Tekirdağ
Kumbağ
Gaziköy
Hasköy
Şarköy

Gönen

Biga
Biga Çayı

Bolayir
Lapseki

Havsa
Uzunköprü
Ergene Çayı
Edirne
Meriç Çayı

Kapıkule
Pazarkule
Kastaniés

Pithio

İpsala
Keşan

Kıpi

Eceabat
Çanakkale
The Dardanelles

Gelibolu (Gallipoli) Peninsula
Gelibolu

E 800
E 80
E 25/110
E 87
E 90

▲ Kapıklıköy & Dereköy
◄ Sofya
◄ Thessaloniki
▲ Kavaklıköy & Dereköy

Ankara & Kütahya ►
Balıkesir & İzmir ►
İzmir ►

tories in the Balkans made their previous homes inhospitable to Turks or Slavic Muslims. This trend was reinforced following the disturbances in Bulgaria during 1989, when hundreds of thousands of ethnic Turks fled to Turkey, though many of the new arrivals subsequently returned to post-Communist Bulgaria.

Thrace

Thrace (Trakya in Turkish), the historic term for the territory bounded by the rivers Danube and Nestos and the Aegean, Marmara and Black seas, is today divided roughly equally among Turkey, Greece and Bulgaria. In ancient times it was home to warlike stock-breeding tribes, whose bizarre religions and unruly habits presented a continual headache for rulers bent on subduing them. Contemporary life is decidedly less colourful, though until the late 1960s nearly all of Thrace was a military security zone and strictly off-limits to foreigners. Most of the area is open to travel now, but all the towns remain heavily garrisoned.

To the south, the flatter land has long since been denuded of trees, while much of the coast has fallen prey to estates of concrete holiday-homes – seasonal barbecue pads for İstanbul's lower middle classes. Inland is staunchly agricultural and in summer a sea of yellow sunflowers, grown for oil, spreads for mile after mile. Further west, in the wetter lands around Üzünköprü, rice is predominant. The north, though, is a different story: rolling hills and dense forests of scrub oak hide itinerant charcoal burners and myriad fish-farms growing rainbow trout. Hidden away across the whole region are open-cast workings extracting the sand and gravel that accumulated on the sea bed that once covered Thrace.

The E80 highway from İstanbul to the main Thracian town of **Edirne** follows almost exactly the route of the Roman and Byzantine **Via Egnatia**, which later became the medieval route to the Ottoman holdings in Europe. Many towns along the road not surprisingly began life as Roman staging-posts, a role continued under the Ottomans who endowed all of them with a civic monument or two. Few places have much to detain you, though you should keep an eye out for various fine **old bridges**, which like the road itself may be Ottoman reworkings of Roman or Byzantine originals. The best of these is the quadruple Büyükçekmece span, crossing the neck of an estuary a few kilometres west of İstanbul and built by the great architect Mimar Sinan in 1563.

Edirne

More than just the quintessential border town, **EDIRNE** – 230km northwest of İstanbul – is one of the best-preserved Ottoman cities and makes an impressive and easily digestible introduction to Turkey. It's a lively and attractive spot of around 120,000 people, occupying a rise overlooking the meeting of the Tunca, Arda and Meriç rivers, a short distance from the Greek and Bulgarian frontiers. The life of the place is derived from day-tripping foreign shoppers, from a growing number of discerning tourists and from the presence of students (the University of Thrace

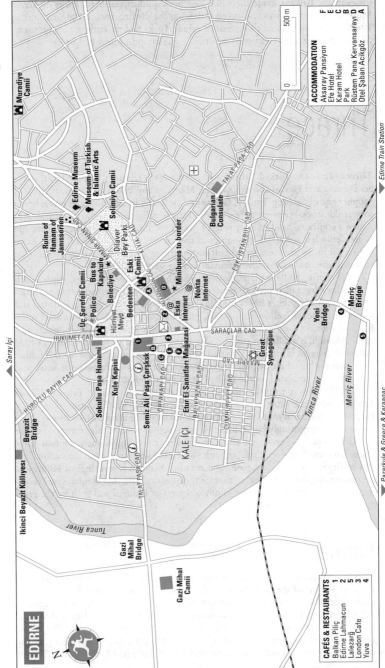

EDİRNE

Otogar, Train Station & İstanbul & Greek Consulate ▲

0   500 m

Saray İçi ▲

Muradiye Camii

Edirne Museum
Museum of Turkish & Islamic Arts
Selimiye Camii

TALAT-PAŞA-CAD

Ruins of Hamam of Janissaries

Üç Şerefeli Camii
Bus to Kapıkule
Police
Belediye
Bedesten
Hürriyet Meyd
Dilaver Bey Parkı
Eski Camii
Minibuses to border
MİMAR SİNAN CAD
KIYIK CAD
Eska Internet @
Nokta Internet @
ESKİ-İSTANBUL-CAD

Bulgarian Consulate

Edirne Train Station ▶

Sokullu Paşa Hamamı
Kule Kapısı
HÜKUMET-CAD
Semiz Ali Paşa Çarşısk
Etur El Sanatları Mağazasi
HOROZLU BAYIR CAD
ORTAKAPI CAD
BALIKPAZAN CAD
MAARİF CAD
CUMHURİYET CAD
SARAÇLAR CAD
Great Synagogue
Yeni Bridge

Meriç Bridge

KALE İÇİ
TALAT-PAŞA CAD

İkinci Beyazıt Külliyesi
Beyazıt Bridge
Tunca River

Gazi Mihal Bridge
Gazi Mihal Camii

Tunca River
Meriç River
Meriç River

Pazarkule & Greece & Karaagac ▶

N

ACCOMMODATION
Aksaray Pansiyon   F
Efe Hotel   E
Karam Hotel   C
Park   B
Rüstem Pana Kervansarayı D
Otel Şaban Acikgöz   A

CAFÉS & RESTAURANTS
Balkan Piliç   1
Edirne Lahmacun   2
Lalezarğ   5
London Cafe   3
Yuva   4

is here). **Downtown**, teeming bazaars and elegant domestic architecture almost distract you from the clutch of striking Ottoman monuments that lifts Edirne out of the ranks of the ordinary. The best of these Ottoman offerings, crowning the town hillock and sufficient reason in itself for a detour here, is the **Selimiye Camii**, the crowning achievement of the imperial architect Mimar Sinan.

Some history

There has always been a settlement of some kind at this strategic point and its military importance has fated it to be captured – and sometimes sacked for good measure – repeatedly over the centuries. Thracian Uscudama was refurbished as Hellenistic Oresteia, but the city really entered history as **Hadrianopolis**, designated the main centre of Roman Thrace by the emperor Hadrian. Under the Byzantines it retained its significance, not least as a forward base en route to the Balkans – or, more ominously from the Byzantine point of view, first stop on the way to attempts on the imperial capital itself. Unsuccessful besiegers of Constantinople habitually vented their frustration on Hadrianopolis as they retreated and a handful of emperors met their end here in pitched battles with Thracian "barbarians" of one sort or another.

The **Ottomans** had by the mid-fourteenth century enmeshed the Byzantines in a web of mutual defence treaties and links by marriage and gained their first permanent foothold on the coast of Thrace. In 1361 Hadrianopolis surrendered to the besieging Murat I and the provisional Ottoman capital was effectively transferred here from Bursa. A century later, Mehmet the Conqueror trained his troops and tested his artillery here in preparation for the march on Constantinople; indeed the Ottoman court was not completely moved to the Bosphorus until 1458. Because of its excellent opportunities for hunting and falconry, Edirne, as the Turks renamed it, remained a favourite haunt of numerous sultans for three more centuries, earning the title *Der-I Saadet* or "Happiness Gate" – when, it's said, there were enough victory celebrations, circumcision ceremonies and marriages to make even Constantinople jealous.

Decline set in during the eighteenth century, prompted largely by an **earthquake** in 1751. During each of the **Russo–Turkish wars** of 1829 and 1878–1879 the city was occupied and pillaged by Tsarist troops; far worse were the Bulgarians, who in 1913 presided over a four-month spree of atrocities. The Greeks, as one of the victorious World War I Allies, **annexed Edirne** along with the rest of Turkish Thrace from 1920 to 1922 and Turkish sovereignty over the city was only confirmed by the 1923 Treaty of Lausanne.

Arrival and information

Buses from elsewhere in Turkey arrive at Edirne's **otogar**, just over 2km southeast of the centre; a free service minibus will whisk you to points opposite the *Belediye* (town hall). The **train station**, a more likely entry point from abroad, is another kilometre out in the same direction; from here, the only transport into the centre is a red city bus, but these are infrequent and a taxi (12YTL) is the easiest option. If you're coming directly **from the Greek or Bulgarian highway border posts**, see the box on "Border crossings", below.

There are two fairly unhelpful **tourist offices** in Edirne: the first at Hürriyet Meydanı 17 (Mon–Fri 8.30am–5pm; ☎0284/213 9208); the second – the office of the Tourism Directorate – at Talat Paşa Caddesi 76 (Mon–Fri 8.30am–5pm, until 7pm in summer; ☎0284/225 5260), about 500m west of the first office, towards the Gazi Mihal bridge. There's also a booth at the Bulgarian (Kapıkule) frontier gate (daily 8.30am–5pm; ☎0284/238 2019). All three outlets supply

Border crossings

At the time of writing, the Turkish–Greek and Turkish–Bulgarian frontier posts are **open 24 hours**. The current trend is for lifting all restrictions on travelling **between Greece and Turkey**, but if in any doubt you can check the current situation at the tourist offices in Edirne before setting out. In **Bulgaria**, the government has lifted the visa restriction for stays of thirty days or less by holders of EU, US, Canadian, Australian and New Zealand passports. The only general proviso is that the expiry date of your passport should not fall within three months of entering the country.

Turkey–Greece

The Turkish frontier post of **Pazarkule**, separated from the Greek one at Kastaniés by a kilometre-wide no-man's-land, is 7km west of Edirne and 2km beyond the last Turkish village of **Karaağaç**.

Red city **buses to Karaağaç** (0.75YTL) run from behind the *Belediye* building in Edirne every twenty minutes; minibuses (1YTL) depart with similar frequency from behind the Rüstem Paşa Kervansarayı. At present, you have to walk the final 2km from Karaağaç to Pazarkule, as there's no dolmuş service.

Alternatively, take a taxi (€10) directly from Edirne **to Pazarkule**. Once through the Turkish post, you'll have to take a Greek taxi to the **Kastaniés** post, as you're not allowed to walk; this applies coming from Greece too – budget on 8YTL per car for the one-kilometre gap. From Kastaniés, on the Greek side, three trains daily, and about as many buses, make the three-hour run down to Alexandhroúpoli, the first major Greek city, between 8am and 1pm, with a couple more later in the day. If all this seems too much bother, compare the more southerly rail and road crossings into Greece described from Kapıkule.

Turkey–Bulgaria

Crossing the **Bulgarian–Turkish border** is slightly less problematic. The vast complex at **Kapıkule**, 18km northwest of Edirne (and 320km south of the Bulgarian capital Sofya) straddles the busy E800 expressway.

Minibuses to Kapıkule (1.25YTL) ply the route half-hourly from 6.30am to 9pm, leaving from behind the Rüstem Paşa Kervansarayı in Edirne. City buses also make the journey for under 1YTL, departing from next to the *Belediye* building. Hakiki Koç runs six **coaches** daily to Kapıkule (2.5YTL), departing from opposite the Bulgarian consulate, while a **taxi** will set you back well over 25YTL. (In the unlikely event that you get stuck at the border, note that there are a few basic motel rooms catering for TIR truck drivers at *Londra Camping* on the Turkish side.)

Balkan Express **trains** depart daily at 2pm from Kapıkule for Bucharest, Sofya and Budapest – you can check current timetables at the tourist offices in Edirne.

tourism ministry brochures and an excellent **map** of Edirne – the latter also sometimes stocked by hotels in town.

Edirne's main annual event is the **Kırkpınar festival** in July (see box on p.231), hosting the famous oil-wrestling. The festival lasts two or three days and is preceded by a couple of days of folkloric exhibitions laid on by the Edirne municipality. For more information, and for tickets to the wrestling events, it's best to contact either tourist office well in advance.

Accommodation

With most hotels booked solid either by truck drivers, Turkish workers on their way back to Germany or carloads of Eastern Europeans, **accommodation** is always tight in Edirne. During the main Turkish holidays and the Kırkpınar festival you'll probably need to book at least a month in advance. Most places are expensive, too, as Edirne's strategic location brings it sufficient, and comparatively undemanding, custom. However, high prices on display in hotel lobbies should be taken with a pinch of salt – bargaining commonly achieves discounts of up to fifty percent. For cheaper options, Maarif Caddesi is lined with reasonable choices, though there are also a few serious dives along here that are best avoided.

Hotels and pansiyons

Aksaray Pansiyon Alipaşa Ortakapı Cad 9 ☎0284/212 6035, ℱ225 3901. Recently-renovated, good-value place with both en-suite and cheaper, waterless, rooms available. ❷

Efe Hotel Maarif Cad 13 ☎0284/213 6166, ⓦwww.efehotel.com. Delightful, if somewhat over-priced, family-run hotel – it's clean and modern, with stylish air-conditioned rooms, satellite TV and an English-style pub on the ground floor. ❺

Karam Hotel Mithtpaşa Mah, Garanti Bankası Sok 6 ☎0284/225 1555, ℱ225 1556. A lively, friendly choice with large rooms in a restored mansion and a basement bar where live traditional Turkish music is performed on weekends. Excellent barbecue dinners are served in a courtyard restaurant. ❹

Park Maarif Cad 7 ☎0284/213 5276, ℱ225 4635. Not quite as spruce as the *Efe*, a few doors down, but nevertheless a clean and calm hotel with a reasonable kebab joint attached. ❹

Rüstem Paşa Kervansarayı İki Kapalıhan Cad 57 ☎0284/215 2489, ℱ212 0462. Restored six-

teenth-century *kervansaray* whose cool, cave-like rooms are set around a pleasant garden-courtyard. Noise is minimal as its substantial walls are quite soundproof, but the decor could do with an update and water supplies aren't all they could be. Staff freely admit to charging higher rates for foreigners, so bargain hard. ❺

Otel Şaban Acikgöz Çilingirler Cad 9 ☎0284/213 1404, ⓦwww.acikgoz.com. Recommended for comfort (rooms have TVs, air conditioning and minibars) and good service. If it's full, try its slightly more expensive sister property around the corner at Tufekciler Çarşısı 76. ❹

Motels and campsites

Fifi Lokanta Mocamp 8km along the E80 towards İstanbul ☎0284/226 0101, ℱ212 9888. Good campsite with en-suite motel rooms (❸) and a pool.

Ömür Camping 8km along the E80 towards İstanbul ☎0284/226 0037. Just past *Fifi*, this is a nice rural spot with space for fifty caravans and a large swimming pool.

The City

You can tour the main sights of Edirne on foot, but as the Ottoman monuments are widely scattered you'll need a full day to do it. Many lie to the north and west of town, deliberately rusticated by the early sultans to provide a nucleus for future suburbs. Because of the depopulation suffered by the city during the last three centuries, urban growth has never caught up with some of them and many have a rather forlorn atmosphere. Still, if the weather's fine, the walk is a pleasure, especially since you'll follow the willow-shaded banks of the **Tunca River** for some distance. Public transport doesn't connect up the more far-flung sites, so hiring a taxi is your only other option.

Eski Camii and the Bedesten

The logical starting point is **Eski Camii**, the oldest mosque in town, right across from the *Belediye*. This boxy structure, topped by nine vaults arranged three-square, is a more elaborate version of Bursa's Lulu Camii. Emir Süleyman, son of the luckless Beyazit I, began it in 1403, but it was his younger brother Mehmet I – the only one of three brothers left alive after a bloody succession struggle – who dedicated it eleven years later. The mosque is famous for its giant works of calligraphy, the most prolific being the large Arabic inscriptions on either side of the front door, one in the name of Allah, the other of Mohammed.

Just across the way Mehmet I constructed the **Bedesten** (closed Sun), Edirne's first covered market, a portion of whose revenue went to the upkeep of the nearby mosque. The barn-like structure with its fourteen vaulted chambers – again indebted to a Bursa prototype – has been restored in the past decade, but modern shops and poor paintwork make the interior drab and unimpressive.

Semiz Ali Paşa Çarşısı and Kale İçi

The other main covered bazaar in Edirne is the nearby **Semiz Ali Paşa Çarşısı** (closed Sun), whose north entrance lies about 250m west, on the corner of Talat Paşa and Saraçlar caddesi. The bazaar was established by Mimar Sinan in 1568 at the behest of Semiz Ali, one of the most able and congenial of the Ottoman grand viziers. A massive fire in 1992 burned out many of its 130 shops, but renovations have been administered with care – particularly impressive is the beautiful multi-domed ceiling.

Just opposite the north entrance looms the **Kule Kapısı** (Tower Gate), sole remnant of the town's Roman/Byzantine city walls; the Ottomans, in a burst of confidence after expanding the limits of empire far beyond Edirne, demolished the rest. The gate was partially restored some years ago and, with a team of archeologists scrabbling around in the excavations, the site promises to become more of a fixture on Edirne's sightseeing list.

West of the Semiz Ali market sprawls the **Kale İçi** district, a rectangular grid of streets dating from Byzantine times and lined with much-interrupted terraces of medieval houses. A stroll through here will uncover some surviving stumps of Byzantine wall.

Üç Şerefeli Camii and the Sokullu Paşa Hamamı

Slightly north of Semiz Ali and Hürriyet Meydanı stands **Üç Şerefeli Camii**, which replaced the Eski Camii as Edirne's Friday mosque in 1447. Ten years in the making, its conceptual daring represented the pinnacle of Ottoman religious architecture until overshadowed by the Selimiye Camii (see opposite) a short time later. Ongoing restorations mean that the courtyard and outer complex are still closed, though the prayer hall has reopened.

△ Oil wrestling at the annual Kırkpınar festival

The mosque's name – "three-balconied" – derives from the presence of three galleries for the muezzin on the tallest of the four whimsically idiosyncratic **minarets**; the second highest has two balconies, the others one, and their bases are all different. Each of the multiple balconies is reached by a separate stairway within the minaret. The **courtyard**, too, was an innovation, centred on a *sadırvan* (ritual ablutions fountain) and ringed by porphyry and marble columns pilfered from

Oil wrestling and the Kırkpınar festival

Oil wrestling (*yağlı güreş*) is popular throughout Turkey, but reaches the pinnacle of its acclaim at the doyen of tournaments, the annual **Kırkpınar festival**, staged early each summer on the Saray İçi islet outside Edirne. The preferred date is the first week of July, but the five-day event is moved back into June if it coincides with Ramadan or either of the two major *bayram*s (religious holidays) following it.

The wrestling matches have been held annually, except in times of war or Edirne's occupation, for more than six centuries and their origins are shrouded in legend. The most commonly repeated story asserts that Süleyman, son of Orhan Gazi, was returning from a battle in 1360 with forty of his men and decided to camp at a village near Edirne. To pass the time the soldiers paired off to wrestle; the last two were unable to best each other after several days of tussling, and in a final elimination match expired simultaneously after midnight. Their companions buried them on the spot and, returning to visit the graves the next season, were astonished to find instead a lush meadow with forty springs (*kırk pınar* in Turkish) bubbling away. Forty is one of the sacred numbers of Islam and the Ottomans needed little encouragement to inaugurate a commemoration.

Despite the less than atmospheric environment of the stadium that now hosts the wrestling, tradition still permeates the event. The contestants – up to a thousand per year – dress only in leather knickers called *kisbet* and are slicked down head to toe in diluted olive oil. Wrestlers are classed by height, not by weight, from toddlers up to the *pehlivan* (full-size) category. Warm-up exercises, the *peşrev*, are highly stereotyped and accompanied by the *davul* (deep-toned drum) and *zurna* (single-reed Islamic oboe). The competitors and the actual matches are solemnly introduced by the *cazgır* or master of ceremonies, usually himself a former champion.

The bouts, several of which take place simultaneously, can last anything from a few minutes to a couple of hours, until one competitor collapses or has his back pinned to the grass. Referees keep a lookout for the limited number of illegal moves or holds and victors advance more or less immediately to the next round until, after the second or third day, only the *başpehlivan* (champion) remains. Despite the small prize purse, donated by the *Kırkpınar Ağaları* – the local worthies who put on the whole show – a champion is usually well set-up in terms of appearance and endorsement fees and should derive ample benefit from the furious on- and off-site betting. In the main, gladiators tend to be villagers from all over Turkey who have won regional titles, starry-eyed with the prospect of fame and escape from a rural rut.

In addition to providing the music of the *peşrev*, the local Romany population descends in force during the Kırkpınar, setting up a combination of funfair, circus and carnival on the outskirts of town. They also have their own **Romany spring festival** (similar to the bigger Takava festival in Kırklareli, p.236), which takes place in the fields around the stadium during the first week of May. The Romany King lights a bonfire on the evening of May 6, and a flaming torch is paraded around to light a number of other bonfires in the area; a dish of meat and rice is given to the gathered picnickers. The next morning, young Romany girls are paraded through the streets on horseback around the Muradiye Camii (where a number of settled Romanies live) to the accompaniment of *davul* and *zurna*, wearing their own or their mothers' wedding dresses.

Roman buildings. The experimental nature of the mosque is further confirmed by its **interior**, much wider than it is deep and covered by a dome 24m in diameter. It was the largest that the Turks had built at the time and, to impart a sense of space, the architect relied on just two freestanding columns, with the other four recessed into front and back walls to form a hexagon.

Right across from the mosque is the sixteenth-century **Sokullu Paşa Hamamı** (daily 6am–10pm; separate wings for men and women; 5YTL, massage 5YTL extra), built by Mimar Sinan, though it's not as friendly, hot or well maintained as it might be.

Selimiye Camii and nearby museums

The masterly **Selimiye Camii**, one of Turkey's finest mosques, was designed by the 80-year-old Mimar Sinan (see box on p.155) in 1569 at the command of Selim II. The work of a confident craftsman at the height of his powers, it's visible from some distance away on the Thracian plain and is virtually the municipal symbol, reproduced on the sides of Edirne's buses, among other places.

You can approach the Selimiye across the central park, Dilaver Bey, then through the **Kavaflar Arasta** (Cobbler's Arcade; closed Sun), which was built by Sinan's pupil Davut and is still used as a covered market, full of household goods and cheap clothing – every day, under the market's prayer dome, the shopkeepers promise that they will do their business honestly. The mosque **courtyard**, approached from the Kavaflar Arasta up a flight of stone steps, is surrounded by a colonnaded portico with arches in alternating red and white stone, ancient columns and domes of varying size above the arcades. Its delicately fashioned *şadırvan* is the finest in the city. The four identical, slender **minarets** each has three balconies – Sinan's nod to his predecessors – and at 71m are the second tallest in the world after those in Mecca. The detailed carved portal once graced the Ulu Cami in Birgi and was transported here in pieces, then reassembled.

But it is the celestial **interior**, specifically the dome, which impresses most. Planned expressly to surpass that of Aya Sofya in İstanbul, it manages this – at 31.5m in diameter – by a bare few centimetres, and Sinan thus achieved a lifetime's ambition. Supported by eight mammoth but surprisingly unobtrusive twelve-sided pillars, the cupola floats 44m above the floor, covered in calligraphy proclaiming the glory of Allah. Immediately below the dome the muezzin's platform, supported on twelve columns, is an ideal place from which to contemplate the proportions of the mosque. The delicate painting on the platform's underside is a faithful restoration of the original, and gives some idea of how the mosque dome must once have looked. The water of the small marble drinking fountain beneath symbolizes life, under the dome of eternity. The most ornate stone carving is reserved for the *mihrab* and *mimber*, backed by fine İznik faïence illuminated by sunlight streaming in through the many windows allowed by the pillar support scheme.

An associated *medrese*, at the northeastern corner of the mosque, is now the **Museum of Turkish and Islamic Arts** (Türk ve İslam Eserleri Müzesi; Tues–Sun 8am–noon & 1–5pm; 2YTL), consisting of fifteen rooms around a pleasant garden courtyard and housing assorted wooden, ceramic and martial knick-knacks from the province. One of the rooms is dedicated to oil wrestling (see box on p.231), including a portrait gallery of its stars, a pair of oil-wrestler's leather trousers and blow-ups of miniatures depicting this 600-year-old sport through the ages.

The main **Edirne Museum** (Tues–Sun 8am–noon & 1–5pm; 2YTL) – the modern building just northeast of the mosque precincts – contains a predictable assortment of Greco-Roman fragments. Its ethnographic section focuses on carpet weaving and other local crafts, including colourful village bridal-wear, which pre-ceded the bland white confectionery that's been adopted from the West.

Muradiye Camii

Northeast of the centre, but simple enough to reach, the **Muradiye Camii** (admis-sion only at prayer times) is an easy ten-minute, down-then-up walk along Mimar Sinan Caddesi from the Selimiye mosque. According to legend Celaleddin Rumi, founder of the Mevlevî dervish order, appeared in a dream to the pious Murat II in 1435, urging him to build a sanctuary for the Mevlevîs in Edirne. The result is this pleasing, T-shaped *zaviye* (dervish convent) crouched on a hill looking north over vegetable patches and the Tunca River; the grassy entry court lends a final bucolic touch. The interior is distinguished by the best İznik tiles outside Bursa: the *mihrab* and walls up to eye level are solid with them. Higher surfaces once bore calligraphic frescoes, but these have probably been missing since the catastrophic earthquake of 1751. The dervishes initially congregated in the *eyvan*s (transepts), which form the ends of the T's cross-stroke; Murat later housed them in a separate *tekke* (gathering place) in the garden.

Along the Tunca River

At Edirne, the **Tunca River** is crossed by the greatest concentration of historic bridges in Thrace, better suited to pedestrians and horse carts than the motor vehicles that jostle to use them. The best way to see them is to take a stroll along the riverbank parallel to the dykes and water meadows of the Tunca's right bank. A good place to start is at the pair furthest upstream, the fifteenth-century **Saray (Süleyman)** and **Fatih** bridges, which join the respective left and right banks of the Tunca with the river island of **Saray İçi**. The island once supported the **Edirne Sarayı**, a royal palace begun by Murat II, which was blown to bits by the Turks in 1877 to prevent the munitions stored inside from falling into Russian hands. Today nothing is left of this pleasure pavilion except the rubble of some baths and a tower, next to which is a modern concrete stadium, venue for the Kırkpınar wrestling matches (see box on p.231).

Following the riverbank west and downstream for half an hour brings you to the double-staged **Beyazit bridge** that crosses another small island in the Tunca River. The seventeenth-century bridge is more commonly known as the Tek Göz Köprüsü ("one-eyed bridge"), referring to its single hump. Across the bridge on the left bank is the **İkinci Beyazit Külliyesi**, built between 1484 and 1488 by Hayrettin, court architect to Beyazit II. This is the largest Ottoman spiritual and physical-welfare complex ever constructed. Within a single irregular boundary wall, and beneath a hundred-dome silhouette, are assembled a mosque, food store-house, bakery, *imaret*, dervish hostel, medical school and insane asylum. Unfortu-nately, most of the buildings are closed to the public these days, though the *imam* or his son may appear in order to give you a short tour (which will mean peering frustratedly through windows and gates). Except for its handsome courtyard and the sultan's loge inside, the **mosque** itself is disappointing, and more interesting is the **medical school** in the furthest northwest corner of the complex. This was conveniently linked to the *timarhane*, or madhouse, built around an open garden, which in turn leads to the magnificent **darüşşifa** (therapy centre). This hexagonal, domed structure consists of a circular central space with six *eyvan*s (side-chambers) opening onto it; the inmates were brought here regularly, where musicians would play to soothe the more intractable cases. Strange five-sided rooms with fireplaces open off three of the *eyvan*s. The *darüşşifa* is now home to the well-intentioned but fairly dull **Trakya University Museum of Health** (Tues–Sun 9am–5pm; 3YTL), boasting a collection of old medical equipment and photographs.

Another twenty minutes' walk south along the river will bring you to the **Gazi Mihal bridge**, an Ottoman refurbishment of a thirteenth-century Byzantine span and hence the oldest around Edirne. Gazi Mihal was a Christian nobleman who became an enthusiastic convert to Islam – hence the epithet *Gazi*, "Warrior for the Faith". His namesake mosque is at the western end of the bridge, from where it's an easy 500-metre stroll back into town.

Eating and drinking

Restaurants cater mainly to passing trade and do little to encourage return custom; most are adequate but not especially cheap. Exceptions include the booths and **street stalls** around Saraçlar Caddesi, serving up the city's speciality, deep-fried liver, as well as every imaginable kind of pudding, pastry and ice cream. You can also get cheap snacks from the acres of **tea gardens** in front of the Selimiye Camii.

Balkan Piliç Saraçlar Cad 14. Plenty of wholesome *lokanta* fare, not just chicken but enticing vegetable dishes and good roast lamb. A plateful of various dishes will cost around 12YTL.

Edirne Lahmacun Salonu Çilingirler Cad 2. Offers a good variety of *pide* and grilled kebabs in a canteen environment (no alcohol) to the local bazaar traders.

Lalezarğ 1.5km south of town (Karaağaç road), on the Meriç River. Unlicensed restaurant with beautiful views of the Meriç and its elegant, honey-coloured bridge. Food – kebabs and *mezes* – is substantial and reasonably priced, served in waterfront gardens. One table is located in the branches of a tree. The licensed *Villa Restaurant* next door is similar. Take the Karaağaç minibus from in front of the PTT, or any red city bus heading south along

Saraçlar Cad.

London Café Saraçlar Cad 74. An unexpected find, this two-storey affair (opposite the PTT) is incongruously decorated with Wild West photographs, cowboy boots and stetsons. There's a wide range of imported alcoholic drinks and a non-Turkish menu including things like chicken schnitzel, spaghetti and burgers.

Yuva 1.3km south of town (Karaağaç road), between the Yeni and Meriç bridges. Friendly place, with inexpensive *mezes* and kebabs, accompanied by *rakı* and (very occasionally) live music. It's one of a line of lively *meyhanes* (taverns) between the bridges, an area dubbed *Bülbül Adası* – "nightingale island" – by the locals. For transport, see *Lalezarğ*, above.

Listings

Banks and exchange There are several banks with ATMs along Talat Paşa Cad, as well as a number of *döviz* offices on and around Hürriyet Meydanı and the Semiz Ali Paşa Çarşısı.
Buses From the *otogar* (☎0284/225 1979), several bus companies, including Kamil Koç, Pamukkale, Varan and Uludar Hakiki Koç, run services to Çanakkale, İstanbul, Kapıkule, Keşan, Kırklareli and Lüleburgaz (see "Travel details" at end of chapter for schedules).
Consulates Bulgarian consulate, Talat Paşa Cad, about halfway to the *otogar* (Mon–Fri 9am–noon; ☎0284/214 0617); Greek consulate, Kocasinan Mah, 2 Sok 3 (Mon–Fri 9am–noon; ☎0284/235 5808) – turn off the main E80 highway opposite the *Çağlar Gazoz* factory.
Hospital Behind the Bulgarian consulate.

Internet access Facilities generally open daily 9am–9pm, at the café in the *Rüstem Paşa Kervansarayı*, as well as the *Eska Internet Café*, just round the corner from the hotel on Çilingirler Çarşısı, and the *Nokta Internet Café*, further down the same street opposite the dolmuş stand.
Police Karanfiloğlu Cad, behind the Üç Şerefeli Camii.
Post office The PTT is on Saraçlar Cad (Mon–Sat 8am–midnight for telephone and telegrams, 8am–8pm for letters, and 9am–5.30pm for full postal services).
Shopping Etur el Sanatları Mağazası, Saraçlar Cad 85, is a classy handicrafts shop, selling a vast range of high-quality products, including inlaid backgammon boards, patchwork quilts, homemade dolls and jewellery.

South of Edirne: Greek border crossings

There's little reason to stop at any point south along the E87 highway as it heads down from **Havsa**, the junction 27km southeast of Edirne. This road does, however, connect **Uzunköprü**, **İpsala** and **Keşan**, one of which you're likely to pass through if in transit to or from Greece.

Üzünköprü

ÜZÜNKÖPRÜ (Long Bridge), a little over 60km south of Edirne, formerly the Thracian and later Greek town of Plotinopolis, gets its current name from the 1.4km-long, 174-arched Ottoman bridge at the north end of town. Built over six hundred years ago, the bridge remains entirely intact, despite occupying a notorious earthquake zone and acting as the town's main access road bearing hundreds of trucks and buses daily – a quite remarkable feat of engineering.

Today the town is an official rail entry and exit post for Turkey – the daily Athens "express" from İstanbul passes through Üzünköprü's station in the early hours of the morning, before crossing the Greek border to **Píthio** where passengers disembark and wait an hour for the connecting Greek service. The Turkish train re-crosses the border and returns to Üzünköprü roughly two hours later, continuing from there back to İstanbul. The line runs through the all but deserted wetlands around the **Meriçnehri River** before crossing the "long bridge", though you're unlikely to see any of it from the train at night.

Üzünköprü station is 4km north of town. If you miss the train, you'll have to take a taxi into the centre where the one-star *Ergene Oteli* (℡0584/513 5438, ℻513 5226; ❷), on the main square, is the only **accommodation** worth considering. It has a reasonable restaurant attached.

İpsala

The main Turkish–Greek road crossing, far busier and somewhat less paranoiac than the Edirne–Kastaniés one, is between **İPSALA**, astride the E25/110 highway, and Kípi in Greece. The two posts here are open 24 hours, but the banking facilities on both sides and the tourist information booth in İpsala (℡0284/616 1577) only operate sporadically, so it's not a bad idea to show up with a certain amount of currency for the country you'll be entering (though if you have dollars or euros, the Turkish immigration officials will be happy to exchange it for Turkish lira). As at the Edirne frontier, there's a 500-metre-wide military zone that you're not allowed to cross on foot; during daylight hours at least, it's fairly easy to arrange a ride over.

From the village of **Kípi** there are six buses daily further into Greece; at the Turkish immigration post there are only taxis available to take you to İpsala.

Keşan

Crossing the border by public transport, it's easier to take a bus to **KEŞAN** (30km southeast of İpsala), whose *otogar* lies 3km north of town. It's a cipher of a place but has frequent bus connections from İstanbul, Edirne and Çanakkale, and into Greece via İpsala. As long-haul bus connections out of Edirne to anywhere but İstanbul are very poor, if you're making for Çanakkale, İzmir or Bursa, you'll almost always have a change of vehicle (with an hour or two's stopover) in Keşan.

Kırklareli

Although it's the capital of Thrace, **KİRKLARELİ** is often overlooked because of its relative proximity to the much larger Edirne. While historically not in the same league, it is nonetheless a pleasant little town clustered around a central main square with enough of interest to warrant at least a couple of hours' visit. It lies 62km east of Edirne: there are hourly **buses** from Edirne's *otogar* to the Kırklareli *otogar*, 1.5km out of town on the İstanbul road, and frequent dolmuşes depart from outside Edirne's *Rüstem Paşa Kervansarayı* to Kırklareli's main square.

The town **museum** (Kırklareli Müzesi; Tues–Sun 9am–12.30pm & 1.30–5pm; 2YTL), on the northeastern corner of the square, neatly presents the history of the area. Pride of place goes to the second-century skeleton of a woman from one of the many local Thracian burial mounds. The museum also offers information about travel to the Neolithic and Iron Age **tombs** found hereabouts; there's a map of the area displayed on the first floor. The easiest tomb to reach, and the only one accessible by public transport, is in the village of Kapaklıköy (itself named after the stone-capped tomb), 8km north along the road to Dereköy; take a Dereköy-bound dolmuş (0.80YTL) from the dolmuş stand in the central square, and you'll find the immense Iron Age tomb in the copse on the far side of the village.

Ottoman Kırklareli is represented by five mosques, of which the fourteenth-century **Hışırbey Camii** on the central square is the most impressive, encompassing both a hamam, with separate entrances for men and women (still operating), and a shopping arcade.

With a large settled Romany population, Kırklareli is also the site of the immensely popular, three-day **Takava festival**, usually held over the first weekend after May 6. Families celebrate the arrival of spring by jumping over small bonfires for luck, while the local authorities organize painting competitions, concerts, bicycle races and a large public bonfire in the town centre on the Saturday night. On the Sunday, buses and coaches transport all and sundry to the banks of the Şeytandere River, southeast of town, for a day-long picnic and more concerts.

The most comfortable **accommodation** in Kırklareli is the two-star *Best Otel Bilgiç* at Şukru Nail Sok 2 (℡0288/214 4671; ❷) just to the east of the square, towards the fruit and vegetable market, which has comfortable en-suite rooms with TV. It also has a licensed **restaurant**, but the food on offer rather depends on how many people are staying in the hotel. The unique *Kırklar Beyoğlu Sineması*, just north of the main square, screens Hollywood **movies** nightly in a converted Ottoman farmhouse.

Lüleburgaz

If you've become a Sinan-ophile, you can visit yet another of his substantial creations, which dominates the town of **LÜLEBURGAZ**, 76km east of Edirne on the main route to İstanbul.

The **Sokollu Mehmet Paşa Külliyesi**, originally commissioned by the governor of Rumeli in 1549, was built in fits and starts and wasn't completed until 1569, during Sokollu's term as grand vizier. What you see today is an imposing mosque and *medrese* abutted by a covered bazaar and guarded by two isolated towers. The mosque proper is peculiar, possessing only one minaret; where the others might be, three stubby turret-like towers jut instead, all joined by a mansard crenellation. The *medrese*, still used as a children's Koran school, is arrayed around the mosque courtyard, entered by two tiny arcades on the east and west sides; in the middle of the vast space stands the late Ottoman caprice of a *şadırvan* (ablutions fountain). The mosque's portico, built to square with the *medrese*, is far more impressive than the interior, and most visitors will soon drift out of the north gate to the **market promenade**, whose shops are still intact and in use. Just outside the gate, a huge dome with a stork's nest on top shades the centre of the bazaar.

Beyond, there was once a massive *kervansaray*, equal in size to the mosque complex. All of it has vanished save for a lone tower, balanced by another, the **Dar-ül-Kura**, at the south edge of the entire precinct, beyond the mosque's *mihrab*. The former **hamam**, across the street from the complex, is now chock-a-block with tiny **restaurants** in its outer bays, though the main dome has collapsed.

There are a few simple but acceptable **hotels** 200m south of Sokollu Mehmet, offering soulless, but very clean en-suite rooms with TV, though there's little point stopping over, given the frequent buses (every 30min or so) to İstanbul or Edirne.

Kıyıköy and the Black Sea coast

KİYİKÖY occupies an idyllic location, perched high on a rocky bluff, overlooking the Black Sea and flanked on both sides by slow-moving rivers and swathes of verdant green forest. It was fortified by the Byzantines around the sixth century, though most of what is still standing dates from the thirteenth and fourteenth centuries. Kıyıköy's Greek population left during the population exchange of the 1920s to be replaced by Bulgarian and Romany Muslims, but many inhabitants still use the former Greek name, "Midye" – after the mussels for which the town is famed. Today, gently crumbling half-timbered houses line the backstreets and part-mended fishing nets hang everywhere.

The main approach to the walled citadel of Kıyıköy is via the narrow south gate, sadly restored with pink cement bricks. The west gate opens onto what used to be the town's **agora**, now housing a pair of tea gardens (of which the *Kartal* also serves beer) and offering superb views to the west. Outside the west gate a road leads down the hill and 300m up the Kazandere River to the impressive **monastery of St Nicholas** – an elaborate structure carved into the rock of the hillside, complete with colonnaded aisles, barrel vaulting and a semicircular apse of tiered seats where the clergy once sat. On the northeast side of the village it's possible to see the part-brick **tunnel**, constructed to allow safe passage down to the harbour in time of siege – the only deep-water anchorage on this part of the coast. A mere fifteen-minute walk west of the village takes you to 2km of unspoilt **sandy beach**, backed by low cliffs oozing fossils.

Practicalities

The village is too tiny to have its own *otogar* and direct **buses from İstanbul**, of which there are two a day (2hr 30min), drop you directly outside the narrow south gate. There are more frequent buses from İstanbul to **Saray**, a sleepy town 29km southwest of Kıyıköy, from where minibuses depart for Kıyıköy every hour.

You shouldn't have much trouble finding somewhere to stay in summer. The town boasts a good number of **pansiyons**, usually on the unoccupied floors of private houses: all are basic, offering shared bathroom and sometimes kitchen facilities, for as little as €7–9 per person a night. Typical of what's available is the *Hulya Pansiyon* (℡0288/388 6016; ❶), signposted to the west of the south gate, offering three-, four- and five-bed rooms with reductions for longer stays. The cliff-top *Deniz Motel and Restaurant* (℡0288/388 6452; ❶) has one-, two- and three-bed waterless rooms and generally fills up quickly at weekends; while the *Palaz Restaurant & Pansiyon* (☎0288/388 6177, ⓦwww.palazpansiyon .com; ❷), outside town on the road to Saray, offers a nice view of cow-filled fields and the beach. West over the Kazandere River are a couple of simple, rubbish-strewn, summer-only **campsites**, but the untidy semi-permanent tents of Turkish families, camped here for the whole summer, have the air of a refugee camp.

Eating out is a more luxurious experience as Kıyıköy is famed for its fish – not only mussels, but locally caught salmon and trout as well. There are several rather good **restaurants** attracting day-trippers from İstanbul, such as the elegant *Yakamoz*, perched on the cliff top by the *Deniz Motel*, and, northeast of the village, the *Tevfiğin Yeri*, offering nice views to the east from its narrow terrace and a meal of *mezes*, salad and fish for about 10–15YTL. The *Liman*, over the way, is a cheaper option.

The Thracian coast

If you're heading west from İstanbul, you don't really outrun the straggling suburbs until the junction where the Edirne-bound E80 splits off from the E25/110, headed for the İpsala frontier station. Fifty-five kilometres beyond the junction, the port of **Tekirdağ** marks the start of the little-visited **Thracian coast**. Here the main E25/110 steers the majority of the traffic inland to Keşan before joining the E87 south to the Gelibolu peninsula. But from Tekirdağ there is an alternative, little-used minor road that also heads eventually to the Gelibolu peninsula, following the coast through a run of fishing villages and small resorts.

Tekirdağ

TEKIRDAĞ, in a hilly setting at the head of a gently curving bay, is a fairly pleasant seaside port, with a few remaining wooden houses and a ferry service to the islands in the Sea of Marmara.

Time to kill between connections could be spent in the sixteenth-century **Rüstem Paşa Camii**, designed by Mimar Sinan and situated opposite the *Belediye* building on Hükümet Caddesi, or in the **Rakoczi Museum** (Rakoczi Müzesi; Tues–Sun 8.30am–4.30pm; 2YTL). Prince Ferenc Rakoczi (1676–1735) was leader of an unsuccessful revolt against the Austrian Habsburgs and the house, where he lived in exile as a Carmelite friar, was converted to a museum in his memory in 1932 by the Hungarian government. Among the exhibits are Hungarian weapons, paintings relating to Rakoczi's life, and his flag.

Down on the shorefront Atatürk Bulvarı, there's a **tourist office** at Eski İskele Yanı 65 (Mon–Fri 8.30am–noon & 1–5.30pm; ☎0282/261 1698), next to the dockside. From here, ferries ply to and from the islands of the Sea of Marmara and on to Erdek on the Kapıdağı peninsula (for ticket details, see p.268). There are at least three car-ferry services to Marmara and Avşa each evening, though out of season the service drops to three a week (weather permitting). The **otogar** is 200m from the ferry landing off Atatürk Bulvarı, on the road to İstanbul.

A few **hotels** stand opposite the ferry jetty: *Yat Hotel*, Ertuğrul Mah Cad 8 (☎0282/261 1054; ❷), off İskele Caddesi, is a reasonable option, where all rooms have toilets and some have full bathrooms. For some reason, Tekirdağ is renowned for its grilled meatballs, which are served in most of the local **restaurants**, though they are barely distinguishable from those sold elsewhere across Turkey. The **local wine** is a more exciting prospect, on sale in shops facing the seafront. The best are mature reds, perhaps in unlabelled bottles, some of which never make it out of the region. The bottling plants 3km to the west of town usually let you sample before buying.

South to Şarköy

To the south of Tekirdağ, and served by regular minibuses from its *otogar*, is a succession of unremarkable and, in the main, overdeveloped resorts, including **KUMBAĞ, HASKÖY** and **ŞARKÖY**. The only one that has managed to retain a good deal of its charm is the pretty fishing village of Hasköy, 25km south of Kumbağ. Here, a pebbly beach is set against rolling, vine-covered hills and a few *pansiyons*, mostly attached to fish restaurants, overlook the harbour.

The Gelibolu peninsula

Burdened with a grim military history but endowed with some fine scenery and beaches, the slender **Gelibolu (Gallipoli) peninsula** – roughly 60km in length and between 4km and 18km wide – forms the northwest side of the **Dardanelles** (Çanakkale Boğazı in Turkish, the ancient Hellespont), the narrow strait connecting the Aegean with the Sea of Marmara. Whether you approach the peninsula from Şarköy or (more likely) Keşan, the road there is pretty, swooping down in long arcs past the Saros gulf.

Site of the 1915 **Gallipoli landings** by the Allied troops, the peninsula contains a mind-numbing series of battlefields and cemeteries that tell of the tragic defeat by the Turkish forces. For Turks the region also holds a great deal of significance, as the Gallipoli campaign made famous a previously unknown lieutenant-colonel, Mustafa Kemal, later to become Atatürk.

Some people visit the peninsula's main town, **Gelibolu**, intending to use it as a base to visit the battlefields. However, **Eceabat**, at the southern end of the peninsula, or Çanakkale (see p.281), across the strait, are much closer to the battlefield sites. If you're intending to join a tour or go under your own steam you'll almost certainly find Eceabat a better bet than Gelibolu.

Touring the battlefields and cemeteries

The **World War I battlefields and Allied cemeteries** scattered along the Gelibolu peninsula are a moving sight, the past violence made all the more poignant by the present beauty of the landscape. The whole area is now either fertile rolling country, or cloaked in thick scrub and pine forest alive with birds, making it difficult to imagine the carnage of 1915. Much of the flatter land is still farmed and ploughing often turns up pieces of rusting equipment, fragments of shrapnel, human bones and even unexploded munitions.

The open-air sites have no admission fees or restricted hours. **Tours of the northern sites** (including the Kabatepe Information Centre) depart from Gelibolu, Eceabat and Çanakkale, and cost between €25–35 per person, depending on the number of tourists around. Tours from İstanbul cost around €75 and should include transport to either Çanakkale or Eceabat and one night's accommodation. Length of tour, departure time and other conditions all vary, so the best policy is to shop around and try to talk to people who have been on specific tours. Check whether any extra costs apply, or if lunch is provided. You'll also want enough time to wander a little, take in the breathtaking beauty of the location and, most likely, swim. Distant sites are often omitted (the focus is very

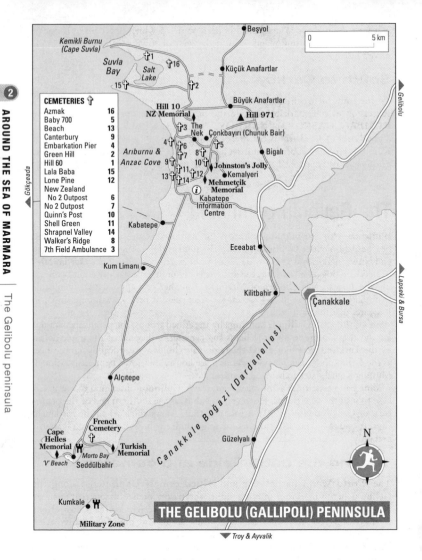

CEMETERIES ⚐

Azmak	16
Baby 700	5
Beach	13
Canterbury	9
Embarkation Pier	4
Green Hill	2
Hill 60	1
Lala Baba	15
Lone Pine	12
New Zealand No 2 Outpost	6
No 2 Outpost	7
Quinn's Post	10
Shell Green	11
Shrapnel Valley	14
Walker's Ridge	8
7th Field Ambulance	3

THE GELIBOLU (GALLIPOLI) PENINSULA

▼ *Troy & Ayvalik*

much on ANZAC), so also check that what you want to see is on the itinerary. All companies are supposed to have Ministry of Tourism licensed guides, who should speak excellent English and have a thorough knowledge of the sites.

You can also make **independent visits** to the sites in the northern and southern parts of the peninsula by a combination of short minibus rides and walking. **Minibuses** run from Gelibolu to Kilitbahir via Eceabat, from Eceabat to Kabatepe village and, less frequently, from Eceabat to Alçitepe via the Kabatepe Information Centre; there's also a sporadic service from Kilitbahir to Seddülbahir. From the Kabatepe Information Centre, you can walk around the main sites to the north inside a couple of hours. At Kilitbahir, minibuses meet the Çanakkale car ferries in summer and take passengers to Alçitepe and Seddülbahir, from where you can tour the surrounding cemeteries and memorials on foot. They also ferry passengers to the Turkish memorial (Çanakkale Abidesi in Turkish).

It's also usually possible to **rent bicycles** in Eceabat, which gives you all the freedom you could possibly require, but be warned – some roads are steep, and can be rough and muddy in winter.

Some history

Soon after the start of World War I it became obvious to the Allies that Russia could not be supplied by sea, nor a Balkan front opened against the Central Powers, unless Ottoman Turkey was eliminated. **Winston Churchill**, in his earliest important post as First Lord of the Admiralty, reasoned that the quickest way to accomplish this would be to force the Dardanelles with a fleet and bombard İstanbul into submission. A combined Anglo–French armada made several attempts on the straits during November 1914, which were repulsed, but they returned in earnest on March 18, 1915. This time they managed to penetrate less than 10km up the waterway before striking numerous Turkish mines, losing half a dozen vessels and hundreds of men. The Allies retreated and command squabbles erupted over allocation of troops to the campaign. The generals saw the western front as paramount, whereas politicians – foremost among them, Churchill – wanted to knock Turkey out of the war first in order to weaken Germany, while at the same time exciting anti-Turkish feelings in Bulgaria and bringing it too into the war.

Regrouped at Mudros harbour on the Greek island of Limnos, the joint expeditionary forces took several months to prepare an amphibious assault on the Turkish positions along the peninsula. During this time the British had no way of knowing that Turkish forces defending the straits were cripplingly under-supplied. Had they attempted it, another naval sprint down the Dardanelles might have succeeded, but instead the delay gave the Turks the chance to strengthen their own defences.

The plan eventually formulated by the British and French commanders called for an Anglo–French landing at Cape Helles, Seddülbahir and Morto Bay at the mouth of the straits, and a simultaneous **ANZAC** (Australia–New Zealand Army Corps) assault at Kabatepe beach 13km north. The two forces were to drive towards each other, link up and neutralize the Turkish shore batteries controlling the Dardanelles.

The Australians landed first at dawn on April 25, 1915, with the British and French making shore around an hour afterwards, followed by the New Zealanders

Anzac Day

Anzac Day, April 25, is the busiest day of the year for the Gelibolu peninsula, as thousands of Australians and New Zealanders arrive to commemorate the Allied defeat, providing a huge annual boost to the local economy. In the days leading up to the 25th Eceabat and Çanakkale start to fill with visitors: Anzac Day tours are organized locally or from just about any travel agent in İstanbul, while all the European overland companies write Anzac Day into their itineraries.

The day itself begins with the **Dawn Service** at 5.30am at Anzac Cove, though most people arrive much earlier to camp out, as the police close all the roads around the grave sites to traffic from 3am. The service used to be a somewhat informal ceremony, but in recent years thousands have attended and the service now features official speeches, prayers and a representative from the Australian or New Zealand forces playing a poignant "Last Post" as the sun rises over Anzac Cove. An hour's breakfast break follows the Dawn Service before the rest of the morning's ceremonies resume – **wreath laying** at the British, French and Turkish memorials, and more services at the Australian memorial at Lone Pine and the New Zealand memorial at Chunuk Bair.

later in the day. The rather hare-brained scheme ran into trouble from the start. Anglo–French brigades at the southernmost cape were pinned down by accurate Turkish fire and the French contingent was virtually annihilated; after two days they had only managed to penetrate 6.5km inland and never managed to move any further. The fate of the ANZAC landing was even more horrific: owing to a drifting signal buoy, the Aussies and Kiwis disembarked not on the wide, flat sands of Kabatepe, but at a cramped and Turkish-dominated cove next to Arıburnu, 2km north. Despite heavy casualties (around 2000 on the first day alone) the ANZACs advanced inland in staggered parties, as the Turks initially retreated. The next day, goaded by their commanders, they managed to threaten the Turkish strongpoint of Çonkbayırı overhead. It was here that one Mustafa Kemal, a previously unknown lieutenant-colonel, rushed in reinforcements, telling his poorly equipped troops, "I do not order you to fight, I order you to die." Amazingly it worked: the ANZAC force never made it further than 800m inland, despite a supplementary British landing at Cape Suvla to the north. With the exception of ferocious battles for the summit in early August, both sides settled into long-term trench warfare. Finally, around Christmas 1915, the Allies gave up, with the last troops leaving Seddülbahir on January 8, 1916. Churchill's career went into temporary eclipse, while that of Mustafa Kemal was only just beginning.

The reasons for the **Allied defeat** are many. In addition to the chanciness of the basic strategy, the callousness and incompetence of the Allied commanders – who often countermanded each other's orders or failed to press advantages with reinforcements – cannot be underestimated. With hindsight you cannot help but wonder why the Allies didn't concentrate more on Cape Suvla and the flat, wide valley behind, skirting the fortified Ottoman heights to reach the Dardanelles' northwest shore. On the **Turkish side**, much of the credit for the successful resistance must go to Mustafa Kemal, then relatively obscure, but later better known as **Atatürk**. His role in the Turkish victory at Çonkbayırı is legendary. Mustafa Kemal seemed to enjoy a charmed life, narrowly escaping death on several occasions and, aside from his tactical skills, is credited with various other extraordinary accomplishments, but primarily that of rekindling morale, by threats, persuasion or example, among often outgunned and outnumbered Ottoman infantrymen.

At various times, half a million men were deployed by defenders and attackers alike; of these well over fifty percent were killed, wounded or missing. Allied deaths were around 52,000 while incomplete records have led to estimates of Turkish dead to be anywhere between 50,000 and 200,000. The carnage among the ANZACs in particular was especially severe compared to the island-nations' populations, but would in fact be dwarfed by the number of ANZACs killed on the western front later in the war. Only around 10,600 lost their lives in the Gallipoli campaign compared with around 60,000 for the entire war. Claims voiced in some quarters that the Allied top brass regarded the "colonials" as expendable cannon fodder have never fully been borne out. Indeed more British and Irish troops died at Gallipoli than ANZACs, with two Irish battalions suffering over fifty-percent casualties on the first day and the 42nd Manchester Division being almost completely wiped out. However, this baptism by blood had several long-term effects: a sense of Australia and New Zealand having come of age as sovereign countries; the designation of April 25 as Anzac Day, a solemn holiday in Australia and New Zealand; and a healthy antipodean scepticism, pending an evaluation of actual national interest in the face of blandishments to join international adventures.

Gelibolu

GELIBOLU – principal town of the peninsula and 35km north of the main battlefield sites – is a moderately inviting, if slightly windy, place perched just where the Dardanelles begin to narrow in earnest. It served as the Anglo–French headquarters during the Crimean War, though the town's history goes back at least as far as the fifth century BC when it was allied with Athens against the invading Persians. It's still a military outpost today, where young Turks on their two-year National Service practice for their passing-out parades at the various military installations around town.

At the heart of town is a colourful, square **fishing harbour**, ringed by cafés and restaurants, its two pools separated by a broad stone **tower**, which is all that remains of the fortifications of Byzantine Callipolis. The fortress was held by an army of rebelling Catalan mercenaries for seven years in the early fourteenth century and later fell to the Ottomans (1354), who rebuilt and expanded it. These days the tower houses the **Piri Reis museum** (Piri Reis Müzesi; Tues–Sun 9.30am–5.30pm; free), dedicated to the legendary fifteenth-century Turkish cartographer (the first man to comprehensively map the Americas), but also containing a small number of local archeological finds and some old photos of the straits. The only other significant monuments are a historic **mosque** in the marketplace and, well inland to the northeast, a few sturdy but otherwise unremarkable Ottoman tombs.

Practicalities

The **ferry jetty** is right at the inner harbour entrance; ferries cross at 3am, 5am, 6.30am, 7.30am and 8.30am, then on the hour from 9am–1am (2YTL, or 8YTL per car) to Lapseki, across the Dardanelles. The *otogar* is 500m out of town on the Eceabat road. Currently, Gelibolu has no tourist office or exchange office, though both occasionally do reopen for business. However, all the main **banks** have ATMs and most will change currency and travellers' cheques, as will the **PTT** kiosk next to the ferry terminal.

For **accommodation**, a short walk up the main street, Liman Caddesi, and then uphill along Taşçılar Caddesi, brings you to the *Otel Dilmaç* (℡0286/566 3212, ℻566 3435; ❷), whose garish pink facade hides well-appointed rooms with TVs and minibars. There's an interesting display of brass ship-fittings in the lobby of the *Hotel Oya* on Miralay Şefik Aker Caddesi, the next street left off Liman Caddesi (℡ & ℻0286/566 0392; ❸): the rooms here are very clean, with TV and fridge, though those at the front with a balcony are twice the size of those at the back. Between the lighthouse and an army camp extends a serviceable **beach**, with a free **campsite** operated by the local municipality. The unprepossessing, old-fashioned *Hotel Yılmaz* (℡0286/566 1256, ℻566 3598; ❸), on Liman Caddesi, should be considered as a last resort to stay in, of merit only really for its daily **tours** of the World War I sites (about 25YTL, including taped commentary and an evening video showing of Peter Weir's *Gallipoli*).

When **eating out**, don't miss the local catch of freshly grilled *sardalya* (sardines), at the excellent *Imren*, to the left of the harbour, which is both cheap and licensed, or the similar *Liman* and *Boğaz* restaurants next door. Expect to pay 15–20YTL for starters, fish and drinks at each of these.

Eceabat

ECEABAT – 40km south of Gelibolu – is less attractive than Gelibolu and smaller than Çanakkale, but is the best base for touring the battlefield sites, whether by yourself or on a tour.

The town doesn't have a proper *otogar* and most **buses** drop you near the ferry jetty, from where **car ferries** run across the Dardanelles to Çanakkale (at 2am & 4am, then on the hour from 7am–midnight; 2.5YTL, or 7YTL per car; 40min). The bus-company ticket offices are right in front of the jetty at Cumhuriyet Meydanı. There's a **PTT booth** by the jetty, changing money and offering a metered phone until 9pm. **Emails** can be picked up at the *Gina Internet Café*, across the road from *TJ's Hostel* on Cumhuriyet Caddesi, and **bike rental** can be arranged at both of these places.

Accommodation is plentiful but you'll need to book well ahead if you want to stay over for Anzac Day. Best budget option in town by far is the backpacker-friendly ⚓ *TJ's Hostel*, Cumhuriyet Caddesi 5 (☎0286/814 3121, ⓦwww.anzacgallipolitours.com; ②), run by the formidable TJ and his Australian wife. The rooms, though small, are clean and tidy and mostly en-suite, and there are several dorm beds available (€6.50). Extras include a laundry, book exchange, screenings of *Gallipoli*, and a lively rooftop bar, with a nightly barbecue-and-beer for 10YTL. TJ and his team also run the recently refurbished *Eceabat* on İskele Meydanı (☎0286/814 2458, Ⓕ814 2461; ③), which offers more upmarket accommodation with large rooms looking out to sea. Also on İskele Meydanı is the *Ece* (☎0286/814 1210; ②) offering simple rooms; the new *Aqua Hotel*, near the jetty, with smart modern rooms (☎0286/814 2458, ⓦwww.heyboss.com; ③); and the *Boss II* (☎0286/814 2311, Ⓔboss@heyboss.com; ②), with adjoining **campsite**, 500m further west up the waterfront and slightly inland.

Eating and, more specifically, **drinking** aren't a problem in Eceabat. There is a line of simple *pide* and *kebap* salons in front of the jetty, plus a smattering of antipodean-named bars around *TJ's Hostel*, easily spotted by the Australian and New Zealand flags hanging outside. By general consensus, the best food in town is served at the *Liman* fish restaurant. at the south end of the promenade.

Battlefield tours

TJ's Hostel runs informative half-day **tours** to the battlefield sites for 35YTL per person, which kick off with a screening of a documentary on Gallipoli, *The Fatal Shore*, and include a picnic lunch and a stop for a swim. For another 35YTL, the battlefield tour can be combined with an additional half-day tour across the Dardanelles to Troy. In addition, the shop in the hostel reception sells a useful battlefield map and guide, plus other Gallipoli-related gear. The Çanakkale-based *Anzac House* and the *Yellow Rose Pansiyon* also run organized tours of the battlefields with pick-ups in Eceabat (see p.281 for more details).

For exploring under your own steam, **local minibuses** depart from in front of the *Atlanta* restaurant for Gelibolu, Kabatepe village (this service can also drop you at the Kabatepe Information Centre) and Alçitepe. There are also services south to Kilitbahir (see below), where you can find regular dolmuşes to the southern battlefield sites.

Kilitbahir and around

The tiny village of **KILITBAHIR**, 5km south of Eceabat, is dwarfed by its massive and perfectly preserved **castle** (Wed–Sun 8.30am–noon & 1.30–6.30pm; 2YTL). Unpublicized, privately run **car ferries** chug across to Çanakkale at regular intervals – generally departing when full – at this narrowest point (1300m) of the Dardanelles. In summer, regular **dolmuşes** meet the Çanakkale car ferries at Kilitbahir and take passengers to Alçitepe, Seddülbahir and the Turkish memorial at the southern end of the peninsula.

The central and northern sites

The first stop on most tours is at the **Kabatepe Information Centre and Museum** (daily 8.30am–5pm; 2YTL), 9km northwest of Eceabat, which contains a well-labelled selection of war memorabilia, including touching letters home, photographs of the trenches, weapons and uniforms. The only sour note is the rather ghastly inclusion of some human, presumably Allied, remains.

The first points encountered along the coast road north of the centre are the **Beach**, **Shrapnel Valley** and **Shell Green** cemeteries – the latter 300m inland up a steep track, unsuitable for all but four-wheel-drive vehicles, and consequently missed out by most tours. These are followed by **Anzac Cove** and **Arıburnu**, site of the first, bungled ANZAC landing and location of the dawn service on Anzac Day. At Anzac Cove a memorial bears Atatürk's famous quotation concerning the Allied dead, which, translated into English, begins: "Those heroes that shed their blood and lost their lives . . . you are now lying in the soil of a friendly country." Looking inland, you'll see the murderous badlands that gave the defenders such an advantage. Beyond Arıburnu, the terrain flattens out and the four other cemeteries (Canterbury, No. 2 Outpost, New Zealand No. 2 Outpost and Embarkation Pier) are more dispersed.

A couple of kilometres north of Arıburnu are the beaches and salt lake at **Cape Suvla**, today renamed Kemikli Burnu ("the bone-strewn headland"), location of another six cemeteries: 7th Field Ambulance, Hill 60 (with its memorial to the New Zealand forces), Green Hill, Azmak, Hill 10 and Lala Bala; all contain mainly English, Scottish, Welsh and Irish dead, with ANZAC graves also in the first two. The roads up here are little more than dirt tracks and most tours don't make it this far.

From Anzac Cove tours go uphill along the road north that roughly follows what was the front line, to the strong points (now cemeteries) scattered around **Çonkbayırı** hill. To the left of this road is **Shrapnel Valley** – the single, perilous supply line that ran up-valley from the present location of Beach Cemetery to the trenches. First up is **Lone Pine** (Kanlı Sırt), lowest strategic position on the ridge and the largest graveyard-cum-memorial to those buried unmarked or at sea. Action here was considered a sideshow to the main August offensive further up Çonkbayırı; a total of 28,000 men died in four days at both points. Just up from Lone Pine is the **Mehmetçik memorial** to the Turkish soldiers who perished and at **Johnston's Jolly** (named after an officer who liked to "jolly the Turks up" with his gun) is a heavily eroded section of **trench**, peaceful now beneath the pine trees.

From here the road forks. To the left is **The Nek** – the scene of Peter Weir's film *Gallipoli* – and the **Walker's Ridge** cemetery. To the right the road continues uphill to Baby 700 cemetery – the high-water mark of the Allied advance on April 25 – and to the massive New Zealand memorial obelisk and the five-monolith Turkish memorial on the crest of **Çonkbayırı** hill (Chunuk Bair). On the Turkish memorial are Atatürk's words and deeds – chief among the latter being his organization of successful resistance to the Allied attacks of August 6–10. The spot where the Turkish leader's pocket watch stopped a fragment of shrapnel is highlighted, as is the grave of a Turkish soldier discovered in 1990 when the trenches were reconstructed. On this part of the front, the trenches of the opposing forces lay within a few metres of each other and the modern road corresponds to the no-man's-land.

To the southern cape

The harbour of **KABATEPE** village, boarding point for the ferry to the Turkish Aegean island of Gökçeada (Imvros; twice weekly in winter; daily in the evening in summer), lies 2km south of the Kabatepe Information Centre. There's a good beach to the north of town – intended site of the ANZAC landing – but if you're after a swim wait until you reach **KUM LİMANİ**, another 3km further south, where an even better strand fringes a warm, clean, calm sea, unusual this far north. There's been little development of this beautiful setting, but you probably won't be alone: a number of tour companies bring their clients here for a dip after battlefield sightseeing. There's recommended **accommodation** at the friendly *Kum Motel* (☎0286/814 1455, ✉otelkum@superonline.com; ❹), which has an attractive bar on the beach. You can camp in the grounds for €7. Call ahead and someone from the motel will pick you up from the Eceabat–Kabatepe dolmuş; otherwise it's a three-kilometre walk from Kabatepe harbour.

The British **Cape Helles Memorial** obelisk adorns the Turkish equivalent of Land's End, 16km beyond Kum Limanı and just past the village of Seddülbahir. From Cape Helles itself, the views south to Bozcaada (Tenedos), west to Gökçeada (Imvros) and east to Asia are magnificent, and abundant **Ottoman fortifications** hint at the age-old importance of the place. Tucked between the medieval bulwarks is an excellent beach, the **V Beach** of the Allied expedition, behind which is a **campsite** – and the biggest of five British cemeteries in the area. A turning just before Seddülbahir leads to the **French Cemetery** above Morto Bay, one of the most striking of all the memorials, with its serried rows of named black crosses, and to the nearby **Turkish Memorial**, resembling a stark, tetrahedral footstool. Locally organized tours rarely venture this far, so if you're intent on seeing these two you'll have to make your own arrangements.

The Southern Marmara shore

The **southern shoreline** of the Sea of Marmara is not as rewarding as the northern one. To the east it consists mainly of a heavily urbanized, polluted dormitory-community for İstanbul. Much of the area was devastated by the **earthquake** of August 17, 1999, in which an estimated 30,000 people were killed – many the victims of rogue builders who ignored building regulations, skimped on materials and miraculously managed to pass official inspections. Since then, hurriedly constructed apartment-blocks have been erected for the tens of thousands who were housed in makeshift tented camps after the quake. Fortunately, **İznik**, historically the most interesting town in the region, suffered little damage. Important as a centre of Christianity and, briefly, capital of the Nicaean Empire, it has many fascinating monuments and merits a stay. To the south, **Bursa**, once one of Turkey's most attractive cities, has succumbed to rapid industrial growth in recent years, bringing great wealth but destroying much of its colourful provincial atmosphere.

Sea bus services from İstanbul provide the quickest access to the region. For example, the bus from İstanbul to Bursa takes a congested five-hour route along the gulf shore through İzmit, whereas it's less than three hours by sea bus and bus via Yalova. Departures are from İstanbul's Yenikapı ferry terminal to **Yalova** (7YTL), **Mudanya** (11YTL) and **Bandırma** (15YTL), as well as to the islands of **Avşa** and **Marmara**. For schedules, see İstanbul's "Travel details", p.219. Using these services, you could see all the sights on the southern Marmara shore over a three- or four-day period, though during July and August, it's advisable to pre-book sea-bus tickets.

Southern Marmara ports and resorts

There's little of compelling interest in the **coastal ports** of the southern Marmara shore, from Yalova to Kumyaka. They like to call themselves resorts – which they are for numbers of locals – and for the most part this is rocky coast, with inland contours softened somewhat by ubiquitous olive groves. **Yalova** itself is the main transport hub, but there's no need to hang around longer than it takes to catch one of the buses outside the ferry terminal that depart for Bursa every half-hour or so (2.25YTL; 1hr). Across the road, dolmuşes to İznik depart every hour on the hour (3.5YTL; 1hr).

Termal

There are regular dolmuşes from Yalova to the famous hot springs at **TERMAL**, 12km to the southwest (just inland from Çinarcik). Although visited by Byzantine and Roman emperors, Termal's springs only became fashionable again at the turn of the twentieth century and most of the Ottoman *belle époque* buildings date from that era.

Atatürk had a house built here, now open as a **museum** (Atatürk Müzesi; Tues–Sun 8.30am–noon & 1–5pm; 2YTL), which preserves a certain rustic charm, its original hand-crafted furniture still in place. Several **hamams** – popular for their beneficial effect on rheumatism and skin diseases – offer communal pools (daily 8am–11pm; 10YTL) with separate compartments for tour groups. Water temperatures reach 65°C, so the best time to visit is in winter when the hot water provides a haven from the seasonal chill. In summer, you'll find yourself swimming, then jumping out to sunbathe in order to cool off.

The spa resort is completely dominated by two luxury **hotels**, both owned by the Yalova Termal Kaplicari hotel group: the *Çinar* and the *Çamlık* (reservations for both ☎ 0226/675 7400, ⓦ www.yalovatermal.com; ❺), whose rooms vary in price according to size, facilities and location. A cheaper alternative can be found nearby in an idyllic location in the village of **ÜVEZPİNAR**, on one of the surrounding hills: the *Dinana* (☎ 0226/675 7668, ⓕ 675 7293; ❹) is family-run and clean, with pleasant rooms all with balconies overlooking the forested mountains, and a restaurant serving simple meals. Üvezpınar is a two-kilometre hike up the road leading from the *jandarma* station to the left of the entrance to Termal, or up steps leading from within the resort itself.

Mudanya

MUDANYA is the closest harbour to Bursa, though the least useful transit point from İstanbul (Yalova is the better option). Bursa and Çanakkale buses and minibuses connect with the arriving ferries from İstanbul. Now rather dull and unappealing, the town's major moment in history was as the place where the provisional armistice between Turkey and the Allies was signed on October 11, 1922, in a nineteenth-century waterside wooden mansion that now houses a small (missable) museum to mark the occasion. More recently Mudanya served as the port of departure for those attending the trial of Kurdish-separatist leader Abdullah Öcalan (currently serving a life sentence as the only inmate on the nearby prison island of İmralı).

Mudanya has one excellent **hotel**: the *Montania*, Eski İstasyon Caddesi (℡0224/544 6000, ⓦwww.montaniahotel.com; ➐), a renovated 150-year-old station building on the seaside esplanade. It has indoor and outdoor pools, a sauna and well-equipped modern rooms, some with sea views. Rates are negotiable out of season.

Kumyaka and Zeytinbaği

KUMYAKA, 7km west of Mudanya, and **ZEYTINBAĞI**, 3km further on, both have **Byzantine churches** that are worth a look. The latter village was the Greek Trilya and the Fatih Camii here is thought to have started life as a thirteenth-century church – it is presently undergoing restoration. A more ruined church just out of town dates from the eighth century. Once you've seen these, you can get a good fish meal by the little anchorage. Both villages are served by bus from Mudanya and Bursa.

İznik

It's hard to believe that **İZNIK**, today a somnolent farming community at the east end of the lake of the same name, was once the seat of empires and scene of desperate battles. But looking around the fertile olive-mantled valley, you can understand the attraction for imperial powers needing a fortified base near the sea-lanes of the Marmara. Today, İznik is firmly a backwater, slumbering away among its orchards and waking only recently to the demands of tourism. Tractors, rather than tour buses, are still the most common sight on İznik's streets. The town's famous sixteenth-century ceramics, the best ever produced

△ İznik tiles

in Turkey, are now all but absent from İznik's museums and mosques – even the tiles sheathing the minaret of Yeşil Camii, the town's most famous landmark, are poor substitutes made in Kütahya. Most people visit İznik as a long day out of İstanbul or Bursa, staying a night at most – just about enough time to sample the town's monuments.

Some history

Founded by Alexander's general Antigonus in 316 BC, the city was seized and enlarged fifteen years later by his rival Lysimachus, who named it **Nicaea** after his late wife. He also gave Nicaea its first set of walls and the grid plan typical of Hellenistic towns; both are still evident. When the Bithynian kingdom succeeded Lysimachus, Nicaea alternated with nearby Nicomedia as its capital until bequeathed to Rome in 74 BC. Under the Roman emperors the city prospered as capital of the province and it continued to flourish during the Byzantine era.

Nicaea played a pivotal role in early Christianity, by virtue of hosting two important **ecumenical councils**. The first, convened by Constantine the Great

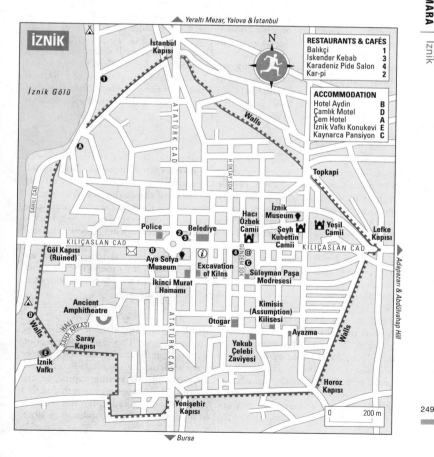

in 325AD, resulted in the condemnation of the Arian heresy – which maintained that Christ's nature was inferior to God the Father's – and the promulgation of the Nicene Creed, affirming Christ's divine nature, which is still central to Christian belief. The seventh council (the second to be held here) was presided over by Empress Irene in 787AD; this time the Iconoclast controversy was settled by the pronouncement, widely misunderstood in the West, that icons had their proper place in the church so long as they were revered and not worshipped.

Nicaea's much-repaired walls seldom repelled invaders and in 1081 the Selçuks took the city, only to be evicted by a combined force of Byzantines and Crusaders sixteen years later. The fall of Constantinople to the Fourth Crusade in 1204 propelled Nicaea into the spotlight once more, for the Byzantine heir Theodore Lascaris retreated here and made this the base of the improbably successful **Nicaean Empire**. The Lascarid dynasty added a second circuit of walls before returning to Constantinople in 1261, but these again failed to deter the besieging Ottomans, who, led by Orhan Gazi, the victor of Bursa, broke through in March 1331.

Renamed İznik, the city embarked on a golden age of sorts, interrupted briefly by the pillaging of Tamerlane in 1402. Virtually all of the surviving monuments predate the Mongol sacking, but the most enduring contribution to art and architecture – the celebrated **İznik tiles and pottery** – first appeared during the reign of Çelebi Mehmet I, who brought skilled potters from Persia to begin the local industry. This received another boost in 1514 when Selim the Grim took Tabriz and sent more craftsmen west as war booty; by the end of the sixteenth century ceramic production was at its height, with more than three hundred functioning kilns. It was to be a brief flowering, since within another hundred years war and politics had scattered most of the artisans. By the mid-eighteenth century the local industry had packed up completely, with products from nearby Kütahya serving as inferior substitutes. İznik began a long, steady decline, hastened by near-total devastation during the 1920–22 war.

The Town

With its regular street plan, İznik is easy to navigate. The main north–south boulevard **Atatürk Caddesi** and its east–west counterpart **Kılıçaslan Caddesi** link four of the seven ancient gates, dividing the town into unequal quadrants. Only enthusiasts will want to walk the entire perimeter of the double **walls**, now missing most of their hundred original watchtowers, but three of the seven portals are worth some time. Heavy traffic has been rerouted through modern breaches in the fortifications to prevent vibration damage to the original openings, now restricted to tractors and pedestrians.

The **lake** provides decent swimming in summer, but the town beaches are scrappy and uninviting; you really need a car to reach the more attractive spots. Both roads out of town along the lakeshore stay close to the water and both offer swimming possibilities at various tiny beaches along the way.

The southeast quadrant

If your time is limited, head directly to İznik's central roundabout, southeast of which is the **Aya Sofya Museum** (Aya Sofya Müzesi; Tues–Sun 8.30am–noon & 1–5pm; 2YTL), housed in all that remains of the Byzantine Church of Holy Wisdom, founded by Justinian. The current structure was built after an earthquake in 1065 and, as the cathedral of the provisional Byzantine capital, hosted the coronations of the four Nicaean emperors. The Ottomans converted it to a mosque directly on taking the city and Mimar Sinan restored it, but the premises were already half-ruined when reduced to their present, sorry condition in 1922.

Inside there's not much to see except some damaged floor mosaics and a faint but exquisite **fresco** of Christ, John and Mary, at ground level behind a glass panel to the left as you enter.

Returning to Kılıçaslan Caddesi, take a right before the tourist office and, opposite the İkinci Murat Hamamı, you'll see the excavations of the İznik **kilns**, still in progress. The site can be entered at any time with the kilns clearly visible; finds from the excavations are on display in the archeological museum (see p.252).

Three blocks east of the kilns, stands the **Süleyman Paşa Medresesi**, built in 1332 – the oldest such Ottoman structure in Turkey and the first example of a school with an open courtyard surrounded by eleven chambers and nineteen domes. Three blocks south of the *medresesi* is the fourteenth-century **Yakub Çelebi Zaviyesi**, founded by the luckless prince slain by his brother Beyazit I at Kosovo in 1389 (see p.264). A block to the east, nothing but foundations remain of the **Kimisis Kilisesi** (Church of the Assumption), the presumed burial place of Theodore Lascaris, which was destroyed in 1922. Nearby is a dank, sunken **ayazma**, or sacred spring.

İznik Vafkı

The **İznik Vafkı**, or İznik Foundation, clearly signposted in the southwest quadrant on Halı Saha Arkası (July & Aug daily 6–11am; Sept–June daily 8am–6pm; ☏0224/757 6025, ⓦwww.iznik.com), was established in 1995 with the dual intentions of researching the early techniques used to produce İznik tiles and restarting production using traditional methods. Today, tiles of extremely high quality are manufactured and sold on site (prices start from €150 each, credit cards accepted); exact replicas of original designs are not reproduced for fear of them being passed off as genuine. During a visit you'll see different production stages and receive a brief history of the İznik *oeuvre*. Occasional workshops are run on request for interested groups, with accommodation in the small hotel on site.

İznik tiles adorn various Turkish company headquarters, while in İstanbul you are likely to see them decorating the stations on the metro line from Taksim to Levant, as well as in the Turkish bath of the *Ritz-Carlton Hotel* and at the new terminal buildings of Atatürk airport. They are also on display in the Montreal Peace Park in Canada.

The northeast quadrant

Just north of Kılıçaslan Caddesi squats the **Hacı Özbek Camii**, the earliest known Ottoman mosque, built in 1333 but much adulterated; the portico was senselessly pulled down in 1939, but is presently being restored by the Ministry of Culture.

Ambling along Kılıçaslan Caddesi you'll soon reach a vast landscaped park to the north, dotted with İznik's most famous monuments. The **Yeşil Camii**, or Green Mosque, erected toward the end of the fourteenth century, is a small gem of a building, its highlight the fantastic marble relief on the portico. Tufted with a stubby minaret that looks back to Selçuk models, the mosque takes its name from the green İznik tiles that once adorned this minaret; they've long since been replaced by mediocre, tri-coloured Kütahya work.

Across the park sprawls the **Nilüfer Hatun İmareti**, commissioned by Murat I in 1388 in honour of his mother, by all accounts a remarkable woman. Daughter of a Byzantine noble (some say of Emperor John VI Cantacuzenos himself), Nilüfer Hatun was married off to Orhan Gazi to consolidate a Byzantine–Ottoman alliance. Her ability was soon recognized by Orhan, who appointed her regent during his frequent absences. The T-form building, whose ample domes perennially play host to storks, is more accurately called a *zaviye* than a mere soup kitchen and is one of the few that never doubled as a mosque. It was originally the meeting place not of dervishes but of the Ahi brotherhood, a guild drawn from the ranks of skilled craftsmen that also acted as a community welfare and benevolent society.

Today the *imaret* contains the **İznik Museum** (Tues–Sun 8.30am–noon & 1.30–5pm; 2YTL), which is sadly lacking in the expected İznik ware. The pieces of fourteenth-century İznik tiles excavated from the town's kilns have been painstakingly restored, but they are all incomplete and there are few of the beautiful sixteenth-century mosque ornaments and massive plates that are commonplace in the museums of İstanbul and abroad. More interesting is an exhibition of **Selçuk tile fragments** found in the area around the Roman theatre and in local kilns – this area was not known to be a centre of Selçuk occupation and it's uncertain whether these tiles were locally produced or imported, although evidence suggests that İznik ware is in part descended from that of the Selçuks. The museum also has such Roman bits as a bronze dancing Pan, some Byzantine gold jewellery and, standing out among the nondescript marble clutter, a sarcophagus in near-mint condition. For a more perilous adventure, and a fine view of Nilüfer Hatun's cupolas, climb the minaret of the adjacent **Şeyh Kubettin Camii**.

The walls and beyond

Closest gate to the Yeşil Camii is the eastern **Lefke Kapısı**, a three-ply affair including a triumphal arch dedicated to Hadrian between the two courses of walls. Just outside is a stretch of the ancient **aqueduct** that until recently supplied the town. It's possible to get up on the ramparts here for a stroll, as it is at the northerly **İstanbul Kapısı**, best preserved of the gates, the outer part of which was constructed as a triumphal triple arch to celebrate the visit of the Roman emperor Hadrian in 124. The inner gate is decorated by two stone-carved **masks**, probably taken from the nearby Roman theatre. Other traces of Roman Nicaea are evident in the southwestern quarter: a course of **ancient wall** delimits the so-called "Senatus court", extending from the surviving tower next to the **Saray Kapısı**, and an all-but-collapsed **theatre** lies just inside the gate.

If time permits, you might walk or drive to the obvious **Abdülvahap hill** 2.5km east of the Lefke Kapısı for a comprehensive view over İznik, its walls, the surrounding olive groves and lake. From March 21 to September 21, when the sun sets between the two distant hills on either side of the lake, the top of this hill is the best place to share a dramatic sunset with picnicking İznik families. The green-painted tomb on top belongs to a certain Abdülvahap, a semi-legendary character in the Arab raids of the eighth century.

Seven kilometres north of İznik in the village of **Elbeyli** is the **Yeraltı Mezar**, a subterranean tomb for which the archeological museum staff in İznik retain the keys. Thought to be the fourth-century burial chamber of a Roman couple (there are two graves here), the single chamber is covered in excellent frescoes, including a pair of peacocks. For a small consideration the museum custodian takes individuals and groups after the museum closes at 5pm. You'll need your own transport, or the willpower to haggle with a taxi driver, for a return trip.

Practicalities

You'll probably arrive at the tiny **otogar** in the southeast quarter, three blocks south of the German-speaking **tourist office**, opposite the *Belediye* on the ground floor at Kılıçaslan Cad 130 (May–Sept Mon–Fri & sometimes Sat 8am–noon & 1–5.30pm; Oct–April Mon–Fri 8.30am–noon & 1–5pm; ☎0224/757 1933). There's an **Internet café** next door to the *Kaynarca Pansiyon* on Gündem Sok. Both men and women can get steam-cleaned at the **İkinci Murat Hamamı** (daily: women 8am–2pm, men 4–10pm; 10YTL) just southeast of İznik's central roundabout and the Aya Sofya Museum.

Accommodation

Rooms, singles in particular, are at a premium and reservations are recommended between mid-June and mid-September – especially at the weekends, when inhabitants of neighbouring towns come to bathe in İznik lake. It's possible to **camp** in the shady site next door to the lakeside *Çamlık Motel* and there's another campsite on the lake just north of the city walls.

Hotel Aydın Kılıçaslan Cad ☎0224/757 7650, ⓦwww.iznikhotelaydin.com. Opposite the police station, with pleasant rooms, many with balconies overlooking the central square. ❸

Çamlık Motel Sahili Cad 11 ☎ & ☎0224/757 1631. Rooms are small but comfortable, with balconies overlooking the lake; there's also an excellent attached restaurant. ❹

Cem Otel Sahili Cad 20 ☎0224/757 1687, ⓦwww.cemotel.com. Pleasant, newly renovated lakeside hotel, with all bedrooms en suite. ❹

İznik Vakfı Konukevi Sahil Yolu Sok 13 ☎0224/757 6025, ⓔinfo@iznik.com. The guesthouse of the foundation dedicated to reviving the town's tile-making heritage (see p.250) is, as you might expect, adorned with all manner of colourful, intricate wall decorations. Rooms are simple but comfortable, and there's a lovely shady garden. ❷

Kaynarca Pansiyon Gündem Sok 1 ☎0224/757 1753, ⓦwww.kaynarca.s5.com. The most appealing midtown budget option, run by English-speaking Ali and his charming family. Dorm beds (€7), as well as en-suite singles, doubles and triples – all rooms have satellite TV, breakfast (€2) is served on the rooftop terrace and there's a kitchen for guests' use. ❷

Eating and drinking

Maple-canopied Kılıçaslan Caddesi has a few good **restaurants**, including two or three good-value *pide* places next to each other near the *Belediye* building. Most outsiders, however, will want to eat **by the lakeshore**, where some of the restaurants are licensed; try grilled or fried *yayın*, the excellent local catfish. For snacks or dessert there are plenty of tea gardens, cafés and ice-cream parlours overlooking the lake.

Balıkçı Sahili Cad 22. Good-value licensed restaurant, with lakeside views and outside tables. Simple grilled or fried fish accompanied by bread and salad costs around 10YTL.

Çamlık Motel Sahili Cad 11. The nicest of the waterside restaurants in a lovely shady setting, dishing up *mezes* and kebabs, including their speciality fish kebab, for around 12YTL a head with beer.

İskender Kebab Kılıçaslan Cad. Fresh *pide*, tremendous local meatballs and steam-tray food, popular at lunchtime with office workers from the nearby town hall. A plate of varied *lokanta*-style dishes will set you back about 7YTL.

Karadeniz Pide Salon Kılıçaslan Cad. Fresh and cheap *pides* washed down with *ayran* – you can watch the food being pulled into shape in the kitchen at the back of this tiny cafeteria.

Kar-pi Kılıçaslan Cad. Fast-food joint that's not a bad place for an air-conditioned break in the middle of the day and makes a change from the male-dominated teahouses; a *lahmacun* (round bread with tomato topping) and salad will cost no more than 4YTL.

Bursa

Draped ribbon-like along the leafy lower slopes of Uludağ, which towers more than 2000m above it, and overlooking the fertile plain of the Nilüfer Çayı, **BURSA** does more justice to its setting than any other Turkish city apart from İstanbul. Gathered here are some of the finest early Ottoman monuments in the Balkans, set within neighbourhoods that, despite being marooned in masses of concrete, remain among the most appealing in Turkey.

Industrialization over the last four decades, and the quadrupling in population to over a million, mean that the city as a whole is no longer exactly elegant. Silk and textile manufacture, plus patronage of the area's thermal baths by the elite, were for centuries the most important enterprises; they're now outstripped by automo-

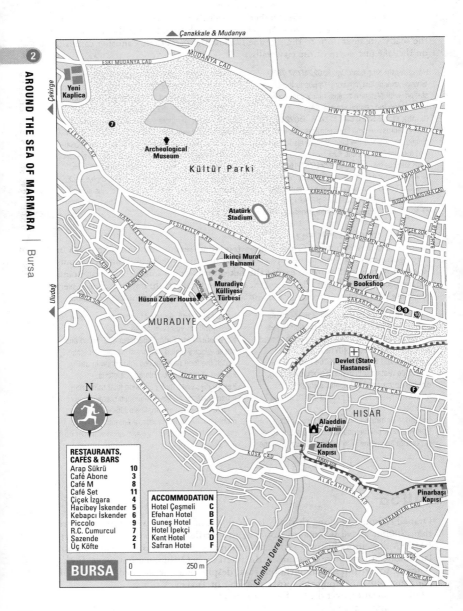

▲ Çanakkale & Mudanya

ESKI MUDANYA CAD
MUDANYA CAD

◄ Çekirge

Yeni
Kaplica

ÇEKİRGE CAD

❼

**Archeological
Museum**

Kültür Parkı

HWY E-23/200 ANKARA CAD

USLU SOK

KIBRIS ŞEHİTLER

MERİNOSLU SOK

DARMSTAD CAD

İLKBAHAR CAD

J SUMER SOK

◄ Uludağ

KAHAOSMAN SOK

HUSÜNÜ MUSTAFA CAD

FIRIN SOK

ÇİÇEK SOK

BAHÇELER SOK

**Atatürk
Stadium**

HAMZABEY CAD

BEŞİKÇİLER CAD

ÇEKİRGE CAD

J DEĞİRMEN CAD

BURSALI TAHİR SOK

BURSACI İZMİR CAD

**Ikinci Murat
Hamami**

YAYLA SOK

İKİNCİ MURAT CAD

**Muradiye
Külliyesi
Türbesi**

ALTIPARMAK CAD

**Oxford
Bookshop**

SAKARYA CAD

❽❾ ❿

Hüsnü Züber House

MURADİYE

KÖSK CAD

KIZLAR CAD

BAĞLI SOK

SAKARYA CAD

HASTALARYURDU CAD

**Devlet (State)
Hastanesi**

ORTAPAZAR CAD

❻

N

ORHANELİ CAD

HISAR

**Alaeddin
Camii**

**Zindan
Kapısı**

KÖSK CAD

**RESTAURANTS,
CAFÉS & BARS**

Arap Sükrü	10
Café Abone	3
Café M	8
Café Set	11
Çiçek İzgara	4
Hacibey İskender	5
Kebapcı İskender	6
Piccolo	9
R.C. Cumurcul	7
Şazende	2
Üç Köfte	1

ALACAHIRKA CAD

**Pinarbaşı
Kapısı**

BAYRAMYERİ CAD

ACCOMMODATION

Hotel Çeşmeli	C
Efehan Hotel	B
Guneş Hotel	E
Hotel Ipekçi	A
Kent Hotel	D
Safran Hotel	F

BURSA

0   250 m

Cılımboz Deresi

SEYDİ NASIH CAD

KESTANELİK CAD

ESKİYOL SOK

SEYDİ NASIH CAD

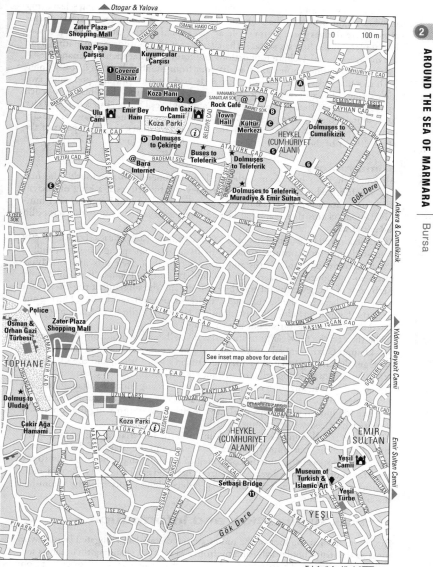

▲ Otogar & Yalova

0   100 m

Zater Plaza Shopping Mall

İvaz Paşa Çarşısı

Kuyumcular Çarşısı

❶ **Covered Bazaar**

Koza Hanı

❸ ❹

Rock Café @ ❷

Ulu Cami

Emir Bey Hanı

Orhan Gazi Camii

Koza Parki

Town Hall

Kültür Merkezi

ⒶⒷⒸ

HEYKEL (CUMHURIYET ALANI) ❺

Dolmuşes to Cumalikizik

❻

✉

ⓘ

Ⓓ **Dolmuşes to Çekirge**

Buses to Teleferik

Dolmuşes to Teleferik

@ **Bara Internet**

Ⓔ

Dolmuşes to Teleferik, Muradiye & Emir Sultan

AROUND THE SEA OF MARMARA | Bursa

▶ Ankara & Cumalikizik

▶ Yıldırım Beyazıt Camii

▶ Emir Sultan Camii

▶

★ **Police**

★ **Osman & Orhan Gazi Türbesi**

Zater Plaza Shopping Mall

TOPHANE

★ **Dolmuş to Uludağ**

★ **Çakir Ağa Hamami**

Koza Parki ⓘ

See inset map above for detail

HEYKEL (CUMHURIYET ALANI)

EMIR SULTAN

★ **Yeşil Camii**

Museum of Turkish & Islamic Art

★ **Yeşil Türbe**

Setbaşi Bridge

⑪

YEŞIL

Gök Dere

Teleferik for Uludağ ▼

255

bile manufacture (both Renault and Tofaş have plants here), canneries and bottlers processing the rich harvest of the plain, and the presence of Uludağ University. Vast numbers of settlers from Artvin province have been attracted by job opportunities at the various factories, while the students provide a necessary leavening in what might otherwise be a uniformly conservative community. Some of this atmosphere derives from Bursa's role as first capital of the Ottoman Empire and burial place of the first six sultans, their piety as well as authority emanating from the mosques, social-welfare foundations and tombs built at their command.

Bursa is sometimes touted as a long day out from İstanbul, but this is really doing both the city and yourself a disservice: it deserves at least one and preferably two nights' stay. The spirit of the place really can't be gauged amid the whisked-in coach parties gawping at the overexposed Yeşil Camii and Yeşil Türbe. Bursa is a good city for walking around – particularly following the recent re-laying of many of the city centre pavements – whether through the hive of the bazaars, the linear parks of the Hisar district or the anachronistic peace of the Muradiye quarter.

Some history

Although the area had been settled at least a millennium previously, the first city was founded early in the second century BC by Prusias I, a king of ancient Bithynia, who in typical Hellenistic fashion named the town **Proussa**, after himself. Legend claims that Hannibal helped him pick the location of the acropolis, today's Hisar.

Overshadowed by nearby Nicomedia (modern İzmit) and Nicaea (İznik), the city stagnated until the **Romans**, attracted by its natural hot springs, began spending lavish amounts on public baths and made it capital of their province of Mysia. Justinian introduced silkworm culture and Byzantine Proussa flourished until Arab raids of the seventh and eighth centuries, and the subsequent tug-of-war for sovereignty between the Selçuks and the Greeks, precipitated decline. During and after the Latin interlude in Constantinople (1204–61), the Byzantines reconsolidated their hold on Proussa, but not for long.

The start of the fourteenth century saw a small band of nomadic Turks, led by one **Osman Gazi**, camped outside the walls of Proussa. After more than a decade of siege, the city capitulated in 1326 to Osman's son, Orhan, and the **Ottomans** ceased to be a wandering tribe of marauders. Orhan marked the acquisition of a capital and the organization of an infant state by styling himself sultan, giving the city its present name and striking coinage. Bursa began to enjoy a second golden age: the silk industry was expanded and the city, now outgrowing the confines of the citadel, graced with monuments.

In the years following Orhan's death in 1362 the imperial capital was gradually moved to Edirne, but Bursa's place in history, and in the hearts of the Ottomans, was ensured; succeeding sultans continued to add buildings, and to be laid to rest here, for another hundred years. Disastrous fires and earthquakes in the mid-nineteenth century, and the 1920–22 war of independence, only slightly diminished the city's splendour.

Arrival, orientation and information

Bursa's position at the foot of the mountain has dictated an elongated layout, with most of the major boulevards running from east to west, changing their names several times as they go. The **otogar** lies 10km north of town on the Yalova road; from here grey-and-blue service buses ferry visitors straight to **Heykel**, the local name for Cumhuriyet Alanı, nominal focal point of the city. Bursa's main **tourist office** (Mon–Fri 8am–noon & 1–5pm; ☎0224/220 1848) is a 200m walk from Heykel, in Koza Parkı, opposite Orhan Gazi Camii, in a row of shops under the north side of Atatürk Caddesi, where you can pick up a reasonable city map.

Bursa's main lengthwise thoroughfare begins life just east of Heykel as **Namazgah Caddesi**, below the district of **Yeşil** and its namesake mosque and tomb. West of İnönü Caddesi it becomes **Atatürk Caddesi** as it passes through the city's central bazaar and hotel district and changes its name again to **Cemal Nadir Caddesi** right below **Hisar**, the nucleus of the Byzantine settlement. After being fed more traffic by Cumhuriyet Caddesi, which divides the bazaar, and by the roundabout at the top of Fevzi Çakmak Caddesi, the boulevard metamorphoses into **Altıparmak Caddesi**, and then into **Çekirge Caddesi** as it heads west past the Kültür Parkı and to the thermal resort of **Çekirge**, 4km west of the centre. However, there are numerous other delightful secondary streets, noted in the city account, all better suited for walking between Bursa's historical sites.

City transport

Though Bursa is narrow, with many points of interest bunched together, it's sufficiently long enough for you to want to consider **public transport** to reach the outlying attractions.

Of the **city buses**, only the #2/A (connecting Emir Sultan in the east of town with Çekirge to the west) and the #3/A (linking Heykel with the Uludağ *teleferik*) are of much use, and you need to buy tickets for them at designated booths. It's often simpler to avail yourself of Bursa's **dolmuşes** instead. Appearing in various colours, the cars all bear destination signs on their roofs, start from fixed points around the city and pick up and let down passengers at places clearly marked with a large "D". If your luggage won't fit in the boot, you'll have to buy a seat for it – still a lot cheaper than a private taxi. Useful routes, many starting at Heykel, are indicated where appropriate in the account of the city, starting on p.258, below; fares are set and average 0.75YTL.

A new **metro line**, linking the Kültür Parkı with outlying suburbs, opened in 2004. Construction of an extension to the town centre is planned over the next couple of years, no doubt creating intense traffic problems until the work is complete.

Accommodation

Reasonably priced hotel beds are generally plentiful in Bursa, not least because it's a little off the backpacking trail and because it's often treated as a day-trip destination from İstanbul. Rich foreigners, particularly Arabs, gravitate toward the luxury spa-hotels 4km out of the centre at **Çekirge**, but there is also a cluster of modest establishments out here, around the Birinci Murat Camii. If you're interested in seeing monumental Bursa, then staying in midtown accommodation, around **Atatürk Caddesi**, makes more sense.

Central Bursa

Hotel Çeşmeli Gümüşçeken Cad 6 ✆ & ✆ 0224/224 1511. Immaculate, extremely welcoming hotel run entirely by women. Rooms have minibars, TVs and fans; buffet breakfast included. ❸

Efehan Hotel Gümüşçeken Cad 34 ✆ 0224/225 2260, ⓦ www.efehan.com.tr. Pleasant three-star comfort in a central location. Extras include minibars and satellite TV. Ask for one of the top rooms for mountain views. ❹

Guneş Hotel İnebey Cad 75 ✆ 0224/224 1404, ⓔ otelgunes@yahoo.com. Cheap, clean and friendly, with centrally heated (though waterless) rooms. ❷

Hotel İpekçi Çancılar Cad 38 ✆ 0224/221 1935. In the bazaar area west of İnönü Cad, with bright, airy and surprisingly quiet rooms. En-suite rooms fall into the next price category up. ❷

Kent Hotel Atatürk Cad 69 ✆ 0224/223 5420, ⓦ www.kentotel.com. The town centre's most prominent hotel offers a high level of comfort – large rooms with satellite TV and minibars – but with a main road in front, a *McDonalds* on one side and a building site on the other, it's apt to get a little noisy. ❻

Safran Hotel Ortapazar Cad, Arka Sok 4 ☎0224/224 7216, ℻224 7219. Beautifully restored wooden house, in an atmospheric part of the old town up on the Hisar. Rooms are modern and there's a good restaurant (see p.265). ❺

Çekirge

Ada Palas Murat Cad 21 ☎0224/233 3990, ⓦwww.adapalas.com. Clean, smart two-star hotel, with a Turkish bath and Jacuzzi. ❹

Atlas Termal Otel Hamamlar Cad 35 ☎0224/234 4100, ⓦwww.atlasotel .com. The full thermal experience for a fraction of the usual price. The *Atlas* has two shiny marble hamams set in a mock Art-Nouveau interior, as well as a reasonable restaurant, garden courtyard and terrace. The bedrooms are comfortable and boast excellent bathrooms. ❸

Hotel Çelik Palas Çekirge Cad 79 ☎0224/233 3800, ⓦhttp://bursa.swissotel.com. The elegance of the hotel's interior – all chandeliers and marble – is slightly let down by its location, right on a

busy main road. The bedrooms all come with a/c, cable TV and hot spring water in the bathtubs, and there's a very good restaurant, but it's the Turkish bath which is the hotel's highlight, with top-to-toe marble and a magnificent domed ceiling. ❽

Demirci Otel Hamamlar Cad 33 ☎0224/236 5104, ℻235 2436. Friendly, unpretentious and good value, with en-suite rooms and a searingly hot hamam in the basement. ❸

Hotel Dilmen Murat Cad 20 ☎0224/233 9500, ⓦwww.hoteldilmen.com. Four-star hotel, with sauna, Turkish bath, rooftop terrace and all the comforts you might expect at this price. Prices are highest at weekends. ❼

Kervansaray Bursa Hotel Çekirge Meyd ☎0224/233 9300, ⓦwww.kervansarayhotels .com. Sumptuous hotel, next to the Old Baths, with an assortment of swimming pools, Turkish baths and saunas. There are five pricey restaurants and a baby-sitting service. ❼

Yat Hotel Hamam Cad 31 ☎0224/233 9335, ℻233 9339. Modern hotel with rooms with TV, plus small garden and Turkish bath. Buffet breakfast included. ❹

The City and around

There's little point in touring Bursa's monuments in strictly chronological order, though not surprisingly many of the oldest ones are clustered just outside Hisar, in today's city centre. The places covered below under each heading can be visited in a leisurely morning or afternoon. If you can't spare this much time, you could just manage to see the most spectacular monuments around the Koza Parkı and at Yeşil in a few rushed hours.

Central sites

Just across from the main tourist office stands the **Orhan Gazi Camii**, whose 1336 foundation makes it the second-oldest mosque in Bursa. Originally built as a *zaviye* for itinerant dervishes, this is the earliest example of the T-form mosque with *eyvan*s flanking the main prayer hall. **Karagöz puppets**, the painted camel-leather props used in the Turkish national shadow-play, are supposed to represent workers who were involved in building the Orhan Gazi Camii. According to legend, the antics of Karagöz and his sidekick Hacıvat so entertained their fellow workmen that Orhan had them beheaded to end the distraction. Later, missing the comedians and repenting of his deed, he arranged to immortalize the pair in the art form that now bears the name of Karagöz.

Just west of Orhan Gazi, the compact **Koza Parkı**, with its fountains, benches, strolling crowds and street-level cafés, is the real heart of Bursa – never mind what they say about Heykel. Though animated through the day and early evening, the plaza empties soon after, with the illuminated fountains dark and still, and the walkways deserted by 11pm.

On the far side of the Koza Parkı looms the tawny limestone **Ulu Cami**, built between 1396 and 1399 by Yıldırım Beyazit I, from the proceeds of booty won from the Crusaders at Macedonian Nicopolis. Before the battle Yıldırım (Thunderbolt) had vowed to construct twenty mosques if victorious. The present building of twenty domes supported by twelve freestanding pillars was his rather

Bursa silk and the cocoon auction

Highlight of the year is the **cocoon auction** of late June and early July, when silk-breeders from around the province gather to hawk their valuable produce. Then, Bursa's Koza Hanı becomes a lake of white torpedoes the size of a songbird's egg; the moth, when it hatches, is a beautiful, otherworldly creature with giant onyx eyes and feathery antennae. You can watch the melee from the upper arcades or, as long as you're careful, the merchants don't mind you walking the floor.

After being sent into a tailspin by French and Italian competition two hundred years ago, the Bursa silk trade has recently experienced a tentative revival. However, the quality of contemporary fabric cannot compare to museum pieces from the early Ottoman heyday and most of the better designs are made up in imported material, which is still better quality than the Turkish. If you're buying silk here, make sure the label says *ipek* (silk) and not *ithal ipek* (artificial silk).

loose interpretation of this promise, but it was still the largest and most ambitious Ottoman mosque of its time. The interior is dominated by a huge *şadırvan* pool in the centre, whose skylight was once open to the elements, and an intricate walnut *mimber* pieced together, it's claimed, without nails or glue. Even less convincing is the tradition stating that the main north portal was remodelled by Tamerlane when he occupied Bursa in 1402–03.

From the north porch you can descend stairs to the two-storeyed **Emir (Bey) Hanı**, originally a dependency of the Orhan Gazi Camii and now home to various offices and shops. A fountain plays under the trees in the courtyard, but with no teahouse or public seating it's not a place to linger. Beyond the Emir Hanı begins Bursa's **covered bazaar** (daily 9am–8pm; closed Sun) whose assorted galleries and lesser *hans* are a delight for shoppers hunting for ready-to-wear clothing, silk goods (scarves to jump suits), towels, bolts of cloth and furniture, all Bursa province speci-alities. The nearby **bedesten** is given over to the sale and warehousing of jewellery and precious metals.

The centrepiece of the bazaar has to be the **Koza Hanı**, or "Silk-Cocoon Hall", flanking the park close to the Orhan Gazi Camii. Built in 1451, when Bursa was the final stop on the Silk Route from China, it's still filled with silk and brocade merchants (plus a few jewellery stores). On the lower level, in the middle of a cob-bled courtyard, a minuscule **mescit** (small mosque) perches directly over its *şadırvan*, while a subsidiary court bulges asymmetrically to the east; there are teahouses and public benches in both.

Bursa's most central **food market** is in the bazaar's Nilüfer Koylu Pasaja, just above Orhan Gazi Camii on Belediye Caddesi. This is the place to stock up for picnics, with an excellent selection of the fruits (strawberries and cherries in spring, peaches and pears in summer), nuts and dairy products for which the region is noted. In the same area, near the *Sazende Restaurant*, handmade lace and other handicrafts are on sale in **Hanamelsanatlar Sokak** ("the street of women's handicrafts"), while flower stalls can be found on İmaret Sokaği. The shopping zone continues east along the narrow, pedestrianized Ukul Sokak, which is lined with shops selling clothes, shoes and household goods.

Another area of the bazaar that has kept its traditions intact despite quake and blaze is the **Demirciler Çarşısı**, the ironmongers' market. This is just the other side of İnönü Caddesi, best crossed by the pedestrian underpass at Okular Caddesi. Stall upon stall of blacksmiths and braziers attract photographers, but be advised that some expect a consideration for posing. From here you can eas-ily continue past a small mosque and some cabinet-makers' workshops to **Fırın**

Sokak, which is lined with some of the finest old dwellings in town. At the end of this short street a bridge spans the **Gök Dere**, one of two streams that tumble through Bursa, forming an approximate eastern boundary for the centre.

Yeşil

Across the stream, it's only a few minutes' walk up to **Yeşil**, as the eastern neighbourhood around the namesake mosque and tombs is known.

Designed by the architect Hacı Ivaz atop a slight rise, the **Yeşil Camii** was begun in 1413 by Çelebi Mehmet I, victor of the civil war caused by the death of Beyazit I. Despite being unfinished – work ceased in 1424, three years after Mehmet himself died – and despite catastrophic damage from two nineteenth-century earth tremors, it's easily the most spectacular of Bursa's imperial mosques. The incomplete entrance, faced in a light marble, is all the more easy to examine for the lack of a portico; above the stalactite vaulting and relief calligraphy you can see the supports for arches never built.

Next you'll pass through a foyer supported by pilfered Byzantine columns to reach the **interior**, a variation on the T-plan usually reserved for dervish *zaviyes*. A fine *şadırvan* occupies the centre of the "T", but your eye is monopolized by the hundreds of polychrome **tiles** that line not just the *mihrab* but every available vertical surface up to 5m in height, particularly two recesses flanking the entryway. Green and blue pigments matching the carpets predominate and praying amid this dimly lit majesty must be something like worshipping inside a leaf. Tucked above the foyer, and usually closed to visitors, is the **imperial loge**, the most extravagantly decorated chamber of all. Several artisans from Tabriz participated in the tiling of Yeşil Camii but the loge is attributed to a certain Al-Majnun, which translates most accurately as "intoxicated on hashish". On the same knoll as the mosque, and immediately across the pedestrian precinct separating them, the **Yeşil Türbe** (daily 8am–noon & 1–5pm; free) contains the sarcophagus of Çelebi Mehmet I and his assorted offspring. Inside, the walls and Mehmet's tomb glisten with the glorious original Tabriz material.

Regrettably, the immediate environs of the two monuments swarm with tour groups: the café nearby overcharges mercilessly for the view and a clutch of converted, vehemently repainted old houses are glutted with souvenir dross. There's not a genuine antique-seller to be found, with the possible exception of one eccentric old man next to the *medrese* (theology academy), which lies 100m from the summit. The academy now houses Bursa's **Museum of Turkish and Islamic Art** (Türk ve İslam Eserleri Müzesi; daily except Mon 8am–noon & 1–5pm; free), set around a pleasant courtyard with fountain, trees and picnic tables. If the museum is short-staffed certain rooms may be closed, but in theory you can view İznik ware, Çanakkale ceramics, kitchen utensils, inlaid wooden articles, weapons and a mock-up of an Ottoman *sünnet odası*, or circumcision chamber. The exhibition of hamam paraphernalia has a local relevance because of the history of bathing in the area, which is probably why Bursa towelling has developed world prominence. In the nineteenth century, however, in place of towels, beautifully embroidered linen cloths were used as wraps. Other signs of wealth were silver bathbowls, bone or tortoiseshell combs, and clogs inlaid with mother-of-pearl, all of which are on display here.

East of Yeşil: to Yıldırım Beyazit Camii

A 300-metre walk east of Yeşil leads to the **Emir Sultan Camii**, lost in extensive graveyards where every religious Bursan hopes to be buried. The mosque was originally endowed by a Bokharan dervish and trusted adviser to three sultans, beginning with Beyazit I, but it has just been restored again after enduring an Ottoman

Baroque overhaul early last century, so you can only guess what's left of the original essence. The pious, however, seem to harbour no doubts, coming in strength to worship at the tombs of the saint and his family.

If you're short of time Emir Sultan Camii is the obvious site to omit: climb down steps through the graveyard instead and cross the urban lowlands to the **Yıldırım Beyazit Camii**, perched on a small hillock at the northeastern edge of the city. If you're coming directly from downtown, this is a substantial hike, so you might want to take a dolmuş (marked "Heykel–Beyazit Yıldırım" or the more common "Heykel–Fakülte"), which passes 200m below the mosque. Completed by Beyazit I between 1390 and 1395, the Beyazit Camii features a handsome, five-arched portico defined by square columns. The interior is unremarkable except for a gravity-defying arch bisecting the prayer hall, its lower supports apparently tapering away to end in stalactite moulding. The only other note of whimsy in this spare building is the use of elaborate niches out on the porch.

The associated **medrese**, exceptionally long and narrow because of its sloping site, huddles just downhill; today it's used as a medical clinic. The **türbe** (tomb) of the luckless Beyazit, kept in an iron cage by the rampaging Tamerlane until his death in 1403, is usually locked. Perhaps the mosque custodians fear a revival of the Ottoman inclination to abuse the tomb of the most ignominiously defeated sultan.

The Hisar

The **Hisar**, Bursa's original nucleus, nowadays retains just a few clusters of dilapidated Ottoman housing within its warren of narrow lanes and some courses of medieval wall along its perimeter.

From where Atatürk Caddesi becomes Cemal Nadir Caddesi in a whirl of traffic, you can climb up to the Hisar plateau via pedestrian ramps negotiating the ancient walls. En route, you'll pass **Zafer Plaza**, a cavernous modern shopping mall, most of it underground but topped by an attractive square and glass pyramid. There are a number of places in here to grab a blast of air conditioning, some cheesecake and a coffee. Alternatively, take a walk along Orhangazi Caddesi, home to a rather contrived artists' colony. Where Orhangazi stops climbing, the **Osman and Orhan Gazi Türbesı** stand side by side at the edge of the fortified acropolis that they conquered. The tombs – post-earthquake restorations in gaudy late Ottoman style – are on the site of a Byzantine church that has long since disappeared except for some mosaic traces near Orhan's sarcophagus.

Far better is the view from the cliff-top **park** sprawling around the tombs and clocktower, with reasonable cafés at the head of the walkways down to Cemal Nadir and Altıparmak *caddesis*. Most of the city's posher shops and cinemas line Altıparmak Caddesi, but for now it's preferable to back away from the brink and explore Hisar itself, where the wreckers took a heavy toll of the vernacular houses before preservation orders went into effect.

You must choose whether to follow signs west to Muradiye, along the most direct route, or to veer inland on a random walk around the neighbourhood. At the southernmost extreme of the citadel you exit at the **Pınarbaşı Kapısı**, lowest point in the circuit of walls and the spot where Orhan's forces finally entered the city in 1326. From there you can stroll parallel to the walls, re-entering at the **Zindan Kapısı**, inside of which is the simple **Alâeddin Camii**, erected within a decade of the conquest and so the earliest mosque in Bursa.

A more straightforward route follows Hasta Yurdu Caddesi until another generous swathe of park studded with teahouses opens out opposite the public hospital. The furthest teahouses have fine views of the Muradiye district, and from the final café and course of wall, obvious stairs descend to the **Cılımboz Deresi**, the second major stream to furrow the city.

Muradiye

Across the stream lies medieval **Muradiye**, where Bursa's best-preserved dwellings line streets at their liveliest during the Tuesday **street market**. If you're coming directly from Heykel, take one of the frequent dolmuşes marked "Muradiye".

The **Muradiye Külliyesi** is easy enough to find and, if you were disappointed by the circus at Yeşil, this is the place to capture the early Ottoman spirit more accurately – while trinket sellers and an antique shop do show the flag, there's no pressure to buy and no coachloads to shatter the calm. The mosque complex, begun in 1424 by Murat II, was the last imperial foundation in Bursa, though the tombs for which Muradiye is famous were added piecemeal over the next century or so.

The ten royal tombs, **Muradiye Külliyesi Türbesı** (daily: May–Sept 8am–noon & 1–5pm; Oct–April 8am–5pm; free), are set in lovingly tended gardens and open on a rota basis; to get into the locked ones you must find the gardener-*bekçi* with the keys – no tip is expected for the service. The first tomb encountered is that of **Şehzade Ahmet** and his brother Şehinşah, both murdered in 1513 by their cousin Selim I to preclude any succession disputes. The luxury of the İznik tiles within contrasts sharply with the adjacent austerity of **Murat II's tomb**, where Roman columns inside and a wooden awning out front are the only superfluities. Murat, as much contemplative mystic as warrior-sultan, was the only Ottoman ruler ever to abdicate voluntarily, though pressures of state forced him to leave the company of his dervishes and return to the throne after just two years. He was the last sultan to be interred at Bursa and one of the few lying here who died in his bed; in accordance with his wishes, both the coffin and the dome were originally open to the sky "so that the rain of heaven might wash my face like any pauper's".

Next along is the tomb of **Şehzade Mustafa**, Süleyman the Magnificent's unjustly murdered heir; perhaps a sign of his father's remorse, the tomb is done up in extravagantly floral İznik tiles, with a top border of calligraphy. Nearby stands the tomb of **Cem Sultan**, his brother Mustafa and two of Beyazit II's sons, decorated with a riot of abstract, botanical and calligraphic paint strokes up to the dome. Cem, the cultured and favourite son of Mehmet the Conqueror, was one of the Ottoman Empire's most interesting might-have-beens. Following the death of his father in 1481, he lost a brief dynastic struggle with the successful claimant, brother Beyazit II, and fled abroad. For fourteen years he wandered, seeking sponsorship of his cause from Christian benefactors who in all cases became his jailers: first the Knights of St John at Rhodes and Bodrum, later the papacy. At one point it seemed that he would command a Crusader army organized to retake İstanbul, but all such plans came to grief for the simple reason that Beyazit anticipated his opponents' moves and each time bribed them handsomely to desist, making Cem a lucrative prisoner indeed. His usefulness as a pawn exhausted, Cem was probably poisoned in Italy by the pope in 1495, leaving nothing but reams of poems aching with nostalgia and homesickness.

A minute's walk from the Muradiye Külliyesi is the **Hüsnü Züber House**, at Uzunyol Sok 3, Kaplıca Caddesi (Tues–Sun 10am–5pm; 2YTL). This former Ottoman guesthouse, built in 1836, sports a typical overhanging upper storey, wooden roof and beams and a garden courtyard. It now houses a collection of carved wooden musical instruments, spoons and farming utensils, many of which were made by Hüsnü Züber himself, the present owner, who inhabits the house still. The main exhibit, however, is the house itself, one of the few of its era to have been well restored and opened to the public.

The Kültür Parkı

From Muradiye it's just a short walk down to Çekirge Caddesi and the southeast gate of the **Kültür Parkı** (token admission charge when entry booths are staffed). Inside there's a popular tea garden, a small boating lake, a disgraceful mini-zoo, and a number of restaurants and *gazino*-style nightclubs. As you stroll, however, it soon becomes obvious that there's no potential for solitude – though courting couples try their best – and no wild spots among the regimented plantations and too-broad driveways.

At the west end of the park, just below Çekirge Caddesi, is the **Archeological Museum** (Arkeoloji Müzesi; daily except Mon 8am–noon & 1–5pm; 2YTL). Inside the museum, exhibits in the right-hand Stone Room vary from the macabre (a Byzantine ossuary with a skull peeking out) to the homely (a Roman cavalryman figurine), but the adjacent hall featuring metal jewellery from all over Anatolia – watch chains, breastplates, belts, buckles, bracelets, anklets, chokers – steals the show. The left wing houses a modest coin gallery and miscellaneous small ancient objects, the best of which are the Roman glass items and Byzantine and Roman bronzes. Oil lamps, pottery, a token amount of gold and far too many ceramic figurines complete these poorly labelled exhibits; while a garden of sarcophagi, stelae and other statuary fragments surrounds the building.

Çekirge

The thermal centre of **Çekirge** ("Grasshopper" – presumably a reference to the natural soundtrack of a summer evening), is another twenty minutes' walk or so along Çekirge Caddesi from the west side of Kültür Parkı. Buses (including the #2/A), as well as dolmuşes (marked "Çekirge"), shuttle to and from the dolmuş stand near the tourist office on Atatürk Caddesi.

Most visitors come here to experience the Çekirge hot springs, which flow out of Uludağ's mountainside and are tapped into by the various hotels and bathhouses. The **Yeni Kaplıca** (New Baths; daily 6am–10pm; 8YTL admission, 60YTL extra for a wash and massage) lie just beyond the Kültür Parkı, accessible by a steep driveway beginning opposite the *Çelik Palas Oteli*. There's actually a clutch of three facilities here: the **Kaynarca baths**, for women only, which is really rather grim and unappealing; the **Karamustafa spa**, for men only; and the Yeni Kaplıca itself, dating in its present form from the mid-sixteenth century, which has a women's section, but is still nothing like as splendid as the men's. According to legend, Süleyman the Magnificent was cured of gout after a dip in the Byzantine baths here and had his vizier Rüstem Paşa overhaul the building. Fragments of mosaic paving stud the floor and the walls are lined with once exquisite but now blurred İznik tiles.

The **Eski Kaplıca** (Old Baths; daily 7am–10.30pm; 8YTL admission, 5YTL extra for a massage), huddled at the far end of Çekirge Caddesi, next to the *Kervansaray Bursa Hotel*, are Bursa's most ancient baths (and much the nicest public bath for women). Byzantine rulers Justinian and Theodora first improved a Roman spa on the site and Murat I in turn had a go at the structure in the late fourteenth century. Huge but shallow keyhole-shaped pools dominate the *hararetler*, or hot rooms, of the men's and women's sections, whose domes are supported by eight Byzantine columns. Scalding (45°C) water pours into the notch of the keyhole, the temperature still so taxing in the main basin that you'll soon be gasping out in the cool room, seeking relief at the fountain in the middle. Afterwards, the bar in the men's *camekan*, where you recuperate swaddled in towels on a chaise longue, serves alcoholic beverages should you wish to pass out completely. Alternatively, head for the swimming pool of the *Kervansaray Bursa Hotel* next door (daily 8am–11pm; 15YTL), where you swim indoors and then under a partition to their heated outdoor section.

On a hillock just west of the thermal centre stands the **Hüdavendigar (Birinci) Murat Camii**, which with its five-arched portico and alternating bands of brick and stone seems more like a church teleported from Ravenna or Macedonia.

Indeed tradition asserts that the architect and builders were Christians, who dallied twenty years at the task because Murat I, whose pompous epithet literally means "Creator of the Universe", was continually off at war and unable to supervise the work. The interior plan, consisting of a first-floor *medrese* above a highly modified, T-type *zaviye* at ground level, is unique in Islam. Unfortunately, the upper storey, wrapped around the courtyard that's the heart of the place, is rarely open for visits.

Murat himself lies in the much-modified **türbe** across the street, complete apart from his entrails, which were removed by the embalmers before the body began its long journey back from Serbia in 1389. In June of that year Murat was in the process of winning his greatest triumph over the Serbian king Lazarus and his allies at the **Battle of Kosovo**, in the former Yugoslavia, when he was stabbed to death in his tent by Miloş Obiliç, a Serbian noble who had feigned desertion. Murat's son Beyazit, later better known as Yıldırım, immediately had his brother Yakub strangled and, once in sole command, decimated the Christian armies. Beyazit's acts had two far-reaching consequences: the Balkans remained under Ottoman control until early in the twentieth century, and a gruesome precedent of bloodletting was established for most subsequent Ottoman coronations.

Cumalikizik

With extra time to spare in Bursa, it's worth taking a trip out to the rural Ottoman village of **Cumalikizik**, 10km east on the Ankara road – easily reached by any dolmuş heading towards Inegöl from the dolmuş stop on Inönü Caddesi. The journey takes around twenty minutes. Documents date the village to 1685, but it is thought to be considerably older, possibly established by the Turkish horseback tribes that flowed into the region during the formative years of the Ottoman principality.

Set on the lower slopes of Uludağ, the cobbled streets are full of dilapidated buildings, leaning brokenly into each other. The Cumalikizik residents once made a living from growing chestnuts, but a virulent disease annihilated the plantation that surrounded the village. Now, raspberries and blackberries are grown instead, but as the young have gradually drifted into Bursa in pursuit of work, Cumalikizik's population has shrunk. The village has pinned its hopes on tourism to survive, promoting itself as a living museum, and after the busy streets of Bursa, Cumalikizik certainly makes a peaceful place to spend a couple of hours, drinking tea and watching the inhabitants gossip on the steps of their decaying houses.

The most prominent sights on arrival are the two enormous plane trees in the square at the entrance to the village where the dolmuş drops you. Following the alleys into the village, you'll find that the roads are only wide enough for pedestrians and pack animals – some are so narrow that two people cannot pass each other – and there is a myriad of fascinating alleyways, dead-ends and cobbled squares to explore. The ground and first floors of the houses harbour the storerooms, stables and inner courtyards; upstairs, the living quarters present bay or lattice windows and wide tiled eaves overhanging the street. Many of the existing original double-front doors are studded with large-headed nails and wrought-iron strips. Neither the **hamam** nor the **mosque** can be dated with any accuracy, though it's thought that they are around three hundred years old. There is a tiny **museum**, with no particular set opening-times – if it's locked, ask anyone to fetch the curator. Inside, there's a ramshackle, but well-meaning, collection of village implements, from old radios, door-knockers and swords, to a pile of rusting farming equipment in the garden. Around the main square at the entrance of the village are a couple of **teahouses** with outside tables and a small bakery selling tasty *börek*.

Eating, drinking and entertainment

Bursa's **cuisine** is solidly meat-oriented and served in a largely alcohol-free environment – reflecting the city's conservative nature. The most famous local recipes are *İskender kebap* (essentially *döner kebap* soaked in a rich butter, tomato and yoghurt sauce) – named after its supposed inventor, İskender (Alexander) Usta, a Bursan chef – and *İnegöl köftesi*, rich little pellets of mince often laced with cheese (when they're known as *kaşaril köfte*) and introduced by Balkan immigrants in the 1930s. If you're hungry, ask for *bir buçuk porsiyon* ("one big portion") as normal-sized portions of either dish are not enough for a meal. The city is also famous for its chestnut-based sweets, and instead of eating Turkish white bread, look out for Bursan *kepekli* (whole bran) loaves at any bakery.

For alcohol with your evening meal, head for the pedestrianized **Sakarya Caddesi** between Altıparmak Caddesi and the walls of the Hisar above, near the clocktower – the former fish market and main street of the Jewish quarter has been reborn as an atmospheric place for an outdoor fish dinner or a drink on a summer's evening. Otherwise, try the **Kültür Parkı**, where you can dine in a peaceful environment and then later take in some Turkish pop at one of the bar-cum-discos, or head up to the overpriced nightclubs in Çekirge's five-star hotels.

Bursa has relatively few nocturnal or weekend events and the student contingent is responsible for any concerts that do occur. The **Kültür Merkezi** or Cultural Centre, on Atatürk Caddesi (℡0224/223 4461), hosts ever-changing art exhibitions and occasional concerts. The **open-air theatre** in the Kültür Parkı is the main venue for the touristy musical performances and folkloric presentations that form a big part of the annual **Bursa Festival** in the last three weeks of July.

Restaurants

Arap Şükrü Kuruçeşme Mah, Sakarya Cad 6 & 29, Tophane. Fish in all shapes and sizes, with beer, wine or *rakı* to wash it down, served at tables on both sides of the cobbled street. Reasonable prices with set meals available from 17.5YTL – typical of places on this quaint pedestrianized street.

Café Abone Koza Hanı, covered bazaar. With its tree-canopied setting in the bazaar's small courtyard, this is the pick of the dozen *pide* ovens, tea booths, *büfes* and tiny restaurants scattered throughout the bazaar. Lunch only, closed Sun.

Çiçek İzgara Belediye Cad 5. The best midtown value for lunch and dinner is this popular place on the upper floor, behind the *Belediye* building (town hall). Flawless service, tableclothed elegance and extremely reasonable prices – the house special *İzgara Köfte* is just 6YTL. Closed Sun.

Hacibey İskender Taşkapı Sok 4, off Atatürk Cad. The original, famous *İskender* salon. It's a tiny, two-storey establishment just off the main square, where the decor is old wood and fake Ottoman tiles and the *İskender* is excellent, but you pay for the ambience.

Kebapçı İskender Unlu Cad 7, Heykel. Another fake Ottoman building, and another claimant to be the inventor of the namesake dish – and that's all they serve, not even salads. It's always packed, even though it's moderately expensive (10YTL

upwards for smallish portions). There's another three-storey branch on Atatürk Cad, near the Kültür Merkezi.

Mercan Restaurant *Kervansaray Bursa Hotel*, Çekirge Meyd, Çekirge. A rooftop restaurant with great views and an outdoor terrace. Dishes include smoked salmon, Chateaubriand and pineapple flambé, but you can expect a bill in the region of 60–70YTL for two, with wine. It's one of five excellent restaurants in this five-star hotel.

R.C. Cumurcul Restaurant Kültür Parkı. One of many relaxed, licensed establishments in the park, where two can eat *mezes* and kebabs, with a bottle of wine, for around 30YTL. Housed in a restored Ottoman building with a large terrace.

Safran Restaurant *Safran Hotel*, Ortapazar Cad, Arka Sok 4, Hisar. Chic little à-la-carte restaurant in a renovated Ottoman mansion. The menu includes cold and hot *mezes*, meat and mushroom stews, good salads, and heavenly sweets such as the *kaymaklı ayva tatlısı* (quince with clotted cream). Expect to pay in the region of 25–30YTL a head for a three-course meal with drinks.

Sazende Restaurant Hamamlar Cad 37, off Belediye Cad. Secluded café set in the small courtyard of a restored Ottoman house (it's also a hotel) in the bazaar, serving a wide selection of cheap workers' dishes, from soup and *pide* to *izgara*.

Üç Köfte İvaz Paşa Çarşısı 3, in the north of the

covered bazaar. The name means "three meat-balls", which is what you get, served up three times over for a portion so the food on your plate is always piping hot. Lunch only, closed Sun.

Cafés and bars

Café M Kuruçeşme Mah, Sakarya Cad 24, Tophane. *Nargile* (hubble-bubble pipe) and coffee bar, with comfortable sofas to smoke from and watch the world go by. This is a good place to try a *nargile* in an easy-going environment.

Café Set Setbaşı bridge, Namazgah Cad, Heykel. Reasonably priced café-bar, which attracts a lively student crowd. Enjoy a beer on the outdoor terrace looking downstream to the next bridge, or on one of the four levels indoors.

Piccolo Kuruçeşme Mah, Sakarya Cad 16, Tophane. Bursa's fashionable youth collect in this trendy bar, hiding behind the sort of windows you can see out of but not into. It serves snacks, but it's better to eat first at one of the surrounding fish restaurants. Stays open late, depending on the mood.

Listings

Banks and exchange There are plenty of banks with ATMs on Atatürk Cad, and exchange offices (Mon–Sat 8am–8pm) in the covered bazaar and on Altıparmak Cad.

Books Good stocks of English-language books and foreign magazines at the Oxford Bookshop, Altıparmak Cad 48–50.

Buses Departures are from the *otogar* (☎0224/261 5400), 10km north of Bursa; regular city buses from Heykel run up there. Kamil Koç, Pamukkale and Varan (and several other companies) run to Ankara, Bandırma, Çanakkale, Erdek, İstanbul (with ferry transfer), İzmir, Kütahya, Mudanya and Yalova. See "Travel details" at the end of the chapter for schedules.

Car rental Avis, Çekirge Cad 139 ☎0224/236 5133; Budget, Çekirge Cad 39/1 ☎0224/223 4204; and Europcar, Çekirge Cad 41 ☎0224/223 2321.

Consulate UK (honorary consulate), Resam Şefik Bursalı Sok, Başak Cad ☎0224/221 2534.

Hamams See p.263, or try the central, historic Çakır Ağa, located just below Hisar on Cemal Nadir Cad (men and women; 6am–midnight; 8YTL); or İkinci Murat, next to the Muradiye tomb complex (Fri & Sun men only, all other days women only; 10am–6pm; 12YTL).

Hospitals Devlet (State) Hastanesi, Hasta Yurdu Cad, Hisar ☎0224/220 0020; and Üniversite Hastanesi, P. Tezok Cad, Hastane Sok, Çekirge ☎0224/442 8400.

Internet access Bursa is well endowed with cybercafés, including *Bara Internet* on Kocaoğlu Sok, and the *Rock Café* on Orhan Sok 10, near Orhan Gazi Camii.

Left luggage At the *otogar*, open 24hr.

Police Police station at Cemal Nadir Cad.

Post office Main PTT branch at the corner of Atatürk and Maksem *caddesi* (daily 24hr for telephone and telegrams, 8am–8pm for letters, and 9am–5.30pm for full postal services).

Uludağ

Presiding over Bursa, the 2543-metre-high **Uludağ** (or "Great Mountain") is a dramatic, often cloud-cloaked massif, its northern reaches dropping dizzyingly into the city. In ancient times it was known as the Olympos of Mysia, one of nearly twenty peaks around the Aegean so named (Olympos was possibly a generic Phoenician or Doric word for "mountain"), and it has a place in mythology as the seat from which the gods watched the battle of Troy. Early in the Christian era the range became a refuge for monks and hermits, who were replaced after the Ottoman conquest by Muslim dervishes.

These days the scent of grilling meat has displaced the odour of sanctity, since Bursa natives cram the alpine campsites and picnic grounds to the gills on any holiday or weekend. Getting there is definitely half the fun if you opt for the **cable car** (*teleferik*), which links the Teleferüç borough of Bursa with the **Sarıalan** picnic grounds at 1635m, where a cluster of *et mangals* (barbecue grillhouses) and *kendin pişin kendin ye* (rent-a-barbecue establishments) await your custom.

Much of the dense middle-altitude forest has been designated a **national park**, though there are only a few kilometres of marked hiking trails. In fact, the best part of the mountain lies outside the park to the east, where a few hours' walking will bring you to some glacial **lakes** in a wild, rocky setting just below the highest summit. The best months for a visit are May and June, when the wild-

△ Skiing near Bursa

flowers are blooming, or September and October, when the mist is less dense. However, due to its proximity to the Sea of Marmara, the high ridges trap moist marine air and whiteouts or violent storms can blow up during most months of the year. **Skiing** is possible from December to March (though it's better earlier in the season than later). There's a dense cluster of hotels, most with their own ski lift, at the 1800m level (a day-pass for each lift costs around 15YTL), and you can rent skis and ski clothes at booths in **Oteller**, as the accommodation and skiing area is known.

Practicalities

To reach the lower cable-car terminus, take a dolmuş labelled "Teleferik" from the corner of Ressam Şefik Bursalı and Atatürk *caddesi*. The wobbly **teleferik** gondolas make the trip up from Teleferüç to Sarıalan every half-hour or so (daily 8am–9pm; 3YTL each way), but are cancelled in high winds; the journey takes just under thirty minutes, with a pause part-way up at Kadıyayla. Try to avoid travelling mid-afternoon, when students make the ascent after school, or at weekends when hour-long queues at either end are the norm. At Sarıalan, at the top, there is an army of dolmuşes waiting to take you to Oteller.

The alternative is to take a **dolmuş** all the way to Oteller, which winds the 32km of paved road up from Bursa's Orhangazi Caddesi. The one-way fee is 3.5YTL per person, though it can occasionally be difficult to muster the necessary number of passengers (six).

You'd follow the same route in your own vehicle, the road veering off above Çekirge and climbing rapidly through successive vegetation zones. Staff at the **Karabelen national park gate**, 20km into the park, charge 3YTL per car when they're in the mood and sometimes have **information** to hand out. The final stretch of road, from just below the gate to the hotels at Oteller, is very rough cobble, designed to prevent drivers from skidding – or speeding – so allow nearly an hour for the trip. In bad weather conditions you will be advised to put chains on your wheels and may not be allowed to make the journey without them.

Accommodation

There's little difference between the four- and five-star resort **hotels** at the road's end in Oteller, but since the national-park campsites are squalid and full in summer and it's too cold to camp in winter, you might want to consider a room. There are some 7500 hotel beds in the area, and while out-of-ski-season rates can dip as low as €40 for a double, in the skiing season (ie, winter) you will find rates of over €200 per night with full board – and no shortage of people prepared to pay.

Hotels worth trying include: the *Ergün* (☎0224/285 2100, ✉info@ergunotel .com; ❻); *Kar Otel* (☎0224/285 1121, ☏224 1123; ❺); *Beceren* (☎0224/285 2111, 🌐www.beceren.com; ❽); *Yazıcı Regency* (☎0224/285 2040, ☏285 2045; ❽); and the *Grand Yazıcı* (☎0224/285 2050, ☏285 2048; ❺). In summer, the *Ergün*, *Beceren* and *Grand Yazıcı* are generally open, but some of the others may be pressed into use as summer English camps for Turkish high-school kids.

Walking routes

From the top of the hotel zone, a jeep-track leads in an hour and a half to a **tungsten mine**. An obvious path, beginning behind the mine's guardhouse, slips up onto the broad but barren watershed ridge, just below the secondary summit of **Zirve** (2496m); follow this trail for an hour and a half to a fork. Right leads to the **main peak** (2543m); the cairned left-hand choice is more rewarding, descending slightly to overlook the first of Uludağ's lakes, **Aynalıgöl**, reachable by its own side-trail a half-hour beyond the junction.

There are some campsites here but none at **Karagöl**, the second and most famous lake, fifteen minutes southeast of the first one, sunk in a deep chasm and speckled with ice floes. **Kilimligöl**, the third substantial lake, is tucked away on a plateau southeast of Karagöl and offers good high-altitude camping. There are two smaller, nameless tarns, difficult to find in the crags above Aynalıgöl.

Returning to Oteller, as long as the weather is good you can stay with the ridge rather than revisiting the tungsten works, passing below the ruined hut on Zirve to meet a faint trail. This soon vanishes and thereafter it's cross-country downhill along the watershed as far as **Cennetkaya**, a knoll above the hotels, served by a marked trail. High above the trees, crowds and jeep tracks here, you just might strike lucky and glimpse patches of the distant Sea of Marmara to the north.

West of Bursa: Uluabat Gölü and Manyas Gölü

The 120-kilometre route west from Bursa to Bandırma is enlivened by two large but shallow lakes, only really accessible by car – though diehard dolmuş enthusiasts may be able to reach them by taking a series of connecting dolmuşes from village to village along the main road. The rarely visited **Uluabat Gölü**, site of the ancient settlement of Apollonia and the diminishing ancient fishing community of **Gölyazı** is 38km west of Bursa, while **Manyas Gölü**, 18km southeast of Bandırma, supports a bird sanctuary where the robust twitcher will appreciate the annual migration as it stops over in April/May and again in November. Neither lake warrants a special visit, but they do provide a break during the tedious drive along the southern Marmara shore.

Uluabat Gölü and Gölyazı

GÖLYAZİ proves to be an atmospheric community of half-timbered houses, with the odd daub of purple or green paint, built on an island now lashed by a causeway to the shore of **Uluabat Gölü**. Bits of Roman and Byzantine **Apollonia** – the lake's alias – have unconcernedly been pressed into domestic service, and extensive courses of wall ring the island's shoreline. On the mainland you can see a huge, ruined Greek cathedral, large enough for a few hundred parishioners. The lake itself, speckled with islets, is only two metres deep, murky and not suitable for swimming, though it does attract a number of water birds.

Appearances would lead you to pronounce Gölyazı the quintessential fishing village: there's a lively open-air **fish market** each morning at the island end of the causeway, nets and rowboats are much in evidence, and the women – who don't appreciate gratuitous snaps being taken of them – patiently mend their traps. All this conceals the fact that pesticide and fertilizer runoff from the surrounding fields is constantly diminishing the lake catch, and a handful of families now emigrate every year.

To get here, you need to keep an eye out for an inconspicuous sign, "Gölyazı", 38km west of Bursa, which marks the six-kilometre side-road to the village. The only **accommodation** is at the *Apollonia Motel* (no phone; ❶) on the landward side of the causeway – it's very rough and ready, and open only if there is an inkling of a demand during July and August. Pick up a room key at the co-managed **restaurant** of the same name at the extreme north edge of the village, where you can sample inexpensive *turna* (lake pike) fresh from a tank. For a couple of dollars (and with proficient Turkish) you can arrange for one of the fisher families to take you out in a small boat to some remote ruins on the nearby islets.

Manyas Gölü

Manyas Gölü attracts visitors mainly because of the national-park bird sanctuary established here in 1938 astride a stream delta and swamps at the northeast corner of the lake. The **Kuş Cenneti National Park** (Kuş Cenneti Milli Parkı; daily 7am–5.30pm; 2YTL) – or "bird paradise" – contains a small visitor centre full of dioramas, labelled in Turkish but with a handy poster giving translations into English, and stocked with stuffed geese, orioles, spoonbills, herons, pelicans, ducks, egrets and owls. Next you're directed to a wooden **observation tower**, with a pair of binoculars, unfortunately not powerful enough for the job in hand. The most spectacular sightings are of pelicans (white and Dalmatian, nesting in May), spoonbills, spotted eagles and night herons, with cormorants and gray herons commonplace. The best months to visit are November – after the first rains and coincident with various migratory species' southward movements – and April to May, when the swamps are at their fullest and the birds are flying north. During these migrations, up to three million birds and some 239 species stop by, including up to five hundred pairs of smew (an Asian duck). You'll have to be satisfied with the observation tower, as there are no walkways or boats provided to get you through or around the delta.

The park and sanctuary is 18km southeast of Bandırma (see below): 13km along the Balıkesir road and then 5km on the signposted side-road. There are no facilities in the park grounds, the closest being a simple **restaurant** with a couple of *pansiyon* rooms by the roadside at Eski Sığırcı, 1.5km before the gate.

Bandırma

BANDİRMA – knocked flat during battles in 1922 and now neighbour to a NATO airbase – is a definite finalist in the ugliest-town-in-Turkey sweepstakes. Given its status as a major transit-point you may well have to spend some time here, but all you really need to know is how to get from one transport terminal to another.

The main **otogar** is on the southern outskirts of town, 800m above the **ferry terminal** (for sea-bus services from İstanbul) and adjoining **train station** (for trains to and from İzmir). If you don't want to walk up the hill or take a taxi to the *otogar*, use the red-and-white city buses labelled "Garaj/600 Evler", which depart from a marquee 200m east of the ferry terminal. Frequent dolmuşes to Erdek leave from outside the ferry terminal.

In the unlikely event that you get stranded here for the night, a number of cheap **hotels** one block up from the ferry terminal, and a couple of mid-range ones on the front, can provide accommodation. Best is the two-star *Hotel Villa Marina* (℡0266/715 1260, Ⓔhotelmarina@ixir.com; ❺) with a rooftop bar and restaurant overlooking the harbour; breakfast costs 7YTL extra. A couple of minutes' walk east of the terminal, centred on the mosque, are a few reasonable **restaurants** dishing up the usual Turkish dishes.

Erdek and the Kapıdağı peninsula

A leafy, cobbled pedestrianized shore esplanade sets the tone for **ERDEK**, tucked at the base of the Kapıdağı peninsula and the closest jump-off point for the Marmara islands (see p.272). It's a pleasant enough town, with its landscaping and patches of park – another of the "İstanbul-by-the-sea" resorts that crowds with the urban middle-class in summer.

Approaching from Bandırma, across the two-kilometre-wide isthmus that joins the peninsula to the rest of Anatolia, you'll have already seen some of the rest of the **Kapıdağı peninsula**, though it's not a promising sight. The shore is almost wholly given over to military facilities, or to campsites firmly oriented toward automobile or caravan custom. The ruins of **ancient Kyzikos**, 3km off the main road, are so negligible that you'd have to be incredibly keen to make the effort to reach them. **Ocaklar**, 5km northwest of Erdek is still the best beach to the north, though development encroaches with every season. **Narli**, a further 4km to the northwest, has a ruined Greek church, and a few small *pansiyon*s, but not much of a beach.

Practicalities

Erdek's **otogar** is by the road in from Bandırma, at the northeast edge of town, and is just a few minutes' stroll away from the waterfront. Almost everything of interest stands either along the shore promenade or just behind it. There's a summer-only **tourist information** kiosk hidden in trees next to the **ferry terminal** (for ferries to the Marmara islands), though it's not always open, and a tiny private office in the *otogar* that offers an accommodation booking service, but unless you speak good Turkish you will struggle to communicate here.

There are **minibuses** out of Erdek to all the main villages, but as traffic is generally light it's probably best to **rent a bike** (around 15YTL a day from outlets all over town).

The **PTT** is on Neyyire Satka, opposite the ferry landing, while one street back from the front are several **Internet cafés**. A number of **shops** on the seafront sell cheap clothes, mostly seconds and overruns.

Accommodation

There's very little reasonable **accommodation** in the town proper – most establishments have been converted to holiday apartments. If you're desperate you

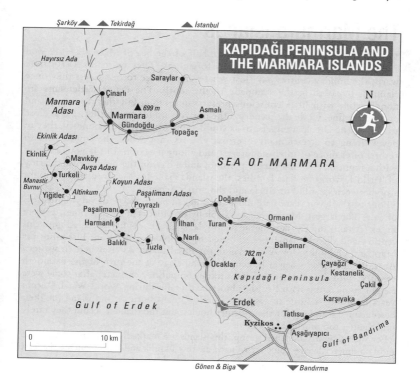

could try either the basic *Saner Hotel* (☎0266/835 7152; ❶), on Neyyire Satka opposite the ferry terminal, or the unfriendly and overpriced *Ümit Hotel*, on Balık Hanı Sokak, behind Cumhuriyet Meydanı (☎0266/835 1092; ❷). Better value is to be had at the out-of-town *Erdek Otel* (☎0266/835 2963; ❷) next to the *otogar*; it has some en-suite rooms and stays open during the winter.

Along the beach, 500m north of town, there must be at least forty establishments – all large affairs aimed at the domestic package market – most of which close in winter. The best value for money is the two-star *Hotel Özgün* (☎0266/835 4722, ℻347 6867; ❸), a friendly establishment, with small well-furnished rooms. Towards the end of the promenade, the *Otel Gül Plaj* (☎0266/835 1053; ❹) is a swish option directly on the seafront, but the deal is half-board only. Top hotel is the luxury, four-star *Agregento* (☎0266/835 4973, ℻835 1399; ❺), with mock-classical trimmings, large indoor and outdoor pools and comfortable air-conditioned rooms. Right at the end of the beach, there's a **campsite**, *Ay Camping* (☎0266/835 4882), which heaves during the summer school holidays.

Eating and drinking

There's plenty of choice when it comes to eating, but nothing that particularly stands out. The seafront strip boasts dozens of small **stalls and cafés** (several on boats moored in the harbour) offering varieties of Turkish fast food, some serving alcohol. One block inland is a predictable array of *pide salonu* and *lokanta*s, though numerous outlets also offer locally produced olive oil, olives and honey.

The Marmara islands

The **Marmara islands** – in the western half of the Sea of Marmara – are well known to Turks, but rarely visited by foreigners. They exist in a 1970s time warp; the holiday centres have lost whatever pretence to trendiness they once claimed, bypassed in the stampede to the south. The major settlements are nondescript, with little conscious preservation ethic, but the swimming and cycling are fine, while the scenery – the horizon studded with islets – is as close to that of the Greek archipelagos as you'll see in Turkey. In all honesty, they're never going to attract many overseas visitors, not when the south Turkish resorts offer more of intrinsic interest and a longer season. But if you're happy with a night or two in a simple pension, and a day on the beach with an army of Turkish working-class families, the islands make for a convenient overnight stop between İstanbul or Bursa and the north Aegean.

Four of the seven islands are inhabited and can be visited with varying degrees of ease. The largest, **Marmara**, was a colony of Miletus in ancient times, as were Erdek (Artaki) and Kyzikos on the peninsula. A Greek identity persisted until this century and the old names are still used by the older generation: Elafonisos for Marmara, Ophioussa for **Avşa**, Haloni for **Paşalimanı**. As elsewhere in western Anatolia, the Greeks began leaving the archipelago at the turn of the twentieth century, with emigration acquiring a more compulsory character after some were caught cooperating with British submarine captains during World War I. Recent years have seen a surge in visits by elderly Greeks born on the island (or their descendants) searching for their former homes, but the islanders claim they rarely find them – too much has changed.

For such a tightly bunched group, the islands are markedly different: Avşa is the most commercialized – some say ruined; the tiny Ekinlik and Paşalimanı are the least spoiled; while Marmara falls somewhere in between. Incidentally, while cars are not expressly forbidden on the islands, neither are they encouraged, making the archipelago relatively quiet by Turkish standards. Finally, if you show up much before June 1 or after September 30, the sea will be cool – and hardly anything open.

Getting to the islands

The islands are accessible by ferry, either directly from İstanbul, from Tekirdağ, or from Erdek, main town of the Kapıdağı peninsula. **Ferry timetables** to the islands are notoriously changeable. Services are predominantly seasonal, with most running over the summer – June to September – and tailing off in April, May and October, before almost grinding to a halt between November and March. Throughout the year, services from Erdek are not as frequent as from Tekirdağ, due to the latter's proximity to the highway to İstanbul. See "Travel details" at the end of the chapter for routes and journey times.

High season sees car ferries running three times a day **from Erdek to Marmara and Avşa** (one early morning, one late morning and one early evening), dropping to one a day or less out of season. Other private, unlicensed car and passenger ferries also run to Marmara and Avşa, as well as **to Ekinlik**, and **Balıklı** and **Paşalimanı** (both on Paşalimanı island), several times a week, but tend to depart only when full. The one-way cost on any of these craft to any of the islands is around 4YTL per person, 25YTL per car.

From Tekirdağ there are up to three passenger boats a day in high season to Marmara and Çinarli on Marmara island, or to Avşa, tailing off to one daily in shoulder season and three times a week out of season, weather permitting (5YTL per person, 15YTL per car). There are also connections on to Erdek.

From İstanbul's **Yenkapı** ferry terminal, there's a summer sea-bus service (daily except Sun at 10.30am; 25YTL) to Marmara and Avşa; in winter, the service drops to twice weekly. In summer there's also an unlicensed private passenger-ferry three times a week **from Şarköy** in Thrace to Avşa and Çinarli on Marmara (10YTL per person).

Marmara

Largest of the islands at roughly 17km by 8km, **Marmara** acquired its name during the Middle Ages thanks to the giant marble quarries (*ta marmara* in Greek) that are still worked on the north shore. Marmara is the ancient Proconnesus, from where the famous blue-grey streaked Proconnesian marble originates, used for many of the columns of Aya Sofya in İstanbul. Sailing in from the south, you'll see the rocky ridge of 700-metre Alyas Dağı, with a ruined Byzantine tower, plunging down to the west tip of the island. Except for its valley-bottom oases, Marmara is bleak – downright windswept and cliff-girt in the north – so most of its villages huddle on the southern, lee shore.

The ferry will stop first at the pretty but facility-less port of Gündoğdu; don't get off here, but wait to reach the main town. This, simply called **MARMARA**, is backed up against a hill with steep, stepped streets penetrating inland, an enchanting setting from a distance, though seen up close its modern domestic architecture is nothing special.

The **beach** is five minutes' walk to the northwest of Marmara town and is sandy, but you'll have to accustom yourself to the extremely low salinity of the Sea of Marmara and the occasional swarms of white jellyfish that plague all the islands from time to time. In cooler weather you might entertain thoughts of hiking up through the mostly barren **interior**, but there are only goat-trails along the ridges and most of the time you'll be restricted to the skeletal network of dirt roads that rings the island.

The only other village equipped to handle visitors is **ÇİNARLİ**, 6km northwest, or a fifteen-minute dolmuş ride along a dirt road from the main harbour of Marmara. Çinarli is a pretty place, with cottage gardens bursting with flowers and a village green shaded by plane trees (*Çınar*) after which the village takes its name, but its 700-metre swathe of sand and pebbles is backed by a scruffy esplanade so it's not particularly private. There's no permanent accommodation in Çinarli, but Turkish families have been known to rent out a few *pansiyon* rooms in busier years, and there are a couple of summer-only fish and kebab restaurants on the front.

East from Marmara, dirt tracks lead several kilometres to the side of the island that has been quarried for centuries. The marble is still today cut into mammoth blocks and transported to the harbour at **Saraylar** – a village in the north of the island populated by migrant quarry-workers from the Black Sea coast. The sole attempt to attract tourists here is a haphazard collection of marble fragments collected together in what is referred to as an open-air museum, though it's little more than a dumping ground for old rocks.

Practicalities

In Marmara town, **ferries** dock at the terminal in the centre from where it's a short walk to the **PTT**, **bank** and a number of small hotels and *pansiyons*. The best **accommodation** is at the far west end of the shore esplanade, facing the sunset. The *Marmara Hotel* (☎0266/885 6140; ❷) has sparse rooms – you share expansive clean marble bathrooms – while the *Şato Motel* (☎0266/885 5003; ❸) has sea-view terraces and a good breakfast, but suffers from noise from the nearby *gazinos*. Next to the jetty and handy for early ferries, the friendly *Murat* (☎0266/885 5222; ❷) has small rooms with shared hot-water bathrooms up the corridor.

Restaurants are fairly unpretentious. The *Şato Motel* serves up a set menu (around 12YTL) that changes each night and the *Birol*, the first establishment over the footbridge from the jetty, has excellent fish, meat and *mezes*. It's slightly more expensive than elsewhere on the island but worth it for the waterside location and good service. Also on the front near the jetty is the *Birsen*, which provides tasty soups and stews – hardly fitting meals for a hot summer's evening, but cheap and filling at 6YTL for a main course.

Avşa

Low-lying and partly covered in vineyards, **Avşa** – around 8km in length and 3–4km wide – is surrounded by beaches and crystal-clear water that are both its *raison d'être* and its curse. The island is heavily developed and virtually a suburb of İstanbul in season, with prime beachfront locations snapped up thirty years ago as holiday homes. The sole cultural point of interest is the abandoned **Aya Triada church**, awash somewhere in the concrete sprawl that is the main town of **TÜRKELİ** – an unruly spread of apartment buildings along the west coast. A promenade dominates the front with its row of cavernous cafés, where families drink tea and play games in the evening.

Taxis and dolmuşes from Türkeli (from next to Hal Çarşısı on Okullar Caddesi) run the 2.5km to **YIĞITLER** on the east coast of Avşa, populated almost entirely by settlers from the former Yugoslavia. One kilometre southeast of the village, there's a large sandy beach called **Altınkum**, overlooked by a couple of summer-only restaurants. For more secluded swimming the only option is to head off by foot to the quieter coves to the south of here.

Practicalities

Ferries dock at the ferry terminal, roughly halfway along the Avşa urban strip, from where small private boats also cross to Paşalimanı – prices and frequency depending entirely on demand. The **PTT** is located to the north of town on Post-hane Caddesi, on the road running uphill parallel to the beach.

Although there's loads of **accommodation**, most fills quickly during high season and tends to be in the form of unremarkable, basic *pansiyon* rooms, often with shared bathrooms, on the spare floors of people's holiday homes. A couple of exceptions include the *Geçim Pansiyon* (T0266/896 1493, W www.gecimpan-siyon.com; ❹), 500m north of the Türkeli ferry jetty, with a wide choice of compact rooms from singles to family-sized, fully-equipped apartments – breakfast and dinner extra and on request – and the friendly, family-run *Yalı Pansiyon* (T0266/896 2085; ❷), immediately south of the jetty on the beachfront, with twelve waterless rooms, but plenty of hot water in the communal bathroom and nice views out to sea.

Restaurants also abound though only the *Yarar* particularly stands out, also south of the jetty on the beachfront – a popular and established diner that opens most of the year, serving seafood and meat dishes from 10YTL. Strangely, despite the island's vineyards, most of the wine on sale seems to come from Bozcaada.

Ekinlik and Paşalimanı

There is little to see or do – never mind anywhere to stay and eat – on Ekinlik and Paşalimanı, but if you are determined to go you can take at least one daily private ferry from Erdek in summer for each of these other two inhabited Marmara islands.

Ekinlik, also known as Kaşık Adası, or "Spoon Island", because of its shape, is little more than a kilometre in length and 500m across. Although there are no beaches, and consequently no tourism development here, the island has a pretty harbourside village. There are several old Greek houses and a ruined church to the left of the jetty. The harbour is full of fishing boats (no pleasure craft, for a change) and is overlooked by a shaded tea-garden.

Again lacking enough beaches to make it the target of development, **Paşalimanı** – irregularly shaped but almost 10km in length – is a sleepy, friendly place, greener than Marmara and Avşa and distinguished mainly by its giant plane-trees. There's very little to attract anyone to **BALİKLİ** village, the "capital", though a few people rent out their spare rooms over summer and occasional day-trippers visit on private boats to drink tea on the jetty before returning to Avşa.

Travel details

Trains

Bandırma to: İzmir (2 daily; 5hr 30min).
Edirne to: Budapest (1 daily; 25hr) via Sofia (10hr) and Bucharest (14hr); İstanbul (2 daily; 5hr 30min).
Üzünköprü to: Athens (1 daily, 17hr). Note: this is not a direct service; connections are made in Thessaloniki.

Buses and dolmuşes

Bandırma to: Balıkesir (hourly; 1hr 45min); Bursa (hourly; 2hr); Çanakkale (hourly; 3hr 30min); Erdek (every 30min; 25min); İzmir (7 daily; 6hr); Manyas

(7 daily; 30min); Yalova (several daily; 3hr).
Bursa to: Ankara (every 30min; 7hr); Bandırma (hourly; 2hr); Çanakkale (hourly; 5hr 30min); Erdek (8 daily; 2hr); İstanbul, with ferry transfer (hourly; 5hr); İzmir via Balıkesir and often Ayvalık (hourly; 7hr); Kütahya (3 daily; 3hr); Mudanya (every 30min; 40min); Yalova (every 30min; 1hr).
Edirne to: Çanakkale (5 daily; 4hr 30min); İstanbul (every 30min; 3hr); Keşan (every 20min; 2hr); Kapıkule (every 30min; 30min); Kırklareli (every hour; 1hr); Lüleburgaz (every 30min; 1hr 15min).
Erdek to: Bandırma (every 30min; 25min); Bursa (8 daily; 2hr).

Gelibolu to: Eceabat (hourly; 50min); Kilitbahir (hourly; 1hr).

İznik to: Adapazarı (hourly; 1hr 30min); Bursa (every 30min; 1hr 30min); İstanbul (1 daily; 3hr 30min); Yalova (hourly; 1hr).

Şarköy to: Edirne (1 daily; 3hr 30min); İstanbul (every 30min; 4hr); Tekirdağ (20 daily; 1hr 30min).

Yalova to: Bursa (every 30min; 1hr); İznik (hourly; 1hr).

Short-hop ferries

Eceabat to: Çanakkale, car ferry (on the hour 7am–midnight, then 2am & 4am; 40min).

Gelibolu to: Lapseki, car ferry (hourly 9am–1am, then 5am, 6.30am, 7.30am, 8.30am; 50min).

Kilitbahir to: Çanakkale, car ferry (according to traffic, 6am–9pm; 10min).

Island & long-haul ferries and sea buses

Services are most frequent in summer (June–Sept), tail off in the shoulder seasons (April–May & Oct) and are greatly reduced during winter (Nov–March).

Avşa to: Erdek (summer 3 daily, winter 1 daily; 3hr); İstanbul (summer 1 daily except Sun; 2hr 45min).

Bandırma to: İstanbul (summer 4–6 daily, winter 2 daily; 2hr).

Erdek to: Avşa (summer 3 daily, winter 1 daily; 3hr); Ekinlik (summer 1 daily, winter 1 weekly; 2hr 30min); Marmara (summer 3 daily, winter 1 daily; 2hr 15min).

Kabatepe to: Gökçeada/Imvros (June–Oct 1 daily, Nov–May 2 weekly; 1hr 30min).

Marmara to: Avşa (summer 3 daily, winter 1 daily; 1hr); İstanbul's Yenkapı terminal (summer 1 daily except Sun; 2hr 45min).

Mudanya to: İstanbul (2 daily; 1hr 45min).

Şarköy to: Avşa (summer 3 weekly; 3hr); Çinarli on Marmara (summer 3 weekly; 1hr 30min).

Tekirdağ to: Avşa (summer 3–4 daily, winter 3 weekly; 3hr 30min); Erdek (summer 2 daily; 5hr 30min); Marmara (summer 3–4 daily, winter 3 weekly; 3hr).

Yalova to: İstanbul's Yenkapı ferry terminal (summer 6–7 daily, winter 2–3 daily; 1hr); Kartal (every 30min; 35min).

The North Aegean

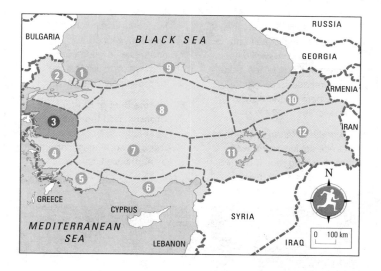

CHAPTER 3 # Highlights

✳ **Troy** The most celebrated archeological site in Turkey boasts a bleak, windswept setting and an enduring mythology. See p.289

✳ **Bozcaada** Small island, famed for its elegant architecture, relaxing atmosphere and especially its wine. See p.286

✳ **Assos** The old town and ancient city occupy a rocky peak, with stunning views of the Aegean and Greece beyond, while its harbour is one of the most picturesque to be found anywhere on the Aegean coast. See p.294

✳ **Ayvalık** Relax in this former Greek fishing-town, with its charming mix of derelict and restored Ottoman houses. See p.299

✳ **Ancient Pergamon** The renowned acropolis has a dramatic setting and wide-ranging ruins that easily rival more famous sights further south. See p.304

✳ **Foça** The former fishing-village is now a popular resort that hasn't forgotten its maritime heritage. See p.313

✳ **Manisa** This working town has some particularly impressive mosques and makes a good base from which to explore the surroundings. See p.315

✳ **Sardis** Seat of King Croesus, and the first city to see the use of coins, these remote ruins warrant a lengthy visit. See p.319

△ Assos Harbour

3

The North Aegean

urkey's **North Aegean** coast sees far fewer visitors than the shoreline further south. There are decent sandy beaches, though the lower sea temperature and lack of a major airport protect the region from widespread development. Most summer visitors are Turks and, while tourism is inevitably important to the local economy, even in August the number of visitors doesn't match those at the country's more renowned destinations. Away from the resort towns, life goes on much as it always has, with farming and fishing providing a livelihood for the bulk of the population.

This area, which roughly constitutes ancient Aeolia, has been settled since Paleolithic times; civilization bloomed early here under the Phrygians, who arrived in Anatolia during the thirteenth century BC. Later waves of Greek colonists established settlements on the coast, leaving the region rich in Classical and Hellenistic remains. Although the sparse ruins of **Troy** in the north don't quite live up to their literary and legendary reputation, the ancient cities of **Assos** and **Pergamon** (modern **Bergama**) display some tangible reminders of the power and wealth of the greater Greek empire. Less visited than any of these is the more isolated Lydian city of **Sardis**, the ancient capital of King Croesus (and Midas before him), one of Aegean Turkey's most impressive archeological sites.

Coming from İstanbul or anywhere else in northwestern Turkey, the most obvious entry point is **Çanakkale** – useful as a base for both the ruins at Troy and the World War I battlefields on the Gelibolu peninsula (see p.239). The road running south from Çanakkale is justifiably characterized as scenic on most maps, with much of the route wooded and gently hilly, giving way to a coastal strip with the mountains of the **Kaz Dağı** range rising behind. Further south, the best stretches of beach lie near **Ayvalık** – the area's longest-established resort – though there are also pleasant resorts and sands along the coastal strip running from **Assos** to **Ören**, on the northern shore of the **Gulf of Edremit**, as well as at the small port towns of **Dikili**, **Çandarlı** and **Foça**. Offshore, the Turkish Aegean islands of **Gökçeada** and **Bozcaada** provide an easy escape from Çanakkale, though many people prefer the charms of smaller islands such as **Alibey**, a good day-trip destination from the resort of Ayvalık.

In general there's less to write home about further **inland**, where a mountainous landscape harbours a few predominantly industrial cities. However, the **İzmir–Bandırma railway line** provides an alternative approach to the region, passing through the otherwise unremarkable provincial capital of Balıkesir (from where there are frequent buses to the Gulf of Edremit and Çanakkale), Soma (a short bus-ride away from Bergama) and **Manisa** – the last a town of some antiquity, often used by visitors as a base for seeing Sardis. Of these inland destinations only Manisa and, further east, the town of **Alaşehir** are really worth any kind of prolonged attention.

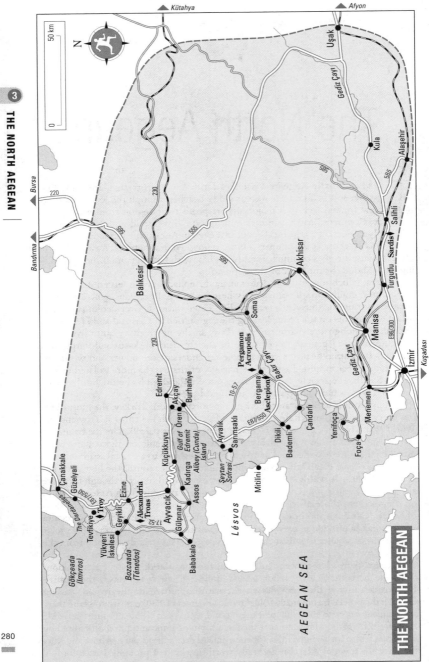

THE NORTH AEGEAN

Çanakkale

Although celebrated for its superb setting on the Dardanelles straits, the functional modern town of **ÇANAKKALE** has little to detain you except for a good archeological museum and a pleasing seafront. However, it is the most popular base for visiting the World War I landing sites (Gallipoli) on the European side of the Dardanelles and for seeing the ruins of Troy. Also, if you're intent on going to the Turkish Aegean islands of Gökçeada or Bozcaada, then Çanakkale makes a convenient jumping-off point.

It's the **Dardanelles** (Çanakkale Boğazı in Turkish) that have defined Çanakkale's history and its place in myth. The area's Classical name, **Hellespont**, is owed to one Helle, who, while escaping from her wicked stepmother on the back of a winged ram, fell into the swift-moving channel and drowned. From Abydos on the Asian side, the youth Leander used to swim to Sestos on the European shore for trysts with his lover Hero, until one night he too perished in the currents; in despair Hero drowned herself as well. Byron narrowly escaped being added to the list of casualties on his swim in the opposite direction in 1810.

In 480 BC Xerxes' Persian hordes crossed the waters on their way to Greece; and in 411 and 405 BC the last two naval battles of the Peloponnesian War took place in the straits, the latter engagement ending in decisive defeat for the Athenian fleet. Twenty centuries later Mehmet the Conqueror constructed the elaborate fortress of Kilitbahir directly opposite the Çimenlik Kale in Çanakkale (which he also built), to tighten the stranglehold applied to doomed Constantinople. In March 1915, an Allied fleet attempting to force the Dardanelles and attack İstanbul was repulsed, with severe losses, by Turkish shore batteries, prompting the even bloodier land campaign usually known as Gallipoli. These days the straits are still heavily militarized and modern Çanakkale is very much a navy town.

Arrival, information and tours

Arriving by **ferry** from Eceabat or Kilitbahir on the Gelibolu peninsula, or from the island of Gökçeada, you'll dock close to the start of Demircioilu Caddesi, which barrels inland, roughly splitting the town in two. Most of what there is to see or do in Çanakkale, except for the archeological museum, is within walking distance of the ferry terminal.

The **otogar** is out on Atatürk Caddesi, the local name for the coastal İzmir–Bursa highway, a fifteen-minute walk from the centre. This is mainly of use for buses to North Aegean destinations, which start and terminate in Çanakkale. However, many buses pass straight through the town centre to cross the straits via ferry and travellers will often find it more convenient to board as they come off the ferry. The bus companies also arrange free transfers to the *otogar* from their respective offices, which lie opposite the tourist office. **Dolmuşes** to Troy run from the minibus garage, opposite the fairground on Atatürk Caddesi.

The **tourist office** on Cumhuriyet Meydanı (May–Sept Mon–Fri 8.30am–7.30pm, Sat & Sun 10.30am–6pm; Oct–April Mon–Fri 8.30am–5.30pm; ☎0286/217 1187, ✉canakkaletourism@hotmail.com), next to the main dock is, in summer at least, staffed by friendly, English-speaking students.

Battlefield and Troy tours

Many people opt to **tour the World War I battlefields** on the Gelibolu peninsula from here. Daily tour-prices fluctuate between 25YTL and 35YTL per person; for details of what to look out for when booking a tour, see p.239. Premier **tour company** is *TJ's Hostel* in Eceabat (see p.244), which you should call for details

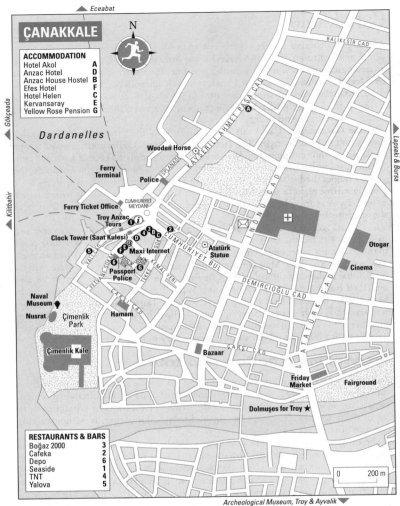

Archeological Museum, Troy & Ayvalik ▼▼

and arrangements. Çanakkale-based tours include *Hassle Free Tours*, operated by the *Anzac House Hostel*, at Cumhuriyet Meyd 61 (see below for details); *Troy Anzac Tours*, just west of the Saat Kulesi (clocktower) at Yali Cad 2 (℡0286/217 5849, ⓦwww.troyanzac.com;) and the *Yellow Rose Pension* (see below for details). All three also offer daily **Troy tours** for around 20YTL, including transport, entry to the site and guide.

Accommodation

Except around Anzac Day, April 25, you'll have little trouble finding a room in town. The most obvious budget options are only a few minutes' walk from the ferry landing. Just south of the tourist office, the Saat Kulesi (clocktower) signals the entrance to a warren of alleys – Fetvahane Sokaıı, Aralık Sokaıı, Yeni Sokak – that are home to various inexpensive hotels and *pansiyons*. Moving across Demircioılu Caddesi, or closer to the water, you'll find the more upscale hotels.

Hotel Akol Kordon Boyu ☎0286/217 9456, ⓦwww.hotelakol.com. Multi-storey, four-star hotel on the seafront north of the main dock offering a decent level of impersonal luxury – good-sized rooms, all with TV and a/c (some with sea views), several restaurants and a roof-top bar. ❻

Anzac Hotel Saat Kulesi Meyd 8 ☎0286/217 7777, ⓦwww.anzachotel.com. Practically opposite the clocktower, this two-star place has neat, plainly decorated en-suite rooms with satellite TV. A roof-top bar is planned, which should add to its charm considerably. ❸

Anzac House Hostel Cumhuriyet Meyd 61 ☎0286/217 5969, ⓦwww.anzachouse.com. Well-equipped backpackers' hostel with basic dorms (€5) and doubles, some without windows. Also a bar and restaurant, Internet access, video room (where *Gallipoli* starring Mel Gibson is shown nightly) and battlefield tours (with one night free to those on the Hassle Free tour; see p.282). ❷

Efes Hotel Fetvahane Sok 15 ☎ & ℗0286/217 3256. Clean, bright and reasonably modern rooms, communal TV room and a homely, friendly feel. Breakfast not included. ❸

Hotel Helen Cumhuriyet Meyd 57 ☎0286/212 1818, ⓦwww.helenhotel.com. Decent mid-range accommodation just back from the front in a narrow building sandwiched between similar establishments. The rooms are pretty basic, but all have private baths and TVs, and there's a good-value hotel restaurant next door. ❹

Kervansaray Fetvahane Sok 13 ☎0286/217 8192. Quiet, polite and friendly family-run affair, housed in a recently renovated 200-year-old mansion with a lovely courtyard garden. No alcohol permitted on the premises. ❸

Yellow Rose Pension Yeni Sok 5 ☎0286/217 3343, ⓦwww.yellowrose.4mg.com. Fifty metres back from the clocktower. Rooms of varying size, though all are stark and basic, as well as dorms (€6) and a disappointing breakfast. Also laundry service, video room, Internet access and battlefield tours. ❷

The Town

The name *Çanakkale* means "Pottery Castle", after the garish Çanakkale ware that finds its way into the ethnographic section of every Turkish museum. Fortunately none of this is conspicuous, the only nod to the local style being in a few appealing, early twentieth-century buildings in the tiny **bazaar** (currently being restored), just south of the nucleus of cheap hotels. There's more interesting shopping at the large **Friday market**, five minutes' walk west on Atatürk Caddesi.

Continue past the bazaar area to **Çimenlik Park**, site of the **Çimenlik Kale** (daily 9am–10pm; free), a fifteenth-century fortress constructed by Mehmet the Conqueror during his march north towards Constantinople. The northern half of the park is given over to the town's **Military and Naval Museum** (Deniz Müzesi; daily except Mon & Thurs 9am–noon & 1.30–5pm; 2YTL). Here you can see archive photos – such as Seddülbahir in ruins after Allied shelling and Atatürk's funeral – as well as military paraphernalia and a model of the Gallipoli campaign. Meanwhile, beached on the park esplanade – from where you get the best views of Çimenlik's sister fort, Kilitbahir, across the straits – is a replica of the minelayer **Nusrat** (same hours and ticket as museum), which stymied the Allied fleet by re-mining at night zones that the French and British had swept clean by day.

An hour should be enough to take in the **Archeological Museum** (Arkeoloji Müzesi; daily except Mon & Thurs 8.30am–noon & 1–5.30pm; 2YTL), nearly 2km from the centre of town; flag down any dolmuş along Atatürk Caddesi labelled "Kepez" or "Güzelyalı". The poorly-labelled collection is strong on brass implements, delicate glass and glazed pottery, unfired lamps and figurines, and wooden objects, most of them from the nearby Bozcaada and Dardanos tumuli. There's also a coin case spanning all cultures from Lydian to Ottoman, but the most exquisite items are the gold and jewellery grave finds, and the bone and ivory work by the exit.

In addition to the museums, the town's main attraction is the waterfront itself with its wide esplanade lined with dozens of cafés and restaurants. It's also home to a replica of the Trojan **wooden horse** (it featured in the 2004 Hollywood film *Troy*), which has been erected in Morrabin Park just north of the ferry terminal.

Eating, drinking and nightlife

Restaurants and **cafés** line almost the full length of the quayside, both north and south of the main ferry terminal, offering a wide variety of dishes, including (inevitably) plenty of fish and seafood. As a simple rule of thumb, the further from the terminal you are, the cheaper the prices, the only exception being the mobile stalls that set up for business every evening just north of the terminal selling roasted corn on the cob for 0.5YTL.

While **nightlife** for locals tends to involve nothing more strenuous than a promenade and a meal along the front, there is a small but surprisingly lively bar scene centred on Fetvane Sokak, a narrow street running south from the clocktower. Aimed mainly at visiting Australians and New Zealanders, some of the bars have live music to compensate for the above-average bar prices. As with accommodation, this all changes around Anzac Day when the sheer weight of numbers alters the area's character beyond recognition.

Restaurants

Boıaz 2000 Saat Kule Meyd. One of the cheapest options, deservedly popular for both lunch and dinner. A dish with rice can cost as little as 3YTL (if you can get a seat).

Cafeka Cumhuriyet Meyd 28. Çanakkale's top gourmet choice, this boasts an elegant indoor dining space and a surprisingly affordable menu featuring modern interpretations of traditional dishes, such as spiced meatballs with herb yoghurt, chili salsa and sautéed potatoes for 7.5YTL.

Seaside Eski Balikhane Sok 3. Perhaps the pick of the cluster of outdoor restaurants immediately south of the ferry terminal, this offers an extensive menu with pasta dishes for around 5YTL, kebabs for 10YTL and fish from around 10YTL.

Yalova Eski Balikhane Sok 31. A wide range of fish and seafood (with most dishes around 10YTL) and a pleasant outdoor terrace with views over the water.

Bars

Depo Fetvane Sokak. The main attraction here is the large outdoor courtyard lined with multi-coloured beanbags, which is as popular with the local youth as with tourists. There's also a small indoor dancefloor.

TNT Fetvane Sokak. A dark cavernous bar with a courtyard restaurant and live music upstairs most evenings.

Listings

Banks and exchange A number of banks and ATMs line Fetvane Sokak and Cumhuriyet Meyd. Opening hours for most banks are Mon–Fri 9am–12.30pm & 1.30–5pm.

Car rental Delta Rent A Car, Cumhuriyet Meyd 21/1 ☎0286/814 1218.

Cinema The cinema below the Gima shopping centre, next door to the *otogar*, shows mainstream releases in English with Turkish subtitles. There's also a much smaller cinema housed within the Belediye İş Merkezi, behind the Atatürk statue.

Internet access At the *Maxi Internet Café* on Fetvane Sokak. The Belediye İş Merkezi also has many smaller Internet shops and cafés, and Inter-net access is available from most of the hotels and hostels, though these tend to be overpriced.

Hospital Hasan Mevsuf Sok ☎0286/217 1098.

Newspapers English-language newspapers from Orka Kitabevi, Yali Cad 5.

Police Kayserili Ahmet Paşa Cad, just north of the ferry terminal.

Post office PTT on İnönü Cad (Mon–Sat 8am–11pm).

Telephones Booths can be found in Cumhuriyet Meyd; there's a small PTT shop within the Belediye İş Merkezi and a Turk Telecom shop on Carsi Cad.

The Turkish Aegean islands

Strategically straddling the Dardanelles, **Gökçeada** and **Bozcaada** were the only Aegean islands to remain in Turkish hands after the 1923 Treaty of Lausanne, which concluded the Greek–Turkish war. Under the terms of the agreement the islands' predominantly Greek inhabitants were exempt from the population exchange of the same year, but after 1937 both Gökçeada and Bozcaada were re-militarized along with the Greek islands of Samothráki and Límnos, and in subsequent decades the Turkish authorities began to assert their sovereignty more forcefully. Though a formal population exchange was never instigated, much of the island's Greek population has left, over the succeeding decades, to be replaced by Turkish settlers. Access to foreigners was banned until 1987 and even now few overseas visitors make their way over from the mainland. What you find, if you make the effort, are inexpensive, basic facilities and good beaches, though both islands are short on banks and exchange shops, so make sure you bring enough cash with you.

Gökçeada

Gökçeada, the larger of the two Turkish Aegean islands, hovers just northwest of the Dardanelles, tantalizingly visible from any of the Gelibolu battlefields. Its previous name, Imvros, most likely derives from "Imbrasos", the pre-Hellenic god responsible for breathing life into infertile land. Today, the barren, hilly island – still heavily militarized – is a hotchpotch of the old and the new, Christian and Muslim. It's also large enough to make your own vehicle necessary. There are local dolmuş services, but they are few and unreliable, barely used by the wealthy Turkish and Greek visitors who make up the bulk of the island's small tourist trade.

During the Gallipoli campaign Gökçeada was occupied by the Allies. General Hamilton's command was based on the island and many troops were ferried from here to the battlefields. Assigned to Turkey for its strategic value after the 1923 peace conference, the island's majority population of seven thousand Orthodox Greeks was more or less left to itself for forty years, save for a token force of a hundred or so Turkish gendarmes and officials. When the Cyprus conflict came to a head in 1964, the Turkish government decided to "claim" the island more pointedly, instituting policies of forced land-expropriation without compensation, heavy garrisoning, the closure of schools for Greek children, settlement of Turkish civilians from the mainland and the establishment of an open prison. These measures were taken specifically to make continued residence for the ethnic Greeks impossible, and they've had the desired effect: today there are only about two hundred Greeks left, the bulk of the population having left for Athens and further afield.

Getting there

In summer there is one **ferry** a day on Friday, Saturday and Sunday to Gökçeada **from Çanakkale** (June–Sept; 2.5YTL each way, 20YTL per car; 3hr), and three ferries a day **from Kabatepe** on the Gelibolu peninsula (July & Aug; 2YTL, or 12YTL per car; 1hr 30min). In winter these times drop to once a week from Çanakkale and twice a week from Kabatepe. However, ferry schedules are notoriously unreliable, so check first at Çanakkale tourist office. Weekend ferries tend to fill quickly in summer, and if you are taking a car over it is advisable to arrive at least two hours before departure. The busiest time to travel is around August 15 when the island's Greek festival is held.

Around the island

Ferries dock at **KUZU LİMANI**, where a dolmuş meets the boat and takes you the 6km inland to the island's small capital, generally known as **GÖKÇEADA MERKEZ**, but also as Çinarli (and, formerly, by the Greek name, Panayia). The grim official architecture on the main drag is complemented by the old Greek vernacular in the backstreets. There are a couple of hotels and restaurants here – including the *Belediye Otel* at Belediye Meydanı (☎0286/887 3375; ❷), with its own good *lokanta*, and the *Pegasus Hotel* on Cumhuriyet Caddesi (☎0286/887 4164; ❷) – as well as two or three huge, shuttered Greek churches. The main square also holds several banks with ATMs.

Most visitors continue a further 5km by dolmuş to the island's former capital of **KALEKÖY** (previously Kastro) on the north shore, where a ruined castle built during Süleyman the Magnificent's reign overlooks a good beach and the Greek island of Samothraki. The island's small **tourist office** is here, next to the harbour (Mon–Fri 8.30am–5.30pm; ☎0286/887 4642). In the centre of town, the *Gökçe Motel* (☎0286/887 4588, ℱ887 2059; ❷) has basic **rooms** with balcony, while the *Yakamoz Pansiyon & Restaurant* on the hill (☎0286/887 2057; ❸) has simple double rooms with rustic charm and a quality restaurant serving things such as *kalamar* (calamari) and *tavuk şiş* (chicken shish). Further up the hill from the harbour, on Barbaros Cad, is the slightly more upmarket *Kale Motel* (☎0286/887 3438, ⓦwww.kalemotel.com; ❸), also with its own good restaurant, while next door is the longstanding favourite, *Kalimerhaba Motel* (☎0286/887 3648, ℱ887 2224; ❸), which also offers decent meals. Along the quay a number of excellent, cheap fish **tavernas** feature roof-terrace seating.

The hamlet of **KALEKÖY ÜSTÜ**, ten minutes up the hill, boasts the restored remains of the oldest church on the island and the *Güzelyali* **restaurant** offering unusually interesting cooking with home-grown vegetables, olives and cheese.

Most of the island's remaining Greek Orthodox population lives 3km northwest of Gökçeada Merkez in **ZEYTİNLİ** (Ayii Theodhori). You'll quickly notice that almost no one here is under sixty, although younger family members do return for regular visits especially during summer. They're understandably bitter about the turn of events and, in the past, have been reluctant to talk to – or be photographed by – outsiders for fear of subsequent Turkish interrogation. These days, though, things are more relaxed, with Turks as well as Greeks turning out in force for the island's **annual festival** of Greek culture held around August 15. The island's most typically Greek village is **TEPEKÖY**, 7km to the west, home of Gökçeada's best and most popular *pansiyon*/taverna, ✻*Barba Yorgo* (☎ & ℱ0286/887 3592, ⓦwww.barbayorgo.com; ❹): this beautifully restored village house is run by the eponymous "Uncle George", a Greek who returned here after years working in İstanbul.

Kefalo Burnu (Kaleköy), the southeastern tip of the island, offers better beaches than those around Kale on Bozcaada (see opposite), but you'll need your own transport if you plan to visit. It also boasts the rusting remains of Allied shipping sunk during the Gallipoli campaign. Nearby, **AYDINCIK** has a good beach, a campsite and lake waters with supposed healing properties.

Bozcaada

The island of **Bozcaada** – formerly known as Tenedos (from Tenes, one of the heroes of the Trojan War) – is a more popular and cheerful place than Gökçeada, if only because it's far less militarized and more architecturally of a piece. It's too close to the mainland to have avoided the attention of Turkish rulers down the ages and the population, as evidenced by a handful of medieval mosques, has historically been about one-quarter Muslim. Covered mostly in vineyards that produce the justly famous Bozcaada **wine**, the island is small enough to walk around, and it has some excellent beaches, though the water is freezing cold until September.

Getting there

Ferries (June–Sept 3 daily, Oct–May 2 daily; 2.5YTL return, 7YTL per car; 1hr 30min) to Bozcaada leave from **Yükyeri İskelesi**, a tiny port with several kilometres of excellent beach, 60km southwest of Çanakkale. Direct dolmuşes from Çanakkale's *otogar* depart three times a day, timed to catch the 10am, 2pm or 6pm ferry.

If you miss the ferry and need to stop over, it's best to hole up in the village of **GEYIKLI**, 5km east of Yükyeri İskelesi, back towards Ezine. Regular dolmuşes ply the short route, though these dwindle considerably after the last ferry crossing. The *Gözde Hotel* here (☎0286/638 5086; ❶) has en-suite **rooms**, while Geyikli also boasts a bank with an ATM and a Thursday street market, where you can pick up the delicious local honey and olives. There is also a **campsite** a few kilometres further down the coast towards Alexandria Troas.

Around the island

The only town, **BOZCAADA** (also known as **KALE** – "castle"), is built on a grid plan along a slight slope. It's surprisingly elegant, with cobbled streets and a good number of preserved old houses with overhanging upper floors. The old Greek quarter extended east from the church to the sea, though nowadays fewer than a hundred elderly Orthodox inhabitants remain. Kale lies in the shadow of its **castle**, which was successively enlarged by Byzantine, Genoese, Venetian and Turkish occupiers, and most recently restored by the archeological service in the 1960s. The result is one of the largest citadels in the Aegean (easily the equal of that at Bodrum) and thankfully it's not a military area, so you can explore every inch – the locals use the keep to graze sheep and the lower courtyard as a football pitch. It also boasts a small **museum** of locally unearthed artefacts (May–Oct daily 10am–1pm & 2–7pm; 2YTL).

The interior of the island consists of gently undulating countryside, flatter than Gökçeada and treeless except for the clumps marking the site of farms. The three best **beaches** are the consecutive strands of Ayazma, Sullubahçe and Habbelle, 7km from Kale on the south coast; take the right at the first fork out of town and then two lefts, or catch one of the half-hourly dolmuşes to Ayazma. Just above Ayazma is an abandoned monastery, home to the *ayazma* (sacred spring) that gave it its name, while closer to the sand are a couple of restaurants. A dirt track leads thirty minutes east to the beach at **Ayiana**, a marvellous site if you're after complete solitude.

Taking the left turn instead at the first fork out of Kale leads to more beaches – narrower and more exposed – on the east shore, along the 4km of asphalt ending at **Tuzburnu**.

Arrival, orientation and transport

Ferries dock at the northeast tip of the island in Kale, where most accommodation is situated. As you leave the quay, the castle is situated nearby, to the right of the town, while to the left, in a tight arc, lies the small fishing **harbour**. Following the main road out of town takes you past the main square on the left, together with a small park often used as an outdoor café. **Dolmuşes** embark on their short journey around the island from behind here. The **PTT** is on the main square, next to the island's only bank, which has an ATM, although it's worth bringing sufficient lira with you, just in case it's out of order.

The *Ada Café* (☎0286/697 8795), one street behind the harbour in town, **rents bikes** for around 15YTL, and also arranges **tours of the island** and hires out camping equipment. Boat excursions and scuba diving are currently outlawed, but accompanying a fisherman on a trip is permitted if the groups are kept small. As this is usually an impromptu affair its best to ask at one of the small fishing boats moored in the harbour.

Accommodation

A haven this convenient not surprisingly fills up in summer, though finding **accommodation** is not a big problem, except at weekends and on public holidays. All the same, advance booking is advisable if you want to stay in anything better than average. There are also numerous **rooms** available in people's houses, advertised as "*ev pansiyon*". Prices vary according to demand, but you can expect to pay from around 16YTL.

The wonderfully quirky ⚑ *Rengigül Pansiyon* on Atatürk Cad (☎0286/677 8171, ⓌWww.rengigul.com; ❹), near the Greek church and clearly signposted from the bank, is highly recommended. The bedrooms of this restored Greek townhouse are decorated with all manner of antiques, artwork and curios (shared bathrooms only) and its artist owner provides a particularly good breakfast. The *Güler Hotel* on the front, to the left of the ferry landing (☎0286/697 8844; ❷) – and its similarly priced annexe, the *Güler Ada* on Alsancak Sok, inland behind the PTT – is clean, modern and pleasant, with breakfast served by the waterside at the hotel. Moving up in price, the *Kaikias Hotel*, on Kale Arkasi behind the castle (☎0286/697 0250, ⓌWww.kaikias.com; ❺), offers large, bright rooms (some decorated with scenes of the Trojan War) in a modern building that resembles a traditional Greek townhouse. *Otel Tena* (☎0286/697 8880, ⓌWww.oteltena.com; ❸), on Ideli Sok, has rooms with TV and shower in a fine old house, though breakfast is not included. The *Ergin Pansiyon* (☎0286/697 8429; ❷), on Şüran Sok, is visible from the coast road as you walk uphill from the castle and has good clean rooms with bathrooms. At the far end of the esplanade behind the harbour, the *Ege* (☎0286/697 8189, Ⓕ697 8389; ❺), on Mektep Sok, is in a partially restored nineteenth-century Greek school: its rooms are of a decent size, all with private bathrooms, and those on the top floor have balconies with nice views.

The upmarket *Thenes* (☎0286/697 8888; ❺), 5km round the coast, south of town at Alaybey, has its own concreted "beach" and rather basic rooms for the price. Beyond here, the *Güler Pansiyon* (☎0286/697 8454; ❷), on Tekirbahçe Mevkii, is beautifully situated on its own strip of beach, with only vines between it and the sea. Rooms are very simple, but guests have use of a kitchen and there are boats to rent. Finally, **Ayazma** beach has a smattering of small **campsites** with attached restaurants, *Paşa Camping* (☎0286/697 8101) being the pick of the crop, well known for its freshly caught fish dishes.

Eating and drinking

There are numerous **restaurants** grouped around the harbour, mostly offering seafood. Of these, *Paşa* is particularly good, offering a quality selection of fresh fish, *güveç* (fish stew) and *mezes* including a fine sautéed calamari. Further east along the harbour street *Lisa's Café* serves an impressive range of wines together with favourites such as *mantı* and mouthwatering chocolate cake – there are occasional exhibitions of paintings here by resident island artists. The most stylish place for evening **drinking** is the *Salhane Bar*, along the coast behind the castle. *Polenta Café*, meanwhile, between the park and the quay, attempts to cater for the European market with Italian coffee and outdoor seating.

Local seafood is usually accompanied by the ubiquitous island **wine**. Traditional grapes include the white Vasilaki and Chavush (sweet table grapes) and the red Karasakez and Karalahna; good brands include Ataol Yunatular and Talay. The

Talay **bottling plant** is at the back of Kale, up the hill behind the school. Though not officially open to the public, it welcomes visitors in an informal sort of a way and its shop sells its own vintages at half shop prices.

Troy

> But Aunt Dot could only think how Priam and Hecuba would have been vexed to see the state it had all got into and no one seeming to care anymore. She thought the nations ought to go on working at it and dig it all up again, and perhaps do some reconstruction, for she belonged to the reconstruction school, and would have liked to see Troy's walls and towers rising once more against the sky like a Hollywood Troy, and the wooden horse standing beside them, opening mechanically every little while to show that it was full of armed Greeks.
>
> Rose Macaulay, *The Towers of Trebizond* (1990)

Although by no means the most spectacular archeological site in Turkey, **TROY**, thanks to Homer, is probably the most celebrated. Known as Truva in Turkish, the remains of the ancient city lie around 20km south of Çanakkale, just west of the main road. It's a scanty affair on the whole, but if you lower your expectations and use your imagination, you may well be impressed. The ruins are now a lot less obscure than previously, with modern scientific methods managing to fill the gaps left by earlier excavations. Recent work has served to clarify the site greatly, to the extent that laypeople can now at least grasp the basic layout and gain a knowledge of the different settlement periods discovered.

Some history

Until 1871 Troy was generally thought to have existed in legend only. The Troad plain, where the ruins lie, was known to be associated with the Troy that Homer wrote about in the *Iliad*, but all traces of the city had vanished completely. In 1868 **Heinrich Schliemann** (1822–1890), a German businessman who had made his fortune in America, obtained permission from the Ottoman government to start digging on a hill known to the Turks as Hisarlık, where earlier excavators had already found the remains of a Classical temple and signs of further, older ruins.

Schliemann was born into a poor Mecklenburg family and became obsessed at an early age with the myths of ancient Greece. Unable to pursue the interest professionally (although he did teach himself ancient Greek, in addition to several modern languages), he amassed his considerable fortune during the Californian Gold Rush of 1849, forsaking commerce at the age of 46 to become the world's most celebrated and successful amateur archeologist.

Schliemann's sloppy trenching work resulted in a certain amount of damage to the site, only rectified by the first professional archeologist to work at Troy, the respected Carl William Blegen, whose excavations began in 1932. Schliemann was also accountable for removing the so-called **Treasure of Priam**, a large cache of beautiful jewellery that was taken back to Berlin and subsequently displayed there until 1941, when it was squirrelled away for safety under Zoo Station. The hoard disappeared during the Red Army's sacking of the city in May 1945; long suspected of having been spirited back to the USSR, it resurfaced spectacularly in Moscow in August 1993 and is now on display in the Pushkin Museum there. A legal tussle between Germany and the Russian Federation to determine ownership is now in progress – as well as careful forensic examination of the precious items to answer allegations that Schliemann fraudulently assembled the treasure from scattered sites in Asia Minor.

Whatever Schliemann's shortcomings, his initial, unsystematic excavations did uncover nine layers of remains, representing distinct and consecutive city developments that span four millennia. The oldest, **Troy I**, dates back to about 3600 BC and was followed by four similar settlements. Either Troy VI or VII is thought to have been **the city described by Homer**: the former is known to have been destroyed by an earthquake in about 1275 BC, while the latter shows signs of having been wiped out by fire about a quarter of a century later, around the time historians generally estimate the Trojan War to have taken place. **Troy VIII**, which thrived from 700 to 300 BC, was a Greek foundation, while much of the final layer of development, **Troy IX** (300 BC to 300 AD), was built during the heyday of the Roman empire.

Although there's no way of being absolutely sure that the **Trojan War** did take place, there's a fair amount of circumstantial evidence suggesting that the city was the scene of some kind of armed conflict, even if it wasn't the ten-year struggle described in the *Iliad*. It's possible that Homer's epic is based on a number of wars fought between the Mycenaean Greeks and the inhabitants of Troy, who, it seems, were alternately trading partners and commercial rivals. Homer's version of events, however, dispensed with these pedestrian possibilities, turning the war into a full-scale heroic drama, complete with bit parts for the ancient Greek gods.

The site

The **site** (daily: May–Sept 8am–7pm; Oct–April 8am–5pm; 10YTL) is signalled by the ticket office – marked "Gişe" – just opposite the dolmuş drop-off point. There's also a small shop here where you can pick up a copy of *A Tour of Troia* by Dr Manfred Korfman, the archeologist who, between 1988 and his death in 2005, oversaw the site's excavation. It consists of two books and a map, which will guide you around with pages of information corresponding to numbers on the signs at the site.

From the ticket office a long, straight road leads to the car park (4YTL) and beyond to the ticket barriers, which mark the site's official entrance. Just to the right stands a 1970s reconstruction of the giant **wooden horse** (which would have delighted Macaulay's fictional Aunt Dot). You can climb a ladder leading up into the horse's belly and look out of windows cut into its flanks (which presumably didn't feature in the original design). The adjacent **excavation house** has a scale model of the site (when it's not out on loan) and an excellent video explaining the history of Troy and the excavations. Just beyond is the ruined city itself, a craggy outcrop overlooking the Troad plain, which extends about 8km to the sea. The circular trail takes you around the site, the twelve panels enlisting the help of schematic diagrams, going some way to bringing the ruins to life. It's a bleak spot, however, leaving you in no doubt as to the thinness of Troy's remains, but as you stand on what's left of the ramparts and look across the plain that stretches out at your feet, it's not too difficult to imagine a besieging army, legendary or otherwise, camped below.

Most impressive of the extant remains are the **east wall and gate** from Troy VI (1700–1275 BC), of which 330m remain, curving around the eastern and southern flanks of the city. The inward-leaning walls, 6m high and over 4m thick, would have been surmounted by an additional brick section. A ramp paved with flat stones from Troy II (2500–2300 BC), which would have led to the citadel entrance, also stands out, as does the nearby partially reconstructed **Megaron Building** (currently protected beneath a giant canvas roof) from the same era, the bricks of which were turned a bright red when Troy II was destroyed by fire. Schliemann, erroneously as it turned out, used the evidence of this fire to draw the conclusion that this had been Homer's Troy and that the items he discovered here made up Priam's treasure.

The most important monument of Roman Troy IX, or Ilium, is the **temple of Athena**, which was rebuilt on a promise of Alexander the Great by his general, Lysimachus, after Alexander himself had visited the temple and left his armour as a gift. Remains found by Schliemann proved the temple to be of the Doric order, and fragments of its coffered ceiling can still be seen on site. The most famous

△ Troy's replica wooden horse

Alexandria Troas

The **ruins of Alexandria Troas**, an ancient city founded by Antigonus I, a general of Alexander the Great, in 300 BC, lie around 30km south of Troy near the holiday village of Dalyan. As with Troy, the ruins, though spread over a vast area, are none too spectacular. Unfortunately, unlike Troy, there's little labelling or organization of the site to help you understand what's there. If you do decide to make the journey, the site can be reached by dolmuş from both Çanakkale and Gülpınar.

relief from the temple, however, depicting Apollo astride four pawing stallions, is now in Berlin. Troy was an important religious centre during Greek and Roman times, and the remains of two other **sanctuaries**, which were also renovated after the visit of Alexander the Great, can be seen at the westernmost point of the site. It's thought that the female deities Cybele and Demeter were worshipped here, because the layout, with altar and grandstand, is similar to the sanctuary in Pergamon.

Practicalities

Çanakkale is the most sensible base for seeing Troy. A couple of companies there offer **guided tours** for around 20YTL (see p.282) and may tell you that there is no dolmuş service to the site. In fact, **dolmuşes** run every twenty minutes from Çanakkale (from the minibus garage, opposite the fairground on Atatürk Caddesi) to the village of **Tefvikiye**, which sits at the gates of the site; it's a thirty-minute ride. If you're moving on further south, the best option is to take the Troy–Çanakkale minibus and jump off at the junction with the main road. From here, you can hop on to any passing southbound bus.

There is **accommodation** in Tevfikiye, in the form of the *Hisarlık Hotel* (℡0286/283 0026, ℻283 0087; ❸), just before the ticket office on the road to the site: it has an attached restaurant and bar, and offers guided tours of Troy.

Gülpınar and Babakale

Heading south of Alexandria Troas you pass through some of the most fertile agricultural land in western Turkey, interspersed with tiny, unspoilt villages and dotted with ancient remains. The beautiful coastal road as far as Gülpınar is flat, well tarmacked and usually deserted, which makes it good for cycling, although you'll need to keep your wits about you as what traffic there is tends to travel at quite a speed. Four dolmuşes a day make the fifty-kilometre trip from Ezine to Gülpınar, where you change for the remaining 9km to Babakale. There's also an infrequent service to Gülpınar from the east, from Ayvacık, which passes out of Assos parallel to the ancient paved road and on through more barren, hillier country marked by attractive villages built of the local andesite rock.

Gülpınar

GÜLPİNAR is notable mainly as the site of the **Temple of Apollo Smintheos**, signposted at the western edge of the village. The shrine is dedicated to one of the more bizarre manifestations of the god, as Lord of Mice. When the original Cretan colonists found themselves harassed by mice, they remembered a previous oracle advising them to settle wherever overrun by the "sons of earth". This they took to mean the rodents, founding the now mostly vanished ancient town of Chryse around the temple. Of the remaining Hellenistic temple, oddly aligned northeast, scarcely more remains, just the platform and some column stumps. It's an atmospheric, lonely site, with detailed on-site explanation panels and is well worth the detour.

Gülpınar itself is a bustling, friendly place, seemingly at odds with its remote position. There are a few reasonable eateries, a couple of beer houses and a single *pansiyon*. However, you might as well push on the 9km southwest to Babakale.

Babakale

The working fishing-port of **BABAKALE** marks the westernmost point of Asia. Despite this notable claim to fame, it remains a low-key place, its sleepy, dusty charms as yet undiscovered by chattering classes of İstanbul who flock to nearby Assos. Referred to in the *Iliad* as Cape Lekton, the village is dominated by a fine eighteenth-century Ottoman **castle** (always open; free), the outer walls and battlements of which have recently been restored.

The village takes its name in part from the castle (or *kale*) and part from a dervish saint (*baba* – literally "father"), whose tomb is in the small graveyard next to the main square. There are some other Ottoman remains, such as a mosque, whose outer walls are curiously decorated with Ottoman gravestones, and a couple of carved marble *çeşme* (drinking fountains). The only local **beach** is about 3km before the port, overlooked by holiday villas, although the rocks on either side of Babakale harbour are ideal for swimming and are well populated with marine life.

Babakale boasts a handful of very reasonable **hotels** ranged on the hillside above the harbour, which tend to fill at weekends, when you may find rooms more expensive. All have their own restaurants offering fresh, locally caught fish. Most reasonably priced is the *Karayel* (☎0286/747 0497, ⓕ747 0358; ❷), which offers basic rooms with bathroom. The next-door *Uran Motel* (☎0286/747 0218; ❸) offers similar facilities, with the added attraction of a rooftop terrace.

Ayvacık

Thirty kilometres south of Ezine lies the market town of **AYVACİK**, gateway to the Classical settlement of Assos. No question but the best time to be in town is Friday – **market day** – when the local people, mostly settled *Yörük* nomads, converge from the surrounding villages to trade their produce at stalls adjacent to the *otogar* and ticket offices. It's a particularly noisy and colourful affair, worth spending some time at between minibus connections: women in traditional patterned *şalvar* (baggy pantaloons) and headscarves sell all kinds of fruit and vegetables, honey, cheese and pre-prepared *börek*. Late April in Ayvacık sees the more extensive annual **Paniyir**, a traditional gathering of the region's nomadic peoples, which revolves around drinking, dancing and horse trading. Although the nomads are nominally Muslim the festival itself is probably descended from pagan celebrations for the arrival of spring, which predate even ancient Greece.

It's not likely that you'll find much else to detain you in town, although Ayvacık is the headquarters of the co-operative **DOBAG carpet project**, based in premises opposite the Elif petrol station on the Çanakkale road, on the outskirts of town. The project has had a profound effect on the Turkish carpet industry (see box on p.294), though it's worth noting that the co-operative only markets its products abroad – carpets sold in the Friday market in Ayvacık (and

DOBAG carpets

The **DOBAG carpet project** was initiated by a German schoolteacher and doctor of chemistry, **Harold Böhmer** who, together with his wife Renate, became interested in Turkish carpets while working in İstanbul in the 1960s. Returning in the 1970s, he started analysing traditional carpet dyes to try and find out why some older rugs were more attractive than newer ones, whose colours either faded to mud grey or remained garish. Böhmer discovered that older rugs used **traditional vegetable dyes**, while many of those made after the 1880s were coloured with **artificial analine dyes**, which had come to Turkey from Europe, primarily Germany.

Next came the more difficult task of trying to find out which plants had produced the more attractive natural colours. For the most part these turned out to grow wild in Anatolia, including: madder (*Rubia tinctorum*), a reed-like plant whose roots produce shades ranging from light red to violet; weld (*Reseda luteola*), one of around twenty plants that can produce yellow dye; as well as extract of oak apples and acorn cups mixed with iron, which produces black. The only exception was the blue produced by natural indigo (from the plant *Indigofera*), which was imported into the region from India as early as Roman times.

In 1981, Böhmer initiated the **Doıal Boya Araştirma ve Geliştirme Projesi** (natural dye research and development project). After devising commercial techniques for the preparation of dyes in a village setting, his newfound methods were taught to the nomads of Ayvacık. The vast majority of plants used in the dyeing process are now farmed in the region (the one exception being indigo).

The project is run as a **workers' co-operative** and under Turkish law only producers are allowed to be members. Thus, it's entirely run by the village women who do all the weaving, as well as choosing their own colours and patterns, adapted from traditional designs. Standards are high, and only carpets that retain their lustre (ie, those made from the best-quality, handspun winter wool and dyes) are accepted by DOBAG. A square metre of a DOBAG carpet has a hundred thousand knots, and consequently costs around €240. A second, similar project has been set up in Yuntdaı, near Manisa.

Although small in themselves, the two projects have had a far-reaching effect on the **Turkish carpet sector**, and it's now almost impossible to find any carpet-seller admitting that artificial dyes have been used in his products. But that doesn't mean they're all natural – many manufacturers simply switched to more sophisticated chemical dyes that give subtler shades and produce the sought-after "faded" effect.

elsewhere in the bazaars of Turkey) may be produced in the area, but are not those of DOBAG. Another co-operative, **Yörük Hale**, sells reliable quality carpets – cheaper than DOBAG – from a small shop opposite the *otogar*.

There are hourly **buses** to the town from Çanakkale as well as a regular service from Ezine, and there's no reason to stay in Ayvacık with Assos (see below) so close; four or five dolmuşes a day run on there from the *otogar*. There are no **banks** in Assos, so Ayvacık is the place to exchange money if you need to.

Assos and around

Situated on and around the ancient Greek city of the same name, **ASSOS**, 25km south of Ayvacık, is a charmingly preserved old village where no new buildings are permitted and old buildings may only be restored using the attractive local stone. **Ancient Assos** sits on top of a steep rocky hill and spreads down the seaward side towards the Aegean. Modern Assos consists of two parts – the village of **Behramkale**, which wraps itself around the top of the hill, and the tiny settlement of former warehouses and fishing cottages grouped around the **harbour** below – but most people, including locals, just refer to it collectively as Assos. Further along the coast, 4km east of Assos, lies the fine shingle beach of **Kadırga**, though getting here can be difficult without your own vehicle.

Undiscovered until the mid-1980s, when it became an inexpensive bolt-hole for the İstanbul literati, Assos these days is anything but cheap. Accommodation prices and availability fluctuate violently – on summer weekends booking in advance is essential, although on weekdays, and in May or late season, you can still find the place close to deserted, with its inimitable charm intact and rooms at realistic prices (though you should still make a point of bargaining). The ruins themselves attract a fair number of coach tours, but thankfully few stop overnight, leaving the village relatively peaceful by evening.

There are four or five **dolmuşes** a day to Assos from Ayvacık. Be warned, though, that during the low season and at slack times they may take a couple of hours to fill, so if there are a few of you waiting it may be worth offering to pay for an early departure (it's roughly 2YTL per person and the minibus won't leave with fewer than eight).

The journey is through beautiful hills covered with olive trees and the Mediterranean oak, whose acorn cups are used to produce a substance for tanning leather, the export of which was the main business of Assos until early last century. The final stretch passes a fourteenth-century, humpback **Ottoman bridge**, built with masonry from the ancient settlement, and then leads up into the village square where local women sell traditional embroidery and women from surrounding *Yörük* villages sell small carpets.

Ancient Assos and Behramkale

According to some sources, Assos was the site of a thirteenth-century BC Hittite colony, although the earliest traces only really date from the eighth century, when Greek colonists from neighbouring Lesbos (Lésvos) established a settlement, later building a huge temple to Athena in 540 BC. Hermias, a eunuch and disciple of Plato, ruled here, attempting to put Plato's theories of the ideal city-state into practice. From 347 to 344 BC Aristotle made his home in Assos as the guest of Hermias, developing his philosophy further before the arrival of the Persians forced him to flee. Assos was also purportedly the source of much of the wealth of Croesus. During medieval times, the Ottomans plundered the town for dressed stone, as did local villagers. The site was only rediscovered in 1880 when it was stumbled on by a 25-year-old American, Francis Bacon. He returned in 1881 to conduct extensive excavations sponsored by the Antiquarian Society of Boston.

Dolmuşes from Ayvacık call first at the upper village, dropping passengers in the small square. From here, it's a short (though extremely steep) walk up the hill to the **Murat Hüdavendigar Camii**, an austere fourteenth-century mosque that probably began as a church, built with stone quarried from the earlier settlement. Beyond is the enclosed site of the sixth-century **Temple of Athena** (open daylight hours; 5YTL), with Doric columns re-erected by an American university archeological team, and a partially rebuilt antique theatre. Unfortunately, both make use of unsightly concrete in places where the original stone proved insufficient. Anyway, it's still beautiful, although overshadowed somewhat by views to Lésvos and over the Gulf of Edremit.

The rest of ancient Assos is a jumble of ruins falling away from the temple, enclosed by the old and partly intact **city wall**, which is accented with towers and quite impressive. The most recognizable part is the old **necropolis**, littered with sarcophagi, which can be viewed on the way down from the village to the harbour.

The two cheapest *pansiyon*s – *Tekin* (☎0286/721 7099; ❷) and *Sidar* (☎0286/721 7047; ❷) – lie on the road back out of the village, but this is one place where it pays to spend a little more, as **accommodation** in the upper village is much better value than down around the harbour. By the bridge is the delightfully laid-back ☂ *Old Bridge House Pension* (☎0286/721 7426, ✉oldbridgehouse@yahoo .com; ❹), owned by a Turkish–Dutch couple who offer tasteful, if somewhat chaotically decorated, rooms in the house itself, as well as cheaper thatched cabins in the small walled garden, and a small dorm (20YTL). In the village itself, just downhill from the ruins, *Timur Restaurant & Pansiyon* (☎0286/721 7449, ✉timurpansiyon@yahoo.com; ❸) has four small double rooms – two with bathrooms – in a beautifully restored 200-year-old house, with a walled garden and restaurant affording superb views over the coastline to Greece. Just around the corner, the *Eris Pansiyon* (☎0286/721 7080, ✉erispansiyon@hotmail.com; ❹), owned by a retired American couple, offers local charm and five rooms with views north over the valley. Take the left lane at the square to find the *Assos Konukevi* (☎0286/721 7081; ❸), whose high-quality apartments have a large lounge, double bedroom and one single bedroom, superb views and a large walled garden. The *Dolunay* (☎0286/721 7172; ❸), next to the dolmuş stop in the centre of the village, is also attractive and comfortable, with an attached restaurant.

For good-value **food** there are a number of cheap *lokanta*s selling typical village dishes such as *mantı* and *gözleme*, washed down with a glass of *ayran*. The *Assos Restaurant*, which overlooks the main square, and the *Kale Restaurant*, on the road leading up to the temple, are both recommended. Pick of the bunch, however, is probably the *Timur Restaurant*, which provides an unforgettable setting for tasty meals or just a drink.

Assos harbour

Having called at the upper village, the dolmuşes from Ayvacık then run down to **Assos harbour**, where they wait for return custom. It's well worth the twenty-minute walk down in any case, for the breathtaking views out over the Aegean to Lesbos. If driving, you'll need to park in the carpark on the final curve before the descent to the harbour (it's about a five-minute walk away) as there's no parking in the town itself. Despite the harbour, there's little yacht trade here and crossing to Greece is illegal, which probably explains the *jandarma* post down on the quayside.

The harbour is very compact with a waterfront area that stretches for just a few hundred metres, alongside which sits a cluster of elegant, old, stone houses, the whole area topped and tailed by two small beaches. Out of season, it's an idyllic resort, though on summer weekends its limited confines struggle to cope with the endless busloads of tour groups.

As all the waterfront properties are hotels of one sort or another, you'll have no trouble locating **accommodation**. A budget option is the *Cakir Pansiyon* (☎0286/721 7148; ❷), with simple, small doubles; it also runs an even cheaper **campsite** (7YTL) set amongst the olive groves at the eastern end of the harbour. Going up a notch, the *Hotel Assos* (☎0286/721 7017; ❹) and the *Behram* (☎0286/721 7016, ⓦwww .behram-hotel.com; ❺), both occupy the same waterfront block near the entrance to the harbour. Both are comfortable and well run, although the *Behram*, which is under the same ownership as the *Old Bridge House* in Behramkale (see above), has the larger rooms and is decorated in a more up-to-date style. For both, it's well worth paying extra for a room overlooking the harbour. Many of the larger hotels offer reasonable half-board options, with the grandest choices being the rather aloof *Assos Kervansaray* (☎0286/721 7093, ℱ721 7200; ❺), next to the beach, with a pool, sauna and courtyard restaurant, and the recently opened, very swanky *Assos Deluxe* (☎0286/721 7017, ℱ721 7240; ❼) with designer, minimalist bathrooms and lavishly appointed bedrooms.

Most of the hotels have good, albeit rather similar, **restaurants**, serving excellent fish meals. The *Fenerlihan*, the *Nazlıhan* hotels, both at the northern end of town, and the *Behram* and *Assos* hotels all have waterfront eateries serving hot and cold *mezze*s for around 3–6YTL and fish and seafood courses for 10–15YTL.

Kadırga

Less than an hour away on foot from Assos harbour is the beach resort of **KADİRGA**. Simply head east along the coastal footpath and cut across the headland by the ugly holiday village. Kadırga is also accessible by a paved four-kilometre road signposted from the upper village.

Kadırga's beach itself is reasonable – over a kilometre of fine shingle – and the resort is yet to be overwhelmed by tourism, though things seem to be heading in that direction, with the recent opening of the vast 256-room *Eden Gardens* resort (☎0286/764 0290, ⓦwww.assosedengroup.com; ❷), with its numerous restaurants, pools and stretch of private beach. Less overwhelming accommodation is provided by the friendly *Assos Park Hotel* (☎0286/721 7163, ⓦwww.assospark.com; ❹), with extensive landscaped gardens, and the *Yildiz Saray* (☎0286/721 7025, ⓦwww.yildizsaray-hotels.com; ❹), that offers double rooms with TV. There are also a couple of **campsites** which rent out tents for around 8YTL a night.

Well worth knowing about, and not properly shown on most maps, is the twenty-kilometre **shore road** east from Kadırga to Küçükkuyu (see below). Though narrow, it is entirely paved, travelled by the occasional dolmuş (or mountain bike) and it allows you to bypass the tortuous mountain curves of the main inland route.

Along the Gulf of Edremit

From Ayvacık, the main Çanakkale–İzmir road winds through pine-forested hills, offering occasional glimpses out across the **Gulf of Edremit**. The road, which is currently being widened and improved, straightens out at **Küçükkuyu**, the first major settlement and the only real town, before continuing past a succession of small resorts to the transport hub of **Edremit** itself.

Küçükkuyu

The small fishing port of **KÜÇÜKKUYU** – 20km southeast of Ayvacık – still has a fleet in evidence, and there are plenty of reasonable seafood restaurants. It's mostly Turkish tourists who swim from the nearby beaches, while on Fridays farmers from the surrounding villages come here to sell their produce at the street market.

The few **hotels** are affordable and never more than a few minutes' walk from the sea: the *Yakamaz Motel* (☎0286/752 6899; ❸) right on the waterfront is worth a try. There are also a few **campsites** in the area, including *Filiz Camping* (☎0286/752 5579), *Truva* (☎0286/752 5206) and *Zeus Motel Camping* (☎0286/752 5068).

East of Küçükkuyu a series of small resorts – one with the baldly descriptive name of Moteller ("motels") – is unlikely to appeal to foreigners. You're best off continuing to Akçay, the next place of any size.

Akçay

From the main road, where long-distance buses will drop you (Edremit-bound dolmuşes continue to the centre), it's about a ten-minute walk into **AKÇAY**, a resort with a pleasant seafront, frequented by middle-class Turks. The hotels, restaurants and discos are packed during the school summer holidays, but deadly quiet out of season. With high demand in peak season, Akçay **hotels** are not particularly cheap. *Otel Linda* at Barbaros Meydanı (☎0266/384 3500, ☎0266/384 2524; ❷) – opposite the PTT – has basic rooms with a balcony and sea view and congenial hosts. *Otel Özsoy* along the waterfront (☎0266/384 1190, ☎384 2190; ❷) offers much the same, but it's just that bit closer to the beach.

The seafront esplanade abounds with cheap fast-food **cafés** and fish **restaurants** – the large *Tuana* is a popular example – while Taner Nuran Sokak in the centre has numerous *lokantas*, *kebab* and *pide salonları*.

Edremit

Easily reached by dolmuş from Akçay, **EDREMIT** is the Adramyttium of the *Iliad*, which was sacked by Achilles. After destroying the town, Achilles kidnapped Chryseis, the daughter of the priest at the Temple of Apollo Smintheos (see "Gülpınar", p.292), only to have her claimed by Agamemnon, leader of the Greek force. This provoked the "wrath of Achilles" (more like a long-drawn-out sulk), one of the major subplots of the *Iliad*.

These days the legends far outshine the reality of the place and you're most likely to stop in Edremit only for services such as the **PTT** and banks, both of which are on Menderes Bulvarı, the main thoroughfare. Edremit is a major public-transport node, with buses to destinations all over Turkey, including services 70km east to the provincial capital of Balıkesir (where you can pick up the İzmir–Bandırma train). The **otogar** is 800m out of town on Yılmaz Akpınar Bulvarı.

Ören

From Burhaniye, 14km south of Edremit, there are dolmuşes to **ÖREN**, another 4km northwest, a small resort popular with Turkish holidaymakers. During the summer you can also reach Ören by boat from Akçay (check with the tourist office in Akçay for current details).

Ören has a beautiful **beach** overlooked by Kaz Dağı, the ancient Mount Ida. It's a much smaller and sleepier town than Akçay, with development restricted to the outlying areas. In the centre there is little new building allowed, leaving space for flower-filled gardens and pine-covered walks between old-fashioned holiday villas. As with Akçay, though, the place is all but deserted once the schools go back. The town has a long history of wine- and olive-oil production, dating back to the Greek occupation, and there's an annual **olive festival** held between August 16 and 18.

There's a **tourist kiosk** (Mon–Fri 8.30am–noon & 1.30–5pm) next to the police station and the small *otogar*, while **accommodation** possibilities are mainly located on Çarşı Caddesi, the street running from the *otogar* to the beach. The *Kösem* (☎0266/416 3230; ❶) is friendly, if a little jaded. Nestling under the pine walkway to the beach is the *Pekcan Motel* (☎0266/416 3180; ❷), with small, but fairly modern rooms. There's also a **campsite**, 300m south of the centre on the main road, best thought of as a last resort.

For good-value food, head for the **market** that runs parallel to Çarşı Caddesi, where stands dish up *pide* and *lahmacun*, baked potatoes and kebabs. At the top of the lane, furthest from the beach, is the *Mesudun* **restaurant** with pleasant outdoor tables. Back towards the beach, the *Ida Yörük Çadiri* is a small café/bar under a large nomadic awning, with low tables, cushioned seating and *nargile*.

Ayvalık and around

AYVALİK, 56km south of Edremit, is growing in popularity with Turkish and European visitors for the charm of its cobbled streets lined with picturesque old Greek houses. In stark contrast to the resorts to the south that have been completely taken over by the holiday trade, the town has retained a fishing fleet, as well as its traditional crafts and markets, and tourism feels like just another string to its bow. The closest good beaches are in the recently developed resort of Sarimsakli, with some remoter, less sandy ones on the island of Alibey, both easily reached from town. Ayvalık is also convenient for ruin-spotting at nearby Bergama – to which there's a fine back-country drive – and stands opposite the Greek island of Lésvos, connected to town in summer by a regular ferry service.

Ayvalık started life as the **Ottoman Greek settlement** of Kydonaie around three or four centuries ago. Both Turkish and Greek names refer to orchards of quince, the rock-hard pear-shaped fruit that grows all round the region but hardly features in its cuisine. In the late eighteenth century the town was granted special concessions by the then grand vizier, Cezayirli Hasan Paşa, who, as a captain in the Ottoman navy twenty years earlier, had been rescued by the Greeks of Ayvalık following a disastrous defeat at the hands of the Russian navy. The town grew to become the most prosperous and imposing on the Aegean coast after İzmir, boasting an academy, a publishing house and around twenty Orthodox churches, many of which still remain. The exchange of populations that followed the Greek–Turkish war of 1920–22 saw the expulsion of the town's Greek Orthodox inhabitants and the conversion of the largest churches into mosques. Ironically, most of the people resettled here after 1923 were Greek-speaking Muslims from Crete and Mytilini (Lésvos), and many of Ayvalık's older inhabitants still speak Greek.

Arrival, information and tours

There are regular direct **buses** to Ayvalık along the main highway, either south from Çanakkale via Edremit, or north from İzmir. Unless explicitly stated these intercity buses will drop you 5km out of town at the Ayvalık highway junction. The main **otogar** is 1.5km north of the town centre, though any red-and-white city bus labelled "Çamlık" will take you into town for about 0.5YTL. Ayvalık is a fairly small place and most of what you'll need is concentrated around **İskele Meydanı**, the small plaza with the Atatürk bust. Northbound buses coming from İzmir usually pass through the square and will drop you here if you ask.

The main **tourist office** is opposite the marina, about 1km south of the square (℡0266/312 3158; Mon–Fri 8.30am–5.30am), although there's also a small summer-only tourist booth on İskele Meydanı (same hours). Just north of the square you'll find the banks, PTT and most midtown bus-company offices.

Regular summer ferries run across to **Alibey** (Cunda) island (see p.303) from the fishing-harbour quay, a vastly preferable route to the circuitous city-bus trip there (across the bridge from the mainland). **Boat tours** around the other local islands also leave from here. They last around six hours, taking in stops for lunch and swimming and sightseeing at Alibey harbour (10YTL, including lunch).

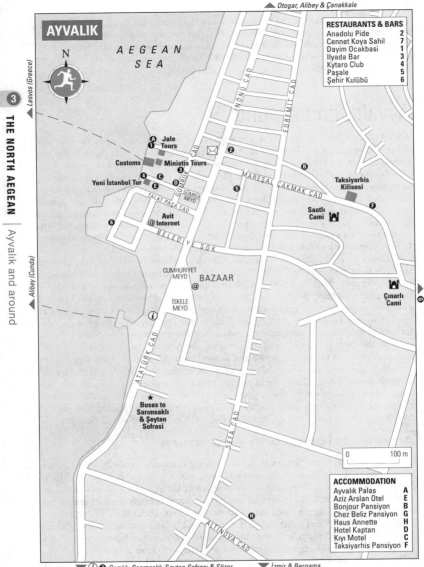

Lésvos (Greece)

Alibey (Cunda)

Ferries to Lésvos

There's a **ferry service to Lésvos** in Greece in summer, but schedules are the least reliable of any of the Greek island–Turkish mainland crossings. Moreover, you have to do the outward and return journeys on the same boat, whether Turkish or Greek, and prices, given the short distance involved, are very high (€50 one way, €60 return; cars €80). Three agencies deal with the crossing (see "Listings", p.302) with six boats a week leaving Ayvalık from May to September (at 9am and returning at 4pm), dropping to just one a week in winter. Departures are from the **ferry terminal** near the Customs building, 250m north of the fishing-harbour quay.

Accommodation

Down by the water, **Gümrük Meydanı**, a once-dilapidated district of old Greek mansions and stone-built warehouses, is being swiftly restored. If hotels around here or in the town's **backstreets** are full, you'll have to extend your search to the south, to the suburb of Çamlık, where a number of modest *pansiyon*s are clearly marked from the coast road (and where the summer villas of late nineteenth-century İzmir Greeks still peek out from between the pines). There are reports of taxi drivers taking unsuspecting tourists to a different hotel than the one requested; a firm yet polite insistence should clear up any "misunderstanding".

The backstreets

Bonjour Pansiyon Maraşal Çakmak Cad, Beşinci Çeşme Sok 6 ☎0266/312 8085. Occupies one of the grandest houses in town; beautifully renovated with a charming courtyard where breakfast is served. ❸

Chez Beliz Pansiyon Maraşal Çakmak Cad 28, Fethiye Mah ☎0266/312 4897, ☎312 4609. Based in the family home of charming ex-actress Beliz, this is a comfortable place (though the rooms are basic, with no en-suites), and there's a nice garden courtyard where lavish dinners are served at 16YTL a head. The hotel is a stiff 10–15min uphill walk from town, but it does hire out bikes. ❸

Haus Annette Neşe Sokak 12 ☎0266/312 5971, ✉annstei@hotmail.com. Occupying a pair of houses near the market, south of the town centre, this is a stylish but basic choice (only one of its eight rooms has a private bathroom), with a plant-filled garden where delicious breakfasts are served by the German owner. ❷

🏃 **Taksiyarhis Pansiyon** Maraşal Çakmak Cad 71 ☎0266/312 1494. One of the best pensions on the Aegean coast, each room harmoniously decorated by Jasmin, the owner, and featuring two terraces and a kitchen for guests. The

serene, former Greek house, immediately behind the church of the same name, also serves as an information centre, bike-rental outlet and book exchange. Booking essential in summer. ❷

Gümrük Meydanı

Ayvalık Palas Gümrük Meyd ☎0266/312 1064, ☎312 7333. Slightly shabby, en-suite rooms with balconies overlooking the sea; buffet breakfast included. It also doubles as the office of the Ayvalık Diving Centre. ❸

Aziz Arslan Otel Gümrük Meyd ☎0266/312 5331, ☎312 6888. One of the cheaper hotels in this area, set just back from the water with ample rooms though fairly nondescript decor. ❷

Hotel Kaptan Balıkhane Sok 7 ☎0266/312 8834, ☎312 1271. These comfortable yet faded rooms are all en suite, some with a/c, a few with sea views, and there's a seaside terrace where breakfast is served. ❹

Kıyı Motel Gümrük Meyd ☎0266/312 6677. Standard-issue 1970s-vintage Turkish hotel, though the rooms try hard to please. Among the cheapest downtown lodgings, it's good value as all rooms are en suite with TVs and minibars. ❷

The Town

Ayvalık presents the spectacle – almost unique in the Aegean – of an almost perfectly preserved Ottoman Greek market town, its essential nature little changed despite the inroads of commercialization. Riotously painted horse-carts clatter through the cobbled **bazaar**, past the occasional bakery boy roaming the alleys in the early morning selling fresh bread and cakes. In the bazaar itself, crafts are still alive and well, as cobblers, copper- and tinsmiths and watch-repairers ply their trades from ramshackle wooden premises. Ayvalık is also famous for its fine yoghurt, cheese and *kepekli* (wholegrain) bread. Thursday is the special **market day**, when the backstreets overflow with produce shipped in from surrounding villages. There's also a daily **fish market** next door to the Alibey ferry terminal, where the local fishermen exhibit the morning's catch. The main **İnönü Caddesi** is the location of numerous factory shops for the region's many olive producers, offering various qualities of olive oil, pickled and salted olives, and rough green olive-oil soap.

There are few other specific sights save for the converted nineteenth-century churches, which punctuate the warren of inland streets. There's little point in asking directions: just use the minarets as landmarks and give yourself over to the pleasure of wandering under numerous wrought-iron window grilles and past ornately carved doorways. The most conspicuous church, Ayios Ioannis, is now the **Saatlı Cami**, renamed after its clocktower. Just north of here and up the hill lies the **Taksiyarhis Kilisesi**, which was never converted into a mosque – it's been closed for years, allegedly awaiting restoration as a museum. Southeast of the Saatlı Cami stands ex–Ayios Yioryios, now the **Çınarlı Cami**, misnamed given that not one of the half-dozen trees gracing its courtyard is a plane (*çınar* in Turkish).

Eating and drinking

The choice of **restaurants** in Ayvalık doesn't quite match the variety of hotels and *pansiyons*. On the seafront, and around the southern end of Gümrük Meydanı, you'll find the usual mix of Turkish fast food, *pide* salons and *lokanta*s, as well as a couple of more expensive fish **restaurants**. Just east of the market on Sefa Caddesi a few **bakeries** produce excellent *helva*-soaked morning pastries. Squeezed amongst the hotels in Gümrük Meydanı the *Ilyada Bar* provides evening **drinks** and a lively backstreet atmosphere, while the nearby *Kytaro Club* has cosy seating overlooking the sea, ideal for watching the last of the sun's rays disappear.

Anadolu Pide ve Kebab Salonu İnönü Cad. Opposite the PTT, this serves nine different sorts of kebab, including *beyti* and *İskender* and delicious *pide*, unbeatable value at 4YTL.

Cennet Koya Sahil 3km south of Ayvalık, on the Sarimsakli road. A worthwhile stop if you're returning late from the beach, this fish restaurant makes an ideal location for an enchanting meal with tables built out over the water.

Dayim Ocakbasi Gümrük Meydanı. Right on the front, this fine kebab restaurant has a large indoor dining area and a terrace on the waterfront. The

kuzu şiş (lamb kebab 10YTL) and *dayim kofté* (meatballs stuffed with cheese 7YTL) are both recommended.

Paşale Down a side street off Mareşal Çakmak Cad. This cosy café/bistro specializes in original homemade *çorba* (soup) recipes alongside the more usual *mercimek* (lentil) and *tavuk* (chicken) choices.

Şehir Kulübuu Gümrük Meydanı. As close to the water as you can be without getting wet, this occupies an idyllic spot at the end of the pier and offers a good range of seafood dishes (mussel salad for 7YTL and octopus salad for 10YTL).

Listings

Banks and exchange All the main Turkish banks have branches in town with ATMs. Currency can be changed at *Gunaydın Döviz* on İnönü Cad, travellers' cheques at the PTT (see below).

Car rental Avis, Talatpaşa Cad 67/B ☎0266/312 2456; Duke, İskele Meyd, opposite the tourist office ☎0266/312 3794; and Light Rent-a-Car, next to the Lésvos ferry terminal ☎0266/312 4959.

Ferry agencies Tickets to Lésvos from: Jale Tours, next to the customs office, Gümrük Cad 41/A ☎0266/312 2740; Yeni İstanbul Tur, next to the *Aziz Arslan Otel* off Cumhuriyet Meyd ☎0266/312 6123; and Miniotis Tours which has an office in the

passage next to the ferry terminal.

Internet Ayvalık has a few small Internet cafés, catering for the games-hungry locals. One of the easiest to find is *Arif Internet* in the Gümrük Meydanı, just across from the *Aziz Arslan* hotel.

Laundry Ak Pak, Edremit Cad 38, is a self-service launderette.

Post office PTT at İnönü Cad, just north of the town centre (Mon–Sat 8am–11pm).

Newspapers There's an astonishing range of English-language newspapers and periodicals on sale at the newspaper booth on Cumhuriyet Meyd.

Sarimsakli

Some of the biggest beaches in the area are 7km south of Ayvalık at **SARIM-SAKLI** ("Garlic Beach"), a local resort accessible by frequent dolmuşes from the stand just south of İskele Meydanı. The sandy shore here is attractive, getting less crowded and developed as you head away from town in either direction along its three-to-four-kilometre length.

You could stay here too – there are plenty of big tourist **hotels** – but, in season at least, most of these cost an arm and a leg. A well-sited budget choice on the waterfront, heading north from the shops, is *Zafer Pansiyon* (⊕0266/324 1760; ❷), with simple, clean rooms. There's a variety of reasonably priced *köfte*, *börek*, soup and *manti lokanta*s on the seafront road, with more pricey **restaurants** on the beach itself. A couple of flash fast-food joints catering to a young Turkish crowd have also sprung up, including the pizza specialist *Brand New Prestij*, on the seafront road.

Şeytan Sofrası

Just before Sarimsakli a right turn leads 3km to the peninsula southwest of Ayvalık. The headland itself levels off at **Şeytan Sofrası** (the "Devil's Dinner Table"). This distinctive rocky outcrop sits virtually at the centre of a vast array of volcanic islands, of which Alibey and more distant Lésvos are just two. In clear weather it's certainly worth the trip here for views, which extend for a hundred kilometres around, and perhaps also to spot otherwise hidden beaches below, to be reached later with your own vehicle. At the northern edge of the headland there's a small cavity in a rock, supposedly Satan's footprint, into which people throw money for luck. More prominent, however, are the numerous votive rags tied onto bushes by the country folk to placate the presiding spirit, Satan or otherwise.

In summer a **bus** leaves for Şeytan Sofrası at around 7pm from the minibus stand near Ayvalık's PTT (returning after sunset), but if you come to watch the sun go down, you'll probably be accompanied by massive crowds intent on the same experience.

Alibey

Across the bay from Ayvalık, the island of **Alibey** – known also as **Cunda Adası** – constitutes either a good day-trip destination or an overnight halt. It's a quieter, less grand version of Ayvalık, with a couple of patches of beach and numerous quayside fish restaurants.

The best way to get here in summer is by **ferry from Ayvalık**: in addition to the daily tour boats, a regular ferry service runs every half-hour (June–Sept; 1YTL each way; 20min) from the quay directly behind the tourist information booth. At other times you'll have to rely on the half-hourly **bus** service from İskele Meydanı, or a **taxi** (at least 20YTL), to cross the bridge linking island to mainland.

Around the island

Behind the island's **harbour** sprawls a grid of sleepy backstreets lined by dilapidated, but still imposing, stone houses – remnants of life before 1922, when Cunda was known as Moskhonissi to its largely Greek-speaking inhabitants. After the Greeks were deported, the island was resettled with Cretan Muslims from around Hania, and you'll find that most people over 50 speak Greek as a matter of course. Recently the place has become the target of middle-class visitors from İstanbul bent on owning an Aegean retreat, with the inevitable consequences.

Halfway up the slope from the waterfront stands the all-but-deserted Orthodox **Cathedral of the Taksiarhis**, its interior retaining a few defaced and faded frescoes. The church was heavily damaged in the earthquake of 1944 and the rumoured restoration has yet to materialize. Above the town on a hill, there's a small, roofless chapel, now used as a stable, from where you can gaze out across the bay to Ayvalık.

The northern half of Alibey, known as **Patriça**, is largely given over to a nature reserve and has some relatively deserted sand and gravel beaches, though as ever they are blighted by the construction of villa complexes and condominiums. Pleasure launches departing from the harbour offer trips to these coves, as well as to an enormous, derelict Greek monastery accessible only by sea.

Practicalities

Ferries dock at the harbour from where everything is only a short walk away. **Accommodation** prices and comfort levels increase toward the waterside, where the best value is on offer at the *Artur Motel* (☎0266/327 1014; ❸), right on the quay, whose rooms sport TVs and fridges. The *Zehra Teyze'nin Evi* (☎0266/327 2285; ❸), further inland by the cathedral, offers decent, if basic, en-suite rooms. Nicest choice by far, though, is the *Ortunç* (☎0266/327 1120, ℉327 2082; ❻), tucked away in a pine forest 4km from the harbour, on the **western shore** of the island, overlooking one of the thirty Blue Flag beaches in the Turkish Aegean. It's run by a retired opera singer, Orhan Tunç, and the recently renovated bungalows and attached restaurant sit nicely in a well-maintained garden. There's also a number of **campsites**, among them *ADA Camping* (☎0266/327 1211, ℉327 2065), 3km southwest of town, which provides good facilities, beach access and slightly overpriced bungalows (❹).

For **restaurants**, the one attached to the *Artur Motel* is excellent and reasonably priced, with a great selection of *meze*s and servings of fresh *kalamari*. Keep an eye out for the inexpensive local seafood speciality, *papalina*, a sort of small, tasty smelt.

The old road to Bergama

The **old road from Ayvalık to Bergama** (75km) takes you through the pine forests and small villages of the Madra Dağı mountain range, and makes a worthwhile alternative to the monotonous main coastal route. With your own vehicle, and a few hours to spare, a pleasant time can be had exploring many of the small villages along the way. The area is famed for its pine nuts and wine, and conceals numerous unexplored ancient remains. The region is fairly remote and the road, particularly in its later downhill stages, is narrow, twisting and demanding. Natural springs appear along the route at regular intervals and are perfectly safe to drink – in fact, a request for bottled water from any of the petrol stations en route will be met with a nonplussed stare.

Around 20km from Bergama, you could stop at the small village of **ÇİNAR** where the *Canli Alabalık* – a small fish restaurant with live trout and a fountain – is to the right of the main village square. If you stop for lunch, you'll have time to take a quick look at the ancient tomb, just outside in the car park.

Bergama

Although frequently touted as a day-trip destination from Ayvalık, **BERGAMA**, site of the **ancient city of Pergamon**, rates a full day or two in its own right. The stunning acropolis of the tyrant, Eumenes II, is the main attraction, but there is a host of lesser sights and an old quarter of chaotic charm to detain you a little longer. Bergama is unpromising at first: the long approach to the centre reveals a dusty modern-looking place, and the monuments to which it owes its reputation are nowhere to be seen. In fact, most of ancient Pergamon is some distance from the modern town and takes a little effort to reach.

Some history

The first recorded mention of Pergamon dates from 399 BC, but the town only gained prominence when it became the base of Lysimachus, one of Alexander the Great's generals. He left some of his accumulated wealth in the hands of his officer Philetarus, who inherited the lot when Lysimachus was killed in battle fighting Syria for control of Asia Minor. By skilled political manoeuvring Philetarus was able to hang onto his new-found riches, passing them on to his adopted son Eumenes, who again defeated the Syrians at Sardis and extended further the domain of Philetarus.

Eumenes, generally recognized as the founder of the Pergamene dynasty, was succeeded in 241 BC by his nephew, Attalus I, whose immediate task was to defeat the Gauls; this he did with the help of the sacrifice of an animal whose liver turned out to bear the word "Victory". Attalus was a cunning ruler – it later emerged that he had secretly imprinted the word onto the liver with a specially made ring – and his authority was soon assured, the fame of his kingdom spreading across the Hellenistic world. Thus installed, he went on to build the **Temple of Athena** and the **Library** in Pergamon.

Attalus's son and successor, **Eumenes II**, consolidated his father's gains, allied himself with the Romans and set about building Pergamon into a great city. He later helped the Romans to defeat the Syrians at the battle of Magnesium, extending his sphere of influence. Under Eumenes II, the gymnasium and theatre were built and the acropolis was secured with a wall. The last king of Pergamon, Attalus III, was less interested in ruling than in chemistry (he spent a lot of time conducting experiments with poisons on criminals), and died after a short reign, perversely leaving his realm to the **Romans**. Under them Pergamon thrived, growing into a city of 150,000 people that was a renowned artistic and commercial centre. With the arrival of the Goths in 262 AD, the city began a gradual decline and passed through the hands of a succession of invaders before falling into ruin.

The German railway engineer **Karl Humann** rediscovered ancient Pergamon in 1871, when he found a strange mosaic in the possession of some local road workers that turned out to be part of the relief from the Altar of Zeus. Humann bought the mosaic from the farmers, gave notice to his Ottoman employers on the rail line and five years later began excavating the acropolis. Work was completed in 1886, and unfortunately most of the finds were carted off to Germany, not least the reliefs from the Altar of Zeus, which you can only view in the Pergamon Museum in Berlin.

Modern-day Bergama has been making the news thanks to the **discovery of gold** in the area. However, far from delighting the local inhabitants, they've been protesting long and hard at its extraction by means of "cyanide leeching" to separate the gold from the native rock.

Arrival, orientation, information and tours

The **acropolis**, the ancient city of the kings of Pergamon, sits atop a rocky bluff towering over modern Bergama, while just out of town, to the west, is the **Asclepion**, the ancient medical centre. The **old town** (site of most of the cheap accommodation) lies at the foot of the acropolis, about ten minutes' walk from

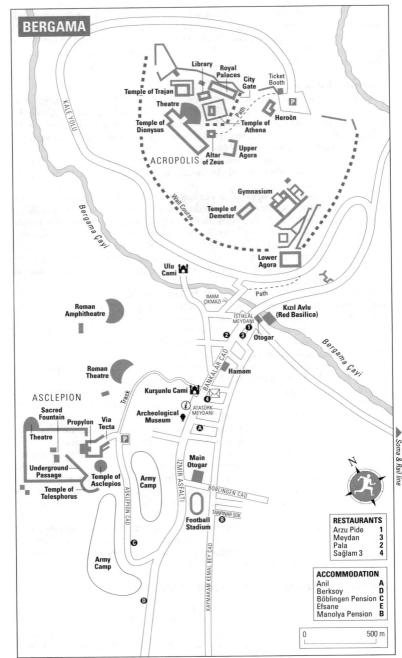

the main **otogar**. If you're visiting on a **day-trip from Ayvalık**, note that the last direct dolmuş back departs from the main *otogar* at 5pm; if you miss it, Dıkılı Ko-op runs a few more dolmuşes back to Ayvalık until about 8pm (with a change and a wait at Dıkılı).

There's a second *otogar* just south of the Kızıl Avlu (Red Basilica) on İstiklâl Meydanı, with bus services to and from points east and north. Most useful are the links with Bursa, and with Soma, 45km away on the main **train** line between İzmir and Bandırma (it's a short taxi ride between Soma's train and bus stations). A Metro service bus links the two *otogar*s, saving you a long walk or a taxi ride.

When **leaving Bergama**, you can easily connect with either the morning or evening trains to Bandırma and the fast ferry to İstanbul – by far the easiest and cheapest way of reaching it from Bergama. The so-called "direct" night buses to İstanbul from the main *otogar*, incidentally, tend to be uncomfortable, slow and expensive.

Information and tours

Bergama's **tourist office** is next to the Archeological Museum on Atatürk Meydanı (summer Mon–Fri 8.30am–7pm; winter daily 8.30am–5.30pm; ☏0232/631 2851), though all it offers are the usual tourism-ministry brochures and a rather feeble map of the town.

As soon as you get off the bus you'll probably be approached by a **taxi driver** offering to ferry you around the ruins for the extortionate sum of €25–30. If there are a few of you, or you're in a hurry, this can make sense, but otherwise it's a bit of a racket, limiting you to one hour at the acropolis (you'll almost certainly want to spend more time there), ten minutes at the Red Basilica and half an hour at the Asclepion.

Accommodation

The town's biggest and most expensive **hotels** announce themselves loudly enough on the approach to town along the İzmir Asfaltı, as do the two local **campsites** (*Caravan Camping* and *Bersoy Camping*, which are signposted just south of the town limits). Bergama's best budget accommodation is located in the old town, though taxi drivers might tell you some places are "closed" or "full" – a quick phone call ahead of your arrival should quash any such claims.

Hotel Anıl Hatuniye Cad 4, off İzmir Asfaltı ☏0232/632 1615, ⓕ632 6353. Very pink and very plush: all rooms have tasteful coordinated furnishings, TVs and air conditioning. **⑤**

Berksoy İzmir Asfaltı, 2km west of town ☏0232/633 2595, ⓦwww.berksoyhotel.com. The most comfortable of the more expensive hotels, with extensive grounds, outdoor pool, tennis court and Internet facilities. **⑤**

Böblingen Pension Asklepion Caddesi 2 ☏0232/633 2153. South of the city centre, this is a decent family-run budget choice on a hill near the Asclepion with large, clean, pleasantly

furnished rooms. **②**

Efsane İzmir Asfaltı 86 ☏0232/632 6351. Large hotel, twinned with the more central *Anıl*, with hardwood fittings and TV in the rooms, plus rooftop pool and bar. The air-conditioned restaurant serves an impressive *meze* selection. **③**

Manolya Pension Tanpinar Sok 11 ☏0232/633 4488, ⓔcafemanolyda@hotmail.com. Small, 23-room, centrally located hotel, behind the main *otogar*, bedecked with Turkish carpets. Some rooms have balcony, TV and air conditioning, and there's a small pool out back. **③**

The Town

The foremost attraction in Bergama itself is the **Kızıl Avlu** or "Red Basilica" (daily 8.30am–5.30pm; 5YTL), a huge redbrick edifice on the river below the acropolis. Originally built as a second-century AD temple to the trinity of

Egyptian gods Serapis, Harpokrates and Isis, it was converted into a basilica by the Byzantines. Early in Christianity it was one of the Seven Churches of Asia Minor addressed by St John in the Book of Revelation – he referred to it as home of the throne of the devil, perhaps a nod to the still-extant Egyptian cult. It's now a crumbling ruin containing a mosque in one of its towers, with the ancient **Selinus River** (today called the Bergama Çayı) passing underneath the basilica via two intact tunnels. Just downstream you'll see a handsome, well-preserved Ottoman bridge, built in 1384; and there are two equally well-preserved Roman bridges upstream.

The area around and uphill from the basilica, north of the river, is given over to the **old quarter** of the town, a jumble of Ottoman buildings, antique and carpet shops, mosques and maze-like streets full of vitality and colour. The antique stalls are full of very beautiful and very overpriced copperware, costing even more than in İstanbul – too many coach tours have had their effect. Similarly, the formerly good reputation of Bergama carpets has been besmirched by too much synthetic dye and machine weaving – beware. However, Tahsin on İstıklâl Meydanı, near the Kızıl Avlu, has a reliable reputation.

Back on the main drag into town you'll find the recently renovated **Archeological Museum** (Arkeoloji Müzesi; Tues–Sun 8.30am–5.30pm; 4YTL), which has a large collection of locally unearthed relics, including a statue of Hadrian from the Asclepion. Many of the statues exhibited mark a shift in style to a more naturalistic technique – incorporating accentuated body shape, form and muscle tone – which allowed for a wider range of expressions, and therefore meaning, to be shown. First developed in Pergamon, this style influenced the later European Baroque style. Also of interest, to the right of the statues, is an impressively complete Roman mosaic of Medusa. There's also a small model of the Altar of Zeus at the acropolis (see overleaf), and a large figurine of Aphrodite holding an oyster shell, found at the nearby site of Allianoi, 18km northeast of Bergama. Unfortunately, the extensive remains of this once important hydrotherapy centre dedicated to Ascelepius, will soon be submerged beneath the vast artificial lake that will be created following the completion of the nearby Yortanlı Dam.

The acropolis

The **acropolis** (daily: 8.30am–5.30pm; May–Sept until 7pm; 10YTL) is readily accessible on foot from the old town – though this is one attraction you may want to reach by taxi or car, at least on the way up, since the path can be difficult to find in that direction. The trail begins on the far side of the second bridge upstream from the Kızıl Avlu, angling obliquely up to the road, crossing which takes you up a fairly steep incline into the lower agora. Set off early, before it gets too hot and, in any case, try not to walk there following the main road, which is steep and not particularly direct, doubling back on itself for about 5km.

Taxis (15YTL) drop you off in the site car-park, by the ticket booth, from where a ramp leads up to the former **city gate**, though this has almost completely disappeared.

Altar of Zeus

The path leads southwest to the huge square **Altar of Zeus**, standing in the shade of two great pine trees. The altar was built during the reign of Eumenes II to commemorate his father's victory over the Gauls, and was decorated with reliefs depicting the battle between the Titans and the gods, symbolizing the triumph of order over chaos (and, presumably, that of Attalus over the Gauls). Even today its former splendour is apparent, though it has been much diminished by the removal

△ Bergama's acropolis

of the reliefs to Berlin. The main approach stairway was on the west, though this is the most deteriorated side today.

The Temple of Athena and the Library

Directly northeast of and exactly parallel to the Altar of Zeus, on the next terrace up, lie the remains of the **Temple of Athena**, dating back to the third century BC. Only some of the stepped foundations on which it was built have survived, although the entrance gate, with the inscription recording its dedication by "King Eumenes to Athena the Bearer of Victories", has been reconstructed in Berlin.

The scanty north stoa of the temple once housed Pergamon's famous **Library**, which at its peak rivalled that of Alexandria. Founded by Attalus II, it came to have a catalogue of 200,000 books. Eumenes II was particularly active in building it up, augmenting the collection by borrowing books from other libraries and not returning them. He is also said to have paid for books by Aristotle and Theophrastus with their weight in gold. Eventually the Egyptian kings, alarmed at the growth of the Pergamon library, which they saw as a threat to their own library in Alexandria, banned the export of papyrus, on which all books were written – and of which they were sole producers – thereby attempting to stem the library's expansion.

In response Eumenes offered a reward to anyone who could come up with a replacement, and the old custom of writing on specially treated animal skins – parchment – was revived, leading to the invention of the codex or paged book, since it wasn't possible to roll up parchment like papyrus. The words "parchment" and the more archaic "pergamene" are both actually derived from "Pergamon". The library was ransacked by Mark Antony, who gave the choicest items to Cleopatra as a gift, but enough remained for it to be consulted up until the fourth century AD.

The Temple of Trajan and around

Still further north and higher up looms the Corinthian **Temple of Trajan**, where Trajan and Hadrian were both revered during Roman times – their busts were taken from the temple and are also now in Berlin. The Germans recently completed the re-erection of the temple columns, plus those from the stoa that surrounded the shrine on three sides. The north architrave is lined with Medusa heads, two of them modern recastings.

Behind the temple are mounds of rubble and collapsed walls – the remains of barracks and the highest reaches of the city's **perimeter wall**. Nearby yawns a cistern with a pillar in the centre, either a level indicator or core of a vanished stairway – this was fed by an **aqueduct**, traces of which are still visible running parallel to a modern one on the hillside to the northwest. Finally, as you begin your descent back down toward the main entrance, you'll pass – east of the library and Athena temple – the extensive but jumbled ruins of the **Royal Palaces**.

The theatre

From the Temple of Athena a narrow staircase leads down to the **theatre**, the most spectacular part of the acropolis. Dating from Hellenistic times, it was cut into the hillside and was capable of seating 10,000 spectators. According to the architectural conventions of the day, the auditoria of Greek theatres were always greater than a semicircle, but at Pergamon the steepness of the site made this impossible, so the architects compensated by building upwards, creating a narrow, sharply raked auditorium with eighty rows of seats. The stage was built from wood and removed after performances – the holes into which supporting posts were driven can still be seen on the terrace at the foot of the auditorium. One of the reasons for the use of a portable stage was to allow free access to the **Temple of Dionysos**, built just off-stage to the audience's right.

The upper and lower agoras

Just south of the Altar of Zeus lies a terrace, formerly the **upper agora** of Pergamon. There isn't much to see today, other than Karl Humann's grave, although this was once the commercial and social focal-point of the city. A path leads down from here to the **lower agora**, where the common people lived and went about their business.

In among the remains of various houses, at the foot of the path to the Lower Agora, is the **Temple of Demeter**, where the local variant of the Eleusinian Mysteries, a cultic ceremony supposed to guarantee a better life after death, was enacted. On the northern side of the temple are the remains of a building containing nine rows of seats with space for about a thousand people, which it's thought were for spectators at the ritual. Below the temple there's a fountain for ritual ablutions and a pit designed to receive the blood of animals sacrificed in the temple. Nearby is a **gymnasium**, spread out over three terraces, where the children of the city were educated. The upper level, with its sports ground, was for young men, the middle was used by the adolescents, while the lower served as a kind of playground for younger children.

Once you've reached the lower agora, it should be a simple matter to find the path from here back down to town – the circular blue waymarks are much easier to see on the way down.

The Asclepion

Bergama's other significant archeological site is the **Asclepion** (daily 8.30am–5.30pm; May–Sept until 7pm; 10YTL), the town's Greco-Roman medical centre. It can be reached along the road starting opposite the PTT, by the Kurşunlu Cami – a drive or walk of 1.5km. Note that the ruins lie within a large and clearly marked military zone, which is closed to traffic at dusk – avoid entering any surrounding army camps and don't take photographs away from the site itself.

The Asclepion was devoted to Asclepios, son of Apollo and the god of healing, who supposedly served as a doctor in the army of Agamemnon during the siege of Troy. According to myth, Asclepios learned how to bring the dead back to life using the blood of the Gorgon that Athena had given to him. Zeus, worried that Asclepios's activities were endangering the natural order of things, struck him down with a thunderbolt but elevated him to the stars in compensation.

In part, the healing methods practised at the Asclepion were ritualistic in nature, with patients required to sleep in the temple in order that Asclepios might appear to them in a dream to relay his diagnosis and suggest treatment. However, dieting, bathing and exercise also played an important role in the therapeutic regime. **Galen** (131–201 AD), the greatest physician of the ancient world, who laid down the basis of much of modern medical science and served as personal physician to the emperor Marcus Aurelius, was trained here.

Much of what can be seen today was built in the reign of the emperor Hadrian (117–38 AD), the early stages of the first- and second-century heyday of the Pergamene Asclepion, when its function was similar to that of a nineteenth-century spa. Some patients came here to be cured of ailments, but for others a visit to the Asclepion was simply a social event, part of the habitual existence of the wealthy and leisured.

The site

From the site entrance, a long, colonnaded sacred way known as the **Via Tecta** leads to the **propylon**, or monumental entrance gate. The propylon was built during the third century AD, after an earthquake that had seriously damaged the complex in the previous century. Northeast of the propylon is a square building that housed a **library** and the statue of Hadrian now on display in the local museum.

To the south of the propylon lies the circular **Temple of Asclepios**, dating from 150 AD and modelled on the Pantheon in Rome. The domed roof of this graceful structure was 24m in diameter and had a circular opening in the centre to allow light and air to penetrate. The floor and walls would have been decorated with mosaics and recesses housed statues of the gods. To the west of the propylon and temple, the broad, open area was originally enclosed by colonnaded walkways, the bases of which can still be seen. At the western end of the northern colonnade is a **theatre** with a seating capacity of 3500, which served to keep patients entertained. At the centre of the open area, the **sacred fountain** still gushes with weakly radioactive drinking water. Nearby, an 80m-long underground passage leads to the **Temple of Telesphoros** (a lesser deity associated with Asclepios) – a two-storey circular building, which, like the Temple of Asclepios, served as a place for patients to sleep while awaiting dream diagnoses. The lower storey survives in good repair.

Eating and drinking

You can eat well in Bergama provided you ignore the large, overpriced tourist **restaurants** along the approach to the Kızıl Avlu. Tour buses will often take you to a particular restaurant, but you're not obliged to eat there. There are a number of good cheap *pide* and kebab options around İstiklâl Meydanı, and some semi-outdoor **beer houses** opposite the archeological museum, near the small terraced public park.

Arzu Pide İstiklâl Meyd. Serves delicious *pide*, topping the usual tomato and cheese *pide* with *çöp şiş* (small scraps of lamb) and good salad.

Meydan Bankalar Cad. Popular local haunt offering a large selection of dishes, including fish, as well as beer and wine.

Pala Mescit Karacac. One of the oldest joints in town, with good-value *köfte* for 3.5YTL. Upstairs at the cramped tables you ring a bell to summon a waiter.

Saılam 3 Hükümeit Cad 89. Specializes in eastern food from the Urfa region, including oven-cooked *kiremit kebap* and *güveç* (meat and veg claypot casserole) as well as *beyti sarma* (a roll of spicy *Adana kebap* covered in unleavened bread, then sliced and served with salad). Garden courtyard out back and rooms upstairs where you dine seated on cushions around low tables.

Dıkılı and Çandarlı

Thirty kilometres west of Bergama and well served by dolmuşes and intercity buses, **DİKİLİ** is a sizable resort with a population of about 10,000. Other than a decent crescent-shaped sandy beach and a promenade lined with cafés and restaurants, there's little of interest unless you arrive in early autumn when local farmers descend on the town with their harvests of raw cotton to sell to wholesalers. Cruise liners occasionally dock in the harbour, allowing their passengers to make day-trips to Bergama and Ayvalık, or head for the beaches to the north. The coast road **north of Dıkılı** takes you near a number of undeveloped resort towns, with the best stretch of sandy **beach** running for about 15km north to Altınova. It is, however, only really accessible if you have your own transport, and there are very few facilities en route.

About half an hour south of Dıkılı is the small fishing port and resort of **ÇANDARLİ**. It occupies a headland that was formerly the site of ancient Pitane, the northernmost Aeolian city, though nothing remains of this. Despite its pedigree, the oldest building in Çandarlı is a perfectly restored fourteenth-century **Genoese fortress** (not open to the public), incorporating recognizable chunks of the ancient city. This is one of several such forts dotting the northwestern Turkish coast and the Greek islands immediately opposite, a reminder of the days when the military and commercial might of Genoa dominated the North Aegean.

The **beach** here is coarse sand and – except in high summer – Çandarlı is not a bad place to get away from the crowds for a day or two. It's remarkably clean and well kept, with a welcoming atmosphere absent in some larger resort towns. The ordinary life of the town centres on the east side of the peninsula, near the bus stop. Here, the lively **market square** (market day is Friday) is surrounded by simple soup-and-*pide* kitchens, beer halls and old Greek houses. There's a **PTT** and a **bank** with an ATM. Hourly **buses** run here from Dıkılı and in summer there's an hourly service between Çandarlı and İzmir (less frequent out of season).

The best budget **accommodation** option – offering basic rooms with shared bathroom – is *Gül Pansiyon* (☎0232/673 3347; ●), close to the beach, a ten-minute walk through the village and past the castle. The *Senger* (☎0232/673 3117; ●), on the seafront past the castle, above the eponymous restaurant, has many repeat customers, particularly Germans, who enjoy its cosily furnished rooms (some with air conditioning and sea views) and buffet breakfast. Or there's the quiet *Samyeli* on the seafront (☎0232/673 3428, ℱ673 3461; ●), also with en-suite rooms, some with air conditioning.

The cheapest places to eat are in town, while most of Çandarlı's fancier **restaurants**, **cafés** and **bars** line the shore road, where the *Kalender Restaurant* serves reasonably priced seafood, with no dish more than 10YTL, and most a lot less. *Pitaneon* is a noisy bar right on the beach, catering mainly for young Turkish weekenders.

Outdoor adventure
travel

From the mighty Toros, running for hundreds of miles parallel to the Mediterranean Sea, through isolated Anatolian volcanic peaks soaring up to 5000m, to the remote alpine Kaçkar behind the Black Sea coast, Turkey is a land of mountains. From charming day walks on the Lycian coast to expeditions up legendary Mount Ararat, there's plenty for walkers and trekkers (not to mention skiers, mountaineers and rock-climbers) to get stuck into.

Water lovers, on the other hand, will be pleased to know that the country has some 5000 miles of coastline, much of it the sparkling azure waters of the Aegean and Mediterranean seas, and water sports are a booming industry. Add plunging mountain rivers, several developed for thrilling white-water rafting, the chance to soar over Cappadocia's unique landscape in a hot-air balloon, or take off from a mountaintop with a paraglider, and you quickly realise that Turkey is a paradise for lovers of outdoor adventure.

Kaçkar mountain scene

Hit the heights

Until recently, only the adventurous few would have ventured to Turkey to walk and trek in its spectacular **mountain ranges**. Fortunately attitudes are changing, and quickly. Mount Ararat, at 5135m the country's highest peak and alleged resting place of Noah's Ark, is ascended regularly every year (see p.923), while many more visit the temperate Black Sea region to trek in the magnificent Kaçkar range (see p.853), with peaks soaring to almost 4000m, glaciers, stunning arrays of alpine flowers and a farming culture little changed for centuries. The compact Aladağlar range (see p.656), with its dramatic limestone peaks, waterfalls and alpine lakes, draws trekkers and mountaineers in equal measure.

Far more accessible are two magnificent **long-distance walking routes** in southwest Mediterranean Turkey, both around some 500km long. The **Lycian Way** (see p.458) winds through pine-forested mountains, dips to secluded coves and charming fishing villages and leads the lucky walker to a succession of wonderfully situated ancient sites. The **St Paul Trail** (see p.608) follows the footsteps of the apostle from the Mediterranean to the Anatolian Plateau, over the lofty Toros mountains and past stunning Lake Eğirdir. Both trails are waymarked using red and white flashes, and give walkers a unique insight into rural Turkish life.

White-water rafting

Canyoning

OK, it's not a water sport in the traditional sense, but you wear a wet suit and invariably get drenched. Abseil down cascading falls, jump into bubbling pools, and generally mess around in the shady depths of a spectacular canyon such as Saklıkent (see p.472), Kaputaş (see p.487) or Kıbrıs in the Lycian mountains (see p.97). Ideal for the congenitally active in the hot summer months, it is best combined with a seaside-based holiday in a resort like Kaş, where you can find reliable companies offering organized one-day (or more) expeditions.

Rock-climbing is in its infancy in Turkey, but several areas are being developed. The best of these is Geyikbayırı, just west of Antalya (see p.96), where a 1.5-kilometre limestone cliff has been bolted to provide (hard) sport-climbing routes. Longer, big-wall routes can be found in the Aladağlar (see p.656).

The wet stuff

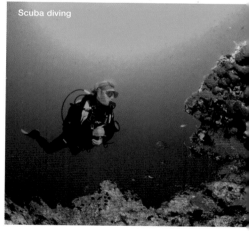

Scuba diving

The sunny weather and clear, warm waters of the southwest Mediterranean make for ideal **scuba-diving**, with reefs alive with barracuda, grouper, damselfish and multi-coloured wrasse, underwater caves and the wreckage of sunken ships to explore. The area is well suited to novice divers, with several reliable companies offering certificated diving courses, and there's plenty to keep the experienced diver happy. Best bases are the charming former Greek fishing villages of **Kaş** and **Kalkan** (see p.492 & p.486), though experienced divers with a love of history may prefer exploring the wrecks of World War I ships off Gallipoli in the north Aegean. **Sea-kayaking** is proving immensely popular, and is an especially great way to explore the indented coastline, islets and shallow, clear waters east of Kaş.

For thrills and spills, the freshwater sport of **white-water rafting** has taken off big-style in southwest Turkey. The **Köprülü** river just east of Antalya, and the **Dalaman** river near Fethiye (see p.538 & p.465), both plunge down from the Toros mountains, offering novice rafters an ideal introduction to the sport (with a trout lunch thrown in). The **Çoruh**, in the northeast of the country (see p.825), is acknowledged to be one of the best rafting rivers in the world – grade five rapids and multi-day programmes through remote country make this a really adventurous trip.

The white stuff

If you're a fan of the white stuff, try one of Turkey's small but rapidly developing **ski resorts**. The best conditions and longest season (Oct–May) are to be found at **Palandöken** (see p.799) close to Erzerum, while the extinct volcanic cone of nearby **Mount Erciyes** (3916m) offers good skiing from December through April (see p.666). Overlooking the Sea of Marmara, **Uludağ** (see p.266) is Turkey's longest-established resort, and very popular with people from İstanbul, as is newer **Kartalkaya** (see p.94). More attractive to those enjoying some winter sun on the southwest Mediterranean coast are the small resorts of **Saklıkent** (see p.472) and, with more reliable snow, **Davraz** (see p.605). Rent a car and head off from the beach into the mountains for an energetic day on the piste.

Paraglider over Ölüdeniz beach

Taking off

Cappadocia in central Anatolia is one the world's most unique landscapes, with its bizarrely sculpted rock pinnacles known locally as "fairy chimneys", plunging valleys and rock-cut churches. Arguably the best way to see this geological wonder is from the air, drifting along in an expertly piloted **hot-air balloon** (see p.634). A dramatic dawn lift-off and a champagne breakfast on touchdown make this the trip of a lifetime – but make sure you've got your credit card handy. If you're after more of an adrenaline rush, try leaping from the mountains behind the bustling resorts of Kaş or Ölüdeniz hanging from a **paraglider** (don't worry, unless you are an expert you'll be in tandem with a professional pilot). Clear air, fabulous views, soaring thermals and dramatic landings either on Ölüdeniz beach or Kaş harbour make this a great experience.

Foça and around

FOÇA – 65km south of Çandarlı – is the modern successor (and linguistically a corruption) of ancient **Phocaea**, founded around 1000 BC by Ionian colonists; it was thus later reckoned a member of the Ionian confederation, despite lying squarely in Aeolian territory. The Phocaeans became renowned seafarers whose enormous, state-of-the-art boats plied the principal trade routes of the Mediterranean throughout the fifth century BC, establishing among other places the city of Massilia, now Marseilles. Powered by fifty oarsmen, the galleys were capable of carrying five hundred passengers or the equivalent in precious metals. On the basis of excavations carried out in 1913, it is claimed that the prodigious Phocaeans also introduced writing into southern France and were responsible for olive cultivation in the Mediterranean basin. In later times, the Byzantines gave Phocaea as a placatory present to the Genoese, who restored its castle and managed to retain the city during the fourteenth century by paying tribute to the Saruhan emirs and later the Ottomans.

The original name *Phocaea* is derived from the ancient Greek word for "seal", an animal that has long lived in the area and whose barking may have given rise to the myth of the sirens luring sailors onto the rocks that features in Homer's *Odyssey*. Today, however, you'll be lucky to see one, as the local colony of **monk seals** now numbers less than a hundred: the colony is protected by Turkey's council of ministers and the target of a World Wildlife Fund conservation project. Frankly you'd have to *be* a seal to really enjoy the sea here, which owing to strong currents and a sharp drop-off is notoriously chilly most of the year. The other fortuitous restraint on development has been the pervasive military presence: Foça is an important naval base, and the land to the north is out of bounds.

None of this has prevented Foça from becoming a favourite summer retreat for İzmir and Manisa people, who own or rent holiday apartments here. They have been joined by a few European tour operators, but the town has accommodated the tourist swell fairly graciously and is still a pleasantly relaxed little place. A boat trip out to the local islets makes a good day-trip, or you can rent transport and head out into the scenic countryside north and east of town.

The Town

Today, sadly, little remains intact of **ancient Phocaea**. Nine kilometres before the modern town, just north of the main road, is the **Taş Kule**, an unusual-looking tomb believed to date from the fourth century BC, squatting beside an Ottoman bridge and a modern cemetery, while a small **ancient theatre** dating from 340 BC marks the east entry to Foça. Some mosaic pavements from a Roman villa, including an almost perfectly preserved portrayal of four Bacchus heads and birds, have been unearthed in what was to be a car park off 193 Sokak near a housing development called the Barişkent Evler. Local legend also maintains that a large black stone is hidden somewhere beneath the streets and those who walk unwittingly over it are destined someday to return to Foça to live.

The oldest structure in Foça itself is the **Genoese fortress** (not open to the public), which has recently been rather crudely restored, with stage-set towers added as a touristic backdrop. More authentic are some wonderful old Greek fishermen's cottages and a few more opulent Ottoman mansions lining the cobbled backstreets. There are also two interesting mosques: the small, unheralded but beautiful, fifteenth-century **Fatih Camii**, and another at the very summit of the castle enclosure, sporting a distinctly lighthouse-like minaret. In the same street as the Fatih Camii are two **hamams**, one of which is 150 years old and has been converted into a bicycle repair shop, while the other continues to operate daily from 8am to midnight.

The castle headland lends Foça an interesting layout, splitting the bay into two smaller harbours: the northerly, more picturesque **Küçükdeniz** (meaning small sea), where most of the action is; and the southern, rather bleak **Büyükdeniz** (big sea), which looks as if it could be anywhere in Turkey, and whose pair of hotel-restaurants is not really recommended, so go only for a view of the huge fishing fleet and the *kale* (castle) on its promontory. Neither bay has a decent beach, with the shore apt to be weedy, although that doesn't stop holiday-makers from setting up their sun loungers on the five metres of slightly grubby shingle exposed at low tide.

Boat trips (May–Sept; around 15YTL) run out from the Küçükdeniz to some of the small islets that dot the coastline to the north of Foça, within an area designated for Special Environmental Protection. Most of the ten boats follow similar itineraries, leaving by 11am returning by 6pm, with three stops for swimming (and lunch) throughout the day.

Practicalities

The town lies 26km west of the main Çanakkale–İzmir road. To reach it, take any İzmir-bound **bus** and ask to be let off at the turning for Foça. From here, a regular **dolmuş** should take you into town. There are also half-hourly direct buses from İzmir itself.

The central square, located at the southern end of the headland between the two bays, is where you'll find the very helpful **tourist office** (May–Sept Mon–Fri 8.30am–6.30pm, Sat & Sun 10am–1pm & 5–8pm; Oct–April Mon–Fri 8.30am–5.30pm; ☎0232/812 1222), opposite a taxi rank. The square also has two **banks** with ATMs. Foça's **otogar** is just south of the square. A pedestrianized road, lined with shops and cafés leads north from the square – you'll find the **PTT** about halfway down on the right – to the *Belediye* (town hall), behind which is a narrow road with two **Internet** cafés, *Kaptan Net* and *Internet Anatolia*. For **car rental**, try *Foça Rent A Car*, Fevzi Paşa Mah 191/7 (☎0232/812 2496), located on the same road.

Accommodation

If you want to stay affordably by the sea, head straight through the town, and north along the long esplanade to where many of the best **pansiyons and hotels** are located. The local **campsites** all lie out of town, on the road to Yenifoça (see below).

Ensar Pansiyon 161 Sok 15 (☎0232/812 1401, ℻812 6159). 200m back from the coast, this nonetheless has sea views from its terrace, with decent-sized rooms and a kitchen for guests. ②

Foçantique Hotel On the long esplanade ☎0232/812 4313, ⊛www.focantiquehotel .com. The town's top choice occupies a lovingly restored nineteenth-century building. Its ten rooms are all furnished with an assortment of antique knick-knacks, rugs and curios, and all sport sumptuous bathrooms (the best of which is a converted hamam). At the front is a modern extension with a stylish breakfast room and roof terrace. ⑥

Fokai At the northern end of the long esplanade ☎0232/812 1765. Quiet and friendly with rooms overlooking the water; highly recommended. ③

Huzur At northern end of the long esplanade ☎0232/812 1203, ℻812 6647. Next door to the *Fokai*, this has nicely furnished rooms and a water-side terrace, though breakfast is not included. ②

Iyigun Pansiyon On the long esplanade ☎0232/812 1182. Decent seafront choice; the rooms have huge windows with good sea views, although the decor could do with updating. ②

Iyon Pansiyon Ismet Paşa Mah 198/8 ☎0232/812 1415, ℮info@iyonpansiyon.com. A very welcoming choice with basic, clean rooms, all with TV and shower, in a restored Greek house, a block back from the sea. There's a kitchen for guests and the friendly owner offers windsurfing lessons for €30 a day. ②

Eating and drinking

Küçükdeniz harbour is lined with fish **restaurants,** mostly along the small esplanade and mostly offering pretty similar fare. Prices for kebabs and *mezes* are marked on boards outside, with main dishes ranging between 7–10YTL, though fish prices vary daily and can be expensive, so check before ordering.

The *Celep* and *Kordon*, on the small square at the southern end of the long esplanade, both offer a good range of fish dishes, including *çipura* (gilt-headed bream, a regional speciality) and lobster. Just south of here, among the trees, the *Sedef* offers the best value in town: try the *kiremit kebap* (lamb cooked on a tile); while *Balik*, on the small esplanade, offers a decent selection of kebabs. Next to the *Kordon*, *Café Neco* is a popular evening hangout for younger residents and also does a good breakfast. The *Nazmi Usta* **ice-cream parlour,** on the long esplanade, serves forty different flavours of home-made ice cream, including mastic gum, and is a firm local favourite.

Around the coast to Yenifoça

The scenic countryside around Foça is ideal for touring by rented car or bike, though any illusions of completely escaping development as the shore heads north are difficult to maintain. Nonetheless, there are some excellent **beaches,** often difficult to access, and a number of basic **campsites** between five and fifteen kilometres from town – namely, *Ferhat, Remzi Nin Yari, Di-Ba* and *Acar Kamping*, in that order as you leave Foça. All have good beaches, with the best at *Acar Kamping*. Further on *Mambo Beach* (no phone; ❷), 2km before Yenifoça, has a bar, campsite, restaurant and *pansiyon*, as well as a decent beach – a far better place to stay than Yenifoça itself.

YENİFOÇA, 23km by road from Foça, maintains a core of old Greek houses, but here the beach is grubby, rocky and suffers from full northern exposure. All in all, the town is merely the turnaround point for heading back to Foça via the **inland road**, past crumbling hamlets abandoned since 1923.

KOZBEYLİ, around 10km before Foça, a small cluster of old Greek village houses centred on a mosque, makes for an evocative stopover. Many of the dilapidated houses and cobbled lanes are now being restored and a few antique shops have sprung up, in anticipation of visitors yet to arrive.

Manisa

The site of the ancient town of Magnesia ad Sipylus, **MANISA** lies about 40km east of Menemen (on the main Çanakkale–İzmir highway) and is easily reached from there, or from İzmir itself, by way of pleasant mountain roads. Over ninety percent of the historic centre was destroyed by the Greek army during its 1922 retreat, but despite this Manisa remains an interesting place with a few fine Selçuk and Ottoman monuments, reminiscent of Bursa as it spills out from the foot of the Manisa Dağı mountain range. This may not seem enough to pull you so far off the main route to the attractions of the central Aegean, but the nearby ruins of Sardis tip the balance in favour of a detour. An overnight stop suggests itself – arriving in Manisa at noon, visiting Sardis in the afternoon and spending the following morning looking around Manisa before moving on. In practice, however, there are limited sleeping and eating options in Manisa and Sardis-bound visitors may prefer to carry on to Salihli, beyond the ancient site.

According to Homer, Manisa was founded after the Trojan War by warriors from the area. Alexander the Great passed through during his campaign, while in 190 BC

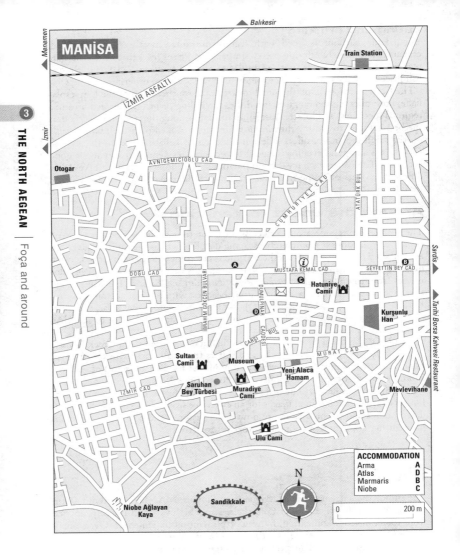

there was a huge battle here between the Romans and the Syrians, under King Antioch III. The day was decided in favour of the Romans by the cavalry of the king of
Pergamon, who was given control over the city as a reward. The town finally came
under direct Roman rule – and entered a period of great prosperity – after the death
of Attalus III of Pergamon. For a short time during the thirteenth century Manisa
was capital of the Byzantine empire, after the sacking of Constantinople by the
Fourth Crusade. In 1313 the city fell into the hands of the Selçuk chieftain Saruhan
Bey; from this century date the earliest of Manisa's surviving monuments. Later, the
Ottomans sent heirs to the throne here to serve an apprenticeship as local governors,
in order to ready them for the rigours of İstanbul palace life.

The Town

Manisa still has a lot to recommend it and the relatively modern town centre, with its extensive parklands, strikes visitors as clean, orderly and prosperous. The principal central attractions in Manisa are three mosques, which you could easily tour in half a day, while a local museum, the remains of the castle and a few other minor sights help to pass any remaining time.

Sultan Camii and around

At the south end of Ören Caddesi, the extension of Ibrahim Gökçen Bulvarı, the **Sultan Camii** was built in 1522 for Ayşe Hafize, the mother of Süleyman the Magnificent, who lived here with her son while he was serving as governor. This rectangular mosque is much wider than it is deep, its single central dome flanked by two pairs of satellite domes. Late Ottoman Baroque paint decoration and a tiny wood-railed pulpit on the west enliven the porch – actually a *son cemaat yeri* (latecomers' praying place). The mosque was once the focus of a large *külliye* (mosque complex) that included a *medrese*, mental hospital and even an official clock-setting shop.

Every year on the third or fourth Sunday of April, the *Mesir Şenlikleri* **Power-Gum Festival** – now well into its fifth century – takes place around the Sultan Camii, to commemorate the occasion when a local doctor called Merkez Efendi concocted a special resin to cure Ayşe Hafize of an unspecified ailment. The gum, or *mesir macunu*, concocted from 41 herbs, is scattered from the minaret by the muezzin to the waiting crowd, who believe that consuming the paste will protect them from pain (especially snake and insect bites) until the next festival. It is also reputed to have an aphrodisiac effect.

Across from the Sultan Camii stands the **Saruhan Bey Türbesi**, the tomb of Saruhan Bey, who took Manisa in 1313, ending Byzantine sovereignty. His army is said to have attacked Sandıkkale, the city's castle, driving a flock of goats with candles on their horns before them to give the impression that a huge army was attacking. The defenders panicked and the castle fell – an event commemorated here by a festival each November 13.

The Muradiye complex

Barely 100m further east along the same side of Murat Caddesi you'll find the **Muradiye Camii**, built for Murat III in 1583–85 while he was governor here. The interior, with its stained-glass windows and relatively restrained decoration – despite the use of 12kg of gold – is impressive: the carved wooden *mimber*, or pulpit, and the sultan's loge are particularly fine, as are the İznik tiles around the *mihrab* and the windows. Unusually, a large women's gallery runs the full length of the cross-stroke of the reverse-T ground-plan, a design more typical of dervish *zaviyes* (hostels), and indeed the mosque, like the Sultan Camii, was originally part of a *külliye*.

Next door to the Muradiye Camii, housed in the former *imaret* (soup kitchen), is Manisa's **museum** (Tues–Sun 9am–5pm; 2YTL), which holds an interesting collection of archeological and ethnological exhibits, including items retrieved from Sardis.

Further along the street, the still-used **Yeni Alaca Hamam** is one of the oldest bath-houses in town. On Thursdays the street itself, Murat Caddesi, is the site of the town's large **market**, where you'll find just about any kind of vegetable or fruit, as well as cheap household items and clothing.

The Ulu Cami and peripheral sites

Manisa's oldest surviving mosque, the **Ulu Cami**, sits on a natural terrace amid a panoramic park 250m above the museum. Built on the site of a Byzantine church in 1366 by Işak Çelebi, the grandson of Saruhan Bey, it is basically a square walled compound divided into two rectangles, with a *medrese* – still functioning as a children's Koran school – tacked onto the west side. Entering the open-roofed courtyard via the ornate portal, you confront the glory of the place, a forest of varied **antique columns**, some "double" and others carrying Byzantine capitals, many presumably recycled from the church that formerly stood on the site. There are more columns in the interior, supporting a very large central dome by means of pointed arches. Back outside, the **minaret** is striped with patterns of green- and grape-coloured İznik bricks. The view out north over the plain is truly spectacular and that alone is well worth the steep climb. For an even more spectacular panoramic view continue further uphill to the fairly unimpressive remains of Manisa's Byzantine citadel, **Sandıkkale**, parts of which date to the eighth and thirteenth centuries.

Follow the maze of streets leading west from here to the foot of Mount Sipylus (Sipil Daı) and you'll eventually come to **Niobe Aılayan Kaya**, the so-called "Weeping Rock of Niobe", in the form of a woman's head from which tears can supposedly be seen issuing every Friday. According to legend, Niobe was the daughter of Tantalus and had seven daughters and six sons. She taunted the nymph Leto – who had only borne the divine twins Apollo and Artemis – for her relative infertility until the latter became jealous and ordered her own offspring to kill Niobe's. Niobe wept for a long time over the bodies of her children until Zeus put an end to her suffering by turning her to rock.

Heading back downhill into town, you could take a detour to the **Mevlevihane** – a former *tekke* or gathering place of the Konya-based whirling-dervish order, the only one in the region – housed in a solid-stone building on the southeastern edge of town.

Practicalities

Upon arrival, walk south away from the **otogar** toward the mountains for about ten minutes until you come to **Doıu Caddesi** – the town's main commercial street, where most of the banks and larger shops are located. The **train station**, with regular daily services from İzmir, lies fifteen minutes north of here, along Atatürk Bulvarı.

Manisa's **tourist office** is on the sixth floor at Mustafa Kemal Cad 606 (Mon–Fri 8am–noon & 1–5pm; ☏0236/231 2541). They should be able to give you a town plan, and may even have someone on hand who can speak English.

On the **accommodation** front, Manisa leaves much to be desired and most of what exists fills with students between mid-September and June. However, the well-signposted *Marmaris Otel*, Anafartalar Mah 3, Sok 10 (☏0236/239 5835, ⓕ239 4686; ❷), is surprisingly good, with presentable modern rooms with TV, but no breakfast. The *Arma* on Doıu Caddesi (☏0236/231 1980, ⓕ232 4501; ❸) in the heart of town is reasonable value, but the rooms are in need of a revamp. The *Otel Niobe* (☏0236/231 3745, ⓕ238 9785; ❷), opposite the *Belediye* building on Sınema Park Caddesi, is cheaper, but rooms catch the full sun in summer. Finally, the *Atlas* at Dumulpınar Cad 22 (☏0236/231 1197; ❷) caters for students and impecunious backpackers alike, with bare, minimally furnished en-suite rooms.

Manisa isn't going to win any prizes in the gourmet stakes either, with little other than the usual range of **kebab and pide salons** and *lokanta*s. However, *Tarihi Borsa Kahvesi*, Borsa Cad 29, comes highly recommended for quality steamtray food and *mezes*. The area around the tourist office features a number of Western-style burger and pizza joints, where pizza and salad should set you back no more than 4YTL. If you're lucky you might find a restaurant offering the traditional autumn dish of stewed quince in *pekmez* (grape molasses), the latter courtesy of the province's vineyards.

Sardis

The ancient site of **Sardis** (Sart in Turkish) lies about 65km east of Manisa and is easily reached from there or from İzmir. It's another of those places in Turkey that is so old that it's difficult to separate history from myth. The area was probably inhabited as far back as 1200 BC and was later settled by the Lydians, descended from native Anatolians and Greek invaders. Sardis grew to be incredibly wealthy thanks to the gold that was washed down from the nearby mountains and caught in sheepskins by the locals. According to legend, the source of these riches was the Phrygian king **Midas**, whose touch turned everything to gold. Unable to eat, his curse was lifted when the gods had him wash his hands in the River Pactolus, which flowed down to Sardis from the south. Wherever the gold came from, the Lydians were happy enough and celebrated their wealth by inventing coinage.

The first coins were issued under the city's most celebrated king, **Croesus**, during whose rule (563–546 BC) the kingdom's prosperity grew, attracting the attention of the Persians under Cyrus the Great. Worried about this threat, Croesus consulted the Delphic oracle as to whether or not he should attack first. The oracle replied that if he did he would destroy a great empire. Croesus went to war and was defeated, and after a two-week siege Sardis fell and Croesus was supposedly burned alive by the victors.

As a Persian city, Sardis was sacked during the Ionian revolt of 499 BC. It made a comeback under Alexander the Great and the Macedonians, but was destroyed by an earthquake in 17 AD. The Romans rebuilt it, having taken it at the same time as Manisa, and the town was the site of one of the Seven Churches of Asia addressed by St John in the Book of Revelation. This didn't save Byzantine Sardis from conquest by Saruhan and destruction at the hands of Tamerlane in 1401, after which the city never really recovered. It only came to light again early this century, when American archeologists began excavating mostly Roman and Byzantine remains.

The road to Sardis

If you're travelling by dolmuş, and fancy a stop on the way, you can visit a 3300-year-old relief, known as the **Taş Suret**, carved into the rock of **Mount Sipylus**, above the road about 7km east of Manisa. It's generally reckoned to be a Hittite version of Cybele, the mother goddess. Ask to be let out at the Akpınar pool and climb a few hundred metres up into the cliffs above the road. The image, none too distinct, is tucked into a five-metre-high niche and was probably placed here in the hope of making the valley of the Gediz River below more fertile.

Mount Sipylus, incidentally, is associated with the ancient king **Tantalus**, whose daughter Niobe was turned into the rock in Manisa. According to legend, Tantalus also had two sons, Pelops and Broteas, the latter of whom supposedly carved this image of Cybele on the mountainside. Pelops ended up being served up in a dish Tantalus prepared for the gods, and narrowly escaped with only his shoulder being eaten. He was later restored to life with a new ivory shoulder and Tantalus was punished by being sent to Hades, where water and food were kept eternally just out of his reach – hence the verb "to tantalize".

The onward journey takes you through an uneventful agricultural landscape. The fertile **Gediz plain**, stretching from Manisa until well past Alaşehir, is totally given over to the cultivation of grapes, particularly sultanas, for which the region is the number-one world producer. Things pick up once the **Boz Daıları** mountain range rears up to the south. When you see the ruins of ancient Sardis, get off at **Sartmustafa**, a small, traditional village centred on a cluster of teahouses, where local farmers like to put their feet up while their wives and daughters work the vineyards.

The sites

There are two main clusters of ruins, both easily reached on foot from the main road. The **first site** primarily made up of the gymnasium and synagogue (daily 8am–5pm; 2YTL), lies just north of the road on the eastern edge of the village and includes the **Marble Way**, a Byzantine shopping street complete with latrines, whose holes and drainage channels are still visible. The various shops are labelled and include a restaurant, an office and a hardware shop. Foundations and low walls with discernible doorways are all that remain, although in some places Greek inscriptions and engraved basins with carved crosses can still be seen.

A left turn leads into the restored **synagogue**, whose walls are covered with impressive mosaics – though these are copies, the originals being housed in the Manisa Museum; the extensive floor mosaics are, however, original. The intact walls and pillars are covered with ornate patterned tiles and explanatory text includes a plaque honouring the donors, mostly North American Jews, for the renovation work.

Almost right next door to the synagogue is the third-century AD **gymnasium and bath complex**, the most prominent building in the city, covering five and a half acres. Its **Marble Court**, the entry from the palaestra to the baths, has been spectacularly restored to its original state when first built in 211 AD. The walls behind the columns would have had marble revetments and the podia would have supported statues, forming a multi-storeyed facade so visually splendid as to suggest that the baths must have been associated with observance of the imperial cult. Behind the court are the remains of a swimming pool and rest area.

From the Sartmustafa village teahouses, a paved track – very poorly marked on the far side of the highway, west of the synagogue – leads 1200m south from the main road to the other main site, the **Temple of Artemis** (daily 8am–5pm; 2YTL). The temple, once among the four largest in Asia Minor, was built by Croesus, destroyed by Greek raiders during the Ionian revolt and later rebuilt by Alexander the Great. Today a baker's dozen of massive Ionic columns, dating from both Hellenistic and Roman times, remain standing, though only two are completely intact. Enough of the foundations are visible to make clear just how large the building, constructed to rival the temples of Ephesus, Samos and Didyma, used to be. In the southeastern corner of the site are the remains of a small brick Byzantine church. Small-scale excavations are continuing beneath a huddle of shelters on a small eastern ridge. More than anything, however, it's the beauty of the setting, enclosed by wooded and vined hills and accented by weird Cappadocia-like pinnacles, that leaves a lasting impression.

Practicalities

Sardis is easily reached by taking the Salihli dolmuş **from Manisa** – or the Salihli bus **from İzmir**. The site can also be reached by **train**: two morning services run from İzmir to Manisa, from where, in turn, there are three services (morning, lunchtime and evening) to Salihli (see below). Taking the train is a more relaxed, though slower, way of doing the trip – trains also return to Manisa a bit later (7.15pm) than the dolmuşes. The dolmuş will drop you on the main highway, at the turn-off for Sartmustafa. The train station is 1km to the north, near the tiny hamlet of Sartmahmut.

As **accommodation** in Manisa is limited, you may prefer to stay instead in **SALIHLI**, a market town 8km beyond Sardis on the İzmir–Afyon road. There's nothing of historical interest here, but it's closer to the ruins. To get out to the site from Salihli, take any of the regular Manisa-bound dolmuşes, which will drop you at the highway turn-off. Salihli's best budget accommodation is at the *Hotel Yener*, Dede Çelak Sok 7 (T0236/712 5003, F714 1562; ❶), just south of the *otogar*, whose front rooms have showers but may suffer a little from traffic noise, especially on market day (Wednesday). Behind the *Yener* is the more upmarket *Berrak*, at Belediye Cad 59 (T0236/713 1452, F713 1457; ❸), while the *Akgül*, clearly visible from the marketplace next to the *otogar* (T0236/713 3737, Wwww .otelakgul.com; ❷), has English-speaking management, rooms with TV and an open-buffet breakfast included. Both places are extremely comfortable.

Travel details

Trains

Balıkesir to: Bandırma (2 daily; 2hr); Kütahya (4 daily; 5hr).
Manisa to: Afyon (1 daily; 10hr); Alaşehir (1 daily 4hr); Ankara (2 daily; 12hr); Balıkesir (3 daily; 3hr); İzmir (5 daily; 1hr 30min); Salihli (3 daily; 1hr 30min); Sart/Sardis (2 daily; 1hr 30min).

Buses and dolmuşes

Alaşehir to: Denizli (4 daily; 1hr 45min); İzmir (hourly; 2hr); Salihli (hourly; 2hr).
Ayvalık to: Balıkesir (hourly; 2hr); Bergama via Dıklı (11 daily; 1hr); Bursa (12 daily; 5hr); Çanakkale (hourly; 3hr 30min); İstanbul (10 daily; 8hr); İzmir (every 30min; 2hr 30min).
Bergama to: Afyon (1 daily; 7hr); Ankara (1 daily; 11hr); Ayvalık (6 daily; 1hr); İstanbul (2 daily; 10hr); İzmir (every 30min; 1hr 45min); Soma (hourly; 1hr).
Çanakkale to: Ayvacık (hourly; 1hr 30min); Ayvalık (hourly; 3hr 30min); Bursa (hourly; 4hr); Ezine (hourly; 1hr); İstanbul (hourly via Thrace; 5hr); İzmir (hourly; 5hr); Lapseki (every 30min; 45min); Troy (every 20min; 30min); Yükyeri İskelesi (3 daily,

timed to meet the Bozcaada ferry; 1hr).
Foça to: Çanakkale (hourly; 5hr); İzmir (hourly; 1hr 30min).
Manisa to: Alaşehir (2 daily; 2hr); İzmir (every 10min; 1hr); Salihli via Sart/Sardis (every 30min; 1hr 30min).

Ferries

Ayvalık to: Alibey (June–Sept, every 30min; 30min); Lésvos, Greece (May–Sept daily, Oct–Apr weekly; 2hr).
Çanakkale to: Eceabat (hourly, on the hour, 7am–3am & 5am; 20min); Gökçeada (June–Sept 1 daily, Oct–May 1 weekly; 3hr); Kilitbahir (every 30min; 10min).
Kabatepe to: Gökçeada (July & Aug daily, Sept–June 2 weekly; 1hr 30min).
Ören to: Akçay (numerous small boats daily in season; 30min).
Yükyeri İskelesi to: Bozcaada (June–Sept 3 daily at 10am, 2pm & 6pm, Oct–May 2 daily; 1hr 30min).

The central and southern Aegean

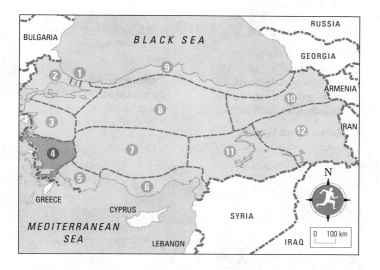

CHAPTER 4 # Highlights

✳ **Altınkum, Çeşme**
Altınkum's remote, sunbaked coves conceal arguably some of the best beaches on the Aegean coast. See p.343

✳ **Birgi** Amble through the evocative streets of a sleepy mountain-village. See p.348

✳ **Selçuk** This small town is an increasingly popular base from which to explore the famous surrounding historical sights, including Ephesus. See p.358

✳ **Priene** Scramble over the ruins of one of the country's best-preserved Hellenistic towns and gaze out over the Meander basin. See p.370

✳ **Heracleia ad Latmos** Former monastic village on Lake Bafa, which has had a compelling hold on the imaginations of modern travellers and the Romantic poets alike. See p.380

✳ **Bodrum** Spend a few days sampling the nightlife at Turkey's most fashionable and sophisticated beach-resort. See p.390

✳ **Aphrodisias** Ongoing excavations at this beautifully sited Roman city are revealing a site to rival Ephesus in grandeur and importance. See p.425

✳ **Pamukkale** Visit the geological oddity that has found its way onto every Turkish tourism poster. See p.429

△ Pamukkale

The central and southern Aegean

T he Turkish **central and southern Aegean coast** and its hinterland have seen foreign tourism longer than any other part of the country. The territory between modern İzmir and Marmaris corresponds to the bulk of ancient **Ionia**, and just about all of old **Caria**, and contains a concentration of Classical Greek, Hellenistic and Roman antiquities unrivalled in Turkey. **Ephesus** is usually first on everyone's list of dutiful pilgrimages, but the understated charms of exquisitely positioned sites such as **Priene**, **Labranda** and **Alanda** have at least as much appeal, if not more.

The landscape can be compelling, most memorably at the eerie lake of **Bafa Gölü**, towering **Samsun Dağı** and the oasis-speckled **Bodrum peninsula**. Towns, however – not least sprawling, polluted **İzmir** – tend to be functional places, best hurried through en route to more appealing destinations. But there are some pleasant surprises inland, particularly **Muğla**, **Birgi** and **Şirince**, the first two unselfconscious Ottoman museum-towns, the last a well-preserved former Greek village still just the right side of tweeness.

The biggest disappointment, however, may be the **coast** itself. Despite the tourist-brochure hype, most beaches are average at best, and west-facing shores are mercilessly exposed to the afternoon winds and waves. Worse still, of the various resort towns on the so-called "Turkish Riviera", only **Bodrum** and **Çeşme** retain a small measure of intrinsic charm. Turkey has embraced *costa*-style tourism with a vengeance and even the shortest and most mediocre sandy stretch is dwarfed by serried ranks of holiday apartments and hastily thrown-up hotels. Much of the development is aimed at the rapidly growing domestic middle-class, since in most locales Turkish law stipulates that holiday properties can only be leased long-term, not sold outright, to foreigners. Belatedly, many local authorities have imposed height limits, so that most new projects are only two (at most three) storeys high.

It takes determination, a good map and, in some places, your own vehicle to get the best out of this coast. **Public transport** is excellent and very cost effective along well-travelled routes, but connections to less obvious places can be frustratingly difficult. The area is well served by **international flights** to İzmir and, in particular, Bodrum, which is now the main gateway to the Aegean resorts. Six of the eight international **ferry/hydrofoil links** with neighbouring Greek islands are found here too, making a visit to or from Greece feasible. The Turkish authorities rarely cause problems for holders of charter tickets who wish to do this.

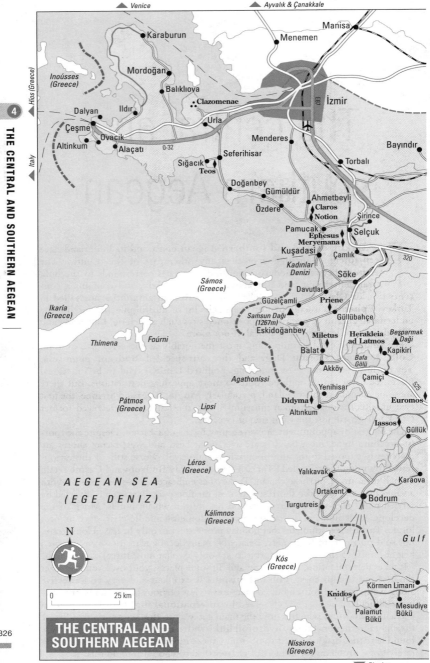

▲ Venice
▲ Ayvalık & Çanakkale

Manisa
Menemen
Karaburun

İzmir

Mordoğan

Balıklıova

Clazomenae

Dalyan   İldır
Çeşme   Urla
Ovacık
Altınkum   Alaçatı   0-32

Menderes

Bayındır

Seferihisar   Torbalı

Sığacık
Teos

Doğanbey

Gümüldür   Ahmetbeyli
Claros
Özdere   Notion   Sirince

Pamucak   Selçuk
Ephesus
Meryemana
Kuşadası   Çamlık

Kadınlar
Denizi
Söke

Davutlar

Sámos
(Greece)
Güzelçamli   Priene
Samsun Dağı   Güllübahçe
(1267m)
Eskidoğanbey   Miletus   Herakleia   Beşparmak
ad Latmos   Dağı
Balat   Kapikiri
Bafa
Gölü
Akköy   Çamiçi
Euromos
Yenihisar

Didyma
Altınkum   Iassos
Güllük

Yalıkavak   Karaova
Ortakent
Turgutreis   Bodrum

Ikaría
(Greece)

Thímena   Foúrni

Agathoníssi

Pátmos
(Greece)   Lipsí

Léros
(Greece)

AEGEAN SEA
(EGE DENIZ)

Kálimnos
(Greece)

Gulf

Knidos   Körmen Limanı
Mesudiye
Palamut   Bükü
Bükü

Kós
(Greece)

Níssiros
(Greece)

▼ Rhodes

N

0   25 km

THE CENTRAL AND
SOUTHERN AEGEAN

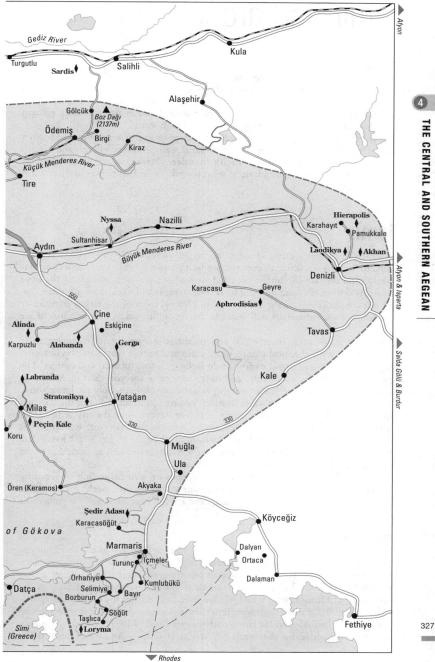

Gediz River

Turgutlu

Sardis

Salihli

Kula

Alaşehir

Gölcük

▲ *Boz Dağı (2137m)*

Ödemiş

Birgi

Kiraz

Küçük Menderes River

Tire

Nyssa

Nazilli

Hierapolis

Karahayıt

Pamukkale

Sultanhisar

Aydın

Büyük Menderes River

Laodikya

Akhan

Denizli

Karacasu

Geyre

Aphrodisias

550

Alinda

Çine

Eskiçine

Karpuzlu

Alabanda

Gerga

Tavas

Labranda

Stratonikya

Yatağan

Kale

Milas

Peçin Kale

330

330

Koru

Muğla

Ula

Ören (Keramos)

Akyaka

Şedir Adası

Karacasöğüt

Köyceğiz

of Gökova

Dalyan

Ortaca

Marmaris

Turunç

İçmeler

Dalaman

Orhaniye

Selimiye

Kumlubükü

Datça

Bozburun

Bayır

Sími (Greece)

Taşlıca

Söğüt

Loryma

Fethiye

▼ Rhodes

İzmir and around

For most travellers, **İzmir** is an unavoidable obstacle on the way to more enticing destinations. But the city is not entirely without interest and it's definitely worth having a look around: its setting and ethnological museum are unique, the seafront has been spruced up and largely pedestrianized in recent years, and the bazaar here offers some of the better shopping in the region. İzmir is also relatively affluent and laid-back, with a burgeoning café-bar and club scene.

The city might also serve as a base for day-trips or short overnight jaunts, either to nearby **Çeşme** and its peninsula – with some well-preserved villages and a beach or two – or to the valley of the **Küçük Menderes River**, where a pair of utterly untouristed old towns give a hint of what the whole of Turkey was like just a few decades ago.

İzmir

Turkey's third largest city and its second biggest port after İstanbul, **İZMİR** – the ancient Smyrna – is home to over two million people. It is blessed with a comparatively mild climate (summer aside) and an enviable position, straddling the head of a fifty-kilometre-long gulf fed by several streams and flanked by mountains on all sides. But despite a long and illustrious history, most of the city is relentlessly modern – even enthusiasts will concede that a couple of days here as a tourist are plenty.

İzmir is a booming commercial and industrial centre, home to major trade expositions, with chemical plants, paper mills and textile works on the outskirts supplanting the traditional export trade in figs, raisins, tobacco and cotton. The people are generally easy-going and have more time for you than in Ankara or İstanbul, a reflection of the prevailing relaxed atmosphere, belying İzmir's size. Yet the city is also home to street hustlers, in part a product of life in the teeming shantytowns that line the banks of the Yeşildere River east of the city centre. This is the grim flip-side of İzmir's development; even in the better-off working-class districts, cloth-weaving sweatshops clank on until late at night. Street hassles are further aggravated by the large numbers of foreign servicemen around, due to the city's role as headquarters of NATO Southeast.

Whether İzmir appeals to you or not depends on you forgetting or ignoring the negatives, at least for the duration of your visit. Certainly nothing can detract from the grandeur of the city's setting, and it's this that may well be your most enduring memory.

Some history

The possibilities of the site suggested themselves as long ago as the third millennium BC, when aboriginal **Anatolians** settled at Tepekule, a hill in the modern northern suburb of Bayraklı (excavated but only of interest to hardcore archeologists). The place has a better claim than most contending candidates as the birthplace of **Homer**, who is said to have lived here during the ninth century BC. Around 600 BC, Lydian raids sent Tepekule into a long decline; it was recovering tentatively when **Alexander the Great** appeared in 334 BC. Spurred by a timely dream corroborated by the oracle of Apollo at Claros, Alexander decreed the foundation of a new, better-fortified settlement on Mount Pagos, the flat-topped hill today adorned with the Kadifekale. His generals, Antigonus and Lysimachus, carried out Alexander's plan after his death, by which time the city bore the name – Smyrna – familiar to the West for centuries after. This and its variants appear to be a corruption of Samornia, an Amazon queen who once had her stronghold on Mount Pagos.

Under the **Romans**, who endowed it with numerous impressive buildings, the city prospered and spread north onto the plain, despite the destructive earthquakes to which the region is subject. It continued to expand with the advent of **Christianity**, spurred by the decline of Ephesus, its nearest rival. The martyrdom of local bishop St Polycarp (156 AD) occurred soon after St John the Divine's nomination of Smyrna as one of the Seven Churches of Asia Minor.

The **Arab** raids of the seventh century AD triggered several centuries of turbulence. **Selçuk** Turks held the city for two decades prior to 1097, when the **Byzantines** recaptured it. The thirteenth-century Latin tenure in Constantinople provoked another era of disruption at Smyrna, with Crusaders, Genoese, Tamerlane's Mongols and minor Turkish emirs jockeying for position. Order was re-established in 1415 by Mehmet I, who finally incorporated the town into the **Ottoman Empire**, his successors repulsing repeated Venetian efforts to retake it. Encouraged by the stability under imperial rule, and despite more disastrous earthquakes in 1688 and 1778, traders flocked to Smyrna (now also known as İzmir), whose population soared above the 100,000-level of late Roman times.

The city was predominantly Christian, mostly Greek Orthodox but with a generous sprinkling of Armenians, Levantine Latins and Sephardic Jews; Muslims rarely made up more than a quarter of the population. It was both the empire's window on the West and a major terminus of the Silk Route from the East: a cosmopolitan entrepôt in which many of the inhabitants were not even Ottoman subjects. The Ottoman ruling class habitually referred to it as *gavur İzmir* or "infidel İzmir" – a necessary evil, within the confines of which the "heathens" enjoyed one of the most cultured lifestyles in the Mediterranean.

Following the defeat of the Ottoman Empire in **World War I**, Greece was given an indefinite mandate over İzmir and its hinterland. Foolishly, a huge Greek expeditionary force pressed inland, inciting the resistance of the Turkish nationalists under Atatürk. The climactic defeat in the two-year-long struggle against Greece and her nominal French and Italian allies was the entry into Smyrna of the Turkish army on September 9, 1922. The secular republic not having yet been proclaimed, the **reconquest of the city** took on the character of a successfully concluded *jihad*, or holy Muslim war, with three days of murder and plunder. Almost seventy percent of the city burned to the ground and thousands of non-Muslims died. A quarter of a million refugees huddled at the quayside while British, American, French and Italian vessels stood idly by and refused to grant them safe passage until the third day.

These incidents are in part attested to by the look and layout of the **modern city**, built from scratch on the ashes. The central boulevards are wide and often tree-lined, the high-rises – except for the forty-storey *Hilton*, the tallest building in town – almost tasteful, but the effect seems sterile, unreal, even melancholy, an almost deliberate exercise in amnesia.

Arrival

Flights arrive at **Adnan Menderes airport**, 18km southeast of the city. From here, use either the sporadic shuttle train (1YTL; 30min) from the airport to Alsancak train station in the north of the city, or the special Havaş airport bus (regular departures 4.45am–8.30/9.30pm; 9YTL; 20–30min depending on traffic), which will deposit you – somewhat more conveniently – on Gaziosmanpaşa Bulvarı. The shuttle trains stop well before midnight, and Havaş coaches cease operating just after the last THY flight, so you may have to rely on a **taxi** (not unbearably pricey if shared between four passengers): 35YTL to downtown İzmir, 80YTL to Selçuk, 115YTL to the centre of Kuşadası.

Long-distance trains pull in at **Basmane station**, almost in the middle of the city, and virtually all of İzmir's affordable accommodation is within walking distance of here. If you're coming from the north on a morning train, and only want to transfer to a bus for Ephesus or Kuşadası, head for the cluster of bus-company offices just north of Basmane, which provide a free shuttle-bus service to the main *otogar*.

The main *otogar*, known as **büyük otogar**, is located next to a large cement works 8km northeast of the centre. If you've got much luggage, it's best to take a taxi (35YTL) into the centre. Otherwise, use one of the buses numbered #601–609 which link the *otogar* with Konak Bus Terminal, the heart of the city's transport system, and stop at Montrö Meydanı and Basmane train station en route. The #54 will also take you to Basmane and on to Konak.

Arriving from anywhere on the Çeşme peninsula, buses halt at either the main *otogar* or at a semi-derelict terminal tucked behind a Shell garage in the coastal suburb of **Üçkuyular**, 6km southwest of downtown. From there, cross the road and take any red-and-white urban bus labelled "Konak", or hail a taxi for approximately 15YTL.

For all departure information, see "Listings", p.341.

Orientation

From Basmane station and Dokuz Eylül Meydanı, two one-way streets – **Fevzipaşa Bulvarı** and **Gazi Bulvarı** respectively – shoot straight west, towards the bay, which is clearly visible from the front steps of the station. North of these streets lies the bulk of the modern city, its largely radial streets wrapped around the vast expanse of the **Kültür Parkı**. From the middle of Gazi Bulvarı, **Gaziosmanpaşa Bulvarı** aims straight for **Cumhuriyet Meydanı**, a seashore half-roundabout with most of İzmir's upmarket tourist facilities clustered around it. The nearby palm-fringed boulevards attract İzmir's cosmopolitan shoppers.

The area south of Fevzipaşa Bulvarı is home to many of the buildings that survived the 1922 fire. The backbone of this district is **Anafartalar Caddesi**, beginning just south of Basmane station and snaking its way to **Konak Meydanı**, where most of the museums and cultural attractions are located. The seashore boulevards, Birinci Kordon (Atatürk Caddesi) and İkinci Kordon (Cumhuriyet Bulvarı), end at Konak Meydanı, too, though three continuation roads – **Mithatpaşa Caddesi**, **Mustafa Kemal Yolu** and **İnönü Caddesi** – follow the gulf to the Üçkuyular bus terminal.

İzmir's core – particularly around Konak – is relatively compact and most points of interest lie close together. Many streets have both a name and a number (where possible we've listed both), but there's no guarantee you'll find either displayed.

Information

There's a **tourist office** in the airport arrivals hall (daily: Nov–March 8am–5pm; April–Oct 8.30am–8.30pm; ☎0232/274 2214), and a **central bureau** at 1344 Sok 2, Pasaport district, across from the Borsa (June–Oct daily 8.30am–7pm; Nov–May Mon–Fri 8.30am–5.30pm; ☎0232/483 5117). The largest and most helpful office, on the ground floor of the *Büyük Efes* hotel, on Gaziosmanpaşa

Bulvarı (☎0232/445 7390), is currently closed while the hotel undergoes renovation, but should reopen some time in 2006. The offices don't book, but only suggest, **accommodation** (mid-range and up), and have been known to run out of their very useful free city-plan. However, programmes for İzmir's various festivals and entertainment venues are kept to hand, with the possibility of ticket sales.

The **tourism police** have a kiosk near the Saat Kulesi (clocktower) in Konak (Nov–March 8am–5pm; April–Oct 8.30am–8.30pm; ☎0232/489 0500). They're generally very helpful and also keep stocks of maps and brochures.

City transport

Walking is much the quickest and easiest way of exploring the city. You are rarely better off taking a bus due to the level of city traffic. **Fevzipaşa Bulvarı** and **Gazi Bulvarı**, in particular, seem to be an almost constant honking mass of congestion. The underground **Metro** line (daily 6am–11pm; 1YTL; 10min) through the southern part of the city does provide a useful (and quick) transport link between Basmane Station (accommodation) and the Konak district (attractions).

Most of the municipality's numbered bus routes are based at the **Konak Bus Terminal** at Konak Meydanı. Two separate organizations, ESHOT and IITC, administer the red-and-white city vehicles between them and tickets are a flat fare of 1YTL; you must buy tickets in advance from white kiosks near most stops. **Ferries** and sea buses to the suburb of Karşıyaka (every 30min; 15min) leave regularly from the nearby Konak City Boat Pier.

For **drivers**, the oddly angled intersections and roundabouts of the modern city are quite confusing to negotiate and there's the added complication of one-way traffic on Gazi Bulvarı (towards the sea) and Fevzipaşa Bulvarı (inland). **Parking** outside of designated car parks and parking areas may appear to be free, but you'll be approached by roving wardens and asked for 1.5YTL. The car park next to the bus terminal costs a flat rate 2.3YTL.

Accommodation

At most times of the year, you should find somewhere to stay very quickly, though street noise (particularly from car horns) is a nearly universal problem. Don't plan on staying overnight during the big annual fair between late August and mid-September, when most hotels are uniformly packed.

The main area for budget hotels is **Akıncı** (also called Yenigün), which straddles Fevzipaşa Bulvarı immediately in front of Basmane train station. The zone to the south, between Fevzipaşa Bulvarı and Anafartalar Caddesi, has traditionally been home to the city's grimmest hotels, though in 2004 it had something of a revamp, with 1296 *sokak* renamed *Otelier Sokağı* (Hotel Street), in an attempt to attract a more upmarket clientele. While there has been some improvement, many of the hotels, behind their charming old wooden facades, are still pretty dire places with chipboard partitions, roach-infested toilets and lobby-lurkers. The hotels on the north side of Fevzipaşa, in an area called **Çankaya**, centred around the pedestrianized 1369 Sokak are a good deal quieter and more appealing. But for out-and-out luxury, you'll have to head for the streets around the seafront **Cumhuriyet Meydanı**.

Akıncı: south of Fevzipaşa Bulvarı

Antik Han Anafartalar Cad 600 ☎0232/489 2750, ⊛www.otelantikhan.com. A real find – this renovated old house on one of the bazaar's busiest streets (it can get a bit noisy) has large, stylish rooms, all with TV and ceiling fans, arranged around a lovely leafy courtyard. ❺

Baylan 1299 Sok 8 ☎0232/483 1426, ⊛http://hotelbaylan.sitemynet.com. Air-conditioned two-star comfort, in spacious rooms with satellite TV furnished to the height of 1970s chic; also

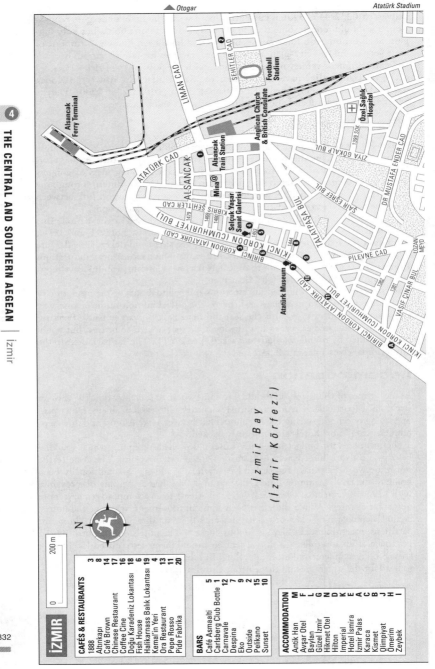

İZMIR

0 — 200 m

N

İzmir Bay
(İzmir Körfezi)

Otogar

Atatürk Stadium

Alsancak Ferry Terminal

LİMAN CAD

ŞEHİTLER CAD

Football Stadium

Özel Sağlık Hospital

Anglican Church & British Consulate

Alsancak Train Station

ZİYA GÖKALP BUL

DR MUSTAFA ENDER CAD

ATATÜRK CAD

Mina@

Selçuk Yaşar Sanat Galerisi

ŞAİR EŞREF BUL

TALATPAŞA BUL

ALSANCAK

KIBRIS ŞEHİTLER CAD

İKİNCİ KORDON (CUMHURİYET BUL)

BİRİNCİ KORDON (ATATÜRK CAD)

PİLEVNE CAD

LOZAN MEYD

Atatürk Museum

VASIF ÇINAR BUL

İKİNCİ KORDON (CUMHURİYET BUL)

BİRİNCİ KORDON (ATATÜRK CAD)

CAFÉS & RESTAURANTS

1888	3
Altınkapı	8
Café Brown	14
Chinese Restaurant	17
Coffee Cine	16
Doğu Karadeniz Lokantası	18
Fish House	6
Halikarnass Balık Lokantası	19
Kemal'in Yeri	4
Ora Restaurant	13
Pepe Rosso	11
Pide Fabrika	20

BARS

Café Asmaaltı	5
Carlsberg Club Bottle	1
Carnavale	12
Despina	7
Eko	9
Outside	2
Pelikano	15
Sunset	10

ACCOMMODATION

Antik Han	M
Avşar Otel	F
Baylan	L
Güzel İzmir	G
Hikmet Otel	N
Hilton	D
Imperial	K
Hotel İsmira	E
İzmir Palas	A
Karaca	C
Kismet	B
Olimpiyat	J
Omerim	H
Zeybek	I

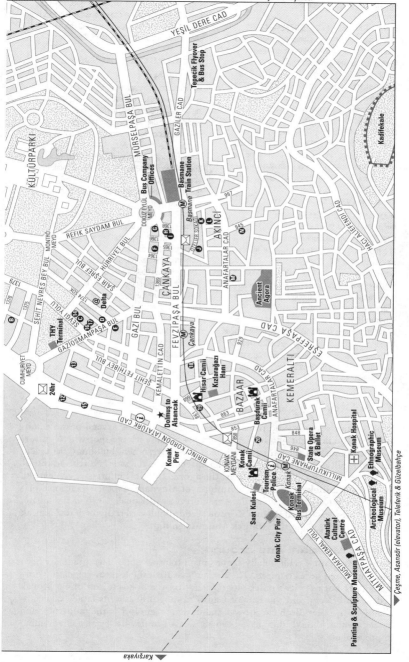

(3.5km)  Otogar & Manisa

Selçuk & Kuşadası

Karşıyaka

Çeşme, Asansör (elevator), Teleferik & Güzelbahçe

333

off-street parking on 1296 Sok. The price includes breakfast. ⑤

Hikmet Otel 945 Sok 25 ⊤0232/484 2672. Quirky and quaint, with a welcoming lobby and communal area, and friendly owners. Centrally heated rooms, available with and without en-suite facilities. ②

Imperial 1296 Sok 54 ⊤ & ⑨0232/483 9771. Better furnished than most budget hotels in this area. The air-conditioned en-suite rooms have TV and minibar. ③

Olimpiyat 945 Sok 2 ⊤0232/425 1269. The cheapest acceptable option in the area; old-fashioned and faded, but reasonably maintained. Some of the forty small rooms only have washbasins, some come with TV. No breakfast. ①

Çankaya: north of Fevzipaşa Bulvarı

Avşar Otel 1364 Sok 8 ⊤0232/441/9552, ⑨441 9624. Rather antiseptically furnished rooms – akin to a motorway motel – though with TV, minibar and air conditioning. ②

Güzel İzmir 1368 Sok 8 ⊤0232/484 6693, ⓦwww.guzelizmirhotel.com. One of the better-value mid-range hotels, though the single rooms with en-suites are tiny. ②

Ömerim Hotel 1368 Sok 4 ⊤0232/445 9898, ⑨441 1777. Nicest of a trio of large hotels under the same management. Large, grandiose, marble lobby and staircase, and accommodating staff, while all the air-conditioned rooms come with TV and minibar. ③

Zeybek 1368 Sok 5 ⊤0232/441 9590, ⑨483 5020. Next door to the *Ömerim Hotel*, this is a less plush, older version, though still with some 1970s charm characteristic of the area. ④

Around Cumhuriyet Meydanı

Hilton Gaziosmanpasa Bul 7 ⊤0232/497 6060, ⓦwww.izmir.hilton.com. Apparently the tallest building on the Aegean coast, the 381-room *Hilton* offers grand rooms (including executive floors), indoor swimming pool, fitness centre, sauna, solarium and massage. ⑧

Hotel İsmira Gaziosmanpaşa Bul 28 ⊤0232/445 6060, ⓦwww.hotelismira.com. Garish pink three-star choice opposite the *Hilton*, offering 72 generic but comfortable rooms, a decent buffet restaurant, a bar and gym. ⑤

İzmir Palas Atatürk Bul 2 ⊤0232/421 5583, ⓦwww.izmirpalas.com.tr. Older, three-star standby with a good seafront location; you should be able to bargain the price down. ⑥

Karaca 1379 Sok 55, Sevgi Yolu ⊤0232/489 1940, ⓦwww.otelkaraca.com.tr. Large, modern hotel, with slick, bilingual staff (it's popular with NATO personnel). Very large, very pink rooms, bristling with mod-cons. Parking available. ⑧

Kismet 1377 Sok 9 ⊤0232/463 3850. Calm location on a leafy sidestreet. A 62-room hotel with a choice of two good restaurants, plus bar, sauna and off-street parking. ⑤

The City

İzmir cannot really be said to have a single centre. Among several possible contenders, **Konak** might win by default, simply because it's the spot where visitors will spend much of their time – lined as it is by government buildings, banks and cultural facilities, and bounded by sea and parkland to the west. North and east of Konak lie the city's extensive **bazaar**, the **agora** – its most impressive ancient site – and the **Kadifekale**, or castle. **Cumhuriyet Meydanı**, another traditional orientation point, lies less than a kilometre northeast of Konak. Beyond the square, the prettified, café-lined **Birinci Kordon** seaside boulevard runs north to Alsancak ferry terminal, passing the **Atatürk Museum** en route.

Konak Meydanı and around

Konak Meydanı – traditionally İzmir's main transport hub – has gradually been landscaped and pedestrianized. The ornate **Saat Kulesi** (clocktower), dating only from 1901 but the city's official logo, stands on the opposite end of the Konak pedestrian bridge from the **Konak Camii**, distinguished by its facade of enamelled Kütahya tiles. Both clocktower and mosque seem lost in the modernity and bustle around, though they have been showcased somewhat by the surrounding improvements.

The area southwest of here forms the undisputed cultural focus of İzmir, home to the Atatürk Cultural Centre and the State Opera and Ballet – see "Arts and entertainment" for both – and virtually all of the city's **museums** (see below).

For good views head for the **Asansör**, located in the heart of İzmir's old Jewish quarter, just off Mithatpaşa Caddesi, about a ten-minute walk southwest from the cultural centre. The elevator is housed in a fifty-metre-high brick tower, which clings to the cliff face. Constructed in 1907, it originally served as a quick route to and from the mansions that once perched on the hill. The lift has since been completely refurbished; the original hydraulic mechanism is on display in the tiny İzmir museum at its base, and at the top is a highly recommended café from where you can look down on narrow streets of crumbling houses.

İzmir's museums

The **Archeological Museum** (Arkeoloji Müzesi; daily except Mon 8.30am–5.30pm; 4YTL), set in the Turgutreis Parkı in Konak, features an excellent collection of finds from all over İzmir province and beyond – well worth an hour or so of your time. The ground floor is largely given over to statuary and friezes of all eras: standouts include an impressively detailed statue of Athena and a headless archaic *kore* (idealized maiden). Most remarkable though are the archaic painted terracotta sarcophagi from Clazomenae (modern day Urla İskelesi on the Çeşme peninsula). The basement contains more large exhibits, while the top floor focuses on smaller objects, with an emphasis on Bronze Age and archaic pottery – more exciting than it sounds, particularly the so-called "orientalized" terracotta and bestiary amphorae from Pitane (Çandarlı). The section of small finds from Erythrae (Ildır) is especially good, as is a case of embossed seals – helpfully displayed with full-colour enlargements – and the Lycian sarcophagi in the garden. The single best piece, though, is a graceful, if peculiar Hellenistic statuette of Eros, clenching a veil in his teeth.

The **Ethnographic Museum** (Efnografya Müzesi; daily except Mon 8.30am–5pm; 2YTL), immediately across from the archeological museum, was built originally as a hospital in 1831 and later served as a poorhouse. Exhibits on the lower floor concentrate on the two types of traditional İzmir house, the wooden Turkish residence and the more substantial "Levantine" (Christian and Jewish merchants') house. There are also reconstructions of a kiln (for making blue beads to ward off the evil eye) and of the first Ottoman pharmacy in the area, as well as dioramas of felt and pottery production, plus a photo and mannequin presentation of camel wrestling and the *zeybeks* – the traditional warrior caste of western Anatolia. The upper floor has a more domestic focus, with re-creations of a nuptial chamber, a sitting room and circumcision recovery suite, along with vast quantities of household utensils and Ottoman weaponry. The galleries finish with flat weavings, saddlebags and fine carpets, accompanied by potted histories of the crafts.

If time is short, the **Painting and Sculpture Museum** (Resim ve Heykel Müzesi; ground floor daily 10am–6pm; upper levels Tues–Sat 10am–5pm; free) is the obvious one to miss. Its lower level hosts changing exhibits, while the two upstairs galleries contain almost two hundred works by Turkish artists, some awful, some decent and most stylistically derivative renderings of pastoral or populist themes reminiscent of Socialist Realism.

Cumhuriyet Meydanı to Alsancak

Cumhuriyet Meydanı, less than a kilometre northeast of Konak, is unremarkable except for the equestrian statue of the Gazi completing his long ride from inland Anatolia and poised in the act of chasing the infidels into the sea. Today the infidels are back, in limited measure, as evidenced by the member-nations' flags undulating in amity outside the NATO Officers and Family Recreation Centre behind the *Hilton* hotel on Sevgi Yolu.

Luxury apartment buildings line the seaside boulevard of **Birinci Kordon** (which doubles back on itself as İkinci Kordon from Alsancak ferry terminal). If you don't fancy walking, you could take one of the **horse-drawn phaetons** that tout for business around Cumhuriyet Meydanı (full tour 25YTL). For several hundred metres either side of Cumhuriyet, the İzmir smart set convenes for drinks and snacks in the evening, while by day, crowds queuing for visas gather outside the German Consulate, housed in one of several substantial buildings that escaped the 1922 destruction. Next door stands the Greek Consulate, ministering surreptitiously to the spiritual needs of the city's few thousand Greek Orthodox inhabitants, descended from those who elected to stay – by laying claim to English or Italian passports – after 1923.

Yet another mansion is the home of the **Atatürk Museum** (Atatürk Müzesi; daily except Mon 8.30am–5.30pm; free), at Atatürk Cad 248, occupying the building where the premier stayed on his visits to İzmir. Room-by-stately-room tours of the first floor are of little interest to foreign visitors – apart, perhaps, from the Comments room where you can read Winston Churchill's uniquely negative appraisal of the statesman.

The Atatürk Museum marks, more or less, the southern margin of **Alsancak**, less affected by the 1922 blaze. Just inland, particularly on 1453, 1469, 1482, 1481 and 1480 *sokak*s, plus the east side of İkinci Kordon, are found entire intact terraces of sumptuous **eighteenth- and nineteenth-century mansions** that once belonged to European merchants, who knew the area as Punta (a term still used). Predictably, these have become targets for gentrification, with expensive eateries and bars opening among the ranks of offices and private homes. One mansion, at Cumhuriyet Bul 252, houses the **Selçuk Yaşar Sanat Galerisi** (June–Sept Mon–Fri 10am–6pm; free), a privately run gallery emphasizing modern Turkish painting and hosting temporary exhibitions.

Returning from Alsancak to the city centre, you unavoidably pass by or through the **Kültür Parkı** (daily 8am–midnight), a forty-hectare lozenge built on the ruins of the pre-1922 Greek quarter. "Culture" in this case means a parachute tower, İzmir TV headquarters, permanent exhibition halls for the city's yearly trade fair, a mini-golf course and funfair, a zoo, an artificial lake, an open-air theatre, plus a dozen *gazino* nightspots and tea/beer-gardens. Only the theatre, occasional venue for summer concerts, is likely to be of interest to foreigners, plus of course the greenery.

Around the bazaar

İzmir's **bazaar**, though a distinct second to İstanbul's, warrants losing yourself in for a half-day or so, and is large enough to include several city districts. **Anafartalar Caddesi**, the main drag, is lined with clothing, jewellery and shoe shops; **Fevzipaşa Bulvarı** and the alleys just south are strong on leather garments, for which the city is famous. İzmir is not, however, known for its carpets – those displayed in the Kızlarağası Hanı (see below) notwithstanding. Any distance away from these principal streets, more mundane merchandise predominates – irrigation pumps, live chickens, canaries and rabbits, plastic pipes, tea sets, olives, pickles, bath tiles and rubber stamps.

In contrast with many other Turkish town bazaars, there is little of architectural interest here, though several late Ottoman mosques are worth a glance in passing. Most of İzmir's commercial wealth resided in harbour warehouses wiped out in 1922; with a pre-Republican population three quarters non-Muslim, there were correspondingly few historic *medrese*s or mosques. One exception, the

Many travellers to western Turkey, and İzmir in particular, are startled by the sight of Africans who are obviously not visitors. They are in fact descendants of the large numbers of Sudanese who were brought to the Ottoman Empire as household slaves, beginning in the sixteenth century.

The most prominent of them, ensconced in the Topkapı Palace, was the Kızlarağası or "Black Eunuch", responsible for the administration of the sultan's harem and, by his very nature, not capable of giving rise to Turkey's contemporary African population. Rather, this is owed to the fact that before World War I virtually every urban household – especially in İstanbul – had a Sudanese manservant and a nanny for the children, often a married couple; any Turkish dictionary still gives "Negro wetnurse" as the primary meaning of *bacı*, today used as a form of address to any woman a few years older than the speaker. Although slavery was formally abolished by Sultan Abdülmecid, many of these domestic slaves chose to remain in the families with whom they had grown up. The sons of the household, and those of the wetnurse herself, were termed *süt kardeşleri* (milk brothers), and between them existed bonds of affection and mutual obligation that usually endured throughout their lives.

After the collapse of the Ottoman Empire, however, the Sudanese were forced to move out on their own, gravitating mostly to southwestern Anatolia, where they occupy secluded villages scattered in the mountains between İzmir and Mersin. To this day, though devout Muslims and fluent Turkish-speakers, they rarely intermarry with other Turks. As in the case of their neighbours the Alevîs (see p.512), this segregation has predictably engendered the sensational allegation that their women earn their dowry for marriage by prostitution, with no shame accruing to the practice.

eighteenth-century **Kızlarağası Hanı** (normal shopping hours; closed Sun), a handsome Ottoman *kervansaray* near the late sixteenth-century Hisar Camii, was restored from the ground up between 1989 and 1993. The vaulted shops inside are overwhelmingly touristy, though there are a few catering to local interests. The shady square in front of **Hisar Camii** is now chock-a-block with eateries and teahouses.

From the agora to Kadifekale

The only surviving pre-Ottoman monument in the flatlands is the **agora** (daily 8.30am–noon & 1–5.30pm; 4YTL), the most accessible of İzmir's ancient sites. From Anafartalar Caddesi turn south onto 943 Sokak, then west onto 816 Sokak where the entrance is to be found on Anafartalar Caddesi next to a multi-storey car park; black-on-yellow signs confirm the way.

The *agora* probably dates back to the early second century BC, but what you see now are the remains of a later reconstruction, financed during the reign of the Roman emperor Marcus Aurelius, after the catastrophic earthquake of 178 AD. It's an impressive site, with water still coursing through ancient ducts and channels. Principal structures, unearthed between the world wars, include a **colonnade** of fourteen Corinthian columns on the west side and an elevated north stoa resting on a vaulted basement. In the eastern part of the area sit hundreds of Ottoman gravestones and earlier fragments of sculpture, the best of which have been removed to the archeological museum. A 25-year excavation programme, which started in 2003, may temporarily close the *agora* to the public – check with the tourist office or the archeological museum.

Rising just southeast of the *agora*, the **Kadifekale**, or "Velvet Castle" (always open; free), visible by night as by day thanks to skilful floodlighting, is slightly disappointing. You could take the #33 city bus from Konak, marked "K Kale", and cover the final 300m on foot, but the best introduction to the citadel is to walk up from the *agora*, the route threading through a once-elegant district of narrow streets and dilapidated pre-1922 houses. Once you reach Hacı Alieffendi Caddesi – probably via 977 or 985 *sokak*s – cross it and finish the climb up the obvious pedestrian stairs opposite, which thread through the city's gypsy quarter.

The irregularly shaped fortress serves as a daytime playground for local kids who'll pester you relentlessly for money. Virtually nothing is visible of its Hellenistic foundations; the present structure dates from Byzantine and Ottoman times. An area in the centre has been excavated revealing some rather scrappy basement dungeons, now half-filled with rubbish. Late afternoon is the best time to go – to wait for the kindling of thousands of city lights below to match the often lurid sunsets over the bay – but the views over the city are unrivalled at any hour. In the warmer months, a **tea/beer garden** operates until late at a prime location under the pines. There are several more along the stretch between the castle gate and the bus stop.

The north shore

Karşıyaka means "the opposite shore" and that's really all this suburb is. Before 1922, its population was about seventy percent Greek Orthodox and it's said that title to much of the land still legally resides with their descendants now in Greece. Karşıyaka provides an excuse for the twenty-minute **ferry ride** across from Konak's jetty, docking next to a waterfront park studded with pubs and snack bars that directly overhang the bay. At evenings and weekends, Karşıyakans turn out here in force to eat the *lokma* (dough fritters) for which the district is famous, for example at *Kemal'in Yeri* on Yala Caddesi across from the ferry dock. The sole monumental destination is the **tomb of Zübeyde Hanım**, Atatürk's mother, some way inland; otherwise the cool breeze on the ride over seems to be most of the point.

The only other destination of interest on the north shore of the bay is the *kuş cenneti* or **bird sanctuary** around the salt-evaporation pans at **Çamaltı**. This is signposted near the Çiğli airfield turn-off, and while there's a commuter train to the Çiğli station, you'll need a taxi or your own vehicle to tour the eight hectares of wetlands.

Eating

Fast-food joints are thick on the ground and a local favourite is pizza served with fried chicken pieces and chips and topped with mayonnaise and ketchup. The obvious budget eateries within sight of Basmane station have tables on the street and offer the usual range of kebabs, *pide* and stews. They're also usually full of transient male travellers with nowhere else to go, making for a pretty depressing – and undistinguished – meal. There's a far better selection of inexpensive outfits in the **bazaar**, but unfortunately most of them close by 7.30pm. Meals eaten close to the Birinci Kordon **waterfront** represent a definite step up in quality and price, though the best hunting-ground by far is among the restored inland mansions of **Alsancak**; restaurants, café-bars, bars and fast-food outlets abound along Kıbrıs Şehitler Caddesi and its sidestreets.

İzmir is particularly noted for its **mussels**, and half a dozen stuffed with rice and pine nuts make a wonderful cheap snack for under 2YTL – don't be conned into paying more. The street vendors are found everywhere, but it's a good idea not to patronize them between late May and early September, when you stand a good chance of food poisoning.

Bazaar

Doğu Karadeniz Lokantası Yeyisel Çıkmazi 39/E. A late-opening (11pm) *meyhane*, just off the beginning of Anafartalar Cad. All male as a rule, but decorous – outdoor seating and impromptu music with your grilled dishes and cold *meze*s.

Halikarnass Balık Lokantası Junction of 870, 871 and 873 *sok*s, overlooking the fountain. A simple fish restaurant near the Bazdurak Camii fish market, where a meal won't cost more than 10YTL.

Pide Fabrika 857 Sok 5/B. Excellent *pide* starting at an incredibly cheap 1YTL a portion.

Between Konak and Alsancak

Café Browne 1379 Sok. On a quiet lane with outdoor seating, serving an excellent range of lunchtime veggie options.

Chinese Restaurant 1385 Sok. Not brilliant, but the least expensive and most central of the city's oriental food outlets, with a good-value set lunch for 17.50YTL.

Coffee Çine 1379 Sok 57, next to *Karaca Hotel*. Multicoloured banquettes, a simple snack menu (sandwiches, pasta and crêpes for around 5–7YTL) and a good selection of flavoured coffees – vanilla, hazlenut, cognac etc.

Ora Restaurant Akdeniz Cad. Popular with students who crowd its pavement tables, this small restaurant-bar makes a lively lunchtime or early-evening pit-stop.

Birinci Kordon and Alsancak

1888 İkinci Kordon (Cumhuriyet Bul) 248. Exquisitely prepared Turkish and Mediterranean seafood served in a restored eighteenth-century mansion.

Altınkapı 1444 Sok 14/A. Good for *döner* and *piliç* (chicken) grills. It's long-established, and popular with the trendy set who, weather permitting, sit outside on the pedestrianized street.

Deniz Restaurant *İzmir Palas Hotel*, Vasif Çınar Bul ☎0232/422 0601. Local favourite offering a sophisticated range of seafood dishes, including a very tasty shrimp casserole for 15YTL. Reservations necessary at weekends.

Fish House Birinci Kordon 174. Deservedly popular seafood restaurant – you'll have to get there early evening to guarantee a seat. Try the fried calamari for 12.5YTL.

Kemal'in Yeri 1453 Sok 20/A ☎0232/422 3190. One of several on this lane, and famous for its excellent (but expensive) seafood; reckon on 25YTL a head. Reservations recomended.

Pepe Rosso Atatürk Bul. In amongst a glut of similar establishments, this stands out by offering a decent selection of authentic Italian pasta dishes in addition to usual seafood staples. Good wine list (they don't serve beer).

Drinking and nightlife

Clustered around the Konak Meydanı are a number of bars offering live Turkish music and dancing. But it's upper **Alsancak** that has blossomed as the district for trendy **nightlife**, with assorted bars and clubs tucked inland along pedestrianized sidestreets invisible from Birinci Kordon. It should be stressed that ownership and themes of each establishment tend to roll over on roughly a two-year cycle, so specific recommendations are subject to change.

△ Eating along İzmir's seafront

A good place to start the evening is at the *Café Asmaalti* on 1453 Sokak, with back-gammon boards, *nargile* pipes, beer etc. From here, it's a good idea just to wander and see what looks lively. Sokaks 1482 and 1480, in particular, are home to dozens of often transitory bars in restored old houses, some of which offer live Turkish music as the evening wears on. *Eko*, on the corner of Pilevne Bulvarı and Cumhuriyet Cad-desi, is popular with expats, and the young and trendy gearing up for a long night out on the town, many of whom will probably end up at the *Carlsberg Club Bottle*, a recently opened Western-style disco with several dance floors.

The cafés, **bars** and upmarket teahouses lining the shore on **Birinci Kordon** (Atatürk Caddesi) are ideal for a quiet drink and a snack while watching the sunset. The best include *Despina* and the appropriately named *Sunset* (which sells pour-your-own 2.5litre kegs of beer for 15YTL) to the north of Cumhuriyet Meydanı, and *Carnavale* and *Pelikano*, to the south, both of which have seafront seating. House and trance together with some Turkish tracks can be heard at the best **club** in town, *Out-side*, situated east of Alsancak on Şehitler Caddesi; cross the railway junction, take a right and follow round past the football stadium and it's on the left.

Arts and entertainment

The **Atatürk Cultural Centre** at Mithatpaşa Cad 92 (Atatürk Kültür Merkezi; ☎0232/483 8520) is home to the local symphony orchestra, which plays regu-larly on Friday evening and Saturday at noon and hosts occasional concerts by "serious" soloists. Tickets are not always sold on the spot – read the hoardings outside the building for directions or ask at the information desk. More varied is the programme offered by the **State Opera and Ballet** (Devlet Opera ve Balesi; ☎0232/484 3692), housed in a wonderful Ottoman Art-Deco specimen on Milli Kütüphane Caddesi, which encompasses everything from chamber music to pop and jazz. Tickets are sold on the premises. Other **classical music concerts** are held at Dokuz Eylül University's Sabanci Cultural Centre, Mithatpaşa Caddesi (☎0232/441 9009 or 441 8477), while with the onset of the hot weather, events move to the open-air theatre in the **Kültür Parkı**.

Most of İzmir's small **cinemas** are located in and around Konak Meydanı, including Çınar in the SSK shopping arcade and Soma, Konak & San on Anafarta-lar Caddesi, to the right of the tourist information booth. Mid-April sporadically sees the holding of the **İzmir International Film Festival**, featuring foreign releases, all shown in their original languages with subtitles. Films are shown at a variety of venues including the Çınar, and İzmir (Cumhuriyet Bul), next to the Dünya bookshop. Finally, the **Alliance Française**, Cumhuriyet Bul 13, and **Centro Italiano**, Kıbrıs Sehil Cad 58, Alsancak, are two more possible venues for exhibitions and film showings.

International İzmir Festival

Linchpin of the summer season is the **International İzmir Festival**, running from mid-June to early July. It's something of a misnomer since many events take place at various restored venues at Ephesus or Çeşme castle. Tickets tend to run to 20–25YTL a head, but fifty-percent student discounts are available and the acts fea-tured are often world-class – past names have included Sarah Vaughan, the Moscow Ballet, Paco Peña, Ravi Shankar and Chris de Burgh. Get this year's programme from the **İzmir Culture Foundation** at Zair Ezref Bul, Park Apt 58/4, 35220 Alsancak (☎0232/463 0300), or from the city tourist offices. **Tickets** are usually available from the State Opera and Ballet box office, the museum in Selçuk, the İzmir *Hilton* or the tourist office in Kuşadası.

Listings

Airlines THY (Turkish Airlines), Gaziosmanpaşa Bul 1/F–G; information ☎0232/484 1220, reservations ☎0232/445 5363. Other airlines include: British Airways ☎0232/441 382; Delta ☎0232/421 4262; KTHY (Cyprus Turkish Airways) ☎0232/422 7164; and Lufthansa ☎0232/422 3622.

Airport Adnan Menderes airport, flight enquiries ☎0232/274 2626. The Havaş airport bus (10 departures daily, 4.45am–8.30/9.30pm; 9YTL; 20–30min) runs from in front of the THY office (see above) 1hr 30min before each domestic THY flight, 2hr before overseas ones (non-THY passengers welcome). Other airline companies occasionally provide a bus transfer; ask when reconfirming your return ticket.

Banks and exchange Many banks have ATMs and offices along Fevipaşa Bul and also in Konak. You can change money round-the-clock at standard bank rates (and commissions) in the PTT (see below) on Cumhuriyet Meyd. Much better are the private exchange booths (Mon–Sat 8.30am–7pm), like Odak Döviz, 1369 Sokak, and Kaynak Döviz, 895 Sok 5/E. Avoid the larger hotels, which offer poor rates.

Books Dünya, Cumhuriyet Bul 143 F/G (mostly English magazines); Elt Haşet, Şehit Nevres Bey Bul 3/B; and ABT1, Cumhuriyet Bul 142/B, next to Dokuz Eylül Universitesi.

Buses The easiest way to reach the main *büyük otogar* is via a free shuttle bus, departing from the company offices ranged around Dokuz Eylül Meyd, the roundabout just north of Basmane station. However, leaving İzmir to the south, it's easy to flag down buses from the pavement along the Tepecik flyover. For the Üçkuyular (Çeşme peninsula) terminal, take any bus from Konak Meyd marked Mithatpaşa or İnönü Cad, including the #5, #86, #169, #216 and #217.

Car rental Avis, Şehit Eşref Bul 18/D ☎0232/441 4417; Budget, Şair Eşref Bul 22/1 ☎0232/441 9224; DeCar, Hürriyet Bul 3/1, Yusuf Dede İş Hana ☎0232/446 0707; Europcar, Airport ☎0232/274 2163; Hertz, 1377 Sok 8 ☎0232/464 3440; Intercity, 1370 Sok 7/1, 2nd Floor, Suite 8 ☎0232/446 0165; Sun, Şehit Nevres Bey Bul 2/D ☎0232/489 9493.

Consulates UK, 1442 Sok, Mahmut Esat Bozkurt Cad 49, an annexe of the Anglican church ☎0232/463 5151; US, Kazim Direk Sok 13, Floor 8, Pasaport district ☎0232/441 2203.

Hamam Some of the cleanest, most secure and best-maintained baths are: Hoşgör, on an alley inland from Mithatpaşa Cad 10, opposite Karataş Lisesi (daily 6.30am–11.30pm; 7YTL; mixed-gender groups by arrangement, otherwise men only); and Sıfalı Lux, Anafartalar Cad (daily 7am–11pm for men, 8am–6pm for women; 10YTL).

Hospitals The most central state hospitals are Alsancak Devlet Hastanesi on Ali Çetinkaya Bul (☎0232/463 6465), and the Konak Hospital (with dental section), across from the ethnographic and archeological museums. Much better are the American Hospital, 1375 Sok (☎0232/484 5360) – staffed with NATO doctors and intended primarily for NATO personnel – and the Özel Sağlık Hastanesi on 1399 Sok, considered the best in town.

Internet *Delta Internet Café*, 1374 Sok; *Mina Internet Café*, 1469 Sok, Alsancak.

Left luggage Inside Basmane station on the right as you enter (daily 7.30am–7.30pm).

Pharmacies In Konak there's Mertsel Ecza Dep, 848 Sok 2/24 ☎0232/483 1649; also try Dogu Ilac Fab, Cetin Kaya Bul 34/1, ☎0232/463 8514; or, in Hatay, Dekim Ecza A.S., 165 Sok 29, ☎0232/232 7090.

Police Tourist Police kiosks on 1207 Sok, Basmane ☎0232/446 1456; in Alsancak next to the hospital ☎0232/464 9360; and in Konak opposite the İş Bank ☎0232/489 0500.

Post office Main PTT office is at Cumhuriyet Meyd (open 24hr); plus branches at 858 Sok, just off 857 Sok, Kemeraltı (Mon–Fri 8.30am–5.30pm, Sat 8.30am–noon) and on Fevzipaşa Bul, 300m west of Basmane train station (same hours). If you don't trust the PTT for shipping souvenirs or personal effects, or can't face the bureaucracy involved, try United Parcel Service, Akdeniz Cad 8/K (office hours), which provides cost-effective air delivery to North America and the UK.

Shopping Traditional Turkish musical instruments are best bought from Bağdat Saz Evi, Kızlarağası Hanı 19/P/22. The best *nargiles* (waterpipes) on the Aegean can be found at İlhan Etike, inside the Kızlarağası Hanı (near Bağdat Saz Evi), or at Mehmet & Osman Kaya, 856 Sok 7/C, in Kemeraltı. The Turkish Ministry of Culture has a shop, Dösim, next to the PTT at Cumhuriyet Bul 115/A, selling high-quality reproductions of Turkish and Ottoman crafts: kilims, silver jewellery and copperware.

Telephones The 24hr Cumhuriyet Meyd PTT has quiet phones, as does the branch at 858 Sok, just off 857 Sok, Kemeraltı.

Çeşme and around

The claw-like mass of land extending west from İzmir terminates near **Çeşme**, most low-key of the central Aegean's main coastal resorts. It's an hour and a half's ride from İzmir along the eighty-kilometre highway, and makes a decent base for the few attractions within shouting distance of town – most notably **ancient Erythrae**, the town of **Alaçatı** and **Altınkum** beach.

The immediate environs of Çeşme are bleak scrubland, the only note of colour introduced by the deeply aquamarine sea and the white of the electricity-generating windmills on the approach to the peninsula. It's a deceptive barrenness: before 1922 the area, almost entirely Greek-populated, was famous for its vineyards and market gardens, nurtured by artesian wells surging up from hundreds of metres below ground level. After 1922, the newly arrived Muslim settlers, mostly from

the Aegean islands, Macedonia or Thrace, turned their goats loose on the farmland and now little remains except for the odd vine or melon patch. Agricultural reclamation is further hampered by the fact that most deep ground-water is now diverted to support the ever-increasing number of villas and five-star hotels on the peninsula's north shore.

The **climate** here is noticeably drier, cooler and healthier than anywhere nearby on the Turkish coast, especially in comparison with occasionally hellish İzmir or muggy Kuşadası. These conditions, combined with the presence of several thermal springs, have made the peninsula a popular resort for over a century. This is the second westernmost point of continental Turkey, subject to currents from the Dardanelles and maritime breezes that make the sea and the nights chilly at any time of the year.

Çeşme

An often sleepy, three-street town of old Greek houses wrapped around a Genoese castle, **ÇEŞME** ("drinking fountain" in Turkish) doubtless takes its name from the many Ottoman fountains, some still functioning, scattered around its streets. Despite guarding the mouth of the İzmir Gulf, it has figured little in recent history other than as the site of a sea battle on July 5, 1770, when the Russian fleet annihilated the Ottoman navy in the straits here.

The place makes an agreeable, brief, stopover on the way to or from Híos in Greece, and it's hard to work up a great deal of indignation about the current scale of tourism here – which, despite the completion of a six-lane dual-carriageway linking İzmir and Çeşme, seems permanently stalled at its present level. There simply isn't enough in and around the town to hold foreigners' interest for even one week of a two-centre package holiday, and Çeşme seems permanently destined for a turnstile role, processing ferry passengers en route to and from Greece or Italy.

Arrival and information

Coming by ferry **from Híos** (Greece), you arrive at the small jetty in front of the castle. The larger ferries **from Italy** (Brindisi and Ancona) use the ferry dock across the bay. For ticket agencies, see "Listings", p.345. Note that the companies operating to Italy suspend departures without notice, or drop services entirely when unprofitable, and it's unwise to advance-purchase a ticket to Italy unless the boat is in harbour, engines running.

Çeşme's small **otogar** is 1km south of the town centre with regular services from İzmir, though local buses serving most nearby destinations including Dalyan, Ilıca and Alaçatı, leave from the eastern end of İnkilap Caddesi.

The helpful **tourist office** (May–Sept Mon–Fri 8.30am–7pm, Sat & Sun 9am–noon & 1–5pm; Oct–April daily 8.30am–noon & 1–5pm; ⓣ 0232/712 6653), by the Customs Office near the quayside, dispenses the usual brochures and town plans, and lets you have a peek at its comprehensive accommodation listings.

Accommodation

Çeşme's popularity as a summer bolt-hole for residents of İzmir means there's a plethora of budget and moderately priced accommodation. The most desirable places to stay are on the hillside to the right of the castle as you face it, or those lining the waterfront to its left. Other options are clustered further south, near the intersection of Çarşı Caddesi and Müftü Sokak.

Otel A Çarşi Cad 24 ⓣ 0232/712 6881, ⓕ 712 6882. Designed and built by its English-teaching owners, this has bright and immaculately kept, spacious en-suite doubles, a sun deck and sea views. The plush interior wouldn't look out of place in a 1970s design catalogue. ➋

Alim Pansiyon Müftü Sok 3 ☎0232/712 7828. Simple place south of the centre with good-value en-suite rooms. ❷

Ertan Otel On the main square ☎0232/712 6795, ☎712 7852. Two-star hotel with sea-facing doubles without balconies, but there's an open-air terrace-bar with great ocean views. ❹

Rasim Palas Ilica, 4km east of Çeşme ☎0232/723 1010. A century-old Greek period-piece, with its own thermal baths preserved because Atatürk once took a cure in the spa-tubs out back; his upstairs room is kept as a shrine. You'll really need your own transport to stay. ❷

Rıdvan Otel By the harbour ☎0232/712 6336, ☎ridvan@superonline.com. Five-storey hotel with spacious, well-maintained, air-conditioned doubles, all with balconies overlooking the square. ❹

Seda Pansiyon Kösk Cad 20 ☎0232/712 6228. This family-run pension, left off İnkilap Cad, is the best in-town budget choice, with breakfast served in its bougainvillea-filled garden. ❷

Tarhan Pansiyon Behind the *kervansaray* ☎0232/712 6599. Friendly place with nine basic en-suite rooms opening onto a small breakfast veranda, offering good views of Çeşme below. ❷

U2 Apartments Muarrem Sok 2 ☎0536/560 7451, ☎ tarhanpansiyon@unimedya.net.tr. Newly built four- or five-person apartments with plain lounge/dining areas and marble self-catering kitchens. ❹

Yalçin Otel Kale Sok 38 ☎0232/712 6981. Higher up the hillside, above the *Tarhan*, this has 18 smart, modern rooms and a terrace with good views over the town. ❷

The Town

The town's three main streets all radiate off **Cumhuriyet Meydanı,** the town's largely pedestrianized main square. **İnkilap Caddesi,** the main bazaar thorough-fare heads off north and east, while **Çarşı Caddesi,** its continuation, saunters south along the waterfront past the castle, *kervansaray* and most of the travel agencies before veering slightly inland. The town's **esplanade** hugs the waterfront to the north passing the small fishing port until it reaches a small crescent of pebbly beach. It's all very pleasant, in a low-key way, but unless you're a fan of nineteenth-century domestic architecture, you'll find that Çeşme's sights are soon exhausted.

You are free to clamber about every perilous inch of the waterfront **castle** (Tues–Sun 8.30am–noon & 1–5.30pm; 3YTL), much repaired by the Ottomans and today home to a small museum containing a paltry collection of finds from nearby Erythrae. The castle's crumbling open-air theatre hosts the **Çeşme Song Contest and Sea Festival** (intermittently held in early July), with performances ranging from the painfully amateurish to mediocre by way of the obscure.

The **kervansaray,** a few paces south of the castle, dates from the reign of Süley-man the Magnificent and has been predictably restored as a "luxury" hotel, though it's anything but. The only other distraction is the huge old Greek basilica of **Ayios Haralambos,** north of the castle on İnkilap Caddesi, now home to an art gallery hosting small exhibitions by local artists (see door for details).

Daily **boat trips** leave from near the fishing port along the coast to local beauty spots. They usually set off at 10.30am, returning at 5.30pm and cost around YTL25, including lunch.

Eating and drinking

Of the three quayside **restaurants** down by the post office, *Papillon's* mix of Turkish and international dishes are about the best of a pricey lot. For better-value seafood and a quieter harbourside location try the *Rıhtım* or the *Marina,* both overlooking the fishing port, or, a couple of minutes' walk further north, *Kerman,* near the beach. About halfway up İnkilap Caddesi, at no. 44, is the *Rumeli Pastanesi,* a local legend, with some of the best **ice cream** – including *sakızlı,* or mastic-resin-flavoured – on the Aegean; their home-made fruit pre-serves (*reçel*) are also on sale. Nearby *Sakarya* is a friendly, modest *lokanta* serving good-value steamtray dishes.

A brief stroll up İnkilap Caddesi reveals a number of **bars** and small discos. One of the more permanent fixtures is the rooftop *SkyBar* on Cumhuriyet Meydanı a stone's throw from the castle, with frequent happy hours, good views and an evening breeze.

Listings

Banks and exchange There are banks and ATMs on Cumhuriyet Meyd and at the western end of İnkilap Cad.

Car rental Sultan, İnkilap Cad 68 (☎0232/712 7395), is about the cheapest; they also rent motorbikes, perfectly adequate for exploring the peninsula. Otherwise, try Avis, Kutludag Sok 14 (☎0232/712 6706).

Ferries Ertürk (☎0232/712 6768, ✆www.erturk .com), opposite the tourist office, runs a morning ferry to Híos and a twice-weekly ferry to Brindisi. Minoan Lines (afternoon boat to Híos) is represented by Karavan Tours, just south of the castle (☎0232/712 7230, ✉karavan@superonline.com). Tamer Tours, Beyazit Cad 15 (☎0232/712 7932), is the representative for the Topaş ferries to Ancona; while Maskot, İnkilap Cad 93 (☎0232/712 7654),

handles Med Link sailings to Brindisi. TDI, at the ferry terminal (☎0232/712 1091), sails to Brindisi. For schedules, see "Travel details" at the end of the chapter.

Hamam Belediye Hamamı on Çarşi Cad, 200m down from the *kervansaray*.

Hospitals Devlet Hastanesi, at the very top of İnkilap Cad, past the turning for Dalyan. However, either the Sağlak Hastanesi in Ilıca (summer only), or the public health centre in Alaçatı (see below), are preferable.

Internet Kalyoncu Internet, İnkilap Cad (daily 9am–8pm).

Police Within the Customs Office building, behind the tourist office ☎0232/712 6627.

Post office The PTT (daily 8am–midnight) is on the waterfront, 300m north of the ferry dock.

South of Çeşme: Alaçatı, Ovacık and Altınkum

For warm, sheltered swimming on largely undeveloped sand beaches, make for the coast **south of Çeşme**, where construction has been slowed since most land belongs to the forestry department or various municipalities. Regular dolmuşes leave from south of Çeşme's tourist office, whenever they are full (in practice every 30min or so), the latest returning at dusk.

Alaçatı

ALAÇATI, 9km southeast of Çeşme, is one of the region's most upmarket resorts, popular with İstanbul's cosmopolitan elite. Formerly a somewhat isolated Greek village unknown to the outside world, its resurgence began when one of the town's charming old stone houses was turned into an upmarket designer hotel, the *Alaçatı Tas*. This proved so popular that, within a few years, it had spawned over a dozen equally stylish and tasteful imitators, not to mention a similar number of gourmet restaurants. Strict building regulations have meant that, in the centre of town at least, this rapid growth has had little effect on the character of the place, and it's still architecturally of a piece. Its old lanes and cobbled streets, particularly on the main throughfare, Kemalpaşa Caddesi, are dotted with antique shops, art galleries and snazzy boutiques selling designer kitchenware. On the town's southern and eastern outskirts, however, whole new streets are currently under construction, which when finished will almost double Aliçatı's size. Although, developers must abide by local regulations, which insist that any new buildings must be in a style in keeping with the old, the expansion cannot help but alter the nature of the town. The town's 300-metre-long sandy **beach** is 4km south, though its rather bleak, windswept sands are only really of interest to those heading for the incongruous five-star beach resort or the large windsurfing centre; the dolmuşes from Çeşme run on here every 45 minutes or so.

Of the town's **hotels**, the ⚓*Alaçatı Tas* (☎0232/716 7772, ⓦwww.tasotel .com; ❽) is still the best. Located at the eastern end of Kemalpaşa Caddesi, this lovingly restored 1890s building has eight large, bright, stylish rooms, all with balconies and air conditioning, and scrumptious breakfasts, featuring home-grown olives and home-made bread and jams, are served on a terrace overlooking the garden and swimming pool. Another good choice is *O Ev*, a hundred yards west (☎0232/716 6150, ⓦwww.o-ev.com; ❽), with chic, modern rooms and a top-notch restaurant with tables set in an ivy-clad courtyard. The *Sailors Otel*, at no. 66 (☎0232/716 8765, ⓔsailors@alacati.com; ❻), is the best **pansiyon** in the area, with spacious wooden-floored, white-and-blue-painted doubles, more reminiscent of Greece than Turkey. Aside from a few cheaper places around the main square, Aliçatı's **restaurants** tend to be very refined affairs. You won't find waiters standing on the street hustling for custom here. At the eastern end of Kemalpaşa Caddesi are three good options: the *Agrilia* is generally regarded to be the pick of the bunch with a lovely rustic dining room and a wide-ranging Mediterranean menu, though the nearby *Lavanta* and *Tuval* are also recommended.

Ovacık

By way of contrast, **OVACIK**, 5km due south of Çeşme, is dusty and half-inhabited, another ex-Greek village on a hill overlooking the straits to Híos. Although regular dolmuşes from Çeşme *otogar* reach the village, the paved road ends here and you'll need your own transport to continue 4km down a dirt road – with a right fork at an old fountain – to the small beach at **Çatal Azmak**. There's a single café here and a better, more isolated, beach another five minutes' walk west.

Altınkum

The best local beaches are those within the coves of **Altınkum**, a series of sun-baked coves 9km southwest of Çeşme, beyond the rather forgettable seaside township of Çiftlik.

Altınkum is easily reached by dolmuş, and between June and September the service continues a kilometre or so from the bus stand at the first cove to the **central cove**, stopping opposite the tiny *jandarma* outpost. This is probably the best beach between Bozcaada and the Turquoise Coast, where multi-hued water laps hundreds of metres of sand and dunes. At one time, it was a stopover on the hippy trail and the cove is still host to a rash of seasonal wooden bars that spring up from the dunes. *Cennet Camping* (☎0532/394 0131; summer only), ten minutes' walk along the beach, is by far the best **campsite** and also rents out tents (€10). Run by the garrulous Okan, and popular with young İzmir weekenders, the site lies within an organic farm, set in gorgeous surroundings just off the beach. The attached **restaurant** is popular at weekends, serving assorted fish dishes (10YTL) and spicy *menemen*. In high season you can **rent kayaks and windsurfers** from the Fun Club on the beach; though it's often windy here, the water is very clear and warm. It's also permissible to camp on the beach.

In high summer you have to walk pretty far to the east to lose the crowds – possibly over the headland to the **easternmost cove**, equal in all respects to the central one. This is accessible along a direct, unsignposted road from Çiftlik (bear left at the north edge of town).

North: Dalyan

The approach to **DALYAN**, 4km north of Çeşme, is announced by a strange, four-storey tower looming over the village's remaining Greek-built houses. This straggly fishing settlement, built on the west shore of an almost completely landlocked harbour, is becoming a popular location for retirement and holiday homes. There are, however, few short-term places to stay, and even less in the way of sandy beach, so for most people a clutch of fish restaurants, appealingly set by the narrow channel to the open sea, will be the extent of Dalyan's interest.

Dolmuşes from Çeşme (every 45min or when full) drop you at the small statue that acts as the main square for the village. Follow the channel round to find a group of locally renowned **restaurants** – the *Liman, Körfez, Köşem* and *Borsa Dalyanköy* – offering (not particularly cheap) *meze* and seafood with outside seating and fine views over the harbour. Less pricey options include the *Levant* and *Sülo Nun Yeri* near the statue. The *Köşem* is also a **hotel**, popular with the yachting and weekend trade (☎0232/724 7358, Ⓕ724 8800; ❸); or try the small family-run *Güven Pansiyon* (☎0232/724 7031; ❶), though breakfast isn't included in the price.

Sığacık and around

Southwest of İzmir, **SIĞACIK** huddles inside a low-slung Genoese castle, with many of its houses built right into the perimeter walls. Otherwise the village is of middling architectural interest and, although you might want to wander the maze of alleys inside, foreigners come to Sığacık primarily for the sake of its good yacht anchorage. Certainly, there are no decent beaches in sight and for a swim you'll need to continue 1.5km over the hill to the west to **Akkum**, a 150-metre-wide sandy cove that's gradually becoming oversubscribed.

The journey to Sığacık by bus is complicated by loop routes and the frequent need to change vehicles. From İzmir or Kuşadası (hourly services from either), you'll find you probably have to change in **Seferihisar**, a large town 40km southwest of İzmir and 6km east of Sığacık – here you can catch a red-and-white *Belediye* bus to cover the remaining distance to Sığacık and Akkum.

The best of Sığacık's **accommodation** is the Dutch-run *Teos Pension* near the castle (☎0232/745 7463; ❷), with well-kept doubles, some with views of the coast, and a decent restaurant and bar. Otherwise there's the *Burç Pansiyon* (☎0232/745 7464, Ⓕ745 7306; ❷), a new building in traditional style, right on the quay. At Akkum there's a **campsite**, *Bungalow Kamping*, on the cape, just past the large *Neptun* windsurfing resort whose patrons crowd out the beach. There are a few fish **restaurants** overlooking the harbour, including the upmarket *Liman*, with quality fish meals for around 20YTL.

Teos

The same road serving Akkum continues for just under 5km to **ancient Teos** (site unenclosed; free). Once one of the most important Ionian cities, Teos was renowned for its colossal temple to Dionysos, deity not only of wine but of the arts and the generative forces of nature. Accordingly, in early Roman times Teos was chosen to host the Guild of Dionysos, the union of all artists, actors and musicians who performed throughout Asia Minor. They soon proved so insufferable that the Teans exiled them to backwaters down the coast. An earlier, more genial embodiment of the Dionysian ethic was the city's famous son, the sixth-century poet **Anacreon**, who choked to death on a grape seed after a long life of wine, women and song.

Appropriately, the second-century BC **Temple of Dionysos** is the most interesting remnant, excavated – with three columns partly re-erected – in a bucolic setting of olive trees and grazing cattle. You can also pick your way

400m northeast to a hillside supporting the **Hellenistic theatre**, though only the stage foundations are left of this, and it's debatable whether it's worth snaking around the wheat fields and buzzing cow-pat flies for the view south over assorted islets to Sámos. About 100m southeast of the theatre you might find the eleven remaining rows of the Roman-era **odeion**. When you've finished sightseeing, call at the small drinks-stand that operates in high season, at the road's end in front of the temple.

Inland: the Küçük Menderes valley

With a spare day, the inland towns and villages of the **Küçük Menderes valley**, southeast of İzmir, are easily seen by public transport, as connections from both İzmir and Selçuk are good. To reach Birgi village, the lake at Gölcük or the conservative town of Tire, you first have to travel via the undistinguished market town of **Ödemiş** – 80km southeast of İzmir – to which there are buses every two hours from İzmir's *büyük otogar*, a three-and-a-half-hour ride. From Ödemiş *otogar* there are hourly services to Birgi and Tire, while six or seven daily dolmuşes to Gölcük leave from the corner of Hatay and Namik Kemal *caddesis*, some 200m from the *otogar*. Failing these, anything plying the mountain road to Salihli passes within 3km of Gölcük and 1km of Birgi, or you'll have to arrange a taxi from Ödemiş (5YTL per car to Birgi, 10YTL to Gölcük).

Birgi

A sleepy community of half-timbered houses lining both slopes of a narrow valley at the foot of Boz Dağ, **BIRGI**, 9km east of Ödemiş, is an excellent example of what small-town Turkey looked like before the wars and cement mania of the twentieth century.

The main thing to see is the **Aydınoğlu Mehmet Bey Camii**, also called the Ulu Cami, an engaging fourteenth-century mosque on the site of an earlier church. It's across the ravine from the Çakırağa Konaği (see below), a little way upstream. Quite a lot of ancient Pyrgion, including a sculpted lion, is incorporated into the exterior walls; inside, it's an understated masterpiece, with the tiled *mihrab* and a single arch betraying a Selçuk influence. Most impressive, though, are the carved hardwood *mimber* and shutters, some of them replacements for those carted off to the Selimiye Camii in Edirne. The sloping wooden roof is supported by a forest of Roman columns, the whole effect more like Spanish Andalucia than Turkey. The minaret features zigzag belts of glazed green tiles, like the Yeşil Cami in İznik, while the dome of the adjacent *türbe* (tomb) of the Aydınoğlu clan is fashioned in concentric rings of alternating brick and the same faïence. A couple of other mid-to late-period Ottoman mosques perch next to or above the stream, along with some ruined baths and a *medrese*, but while these add to the atmosphere of the place none can compare to the Ulu Cami.

Birgi's houses – ensembles of wood and either brick, stone, lath-and-plaster or half-timbered mud – run the gamut from the simple to the sumptuous. Many are dilapidated, but the restored eighteenth-century **Çakırağa Konağı** (Tues–Sun 9am–noon & 1–6pm; 2YTL) operates as a museum and has some explanatory panels in English. Built by one Zerif Aliağa in 1761, the mansion is one of the best surviving specimens of those built in the wake of the decentralizing reforms of the eighteenth century, which allowed local potentates (the *derebeys*) to rule and live in grand style. Many have burned down or simply rotted away owing to the widespread use of wood in coffered and painted ceilings, lattices and built-in cupboards (*mısandras*). Most *konaks* were two-storeyed, but the slope here dictates a three-storey plan: the ground floor in stone, the upper floors in lath-and-plaster. The extensive and vivid murals depict stylized skylines of favourite coastal cities; the presence or absence of particular structures allows dating of the paintings to the nineteenth century.

Birgi has little **accommodation**: by far the best is the delightful 🗛 *Birgicek Hanı* (☎0232/762 6437, ℻762 6405; ❹), which offers charming antique-strewn rooms and delicious home-cooked meals.

Gölcük

GÖLCÜK, 20km north of Birgi, is just about the last thing you'd expect to see in the Aegean region: a six-acre alpine **lake** in a wooded cavity tucked nearly halfway up 2129-metre Boz Dağ. The coolness and the greenery make it a favourite local summer and winter retreat. The lakeshore itself is surprisingly undisturbed, probably because swimming in the reedy, murky waters is forbidden.

Many come just for the day to eat **catfish** (*yayın* in Turkish) at the *Rıhtım Restaurant*, which has a gazebo built on stilts over the water. **Accommodation** is limited and liable to fill in high season: the very large lakeside *Otel Prenses* (☎0232/558 1115, ℻558 1148; ❸) is excellent value, with extensive grounds, large rooms, some with balcony views of the lake, and half-board facilities (with excellent chicken and lamb *şiş* and *köfte* meals); it's open all year. Alternatively, the nearby *Gölcük Otel* (☎0232/558 1333; ❷; closed in winter) has clean, simple rooms.

Tire

Thirty kilometres across the valley floor from Ödemiş, **TIRE**, clustered at the base of Güme Dağı, is an altogether different proposition. Much fought over by Byzantines and Selçuks, it eventually became one of the Aydınoğlu clan's first important strongholds, and the conservatism and religious fervour of the inhabitants is still apparent (and disparaged by secular Turks). If you've had an overdose of the touristed coast, Tire makes the perfect antidote – though being stared at may be part of the experience.

There are hourly **dolmuşes** here from Ödemiş. The **old quarter** with its rickety houses is uphill from the main traffic roundabout in the northwest of town; you might have a look at the map posted outside the **museum** (daily except Mon 8.30am–noon & 1–5pm; 1.25YTL), but the best strategy is just to wander around. First, find the **Yeşil Imaret Zaviyesi**, also known as the Yahşi Bey Camii, built in 1442 by a general of Murat II as the core of a dervish community. An unusual scallop-shell half-dome looms over the *mihrab*, as does stalactite vaulting over the front door. No other monument cries out for attention – your main impression will be of a staggering number (reputedly 37) of indifferently restored Ottoman mosques, and older *türbes* or tombs, including two by the *otogar*.

Tire's atmosphere is, however, considerably enlivened by a large Gypsy presence from the surrounding villages, most in evidence at the weekly **Tuesday market**, reputedly the best in the Aegean region. The Gypsies are probably the source of the lace articles sold in the bazaar, and of the local horse-cart painting technique, imitated by some wealthy city-dwellers on their kitchen cabinets.

The heart of ancient Ionia

Although ancient **Ionia** – including half of the historic league of thirteen cities known as the Panionium – extended north of the Çeşme peninsula, what the term usually evokes is the often startlingly beautiful territory around the deltas of the Küçük and Büyük Menderes rivers. Few other parts of Turkey can match this region for the sheer concentration of ancient cities, which in their time were at the forefront in the emergence of the sciences, philosophy and the arts.

The Ionian coast was first colonized by Greek-speakers in the twelfth century BC and the culture reached its zenith during the seventh and sixth centuries BC. Enormous advantages accrued to those who chose to settle here: an amenable climate, fertile, well-watered terrain, and a strategic location between the Aegean – with its many fine harbours – and inland Anatolia. Local development was only temporarily hampered by the Persian invasions, Alexander the Great's contrary campaigns, and the chaos following his death, and under the Romans and the Byzantines the region perked up again. Indeed, urban life here might have continued indefinitely were it not for the inexorably receding coastline – thanks to the two silt-bearing rivers. By mid-Byzantine times virtually all of the Ionian cities had been abandoned, and with the declaration of Christianity as the state religion, religious centres and oracles met a similar fate.

Today's inhabitants have found the silver lining to the cloud of the advancing deltas, cashing in on the rich soil brought down from the hills. Vast tracts of cotton, tobacco, sesame and grain benefit from irrigation works, while groves of pine, olive and cypress, which need no such encouragement, adorn the hills and wilder reaches. And the sea, though more distant than in former times, still beckons when tramping the ruins palls. Indeed, tourism is now threatening to outstrip agriculture as a means of making a living.

This is nowhere more obvious than in **Kuşadası**, an unabashedly utilitarian base for excursions to the major antiquities. The main show of the area is undoubtedly the ensemble of ruins that span numerous eras: most notably at **Ephesus**; at **Priene** – perhaps the most dramatic site of all the Ionian cities; at **Miletus**, further south – probably the least impressive; and at **Didyma**, with its gargantuan temple. The beaches near these ruins unfortunately tend to be functional at best and always exposed; the immensely popular exception is **Altınkum**, now a densely developed and tatty package-holiday venue.

Kuşadası

KUŞADASİ is a brash, mercenary and unpleasant Las Vegas-on-Sea that extends along several kilometres of coast and well inland. In just three decades its population has swelled from about 6000 to almost 40,000, though how many of these are year-round inhabitants is debatable.

The town – whose name means "Bird Island" – is many people's introduction to the country: efficient ferry services link it with the Greek island of Sámos, while the resort is an obligatory port of call for Aegean cruise ships, which disgorge vast crowds in summer, who delight the local souvenir merchants after a visit to the ruins of Ephesus just inland. Not to be outdone by Bodrum and Marmaris, and in a studied attempt to siphon off some business from the Greek islands opposite,

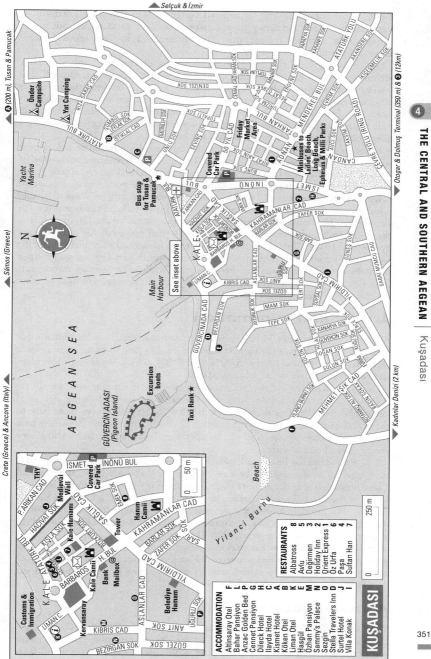

▲ Selçuk & İzmir

◀ (200 m), Tusan & Pamucak
◀ Samos (Greece)
◀ Crete (Greece) & Ancona (Italy)

N

Yacht Marina

A E G E A N   S E A

Main Harbour

Excursion boats

GÜVERCIN ADASI
(Pigeon Island)

Taxi Rank ★

Yilanci Burnu

Beach

Önder
X Campsite

▲ Yat Camping

Bus stop for Tusan & Pamucak

See above

See inset above

Friday Market Area

Covered Car Park

Minibuses to Ladies' Beach, Long Beach, Ephesus & Milli Park

▼ Otogar & Dolmuş Terminal (350 m) & ⑤ (12km)

▼ Kadınlar Denizi (2 km)

0   50 m

0   250 m

ACCOMMODATION
Altınsaray Otel   F
Bahar Pansiyon   L
Anzac Golden Bed   P
Cennet Pansiyon   G
Dilek Hotel   H
İlayda Hotel   C
Kısmet Hotel   A
Köken Otel   B
Liman Otel   E
Hasgül   K
Özhan Pansiyon   M
Sammy's Palace   N
Sezgin   O
Stella Travelers Inn   D
Surtel Hotel   J
Villa Konak   I

RESTAURANTS
Albatross   8
Avlu   5
Değirmen   3
Holiday Inn   2
Orient Express   1
Öz Urfa   6
Paşa   4
Sultan Han   7

KUŞADASI

Customs & Immigration

THY

Medieval Wall

Covered Car Park

Kale Hamamı

Tower

Kale Camii

Kervansaray

Bank @ Mailbox

Hanım Camii

Belediye Hamam

the local authorities have also constructed a huge yacht marina at the north end of town. It's the largest and best-equipped marina northwest of Marmaris, but it can't help but seem a strange venture, since the coast nearby is largely exposed leeward shore and unsuitable for cruising.

Not surprisingly, all this rapid development has affected local attitudes. New arrivals are besieged by touts offering accommodation, carpets and so forth, and unaccompanied women should be prepared for the shock of being singled out as targets. Reasons to stay here include the excellent connections to nearby attractions, the adjacent beaches and the lively and comparatively sophisticated nightlife, rather than the town's minimal charm. However, if beer-guzzling holiday-makers leave you cold, you might prefer Selçuk as a base.

Kuşadası's origins are obscure; no proven trace has been found of any ancient settlement. The Venetians and Genoese renamed the Byzantine anchorage of Ania as Scala Nuova when they established the harbour here to replace Ephesus's silted-up one, but only in the Ottoman era did the port acquire its current name, derived from the small fortified islet – Güvercin Adası, or "Pigeon Island" – tethered to the mainland by a causeway. The little castle on the island is actually the southernmost of several Aegean fortresses built by the Genoese during the fourteenth and fifteenth centuries. Sepia-toned postcards for sale, reissued by the local Lions' Club, show the town as it was from the 1920s until the 1950s: handsome, tiered ensembles of tile-roofed nineteenth-century houses grouped in distinct neighbourhoods (of the Jews, the Greeks, the Muslim immigrants from Crete or the Peloponnese) – especially poignant souvenirs in light of what has transpired here since the 1970s.

Arrival and information

Arriving by **ferry** from Sámos, you'll exit customs directly onto Liman Caddesi, and walk right past the **tourist office** at no. 13 (June–Sept daily 8am–5pm; Oct–May Mon–Fri 8am–5pm; ☎0256/614 1103), which hands out town plans and keeps exhaustive lists of accommodation.

The **long-distance otogar**, where you're dropped if coming from the south, is over a kilometre out, past the end of Kahramanlar Caddesi on the ring road (*çevre yolu*) to Söke. **Local dolmuşes**, labeled "Şehir Içi", travel from here to the centre of town, stopping at the corner of Atatürk and Inönü *bulvarı*s, where you can also pick up services to the northern Tusan beach and its southern annex of Kadınlar Denizi.

If you're bound for Izmir on Elbirlik's frequent shuttle service, you really have to trudge out to the *otogar* to be sure of getting a seat, since they often sell out. These buses pass also the **airport** gate, 700m from the terminal proper; ask to be let off at *havalimanı kavşağı* ("airport junction"), and allow an hour and a half for the trip. Taxis usually wait to transfer you the final distance from the junction to the airport, and you pay 5YTL maximum per car. A taxi between Kuşadası and the airport will cost you a staggering 100YTL.

Drivers have a choice of **car parks** in the centre of town, including an open-air park on Atatürk Bulvarı and a covered car park on Inönü Bulvarı, both of which cost a flat 3YTL. Illegally parked vehicles will be towed to a remote pound and drivers fined a minimum of 35YTL.

Accommodation

The tourist office lists over 400 **hotels and pansiyons** of all categories in Kuşadası, though some of these are used as brothels. One area for reasonably priced, hygienic accommodation is just south of the Kale – the core of the town – uphill from

Barbaros Hayrettin Bulvarı, particularly the upper reaches of Yıldırım, Aslanlar and Kıbrıs *caddesi*s. For a relatively central location with a sea view, try Bezirgan Sokak, above Kıbrıs Caddesi, reached quickest via the stairs behind the Orient Bazaar shopping centre, although it's a steep climb if you're carrying luggage. For more comfort, there are a number of sea-view establishments scattered along the entire length of the shore road. Kadınlar Denizi (Ladies' Beach) may suggest itself as a cheap and cheerful base, but accommodation here can be squalid, and the poor beach can't compensate for its relative remoteness.

It's advisable to choose from the hotels and *pansiyon*s we recommend below, as we have received serious complaints about a number of establishments and proprietors, particularly those who tout at the *otogar* or the pier.

Bezirgan Sokak

Hasgül Bezirgan Sok 53 ☎0256/614 3641. At the quiet end of Bezirgan Sok, beyond the co-managed *Hotel Stella*. Some of the plainly decorated rooms overlook the bay; there's a terrific roof terrace, friendly staff, plus use of the *Stella*'s pool. ❷

Stella Travelers Inn Bezirgan Sok 44 ☎0256/614 1632, ⓦwww.stellatravelersinn.com. This former two-star hotel has been transformed into a decent backpackers hostel with good-sized dorms (€9), double and triple rooms, a rooftop bar with views of the harbour, a swimming pool, Internet access and laundry service. Breakfast not included. ❸

Kıbrıs Caddesi and Kale

Bahar Pansiyon Cephane Sok 12, Kale ☎0256/614 1191. Down in the flatlands in an area better known for nightlife than quiet sleep, but the double glazing in the well-appointed, air-conditioned rooms keeps the noise at bay. Closed in winter. ❸

Liman Otel Kıbrıs Cad, Buyral Sok 4 ☎0256/612 3149, ⓕ614 6913. Very friendly service, fair-sized rooms, some with air conditioning and tiled bathrooms, in a small, modern building. It's central but relatively calm; ask for a sea-facing room. ❸

Özhan Pansiyon Kıbrıs Cad 5 ☎0256/614 2932. Small but reasonably kept *pansiyon*, whose quiet doubles with neutral decor represent good value. A nice terrace bar and heating in winter. ❷

Sammy's Palace Kıbrıs Cad 14 ☎0256/612 2588, ⓦwww.hotelsammyspalace.com. This large hostel, favoured by antipodeans, has cramped dorms (a rather pricey €12), basic doubles, and a rooftop restaurant/bar commanding enviable views of the shoreline. It's well organized, with Internet and laundry facilities, and a street-level travel agent. ❷

Surtel Hotel Atatürk Bul 20, Hacivat Sok ☎0256/612 0606, ⓔsurtel@kusadasi.net. Three-star comfort on a pedestrian alley bordering the *kale* wall. Attractively designed complex with a shaded café, large pool and restaurant. Rooms are spacious and comfortable, if rather heavy on the chintz. ❹

Yıldırım, Aslanlar and Kahramanlar caddesis

Anzac Golden Bed Aslanlar Cad, Uğurlu Sok 1 ☎0256/614 8708, ⓦwww.kusadasihotels .com/goldenbed. Signposted from Yıldırım Cad, this laid-back, friendly and quiet *pansiyon* is nicely decorated with kilims and home furnishings. Good views from both the balconied rooms and the rooftop breakfast terrace. Book ahead in high season. ❸

Cennet Pansiyon Yayla Sok 1, corner of Yıldırım Cad ☎0256/614 4893. Spotless *pansiyon* with a small garden. *Table d'hôte* meals available by advance arrangement. ❷

Dileck Hotel Kahramanlar Cad 73 ☎0256/614 9262, ⓦwww.dilekhotel.com. A centrally located hotel with a small pool, spacious dining area and well-stocked bar. Doubles are fairly minimally furnished, with dark-wood fittings, tiled floors and air conditioning. Tours offered. ❹

Sezgin Hotel Aslanlar Cad 68 ☎0256/614 4225, ⓔsezgin@ispro.net.tr. Run by the energetic Sezgin ("Mr Flash") and his multilingual staff, this extremely well-organized hotel, popular with backpackers, has a breakfast garden with pool, satellite TV, Internet facilities, and a wide range of other services including airport pick-up and a ten-percent discount on Sámos tickets.❷

🏃 **Villa Konak** Yıldırım Cad 55 ☎0256/612 2170, ⓦwww.villakonakhotel.com. Lovely converted old house with delightful rambling gardens, thick with magnolia and citrus trees. The large, stylish bedrooms are decorated with an assortment of antiques and there's a good restaurant. ❺

On the seafront

Altınsaray Otel Yılancı Burnu Sok ☎0256/614 4939, ⓦwww.hotelaltinsaray.com. Attractively set in landscaped gardens; with a *faux* İznik-tiled atrium and dining room. Only some of the smallish rooms have balconies overlooking the medium-sized pool, but the beach isn't far away. ❸

Ilayda Hotel Atatürk Bul 40 ℡0256/614 3807, ⓦwww.hotelilayda.com. Rather boxy-looking sea-front hotel of 1970s vintage but well maintained; the surprisingly quiet rooms have sea views, TV and air conditioning. ❹

Kismet Hotel Yacht Marina ℡0256/618 1290, ⓦwww.kismet.com.tr. Part owned by Hümeyra Özbaş, a princess descended from the last Otto-man sultan, this elegant spot inhabits a different universe from the rest of the town's hotels. From its lovely landscaped gardens, set high above the yacht marina, Kuşadası looks peaceful and almost beautiful. Ordinary rooms resemble small suites, while "de luxe" rooms are palatial, and there's a private lido and tennis court. ❽

Köken Otel İstiklâl Cad 5 ℡0256/614 1460. Set back just inland from noisy Atatürk Bul, this small, friendly two-star hotel has balconied rooms with sea views. ❸

Campsites

Önder Atatürk Bul 74, behind the Yacht Marina ℡0256/618 1590, ⓕ618 1517. Popular, reason-ably priced place with good facilities, including tennis courts, a swimming pool and restaurant. Open all year.

Yat Kamping Atatürk Bul 76 ℡0256/618 1516, ⓦwww.campingturkey.com. Just south of *Önder* campsite and offering much the same fare – tents for hire, a caravan area, a swimming pool, restau-rant and laundry service. Open all year.

The Town

Liman Caddesi runs 200m from the ferry port up to the sixteenth-century **Öküz Mehmet Paşa Kervansaray**, restored as a luxury hotel where themed "Turkish Nights" concerts are held. To the right is the Orient Bazaar shopping centre, while to the left is Atatürk Bulvarı, the main harbour **esplanade**. Barbaros Hayrettin Bulvarı is a pedestrian precinct beginning next to the *kervansaray* and homing in on a little **stone tower**, a remnant of the town's medieval walls. To the left as you ascend lies the **Kale district**, huddled inside the rest of the walls, with a namesake mosque and some fine traditional houses that help lend the town what little appeal it has – most of these have been done up as restaurants and bars. Bearing left down Sağlık Caddesi takes you along the rear of Kale, where bits of old wall (including the landscaped stretch parallel to Hacivat Sokak) are visible; bearing right leads up towards some of Kuşadası's more desirable *pansiyons*, scattered among the largest neighbourhood of handsome old dwellings. Continuing straight on, the walkway (emblazoned with a sign "Old Bazaar") changes its name to Kahramanlar Caddesi, dividing (the left fork becomes Adnan Menderes Bulvarı) just past the Hanım Camii. **Market day** is Friday, with the market area north of Adnan Menderes Bulvarı inevitably skewed by tourist interests.

Out across the causeway, **Güvercin Adası** presents a series of landscaped ter-races within its fortifications, dotted with tea gardens and snack bars – good spots to wait for an afternoon ferry to Greece. Swimming off the islet is rocky; for the closest decent sand, head 500m further south to the small beach north of **Yılanci Burnu**, or patronize one of the **day-trips** offered by excursion boats moored along the causeway. Most offer a similar itinerary, leaving at 9am, visiting three isolated beaches and returning by 4pm. The price usually hovers around 25YTL; chat with the skippers first before you make your choice.

The beaches

There's a small stretch of artificial beach in the town centre between the main harbour and the yacht marina, although this is pretty grubby and, in high season, crowded almost beyond belief. Kuşadası's most famous beach, **Kadınlar Denizi** (Ladies' Beach), just under 3km southwest of town, is a slight improvement but gets equally congested in summer. Dolmuşes (labelled "Ladies' Beach") trundle

△ Ladies' Beach, Kuşadası

south along the seafront past Güvercin Adası, and continue on to **Paradise Beach**, just one cove further along, which is smaller and quieter with only a few bars.

Tusan beach, a long stretch of hard-packed sand, 5km to the north of town, is probably more worthwhile, despite noise from the coast road; the *Tusan Hotel* at the northern end rents out all manner of watersports equipment. This area is also home to two of the largest waterparks in Turkey, Adaland (☎0256/618 1252, ⓦwww.adaland.com) and Aquafantasy (☎0232/893 1111, ⓦhttp://aquafantasy .com), both of which have all the chutes, slides and wave pools you could possibly want. All Kuşadası–Selçuk minibuses pass by.

Much the best beach in the area is **Pamucak**, at the mouth of the Küçük Menderes river, 15km north of town, a little way off the route to Selçuk. The dolmuş from Kuşadası's Atatürk Bulvarı to Selçuk (every half-hour) stops at the northern end of the beach. The main disadvantage of this exposed, four-kilometre-long stretch of sand is that it can't be used if the wind is up. Popular principally with local families, it's scarcely developed except for the two enormous complexes situated near the far south end.

Eating

The vast majority of **restaurants** here are aimed squarely at package holiday-makers and the hordes of tourists coming off cruise-liners – you'll have no trouble finding somewhere to serve you a full English breakfast at any time of day. However, authentic local cuisine can be found, and it tends to be cheaper than the foreign fare aimed at tourists. For quality fish dishes, locals recommend one or two restaurants overlooking the harbour and ferry terminal, though prices can be daunting. Better value is offered by the establishments located inside the castle on Güvercin Adası.

Kale area

Avlu Cephane Sok 15/A. You'll do no better for traditional Turkish food than this unlicensed place with rear-courtyard seating. It serves low-priced grilled lamb and steamtray specialities for around 5YTL.

Öz Urfa Kebapçısı Cephane Sok 9. Well regarded locally for its authentic Turkish dishes; particularly geared towards grilled meat. Expect to pay 7.5YTL per dish. Licensed.

Paşa Cephane Sok 21. Entertaining family affair

set within the confines of a picturesque courtyard. Recommended for its seafood and very cheap *meze*s.

Sultan Han Bahar Sok 8. Decent seafood restaurant in amongst the maze of narrow alleyways just back from the front. Prices are reasonable (around 10YTL for fish, though check before ordering) and there's a nice outdoor courtyard.

South of the tower

Albatros Restaurant Emek Sok 4, Belediye Dükkanları Zabıta Karşısı. Squeaky clean unlicensed restaurant (the sign is obscured by a huge climbing vine), which serves outstanding stews and the like for just over 5YTL, each accompanied by a complimentary dish of pickled chilli.

Holiday Inn Restaurant Kahramanlar Cad. Popular with discerning locals and tourists alike, this eastern Turkish outfit has made a name for itself

with its array of kebabs, including the two-person *Vali Kebap* of lamb, beef and chicken served with rice, salad and chips for 17YTL. Licensed.

Orient Express Adnan Menderes Bul 17/1. A small, friendly, Dutch-run establishment with a nice garden. One of the better, more popular restaurants catering for the tourist trade, with fodder including pasta or steak and chips.

Saraydamları

Değirmen Davutlar Yolu 4, 3km from Davutlar, 12km south of İzmir ☎0256/681 2150. Meticulous re-creation of an old mill, built from traditional and salvaged materials, with a menu featuring seldom-seen household breads, noodles and stews, as well as selections from the grill (around 20YTL), with chicken and duck raised on the premises. Summer tables on the lawn overlook an artificial lake. Booking advised. Open all year.

Drinking and nightlife

After-dark activity in Kuşadası is distributed over perhaps three dozen **bars**, clumped into distinct groups: a dwindling number of arty, genteel bars of the Kale district; their more energetic neighbours, featuring live music sung in either Turkish or English; and Irish/British pubs with karaoke gear and recorded house and techno tracks, culminating in the downmarket, foreigner-dominated "Barlar Sokak" area. If you pace the streets named below, guided by the cranked-up sound systems, you'll certainly find something to suit.

The most durable of the **Kale** watering holes, and congenial environments for meeting educated Turks on holiday, include the perennially popular *She*, at the corner of Bahar and Sakarya *sokak*s. Dancers will want to gravitate towards the large two-floor open-roofed *Ecstacy* nearby at Sakarya Sok 10, which is flanked by several decent bars including the English-owned *Taps* and the appropriately named *Another Bar*. *Ankara* on Cephane Sokak is a good representative of a live Turkish-music venue, while the *Big Bang Rock Café* at Kışla Sok 27 is true to its name.

Just off the foot of Yıldırım Caddesi, Eskipazaryeri Sokak has been officially renamed **Barlar Sokak** (Bar Street), as the entry arch proclaims. The decibels emanating from the dozen or so "Irish" and "London" pubs are deafening, with the Union Jack T-shirt brigade and rugby-song choirs out in force. If this seems at all desirable then *Jimmy's Irish Bar* is probably a good place to start and one of the few bars here actually owned by a Kuşadasın.

Listings

Banks and exchange There are ATMs on Liman Cad by the tourist office and on Barbaros Hayrettin Bul, where you also find a few *döviz* offices.

Books Kuydaş, İnönü Bul 8/B, for secondhand English-language books, newspapers, magazines, CDs and tapes, and nautical charts.

Car rental Offices cluster along İnönü Bulvarı, just back from the sea; standard walk-in rates of around €70 a day can be bargained down to €30–50 at slack times. Outlets include: Avis,

Atatürk Bul 26/B ☎0256/614 4600; Budget, Sağlık Cad 58 ☎0256/614 4956; Katar, İnönü Bul 58 ☎0256/613 2346; and Start, İnönü Bul 6/1 ☎0256/614 3126.

Ferries The main agency for *Sultan 1*, the Turkish morning boat to Sámos, is Azim Tours, Liman Cad, Yayla Pasajı (☎0256/614 1553, ⊛www.azimtours .com), though any travel agent in town should be able to sell you a ticket. All other boats, including the Greek afternoon ferry and the twice weekly hydrofoil are handled by Diana Travel, Atatürk Bul 80 (☏0256/618 1800, ⊛www.dianatravel.com). A return costs €35, considerably more if you stay overnight as you'll have to pay both an exit tax from Greece and an entry tax to Turkey. For schedules and prices, see "Travel details" at the end of the chapter.

Hamams Kale Hamamı, behind the Kale Camii, is very touristy, Belediye Hamam on Yıldırım Cad slightly less so. Both open daily 9am–9pm and are expensive at 25–35YTL.

Hospital The state hospital is at Atatürk Bul 32 (☏0256/613 1616), near the park.

Internet M@ilbox Internet Café, Barbaros Hayrettin Bul, 1st floor (daily 9am–8pm).

Laundry Can Laundry, Özgür Sok 8, off the south side of Adnan Menderes Bul.

Post office The PTT is on Barbaros Hayrettin Bul (May–Sept 24hr; Oct–June 8am–midnight).

Tours and travel agencies *Sammy's Palace* (see "Accommodation" above) organizes day-tours to some of the more popular tourist destinations, such as Ephesus (€35), Pamukkale (€30) and combined trips to Didyma, Miletus, Priene (€30). Other recommended travel agents include Sisan Tours, Yıldırım Cad 17 (☏0256/614 1188, ⊛www.sisantours.com), and Anker Travel, Ismet İnönü Bul 14 (☏0256/612 4598, ⊛www.ankertravel.com).

Dilek Yarımadası Milli Parkı

The imposing outline of **Samsun Dağı**, otherwise known as Dilek Dağı (the ancient Mount Mycale), dominates the skyline south of Kuşadası and may inspire notions of a visit. Regular dolmuşes (8am–dusk; 1hr) make light work of the 28-kilometre trip to the national park established around the mountain.

The **Dilek Yarımadası Milli Parkı** (spring & autumn daily 8am–5pm; summer daily 8am–6.30pm; winter closed; 3YTL, cars 4YTL) was set aside in 1966 for, among other reasons, the protection of its thick forest and diverse fauna, which is said to include rare lynx, jackal and wild cats. However, you are unlikely to see any of the species in question, since much of the 28,000-acre park is an off-limits military zone; try to walk out towards the tempting bits at the very tip of the peninsula and armed conscripts will bar the way.

Arguably, the park performs its function as a wildlife preserve better than it does that of an all-purpose recreation area. The undeniable beauty of the terrain, certainly the most unspoiled along the Turkish Aegean, is owed entirely to the military presence. The most visited portion of the unrestricted zone consists of a ten-kilometre stretch of mostly paved road beyond the entrance and four good, but often windswept, beaches along it – **İçmeler** (hard sand shaded by plane trees), just beyond the gate; **Aydınlık Koyu** (pebbles); **Kavaklı Burun** (pebbles); and the last and prettiest one, **Karasu** (700m of pea gravel). Each beach has its own small snack bar or drinks kiosk operating in high season.

Immediately past Karasu the onward dirt track is signposted as "Yasak Bölge", and armed patrols will turn you back should you venture further. A lone jeep track, gated against wheeled traffic and signposted as "Kanyon", complete with walking-man symbol, does saunter inland between Aydınlık and Kavaklı beaches, curling up to the **summit ridge** east of 1237-metre Samsun Dağı (Dilek Tepesi).

Better access to the ridge is possible by trail from **ESKIDOĞANBEY**, a village to the south. This is an all-day outing, best done in spring or autumn to avoid the heat. Chances of wildlife-spotting, particularly badgers, jackals and birds of prey, are probably better here than within the confines of the national park on the other side of the mountain. Since the closure of most short-term accommodation in Eskidoğanbey, walkers tend to take an early dolmuş to one or other of the trailheads, hike over the mountain, and take an evening dolmuş back to Söke or Kuşadası from the walk's endpoint.

There are no facilities for staying overnight in the park, though it does provide WCs, barbecue areas and a small café. The closest *pansiyon*s and hotels, pitched at Turkish visitors, are in and around **GÜZELÇAMLI**, a village 1km outside the reserve boundaries. The pebble beaches 300m below Güzelçamlı are not as good as those in the park, and are hemmed in by massive over-development.

Selçuk and around

A laid-back farming town only two decades ago, **SELÇUK** has been catapulted into the limelight of premier-league tourism by its proximity to the ruins of Ephesus. The flavour of tourism here, though, is markedly different from that at nearby Kuşadası; its less prestigious inland location, good-value accommodation and ecclesiastical connections (not least, the burial place of St John the Evangelist) make it a haven for a disparate mix of backpackers and Bible Belters. Some may find this characterization a bit harsh, but it's not meant as out-and-out disparagement – it means, among other things, that the numerous carpet-shop hustlers and accommodation touts here have a more realistic idea of their audience's financial limits.

Although evidence of settlement as early as 2000 BC has been found atop Aya-soluk hill (a feature used as Selçuk's logo), the town only really flourished as a Byzantine enterprise during the fifth century AD, after the harbour of adjacent Ephesus had completely silted up. Like Birgi and Tire, the place was later a haunt of the Aydınoğlu clan, who yielded to the Ottomans in the early fifteenth century. Despite a role in the events of the early Church, including key events in the life of Paul, John and (supposedly) the Virgin, local Christianity thereafter was mostly restricted to the village of Kirkince, now Şirince (see p.364). In this century, the town's demographic profile has become an uneasy mix: of Rumeliot (south Balkan) and Bosnian emigrants, who arrived in successive waves between 1890 and 1960; settled Yörük nomads wont to idle in the teahouses; and Kurds and gypsies. Each group has its own designated quarter, socializing little with the others.

Arrival and information

At the base of the castle hill and across the busy E24/550 highway (known as Atatürk Caddesi in town), a replica of one of the statues of Artemis from the town museum marks the start of a pedestrian precinct, with Cengiz Topel Caddesi its main throughfare. This leads east to the **train station**, from where there are seven daily connections to İzmir, two to Denizli and one each to Afyon, Isparta and Söke. Along the way you'll pass the **PTT** and several of the town's restaurants and bars. Following Atatürk Caddesi a bit further south brings you to the **otogar**; it's worth knowing that the Elbirlik shuttle between Kuşadası and İzmir airport always makes a stop on the main highway.

On the western side of Atatürk Caddesi, on the corner of the central park and Uğur Mumcu Caddesi (or Love Street as the sign proclaims), the cheerful **tourist office** (May–Sept daily 8.30am–noon & 1–5.30pm; Oct–April Mon–Fri 9am–noon & 1–5.30pm; ☎0232/892 6328) has extensive lists of accommodation. You will find the tourist office to be a more disinterested source of intelligence than the rug boys and *pansiyon* promoters (often one and the same person) who mob every bus arrival, sometimes boarding them at the town limits to deliver their sales pitch. Subsequent hustles are more refined, and some include the time-honoured offer of a lift to Ephesus and loan of a site guidebook – bracketed by "coincidental" stopovers at a relative's carpet shop for tea and a "chat".

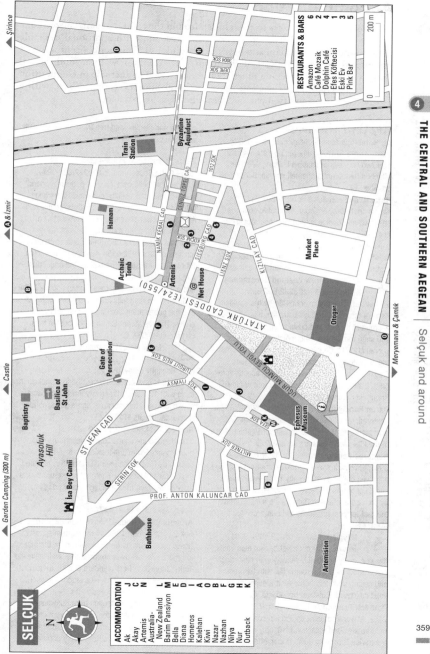

Accommodation

Most recommended places to stay cluster around the central pedestrianized zone or just west of Atatürk Caddesi, near the museum, with additional desirable establishments scattered on and beyond Ayasoluk hill. Another concentration of *pansiyon*s is found in the east of the town – five minutes' walk beyond the rail line – where life is lived at a more traditional pace. The increase in competition between Selçuk's hotels is good news for hotel hunters, though those with a "stork-view" option often charge a premium for the privilege.

Around the museum

Ak Hotel Uğur Mumcu Sevgi Yolu 14 ☎0232/892 2161, ✆892 3142. Family-run operation spread over two (somewhat shabby) buildings with an attached restaurant and small garden. Bargaining possible. ❷

Hotel Akay Serin Sok 3 ☎0232/892 3172, ⓦwww.hotelakay.8m.com. Affordable boutique-style two-star choice spread over two properties with standard and superior rooms, all with balconies overlooking a garden. Fine views of the mosque, castle and basilica from its cushioned rooftop restaurant and bar. Swimming pool. ❸

Australia-New Zealand Guesthouse Miltner Sok 17 ☎0232/892 6050, ⓦwww.anzguesthouse.com. Run by the ebullient Harry, a returned Turkish-Australian, this *pansiyon* is proud of its rug- and cushion-covered courtyard and snug rooftop bar, where nightly barbeques are served (12YTL). Doubles (with private bathrooms), triples (without) and dorms (€7.50) available. Also offers tours to Ephesus (35YTL), scooter hire (35YTL a day), and lends out bikes free of charge. Breakfast not included. ❷

Barım Pansiyon 1045 Sok 34 ☎0232/892 6923. Restored, rambling old house complete with its own stork's nest and a lush courtyard/garden. Most of the kitschy doubles are en-suite. ❷

Homeros Pension Asmalı Sok 17 ☎0232/892 3995, ⓦwww.homerospension.com. Split over two adjoining buildings this family-run pension has a choice of rooms, all nicely decorated and furnished by their carpenter son Derviş. Fine sunsets from the roof terrace; breakfast and home-cooked meals extra. ❸

Nilya 1051 Sok 7 ☎0232/892 9081, ⓦwww.nilya.com. Set behind high walls, this is a lovely, tranquil hideaway with charmingly cluttered kilim-strewn rooms (all with bathrooms and ceiling fans) laid out around a peaceful, tree-lined courtyard. Excellent breakfasts. ❹

Outback Pension 1045 Sok 45 ☎0232/892 2452, ⓦwww.outbackpension.8m.com. Friendly, moderately sized establishment, ably run by Mark, a returnee Turk from Down Under, offering en-suite doubles and singles, and free transport to Ephesus and local beaches. ❷

East of Ayasoluk

Hotel Bella St Jean Cad 7 ☎0232/892 3944, ⓦwww.hotelbella.com. An ever-popular readers' favourite near the basilica gate, this offers good-value, nicely decorated rooms with balconies and American power-showers. Good views of local stork-nests from the rooftop restaurant. ❸

Kalehan Hotel İzmir Cad, 5min north of central junction ☎0232/892 6154, ⓦwww.kalehan.com. Bit of a tour mill, but luxurious for the price, this large complex of three Ottoman-style houses is laid out around a central rose garden and pool. The bedrooms are tastefully furnished (most with a/c) and the public areas are littered with antiques and curios. The restaurant is one of the best in town (set menu 20YTL). ❺

Nazar Hotel Eski İzmir Cad 14 ☎0232/892 2222, ⓦwww.nazarhotel. com. Recently renovated, this good-value family-run place is now one of the best budget choices in town with 13 clean, attractively furnished rooms, a new courtyard and pool area, and a good rooftop restaurant (meals 12YTL). ❷

Nazhan 1044 Sok 2 ☎0232/892 8731, ✆nazhan@superonline.com. A delightful small house packed with antiques and bric-a-brac, chosen by Nazhan and Kemal when they escaped the rat race of İstanbul. Each of the five doubles is individually decorated to a high standard. ❹

Around the *otogar*

Artemis Guest House ("Jimmy's Place"), 1012 Sok 2 ☎0232/892 1982, ⓦwww.artemisguesthouse.com. In swish new premises near the market place and run by an irrepressible, well-travelled Turk, "Jimmy's" offers standard and luxury (plushly furnished) en-suite rooms, plus laundry, kitchen, garden, pool, Internet access, and cheap breakfasts (6YTL). Will arrange collection from Kuşadası ferry. Book ahead. Standard rooms ❶, luxury rooms ❸

Kiwi Pension Kubilay Cad 26 ☎0232/892 4892, ⓦwww.kiwipension.com. Deservedly popular backpackers', 5min south of the bus station. Basic but clean rooms (ask to look around as some are better than others) with balcony, and dorm beds (€7). Also has a swimming pool, located separately in the orchards on the road to Ephesus. Large breakfast included. ❸

East of the train station
Diana Pension 3004 Sok 30, Zafer Mah ☎0232/892 1265, ✉jesseakin@hotmail.com. A small, quality pension with good views of Selçuk, popular with mature tourists. Run by the accommodating Jesse; some of the comfortable, homely rooms have air conditioning. ❷
Nur Pansiyon 3004 Sok 16, Zafer Mah ☎0232/892 6595. Run by a widow, Sükran Kiraci, and particularly appropriate for single women trav-

ellers. An optional breakfast is served in the garden, with excellent cheap evening meals available too. Will collect arrivals from the *otogar*. ❶

Campsites
Dereli Motel and Kamping Pamucak beach, 7km west of Selçuk ☎0232/893 1205. Large campsite set amongst palm trees, right on the beach; with attached restaurant and simple bungalows (❷) you could almost be in Thailand. Can arrange pick-up from *otogar* though the Pamucak dolmuş drops at entrance. Open all year.
Garden Camping Selçuk, 300m beyond İsa Bey Camii ☎0232/892 6165, ✆892 2997. Shady, grassy campsite where you can pitch your tent for €7 (used by caravans and tourers, too). Open all year.

The Town

Selçuk offers a variety of antiquities from diverse eras (not least in its excellent Ephesus Museum), which can easily be toured in a single day. The town's sights are numerous and interesting enough to warrant another night's stay after visiting Ephesus, especially if you also plan on heading out to the shrine at Meryemana or the hill-village of Şirince.

Ayasoluk Hill
Lodestone of settlement in every era, **Ayasoluk** hill (daily 8am–6.30pm; 4YTL) is the first point you should head for. You enter the site through the **Gate of Persecution**, so called by the Byzantines because of a relief of Achilles in combat that once adorned it, mistakenly thought to depict a martyrdom of Christians in the amphitheatre of nearby Ephesus.

St John the Evangelist – or "Theologian" as the Greeks knew him – came to Ephesus in the middle of the first century. He died here around 100 AD and was buried on Ayasoluk Hill, whose name is thought to be a corruption of "Ayios Theologos". The sixth-century Byzantine emperor Justinian decided to replace two earlier churches sheltering John's tomb with a basilica worthy of the saint's reputation, and until destruction by Tamerlane's Mongols in 1402 it was one of the largest and most ornate Byzantine churches in existence.

Today, various colonnades and walls of the **Basilica of St John** have been re-erected, courtesy of a religious foundation based in Lima, Ohio, giving just a hint of the building's magnificence in its prime. The purported tomb of the evangelist is marked by a slab on the former site of the altar. Beside the nave is the **Baptistry**, where fundamentalist tourists may pose in the act of dunking for friends' cameras. The restored **Byzantine castle** on top of the hill, which is the first part of the town to come into view as you arrive from the north, is currently closed following the partial collapse of one of its walls.

The Ephesus Museum
The **Ephesus Museum** (Efes Müzesi; daily 8.30am–noon & 1–7pm, winter closes at 5pm; 4YTL) is permanently packed with visitors, but is well worth setting aside the time to visit. Its galleries of finds are arranged thematically rather than chronologically which helps to present the ancient city as a living space rather than just a repository of artefacts, although be aware that the labelling is often

quite vague and, in places, incomplete. The first, small-finds hall contains some of the most famous bronze and ceramic objects in the collection, including Eros riding a dolphin, effigies of the phallic gods Bes and Priapus, a humane bust of the comedian Menander, and various excellent miniatures from the Roman terrace houses at Ephesus, one of which is re-created here and inhabited by costumed cardboard cut-outs.

Beyond here, past some relief and free-standing statuary from the fountains of Ephesus, there are a couple of courtyards, containing sarcophagi, column capitals and stelae, from which steps lead down to another courtyard with attractive fountains and a small souvenir stall.

Continuing through the main galleries, you'll enter a hall devoted to tomb finds and mortuary practices. Just beyond this is the famous **Artemis room**, with two renditions of the goddess studded with multiple testicles (not breasts, as is commonly believed) and tiny figurines of real and mythical beasts, honouring her role as mistress of animals. At Ephesus, Artemis adopted most of the attributes of the indigenous Anatolian mother-goddess Cybele, including a eunuch priesthood – the stone testicles possibly symbolize the ultimate votive offering.

The last gallery houses friezes and busts from imperial cult temples – the strangest fragments a giant forearm and head, the latter misshapen and infantile, part of a five-metre statue of Domitian (emperor 81–96 AD), and a small space set aside for touring exhibitions.

The Artemision

Beyond the museum, 200m along the road toward Ephesus and to the right, are the scanty remains of the **Artemision**, or the sanctuary of Artemis (daily 8.30am–5.30pm; free). The archaic temple here replaced three predecessors dedicated to Cybele, and was itself burned down in 356 BC by Herostratus, a lunatic who (correctly) reckoned his name would be immortalized by the act. The massive Hellenistic replacement was considered to be one of the Seven Wonders of the Ancient World, though this is hard to believe today: the Goths sacked it in 263 AD and the Byzantines subsequently carted off most of the remaining masonry to Ayasoluk and Constantinople, leaving just a lone column (re-erected in modern times) amid battered foundation blocks. It took the English archeologist J.T. Wood six years of trial soundings in the mud to locate the temple's foundations in 1869. Constant pumping is necessary to keep the area from flooding, and in winter the ducks come here for a swim anyway.

İsa Bey Camii

The **İsa Bey Camii** is the most distinguished of the various Selçuk monuments, the style that gives the town its name. It's a late fourteenth-century Aydınoğlu mosque and it represents a transition between Selçuk and Ottoman styles, with its innovative courtyard – where most of the congregation would worship – and stalactite vaulting over the entrance; the contemporary Ulu Cami in Manisa, though much smaller, is conceptually quite similar in its use of a courtyard. Although recently restored, the İsa Bey's two minarets were snapped off long ago and the ablutions fountain in the court is missing. If you can get inside the main hall, you'll see a high, gabled roof supported by Roman columns and some fine tile-work in the south dome. Just south of the mosque are the fenced-off remains of a fourteenth-century **bath-house**, which can be seen from Prof A Kaluncur Caddesi.

Eating, drinking and entertainment

Virtually all Selçuk's **restaurants** are found in the town centre, and tend to be rather similar: they are not nearly so exploitative as some in Kuşadası, though not as refined either. Good-value establishments along and around the pedestrian-ized Cengiz Topel Caddesi include *Efes Köftecisi*, which serves up good, simple and cheap steamtray specials, and the relatively elegant *Eski Ev*, offering good Turkish home-cooking in a leafy courtyard. It's not every restaurant that can offer views of one of the Seven Wonders of the Ancient World, but *Amazon*, on Prof A Kaluncur Cad, a stylish, modern dining room just around the corner from the museum, can oblige from its pavement tables. It's English-owned (hence the appearance of prawn cocktail on the menu), but serves decent kebabs and steaks for around 10YTL. Otherwise, several of the town's hotels – most notably the *Kalehan* – operate decent dining rooms that are open to the public.

After-hours tippling takes place at several noisy **pubs** near Cengiz Topel Caddesi. The *Pink Bar* and *Dolphin Café* have tables spilling out onto Siegburg Cad and are good for late-night carousing, while *Café Mozaik*, around the corner, offers the more sedate charms of *nargile* pipes and comfy floor-cushions.

For formal entertainment, the second or third week of July sees the **Ephesus Festival**, with various international music and dance performances occurring nightly at the Ephesus amphitheatre. Enquire at the tourist office for details and tickets (around 35YTL). Mid-January brings **camel-wrestling bouts**, between huge male camels, at the edge of town.

Around Selçuk

The main draw in the region is the ancient city of Ephesus (p.365), not to be missed if you are staying in Selçuk. However, a few other local diversions are worth considering, including the evocative village of **Şirince**, nestled in the hills 8km to the east. It's increasingly becoming a weekend bolthole for wealthy Turks and makes for an easily attainable day-trip. **Meryemana**, on the other hand, only of any real interest to those on a biblical tour, requires your own transport or a taxi.

Meryemana

Eight kilometres southwest of Selçuk, beyond Ephesus and just below the summit of Bülbül Dağ, stands **Meryemana** (dawn–dusk; 10YTL, plus car-park fees), a monument to piety and faith. Though most orthodox theologians maintain that the Virgin Mary died and was buried in Jerusalem, another school of thought holds that the mother of Jesus accompanied St John the Evangelist when he left Palestine in the middle of the first century on his way to Ephesus.

After the medieval turmoil around Ephesus nobody from abroad was inclined to delve further into the matter until **Catherine Emmerich** (1774–1824), a German nun and seer who never left her country, recorded her visions of a small stone house, where, she claimed, the Virgin had lived her last years. In 1891 Lazarist priests from İzmir decided to follow her descriptions and discovered a building that matched them – and which, in its role as the **chapel of Panayia Kapılı**, was already a focus of adoration by the Orthodox Greeks of nearby Kirkince (now Şirince) especially on August 15, the Feast of the Assumption. Things mushroomed predictably from there, spurred by a papal visit and imprimatur in 1967, and today the place is on the checklist of pilgrims from around the world.

The site is enclosed within a municipal park and subject to a generous dose of commercialism – though the dense forest and fountain are pleasant enough. The **house** itself, now a chapel aligned unusually southwest-to-northeast, probably dates from early Byzantine times, though its foundations may indeed be first-century. It overlooks a beautiful wooded valley and two terraces where a spring gushes forth; nearby, tree branches are festooned with the votive rag-scraps left by Muslim pilgrims, for whom *Meryemana* (Mother Mary) is also a saint. Whatever you may believe about the historical likelihood of this being Mary's last home, the shrine is a tribute to the tenacity of mother-goddess veneration in Anatolia.

The site is accessible only by private car or taxi (or, if you're really determined, on foot, but it's a good hour's walk). If you want to come, it makes sense to combine a visit with a day at Ephesus, whose upper entrance is 5km to the north; see p.365 for details.

Şirince

ŞIRINCE, a well-preserved, originally Greek-built hill-village, situated 8km east of and above Selçuk, has a history going back 600 years. The village's lush orchards and vineyards are now worked by Muslim settlers from near Thessaloníki, who make assorted wines that pack quite a punch – you can taste and buy them at any of the village's many wine shops. Dido Sotiriou, chronicler of the Greek Asia Minor experience and its post-1922 aftermath, visited here in 1990; much of her classic novel *Farewell to Anatolia*, perennially popular in Turkey, was set in the village. Not surprisingly, the place has become a target of tour groups, and on summer weekends, with local hawkers out in strength, it does a passable imitation of a hill-top Kuşadası. In particular, beware of invitations to private homes, which invariably serve as pretexts to foist lacework on you. Out of season, however, it's a much more pleasant and relaxed place and genuinely lives up to its reputation as one of the region's most idyllic villages.

At the edge of Şirince stands a late nineteenth-century **church**, with a pebble-mosaic floor, plaster relief-work on the ceiling and wooden vaulting – though much is crumbling away. Nearer the middle of the village there's a larger stone **basilica** dating from 1839 and restored as an art gallery. But the main point of a visit is the idyllic scenery and the handsome domestic architecture, which, since the late 1980s, has attracted wealthy urban Turks in search of characterful vacation homes.

Six or seven daily **dolmuşes** leave from Selçuk's *otogar* between 8.30am and 5pm, and drop you in the centre of the Şirince village, where nothing is more than a few minutes' walk away. You could stay overnight here, though **accommodation** prices are relatively high: in the centre of town, *Erdem Evleri* (☎0232/898 3069; ❹) has lovely rooms in a restored old house furnished with antiques and boasts the only espresso machine for miles; while the *Nişanyan Evleri* (☎0232/898 3117, ⓦwww.nisanyan.com; ❻) is a restored mansion with serene views and superb singles and doubles, five minutes up on the eastern slopes at the end of a dirt track above the town. Travel-writer owners Sevan and Müjde also have a number of four-person apartments in the village (❻), some with *kerevets* (built-in wooden beds) and designer bathrooms.

There are half a dozen **restaurants** – such as the well-established *Koy* – clustered around the main square at the east end of the village's single-lane bazaar. Alternatively, the Artemis Restaurant enjoys a spectacular setting in a former school overlooking the valley at the entrance to the village, and offers an excellent Turkish menu (mains are 7–10YTL), as well as a wide range of local wines.

Çamlık Open-Air Rail Museum

Some 12km south of Selçuk on the main highway to Aydın, the village of **ÇAMLIK** is the site of the **Çamlık Open-Air Rail Museum** (Buharlı Lokomotif Müzesi; open daily; 2YTL), 50m southwest of the road after the village-limits sign. The museum occupies the sidings of a former train-works and exhibits include more than two dozen steam locomotives, many pre–World War I; the majority are German-made but there are also British, American, Czech, French and Swedish models. The locomotives are rust-proofed and mounted on sections of track, and you are free to clamber up into the cabs and to operate the hand-wound turntable around which a half-dozen of the most impressive are grouped. Other rail vehicles – such as handcarts and cranes – are also on display. A particularly scenic, if slow, way of reaching the museum is by taking one of the three daily Selçuk–Aydın trains, and getting off at Çamlık station. The museum itself is a further 1km walk away in the town's former station, which fell into disuse following the rerouting of the İzmir–Aydın mainline.

Ephesus

With the exception of Pompeii, **EPHESUS** (Efes in Turkish) is the largest and best-preserved ancient city around the Mediterranean; and, after the Sultanahmet district of İstanbul, it's the most visited tourist attraction in Turkey. The ruins are mobbed for much of the year, although with a little planning and initiative it's possible to tour the site in relative peace. Certainly, it's a place you should not miss, though you may come away disappointed at the commercialization and the extent of areas that are off-limits. You'll need two to three partly shady hours to see Ephesus, as well as a bottle of water – the acres of stone act as a grill in the heat of the day, and the water sold from the on-site kiosks is expensive.

Some history

Situated by a fine harbour at the terminus of overland trade routes, and beneficiary of the lucrative cult of the Anatolian mother-goddess Cybele/Artemis, Ephesus led a charmed life from earliest times. Legends relate that **Androclus**, son of King Kodrus of Athens, had been advised by an oracle to settle at a place indicated by a fish and a wild boar. Androclus and his entourage arrived here to find natives roasting fish by the sea; embers from the fire set a bush ablaze, out of which charged a pig, and the city was on its way. The imported worship of Artemis melded easily with that of the indigenous **Cybele**, and the Ephesus of 1000 BC was built on the north slope of Mount Pion (Panayır Dağı), very close to the temple of the goddess.

The Ephesians needed their commercial wealth, since they rarely displayed much common sense, military strength or political acumen. When the Lydian **King Croesus** appeared in the sixth century, the locals could muster no other defence than to rope off the Artemis temple and retreat behind the barrier. Croesus, perhaps amused by this naivety, treated the city leniently and even contributed to the temple. Still unfortified and ungarrisoned, Ephesus passed back and forth between Greek and Persian interests until the Hellenistic era.

Alexander the Great, on his visit in 334 BC, offered to fund the completion of the latest version of the Artemis shrine, but the city fathers tactfully demurred, saying that one deity should not support another, and dug deeper into their own pockets. Following Alexander's death his lieutenant **Lysimachus** moved the city to its present location – necessary because the sea had already receded considerably – and provided it with its first **walls**, traces of which are still visible on Panayır Dağı and Mount Koressos (Bülbül Dağı) to the south.

In subsequent centuries, Ephesus displayed flashes of its old fickleness, changing allegiance frequently and backing various revolts against Roman rule. Yet it never suffered for this lack of principle: during the Roman imperial period it was designated the **capital of Asia** and ornamented with magnificent public buildings – the ones on view today – by a succession of emperors. Ephesus's quarter-million population was swelled substantially at times by the right of sanctuary linked to the sacred precinct of Artemis, allowing shelter to large numbers of criminals. Of a somewhat less lurid cast was the more stable, mixed population of Jews, Romans, and Egyptian and Anatolian cultists.

Despite, or perhaps because of, this, **Christianity** took root early and quickly at Ephesus. St John the Evangelist arrived in the mid-first century, and **St Paul** spent the years 51–53 AD in the city, proselytizing foremost among the Jewish community. As usual, Paul managed to foment controversy even in this cosmopolitan environment, apparently being imprisoned for some time – in a tower bearing his name near the west end of the walls – and later provoking the famous silversmiths' riot, described in Acts 19:23–20:1. Paul preached that the silver votive images of Artemis were not divine. The head of the silversmiths' guild, seeing his livelihood threatened, assembled his fellows in the amphitheatre where they howled "Great is Artemis of the Ephesians!" – as well as calling for the apostle's blood. The authorities managed to calm the crowd, but Paul was obliged to depart for Macedonia.

Under the Byzantines, Ephesus was the venue for two of the **councils of the Church**, including one in 431 AD at which the Nestorian heresy (see p.918) was anathematized. However, the general tenor of the Byzantine era was one of decline, owing to the abandoning of Artemis-worship following the establishment of state Christianity, Arab raids and (worst of all) the final silting up of the harbour. The population began to siphon off to the nearby hill crowned by the tomb and church of St John, future nucleus of the town of Selçuk, and by the time the Selçuks themselves appeared the process was virtually complete.

Visiting the site

Approaching the **site** (daily 8.30am–6.30pm; winter closes 5.30pm; last ticket 30min before closing; 15YTL, 4YTL parking fee) **from Kuşadası**, get the dolmuş to drop you at the *Tusan Motel* junction, from where it's another easy kilometre to the lower entrance and ticket office. **From Selçuk**, many of the hotels offer free transport, or a taxi costs around 6YTL. Alternatively, you could walk the 3km, although you'd have to fend off the constant entreaties of the horse-drawn-cab drivers who ply the route (10YTL per cart): the first 2km of the walk along a mulberry-shaded lane paralleling the busy highway are rather pleasant, the final 1km along a narrow hill with no pavement, less so. There is also a second, **upper entrance** on the southeastern side of Ephesus, on the way to Meryemana – perhaps a more sensible route in summer since it enables you to walk downhill through the site (tour buses tend to drop their clients here, retrieving them at the lower gate). Visiting Meryemana first by **taxi from Selçuk** will allow you to use the upper gate: 40YTL (per car) should include a half-hour wait at "Mary's house", then a final drop-off at the top of the Ephesus site.

The Cave of the Seven Sleepers

Before reaching the lower entrance, you can detour left off the approach road after 300m and then proceed about 1km to visit the **Cave of the Seven Sleepers**, the focus of a touching legend. Seven young Ephesian Christians, refusing to sacrifice to the second-century emperor Decius, took refuge in this cave, were walled in by the imperial guard and fell into a deep sleep. An earthquake shattered the wall and woke them; upon ambling down to town for food, they discovered that two hundred years had passed and that Christianity was now the state religion. When the seven men died soon after – presumably from shock – they were re-interred in the grotto, and a commemorative church was built over their graves.

The place is in fact an extensive network of catacombs backed into the hillside on several levels, which was used until late Byzantine times. Only the lower level can currently be visited, with the rest of the complex tightly fenced and only visible from the perimeter path that snakes above it. On the approach road you run

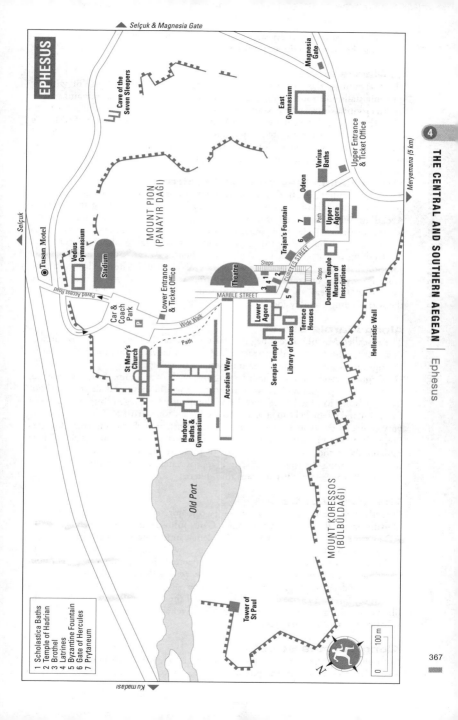

EPHESUS

1 Scholastica Baths
2 Temple of Hadrian
3 Brothel
4 Latrines
5 Byzantine Fountain
6 Gate of Hercules
7 Prytaneum

Selçuk & Magnesia Gate

Magnesia Gate

Cave of the Seven Sleepers

East Gymnasium

Upper Entrance & Ticket Office

Varius Baths

Odeon

Selçuk

Tusan Motel

Vedius Gymnasium

Stadium

MOUNT PION (PANAYIR DAĞI)

Trajan's Fountain

7

Upper Agora

Path

6

Meryemana (5 km)

Paved Access Road

Lower Entrance & Ticket Office

Steps

Theatre

1
4
2

CURETES STREET

Car & Coach Park

Wide Walk

MARBLE STREET

3

5

Domitian Temple

Museum of Inscriptions

Steps

St Mary's Church

Path

Lower Agora

Terrace Houses

Hellenistic Wall

Arcadian Way

Serapis Temple

Library of Celsus

Harbour Baths & Gymnasium

Old Port

MOUNT KORESSOS (BÜLBÜLDAĞI)

Kuşadası

Tower of St Paul

0   100 m

N

a gauntlet of *gözleme* and *çay* stalls, rather more relaxed and pleasant than those crowding the entries to Ephesus proper.

St Mary's church

The first hint of the city, well before you reach the tacky parking lot with its souvenir stalls and tour buses, is the rather eroded (and pilfered) remains of the **Vedius gymnasium** and the **stadium**, funded by Nero. Once past the entry gate, take a sharp right along a path signed "Meryem Kilisesi", which leads to **St Mary's church**, an absurdly elongated hotchpotch constructed between the second and fourth centuries AD. The building, originally a Roman warehouse, was the venue of the ecumenical council in 431 AD; its baptistry is in good condition.

The Arcadian Way and the theatre

Beyond the church, the **harbour baths** and **gymnasium** are prominent, but overgrown and difficult to explore. They are usually approached along the splendid **Arcadian Way**, so named after the fifth-century Byzantine emperor Arcadius who renovated it. Today tree- and bush-fringed, it's a forlorn echo of the era when it was lined with hundreds of shops and illuminated at night – although its neglect is refreshing when compared to the ancient **theatre**, brutally restored to provide additional seating for the various summer festivals, with material that would be more appropriate buttressing a California freeway flyover. If you bother to climb past the 20,000 seats of half-modern masonry to the top, it's for the views over the surrounding countryside.

Along Marble Street

The so-called **Marble Street** begins near the base of the theatre and heads almost due south; wheel-ruts in the road and the slightly elevated colonnade remnant to the right indicate that pedestrians and vehicles were kept neatly separated. Also to your right as you proceed is the **lower agora**, with an adjoining **Serapis Temple**, where the city's many Egyptian merchants would have worshipped. About halfway along Marble Street, metal stanchions protect alleged "signposting" – a footprint and a female head etched into the rock – for a **brothel**. It's located in the very centre of the Roman city, at the junction with the other main street, Curetes Street (see below), named after a caste of priests at the Artemis shrine. Little remains above chest height at the house of pleasure, but there are some fine floor mosaics denoting the four seasons, and (appropriately enough) one of the priapic figurines in the Selçuk museum was found here.

The Library of Celsus

Directly across the intersection of the two major streets looms the **Library of Celsus**, originally erected by the consul Gaius Julius Aquila between 110 and 135 AD as a memorial to his father Celsus Polemaeanus, who is still entombed under the west wall of the structure. The elegant, two-storey facade was fitted with niches for statues of the four personified intellectual virtues, today filled with plaster copies (the originals are in Vienna). Inside, twelve thousand scrolls were stored in galleries designed to prevent damp damage – a precaution that didn't prevent the Goths burning them all when they sacked the area in 262 AD. Abutting the library, and designed to provide entry to the lower agora, is the restored triple **gate of Mazaeus and Mithridates**.

Along Curetes Street

Just uphill from the Roman city's main intersection, a **Byzantine fountain** looks across **Curetes Street** to the public **latrines**, a favourite with visitors owing to

△ The Library of Celcus

the graphic nature of their function. Continuing along the same side of the street, you'll come to the so-called **Temple of Hadrian**, actually donated in 118 AD by a wealthy citizen in honour of Hadrian, Artemis and the city in general. Currently a drinks stand occupies its left side. As in the case of the library facade, most of the relief works here are plaster copies of the originals, which reside in the Selçuk museum. The two small heads on the arches spanning the four columns out front are of Tyche and possibly Medusa, respectively installed for luck and to ward off evil influences.

Behind and above the temple sprawl the first-century **Scholastica baths**, named after the fifth-century Byzantine lady whose headless statue adorns the entrance and who restored the complex. There was direct access from here to the latrines and thence the brothel, though it seems from graffiti that the baths, too, were at one stage used as a bawdy house. Clay drainage pipes are still visibly lodged in the floor, as they are at many points in Ephesus.

The terrace houses

On the far side of Curetes Street from the Temple of Hadrian lies a huge patterned **mosaic**, which once fronted a series of shops. Behind this, housed in a protective plexiglass-and-steel shelter, are the famous **terrace houses**: 62 rooms comprising one of the world's best preserved Roman domestic environments. The houses are currently closed for restoration, but are due to reopen in late 2006.

The first house is built around an atrium with a fountain, paved in black-and-white mosaics; a room leading off this to the east has walls covered in murals, including one of Hercules battling the river-god Achelous. In the second dwelling, the central court features a fine mosaic of a triton cavorting with a nereid; just south of this, in an overhead vault, Dionysos and Ariadne are depicted in an excellent glass mosaic, which, while damaged, is still recognizable. Excavations of the large central dome, part of the Dionysus House built in 588 BC, revealed the tiny golden figurine of an Egyptian priest, now on display in the Selçuk museum.

To the upper entrance

Returning to Curetes Street, you pass **Trajan's Fountain**, whose ornamentation has been removed to the museum, and then the street splits just above the **Hydreion** (another fountain) and the **Gate of Hercules**, where a remaining column relief depicts the hero wrapped in the skin of the Nemean lion. Bearing right at the junction takes you to the **Domitian Temple**, of which only the lower floor of the complex is left intact, housing a **Museum of Inscriptions** (currently closed).

The main thoroughfare skirts the large, overgrown **upper agora**, which lies opposite the civic heart of the Roman community – the **prytaneum**. This housed the inextinguishable sacred flame of Ephesus and two of the Artemis statues in the Selçuk museum, in spite of Hestia (Vesta) being the presiding goddess; it also served as the reception area for official guests.

The adjacent **odeon**, once the local parliament, has been as insensitively restored as the main theatre, though presumably the 27 rows of seats are the original number. The **Varius baths** mark the end of the paved Roman street-system, and also the location of the upper site entrance. Beyond the gate huddles the massive **east gymnasium**, next to which the **Magnesia Gate** signals the true edge of the old city. The asphalt road here leads 5km south to Meryemana (see p.363), but you'd have to hitch or hope for a passing taxi – it's too steep and car-infested a walk to be enjoyable.

Priene

Perched on a series of pine terraces graded into the south flank of Samsun Dağı, 35km south of Kuşadası, the compact but exquisite site of **Priene** enjoys a situation that bears comparison with that of Delphi in Greece. The original settlement, legendarily founded by refugee Athenians and dating from perhaps the eleventh century BC, was elsewhere in the Meander basin; the townspeople, following the receding shoreline – now just visible to the west – re-founded the city on its present site during the fourth century BC, just in time for Alexander to stop in and defray the cost of the principal temple of Athena. The Panionion sanctuary, cult centre of the league of Ionian cities, had always lain in Priene's territory, just the other side of Samsun Dağı; as a result its priest was usually chosen from Priene, whose secular officials also presided over the regular meetings of the confederacy. Under Roman – and later Byzantine – rule, however, the city enjoyed little patronage from the emperors, with the result that Priene represents the best-preserved Hellenistic townscape in Ionia, without any of the usual later additions. The town was laid out by Hippodamus, an architect from nearby Miletus, who favoured a grid pattern made up of various *insulae* (rectangular units), each measuring roughly 42m by 35m. Within each rectangle stood four private dwellings; a public building had its own *insula*, sometimes two.

The site

The **site** (daily 8am–6.30pm, winter closes 5.30pm; 2YTL, parking 2YTL) lies a few hundred metres west of the village of Güllübahçe (see "Practicalities", p.372). There's a site map posted at the entrance, but the labelling is incorrect and, in many cases, confusing. From the entrance, it's a good steep walk up the hill to the Northeast Gate into the city. Priene is a much less visited site than Ephesus, hence all the lizards scampering around between the ruins, and its isolation gives it a lonely, faded grandeur that Ephesus lacks. Ephesus' heaving crowds, however, make it easy for you to imagine it as a lively, bustling metropolis, whilst it's difficult to regard Priene as anything other than a crumbling ghost-town.

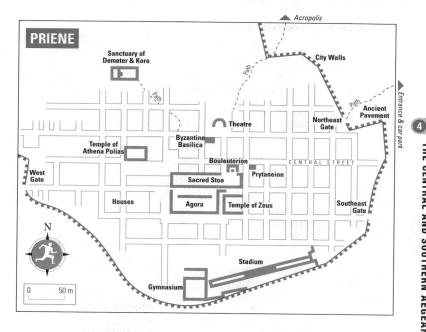

South of the central street

The first easily distinguished civic monument, more or less in the centre of the site, just south of the central street, is the square **bouleuterion** or council chamber, the most intact in Turkey, consisting of seats on three sides enclosing the speakers' area, together with a sacrificial altar.

Just east of the bouleuterion are the scantier remains of the **prytaneion**, or town administration offices, with traces of a dining area for the highest municipal officials. On the next terrace down lie the **Temple of Zeus**, the **agora** and the **sacred stoa**, once graced by outer and inner series of Doric and Ionic columns, though nothing is left above knee level of any of these. The commanding views, however, suggest that this was the heart of public life in the city.

Clearly visible below, reached by way of a stairway from the agora, are the **gymnasium** and **stadium** – relatively neglected parts of the site due to the shadeless climb back up entailed by a visit. Some of the gymnasium walls are decorated with still-visible graffiti; nearby are **bathing basins**, complete with gutters and lion-head spouts, for use after athletics. On the west side of the stadium there are a few sets of **starting blocks** for foot races; spectators watched from the north side of the 190m-by-20m area, where some seats are still discernible.

Heading west down a gentle slope off the central street brings you into the midst of the densest surviving residential district in Priene, where thick walls stand up to 1.5 metres in some places. Though many of the **houses** are choked by pine and shrubbery, others permit entry. The usual ground plan was that of a narrow passage leading to a large central court, surrounded by various rooms. The discovery of occasional stairways demonstrated that some dwellings had two storeys. Priene's **west gate** marks the end of both the main street and the blocks of houses.

North of the central street

The city's most conspicuous monument, the **Temple of Athena Polias**, stands two terraces above the main residential street. The temple took more than two centuries to complete and, in its time, was considered the epitome of Ionic perfection; a manual written by its designer Pytheos was still considered standard reading in Roman times. Five of the original thirty Ionic columns were re-erected in the 1960s and at certain seasons of the year they catch the sunset and glow in the dusk long after the rest of the archeological zone has been plunged into darkness. The rest of the columns lie in sections scattered around the site like enormous stone cogs.

Directly north of the Athena temple, reached by a faint trail through the pines, is the **Sanctuary of Demeter and Kore**, on the highest terrace of the urban grid. Other than the foundations – a good century or two older than those of any other shrine in Priene – little is visible today besides the few Doric column stumps and a pit for catching the blood of sacrificial animals.

The **theatre**, a little way southeast, is by contrast in an excellent state of preservation, its layout and seating (for 5000, Priene's entire population) unchanged from the Hellenistic original. Most prominent are five larger-than-average marble thrones for the municipal dignitaries. The stage buildings were extensively modified during the second century AD – virtually the only Roman tampering with Priene's public buildings. Just behind them are the waist-high remains of a **Byzantine basilica**.

If you're keen on scrambling and the weather is not too hot, take the path beginning above the theatre, which leads in stages to the **acropolis**, on the bluff known as Teloneia in ancient times. A head for heights is useful as the path dwindles, after passing an aqueduct and some cisterns, to a series of paint-splodge-marked steps and goat traces zigzagging steeply up the cliff. Allow an extra hour and a half for the round trip.

The mandatory exit from the site is the former **main (northeast) gate**, still mostly intact.

Practicalities

All-in tours can be arranged from Selçuk hotels and hostels, and are a good idea if time is limited. The tour usually includes a reasonable guide with a 9.30am pick-up from your hotel, a lunch stop and a 5pm return. The itinerary is open to alteration but often starts at Priene moving on to Didyma (p.375) and saving the shadeless Miletus (see below) until last. Prices average around €30 but it's worth shopping around as they do vary enormously.

Dolmuş services to Priene require a change of vehicle at Söke, 24km southeast of Kuşadası and 44km south of Selçuk. Making connections is pretty hassle-free: you'll be deposited right next to vehicles leaving for Priene, Miletus and Didyma. The hourly **dolmuşes from Söke** take twenty minutes to reach the very spread-out village of **Güllübahçe**, scattered 200 to 700m east of the ruins.

It is tempting to save a visit to Priene for late afternoon, when it is at its most beautiful, but staying overnight can be a problem. There are only a couple of small **pensions** in the village, including the *Priene* (☏0256/547 1725; ❷), which offers very reasonable en-suite rooms as well as camping space but requires advance booking in high season. Of the handful of **restaurants**, the best is *Pınar*, at the far west end of the village, right below the site car-park, though *Şelale*, in the village centre, has a wider menu.

Miletus

The position of **MILETUS** (Milet in Turkish), on an eminently defendable promontory jutting out into the ancient Gulf of Latmos, once outshone that of Priene. However, its modern setting, marooned in the seasonal marshes of the Büyük Menderes, is dreary, and there's little left to bear witness to the town's long and colourful past. Only the theatre, visible from some distance away, hints at former glories (and even this is often submerged under water in winter). Up close, the site is a confusing juxtaposition of widely scattered relics from different eras, often disguised by weeds, mud or water, depending on the season. Ironically, even the grid street-plan championed by native son Hippodamus has largely failed to survive, swept away by the Romans and geological processes. If you're pressed for time, this might be the Ionian site to miss.

Some history

Miletus is at least as old as Ephesus and far older than Priene; German archeologists working locally since the 1890s have uncovered remnants of a Creto-Mycenaean settlement from the sixteenth century BC. Ionian invaders made their first appearance during the eleventh century, and by the seventh century BC Miletus was in the first flush of a heyday that was to last more than two hundred years, when the city was able to repulse the advances of the Lydians and found colonies all over Anatolia. It was also a highly evolved cultural centre, with a roll call of scholars and thinkers that included the mathematician Thales and the courtesan-orator Aspasia, friend of Socrates and Pericles.

While not strong enough to completely avoid Persian domination, Miletus did manage to secure favourable terms as an equal, and even took the opportunity to

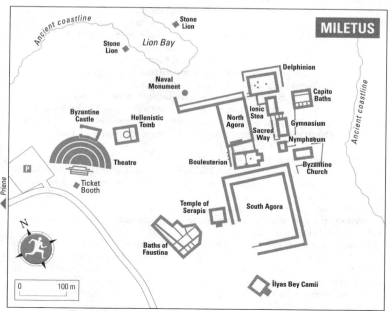

Museum & South Entrance ▼ *Akköy & Didyma*

appropriate the nearby oracle of Didyma. But with Athenian instigation, the city was unwisely persuaded to take command of the abortive Ionian revolt against the Persians between 500 and 494 BC. After the rebels were finally defeated in the naval battle at nearby Lade Island, Darius punished the ringleader severely with wholesale massacre and pillage.

Within fifty years Miletus was rebuilt some distance to the northeast of its original site, but it was never again to be as great – or as independent. Alexander saw fit to "liberate" the city from a new, short-lived occupation by the Persians and their allies, including a huge fleet anchored hard by which sat motionless, perhaps in awe of the Macedonian's mystique. Later it was bequeathed to the Romans, under whose rule it enjoyed a brief renaissance – most of what you see today is a legacy of various emperors' largesse. The Byzantine town stubbornly clung to life, producing Isidorus, architect of İstanbul's Aya Sofya. In the ninth century Miletus was already dwindling and by the time the Menteşe emirs, and then the Ottomans, took control, there was little left to prize.

Visiting the site

The site lies 45km south of Selçuk and access by public transport is fairly easy from Söke (see "Priene: Practicalities" on p.372): all dolmuşes bound for Balat (2km from the ruins), Akköy or Altınkum run past Güllübahçe (for Priene) and Milet; the journey from Söke takes 40 minutes. At Akköy, 6km to the south, there are simple eateries (but no accommodation); otherwise some expensive snack-bars cater for a tour-bus clientele near the **site entrance** (daily: summer 8.30am–7pm; winter 8.30am–5.30pm; 2YTL). Note that the **museum**, 1km south of the main ticket booth, is currently closed following the theft of various artefacts and is likely to be relocated to Didyma in the future.

Theatre and castle

The most obvious attraction at Miletus is behind the ticket stall: a **theatre**, whose Hellenistic base was modified and enlarged during the second century AD to a capacity of 15,000. One of the first things you'll see on the orchestra floor is a stone block with two griffins carved in relief, one playing a lyre. The centre of the front row sports two pillars that once supported the emperor's canopy. Further up, the vaulted exit passageways are enormous and virtually intact; unfortunately the area above the *diazoma* (dividing terrace) is now off-limits.

An eighth-century **Byzantine castle** and some contemporaneous ramparts surmount the theatre, giving a marvellous 360-degree view over the flood plain, and the chance to get your bearings on the rest of the site. Visible on the plain a kilometre or so to the west is a scrubby hill, formerly the **Island of Lade**.

The harbour area

Descending from the walls, you pass a **Hellenistic tomb** featuring a circular burial chamber in the middle. Further east, a round base is all that remains of the **naval monument**, commemorating an unknown victory of the first century BC, that once overlooked the most impressive of Miletus's four harbours, the "Lion Bay", so called for the two **stone lions** that guarded the entrance – now embedded up to their haunches in marsh silt.

The end of the tongue-shaped bay was lined by a colonnade that extended east to the sixth-century **Delphinion**, dedicated to Apollo Delphinius, patron of sailors, ships and ports. Not surprisingly in such a maritime community, it was the most important religious establishment in town. Today you can still see the foundations of altars or semicircular benches and the enclosing colonnade. Immediately south squat some incongruous **Selçuk baths**.

Along and around the Sacred Way

Both the Delphinion and baths stand at the north end of a handsomely paved **Sacred Way**, which in its time linked Miletus with Didyma; after a rainy winter, though, it's likely to remain submerged for some months. On the same side of the pavement as you walk south stands a first-century AD **Ionic stoa**, conspicuous owing to its rather clinical partial restoration, which partly shields the enormous **Capito baths** and a **gymnasium** of the same era. The most satisfying monument east of the Sacred Way is the **nymphaeum**, the largest public fountain of Miletus, once extremely ornate but now standing at barely half its original height. Just south of here are the ruins of a sixth-century **Byzantine church**.

On the west side of the pavement, beginning at the harbour, are the jumbled and overgrown remains of the so-called **north agora**. Marginally more interesting is the second-century BC **bouleuterion**, which faces the nymphaeum. The Sacred Way skirts the **south agora**, unexcavated except for a monumental gateway, which was carted off to Berlin in 1908. West of the *agora* are the recessed premises of a third-century AD **Temple of Serapis**, where you can make out a bas-relief representation of the deity Serapis Helios on a fallen pediment.

The Roman **Baths of Faustina** (Marcus Aurelius's wife), west of here at the foot of the theatre hill, are distinctive for their position at an angle to what remains of the urban grid – and for their good state of repair. The most engaging sight inside is the two spouts that once fed the cold pool: one in the form of a now decapitated statue of local river-deity Meander, the other an intact lion-head.

İlyas Bey Camii

About 200m to the south and marked by dense vegetation, the early fifteenth-century **İlyas Bey Camii**, built by that Menteşe emir to give thanks for his safe return from captivity by Tamerlane, is arguably more interesting than anything at the ancient site except the theatre. The mosque, dressed entirely in marble pillaged from the ancient city, lost its minaret in the 1958 earthquake that levelled nearby Balat, but otherwise fared well, retaining its fine carved-marble *mihrab*, stalactite vaulting and Arabic inscriptions. The entrance is particularly enchanting, with a carved marble screen flanking the door and triple bi-coloured arches just out-side. There was once a *medrese* and *imaret* adjacent, but only a peaceful, neglected courtyard with some adjoining cells and head stones has survived. It's a serene and contemplative corner, more frequented by storks than humans.

Didyma and around

By the time you reach **DIDYMA** (Didim in Turkish) site fatigue might be beginning to set in. However, the oracular sanctuary of Apollo, though half-ruined and besieged throughout the middle of the day by swarms of tour groups, rarely fails to impress. The best time to visit – and the hour when, having worked their way through either Priene or Miletus or both, many people tend to show up – is late afternoon or early evening, when the masonry glows in the sunset. The other great advantage of a visit is being able to combine seeing the ruins with hitting the nearby beach at **Altınkum**, just 5km to the south.

Some history

An oracle and shrine of some sort apparently existed at Didyma long before the arrival of the Ionian settlers in the eleventh century BC – the name itself is an ancient Anatolian word – but the imported **cult of Apollo** quickly appropriated whatever previous oracle, centred on a sacred well and laurel tree, had worked here. Didyma remained a sacred precinct, under the jurisdiction of a clan of priests originally from Delphi, and was never a town as such, though it eventually became a dependency of nearby Miletus. Every four years the sanctuary was also the venue for the Didymeia, a festival of music and drama as well as athletics.

The Archaic shrine, begun during the eighth century BC, was finished within two hundred years, and though similar in design to the current structure, it was half the size. After their defeat of the Ionian revolt in 494 BC, the Persians destroyed this first temple and plundered its treasures, including the cult statue of Apollo. The oracle puttered along in reduced circumstances until Alexander appeared on the scene, when the cult statue was retrieved from Persia and a new temple (the one existing today) commissioned.

Despite continuing subsidy from the Romans, work continued at a snail's pace for more than five centuries and the building was never actually completed – not entirely surprising when you consider the formidable engineering problems presented. In the end Christianity put paid to the oracle, and when the edict of Theodosius in 385 AD proscribed all pagan practices, construction ceased for good, after which a medieval earthquake toppled most of the columns. Inhabitants of the Greek village of Yeronda (the Ottoman name for the hamlet overlooking the temple precinct) helped themselves liberally to the ancient masonry in their midst, and blocks from the site can still be seen incorporated into some of the older village houses.

At its zenith Didyma was approached not only from Miletus but also from Panormos, a cove 6km west, via a sacred way whose final stretches were lined with statuary. Neither pavement nor statues are visible today, the latter having been spirited away to the British Museum in 1858.

The site

Entry to the **site** (daily 8am–7pm, closes 5.30pm winter; 2YTL) is now by way of a gate to the north of the enclosure. At the bottom of the steps look out for the **Medusa head**, which fell from a Roman-era architrave and is now the unofficial logo of the place, repeated ad infinitum on posters and cards all over Turkey.

Pilgrims would first visit a **well** below the resting place of the Medusa head and purify themselves, then approach a still-prominent **circular altar** to offer a sacrifice before proceeding to the **shrine** itself. Even in ruins this is still intimidatingly large – the surviving column stumps alone are considerably taller than a man, and in its nearly complete state it must have inspired reverence. The effect was accentuated by the shrine's position on a steep, stepped base and enclosure in a virtual forest of 108 Ionic **columns** – though only three of these stand to their original height. The remaining twelve stumps supported the roof of the entry porch, reached by a steep flight of steps, where supplicants would deliver their queries to the priest of Apollo, who would reappear after a suitable interval on a terrace some six feet higher to deliver the prophetess's oracular pronouncement. Questions ranged from the personal to matters of state; prophecies were recorded and stored for posterity on the premises. The cult statue of Apollo, his sacred laurel and the sacred well were formerly enclosed in a miniature shrine of which only traces remain – though the **well** itself is still obvious, roped off to prevent accidents. As at Delphi in Greece, prophecies were formulated by a priestess, who either (accounts disagree) drank from, bathed in or inhaled potent vapours from the waters. Her subsequent ravings were rephrased more delicately to those waiting out front.

Petitioners did not normally enter the inner sanctum, except to watch the goings-on of the Didymeia from a monumental stairway providing access to the terrace from the interior. The steps still bear spectators' graffiti, though the terrace is currently off-limits – you enter the sanctuary proper by means of twin tunnels to either side. The innermost court was never roofed, though the height of the walls once exceeded 20m; today they're half that height.

Practicalities

Hourly **dolmuşes** and full-size buses cover the route between Söke and Altınkum beach (see below) via **Didim village**, the modern name for Didyma. It's a fifty-minute ride to the village; ask to be dropped off at the junction 200m from the ruins, otherwise buses will continue on to the *otogar*, 2km out of Didim village to the west. The village itself is something of a tourist trap, crammed with souvenir shops, and all three of the **restaurants** across from the archeological zone are expensive and poor in quality. For a good feed at reasonable prices, walk a kilometre northeast to **Yenihisar**, a much larger, more untouched village, where the *lokanta*s are less touristy and a bit more authentic.

Accommodation is limited to basic rooms at the *Pension Oracle* (℡0256/811 0270; ❷), offering breakfast on a terrace directly overlooking the ruins, or the more comfortable, characterful ⚑ *Medusa House* (℡0256/811 0063; ⓦwww .medusahouse.com; ❼), nearby: run by a German–Turkish couple, it features rustic rooms in a restored old building with a lovely rambling garden.

South of Didyma: Altınkum

Five kilometres south of Didyma, the information placard at the road's end in **ALTINKUM** says it all, listing well over a hundred hotels and *pansiyon*s arrayed behind a single kilometre of beach split by a headland. In midsummer it's standing room only on the sand, but at least it lives up to its name ("golden sand" in Turkish): a gently sloping beach with no surf, ideal for children and in total contrast to the exposed coast on the other side of Didyma. Of late the place has become the Turkish equivalent of the Costa del Sol, with a large British package presence that has engendered a rash of "English" eateries with food (and prices) the way Turks imagine Brits like it ("Roast Beef and Yorkshire Pudding", as well as the widely advertised, and totally inedible, "T-bone steaks").

Altınkum is essentially the shore annex of Yenihisar (see above), which is where you'll find most of the amenities (such as proper shops). However, to the right of the T-junction marked by the accommodation placard there's a **bank** and **PTT** as well as a sporadically staffed **tourist information** booth further along. The least expensive **pansiyons**, such as the *Ankara* (℡0256/813 6895, ⓕ813 7626; ❶) – not including breakfast – and the *Agais* (℡0256/813 1379; ❷), can be found on the upper, parallel street behind the far western jetty, but these are usually block-booked by Turkish families in season. Lodgings to the east of the accommodation placard are considerably more upmarket, though not much more expensive: try the *Göçtur* (℡0256/813 2740; ⓦwww.gocturhotel.com; ❷) and the *Majestic* (℡0256/813 4615, ⓕ813 5018; ❸).

Ancient Caria: the coastal regions

In antiquity, **Caria** was an isolated, mysterious region purportedly inhabited by barbarous people indigenous to the area (a rarity in Anatolia), speaking a language distantly related to Greek. Following the advent of Alexander, and the Hecatomnid dynasty at Halicarnassus, Hellenization proceeded apace and the differences between the Carians and their neighbours diminished. After the Byzantine period, and the fifteenth-century absorption of the local Menteşe emirate by the Ottomans, the region again assumed backwater status. Until the early republican years, internal exile to the coast here was an habitual and feared sentence for political offenders. In a strange echo of the ancient tendency, the dialect of **Muğla province** – whose territory corresponds almost exactly to that of coastal Caria – is still one of the most eccentric and difficult to understand in the entire country.

Bafa Gölü (or Lake Bafa) and ancient **Heracleia ad Latmos** on its northeast shore make a suitably dramatic introduction to coastal Caria. **Euromos** and **Labranda** are two of the more satisfying minor ancient sites in Turkey, and both can be seen from **Milas**, the nearest substantial town. Nearby, at **Stratonikya**, a once-untouched ancient metropolis is almost engulfed by a lignite quarry. Southeast of Milas, **Peçin Kale** constitutes a Turkish oddity – a ruined medieval city, in this case the Menteşe capital. **Ören**, still further southeast on the same road, is another rare beast: an attractive coastal resort that has not yet been steamrollered by modern tourism. Southwest of Milas, however, neither **ancient Iassos**, nor the small resort of **Güllük**, live up to their hyped reputations. Most visitors bypass Güllük in favour of **Bodrum** and its peninsula, very much the big tourist event on this coast, with tentacles of development creeping over every available parcel of surrounding land – though what attracted outsiders to the area in the first place still shines through on occasion.

Moving on, **Muğla** makes for a pleasant stopover if you're passing through: one of the best-preserved Ottoman townscapes in Turkey, coexisting with an unobtrusive, well-planned new city.

Further south, **Marmaris** is another big – and rather overblown – resort, from which the **Loryma (Hisarönü) peninsula** beyond, bereft of a sandy shoreline but blessed with magnificent scenery, offers the closest escape. As a compromise, **Datça** and its surroundings might fit the bill, with some remote beaches nearby more rewarding than the much-touted ruins of ancient **Knidos**.

Bafa Gölü

Bafa Gölü (Lake Bafa), one of the most entrancing spectacles in southwestern Turkey, was created when silt deposited by the Büyük Menderes river sealed off the Latmos gulf from the sea. The barren, weirdly sculpted pinnacles of ancient **Mount Latmos** (Beşparmak Dağı) still loom over the northeast shore, visible from a great distance west. Numerous islets dot the 100-square-kilometre lake, most of them sporting some sort of fortified Byzantine religious establishment, dating from the lake's days as an important monastic centre between the seventh and fourteenth centuries.

△ Lake Bafa

Bafa's separation from the sea is not perfect: canals link the lake's west end with an oxbow of the Büyük Menderes close by. As a result, the water is faintly brackish and fish species tolerant of both salt and fresh water shuttle back and forth, spawning in the lake. The most important are *levrek* (bass), *kefal* (grey mullet), *yayın* (catfish) and *yılan balığı* (eel), although overuse of the lake's water by local farmers has caused its level to fall by more than 2m in recent years and the fish numbers are decreasing. Stocks are currently still high enough, however, to support the arrival throughout the year of more than two hundred species of migratory wildfowl, including the endangered crested pelican, of which there are believed to be less than two thousand left in the world. During dry years the water level falls even further and the weeds that hover in the shallows can burgeon, making access difficult – which is a shame since the water temperature is ideal for swimming.

Practicalities

Bus services past the lake are frequent, but Söke–Milas dolmuşes (every 30min) are more flexible than the big coaches in terms of stopping. The southern shore of Bafa, which the main highway follows, is the location of a few combination **campsite-pansiyon-restaurants**, best thought of as a serene setting for lunch (at least for those in their own vehicle). Heading east, the most acceptable of these are the basic, five-roomed *Ceri'nin Yeri Pansiyon* (☎0252/512 4498; ❶), run by proprietor Ceri, with a restaurant menu that varies with the day's catch, and the *Club Natura Oliva* (☎0252/519 1072, ⓦwww.clubnatura.com; ❺), a German-owned establishment with thirty large, if somewhat spartan rooms, in nine houses, all with balconies overlooking the lake. There's also a restaurant serving a wide range of dishes (including several vegetarian choices), with guided hikes of the local area offered.

Swimming is best from the far side of the monastery-capped islet, which in dry years is joined to Ceri's restaurant by a muddy spit. On the islet, some flattish rocks offer a weed-free corridor out onto the lake when the water level is normal. Failing that, dive off the end of the wooden jetty constructed to outrun the weeds.

Heracleia ad Latmos

Across Lake Bafa, most easily seen from the *Ceri'nin Yeri pansiyon*-restaurant, is a patch of irregular shoreline with a modern village, Kapıkırı, whose lights twinkle at the base of Mount Latmos by night. This is the site of **Heracleia ad Latmos** (Heraklia in Turkish) one of Turkey's most evocatively situated ancient cities.

A settlement of Carian origin had existed here long before the arrival of the Ionians, and Carian habits died hard, though Latmos – as it was then known – had far better geographical communication with Ionia than with the rest of Caria. Late in the Hellenistic period the city's location was moved a kilometre or so west, and the name changed to Heracleia, but despite adornment with numerous monuments and an enormous wall it was never a place of great importance. Miletus, at the head of the gulf, monopolized most trade and already the inlet was beginning to close up.

Heracleia owes its fame, and an enduring hold on the romantic imagination, to a legend associated not with the town itself but with Mount Latmos behind. **Endymion** was a handsome shepherd who, while asleep in a cave on the mountain, was noticed by Selene, the moon goddess. She made love with him as he slept and in time, so the story goes, bore Endymion fifty daughters without their sire ever waking once. Endymion was reluctant for all this to stop and begged Zeus, who was also fond of him, to be allowed to dream forever; his wish was granted and, as a character in Mary Lee Settle's *Blood Ties* flippantly observed, thus became the only known demigod of the wet dream. Later, Christian hermits who settled in the vicinity during mid-Byzantine times cleaned up Endymion's act, so to speak – in their version he was a mystic who after a lifetime of "communing" with the moon had learned the secret name of God. Once a year the anchorites, leaving their homes on the island cloisters, or in various caves on Latmos, converged upon an ancient tomb believed to be Endymion's. The sarcophagus lid would be opened and the bones inside would emit a strange humming noise, said to be the deceased saint's attempt to communicate the holy name.

The monastic communities, after producing a few minor saints, were dispersed for good early in the fourteenth century and little is now left of any of the Byzantine monuments. But when a full moon rises over the serrated peaks across the water, it is easy to suspend disbelief in all the legends pertaining to the place. Indeed Endymion's fate has exercised a fascination on many subsequent eras: Shakespeare declared "Peace, ho! The moon sleeps with Endymion/And would not be waked!", and four centuries later Keats added: "What is there in thee, Moon! that shouldst move my heart so potently? . . . Now I begin to feel thy orby power/Is coming fresh upon me."

The site

Arriving by car, park your vehicle either next to the *Agora Pansiyon* (see "Practicalities", below) or in another area about 200m up the hill. The site is not enclosed, though you may have to pay 4YTL **admission** if the warden is in the ticket booth.

The crudely signposted **bouleuterion** lies 100m to the east of the first parking area, though only the retaining wall and some rows of benches are left of the second-century BC structure. The **Roman baths** visible in the valley below, and a crumbled but appealing **Roman theatre** off in the olives beyond, can be reached via an unmarked trail starting between the first and second parking areas. The path up to the **hermits' caves** on Mount Latmos begins at the rear of the second parking area. Stout boots are advisable, as is a cool day in early spring or late autumn

– for a place still so close to the sea, Heracleia can be surprisingly hot and airless. Similar cautions apply for those who want to trace the course of the **Hellenistic walls**, the city's most imposing and conspicuous relics, supposedly built by Lysimachus in the late third century BC.

The *Agora*'s restaurant looks south over the **Hellenistic agora**, now mostly taken up by the village schoolyard; its south edge is buttressed by a row of **shops**, whose downhill side stands intact to two storeys, complete with windows. From the *agora* grounds you've a fine view west over the lake and assorted castle-crowned promontories. A box-like Hellenistic **Temple of Athena** perches on a hill west of the *agora*; less conspicuous is an inscription to Athena, left of the entrance.

From the *agora* a wide, walled-in path descends toward the shore and the final quota of recognizable monuments at Heracleia. Most obvious is the peninsula – or, in wet years, island – studded with **Byzantine walls** and a **church**. A stone causeway half-buried in the beach here allowed entrance in what must have been drier medieval times. Follow the shore southwest to the *Zeybek* restaurant, strategically astride another promontory, and then continue along its access drive to the junction with a slightly wider track. Across the way you should see the tentatively identified Hellenistic **Sanctuary of Endymion**, oriented unusually northeast to southwest. Five column stumps front the structure, which has a rounded rear wall – a ready-made apse for later Christians – with sections of rock incorporated into the masonry.

Striking out across the pasture opposite the Endymion shrine, and skimming the base of yet another Byzantine castle, you arrive at the ancient **necropolis**, which consists of a few dozen rectangular tombs hewn into boulders on the shore. Many are partly or completely awash, depending on the water level.

Practicalities

The most common access to Heracleia is by **boat** from *Ceri'nin Yeri* (see "Bafa Gölü: Practicalities" on p.379). Tours generally depart between 9.30 and 10.30am, take twenty minutes to cross the lake, and allow just under two-and-a-half hours at the ruins – enough for a look around and a quick meal. Reckon on paying about 8–10YTL a head round-trip, assuming a group of at least ten people, plus site admission.

Alternatively, if you have your own vehicle, drive east to Çamiçi village (6km beyond *Ceri'nin Yeri*) and then turn left at the signpost ("Herakleia"). The ten-kilometre paved road leads through fields and finally a wilderness of Latmian boulders to the modern village of **KAPIKIRI**, built higgledy-piggledy among the ruins. Scattered in and around Kapıkırı are a few simple **pansiyons** and **restaurants**, and a campsite. The opening periods of most establishments are erratic to say the least, though most will open for the main May to September period. *Selene's*, near the waterfront (☏0252/543 5221, ⓦwww.bafalake.com; ❷), is a good choice with basic rooms and a lakeside restaurant: it can also organize boat trips on the lake. Alternatively, the *Agora Pansiyon* (☏0252/543 5445, ⓦwww.herakleia.com; ❺) has basically furnished doubles and a restaurant arranged around a verdant garden, while the lakeside *Zeybek Restaurant-Camping* (☏0252/543 5158) has good views and serves moderately priced fish.

Milas

A small, initially nondescript town of some 35,000 people, and major regional transport hub, **MILAS** is too often given short shrift by tourists intent on reaching the fleshpots of Bodrum as quickly as possible. This is a shame, for although it's unlikely that most foreigners would want to stay the night here, there are enough sights of interest to fill a few hours between buses.

First impressions – sprawling apartment buildings on the outskirts, traffic congestion in the bazaar – are not reassuring, but a stroll around reveals beautiful old houses tucked away behind the main thoroughfares. The town's market is at its best on Tuesdays, when organized tours visit from Bodrum. The local specialities – honey, olives and earth-toned carpets – are sold here; in winter and spring the stalls sell freshly picked wild herbs and sweet-tasting purple carrots.

Milas – or **Mylasa**, as it was formerly known – was an important Carian centre (its original location was at the nearby hill of **Peçin Kale**), but it was the Halicarnassus-based Hecatomnid dynasty that really put it on the map. The nearby quarries provided ample marble for numerous public monuments, while increased control over the sanctuary at Labranda brought the city additional benefits. Mylasa's assignment by the Roman republic to the jurisdiction of Rhodes in 190 BC was too much for the locals to stomach and they rebelled within twenty years, declaring a brief independence which lasted for two more decades before eventual incorporation into the Roman Empire. Details of the Byzantine period are obscure, but the city experienced a resurgence during the fourteenth century when the Menteşe emirs, a Turcoman clan, made it the capital of their realms in southwestern Anatolia.

The Town

An elaborate early Roman tomb known as the **Gümüşkesen** (literally "cuts-silver") is the most obviously impressive relic of ancient Mylasa. The way there is poorly marked from the town centre, but the monument is easy enough to find by heading 500m west along Kadıağa Caddesi, which soon becomes the slightly sloping Gümüşkesen Caddesi. There are no formal visiting hours nor an admission fee to the landscaped site, which lies in a slight depression south of Hıdırlık hill.

The monument consists of a square burial chamber surmounted by a Corinthian colonnade with a pyramidal roof – a design presumed to be a miniature of the now-vanished mausoleum at Halicarnassus. The ceiling sports elaborate carvings and some flecks of paint; a hole in the floor allowed mourners to pour libations into the sepulchre below.

Milas's lively tradesmen's **bazaar** covers the western slopes of Hisarbaşı hill, which has been the focus of settlement in every era. Once past the warren of alleys perpendicular to the main Cumhuriyet Caddesi, veer up to the summit and the late Ottoman **Belen Camii**. Immediately to its right stands the eighteenth-century **Çöllühanı**, one of the last semi-functioning, unrestored *kervansarays* in western Turkey. Leaving here, go through the archways of the more modern *han* opposite and continue downhill to the grounds of the fine, grey-marble, late fourteenth-century **Firuz Bey Camii**, erected by the Menteşe emirs using bits of the ancient town.

Back past the Çöllühanı, heading southeast behind the PTT, there's a district of sumptuous **old houses**, the finest in Milas, built from the wealth engendered by tobacco and cotton during the nineteenth century, when the town boasted large Greek Orthodox, Armenian and Jewish populations. One of the finest houses on the hill is at Tabakhane Cad 9/A, which still boasts particularly impressive stone carving around the door. Watch for yellow arrow-signs with the legend "Uzunyuva" (Tall Nest) and the single Corinthian column, adorned with a stork's nest (hence the name), announcing the first-century BC **Temple of Zeus**, adjacent to which a sign cryptically reads "Kutsal Alan" (Holy Clearing). Much of the foundation has been incorporated into later houses, with pieces of carved masonry often reused as keystones above doors.

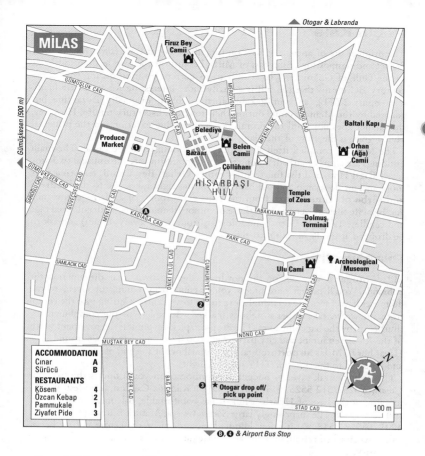

Downhill from here you'll pass a huge stretch of ancient **city wall** and at the bottom of the slope an **Ottoman bridge** with an inscribed plaque. Across the bridge, a few minutes' walk past the **Orhan (Ağa) Camii**, oldest of the town's mosques (1330), stands the **Baltalı Kapı** (Gate-with-Axe) – the largest remaining section of the city walls. The axe in question, a double-headed attribute of Zeus, is faintly carved on the north-facing keystone.

The late fourteenth-century **Ulu Cami**, further south along Şair Ulvi Akgün Caddesi, is perhaps even more engaging, an exotically asymmetrical building incorporating a vast quantity of plundered antiquities. Kufic inscriptions adorn the lintels, and a peculiar staircase leads up over the front door to a short and stubby minaret. In addition, the building has gables, buttressing and a dome over the *mihrab* end, and the whole effect is more that of a Byzantine church than a mosque.

Across the street, the **Archeological Museum** (Arkeoloji Müzesi; daily 8.30am–noon & 1–5.30pm; 4YTL), labelled almost exclusively in Turkish, has a sparse collection considering the size of the hall – merely pottery and figurines from the immediate environs of Milas, plus two cases of mediocre gold diadems and slightly better jewellery. More interesting is the garden, which contains a large collection of ancient Jewish gravestones.

Peçin Kale

The original site of ancient Mylasa on the hill of **Peçin Kale** (*Beçin Kale* in local dialect and signposting), 5km east of Milas, lies just off the road leading southeast to the Gulf of Gökova. Mylasa's shift to its current position during the fourth century BC means that the hill is actually more interesting for its **castle** (daily 8am–8pm; 2YTL), an unmistakable fortified bluff, originally Byzantine but adapted by the Menteşe emirs during their fourteenth-century tenure. However, the citadel does not fulfil the promise of its imposing exterior and the principal saving grace is the view of the plain, 200m below.

The Menteşe complex itself lies about 400m south from the castle. The main buildings are clearly marked: among the most interesting are the unusual two-storeyed **Kızıl Han**, and the fourteenth-century **Orhan Bey Camii**, featuring a far more ancient doorjamb and old hamam. Bearing right takes you to the **medrese and türbe of Ahmet Gazi**, from the same era – tombs of a Menteşe governor and his wife that are venerated as those of minor Islamic saints, with coloured rags and candles. Take any Ören-bound dolmuş from town (every 45min) and ask to be dropped at the *Beçin Kale* turn-off.

Practicalities

Milas's **otogar** is way out on the northern edge of town, near the junction for Labranda. You'll be left here unless you've come from Güllük or Ören, whose dolmuşes have a separate **terminal** close to the town centre. Getting into the centre from the *otogar*, take either a dolmuş marked "Şehir İçi" or the complimentary shuttle run by the big companies. The drop-off/pick-up point is the pavement south of the *Köşem* restaurant and city park; there's no fixed rank – just wait around. The Havaş bus to **Milas airport** stops at the roundabout at the end of Atatürk Bulvarı and is geared to the times of THY internal flights.

The only central, savoury budget **accommodation** you'll find is the two-star *Çınar* (T0252/512 5525, F512 2102; ❸) on Kadıağa Caddesi, just west of a T-junction at the base of Hisarbaşı hill; it has comfortable, balconied rooms but is still no bargain. The surprisingly large *Sürücü Otel* on Atatürk Bulvarı (T0252/512 4001, F512 2548; ❷) is a few hundred metres out of the centre but far better value; its attached restaurant and café are frequented by students from the nearby university.

Simple **lunches** can be had at the *Pamukkale Pide Salonu*, near the market, where you can get a *pide* and a drink for less than 4YTL, or at several nearby hole-in-the-wall joints. Another good midday option is the *Özcan Kebap Salonu*, halfway up the main thoroughfare, Cumhuriyet Caddesi. The *Köşem* near the park and the *Sürücü Hotel*'s **restaurant** are licensed and not too expensive, while the *Ziyafet Pide*, opposite the school, serves enamel-corroding spiced *pide*.

Euromos, Labranda and Stratonıkya

A short distance northwest of Milas lie two impressive Carian ruins that, together, make a good day out from the town. **Euromos** is easily reached by public transport, although you really need your own vehicle to visit isolated **Labranda**, as dolmuşes only take you halfway. To the east of Milas lies the ancient Roman city of **Stratonıkya**, again one for those with their own transport and a passion for ruins.

Euromos

Two-thirds of the way between Bafa Gölü and Milas, 4km southeast of the town of Selimiye, a Corinthian Temple of Zeus, north of the road in an olive grove, is virtually all that remains intact of the ancient city of **Euromos** (daily: May–Sept 9am–7pm; Oct–April 9am–5.30pm; 4YTL if warden present). However, it's sufficiently unusual – only two other temples in Turkey are in a comparable state of repair – to justify a detour.

You can get to the site **from Milas** by taking a dolmuş towards Selimiye (every twenty minutes between 7am and 7pm). If you are returning by public transport be warned that Selimiye–Milas dolmuşes, often full by this point, may refuse you. Be prepared to walk the 4km back to Selimiye to find one at the start of its run.

There was a sanctuary to a native Carian deity on this spot as early as the sixth century BC, together with a city originally known as Kyromus. By the fourth century, under the Hellenizing influence of nearby Halicarnassus, the name had changed to Euromos and the cult of Zeus had merged with that of the earlier god. The city attained its greatest importance during the Hellenistic and Roman periods, when it nearly rivalled nearby Mylasa, but by Byzantine times it had sunk back into obscurity.

The **Temple of Zeus** is a legacy of the generous Roman emperor Hadrian, though the fact that several of the remaining columns are unfluted suggests that the shrine was never finished. Of the original 32 columns, arranged six by eleven, only sixteen remain, though all of these are linked to one or more neighbours by portions of the architrave. The city itself was built several hundred metres to the northwest of the temple, but the only easily found trace of it is a stretch of wall with a **tower**, up on the ridge overlooking the sacred precinct. The city's badly eroded **amphitheatre** lies about ten minutes' walk north, on the far side of the ridge, down and right from the tower.

Labranda

The sanctuary of Zeus at **Labranda** (Labraynda in Turkish), perched in splendid isolation on a south-facing hillside overlooking the plain of Milas, is arguably the most beautifully set archeological zone of ancient Caria. It's also one of the least visited – it takes a very sturdy tour bus to brave the horrendous road in. The site lies over 15km north of Milas, but dolmuşes only go as far as the hamlet of **Kargıcak**, roughly halfway, beyond which you must walk or beg lifts from passing trucks. The road, though fully asphalted, is still a difficult drive with the gradient at times punishing and mud a problem. A **taxi from Milas** will set you back the better part of 25YTL.

Excavations since 1948 have turned up no finds older than the seventh century BC, but it seems certain that some god was venerated here long before that. Oddly enough, the agreeable climate 600m up, coupled with a perennial spring, never prompted the founding of a city, but instead nurtured a grove of sacred plane trees that eventually became the precinct of Zeus Stratios (the Warlike), alias Zeus Labrayndus (the Axe-bearing), after his depiction on fourth-century coins struck at nearby Mylasa. The fourth-century BC Hecatomnid rulers of Halicarnassus and Mylasa did much to promote the cult, endowing various structures at the sanctuary that can still be seen. However, the priests of Zeus retained a large degree of autonomy, exerting their independence to advantage during the chaotic years after the death of Alexander. Roman and later Byzantine rule brought few material benefits to Labranda, and the place was finally abandoned during the late eleventh century.

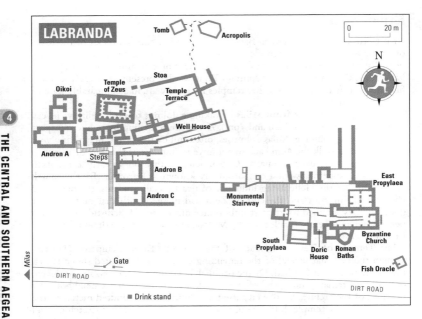

The site

Just when you're beginning to wonder if you've made a wrong turn, a clump of poplars – replacing the long-vanished plane trees – heralds the location of the springs that still supply some of the water for modern Milas. A drinks stall and some beehives stand opposite the artificial terraces of the **sanctuary** (daily 8am–8pm; 4YTL) and the rickety wooden gate giving onto them. The warden's family lives on the premises, and the children will usually escort you through the principal monuments in the following order, though they can only speak Turkish. In any case, the site is well marked and there's a helpful map-placard.

After skirting some unidentified ancient buildings, you climb up to the so-called **Andron A** – one of three such constructions at Labranda, used for sacred banquets held at the shrine. While roofless, it is otherwise complete, and includes a windowed niche in the back. Immediately adjacent are the **oikoi** (priests' residences), fronted by four Doric column stubs. Like the Andron A, this was another foundation of the Hecatomnids, though authorities disagree on whether it was the actual quarters of the cult priests or merely the repository of temple records.

The **Temple of Zeus**, originally laid out in the fifth century and rededicated by Idrieus, sprawls east of here. None of it stands more than knee high, yet it is appealing, especially when viewed from the near edge of the temple terrace, lined with the rudiments of a stoa. From its far corner a path leads up to the ruined **acropolis** and – more importantly – to a massive fourth-century **tomb** thought to be that of Idrieus and his family. This is divided in two, with three sarcophagi in the rear chamber and a damaged pair up front.

Just below the south rim of the temple terrace is the recessed **well house**, the original exit point of the spring; just across the flat area from here are **Andron B**, donated by Mausolus and relatively intact, and **Andron C**, a Roman contribution that has not weathered the ages as well.

From the level area in front of Andron C, it's a short distance to the prominent **monumental stairway** descending to the lowest terrace at the site. A right turn at the bottom of the steps leads to the **south propylaea**, one end of the sacred way to Mylasa, patches of which can still be followed; straight ahead takes you to the more prominent **east propylaea**, terminus of a processional way, long disappeared, from Alinda. Wedged in between the two propylaea are the remains of a so-called **Doric house**, some adjoining **Roman baths** and a **Byzantine church**, beyond which are the probable foundations of Labranda's famous **fish oracle**. The resident fish, bedecked with jewellery according to several ancient sources, were thrown bits of food by their custodians. Depending on whether they accepted the morsels or not, the enquirer's fortunes were in the ascendant or the decline.

Stratonıkya

The ancient city of **Stratonıkya** (Stratoniceia in Turkish), 25km east of Milas, would be more acclaimed if it weren't for a giant, adjacent lignite quarry, whose noise and dust considerably reduce the peace and tranquillity. That the site continues to exist at all is a tribute to the Ministry of Culture's obstinacy in the face of the coal company's demands to swallow it up.

The archeological zone occupies the site of tumbledown **Eskihisar village**, nearly all of whose population have moved 3km west to a new settlement. Still, if you have your own vehicle (there's no public transport) and time to spare, the ruins are worth a visit. Signs direct you through the crumbling houses, themselves worthy museum pieces of 1930s' architecture, past the abandoned teahouse and vandalized mosque to a parking area beside the makeshift museum (see below); 4YTL **admission** is payable when the portakabin is staffed.

Stratonıkya was a third-century BC Seleucid foundation, but its heyday occurred during the Roman imperial period, so everything you can see now dates from that time. A few paces north of the empty teahouse is the Roman **gymnasium**, an elaborate structure with a colonnaded semicircular chamber sandwiched between three quadrangles of massive masonry. At the edge of the village, overlooking the opencast mine, is the **north city gate**, flanked by a lone, unfluted Corinthian column, just outside of which is a fragment of a **sacred way** that once led to a shrine of Hecate at nearby Lagina. By the pavement stands a **subterranean tomb** in good condition, the sole survivor of a necropolis, which, like the sacred way, has been sacrificed to mining interests. Bits of the substantial **city wall** are incorporated into houses on the west side of Eskihisar, with more chunks visible marching up the hillside to the south.

On the opposite side of the village is the most imposing remnant, a vast rectangular precinct identified either as a **bouleuterion** or a **shrine of Serapis**. The first thing you'll see is an isolated, rectangular **monumental gateway** erected a few metres west, but currently entry is via twin staircases bored through the south and north side-walls; the north wall's interior is covered with inscriptions. Its possible role as a council house is supported by the five rows of seats, overlooking the countryside to the east. Southeast of here, the garden of an ochre-stained building serves as an impromptu **museum–cum–warehouse**, where finds from the excavation have been temporarily stored.

Ören

ÖREN is an endangered Turkish species – a coastal resort that's not completely overdeveloped. It's virtually the only sizable village on the north coast of the gulf of Gökova, and owes its pre-tourism history to the narrow, fertile, alluvial plain adjacent, and the lignite deposits in the mountains behind.

The route there is inauspicious, the landscape defaced by two giant power-plants built with Polish aid. These installations are also one of the reasons tour operators have not seen fit to develop the area, although the industrial scenery of stacks and opencast mining stops well short of Ören itself, and pollution has not yet affected the crystalline waters offshore. Overall Ören makes a great hideout from the commercialism that has engulfed the rest of the coast, and is an excellent spot to recuperate from the rigours of overland travel. People, mostly from Ankara, come to stay for weeks on end: a single day is really pointless, and since there are fewer than 250 beds to go around, the place fills up in high season, when reservations are strongly advised.

The upper village and ancient Keramos

The **upper village**, on the east bank of a canyon mouth exiting the hills, is an appealingly homogenous settlement, scattered among the ruins of **ancient Keramos**. You can easily make out sections of wall, arches and a boat slip, dating from the time when the sea (now 1km distant) lapped the edge of town. Excavations are in progress, with some archeological fragments housed in a small fenced-off area, but a do-it-yourself tour through the village's old, mostly Ottoman Greek, houses should turn up some interesting oddments. The new resort area down on the coast (see below) has little in the way of relics, save for sections of column carted off from the main site by *pansiyon* owners for use as decoration.

The upper village has **shops** and a **post office** but no bank. Most **dolmuşes** from Milas continue the final short distance to the beach. For those driving themselves, a 45-kilometre **road** of sorts continues east from Ören past unspoiled, spectacular canyonland to the resort of Akyaka (see p.408), but only the first 8km or so at each end have been widened or improved in any way, leaving a horrendous middle section capable of shearing off exhausts: explore at your own risk.

The beach

The **beach** is a more than acceptable kilometre of coarse sand, gravel and pebbles, backed by handsome pine-tufted cliffs; in clear weather you can spy the Datça peninsula opposite. Once there was a working harbour at the east end of the town, but since lignite is now burned locally rather than being shipped out, the lignite-loading conveyor has been demolished and what's left of the jetty now serves a few fishing boats and the occasional wandering yacht.

Practicalities

Dolmuşes from Milas take an hour to reach Ören. Having passed through the upper village you'll be dropped at the beach. Should you plan on **staying**, the best mid-range option is the *Hotel Alnata* (℡0252/532 2813, ℻532 2381; ❹), at the west end of the beach, with large, stylish rooms, a garden and pool. The *Kardelen* (℡0252/532 2678; ❸) is another good choice, though its slightly inland location is a drawback. Other alternatives include the beachfront *Yalı Motel* (℡0252/532 2227; ❷); the *Kerme* (℡0252/532 2065; ❷), with a rudimentary **campsite**, simple wooden cottages and attached seafood and kebab restaurant down on the shore; and the rather plain *Yıltur Motel* (℡0252/532 2108, ✉yiltur@smallhotels.com.tr; ❷), in a rambling old compound at the far eastern end of the beach by the jetty.

Some of the hotels operate unassuming **restaurants**. Alternatively, there's *Çorumlunun Yeri* on the seafront, with tasty fish *mezes* and kebabs, or the nearby *Palmiye* café.

Iassos

Covering a headland almost completely surrounded by the gulf of Asim (Asin in local dialect), **Iassos** would seem, from a glance at the map, to promise great things. Alas the ruins, after the first few paces, fizzle to virtually nothing, and swimming in the sumpy coves nearby is hardly an inviting prospect. Only the excellent local fish, the best reason to visit, represents an unbroken tradition from the past.

Maritime stories abound at Iassos. In Hellenistic times the city's coinage even depicted a youth swimming with a dolphin that had befriended him. A more repeated tale concerns an itinerant musician that held his audience's attention until the ringing of the bell announcing the opening of the Iassian fish market. At that, the townspeople rose and trooped out, except for a partially deaf gentleman. The singer approached the man to compliment him on his manners; the deaf one, on understanding that the market had begun, hastily excused himself and fled after his peers.

The adjacent soil has always been poor and from very early times Iassos must have attracted settlers, and made its living, by virtue of its good anchorage and fisheries. Traces of Minoan and Mycenaean habitation from as far back as 1900 BC have been found, though the city was damaged so badly during the Persian, Peloponnesian and Mithridatic wars that it never amounted to much until Roman imperial rule. Particularly during the second century AD, Iassos recovered substantially, and most of what can be seen today dates from those years. During the Byzantine era the city ranked as a bishopric, reflected by the presence of two basilicas. The hilltop castle was a medieval foundation of the Knights of St John, and after the Turkish conquest the place was known as Asimkalesi (Asim's Castle), Asim being a local *ağa* (feudal lord). The poor condition of most antiquities here can be attributed to the Ottoman policy of loading all easily removable dressed stone onto waiting ships for transfer to building sites in İstanbul.

The site

On entering the modern village of Kıyıkızlacık, next to the ruins, you first pass a Roman mausoleum, arguably far more interesting than anything within the city walls and now in service as the site **museum** (erratic hours; 4YTL). Inside, the star exhibit is a Corinthian temple-tomb resting on a stepped platform.

At the principal **site of Iassos** (always open; 4YTL admission when staff present), things start promisingly enough as you cross the isthmus beyond the mausoleum to the **dipylon** (gate) in the **Hellenistic city wall**, repaired by the Byzantines. Once inside, the well-preserved Roman **bouleuterion**, with four rows of seats, lies immediately to your right. On your left, the **agora** has undergone a partial restoration of its Roman colonnade; at the south corner of the square is a rather obscure rectangular structure known as the **Caesarium**. Southeast of the castle there's a Roman **villa** with blurry murals and extensive floor mosaics, the latter hidden under a layer of protective sand. Close by, a wide stairway descends to the foundations of a small **Temple of Demeter and Kore**, while beyond is a partially submerged defensive **tower**.

From beside the tower a narrow but definite path threads past the large **stoa of Artemis** on the right, before reaching the meagre hillside **theatre**, of which only the cavea walls and stumps of the stage building remain – the fine view over the northeast harbour partly compensates. Continue around, or (better) through, the obvious **castle**: there's little to see within the medieval walls, though again the panorama from atop the ramparts is excellent.

There's an hourly dolmuş service to Kıyıkızlacık **from Milas**, 15km to the east. The turning is 8km west of Milas – a pretty drive, narrow but paved all the way, first across a plain planted with cotton, then through pine- and olive-studded hills. With your own transport you can approach **from Bodrum**, 40km to the south-west, on the narrow, but fair-standard dirt road beginning 3km north of Koru on the Bodrum–Milas road; just near a Petrol Ofisi station, a black-on-yellow sign announces "Iasos 17".

The other option is to take an **excursion boat from Güllük**, a small resort 27km southeast of Milas, from whose jetty trips depart daily (May–Sept; 12YTL), almost always including a swimming stop at a beach only accessible from the water. This is certainly a bonus, since there are no beaches worthy of the name accessible by foot or vehicle anywhere near Iassos.

In Kıyıkızlacık village, four or five **restaurants** specialize in fish, in particular the cheap and excellent local *çipura* (gilthead bream); best of the bunch is the *Dilek*, behind the touristy *İasos Deniz* on the waterfront. There are a few summer-season **pansiyons** up the hill; most eateries and lodgings overlook the rather murky fishing and yacht harbour.

Bodrum and its peninsula

In the eyes of its devotees, **BODRUM**, with its low-rise whitewashed houses and subtropical gardens, is the longest established, most attractive and most versatile Turkish resort – a quality outfit in comparison to its upstart Aegean rivals, Marmaris and Kuşadası. However, its recent, almost frantic attempts to be all things to all tourists have made it hard to tell the difference, while the controlled development within the municipality – height limits and a preservation code are in force – has resulted in wholesale exploitation of the nearby peninsula, until recently little-disturbed. The new airport at Milas enables easier access for both tourists and İstanbul-based weekenders, the latter's fondness for the area inflating prices in general.

The Bodrum area has long attracted large numbers of Britons, both the moneyed yacht set and the charter-flight trade. Most of the big UK package-tour operators are active here, which can be either reassuring or offputting, depending on your viewpoint. If you want waterborne distractions laid on by day and some of the most sophisticated nightlife in Turkey (complete with important DJs and lager louts), then Bodrum town, and Gümbet in particular, will probably suit. If you're after a coastal backwater with some vestiges of local character, then peninsular outposts such as Gümüşlük and Akyarlar more closely answer to the description.

Some history

Bodrum was originally known as **Halikarnassos** (Halicarnassus), colonized by Dorians from the Peloponnese during the eleventh century BC. They mingled with the existing Carian population, settling on the small island of Zephysia, which in later ages became a peninsula and the location of the medieval castle. Along with Knidos, Kos and the three Rhodian cities of Lindos, Kamiros and Ialyssos, Halicarnassus was a member of the so-called Dorian Hexapolis, whose assembly met periodically at the sanctuary of Triopian Apollo at Knidos. At some point during the sixth century BC Halicarnassus was expelled from the confederation, on the pretext that one of the city's athletes had failed to show proper reverence to the god. In reality, the increasingly Ionian character of Halicarnassus offended the other five cities.

Later, the city came under Persian influence, while managing to retain considerable autonomy. Halicarnassus' most famous son, **Herodotus** (484–420 BC), chronicled the city's fortunes in his acclaimed *Histories*. Eventually direct Persian rule was replaced by that of the **Hecatomnid satraps**, a capable if rather inbred dynasty, the most renowned of whose rulers was **Mausolus** (377–353 BC), a leader who greatly increased the power and wealth of what in effect was a semi-independent Carian principality. An admirer of Greek civilization, Mausolus spared no effort to Hellenize his cities, and was working on a suitably self-aggrandizing tomb at the time of his death – thereby giving us the word "mausoleum". **Artemisia II**, his sister and wife, completed the massive structure, which came to be regarded as one of the Seven Wonders of the Ancient World. Like her ancestor Artemisia I, she distinguished herself in warfare, inflicting a humiliating defeat on the Rhodians, who were tricked into allowing her entire fleet into their port.

In 334 BC the rampaging Alexander's arrival coincided with a bitter succession feud between Artemisia's heirs. The Macedonian armies wreaked such havoc that the city never fully recovered, and its population was dispersed throughout Caria over the next two chaotic centuries. After a period of little importance under the Roman and Byzantine empires, and brief shuffling among Selçuk, Menteşe and Ottoman occupiers, the **Knights of St John** slipped over from Rhodes in 1402 and erected the castle that is now Bodrum's most prominent landmark. Urgently needing to replace the fortress at Smyrna destroyed by the Mongols, the Knights engaged the best military engineers of the era to construct their new stronghold on the promontory. The name *bodrum*, meaning "cellar" or "dungeon" in Turkish, probably pays tribute to the stronghold's subterranean defences. After Süleyman the Magnificent compelled the Knights to depart in 1523, the castle's history was virtually synonymous with that of the town until early this century.

Arrival, orientation and information

International and domestic **ferries** (from Marmaris, Datça, Dalyan, Kós and Rhodes) dock at the jetty west of the castle. Buses drop you at the **otogar**, 500m up Cevat Şakir Caddesi, which links Belediye Meydanı with the main peninsular highway and divides the town roughly in two. Transfer to and from the Milas/Bodrum **airport**, 35km northeast of town can be tricky. THY customers can take a shuttle bus, but must book at the THY office (see "Listings" on p.400) at least two hours before the flight. Otherwise the only other option is taking a taxi, which costs at least 40YTL.

Cevat Şakir's approximate pedestrianized continuation, Kale Caddesi, defines one edge of the bazaar, huddling in the shadow of the medieval castle. Kale Caddesi ends at İskele Meydanı, officially known as Barış Meydanı and home to the generally unhelpful **tourist office** (May–Sept Mon–Fri 8am–5.30pm; ☏0252/316 1091).

Northwest of Cevat Şakir Caddesi is the service-oriented side of town. Most travel, yacht- and car-rental agencies, plus the bus-company offices, line Neyzen Tevfik Caddesi, which takes off from Belediye Meydanı. Its most important sidestreets, especially when hunting for accommodation, are Menekşe Sokağı and Türkkuyusu Caddesi.

Driving is difficult in Bodrum, made all the more so by a strict, anticlockwise one-way system; you enter town via Cevat Şakir, proceed west along Neyzen Tevfik, curl north towards Turgutreis Caddesi via one of several minor streets and then proceed east again. Türkkuyusu Caddesi and Hamam Sokağı are northbound (uphill) only. On the eastern side of town, Atatürk Caddesi is westbound only. **Parking** is even more frustrating: shelling out for car-park fees or, even worse,

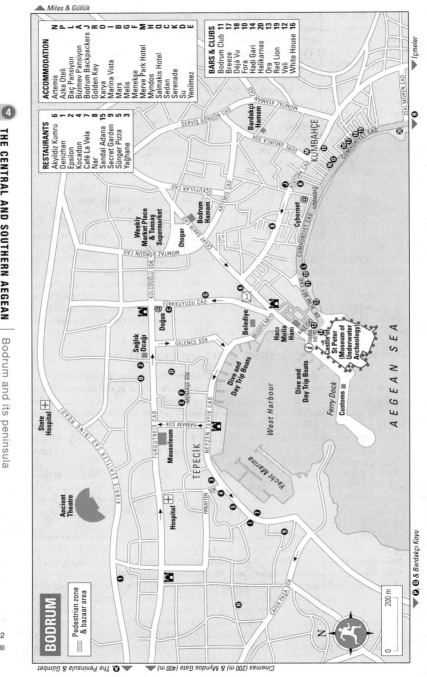

BODRUM

Pedestrian zone & bazaar area

ACCOMMODATION
Artemis — N
Azka Oteli — P
Baç Pansiyon — L
Bizimev Pansiyon — A
Bodrum Backpackers — J
Golden Key — R
Karya — O
Marina Vista — I
Mars — B
Melis — G
Menekşe — F
Merve Park Hotel — M
Myndos — H
Salmakis Hotel — Q
Sedan — C
Serenade — K
Su — D
Yenimez — E

RESTAURANTS
Akyıldız Kumru — 6
Denizhan — 1
Epsilon — 2
Kocadon — 4
Café La Vela — 7
Nar — 8
Sandal Adana — 15
Secret Garden — 9
Sünger Pizza — 5
Yağhane — 3

BARS & CLUBS
Bodrum Club — 11
Breeze — 17
Déjà Vu — 18
Fora — 10
Hadi Gari — 14
Halikarnas — 20
Ora — 19
Red Lion — 13
Veli — 12
White House — 16

▲ Milas & Güllük

► İçmeler

Weekly Market Place & Tansaş Supermarket

State Hospital

Ancient Theatre

Mausoleum

Hospital

Sağlık Ocağı

Doğuş

Otogar

Bodrum Hamam

Bardakçı Hamam

Belediye

Haci Molla Hani

Castle of St Peter (Museum of Underwater Archeology)

Dive and Day Trip Boats

Dive and Day Trip Boats

Ferry Dock

Customs

West Harbour

Yacht Marina

AEGEAN SEA

KUMBAHÇE

TEPECİK

DERVİŞ GÖRGÜN CAD
MÜMTAZ ATAMAN CAD
DERE UMURCA SOK
ATATÜRK CAD
CUMHURİYET CAD
ZEKİ MÜREN CAD
ÜÇKUYULAR CAD
ARTEMİS CAD
KEMAL ŞAKİR CAD
MÜMTAZ GÖRGÜN CAD
KULCUOĞLU SOK
TÜRKKUYUSU CAD
GELENCE SOK
BELEDİYE MEYD
NEYZEN TEVFİK CAD
HAMAM SOK
MENEKŞE SOK
TURGUTREİS CAD
HİKAYTEN SOK
KIBRIS ŞEHİTLER CAD / RİNG ROAD
CAFER PAŞA SOK
İSKELE MEYD
CEVAT ŞAKİR CAD / DR ALİM BEY CAD
ADLİYE SOK
ADNANBAŞI
CYBERNET

N

200 m
0

◄ ▲ The Peninsula & Gümbet
▲ Myndos Gate (400 m)
► & Bardakçı Koyu
Cinemas (200 m) &

getting a vehicle out of impoundment is disheartening, so we've noted accommodation with parking space.

Accommodation

Desirable accommodation tends to concentrate in three main areas: in **Kumbahçe Mahalle**, near the beach and bars of Cumhuriyet Caddesi; in **Tepecik** district, along or just off Neyzen Tevfik Caddesi (passably quiet); and on the convenient and usually peaceful **Türkkuyusu Caddesi**, winding up from Belediye Meydanı. There are also several desirable locales along, or just off, **Turgutreis Caddesi**, as well as behind **Bardakçı Koyu**, the first sandy bay southwest of the town centre. Accommodation at **Gümbet**, 2km west, virtually a suburb of Bodrum, is heavily package-oriented, with hotels block-booked from overseas, but there are one or two independent possibilities.

Prices tend to be higher than elsewhere in Turkey, particularly in July and August, when advance reservations are recommended. Out of season most hotels (except those with central heating) are closed. Air conditioning is a distinct bonus in midsummer, when the less expensive *pansiyon*s tend to be airless shoeboxes. There are few places to **camp**: the *Dönen Pansiyon* (off Türkkuyusu Cad) allows pitching of tents in its garden, but otherwise *Camping 86* in Akyarlar (see p.403) is the most convenient place.

Kumbahçe Mahalle

Artemis Cumhuriyet Cad 117 ☎0252/316 1572, ⓦwww.artemispansiyon.com. Some of the air-conditioned rooms at the front can be noisy, but all are very comfortable with good views across the bay, and there's a rooftop breakfast bar and a ground-floor café. ❸

Baç Pansiyon Cumhuriyet Cad 14 ☎0252/313 1602, ⓔbacpansiyon@turk .net. This luxurious, but surprisingly affordable, boutique hotel is located right in the heart of the action, in amongst a glut of bars, restaurants and shops. The stylish rooms are all double-glazed, cutting out much of the noise, and those at the rear have balconies with views of the castle. ❹

Bodrum Backpackers Atatürk Cad 318 ☎0252/313 2762, ⓦwww.bodrumbackpackers .com. Big, noisy, bustling backpackers' favourite offering clean, well-kept dorms (€6.50), a few double rooms, a roof terrace, Internet access, laundry service and a "British Bar" with a big screen showing an endless succession of football matches. ❷

Golden Key Şalvarağa Sok 18 ☎0252/313 0304, ⓦwww.goldenkeyhotels.com. Small luxury hotel at the far eastern end of the seafront with seven lavishly furnished rooms, all with sea views, three with their own garden. It also has its own private stretch of beach and an excellent restaurant. Parking available. ❽

Karya Cumhuriyet Cad 127 ☎0252/316 1535. Right in the centre of the bar zone overlooking the town's narrow strip of beach, this has well-appointed rooms, many with ceiling fans and satellite TV, but is unavoidably noisy. Air-conditioned rooms have central heating in winter (when prices drop a little). ❹

Merve Park Hotel Atatürk Cad 73 ☎0252/316 6559, ⓦwww.mervepark.com. Small, cultivated and stylish. The attractive doubles are fitted out with antiques, wood carvings and marble bathrooms. There's a nice pool too. Parking available. ❻

Serenade Atatürk Cad 55 ☎0252/316 0800, ⓦwww.bodrumserenade.com. Swish boutique hotel just back from the seafront with large, sound-proofed rooms, all with TVs and a/c. ❺

Türkkuyusu Caddesi

Melis Türkkuyusu Cad 50 ☎0252/316 0560. Set back from the street, with a garden and popular bar. It's where Aussie backpackers tend to go straight off the boat from Kós. ❸

Sedan Türkkuyusu Cad 121/A ☎0252/316 0355. A slightly shabby 1970s-vintage *pansiyon* built around a courtyard superbly shaded by lush vines. There's a choice of rooms with or without en-suite facilities, and limited parking. ❷

Tepecik

Marina Vista Neyzen Tevfik Cad 226 ☎0252/316 2269. Fancy stark-white luxury hotel opposite the yacht marina. All its eighty-plus rooms have TVs, a/c, and very elegant bathrooms. There's also a swimming pool, restaurant and games room. ❽

Menekşe Menekşe Çıkmazı ☎0252/316 0537. Good-value rooms set in peaceful gardens. There's limited parking (and stroking the numerous pets is free!). The street is the continuation of Menekşe Sok. ❷

Myndos Myndos Cad 1 ☏ 0252/316 3080, ✉ myndos@hotelmyndos.com. Medium-sized three-star hotel, which features in some package-tour brochures. Both an adult and toddlers' pool, indoor and outdoor restaurants and tennis court. The small but inviting rooms are all air-conditioned; the price is for half-board accommodation. Parking available. ❹

Yenilmez Menekşe Çıkmazı ☏ 0252/316 2520. Central, quiet, modern *pansiyon* with a nice garden; a good option if the next-door *Menekşe* is full. It doesn't serve breakfast, though there's a kitchen for guests. ❷

Turgutreis Caddesi

Mars Turgutreis Cad, İmbat Çıkmazı 20 ☏ 0252/316 6559, 🖷 316 1610. Most evocative of three small hotels clustered here, with simple rooms, a small pool, and a mostly French clientele. ❷

Su 1201 Sok, off Turgutreis Cad ☏ 0252/316 6906, 🖳 www.suhotel.net. A large well-equipped complex laid out around one of the biggest pools in town. The cheery multi-coloured rooms all have balconies overlooking the central courtyard where there's a lively bar. The hotel is inaccessible to cars (which helps to keep the noise levels down), although it does have its own parking around the corner. The hotel also has a couple of very luxurious apartments near the mausoleum (€100). ❻

Bardakçı Koyu

Azka Oteli ☏ 0252/316 8992, 🖳 www.azkaotel .com. Five-star comfort right on the best part of the beach, with large pool and sun terrace. The over-priced rooms are reminiscent of a quality English B&B; try and get a double in the terraced north wing, facing the garden. ❼

Salmakis Hotel ☏ 0252/316 6506, 🖳 www. salmakis.com.tr. Large four-star complex with a range of decent doubles as well as unit apartments with mock-village rustic decor, on several levels. Has a share of the beach just down from the *Azka*, as well as its own enormous pool, complete with landscaped islets. Rooms ❹, apartments ❻

Gümbet

Bizimev Pansiyon Meneres Cad 47 ☏ 0252/313 7249. Small, basic doubles, adequately furnished (breakfast extra) and close to Gümbet's day- and night-time distractions. ❷

The Castle of St Peter

Sitting on a promontory splitting the inner and outer harbours, Bodrum's main landmark is the **Castle of St Peter**, now home to the town's cultural centrepiece, the **Museum of Underwater Archaeology** (Tues–Sun 8.30am–noon & 1–5pm; 10YTL). Despite the relentless commercialization of the grounds, the museum is well worth visiting, with its array of towers, courtyards and dungeons, as well as separate museums displaying underwater finds from various wrecks.

The castle was built by the Knights of St John over a small Selçuk fortress they found on the site. An initial circuit of walls was completed in 1437, though as the new science of artillery ballistics advanced the garrison saw fit to add more walls and moats, particularly on the landward side. Given their powerful fleets, the Knights had less fear of attack by sea. Fourteen water cisterns were provided to guarantee self-sufficiency in the event of siege, increasingly probable after 1453 when the citadel became the sole Christian stronghold in Anatolia. Work proceeded slowly and the finishing touches had just been applied in 1522 when Süleyman's capture of the Knights' headquarters on Rhodes made their position here untenable. Bodrum's castle was subsequently neglected until the nineteenth century, when the chapel was converted to a mosque, the keep to a prison, and a hamam installed. During a siege in 1915, shells from a French battleship levelled the minaret and damaged various towers. The Italians repaired most of the harm done during their brief postwar occupation, though the place was not properly refurbished until the 1960s, when it was converted into a museum.

△ The Castle of St Peter, Bodrum

The lower courtyard and chapel

Initial entrance is no longer via the **north gate**, facing Barış Meydanı, but through the **west gate**, looking on to the water. Once inside the west moat, you'll notice bits of ancient masonry from the mausoleum incorporated into the walls, as well as some of the 249 Christian coats of arms.

Stairs lead up to the seaward fortifications and then into the **lower courtyard**, where strolling peacocks congregate around a small drinks stall, the first of a number scattered strategically across the huge grounds. On the left, a linear display on amphora production culminates in the "**medieval shop**", actually a pretext to sell unusual aromatic oils, herbal samples and souvenir foodstuffs.

To the right, the **chapel** houses a fascinating reconstruction of a seventh-century Byzantine ship, whose remains were excavated off Yassıada. The display, incorporating the salvaged hull, shows how such ships were loaded with cargoes of amphorae. A building at the base of the **Italian Tower** holds a small glass collection, mostly Roman and early Islamic work, displayed in odd reverse illumination.

The Glass Wreck Hall and Uluburun Wreck Hall

There's a more substantial display in the so-called **Glass Wreck Hall** (Tues–Fri 10–11am & 2–4pm; 4YTL separate admission), which houses a Byzantine ship-wreck and cargo found 33m down at Serçe Limanı in 1973. Dating from 1025, this was a peacetime trading vessel plying between Fatimid and Byzantine territories. The craft – tubby and flat-bottomed to permit entry to the Mediterranean's many shallow straits – is displayed in a climate-controlled environment, though only twenty percent of the original timbers are preserved. The rest is a mock-up, loaded with a fraction of the cargo: two tonnes of raw coloured glass, finished glassware and tamped-down broken shards intended for an early recycling programme. The archeologists' main task, which took eleven years to complete, was to separate

395

15,000 fragments into the three categories. When she sank, the ship was apparently headed for skilled glass workshops along the Black Sea and returning empty pots to their owners – a frugal bunch, it would seem, as the amphorae were being used long after their spouts and handles had been badly damaged. Also displayed are the personal effects of the passengers and crew, including gaming pieces, tools and grooming items. All told, it's a well-labelled and well-lit exhibit, worth the extra expense if you can coincide with the restricted opening hours.

The **Uluburun Wreck Hall** (Tues–Fri 10–11am & 2–4pm; free) on the east side of the castle precinct houses the local Bronze Age and Mycenaean collection. It features artefacts recovered from three Aegean wrecks, including finds from the Uluburun site near Kaş.

The Carian Princess Hall

On the next level up, the linked Italian and French towers are now home to a gift shop. Just beyond, the **Carian Princess Hall** (same hours as castle; 4YTL separate admission) contains artefacts from an ancient tomb found miraculously unlooted during hotel-building works in 1989. The sarcophagus, with its skeleton of a Carian noblewoman who died in the fourth century BC, is on view, along with a scant number of gold tomb finds, which were almost certainly imported, as the metal is not found locally. Items buried with her include the lady's favourite drinking cup and an elaborate diadem with floral motifs, which lends credence to the supposition of royalty.

The English Tower, upper courtyard and dungeon

The **English Tower**, at the southeast corner of the castle precinct, is a bald attempt to pander to Bodrum's major foreign constituency. Inside is a themed cafeteria, around which assorted standards of the Order of St John and of their Muslim adversaries compete for wall space with an incongruous array of medieval armour and weapons. Many visitors attempt to decipher extensive swathes of Latin graffiti incised into the window jambs by bored knights.

Finish your tour by crossing the **upper courtyard**, landscaped like much of the castle grounds with native flora, to the **German Tower**, with an exhibition of Ottoman royal *tuğra*s (seals), and the **Snake Tower** – named for the serpent relief plaque over the entrance.

East of these, it's possible to make a long, dead-end detour, past a horrible diorama on galley slavery, to the lowest exhibit in the Gatineau Tower. This, the Knights' former **dungeon**, is adorned with dangling chains and bathed in lurid red light, while an infernal blacksmith fashions fetters to the sound of prerecorded moans and sighs. In case you missed the point, an original Latin inscription over the door reads "Here God does not exist".

The Town

The castle neatly divides the town into two contrasting halves: to the west is the more genteel area that surrounds the spruced-up yacht marina, with its upmarket hotels and restaurants; while to the east is the town's party zone where you'll find the highest concentration of bars and restaurants. Immediately to the north of the castle lies the **bazaar**, most of which is pedestrianized along its two main thoroughfares of Kale Caddesi and Dr Alim Bey Caddesi; traffic enters the dense warren of streets to the southeast via Atatürk Caddesi, 200m inland. East of the spot called **Azmakbaşı** (Creek Mouth), Alim Bey becomes Cumhuriyet Caddesi (the two roads are jointly referred to locally as **Uzunyol** – Long Street), which overlooks a thin strip of somewhat scrubby beach: despite its less than pristine appearance, it's packed to bursting with sunbathers during the day.

Bodrum in literature and music – and in drag

In recent years Bodrum has become something of a magnet for Turkish bohemian types. The earliest arrival was the writer-to-be **Cevat Şakir Kabaağaçlı**. He had just been paroled in 1921, after serving half of a fourteen-year manslaughter sentence for killing his father, a wealthy pasha, when he was internally exiled here in 1925 for three years on charges of sedition. He persistently declined to make any public comment on the patricide, but for most of the balance of his long life (1893–1973) he voluntarily remained in Bodrum, devoting himself to the welfare of the area, in particular to the preservation of its monuments (he once wrote to the British Museum demanding the return of the Halicarnassian artefacts pillaged by Charles Newton). He also recorded the lore and legends of the local seafarers, penning several collections of short stories based on these conversations under the *nom de plume* "Fisherman of Halicarnassus". To him is also owed the concept of the *Mavi Yolculuk*, or "Blue Voyage", the title of a work of his describing his week-long Aegean forays from the 1920s until the 1950s on a primitive sponge-fishing boat. Kabaağaçlı is buried on a hill overlooking the bay of Gümbet, having died some years before his bohemian sea voyages with like-minded disciples had become the money-spinning *gület* cruises of today and the inspiration for a biopic *Blue Exile* (1994), starring Hanna Schygulla as one of his three wives.

Ahmet and Nesuhi Ertegün, two more prominent Bodrum habitués, were the sons of the Turkish ambassador to the US during the 1930s and 1940s, and caught the jazz bug while living in America. Both later became big-time recording executives, establishing Atlantic Records, which, in the early 1960s, launched the careers of (among others) Charles Mingus, John Coltrane and the Modern Jazz Quartet. The Ertegüns were influential in the process of introducing jazz to Turkey, and their careers go a long way toward explaining the music's popularity among the Turkish middle and upper classes. Nesuhi died in 1989, but his brother still occasionally visits the family villa in Bodrum.

Another long-term local villa-owner was **Zeki Müren**, foremost among a bevy of widely acclaimed transvestite pop singers in Turkey. He lived in Bodrum – and circulated out of drag – from the 1970s until his death in 1996, and has a street named after him, appropriately enough leading to the biggest disco in Turkey. His house is now a small **museum**, Zeki Müren Caddesi 19 (Tues–Sun 9.30am–5.30pm; 4YTL), filled with memorabilia from his life, including his flamboyant stage costumes.

From landscaped Belediye Meydanı, stroll up Türkkuyusu Caddesi towards Turgutreis Caddesi. Turn right to find the **market** (produce on Thursday and Friday, clothes on Tuesday), in the fairgrounds behind the *otogar*, though don't count on unearthing any stupendous bargains. Bear left instead down Turgutreis Caddesi and you pass through a small district of **old stone houses** with courtyards that give some hint of what pre-tourism Bodrum was like.

Roughly 400m west along Turgutreis Caddesi lies all that's left of the **Mausoleum** (Tues–Sun 8.30am–noon & 1–5.30pm; 4YTL). Designed by Pytheos, architect of the Athena temple at Priene, the complete structure measured 39m by 33m at its base and stood nearly 60m high. A colonnade surmounted the burial vault and supported a stepped pyramidal roof bearing a chariot (now in the British Museum) with effigies of Mausolus and his sister-wife Artemisia. Most available vertical surfaces were adorned with friezes and statues executed by some of the best sculptors of the age.

The tomb stood essentially intact for over sixteen centuries before being severely damaged by an earthquake. The Knights of St John finished its destruction between 1402 and 1522 by removing all the cut stone as building material, and burning much of the marble facing for lime. Happily for posterity, they used most of the friezes for decorating their castle. When Stratford Canning, British

Boat trips around Bodrum

It's almost impossible to miss the touts for **boat trips** in Bodrum and, if you're not planning to tour the area by land, they are worth taking advantage of, since swimming anywhere near the pair of polluted town bays is inadvisable. Most of the craft are concentrated on the west harbour, and a typical day out starts between 9.30 and 10.30am and finishes between 4 and 5pm, costing roughly 25YTL per person in a minimum group of seven (lunch extra). Itineraries vary little, with most boats visiting a fixed list of attractions in the following order.

First stop is usually **Kara Ada**, a sizable island southeast of town, where you bathe in some hot springs issuing from a cave at the island's margin. Next halt is the **Akvaryum**, a snorkellers' venue in the Ada Boğazı (Island Strait) near Gümbet, with claimed optimal underwater visibility of 30m; the fish, however, usually seem to be frightened off by the crowds of humans and motor noise. The final moorings, also accessible by land, tend to be two of the following attractions: **Kargı** beach, where you can ride camels, **Bağla** cove and **Karaincir** bay. Some craft head east from Kara Ada to visit **Orak Adası** and **Yalıçiftlik** beach instead.

Ambassador to the Sublime Porte, noticed them there in 1846, he obtained permission to ship them to the British Museum. Eleven years later Charles Newton discovered the site of the mausoleum and unearthed the statues of Mausolus and Artemisia, plus portions of the chariot team, which went to join the other relics in London.

Not surprisingly the mausoleum in its present condition ranks as a disappointment, despite diligent and imaginative work by Danish archeologists. Little is left besides the precinct wall, assorted column fragments and some subterranean vaults probably belonging to an earlier burial chamber. In a shed east of the foundation cavity are exhibited plans and models, as well as a copy or two of the original friezes in England.

By way of contrast the **ancient theatre**, just above the main highway bounding Bodrum to the north, has been almost overzealously restored and is now used during the September festival. Begun by Mausolus, it was modified in the Roman era and originally seated 13,000, though it has a present capacity of about half that. The so-called **Myndos Gate**, west of the junction of Turgutreis Caddesi and Cafer Paşa Caddesi, is the best surviving section of Mausolus's ambitious city wall, though remains of five towers are spread round the town.

Eating

Almost everywhere in Bodrum you pay over the odds to eat out, especially if you're close to the water or in a chi-chi restaurant. Elsewhere, dismal dives offering greasy British food abound and the majority of new places only last a season or two before changing name, style and management. However, if you know where to look, the dining scene isn't all bad.

A good place to start is the vine-covered **Meyhanelar Caddesi** in the bazaar where a number of small restaurants all vie with each other to offer you the traditional Turkish experience. Anywhere else, especially overlooking either bay, you can expect a considerable jump up in price. There is a cluster of upmarket restaurants near the marina that, considering the standard of cuisine, are reasonably good value, certainly when compared with the numerous costly fish and kebab establishments on the seaward side of **Dr Alim Bey Caddesi**. The landward side of the same street and the small square are home to an ever-changing array of fast-food and pizza joints – none of which offers anything like good value for money, but most of which are licensed. If you have the inclination and the funds, you can eat Chinese, Thai, Italian, Indian and even Mexican cuisine in Bodrum – often in the same restaurant.

Akyildiz Kumru ve Kebap Salonu Cevat Şakir
Cad, Çarşl Sok 29. Inexpensive, good-quality kebab
salon a couple of hundred yards back from the
front, run by two ebullient local brothers.
Denizhan Turgut Reis Yolu ☎0252/363 7674.
West of town, past the antique theatre, this is well
worth the trip if you fancy spoiling yourself. You
can watch the dishes, which include huge, lavish
kebabs, being prepared in the glassed-off kitchen
in the centre of the restaurant. Main courses from
8–14YTL.
Epsilon Türkkuyusu Mah, Keles Cikmazi 5
☎0252/313 2964. Gourmet courtyard restaurant
with daily European and Turkish specialities; count
on 12–15YTL for a main, considerably more for the
vintage wine.
Kocadon Saray Sok ☎0252/316 3705. Traditional
Ottoman cuisine served up in an elegant cobbled courtyard. Stick with the *mezes* for 8–12YTL
unless you want to break the bank.
Café La Vela Neyzen Tevfik Cad 5 ☎0252/316
1229. Despite its upmarket clientele and fancy surroundings by the yacht marina, this Italian eaterie
is perfectly affordable – sandwiches and pizzas
from 7YTL, mains from 10YTL, and if you fancy
pushing the boat out, steak in port for 14YTL.
Nar Atatürk Cad 27. Small, unpretentious kebab

and *pide* joint, with tasty woodfired pizzas (7YTL);
caters mainly for the passing pub crowd.
Sandal Adana Kebap House Atatürk Cad 76/D.
For authentic eastern Turkish cuisine, especially
grilled chicken and *köfte*, try this well-established
restaurant, which sits on a landscaped plot, making the most of its insalubrious roadside setting.
Typically 15YTL a head.
Secret Garden Sanat Okullu Cad, 1019 Sok
☎0252/313 4479. Situated in the romantic, walled
garden of an old house, this exclusive restaurant
offers international cuisine, with meals for around
40YTL.
Sünger Pizza Neyzen Tevfik Cad 218. Cheap,
cheerful, popular pizza restaurant, with excellent
views from its rooftop; justifiably packed with
yachties and locals most evenings. Delivery service
available.
Yağhane Neyzen Tevlik Cad 170
☎0252/313 2732. The burning torches
outside this former olive-oil factory make this
refined restaurant easy to spot: the distinguished
old building is festooned with bougainvillea and the
menu thick with Mediterranean influences. A two-
course meal without wine costs under 20YTL, with
the Roquefort, mushroom and spinach crêpes with
sweet tomato salsa (12YTL) recommended.

Drinking, nightlife and entertainment

There must be over sixty places to drink and dance in Bodrum, most of them lining Dr Alim Bey Caddesi (where many of the bars on the seaward side lead straight
through to a waterfront area) and its continuation, Cumhuriyet Caddesi. All get
packed and sweaty of a summer night. Many are seasonal establishments, consisting of just a bar with a small dance-floor, and few have cover charges, though
drink prices are high. The busiest time of the night is from 11pm to 3am.

Bars and clubs

The ultimate experience is *Halikarnas* (☎0252/316 8000, ⓦwww.halikarnas
.com.tr) at the eastern end of Cumhuriyet Caddesi, where a 30YTL cover charge
(35YTL on Friday and Saturday) and proper dress sees you in with the beautiful
people, up to 5000 of them on the mammoth dance-floor. The external laser
show, frequently aimed at the castle, and the illuminated 15-metre water fountain
outside the club, are free.

West of *Halikarnas*, en route to Azmakbaşı, are a glut of similar dance-bars
including *Déjà vu*, *White House* and *Breeze*, all offering happy hours and last season's chart hits, and the well-established *Red Lion*. Further west, along Alim Bey
Caddesi, is *Fora*, which has a waterfront dance-floor with views of the castle.
Almost next door is the boarding area for *Halikarnas*' main rival, the *Bodrum
Club* (☎0252/313 3600, ⓦwww.clubbodrum.com; 35YTL), a nightclub on a 2000-
person capacity catamaran that sets sail every night at 1am for a four-hour disco
on the ocean waves; advance tickets may be necessary in peak season. Also near the
western end of Alim Bey, is the *Ora* disco and the popular "live blues" bar, *Veli*,
one of the longest lived of Bodrum's watering holes, attracting an older, Turkish

crowd. At the far western end of Alim Bey, near the tourist office, stands *Hadi Gari*, an acclaimed music-bar in an old fig-warehouse.

Cinemas

Bodrum has two fully fledged **cinemas**: the Karia Princess (Candlıdere Sok 15), in the basement of the eponymous hotel, and the outdoor Sinema Bodrum, 100m to the east, with screenings most nights in summer at least an hour after dark (usually 10pm). Films have the original soundtrack and Turkish subtitles; playbills are posted at strategic locations.

Bodrum Festival

During early September a Turkish **music and arts festival** livens things up in central Bodrum. Although centred on the castle and its immediate environs, processional floats and other eye-catching displays parade along the main Neyzen Tevfik Caddesi. Numerous organized events take place during this period; check with the tourist office for this year's details.

Listings

Airlines THY (Turkish Airlines), Kıbrıs Şehitleri Cad 82/2/22 ☎0252/317 1203. THY ticket-holders can book here for the shuttle bus to Milas airport.

Banks and exchange *Döviz* houses are ubiquitous (daily 10am–11pm), or use the ATMs of any main bank, including Pamukbank, Garanti Bankası, Yapı Kredi or Akbank, found especially along Dr Alim Bey Cad and Cevat Şakir Cad (Mon–Fri 9am–noon & 1.30pm–5pm).

Books There's only one proper bookstore (as opposed to purveyors of tourist literature): Bodrum Kitaplişi, Cumhuriyet Cad, Adliye Sok 4.

Carpets Etrım and Mumcular, east of Bodrum, are the target of special-interest tours to the "carpet villages" where the tawny-hued Milas carpets are woven.

Car rental Airtour, Atatürk Cad 198 ☎0252/316 5927; Avis, Neyzen Tevfik Cad 92/A ☎0252/316 2333, and at Milas airport domestic terminal ☎0252/316 0201, international terminal ☎0252/523 0203; Budget, Neyzen Tevfik Cad 96/A ☎0252/316 7382; DeCar, Neyzen Tevfik Cad 236/B ☎0252/313 2151; Europcar/InterRent, Neyzen Tevfik Cad 48 ☎0252/316 5632; Hertz, Neyzen Tevfik Cad 232 ☎0252/318 1053; Sun, Neyzen Tevfik Cad 82/A ☎0252/316 4385; and Unicar, Neyzen Tevfik Cad 80 ☎0252/316 6252.

Consulate Honorary British Consulate, Fevzi Çakmak Cad, 1314 Sok 6/8 ☎0252/319 0093, ⓔhonconbod2@superonline.com.

Diving Most of the long-running outfits listed below offer courses, tours and servicing. Aquapro, Nimets Cad ☎0252/313 8693 or 313 1341; Yunus Scuba School, Menekşe Çıkmazi 2/A ☎0252/316 5890, ⓔyunusscuba@superonline.com.tr; Swedish-run Poseidon, Neyzen Tevfik Cad 80/A ☎0252/313 8727, ⓔposeidon@poseidon.com;

and Aegian Pro Dive Centre, Neyzin Tevfik Cad 212 ☎0252/316 0737, ⓦwww.aegeanprodive.com. For equipment sale or spares, try Bodrum Dive Store, Kıbrıs Şehitler Cad, Alaman Centre E/3 (☎0252/316 0493), or Derin Diveshop, Atatürk Cad 5 (☎0252/313 0173).

Ferries and hydrofoils There are domestic services to Marmaris, Dalyan and Datça as well as the short hops to Kós and to Rhodes in Greece; see "Travel details" at the end of this chapter for schedules and prices. Buy tickets from the two agencies just outside Customs on the jetty: Bodrum Express (☎0252/316 1087, ⓦwww.bodrumexpresslines.com) for hydrofoils; and Bodrum Ferryboat Association (☎0252/316 0882, ⓦwww.bodrumferryboat.com) for ferries.

Hamam Bodrum Hamam on Cevat Şakir Caddesi opposite the *otogar* (daily segregated bathing 6am–midnight) and Bardakçi Hamam on Dere Umurca Sok (daily 8am–8pm; later in summer according to demand).

Hospitals The English-speaking Karia Medical Centre, Kıbrıs Şehitler Cad 97 (☎0252/313 6233), and Medicare, Hamam Sok 4 (☎0252/316 7051), both promise 24hr, seven-day attention. The State Hospital (Devlet Hastanesi; ☎0252/313 1420) is 300m east of the theatre on the ring road Kıbrıs Şehitler.

Internet access Cybernet Internet Café, Dr Alim Bey Cad; Doğus Internet, Türkkuyusu Cad.

Laundry Mavi, Turgutreis Cad, Davutlar Sok 3.

Pharmacies Marina, Neyzen Tevfik Cad ☎0252/313 0007.

Police Dr Alim Bey Cad ☎0252/316 8079.

Post office PTT at Cevat Şekir Cad (open daily 24hr).

Supermarkets Migros, near the turning for

Gümbet; Tansaş, by the *otogar*.

Yachting and tours Most set cruises hug the scenic Gökova gulf coast en route to Marmaris, though individual itineraries are catered for. Akustik Travel and Yachting, Neyzin Tevfik Cad 200 (☎0252/313 8964, ⓦwww.travelbodrum.com), is a long-running outfit specializing in custom yacht tours and car rental. S&J Travel & Yachting, Neyzen Tevfik

Cad 218/A (☎0252/316 0561, ⓦwww.sjyachting .com), specializes in custom-itinerary *gület* hire; minimum six days, with a crew of 2–4 (including a cook). The main alternatives, with weekly scheduled departures, are Aegean Yacht Services, Paşa Tarlasi Cad 21 (☎0252/316 1517, ⓦwww .aegeanyacht.com); and Fora Tourism & Yachting, Neyzen Tevfik Cad 210 (☎0252/316 4664).

Around the peninsula

There is more of interest and beauty in the rest of the **Bodrum peninsula** than the often dreary environs of the town, and no matter how long or short your stay, some time spent there is worthwhile. The north side of the peninsula tends to be greener, with patches of pine forest; the south, studded with tall crags, is more arid, with a sandier coast.

The population on the peninsula was largely Greek Orthodox before 1923 and villages often still have a vaguely Hellenic feel, with ruined churches, windmills and old stone houses that even the most brazen new developments attempt to imitate. The landscape in general, with bare rock (and sometimes castles) at the higher elevations, and vast oases along the streambeds and shore, is not unlike that of the islands of Pátmos, Léros or Kálymnos across the water. An exotic touch is lent by the ubiquitous, white-domed *gümbets* (cisterns) and by the camel caravans – not mere tourist photo ops, but working draft animals, especially during the off-season.

There is also a relatively high concentration of serviceable **beaches**, with Bitez, Ortakent and Gümüşluk recently being awarded Blue Flag status for cleanliness. Virtually every resort of any importance is served by **dolmuş** from Bodrum's *otogar* (see "Travel details" at the end of the chapter for schedules), though few services allow travel between villages without first returning to Bodrum. The account of the coastline that follows covers the south, west and north shores in a clockwise direction from Bodrum.

Gümbet

Roughly 2km west of Bodrum on the peninsula's south shore, **GÜMBET** is the closest proper resort to the town – indeed, almost a suburb – and its 600-metre, tamarisk-lined, gritty beach is usually packed, with parasailing, ringo-ing and water-skiing taking place offshore. Development here is exclusively package-oriented with large hotels and *pansiyons* – a hundred of them on the gradual slope behind, with more springing up – catering for the rowdy, mainly English, 18-to-30 crowd that has effectively claimed this bay. The nightlife as transient as its clientele and rivals Bodrum in number of bars and clubs, if not in quality of its clientele – a taxi fare back to town will set you back 12–25YTL depending how early in the morning it is.

Bitez

BİTEZ (Ağaçlı), the next cove west, 10km from Bodrum, is a little more staid and upmarket, and (along with Farilya) seems to have adopted Gümbet's former role as a windsurfing and sailing centre. There are a number of reasonable watering holes for the yachties, but the beach is negligible, even after artificial supplementing. Of the thirty-plus **hotels** here, the well-designed, four-star *Okaliptüs* (☎0252/363 7780, ⓦwww.okaliptus.com.tr; ❻), nestled in a grove of tangerine trees with its own small stretch of beach and pool, is probably the pick of the bunch. A cheaper option is the *Billur Pansiyon* (☎0252/363 7849; ❷) at the back of the village.

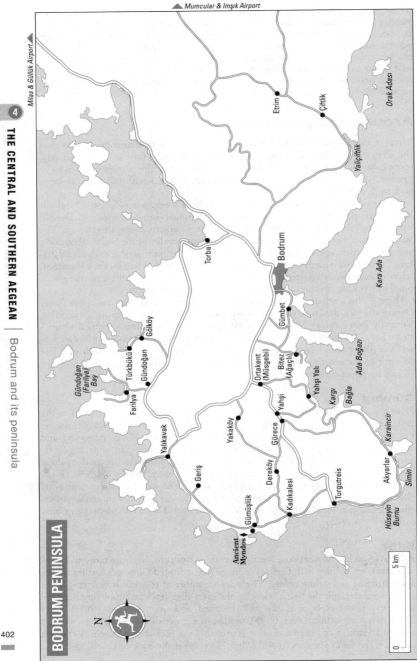

BODRUM PENINSULA

Mumcular & Imşık Airport

Milas & Güllük Airport

Etrim

Çiftlik

Orak Adası

Yalıçiftlik

Kara Ada

Torba

Bodrum

Gümbet

Gölköy

Türkbükü

Gündoğan

Gündoğan
(Farilya)
Bay

Farilya

Ortakent
(Müsgebi)

Bitez
(Ağaçlı)

Yahşi Yalı

Ada Boğazı

Yahşi

Kargı

Bağla

Yalıkavak

Yakaköy

Gürece

Karaincir

Geriş

Dereköy

Kadıkalesi

Turgutreis

Akyarlar

Şimin

Gümüşlük

Ancient
Myndos

Hüseyin
Burnu

N

0   5 km

Ortakent, Yahşi and around

The south-peninsular trunk road continues to **ORTAKENT** (still known by its old name Müsgebi), an inland village crowned by the early seventeenth-century Mustafa Paşa tower and blessed with abundant water and orchards. From both Ortakent and **YAHŞI**, the next settlement, paved drives wind down several kilometres through oases to the longest, though not necessarily best, beach on the peninsula at **Yahşi Yalı**. Its two-kilometre length is closed to wheeled traffic, and the clutter of shops, mediocre restaurants, motels and small hotels can make access problematic if you're not actually staying here. The resort is pitched almost totally to Turkish families, with a scattering of Czech and Russian tour groups. If you do choose **to stay**, you may as well plump for the top end of things here: the three-star *Club Petunya* (Ⓣ0252/348 3272, Ⓦwww.clubpetunya.com; ④) is right on the beach, with lodging in separate garden buildings. It's available through a couple of British package specialists, most consistently Sunquest (see p.31). Dolmuşes to the beach are marked "Ortakent Yahşi Sahil" or "Yahşi Yalı".

Kargı, Bağla and Karaincir

Beyond Yahşi, a turning flanked with hotel signs at Gürece leads high above **Kargı** – a beach more commonly reached by boat from Bodrum and known as "Camel Beach", since this is where day-trips stop for a spot of camel riding. The beach and bay are sandy and gently sloping, overlooked by the ubiquitous villas and a handful of fish restaurants. The main **accommodation** option is the four-star *Javelin Hotel* (Ⓣ0252/348 3541; ⑤).

Bağla, the next cove on, initially seems off-putting, with a water tank resembling an airport control-tower planted amidst the villas that cover the cape. But if you've arrived with your own transport, persevere by going straight past the old Greek chapel to the beachfront parking space, rather than following signs to the fee-parking at a pair of mediocre restaurants. The sand here is the softest in the vicinity of Bodrum; accordingly, excursion boats arrive in force by noon.

Karaincir, the next bay with public access, is nearly as good – 600m of sand guarded by a pair of headlands that marks the most westerly point visited by the Bodrum excursion boats. Canoes and windsurfing boards can be rented, and while mid-beach is completely crowded out by sunbeds and umbrellas, the south end of the strand inexplicably remains in its wild, natural state. The adjacent *Dorya* and *Bal Mahmut* **restaurants** divide most of the custom between them, with a handful of cafés and bars further south hemming in the beach a bit claustrophobically. Of the few simple **motels** up by the main road, the *Bizimtepe* (Ⓣ0252/393 6343, Ⓦwww.hotelbizimtepe.com) is recommended, with either air-conditioned doubles (③) or four-person apartments (€50) available.

Akyarlar and beyond

Surrounded by eucalyptus trees, **AKYARLAR** (the former Greek port of Kefalouka), 30km from Bodrum, is more of an actual village – albeit one surrounded by estates of concrete villas – with a stone jetty, yacht harbour and mosque. The often breezy conditions here make it cooler and more comfortable in summer than sweaty Bodrum. Akyarlar's beach is small and hardpacked, mostly given over to windsurfing, but with both Karaincir and, in the opposite direction, the sandy cove at **Simin** – below the *Simin Hotel* – within walking distance, this is no great loss.

More to the point, Akyarlar is your passport to good local eating, with cuisine and a clientele far more Turkish, and prices far lower, than anywhere east of here. Current favourite **restaurants** include *Kücük Ev*, good for both meat and fish dishes, those attached to the *Akyarlar* and *Kılavuz* motels, and the *Mehtap*, particularly popular for fish. For **accommodation**, the *Kılavuz* (Ⓣ0252/393 6006; ③), the *Babadan* (☏0252/393 6002; ❸), with simple rooms, some with sea views, and the *Candan* (☏0252/393 6035; ❷) offer the best value. There's **camping** at *Camping 86* (☏0252/393 6233).

Beyond Akyarlar the coast is lined with villas (and a very few *pansiyons*), all of which stare across at nearby Kós (just two nautical miles away) and assorted Turkish islets. The good **beach** on the peninsula's southwesternmost cape is partly occupied by the Armonia time-share village, but the far end, under the **Hüseyin Burnu** lighthouse, offers free access and is popular with Turkish free-campers and caravanners, as well as a few German windsurfers, who repair to the *Fener* **restaurant** for sustenance. The food is not that great, but it's still the only place for a bite between here and Turgutreis.

Turgutreis

Once the road rounds the point to skirt the peninsula's west shore, the wind becomes stronger and the sand disappears, with nothing aside from villas until **TURGUTREİS**, the peninsula's second largest town. Frequent dolmuşes ply the route between here and Bodrum, 18km east. As a strictly package resort, this is not the best place to experience authentic local culture, although its Saturday market does attract locals from far and wide. The town itself is a sterile grid of streets packed with over a hundred hotels that leads down to a cobbled esplanade and a small exposed beach. The new yacht marina has, as yet, failed to lift the town's image in a more upmarket direction, athough the planned Bodrum Express Lines ferry service to the nearby Greek islands of Kalymnos and Patmos may help. Of the **hotels**, the *Ceylan* (☏0252/382 2376; ❷) is one of the cheapest, offering en-suite rooms but no breakfast; or try the nearby, jointly-run *Monalisa* (☏0252/382 3361; ❹) and *Korton pansiyons* (☏0252/382 2932; ❹), which also offer half-board accommodation.

Kadıkalesi

A recently asphalted side-road starting by the Turgutreis *otogar* leads north to better things, through a fertile landscape of the tangerine groves for which the region is famous. After 4km you reach **KADİKALESI**, with its long, partly protected sand beach and unbeatable views over to assorted islets. The old Greek church on the hill is the most intact around Bodrum, but of the village's namesake "judge's castle" there seems to be no trace. As with Turgutreis, there is little **accommodation** available if you haven't arranged it in advance. Your best bet is the friendly *Club Blue Bodrum* (☏0252/382 2017; ⓦwww.clubluebodrum.com; ❹), boasting a swimming pool and watersports equipment in addition to comfortable rooms. The beach is overlooked by a couple of fish restaurants.

Gümüşlük

If you've had a bellyful of villa phalanxes, then sleepy **GÜMÜŞLÜK**, 2km past Kadıkalesi or 6km along a direct road from a turning at Gürece, is perhaps the best bet. Easily the nicest spot on the peninsula (40min by dolmuş from Bodrum), it partly occupies the site of **ancient Myndos**, so most new development has been prohibited by the archeological service. The majority of the sparse ruins litter the flat isthmus that links a giant, towering cape to the rest of the peninsula; you can scrabble around the unrestricted site, assisted by a placard map. Yachties are drawn here by the excellent deep anchorage between the headland and Tavşan Adası (Rabbit Island), with more traces of ancient Myndos; the rabbits are shy, and only emerge at night. The kilometre-long sand and gravel **beach** extending south of the island is less protected but still attractive, with watersports gear for rent.

Among a bare handful of low-key **pansiyons**, those that cater well to independent travellers include the *Sisyphos* (℡0252/394 3016; ❺), at the south end of the beach, with a decent terrace restaurant and lush grounds. Mid-beach are the humble but recommended *Hera Pansiyon* (℡0252/394 3065; ❸) and the *Gümüşlük Motel* (℡0252/394 3045; ❸), with standard doubles, some with sea views. The UK holiday operator Tapestry (see p.52) controls the best of the very characterful **self-catering villas** at the north end of the beach, overlooking the most sheltered part of the bay. Their presence has resulted in a surprising concentration of well-stocked shops in the shoreline hamlet. The actual village of Gümüşlük lies 2km inland, from where you can climb to an abandoned ridge-top monastery.

A dozen waterfront **restaurants** cater primarily to yacht passengers and seasonally resident Turks. Most are outrageously priced, with expensive *meze* and obligatory service charges, but of a good standard, specializing in freshly-caught fish. *Ali Reza* is the most established, with *Soğan Sarmısak* a newer establishment, while the nearby *Batı* does meat as well as fish, and has its own *pide* oven.

Yalıkavak

In general, the north flank of the peninsula, served by a loop road out of Ortakent (or the narrower coastal route from Gümüşlük) has poor swimming and a relative lack of facilities. The trip over to **YALIKAVAK** – 20km from Bodrum – with glimpses of sea from a windmill-studded ridge, is possibly more worthwhile than the destination itself. Formerly the area's main sponge-fishing port, it has now been ruthlessly gentrified with its shorefront windmill marooned in a pedestrian zone that extends through most of the commercial district; vehicles can get little further than the small *otogar*.

There are just a handful of **hotels** along the town's scrappy stretch of coast, most notably the cheap but noisy *Yalıkavak Pansiyon* (℡0252/385 4035; ❶). The hills above the town, however, are home to two of the region's swishest establishments, both with fabulous views over the coast: the ⚘*Lavanta* (℡0252/385 2167, ⓦhttp://lavanta.com; ❻) has luxury suites and a top-notch restaurant set in pristine gardens, while the designer boutique *4Reasons*, 2km northwest of town (℡0252/385 3212, ⓦwww.4reasonshotel.com; ❻), is all stark white walls and ultramodern accessories, with an excellent poolside restaurant. The town's best **restaurant**, the *Değirmenci* (℡0252/385 2419) is next to the windmill, and offers a reasonbably priced Mediterranean menu, with *meze*s and sandwiches from 7YTL, and steak and fish from 10YTL.

Gündoğan

GÜNDOĞAN (also known as Farilya), three bays east and surrounded by pine forest, represents something of an improvement on Yalıkavak. The long, mostly narrow but serviceable beach, divided by a small harbour, is little impinged upon by the surrounding villas. The tour company Nielson Sailing maintains a big presence here, with its windsurfers and small craft; the constant breeze does not, however, prevent swimming. Restaurants and bars (mostly indifferent) extend right of the anchorage, while **accommodation** options cluster to the left. Of these, the most reasonably priced is the *Gürkaya* (℡0252/387 7007; ❷), overlooking the beach, while the *Yılankaya Motel* (℡0252/387 8037; ❸) has air-conditioned rooms.

For a taste of the local Ottoman heritage, you can walk a kilometre inland to **Gündoğan village** proper, where there's a ruined monastery to climb to.

Gölköy and Türkbükü

The turning for **GÖLKÖY**, 1km further east, is easy to miss. Development here is low-rise, with the improbably slender beach doubling as the shore path. Swimming platforms have been erected for diving into the cold, clear water by the half-dozen **motels**, which include the *Sahil Motel* (T 0252/357 7117; ⑤), the *Antik* (T 0252/357 7114; ④), and *Kaktüs Çiçeği*, on the beach (T 0252/377 5253, F 377 5248; ⑥). The last has only sixteen rooms and booking in advance is essential, as many guests return every year.

TÜRKBÜKÜ, aka the St Tropez of the peninsula, lies just around the corner and on the same dolmuş route, but has lost what little beach it had following enlargement of the quay – everyone swims from platforms. The clientele is over-whelmingly from the İstanbul moneyed and media set, who often come ashore from their yachts at anchor – the indented local coast and island provide shelter for even more craft than at Gümüşlük. Much of the **accommodation** here is una-shamedly luxurious and expensive. If you've got a spare €225 a night to spend, you can get yourself one of the cheapest suites at the lavish *Ada Hotel* (T 0252/377 5915, W www.adahotel.com; ⑥), set on a hill overlooking the town. The town's restaurants have a reputation for excellence, but are equally pricey. Otherwise, the only points of interest in Türkbükü are a ruined church and some partially collapsed rock-tombs.

Muğla and around

Muğla, capital of the province containing several of the biggest resorts on the Aegean, is something of a showcase town and an exception to the Turkish rule of dire urban architecture. It's also the closest town to **Akyaka**, the first coastal settlement you encounter at the bottom of the winding grade descending south from Muğla's plateau.

Muğla

MUĞLA's well-planned modern quarter incorporates spacious tree-lined bou-levards and accommodates some hillside **Ottoman neighbourhoods** that are among the finest in Turkey. A leisurely stroll through the lanes of well-maintained eighteenth-century white houses, with their tiled roofs, beaked chimneys and ornate doors, is well worth half a day.

The **bazaar**, encompassing a grid of neat alleys nestling at the base of the old res-idential slope to the north, is divided roughly by trade (blacksmiths predominat-ing). South of the bazaar is the **Ulu Cami**, built in the fourteenth century by the Menteşeoğlu emir, İbrahim Bey. The serene **Yağcılar Hanı**, a restored *kervansaray* located on Kursunlu Caddesi, contains carpet shops and *çay* stalls, while a second restored *kervansaray*, **Konakaltı Hanı**, on General Mustafa Muğlali Cad, is in use as an art gallery. Meanwhile, the town's **museum**, on Yatağan Eskişer Caddesi (daily except Mon 8.30am–5.30pm; 2YTL), houses a collection of locally found dinosaur fossils, including prehistoric rhino, giraffe, horse and elephant.

Practicalities

The large **otogar** lies 400m southwest of the centre on Zübeyde Hanim Caddesi, and is served by regular services from Bodrum, Fethiye and Marmaris. Muğla's **tourist office**, Cumhuriyet Bul 24 (summer Mon–Fri 8am–7pm; winter Mon–Fri 8am–noon & 1–5.30pm; T 0252/214 1261), is a fifteen-minute walk from the *otogar*, and willingly provides pamphlets and maps. Banks with ATMs can be found on the central roundabout and İnönü Caddesi, and there's an Internet café, *Sun Internet*, on Ismet Çalak Caddesi.

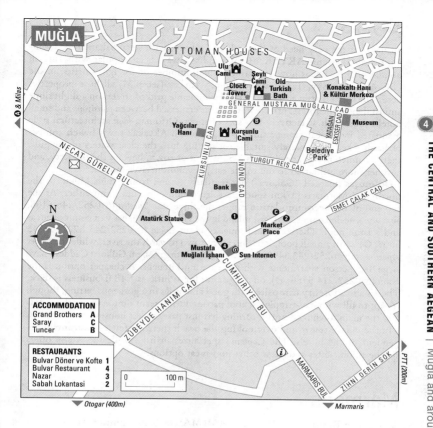

Accommodation covers the two extreme ends of the price range, with little choice in the middle, but since Muğla is not exactly deluged with tourists, this shouldn't be a problem. The quietest and least expensive mid-range option is the *Otel Saray* (☎0252/214 1950, ℉214 3722; ②), facing the produce market but dead calm at night, with comfortable rooms with baths and balconies. A good-value cheapie to the north is the *Tuncer Hotel* at Kütüphane Sok 1 (☎0252/214 8251; ②). If you're going to splash out try the *Hotel Grand Brothers* (☎0252/212 2700, ℉212 2610; ⑤), 1km on the road west out of town, complete with swimming pool, sauna and its own hamam.

Eating out in Muğla is unlikely to be memorable, with plenty of average *lokanta*, kebab and *pide* options. In the Mustafa Muğlali Işhanı (a large office and shopping complex), the licensed *Bulvar Restaurant* is popular at lunchtimes, with a good line in spit-roasted chickens, but very limited *meze* and steamtray food. Next door, and serving excellent *döner* and kebab, is the more upmarket *Nazar*. A cheaper, more versatile option is the nearby *Sabah Lokantasi*, opposite the *Otel Saray*, licensed and serving *meyhane* fare and *hazır yemek* at pleasant outdoor seating opposite a fountain. Otherwise, the *Bulvar Döner ve Köfte* restaurant on İnönü Caddesi offers a good range of kebabs.

Akyaka

Situtated at the very head of the Gulf of Gökova, with steep Sakara Tepe looming overhead, scenic **AKYAKA** (Gökova) has always been popular with Turkish holiday-makers but is now attracting a small number of foreign tourists; in the UK, Anatolian Sky, Tapestry and Simply Turkey (see p.31) all have properties here. The town is arrayed along an unobjectionable grid of streets on a slight slope amidst dense pine forest; private villas are interspersed between *pansiyons* and small hotels, most built attractively in a sort of mock-Ottoman-*köşk* architectural style mandated by a local preservation code. Although Akyaka's town **beach** consists of hardpacked sand, merely suitable for getting into the clear waters of the gulf, there's a much better gravel beach 2.5km west of town, beyond the old jetty, and another more utilitarian strand to the east, beyond the river mouth.

Dolmuşes (marked "Gökova") ply regularly to and from Muğla (30km to the north) and Marmaris (37km south), a thirty-minute journey from either. At the top end of the **accommodation** range, the three-star *Yücelen* (☎0252/248 5108, ⓦ www.yucelen.com.tr; ❺), just inland in the village centre, has vast common areas and a large pool. The cosier and squeaky-clean *Engin* (☎0252/243 5727, ⓕ243 5609; ❷), with a small pool, is in the east of town towards the river, while the *Server Apartments* (☎0252/243 5497, ⓔserver@akyaka.org; ❸), on Gökova Caddesi, have large 4–5 person apartments with self-catering kitchens. A cheaper option is the *Fatih* (☎0252/214 5786; ❷), offering suites for as little as €18 if business is slack. There's also a forestry **campsite** with good amenities in a gorgeous setting, though it's apt to fill with day-tripping school parties during term time – to get there, follow the main town road north, turning left just past the last houses.

In the village centre and overlooking the beach there are few **restaurants** independent of the hotels. The *Captain's* specializes in fish, while the *Köşem* offers spaghetti, omelettes and a few other non-meat options.

Marmaris

Along with Kuşadası and Bodrum, **MARMARIS** is the third of Turkey's less-than-holy-trinity of hugely overdeveloped Aegean resorts. Boosters call it *Yeşil Marmaris* – "Green Marmaris" – which it certainly is, but they omit mention of the humidity, the ferocious mosquitoes and the amorphous concrete sprawl that extends for nearly 10km around the bay. Development has dwarfed the old village core of shops and *lokantas* lining narrow, bazaar-like streets, an intricate warren contrasting strongly with the European-style marina and waterfront. According to legend, the place was named when Süleyman the Magnificent, not finding the castle here to his liking, was heard to mutter "*Mimarı as*" ("hang the architect"), later corrupted to "Marmaris" – a command that ought perhaps still to apply to the designers of the seemingly endless apartments and hotels.

Marmaris's **Netsel Yacht Marina**, Turkey's largest, has more than anything else shaped the town's character – this is the main base for most yacht charter organizations operating on the Turquoise Coast. Proximity to Dalaman airport also means that both foreign and domestic tourists pour in nonstop during the warmer months, and – the Netsel Marina aside – the town remains very much a downmarket package resort.

Marmaris's **history** has been determined above all by the stunning local topography: a deep, fjord-like inlet surrounded by pine-cloaked hills. This did not seem to spur ancient Physcus, the original Dorian colony, to any growth or importance, but Süleyman comfortably assembled a force of 200,000 here in 1522, when launching the successful siege of the Knights of St John's base in Rhodes. Shortly after this campaign Süleyman endowed the old town nucleus with the tiny castle and a *han*. In 1798 Nelson's entire fleet sheltered here before setting out to defeat Napoleon's armada at the Battle of Aboukir Bay in Egypt.

Arrival and information

Marmaris's **otogar** is 2km outside the town centre on the Muğla road. A regular dolmuş service runs from the *otogar*, down the main Ulusal Egemenlik Caddesi, stopping outside the huge Tansaş shopping centre – from where all the town's **dolmuş** services start. The Havaş **airport bus** from Dalaman airport leaves you in front of the THY office on Atatürk Caddesi, the long shore road also known as Kordon Caddesi. Marina Taxi has a booth in the Netsel Yacht Marina and will run you to Dalaman for around 80YTL. Drivers should note that no **parking** is allowed anywhere

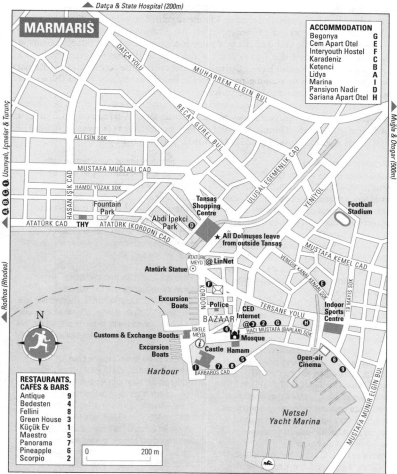

▲ *Datça & State Hospital (200m)*

MARMARIS

ACCOMMODATION
Begonya	G
Cem Apart Otel	E
Interyouth Hostel	F
Karadeniz	C
Ketenci	B
Lidya	A
Marina	I
Pansiyon Nadir	D
Sariana Apart Otel	H

DATÇA YOLU

MUHARREM ELGIN BUL

RECAT GÜREL BUL

◄ **Ø, Ø, Ø, Ø** Uzunyalı, İçmeler & Turunç

ALİ ESİN SOK

MUSTAFA MUĞLALI CAD

IŞIK CAD

HASAN CAD

HAMDİ YÜZAK SOK

Fountain Park

ATATÜRK CAD **THY**

ATATÜRK (KORDON) CAD

Abdi İpekci Park

Tansaş Shopping Centre

ULUSAL EGEMENLIK CAD

YENYOL

Football Stadium

MUSTAFA KEMEL CAD

★ **All Dolmuşes leave from outside Tansaş**

ATATÜRK MEYD. **@ LinNet**

Atatürk Statue ◉

KORDON

VENEDIK KANAL KENARI SK

19 MAYIS SOK

Ê

Excursion Boats

F

Police

CED Internet

@

BAZAAR

TERSANE YOLU

Indoor Sports Centre

Customs & Exchange Booths

İSKELE MEYD.

ℹ

Excursion Boats

Castle **Hamam**

HACI MUSTAFA (BARLARI) SOK

Mosque

Open-air Cinema

Ø Ø

N

Harbour

BARBAROS CAD

MUSTAFA MÜNİR ELGIN BUL

RESTAURANTS, CAFÉS & BARS
Antique	9
Bedesten	4
Fellini	8
Green House	3
Küçük Ev	1
Maestro	5
Panorama	7
Pineapple	6
Scorpio	2

Netsel Yacht Marina

0 ——— 200 m

◄ *Rodhos (Rhodes)*

► *Muğla & Otogar (500m)*

Cennet (Nimara) Adası, Aktaş & Ada Ağzı ▼

along the Kordon, but the Tansaş supermarket has a large multistorey car park which is free if you produce a receipt for shopping, otherwise 3YTL a day.

Arriving by **ferry** from the Greek island of Rhodes or **hydrofoil** from Bodrum, you dock by İskele Meydanı, on one side of which stands the extraordinarily knowledgeable **tourist office** (summer daily 8am–8pm; winter Mon–Fri 8am–noon & 1–5pm; ☏0252/412 1035), dispensing town plans, bus schedules and accommodation lists. This is also the best place for details of the current **boat charter** prices (see box on p.413). **Boat-taxis** to İçmeler and Turunç leave from in front of the tourist office (5–8YTL one way).

Accommodation

Although there is no concentration of *pansiyon*s or small hotels in Marmaris, some apart-hotels have sprung up in the area inland from the marina, while a handful of very basic establishments (and a youth hostel) survive in the **town centre**. Better value for money can be had out at the west end of the Kordon, close to where **Kemal Seyfettin Elgin Bulvarı** splits away to run parallel to **Uzunyalı** beach. Further west, some three hundred hotels line the five-kilometre palm-fringed strip, with the luxury, all-inclusive complexes – the *Grand Azur, MGM, Altsnyunus, Grand Yazıcı* and *Iberotel* – clustering at the far end. For the best value here, try the seafront establishments in the neighbourhood of the *Turban Hotel*, at the edge of the built-up area, or head a few blocks inland. **Kenan Evren Bulvarı**, incidentally, is the continuation of Kemal Seyfettin Elgin Bulvarı running parallel to the beach but slightly inland. Note that accommodation is tight during the yachting regatta in the second week of May.

Your best bet for **camping** near the centre is to stroll along Uzunyalı beach and see who's operating this year between the building sites. Alternatively, 1.5km east of Marmaris, past the Günnücek forestry reserve, are *Dimet Camping* (☏0252/413 3905) and *Pekuz Camping* (☏0252/413 1061), both open all year.

Town centre

Hotel Begonya Hacı Mustafa Sok 101 ☏0252/412 4095, ☏412 1518. Delightful renovated barn with designer architecture, air conditioning and enclosed garden; it's double-glazed against loud music from nearby (and, indeed the hotel's own) bars. **④**

Cem Apart Otel Venedik Kanal Kenari Sok 25/12 ☏0252/413 1725, ☏413 1726. Self-catering units (sleep four) with averagely furnished rooms but well-fitted kitchens, arranged around a rather small pool and sauna. **④**

Interyouth Hostel 1 42 Sok 45 ☏0252/412 3687, ☏interyouth@turk.net. IYHF-accredited hostel within the covered bazaar. Clean, comfy but bare double rooms as well as dorms (€6) – it's hopelessly overcrowded in season. There's also an Internet café and various short-term meal deals, such as free pasta for lengthy stays. **②**

Hotel Marina Barbaros Cad 37 ☏0252/412 6598, ☏www.marmarismarinahotel.com. Neat rooms with intricate wooden ceiling designs (and surprisingly little street noise). The telescopes on the rooftop breakfast bar/restaurant command breathtaking views of the bay. **④**

Pansiyon Nadir Kemerati Mahalesi ☏0252/412 1167. As cheap as the town's accommodation gets, with clean simple rooms with en-suite bathroom (and hot water). For an extra €6, the adjacent *Hotel Nadir* has similar rooms but with TV and a/c. **①**

Sariana Apart Otel 24 Sok 4 ☏0252/413 6835, ☏www.marmarishotel.com. Suites containing a starkly furnished double bedroom, modern bathroom, lounge and kitchen, as well as access to the hotel bar and pool. **⑤**

West of the centre

Hotel Karadeniz Atatürk Cad (Kordon) 68 ☏0252/412 3642, ☏412 1064. Comfortable, well-run hotel (200m off our map) offering all the usual amenities. Rooms are large and bright, but the best aspect is its convenient location, just across from the beach. **④**

Ketenci Hotel Kemal Seyettin Elgin Bul ☏0252/412 6395, ☏412 8996. Slightly inland (600m off our map) with modern rooms with balcony. Boasts a fair-sized pool and a restaurant. **④**

Hotel Lidya Kenan Evren Bul ☏0252/417 3350, ☏412 1478. The oldest luxury hotel in Marmaris (800m off our map) still has the most character and smoothest service, despite its vast size. There are 385 well-equipped rooms, and good beach facilities, complete with a nightclub on site. **⑤**

△ Day-trip boats in Marmaris

The Town

Ulusal Egemenlik Bulvarı, where you'll find the town's huge Tansaş supermarket, cuts Marmaris roughly in half, and the maze of narrow streets to the east of it is home to most of the monuments and facilities of interest to the average tourist, including the castle, bazaar, banks and PTT. Numerous travel agencies and bus-company ticket offices cluster a hundred or so metres to either side of **Atatürk Meydanı**, the seashore plaza at the southern end of Ulusal Egemenlik Bulvarı. Further west the weekly **Friday market** is held behind the THY office, where women from surrounding villages sell a range of home-made goodies, including delicious jams.

Little is left of the sleepy fishing village that Marmaris was a mere two decades ago. The **bazaar**, including its diminutive *kervansaray*, now rivals those at İstanbul and Kuşadası in its array of glitzy kitsch on offer, and only the **Kaleiçi** district, the warren of streets at the base of the tiny castle, offers a pleasant wander. The **castle** itself (daily 8am–noon & 1–5.30pm; 2YTL) is open as a fully stocked museum with clearly annotated displays of local finds; it also serves as a venue for events during the May festival.

In any case, you don't come to Marmaris for cultural edification, and you swim off the badly polluted **Kordon beach** at your peril – though this doesn't seem to deter the hundreds of bathers who use it daily. It's far better to take a dolmuş (regular services from Ulusal Egemenlik Bulvarı) or boat-taxi (see opposite) out to **İçmeler**, 9km west of Marmaris, whose old village core survives precariously at the far edge of the recently developed resort. Here the sand is coarse but cleaner than at Kordon, as is the sea.

Boat excursions

Day-trips usually visit highlights of the inner bay, not venturing much beyond the straits separating Cennet and Keçi islands. Most skippers will take you to a beach on the north side of Cennet Adası, and to caves on the south shore, then complete the day with a visit to Kumlubükü or Turunç coves (see "Around Marmaris", pp.416–417). Since all these spots are fairly difficult to reach by land, it's worth the effort – and the price of around €20 per person may include a full lunch. The boats are moored along the southern end of Kordon Caddesi and the castle peninsula, and leave at 9am during the May to September summer season.

One offer that you definitely can refuse is an **excursion to Kaunos** (see p.466) from Marmaris: because of the distance involved, you'll spend six-plus hours sailing and, at best, two hours sightseeing. Kaunos is more usually reached from Dalyan or as part of a lengthy cruise.

Eating

Getting a decent meal at a reasonable price is something of a challenge in Marmaris. In town, the **restaurants** around the bazaar tend to offer fast food and English dishes. Simple pizzerias and other spots serving light meals abound along the Kordon and further west, where homesick Brits seek relief at various English-named outfits serving indifferently cooked "English" food. East of the castle, the waterfront spots along Barbaros Caddesi change names, management and cuisine frequently – here, a meal with wine will run to around 35YTL a head, more if you eat the seafood.

Antique Overlooking Netsel Yacht Marina ℡0252/413 2955. Smart Italian restaurant offering cosy atmosphere and impeccable service for about 45YTL per person. Book ahead as this place is busy in season.

Bedesten Café Below the mosque in the bazaar. Lovely courtyard oasis for coffee and a *nargile* (waterpipe). With a choice of chairs or traditional cushions, and a trickling fountain, it's an "ethnic" kind of place aimed at tourists, but is at its best at night when the daytime awning is drawn back to reveal a star-studded view.

Fellini Pizza On the waterfront. Popular, no-nonsense pizzeria, particularly recommended for its vegetarian options.

Küçük Ev İçmeler, 9km west of Marmaris. One of the area's longest-running restaurants, serving a wide selection of *hazır yemek* (set meals) for 15–30YTL per head, including beer.

Maestro Barbaros Caddesi. Its menu may be a typical "calling all cuisines" affair – steak, pizza, pasta, kebabs etc – but this gets the nod for its extensive vegetarian choices. Mains YTL8–12.

Pineapple Netsel Yacht Marina ℡0252/412 0976. Ever-popular dressy Turkish/English eaterie, famous for its barbecued lamb (18YTL). With an attached English pub upstairs, things can get a bit noisy.

Drinking, nightlife and entertainment

Most of Marmaris's tippling takes place along **Hacı Mustafa Sokağı** (or Barlar Sok), which in recent years has become a fully fledged "Bar Street" along the lines of those in Kuşadası and Bodrum. More than two dozen **bars and clubs** here feature increasingly sophisticated designer profiles and various sorts of (usually live) music, often in spacious inner courtyards. Names and favourites change yearly, if not more often, though a couple of long-termers include *Green House* and *Scorpio*. Up above, behind the castle, the *Panorama* bar offers the best views. The yachties expand their liver capacities during the happy hour at a group of pubs and upmarket restaurants within the Netsel Yacht Marina.

An **open-air cinema**, behind the *Keyif Bar* at the western end of the marina, shows original-language international releases with Turkish subtitles. An annual **yachting and arts festival** takes place in the second week of May, aimed primarily at those of the sailing fraternity, and there's a large **yacht race** during the first week of November. For further details contact the Marmaris Yacht Club (℡0252/412 3835, ⓦwww.miyc.org).

Coastal boat charters

Chartering either a **motor schooner** (*gület*) or a smaller **yacht** out of Marmaris will allow you to explore the convoluted coast between Bodrum and Kaş. Especially out of high season, the daily cost isn't necessarily prohibitive – no more than renting a medium-sized car, for example – and in the case of a *gület*, a knowledgeable crew will be included. Virtually all the shore described in this chapter and the next is accessible by boat, and there are also many other hidden anchorages.

You can pre-book a yacht charter through **specialist holiday operators** (see Basics for details), or you can make arrangements on the spot; though prices are always quoted in euros or US dollars, it's possible to pay in Turkish lira. Substantial deposits are required – usually fifty percent of the total price.

The best option for individual travellers or small groups is a **cabin charter**. Several companies set aside one schooner whose berths are let out individually. The craft departs on a particular day of the week with a fixed itinerary of seven days. Prices depend on demand but in April, May and October are around €320 per person, including all food and watersports equipment – excellent value. From June to September the cost jumps to over €400.

If you can assemble a large group, and have more time at your disposal, consider a **standard charter** of a twenty-metre motor schooner. A group of twelve, for example, will pay around €30 each daily during May or October, not including food or sporting equipment, and over €50 from June to September. Companies often offer to supply food from about €15 per person per day, though you'd spend about the same eating two meals a day on shore. Probably the best strategy is to dine in restaurants at your evening mooring and to keep the galley stocked for breakfast and snacks. If you tip the crew appropriately they're usually happy to shop for you. One of the oldest and more reliable **charter agencies** in Marmaris is Yeşil Marmaris, Barbaros Cad 11 (T0252/412 6486, Wwww.yesilmarmaris.com).

For the greatest degree of independence, so-called **bareboat yacht charter** is the answer. Prices range from €1400 for the smallest boat in the off-season, to €5200 for the largest in high season. This assumes that at least one of your party is a certified skipper; otherwise count on at least €110 a day extra (plus food costs) to engage one. For bareboat yachts, one of the larger local operators is Offshore Sailing at the Albatros Marina, 3km east of Netsel Marina (T0252/412 3430, Wwww.offshore-sailing.net).

Listings

Airport THY has a Havaş service bus to Dalaman airport, 90km east, departing from its office at Atatürk Cad 50/B (T0252/412 3751) 2hr 45min before flight departures. In addition, the Marmaris *Belediyesi* runs two daily buses to the airport.

Banks and exchange Assorted *döviz* booths along the Kordon and near the ferry jetty stay open late (sometimes until 9.30pm), including Sundays and holidays. Marmaris is also well endowed with credit/debit-card-accepting ATMs.

Bike and jeep rental Yoshimoto (T0252/417 6237, Wwww.yoshimoto.de) delivers rental bikes (from €65 a day) to your hotel (and organizes guided motorbike safaris throughout Turkey, starting at €1180). Çağdaş Tour, behind 10 Kordon (T0252/412 4125), rents bikes and cars; Best Motor, Kemal Elgin Cad opposite the *Balim Otel*

(T0252/412 4361) for bikes, mopeds, motorbikes and jeeps.

Books Arkadaş Kitap, in front of the Sabaci High School on Kordon, has a selection of secondhand books in English, French and German; Hittite, Hacı Mustafa Sok, is a book and music store; NET, in the bazaar, stocks nautical charts of the area; Şehrazat, across from Hacı Mustafa Sok 49, behind the castle, has some used English books to trade; and Marmaris International Bookstore, Talat Paşa Sok, has a selection of current English bestsellers.

Buses The main bus companies – Varan, Ulusoy, Pamukkale, Kamil Koç, Hakiki Koç – all have offices in or around Tansaş shopping centre at the Kordon Caddesi end of Ulusal Egemenlik Bul, and all run courtesy buses to the *otogar* to connect with their company's major routes.

Car rental Airtour, Kenan Evren Bul, Alter Sok 18/A ☎0252/412 3963; Avis, Kordon Cad 30 ☎0252/412 2771; DeCar, Ulusal Egemenlik Cad, Rodoslu Kemal İş Hanı 13 ☎0252/413 4669; Europcar/InterRent, Kordon Cad 12 ☎0252/412 2001; Hertz, İskele Meyd ☎0252/412 2552; Intercity, İskele Meyd 41 ☎0252/413 0106; LeMar, Kemal Seyfettin Elgin Bul 4 ☎0252/412 3222.

Consulate Honorary British Consulate, c/o Yeşil Marmaris Tourism & Yachting, Barbaros Cad 11, near the marina ☎0252/412 6486 or 24hr ☎0532/262 7661.

Ferries and hydrofoils From April to October there's a twice-weekly domestic hydrofoil to Bodrum via Gökova Bay and daily hops to Rhodes in Greece; there's also a twice-weekly car ferry; see "Travel details" at the end of this chapter for schedules and prices. Authorized agents include Yeşil Marmaris, Barbaros Cad 11 (☎0252/412 6486, ⓦwww.yesilmarmaris.com), and Engin Turizm, G. Mustafa Muğlalı Cad 16, 3rd Floor (☎0252/412 6944).

Hamam There's an old one in the rear of the bazaar at Eski Cami Arkası 3 (daily 8am–midnight for both sexes; 12YTL), and the newer touristic Armutalan Hamam, off the Datça road, 1km north of the town centre (daily 8am–11pm; 20YTL).

Hospitals The state hospital is at the junction of Yunus Nadı Cad and the Datça road ☎0252/413 1445; Ahu Hetman private hospital is in Armutalan suburb, 167 Sok ☎0252/ 413 1415.

Internet Lin Net, Atatürk Cad 36, opposite the Atatürk statue; and CED Internet, just back from the waterfront.

Laundry Marmaris laundry is located in the street behind the *Gün Café*, in front of the castle.

Pharmacies The most central ones are: Dee Pharmacy, Datça Yolu E Devlet Hastane ☎0252/412 3230; Ebru Pharmacy, Hasan Isik Cad, 103 Sok 49 ☎0252/413 6666; and Fulya Pharmacy, K. Elgin Bul 53/3 ☎0252/412 9314.

Police On Kordon Cad, next to the government house ☎0252/412 1872.

Post office PTT is within the bazaar on 49 Sok (mail services until 6pm, phones 24hr).

Rafting Alternatif Turizm, Çamlık Sok 10/1 (☎0252/417 2720, ⓦwww.alternatifraft.com), offers regular springtime whitewater-rafting trips on the Dalaman river, plus river and sea kayaking, and tailor-made Turkey-wide outdoor-sports packages. Prices range from 5-day Coruh Rafting expedition (northeast Turkey) from €600, to 1-day sea kayaking on Köycegiz Lake from €100.

Around Marmaris: the Rhodian Peraea

In ancient times the peninsula extending from the head of the Gulf of Gökova to a promontory between the Greek islands of Symi and Rhodes was known as the **Rhodian Peraea** – the mainland territory of the three united city-states of Rhodes, which controlled the area for eight centuries. Despite this, and the fact that the natives were granted full Rhodian citizenship, there is little evidence of the long tenure. The peninsula was (and still is) a backwater, today known as the **Hisarönü peninsula** – or the Loryma or Daraçya peninsula, depending on which map you look at or yacht skipper you ask. In fact, yachts have up to now been the principal means of getting around this irregular landmass and, although a proper road was completed in 1989, the difficulty of access has so far kept development to a minimum.

North: the Gökova gulf shore

The pristine shores of the **Gulf of Gökova** were badly affected by a massive forest fire in 1996, which roared along the southerly shore between the Muğla–Marmaris road and the Marmaris–Datça highway, reducing thousands of forested acres to ashes. Fortunately, natural regrowth and a reforestation policy have redressed much of the damage, though obvious remaining signs are the older trees, which bear visible scorching.

In Marmaris you'll probably notice signs pitching an excursion to "Cleopatra's Isle". This is actually **Sedir Adası** (Cedar Island), an islet near the head of the Gulf of Gökova, which still sports extensive fortifications and a theatre from its time as Cedreae, a city of the Peraea. More evocative, however, is its alleged role as a trysting place of Cleopatra and Mark Antony, and the legend concerning the island's beach – the main goal of the day-trips; the sand was supposedly brought from Africa at Mark Antony's behest, and indeed analysis has shown that the grains are not from local strata. To preserve the sand, strict regulations control the beach's use: visitors are forbidden from removing the sand and are even obliged to take a footbath before they leave to remove any possible lingering grains.

The usual way of getting to the island is by tour boat, departing between 10 and 11am from **Çamli İskelesı**, 6km down a side-road beginning 12km north of Marmaris, reachable either via a tour-operator's shuttle bus or the hourly dolmuş from Marmaris. The boats return at 4 or 5pm. As well as the obvious jaunt to Sedir Adası, boat trips also leave from here to **İNGİLİZLİMANI**, a beautiful inlet reachable only by sea. It got its name ("English Harbour") from a World War II incident when a British ship sought shelter from pursuing Germans in these nominally neutral waters.

Boats based at Çamlı İskelesı also call at **KARACASÖĞÜT**, accessible by land via a side road 11km north of Marmaris. It's 13km (the occasional village-bound dolmuş will take you the first 11km) to this almost landlocked bay, girded by willows, with the wall of mountains north of the open gulf as a backdrop. It's a big yacht and *gület* haven, and you can watch the action from several restaurants overlooking the bay. The main beach, alas, is muddy and has two creeks draining onto it, so you can really only swim off the purpose-built platform jutting out into the water, well away from the boats and the shore.

South to Bozburun

Overland access to the bulk of the **Hisarönü peninsula** is by way of a paved road, which branches south from the main Datça-bound highway, 21km west of Marmaris, and describes a loop back to Marmaris via Selimiye, Bayar, Turunç and İçmeler. **Dolmuşes** from Marmaris leave several times daily for Orhaniye, and there are three daily services to Bozburun.

Orhaniye and Selimiye

ORHANİYE, 9km off the main highway, is visited mostly for its yacht anchorage. The beach here is confined to muddy, sumpy shallows, though further out in the bay lurks a celebrated curiosity: a long, narrow, submerged sandspit known as **Kızkumu** (Maiden's Sand) extends halfway across the bay that gives anyone who walks on it the appearance of "walking on water". Legend asserts that a local beauty, menaced by raiding pirates, filled her skirts with sand and attempted to escape across the water by creating her own causeway, but upon exhausting her supply at mid-bay, drowned herself rather than surrender her virtue to the marauders. Another version has her attempting to escape an unwanted arranged marriage to a rich landowner's son. There are two small **hotels** and a mere half-dozen *pansiyon*s of note here, including the clean *Palmiye Motel* (☏0252/487 1134; ➌).

SELİMİYE, 9km further south, is the next coastal village where visitors tend to stop, again mostly by yacht. The remains of an Ottoman fort overlook the port here, at the head of an all-but-landlocked arm of the giant Delikyol bay. Numerous quayside restaurants are aimed mostly at the passing boat trade, as are the pleasant *pansiyon*s that have sprouted since the road was paved. **Accommodation** may fill in season, so pre-booking is a good idea – try the *Beyaz Güvercin* (☏0252/446 4274, ⓦwww.beyazguvercin.com; ➌) or the *Hotel Begovina* (☏0252/446 4069, ⓦwww.begovina.com; ➍). Several daily dolmuşes leave Bozburun (below) for Selimiye from May to September, though outside the summer season the service is somewhat erratic.

Bozburun and beyond

BOZBURUN, 7km over the hill from Selimiye, is not much more than a yacht harbour: yacht repairs and supplies are conspicuously on offer, and *gület* boatyards occupy a large area. The settlement itself is undistinguished, slumbering in dusty heat six months of the year, but its setting, on a convoluted gulf with a fat islet astride its mouth and the Greek island of Sími beyond, is startling.

The place is unlikely to go the way of Datça (see p.417), since there is precious little level land for villas, even less fresh water and absolutely no sand beaches. Nonetheless Bozburun has long been an "in" resort for various eccentrics – ex-journalists turned bartenders, recording executives turned restaurant proprietors, diehard Turkish hippies – who collect in this most isolated corner of coastal Turkey.

In high season **pansiyon** proprietors will collar you as you alight from the thrice-daily dolmuş from Marmaris. *Suna Pansiyon* (T 0252/456 2119; ❷), which offers doubles with bathroom and kitchen access, is good value. If you fancy something more upmarket call for a boat to ⚓ *Sabrina's House* (T 0252/456 2045, W www .sabrinashaus.de; ❺), a German-run, television- and traffic-free idyll set on the far edge of the harbour; this tasteful haven in burgeoning gardens has huge bright and airy suite-like units and (of necessity) an excellent restaurant (meals around 25YTL). Without the free boat shuttle, it's a thirty-minute walk to *Sabrina's*, partly along the road signposted to "Hotel Mete". Overlooking the shore, the *Pembe Yunus* (the name translates as "Pink Dolphin"; T 0252/456 2154, W www .pembeyunus.net; ❸) is a popular, cheaper alternative, with modest single and double en-suites and a renowned waterfront fish **restaurant** (25YTL for guests). It's the best of the fifteen or so quayside restaurants here, which offer a variable range and quality of food and service. The trendy set, whether Turkish landlubbers or yachties, gathers at the *Möwe Bar*, run by yet another refugee from the İstanbul rat race.

The boat day-trips advertised in Bozburun rarely leave the confines of the bay. Instead, in cooler weather, you could walk east one valley to **SÖĞÜT**, essentially a farming oasis with a minimal shore settlement boasting two restaurants and a couple of *pansiyons*. The dolmuş serving Söğüt terminates at **TAŞLICA**, a hilltop village girded by almonds and olives sprouting from what's otherwise a stone desert. From the square where the dolmuş minibus leaves you, a three- to four-hour trail leads south to ancient **Loryma**, where a Rhodian-built fort overlooks the magnificent harbour of **Bozukkale** – which in turn holds several restaurants. If you don't want to walk back the same way, you just might be able to hitch a boat ride out from here.

The east coast of the Hisarönü peninsula

From Selimiye, the main loop road climbs inland to **BAYİR**, a mountain village spread across an amphitheatre of rocky terraces, whose distinctive feature is a 2000-year-old tree on its main square. A local tradition states that circling it seven times will prolong the walker's life, a myth not gone unnoticed by the troop of jeep safaris that regularly invade. A side-road leads the 3km down from here to **Çiftlik** bay, a once-isolated beach now dominated by a huge holiday village. Occasional dolmuşes do brave the route from Turunç, but their infrequent times make having your own transport the only practical option.

Turunç

The main route curls north back towards Marmaris, with another spur road leading down to **TURUNÇ**, which, since the late 1980s, has been transformed from a few farms and two ramshackle restaurants into an exclusive package venue. It's stunningly beautiful, boasting a 500-metre beach of coarse sand, backed by impressive, pine-tufted cliffs. These are now dotted with hotels and villas, some of whose residents commute to sea level using cogwheel chairlifts. The *Diplomat* self-catering beachfront apartments and *Dereözü Elveri*, a small property set in lush pine forests just inland, can both be booked through UK-based Tapestry Holidays (see p.32) Three walk-in **hotel** options are the air-conditioned *Özcan Hotel* (T0252/476 7014, F476 7710; **❹**) and the *Zeybek Hotel* (T0252/476 7014, F476 7710; **❸**) and the *Merhaba Motel* (T0252/476 7285; **❸**); owners of the latter also run the *Minem* restaurant-bar on the beach. **Pensions** include the *Gül Pansiyon* (T0252/476 7003; **❸**) and the overpriced *Çınar Motel* (T0252/476 7088; **❸**), both with en-suite doubles and kitchen access.

A spur road (and sometimes a dolmuş) heads south, past ancient **Amos** (only Hellenistic walls and theatre remain) to **KUMLUBÜKÜ**, another large bay with decent amenities. Along with the Çiftlik bay, 4km southwest of here by rough tracks or paths, it's the only really big patch of sand on the whole peninsula.

The Datça peninsula

Once past the turning for Bozburun, the main highway west of Marmaris ventures out onto the elongated, narrow **Datça (Reşadiye) peninsula**. There are glimpses through pine gullies of the sea on both sides, and the road is fiendishly narrow and twisting and it's inadvisable to use it at night. Ongoing roadworks are continuing to straighten out some of the more treacherous bends, and delays of one to two hours can sometimes be experienced. There's nothing until **Datça** town except two private **campsites**: *Öz-Il Kamping* (T0252/723 3457) on Karaincir Beach, and *Aktur* **campsite** (T0252/724 6168), 18km before Datça behind a larger, sandy beach.

Beyond Datça the peninsula broadens considerably, and the scenery – almond or olive groves around somnolent, back-of-beyond villages at the base of pine-speckled mountains – is quite unlike that which came before. Towards **ancient Knidos**, the ancient site on the western cape, of the 32km of road beyond **Reşadiye** village the 24km to Yazıköy are paved, but the last 4km are appalling, although an ordinary car with good clearance should make it in dry weather.

Datça

Too built-up and commercialized to be the backpackers' haven it once was, **DATÇA** is still much calmer than either Bodrum or Marmaris. It's essentially the shore annex of inland Reşadiye village but under the ministrations of visiting yachtspeople and tour operators it has outgrown its parent. Still, partly due to low local accommodation standards and the difficulty of access, prices are noticeably lower than in Bodrum or Marmaris, and most villa development lies out of town to the east. Carpet shops are big news with several in town aimed at the yacht and package trade.

Life in and around Datça mostly boils down to a matter of picking your swimming or sunbathing spot. The **east beach** of hardpacked sand, known locally as Kumluk, is oversubscribed but has some shade. The less crowded **west beach**, mixed pebble and sand and called Taşlık, is acceptable and gets better the further you get from the anchored yachts.

In contrast to the scenery on the drive in, the immediate surroundings of Datça are quite barren, softened only by a mineral-spring-fed small **lake** halfway along the west bay. Warm water seeps from the lake bed, 2m down, making swimming here nicer than in the sea, and a line of appealing café-bars overlooks the stone dam that augments the water level.

Arrival and orientation

Apart from its setting, Datça's most striking feature is its layout: a single, kilometre-long high street meandering between two sheltered bays separated by a hillock and then a narrow isthmus, finally terminating at a cape. Along the way in you pass – more or less in this order – the **PTT**, most of the main **banks**, the tiny tourist office, a traffic circle dominated by a large tree, with **taxi rank** and **bazaar** grounds (Fri & Sat) adjacent, and **travel agencies**.

The **tourist office** (Mon–Fri 8am–6pm; ☎0252/712 3163) is hidden away in a large cream-coloured government building on the high street – identifiable by the police vans parked outside. It can supply maps and lists of accommodation for the whole peninsula.

The nine or so daily **buses** to and from Marmaris stop at the Pamukkale bus company office, just back from the harbour. Datça also has a small *otogar* on the outskirts of town, near the *jandarma* post; if you end up here **taxis** and service buses will compete to take you into town, but it's only a fifteen-minute walk. Except in high season, few of the big bus companies reach Datça, and you might be best off taking a short-hop dolmuş to either Marmaris or Muğla, from where there will be more frequent onward departures.

Ferries and **hydrofoils** from Bodrum arrive at Körmen Limanı, 9km to the north; your ticket includes a shuttle bus service into Datça. It's worth taking the boat at least in one direction to avoid duplicating the wild bus journey in from the east. From Körmen Limanı there are once-a-week direct return ferries to the Greek islands of Kós (Mon), Rhodes (Sat) and Sími (Sat). You'll also find small charter boats in Datça offering trips to Knidos (about 16YTL) and Koytur (about 35YTL).

Accommodation

Accommodation, although limited, is generally sufficient to meet demand. The most obvious desirable location is the hillock separating the two bays, where there are several *pansiyon*s to choose from, including the *Huzur* (☎0252/712 3052; ❸), with the most modern rooms and an attractive terrace, and the *Karaoğlu* (☎0252/712 3079; ❷), with the best sea view and a pleasant attached restaurant. *Yılmaz Pansiyon* (☎0252/712 3188; ❷), close to the beach strip, is cheaper, though it doesn't serve breakfast.

The small, friendly **campsite**, *Ilıca Kamping* (☎0252/712 3400; open all year), perfectly located at the far end of the beach, is an ideal spot to relax, with a good restaurant, bar, and serene views, five simple two-person bungalows (❶) and room for 27 tents.

Out **on the cape**, formerly an island called Esenada, the aging *Dorya Motel* (☎0252/712 3614, ℱ712 3303; ❹) is home to such package trade as Datça gets. Rooms are hardly state of the art, but the place does offer well-kept gardens and common areas, a pool and a private lido. But probably the smartest choice in town is the *Villa Tokur* (☎0252/712 8728, ℱ712 8729; ❹), up **on the hill** with unparalleled views of the beach, run by a Turkish–German family, with pool and nicely tended garden.

Eating and drinking

Various cafés overlooking the east beach offer full **breakfast** for as little as 4YTL. Othwerwise, Datça's **restaurants** are fairly indistinguishable in terms of price and quality. The *Iskele*, *Karaca* and *Kapani Yeri*, on the bluff overlooking the harbour, and the *Hüsnünün Yeri*, down on the fishing-boat dock, offer the usual list of kebabs and fish. Cheaper places include the nicely decorated *Defne Pide Salonu* on the main drag and inland sidewalk eateries such as *Zekeriya Sofrası*, *Korsan*, *Valentino* and *Kemal*, on the west side of the main thoroughfare. Further inland from the main drag, the *06 Aspava Restaurant*, offering *pide* and kebab specialities from Adana at 3–5YTL a head, is a local favourite.

The most frantic activity you'll find in Datça is after dark at the handful of small **music pubs** and **bars** along the west harbour and beyond on the west beach. Among others there's *Bambu Bar* and *Bolero*, with *Eclipse* perhaps being the most popular of the lot.

Boat trips

The local **boat trips** advertised on the west harbour make a good day out. Groups generally depart between 9 and 9.30am, returning between 5 and 6pm. Standard stops include Palamut Bükü, Domuz Çukuru, Mesudiye Bükü and ancient Knidos – most of which are detailed below. The going price per person, excluding lunch (usually in a restaurant at Palamut Bükü) and allowing three swim stops, is around 18YTL, which compares well, for example, with the price of taking a taxi to Knidos.

Eskidatça

Two kilometres from Datça, back on the road towards Marmaris, a left turn takes you along a minor paved road to the original hamlet, **ESKIDATÇA**. The cobbled road leading into the hamlet passes the teahouse before splitting into two, up and down hill. The sleepy maze of alleys – used mainly by cows – and ancient stone-built farmhouses have lately become a haven for artists and writers, who have renovated many of the delapidated country homes. One such example is now the *Antik Bar and Restaurant*, with a walled garden.

West to Knidos

Some 9km west of Datça signs point down the five-kilometre side road to the shore hamlet of **MESUDIYE BÜKÜ**. There is an occasional dolmuş to Mesudiye from Datça, leaving from the traffic circle. Accommodation prices here are slightly cheaper than in Datça, but not much happens after dark. Choose from the *Yıldırım Motel* (☎0252/728 0221, ℻728 0224; ❷), the German-speaking *Hoppala* (☎0252/728 0148; ❷) and the *Özdemir Pansiyon* (☎0252/728 0128; ❸), the last with air-conditioned rooms and decent attached restaurant.

HAYİT BÜKÜ, one cove east with the necessary road-fork left well marked, hasn't such a good beach, but the bay itself is well protected by a scenic, clawlike headland to the west. Accordingly, the place sees lots of boat traffic and there's a large dock, a few restaurants and some **motels** – such as the *Ogün Pansiyon* (☎0252/728 0033; ❷) and the *Gül Pansiyon* (☎0252/728 0027; ❷), where breakfast is around 5YTL extra.

Nine kilometres of coast road, rough but just passable in an ordinary car in low gear, links Mesudiye with **PALAMUT BÜKÜ**. Most vehicles (but no dolmuşes) take the main road to the point in Yaka Köyü, about 20km out of Datça, where a side road drops 4.5km south to Palamut. Without your own transport you'll need to take the dolmuş which leaves from behind the Ziraat Bankası in Datça. The stark setting is balanced by a kilometre-long beach of tiny pebbles lapped by brisk, clear water, with an islet offshore. Of a handful of **pansiyons**, mostly occupied for weeks on end by Turkish families, one of the most appealing is the *Bük* (☎0252/725 5136; ❷), at the far eastern end of the bay. The only drawback is that most **restaurants** are well to the west, by the harbour.

The Aphrodisiac cult at Knidos

Like several cities in Asia Minor, Knidos was a Peloponnesian Dorian foundation, circa 1000 BC, its original site located near present-day Datça. The famous shrine of Apollo, religious focus of the Dorian Hexapolis, is thought to have been above today's Palamut Bükü. During the middle of the fourth century BC Knidos was moved to its present location – a shrewd step, taking advantage of the enforced stays of ships sheltering here from high local winds. The new town was built on both the tip of the mainland and what was then an island to the south. In ancient times the two were joined by a causeway, sluiced by a bridged channel, but the channel has long since silted up.

Undoubtedly Knidos's most famous "citizen" was an inanimate object, the **cult statue of Aphrodite** by Praxiteles, the first large-scale, freestanding nude of a woman (modelled by the famous Athenian courtesan, Phryne). This adorned the new city from its earliest days and became, even more than the menacing winds, Knidos's chief source of revenue. Set up in a sanctuary so that it could be admired from every angle, the marble Aphrodite attracted thousands of ancient tourists, not all of them mere art-lovers. According to legend the statue bore a dark stain in its crotch, not a flaw in the marble but the result of a youth conceiving such a passion for it that he hid in the temple until after closing time and made love to the effigy.

After paying their respects to the image, more conventional pilgrims were wont to observe the rites of love with one of the sacred prostitutes who worked in the temple precincts. Subsequently, customers bought tacky pornographic souvenirs, whose nature will be familiar to anyone who has browsed a postcard rack or gift shop anywhere in the modern Aegean. All this licence was – perhaps predictably – too much for the Byzantine Christians, who destroyed Praxiteles' Aphrodite along with the temple, though the aptly named Iris Love, chief of the American archeological team, claims to have discovered the goddess's head in a vault at the British Museum. Copies and incomplete versions of the statue still exist in New York, Paris, Rome and Munich.

Knidos

Hard as it is to believe from its current state, **Knidos** (Cnidus), out on windlashed Tekir Burnu (the Cape Krio of antiquity), was one of the most fabled and prosperous cities of antiquity. With its strategic location astride the main shipping lanes of the Mediterranean it was a cosmopolitan city, and illustrious personalities hailing from here were legion. In its heyday it was also home to an eminent medical school, rival to the Hippocratic clinic across the straits on Kós. However, the city was most notorious for a splendid statue of Aphrodite and the cult (and sacred brothels) that surrounded it.

The catch is that very little remains of this former greatness, and it's probably not worth punishing any vehicle for the full distance from Datça to see it. At least until ongoing excavations are completed, a short halt on a **boat trip** (see opposite) is all that the site will merit for most visitors. You could take a **taxi from Datça**, but this will cost at least 50YTL, and give you only an hour at the ruins.

Arriving by boat you dock in the south bay, backed by a single restaurant and a police post. Leave vehicles at the small **car park**; a nearby sign requests that, although the site is unenclosed, you should observe the official **visiting hours** of 8am to 7pm and pay admission – YTL4 – if the keeper is manning his booth.

The site

With the ruins still under excavation, the site-plan placard near the entrance is of little use, though labelling and signposting have improved in recent years. The overwhelming first impression is of an enormous, weedy mess, booby-trapped with deep, unguarded trenches, though the windswept setting is undoubtedly dramatic.

Most of Knidos's public buildings were on the mainland side and of these the **Hellenistic theatre**, overlooking the south anchorage, is the best preserved. A military watchtower on the ex-island confirms that most of it is off-limits; visit instead the two **Byzantine basilicas**, one huge with extensive mosaics, overlooking the north harbour. Hellenistic Knidos was laid out in a grid pattern, though the hilly site necessitated extensive terracing, retaining walls and stairways. Clambering along these, you can take a self-guided tour by following arrow-signs to the agora (by the north port), the bouleuterion, a Corinthian temple, a purported sundial and an unidentified mosaic floor. Of the Aphrodite shrine, on the very highest terrace, there remains only the circular foundation of either an altar or perhaps the tholos (round portico) where the image of the goddess was displayed.

Inland Caria

Away from the coastal regions, the major settlements in ancient Caria tended to be concentrated along the upper reaches of the Meander river, now the Büyük Menderes, and its tributaries, particularly the Marsyas – today's Çine Çayı (Çine river). Its old name, the **Marsyas**, commemorates a legend concerning the satyr Marsyas, a devotee of the mother-goddess Cybele. Upon finding a deer-bone flute discarded by Athena, he became entranced by its sound as he played in Cybele's processions, and was so bold as to challenge Apollo to a musical contest. The god accepted on condition that the winner could impose the punishment of his choice on the loser. Marsyas lost; Apollo tied him to a pine tree near the source of the stream that would bear his name, and flayed him alive.

Aydın, a pleasant town easily reached from Kuşadası, is the base of choice for visiting ancient **Nyssa**, and also **Alinda**, **Alabanda** and **Gerga**, the archeological sites of the Çine valley. Of these, only Alinda is anything like required viewing, and it is also the easiest to reach by public transport. The other two are pretty remote and for most visitors don't repay the effort involved in driving (or, in the case of Gerga, walking) out to them. Further east, **Aphrodisias**, on a high plateau south of the Büyük Menderes, is similarly isolated, but buses are more obliging since it's fast becoming the archeological rival of Ephesus in the southwest Aegean.

Still further inland, the functional city of **Denizli** has transport connections in every direction, most obviously with **Hierapolis/Pamukkale**, an ancient site cum geological prodigy that's the star of every other Turkish tourist poster ever produced. Whether it figures as the high or low point of your stay depends on your temperament, but if escape becomes imperative, minor attractions such as **Laodiceia** and **Akhan** are conveniently close.

Aydın and around

Aydın is a modern provincial capital, with clean, tree-lined main boulevards and a smattering of older buildings in the centre. Despite its rather dowdy accommodation choices, its excellent dolmuş services make it the obvious jumping-off point for the area's ancient ruins – Nyssa to the east, and the sites of the Çine valley (Alinda, Alabanda and Gerga), scattered either side of the scenic road south to Muğla.

Aydın

AYDİN started life as Tralles, the distinguished ancient town founded, according to legend, by colonists from the Greek Argive and Thrace; the site of the original settlement was a plateau northwest of today's city. Despite its good natural defences Tralles submitted, or fell, to whichever conqueror was currently traipsing through Asia Minor, but enjoyed a period of prosperity during the Roman imperial period, even eclipsing neighbouring Nyssa.

Contemporary Aydın's biggest attraction is currently off-limits since the site of **ancient Tralles** lies in a military zone at the northern end of Serbetçi Caddesi, 1km north of town. For the time being visitors will have to make do with **Üçgöz**, literally "three eyes", three arches situated on a small hillock just outside the military zone. Excavations here have yet to be carried out, but according to locals it is all that remains of three vaults, themselves part of the gymnasium of Tralles.

On Gazi Bulvarı, next to the sports centre, lies Aydın's other main pull, the **museum** (daily except Mon 8am–noon & 1–5.30pm; 2YTL), which has a wide collection of local finds, displayed chronologically. Notable exhibits include a bust of Athena and a statue of Nike, as well as coins, terracotta fragments and idols. The grounds house an extensive range of larger finds from Tralles, including column capitals and parts of recovered statues.

The only other buildings of note are two seventeenth-century mosques: the **Süleyman Bey Camii**, across from the pleasant, mosaic-paved central park, and the **Ahmet Şemsi Paşa Camii** on Adnan Menderes Bulvarı. Otherwise, there's nothing to see except the bizarre fig sculpture about 100m west of the *otogar* – Aydın is famous for its figs (and olives) and you'll see dried figs on sale almost everywhere.

Practicalities

The **otogar** is 700m south of the centre on the main highway, just west of a large roundabout and the **tourist office** (Mon–Fri 8am–5.30pm; ☎0256/225 4145), which offers excellent city maps; the *otogar* is connected with the centre of town by complimentary shuttle bus. Adnan Menderes Bulvarı shoots straight up to the heart of town, where the **train station** (services from İzmir and Denizli) and **PTT** face each other, just west of the central square organized around Altsan 1 Caddesi. Hükümet Bulvarı, Menderes's narrower continuation, climbs past the bulk of the hotels and restaurants before intersecting Gazi Bulvarı, Aydın's main east–west thoroughfare and home to the **dolmuş station**.

Accommodation is neither inspiring, nor particularly cheap. The best is found at the *Özlü*, Adnan Menderes Bul 71 (☎0256/213 2988, ℱ225 3371; ❷), where rooms come with TV. Otherwise there's the *Kabaçam*, Hükümet Bul, 11 Sok 2/B (☎0256/2252794; ❷), with reasonable en-suites, also with TV; or the similar but slightly more worn *Baltaçı*, Gazi Bulvarı, 3 Sok (☎0256/225 1320; ❷).

You'll find most of the **eating** options tucked in the backstreets around the bazaar, west of Hükümet Caddesi. The *Şanlıurfa Kebap Salonu* is better than most with large şiş and çöp kebabs.

Nyssa

Awash in a sea of orange groves in the hills above the Büyük Menderes valley, ancient **Nyssa** is rarely visited – and except for its theatre, bouleuterion and unusual layout, there is little to interest nonspecialist visitors. What's left above ground is mostly numerous arches of inferior masonry.

Originally founded by Peloponnesians, the city flourished from the first century BC until the third century AD, and subsequently remained an important Byzantine community. During the Roman era it was famous as an academic centre, attracting pupils from throughout Asia Minor. Strabo, while not a native, studied here and left detailed accounts of the city, which can still be partly verified, even in Nyssa's present ruinous condition.

The archeological zone lies 2km above **Sultanhisar**, the modern successor to Nyssa, 32km east of Aydın and astride major bus and rail routes; dolmuşes run here every thirty minutes from Aydın. Sultanhisar has simple eateries, but no public transport up to the ruins themselves.

The site

The paved access road from the ticket office (always open; 2YTL during daylight hours) leads into a small car park flanked by picnic tables. Just north of here lies an excellently preserved **Roman theatre** with a capacity of well over 5000 – a structure that is slowly being taken over by wild olives sprouting amidst the seats. The paved road continues another 300m uphill to the start of the 200-metre walk to the **bouleuterion**, where twelve semicircular rows of seats face out onto an area graced with a **ceremonial basin** and **mosaics**.

Strabo described the city as built on both sides of a steep ravine, and some of the monuments that he listed are still clinging to the banks of the canyon. A path just to the east of the theatre descends to the mouth of an enormous, 115-metre-long **tunnel** burrowing under the car park. Beyond the southern exit are the remains of two **bridges** linking the halves of Nyssa, and the virtually unrecognizable rubble of a stadium and a gymnasium, well recessed into the flanks of the gully and both currently off-limits. The tunnel, in addition to functioning as a simple storm drain, could be used to fill the stadium with water for mock naval battles.

To the west of the access road, reached by another path beginning 100m north of the guard post, stand the remains of some **baths** (adjoining the theatre) and a **library**, alleged in many sources to be the most important in Asia Minor after the one in Ephesus. You wouldn't know it from today's muddled, two-storey building, lost in more olives.

Alinda

Alinda, the first and best of the ancient ruins in the Çine valley, south of Aydın, crowns a huge bluff that dominates the area, and is closely linked with a colourful episode in the life of Alexander the Great. Ada, the sister of King Mausolus of Halicarnassus, after losing the battle for succession to the Hecatomnid throne during the middle of the fourth century, was exiled to Alinda, then a mere fortress, where she awaited an opportunity to reverse her fortunes. A few years later, upon the arrival of Alexander, Ada offered to surrender Alinda and all her personal resources in exchange for his aid in regaining her royal position. Her proposal was accepted, and Alexander holed up in Alinda for some time, preparing their combined – and eventually successful – siege of Halicarnassus. During this period they became close friends, and it seems that Ada even adopted Alexander as her son. After their victory Ada was left to rule over most of Caria, but she was the last of the remarkable Hecatomnid line; little of consequence occurred locally after her death.

Getting there

Though the site of Alinda lies 28km off the main highway, a total of 58km from Aydın, public transport connections are decent. There are direct dolmuşes from Aydın to **KARPUZLU**, the fair-sized town at the base of the ruins. Or you can use an Aydın–Çine dolmuş (departing across the road from Aydın tourist office, and from the *otogar*) and change vehicles in Çine town. The last direct service back from Karpuzlu to Aydın leaves at 4pm, to Çine at 5.30pm. If you end up having to stay in **ÇINE**, the squeaky-clean *Alabanda* (☎0256/711 7949; ❶), opposite the tiny *otogar*, offers en-suite rooms with TV, but no breakfast. In Karpuzlu there are several adequate restaurants, but only one bare-bones hotel.

The site

From the little square where the dolmuşes stop, follow the signs 400m up a dirt track to the unfenced **site** (always open; 2YTL charged during daylight hours) and car park. Close by, the oldest houses of Karpuzlu merge into ancient masonry just below the monstrous **market building**. One hundred metres long, this was originally three storeys high, with hefty interior columns; now only two floors stand, but these are in perfect condition, and, like so much Carian stonework, bear a strange resemblance to Inca construction half a world away. Cross the open agora behind to some courses of wall, where an obvious serpentine path leads up to the well-preserved **theatre**, retaining two galleries and most of its seats. These face south, giving superlative views over Karpuzlu and its valley. From here, continue further north up the hill, where an impressive, two-storey **Hellenistic watch-tower** surveys a patchwork of fields and trees, with rings of mountains up to 50km distant. The flat space around the tower is peppered with cistern mouths and partly collapsed tunnels that supposedly once led to the lower levels of the city. Walk west along the neck of the ridge, past the foundations of **acropolis houses**, until you reach a gap in the **city walls**; just beyond are a couple of specimens from Alinda's extensive **necropolis**.

Alabanda

Although originally a Carian settlement, **Alabanda** figures in history only briefly as a Roman city, notorious for its scorpions. Today there is not much on view at all, and the site, 8km west of Çine, is perfunctorily signposted and served only by an infrequent dolmuş from Çine. Only the old **bouleuterion**, north of the road, is obvious, its walls standing up to 6m high. The **theatre**, up in the village across the road, has almost disappeared – houses have been built up against it, and vegetables are being raised in the old stage area.

Gerga

Near the headwaters of the Çine Çayı, the valley narrows to a defile known as the Gökbel pass. The deserted landscape, with the water far below tumbling over huge boulders, is evocative of Marsyas and his fate – and hides **Gerga** (40km southeast of Aydın), the most mysterious ancient site in Caria.

Twelve kilometres south of Eskiçine, the graceful **İncekemer** Ottoman bridge spans the gorge. Dolmuşes from Çine run past frequently, as do buses bound for Muğla, Marmaris and Fethiye, but you'll have to specify carefully that you want to get off at the bridge. There's parking space at the roadside. From here, it's an hour and a half's **walk to Gerga**. Cross the bridge, then another flimsy cement one across a tributary, and stay with the main trail, which soon becomes a dirt track. After 25 minutes you'll reach the village of İncekemer Mahalle, split in two by yet another watercourse. Change to the west bank of this, maintain a northerly course and continue up the small valley between the big ridge and a smaller rock plug to the east. Near the top, make a hairpin left over a slight saddle to reach some drystone walls and thornbush barriers for livestock. Just past this is a small farm at the base of a terraced hillside, on which stand the remains of Gerga.

Virtually nothing is known for certain about Gerga, other than that it is of very early Carian vintage, with crude, monolithic masonry supposedly dating from the Roman era. At first sight it would appear to have not been a town, but a sacred precinct like Labranda. The most conspicuous item is a **tomb–temple** in the form of a house, in perfect condition, despite its current usage as a cowshed. Its stone roof is intact and on the lintel "GERGAS" is inscribed in Greek lettering – which some archeologists theorize is not the place name but that of an obscure Carian deity. You actually enter the site between two upright, flattened **monoliths**, irregularly shaped like African termite nests; adjacent is a large lustral **basin** carved from living rock. A giant headless **statue** lies on the ground beyond the tomb-temple, and at the far edge of the main terrace are two purported **fountains**: one backed into the hillside, the other freestanding and bearing another "GERGAS" legend. While none of the individual structures is that impressive, the total effect and the outlandish location is unsettling.

Aphrodisias

Situated on a high plateau over 600m above sea level, ringed by mountains and watered by a tributary of the Büyük Menderes, **Aphrodisias** is among the most isolated and beautifully set of Turkey's major archeological sites. Acres of marble peek out from among the poplars and other vegetation that cloaks the remains of one of imperial Rome's most cultured Asian cities. Late afternoon visits have the bonus of often dramatic cloud formations, spawned by the elevation, and the attendant dappled lighting.

△ Aphrodisias

Some history

Aphrodisias was one of the earliest occupied sites in Anatolia. Neolithic and Bronze Age mounds have been found here, including the artificial hill supporting the theatre. There has also been a **fertility cult** of some sort here for just as long, fostered by the agricultural associations of the river valley. The Assyrian goddess of love and war, Nin, became syncretized with the Semitic Ishtar, whose attributes were eventually assumed by the Hellenic Aphrodite.

Despite a strategic position near the meeting point of ancient Caria, Lydia and Phrygia, and its proximity to major trade routes, Aphrodisias for many centuries remained only a shrine, and never really grew into a town until the second century BC. The citizens of Aphrodisias were amply rewarded for their support of the Romans during the Mithridatic revolt. Many special privileges – including the right of sanctuary within the Aphrodite temple precincts – were granted, and the rapidly burgeoning city was heavily patronized by various emperors, becoming a major cultural centre. It was renowned in particular for its school of sculpture, which took advantage of nearby quarries of high-grade marble, and Aphrodisian works adorned every corner of the empire, including Rome itself.

Perhaps because of this fixation with graven images, not to mention the lucrative cult of Aphrodite (similar to that at Knidos), paganism lingered here for almost two centuries after Theodosius proscribed the old religions. Even following conversion of the Aphrodite shrine to a more decorous basilica, and a change of name to Stavropolis (City of the Cross), the Christianity professed here tended toward heretical persuasions.

The reputation of its love cult had served to protect Aphrodisias since its inception, but by the fourth century AD a wall had become necessary. This failed singularly, however, to stave off the effect of two earthquakes and sundry raids, and decline was the dominant theme of Byzantine times. The town was abandoned completely during the thirteenth century, its former glories recalled only by the Ottoman village of Geyre – a corruption of "Caria" – among the ruins. Romantic travellers dutifully stopped, sketched and copied inscriptions, but none suspected the wealth of relics hidden from view.

First French, then Italian researchers poked rather desultorily below the surface early last century, but it is only since 1961 that work by a New York University team under Dr Kenan Erim has permitted a fuller understanding of the site. Dr Erim's death in 1990 (he is buried on the site) marked the end of an era; currently no new monuments are being uncovered, with ongoing work concentrating on consolidation, cleaning and documentation of inscriptions. The intention is to render Aphrodisias on a par with Ephesus and the eventual results will certainly be spectacular, though for now some of the site's more interesting areas remain off-limits.

The site

A loop path around the **site** (daily: summer 8am–7pm; winter 8am–5.30pm; 7YTL) passes all of the major monuments, though at the time of writing only the stadium, theatre, odeion, council houses and the temple of Aphrodite have completely unrestricted access.

First stop is the magnificent, virtually intact **theatre**, founded in the first century BC but extensively modified by the Romans for their blood sports three centuries later. At the rear of the stage building are chiselled imperial decrees affecting the status of the town. Still further behind the stage is a large square, the **tetrastoön**, originally surrounded by colonnades on all sides, and one of several meeting places in the Roman and Byzantine city. South of the tetrastoön lies a large baths complex.

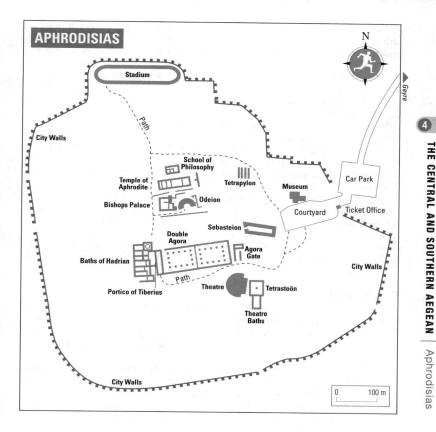

The path skirts the north flank of the theatre, right under the hill's summit; down and to the north you may often see workmen pottering about in the **Sebasteion** – two parallel porticoes erected in the first century AD to honour the deified Roman emperors – and the **double agora**, two squares ringed by Ionic and Corinthian stoas. Numerous columns still vie with the poplars, and the whole area is bounded to the southwest by the **Portico of Tiberius**, which separates the agora from the fine **Baths of Hadrian** (currently out of bounds), preserved right down to the floor tiles and the odd mosaic.

North of the baths, several blue-marble columns sprout from a multi-roomed structure commonly known as the **Bishop's Palace**, from its presumed use during Byzantine times. However, its ground plan, particularly the large audience chamber, is typical of a governor's residence in Roman provinces and that is certainly how the building began life. East of here huddles the Roman **odeion**, with nine rows of seats. Since the many earthquakes have disrupted the local water table, the orchestra is prone to springtime flooding, and today frogs often croak where concerts were once given and the city council deliberated.

A few paces to the north, fourteen columns of the **Temple of Aphrodite** are all that's left of the city's principal sanctuary. The Byzantines mangled not only the idol within but also the ground plan when they converted it to a basilica during the fifth century, so considerable detective work was required to re-establish the first-century BC foundations. Even these were laid atop at least two older structures, with evidence of mother-goddess worship extending back to the seventh century BC. The Hellenistic/Roman sanctuary had forty Ionic columns arranged eight by thirteen, with the cult image erected in the main hall. The Byzantines removed the columns at each end of the temple, fashioning an apse to the east, an atrium and baptistry on the west, and it's this architectural pastiche you see today. Immediately north is the so-called **School of Philosophy**, tentatively identified, like the bishop's palace, on the basis of resemblance to other such structures elsewhere.

The northernmost feature of the site, 200m off the main path, is the 30,000-seat **stadium**, one of the largest and best preserved in Anatolia. Under the empire, and with official encouragement, many cities of Asia Minor held periodic festivals in imitation of the major Greek competitions. Those at Aphrodisias were a version of Delphi's Pythian Games, with sporting, musical and dramatic events.

Returning to the main loop trail, the last thing you'll notice before exiting onto the museum square is the recently re-erected **tetrapylon**, a monumental gateway with two double rows of four columns, half of them fluted, supporting pediments with intricate reliefs. This second-century AD edifice is thought to mark the intersection of a major north–south street with a sacred way heading toward the Aphrodite shrine.

The museum

An earthquake in 1956 damaged the old village of Geyre, giving the authorities a timely pretext to relocate the villagers 1.5km to the north and begin excavations. The old village square is now flanked by the archeologists' quarters and by the attractive **museum**, whose collection consists almost entirely of sculpture recovered from the ruins.

Given that Aphrodisias met most of the demand for effigies under the empire, even what remains after the loss of originals and the spiriting away of works to city museums is considerable. The so-called "Aphrodite Hall" contains statuary related to the cult, a rendition of the goddess, much defaced by Christian zealots, occupying the position of honour. In the "Penthesileia Hall", a joyous satyr carries the child Dionysos in his arms. The "Melpomene Hall" contains a wrenching version of the muse of tragedy, together with two suitably loutish-looking boxers – ironically lacking their hands – and the completely intact, quasi-satirical portrait of Flavius Palmatus, Byzantine governor of Asia; with a small head and thick body, he was an ugly, malproportioned man, but, judging from the facial expression, one you crossed at your peril. Recent notable additions to the collection include the remounted, so-called "Zoïlos" friezes and portrait busts of various philosophers. The first (or last) notable item you'll pass is a version of Nike carrying a trophy, opposite the souvenir stall.

Practicalities

Aphrodisias is situated 13km southeast of **KARACASU**, the nearest sizable town, which lies 25km from the E24/320 highway between Aydın and Denizli. From the highway, you'll need to change transport at **NAZILLI**, whose *otogar* sits just north of the highway on the west edge of town. If coming by train, exit Nazilli station and turn right onto the main town thoroughfare, or follow the tracks southwest – they pass very near the bus stand. **Dolmuşes to Karacasu** depart from the rear of the Nazilli *otogar*; during warmer months the route may extend to Geyre, the village next to the ruins. Best bet for accommodation in Nazilli, if required, is the two-star

Metya Hotel (℡0256/312 8888, ℱ312 8891; ❷). In Karacasu there is only the grimmest of dormitories, built directly over the small bus-terminal building.

Whatever happens, try to avoid getting stranded at Aphrodisias – a distinct possibility after 6pm, even in summer. A round trip by **taxi from Karacasu** will cost you 25YTL, double that if you have to take it all the way back to the Nazilli–Denizli highway. If you are going to get stuck, you're best off doing so at **GEYRE**, next to the ruins, where the simple *Chez Mestan pansiyon*-campsite (℡0256/448 8046; ❷), 600m from the site on the main highway, has basic waterless doubles; the more comfortable *Aphrodisias Hotel-Restaurant-Camping* (℡0256/448 8132, ℱ448 8422; ❷) is 1km west of *Chez Mestan*, with good en-suite rooms and a rooftop restaurant.

The other option for visiting the site is to take a **tour** organized through one of the pensions in Pamukkale (see p.431), for which the going rate is around 25YTL.

Pamukkale and around

As you approach the UNESCO World Heritage site of **Pamukkale** from Denizli, a long white smudge along the hills to the north suggests a landslide or opencast mine. Getting closer, this resolves into the edge of a plateau, more than 100m higher than the level of the river valley and absolutely smothered in white **travertine terraces**. Some are shaped like water lilies, others like shell-bathtubs with stalagmitic feet, with the simplest ones resembling bleached rice-terraces out of an oriental engraving. The Turks have dubbed this geological fairyland *Pamukkale*, or "Cotton Castle".

The responsibility for this startling natural wonder rests with a spring, saturated with dissolved calcium bicarbonate, bubbling up from the feet of Çal Dağı beyond. As the water surges over the edge of the plateau and cools, carbon dioxide is given off and calcium carbonate precipitated as hard chalk (travertine). What you see now has been accumulating for millennia, as slowly but surely the solidified waterfall advances southwest. Seen at sunset, subtle hues of ochre, purple and pink are reflected in the water, replacing the dazzling white of midday. The spring itself emerges in what once was the centre of the ancient city of **Hierapolis**, whose ruins would merit a stop even if they weren't coupled with the natural phenomenon of the terraces.

The hotels here at one time siphoned off the precious mineral waters for their own heated pools, thus damaging the terraces further downstream. Those establishments that once stood above the travertines have been demolished, and the waterflow to the rest is now strictly rotated in order to preserve the site and also to allow the greatly diminished deposits to "regrow". Present restrictions on access to the travertine terraces mean that visitors are confined to the major pathways around the site and can visit only a handful of the smaller pools on the furthest southern edge of the terraces.

Some history

The therapeutic properties and bizarre appearance of the hot springs were known about for thousands of years before an actual town was founded here by one of the Pergamene kings during the second century BC. After incorporation into the Roman Empire in 129 BC, development proceeded apace, spurred by minor industries in wool and metals, plus a health spa practically the equal of the present one. Hierapolis seems to have enjoyed considerable imperial favour, especially after catastrophic earthquakes in 17 AD and 60 AD. No fewer than three emperors paid personal visits, stimulating local emperor-worship alongside the veneration of Apollo and his mother Leto, who was venerated in the guise of Cybele.

The presence of a flourishing Jewish community aided the rapid and early establishment of Christianity here. Hierapolis is mentioned in Paul's Epistle to the (neighbouring) Colossians, and Philip the Apostle is thought to have been martyred here, along with his seven sons. However, as at Aphrodisias, paganism lingered well into the sixth century, until a zealous bishop supervised the destruction of the remaining focuses of ancient worship and the establishment of nearly one hundred churches, several of which are still visible.

Hierapolis slid into obscurity in late Byzantine times, nudged along by Arab and Turcoman raids. After the Selçuks arrived in the 1100s, the city was abandoned, not to figure much in the Western imagination until Italian excavations began in 1957. A mere six decades have sufficed to re-create, if not the monumental taste, then certainly the commercialism of the Roman period.

Pamukkale Köyü

PAMUKKALE KÖYÜ, a once-sleepy village at the base of the cliff, is where most foreign travellers stay. In recent years, the village has acquired a rash of discos, carpet shops, hustlers and wretched restaurants in its centre. Despite all this, it's still a rural settlement, partly dependent on cotton; beyond the main drag, especially in the lower neighbourhood away from the travertine, little outward change is evident. For any nocturnal peace, it's better to stay on the outskirts, whose limit seems to have stabilized about 500m west of the road leading up to the south gate of the ruins.

Arrival, information and transport

Most travellers arrive from the agricultural town of **Denizli**, 20km to the south, from where **dolmuşes** labelled "Pamukkale/Karahayat" set off from a rank on the west edge of the *otogar*; the last departure in either direction is around 11pm in summer (9pm for Karahayat), much earlier in the cooler months. A **taxi from Denizli** will set you back 15YTL per car-load; or consider ringing one of the recommended *pansiyon*s, who are often able to fetch you for free (or at least for a reasonable charge).

There are also **long-distance bus connections** between Pamukkale Köyü and most of the larger resorts – Kaş, Marmaris, Kuşadası and Fethiye, among other places – up to several times daily, although the buses are really minibuses and not air-conditioned. Several bus companies, including Pamukkale, have ticket offices in the village, but be sure that the fare and itinerary include a shuttle to the Denizli *otogar* (you'll rarely get through-service, except perhaps in peak season).

Accommodation and eating

There's been a vigorous winnowing of excess capacity in Pamukkale Köyü, spurred by falling tourist numbers, with substandard (ie non-en-suite) outfits folding. You should still be prepared for the attentions of the notorious local accommodation **touts**, rivalling those at Selçuk and Kuşadası for their aggression and mendacity. An advance telephone call to one of the establishments mentioned below, and a word to the touts that you have prepaid by credit card, should solve any problems. In any case, it's well worth arranging a room in advance as the various establishments, well aware of the touts' ploys, may offer to fetch you from Denizli or meet you in the village if informed of your arrival time. Most lodgings in the village are open all year and advertise the presence of a **swimming pool**, but by the time the mineral water has made the long trip down from the

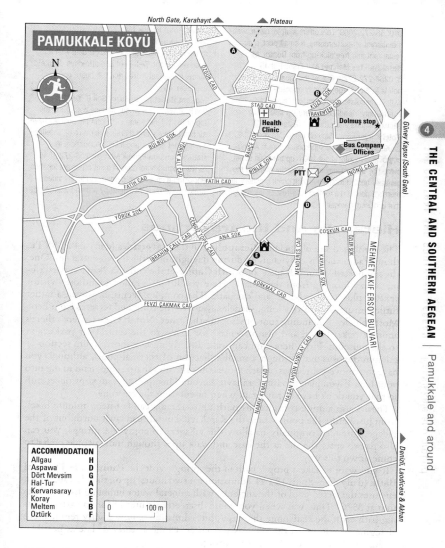

PAMUKKALE KÖYÜ

North Gate, Karahayıt ▲   ▲ Plateau

ACCOMMODATION

Allgau	H
Aspawa	D
Dört Mevsim	G
Hal-Tur	A
Kervansaray	C
Koray	E
Meltem	B
Oztürk	F

0   100 m

Güney Kapısı (South Gate) ▶

Denizli, Laodicea & Akhan ▶

cliff it's distinctly cool and murky – a summertime pleasure only. **Eating out**, the situation is almost uniformly dire. Service is slack and prices nearly double what they'd be elsewhere. You'll usually get better value from your *pansiyon* or motel, some of which offer half-board rates.

Allgau Backstreet near junction of Korkmaz Cad and Mehmet Akif Ersoy Bul ☎0258/272 2250, ✉allgau@hotmail.com. At the remote south end of the village, run by the most relaxed, genuine owners in town. Basic rooms overlook the garden and pool, or there are wooden bungalows and tent

space. ❷

Aspawa Menderes Cad ☎0258/272 2094. With an off-street mineral pool, a choice of single, double or triple rooms (with or without a/c, particularly good breakfasts (3YTL), and satellite TV. ❷

Hotel Dört Mevsim Hasan Tahsin Kubilay Cad 19

431

⊤0258/272 2009. This offers simple, clean, well-maintained en-suite rooms, a small pool, a decent restaurant and free pick-up from Denizli. ❸

Hotel Hal-Tur Mehmet Akif Ersoy Bul 45 ⊤0258/272 2723. One of the most prestigious hotels in the village, directly opposite the terraces, with immaculate a/c rooms with satellite TV. It's surprisingly friendly and there's a swimming pool, Jacuzzi, sauna and attached restaurant. ❹

Hotel Kervansaray Alley off İnönü Cad ⊤0258/272 2209, ⓔkervansaray@superonline.com.tr. A long-standing favourite, about 200m up the main street, owned by the welcoming Kaya family. Many of the centrally-heated rooms overlook creek greenery, and there's a pool and a rooftop café-restaurant (though this is closed in winter). ❷

Koray Hotel Pamuk Mah 27 ⊤0258/272 2222, ⓦwww.korayhotel.com. Popular, small hotel built around a non-mineral pool and garden, with a good restaurant. Well-kept and attractive double rooms (breakfast extra), and full-board options available. ❸

Meltem Guesthouse Kuzey Sok 9 ⊤0258/272 2413, ⓦwww.meltemguesthouse.com. Near the top of the village: some of the simple doubles have air conditioning, and there's a dorm (€8), satellite TV, Internet access and local information. ❶

Öztürk Pension Pamuk Mah ⊤0258/272 2838, ⓦwww.ozturkhotel.com. A quiet off-street location, enclosing a small pool-garden and lovely vined breakfast terrace. Managed by a friendly family. ❸

Hierapolis and the travertines

The combined site of ancient **Hierapolis** and the **travertines** (daily 24hr; 5YTL, though admission is only charged during daylight hours) has two entrances. One, the signposted "Güney Kapısı" or **South Gate**, is at the end of a 2km road describing a lazy loop up from the village. Here you'll find a rather grandiose "visitor centre" plus a ticket booth and car park. The complex seems, however, a rather futile gesture, as you've a long, shadeless walk to the ruins and terraces from here. Most vehicles – including tour buses – use the other, **North Gate** (where's there's another ticket booth and visitor centre) for access to the central car parks next to the museum. From here, you can walk directly upon a short, 250m section of calcium deposits and through a small collection of thermal pools, although you have to remove your shoes, which means the calcium's sharp ridges tend to dig into your feet. If you plan to visit Karahayıt, beyond Hierapolis, retain your ticket stub so that you don't have to pay again when re-entering the fee zone.

There's also a quite conspicuous **path** up to the plateau (a fifteen-minute hike), from just before the point where the Karahayıt-bound road curls north out of the village. Intended originally to allow the villagers to enjoy the springs, you can also pay to enter the site at the base and walk up – though most people prefer to come down this way.

If you want to take a proper bath in the springs, visit the **Pamukkale Thermal Baths** (daily 8am–8pm; 18TYL admission for two hours) up on the plateau, which encloses the sacred pool of the ancients, with mineral water bubbling from its bottom at 35°C. Time was when you could discreetly saunter in for an early-morning bath with the staff none the wiser, but admission is now highly regimented; changing rooms are to the right as you enter. Come as early or late as possible; midday is the province of large tour groups.

On your way to the pool you'll pass the **tourist office** (daily in season 8am–noon & 1.30–7.30pm; ⊤0258/264 3971), principally useful for its combined map of the site and village, and the **museum** (daily except Mon 8am–8pm; 2YTL), housed in the restored second-century AD baths. Its rather disappointing collection consists primarily of statuary, sarcophagi, masonry fragments and smaller knick-knacks recovered during excavations at Hierapolis. Behind the museum is a large sixth-century **basilica**, probably the Byzantine-era cathedral, with two aisles sandwiching the nave.

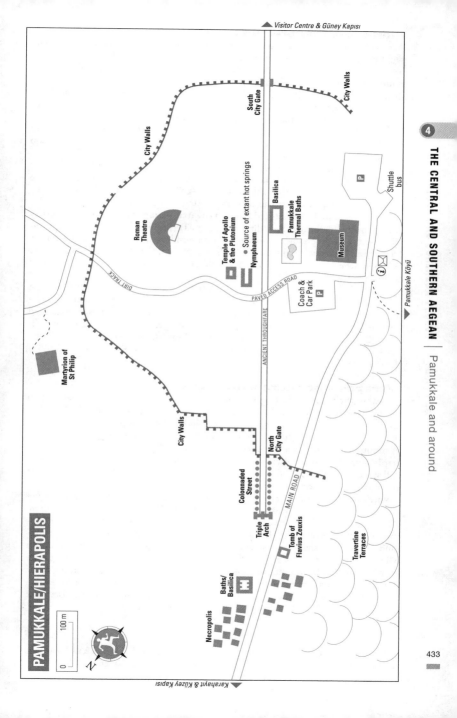

PAMUKKALE/HIERAPOLIS

0   100 m

N

▲ Visitor Centre & Güney Kapısı

City Walls

City Walls

South City Gate

Roman Theatre

Temple of Apollo & the Plutonium

● Source of extant hot springs

Nymphaeum

Basilica

Pamukkale Thermal Baths

Museum

P

Shuttle bus

▶ Pamukkale Köyü

i

PAVED ACCESS ROAD

Coach & Car Park

P

DIRT TRACK

ANCIENT THROUGHFARE

Martyrion of St Philip

City Walls

Colonnaded Street

North City Gate

MAIN ROAD

Triple Arch

Tomb of Flavius Zeuxis

Travertine Terraces

Baths/ Basilica

Necropolis

▲ Karahayıt & Kuzey Kapısı

Hierapolis: eastern monuments

Access to the **eastern monuments** of ancient Hierapolis is via a narrow road winding up between the main car park and the museum. The first break – it can hardly be called a gate – in the roadside fence gives access to a **nymphaeum**, or fountain-house, the **Temple of Apollo** and the adjacent **Plutonium**. The Apollo shrine in its present, scanty form dates from the third century AD, though built on a second-century BC foundation. The grotto of the Plutonium, a quasi-oracular site sacred to the god of the underworld, is today a small, partly paved cavity beyond which you can hear rushing water and an ominous hissing – the emission of a highly toxic gas, probably a mixture of sulphurous compounds and carbon dioxide, capable of killing man and beast alike. In ancient times the eunuch priests of Cybele were reputedly able to descend into the chasm with no ill effect; whether this was a result of their anatomical deficiency or some less obvious ruse is unknown. Today, a formidable metal cage-grille keeps daredevils out – before this was installed, two Germans died attempting to brave the cave.

The next feature is the restored **Roman theatre**, dating from the second century AD. Admittedly, theatres are a dime a dozen in Turkey but this one is in exceptionally good shape, including most of the stage buildings and their elaborate reliefs. During the **International Pamukkale Song Festival** (late June) performances are held here: the 46 rows of seats can still hold up to 7000 spectators comfortably, as against the former capacity of 10,000.

After seeing the theatre, return to the dirt track and follow it further east past a stretch of the **city walls**, turning left onto a smaller path and eventually halting before the **Martyrion of St Philip**, built in honour of the apostle, martyred here in 80 AD. This fifth-century structure, comprising many rectangular cells converging on a central octagonal chamber, was almost certainly not Philip's tomb, nor even a church, but probably the venue for festivals and processions on the saint's day.

Hierapolis: northern monuments

Arguably the most interesting part of the city is the **colonnaded street**, which once extended for almost 1km from a gate 400m southeast of the sacred pool to another breach in the north wall. This thoroughfare, parallel to the plateau's edge, unevenly bisected the grid plan of the Hellenistic city and terminated at each end in monumental portals a few paces outside the walls. Only the northerly one, a **triple arch** flanked by towers and dedicated to the emperor Domitian in 84 AD, still stands. The short stretch of intact paved way, flanked by numerous re-erected columns, was the commercial heart of the city.

North of Domitian's triple arch, on the east side of the road, stands the squat bulk of some second-century AD baths, converted 200 years later into a **basilica**. Slightly closer to the archway, west of the asphalt, is the elaborate **Tomb of Flavius Zeuxis**, a prominent Hierapolitan merchant – the first of more than a thousand tombs of all shapes and sizes constituting the **necropolis**, the largest in Asia Minor and extending for nearly 2km along the road. The more sumptuous ones bear epitaphs or inscriptions warning grave-robbers of punishments awaiting those caught, and there are even forecourts with benches for visits by the deceased's relatives. Nowadays, camels and their drovers, instead of tomb-desecrators, lurk among the tumuli.

Karahayıt

Dolmuşes cover the 7km or so from the lower village to **KARAHAYİT**, famous for its *Kırmızı Su* (Red Water). These hot (55°C), iron-rich springs well up from within a single, blunt-topped rock formation and then flow, considerably cooled down, into a large rustic pool flanked by a tasteful tea garden and some small souvenir shops; use of the pool is free.

Karahayıt is a very different experience to Pamukkale Köyü: it's patronized almost exclusively by Turkish families from Konya and other conservative Anatolian cities, intent on finding a thermal cure for various maladies; alcohol is difficult to locate and sunbathing in public is frowned upon. As at Pamukkale, however, overzealous tapping of the thermal springs by the various *pansiyons* has led to a similar reduction in flow and threats by the authorities to close down, or at least regulate, the offending establishments.

The *pansiyons* and **hotels** all offer either en-suite thermal baths or communal pools, the friendliest and cheapest being *Albay Pension* (☎0258/271 4065; ❶). *Yeşil Dere*, which keeps live trout for its **restaurant**, has the only **campsite** in the area.

Laodiceia and Akhan

Just off the road linking Pamukkale and Denizli are two minor sites, ancient **Laodiceia** and the remains of the Selçuk *kervansaray* at **Akhan** – either worth a short detour if you've time or your own vehicle.

Laodiceia

Thirteen kilometres south of Pamukkale, a black-on-yellow marker points 500m west to a placard detailing the delights of "Laodikya", the site of **ancient Laodiceia**. This covers an elevated tableland squeezed between two river valleys, the bleak melancholy of the meagre remains accentuated by tractor furrows and power pylons. It's a setting redeemed principally by perennially snow-covered Honaz Dağı (2571m) to the southeast, matched in miniature by the white strip of Pamukkale to the north.

Founded by the post-Alexandrian Seleucid kings in the mid-third century BC at the junction of two major trade routes, Laodiceia came under Roman rule at the same time as the other cities of Caria. It later became an important bishopric during Byzantine times, only beginning its final decline after a fifth-century earthquake. Shortly after the Selçuk conquest the city was abandoned in favour of nearby Denizli.

As befits a settlement of mostly Roman importance, the visible ruins date from that era. The track starting at the orientation placard dwindles away in the centre of the plateau, next to the rubble of a **nymphaeum**. Southeast of here, at the edge of the site, is the 350-metre-long **stadium**, the largest in Asia Minor but in parlous condition, constructed in the first century AD under the emperor Vespasian. Overlooking it are the fairly substantial remains of a Hadrianic **gymnasium** and **baths complex**. These, and the archeological zone in general, have suffered from systematic masonry pilferage in recent times; engravings from the 1820s show monuments standing to twice their present height. Return to the nymphaeum once more and cross the rudimentary track to find the foundations of an **Ionic temple**. Continue a short distance north and begin pacing the edge of the upland to find, in quick succession, the **small theatre** – facing northwest and with many seats intact – and the **large theatre**, facing northeast over the modern village of Eskihisar.

Akhan

It's possible to walk the 3km between Laodiceia and the Selçuk *kervansaray* of **Akhan**. Upon reaching the E24/320 highway (the main Denizli–Afyon road), turn left and proceed 1.5km to the lightly restored structure tucked just north of the asphalt, on the west bank of a creek. If you enter the modern village of Akhan, you've gone too far. The rectangular structure encloses a courtyard, with arches to either side, and a covered hall at the rear. An inscription over the front gate, which looks southeast over the stream and a peach orchard, declares that the building was completed in 1252–1253, under the reign of the sultan İzzedin Kaykavuş.

Travel details

Trains

Denizli to: Afyon–Eskişehir–Haydarpaşa– İstanbul (1 daily; 14hr 30min); Afyon (1 daily; 5hr 30min).

İzmir (Basmane) to: Denizli (3 daily, via Aydın & Nazilli; 6hr); Manisa–Balıkesir–Bandırma (3 daily; 6hr 30min; ferry connection at Bandırma for İstanbul); Manisa–Balıkesir–Kütahya–Ankara (2 daily, both with couchettes or full sleepers; 14–16hr); Manisa–Balıkesir–Kütahya–Eskişehir (3 daily; 9hr 30min–11hr); Ödemiş (1 daily; 3hr); Selçuk (2 daily; 1hr 45min); Söke via Selçuk (3 daily; 2hr 15min).

Selçuk to: Aydın (3 daily; 1hr); Denizli (2 daily; 4hr 15min); İzmir Basmane (6–7 daily; 1hr 45min).

Buses and dolmuşes

The schedules below are for the summer season; out of season (Nov–April), the number of buses and minibuses drops drastically.

Aydın to: Alinda via Karpuzlu (hourly; 1hr); Ankara (4 daily; 9hr); Çine (15 daily; 35min); Denizli (every 30min until 7pm; 2hr); Fethiye (hourly; 5hr); Konya (4 daily; 9hr); Marmaris (hourly; 3hr); Nazilli (every 30min; 45min); Söke (every 30min; 50min); Sultanhisar (every 30min; 30min).

Bodrum to: Ankara (4 daily; 11hr); Bitez (every 30min; 15min); Fethiye (6 daily; 5hr); Gölköy (hourly; 30min); Gümbet (every 15min; 10min); Gümüşluk (every 30min; 40min); Gündoğan via Torba (hourly; 25min); İstanbul (20 daily; 12hr); İzmir (hourly; 3hr 30min); Marmaris (hourly; 3hr 15min); Muğla (hourly; 2hr 30min); Ortakent (every 30min; 20min); Pamukkale (2 daily; 5hr); Turgutreis (every 30min; 25min); Yahşi Sahil (every 30min; 20min); Yalikavak (10 daily; 25min).

Datça to: Ankara (several daily; 13hr); İstanbul (several daily; 16hr); Marmaris (9 daily; 2hr); Mesudiye (several daily; 30min); Muğla (11 daily; 3hr 15min).

Denizli to: Antalya via Burdur/Korkuteli (14 daily; 5hr 30min); Bodrum via Kale/Muğla (2–3 daily; 4hr 30min); Konya via Isparta and Eğirdir (several daily; 7hr 15min); İzmir (every 30min; 4hr); Marmaris via Kale/Muğla (8 daily; 3hr 30min); Tavas (hourly until 6pm; 40min); Yeşilova, for Salda Gölü (8 daily; 1hr 30min).

İzmir to: Afyon (5 daily; 5hr); Ahmetbeyli (at least 8 daily; 1hr 20min); Ankara (11 daily; 8hr); Antalya via Aydın and Burdur (hourly; 7hr); Aydın (every 30min; 2hr); Ayvalık (every 30min; 2hr 30min); Bergama (every 30min; 1hr); Bodrum (hourly; 4hr); Bursa (hourly; 7hr); Çandarli (6 daily; 2hr); Çanakkale (6 daily; 5hr 30min); Çeşme (every 15–20min; 1hr 30min); Datça (several daily; 7hr); Denizli (hourly; 4hr); Edirne (6 daily; 12hr); Fethiye (12–18 daily; 7hr); Foça (every 30min; 1hr 30min); Gümüldür (hourly; 1hr 40min); İstanbul (hourly; 10hr); Kuşadası (every 30min; 2hr); Manisa (every 15min; 45min); Marmaris (hourly; 5hr); Milas (hourly; 3hr); Muğla (hourly; 4hr); Ödemiş (every 2hr; 3hr 30min); Salihli (hourly; 1hr 30min); Sart (hourly; 1hr 30min); Seferihisar (at least hourly; 1hr); Selçuk (every 20min; 1hr 40min).

Kuşadası to: Aydın (hourly; 1hr 15min); Antalya (2 daily; 8hr); Bodrum (4 daily; 3hr); Dilek Yarımadası National Park (every 30min; 40min); İstanbul (5 daily; 11hr); Menderes airport (every 20min until 9pm; 1hr 30min); İzmir (every 30min; 2hr); Pamukkale (12 daily; 3hr 30min); Seferihisar (hourly; 1hr 30min); Selçuk (every 20min; 30min); Söke (every 30min; 40min).

Marmaris to: Akyaka (every 30min; 30min); Ankara (14 daily; 13hr); Antalya (5 daily; 6hr); Bodrum (hourly; 3hr 15min); Bozburun (3 daily; 1hr 15min); Datça (9 daily; 2hr); Denizli (6 daily; 3hr 30min); Fethiye (hourly; 2hr 45min); İstanbul (4 daily; 11hr); İzmir (17 daily; 5hr); Orhaniye (several daily; 35min); Ortaca (hourly; 1hr); Selimiye (3 daily; 50min); Tavlica (1 daily; 1hr 40min); Turunç (hourly; 20min).

Milas to: Bodrum (hourly; 2hr); Denizli (13 daily; 2hr); Euromos (hourly; 15min); Güllük (every 30min; 35min); İzmir (every 30min; 4hr 30min); Muğla (hourly; 1hr 15min); Ören (at least 6 daily; 1hr); Selimiye (hourly; 20min).

Muğla to: Akyaka (every 30min; 30min); Fethiye (12 daily; 2hr 30min); Köyceriz (hourly; 50min); Marmaris (every 30min; 1hr).

Nazilli to: Geyre (6–7 daily; 50min); Karacasu (6–7 daily; 40min).

Selçuk to: Kuşadası (every 20min until 10pm; 30min); Tire (every 20min; 40min).

Söke to: Altınkum (hourly; 50min); Bafa Gölü (every 30min; 30min); Balat (several daily; 40min); Didyma (hourly; 50min); Dilek Yarımadası National Park (every 30min; 40min); Güllübahçe (hourly; 20min); Güzelçamlı (every 30min; 40min); Milas (every 30min; 1hr 20min); Miletus (several daily; 40min); Priene (hourly; 20min).

Domestic ferries and hydrofoils

All schedules also apply to the reverse itinerary, and are valid during the May–October season only. The first two services are currently operated by Bodrum Express Lines, which quotes prices exclusively in euros, though you can pay in Turkish lira. The Datça services are run by Bodrum Ferryboat Association.

Bodrum to: Marmaris (4 weekly; 2hr). €25 one way, €30 open return.

Dalyan to: Bodrum (4 weekly; 1hr). €35 one way, €40 open return.

Datça to: Bodrum (2 daily; 2hr). Services arrive at and depart from Körmen Limanı, 9km north of Datça; shuttle bus included in price; 15YTL one way, 25YTL open return, 45YTL for a small car.

Ferries and hydrofoils to the Greek islands

Turkish vessels normally leave in the morning – usually between 8 and 9am – returning from Greece between 4.30 and 5.30pm, depending on the time of year; Greek craft arrive between 9 and 10am and return between 4 and 5pm. For a morning boat you must bring your passport to ticket agencies the evening before – or, failing that, at the crack of dawn – so that your name is recorded on a passenger manifest; for an afternoon boat it should be enough to hand over your papers two hours before sailing time. In high season the boats occasionally sell out a day in advance, and schedules are subject to alteration depending on demand and season.

Fares are overpriced for the distances involved (though there may be significant reductions in slow seasons). This is partly because Turkish ports demand departure and arrival taxes from passengers, while all Greek ports hit any passenger staying overnight with stiff departure taxes. The overnight prices do not include the cost of Turkish visas required by various nationalities. Taking a small car over on a ferry costs 60–120YTL one way depending on the port; combivans and other overland vehicles can cost almost double. Advance booking is essential, since the boats often hold only two or three vehicles. All the ferries below quote prices in euros, though you can pay in Turkish lira.

Bodrum–Kós Ferries (6–12 weekly, 1 or 2 weekly in midwinter; 45min; €23 day return); Hydrofoils (daily in summer; 20min; €33 day return).

Bodrum–Rhodes twice weekly in summer; 2 hr 15min; €45 one way, €50 open return including taxes.

Çeşme–Híos May–Oct 2–5 weekly; Nov–April 1 weekly; 1hr; €35 one way (no Turkish tax), €50 open return (the latter includes Greek tax).

Kuşadası–Sámos Ferries (twice daily May to late Oct, 1 weekly in midwinter; 1hr 30min); Hydrofoils (2–3 weekly; 45min). Both hydrofoils and ferries €25 one way, €55 open return (plus €14 Turkish tax, plus €19 if you stay overnight in Greece).

Marmaris–Rhodes Hydrofoils (twice daily May–Oct, 1 or 2 weekly in midwinter; 1hr 15min; €26 one-way (includes Turkish tax), open return €37 (plus €14 Turkish port tax and €19 Greek port tax); Car ferries (May–Oct weekly; 2hr; small car €180).

Ferries to Italy

Çeşme–Ancona mid-March to mid-Oct weekly, usually Wed; 65hr; €160 single (€30 port tax); small car €160 (€40 port tax).

Çeşme–Brindisi mid-June to mid-Sept 2 weekly; late June to mid-Sept 2 weekly on Med Link Lines; 31hr; one-way fares are €110 per passenger for a middling cabin, including taxes and meals, plus €145 for a small car.

Flights

Bodrum (Milas) to: İstanbul (summer 7–8 daily; winter 10 weekly); Antalya (1 daily).

Denizli (Çardak airport) to: İstanbul (1 daily).

İzmir to: Ankara (5 daily); Antalya (6 daily); Dalaman (1 weekly; 1hr); İstanbul (13 daily).

The Turquoise Coast

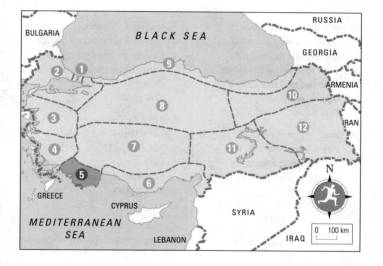

CHAPTER 5 # Highlights

✳ **Kaya Köyü** This abandoned Greek Orthodox village near Fethiye is a moving relic of the population exchange of 1923. See p.452

✳ **Paragliding at Ölüdeniz** A thrilling (if pricey) way of appreciating the stunning lagoon and beach. See p.456

✳ **The Lycian Way** The long-distance trail – passing spectacular coves, ruins and mountain wilderness – makes an ideal low-season activity. See p.458

✳ **Çıralı** Unspoilt nature-lovers' paradise with a turtle-nesting beach, an ancient city at the south end and the spectacular foothills of Tahtalı Dağ just inland. See p.517

✳ **Tlos** Perhaps the most dramatically sited of the numerous ancient cities of Lycia. See p.469

✳ **Patara** Ancient ruins enhanced by an enormous sandy beach, one of the longest in the Mediterranean. See p.479

✳ **Kaş** Opposite the Greek islet of Kastellórizo, this is one of the most congenial resorts on the coast, with some of the best scuba-diving in the Med. See p.488

✳ **Kekova** The eerie seascapes and submerged ruins of this inlet system make an ideal sea-kayaking venue. See p.499

△ Ruins at Tlos

The Turquoise Coast

urkey's southwesternmost shore is dominated by the Baba, Akdağ and Bey ranges of the Toros mountains, which drop precipitously to a road running mostly parallel to the sea, its curves sometimes skimming just above the water; this is the **Turquoise Coast**, noted for its fine beaches and beautiful scenery. Along here, and some distance inland, lay the ancient kingdom of **Lycia**, peopled by an independent race who bequeathed a legacy of distinctive rock tombs to Turkish tourism.

Until the late 1970s there was no continuous paved road through these parts, and most seaside settlements were reachable only by boat. Many of the most attractive bays and islands are still inaccessible to vehicles, with yachting and *gület* trips accordingly popular. But roads in the area have vastly improved since the late 1990s, penetrating to hitherto idyllic, isolated bays such as Kekova, Adrasan and Çıralı. However, there's a chance that the impact of large-scale development will be minimized by official decrees – certainly, the height of new buildings has been restricted, nearby archeological sites and wildlife habitats often prompt special protection measures, and touting in the streets and at *otogar*s is not yet at the level of Kuşadası, Selçuk or Pamukkale. And the increased overland accessibility is a blessing if you're reliant on public transport rather than a yacht.

The usually excellent **Highway 400** runs from Marmaris to Antalya, linking most of the major sights along the way, and offering occasional panoramic views. A bypass between Göcek and Kalkan has diverted traffic away from intervening villages and shaved the travel time between Fethiye and Patara to about an hour, while in the opposite direction a new tunnel being built between Göcek and Dalaman will knock another fifteen minutes off the journey time. The Turquoise Coast is best approached via **Dalaman airport**, to which there are regular direct international flights from April to November (and, occasionally, in winter), as well as domestic flights from İstanbul.

At the far west of the region, **Dalyan** is renowned for its sandy beach – a breeding ground of loggerhead turtles – and the nearby ruins of **Kaunos**, as well as being an attractive small resort in itself, though now – as throughout the region – sales of holiday homes are beginning to overtake conventional tourism as a money-spinner. East of here, **Fethiye** is the Turquoise Coast's most central resort and largest town; along with the nearby lagoon of **Ölüdeniz**, it's well placed for access to some of the best of the area's numerous and spectacularly sited Lycian ruins. **Oenoanda**, **Pınara**, **Tlos** and **Sidyma** lie close to Fethiye in dramatic mountainous locations, while further southeast **Patara** abuts one of Turkey's best beaches, making it easy to combine a sea-and-sun holiday with cultural forays to the **Letoön** sanctuary and **Xanthos**. Other convenient bases for outings are the resorts of **Kalkan** and **Kaş** to the east, both far smaller than Fethiye and pitched at slightly different clienteles.

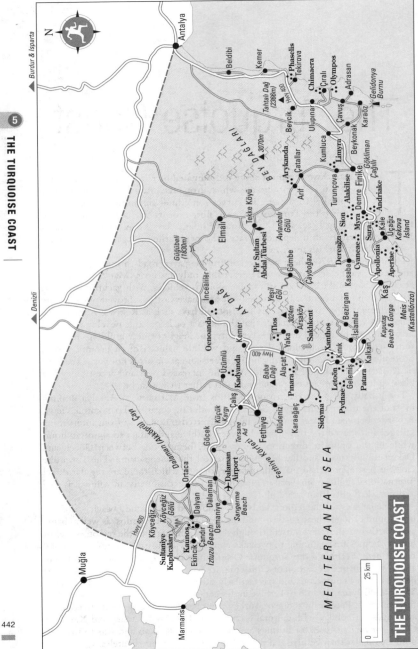

442

THE TURQUOISE COAST

MEDITERRANEAN SEA

| 0 | 25 km |

N

Burdur & Isparta

Denizli

Muğla

Marmaris

Antalya

Beldibi

Kemer

Phaselis

Tekirova

Chimaera

Çıralı

Olympos

Adrasan

Gelidonya Burnu

Tahtalı Dağ (2366m)

Hwy 400

Beycik

Ulupınar

Çavuş

Karaöz

3070m

Arykanda

Çatallar

Kumluca

Limyra

Beykonak

BEY DAĞLARI

Arif

Turunçova

Alakilise

Gökliman

Çağıllı

Andriake

Andriake

Tekke Köyü

Avlanbeli Gölü

Sion

Myra

Sura

Apollonia

Aperlae

Kale

Uçağız

Kekova Island

Elmalı

Pir Sultan Abdal Türbesi

Gömbe

Çayboğazı

Dereağzı

Cyaneae

Kasaba

Kaş

Gügübeli (1830m)

İncealiler

Yeşil Göl

3024m

Bezirgan

İslamlar

Meis (Kastellórizo)

AK DAĞ

Oenoanda

Kemer

Tlos

Yaka

Arsaköy

Saklıkent

Xanthos

Kalkan

Kaputaş Beach & Gorge

Üzümlü

Baba Dağı

Alagat

Kınık

Gelemiş

Patara

Dalaman (Akköprü) Çayı

Kadyanda

Çalış

Pınara

Letoön

Pydnae

Küçük Kargı

Göcek

Öludeniz

Karaağaç

Sidyma

Fethiye

Tersane Ad.

Fethiye Körfezi

Dalaman Airport

Dalaman

Ortaca

Sarıgerme Beach

Osmaniye

Dalyan

Köyceğiz

Köyceğiz Gölü

Sultaniye Kaplıcaları

Kaunos

Ekincik

Çandır

İztuzu Beach

Hwy 400

To the east, **Finike** is the next major town; although far less successful than Fethiye as a tourist centre, it still makes a good starting point for a precipitous inland route that takes in the sites of **Limyra** and **Arykanda** on the way up to the high plateau of **Elmalı**. The rarefied air and marvellous setting repay the trip, especially if a return loop to the coast is made via **Gömbe**, jumping-off point for the alpine attractions of **Akdağ**.

Beyond Finike, the scenery becomes increasingly spectacular as you enter a densely forested area on the slopes of **Tahtalı Dağ**, officially designated a national park, before passing the sites of ancient **Olympos** – set close to more good beaches at **Adrasan** and **Çıralı** – and ancient **Phaselis**. Thereafter, however, a string of functional (not to say dreary) purpose-built resorts dominated by German and Russian holiday-makers lines the approach to Antalya and the Mediterranean coast (see Chapter 6).

Some history

The mountainous, rugged territory of **Lycia** (Likya in Turkish) lies south of a line drawn roughly between Antalya and Köyceğiz Gölü. The peaks of the Bey Dağları and Akdağ, each exceeding 3000m in altitude, form the core of the region, and have always isolated it from the rest of Anatolia. Relatively secure in their mountain fastness, the Lycians – now thought to be an indigenous, pre-Hittite people rather than (as previous theories proposed) Cretan immigrants – hold a distinctive place in ancient Anatolian history. Their notoriously fierce desire for independence prompted the citizens of Xanthos on two separate occasions to make a funeral pyre of their own city and burn themselves alive, rather than be conquered. They also had their own language and customs; for example, Herodotus wrote that (unusually) "they reckon their lineage not by their father's but by their mother's side". The main ancient cities or conurbations of smaller towns organized themselves together against external authority as the **Lycian Federation**. This was a democratic grouping consisting of 23 voting units, charged with electing national officials and municipal authorities and, until control of Lycia was assumed by imperial Rome, making decisions of state. The Lycians are first mentioned in Homer's *Iliad*, in which they fought as allies of the Trojans. Later, in the sixth century BC, the region was subdued by the Persian general Harpagus, but was then largely left to govern itself.

From 454 BC, after the Athenian general Kimon had cleared all Persian garrisons from the Mediterranean coast, the Lycians became members of the Delian League, a maritime alliance that required them to pay tribute to Athens. The League ceased to exist after the Peloponnesian War ended in 404 BC and Lycia again fell under Persian domination, although this did not mean that it entirely accepted vassal status. Alexander the Great arrived in 333 BC and, after the conquest of Halicarnassus, secured the surrender of Lycia without further trouble; following his death Lycia was ruled by Alexander's general, Ptolemy, also king of Egypt. During **Ptolemaic rule** in the third century BC the native Lycian language was replaced by Greek and the cities adopted Greek constitutions. The Ptolemies were defeated by Antiochus III in 197 BC, who in turn was bested in 189 BC by the Romans, who handed the kingdom over to the Rhodians. The Lycians bitterly resented Rhodian control and succeeded in 167 BC in having this administrative relegation revoked.

Thereafter, the Lycians enjoyed over two centuries of semi-independence, during which time their Federation came back into prominence, resisting attack once again by the Pontic (Black Sea) king Mithridates in 88 BC and being subsequently rewarded by Rome for their loyalty. During the Roman civil wars, Lycian reluctance to assist Brutus led to the destruction of Xanthos, and although Antony later reconfirmed the autonomy of Lycia, in 43 AD the region was joined to Pamphylia in a larger Roman province. **Roman imperial rule** was not unduly harsh. Indeed, the area reached its maximum ancient population of about 200,000, a figure not again equalled until the twentieth century, and the cities were graced by the Roman civic architecture that constitutes most of the ruins on view today.

During the fourth century the province was divided by Diocletian and a period of Byzantine-supervised decline set in, a process helped along by Arab raids in the seventh and eighth centuries. From this point on, the history of the region resembled that of the rest of western Anatolia, where, after the establishment of Selçuk Turk sovereignty during the eleventh and twelfth centuries, and an interlude of minor emirates, a more durable Anatolian Muslim state was installed by the **Ottomans**. They continued a pattern of moving nomadic Turkic tribes into the Lycian uplands, leaving the coast to pirates and local chieftains, until in the eighteenth century the sultan ordered its settlement by more tractable, productive Greek Orthodox colonists from the offshore islands.

Fethiye

FETHIYE is the inevitable fulcrum of the Turquoise Coast, and a hub of its burgeoning real-estate industry, though it remains a lively, Turkish market town of nearly 60,000; in contrast to nearby Kaş, Fethiye has been able to spread north along the coastal plain here. The transport and marketing of oranges and tomatoes is almost on an equal footing with tourism, though chromium ore – a major Fethiye-hinterland product – is no longer shipped from here but from nearby Göçek. Fethiye occupies the site of the ancient Lycian city of **Telmessos**, and some impressive rock-tombs are an easy stroll from the centre, itself enlivened by a Hellenistic theatre.

Fethiye also makes a convenient base for the nearby beaches at Çalış, Ölüdeniz and Kıdrak, while a short drive or long walk out of Fethiye brings you to the ghost village of Kaya Köyü. There's also a good supply of rugged local coastline accessible by boat; the **Gulf of Fethiye** is speckled with twelve islands, and a favourite strategy is to embark on a one-to-four-day boat tour from Fethiye harbour, in search of secluded coves in which to swim, fish and anchor for the night.

Some history

Nothing much is known of the **origins of Telmessos**, except that it wasn't originally part of the Lycian Federation; indeed, in the fourth century BC the Telmessans actually fought against the Lycians. It may be that Pericles, a Lycian dynast, subsequently subdued the Telmessans and allowed them into the Federation – Lycian inscriptions have been found in the city, and it is known that during the Roman imperial era the city was part of the Federation, if unique in having good relations with Rhodes.

Like most Lycian cities, Telmessos was captured by Alexander in 334–333 BC, but lost not long after. The city was recaptured by one of Alexander's companions by a famous ruse: Nearkhos the Cretan asked permission to leave a number of captive women musicians and boys in Telmessos, but the women concealed weapons in their musical-instrument cases, and the prisoners' escort used them to seize the acropolis. In the eighth century, the city's name was changed to **Anastasiopolis** in honour of a Byzantine emperor. This name gave way to **Makri** in the following century (Meğri in Turkish), and – after the expulsion of the predominantly Greek Orthodox population – became Fethiye during the 1930s, in honour of a local

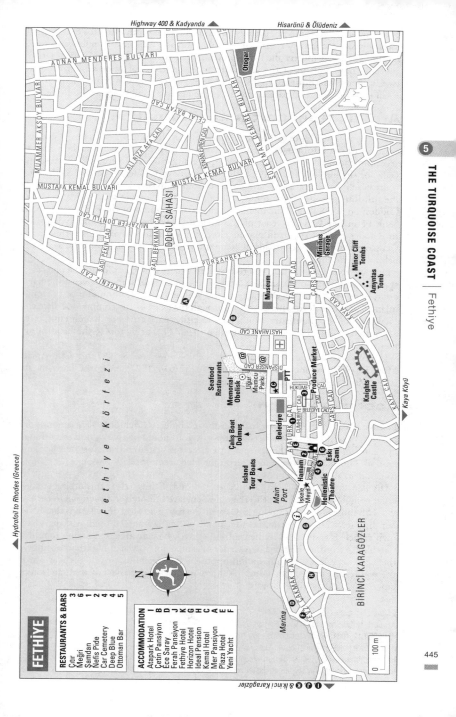

▲ *Highway 400 & Kadyanda*   ▲ *Hisarönü & Ölüdeniz*

▲ *Hydrofoil to Rhodes (Greece)*

F e t h i y e   K ö r f e z i

FETHİYE

RESTAURANTS & BARS

Çıtır	3
Meğri	6
Şamdan	1
Nefis Pide	2
Car Cemetery	4
Deep Blue	4
Ottoman Bar	5

ACCOMMODATION

Atapark Hotel	I
Çetin Pansiyon	B
Ece Saray	D
Ferah Pansiyon	J
Fethiye Hotel	K
Horizon Hotel	G
Ideal Pension	H
Kemal Hotel	C
Mer Pansiyon	A
Plaza Hotel	E
Yeni Yacht	F

N

0   100 m

BİRİNCİ KARAGÖZLER

Marina

Main Port

Island Tour Boats ▲

Çalış Boat Dolmuş ▲

Seafood Restaurants

Memorial Obelisk

Uğur Mumcu Parkı

İskele Meyd.

Hellenistic Theatre

Hamam

Eski Cami

Produce Market

Belediye

PTT

HÜKÜMET

Knights' Castle

Museum

Minibus Garage

Minor Cliff Tombs

Amyntas Tomb

DOLGU SAHASI

ADNAN MENDERES BULVARI

MUAMMER AKSOY BULVARI

ALİ RIZA AKA CAD

MUSTAFA KEMAL BULVARI

CELAL BAYAR CAD

SÜLEYMAN DEMİREL BULVARI

KENAN EVREN CAD

MUSTAFA KEMAL BULVAR

MUZAFFER DONTUL CAD

SADİ PEKİN CAD

SADİ BEKMAN CAD

AKDENİZ CAD

PÜRSAHBEY CAD

HASTAHANE CAD

DİSPANSER CAD

ATATÜRK CAD

CUMHURİYET CAD

BELEDİYE CAD

OKUL CAD

ÇARŞI CAD

ÇARŞI CAD

KAYA CAD

KAYA CAD

ATATÜRK CAD

▲ **①, ⑨, ⓚ & İkinci Karagözler**

▶ *Kaya Köyü*

pilot and war hero named **Fethi Bey**. Uniquely on the south Turkish coast, a small local Jewish community remained here undisturbed well into Republican times, though they had mostly died out or emigrated to Israel by the 1950s. Hardly anything now remains of the ancient or medieval city, partly because it suffered two immense **earthquakes** in 1857 and 1957, which toppled much of the town – whose rubble lies compacted under the present quay and shoreline boulevard.

Arrival, transport and information

The **otogar** is over 2km east of the town centre at the junction with the Ölüdeniz road. Short-haul **dolmuşes** run almost constantly from here as far as the popular accommodation district of Karagözler, sparing you the three-kilometre-plus walk, or shelling out for a taxi. Other dolmuşes to Ölüdeniz, Göcek, Saklıkent, Çalış beach and Kaya arrive at and leave from underneath wooden marquees at the **minibus garage**, about 500m east of the central market area, south of Çarşı Caddesi on 136 Sokağı. The main **taxi ranks** are found near the PTT, and beside Şehit Fethi Bey Parkı, in front of the ancient amphitheatre. Seasonal **hydrofoils** to Rhodes dock at the main marina jetty, while **dolmuş boats** link Fethiye and Çalış regularly in season (daily 9.30am–midnight), departing from the seafront behind the *Belediye*.

Driving your own vehicle, you're forced to adhere to what is in effect a one-way system: westbound on **Atatürk Caddesi**, the main road leading toward the harbour, lined with most services and official buildings, and eastbound mostly along inland **Çarşı Caddesi**, which threads through the heart of the commercial district. **Parking** can be a nightmare: you'll have to either park out near the museum, buy a windscreen chit from a parking warden (3–4YTL), or patronize the handful of fee-paying *otopark*s.

There's a **tourist office** (May–Sept daily 8am–noon & 1–7pm; Oct–April Mon–Fri 8.30am–noon & 1–5.30pm; ☎0252/614 1527), near the harbour at İskele Meydanı 1, though it is pretty useless.

Accommodation

Fethiye has a range of lodging for all tastes and budgets, including a fair amount of business hotels. Unlike other coastal resorts, you should be able to find something even in high summer, though perhaps after considerable trudging or phoning around. Unless otherwise stated, recommended accommodation is open (or claims to be open) all year round.

Divided into Birinci (First) and İkinci (Second) **Karagözler**, this desirable and quiet neighbourhood is home to the oldest enclave of hotels and *pansiyon*s in Fethiye, with most premises enjoying a view of the bay. The only drawback is that it's a fair distance west of the transport terminals and restaurants, though parking your own vehicle is easier than in the centre. Fethiye's **bazaar area**, extending roughly two blocks to either side of Çarşı Caddesi, can be noisy even at night; accordingly there are very few accommodation options left hereabouts. A few paces toward the **water**, and then north along the shoreline of **Dolgu Sahası** district, are some quieter, more expensive choices.

Karagözler

Atapark Hotel Shore road, İkinci Karagözler ☎0252/612 4081, @www.atahotels.com. The second best hotel in town after the *Ece Saray*, with hamam, fitness centre, restaurant, small pool and Internet café, though only the larger, pastel-coloured sea-view rooms are worth the money. **⑥**

Ece Saray Marina quay, Birinci Karagözler ☎0252/612 5005, @www.ecesaray.net. Indisputably the top lodging in central Fethiye, this mock-traditional low-rise hotel occupies impeccably landscaped grounds in a quiet corner of the shore esplanade. The plush rooms all enjoy a sea view, and common facilities include a spa, fitness centre, infinity pool, two bar/restaurants and of course the private marina. Good value for the facilities on offer. ⑧

Ferah Pansiyon (Monica's Place) Ordu Cad 21, İkinci Karagözler ℡0252/614 2816, ⒲www .ferahpension.com. Part of a chain of Turkish backpackers' hostels, with dorm beds (€5) or basic doubles and triples, pick-up service from the *otogar*s, Internet access, and optional evening meals. There's a sea view, despite its location one block inland. ②

Fethiye Hotel Ordu Cad 16, İkinci Karagözler ℡0252/614 6813, ⒡614 3663. Fairly comfortable, small hotel with bay views and a large pool-garden, though it's dominated by tour companies most seasons. ④

Horizon Hotel On the back road to Kaya, Birinci Karagözler ℡0252/612 3153, ⒡612 3154. Small, slightly odd hotel (there are portholes instead of windows in the rooms), but well renovated in marble and pastel trim, with TV and a/c fitted throughout. A small pool and rooftop bar-restaurant clinch the deal. ④

Ideal Pension Zafer Cad 1, Birinci Karagözler ℡0252/614 1981, ⒲www.idealpension.net. A fairly quiet, well-sited budget outfit, whose small, basic en-suite rooms have carpets and balconies, and double beds for couples. A roof terrace serves Western-style breakfasts (charged extra), and there's an on-site laundry and Internet access, plus friendly family management. ②

Yeni Yacht (Yacht Plaza) Hotel Opposite the yacht marina, Birinci Karagözler ℡0252/612 5067, ⒲www.yachtplazahotel.com. Aspires like its grander neighbour the *Ece Saray* to be a self-contained seaside resort, with private jetty, lush bay-side breakfast garden and fair-sized pool. Rooms are plainer than the common areas, but perfectly serviceable. ⑤

The bazaar and waterfront

Çetin Pansiyon 510 Sokağı, Dolgu Sahası ℡0252/614 6156, ⒡614 7794. Oblique sea views and a ground-floor terrace-bar at this welcoming *pansiyon*, run by brothers Şaban and Ramazan, more or less opposite the DSİ (Water Board) building. Rooms without breakfast or a/c are cheaper. ②

Kemal Hotel Behind the PTT ℡0252/614 5010, ⒲www.hotelkemal.com. Cheerful, air-conditioned rooms, many with sea views; doubles are small but balconied, suites larger but balcony-less. That said, its main virtue is a convenient and fairly quiet location. ④

Mer Pansiyon Akdeniz Cad, Dolgu Sahası ℡0252/614 1177, ⒲www.merpansiyon.com. Welcoming, German-Turkish-run outfit with pleasant breakfast salon and carpeted a/c rooms, the front ones with sea-view balcony. They also have a large apartment to rent on Şövalye Adası. ③

Plaza Hotel Corner Atatürk Cad and Çarşı Cad ℡0252/614 9030, ⒡614 1070. A good fallback hotel, amenable to bargaining at slow times. The roof/breakfast terrace is the high point here; double-glazed rooms are on the small side (except the "suites", really quads), and few have balconies, though all have a/c, TV, phones. Parking is at the municipal lot opposite. ③

The Town

The remains of ancient **Telmessos** are obvious as soon as you arrive in Fethiye. Covering the hillside above the bazaar area are a number of Lycian rock tombs, striking in their proximity to the city and in the grandeur of their setting. Most notable – and worth a closer inspection, despite swarms of children who will offer to guide you there unnecessarily and then demand money – is the **Amyntas Tomb** (daily 8.30am–sunset; 4YTL), so called because of the inscription *Amyntou tou Ermagiou* (Amyntas son of Hermagios) carved in Greek letters on the wall of the tomb. To get there, take any of the lanes leading south from Kaya Caddesi (cars can make it up), which give onto 115 Sokağı running along the base of the fenced-in archeological area. The tomb porch consists of two Ionic columns surmounted by a triangular pediment, carved in close imitation of a temple facade – even down to simulating the bronze nails with which the door frames were studded – giving an excellent impression of what the original wooden temple porches would have looked like. The tomb would have been entered through the bottom right-hand panel of the doorway, but this was broken by grave robbers long ago.

Behind the tourist office and main quay sprawls the conspicuous Hellenistic **theatre**, excavated only since 1994. Much of its masonry was carted away after the

1957 earthquake for construction material, so it's rather frayed at the edges. Benefit concerts are sometimes staged here in season to help raise funds for a complete restoration of the stage building and seating, though the process is completely stalled at present.

There's not all that much else to see in Fethiye, although you can visit the remains of the medieval fortress, the so-called **Knight's Castle**, on the hillside behind the harbour area. The path to the castle leads off Çarşı Caddesi through backstreets up to the acropolis, affording good views of the town on the way. The fortress is attributed to the Knights of St John, but a variety of architectural styles suggests additional work on the part of Lycians, Greeks, Romans, Byzantines and Turks. The Gypsy shantytown formerly built around the walls has been cleared to make way for a future park, whilst the walls themselves will be restored if an EU grant materializes.

Tucked away inconspicuously amongst various schools, Fethiye's **museum** (Tues–Sun 8.30am–5pm; 2YTL) is poorly labelled, dark and small, but worth a visit for its troves of coins, jewellery, statue fragments and pottery. Its most compelling exhibit is a stele found at the Letoön (see p.475), dating from 358 BC, which was critically important in deciphering the Lycian language. This stone slab is covered in a trilingual text in Lycian, Greek and Aramaic concerning a sanctuary in Xanthos dedicated to the mythical god-king, Kaunos, supposed founder of the eponymous city. There's also the "Stele of Promise", an example of a custom particular to northern Lycia, a votive offering to the god Kakasbos. Highlight of the small ethnographic section is a nineteenth-century Greek carved door.

Finally, another huge stele – or rather nocturnally illuminated **obelisk** – of a different sort dominates waterfront Uğur Mumcu Parkı. A pet project of the MHP (Nationalist)-run municipality, it was erected in 2001 to honour locals killed during the long-running PKK insurrection. Local outcry converted it to a general servicemen's memorial for all recent conflicts.

Boat tours and cruises

The standard-issue, multi-island, one-day **boat tours** cost about €14 a head. Just turn up at the quayside for daily departures between May and October, usually leaving at around 10am and returning at 6pm. However, these one-day trips tend to be rushed, taking in a set repertoire of relatively spoilt islands, with little time at each. It's far better to charter your own boat and crew to take in just one or two selected islands. If you've more time, sign on for one of the **cabin cruises** which depart at least five times a week in season. Four-night, three-day itineraries head either west to Marmaris via Göcek and Ekincik (less popular but more scenic), or more commonly four-day cruises run east, with overnights near or at Gemile Adası, Kalkan and Kekova before a final minibus shuttle from Demre to the treehouse lodges at Olympos (see p.514): allow €120–150 per person, including full board and drink (excluding alcohol). Paying over €140, and boarding only owner-operated craft, is recommended to ensure quality; also make sure you check the craft carefully before handing over your cash, and talk to returning clients – complaints about everything from blocked toilets to abusive crew to hidden extra charges are common. Two Fethiye **outfitters** which have generated positive feedback are Big Backpackers (☎0252/614 1981 or 0532/235 2978, ⓦwww.bigbackpackers. com) and the well-established, Australian/Turkish-run Before Lunch (formerly Almila; ☎0252/614 0052 or 0535/636 0076, ⓦwww.beforelunch.com), which runs six- and nine-cabin boats and is noted for its good meals.

Scuba diving at Fethiye

After years of over-hyping, when fourteen dive schools competed here, just a handful of bona fide **scuba-diving operators** remain in Fethiye. Despite their optimistic brochure promotion, there are few if any fish to be found in local waters; ruthless over-fishing with dynamite and drag-nets has seen to that. What the gulf *can* offer is reasonable visibility, coral and other invertebrates, walls and rock formations, and submerged ruins, artefacts and caves. Two outfits to try are Dolphin Diving Centre, whose boat is moored on the quay behind the post office (℡0535/717 3130), or the nearby Diver's Delight, Dispanser Sok 25, Cumhuriyet Mahallesi, near the memorial obelisk (℡0252/612 1099, ⓦwww.diversdelight.com). Prices for trips and courses are usually quoted in sterling, with two-dive day rates starting at £39, while PADI five-day courses cost £235, and CMAS two-star certification £230.

Eating and drinking

The best option for eating in Fethiye is to head for the spruced-up central courtyard of the **fish and produce market**, and buy the fish of your choice (best selection before 7pm) from the central stalls, then take it to be cooked at one of several *meyhane*s around the perimeter (€2.50 fee): ⚘ *Çıtır* at the northeast corner is competent and savoury, with a good range of *mezes*, and your total outlay (including fish, cooking fee with a modest intake of beer) shouldn't exceed 17YTL a head. The market square is a lovely, traffic-free environment with views up to the castle, but if you want to eat fish by the sea, the only option is a row of seafood **restaurants** behind Uğur Mumcu Parkı, though they aren't nearly as good value as the central market. Alternatively, the long-running doyene of local eateries, *Meğri*, just off Çarşı Cad 23/A (supposedly 24-hour), is acceptable for home-style Turkish dishes and puddings, though avoid its blatantly touristy and overpriced annexe at Likya Sok 8–9. Less expensive, alcohol-free meals can be had at *Şamdan*, Tütün Sok 3, with a good range of grills, *hazır yemek* and puddings (closes by 8pm), or at the ever-popular *Nefis Pide* at Eski Cami Sok 9, which also serves a range of excellent kebabs and meat dishes at indoor/outdoor tables.

Most of Fethiye's **drinking venues** are in the old bazaar. A well-established favourite is *Car Cemetery Bar* at the south end of Hamam Sokağı, with the almost adjacent *Deep Blue* getting good marks for conviviality and staying open until 3am. Nearby on Karagözler Sokağı, the *Ottoman Bar* offer *nargile*s as well as drinks and dancing.

Listings

Airline THY is represented centrally by Fetur, Atatürk Cad 72 ℡0252/614 2443; the service bus to Dalaman airport for THY flights costs 15YTL.
Banks and exchange Beware souvenir shops and storefronts that promise cash advances on credit cards – short-changing is common. Stick to authorized venues, such as the PTT, banks and *döviz* dealers, most of which are near the market square, including Dikmen at Atatürk Cad, Belediye İşhanı 21. ATMs cluster within a few yards of each other at the west end of Atatürk Cad.
Books Imagine, Atatürk Cad 18/B, has a very limited stock of new tourism-related titles; there's also a secondhand stall opposite the mooring of the *Sufi*

boat, near the *Belediye*.
Car rental Hi-Car, at the yacht marina ℡0252/614 7434; Oscar, Dispanser Sok 23 ℡0252/612 7778, ⓦwww.oscarrentacar.com; Sixt, Hillside Club Resort ℡0252/614 7593; Telmessos, Dispanser Sok 24/A ℡0252/614 6223, ⓦwww.telmessos .com.
Hamam At Hamam Sok 2 (daily 7am–midnight; 15YTL); usually lukewarm and touristy, this is not a particularly good introduction to Turkish baths.
Hydrofoil From May to October, hydrofoils run almost daily directly to Rhodes in Greece (journey time 1hr 30min); current price about €65 return. For exact schedules see "Travel details" at the end

of the chapter, and contact designated agent Yeşil Dalyan (see below).

Internet The most central Internet cafés are Millennium, on 503 Sok, and the nearby Line Bilgisayar, on 500 Sok.

Motorbike rental Abalı, just behind the theatre roundabout ☎0252/612 8812; Toros at the marina ☎0252/614 1648.

Post office Main PTT is on Atatürk Cad (Mon–Sat 8am–midnight, Sun 9am–7pm).

Shopping Fethiye has the above-cited food market located between Cumhuriyet Cad and Tütün Sok in the centre of town – adjacent is a district with plenty of fake designer clothes, perfume and badly cured leather; fake or adulterated saffron and honey (plus the odd pickpocket) abound too. Repu-

table honey is available at Fen İş Bal Evi, Çarşı Cad 150/A. Main market day is Tuesday, when villagers from surrounding districts flood into town with their produce; peak hours 10.30am–1pm. The place to hunt for carpets, leather and silver is Paspatur district, especially to either side of Hamam Sokağı. Supermarket chains Tansaş and Migros have small branches just inland from Atatürk Caddesi, near the PTT; there's a larger Migros at the outskirts.

Travel agents Lama Tours by the hamam (☎0252 614 4964), and Labranda Tourism, Atatürk Cad 78/2 (☎0252/612 0323), handle tickets for all airlines; Yeşil Dalyan at Fevzi Çakmak Cad 168 opposite the main jetty (☎0252/612 4015), is the sole outlet for hydrofoil tickets to Rhodes.

Around Fethiye

Easily reached on a day-trip from town are a variety of attractions: an ancient Lycian city (**Kadyanda**) in a spectacularly remote setting, the huge abandoned village of **Kaya Köyü**, and a handful of popular if variable beaches, ranging from long **Çalış** to tiny **Gemiler**. Most of these sites are well connected by public transport in season, and a few can even be reached on foot from Fethiye.

Kadyanda

Under an hour's drive north of Fethiye, the ruined mountain-top city of **Kadyanda** dates back at least 2500 years, but has only seen tourists for the last decade or so. It's accessible on a broad, well-marked road from a roundabout on the bypass highway, northeast of Fethiye, and the initial, paved 16km to **ÜZÜMLÜ** village (served by sparse public transport) are quickly covered. This attractive village has so far made little of its proximity to the ruins, other than an acceptable **restaurant** opposite the mosque and a low-key trade in its fine cloth goods known as *dastar*. At the crossroads here, turn left at the usual black-on-yellow sign, then proceed 3.5km more on a narrow paved road to just beyond the summit of a pass with a view of Akdağ. Now bear right, following another "Kadyanda" sign, to negotiate well over 5km of widened, improved dirt track to a small car park in the pines below the site. With local assistance you might be able to find the old direct **path from Üzümlü** (1hr-plus), which shortcuts all but the last 2km of the road and goes via some little-visited rock tombs.

At **the site** (unfenced, always open; 4YTL if warden present), an arrow points you to the start of a self-guided tour along a graded loop path. First you bear south, past numerous vaulted tombs of the **necropolis**, then close to presumed bits of the **city wall** on the left, followed by a climb to a false summit with a long, partly preserved **agora**, and the first views of Fethiye. At the true top of things, matters fall into place with the highlight of the site: a long, narrow **stadium**, with seven rows of its seats surviving. Steps in the seats lead up to a huge jumble of masonry, all that's left of a **temple** to an unknown deity. On the opposite side of the stadium stand the substantial **Roman baths**, with their polygonal masonry and entry archway. At the northeast edge of the stadium, a flat expanse is pierced by the mouth of a deep cistern that supplied the city with rainwater – one of many, so beware holes in the ground.

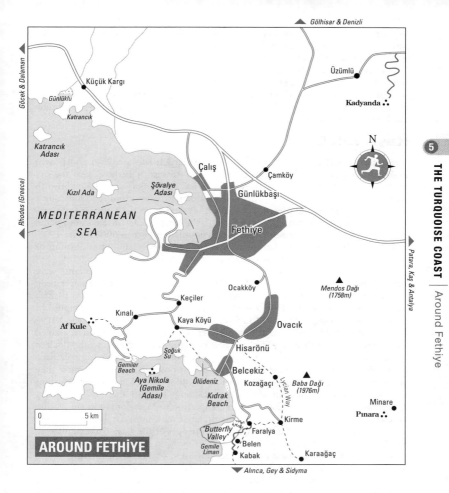

Finally the path angles south to the best-preserved stretch of **city wall**, punctuated by windows and affording incomparable views of the ridges on the horizon and the forested valleys in between. Crossing the top of a square bastion, you look down into the **theatre**, which retains its rear facing and stage wall (doubling as part of the city fortification), plus many of its seats – though like most of the site it's only partly excavated. The descent to the road completes a leisurely 45-minute walk through superb mountain scenery – good reason alone for a visit.

Çalış beach

If you're here specifically for a beach holiday, **Çalış**, some 5km north of central Fethiye, might do the trick. There's a direct road there from town along the coast, as well as boat dolmuşes, though ordinary dolmuşes arrive there in a roundabout way from the main highway via Günlükbaşı suburb. Their final stop is way at the north end of the resort, near the *Seril* hotel; the Çalış esplanade itself is off-limits for cars. Çalış's gravelly sand extends for 2km, with views over the bay islets to the sunset, but it's prone to pummelling in summer from wind and waves, making the water very murky if not downright filthy.

Çalış itself is essentially a tourist ghetto of leather shops, mini-markets, mediocre restaurants and downmarket hotels, overrun in season by a somewhat elderly British and Dutch clientele, who subsequently return in large numbers to buy retirement homes here. The navigable channels and marshes just inland are picturesque but breed swarms of mosquitoes.

Kaya Köyü

The deserted settlement of **KAYA KÖYÜ**, the largest late-medieval ghost town in Asia Minor, is located on the side of a hill southwest of Fethiye, near the site of ancient Karmylassos. It was known as **Levissi** (or Livissi) after the eighteenth century, when it was settled by Greek Orthodox Christians from the Dodecanese islands just offshore; the present appellation is taken from the rather inappropriately named Kaya Çukuru or "Stone Gulch", the small but fertile adjacent upland (altitude 200m) that partly supported a local population of over 6000 before 1923, and still produces substantial crops of tobacco and grain – and, after autumn or spring rainstorms, spectacular mass migrations of toads.

The place has been abandoned since then, when its Christian inhabitants were exiled, along with more than a million others, to a country that had never been their homeland. Kaya is one of the most dramatic and moving sites on the Turkish coast, putting into painful relief the human suffering involved in the compulsory **population exchange** (see p.951 in Contexts). Despite the horrors of the 1919–1922 Greco–Turkish war, relations between Christian and Muslim remained good hereabouts, with local "Turks" accompanying the "Greeks" to the dock at Fethiye to bid them farewell. Tales still circulate of the Greeks having entrusted their neighbours with treasure chests against their possible return; of course they never did come back, but the caskets remain unopened. Macedonian Muslims were sent here to occupy the abandoned buildings but, for the most part, they didn't stay, considering the land poor in comparison to Macedonia and emigrating instead to points as far-flung as Australia. In any event, most locals currently live in the hamlets of Keçiler and Kınalı, at the far fringes of the Kaya Çukuru plateau, overlooked by the ruins.

All you can see now of Kaya is a hillside (admission 4YTL, when entrance booths staffed) covered with almost a thousand ruined dwellings – all of them with fireplaces and cisterns more or less intact – and the attractive **Panayia Pyrgiotissa** basilica (or Kato Panayia), the most important of three churches here, to the right of the main path, about 200m up the gentle slope from the road. The church, dated 1888 by a floor mosaic, retains some of its marble altar screen and murals, including faces of Christ and the apostles over the altar, but the general state of dereliction merely serves to highlight the plight of the village. A particularly grisly item in the southwest corner of the church precinct is the **charnel house**, piled high with human leg bones; the departing Greeks took the exhumed skulls of their ancestors away with them.

As with most other remote, abandoned Greek villages, proper title deeds for individual Kaya properties were never issued by the Republican Turkish government. In 1988, mass acquisition of the village houses for package-holiday accommodation was threatened, though development plans have been withdrawn and a preservation order slapped on the valley to protect it. Nowadays, only five percent of agricultural land area may be built on and only archeologically approved restoration – including, potentially, the two largest churches – is allowed. The old village remains the focus of Greco–Turkish **reconciliation festivals**, with its Greek diaspora visiting regularly from Greece; Orthodox Patriarch Vartholomeos himself stayed here at the start of the new millennium. The place has again been in the spotlight since Louise de Bernières disguised it as Eskibahçe, the setting for most of his 2003 epic *Birds Without Wings* (see "Books", p.1043).

Practicalities

A paved nine-kilometre road – plus a cobbled **path**, still two-thirds intact, which significantly shortcuts it – climb up from behind the castle in Fethiye towards Kaya Köyü (about two hours' walk). By **dolmuş** from the main terminal, however, it's a fifteen-kilometre journey, taking a roundabout route via the twin resorts of Ovacık and Hisarönü, whose tendrils end around 4km east of the village. You can easily continue on foot **from Kaya Köyü to Ölüdeniz**; see the box on p.457 for directions.

There are a number of **accommodation** choices at the edge of the village or slightly beyond. Cheapest is the simple *Selçuk* (☎0252/618 0075; ❷), south of the mini-roundabout beside the central teahouse. Some 500m along the road to Kınalı, in lovely grassy grounds, you'll find *Villa Rhapsody* (☎0252/618 0042 or 618 0049, Ⓦwww.villarhapsody.com; closed Dec–April; ❸), whose stark rooms of varying sizes are softened by pale carpets. There's also English-speaking management, and a bar-restaurant around the large pool. In Kınalı hamlet, 2km west of Kaya Köyü, the best of several local restoration projects can booked through

△ The abandoned village of Kaya Köyü

Tapestry Holidays (see p.32): accommodation is in six old houses which have been exquisitely refurbished with many original features preserved. Alternatively, on the north slope of the valley in the hamlet of Keçiler stand four high-standard two-bedroom villas arrayed around a figure-eight-shaped pool. Run by Bridget and Tim Ives (℡0252/618 0157, ⓦwww.turkeyvillas.com), the villas cost £500–700 a week each, and the Ives provide all assistance necessary in arranging flights and other logistics.

Central Kaya has about a dozen **cafés** and simple **restaurants**, many strategically straddling the paths into the ruined town, but few are particularly memorable. *Bülent'in Yeri*, on the through-road near the colonnaded cistern, is fine for a quick snack of fair-priced *saç böreği*. For a superlative, not-for-the-squeamish carniverous feed (plus limited *mezes*), head for ⚡ *Cin Bal*, well-signposted at the eastern edge of the village, where whole hung sheep form much of the indoor decor; summer seating is in the attractive outdoor garden, while the huge winter hall – often packed with locals – is kept cosy by the fact that each table has its own grill-fire-place. This is a *kendin pişin kendin ye* place, where you buy superb lamb by the kilo and then cook it yourself at a tableside barbeque. Good *mezes*, vegetable garnish and reasonably priced drink complete the experience. Incidentally, the name ("Honey Gin") comes from the late founder's variety of bootleg hooch.

Af Kule, Gemiler and Aya Nikola

About 1km beyond Kınalı, there's a turning west for the isolated ruined monastery of **Af Kule**; the sign says "800m" but it's more like 1km to the road's end, where you bear up and right onto the broad, obvious donkey-track. Alternating blue-paint arrows and red dots encourage you on the climb west–northwest until you top a ridge, 25 minutes from the Gemiler-bound road, and then plunge down five minutes more in zigzags to the roofless but otherwise intact monastery on its terrace, overawed by a cliff. Wedged into this are a couple of chapels; stone steps lead to the higher hermitage which, though now without any frescoes, is well worth the ascent.

Isolated **Gemiler** beach lies 8km southwest of Kaya Köyü along a well-marked gravel-stabilized track, not served by any public transport. Despite what you may read elsewhere, it is not possible to walk directly from Kaya to Gemiler – the intervening terrain is steep and dangerous. Instead, you first proceed past Kınalı, and then use the paint-blob-marked trail down from the top of the gully, 200m past the point where the road starts its descent.

Gemiler's only amenities are half a dozen semi-legal **snack-shacks** – none of them up to more than *gözleme* and soft drinks, except the far left one as you face the sea, which does overpriced fish and salads. The beach itself (not always clean) is divided up by small jetties and sun-bed concessions (you pay 2YTL to park as well); the water offshore can be murky, but offers decent snorkelling in autumn, and is popular with local kayakers.

Just offshore at Gemiler looms a prime destination of local boat trips: **Aya Nikola (Gemile) Adası** (admission 4YTL, if warden present), an island and yacht anchorage on which stand prominent remains of several eras, including a few rock tombs, a seventh-century Byzantine monastery and a later, ruined hamlet complete with a nineteenth-century church. The island's environs, along with Ölüdeniz, were used in the late 1990s as the location for a satellite-TV-movie version of *The Odyssey*, starring Greta Scacchi. Without a boat, all you can do is walk from Kaya Köyü to the bay of Soğuk Su directly opposite Gemile island, over the obvious saddle with the little white chapel, in about forty minutes – see p.457 for more walk directions.

Ocakköy, Ovacık and Hisarönü

More or less due south of Fethiye are a string of resorts that, despite inland settings, now get the lion's share of tourist overnights in the Fethiye area. **Ocakköy** has some claim to architectural distinction, but **Ovacık** and **Hisarönü** are functional dormitories at best, with water in this arid environment pumped up a pipeline from the plain around Fethiye.

Ocakköy

The main road southeast out of Fethiye climbs to a pass, where a signposted dirt-track leads 2km west to an abandoned Ottoman shepherd's hamlet, **OCAKKÖY**, which served as the winter quarters for the village of Ovacık (see below). The ex-hamlet has metamorphosed into ⚐ *Ocakköy* (☏0252/616 6157, ⓦwww.ocak-koey.de), a development of some thirty individually styled, self-catering, restored stone cottages dotting the hillside, plus more conventional rooms or apartments set around three swimming pools (two reserved for adults only). The cottages enjoy commanding views over the agricultural plain to Baba Dağı, the ancient Mount Antikragos, and make for a wonderfully peaceful stay, aside from the occasional disco-thump from Hisarönü. This is one of the few resorts in Turkey that actively caters for disabled clients, with wheelchair ramps and harness slings for lowering yourself into one of the pools, and it's also good for kids, as there's a crèche and designated family pool. Most units are available exclusively through Tapestry Holidays (see p.32) from early May to late October, though for the rest of the year you can secure a cottage on a self-catering basis (❹), as there's no bar or restaurant service in winter; heat is provided by the working fireplaces.

Ovacık and Hisarönü

Just beyond the pass, the straggly, linear village of **OVACİK** seems to consist entirely of estate agencies, villas and about a hundred *pansiyon*s and small hotels that have been largely snapped up by tour operators – surprisingly, in view of its inland, roadside location and the decidedly modest endowments of many of these establishments. Folk tend more to stay in Ovacık and do their partying in **HISARÖNÜ**, which (with fifty or so more lodgings) nominally lies 1.5km along the side road to Kaya and Gemiler. Once a tiny hamlet, it has spread to be almost contiguous with Ovacık and now offers all the dubious delights of a landlocked concrete resort: pulsing sound-systems, lanes pedestrianized by night, and a remarkable number of walk-in, 24-hour clinics with English-speaking staff for attending to those afflicted by "Turkey tummy" or who fell asleep drunk in the sun.

Some of the highest standard **accommodation** here, well south of the "seething" zone and thus calm, is at the four-star *Montana Pine Resort* (☏0252/616 7108, ⓦwww.montanapine.com; ❺; closed Nov–March). It's a sympathetically designed complex, with large rooms and good bathrooms (though the bedroom fittings are showing their age), one of the best breakfasts on the Turquoise Coast and no fewer than three pools. Just about the southernmost building here – catering to a vastly different market – is the *Sultan Motel* (☏ & ⓕ0252/616 6261; ❸), built right at the start of the Lycian Way (see box, p.458) and acting as a **lodge** for trekkers at the start or end of their journey; the spartan, balconied cottages just uphill from a large pool vary considerably in decor and are arranged as twin, triple or dorms.

Given the quick-buck nature of the place, few **restaurants** stay in business more than a season, and the general profile is of bad, identikit places serving "steak &

chips" priced in pounds, and bars with names like *Delboy's* or *English Rose*. The only place with any Turkish atmosphere is the *Mehtap Çorba Salonu*, out on Hisarönü's bypass road. If you're staying at Kaya Köyü or Ölüdeniz (see below), Hisarönü's main utility is the presence of a free-standing bank **ATM**, and competitive **car rental** outlets: Explora (℡0252/616 6890, Ⓦwww.exploratravel.com) is particularly recommended for the good condition of its cars.

Ölüdeniz and beyond

Ölüdeniz, 10km south of Fethiye, is the azure lagoon that features on every second Turkish travel poster (dawn to dusk; admission to the fenced national park 3YTL per person, 8–13.50YTL per car depending on size; sun-lounger and umbrella rental 5YTL). Its warm, if occasionally turbid, waters make for pleasant swimming even in April or May, and serve as a protected venue for a spin in a rented kayak or pedalo (motorized sports are only allowed in the open sea). However, the environs of this once-pristine lagoon, whose name translates as "Dead Sea" in Turkish, rank as one of the country's most popular resorts, and since the late 1980s its beaches – both the spit enclosing the inlet (mostly Turks) and the more exposed strand of **Belcekiz** (mostly foreigners) – reach saturation level on summer weekends. At such times, it's perhaps worth avoiding Ölüdeniz altogether in favour of the **Kıdrak** forest-service beach (admission 3YTL per person; parking 4.5YTL), 3km east of Belcekiz beside the ultra-posh *Club Lykia World* (German all-inclusive tours only). Kıdrak is cleaner and less commercialized than Belcekiz, with just a small snack-bar and a seasonal sun-bed/umbrella concession (there's natural shade in the pines if required).

Both Belcekiz and Kıdrak serve as landing-pads for **paragliders**, who are kitted out by several beachfront outfits for a hefty €85–100 and taken to a point near the summit of 1976-metre Baba Dağı for launching – best visibility is in autumn. Despite frankly inflated rates, the sport goes from strength to strength locally, as it is reputedly the second best spot worldwide to indulge: Sky Sports (℡0252/617 0511, Ⓦwww.skysports-turkey.com) is the most heavily publicized and longest established outfit.

A more predictable repertoire of **boat trips** – to remote coves, islets and Byzantine ruins – is also on offer, though beware limp lunches, guide fatigue and stops missed out or rushed. The cheapest (2–3 daily dolmuş boats; 11YTL return) and most popular destination is the beach and limestone canyon just inland dubbed **Butterfly Valley** (Kelebek Vadisi in Turkish) after the many species that flutter about during the right seasons. There's also a waterfall (5YTL admission; 20min inland) and the beach itself, which is frequented by an uneasy mix of day-trippers sipping vastly overpriced beers at the café and time-warped hippies staying in the primitive treehouse or bungalow accommodation here.

Practicalities

By far the most attractive approach to Ölüdeniz is **on foot from Kaya Köyü** (see box, opposite); though frequent **dolmuşes** (every 15min, 15min journey) make the trip here from Fethiye until late at night. The dolmuşes drop you just behind the beach, between the *jandarma* post and the pedestrian promenade of Belcekiz.

Accommodation

Most accommodation clusters behind gentrified Belcekiz beach with its broad, landscaped promenade. Of the rough-and-ready **bungalow–treehouses** that set up shop here for the hippie vanguard during the late 1970s, only one survives:

This mostly downhill walk takes you from Kaya village to the northwest shore of the lagoon in about ninety minutes, with another thirty minutes separating you from the dolmuş stop. The route begins in Kaya from the easterly Yukarı Kilise (aka Taksiarhis), and is fairly well marked by rust-red paint blobs; don't trust blue ones, nor those leading you over the pass with a windmill and chapel. The proper path climbs somewhat faintly to a plateau within fifteen minutes, then levels out through pine woods for another twenty minutes, before reaching fine overviews of Aya Nikola and Soğuk Su, and a stretch of well-engineered, cobbled, descending path. This ends at some charcoal-burners' flats, with a less distinct path to a large rectangular cistern just beyond, before the head of a ravine. Here the trail appears to split; the left-hand option is easier going. Just under an hour along both routes converge before you reach an obvious pass with some pine-studded rocks on the right, affording the first eye-full of the lagoon. From here you've an uncomplicated, if sharp, drop to the first umbrella-and-sun-bed concession on the shore.

Oba Hostel (℡0252/617 0470, ⓦwww.obahostel.com), about 300m inland, with a variety of budget accommodation – either plain cabins and a dormitory "treehouse" (€5 per person) or en-suite chalets (❷) in a pleasant garden setting – as well as Internet facilities. A trio of tent/caravan **campsites** abut the north shore of the lagoon, just below the *Hotel Meri*. The *Hotel Meri* (℡0252/617 0001, ⓦwww .hotelmeri.com; ❾; closed Nov–March) is the only bona fide **hotel** around the lagoon itself, sited on a forested hillside overlooking Ölüdeniz. Cog-and-pinion elevators take you up through the gardens, from the level of the private beach, annexe buildings and heart-shaped pool, to the main body of rooms. These mostly have sea views and large balconies; room rates, though steep, are for full board: it is often cheaper to book through various UK tour operators (see p.31), or to come in April or October (❻), or May, June or September (❼). At Belcekiz, next to the *Help Bar* but quiet despite this, is the 2004-built ⚓*Oyster Residences* (℡0252/617 0765, ⓦwww.oysterresidences.com; ❽). The sixteen large, wooden-floored rooms with their quality textiles are arranged around a pool with wooden decking; breakfast, featuring smoked salmon and eggs, is a highlight.

In the former orchards behind Belcekiz and on the slopes flanking the road in, there must be three-score other motels, hotels and makeshift camps. Peaceful, good-value choices not monopolized by packages include the *Hotel Bronze* inland from *Oba Hostel* (℡0252/617 0107, ⓦwww.hotelbronze.com; ❹), with simple but air-conditioned rooms around a pool terrace; and the *Aygül Hotel* halfway back to Ovacık (℡0252/617 0086, ⓔinfo@aygulhotel.com; ❸), whose plain rooms are offset by the eyrie-like hillside setting and large pool.

Eating, drinking and nightlife

Eating out in the Ölüdeniz area is generally bland, forgettable and (predictably) not cheap. A sterling exception is the durable, fair-priced *Kumsal Pide*, at the east end of Belcekiz pedestrianized esplanade, where the *mezes* are above average in quality and size, and a *düble pide* easily feeds two; it's open all year, and has a **bowling alley** in the basement, surely the only one for miles. Honourable mentions also go to the restaurant at the *Oba Hostel*, which is tasty enough, gets some Turkish patronage and isn't vastly overpriced; while the *Secret Garden*, predictably hidden away in the back lanes of Belcekiz, has a good line in *tandır kebap* and sea bass baked in a salt crust; booking in season suggested on ℡0252/617 0231.

Nightlife tends to be late and loud. The most obvious beachfront spots are *Help Bar-Brasserie* (the food's exorbitant), and its nearby first-floor rival, the *Buzz Beach Bar*.

Inaugurated in early 2000, the **Lycian Way** is a long-distance trail running parallel to much of the Turquoise Coast. It begins above Ölüdeniz, at Ovacık, and ends just shy of Antalya, taking in choice mountain landscapes and seascapes en route, with many optional marked detours to points of interest, typically Roman or Byzantine ruins not found in any conventional guidebook. In theory it takes about **a month to complete** – though it's expected that walkers will sample it in stages rather than tackling the whole trail at one go. Some of the wildest sections are between Ovacık and Gavurağili, above the Yediburun coast, and between Kaş and Üçağız; descriptions of the best of these routes are given below and on p.497. **Elevation** en route varies from sea level to 1800m on the saddle of Tahtalı Dağ. October (pleasantly warm) or April and May (when water is plentiful and the days long) are the best **walking seasons** along most of the way, with summer out of the question.

The Lycian Way uses an assortment of **surfaces**, from cross-country boulder-hopping to brief stretches of asphalt, by way of forested paths, cobbled or revetted Byzantine/Ottoman roads and tractor-tracks. While the entire distance is marked with the conventional red-and-white blazes used in Europe, plus occasional metal "street furniture" giving distances to the next key destination, waymarks are often not there when you need them most. Some patches have not been entirely cleared of fast-growing scrub, and may close up again within a few years unless used; additionally, sometimes villagers block the route with piled, cut gorse, though volunteer marking and cleaning parties have recently removed most obstacles, and further waymarking "parties" are planned. Kate Clow, who originally marked the Lycian Way, also adapted the Turkish military's ordnance survey 1:50,000 maps, so a reasonably accurate **guide-booklet-with-map** called *The Lycian Way* is available, which indicates points for water, camping, and (somewhat obsoletely) overnighting indoors. Hard-wearing and waterproof, the map often saves the day, as trail descriptions can be vague at precisely the points where waymarks are missing; also be aware that elapsed timings in the text are for those with a full pack, so deduct about 25 percent when doing sections as day-hikes. The English-language version is on sale at select outlets such as Imagine in Fethiye, the lone computer/CD shop in Hisarönü, the *Merhaba Café* in Kaş and (overseas) at speciality travel stores like Stanfords in the UK. A **website**, ⓦ www.thelycianway.com, offers updates on route conditions and the opportunity to add comments of your own or sign up for a maintenance party.

Beyond Ölüdeniz: along the Lycian Way

South of Kıdrak lies some of the least exploited coastline in Turkey: the **Yediburun** or "Seven Capes" headlands, with a number of isolated villages just inland. Since the early 1980s dirt roads have been pushed to most, though not yet all, of them, and for many points the **Lycian Way** long-distance trail remains the most straightforward method of access. Below, we cover the first 25km of the route between Ovacık and Kabak, at the current end of the dirt-road system, though the directions are given in the reverse order to those in the Lycian Way guide booklet – ie, *from* Kabak. This makes for a lengthy, lightly laden **day-walk** of six and a half hours, though with rests, lunch stop and safety margin for getting lost you'd be wise to allow eight. To reach Kabak and the start of the walk, you'll need to get the earliest of the three daily **minibuses from Ovacık** to Kabak via Faralya, a hair-raising forty-minute journey careering partly along the edge of the Kelebek Vadisi.

Kabak to Farlaya

The bus will drop you off at the turnaround in **KABAK**, where the lower alternative of the east-bound Lycian Way leads down within half an hour to the fine sandy beach of **Gemile Liman**. En route it passes through or near three recommended **trekkers' lodges**: the *Olive Garden* (℡0252/642 1083; ❸ half-board only), opened in 2005 and with the best views and congenial management; the *Full Moon* (℡0252/642 1081; ❸ half-board only) at the end of the road, with a hillside pool and strategically-placed bar; and *Turan's Camp* (℡0252/642 1227, Ⓦwww .turancamping.com; ❸ half-board only), slightly inland from the beach, with wild boar on the menu, yoga programmes and a large plunge-pool.

Begin your Lycian Way hike with a steady twenty-minute climb north past fields and through open woodland to a track; bear right and carry on 25 minutes more, with little altitude change, through high grain fields (and no shade) before dropping to a canyon with a powerful spring draining past **BELEN** hamlet (which isn't shown on the Lycian Way map). Just past the spring, bear right and up onto the resumed path, climbing twenty minutes to the last saddle between Belen and Faralya village. From the pass you've a fifteen-minute descent to the road again – there's a sharp elevation drop, but along a gorgeous forest path with cobbled surface.

Turn right and continue another quarter-hour along the dirt road through the Hisar *mahalle* of Uzunyurt, still known universally by its Ottoman name of **FARALYA**, set magnificently part way up the slopes of Baba Dağı, with views across to Rhodes on clear days. Along the way you'll pass the non-vehicle lane leading downhill to *George House* (℡0252/642 1102, Ⓦhttp://georgehouse.site-mynet.com; ❶), providing basic, mattress-on-the-floor treehouse-style **accommodation** and largely vegetarian meals pitched at trekkers, and – 500m further – the *Gül Pansiyon* (℡0252/642 1145; ❷), by the bus stop, which also does slightly pricey trout meals. You're far more likely to get a meal or bed on spec at either of these places than at the area's most prestigious accommodation, just up the resumption of the trail proper: ⚘ *Değirmen/Die Wassermühle* (℡0252/642 12 45, Ⓦwww.natur-reisen.de; ❻; closed late Oct–March), where you'll be lulled to sleep by the sound of mill-race water. Seven comfortable apartments (❼ half-board only) and two conventional rooms (❻ half-board only) are grouped around a restaurant (meals usually for guests only), the restored mill and a stone-crafted swimming pool; minimum one-week stays are usually required. All three establishments are perched just above "Butterfly Valley", difficult to reach from this upstream end unless you're an experienced scrambler; the path – such as it is – is much easier climbed from the day-trippers' beach.

Faralya to Ovacık

The Lycian Way continues sharply uphill and north from *Değirmen*, leaving the stream canyon after twenty minutes; then it's ten minutes more along a steadily broadening forest track, through welcome shade, to a fountain. Some 45 minutes from Faralya, having passed fields on the left, a goat-pen and a second cistern-spring, the path resumes to bring you to the mosque at the centre of **KİRME** village (no facilities), flanked to the east and north by pine-flecked cliffs but open to the south.

It's a ten-minute climb up to the spring and mulberry trees by the road serving the village, where you turn left (north) and then are obliged to follow the road for more than an hour to the next village of **KOZAĞAÇİ** – there's a fifteen-minute path shortcut at one point, though red-and-white waymarks may be deficient. They continue to be so around Kozağaçı (last spring water) where, once clear of the village, it's vital *not* to be lured into following a green-dot-marked path up Baba Dağı, but stay with the trail that contours around the hillside, past a modern house, to a saddle and spectacular views over the whole coast from Ölüdeniz to the Dalyan area.

From this point a well-engineered **corniche route**, partly cobbled and doubtless of medieval vintage, drops sharply along fairly shadeless hillside – 45 minutes, an hour, and 75 minutes along respectively you'll pass *sarnıç* or rain cisterns (for emergency use only). About ninety minutes from Kozağaçı, the route flattens out and even climbs momentarily, but there's shade once again. Two hours from Kozağaçı another cistern marks the trailhead where a track system stops and vehicles can pick you up; otherwise it's another 900m to the paved **Ovacık–Ölüdeniz road**, and the *Sultan Motel* (see p.455).

Göcek and around

Set at the far northwest corner of the Gulf of Fethiye (formerly the Gulf of Sko-pea), **GÖCEK** is an obligatory stop on yacht or *gület* tours despite some rather off-putting industrial installations to one side of the bay. It has become very trendy with both foreigners and Turks, with the late President Özal himself vacationing here on occasion during the 1980s (the main street is now named after him). While there's no beach to speak of, the passing boat trade has resulted in an astonishing concentration of facilities for such a small place: laundries, a chandlery, a half-dozen posh souvenir shops and several bank ATMs along, or just off, the main inland commercial street, much of which is permanently closed to traffic. The meticulously landscaped, lawn-fringed shore esplanade is car-free too, and venue for one of the best-attended evening promenades on this coast.

The nearest proper beaches lie some 10km east of Göcek along Highway 400 at Küçük Kargı. Here two pebble bays, **Günlüklü** and **Katrancı**, are served by the Kargı–Yanıklar–Fethiye minibuses and have forest backdrop, rudimentary snack bars and no-frills campsites.

Practicalities

About a half-dozen daily **dolmuşes** link Fethiye with Göcek, leaving you at the main car park just off the inland shopping street. If you are seized by the urge to stay – and it does makes a convenient last overnight stop before a flight home from Dalaman – you have some ten **pansiyons** to choose from, plus several **hotels** or apart-hotels. Basic *pansiyon* digs include the air-conditioned *Ünlü* (℡0252/645 1170; **❸**) and the nearby, plain *Tufan's* (℡0252/645 1334; **❷**), overlooking the less busy, west end of the quayside. For a better standard, go for the *Yıldırım Pansiyon* (℡0252/645 1189; **❹**), further west; the *A&B Home Hotel* (℡0252/645 1820, Ⓦwww.abhomehotel.com; **❺**), on the inland side of the main street, with a pool and superior breakfasts; or, best of all – though well inland behind the *Nirvana* complex – the *Yonca Resort* (℡0252/645 2255, Ⓔyoncaresort@superonline.com; **❺**), an intimate, antique-furnished eight-room inn with a small pool and rustic impedimenta in the garden. Other comfortable lodgings here tend to be the exclusive province of UK package companies.

The trendy set has had a deleterious effect on many of the half-dozen or so, occasionally precious waterside **restaurants**, with obligatory service charges and miniature portions even by Turkish resort standards – this tends to be accentuated the closer you get to the Port Göcek Marina. However, *Mosaic* on the western half of the pedestrianized front (relative to Port Göcek) boasts elegant cooking with French flair – about 22YTL a head with a modest intake of alcohol, but worth it. Nearby *Özcan* is considered tops for a *meze*-based meal but unhappily raises touting for custom to a coarse art, and the nearby waterfront *Yelken* has just as good *mezes*, fish and steaks. Just inland, but still in the pedestrian zone, *Antep Sofrası*, between *Ünlü* and *Tufan's pansiyon*s, specializes in quality kebabs and *lahmacun* at (for Göcek anyway) budget prices.

Among a handful of **bars**, the most civilized is *Dr Jazz* next to *Mosaic*, with poster decor and a jazz soundtrack. Alternatively, the contemporary bistro-bar *Café West*, near the *Deniz Hotel*, is popular with yacht crews and serves good breakfast and other light meals at tables out front, as well as offering **Internet** access, newspapers and magazines.

Dalaman and Sarıgerme

The main town west of Fethiye is bleak, dusty, grid-planned **Dalaman**, home to the southern Turkish coast's main airport, one of the country's two open prisons and not much else. Visitors flying in for resort holidays will see little of the town, and the sole reason for anyone to pass through is to reach **Sarıgerme** beach, 15km southwest of Dalaman. Even then there's a more direct side-road from Highway 400, just east of Ortaca, marked with the regulation black-on-yellow signs.

Dalaman

Dalaman airport (flight enquiries ℡0252/792 5291) has a 24-hour tourist information desk and round-the-clock banking facilities, including an ATM, as well as two **car rental** booths: Avis (℡0252/792 5118) and Europcar (℡0252/792 5117). Be aware that domestic flights and international charters arrive at separate buildings. There are no public-transport links from the airport, so barring a transfer coach or rental car you'll have to take a taxi 5.5km along Kenan Evren Bulvarı into town (about 12YTL); if you're bound for Dalaman's **otogar**, 5.5km further out of town on Highway 400 just west of the main roundabout, budget 12YTL more. At those rates, if you're arriving on a THY domestic flight, it's worth coinciding with the *servis araba* to Fethiye or Marmaris, which costs much the same.

With both Göcek (see opposite) and Sarıgerme (see overleaf) so close, there's absolutely no reason to patronize either the handful of shabby *pansiyon*s in town or the overblown businessmen's hotels lining Kenan Evren Bulvarı. As part of their "rehabilitation", low-risk convicts from the local prison run a clinical-decor **restaurant** attached to a chicken farm (it's on the right, next to the prison gate, as you enter town from the north) – so the menu's strictly roast chicken and rice, at rock-bottom prices with friendly service. Another establishment worth patronizing is the **travel agency** Yabancı Services, at Gazi Bul 102 (the airport approach road; ℡0252/692 3613, ⓦwww.yabanci.com), run by Alison Grundy; she can arrange one-way and return charters back to the UK from Dalaman, Bodrum, İzmir or Antalya.

Sarıgerme

Sarıgerme is not quite as long as İztuzu beach near Dalyan but just as scenic, fringed at its western, developed end with pines and offering sweeping views east past the mouth of the Dalaman Çayı toward the mountains near Fethiye. Just offshore, **Baba Adası**, capped by a crumbling, tree-obscured stone pyramid thought to be an ancient lighthouse, only partly protects the beach from the prevailing strong southwesterly winds that make Sarıgerme better for sailing sports than swimming. The water is likely to be cleaner than at İztuzu, though colder too owing to freshwater springs that dribble into the sea near the westernmost cove.

The fact that several enormous luxury complexes are set well back from the sand confirms that Sarıgirme is a loggerhead-turtle-nesting beach, though new construction on the ridge overhead has made a mockery of the Environment Ministry's guidelines for such protected areas. Cars are banned from the attractively landscaped park in the pines just behind, to which entering pedestrians are charged a fee during daylight hours. But sun-beds and umbrellas are there a-plenty (most of them affiliated with the tour-group-dominated hotels inland), as well as watersports and diving on offer at two outlets (pitched in German and priced in euros). Aside from a drinks stall and rudimentary snack cantina in the park, there's no food, so it's best to bring a picnic to spread on the tables provided.

Dalyan and around

The landscape to the west of Fethiye more than holds its own in scenic appeal, and the newly widened and straightened Highway 400 has reduced access times. Westbound buses from Dalaman continue to Ortaca, from where plentiful minibuses make the twenty-minute journey to the little town of **Dalyan**, 13km off Highway 400 and a good base for the surrounding attractions: the ancient site of **Kaunos** downriver from Dalyan, **İztuzu beach**, the beautiful freshwater lake of **Köyceğiz** with its shoreline hot springs, and the remote but increasingly frequented bay of **Ekincik**.

Dalyan

DALYAN first achieved a measure of international fame in 1986, when its "turtle controversy" blew up into a major battle against developers, who wanted to build a luxury hotel on nearby İztuzu beach, a breeding ground for the loggerhead turtle (*Carretta carretta*). Conservationists succeeded in halting the scheme, and now the beach is statutorily protected between May and October, when the eggs are laid.

In the wake of this campaign, the town hoped to present itself as ecologically correct, but its mess of *pide salonları*, carpet shops, T-shirt vendors and loud bars has proved little different from most other mainstream resorts. The **turtle motif** has been commercially harnessed ad nauseam: there's a turtle statue in the main square; restaurants, car rental outfits and *pansiyons* are named after the creatures; they appear on postcards, T-shirts and taxi doors; and you can even buy ceramic statuettes of the infant turtles hatching. Second-home sales have rocketed in the area, and the town centre is now crammed with multiple estate-agents, DIY shops and a large Migros supermarket.

Otherwise life in Dalyan revolves around the **Dalyan Çayı**, the river that flows past the village linking the Köyceğiz lake and the sea. Many choice *pansiyons* line the east bank of the river, and the boats that putt-putt up and down it – navigating swathes of reeds reflected bright green in the water – are the preferred means of transport to all of the major local sites. Craft heading downstream pass a series of spectacular fourth-century **rock tombs** set into the cliff on the west bank, many of them temple-style with two Ionic columns, similar to those at Fethiye.

Arrival, information and transport

Arriving **dolmuşes** from Ortaca – and far less frequently from Marmaris or Fethiye – drop you at the terminal just behind the centrally placed **PTT** (daily: June–Sept 8am–10pm; Oct–May 8am–7pm), near which are several bank **ATMs**. There's also a **tourist office** housed in a tiny storefront near the *Belediye* (April– Nov Mon–Sat 9.30am–noon & 2–6pm), though the website ⓦ www.dalyan.co.uk

(affiliated to Kaunos Tours; see below) is more useful, especially the unvarnished restaurant reviews.

Dolmuş boats to the river end of İztuzu beach (5YTL return; 40min) depart from Kordon Boyu, opposite the mosque. In season, most have left by 10.30am, though there may be one more at 2pm. They return every half-hour or so between 3pm and sunset. Otherwise, there are peak-season **minibuses** (every 30min) along the 13km road to the east end of the strand. Many of the *pansiyon*s along the river (see "Accommodation" below) also have their own small motorboats providing a once-daily service to the beach for a nominal fee.

Renting a **mountain bike** in town is another possible strategy for getting around, at least in the cooler months. They're available both at the better package hotels and at certain travel agents, for no more than 10YTL a day. Best route for a **bike ride** is to İztuzu beach: there's one nasty hill en route, with *ayran* and *gözleme* stalls to pause at for refreshment in the hamlet of Gökbel. This land route is recommended at least once, as you loop around the Sulungur lake and get glimpses of marsh and mountain not possible amid the claustrophobic reed beds of the Dalyan Çayı. The unpublicized **rowboat ferry** (1.5YTL round trip) at the river end of Yalı Sokağı provides access to the ruins at Kaunos – not a bad target for a sunset stroll. You could take a bike across too – the rowboat ferry should take you after some grumbling – in order to cycle to Kaunos and beyond along an extensive system of dirt tracks.

Accommodation

Many of the most desirable *pansiyon*s are scattered around a swelling in the river locally referred to as the "göl" (lake), though you'll have little hope of a vacancy in high season without calling well in advance. They're on or just off **İskele (Maraş) Caddesi**, which heads from the middle of town to a dead end nearly 2km south, opposite the fish processing plant. A second cluster of *pansiyon*s lines **Ada Sokağı**, the dirt side-track off İskele Caddesi, leading west through the area known as Maraş Mahallesi. All of the options here, except for the *Palmyra*, are set in beautiful "lake-front" orchard-gardens, with breakfast served at riverside terraces, and hygienic river swimming off the same structures. To reach either of these areas, take the signposted **İztuzu road** – home to most of the more comfortable hotels – and then bear right at the second junction (this gets you around a one-way system and nocturnal street closures for pedestrians).

Mosquitoes are a major plague everywhere, so bring anti-bug juice, an electrification mat or a mosquito net, since your accommodation may not have window screens or provide such repellents. Very few places are open all year – most accommodation closes from November to March – while anything styling itself a hotel is likely to be monopolized by tours for much of the season.

Riverview establishments

Hotel Caria Yalı Sok, off İskele Cad ☎0252/284 2075, ℱ284 3046. Near the rowboat ferry – about half the large, air-conditioned rooms here have river views, and there's also a rooftop breakfast terrace overlooking the rock tombs. ❸

Çınar Sahil Pansiyon Yalı Sok, off İskele Cad ☎0252/284 2117. Across the street from *Hotel Caria*, set in a small citrus grove and perhaps the best budget choice with clean, airy one-, two- or three-bedded rooms and a rooftop breakfast terrace. ❷

Göl Hotel North of the central park; follow Kordon Boyu ☎0252/284 20 96, ℱ284 2555. Plain, medium-sized rooms in a pleasant environment, with the usual roof terrace. Room balconies allow a partial river view, and there's street parking. ❸

Prince of Kaunos Hotel Upriver from the mosque; follow Kordon Boyu past the *Göl Hotel* ☎0252/284 5230, ℱ284 2604. A kitsch lobby belies cheerful air-conditioned rooms, most with mountain or river views, decked out with coloured curtains and pastel furniture. Some tours stay here, but on-spec clients are welcome to try their luck. ❹

İskele Caddesi

Aktaş Pansiyon 400m south of Yalı Sok
☎0252/284 2042, ⓕ284 4380. Half the rooms
have views of the rock tombs across the river,
though top-floor ones lack balconies and, despite
air conditioning, can get oven-like in summer. Self-
catering kitchen facilities available. ❸

🏃 **Asur Oteli/Assyrian Hotel** South end of
İskele Cad ☎0252/284 3232, ⓦwww
.asurotel.com. Dalyan's best hotel is a landscaped
complex popular with tour companies. Award-
winning architecture and pleasant, if small and
slightly dark hexagonal rooms, some with double
beds and all with a/c, contemporary bathrooms,
and river and mountain views. There's a private
beach-shuttle boat and decent food at the open-
buffet restaurant, while an annexe of two-bedroom
apartments is available just inland. Rates drop
sharply in low season. Rooms ❻, apartments ❼

Ada Sokağı

🏃 **Happy Caretta Hotel** ☎0252/284 2109,
ⓦwww.happycaretta.com. Somewhat
bumped-up rates, though you'll appreciate the
thick walls on the oldish building (which keep the
ten doubles and four family rooms cool in summer
– there's also a/c), and a kind managing family. Proprietress İlknur speaks English. Attractive
upstairs lounge with fireplace for winter (it's open
all year); evening meals on request. ❹
Lindos Pansiyon ☎0252/284 2005, ⓔlindos@
superonline.com. Well-appointed rooms with rare
double beds and proper shower cabins, as well
as a family studio; rooms with a/c are a category

higher. Also a pleasant lounge for cool weather,
free canoes available, and genial management
by English-speaking Levent Sünger. İztuzu-bound
boats can be flagged down here. ❷
Palmyra Hotel End of Ada Sok ☎0252/284 4550,
ⓦwww.Pansion_Palmyra.com. Partly a/c, well-
appointed rooms set back slightly from the river,
but the rural grounds have their own dock. ❸

İztuzu road

Kervansaray Arıkan Karakol Sok ☎0252/284
2487, ⓔhotelarikan@hotmail.com. Mock-Ottoman-
style three-star with variable rooms – doubles to
apartments, a tiny pool, and an on-site hamam. ❹
Manzara Villas Eastern edge of town, 1km from
centre; ring for directions ☎0252/284 4465, in
UK ☎01304/375093, ⓦwww.manzara.co.uk.
Three well-designed six-person villas around a
pool-garden, set in open country with a view of
the "Sleeping Giant" mountain, make an excellent self-catering choice for families, though good
breakfasts are available. Genially run by expatriate
Clare Baker, whose UK branch will provide help in
securing flights and car rental. Rates are quoted
weekly, from £240–300/week for a double room,
£450–600/week for 6 (with 10 percent discount for
Rough Guide readers).
Metin Erkul Sok 14, continuation of Yalı Sok, east
of İskele Cad ☎0252/284 2040, ⓦwww.met-
inhotel.com. Two-star hotel, with spacious fanned
or a/c rooms (though views only of the pool court),
and large common areas (including sauna). It's currently UK-package-dominated, though you might
strike lucky if you ring independently. ❹

Eating and drinking

As a rule, town-centre **restaurants** in Dalyan are pricey, bland and Anglicized
– touts yell "spaghetti!" and bread comes with pots of butter, pub-style. So it's
fairly futile to expect much in the way of Turkish culinary authenticity or generous portion size, and overall you're better off dining on the outskirts of town or in
the open countryside. The lone exceptions are *Metin Pide*, at the start of the İztuzu
road, with proper portions of meat, fish and *meze* as well as the namesake *pide*, served
either in the spartan indoor premises or in the garden across the street; and the *Atay
Dostlar Sofrası*, just shy of the river and diagonally across from the boat co-op office,
an inexpensive, licensed *hazır yemek* place with a number of grilled dishes. *Ali's*,
behind the mosque, is the closest Dalyan has to a lively night-time *meyhane*, though
there seems to be one price scale for Turks and another for foreigners. In summer,
the best local eatery is *Saki*, on the riverbank by the Kaunos rowboat jetty, specializing in Turkish vegetarian dishes and stocking organic wines. Working a longer
season, and popular with middle-class Turks for its authentic, affordable Turkish
dishes, is *LeyLey*, about 1500m out on the Ortaca-bound road; if you don't have
transport, ring ☎0252/284 4669 for their free shuttle. Finally, the *Gölbaşı*, about
halfway to the beach on the İztuzu road, also lays on a minibus service and does
superb **breakfasts** with real coffee and fresh orange juice. Other venues for break-

fast and sweets include *Fruit Bar* down İskele Caddesi, serving fresh fruit concoctions and crêpes with *dondurma*, as well as souvenir home-made jams, or *Gerda's Waffles*, a little booth with outdoor seating near the *jandarma* post.

Nightlife in the handful of bars along the upper reaches of İskele Caddesi, and around the town centre, is fairly self-evident; as format and ownership changes almost yearly, just choose according to the noise level and the crowd. One of the more durable ones is *Blues Bar*, on the river side of İskele Caddesi, south of Yalı Sokağı, with live music most nights in summer. There are numerous **Internet cafés** in the centre, which come and go.

Tours and activities

The most popular local outing is the **day-tour** offered by the motorboat co-op based on the quayside. These excursions – usually departing by 10.30am – take in thermal springs on Köyceğiz lake, Kaunos ruins and the beach, and are good value at about 7YTL a head (assuming eight to ten passengers), but a bit rushed for a return by 6pm. If you prefer to dictate the pace, you can **custom-rent** a whole boat, which costs around 90YTL for an entire day for groups of up to a dozen. Half- or two-third day-trips – say for a visit to the ruins and the Ilıca mudbaths – can also be arranged.

Many of the riverside *pansiyon*s will take you on **evening boat trips** upriver to sit and watch for the silent dark shapes of freshwater terrapins surfacing for air. You can sometimes get such boats on a self-skippering basis; usually, though, you'll only be entrusted with a canoe or rowboat.

Kaunos Tours near the PTT (☎0252/284 2816, ⓦwww.kaunostours.com) **rents cars** and organizes **adventure trips** – canyoning, scuba diving (at nearby Ekincik; see p.468), horse riding, mountain biking, sea kayaking and river rafting on the Dalaman Çayı (aka Akköpru Çayı) – one of the best such rivers in the country until a proposed dam is completed – though most of this is subcontracted to Alternatif Turizm in Marmaris (see p.414). Most excursion days are €40 except for rafting which is €50, including lunch and transfers.

△ Dalyan's rock tombs

Kaunos

The excavation of ancient **Kaunos** began in 1967 and still takes place each August, sometimes using labour from the low-security prison at Dalaman. While the ruins are minimally labelled and by no means spectacular, the site is one of the most pleasant and underrated minor attractions on this coast, swarming with wildlife (not least mosquitoes), including herons and storks in summer, flamingos in winter, plus small terrapins, tortoises, snakes and nodding lizards in all seasons.

Arriving by **tour boat**, you disembark either at the fish weir or at another jetty on the opposite side of the rock outcrop supporting Kaunos's acropolis. The fish caught (*dalyan* means weir) are mostly grey mullet and bass, and a fragmentary inscription found at Kaunos suggests that the river has been exploited for food since ancient times. From either landing point it is a ten-minute walk up to the **site** (daily dawn to dusk, but unenclosed; 4YTL when warden present).

It's also easy to walk to Kaunos, using the **rowboat ferry** from Dalyan (see p.463), which lands just under the cliff-hewn temple tombs on the west bank. The ferry is intended mostly for the inhabitants of Çandır, the closest village to ancient Kaunos, and a quarter-hour's stroll from Dalyan. It is also possible to **drive to Kaunos** from Köyceğiz via the Sultaniye baths and Çandır; but the road beyond the hot springs, while paved, is potholed, meandering and indirect.

Some history

Although Kaunos was a Carian foundation of the ninth century BC, the city exhibited various Lycian cultural traits, not least the compulsion to adorn nearby cliffs with typically Lycian rock-tombs. Kaunos was also closely allied to the principal Lycian city of Xanthos, and when the Persian Harpagus attempted to conquer the region in the sixth century BC, the two cities were the only ones to resist. Kaunos began to acquire a Greek character under the influence of the Hellenizing Carian ruler Mausolus – an apparently successful campaign, since no Carian words have been found on inscriptions here. Subsequently, the city passed from one ruler to another: to Ptolemy after Alexander's death; then to the Rhodians; and finally, after fierce resistance to Rhodes, to indirect Roman imperial administration.

Besides its fish, Kaunos was noted for its figs, and for the prevalence of malaria among its inhabitants; the fruit was erroneously deemed to be the cause of the disease by outsiders, rather than the anopheles mosquitoes that, until 1948, infested the surrounding swamps. Another insidious problem was the silting up of its harbour, which continually threatened the city's substantial commercial interests. The Mediterranean originally came right up to the foot of the acropolis hill, surrounding Kaunos on all sides apart from an isthmus of land to the north. But the Dalyan Çayı has since deposited over 5km of silt, leaving an expanse of marshy delta in its wake.

The site

Much of Kaunos is yet to be unearthed, despite the long-running excavation, and not every individual monument is labelled. North of the city extend well-preserved stretches of **defensive wall**, some of which is thought to have been constructed by Mausolus early in the fourth century BC. Just below the **acropolis** outcrop, crowned by a medieval and Hellenistic fortified area, the second-century BC **theatre** is the most impressive building here. Resting against the hillside to the southeast, in the Greek fashion it's considerably greater than a semicircle and retains two of its original arched entrances. Between here and the Byzantine church, a **temple to Apollo** has recently been identified.

Northwest of the theatre and Apollo temple, closer to the upper ticket booth, the **Byzantine basilica** and the city's **Roman baths** are also in excellent condition, and an observation platform has been erected near the basilica. A paved stone street leads downhill from the baths to an ancient **Doric temple**, consisting most obviously of an attractive circular structure, possibly an altar, sacred pool or podium, flanked by bits of a re-erected colonnade. A path continues to the **agora**, on the lowest level, which boasts a restored **fountain–house** bearing an inscription to Vespasian, at the end of a long **stoa**. The ancient **harbour** is now the Sülüklü Gölü, or "Lake of the Leeches". According to ancient observers the lake was barred by a chain in times of danger; nowadays it's merely dive-bombed by feeding waterbirds.

İztuzu beach

Tourism and turtles have been made to coexist uneasily at superb, packed-sand **İztuzu beach**, which stretches southeast from the mouth of the Dalyan Çayı. You should remain wary of **turtle nests**, which are easily trampled on; turtle tracks – scrapings in the sand where the creatures have hauled themselves up onto the beach to lay their eggs – are visible in June and July. The beach and marshes immediately behind are often alive with other wildlife too, including lizards, snakes, crabs, terrapins and tortoises, and its approach road is lined with profusely flowering oleander bushes, as well as deformed trees showing the effects of high winter winds.

Whether you go to the road's end (May–Oct car park 3YTL; barrier, 2km before booth, shuts at dusk) or the river-mouth end of İztuzu beach, the biggest problems are the lack of shade and the poor eating options. Bring some sort of sun protection and consider renting an umbrella from one of the drink-*gözleme*-and-ice-cream kiosks. There are only a few kiosks, at either end of the beach, and their menus are fairly pricey (eg 4YTL for a *gözleme*) as well as limited, so you'll probably want to bring some food, too. Umbrellas, whose masts damage the turtle nests, are not permitted from a line of squat marker-stakes down to the sea, and all access to the beach is banned between 8pm and 8am in summer – though these rules appear to be flouted regularly.

During the day the entire four-kilometre length of the beach is open to the public (it takes about half an hour to jog it from end to end); owing to wind exposure the water can be choppy and murky, but the gently shelving seabed makes this spot excellent for children. Alternatively, you could be ferried across the river mouth to a smaller, more peaceful beach shaded by some pines (swimming in the current-laced river mouth is discouraged).

Ilıca and Sultaniye Kaplıcaları

Ten minutes upriver from Dalyan in the direction of Köyceğiz are the **Ilıca thermal baths**, a series of open-air mud pools (2YTL) worth investigating on a boat trip. These springs are supposed to increase male potency and cure rheumatism or gynaecological problems; temperatures approach 40°C. Note, however, that the total area is small, and in season gets packed during the day with tour groups – you're better off going at an odd hour, or convincing your skipper to take you to a second, more remote set of hot springs, further upstream toward the lake.

These, the **Köyceğiz Sultaniye Kaplıcaları**, are also accessible by a paved, eighteen-kilometre road from Köyceğiz (see below); follow signposting for Ekincik on the west side of Köyceğiz town, and then veer left to follow signs for Çandır and the Sultaniye Kaplıcaları. The **main baths** themselves (3YTL), housed in a conspicuous white-domed structure right on the lakeshore, are claimed to be open around the clock despite the nominal posted hours of 6am to 10pm. However, 11am to 6pm is set aside for *tur* (ie mixed bathing), while at other times there are roughly alternating hours for men and women who are expected to take the plunge nude. The dome shelters a large round pool with a naturally rocky and uneven bottom, from which the water wells up at 39–41°C; it's best appreciated at night or during the cooler months, otherwise you'll be needing to dive into the adjacent lake periodically. The modern chamber has walls marble-lined to waist height, but ancient masonry at the pool rim is evidence that the baths have been present in some form at least since Roman times.

Around the dome structure are scattered a number of **open-air pools** (also 3YTL): one hot (beside the bar), one cold, and one muddy-bottomed (beside the snack-café). If you can't tear yourself away, it's also now possible to stay the night at basic **chalets** (❷) up in the hillside pine trees – ask the attendant.

Köyceğiz

KÖYCEĞIZ, 23km north of Dalyan, is a sleepy little lakeside town long been eclipsed touristically by its rival across the lake. Nevertheless, it boasts a healthy economy, based on local cotton, olive, logging and citrus cultivation, while its position on the scenic, ten-metre-deep **Köyceğiz Gölü** – once a bay open to the Mediterranean that became dammed by silt deposits – gives it a further source of income in the shape of the fish who swim up the Dalyan Çayı to spawn here.

Practicalities

There's no great advantage in staying here over Dalyan, other than the better transport connections – Dalyan, Muğla and Marmaris are served by regular minibus – though you could use it as an alternative base for visiting the ruins at Kaunos. There's a PTT, an Internet café just opposite, and at least one bank ATM. The **tourist office** on the main square (Mon–Fri 8.30am–noon & 1.30–5pm; ☏0252/262 4703) can advise on excursions and accommodation.

Of the three central **lakefront hotels**, two are overpriced and fairly grim; the happy exception is the welcoming *Alila Hotel* (☏ & ☏0252/262 1150; ❸), with carved ceilings in its well-kept common areas, varied bedrooms (including family suites sleeping five), heating/air conditioning, and a decent lakeside restaurant. Alternatively, choose from among a handful of establishments **west of the centre**, listed in the order you encounter them. First there's the *Tango Pension* on Aliihsan Kalmaz Caddesi (☏0252/262 2501, Ⓦwww.tangopension.com; open all year; ❷), on the "Fez Bus" circuit of backpackers' hostels, with minimalist, if en-suite, heated rooms or dorms (€7) and bikes for rent; second, the older, less noisy *Fulya Pansiyon* on the same street, within sight of the lake (☏0252/262 2301; ❷); next, the slightly more elaborate rooms of the waterside *Flora Motel & Pub*, Cengiz Topel Cad 110 (☏0252/262 3809, Ⓦwww.florahotel.info; ❸), with a lakefront terrace, free airport transfers and river-rafting arrangements; and finally the nearby, waterside, German-owned *Panorama Plaza Hotel* at Cengiz Topel Cad 69 (☏0252/262 3773, Ⓦwww.panorama-plaza.net; ❹), with the best-standard rooms – including large, fancy bathrooms and tiny balconies – a pool and watersports on the lake.

There are a bare handful of **restaurants** in the centre, but these are usually so dire that you should arrange evening meals with your *pansiyon* – both the *Tango* and the *Flora* are particularly geared up for this.

Ekincik

The idyllic **bay of Ekincik** lies 38km southwest of Köyceğiz, the road there mostly paved and wide except near Hamit Köy. There are several daily minibuses from Köyceğiz, but most visitors arrive by boat – either on their own yachts, or with craft of the motorboat co-op based here. As part of the conservation measures instituted at İztuzu beach, boats of any sort were forbidden to anchor the night at the river mouth there, and Ekincik was chosen both as a yacht anchorage and as a base for shuttling yachties to the Kaunos ruins. This, and the new road in, have spurred development in the Ova *mahalle* of very scattered **EKINCIK** village, mostly in the form of a cluster of beachfront **hotels**. Best, oldest and most aesthetic of three here is the *Ekincik* (℡0252/266 0203, ℻ 266 0205; ❹) at mid-beach, where the fair-sized, pine-and-white-tile rooms have air conditioning, balconies and sea, hill or garden views. Inland, but still with sweeping sea views (especially from the rooftop restaurant), top choice is the *Akdeniz* (℡0252/266 0255; ❷), with large if eccentrically laid-out rooms and a kindly managing family who may open off-season (they live on site). There's a summer-only **campsite** run by the Yıldız family, the *Gold Star* (℡0252/266 0241), towards the quieter east end of the bay.

The tan-sand **beach** itself is superb, another turtle-egg-laying venue, with good snorkelling and scuba diving at **Maden İskelesı**, on the far eastern end of the beach near a system of submarine caves. Another favourite local activity is the walk to or from **Çandır village**, on a mostly preserved old trail affording spectacular sea views, which takes under three hours. The only catch is getting back to your start-point, done either by retracing your steps or getting an expensive ride with the boatmen's co-operative.

The Xanthos valley

East of Fethiye lies the heartland of ancient Lycia, home to a number of archeological sites, including the two ancient citadel-cities of **Tlos** and **Pınara**, on opposite sides of the **Xanthos river valley**. They were both important settlements, having three votes each in the deliberations of the Lycian Federation, but Tlos had the geographical advantage, lying above a rich, open flood-plain and sheltered to the east by the Massicytus range (today's Akdağ); Pınara's surrounding hilly terrain was difficult to cultivate. Even remoter and less fertile is mysterious **Sidyma**, up on the ridge separating the valley from the Mediterranean. All these cities were unearthed by the English traveller Charles Fellows between 1838 and 1842, during the same period as his work – or pillaging, as some would have it – at **Xanthos**, though he seems to have left unmolested the nearby religious sanctuary of **Letoön** and the naval fortress of **Pydnae**.

The seventy-kilometre stretch of road as far as Kalkan, for the most part following the valley of the ancient Xanthos river (now the Eşen Çayı), is still an immensely fertile area, home to fields of cotton and maize and a wide variety of fruit. Plans for a local airport have thankfully never been realized and this, in tandem with archeological restrictions, has helped to keep growth at **Patara**, the main resort here, modest by Turkish coastal standards. Between Tlos and Patara, the magnificent river gorge of **Saklıkent** is easy to visit by dolmuş or with your own vehicle, though of late it's become something of a tourist circus. Isolated-ruins buffs can instead visit the unpromoted, unspoilt Lycian city of **Oenoanda**, high in the mountains north of Tlos.

Tlos

One of the most ancient of the Lycian cities, **Tlos** is situated beside the modern village of Asarkale. It is referred to in Hittite records of the fourteenth century BC as "Dalawa in the Lukka lands", and the discovery on the site of a bronze hatchet dating from the second millennium BC confirms the long heritage of the place.

However, little else is known about its history, although it was numbered among the six principal Lycian cities.

The ruins themselves, while reasonably abundant, are in many cases densely overgrown or even farmed, so that the precise identification of buildings is debatable. The setting is undeniably impressive, a high rocky promontory that affords excellent views of the Xanthos valley. The acropolis hill is dominated by a Turkish fortress from the Ottoman period, the residence of a nineteenth-century brigand and local chieftain, Kanlı ("Bloody") Ali Ağa, who killed his own wayward daughter to defend the family reputation. Now used as a football pitch and pasture, it has obliterated all earlier remains on the summit. On its northeast side, the acropolis ends in almost sheer cliffs; on the eastern slope are traces of the Lycian city wall and a long stretch of Roman masonry.

There's patchy **public transport** the full distance to Tlos, provided by Saklıkent-bound minibuses from Fethiye, which occasionally detour to the site. Tlos is, however, firmly established on the organized-excursion circuit, so you shouldn't have to shell out for a private taxi. Under your own steam, **from Fethiye** veer left 22km out of town towards Korkuteli, and once over the Koca Çayı bridge, bear immediately right onto the marked side-road to both Tlos and Saklıkent. Some 8.5km along, turn left (east) onto a signposted paved minor road; it's 4km up here to the base of the acropolis hill – which stays in constant view. In spring the route up, with snow-streaked Akdağ as a backdrop for the purple of flowering judas trees, is spectacularly beautiful. Coming **from Patara**, at Alaçat take the eastbound road marked "Saklıkent 15km"; when you reach a T-junction, with "Saklıkent" signposted opposite a mini-market for the right turning, bear left (north) instead, following a "Tloss" sign, for just over 2km until another "Tloss" sign points up the 4km of final approach.

The site

Entry to **the site** (unenclosed; admission 4YTL when staff present) is via the still-intact northeastern city gate, next to the guard's portakabin.

Cobbled stairs ascend to the main **necropolis**, consisting of a few free-standing sarcophagi and a complex of rock-cut house-tombs, one of which was discovered intact as recently as October 2005, yielding treasure soon to go on display at the Antalya museum (see p.533). If, however, you walk along a lower, level path from the gate, outside the city walls, you reach a second group of rock tombs; dip below and right of these along a zigzagging trail to reach the best of the graves, the **Tomb of Bellerophon**, at the northern base of the hill. Its facade was carved to resemble that of a temple, with roughly hewn columns supporting a pediment, and three carved doors. On the left wall of the porch is the relief that gives the tomb its name, representing the mythical hero Bellerophon riding the winged horse Pegasus, while facing them over the door is a lion – probably meant to stand guard over the tomb. Apparently one of the ruling families of ancient Tlos claimed descent from Bellerophon, so it can be assumed that this was the burial place of royalty. Be warned, however, that it's a fifteen-minute scramble down, requiring good shoes, with a ladder ascent at the end, and both figures, especially the lion's head, have been worn down by vandals and the elements.

Between the east slope of the acropolis hill and the curving onward road is a large open space seasonally planted with peas, corn or hay, thought by some to be the site of the **agora**. Close to the base of the hill are traces of seats that were a part of a stadium which, unusually, lay parallel to the marketplace. The opposite side of the agora is lined by a long, arcaded building presumed to be the **market hall**, with interior arcades.

Well beyond this, reached by a broad path off the main eastbound road, lie the **baths**, where the sound of running water in nearby ditches lends credence to its identification. This is a romantic vantage point, and perhaps the best bit of Tlos: three complete **chambers**, one with an apsidal projection known locally as **Yedi Kapı** (Seven Gates), after its seven intact windows, which provide an atmospheric view of the Xanthos valley. This is currently off-limits due to excavations designed to uncover the fine marble floor, which have also revealed a large, possibly Christian, cemetery.

Just east of the approach path to Yedi Kapı are the remains of a Byzantine **basilica**, and southeast of this another open space believed to be the true site of the city's agora. Just north of the modern through-road stands a magnificent second-century BC **theatre**, with 34 rows of seats remaining. The stage building has a number of finely carved blocks – including one with an eagle and a garlanded youth – and its northern section still stands to nearly full height, vying with the backdrop of mountains.

Practicalities

Right opposite the ticket booth there are a couple of simple snack **cafés** run by the villagers of Asarkale. From the theatre just east, the onward road continues 3km uphill to several trout restaurants in the village of **YAKA**. Of these the most famous is the *Yaka Park*, formerly a watermill, where at the bar your drink is chilled in a sluice through which your potential dinner swims by. However too many tours have had an effect, and *Rifat's Garden*, 1km or so further, currently has the edge in terms of quality and service.

You can also **stay** overnight locally at the ⚜ *Mountain Lodge* (℡0252/638 2515, Ⓦwww.themountainlodge.co.uk; open winter also by appointment), just under 2km down the road from the ruins entrance. Choose between well-appointed, carpeted, high-ceilinged en-suites in the garden annexe (❹), or four air-conditioned luxury units (❺) in the wing overlooking the pool and bar. Engaging proprietor Melihat prepares fine evening meals in an area thin on non-trout-based cuisine, served in the wood-beamed and stone pub-restaurant with a fire for the cooler months. She also organizes treks in the area and is knowledgeable about local flora.

Oenoanda

Ancient **Oenoanda**, about 50km northeast of Tlos, was one of the northernmost and highest (at 1350–1450m elevation) of the Lycian cities. Set in wild mountain country, it's one of the more obscure archeological sites in the region but, as an unspoilt example of how all Lycian cities were before tourism, thoroughly rewards the considerable effort involved in reaching it (your own transport is essential).

The **history** of Oenoanda is hardly less obscure, with no account of it predating the second century BC. It was most renowned as the birthplace of Diogenes the second-century AD Epicurean philosopher (not the Athenian cynic); to him is attributed a lengthy inscriptionary discourse, the longest such in antiquity, fragments of which are scattered across the site, most visibly around the agora and "esplanade". Oenoanda was first surveyed by a British archeological team in 1996 and is set for more vigorous excavations in the future. With luck, the pending digs will be able to find – and reassemble – Diogenes' text to its full estimated length of over 60m, as well as confirm identities of the various structures. Until then, Oenoanda remains a vast, romantic jumble of tumbled masonry, lintels, statue bases, column fragments, cistern mouths and buried arches, overgrown with a mixed forest of juniper, kermes oak and cedar, frequented only by squirrels and the occasional hunter or shepherd.

The site

To **reach the site**, proceed as if you were travelling from Fethiye to Tlos (see "Tlos" on p.470), but where you would turn right for Tlos and Saklıkent, instead continue straight along Highway 350. Some 34km northeast of the river bridge at Kemer, bear right (east) onto a side road marked for Seki and Elmalı, where a fine Ottoman bridge in the Seki Çayı by the modern asphalt is the most durable indicator. Exactly 1100m along, turn south on a yet more minor road (the sign is rusted over); 800m down this, veer right at an unmarked fork to proceed 1.5km more to the village of **İncealiler**, visible at the base of the slope to the south. Turn right at the phone box and standard archeological-service sign – do not follow the river further upstream – and park by the **coffeehouse** in front of you.

Head up the main pedestrian thoroughfare among the village houses, then near the top of the grade, bear right at two heaped boulders onto a narrower track, that soon dwindles to a path, running parallel to a tributary stream. Continue west towards the escarpment in front of you, where the first free-standing **tombs** poke reassuringly up. The path describes a broad arc left (south) around the top of the stream valley, forging through the low scrub.

Some 45 minutes from the coffeehouse, the trail fizzles out at the ridgeline as you meet the polygonal masonry of the massive south-to-north **aqueduct** that supplied the city, whose bluff-top site inclines gently to the south but is quite sheer on all other sides. Slip through a gap in the aqueduct, with tombs of the **necropolis** flung about on every side, and veer right along the ridge to meet Oenoanda's massive Hellenistic **city wall**, with an arched window; the way through is well to the left of this, by a strong hexagonal **tower** with archers' loopholes. Some ten to fifteen minutes' walk cross-country north from this, keeping just east of the ridge line, brings you to the large flat paved area of the **agora**; just beyond this stands an unidentified structure, possibly a **baths**, with an apse on the northwest wall and an arch dividing two of the rooms. Just northeast of this, a gate in the **Roman wall**, longer but much lower than the Hellenistic one, opens onto a vast flat area, tentatively dubbed an **"esplanade"**, with traces of stoas to either side. Northwest of the presumed baths, a structure with a three-arched facade – possible a **nymphaeum** or small **palace** – precedes the partly preserved **theatre**, its fifteen or so rows of seats taking in fine views of the Akdağ summits.

Saklıkent

Back on the main country road below Tlos, as you head south, the gauntlet of *saç böreği*, *gözleme* and *ayran* stands confirms that you're en route to the hugely popular **Saklıkent gorge**, the most dramatic geological formation in the Xanthos valley. After 9km, you bear left for just over 3km to the gorge mouth, 44km out of Fethiye. There's a regular minibus service in season – look for vehicles marked "Kayadibi/Saklıkent" at Fethiye's dolmuş *otogar*.

The mouth of the gorge is deceptively modest; to reach it leave the road bridge for a 150-metre pedestrian **walkway** (open during daylight hours; 2.25YTl) spiked into the canyon walls, ending at the **Gökçesu/Ulupınar springs**, which bubble up under great pressure from the base of the towering cliffs, exiting the narrows to mingle eventually with the Eşen Çayı. It's a magical place, seemingly channelling all the water this side of Akdağ, though made somewhat less so by the tatty tea-and-trout stalls just downstream outside the gorge – and by the regular descent of coached-in tour groups from Fethiye and other resorts. Many of the **restaurants** suspended on wood platforms above the cascades were destroyed by winter flooding some years back and have never been rebuilt.

Beyond this point, the water-sculpted chasm extends 18km upstream, though further progress for all except rock-climbers is blocked after about 2km by a boulder slide. If you want to explore up to that point, it's initially a **wading** exercise – take submersible shoes, or rent a pair here. The entire length of the gorge was first descended in 1993 by a technically equipped **canyoning** expedition who took eighteen hours (bivouacking halfway), and required frequent abseils down dry waterfalls and thirty-metre rock stacks. This trip is now offered on a custom basis, during summer only, by certain adventure outfits in Kaş (see p.495).

With your own vehicle, it's easy to continue from the gorge mouth down the unsignposted road to Xanthos, the Letoön or Patara (all described later in the chapter); proceed over the road bridge past the half-dozen trout restaurants and the treehouse-format *Saklıkent Gorge Camp* (☎ 0252/659 0074, ⓦ www.saklikentgorge .com; ❷ half-board only), which arranges rafting locally, to follow the paved road along the left bank of the river. After twelve rather lonely, unmarked kilometres, you reach Palamut village; bear right at the fork immediately beyond Çavdır, the next village, and, 7km past Çavdır, you join the new highway through the Xanthos valley. Bearing left leads to Patara and (eventually) Kalkan; cross the highway and continue on the narrower road to reach Xanthos after a kilometre or so.

Pınara

About 45km southeast of Fethiye on Highway 400 towards Patara, you'll see the well-marked turning west (right) for ancient **Pınara**. Practically nothing is known about this city, inscriptions discovered at the site being singularly uninformative. According to the fourth-century Xanthian historian Menekrates, it was founded to accommodate the overflow from Xanthos. Later on, however, Pınara – whose name means "something round" in the Lycian language, presumably because of the shape of the original, upper acropolis – grew to become one of the larger Lycian cities, minting its own coins and earning three votes in the Federation.

It's just over 3km from the start of the side road to the edge of Minare village (one café, one restaurant, but no public transport), from where 2.2km more of signposted but steep dirt track leads to the start of the ruins. You can hike this final distance in about half an hour, though you'll be buzzed by traffic in summer since Pınara is beginning to feature on formal tours.

Approaching the site, the **cliff** on which the original city was founded is unmissable, practically blocking out the horizon – indeed it's worth the trip up just to see this towering mass, whose east face is covered in rectangular openings, thought to be either tombs or food storage cubicles. These can only be reached by experienced rock-climbers and it's hard to fathom how they were ever cut in the first place.

The site

The main part of the ruins of Pınara (unenclosed; admission 4YTL when guard present) are situated on the lower acropolis hill, to the east of the cliff, where the city was relocated quite early in its history, when defence had become less of a priority. The **lower acropolis** is overgrown and most of its buildings are unidentifiable, though the access track has been extended to a point almost level with it.

Pınara's **tombs** are probably its most interesting feature, especially a group on the west bank of the seasonal stream that tumbles through the site. On the east side of the lower acropolis hill (follow a path marked with arrows on metal signs), the so-called **Royal Tomb** is unique for its detailed if well-worn carvings on the walls of its porch, representing four walled cities with battlements, gates, houses and tombs, plus one or two human figures; a frieze survives above, showing a large number of people and animals in a peaceable scene – perhaps a religious festival. Inside there is a single bench, set unusually high off the ground, suggesting that it was the tomb of just one person, probably of royal blood.

On the same side of this lower hill but higher up, reached by a direct path north from the Royal Tomb, there's a house-tomb with a roof in the form of a gothic arch, at whose point is a pair of stone **ox horns** thought to ward off evil spirits. This stands near the top of the lower acropolis, and at the eastern edge of the presumed **agora**. Just north of the horned tomb, under the welcome shade of a dense growth of pines, the massive foundations of a **temple** to an unidentified god overlook the theatre (see opposite). Hairpinning back south, a level path threads between the pigeonholed cliff and the lower acropolis, first past a very ruinous but engaging **odeion**, then through a chaos of walls, uprights, heart-shaped column sections and tombs clogging the flattish area between the heights: there's nothing identifiable, but this was clearly the heart of the city.

At the far south end of this little plateau, two sarcophagi flank a man-made terrace and a sharp drop to the stream valley. About the only building that can be identified here with certainty by its apse is a **church**. Above this juts a strange, intact **tower**, identified by some as a tomb but more likely to have been a guard-house controlling the way to the upper citadel, and offering a fine vantage point for making sense of the jumbled town. From the terrace, the path descends to the canyon floor, passing more rock tombs and a wonderful permanent spring – which moves down-canyon as the year progresses – en route to the car park.

Northeast of the town, easily accessible along a marked side-track from the main track passing the base of the lower acropolis, is the well-preserved **theatre**, backing into a hill and overlooking a tilled field as well as the "Swiss cheese" cliff; small but handsome, and never modified by the Romans (on-site signage to the contrary), it gives an idea of Pınara's modest population.

Sidyma

Sidyma is the most remote of the Xanthos valley's ancient cities – and indeed, sited halfway up the ancient Mount Kragos (the modern coastal peak of Avlankara Tepesi), is scarcely in the valley at all. Contrary to some reports, it's a rewarding and understated site in a striking landscape astride the Lycian Way. Like most of the region's antiquities, Sidyma was only "rediscovered" by Europeans during the mid-nineteenth century, and has been scarcely visited since – certainly it has never been properly excavated.

From Highway 400 take the turning marked for Eşen and "Sidyma, 13km", just north of a side road for Kumlova and Letoön. Proceed 6km to an unmarked junction on the dirt-road system, and turn left (south); it's just over 2km to the first buildings (including the conspicuous primary school) of **Dodurga** village, and another 3km to road's end in Dodurga's Asar Mahallesi, where two mulberry trees flank the ruins of the agora and a Lycian Way metal signpost. All but the last 2km are paved, and any vehicle should be able to make the climb. Trekking southeast on the **Lycian Way**, it's a day-and-a-half's march from Kabak to Sidyma, via Alınca.

The site

The *mahalle*'s mosque occupies the site of the baths, and reuses pillars from the agora's stoa. Indeed the principal charm of the place is the way in which ancient masonry crops up everywhere: incorporated into house corners, used as livestock troughs, or just sprouting incongruously in dooryards next to satellite dishes. An exceedingly ruined **castle**, garrisoned into Byzantine times, sits on a hill to the north; scattered in the fields to the east, and requiring some scrambling over walls to reach, is the **necropolis**, comprising a variety of tomb types, though most have angular gabled roofs rather than the "Gothic" vaulted ones seen elsewhere. Near the centre of the agricultural plain is a group of remarkable, contiguous tombs: one has ceiling panels carved with rosettes and human faces, while the adjacent tomb has a relief of Eros on its lid and Medusas at the ends (a motif repeated elsewhere). Another spectacular cluster, including a two-storeyed one, covers the low ridge beyond the fields. In the middle of the necropolis stands an enormous, fairly intact, square structure – probably a Roman-imperial **heroön** or temple-tomb – with a walled-up doorway on the north side.

Practicalities

The closest tourist facilities are in hillside **ALİNCA**, which can be reached by returning to the unmarked junction and heading southwest through Boğaziçi and then northwest. Just off the Lycian Way at the top of the village, stands the pricey *Dervish Lodge* (☎0252/679 1142), with views to die for and accommodation ranging from small gazebos (at €35 per person half-board) to standard doubles (€60 per person half-board). Probably better value, though much further off the trail, is *Black Tree Cottages* (☎0252/679 1105, ⓦwww.blacktree.net; closed Oct–March) in **KARAAĞAÇ**, 3.5km beyond. These occupy extensive if rather bleak grounds, 1100m up, with rare Baba Dağ cedars growing overhead; the accommodation comprises an old restored trekkers' lodge (16 beds at €8 a head) and nine newer free-standing cottages, well built in local stone and pine, accommodating four to seven people (£280 a week for 1-bedroom, £380 a week for 3-bedroom). There's a swimming pool, tennis courts and restaurant-bar that serves simple lunches if you show up on spec. A decent though unmarked, non-Lycian Way trail links Karaağaç with Kirme. Perhaps the best lodging in the area, however, is in **GEY**, a three-hour trek southeast of Alınca or 8km by road from Sidyma. Here Leon and Semra's ☆ *Yediburunlar Lighthouse Guesthouse* (☎0252/679 1001; ❻ half-board) has all the sweeping views of a lighthouse, but is in fact a new stone-and-wood built, four-room boutique inn with all comforts including a pool; a trekkers' annexe is under construction as the main building is often taken up by package companies.

The Letoön

The Letoön, shrine of the goddess **Leto**, was the official religious sanctuary, oracle and festival venue of the Lycian Federation, and the extensive ruins remaining today bear witness to its importance. The site lies 16km south **from Pınara** along the old road (less on the new highway), the turning marked with a "Kumluova, Karadere, Letoön 10" sign. Driving instead **from Patara**, leave Highway 400 at the Kınık/Xanthos turning; clear Kınık town and cross the Eşençay bridge; then descend into pines and take a hairpin left turn marked by a "Letoön 4" marker. There's a **dolmuş from Fethiye** to Kumluova, the village beside the site: get off in the village centre near the signposted turn-off to the Letoön, a few hundred metres' walk away.

Some history and mythology

Following the demise of the Lycian Federation, the sanctuary became Christianized during Byzantine times, and wasn't abandoned until the Arab raids of the seventh century. The Letoön was initially rediscovered by Fellows in 1840, although French-conducted excavations didn't begin until 1962, since when it has been systematically uncovered and labelled. The latest phase of the excavations, which take place annually in September and October, are aimed at a partial reconstruction of the main temple here.

The nymph Leto was loved by Zeus and thus jealously pursued by Hera, his wife. Wandering in search of a place to give birth to her divine twins (Apollo and Artemis), Leto approached a fountain to slake her thirst, only to be driven away by local herdsmen. Leto was then led to drink at the Xanthos river by wolves, and so changed the name of the country to Lycia, *lykos* being Greek for wolf. After giving birth to her children, she returned to the spring – on the site of the existing Letoön, and forever after sacred to the goddess – to punish the insolent herdsmen by transforming them into frogs.

The name Leto could be derived from the Lycian word *lada* (woman), and it is conceivable that the Anatolian mother-goddess, Cybele, was worshipped here before her. Another similarity between the two goddesses is their connection with incestuous mother–son unions, something thought to have been common in Lycian society. Most famous of all the prophecies supposed to have been delivered at the Letoön was that received by Alexander the Great, informing him that the Persian Empire would be destroyed by the Greeks.

The site

Since excavations of **the site** (daily: summer 8am–7.30pm; winter 8.30am–5pm; 4YTL) began, the remains of three temples, a nymphaeum and two porticoes have been uncovered, as well as a number of interesting **inscriptions**. One of these stipulates conditions of entry to the sanctuary, including a strict dress-code of simple clothing and prohibiting rich jewellery or elaborate hairstyles. Another important inscription, found on the rock-shelf east of the temples, is a trilingual text in Lycian, Greek and Aramaic, referring to the establishment in Xanthos of a cult of the Kaunian deity Basilens ("King"), which proved invaluable in deciphering the Lycian language.

The low ruins of the three **temples** occupy the centre of the site, beyond the relatively uninteresting (and waterlogged) agora. The westernmost of them, straight ahead as you stand with your back to the entrance, bears a dedication to Leto. Once surrounded by a single colonnade with decorative half-columns around the interior walls, it dates back to the third century BC. Three columns and an architrave on the north side of the structure have currently been reconstructed; though the masonry may seem jarringly garish it was, in fact, sourced from the original marble quarry near modern Finike. The temple in the centre is a fourth-century BC structure, identified by a dedication to Artemis; its northern part incorporates a rocky outcrop. The easternmost temple was similar in design to the temple of Leto, surrounded by a Doric colonnade with half-columns around its interior. The reproduction **mosaic** on the floor of this temple – the original is now in the Fethiye museum (see p.448) – depicts a lyre, bow and quiver with a stylized flower in the centre. This suggests that it was dedicated to Artemis and Apollo, since the bow and quiver were symbols of Artemis, and the lyre that of Apollo. Not surprisingly, these children of Leto, legendarily born in the Xanthos valley, were the region's most revered deities. The style of architecture and mosaic date the temple to the second and first centuries BC.

Beyond the three temples, to the southwest, extends a **nymphaeum**, which consisted of a rectangular structure with two semicircular recesses on either side, with niches for statues. The remains of the building are bordered by a semicircular paved basin with a diameter of 27m, now permanently flooded by the high local water-table and full of terrapins and noisy frogs. A **church** was built over the rectangular section of the nymphaeum in the fourth century, and destroyed by Arab invaders in the seventh, so that only its outline is now discernible. Similarly, the notable stork mosaic on its floor is, alas, headless and apt to be covered by grass and sand.

Returning to the car park at the entrance, you'll come to a large, well-preserved Hellenistic **theatre** on the right, entered through a vaulted passage. Sixteen plaques, adorned by comic and tragic **masks in relief**, decorate the northeast entrance to this passage, while nearby sits an interesting Roman **tomb** with a relief representation of its toga-clad occupant.

Pydnae

Dolmuşes from Kumluova village (labelled "Kumluova–Karadere" run the 7km southwest to the end of the paved road (and dolmuş stop), where the ancient **fortress of Pydnae** is obvious on the right, on the far side of the Özlen Çayı. To reach the fortress itself, you'll need to continue to the end of the onward mud-and-sand track (best with a 4WD) that leads to the beach (no facilities) at the stream mouth. Cross the rickety footbridge here, and head up behind the single dwelling and greenhouses to pick up Lycian Way markers, which lead to – and through – the fortress gate within twenty minutes.

Pydnae was a small naval base at the extreme northwestern end of the much larger, deeper bay that once existed between here and Patara, before the Özlen and Eşen streams silted it up. The irregularly shaped precinct is built of almost perfectly preserved, Hellenistic **polygonal masonry**, with steps leading up to the walls at various points and, every so often, square towers with loopholes for archers. The most recent structure inside, and the only one besides a roofless **cistern** with its walls still rendered, is a Byzantine **church**, its arched apsidal window overlooking the reedy marshes where fleets once anchored.

Xanthos

The remains of the hilltop city of **Xanthos**, with their breathtaking views of the Xanthos river – now the Eşen Çayı – and its valley, are among the most fascinating in the whole of Lycia. The site was first made familiar to the British public in 1842, when traveller Charles Fellows visited and carried off the majority of its movable art works, just four decades after the Elgin marbles had been similarly pillaged. It took two months to strip the site of its monuments, which were loaded onto the HMS *Beacon* and shipped to London. The most important construction discovered at ancient Xanthos, the fourth-century Nereid Monument, a beautifully decorated Ionic temple on a high podium, is now in the British Museum, along with many other monuments and sculptures. However, enough was left behind here to require a two-hour visit. Afternoons are scorchingly hot even by Lycian standards – try and go earlier or later in the day.

Buses or (more likely) **dolmuşes** between Fethiye and Patara will drop you off in Kınık, less than 2km beyond the southerly Letoön turn-off, from where it's a twenty-minute uphill walk. Alternatively, Xanthos features in the repertoire of virtually every tour company pitching **organized excursions**, usually in tandem with the Letoön.

Some history

Part of the fascination of a visit to Xanthos lies in the city's history, which was dominated by the mercurial fortunes and temperament of its inhabitants. In mythology the city was connected with the story of Bellerophon and Pegasus (see "Olympos and Çıralı", p.515). King Iobates – who initially set impossible tasks for Bellerophon and later offered him a share in his kingdom – ruled here, and the city was the home of the grandson of Bellerophon, Glaucus, who was described in *The Iliad* as hailing "from the whirling waters of the Xanthos".

Archeological finds from the site date back to the eighth century BC, but the earliest historical mention of the city dates from 540 BC and the conquest of Lycia by the Persian general Harpagus. From Caria he descended into the Xanthos valley and, after some resistance, subjected the city to siege. The Xanthians' response was the first local holocaust, gathering their families and making a funeral pyre with their household belongings. The women and children died in the flames, and the men perished fighting, the only surviving citizens being eight families who were out of town at the time.

The subsequent fate of Xanthos resembled that of the rest of Lycia, with Alexander succeeding the Persians, and in time being succeeded by his general Antigonus and then by Antiochus III. After the defeat of Antiochus, Xanthos was given to Rhodes along with the rest of Lycia.

The second Xanthian holocaust occurred in 42 BC during the Roman civil war, when Brutus besieged the city, causing the citizens again to make funeral pyres of their possessions and cast themselves into the flames. Xanthos prospered anew in Roman imperial times, and under Byzantine rule the city walls were renovated and a monastery built.

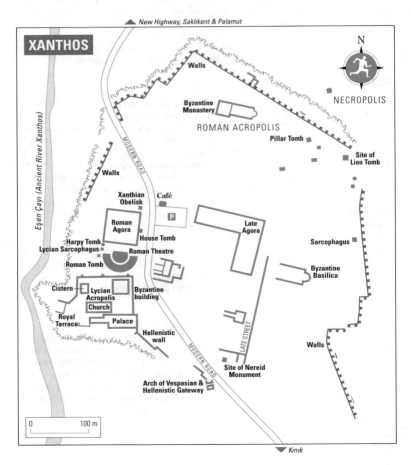

The site

The **site** is unfenced (except for the theatre area), but officially open 8am to 7.30pm in summer, 8.30am to 5pm in winter; the warden stationed at the car-park souvenir stall will collect 4YTL admission, plus parking fees.

Very close to the entrance booth, west of the road, stands the monumental **Arch of Vespasian** and an adjoining **Hellenistic gateway**, the latter bearing an inscription recording that Antiochus the Great dedicated the city to Leto, Apollo and Artemis, the national deities of Lycia. Further up, east of the road, the former location of the **Nereid Monument** is marked by a plaque.

West of the car park, at the top of the access road, the Lycian acropolis and the Roman agora sandwich the Roman theatre, beside which are two conspicuous Lycian monuments. To the north looms the so-called **Harpy Tomb**, once topped with a marble chamber removed by Fellows; this has since been replaced by a cement cast of the original. The paired bird-women figures on the tomb's north and south sides have been identified as harpies, or – more likely – sirens, carrying the souls of the dead (represented as children) to the Isles of the Blessed. Other reliefs each side portray unidentified seated figures receiving gifts, except for the west face where they are regarding opium poppies. Beside the Harpy Tomb a **Lycian sarcophagus** stands on a pillar, an unusual structure thought to date from the third century BC. Traces of a corpse and some third-century pottery were found inside the tomb, along with a sixth-century BC relief – thought to have been brought from elsewhere – depicting funeral games.

Just northeast of the agora looms what's popularly known as the **Xanthian Obelisk**. It is in fact the remains of another pillar tomb, labelled as the "Inscribed Pillar" and covered on all four sides by the longest known Lycian inscription, which runs to 250 lines and includes twelve lines of Greek verse. Since the Lycian language hasn't been completely deciphered, the understanding of the inscription is based on this verse, and on proper names appearing in the text, which tells the story of a champion wrestler who went on to sack many cities, and generally glorifies his family name.

The nearby **Roman theatre** was built on the site of an earlier Greek structure and is pretty complete, missing only the upper seats, which were incorporated into the Byzantine city wall. Behind the theatre, overlooking the Xanthos valley, lies the **Lycian acropolis**, in whose far southeastern corner are the remains of a square building believed to be the palace of the early Xanthian kings destroyed by Harpagus. Beneath the protective sand you can find patches of sophisticated mosaic, which indicate Roman or Byzantine use of the acropolis; there are also water channels everywhere underfoot plus a huge cistern, suggesting an advanced plumbing system and a preoccupation with outlasting sieges.

Walk east from the car park, then south through the so-called **late agora** to a **Byzantine basilica**, currently fenced off but easy enough to enter – beware the unauthorized guides offering useless, incomprehensible and overpriced "tours" of its grounds. The basilica is distinguished by its extensive abstract **mosaics** – the best in western Turkey – and a *synthronon* in the semicircular apse. On the hill north of here is the **Roman acropolis**, at the eastern side of which are a number of freestanding **sarcophagi**, and above, cut into the hillside, a group of picturesque **tombs** mainly of the Lycian house (as opposed to temple) type. A well-preserved early **Byzantine monastery**, containing an open courtyard with washbasins along one side, is located to the north of the acropolis hill.

Patara and Gelemiş

Patara was the principal port of Lycia, famed for its oracle of Apollo, and as the birthplace during the fourth century AD of St Nicholas, Bishop of Myra (aka

Santa Claus). Today, however, the area is better known for its huge white sand **beach**, served by the *pansiyons*, bars and restaurants in the village of **Gelemiş** almost 3km inland. The beach is a summertime turtle-nesting area, off-limits after dark (May–Oct), while in winter the lagoon behind attracts considerable bird life from inner Anatolia. Conservationists, backed by the Ministry of the Environment, have won the fight to exclude villas from the cape at the southeast end of the strand, while the protected archeological status of the area seems to have put a stop to most new building at Gelemiş – indeed there have been repeated official threats to raze the entire settlement. Plans for a local airport have been shelved, with a change of venue to Çukurbağ, above Kaş, contemplated if tourist numbers (and the Turkish economy) ever revive sufficiently. As part of a new-found "green" image, horse riding and walking in the hills to the east are now promoted, using both the Lycian Way and other trails.

Gelemiş lies south of Highway 400, down a paved side-road beginning by a prominent rock outcrop; the turn-off is signposted about midway between the villages of Ovaköy and Yeşilköy. **Minibuses**, stopping in the centre near the PTT, arrive every half-hour from Kalkan – from Fethiye there are around fifteen a day – and many of these continue past the ruins of Patara to the beach at the road's end. Be aware that long-haul buses may only call at the junction with the main road, 3.5km north of the village.

Some history

Numerous myths concern the Greek origins of the city of Patara, but in fact the city was Lycian from the beginning, as evidenced by coins and inscriptions spelling out an un-Hellenic PTTRA. The city was famous for its temple and oracle of Apollo, which was supposed to rival the one at Delphi in accuracy, probably because Apollo supposedly spent the winter months in the Xanthos valley. However, no verifiable traces of this temple have ever been found.

Patara played an important part in Lycian and Hellenistic history, being used as a naval base during the wars between Alexander's successors. Later, in 42 BC, Brutus threatened the Patarans with a fate similar to that of the Xanthians (see p.478) if they didn't submit, giving them a day to decide. Plutarch wrote that Brutus released the women hostages in the hope that they would lessen the resolve of their menfolk. When this didn't work, Brutus freed all the remaining hostages, thereby proving his amiability and endearing himself to the Patarans, who subsequently surrendered. Whatever his tactics, his chief motive for taking the city was suggested by the fact that he took no prisoners, but merely ordered that all the city's gold and silver should be handed over.

Patara

At the far southern edge of Gelemiş village, a lockable gate and ticket booth controls vehicle access to both beach and **archeological site** (daily: May–Oct 8.30am–7.30pm; Nov–April 8.30am–5pm; 2YTL) some distance beyond. Although the ruins are unfenced, you are technically not allowed in on foot outside the official opening times.

Much of the site has never been fully excavated, and by and large it presents a spectacle of numerous unidentified and badly overgrown walls in polygonal masonry. Few clear paths link individual ruins, which often means repeated, irritating backtracking to the main road. There are also no facilities or shade – bring water, stout shoes and a head covering during summer.

Two kilometres from the village, the entrance to the city is marked by a triple-arched, first-century AD **Roman gateway**, almost completely intact. To the west of the gate rises a little hill where a head of Apollo was discovered, prompting speculation that this was the site of the temple of Apollo. Just outside the gate, a **necropolis** is currently being excavated every summer by a Turkish team led by Fahri Işik from Akdeniz University in Antalya.

South of the hill sits a **baths complex**, similar to the one at Tlos, with arches and five rectangular apsidal windows, and the foundations of either a **basilica** or an extension of the baths, to which an exotic touch is lent by a shady palm grove sprouting up from the flooring and almost totally obscuring it. To the west of these, tacked onto the longest surviving extent of the **city walls** – and difficult to reach – is an attractive second-century **temple**. While too small and simple to be identified as the city's famous Apollo shrine, it has a richly decorated seven-metre-high door-frame – its lintel long on the point of collapse – leading into a single chamber. Further south, reached by a different track from the main road, are more **baths**, built by the emperor Vespasian (69–79 AD), which impress mainly by their squat bulk. Just west of these is a large **paved area**, either the main agora or a processional street, with its north end partly submerged by the high local water-table, and a growing number of stubby columns being re-erected by the excavators.

The **theatre** sits southwest of these baths, under the brow of the acropolis hill and easiest reached by yet another track heading off the main road, a few paces before the beach car park. The cavea has been cleaned of sand to reveal eighteen rows of seats up to the diazoma (dividing walkway) and a dozen or so more beyond. The partly intact stage building is slowly being pieced together; on its exterior you can read a Greek inscription ascribing the erection of the stage to a woman, Vilia Prokla, and her father, both citizens of Patara. The funding for it was approved by the local council, which is thought to have been convened in the recently exposed **boueuterion** (locked but views through the gate) between the theatre and the agora, with its horseshoe array of seating.

South of the theatre a reasonable path climbs uphill to the city's **acropolis**. At the top lurks an unusual rectangular pit, some ten metres across, with a pillar (for measuring water level) rearing out of the bottom and badly damaged stairs down its side. Since it doesn't overlook the old harbour, the pit was almost certainly a **cistern**, and not the **lighthouse** as originally supposed; that is iden-

▲ Patara beach

tified as the square, arched tower, its top collapsed, on the west side of the hill, which still has a fine view over the sea, beach and brackish swamp that was once the **harbour**. The latter silted up gradually in the Middle Ages and was subsequently abandoned, separated today from the beach by 300-metre-wide dunes stabilized by introduced mimosa and fencing. On the far side of the stagnant port, across the dunes, are the bulky remains of **Hadrian's granary**.

The beach

The **beach** of fine white sand at Patara (same ticket and admission policy as ruins) ranks as one of the longest continual strands in the Mediterranean: 9km from the access road to the mouth of the river (accessible from Gelemiş by a side road labelled "Çay Ağzı"; see below), then almost 6km further to the end. Rather than making the hot, half-hour stroll out from the centre of Gelemiş in summer, most people flag down a **beach dolmuş** or take advantage of tractor-drawn transport laid on by the hotels. Parking at the road's end is very limited, as the archeological authorities have refused permission to expand the space. The only facility is a wooden stall out on the sand selling snacks, drinks and renting out beach paraphernalia: it has a very limited menu, however, and exorbitant prices (15YTL for sun beds and umbrella rental), so come prepared.

In season it gets crowded in the immediate vicinity of the beach entrance, but a walk along the dunes toward the river and the Letoön brings you to more than enough solitary spots – and a few unharassed colonies of nudists. Spring and autumn swimming is delightful, but in summer the exposed shoreline is sometimes battered by a considerable surf (at least by Mediterranean standards).

If you wish to visit the beach after the Patara gate has closed – to watch the sunset, for example – you'll need to use the side road to **Çay Ağzı** ("River Mouth"), marked inconspicuously between Gelemiş and Highway 400, next to the rock outcrop, where a small sign indicates "Çay Ağzı 5" (though it's nearer 6km). The beach here isn't as nice as at Patara, nor are there any facilities.

Gelemiş

GELEMIŞ itself consists of little more than a busy T-junction, with a main, crescent-shaped neighbourhood threaded by a single twisting high-street extending west, then climbing northwest onto a small hill. Before 1950, the entire area was highly malarial and the nomadic *Yörüks* who had settled here spent the hottest months up in the healthier mountain village of İslamlar, near Gömbe. Subsequently, a lake immediately northeast of Highway 400 (still erroneously shown on many maps) was drained by a canal, and the Patara swamp shrunk by eucalyptus plantations in the village centre.

It's worth noting, however, that Gelemiş is under threat from a currently dormant Ministry of Culture proposal to evacuate and demolish the entire village, as part of its general policy of "cleaning up" the environs of archeological sites. A petition and campaign from hoteliers and satisfied prior clients, and a three-day "strike" by local shopkeepers and taverna proprietors, forced the ministry to back down in 2001, but what's seen locally as a "death sentence" could be revived at short notice.

In the meantime, **accommodation** here is a buyers' market as Gelemiş has an excess capacity of (sometimes shoddy) lodgings, with package allotments relatively scarce. The most desirable premises are either on the ridge to the east of the T-junction, or on the western hill above. It is possible to walk from this latter neighbourhood past the west shore of the swamp and Hadrian's granary to the beach in about twenty minutes, but this puts you out on a part of the dunes devoid of facilities, and this route is best used as an interesting alternate return to the village at day's end.

Independent choices for eating out are somewhat limited and you're often best off arranging to be fed at your accommodation; cuisine tends to be sustaining rather than *haute*. The most reliable and durable **restaurants**, in no preferential order, are those attached to the *Lumière*, the *Golden* and the *Flower pansiyons*, with a clutch of more adventurous but changeable outfits next to the central park and playground. If standard Turkish hotel **breakfasts** don't start the day well for you, try one of the two unusually tasty *gözleme* stalls next to the *Golden Pansiyon*. On Gelemiş "high street" are a number of fairly well-established **bars** – the best are *Sarpedon*, with a 1970s and 1980s soundtrack and a hearth fire in cooler months; *Medusa*, whose proprietor Pamir is involved with local environmental issues and runs a very basic **campsite** out back; and the quirky *Flintstones*, on the beach road a bit before the ticket booth, with cheapish beer, reggae soundtrack and inexpensive snacks. There's even a small local **travel agency** in the basement of the *Golden Pansiyon*: Gelemiş Turizm (ⓣ0242/843 5105), offering trekking trips in addition to the standard Xanthos canoeing and archeological excursions.

Accommodation

Ferah Hotel ⓣ0242/843 5180, ⓔferahhotel@hotmail.com. On the western hill, with large, well-maintained, partly a/c rooms and an unusually pleasant garden restaurant. ❸

Flower Pension ⓣ0242/843 5164, ⓦwww.kircatravel.com. Of the few establishments along the approach to the village from Highway 400, this is the only one worth considering. West of the road as you enter Gelemiş, this en-suite *pansiyon*, run by Ayşe Kırca, has a breakfast terrace overlooking a lush garden. ❷

Golden Pansiyon ⓣ0242/843 5162, ⓦwww.goldenpension.com. Arif Otlu caters to those on a budget with fairly large, 2004-renovated rooms (some balconied, all double-glazed and a/c), located very centrally. The restaurant here sometimes has trout or ocean fish on the menu. Uniquely here, open all year. ❷

Lumière ⓣ0242/843 5043. Downhill but set well back from the through road, close to the T-junction, offering variable-sized, pastel-decor rooms with kilims and proper stall showers, and a pool-terrace restaurant. ❷

Mehmet ⓣ0242/843 5032, ⓦwww.mehmeta-parts.com. On the eastern ridge, offering plain, medium-sized rooms (❸) with balconies, some overlooking a pool and restaurant, plus three well-appointed apartments (❹).

Merhaba Hotel ⓣ0242/843 5199, ⓦwww.merhabapatara.com. Up on the easterly ridge amongst the trees, just before the archeological zone, this scores more for its sunset and sea views (most reliably from the rooftop restaurant) and peaceful environment than the 1980s-basic rooms themselves, though there are also a few a/c family suites. ❹

Patara View Point Hotel ⓣ0242/843 5184 or 0533/350 0347, ⓦwww.pataraviewpoint.com. Muzaffer Otlu's and Anne-Louise Thomson's hotel has an unbeatable setting on the easterly ridge. The rooms have mosquito nets, balconies and heating/a/c, there's a tractor shuttle to the beach, a pool-bar where breakfast is served, Internet access and a Turkish-style night-time terrace. They're open all year by arrangement, with advantageous weekly rates. Credit cards accepted with a 2 percent surcharge. ❹

Zeybek 2 Pansiyon ⓣ0242/843 5141, ⓔzeybek-pension2@hotmail.com. A vine-shrouded premises occupying the best position on the western hill; the rooms have fans, and the owners are generally willing and helpful. ❶

Kalkan and around

Thirteen kilometres beyond the turn-off for Patara, the former Greek village of Kalamaki, now **KALKAN**, appears to cling for dear life to the steep slope on which it's situated. Occasionally the older, stone-built houses lose their fight with gravity, as happened during the severe 1957 earthquake, traces of which are still discernible in a few unrepaired buildings of the original village core to the east. Tourism and real-estate sales, though now the lifeblood of the place, are fairly new phenomena: until the late 1970s both Kalkan and its neighbour Kaş eked out a living from charcoal burning and olive growing. The locals benefiting from the initial boom were those too poor to spend the summer tending grain and apples on the huge plateau around the mountain village of Bezirgan, and who therefore were on hand to staff the new establishments; the richer residents sold up their seaside property without realizing its value. Until the mid-1980s, Kalkan had a distinctly bohemian atmosphere, serving as an escape from the often oppressive conditions in larger Turkish cities after the 1980 coup. It was the sort of place where Rudolph Nuryev could come ashore from his private yacht one rainy winter night and play a two-hour video of himself dancing naked for those assembled in one of the three existing bar-restaurants of the time.

Today, dancing in the buff is probably the last thing on the agenda of the relatively wealthy, sedate and overwhelmingly British clientele; since the millennium conventional tourism has morphed into residential tourism, and Kalkan into an upmarket expat colony of about 1200 (out of a total population of 4000) with European prices to match. Two dozen estate agencies have thus far sold six hundred flats or villas to foreigners for crazy money, with nearly as many more still unsold; runaway, generally unaesthetic development, encouraged by a gung-ho mayor, has scarred the hillsides and is threatening to uproot the last of the local olive groves. The rise and rise of the second- (or only) home industry has cut a huge swathe through the small boutique hotels which used to be Kalkan's lifeblood but have now shut or been converted to apartments; many hoteliers, seeing the writing on the wall, turned contractor and sold properties to their former clients. Lingering elements of the package-holiday trade monopolize most of the better remaining short-term accommodation, and ensure that Kalkan remains more exclusive – and more twee – than nearby Kaş.

If you can accept this all-pervading social profile – and the lack of a sandy beach – Kalkan makes a good base from which to explore Patara, Xanthos and the Letoön, while **excursions** east along the coast or inland to the Toros mountains can occupy another day or so.

Arrival, transport and services

Minibuses stop near the top of the bazaar, near the taxi rank; long-distance **buses** will leave you at the top of the built-up area, at the junction with the spur road into town. There's no tourist office in Kalkan, though there's a single **bank** with ATM next to the **PTT** (open daily in season, also with metered phones until midnight). There are four or five **car rental** outlets, plus a single motorbike franchise, though scooters are only suitable for short jaunts to Patara and Kaş.

Accommodation

A handful of surviving *pansiyon*s are located in the converted old buildings lining the central grid of cemented lanes – a district known as **Yalıboyu** – that drops from **Hasan Altan Sokağı** down to the harbour. There is also a district of newer, purpose-built hotels extending a kilometre or so west from the edge of town along **Kalamar Yolu**, which heads towards Kalamar Bay. Most of these establishments are block-booked in season by tour operators; larger room sizes, and usually the presence of a swimming pool, offset the disadvantage of a hefty walk into town. The closest recommendable accommodation actually on **Kalkan Bay** is 3.5km out of town, on the east (left-hand) shoreline. Unless otherwise indicated, all lodging is open May to October.

Yalıboyu

Balıkçı Han 2 On the waterfront, central ☎0242/844 3075. Although the parent hotel has

been sold for conversion into flats, its annexe survives to the east with several tranquil, air-conditioned, 40-square-metre suites (including two galleried family units), overlooking the ravine and sea. **⑤**

Çetinkaya Pansiyon On the waterfront, far east end ☎0242/844 3307. Large (for central Kalkan) rooms, with varying numbers of beds and air conditioning or fan. The breakfast terrace has a harbour view. **④**

Daphne Pansiyon Above the ex-church mosque, opposite fountain plaza ☎0242/844 2788, ✉daphne_kalkan@hotmail.com. Five simple but large and tastefully decorated double rooms, all with balconies, partial sea views and a/c. Open all year. **③**

Stone House On the waterfront, east end ☎0242/844 3076, ⓦwww.korsankalkan.com. Three large, well-appointed rooms plus a self-catering apartment in this restored house, with an affiliated seafood restaurant. **④**

White House Near top of lane leading up from the east end of waterfront ☎0242/844 3738 or 0532 443 0012, info in winter from UK ☎020/7350 2161. Turkish (Halil)–English (Marion)-run *pansiyon* with large, airy rooms in a variety of formats, from single to quad. Although only four of the ten have balconies, pool privileges are arranged elsewhere and the roof terrace is one of the best in town. Single travellers get a good deal too. **④**

Hasan Altan Sokağı and inland

Çelik Pansiyon Süleyman Yılmaz Cad 6, one block up Altan Sok ☎0242/844 2126 or 0535/224 3846. Long-established cheapie, with basic en-suite rooms and a dazzling terrace view for breakfast. Open all year. **②**

🏃 **Türk Evi (Eski Ev)** Near top of perpendicular lane heading up from Süleyman Yılmaz Cad ☎0242/844 3129, ⓦwww .kalkanturkevi.com. Wonderfully refurbished old house with welcoming common areas, wooden floors upstairs and tiled-floor units downstairs, all with mosquito nets and kilims and some with fireplaces. Open wintertime by arrangement (there's no other heating – or cooling); the road into town passes just up the hill, for easy car access. Discounts for long stays; otherwise **③–④**

Kalamar Yolu

Aldi Hotels 500m along Kalamar Yolu ☎0242/844 3681, ✉aldihotels@hotmail.com. A group of four contiguous, comanaged units at the quiet end of a descending cul-de-sac, furnished to a high standard. All except the *Diva Hotel* (**③**) have ample sea views over the surrounding olive groves; you pay extra for an unobstructed panorama at the *Dionysia* (**④**). The more sumptuous, self-catering *Diana Aparts* and the one-family *Villa Diana* (both **⑤**) are usually block-booked by UK package companies.

Kalkan Regency Hotel 1km along Kalamar Yolu ☎0242/844 2230, ☏844 2290. Indisputably the town centre's best hotel, usually dominated by UK packages, but there's some chance of a 2003-renovated room if you turn up in May or October. Well-laid-out grounds, in a prime position, feature an enormous pool, billiard table, fitness centre, hamam (included in rates) and on-site restaurant. The large rooms are carpeted, with tiny balconies. **⑦**

Meldi Hotel 800m along Kalamar Yolu, seaward side ☎0242/844 2541, ⓦwww.meldihotel. com. Fair sized rooms, all with up-to-date bathrooms and small balconies, either with garden or mountain views; breakfast is served next to the decent-sized pool. Mostly filled with UK packages (currently bookable through Tapestry Holidays; see p.32). **⑤**

Viewpoint Villas 1km along Kalamar Yolu, uphill side ☎0242/844 3642, ⓦwww.pataraviewpoint .com. A group of six villas arranged around a pool and equipped to a very high standard – Jacuzzi, full kitchen, fireplace in sitting room, etc – each sleeping 4–5. Managed by the *Patara View Point Hotel* (see p.483); £675/week per villa in high season.

Mahal Lido

🏃 **Villa Mahal** 3.5km east of town ☎0242/844 3268, ⓦwww.villamahal .com. Although there is road access, a free-to-guests boat shuttle from the harbour is the best way to approach Kalkan's most exclusive, tasteful lodging, with rooms costing €150–250. A segmented veranda wraps itself around the ten irregularly-shaped standard rooms, while steps lead down past an infinity pool to the sea and lido – about the only one in Kalkan directly linked to accommodation, though open to the public for the sake of its popular restaurant. There's also a suite and two detached cottages – including the "Cliff House" with a private pool – furnished in the same designer-minimalist decor, with the multi-terrace setting among olive trees guaranteeing privacy. **⑧**

Eating and drinking

Restaurants are scattered fairly evenly throughout town, though bars tend to cluster either just above the seafront or along Hasan Altan Sokağı, which after dark

Scuba diving near Kalkan

Kalkan has several locally based dive operators: **Dolphin Scuba Team** (☎0242/844 2242 or 0542/627 9757, ⊛www.dolphinscubateam.com), **Barrakuda Dive Center** (☎0242/844 3955 or 0536/269 2181, ⊛www.dive-turkey.com) and **Island Divers** (☎0242/844 1267 or 0533/689 7023, ⊛www.islanddivers.net) are all on or near the yacht-harbour quay. **Prices** compare well to Fethiye, with a two-dive day typically £37, and a PADI Open Water course £240.

Most of the hundred or so local **dive sites** are a 45-minute boat-ride away, around the islets plainly visible at the mouth of the bay: Yılan Adası (Snake Island), immediately south of Fare Adası (Mouse Island), and the remoter islets of Heybeli and Öksüz. Beginners dive the shallows at the north tip of "Snake", and virtually the entire perimeter of Heybeli. More advanced divers are taken to a dramatic wall, alive with barracuda, grouper and myriad smaller fish, between 20m and 50m at the south tip of "Snake", to a number of reefs off Heybeli and Öksüz or to sand-bottom caves on the mainland with their entrances at 25m. But by far the most spectacular calm-weather dive site, for intermediate and advanced divers, is so-called "**Wreckers Reef**", southeast of Kalkan, off İnce Burun. Here, in 15m of water, are the mangled remains of the *Duchess of York*, built in Hull in 1893 and sunk sometime after 1920 – her bell is on show at Barrakuda Dive Center. However, rather more interesting is another larger, older, mystery craft, broken into three sections at depths of 35–60m, and with teak-plank decking, intact winches and a vast cargo of lead ballast. The reef is wrongly marked on most nautical charts and fairly regularly claims new victims. Except in the caves with their chilly freshwater seeps, **water temperatures** are a comfortable 18–29°C; the sea warms up abruptly in mid-May with a current change, and stays warm into November. **Visibility** is typically 20–30m.

becomes the main pedestrianized drag linking the bus stop with the village centre. Restaurant prices here, however, are stratospheric – potentially over 58YTL a head – for bland British comfort-food and curries; the fact that most restaurants have dropped their old Turkish names for the equivalent in English is a telling comment indeed.

Of several **waterfront restaurants**, the longest established and most consistent are *Deniz* (aka *Pala'nin Yeri*), the *Korsan* and its sister establishment *Fish Terrace*, all near the east end of the quay. Heading **uphill and inland**, *Foto'nun Yeri*, just below the taxi rank on Hasan Altan Sokağı, is a good, though pricey, platform-seating venue for *mantı* and *gözleme*. For the same price (18YTL) you'll probably do better two lanes over at *Belgin's Kitchen*, popular for its cavernous mock-nomad decor and live Turkish evenings; the limited menu's not bad either, featuring such delights as *mantı* and *çiğ börek*. **Up near the PTT** is where the locals mostly eat; here the *Ali Baba* is popular at lunchtime, whilst the nearby *Bezirgan's Kitchen* (supposedly 24hr) costs a tad more for home-style cooking but has more atmosphere, including a wood fire in the cooler months and a resident, free-range parrot. Established **bars** include the long-lived and loud *Yalı*, up at the top of Yalıboyu, ideal for a pre-dinner drink, and the *Yacht Point* down on the quay, with variable music but generally hopping late on an August night.

The beaches

Kalkan itself has an artificially supplemented **pebble beach** called **Kömürlük**, just at the east edge of town; it's pleasant enough and the water is quite clean and chilled from freshwater seeps, with one spring spilling onto the beach itself from just inland. Although bigger than it looks from afar, it still gets hopelessly full in summer, when you'll probably want to use the swimming platforms or **lidos**, with names such as Likya, Kalamar and Mahal, that dot the flanks of the bay – reasonably priced shuttle boats take you to them. The only other bona fide beach within walking distance is a coarse-pebble one well southwest on the coast, which the Lycian Way visits on its course between Gelemiş and Akbel saddle 2km northwest of Kalkan.

The 26km of road east from Kalkan to Kaş follows the harsh karstic coastline, the thin soil stained red from traces of metallic ores, with the Greek isles of Kastellórizo and Rhó increasingly visible out to sea. Just under 6km along you cross the **Kaputaş Gorge**, a deep canyon leading back into the cliffs (canyoning trips are arranged in Kaş). Steps from the roadside parking area – where there's a *jandarma* post, and signs warning you not to leave valuables in cars – take you down to **Kaputaş beach**, a 150-metre-long expanse of pebble and blonde sand that is normally fairly crowded, given the poor quality of any beaches closer to Kalkan or Kaş. Kaputaş has served as the backdrop for innumerable TV advert shoots, and unless there's been a southerly storm the water is crystalline. The closest reliable facility is Ali Taylı's welcoming *Ada Fish Restaurant*, some 500m east of Kaputaş, which does a bumping summer trade thanks to the fresh and reasonably priced (30–35YTL a kilo) fish bought in daily at 8am; if you're taken with the spot, there are basic, non-air-conditioned, en-suite **rooms** downstairs (☎0535/947 5478; ❶) overlooking the Sidek peninsula and its Byzantine ruins.

Inland: İslamlar and Bezirgan

The closest mountain settlement to Kalkan is **İSLAMLAR**, 5km north of Highway 400; make the turn inland at Akbel, with its depressing rows of post-earthquake prefabs. The old name of Bodamya – Ottoman Greek dialect for "rivers" – is still in use, and the high, cool village is indeed alive to the sound of falling water, used to power mills and nurture half a dozen or so trout-farm **restaurants**. Each has its own loyal partisans – particularly *Çiftlik*, the remotest one at the top of the village, and *Değirmen* with a working mill in the basement grinding locally grown sesame seeds, which you can ask to have served with *pekmez* or grape molasses – but the menus all tend to be fairly identical, with smallish trout priced at about 5YTL each. *Mahmut's* (open all year, credit cards accepted) in the centre is the most polished and slightly pricier, but worth it for the grilled-vegetable-and-rocket side garnish and decent service.

Continuing above İslamlar, about 5km along you hit the main Kalkan–Gömbe road; bear right (southeast) for a pleasant forty-odd-kilometre loop back to Kalkan via the upland *ova* (plateau) of **BEZIRGAN**, famous in the past for its horses, but today devoted to sesame, chickpeas and orchard crops – the fertile plain was once a prehistoric lake, and there's a sprinkling of Lycian rock tombs and an ancient citadel on the hill flanking the Lycian Way's entrance to the valley. At the northwest edge of the two-*mahalle* village (and signposted at the *ova*'s north end) is Turkish Erol and Scottish Pauline's excellent, 150-year-old village-house **inn**, ⚐ *Owlsland* (☎0242/837 5214 or 0535/940 1715, ⓦwww.owlsland.com; closed Dec–Jan; ❺, or ❻ half-board), named after the Scops and little owls resident in the nearby almond trees. It lies about 1.5km off the Lycian Way, making it a logical stop on the trek; Erol is a mean cook and you're well advised to have half-board. At 720m elevation, you'll need the woodstoves in the minimally restored rooms to stay warm during spring or autumn.

Alternatively, by studying the Lycian Way map, you can fashion a **loop walk** with the *ova* as pivot; only 1.6km separates the two debouchements of the path onto the ascending road from Kalkan, and indeed this circular walk is offered locally as an organized outing. If you don't join a tour, you can take a minibus from Kalkan's top junction to Bezirgan – there are two daily from Kınık bound for Gömbe – and then walk back to Kalkan in about three hours.

The main road **north from Bezirgan** makes for a lovely drive, passing great stands of *katran* ("Lebanon" cedar) and the *ova* of Akyazı, comprising the flood-plain of the Koca Çayı, which eventually becomes the Saklıkent Gorge, with the three-thousand-metre-high ridge of Akdağ closing the skyline to the northwest. You link up with the Kaş–Gömbe route just past Sütleğen.

⑤ Kaş

Tourism has utterly transformed **KAŞ**. It first sprang to prominence after about 1850, and until 1923 was a Greek-populated timber-shipping port known as Andifli. It's always been appealingly nestled in a curving bay – the name Kaş means "eyebrow" or "something curved" – with a backdrop of vertical, 500-metre-high cliffs peppered with rock-tombs, and startling, head-on views of Greek Kastellórizo. But what was a sleepy fishing village until the early 1980s has become a holiday metropolis, whose permanent population of 8000 is vastly outnumbered in summer by the vacationers on whom locals depend for a living. Attitudes towards outsiders have inevitably hardened – the *otogar* is predictably well patrolled by accommodation touts – though they're not yet like those encountered at Selçuk or Pamukkale. Residential tourism is not so developed as at Dalyan or Kalkan, so Kaş remains less snooty, more youth-oriented and more cosmopolitan; aspiring İstanbul and Ankara yuppies flock here, while amongst foreigners it's still firmly established on the backpackers' trail.

Kaş has also long been a major halting point on "Blue Cruise" itineraries, and **yacht and gület culture** is as important here as at Kalkan – with day-trips available for the less well-heeled. For private yachts, a new marina is being built at Bucak Limanı (formerly Vathy), the long fjord west of town, wedged between Highway 400 and the Çukurbağ peninsula, which extends 5km southwest of Kaş.

There's no beach to speak of in Kaş itself, or anywhere nearby, which together with the lack of a really convenient airport, has spared the town the full impact of modern tourism. Indeed, if you're not looking for antiques and carpets, at first glance there seems little to keep you here. However, the town gets lively at night, since shops stay open until 1am in season – and the various bars much later than that. If you don't have your own transport, Kaş also makes a handy base from which to reach Kekova and nearby Patara, and various types of **adventure tourism** are beginning to take off. The modern town is built atop the site of ancient **Antiphellos**, whose remaining ruins still speckle the streets, as well as covering the base of the peninsula to the west.

Arrival, information and transport

All buses and dolmuşes arrive at the **otogar** at the top inland end of Atatürk Bulvarı (also known as Elmalı Caddesi). The **tourist office** is at waterfront Cumhuriyet Meydanı 5 (April–Oct Mon–Fri 8.30am–noon & 1–7pm, Sat & Sun 10am–noon & 1–7pm; Nov–April Mon–Fri 9am–noon & 1–5pm; ☎0242/836 1238), stocking glossy brochures as well as hotel lists, though rather short on any other information. Central Kaş is small enough to get around on foot, with **parking** (fees payable) largely limited to the harbour quay, and behind the old market square. There's a public **shuttle service** around the Çukurbağ peninsula's loop road, provided by hourly minibuses labelled "Yarımada-şehiriçi"; traffic is no longer allowed to pass directly from town along Necip Bey Caddesi to the Çukurbağ peninsula, but must go the long way around, via Bucak.

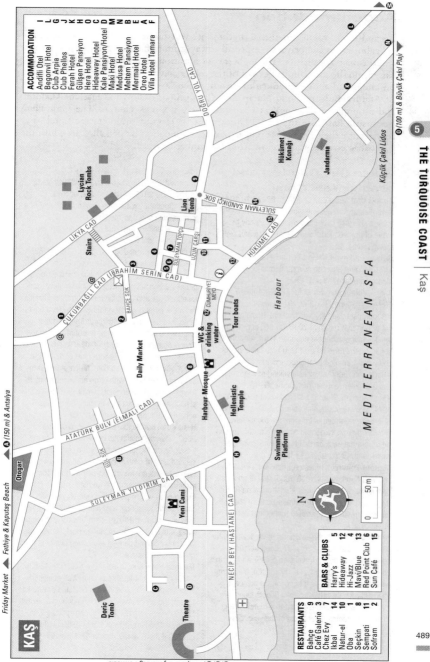

KAŞ

ACCOMMODATION

Andifli Otel	I
Begonvil Hotel	L
Club Arpia	G
Club Phellos	J
Ferah Hotel	K
Gülşen Pansiyon	H
Hera Hotel	C
Hideaway Hotel	O
Kale Pansiyon/Hotel	D
Maki Hotel	M
Medusa Hotel	N
Meltem Pansiyon	B
Mermaid Hotel	E
Oreo Hotel	A
Villa Hotel Tamara	F

RESTAURANTS

Bahçe	9
Café Galerie	3
Chez Evy	7
İkbal	14
Natur-el	10
Oba	1
Seçkin	8
Sempati	11
Sofram	2

BARS & CLUBS

Harry's	5
Hideaway	12
Hi-Jazz	4
Mavi/Blue	13
Red Point Club	6
Sun Café	15

Accommodation

Because of the town's nocturnal rhythms, it's worth hunting a bit out of the centre for calm, views and privacy – especially away from traffic-clogged Atatürk Bulvarı and the main bar district. The highest concentration of desirable hotels and *pansiyons* within the town limits lies east of the centre, beyond the cluster of government buildings and above **Küçükçakıl beach**; an enclave of budget lodgings lies west of Atatürk Bulvarı, along **Necip Bey Caddesi** (also known as Hastane Caddesi) and around the hilltop Yeni Cami, formerly a Greek church. The **Çukurbağ peninsula** has since the mid-1990s acquired a crop of multi-starred hotels, but few deserve their rating. Most in-town accommodation is open all year, whilst the Çukurbağ establishments close from November to April.

Necip Bey Caddesi and around Yeni Cami

Andifli Otel Necip Bey Cad 17 ☏0242/836 1042. Seventies-style outfit with shared bathrooms, though charging contemporary rates strictly by virtue of the wonderful sea-view terrace and sea-facing rooms. ❷

Gülşen Pansiyon Necip Bey Cad 21 ☏0242/836 1171. Modern affair on several floors; lucky balconied rooms face the sea. ❷

Hideaway Hotel Eski Kilise Arkası 7 ☏0242/836 1887, ⓔhideaway @superposta.com. Ex-backpackers' hostel which got a thorough refurb in 2003–04 and is now the most salubrious budget option in town. Air-conditioned rooms have all-new tiled baths plus marble and wood trim; common areas include a small plunge pool, Internet access, willing management and a popular roof-bar/restaurant. ❸–❹

Kale Pansiyon/Hotel 11 Kilise Mevkii ☏0242/836 4074, ⓦwww.guletturkey.com. Two-wing complex with largely German patronage; the rooms have cheerful marble, wood and white-tile decor, the sea view from the back garden is unobstructed. Open year-round. ❸ pansiyon, ❹ hotel

Meltem Pansiyon Sidestreet between Elmalı Cad and Yeni Cami ☏0242/836 1055. One of about six *pansiyons* clustered here and just uphill on Recep Bilgin Cad. This gets the thumbs-up from readers for a warm welcome, sizable rooms and decent breakfasts. ❶

Oreo Hotel Yaka Mahallesi, north of the town centre ☏0242/836 2220 or 836 3737. Good-standard hotel managed by BT Travel (see p.495), and apt to be occupied by sporty types. Over half of the rooms have sea views, there's a big pool and adjacent shady garden for breakfast, and good suppers are available by arrangement, next to a roaring fire in the cooler months. Open most of the year. ❹

Küçükçakıl beach

Begonvil Hotel Koza Sok, about halfway along ☏0242/836 3079, ⓦwww.hotelbegonvil .com. "Boutique" hotel, side-facing at the end of a terrace, with small-to-medium, cheerfully tasteful rooms; all enjoy some kind of view and are air-conditioned, and some have double beds. ❹

Club Phellos Hotel Doğruyol Sok 4 ☏0242/836 1953, ⓦwww.hotelclubphellos.com.tr. The best-standard town-centre hotel: medium-sized rooms are all air-conditioned, with sea/island views, terracotta floors and (usually) mini-bathtubs. Facilities include a large pool, sauna/fitness centre, a pool table, and adequate parking out front (a major issue in peak season). Slight discount offered to *Rough Guide* readers. ❼ Half-board only

Ferah Hotel Küçükçakıl shore road ☏0242/836 1377, ⓦwww.hotelferah.com. Much better-than-average small hotel, with large air-conditioned rooms, a friendly managing family, on-site scuba school, and breakfast and evening barbecues served by the pool; open all year. ❹

Hera Hotel Küçükçakıl shore road ☏0242/836 3062, ⓦwww.lycianhotel.com/hera. Despite the kitsch Greek facade and lobby, it's considered second only to *Club Phellos* as prime in-town digs, with a fitness centre and on-site hamam. The rooms vary considerably – go for the larger front-facing ones where possible. Open all year. ❼

Maki Hotel Koza Sok, east end ☏0242/836 3480, ⓦwww.kasmakihotel.com. Largish a/c rooms, most with a view, a small plunge pool, lift and private underground parking are selling points at this quiet, end-of-the-road hotel. ❹

Medusa Hotel Küçükçakıl shore road ☏0242/836 1440, ⓦwww.medusahotels.com. Well-equipped, well-run three-star hotel with a pool and private lido, though the a/c rooms – some with double beds and island views – are rather small and spartan, with elderly baths. Four-person family suites on the roof offer a bit more space. Rooms ❹, suites ❺

Çukurbağ peninsula

Club Arpia North-shore loop road, Gazeteciler district, 7km out of town ℡0242/836 2642, ✉arpia@bougainville-turkey.com. Rooms are well-kept, but the place really scores for its sunset views, private shoreline lido and poolside restaurant (there's a better-than-average breakfast and open buffet supper). Bookable direct or through Bourganville Travel in town (see "Listings"). Easter to mid-Nov. ❹

Mermaid Hotel South leg of loop road, 5km out ℡0242/836 2668, ℻836 2618. Balconied, limited-view rooms at this self-styled "boutique hotel" are on the small side, but appealingly furnished and a/c. Common areas, filled with antiques, are grander, while the pool and setting are very pleasant. Open all year by arrangement. ❼ half-board.

Villa Hotel Tamara Southwest end of peninsula ℡0242/836 3273, ✉tamara1@ixir.com. Attractive, stone-clad hotel with eighteen large standard rooms (❼), eight suites (❽; €140) and three honeymoon suites (❽; €160;) in stylishly varied decor. The hot water is reliably boiler-generated (not solar-heated), there's a salt-water pool in a superb hillside setting, though meals other than breakfast are best taken elsewhere. Claims to be open all year.

Camping

Kaş Kamping Necip Bey Cad, 1km west of town, just past the amphitheatre ℡0242/836 1050. Long a favoured link in the Hippie Trail to Asia, the local campsite is perennially for sale, but while it survives in its present format, there's a swimming platform, lively bar-restaurant, caravan space and A-frame cabins (❷) for the tentless.

The Town

Ancient **Antiphellos** was the harbour of ancient Phellos, way inland near the modern village of Çukurbağ and one of the few Lycian cities to bear a Greek name (*phellos* means "cork oak"). Excavations at Kaş have unearthed a settlement dating back to at least the fourth century BC, although Antiphellos only gained importance in Hellenistic times, when an increase in seagoing commerce meant it thrived while Phellos withered. By the Roman era, it was the most important city in the region, famed particularly for its sponges, which Pliny mentioned as being exceptionally soft.

The remains of the ancient city are few and scattered, but what's on show is quite impressive. Out of town, 500m along Necip Bey Caddesi from the harbour mosque, sits a small, almost complete Hellenistic **theatre** with 26 rows of seats, well used by those watching the sunset. The theatre never had a permanent stage building, but in modern times a curved wall was built in place of a stage to provide a backdrop for local wrestling matches.

Above and behind the theatre, 100m away on the top of a hill, stands a unique **Doric tomb**, the so-called Kesme Mezar, also almost completely intact. Its single chamber forms a slightly tapering cube cut from the rock on which it stands. The two-metre-high entrance was once closed by a sliding door, but can now be entered in order to examine the bench at the back (on which the body would have been laid out), decorated by a frieze of small female figures performing a dance.

The most interesting of the sarcophagi to have survived local pilfering for building materials is the **Lion Tomb** at the top of the Uzun Çarşı. This towering structure has two burial chambers, the lower one forming a base for the Lycian sarcophagus above it. On the side of the lower chamber is an undeciphered Lycian inscription, written in a poetic form similar to that of the inscribed obelisk at Xanthos. The tomb's name derives from the four lifting bosses (projecting bits of masonry used to remove the Gothic-style lid from its base) in the shape of lions' heads, resting their chins on their paws.

The beaches

Considering that Kaş is a major Turkish resort, local natural beaches are surprisingly poor; those few on the north shore of Bucak Limanı are muddy and give

The Mediterranean around Kaş has arguably the best visibility (up to 30m) and greatest variety of sea life of the entire Turkish coast, as well as the shortest transfer times to dive sites. These are facts not lost on Turkey's divers, who descend in force during summer or over any long weekend year-round. There are ostensibly ten or so dive operators in town, many operating out of the basements of Küçükçakıl hotels, but in terms of boat comfort, safety standards, quality equipment and language/thoroughness of instruction, only two companies really rate consideration: **Sun Diving** at Liman Sok 10, on the west side of the harbour (☎0242/836 2637, ⊛www.sundiving.de), and **BT Diving**, part of Bougainville Travel, Çukurbağlı (officially İbrahim Serin) Cad 10 (☎0242/836 3737, ⊛www.bougainville-turkey.com).

Because of the brief shuttle time to sites, it's quite feasible to dive only in the morning or afternoon, and accordingly **prices** are per dive rather than per day. Both recommended operators advertise single dives at £20 (£14 if you bring your own gear except tanks/weights), making this about the least expensive place to dive in Turkey. A PADI Open Water course will cost about £205, Advanced Open Water £140, plus £25 for course materials (a PADI requirement worldwide).

Dive sites

There are close to sixty dive sites in the area, with lots of new discoveries since the millennium; many of these are on the flank of the Çukurbağlı peninsula, with most of the others around the islets at the marine frontier with Greek Kastellórizo. **Beginners** might visit a tunnel at 15m and a shoreline cave fed by an icy freshwater spring in Bayındır Limanı, or the shallower reaches of "Stone Edge" or Güvercin Adası, areas off the Çukurbağ peninsula. **Moderately experienced** divers may be taken to the site known as "Canyon", where beginning in four-metre depths they drop through the namesake formation past a reasonably intact Greek cotton-carrying freighter that ran aground here in the 1960s. This was later dynamited to remove the navigational hazard, with its stern lodging in 35m of water. Next there's a traverse of a big-wall dropoff, and then a return north with prevailing currents via a tunnel system at 15–18m. Only **advanced** divers using nitrox or triox tanks can visit the wreck of a World War II bomber shot down between Kaş and Kastellórizo, resting nearly intact in 65m of water at the site called "Flying Fish", just beyond "Canyon".

Fish you're likely to see – at their best in August or September – includes grouper, barracuda, amberjack and the occasional ray; smaller species typically seen include cardinal fish, damselfish, parrotfish, flying fish, ornate wrasse and schools of bream or pandora.

onto sumpy water. In town itself, **Küçükçakıl** has been pretty much taken over by the hotels facing it, which have installed snack-bar and sun-bed concessions and fitted the shoreline with flagstone or wood-deck lidos – though the public is welcome to patronize the loungers and bars. **Büyük Çakıl**, just over a kilometre east of town, is a small (60m wide), shingle-and-sand cove with a handful of snack bars that gets crowded out. For more space, take a water dolmuş (hourly low season, every 20min peak times; 5YTL one way, 7YTL return) to **Limanağzı**, the next, large bay to the southeast, with snack bars and sun-beds behind each of three swimming areas. Leaving town to the west, the **Çukurbağ peninsula** gives good views of the Greek island Kastellórizo, and is lapped by clear, aquamarine water, but again has no beaches to speak of, only more hotel-built lidos where you can clamber into the water unmenaced by the ubiquitous sea urchins. The best of the lidos is below the *Aquarius Hotel* facing Meis, which is open to the public but sun-bed fees are payable. The nearest really decent beach is **Kaputaş**, 21km towards Kalkan, described on p.487.

△ Kaş

Boat tours and Kastellórizo

Boatmen at the harbour offer standard full-day tours (depart 10am, return 6pm) to either **Kekova** or to **Patara** (from 23YTL per person, including lunch). **Custom tours** in a boat taking six to eight people start at 210YTL a day at the beginning of the season (April and May), reaching 360YTL in a busy year by late season (Aug and Sept).

Day- (or one-way) trips to the **Greek island of Kastellórizo** (see below) operate on a demand basis, daily Monday–Friday in peak season, perhaps twice weekly in winter, but never at weekends when the customs is closed. Turkish craft depart Kaş at 10am, although there is usually an extra, unpublicized Greek boat to Kastellórizo on Friday and Monday evenings. Journey time is about forty minutes, and unless you arrange otherwise the return tends to be around 1–1.30pm, giving barely enough time for lunch on Kastellórizo (many passengers are only concerned with securing new entry visas for Turkey). You should never pay more than €32/53YTL round trip per person, and at slow times with stiff bargaining you may well pay as little at €24/40YTL. One recommended captain is Selahattin Çıplak (℡0537/674 5572).

Kaş is an official entry/exit port for Turkey, but Greek Kastellórizo is not – though the Greek authorities have no basis in law for preventing EU nationals from landing in Greece. Non-EU nationals may be forbidden from leaving Kastellórizo until their personal details are faxed to Athens for confirmation that they aren't heinous criminals; this petty harassment becomes slightly more understandable when you learn that this is a major smuggling corridor. To go across legally, you'll need to surrender your passport to the arranging travel agency or boat captain the night before; returning to Kaş from Kastellórizo, no fresh visa fee is payable as long as you have time left on your existing multiple-entry visa.

Kastellórizo

The picturesque port of the Greek island of **Kastellórizo**, called Meis in Turkish after the Greek alternate name (Meyísti), lies just over three nautical miles off the

Turkish coast. It is among the smallest inhabited islands of the Dodecanese archipelago, a haven for yachties and a favourite place to nip across to for renewing three-month Turkish tourist visas. You'll find complete coverage of the island in *The Rough Guide to the Dodecanese and the East Aegean* but it's worth saying here that there are at least two weekly onward boats to Rhodes most of the year, plus three to five weekly flights on a puddle-jumper aircraft. If you just miss a departure, a couple of days on the island will be time well spent, with affordable seafood, walking opportunities and adequate nightlife on offer.

Eating and drinking

There are many excellent **restaurants** in Kaş, though few actually face the waterfront, and those that do are prone to scams and ripoffs – two in particular to avoid are *Smiley's* and *Mercan*.

Bahçe Uzun Çarşı. The broadest range of cold and hot *mezes* in town, served in the garden (*bahçe* in Turkish). Mains in comparison are almost incidental, though their *ayva tatlısı* is a fitting finale. Open May to early Nov.

Café Galerie Çukurbağlı Cad 12. Just three tables inside, and three out, but all likely to be occupied because of the best Austrian-style coffees and pastries – at Austrian prices.

Chez Evy Terzi Sok 2, off Süleyman Topçu Sok ☎0242/836 1253. A worthwhile splurge (41YTL each, plus any wine) sees French country recipes meet Turkish flavours. The result is happier and more generous than you'd expect – the pepper steak and (in autumn) wild boar are to die for – while Evy herself, who used to cook for the rich and famous on their private mega-yachts, is one of the characters of Kaş. Booking for the garden seating is necessary in season; otherwise wait for a table, or have a nightcap, in the rustic bar. Supper only; open much of the year.

Ikbal Süleyman Sandıkçi Sok 6. Intimate (just 12 tables) garden bistro in a quiet lane. Good value for *nouvelle* Turkish cuisine and wine. Open May–Oct.

Natur-el Gürsoy Sok, off Uzun Çarşı. Both outdoor seating and a lovely interior upstairs for the cooler months. Besides Turkish snacks such as *mantı, su böreği* and *çiğ böreği*, there's an

ambitious – and not uniformly successful – range of mains such as *hunkâr beğendi* and *cevizli nar tavuk* (chicken in walnut and pomegranate sauce). Friendly, low-key service; a good choice for vegetarians. Booking suggested on ☎0242/836 2834.

Oba Çukurbağlı Cad 8, near the PTT. Licensed diner that's ace for simple home-style soups and *sulu yemek*, though portions are on the small side; equally pleasant garden or indoor seating.

Seçkin Atatürk Bul 2, behind the Harbour Mosque. The best of a cluster of three similar budget-priced, unlicensed outfits pitched mainly at locals, this does *döner kebap* and a few *sulu yemek* by day, plus *işkembe* and *paça* soups as hangover tonics after midnight (when it's busiest). It also serves great traditional desserts like *kabak tatlısı* topped with *kaymak* or *dondurma* at any hour. Indoor, garden and sidewalk seating; open around the clock.

Sempati Gürsoy Sok. Since opening in 2002 this has garnered a reputation for excellent meat dishes accompanied by a few selected *mezes*, such as *arnavut ciğer* and *mücver*, plus four varieties of *rakı*.

Sofram Bahçe Sok 1, on the corner of the old market square. A mix of affordable *sulu yemek*, grills, *pide* and puddings at this licensed lunchtime favourite, with a pleasant atmosphere despite the workaday location.

Nightlife

A varied, crowded, sometimes high-decibel **nightlife** – easily the best on the Turquoise Coast – is what makes Kaş for many visitors.

Harry's Bar Çukurbağlı Cad 13. Gets going early in the evening, offering an Edward-Hopperish view from outside into the minimalist bar, with ceiling fans and neon logo, as well as free wi-fi access for the price of drink or two.

Hideway Cumhuriyet Cad 16/A officially, actually in a lane off the old market square. Easily the coolest garden bar/café in town (open only May–Nov); vintage rock and blues soundtrack, divan and table seating, romantic lighting and ever-popular

(if somewhat pricey) Sunday breakfast.
Hi-Jazz Zümrüt Sok 3. The designated local jazz venue, though the playlist gets less vintage and more daring towards the small hours.
Mavi/Blue Cumhuriyet Medanı. The oldest bar-café in town: 25 years ago it was a coffeehouse where retired fishermen played backgammon, now it's musical, young and trendy from mid-afternoon until morning.

Red Point Club Süleyman Topçu Sokağı. Kaş's premier after-hours dance club in an old barn, packed solid after midnight despite a fairly spacious dance-floor for the sake of DJ-spun rock and soul. Tables out in the lane during summer.
Sun Café Hükümet Caddesi. Musical *meyhane*, where the emphasis on food has been eclipsed by live music gigs, which dominate proceedings after 11pm.

Shopping

The upmarket tourist industry in Kaş centres on the **Uzun Çarşı** (Long Market), and that's exactly what it is – an uninterrupted bazaar of crafts and designer clothing shops with a selection (and prices, of course) that would fit right in at any European city-centre mall. While overseas labels produced under licence are easy to come by, there are also local designers tailoring to order from hand-woven fabrics produced in nearby villages. You can best view such raw cloth at the slightly shabby, but lively, weekly **Friday market**, at the edge of town en route to Bucak Limanı. The old market in the town centre has become a park (and car park), but still has a wide variety of shops on its perimeter.

The **antique shops** along Uzun Çarşı are all of similar quality, so none are particularly worth singling out; carpets, clothing, jewellery, metal antiques and kitsch knick-knacks predominate. Off Uzun Çarşı, the Old Curiosity Shop near the post office at Bahçe Sok 3/B, has a museum-like collection of not-very-portable but unique objects aimed at second-home owners.

Finally, Kaş has the only "**supermarkets**" between Fethiye and Kemer near Antalya, both at the junction on Atatürk Bulvarı opposite the *otogar*: Gen-Pa and a mini-Migros. Neither can compare in size with their counterparts in the larger towns, but if you're after a choice of quality wine, exotic foodstuffs or trekking staples, these are the places.

Listings

Banks and exchange Yapı Kredi ATM behind the Harbour Mosque; Halkbank and İş Bankası ATMs on Atatürk Cad; Ziraat Bankası, next to the PTT.
Books, magazines and recordings The *Merhaba Café* on Çukurbağlı Cad, towards the PTT end, sells foreign newspapers and books, as well as quality postcards, in addition to gourmet cakes and expensive coffee; Merdiven Kitap Evi on İlkokul Sok 4/B has used paperbacks and a few new dictionaries and guidebooks. Dem Müzik Evi at Atatürk Bul 9/C keeps a good selection of the best Turkish folk, *özgun* and devotional music.
Internet Netcafé, top end of Çukurbağlı Cad, past the PTT on the right; also Magicom, nearby.
Laundry Rose, Süleyman Topçu Sok; also a booth on the quay.
Paragliding The cliffs above Kaş are beginning to rival Ölüdeniz as a paragliding venue, and it's marginally cheaper here. Contact the local branch

of Skysports (☎0242/836 3291); expect to pay €65–75.
Taxis Main ranks are in the old market square, and at the base of the jetty.
Travel agents The British/Turkish-run ⚓ BT Adventure & Diving/Bougainville Travel, Çukurbağlı Cad 10 (☎0242/836 3737, ⓦ www.bougainville-turkey.com), is the foremost adventure-travel agency in the area for diving, mountain treks, canyoning and sea-kayaking, though they also offer more conventional excursions. Dragoman, Uzun Çarşı 15 (☎0242/836 3614, ⓦ www.dragoman-turkey.com), offers similar outings but is more Francophone-orientated.
Water Delicious and potable, straight from the limestone mountains around Gömbe, available free at taps by the Harbour Mosque; the Saklıkent pipeline water is considered only fit to wash in.

North of Kaş: Akdağ and Yeşil Göl

When sea-level pleasures at Kaş pall, especially in excessively hot weather, there's no closer escape than the cool heights of the **Akdağ range**, which soars to over 3000m in the space of 20km. The standard jump-off point for excursions into the mountains, and one easily reached by public minibus from Kaş, is **Gömbe**, a small town 60km north of Kaş, on the road to Elmalı. This provides access to **Yeşil Göl**, Lycia's only permanent alpine lake, and also serves as a first stop for anyone intending to climb the **peak of Akdağ** itself, a three-hour climb above the lake.

Gömbe

The ninety-minute ride up from Kaş is mostly shaded by extensive pine forests, which yield to vast apple orchards as you approach **GÖMBE**. No commercial maps yet show the huge **Çayboğazı reservoir** which has re-routed any approach from the south – drivers should avoid the circuitous bypass road by going right over the dam-top road. Gömbe, the ancient Comba (nothing remains), is famous for a festival of the local Tahtacıs, which happens in June, and another farmers' fair during the latter half of August.

Around the main *Belediye* square are three simple but adequate **restaurants**, all with similar bean-soup-and-*köfte* menus – the *Şafak* is licensed, but the *Çörekçi* is friendlier and more savoury – a few *dondurma* parlours on summer evenings, plus three **pansiyons**, mostly on the hillside south of the square. Of these, fanciest is the en-suite *Paşa* (☎0242/831 5208; ❷), though the nearly adjacent *Akın* (☎0242/831 4117; ❶) is adequate and clean, with shared bathrooms.

Yeşil Göl and Akdağ

Most people come to Gömbe to visit **Yeşil Göl** (Green Lake), a short distance west and the only permanent body of water in the generally arid, karstic Akdağ sierra. Tucked into the east flank of Akdağ at about 1850m elevation, Yeşil Göl is a large, clean and fairly deep tarn at its best between April and June; the earlier in spring you show up, the finer the **wildflower** displays. The southern shore of the lake has enough (slightly sloping) turf for a handful of tents, should you wish to **camp** the night – advisable if you plan to traverse Akdağ (see p.498).

To reach the lake, it's best to have your own transport (2WD vehicles passable with care, but preferable to have 4WD), but the following directions apply equally to hikers. Leave the square heading north and turn left immediately after crossing the river bridge, then take the second paved right, and begin climbing. Zigzags take you to the Çukurbağ Köyü mosque; turn left here and keep an aqueduct, and phone lines, parallel to your track – confirm directions by asking for the track to "Subaşı Yayla".

Exactly 6.2km above the central Gömbe bridge, half an hour's low-gear driving around wash-outs, ruts, boulders and treefalls, just above the highest gnarled junipers, you'll reach a widening in the track beside a vigorous stream, near the start of the aqueduct. Some 500m past this widening is another parking place, flanked by a brick privy with four squat-slots; immediately beyond a landslide blocks the track. Down in the stream ravine a cement pedestrian bridge gives the only safe access to the far bank, where faint paths lead up to another non-vehicular track, blocked off by boulders at its turn-off from your original track – assuming the landslip is ever cleared, you could wrestle a car this far as the main motorable track executes a hairpin across the ravine, upstream from the privy. In either case, follow this rougher track past some rudimentary shepherds' huts and corrals; immediately after this leave the track for proper paths over a gentle saddle that emerges abruptly at an overlook for the lake (maximum 30min from the privy).

The following portion of the Lycian Way begins in Kaş and will take most walkers two full days (or three shorter days) to complete. Outside of the April grazing and charcoal-making seasons, it's one of the lonelier sections of the route, so you need to be fairly self-sufficient (sleeping bag, stove, food, probably a tent), and carry at least two litres of water per person from the outset, topping up at every opportunity. Done as a two-day hike, it's a strenuous 9hr 30min second day from the suggested campsite, with a very early start required to enjoy both the ruins en route and a soft bed in Üçağız before dark.

Take a taxi to the end of the asphalt road at **Büyü Çakıl** and follow the dirt track away from the last houses. Over the first hour this dwindles to a good path leading to a long, flat field above **Bayındır Limanı**, after which there's a rougher, cross-country hour to the rocky double bay of **Çoban Plajı**, facing Kastellórizo. From here an easier herders' path leads in 45 minutes up to a shady saddle, with a subsequent gradual descent for 45 minutes more, paralleling the coast, to ruined cottages at **Ufak Dere** cove (poor-to-average swimming). This makes a good lunch stop. From Ufak Dere, ascend 45 minutes on a mix of tracks and paths to another pass where Kastellórizo is visible for the last time, and there's an apparently abandoned, unlocked house with a cistern inside – the first reliable water en route, for which you'll need parachute cord and a container-with-handle to fetch. From here, the trail descends half an hour to a point where you can divert right (seaward) onto a marked-as-"wrong-way" path, which leads quickly to some charcoal-burners' flats under shady pines by the sea. This makes a wonderful **campsite**, with fine swimming in the bay here. Resuming progress, you've another hour-plus on a sometimes indistinct path to the next "beach", with poor bathing, and the possibility of camping in the olive groves just inland; swimming is better off the rocks some 45 minutes ahead. There the route veers inland up a valley for half an hour to a third pass with a reliable, deep well (equipment required, as above) and the remains of an ancient watchtower. Next you skirt the hill above, either to its left or right (the waymarks go anticlockwise), to emerge on a jeep track leading to **Boğazcık** village (another hour to get there); there's water here, but no other facilities. The Lycian Way proper veers off east before actually reaching the village, onto an ancient path giving access within 45 minutes (including a 15-minute detour) to ancient **Apollonia** (see p.502). After visiting Apollonia, continue south on either the marked or "wrong-way" route (they converge) for 2hr 15min to ancient **Aperlae** (see p.502). Do not be surprised if you share the path with a camel or two – the authorities have forbidden road construction in this archeologically rich area, and working (as opposed to tourist-attraction) camels are the most efficient transport for the shepherds who keep animals on the Sıcak peninsula. From Aperlae, cross the isthmus of the Sıcak peninsula on level ground, arriving after half an hour at the two restaurants at the jetty here – one of them belonging to Ramazan, one of the last local camel-drivers. You could camp behind the buildings, especially if you ate a meal here. The onward trail is initially faint and counterintuitive, veering briefly northwest away from the water, marked at first only by plain red paint dashes. Subsequently it becomes more distinct in the red dirt, and conventional two-colour blazes reappear. Near some cottages on a ridge, angle towards the northeast edge of the *ova* here – *don't* take tempting traces marching down the centre – to reach simple shelters used by charcoal-burners. Resumed waymarks lead you up onto the true left bank of the ravine draining from the *ova*, about an hour beyond the restaurants, for your first view of the **Üçağız bay**; the *ova* pastures with their cowpats – and flies – are left behind. Go through a fence into olive-grove terraces, where path and waymarks vanish again; make your way, with rough ground underfoot, as best you can, to the shore (1hr 45min from restaurants), making sure to head for the left (north)-most inlet of the double-pronged bay ahead. The route, now essentially cross-country, hugs the shore for the final 45 minutes to the first buildings of **Üçağız**.

Climbing Akdağ

If you intend to **climb the peak** of Akdağ (3024m), retrace your steps to the main motorable track and proceed west; after about ten minutes you pass a quadruple-spouted spring. After a few bends, and now high above the stream-bed, you adopt the true right bank (facing the direction of flow) of the watercourse. When you reach a tributary coming from the south, turn to follow it, keeping to the true left bank. The summit ridge will be ahead, on your right; soon you should pick up a distinct, cairned path that will take you all the way to the top, a two-and-a-half-hour hike one-way with a daypack, from the spring. The **summit cairn** contains a "guestbook" to sign, and the views over the snow-flecked badlands are superb. An ice-axe is most useful until June or July (depending on the preceding winter), and you'll need an adequate water bottle in any season.

If you wish to do a complete **traverse of the range**, you'll have to plan on an overnight stop somewhere on the mountain. The classic descent is to **Arsaköy** (with a basic village inn and two places to eat) on the west flank of Akdağ, from where a wonderful cobbled path descends for a couple of hours towards Saklıkent before disappearing under a bulldozer track.

Dereağzı

About 30km northeast of Kaş, some imposing ruins at **Dereağzı** – an enormous, half-intact Byzantine church, and a strong Byzantine castle built atop a much earlier fortification – are a worthy destination for anyone with their own transport. The latter guarded a strategic narrows (Dereağzı means "valley mouth" in Turkish) in the easiest route for shipping grain and cedar wood to Andriake (see p.507) from the rich upland plains of Elmalı and Kasaba.

To get there, take the road to Gömbe and turn east at Kasaba village, following signs to Çatallar, and then proceed for just over 8km to Dirgenler village. At a crossroads here, a sign points left to three villages; you go right onto a gravel track towards a pine-studded ridge. After 2.8km, you reach the head of a gorge, with some rock tombs visible, and a small water-pumping station in a concrete shed; this is the point where the Kasaba plateau begins draining towards the sea. The abrupt, roughly triangular hill on your right turns out to be covered in ruins of a castle, barely noticeable from afar.

The castle

From just before the pumping station, faint goat paths angle southwest to become the old Byzantine path – still the only way up – leading within twenty minutes to the overgrown **main gate** in the northwest-facing wall. Once up and in, you fully appreciate the amazing site, not unlike those of the Cathar castles of Languedoc: the southwest-to-northeast ridge is essentially a knife-edge, and the entire fortified hill is lapped by two rivers, the Kasaba and the Karadağ, which mingle at the southeast tip to form the Demre Çayı.

The ancient Lycians first built this castle during the sixth to fifth centuries BC, using polygonal, unmortared masonry, or occasionally even hewing into the rock strata. After the devastating Arab wars of the eighth century AD, the Byzantines improved and enlarged it during the ninth and tenth centuries, using their preferred mortared-rubble technique. In particular they added the half-dozen triangular or rectangular **bastions and towers** still visible on the lowest, northwest wall, the castle's weakest side. American surveys and explorations from 1974 to 1981 revealed two more inner layers of defence as one proceeds to the summit, complete with a **church**, plus dozens of **cisterns** and water-collecting channels.

Down in the Karadağ gorge, most of the area's Lycian **rock tombs and sarcophagi** are on the east bank of the stream, near the passage of an **ancient road** with numerous steps. This road can still be trekked along for about 5km, though since the bulldozing of a modern dirt road through the gorge there's less enjoyment to be derived from this.

The church

From the water-pumping station you can walk northwest on a river-bank track along the Karadağ (flippantly called the Boklu or "Shitty" creek by locals, after its algae infestation) to a point just opposite the knoll-top church where channels in the marsh narrow enough for you to cross. The huge **church**, dating from the same time as the castle reconstruction, was clearly funded from the imperial capital, given its size and the richness of its marble decoration (now all in Antalya's archeological museum). Unusual in plan and design, it has two curious, free-standing hexagonal structures, one at the apse end and one where the narthex presumably was. The brick-and-rubble church was the focus of quite a large town, which disappeared within two hundred years of its foundation; oddly neither the Byzantine nor Lycian name for Dereağzı is known, since no identifying inscriptions or coins have been found.

From the pumping station, you can make a circuit back to the coast by following the fairly smooth vehicle track downstream **along the Demre Çayı**; it's 23km, the last 4km paved, and passable to most cars except perhaps at high water in spring (there's one river ford). Near the end, ancient watchtowers flank the widening valley on either side.

The Kekova region

Some of the most beautifully situated ruins on the south coast are in the area known as **Kekova**, after the eponymous offshore island. It's a stretch of rocky coastline littered with remains of Lycian settlements, some now submerged under the translucent waters of the calm, shallow, almost landlocked gulf here. Since the early 1990s land communications – both by road and by trail – have been improved, so the region is no longer the exclusive preserve of boat and yacht tours. Many Lycian ruins can be easily visited from the inlet-shore village of **Üçağız**, while inland lie the neglected remains of **Apollonia**, a dependency of coastal Aperlae, and the substantial ruins of **Cyaneae**.

Üçağız

The central village for the region is **ÜÇAĞIZ,** 38km from Kaş and connected to Highway 400 by a surfaced, twenty-kilometre road. Thus its quiet days are past: carpet, antique and jewellery shops have sprouted, boat-trip touts swarm around you on arrival (or pretend to be hitchhikers on the road in), and you've little hope of finding one of the hundred-odd beds unoccupied in July or August. Most of the surroundings have been designated an archeological site, which should protect Üçağız from unseemly concrete expansion by limiting the number of new buildings. And indeed its essential village identity has yet to be completely supplanted – out of season the place is still idyllic.

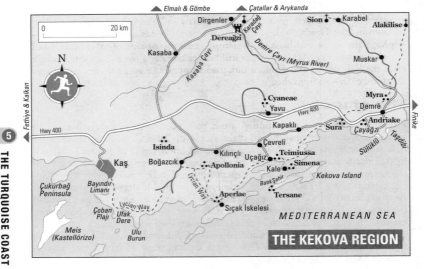

THE KEKOVA REGION

Practicalities

There's just one daily **dolmuş** from Demre, geared to villagers', not tourists',
needs (ie: out in the late afternoon, back in the morning). Üçağız's **pansiyons** are
simple, but often fairly pricey considering the remote location and lack of a beach.
Although fresh water has been piped in from the environs of Gömbe, hot showers
can still be erratic. The best and most secluded places both lie at the west end of the
village. The stone-clad *Kekova* (℡0242/874 2259; ❹) has relatively palatial air-conditioned rooms and a shared wrap-around balcony. Just beyond, the ⚓ *Ekin Hotel*
(℡0242/874 2064 or 0534/936 7783) sports a pleasant garden, clean, airy rooms in
the original building (❸) and a newer extension at the back (❹) housing suites, with
all-important insect screens plus air conditioning: it's run by cultured brothers Ali
and Yusuf with a well-developed service ethic. The best budget option is the *Nergiz*
(℡0242/874 2041; ❷), partially en-suite and run by the friendly Alıçavuzoğlu family; it's unmarked, but just opposite the primary school.

None of the several waterside **restaurants** offer especially good value: the most
tolerable and durable is the *Liman Marina* (aka İbrahim's), where drinks and *mezes*
are reasonably priced, though mains are expensive.

Around Üçağız

Until the road was built, the Lycian remains that surround Üçağız were visited by
few apart from hardy goats and archeologists. Teimiussa – and if you like walking,
Simena and Aperlae – can be reached on foot from the village, but sooner or later
you'll go on a **boat trip**, the main thing to do at beachless Üçağız. Destinations
and prices are fairly standard: €8 per boat to take in nearby Kale (Simena) and
Kekova island; €20 to Andriake port or Aperlae ruins; and just under €6 for a
one-way shuttle to Kale (the walk back takes 45min over rocky terrain, preferably
on a cool day).

Üçağız translates as "three mouths" in Turkish, and the old Greek name of
Tristomo, meaning exactly the same thing, is still recognized. The three apertures
in question are the straits at each end of the island opposite, plus the entry to the

Bougainville Travel in Kaş (see p.495) remains the principal organizer of **sea-kayaking day-tours** in the Kekova area, a wonderful, low-impact way of appreciating the eerie seascapes. They have the further advantage of allowing you to approach the shoreline, and the Batık Şehir in particular, much closer than the glass-bottomed cruise boats do, and also of using narrow, shallow channels off-limits to larger craft – which are, incidentally, your main threat, as you must be wary of their wake. With a suitable head covering and a water bottle secreted under your apron, you'll tolerate all but the hottest summer days, even wrapped inside a life vest. Trips often begin with a motorized tow from Üçağız to the starting point of your choice, for example Tersane; outings can be as long or short as stamina allows. Per-person rates, including a transfer from Kaş to Üçağız and a picnic lunch, are approximately €40 for a day's excursion.

lake-like gulf, at whose rear the village is situated. **Kekova island** itself boasts the area's only beach, plus the best of the ruins, most of which are submerged but visible below the sea. The ruins of the ancient town of **Aperlae** are found on the other side of a peninsula to the west of Üçağız, while at the east edge of the village stand the fortified acropolis and tombs of another small Lycian settlement – **Teimiussa**. A little way beyond lies the village of **Kale** and the castle at **Simena**, clearly visible on the horizon. Several small islands, quarried in ancient times to near sea level, dot the bay.

Kekova island

The most romantically situated local antiquities are those submerged along the northern coast of **Kekova island**, known as Batık Şehir (Sunken City) locally, and to date not identified with any ancient city. The underwater remains of stairs, pavements, house walls and a long quay wall can all be seen; however snorkelling or even just swimming are banned to prevent the removal of antiquities from the area, and most boatmen won't approach the rocky shoreline (the best view is from a kayak; see box, above). Near the southwest tip of the island, at the spot known as Tersane (Dockyard), looms the apse of a long-vanished church, in whose shadow bathers spread their towels on fine shingle; unhappily, much of the apse collapsed during a particularly violent storm in February 1996.

Teimiussa

Ancient **Teimiussa** is easily reached from Üçağız's *Kalealtı* restaurant, immediately below and beside it. Nothing is really known about the history of the place, but inscriptions indicate that it was occupied in the fourth century BC. The site, which suggests a settlement without walls and few or no public buildings, consists mainly of a good scattering of rock tombs; some of these have semicircular benches cut into their bases – convenient for pondering mortality as you stare out to sea, and probably used by the ancients when visiting their deceased relatives with *nekro-deipna* (food for the dead). On the hill above squats a small fort or tower, about the size of a house, while far below at sea level you can try to hunt for the tiny, rock-cut landing stage.

Kale and Simena

A ruined castle of the Knights of St John – and the village of **KALE** below it – are a ten-minute boat ride, or a longer kayak-paddle or walk from Üçağız. The secluded village itself is the haunt of Rahmi Koç, scion of a wealthy Turkish industrialist family, who donated a school in conjunction with restoring an old house here as a holiday retreat. Even for lesser mortals, Kale makes a lovely place to stay – it's another protected archeological zone, with no permanent new buildings permitted – though some rustic-looking **pansiyons**, overlooking the sea and a marooned sarcophagus, are pricey for what you get. The best three are the *Kale Pansiyon* (☎0242/874 2111, ℱ874 2110; ❹), occasionally taken up by British package agencies; *Nesrin's Bademli Ev* (☎0242/874 2170; ❹), a charming, three-unit inn with fireplaces in the wood-and-stone rooms, and, just up the slope from this, the *Mehtap Pansiyon* (☎0242/874 2146 or 874 2077, ✉info@mehtap-pansiyon.com; all year; ❸), with ten plain but air-conditioned, wood-floored rooms. It also has **camping** space available and good suppers served on the plat-form-terrace. Most of the six or seven waterfront **restaurants**, which have had a long and jading acquaintance with the tour-boat trade, charge a set price for a fill-your-plate *meze* buffet.

The climb to the acropolis of ancient **Simena** (unenclosed; 4YTL when warden present) is steep but brief, and worth it both for the views as well as for the medi-eval **castle** itself, whose castellated ramparts are in good condition, partly resting on ancient foundations. Inside the Knights' castle is a fifteen-metre-wide **theatre** carved into the living rock, large enough for perhaps two hundred people; on the eastern slopes of the hill, off the path, stand some well-preserved **sarcophagi**. Brace yourself for being followed all the way up and down by children peddling printed headscarves, and village women pressing oregano into your hands or offer-ing guiding services in exchange for a consideration.

Aperlae

Southwest of Üçağız lies the site of **Aperlae**, a forty-minute boat ride to a landing stage with two restaurants, followed by a half-hour walk; it's also accessible via the Lycian Way. Its remoteness means that the site is practically deserted, though there's a cluster of modern houses at Sıçak İskelesı, beside the ruins. The remains of the **city walls** are fairly well preserved and easily identified – they bisect the hillside and enclose a rectangular area, with the sea lapping the southern side; the **necropolis**, as is usual, lies almost entirely outside the walls. As at Kekova, sub-sidence has submerged the harbour quarter, but swimming and snorkelling here is thus far unrestricted. If you follow the line of the old **quay**, now in 1–2m of water and indented at 15-metre intervals for the mooring of ships, you can easily see heaps of pottery shards, amphora necks, terracotta floor-tiles and shell-mid-dens from the ancient murex-dye industry, all encrusted together. There are also building foundations in rows divided by narrow **streets**, including a small section of intact pavement near the shore.

In the absence of competing hypotheses, it's assumed that Aperlae was a Lycian city – a theory supported by Lycian coins with inscriptions "APR" and "PRL" that have been found. By imperial Roman times, Aperlae definitely headed a league of four cities, the others being Simena, Apollonia and Isinda (near modern Belenli).

Apollonia

If Aperlae is neglected, unexcavated **Apollonia** is even more so. It can be reached on foot, either from Boğazcık, by a spur from the Lycian Way (see box on p.458), or part way by a two-kilometre track from the modern village of **Kılınçlı** (alias Sıçak) on the Üçağız-bound road.

Apollonia is mainly known for its superb **necropolis**, which spikes the lower northeast slope of the hill on which the city is found, facing Kılınçlı. There is one conventional sarcophagus with extravagant Gothic-type details, but most distinc-tive are a half-dozen or so **pillar tombs**, considered the ur-burial method of the ancient Lycians, and proving Apollonia's antiquity. Isolated from the other tombs, at the west end of the hill facing Boğazcık, stands an unusual **carved tomb** on two levels. But there is more to see here in the acropolis, which at its east end appears to be double: a much older stockade inside a Byzantine citadel. Particularly on the southwest flank, the **city walls** – made of unusually large quadrangular and pentagonal blocks – are pierced by windows and a gate. From atop the inner, ancient fort, you look west over a well-preserved **Byzantine church**, possibly of the sixth or seventh century; just west of this, overgrown but in a fair state of preservation, is a lovely little **theatre**. The views from the hill, whether inland to the Lycian mountains or out to sea, are the icing on the experience.

Cyaneae

East of the turn-off for Üçağız, Highway 400 enters a stretch of wild, inhospitable countryside, whose bleak aspect appeals only to the herds of sheep and goats grazing it. In antiquity, however, this region was scattered with small settlements, the most interesting nowadays being **Cyaneae** (Kyaneaı in Turkish signage), 23km from Kaş in the hills above the village of **Yavu**. The name Cyaneae/Kyaneaı derives from the ancient Greek for "dark blue" – also the origin of the word cyanide – but it's uncertain why the city was given this name. The contemporary nickname, "city of sarcophagi", seems more apt, since the Lycian and Roman sarcophagi studding the site are the most numerous of any city in the region, and the main reason to visit. Little is known about Cyaneae's **history**, apart from the fact that it was the most important settlement in the region between Myra and Antiphellos (modern Kaş), and linked by a direct road to the harbour of Teimiussa, 12km away as the crow flies. It prospered in Roman times, and was the seat of a bishopric in the Byzantine age.

From Yavu village centre there's a signposted, two-kilometre **path to the site**; the hike up only takes about 45 minutes but the route is extremely steep. Rather easier is an unmarked four-kilometre **dirt road** that takes off from the north side of Highway 400, precisely 1km west of the side road to Yavu; the last stretch of this track is quite rough, but negotiable with care in an ordinary 2WD car. It's possible to take a **local guide** along, but not strictly necessary; it is they who've had a hand in misleadingly signposting the slip road to Yavu as "Kyaneaı 4", and keeping the dirt track unsignposted. Guides can be found at a marked "tourist office" in the village, and charge €15 per party, though they can be negotiated down. The only other facility, on Highway 400 about 500m in the direction of Demre, is the Çeşme **restaurant** (open in season only).

The site

On the left of the path up from the village are some of the oldest and most interesting of Cyaneae's **tombs**, lining either side of a passage that may have been part of the ancient road. The most impressive – a sarcophagus carved completely from the rock on which it stands – lies south of the road. The Gothic-arch "lid", cut from the same piece of rock, has two lions' heads projecting from each side. Near the top of the path, keep an eye out for a subterranean shrine or tomb with six columns.

Below the city, fairly inaccessible on the south face of the hill, stands an impressive **temple-tomb** whose porch has a single free-standing column and, unusually, a recess above the pediment in which a sarcophagus has been installed. According to an inscription, this was reserved for the bodies of the head of the household and his wife, while the rest of the family were buried in the tomb.

The hilltop **acropolis** is surrounded on three sides by a wall, the south side being so precipitous that it didn't need protection. The buildings inside are in

△ Lycian tombs near Kekova

a ruined state and covered with vegetation, but several have been more or less tentatively identified, including a library, baths and two Byzantine churches, one with a lengthy inscription by the door. Near the summit is a tomb with a relief of a charioteer driving a team of four horses. The city had no natural spring nearby, so vaulted cisterns and reservoirs square-cut from the living rock are ubiquitous.

To the west of the summit, on the far side of the area used for parking, stands a moderate-sized **theatre** with 23 rows of seats still visible, divided by the diazoma. Its upper rows make ideal vantage points to survey the western walls of the acropolis, the Kekova inlet to the south, and a row of sarcophagi flanking an ancient path linking the theatre and the acropolis. Mainly Roman, these tombs tend to be very simple, with rounded lids and crests, but include a few lion-head bosses too.

Demre and around

East of Yavu, Highway 400 swoops down in a well-graded arc towards the river-delta town of **Demre**, focus of some of the more intriguing sites in Lycia. It's worth pausing here in order to see the **Church of St Nicholas** – best observed in peace and quiet before 9am or after 5pm, when Demre is practically empty of visitors. Nearby attractions include the ancient city of **Myra**, just to the north, and the ancient harbour of **Andriake** and Apollo oracle at **Sura**, a little way south (you pass close to both approaching from the west).

Some history

Myra was one of the most prominent members of the Lycian Federation, and retained this importance throughout the Middle Ages because of its associations with the bishop **St Nicholas** (aka Santa Claus). An ancient tradition asserts that the city's name derives from the Greek word for myrrh, the gum resin used in the production of incense. Although no record of the manufacture of this unguent is recorded, the emperor Constantine Porphyrogenitus described the city as the "thrice blessed, myrrh-breathing city of the Lycians, where the mighty Nikolaos, servant of God, spouts forth myrrh in accordance with the city's name". There is also a tale that when the tomb of St Nicholas was opened by Italian grave robbers, they were overwhelmed by the smell of myrrh emanating from it.

Despite its subsequent fame, there is no mention of Myra in records before the first century BC. In 42 BC the city distinguished itself with typically Lycian defiance by refusing to pay tribute money to Brutus; Brutus's lieutenant had to break the chain closing the mouth of the harbour at Andriake – the city's port – and force his way in. Subsequently, Myra had an uneventful if prosperous history until its abandonment in the fourteenth century, treated well by its imperial overlords and receiving its highest accolade when the Byzantine emperor Theodosius II made it capital of Lycia in the fifth century.

By then the city's fame had been much enhanced by one of its citizens, namely St Nicholas, born in Patara late in the third century AD and later appointed bishop of Myra. He is supposed to have slapped the face of the Alexandrian heretic Arius at the Council of Nicaea in 325 AD, although his Western identity as a genial old present-giver is perhaps more familiar, arising from the story of his kindness to the three daughters of a poor man who were left without a dowry. Nicholas is credited with throwing three purses of gold into the house one night, enabling them to find husbands instead of selling themselves into prostitution. Many posthumous miracles were attributed to the saint, but little is actually known about the man. However, it has been established that after his death he was buried in the church in Demre now dedicated to him, and it is also widely believed that in 1087 his bones were carried off to Italy by a group of devout raiders from Bari (although the Venetians and Russians lay dubious claim to a similar exploit). Demre is still proud of its connection with St Nicholas (*Noel Baba* or "Father Christmas" in Turkish); every December 6 (the saint's feast day) a special mass is held in his church, attracting pilgrims from Greece, Italy and (especially) Russia, though these also take place on random Sundays throughout the year.

Demre

DEMRE (officially called, and signposted as, Kale) is a rather scruffy little place, too far away from the coast to merit a "seaside" tag, and afforded more midday attention by Russian tour parties than it can really handle. Tourism has always been dwarfed by the main local business of growing citrus fruit and tomatoes, whose greenhouses – spread below as you descend the escarpment to the west – make the town seem bigger than it really is. Unlike other nondescript towns on the coast from here to Antalya who juggle sun-and-wave motifs in their municipal logos, Demre is unequivocal about its priorities and self-image: a giant tomato occupies most of its coat-of-arms, though lately a silhouette-bust of Father Christmas has also crept in, and the town centre is absolutely overrun with Santa kitsch.

The Church of St Nicholas

The **Church of St Nicholas** (daily: May–Oct 8.30am–7pm; Nov–April 8.30am–5/6pm; 5YTL) dominates the centre of Demre, situated on the right of pedestrianized Müze Caddesi as you head west. Despite the erection of a horrible synthetic protective canopy to one side, the building remains evocative of the life and times of its patron saint, even if the myths surrounding him are more romance than fact.

The beatification of Nicholas occurred after visitors to his tomb reported miraculous events, and Myra soon became a popular locus of pilgrimage. A monastery was built nearby during the eleventh century and, even after the Italian merchants stole the bones of the saint, the pilgrimages continued; indeed, it is thought that the monks simply designated another tomb as that of St Nicholas, and would pour oil through openings in the top and collect it at the bottom, to sell to pilgrims as holy secretions.

The contemporary church has little in common with the fourth-century original, which was rebuilt by Constantine IX in 1043, probably after its destruction by occupying Saracens. Today's shrine is basically a three-aisled basilica in form, with a fourth added later. In 1862 Russian Tsar Nicholas I had the church renovated, installing a vaulted ceiling instead of a cupola in the central nave, along with a belfry – both unheard of in early Byzantine architecture. Turkish archeologists have carried out more recent restoration in order to protect the building, such as the addition of the small stone domes in the narthex.

Perhaps the most typical Byzantine feature is the **synthronon** or bishop's throne in the apse, a relatively rare sight in Turkish medieval buildings since most were removed when such churches were converted into mosques. Some of the patchy interior **frescoes** have been restored recently; the best and clearest, in the dome of the north transept, is a *Communion of the Apostles*. **Mosaic floor** panels, mainly comprising geometric designs, adorn the nave and south aisle, while among the pieces of masonry near the entrance is one carved with an anchor – Nicholas is the patron saint of sailors as well as virgins, children, merchants, scholars, pawnbrokers and Holy Russia. His supposed **sarcophagus**, in the most southerly aisle as you face the bishop's throne, is worth a look, although not considered genuine. The tomb from which the saint's bones were stolen was reportedly located under a stone pavement – and, more significantly, on this one there are marble statues representing a man and a woman (obviously a couple) on the lid.

Practicalities

All buses and dolmuşes drop you at the fairly central **otogar**. There's a single surviving **pansiyon** out of town on the way to ancient Myra – the *Kent* (☎0242/871 2042; ❷) – though this is more of use to trekkers on the Lycian Way. More central **hotels** include the *Grand Hotel Kekova*, east of the centre opposite the PTT (☎0242/871 3462, ☎871 5366; ❹). Among a bare handful of **restaurants** downtown, the unlicensed *İpek*, on the same side of Müze Caddesi as the church, is popular with locals for its good, inexpensive *pide*, grills and *sulu yemek*.

Myra

The remains of ancient **Myra** (daily: April–Oct 8.30am–7.30pm; Nov–March 8.30am–5pm; 5YTL) are a two-kilometre walk or drive north of Demre's town centre, and form one of the most easily visited Lycian sites. Accordingly it's packed with tours even in off-season, let alone the summer, when the best times to visit are either early morning or after 5.30pm. You will still have to run a gauntlet at all times of overwhelming tourist tat lining the access walkways, plus local kids selling oregano sprigs and unneeded guide services.

Apart from the highlights – a large theatre and some of the best examples of house-style rock tombs to be seen in Lycia – most of the city is still buried. The **theatre** was destroyed in an earthquake in 141 AD but rebuilt shortly afterwards; the rock face behind it being vertical and unable to support the cavea, the structure had to be constructed with masonry on either side, although its back rests against the cliff. The theatre is flanked by two concentric galleries covering the stairs (still intact), by which spectators entered the auditorium. Lying around the orchestra and just outside are substantial chunks of carving that would once have decorated the stage building, including several depicting theatrical masks, a bust of a woman and a Medusa head.

The main concentration of **tombs** (currently off-limits) stands to the west of the theatre. Most of the tombs are of the house type, supposed to imitate Lycian dwelling-places, even down to the wooden beams supporting the roofs. Some are decorated with reliefs, including warriors at the climax of a battle, a naked page handing a helmet to a warrior, and a funerary scene.

The second group of tombs, called the **river necropolis**, is around the side of the second long ridge on the right as you stand with your back to the theatre stage. To get there, leave the main site, turn left off the final access drive onto the main approach road, and continue inland for 1.5km. Here a monument known as the "**painted**" **tomb** (though it no longer retains any pigment) features the reclining figure of a bearded man and his family in the porch, and outside on the rock face what is presumed to be the same family, dressed in outdoor clothes. To the east of the theatre, below the acropolis hill, lie the remains of a brick building whose identity is unknown, although it preserves an inscription on a Doric column concerning a ferry service that operated between Myra and Limyra in imperial Roman times.

The coast near Demre

The port of the ancient city of Myra, **Andriake**, lies well over 2km southwest of Demre, and nearly 5km from Myra itself. To get there (there's no public transport), head west out of Demre towards Kaş, and then bear left, following black-on-yellow signs, when the main highway begins tackling the grade on the right bank of the stream leading down to the sea. Another kilometre beyond the site lies the modern anchorage of **Çayağzı** ("Rivermouth"), site of a reasonable beach and start-point for boat trips to the Kekova region. There's a far better beach at **Sülüklü**, however, 3km east of Andriake and accessible by a paved side-road.

Andriake

Ancient **Andriake**, built on either bank of the ancient Androkos river, was the site of **Hadrian's granary**, vital not only to Myra but to the whole Roman world, since its contents were sent to Rome to be distributed around the empire. The substantial remains of the building can still be seen south of today's river, which runs parallel to the road between Demre and the beach. The granary – built on the orders of Hadrian between 119 and 139 AD, and very similar to the one at Patara – consists of eight rooms constructed of well-fitting square-cut blocks. The outer walls still stand to their original height, giving a clear idea of the impressive overall size of this structure. Above the main central gate are busts of Hadrian and what is thought to be his wife, the empress Sabina. Another decorative relief on the front wall, near the second door from the west, depicts two deities of disputed identity, one of whom is flanked by a snake and a griffin, while the other reclines on a couch.

Çayağzı and Sülüklü

Çayağzı offers a rather average sandy beach and a half-dozen snack-shacks opposite the main quay, though the shacks operate fitfully, as does the lone full-service restaurant on the far side of the pedestrian bridge. This is still a working fishing-port, with an active boatyard, and it's possible to get a **boat** from here to the Kekova area, a 45-minute journey, followed by the standard tour of the underwater ruins at Kekova island. You'll need a boatload (10–15 people) – although some owners (who tout aggressively on your arrival) will take individuals or couples for around 16YTL.

The only other reason to come to Çayağzı is for a swim. The beach is fairly short, but broad and duney – though also trash-strewn and prone to algae slicks, which, together with the Kaş–Demre highway passing just overhead and the area's status as an archeological zone, perhaps accounts for the minimal development here. However, the beauty of the skyline to the west cannot be underestimated, where parallel ridges – as in a Japanese print – march down to Kekova.

There's much better swimming and beachcombing, however, at **Sülüklü**, reached via the narrow, initially uphill road beginning near Hadrian's granary. Although it's a more exposed bay than Çayağzı, the water and 700m of sand are cleaner, with two or three simple restaurants just behind. Demre's "town beach" at **Taşdibi**, just the other side of the headland closing off Sülüklü, is more protected but consists of coarse pebbles.

Sura

Marginally more accessible than Andriake is the ancient Apollo oracle at **Sura** (unrestricted access; free), which is reached either from the direct Üçağız–Kapaklı–Andriake road, just before it joins the new highway looping high above Andriake en route to Demre, or via the Lycian Way. Sura is little visited and unspoilt, except for a large, illicit rubbish-tip by the edge of the road just west, which is slowly polluting the marsh below – and presumably the beach. Incidentally, do not be tempted to try reaching the oracle from Çayağzı beach; you will founder in the marsh, and there is no usable trail along the rocky hillsides enclosing it to either side.

Unlike Patara, Sura was never a city, merely a sacred precinct with only priests resident. The **acropolis**, rising very modestly above the level of a small plateau here, had a square outer perimeter wall (with stubs of watchtowers still visible on the north), and on the west side a peculiar twelve-chambered keep, possibly a hostel for pilgrims. Just southeast of this was a presumed **priestly residence**, today only discernible as a large rock-cut terrace; a few paces west of this, a rock-cut **stairway** (still partly preserved) descended the sheer cliff face beyond the keep to the vicinity of a **sacred spring**, which still flows. Close to this, plainly visible from afar in the mud-flats, is the well-preserved **Temple of Apollo Surios**, together with the spring which was the focus of the ancient oracle.

This, according to ancient writers, was most peculiar in form and function. Supplicants arrived bearing spits of roasted meat, which they presented to priests awaiting them in a sacred grove by the shore; though the temple is now 1.5km inland, in ancient times the sea came almost up to its door. The priests would then throw the meat into a "whirlpool" in the sand, apparently a place where freshwater springs welled up in the tidal stream-mouth; every surge of the sea would bring numerous fish, attracted by the meat. Then the pilgrims' fortunes would be proclaimed on (accounts differ) either according to whether the fish accepted or rejected the meal, or by the species and behaviour of the fish. The extra springs can still be seen rippling the surface of the stream in front of the temple, and in coastal Turkey quite large ocean fish – sea bass and mullet – are tolerant of brackish conditions, though the "whales and sawfish" of the ancient authors are perhaps fantastic. After the suppression of pagan oracles towards the end of the fourth century AD, two **Byzantine churches** sprung up here: one behind the temple, one up in the acropolis.

Finike

A twisty half-hour drive beyond Demre, the harbour town of **FINIKE**, formerly Phoenicus, no longer preserves evidence of its past, and has little to suggest an illustrious future either. Highway 400 has been a double-edged sword for Finike: its local completion during the 1960s, long before the Finike–Antalya and Kaş–Kınık stretches were opened, provided the town with a much-needed link between the port and inland citrus groves, the mainstay of the local economy (an orange figures in the municipal logo). But this busy thoroughfare has also ruined Finike aesthetically by cutting its centre off from the beach and disturbing the peace of this potentially attractive place.

The town used to be deserted in summer as its residents headed up to the *ova* around Elmalı, but now concrete constructions obscure the view of the bay, and they vastly outnumber the few remaining Ottoman houses, mostly found inland. Finike's **marina** has become very busy, attracting *gülets* and private yachts put off by Antalya's high docking fees and distance from the best cruising coasts. But if you're not on a boat, the only reason to stay is for easy access to a pair of nearby ancient cities: Arykanda and Limyra (see p.510).

Finike's main **beach**, extending 4km east of town, has little to recommend it other than sandiness and length: it's not terribly scenic, clean or protected from wind and waves, and it's backed by the suburb of **Sahilkent** with its vast numbers of apartment blocks and lodging pitched at weekending Turks. For calmer swimming, there are two prettier pebble coves – **Gökliman** (4km west) and **Çağıllı** (8km west) – between Finike and Demre.

Practicalities

Finike's **otogar** is centrally situated, just off Highway 400, 300m along the road to Limyra, Arykanda and Elmalı. Those heading east should note that the town has the last **banks** with ATMs before Kemer (bar unsightly Kumluca). The **hamam**, by the bus station, is modern and well maintained.

As at Demre, there's relatively little choice in terms of **accommodation**. Your best option, up a long flight of steps on the hill 150m south of the *otogar*, is the *Paris Hotel-Pansiyon* (☎0242/855 1488; ❷), a pleasant place with some plumbed rooms, and a terrace with a good view of Finike bay. The friendly managing family speaks French and English, and operates a rooftop restaurant in summer. Otherwise, try the medium-sized, basic *Şendil* (☎0242/855 1660; ❷), also with a roof terrace and well signposted in a quiet spot 300m inland from the shoreline park. For greater comfort, the *Bahar Otel* (☎0242/856 2020; ❸) is right in the town centre.

Eating options in Finike are similarly limited, if mostly licensed: the *Deniz*, a few steps west of the PTT, is an old standby, though portions tend to be small even by Turkish standards. The best all-rounder is *Birlik* (near the *Bahar Otel* across from the Ziraat Bankası), open 24 hours and with good grilled fish plus a few *mezes* and soups (though slightly bizarre service). Certainly the most pleasant environment is provided by the *Petek*, with a summer terrace overlooking the yacht drydock (if not actually the water); the wood-stove-equipped winter salon doubles as the yachties bar and club, and the food's not bad either.

Limyra, Arykanda and Elmalı

The route **inland from Finike to Elmalı** (Highway 635) is an hour and a half's uphill drive along a precipitous mountain road, made especially terrifying by the cavalier attitude of the numerous truck drivers who hurtle up and down it with timber or loads of produce from the local orchards. On the way up it's worth stopping to visit two beautiful mountain sites, **Limyra** and **Arykanda**.

Limyra

The site of **Limyra** is the less impressive of the two – though it is being re-excavated under Austrian supervision and is easily accessible if you have just a cycle or a motorbike. It's about 10km north of Finike, 3km from the Finike–Elmalı highway: turn off at the village of Turunçova and head east down a signposted road. Any Finike–Elmalı dolmuş can drop you off at Turunçova, from where you'll have to walk the remaining distance. There's a car park and village of sorts at the site itself, complete with pesky children.

Limyra had a promising start: founded in the fifth century BC, the city was made capital of Lycia by local ruler Pericles in the fourth century. From then on its fortunes were broadly the same as other Lycian cities, and it didn't make much of an appearance in the history books until 4 AD, when Gaius Caesar, grandson and adopted heir of Augustus, died here on his way home from Armenia. During Byzantine times it became the seat of a bishop, but suffered badly during the Arab raids of the seventh to ninth centuries and was largely abandoned. A peculiar feature of the site, noted in antiquity, is the vigorous spring-fed river, typical of this kind of rock strata, that emerges suddenly at the base of Tocak Dağı; apparently there was a fish-oracle here too, similar in concept to the one at Sura (see p.508).

The main settlement, and consequently most of its public buildings, lay at the foot of the hill, but now few traces of ancient buildings are visible on the flatlands among the branches of the river, and the ruins mostly consist of several hundred **tombs**. The southern slope of the mountain is covered by tombs cut into the rock face; above is a fortified **acropolis**. On the left of the road from Turunçova, the western **necropolis** includes an impressive two-storey tomb in a citrus grove. North of the road looms a **theatre** dating from the second century AD, behind which is a free-standing fourth-century sarcophagus with an inscription in Lycian announcing it as the tomb of Xatabura, thought to have been a relation of Pericles (the founder of the Lycian Federation). Among its abundant relief carvings are a funeral feast, on the south side, and on the west a scene depicting the judgement of Xatabura, pictured as a naked youth.

At the top of Tocak Dağı, north of the site, stands the most interesting **tomb** of all, signposted as the "Heroon" from the theatre. It's about a forty-minute climb to get there, up the path leading from the back of the village, but worth the effort – swarms of local children will offer their unnecessary services as guides. This mausoleum is probably that of Pericles, who saved Lycia from the ambitions of Mausolus in the fourth century. The tomb divides into two parts: a lower grave chamber, and the upper chamber styled like a temple, with a row of four caryatids at front and back. The figures of the frieze, which show the hero mounting his chariot, indicate the blend of Greek and Persian influences on later Lycian art.

Arykanda

Arykanda lies 34km north of Finike, on the right-hand side of the road; if you're coming directly from Kaş, make use of the short cut between Kasaba and Çatallar, 4km below the ruins, which is entirely paved and fairly broad despite pessimistic depictions on obsolete touring maps. Travelling by minibus, you should ask to be dropped off at the village of **Arif**, from whose top end it's a one-kilometre signposted walk to the ruins along a side road passable to any car. At the end of the line you'll find toilets, water taps, and a double parking area, but as yet no fencing or ticket booth (though 4YTL admission is charged when the warden is present). Individual monuments are scattered and unlabelled, though there is a good site plan by the entrance.

Finds here date back to the fifth century BC, but the typically Lycian "-anda" suffix suggests that the city may have been founded a millennium earlier. Although Arykanda was a member of the Lycian Federation from the second century BC, its inhabitants were chiefly renowned for their sloth and profligacy: when Antiochus III tried to invade Lycia in 197 BC, they reputedly took his side in the hope of reaping financial benefits to help repay their debts. Christianity gained ground here in the third century, as proved by a copy of a petition to the emperor Maximinus, in which the Arykandans request that the "illegal and abominable practices of the godless (pagans)" be suppressed. The city continued in a much-reduced form until the eleventh century, mainly confined to the area just to either side of today's main through-path.

Arykanda's setting is breathtaking, comparable to Delphi in Greece; it occupies a steep, south-facing hillside overlooking the major valley between the Akdağ and Bey mountain ranges. A pronounced ravine and a series of power pylons divide the site roughly in half. The first thing you'll see, beside the lower parking area, is a complex structure variously dubbed "Naltepesi" or "**lower acropolis**"; entered by a right-angled stairway, its function is not yet completely understood, but you can make out a small bath-house and presumed shops. North of the same parking area sprawls a large **basilica** with extensive mosaic flooring under tin-roof shelters posed over each aisle, and a semicircular row of benches (probably a *synthronon*) in the outer apse. Another, smaller one, lying parallel just inside, suggests eighth-century destruction and subsequent more modest rebuilding; on a terrace just below is another, unidentified mosaic-floored building. But the most impressive sight as you arrive, looming to the east, is the ten-metre-high facade of the **baths**, with numerous windows on two levels, and apsidal halls at each end – the westerly one with a still-intact plunge pool, the easterly one with stacked hypocausts; the **gymnasium** lies just beyond.

Other constructions worth seeking out include a small **temple** or tomb above the baths complex (one of three "monumental tombs" on the site plan) that was adapted for Christian worship – on the east wall is the Greek inscription "Jesus Christ is Victorious" and a crude cross; there are more Roman or Byzantine mosaics in the tombs or temples immediately east of the Christianized one. West of the ravine and power lines, and above the agora – whose engaging odeion has been defaced by horrible new marble cladding – an impressive **theatre** retains some twenty rows of seats divided by six aisles, plus a well-preserved stage building. Above this sprawls a short but attractive **stadium**, with several rows of seats exposed.

Elmalı

The 1100-metre-high plain around Elmalı is the biggest stretch of arable land in upland Lycia, an important centre for harvesting apples, potatoes, sugar beets and chickpeas – and, until recent conservation edicts, the cedars of the Beydağları as well. **ELMALİ** (literally, "apple-ish"), dominated by nearby snowcapped Elmalı Dağı (2296m), is a town of 15,000, notable for its domestic architecture: a number of houses in the hillside old quarter are beautiful Ottoman timber-framed *konaks*, though many are in precarious condition, and all are greatly outnumbered by the straggly sprawl of the new town. The air is cool and fresh even in summer, with a faint smell of wood smoke, and Gömbe (see p.496) is even easier to reach from here than from Kaş.

The Tahtacıs

The so-called **Tahtacılar** or "Board-Cutters" are a secretive and much-maligned group who are in fact Alevîs, a sect closely related to Shiism and specifically the Bektaşi dervish order. They are descended from remnants of the army of Shia Shah Ismail, who was defeated by Sultan Selim I at the Battle of Çaldıran in 1514. Like all good heretics before and since, the stragglers retreated high into the mountains, out of reach of their enemies, and today occupy villages in a wide montane crescent, extending from Edremit to Adana, with a special concentration in the Toros ranges. Their present name commemorates the professions of logger and wood-carver that many of them have followed in recent centuries; such Tahtacıs are semi-nomadic, under summer contract to the Forest Service, with whole villages sent to fell trees in areas that change from year to year.

While the allied Bektaşis have their spiritual centre at central Anatolian Hacıbektaş, and an important pilgrimage shrine near Elmalı (see below), the Tahtacıs still maintain a seminary at Narlıdere outside İzmir. Their **beliefs**, which they can be reluctant to discuss with outsiders, share most of the tenets of Alevîsm: stress on inner purity of observance rather than external ritual, or abstention from alcohol; interdenominational tolerance and disdain of materialism; and relatively equal status for women. They are abhorrent to orthodox Sunni Muslims, who in recent decades constructed mosques – often at gunpoint – in previously mosque-less Alevî villages. Their free-thinking has often also brought them into (sometimes violent) conflict with the authorities. The Tahtacı/Alevî attitude towards women has engendered the most scurrilous slanders (principally nocturnal drunken orgies), and for visitors, it is the boldness of the unveiled women – who are not shy about addressing strangers – that is the most reliable clue that you are in a Tahtacı area, and a welcome change after the po-faced sexual segregation of mainstream Turkish village society.

Elmalı has a fine Classical Ottoman mosque, the early seventeenth-century **Ömerpaşa Camii** (open prayer times), whose exterior is decorated with beautiful faïence panels and inscriptions; the interior is disappointing, while the mosque *medrese* now serves as a library. Further up the main street is all that remains of a Selçuk mosque, a stubby piece of masonry that was once the base of a minaret. To the northwest, in the street behind the former *medrese*, you'll find the well-disguised sixteenth-century **Bey Hamamı**, regrettably poorly run and not recommended.

The town comes alive for its Monday **market**, the best and least touristy in the region, and its notable **wrestling competition**, held for three days in a purpose-built stadium during the first week of September. If you want to stay – not that there's any need to – there's one surviving central **hotel**, the *Arzu* (☎0242/618 6604; ❸) just uphill beyond the mosque. There are no full-service **restaurants** in the town centre, only a few *pastanes*.

With your own transport, you can head northwest beyond Elmalı to the **Güğübeli**, an 1830-metre pass at the north end of the Akdağ massif. The pass provides a worthwhile short-cut west to the Fethiye area, with fine views east to the Beydağları and west to the mountains behind Fethiye. It's a forty-minute climb through a river canyon, past tufts of juniper and the odd pastoral pen, while the descent southwest to Highway 350 via Seki passes the side-turning for Oenoanda (see p.471). Though well-paved, this is considered a minor road, and not kept snow-ploughed from late December to mid-April, when chains will usually be needed.

Pir Sultan Abdal Türbesi

For further insight into Alevî/Tahtacı beliefs (see box, opposite), you'd do well to make your own pilgrimage to the *türbe* of **Pir Sultan Abdal Musa**, a four-teenth-century poet-saint who is second only to Hacı Bektaş Veli in the Alevî pantheon. The tomb (open reasonable hours) stands at the southeast edge of well-signed Tekke Köyü, 15km south of Elmalı, set amidst an old graveyard, with the Beydağlar on the skyline to the east. In the inner chamber, the saint's sarcophagus lies beside those of his father, mother, sister and favourite disciple Gaygusus Sultan. The outer portico is festooned with posters of various figures in the history of Alevîism and its affiliate Shiism: Hacı Bektaş Veli with his familiars the lion and the stag, the Battle of Kerbala with graphic martyrdoms of Ali's sons Hussein and Hassan, plus the Twelve Imams.

The Olympos coast

East of Finike, the coast road barrels dead straight past the beach before turning ninety degrees to enter Kumluca, an unattractive market town worth a stop only during its late-January camel-wrestling matches. Beyond Kumluca, Highway 400 curls up into the **Beydağları National Park**, comprising a spectacular sequence of densely pine-forested ridges and precipitous bare cliffs. Hidden at the mouths of canyons plunging toward the sea are two of Lycia's more unspoiled beach resorts: **Adrasan** and **Olympos/Çıralı**. If you're heading towards either by car, forgo the main highway in favour of the narrow but paved side-road that veers off at the east edge of Kumluca, signposted "Beykonak, Mavikent". This scenic short-cut rollercoasters through forested valleys and along dramatic coastline to **Gelidonya Burnu**, with its lighthouse and scenic flanking sections of the Lycian Way, before emerging at Çavuş, the nearest proper village to Adrasan and Olympos. The only trick en route involves turning left (north) at a signposted junction near the out-skirts of Karaöz, the last bay and village before Gelidonya Burnu.

Gelidonya Burnu

From Karaöz, an obvious dirt road beginning at the small pebbly beach heads south towards the cape, parallel to the coast. Taxis or buses won't get any further than about 3.5km along, should you be thinking of arranging a pick-up shuttle later (a popular strategy with walking groups). About 6.5km from Karaöz, leave the track in favour of the marked **Lycian Way**, now a steadily rising path through oaks and pines; from the trailhead it's just under an hour with a daypack (round-trip) to the picturesque **lighthouse** just above Taşlık Burnu (as **Gelidonya Burnu**, the "Swallow Point" of the ancients, has been officially renamed). French-built in 1936, it figures prominently on the back cover of the Lycian Way guidebook. The lighthouse is not currently inhabited, though if you're here at dusk you may meet the keeper who bikes out from Karaöz to light the lamp daily. Beyond the cape straggle the treacherous **Beş Adalar** (Five Islands), shipping hazards that have caused many a wreck, including an ancient one which yielded a vast amount of treasure to archeological divers during the 1960s.

North of the lighthouse stretches a ruggedly scenic section of the Lycian Way, threading deserted hillside between the sea and a thousand-metre-high ridge, on its six-hour course to Adrasan (path or cross-country except for the last hour). It's probably best not attempted alone, but walking this bit has become a fairly popular organized group outing, so in any case you'll probably have company.

Adrasan

Some 18km beyond Kumluca on Highway 400, the first side-road to Olympos (see p.514) provides an alternative route to Çavuş village and the bay of Adrasan. Whether you arrive at the central junction in Çavuş from this direction, or from Mavikent, you'll turn east onto the seaward road (marked "Sahil"), following hotel placards for 4km more to emerge at the attractive, relatively peaceful beach resort of **ADRASAN**. This falls within the confines of the national park, which as much as anything else has acted as a healthy brake on development here.

You can get here directly by a lone late-afternoon **bus from Antalya** (it goes back at 7am the next day), arriving in time to stay at one of the two dozen *pansiyon*s and hotels dotted along the length of the beach, or along the stream meeting the sea at the north end, under the shadow of pointy Musa Dağı. Most of the fancier **hotels** (though the term is only relative), formerly aimed exclusively at British package tourists, are sited at the south end of the strand, near the jetty. One of the best, with a large pool and its own patch of beach, is the well-kept *Ford* (℡0242/883 1098, ℻883 1026; ❺; closed Nov–April), the last establishment in the row, with English-speaking management and rooms always held back for walk-ins. Slightly inland along the southerly approach road, on a hillside amidst the pines, the *Eviniz Pansiyon* (℡0242/883 1110, ⓦwww.eviniz.de; closed Nov to mid-May; ❻) offers a pleasant pool terrace, indoor restaurant and views over the plain to the sea. At the far north end of the beach, where the road turns inland to become the northerly access drive following the stream (joining the main road in at the Çakmak Camii), are two more worthwhile choices: *Golden River Hotel* (℡0242/883 1190, ⓦwww.goldenriveradrasan.com; ❹), closest to the beach, with large if basic, white-tiled rooms, and (best of all) the much newer *Hotel Aybars* (℡0242/883-1133 or 0532/314 1887, ⓦwww.aybarshotel.com; ❹, ❺ half-board), with large, air-conditioned, balconied rooms overlooking lush grounds and a decent restaurant. It's open in winter, December to March, by arrangement only; Aysın, on the mobile number given, speaks good English.

The *Golden River* and *Aybars* hotels, and several **restaurants** on the east bank of the enchanting watercourse, are all accessed by wobbly suspension bridges; diners are seated by, or even in, the streambed, where some of the hundreds of local ducks come to cadge your spare bread. None are really worth singling out, but competition also ensures that none are grotesquely expensive or greasy. Back on the south end of the beach, *İrfan Korkmazer'in Yeri* restaurant, on the south esplanade, is the most popular establishment with locals, and is reliably open in spring and autumn.

A popular **boat-trip** destination is **Ceneviz Limanı**, a cliff-girt bay beyond Musa Dağı that's inaccessible on foot. There's also a small, German/Turkish-run **scuba centre** at mid-beach, Diving Center Adrasan (℡0242/883 1353, ⓦwww.diving-adrasan.com; closed Feb to late March), which arranges accommodation locally as part of its dive packages (CMAS/PADI certification from €280; 10-dive package €200), though Ceneviz Limanı itself is off-limits to divers for archeological/military reasons.

Olympos and Çıralı

From Highway 400, two marked side-roads provide access to the ruins of the ancient Lycian city of **Olympos**. After 8km, the southerly road (marked "Olympos 11, Adrasan (Çavuşköy) 15") becomes a three-kilometre rough dirt-track ending at a car park and inland ticket booth for the ruins (see "The site of Olympos", opposite). Just upstream from here in the **Olympos valley** are a dozen-plus *pansiyon*s or "treehouse" lodges – a legendarily popular base with Anglophone backpackers. The northerly turning off Highway 400, 800m north of the southerly one and signposted "Çıralı 7, Yanartaş, Chimaera", leads down to the hamlet of **Çırali** on the coast, which also has food and accommodation, and easy access to the ruins by a short stroll south along the beach. Above the Çıralı coastal plain, on the toes of nearby Tahtalı Dağ, burns a perpetual flame, fed by natural gases issuing from the ground. Since antiquity this has been called the **Chimaera**, a name it shares with a mythical fire-breathing monster supposed to have inhabited these mountains.

There is a single daily direct minibus **from Antalya** to Çıralı, running Monday to Saturday in the late afternoon, returning the next day at 6.30am, as well as two buses a week **from Kumluca**. Between May and October, a **connecting minibus** runs from the respective main-road turn-offs to Çıralı (6 daily) and Olympos (almost hourly). At other times of the year the minibus only departs from either end of its run when full, so you may have to shell out for a taxi (16YTL) to cover the 7km of side road. Alternatively, some of the more commercially minded lodges lay on a complimentary **shuttle bus service** two or three times daily to the Olympos-valley accommodation.

Some history

Nothing is known about the origins of Olympos, but the city presumably took its name from Mount Olympos, thought to be present-day Tahtalı Dağ, 16km to the north – one of over twenty mountains with the name Olympos in the Classical world. The city made its historical debut during the second century BC, when it was minting its own coins. Strabo the historian wrote in 100 BC that Olympos was one of six cities in the Lycian Federation that had three votes, attesting to its importance.

The principal deity of Olympos was Hephaestos (Vulcan to the Romans), god of fire and of blacksmiths. He was considered a native of this region, and the remains of a temple dedicated to him can be found near the Chimaera; fines for damage to local tombs were payable to the temple treasury. In the first century BC, the importance of Hephaistos diminished when Cilician pirates led by Zenicetes overran both Olympos and nearby Phaselis and introduced the worship of Mithras, a god of Indo-European origin, whose rites were performed on Mount Olympos. Zenicetes made Olympos his headquarters, but in 78 BC he was defeated by the Roman governor of Cilicia, and again in 67 BC by Pompey, after which Olympos was declared public property. The fortunes of the city revived after it was absorbed into the Roman Empire in 43 AD, and Christianity became prominent. Olympos was used as a trading base by the Venetians and Genoese in the eleventh and twelfth centuries – thus Ceneviz Limanı or "Genoese Harbour" just to the south – but was abandoned in the fifteenth century as the Ottomans dominated the Mediterranean.

The site of Olympos

There are two entrances to the **site of Olympos** (daily: April–Oct 8am–7pm; Nov–March 9am–5.30pm; 2YTL): one inland, at the end of the southerly approach road, and another (where the guards are reportedly not as vigilant) about fifteen minutes' walk south along the beach from Çıralı. As at Patara, nocturnal "raids" of the ruins are expressly forbidden. It's potentially an idyllic site, located on the banks of an oleander- and fig-shaded stream running between high cliffs. Alas, a decade or so of backpackers littering or sleeping rough in the site (despite notices forbidding both) has seen the water muddied or worse, and the turtles, ducks and frogs that used to live here now make themselves scarce. The scanty ruins line the banks of the stream, which rarely dries up completely in summer, owing to three freshwater springs welling up on the north bank, quite close to the ocean.

The first things you'll notice are extensive **Byzantine-Genoese fortifications** overlooking the beach from each creek bank, just twenty to thirty metres up the crags. At the base of the fort on the north bank are two **"harbour tombs"**, recognizably Lycian in form, with a touching epigraph on a ship captain – complete with boat in relief – translated for viewers. Further along on the south bank stands part of a quay wall and an arcaded **warehouse**; to the east on the same side lie the walls of a Byzantine **church**; while in the river itself is a well-preserved pillar from a vanished **bridge**. Back in the undergrowth there is a **theatre**, its seats mostly vanished.

The north bank of the river has the most striking ruins. On the hill to the east of the path to the beach looms a well-preserved marble **door-frame** built into a wall of ashlar masonry. At the foot of the carved doorway is a statue base dedicated by an inscription to Marcus Aurelius, with the dates 172–175 AD. East of the portal hide a Byzantine **villa** with mosaic floors, a mausoleum-style **tomb**, and a Byzantine **aqueduct** that carried water to the heart of the city. The aqueduct overlaps the outflow of one of the aforementioned springs; follow it upstream, past the mausoleum-tomb, to the villa. Though paths have been hacked through the jungly vegetation beyond the portal, the aqueduct trough remains your best bet for clear navigation.

The Chimaera

North of Olympos, in the foothills of Tahtalı Dağ, the eternal flame of the **Chimaera** is about an hour's stroll from Çıralı village; it's also possible to drive to the bottom of the ascent and walk from the car park (about 20min; 2YTL admission). Tracks to the trailhead are well signposted, though the path up (now part of the inland alternate Lycian Way) has been garishly fieldstoned, with awkward step intervals, on its way to a Byzantine chapel and Tholos of Hephaestos as well as the flame. The climb is most rewarding (and coolest) as dusk falls, since the fire is best seen in the dark; some people make rag-torches and ignite them from the flames, using them to light the path on the way down. Most of the Olympos-valley treehouse-lodges organize recommended nocturnal visits, with transfer by tractor-drawn carriages.

The Chimaera, a series of flames issuing out of cracks on the bare hillside, is one of the most unusual sites in the whole of Lycia. It's not certain what causes the phenomenon; surveys have detected traces of methane in the gas but otherwise its make-up is unique to this spot. The flames can be extinguished temporarily if covered over, when a gaseous smell is noticeable, but will spontaneously re-ignite.

What is known, however, is that the fire has been burning since antiquity, and inspired the local worship of Hephaestos (Vulcan), generally revered in places where fire sprang from the earth. The mountain was also the haunt of a fire-breathing monster with a lion's head and forelegs, a goat's rear end, and a snake for a tail: the Chimaera. Its silhouette, incidentally, has long been the logo of the state-run *Petrol Ofisi* chain of Turkish filling stations.

Legend relates how **Bellerophon** was ordered by Iobates, king of Xanthos, to kill the Chimaera in atonement for the supposed rape of his daughter Stheneboea. With the help of the winged horse Pegasus, Bellerophon succeeded, killing the beast from the air by dropping lead into its mouth. Later, Bellerophon was deemed to have been falsely accused, and avenged himself on Stheneboea by persuading her to fly away with him on Pegasus and flinging her into the sea. He finally got his own just desserts when he attempted to ascend to heaven on Pegasus, was flung from the magical horse's back and, lamed and blinded, forced to wander the earth as a beggar until his death.

Olympos valley

The main drawback to basing yourself in the **Olympos valley** is that you're still some way from the beach, and need to pay for admission every time you cross the archeological zone for a swim. What's more, it's very much a narrow-minded overlanders' "ghetto", despite pretensions to superiority over conventional package tourists. The chief attraction seems to be the cheap beer, and groups of Aussies duly take their evening promenade along the road, bottles in hand, to a soundtrack of reverberating rock music. During the two weeks before or after ANZAC day, when any self-respecting Ozzie or Kiwi will be paying homage at Çanakkale, don't expect any vacancies. Prices at all establishments listed below are ❷ for a shared-bath treehouse, and ❸ for en-suite bungalows (on a half-board basis); dorms (where available) and camping space usually cost €7–10 per person. Many of the lodgings hire travellers to wash up, make beds and cook on a casual basis – as ever, illegal in Turkey, but a good stopgap if funds are running low.

The most treehouse-like of the **lodges**, and thus the first to fill, are: *Kadir's*, furthest from the ruins (T 0242/892 1250, W www.kadirstreehouses.com), with the liveliest bar in the valley; *Bayram's*, nestled in an orange grove closest to the ruins, with Internet access (T 0242/892 1243, W www.bayrams.com); and *Türkmen*, in between the two, near the stream ford (T 0242/892 1249, W www.turkmenpension.com), the most comfortable of the trio. Of more upmarket and (relatively) quiet establishments, the *Şaban* opposite *Türkmen* (T 0242/892 1265, W www.sabanpension.com) doesn't play constant music, but does have better-than-average food, more personable management and Internet access.

Çıralı

Since 1990, tourist development has taken off noticeably at **ÇIRALI**. Three hotels and almost forty *pansiyon*s have sprung up along the approach road and behind the three-kilometre **beach**, between the Ulupınar stream which meets the sea here and the low hills to the north. Loggerhead and green sea **turtles** still use this formerly deserted bay to lay their eggs. The Turkish Society for the Protection of Nature maintains a seasonal information booth here – when it's shut, their message remains posted: don't camp on/illuminate/dig up/litter the beach during the summer nesting season.

The best **accommodation** is listed below: there's no formal **campsite**, and as rough camping is actively discouraged (because of the turtles), some *pansiyon*s offer space for tents. After long-running disputes between the forestry and archeological services on the one hand, and local proprietors on the other, the beachfront **restaurants** have been moved back a token few metres from the sand, and seven or eight survivors – stretching in a line north of the river-mouth – seem here to stay. Of these, the best and most popular – if surprisingly pricey – are the *Orange Home*, the *Azur* and *Karakuş*; while south of the river-mouth, where parking is very limited (fee collected by roving warden), the most durable snack-bar is *Olympos Yavuz*, one of two adjacent rivals strategically straddling the sandy path to the ruins (vehicles not allowed beyond this point).

Hotels and pansiyons

Arcadia T 0242/825 7340, W www.arcadiaholiday.com. Towards the north end of the beach, and one of the few establishments actually abutting it, this Canadian-Turkish-managed establishment has five superb all-wood chalet-suites well spaced on its lawn, with recessed lighting, Internet access, modern baths and coffee machines. Half-board only. ❼

Barış Pansiyon T 0242/825 7080. Just behind the beach near the restaurants, this has ample parking and a choice of spartan, older en-suite rooms and a new wing of half-air-conditioned, half-balconied units (priced a category higher). ❸–❹

Emin Pansiyon T 0242/825 7320, W www.eminpansiyon.com. On the beach road, two doors past *Odile Hotel*. A mix of cement and wood-built chalets, with plenty of orchard and/or lawn between

△ Çıralı beach

the rows. Superior breakfasts include omelettes, quince jam and *pekmez* made from *tahin* or *harubu* (carob syrup). Friendly family management. ❹

Jasmin Pension ℡0242/825 7247, ⓦwww.cirali .de. Characterful rooms with en-suite bathrooms in the main building, thoroughly overhauled in 2004, and two more rooms in a modern annexe. There's a pleasant, wood-floor-and-dirt-terrace bar/restaurant/lounge area offering vegetarian suppers, flat bread and home-made apricot jam at breakfast, plus a paperback trading library. ❹

Myland Nature Pansiyon ℡0242/825 7044, ⓦwww.mylandnature.com. North end of beach strip, between *Odile* and *Arcadia*. Rather steeply priced for the ordinary wood chalets with hammocks outside, set in six acres of orchard, but you're paying for the organically grown food, photo

seminars, yoga course, massage and other activities on offer. Closed Jan–Feb. ❻

Odile Hotel Just past mid-beach. ℡0242/825 7163, ⓦwww.otel-odile.com. Keen management, a mixed clientele and 36 large, decently equipped units around a pool garden where the landscaping has finally grown in, make this good value. Credit cards accepted; closed Nov–Feb. ❺

Olympia Tree House ℡0242/825 7351, ⓦhttp:// olympiatreehouse.freeservers.com. If you want the treehouse experience without the juvenalia prevalent in the Olympos canyon, come instead to this friendly spot just north of the Ulupınar stream-mouth. Of the twelve units-on-stilts, two are relatively luxurious, the others basic, all are plumbing-less; tent space provided summer only. Open April to mid-Nov. ❸

Beycik, Ulupınar and Tahtalı Dağ

The formerly rural village of **BEYCIK**, about 17km inland, up a side road from Highway 400 just past the Ulupınar turning, has been transformed by wealthy

Turks buying land here to take advantage of the superb views – it's currently a bit of a mess, with bulldozer scrapings, half-built villas and gouged pavement everywhere. The main bright-spot is *Villa il Castello* (☎0242/816 1013, ⊛http://villacastel.hypermart.net; ❹), well-conceived, comfortable **accommodation** with a pool, fitness centre and stylish bar-restaurant, where you can get a decent cappuccino among other things. The nine large, well-appointed suites can fit two kids and two adults and, at 1000m elevation, are heated but not air-conditioned.

Elsewhere, meals can be found very close to the northerly turning to Çıralı from Highway 400, at a half-dozen restaurants in the tiny, wooded hill-hamlet of **Ulupınar** with its many trout farms. The best one, downhill by the gushing spring, is *Botanik*; it's no stranger to coach tours, but the quality and value are good, with plenty of decent *meze*s and meat dishes in addition to the expected trout.

The inland variant of the Lycian Way links Çıralı with Beycik, making the village the logical start-point for ascents of 2366-metre **Tahtalı Dağ**. It's possible to do this as a day-hike in a very arduous eight-hour round trip, but a full traverse to Yayla Kuzdere, Gedelme and beyond along the Lycian Way, with at least one overnight outdoors, is recommended. There are good campsites and water just over the saddle visible from Beycik, at **Çukur Yayla**. The peak itself will have snow from late November through early May in a wet year, and is prone to marine-generated white-outs at any time, so an appropriate level of mountaineering skills and equipment are required for the summit ascent. Despite the area having national-park status, work has begun on a cable car up from the Tekirova resort, and unsightly pylons now dot the formerly unspoilt landscape, with the summit also earmarked for a projected ski area.

On to Antalya

Heading north from Olympos, there is very little reason to stop before Antalya. The overdeveloped and overpriced package resorts along this stretch of coast – notably Tekirova, Kemer, Göynük and Beldibi – leave a lot to be desired, and only the extensive ruins of the ancient city of **Phaselis** will tempt you off the main road. With regular buses out of Antalya in this direction, the only reason to stay overnight hereabouts is the *Sundance Nature Village*, at the north edge of Tekirova behind the southwest beach of Phaselis, on the coastal variant of the Lycian Way (☎0242/821 4165, ⊛www.sundance.web.tr; ❷). This complex of bungalows and treehouses, set amongst 120 partly pine-forested acres, also offers a widely praised restaurant using produce from its own gardens, horseback riding, trekking and tent space.

Phaselis

The ruins of ancient **Phaselis** (daily: summer 8am–7pm; winter 8am–5.30pm; 10YTL, plus 3YTL per car), just off the highway, 3km north of the German-dominated resort of Tekirova, are magnificently situated around three small bays, providing ample opportunity to contemplate antique architectural forms from a recumbent position on one of the beaches. The natural beauty of the site, the encroaching greenery, the clear water of the bays, and the seclusion, all make for a rewarding half-day outing – though you may wish to bring a picnic if you don't fancy patronizing the snack-caravans at the beachside car-park.

Some history

Phaselis was not always part of Lycia; situated at the border with Pamphylia, the city at certain points in its history was decidedly independent. According to legend, Phaselis was founded in 690 BC by colonists from Rhodes, and until 300 BC inscriptions were written in a Rhodian variety of the Dorian dialect.

The Phaselitans were great traders; they are supposed to have bought the land on which the city was founded with dried fish, and a "Phaselitan sacrifice" became proverbial for a cheapskate offering. They further earned themselves a reputation as venal scoundrels because at one point, needing funds, they sold Phaselitan citizenship for a pittance, attracting undesirable elements from all over Asia Minor. The city's trading links apparently stretched as far as Egypt, and their coins commonly depicted the prow of a ship on one side and the stern on the other.

Along with most of the rest of Asia Minor, Phaselis was overrun by the Persians in the sixth century, and was not freed until 469 BC. By that time, they had begun to feel loyalty to their imperial overlord, and it was with some difficulty that the Athenian general Kimon "liberated" them, making the city part of the Athenian maritime confederacy along with Olympos.

In the fourth century, Phaselis demonstrated its autonomy (or perhaps its perversity) by providing help to Mausolus, the satrap – or principal governor – of Caria, in his attempt to subdue the Lycian kingdom. Further evidence of Phaselitan sycophancy in their approach to authority was their behaviour toward Alexander the Great in 333 BC: not content with just surrendering their city to him, they also proffered a golden crown.

Phaselis became part of the Lycian Federation during the second century BC, but was soon, like Olympos, overrun by Cilician pirates. Although it was accepted back into the Federation afterwards, their long occupation of the city reduced it to a mere shell, with a much reduced, penniless population. After the *Pax Romana* came into effect, Phaselis distinguished itself with yet more obsequiousness: when Emperor Hadrian visited in 129 AD during a tour of the empire, statues were erected, a forum was constructed, and a gateway dedicated to him.

The site

The paved, one-kilometre side road that leads to the city from Highway 400 passes under a bluff on the left with a **fortified settlement** enclosed by a wall of Hellenistic masonry, the northernmost section of which has a tower and three archery slits. Though it can't compare in grandeur to several sites on the Pamphylian coast, or even to nearby Arykanda, there's certainly enough to see at the main site, which served as a location for filming *Jason and the Argonauts* in 1999. The most obvious landmark is the substantial and elegant remains of a Roman **aqueduct**. Supposed to have been one of the longest such conduits in the ancient world, it took water from a spring within the northern fortifications almost as far as the south harbour. To one side is a **bath-gymnasium** complex, with a geometric-mosaic floor in one room.

Arranged around a 400-metre-long promontory behind which most of the fan-shaped city is situated, Phaselis's three **harbours** are immediately obvious, and an ideal means by which to orient yourself. They served the city's extensive mercantile activities, particularly the export of local timber and botanical oils. The **north harbour** was too exposed to be used commercially, except in very favourable conditions, but it preserves the remains of an ancient quay on its south side. It offered an easy landing-point for aggressors, however, so the crest of the cliffs above were well fortified. This three-metre-wide wall now lies submerged, but is still intact. The middle or **city harbour** has a strong sea wall, since it is exposed to the north and east, and the eighteen-metre-wide entrance could be closed off. Today it's a sheltered swimming cove with a small beach and shallow water. The largest port, the **southwest harbour**, was protected by a 180-metre-long breakwater, most of which is now submerged. It provided docking for larger trading ships of up to a hundred tons, and now sees numerous yachts and *gület*s calling for the sake of its fine, large beach.

Between the harbours the promontory **acropolis** is covered in the very overgrown ruins of ancient houses and round cisterns. The main axis of the city is the **paved avenue**, which crosses the neck of the promontory, linking the south and middle harbours; partway along it kinks slightly at a rectangular plaza, thought to be the heart of the **agora**. At the southern-harbour end, a monumental **gateway** was constructed during 129–131 AD, like the agora, in honour of Hadrian's visit. Built of grey-white marble blocks, it bore a dedication to the emperor, though now only the foundations and tumbled masonry survive.

The well-preserved, second-century AD **theatre**, looking towards Tahtalı Dağ from between the acropolis and the main street, could hold around 1500 people. There are three large doors above present ground-level, which probably led onto the stage. Just visible below these are a row of five smaller doors that would have opened into the orchestra beneath the stage, and were possibly used to admit wild animals.

Travel details

Buses and minibuses

The schedules below are greatly enhanced in season by the 24-seat minibus service of the Patara Ko-op, which plies the coast between Fethiye and Finike, and of the Batı Antalya Ko-op, which shuttles almost constantly between Kaş and Antalya.

Dalaman to: Antalya (2 daily in summer; 6hr inland route); Bodrum (5 daily; 3hr 30min); Denizli (2 daily; 4hr 30min); Fethiye (twice hourly; 1hr); İstanbul (2 daily; 14hr); İzmir (14 daily; 5hr); Kaş (4 daily; 3hr); Marmaris (12 daily; 2hr); Muğla (18 daily; 2hr); Ortaca (twice hourly; 20min).

Dalyan to: Fethiye (2 daily; 1hr); Göcek (2 daily; 30min); Marmaris (2 daily; 2hr). NB: All these services depart before noon – for more choice take a local minibus to Ortaca.

Demre to: Elmalı (5 daily; 2hr); Fethiye (6 daily; 4hr); Finike (hourly; 30min); Kaş (hourly; 1hr); Üçağız (1 daily; 45min).

Elmalı to: Antalya (9 daily; 2hr); Demre (6 daily; 1hr 30min); Finike (twice hourly; 1hr 15min); Kaş (3 daily; 2hr 30min).

Fethiye to: Antalya (8 daily; 4hr by inland route, 7hr by coast); Bodrum (6 daily; 4hr 30min); Denizli (5 daily; 4–6hr – ask for express route); İstanbul (3 daily; 14hr); İzmir (twice hourly; 7hr); Kaş (15 daily; 2hr); Marmaris (hourly; 3hr); Pamukkale (several daily; 5hr); Patara (15 daily; 1hr 15min).

Finike to: Antalya (twice hourly; 2hr 15min); Demre (hourly; 30min); Elmalı (twice hourly; 1hr 30min); Fethiye (13 daily; 4hr); Kalkan (2 daily; 2hr); Kaş (7 daily; 1hr 15min).

Kalkan to: Antalya (7 daily; 4hr 30min); Bodrum (1 daily; 6hr); Fethiye (every 30min; 1hr 30min); İstanbul (1 daily; 15hr); İzmir (3 daily; 8hr); Kaş (every 30min; 30min); Marmaris (2 daily; 4hr 30min).

Kaş to: Antalya (6 daily; 4hr); Bodrum (3 daily; 6hr 30min); Fethiye (15 daily; 2hr 15min); Gömbe (3 daily; 1hr 30min); İstanbul (2 daily; 12hr); Marmaris (4 daily; 5hr); Pamukkale (2 daily; 8hr); Üçağız (1 daily; 45min).

Ortaca to: Antalya (2 daily; 7hr coastal route); Bodrum (5 daily; 4hr); Dalaman (twice hourly; 20min); Dalyan (25 daily; 20min); İzmir (10 daily; 5hr 30min); Kaş (5 daily; 3hr 30min).

Patara to: Antalya (8 daily; 5hr 15min); Fethiye (8 daily; 1hr 15min); Kalkan (10 daily; 30min); Kaş (10 daily; 1hr). NB: Many of these services depart from the main road, not the village centre.

International hydrofoils

Fethiye to: Rhodes (daily May to early Oct; 1hr 30min). Ticket price approximately €65 return.

Flights

Dalaman to: İstanbul (June–Sept 3–4 daily, April, May & Oct 2 daily, Nov–March 1 daily; 1hr 15min).

6

The Mediterranean coast and the Hatay

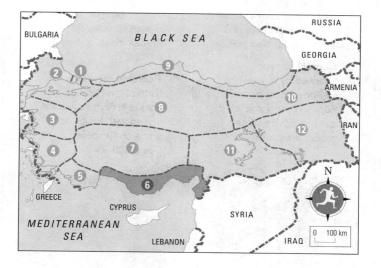

CHAPTER 6 # Highlights

* **Kaleiçi** Antalya's old quarter, clustered around a charming harbour, is great for nightlife and shopping. See p.531

* **Termessos** Arguably the most dramatically situated of all Turkey's ancient sites, perched on the edge of a precipitous gorge. See p.538

* **Aspendos** Stunningly preserved Roman theatre, the impressive venue for an annual opera and ballet festival. See p.543

* **Köprülü canyon** Spanned by a graceful Roman bridge, the Köprülü river gorge is ideal for novice whitewater rafters. See p.545

* **Side** Watch the sun set behind the elegant columns of the Athena temple on Side's seafront. See p.546

* **Göksu delta** The atmospheric flatlands of the delta are a haven for the Dalmatian pelican and loggerhead turtle. See p.564

* **Antakya's Archeological Museum** Don't miss the immaculately preserved collection of Roman mosaics. See p.583

* **Regional cuisine** For a taste of the Hatay try the unique fiery muhammara, served with flat bread and a chilled beer. See p.585

△ Section of mosaic from Antakya museum

6

The Mediterranean coast and the Hatay

T he **Mediterranean coast** of Turkey, where the Toros (Taurus) mountain range sweeps down to meet the sea, broadly divides into three parts. The stretch from Antalya to Alanya is the most accessible, with the looming presence of the Toros range separated from the sea by a fairly broad coastal strip. Once beautiful, intensive agriculture, particularly cotton growing, and package tourism have taken an enormous toll on the environment here. East of Alanya, the mountains meet the sea head-on, making for some of Turkey's most rugged stretches of coastline, where hairpin bends and mountain roads can make travel an agonizingly slow process. As a result, this is the least developed and unspoiled section of Mediterranean coastline. Further east the mountains finally recede, giving way to the flat, monotonous landscape of the Ceyhan river delta, made even more dreary by relentless urban and industrial sprawl. South and east of here, turning the corner towards Syria, the landscape becomes more interesting, as the Amanus mountain range dominates the fertile coastal plain, with citrus crops and olives the mainstay of the economy.

The bustling, modern city of **Antalya** is the region's prime arrival and junction point. East of here, in the ancient region of Pamphylia, the ruins of four cities – **Perge**, **Sillyon**, **Aspendos** and **Side** – testify to the sophisticated civilization that flourished during the Hellenistic period. Perge and Aspendos, in particular, are both well-established day-trip destinations from Antalya, while the modern town of Side has become a package-tour resort, albeit a highly enjoyable one.

Seventy kilometres east along the coast, the former pirate refuge of **Alanya** – now a bustling tourist centre – is set on and around a spectacular headland topped by a Selçuk citadel. Continuing east, the best places to break your journey are **Anamur**, where a ruined Hellenistic city abuts some of this coast's best beaches, and **Kızkalesi**, whose huge Byzantine castle sits 200m from the shore of a sandy bay. Kızkalesi also makes a good base from which to explore the ancient city of **Uzuncaburç**, a lonely ruin high in the Toros mountains.

Beyond Kızkalesi is the fertile alluvial delta known as the **Çukurova**, where the Ceyhan river spills down from the mountains and meanders sluggishly into the eastern Mediterranean. This end of the coast – characterized by concentrations of industry and low-lying cotton plantations – has very little to recommend it. **Mersin** has regular ferry connections to northern Cyprus; **Tarsus**, the birthplace of St Paul, has few surviving reminders of its long history; while **Adana**, one of the country's largest urban centres, is a hectic staging-post for journeys further east.

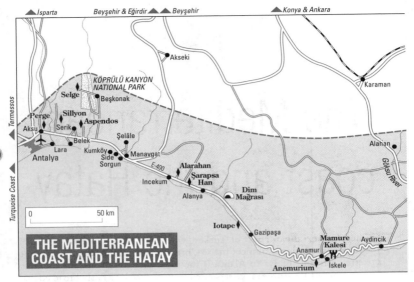

Akseki

KÖPRÜLÜ KANYON
NATIONAL PARK

Karaman

Selge   Beşkonak

Perge   Sillyon

Aksu   Serik   Aspendos

Belek   Şelâle

Lara   Kumköy   Manavgat   Alahan

Antalya   Side   Sorgun   E-400   Alarahan

Şarapsa
Han

Incekum   Dim
Mağrası

Alanya

Iotape   Gazipaşa

Mamure
Kalesi   Aydıncık

Anamur

Anemurium   İskele

Termessos

Turquoise Coast

Göksu River

Alahan

0   50 km

**THE MEDITERRANEAN
COAST AND THE HATAY**

From Adana, routes head north to the central Anatolian plateau (see Chapter 7) or east to the Euphrates and Tigris basins (Chapter 11), though this chapter turns its attention south, towards the area formed by the curve of the coast down towards Syria. This is the **Hatay**, a fertile, hilly region where different cultures have met – and often clashed – in their efforts to dominate the important Silk Route trade. **Antakya** is the Hatay's main centre and the best starting point for exploring the region, though cosmopolitan **İskenderun** makes for a surprisingly agreeable base. From Antakya there are frequent dolmuş connections to **Harbiye**, site of the Roman resort of Daphne, and to the town of **Samandağ**, from where you can visit Armenian **Vakıflı** and what's left of the ancient Roman port of **Seleucia ad Piera**.

Antalya to Alanya

The western part of the Turkish Mediterranean coast – between Antalya and Alanya – is topographically a potential delight, with the lush Pamphylian plain fronted by sandy beaches and backed by the towering Toros range. Unfortunately this entire coastal belt has been virtually subsumed by development. A four-lane highway now runs right behind many of the beaches, all-inclusive hotels and holiday-village complexes in various stages of completion mar both the beach and its hinterland. Market towns that once served the local farming communities have burgeoned into messy sprawls of concrete providing for the tourism industry. It is

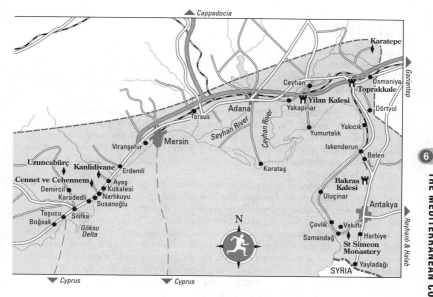

hard to imagine that this region was once ancient **Pamphylia**, a loose federation of Hellenistic cities established by incomers from northern Anatolia. According to ancient Greek sources, Pamphylia was settled by a "mixed multitude" of peoples following the fall of Troy around 1205 BC. It played a relatively minor role in the history of Anatolia, never even attaining local military significance, and the Pamphylian cities were fought over for centuries by stronger neighbours, amongst them the Lydians and Persians. To an extent, the Pamphylians profited from this, playing off one would-be invader against the next, while continuing to run their own affairs, regardless of who exercised ultimate control. In later years, Mark Antony was sent to take charge of the region, treating it as his personal domain until defeated by Octavius Caesar at the battle of Actium in 31 BC, after which Pamphylia was formally absorbed into the Roman Empire under the Pax Romana.

With its massive international airport, the booming city of **Antalya** is the gateway to the region. Now a fully fledged resort, it is worth visiting for its restored old town and marvellous archeological museum. The nearest (and most fascinating) ruined city is **Termessos**, perched on the saddle of Mount Solymos overlooking the Antalya gulf. The four surviving ruined cities of Pamphylia also rival the beaches as tourist magnets, with **Perge** and **Aspendos** the best preserved and most evocative sites. In between these two, the less intact, earthquake-wracked remains of **Sillyon** are harder to reach. Further along the coast, **Side** is one of the region's major resorts, though the striking ruins of its ancient city are fast being overshadowed by the rapidly growing tourist facilities. It remains, however, the ideal place if you're after beach action and holiday nightlife.

Alanya, the next sizable centre, has also seen an explosion of hotel building and tourism-related commerce over the last few years, but has retained an attractive old quarter. Away from the coast, the **Köprülü Kanyon** national park and the ruins of ancient **Selge**, easily accessible from Antalya and Side, make a delightful day's excursion.

Antalya

Turkey's fastest growing city, **ANTALYA** is blessed with an ideal climate (except during the searing heat of July and August) and a stunning setting atop a limestone plateau, with the formidable Beydağları looming to the west. In the heart of town, the pretty yacht harbour huddles below the Roman walls, while behind the new buildings the crescent of Konyaaltı bay curves to the industrial harbour 10km west of town. Despite the sometimes grim appearance of its concrete sprawl, Antalya is an agreeable enough city to live in, but the main area of interest for outsiders is confined to the relatively tiny and central old quarter within the Roman walls, known as the Kaleiçi (or "within the castle"). Three or four days in town – including half-day excursions to the nearby ruins of Termessos, Perge and Aspendos – should be sufficient.

Antalya was founded as late as the second century BC by Attalus II of Pergamon, and named **Attaleia** in his honour. The Romans did not consolidate their hold on the city and its hinterland until the imperial period, at the conclusion of successful campaigns against local pirates. Christianity and the Byzantines got a similarly slow start, though because of its strategic location and good anchorage Antalya was an important halt for the Crusaders. The Selçuks supplanted the Byzantines for good early in the thirteenth century, and to them are owed most of the medieval monuments visible today (albeit some built on Byzantine foundations). Ottoman Antalya figured little in world events until 1918, when the Italians made it the focus of their short-lived Turkish colony.

Arrival, orientation and information

Both **buses** and intertown **dolmuşes** use the *otogar*, about 7km north of town on the Ankara road; bus companies have their own service buses, which will deliver you to the town centre, and there is also a blue-and-white municipal bus marked "Terminal" linking the *otogar* with the centre. Whichever you use, alight either near the Atatürk statue for pensions on the west of the old city, or at the *Belediye* (Town Hall) corner for pensions on the east side.

Buses for Kemer and the westbound coast road for Kaş and Kalkan arrive at and depart from opposite the *Falez Hotel* on 100 Yıl Bulvarı, 2km west of the centre. Inbound buses arrive just around the corner near the Devlet Hastane (State Hospital), and from the intermediate roundabout frequent dolmuşes take you to the town centre – look out for those marked "Kale Kapası" and "Işıklar".

West of the *Falez Hotel* is the main harbour and dock where **ferries** arrive from Venice – it's 10km from the centre of town and there is no dolmuş service, so you'll have to take a taxi to the centre. Antalya's lushly landscaped **airport** stands at the centre of a maze of motorways some 12km east of the city. Taxis into town cost about 20YTL per car during the day and 30YTL between midnight and 6am, or take the Havaş airport bus, which drops off outside the post office on Güllük Caddesi, 600m west of Kaleiçi. If you arrive from abroad, you will land up at one of the two international terminals, from where a taxi is the only option.

Orientation and information

The main entrance – the **Kalekapısı** (literally, "the gate of the city") – to the **Kaleiçi** (old quarter) is marked by the Saat Kulesi (clocktower). The clocktower itself lies opposite a pool and fountain at the southern end of the **Şarampol** (Kazım Özalp Caddesi), now a pedestrian shopping area. A tramway circles the old quarter and runs along the sea front; **tram services** are every half-hour (0.80YTL) and departure times are posted at the tram stops. South from Kalekapısı, the

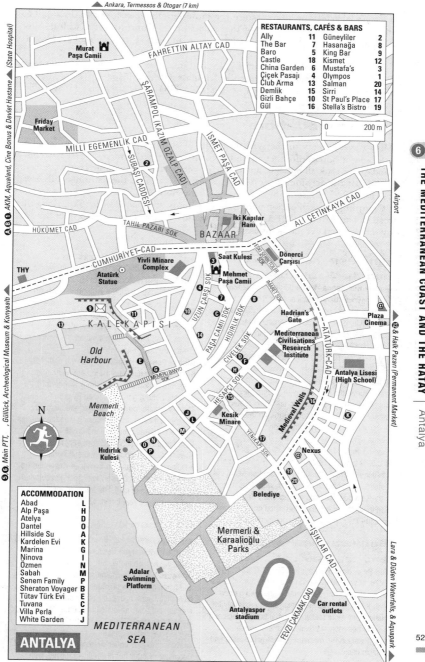

Kaleiçi's labyrinthine alleys lead to the most desirable pensions and downhill to the harbour. To the west along the waterfront is **Cumhuriyet Caddesi**, later Akdeniz Bulvarı, which gives access to the landscaped park behind **Konyaaltı** beach.

The **tourist office** is (temporarily) located in a wooden booth on Cumhuriyet Caddesi, opposite the southern end of Güllük Caddesi (Mon–Fri 8am–noon & 1–5.30pm, Sat & Sun 9am–5pm; ⊕0242/243 4384). Free city maps are available, but little else.

Accommodation

Most travellers stay in the walled quarter of **Kaleiçi**, in old houses restored as *pansiyon*s or hotels, often set around attractive courtyard gardens. There is accommodation to suit all budgets, and prices are often heavily discounted out of season. Note that the accommodation here, particularly around the harbour-walls area, can be subject to late-night noise from nearby clubs.

Camping is not an option within the city limits. *Camping Bambus*, 3km along the road to Lara (⊕0242/321 5263), is oriented towards caravanners, but does have its own beach and decent facilities.

Between the old harbour and the Saat Kulesi

Marina Residence Mermerli Sok 15 ⊕0242/247 5490, ⊛www.marinaresidence.net. The last word in luxury, murals and marble. It's a tasteful place with excellent views over the harbour, a raised glass-walled pool alongside the garden bar, and appetizing food. ❻

Tütav Türk Evi Otel Mermerli Sok 2 ⊕0242/248 6591, ⊛www.turkevievi-otelleri.com. A good-value option, set in the old walls above the harbour, with superb views from the attached restaurant. It's tastefully restored, though some find its mock-Ottoman interior decor a little stuffy. The lovely pool is a real bonus. ❺

Tuvana Hotel Karanlık Sok 18 ⊕0242/247 6015, ⊛www.tuvanahotel.com. Top-notch hotel fashioned from a beautifully restored series of old houses. The characterful rooms, with intricately carved wooden ceilings and carefully draped windows, are individually furnished and come with satellite TV, minibar and air conditioning. ❼

Between Hadrian's Gate and the Kesik Minare

Alp Paşa Hotel Hesapçı Sok 30–32 ⊕0242/247 5676, ⊛www.alppasa.com. Lush conversion of an Ottoman mansion, set around a cramped garden with a tiny pool. The cheapest rooms are nicely furnished; pay more and you'll get antique fittings and marble bathrooms. Excellent buffet meals attract non-guests in the evenings. A well-established and reliable choice. ❻

Atelya Pansiyon Civelek Sok 21 ⊕0242/241 6416, ⊛www.atelyahotel. com. Excellent restoration of two connected Ottoman houses set around a delightful courtyard – complete with a stir-crazy tortoise and a bar. The hotel boasts three annexes, the most recently restored of which has individually furnished rooms, each named after a sultan – rooms here are a little more expensive. ❹

Ninova Pension Hamit Efendi Sok 9 ⊕0242/248 6114, ⊛www.ninovapension.com. Very quiet, elegantly restored house, with a wonderful verandah and a garden shaded by citrus trees. The hospitable Armenian owner has tastefully refurbished each room, exposing wooden ceilings and bare boards. Recommended. ❹

Villa Perla Hesapçı Sok 26 ⊕0242/248 9793, ⊛www.villaperla.com. Very authentic Ottoman building, with antique furnishings in eleven individually styled rooms, plus an atmospheric courtyard garden with small pool. The attached restaurant has a very good reputation. ❺

Between the Kesik Minare and the Hıdırlık Kulesi

Abad Otel Pansiyon Hesapçı Sok 52 ⊕0242/247 4466, ⊛www.abadotel.com. This well-converted old house has a family atmosphere, friendly staff, and fish tanks in the breakfast room. Simple rooms have tiled floors, both ceiling fans and air conditioning, and basic en-suite bathrooms. ❸

Dantel Pansiyon Zeytin Geçidi 4 ⊕0242/247 3486, ⊜dantelhotel@hotmail.com. Immaculate conversion buried under overgrown bougainvillea. Rooms are simply but tastefully furnished, with nostalgic pictures of old İstanbul on the walls, have TV and air conditioning, and the bathrooms are spotless. Tasty evening meals (including shrimp casserole) are good value and served on the rooftop terrace. ❹

🏃 **Özmen Pansiyon** Zeytin Çıkmazı 5 ⓣ0242/241 6505, ⓦwww.ozmenpension .com. Extremely well run by the energetic Aziz and his German wife, it boasts airy, spotless, air-conditioned rooms and a lovely breakfast terrace with views over the bay. Aziz will collect you from the airport for €15 or the *otogar* for €8. ❷

🏃 **Sabah Pansiyon** Hesapçı Sok 60 ⓣ0242/247 5345, ⓦwww .sabahpansiyon.8m.com. Run by three friendly brothers, this backpacker-oriented joint offers an informal information service (in English), good-value car rental, tours, fine food, cheap beer, email access and satellite TV. All rooms now boast air conditioning, most have TV and a CD player, and the white walls and curtains set off the kilim-strewn tiled floors. Great value. ❷

Senem Family Pansiyon Zeytin Geçidi Sok 9, near Hıdırlık Kulesi ⓣ0242/247 1752. Run by a lively and charming Turkish couple, this modern pension has a family atmosphere, clean rooms with whitewashed walls and flowery curtains, and simple en-suite facilities. The rooftop breakfast bar affords wonderful views of the sea and mountains. ❷

White Garden Pansiyon Hesapçı Geçidi 9 ⓣ242/241 9115, ⓔwhitegardenantalya@yahoo .com. IYHF-affiliated and geared towards backpackers – the modern en-suite rooms are fairly small, with white walls and tiled floors, but the staff are very helpful and there's a quiet garden. ❷

East of Atatürk Bulvarı

Kardelen Evi Haşım İşcan Mah, 1297 Sok 14 ⓣ242 2431148, ⓔnicholas66@e-kolay.net. Two self-contained apartments in a restored house in the quiet backstreets off Atatürk Cad. Both accommodate up to four people in traditionally furnished and decorated rooms. Weekly rental from €100 per apartment.

West of the city centre

Hillside Sü Konyaltı 07050 ⓣ0242/249 0700, ⓦwww.hillside.com.tr. A minimalist triumph or the sterile apogee of modernism? Whatever your opinion, there is no doubt that this hotel – all white save for the massive, glittering mirrored disco-balls that dominate the atrium – is a bold exercise in interior design. The setting, at the western end of the Kültür Parkı, is superb, as is the Olympic-length pool. Room rates vary from €212 to €280, prices which appear to prove that less does in fact equal more. ❽

Sheraton Voyager 100 Yıl Bul ⓣ0242/243 2432, ⓦwww.airliner.de/ittantalya.html. Lush gardens surround an ocean-liner-style curve of concrete, the foyer glitters with polished brass, glass and crystal, and the huge rooms are marvellously opulent. Two restaurants, two pools, sauna, Jacuzzi and every other facility you'd expect for the price (which is a minimum of €150, rising to €180 for rooms with a sea view). ❽

The City

The best place to start exploring the old town, Kaleiçi, is from the old harbour, where the once-crumbling quays have been rebuilt, gardens laid out and the harbour walls and a mosque restored. Most attractions are within walking distance of each other, but jump on the tram or a dolmuş to visit the excellent archeological museum.

Kaleiçi

Inevitably, the authentic atmosphere of the **old harbour** has been sacrificed to the redevelopment – the harbour is now mainly home to day-trip boats, some charter *gület*s and a very few fishing boats, but on balance, the venture seems to have been a success, and the area is popular with tourists and locals alike.

From the harbour, head uphill along Uzun Çarşı Sok, past souvenir and carpet shops and the eighteenth-century **Mehmet Paşa Camii**. Along the way, you might want to stop off at the tiny garden of the local arts society, known as **ANSAD**, for a cool drink or to check notice boards advertising concerts, slide shows and even Sunday treks. At the northern end of Uzun Çarşı Sok is **Kalekapısı** (Castle Gate), where the **Saat Kulesi**, a Selçuk tower with inset Roman column drums, is built into a section of the old walls. Kalekapısı is overlooked by the **Yivli Minare** or "Fluted Minaret", erected during the thirteenth-century reign of the Selçuk sultan,

△ Yivli Minare, Kaleiçi

Alâeddin Keykubad, and today something of a symbol of the city. The adjacent mosque is still in use, with the area in front doubling as an informal bazaar and open-air café, with good views over the bay. Facing the café is an early, plain **Selçuk han** whose crumbling walls have been "restored", a rather grand term for encasing the ruins in glass. Above this area, but accessed from Cumhuriyet Caddesi, is an old baths, now the Fine Arts Gallery, which sometimes hosts interesting exhibitions; the original foundation was built on top of a church. Next door is a **türbe** (tomb) from 1377.

From Kalekapısı, bear right and right again onto Atatürk Caddesi, and you'll soon draw even with the triple-arched **Hadrian's Gate** (Üç Kapılar), recalling a visit by that emperor in 130 AD. Hesapçı Sokak, the quietest entry to Kaleiçi, also begins at Hadrian's Gate and if you follow it through the old town, you'll pass its restored Ottoman houses, many of which have been turned into pensions, trinket shops or restaurants and bars. Right off Hesapçı Sokak, on Kocatepe Sokak, is the well-signposted **Mediterranean Civilisations Research Institute** (Mon–Sat 9am–5.30pm; 1.5YTL), set in two restored Ottoman houses built around courtyard gardens. Behind one house is the restored garden church of St George, which is used for exhibitions often made up of items from the private collection of the Koç family, Turkey's richest, who sponsor the institute. The second house contains a marvellous library of books on archeology and antiquities; treasures include original editions of the engravings made by the archeologist-cum-explorer Texier when he investigated Asia Minor for the French government in the 1840s. There are also excellent reference materials and yearbooks on local archeological activities and projects sponsored by the institute. Experts will want to spend some time here nosing through the rarities, but even amateurs will find the English-speaking archeological staff helpful in finding books about local sites.

About halfway along Hesapçı Sokak stands a tower and attendant buildings known collectively as the **Kesik Minare** (Broken Minaret), an architectural anomaly that's done successive duty as temple, church and mosque: compare the reused Roman capitals with later Byzantine ones.

Beyond the Kesik Minare, you emerge above the sea and turn left to reach the adjoining **Mermerli** and **Karaalioğlu** parks, which contain a number of tea gardens as well as the **Hıdırlık Kulesi** in the northwestern corner. This round Roman tower is the best place in town to watch the frequently spectacular sunsets over the snow-capped mountains across the gulf of Antalya. Return to the harbour past the *Mermerli* restaurant, which has a private staircase down to the only city-centre beach, **Mermerli**, where you can swim for 8YTL. The **Adalar** swimming area (5YTL), reached via steep steps from Karaalioğlu park, with decking on the rocks and ladders into the sea, is a better alternative. The staff are friendly, drinks and snacks reasonably priced, and the views across the bay magnificent.

Antalya's two permanent markets are the **Pazar**, at the southeast corner of Şarampol, selling mainly gold, clothes and shoes, and the **Halk Pazarı** (People's Market), a permanent market a ten-minute walk east of Hadrian's Gate, slated for massive redevelopment, and already selling more fake designer clothes and tourist-oriented souvenirs than it does fruit and vegetables. The **Altın Pazarı** (Gold Bazaar) in the İki Kapılı Hanı, behind the Pazar, has been restored and is now open for business, selling local cotton fabrics and furnishings as well as gold.

The Archeological Museum

The one thing you shouldn't miss while in Antalya is the city's **Archeological Museum** (Arkeoloji Müzesi; Tues–Sun 8.30am–5.30pm; 15YTL), situated on the western edge of town at the far end of Kenan Evren Bulvarı. It's one of the top five archeological collections in the country, and it's well worth spending half a day there. To reach it from the city centre, take any dolmuş labelled "Müze" or "Liman" – departing from one of the "D" signs along Cumhuriyet Caddesi – or take the westbound tramway to its last stop, Müze.

At the museum entrance, a small children's section, primarily used for school groups, provides the opportunity for play with old tools and pots, and past this, the well-lit galleries are arranged both chronologically and thematically. Standing out among the early items are a cache of **Bronze Age** urn burials from near

Elmalı, and finds from an unusually southerly **Phrygian tumulus**, with the trademark Phrygian griffin-head much in evidence. Ancient metalworking skills are also showcased in some fine silver plate, three superb belts and several silver and ivory Phrygian figurines sporting droll yet dignified expressions. All date from the eighth and seventh centuries BC and are among the museum's worthiest treasures.

It's quite a jump in time to the next galleries, which contain many second-century AD **statues from Perge**: a complete pantheon in unusually good condition has been assembled. Opening off from here is a room filled with smaller pieces, including perfume flasks, bronze statuary and lamps, and an underwater case showing miscellaneous finds from wrecks, as well as yet more Perge statuary honouring the various demigods and priestesses of the Roman imperial cult. Best exhibits of the adjoining sarcophagus-wing are two almost undamaged coffers depicting the **life of Hercules**. In the building's corner hall, mosaics, including one depicting Thetis dunking Achilles in the Styx, are in fair to good condition but crudely executed; a **gaming board** nearby, recovered from Perge, is more unusual. The corner hall leads into a gallery dedicated to **theatre friezes** and statues from Perge. The all-over marble tiling doesn't show them off to their best advantage, but the display, which includes statues of gods and emperors and a frieze showing battles between heroes and sea monsters, is marvellous.

A narrow room adjoining the mosaic hall is devoted to **icons** recovered after 1922 from various churches in the Antalya area. They're mostly of recent date, and popular in style, but unusually interesting for their rarely depicted themes and personalities. At the centre of the collection is a reliquary containing what are purported to be the bones of **St Nicholas of Myra** (see p.505). Near this is a case containing early Byzantine church silver, including a gilt thurible from the monastery of Sion in the hills behind Myra, found in 1963 by villagers at Kumluca after presumably being hidden or lost during a pirate raid. However, the majority of the unique hoard discovered by the villagers was taken abroad in somewhat clandestine circumstances, and is now on show at Dumbarton Oaks Research Library in Washington, DC.

The collection is rounded out by an **ethnography** section, a hotchpotch of İznik ceramics, kitsch glass lamps, smoking and writing implements, household goods, weapons, dress and embroidery, weights and locks, musical instruments and a fine Arabic map of the Middle East. A diorama of nomad life is followed by a collection of socks and carpets.

Besides the collections, there's a bookshop, a **café** and a pleasant shady garden scattered with some fine overspill sculptures and tombs. Crossing the road from the museum reveals wide views of Konyaaltı bay and a precarious path that leads down to Konyaaltı beach (see below).

Boat trips, beaches and waterfalls

Boats by the harbour in Kaleiçi offer a variety of half- and full-day local tours, all of which take in the best views of the Düden waterfalls (see below), plus a combination of local beaches, swimming, cruising the gulf and a barbecue lunch. Some also offer evening entertainment in the shape of moonlit buffets and belly dancing. Prices vary according to the number of people, season and itinerary, but you can expect a half-day trip to cost from around €10 per person, more for evening cruises with entertainment.

Antalya's lengthy western beach, **Konyaaltı**, now spruced up, is finally beginning to live up to its dramatic situation between Antalya's cliffs and the Beydağları mountains. It's shingle, rather than sand, but it's clean and well maintained. Entry

6

to the beach is free, and loungers and umbrellas are available for a modest fee. Those with children should be aware that the beach shelves quite steeply and there is a slight tow from west to east. A pleasant **promenade** lined with palm trees and cafés backs the beach. Konyaaltı is easiest reached by the west-bound tram – get off at the terminus (just past the archeological museum) and follow the road down the steep hill (five minutes' walk).

Lara beach, 10km southeast of town and reached by dolmuşes running along Atatürk Caddesi, has fine sand but is enclosed by a forbidding fence and accessible only for a small fee. The lower **Düden waterfalls** reach the ocean at Lara, though to see them to full advantage you'll need to take a boat tour from the old harbour. The upper cascades, some 9km northeast of town, are served by dolmuş but are barely worth visiting.

The secluded **Kurşunlu waterfalls** (daily 9am–8pm; 1YTL), 18km northeast from Antalya off the Isparta road, can be reached by dolmuş or *Belediye* bus from a bus stop on the northern edge of the Halk Pazar. The inviting green pool into which the high falls cascade is forbidden to swimmers. An unmarked, but easy-to-follow, walking trail from here follows the riverside in a two-hour circular loop, passing the fishing retreat of one of Turkey's ex-presidents.

Eating

Antalya is full of cafés and restaurants and good places can be found all over town, but especially in **Kaleiçi** and along **Atatürk Bulvarı** and **İşıklar Caddesi**. We've picked out some of the best choices, across all budgets, below. For the local speciality – *tandir kebap*, clay-roasted mutton – visit **Eski Serbetçiler Içi Sokak**, a narrow street running down the west side of the Dönerci Çarşısı (see "Atatürk Bulvarı and İşıklar Caddesi", below), crammed with restaurants, many with pavement tables.

Local street markets are open nearly every day in some part of the city and have a staggering array of fresh local produce at knockdown prices. The biggest is the **Friday market** off Milli Egemenlik Caddesi, while on Sundays, head northwest of the main PTT and ask for the *Pazar Pazar* – **Sunday market**.

Kaleiçi

Castle Restaurant To the right of the Hıdırlık Kulesi, on the cliff top. A café-bar with the best views in Antalya and cooling up-draughts for the very popular clutch of tables set right on the cliff edge. It serves *mezes*, kebabs and cold beer and is much favoured by Antalya's young lovers. A meal with beer will set you back around 12YTL. Recommended.

Gül Kocatepe Sok. Foreign-owned restaurant-bar next to the taxi stand, serving fresh *mezes* and casseroles, plus beer and a range of wine. Expect to pay around 15YTL for a meal with drinks. The cool, stone-walled interior is atmospheric, and the service excellent.

Hasanağa East of Paşa Camii Sok, near Hadrian's Gate. With tables set out under a canopy of citrus trees in a charming courtyard garden, and very popular with the locals, this is a good choice for an intimate evening meal. Black Sea dishes form an excellent addition to the Mediterranean cuisine on offer – try the spicy red-cabbage soup followed by fresh *hamsi* (sardines). A decent meal with a beer

or the house wine shouldn't cost more than 20YTL. Traditional live-music sessions at weekends.

Mustafa's Under the Saat Kulesi, at the entrance to Kaleiçi. Only in business here between midnight and 5am, this mobile stall sells tasty *köfte* and *kokoreç* (rolled lambs'-intestines, grilled, heavily spiced and far tastier than you might expect). Help yourself to the array of tomatoes, onions, parsley, lettuce and rocket. With an *ayran* or two it makes for a perfect stop after a night on the town.

Sirri Restaurant Uzun Çarşısı Sok. Atmospheric courtyard restaurant specializing in fish dishes and *guveç*, an appetizing meat and vegetable casserole served piping hot in a clay bowl. It's not cheap – a full meal will cost around 30YTL (more for fish, sold per kilo and varying widely in price according to species and season) with drinks, but the quality and service are excellent.

St Paul's Place Just off Yenikapi Sok. Attached to the American-run evangelical church, a fine café serving delicious coffees (2.5YTL), cookies and cakes. You can also check out the extensive library (not all of it religious). Closed Sun.

Atatürk Bulvarı and İşıklar Caddesi

Dönerci Çarşısı Corner of Atatürk Cad and Cumhuriyet Cad. A "*döner*-sellers' market" – fast-food joints under one roof, devoted to kebabs, *köfte* and *kokoreç*. Some sell *midye* (mussels) in season. A meal here should cost less than 5YTL.

Güneyliler West of Şarampol, just north of the *Kışlıhan Hotel*. This bustling, spotlessly clean restaurant serves excellent *lahmacun* and kebabs (preceded by a complimentary helping of salad, flat bread and spicy *çiğ köfte*) and is always packed with locals. A substantial meal can be had for around 8YTL.

Salman İşıklar Cad. Air-conditioned coffee bar–patisserie at the Atatürk Bul end of the street, with a good range of *poğça* (plain and filled savoury breads), *baklava*, continental-style cakes and tarts – plus a salad bar.

Stella's Bistro İşıklar Cad. Close to the *Salman*, and one of the few places in Antalya with a non-Turkish menu: pasta and steak for lunch and dinner, and afternoon tea with cream cakes. Prices are high, around 30YTL for a meal including drinks, but service is immaculate.

West of the centre

Baro Cliff-top park south of Cumhuriyet Cad. A short walk from Kaleiçi, but worth the effort for the quality of the food, the lower prices and the superb views. A popular restaurant offering a huge range of buffet *meze*s, a good *Osmanli Tabagi* (casserole) main course (6YTL) and live folk music on Friday and Saturday evenings.

China Garden Just off Cumhuriyet Cad, on the way to the archeological museum. Antalya's best Chinese restaurant. A set meal will cost around 12YTL, a beer 4YTL, and the views from the cliff-edge terrace are breathtaking.

East of the centre

Kismet Halk Pazarı. Ten minutes' walk from Hadrian's Gate, with a cheerful pine-clad interior enlivened by kitsch, fish-oriented pictures, and tables spilling out onto the market alley. Fish starters (6–8YTL) include pickled anchovy, mussel salad and fried squid with cheese. Grilled main fish-dishes are around 10YTL per portion, the recommended *hamsi tava* (fried sardines) only 6YTL.

Drinking and nightlife

Much of Antalya's **nightlife** is concentrated around the harbour area, with its myriad bars, clubs and discos. Bars are often open all day and keep going until 4 or 5am, discos from around 8pm to 4am. There are also plenty of places to listen to live **Turkish music** in Antalya, particularly *halk*, *türkü* and *özgün*. At these venues you sit at a table and a waiter will take your order for drinks and *çerez* (a mix of salted nuts, sunflower seeds and roasted chickpeas). Keep an eye out for fly posters advertising the concerts of the bigger stars of the Turkish music scene, who often play the **Açık Hava Tiyatro** (open-air theatre) situated at the eastern end of Konyaaltı beach. Tickets can be bought from an open-air stall at the northeast end of Atatürk Bulvarı, priced from 13YTL and upwards depending on the popularity of the act.

Bars and clubs

Ally Kaleiçi. A complex of bars and a disco on the Roman walls, with an impressive laser show cutting the night sky across the water; but it is prohibitively expensive (16YTL) by local standards, and very unpopular with guests in nearby pensions.

The Bar, aka **Rock Bar** Uzun Çarşışı Sok. Favoured by students from the local university and Antalya's grunge contingent. Surprisingly passable live rock acts play in a crowded, smoky, upstairs room most weekends. Take a breather and get in some conversation in the downstairs bar, set in a pleasant courtyard garden.

Club Arma Kaleiçi Yat Limanı. Affluent restaurant cum dance club on the west side of the harbour. A spacious, colonnaded dining area in an old, stone-built warehouse serves expensive fish dishes. The dance area is on a terrace perched right at the sea's edge. Come here to watch Antalya's rich set enjoy an evening out.

Demlik Zafer Sok 16. A decent alternative to the Gizli Bahçe, especially if you're not bothered about listening to rock. Tables set under orange trees in a quiet walled garden, and beers for 3.5YTL.

Gizli Bahçe Kaleiçi, off Paşa Sok. Well-hidden student-oriented bar (ask for the Karatay Medresesi to locate it), beers at 3.5YTL (served with a free helping of salted popcorn), a limited fast-food type menu, rock music and shady garden.

King Bar Kaleiçi. Just behind the waterfront – a good bet for those whose tastes fall between low rock dives and large dance venues, with varied music, a small dance-floor and beers for around 5YTL.

Olympos *Falez Hotel*, 100 Yıl Bul. The huge club in the hotel basement has a superb laser show and trilingual DJs playing mostly Eurodisco to a smart Turkish clientele.

Turkish music

Çiçek Pasajı Uzun Çarşısı Sok. Recently revamped, with tiered seating areas surrounding a central well where the musicians play. It is the best place in town to catch live Turkish music, situated a couple of hundred metres down from the clock-tower. There's a small terrace with views over Kaleiçi and the bay.

Entertainment and festivals

The Hasan Subaşı Kültür Parkı – also known as AKM or **Atatürk Kültür Merkezi** – is a complex of two theatres and a pyramid-shaped glass exhibition centre set in a cliff-top park, 3km west of the centre. It's about 300m down 100 Yıl Bulvarı past the *Sheraton* and *Falez* hotels; dolmuşes from the town centre marked "Adliye" or "AKM" pass the gates. With its tea gardens and children's playgrounds, the park is a favourite spot for joggers, roller-bladers and Sunday strollers, while the theatre complex stages the occasional classical concert and shows American films. Below the park, backing Konyaltı Plajı, is the **Beach Park**, a landscaped complex of restaurants, cafés, bars and clubs and a seasonal open-air cinema.

Antalya also has two waterparks with numerous slides, chutes and wave pools. **Aqualand** (May–Oct 9am–dusk; 17YTL, 13YTL children), on the southwestern edge of the Kültür Parkı, is reached by the same dolmuşes. At the attached **Dolphinland** it's possible to swim with a dolphin for €60. The original **Aquapark** (daily 9am–dusk; 17YTL), behind the *Dedeman* hotel, east of the centre, is reached by Lara-bound dolmuşes.

The most convenient **cinema** is the Plaza, under the Antalya 2000 building, between Hadrian's Gate and the Halk Pazarı, which has three air-conditioned screens. The Prestige on the Lara road has five screens. For the ultimate experience the eight-screen Cine Bonus in the Migros centre out beyond the Kültür Parkı has double and reclining seats. Antalya plays host to a major international **film festival**, the Altın Portakal or Golden Orange (usually the week spanning the end of September and the beginning of October). The AKM, Cine Bonus and Beach Park (this last is open-air) cinemas show the films entered for the various categories and the Kültür Parkı hosts receptions and parades of the stars. A fine selection of world cinema is showcased, as well as the best of Turkish movies. All films are subtitled in English as well as Turkish. Antalya is also crowded during the **Aspendos Opera and Ballet Festival** (see box on p.545 for details).

Listings

Airlines THY, Konyaaltı Cad 24, Antmarın İş Merkezi ☎0242/243 4383, reservations ☎444 0849; Onur Air, Çağlayan Mah, 2055 Sok 20, Barınaklar ☎0242/324 1335; Atlas Jet, İşıklar Cad 53/A ☎0242/444 0387.

Airport General information ☎0242/330 3030, flight enquiries ☎0242 330 3600.

Banks and exchange There are banks with ATMs and *döviz* offices throughout the city, and some *döviz* offices on Şarampol even open on Sundays (though most operate Mon–Sat 9am–7pm). You can also exchange currency at the PTT (see below).

Books The Owl Bookshop, Akar Çeşme Sok 21, off Hesapçı Sok in the old town, has an excellent selection of mainly English-language secondhand books. Ardiç, in the Seleker shopping mall on Gül-lük Cad, is the best place to buy English-language guides and novels.

Buses You can reach almost all provincial capitals in Turkey direct from Antalya *otogar*. Major companies such as Kamil Koç, Akdeniz and Metro, have ticket offices in town, especially on Subaşı Cad, and their own shuttles servicing the *otogar*. Minor companies such as Göreme Tur (for Cappadocia) are "minded" by the majors; see the destinations and company logos on the bus office windows. Important local companies are Antalya Tur (Fethiye and Kaş/Kalkan ☎0242/331 1086) and Gürman (Eğirdir/Isparta ☎0242/331 1050). Some pensions in the old town sell or book bus tickets.

Car rental There are numerous car-rental agencies in Kaleiçi, and many more on Fevzi Çakmak Caddesi, near Antalyaspor's stadium. In July and August, book your car well in advance; at other times, bargain hard. Try the *Sabah Pansiyon* (see "Accommodation"), Mithra Travel (see "Tours", below), or Hertz out at the airport on ☎0242/330 3848.

Consulate UK, Gençlik Mahallesi, 1314 Sok, Elif apt 6/8 (☎0242/244 5313), to the right of and behind the *Talya Hotel*, off Fevzi Çakmak Caddesi.

Ferries The Turkish Maritime Lines office, for tickets for the fortnightly ferry to Venice, is at Konyaaltı Cad 40/19 (☎0242/241 1120).

Hamams In Kaleiçi, try Nazır on Hamam Aralığı Sok, behind the Mehmet Paşa mosque – built in 1611 and still going (daily: men 6–10am, women 10am–5pm, mixed 5pm–midnight; 10YTL bath only, 32YTL for a two-hour soak and massage.

Hospital State Hospital (Devlet Hastane) and outpatients' clinic, Soğuksu Cad ☎0242/241 2010; University Teaching Hospital (Tip Fakultesi), Dumlupınar Bul ☎0242/227 4480.

Internet Try Baryum Bilgisayar in the Antalya 2000 building on Recep Peker Caddesi, above the Plaza cinema.

Laundry Both Sempatik and Mutlu Çamışırhane are on Sakarya Sok, facing the Kesik Minare.

Left luggage There's a 24-hour office marked "Emanet" at the *otogar*; items priced by size and value.

Police Tourist Police, Emniyet Müdürlüğü, Yat Limanı, Kaleiçi ☎0242/243 1061.

Post office The main PTT is at Güllük Cad 9 (daily 9am–5pm for exchange and letter service; 24hr for phones). A kiosk near the clocktower in the old city caters to tourist needs.

Shopping Although traditional take-home items are rugs and leather, you'll find that jeans, gold, and designer-label clothes and shoes are a better bet these days. Check out the boutiques along Atatürk and Işıklar *caddesis* and in the new Migros centre for the real thing; try Cumhuriyet Cad (past Güllük Cad) or the Halk Pazarı for fakes.

Tours Whitewater rafting on the Köprülü river is a full-day excursion from Antalya. The most reliable company is Medraft (☻www.medraft.com, ☎0242/312 5770). A day's rafting, including transfers and meal, costs €40. There are dozens of competitors, some considerably cheaper, but usually the guides are not so experienced, the equipment less well maintained and the meal not so substantial. Many Antalya travel agents will book rafting trips for you – try Akay on Cumhuriyet Cad, Maki on Uzun Carşi Sok, as well as many Kaleiçi *pansiyons* – for around €40 per person. Mithra Travel, Hesapçı Sok (☎0242/248 7747, ☻www.mithratravel.com), in the old city, organizes one- or two-day treks (from about €20 per person per day) in the limestone massifs overlooking Antalya, and can also arrange self-guided walks where its staff book the accommodation and provide you with maps and instructions; prices vary according to group size. It also offers car rental.

Yachting Some yachts are open to charter for groups of four to twelve. Ask around at the harbour during the slow spring season and you could get a bargain cruise for the same price as hotel bed and board.

Termessos

Situated over a thousand metres above sea level 30km northwest of Antalya, the ancient site of **Termessos** is one of Turkey's prime attractions. Indeed, its dramatic setting and well-preserved ruins, tumbling from the summit of the mountain and enclosed within the boundaries of a national park – the Güllük Dağ Milli Parkı – merit a considerable journey.

Despite its close proximity to Lycia, Termessos was actually a Pisidian city, inhabited by the same warlike tribe of people who settled in the Anatolian Lakeland, around Isparta and Eğirdir, during the first millennium BC. The inhabitants of Termessos originally named themselves after the nearby mountain of Solymus – today's Güllük Dağ; their language, of which no surviving inscriptions remain, was a dialect of Pisidian, which Strabo called Solymian. The first mention of the

Solymians comes in the ancient myth of Bellerophon and Pegasus, when Bellerophon, after defeating the monster of the Chimaera, was sent to fight them. The first appearance of the Solymians in history proper was in 333 BC, when Alexander the Great made an attack on the city and was repelled. Fourteen years later, Termessos played an interesting part in the history of the region when Antigonus – one of Alexander's successors – was challenged by Alcatus for command of the region. The Pisidians supported Alcatus, and he took refuge in Termessos. The elders of the city, however, saw the possible dangers involved in defying Antigonus and laid a trap for Alcatus, preparing to take him captive. Alcatus committed suicide; his body was delivered to Antigonus, but after three days it was rescued and reburied in Termessos.

Unlike that of its Lycian neighbours, much of the history of Termessos is characterized more by attack than defence, and in the third and second centuries BC the Termessians first took on the Lycian Federation, then their neighbours in nearby Isinda. The city's position, commanding the road from the Mediterranean to the Aegean, gave Termessians the opportunity to extract customs dues from traders; a wall across the valley is believed to be the site of their customs post. Later, in 70 BC, Termessos signed a treaty of friendship with Rome, under which they were exempted from the jurisdiction of the governor – an independence that they proudly expressed by never including the face or name of a Roman emperor on their coinage. The city must have been abandoned quite early, probably after earthquake damage in 243 AD, and has only been surveyed, never excavated.

The site

A thorough exploration of rugged Termessos (daily 7.30am–7.30pm; 4YTL entry to the forest park, another 4YTL to the site itself) can be quite strenuous. Sturdy footwear and a supply of water are advisable, and you should time summer visits to avoid the midday sun. After checking the site map at the car park you'll need to climb a good twenty minutes before you reach the first remains of any interest, although on the way you'll pass a number of well-labelled, though mainly inaccessible, ruins, including the aqueduct and cistern high on the cliff-face to the left of the path.

The second-century AD **King's Road** was the main road up to the city, close to which the massive lower and upper **city walls** testify to a substantial defence system. The central part of the city is beyond the second wall, to the left of the path. Its surviving buildings, formed of square-cut grey stone, are in an excellent state of repair, their walls standing high and retaining their original mouldings. In part, this is due to the inaccessibility of the site; it's difficult to imagine even the most desperate forager coming up here to pillage stone.

The first building you reach is the well-preserved **gymnasium**, with a baths complex alongside. This, however, is far overshadowed by the nearby **theatre**, one of the most magnificently situated in Turkey, with the mountain climbing behind and a steep gorge dropping to its right. Greek in style, it had seating space for 4200 spectators, and wild animals were released into the orchestra from a basement under the later, Roman-built, stage. Some of the seats are missing, but otherwise it's in a good state of preservation.

To the west of the theatre is the open grassy space of the **agora**, at the far end of which is a **mausoleum**, approached up a broad flight of steps, with a six-metre square platform – at the back of which a grave pit is sunk into the rock. Its unusual position on the marketplace suggests that the tomb belonged to an extremely eminent citizen, and it has even been suggested that this could be the tomb of Alcatus, the pretender to the governorship of Pisidia – though the tomb on the hill above (see below) is generally accepted as more likely. On the far side of the agora from the theatre stands a smaller theatre or **odeion**, which, according to inscriptions, was used for horse and foot races, races in armour, and – by far the most frequently held – wrestling. The walls of the building stand to almost ten metres. Surrounding the odeion are four **temples**, only one of which – that of Zeus Solymus, god of war and guardian of the city of Termessos – is in a decent state of repair, with walls standing to over five metres and a bench at the back for statues. Two of the other three temples on the southeast side of the odeion – the two with portals still standing – were dedicated to the goddess Artemis.

Following the trail up the hill from here brings you to a fork, the left-hand path of which continues on to the **necropolis**, where you'll see an incredible number of sarcophagi dating from the first to the third centuries AD. Most are simple structures on a base, though there are some more elaborate ones, with inscriptions that describe the penalties for their violation. If you climb as far as the fire lookout tower, you're rewarded with incredible views over the adjoining valley, rumoured to be the stopping place of Alexander the Great when he planned his assault on Termessos.

Returning downhill, take the left-hand fork for several hundred metres to the so-called **Tomb of Alcatus** – widely accepted as the mausoleum of the general. The tomb itself is cave-like and undistinguished, but the carvings on its facade are remarkable, particularly one depicting a mounted soldier, with a suit of armour, a helmet, a shield and a sword – the armour of a foot soldier – depicted lower down to the right of the figure. The tomb and reliefs are consistent with the date of Alcatus's death, and the figure in the carving wears armour identical to that of Alexander the Great in a mosaic of the battle of Issus in the Naples archeological museum.

Practicalities

Antalya, 30km southeast, is the most obvious base for visiting Termessos. To get there **by car**, take the Burdur road out of Antalya, turning left after 11km towards Korkuteli. The left turning to Termessos is marked off the Korkuteli road after about 14km, from where a track leads 9km up through the forested national park to the site. Using **public transport**, you need to take a bus (hourly) headed for Korkuteli as far as the beginning of the forest track, from where you can take one of the taxis (around 16YTL including waiting time and return to main road) that tout for business here.

The Pamphylian cities

The twelfth century BC saw a large wave of Greek migration from northern Anatolia to the Mediterranean coast. Many of the incomers moved into the area immediately to the east of Antalya, which came to be called **Pamphylia**, meaning "the land of the tribes", reflecting the mixed origins of the new arrivals. Pamphylia was a remote area, cut off from the main Anatolian trade routes by mountains on all sides; nevertheless four great cities grew up here – Perge, Sillyon, Aspendos and Side.

The first recorded mention of the region dates from the sixth century BC, when Croesus, the last king of Lydia, absorbed Pamphylia into his realm. When Croesus was defeated by the Persians in 546 BC, the Persians assumed control of the area. This alarmed the Greeks, who attempted to gain control of Pamphylia, resulting in a series of wars, with the Pamphylians fighting on the side of the Persians. With the exception of Sillyon, Pamphylia eventually fell to Alexander the Great. After his death the region became effectively independent, though nominally claimed by the various successor kingdoms that inherited Alexander's realm. During the first century BC the Romans, annoyed by the activities of the Cilician pirates operating from further along the Mediterranean, took control of the coast. Their rule ushered in three centuries of stability and prosperity, during which the Pamphylian cities flourished as never before.

If you want to visit the main Pamphylian sites in a single day a **taxi** is the best option, and should cost around €60 for the day (check out the rank at the southern end of Atatürk Bulvarı in Antalya, which lists prices for various destinations on a wooden board). The bus tours (€25–40) organized by various agents in Antalya's Kaleiçi district seldom include Selge (see p.546), but do include tedious stops at out-of-town gold and carpet shops.

Perge

About 15km east of Antalya, the ruins of **Perge** can be reached by taking one of the frequent dolmuşes or *Belediye* buses (every 20min or so) to the village of Aksu on the main eastbound road; these are best boarded at the roundabout at the north end of Dr Burhanetin Onat Caddesi, a five-minute walk east of the Halk Pazarı. From the village it's a fifteen-minute walk to the site itself, though you may be able to flag down a dolmuş from the village if you don't want to walk.

At the top of the hill is the **site entrance** (daily 9am–noon & 1.30–5pm; 10YTL) and car park, marked by a cluster of souvenir stalls and soft-drinks stands. It's an enticing spot, the ruins expansive and impressive, and you could easily spend a long afternoon looking around. Substantially more of the city survived until 1922, when, according to some accounts, the theatre was more or less intact. However, a 1920s construction boom in the nearby village of Murtunas led to the readily available supplies of stone at Perge being pillaged by local builders.

Some history

Perge was founded around 1000 BC and ranked as one of the great Pamphylian trading cities, despite the fact that it's nearly 20km inland – a deliberate defensive siting so as to avoid the unwanted attentions of the pirate bands that terrorized this stretch of the Mediterranean. Later, when Alexander the Great arrived in 333 BC, the citizens of Perge sent out guides to lead his army into the city. Alexander was followed by the Seleucids, under whom Perge's most celebrated ancient inhabitant, the mathematician Apollonius, lived and worked. A pupil of Archimedes, Apollonius wrote a series of eight books describing a family of curves known as conic sections, comprising the circle, ellipse, parabola and hyperbola

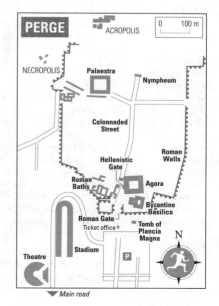

– theories that were developed by Ptolemy and later by the German astronomer Kepler. Most of the city's surviving buildings date from the period of Roman rule, which began in 188 BC. After the collapse of the Roman Empire, Perge remained inhabited until Selçuk times, before being gradually abandoned.

The theatre and stadium

Just beyond the site entrance, the **theatre** has been closed for repairs for some time. It was originally constructed by the Greeks, but substantially altered by the Romans in the second century AD. Built into the side of a hill, it could accommodate 14,000 people on 42 seating levels rising up from the arena and was the venue not only for theatrical entertainment, but also for gladiatorial displays. To the northeast of the theatre is Perge's massive horseshoe-shaped **stadium**, the largest in Asia Minor at 234m by 34m, with a seating capacity of 12,000. Because the stadium was built on level ground it was necessary to provide massive supporting pillars and arches. The spaces between these arches were divided into about thirty huge rooms (housing shops and businesses), many of which are still intact, giving a good impression of the scale of the whole stadium complex.

The walled city

In places, stretches of the Seleucid walls have survived, giving some indication of the extent and ground plan of the original city. Just in front of the outer gates is the **Tomb of Plancia Magna**, a benefactress of the city, whose name appears later on a number of inscriptions. Passing through the first **city gate**, you'll see a ruined **Byzantine basilica** on the right, beyond which lies the fourth-century AD **agora**, centred on a ruined temple. To the southwest of the agora are the excavated **Roman baths**, where a couple of the pools have been exposed. Across the cracked surface of the inlaid marble floor, the original layout of frigidarium, tepidarium and caldarium can – with the help of a few signs – still be discerned. Also visible in places are the brick piles that once supported the hypocaust floor of the baths, enabling warm air to circulate underneath.

At the northwest corner of the agora is Perge's **Hellenistic Gate**, with its two mighty circular towers, the only building to have survived from the Hellenistic period. Behind, the horseshoe-shaped court and ornamental archway were both erected at the behest of Plancia Magna, the former once adorned with statues – the bases of a number of which were found during excavations carried out during the mid-1950s. Beyond is the start of a 300-metre-long **colonnaded street**, with a water channel running down the middle and the shells of shops to either side. Walking along it, you'll be able to pick out the ruts made by carts and chariots in the stone slabs of the roadway. Also visible are a number of reliefs near the tops of the columns, just beneath the capitals, one of which depicts Apollo, while another shows a man in a toga, offering a libation at an altar. At the end of the street is the **nymphaeum**, an ornamental water outlet from where a stream splashes down into the water channel below. Above here is the **acropolis** – probably the site of the original defensive settlement, of which little has survived. To the west of a crossroads just before the nymphaeum is a **palaestra**, dating from 50 AD, according to an inscription found on its south wall. West of here, archeologists have found a **necropolis** leading from one of the city gates, sarcophagi from which can now be seen in the Antalya archeological museum.

Sillyon

About 7km east of Perge are the ruins of the ancient city of **Sillyon**, also dating from about 1000 BC, although much less intact than those at Perge. Situated on top of a table-like hill, its strategic position enabled it to repulse an attack by Alexander the Great, who never succeeded in capturing it. These days, it doesn't seem to attract as many visitors as some of the other Pamphylian sites, partly because it's impossible to reach by public transport, and perhaps because of the landslide in 1969 which swept about half of it away.

To get there by car **from Perge**, head back to Aksu village and follow the coastal road, taking a signposted left turn about 7km east of the village. From here a road leads 8km inland to the small modern settlement of **Asar Köyü**, from where an unsignposted dirt track leads to the site itself. It's possible that some of the villagers may offer to guide you around, which can be quite useful as they will alert you to the presence of hazardous unfenced cisterns.

The site

The site is unfenced and entry free. You can climb up to the acropolis by way of a ramp leading from the **lower gate** up the western side of the hill. To the left of the gate are the foundations of a **gymnasium**, used as a bishop's palace in Byzantine times and now home only to sheep. At the top of the ramp you'll find a large and well-preserved city gate and, scattered around the rest of the hilltop, a number of buildings of indeterminate age and function. The largest is a late **Hellenistic structure** with several arched windows in its upper storeys that later served the Selçuks as a fortress. Just to the south is a long hall-like building, possibly a former gymnasium, in which you can see the slots and holes used to hold wooden shutters in place in the window frames. East of here lies a building with a 37-line **inscription** carved into its stone doorjamb – the only surviving written example (apart from a few coins) of Pamphylian, the Greek dialect spoken in this area until the first century AD.

The most interesting part of the acropolis is the area around the ruined **theatre**, which offers graphic visual evidence of nature's erosion of the man-made past. Following the 1999 earthquake, only the top few seats remain, the rest of the structure now lying scattered across the plain below – the huge blocks you can see were once part of the seating terraces. Further east are the foundations of a number of **houses** and part of a **temple**.

Aspendos

Returning to the main road, head east for **Aspendos**, whose theatre is probably the best preserved in Asia Minor – it's still used to stage the annual Aspendos Opera and Ballet Festival. In summer, there are regular **dolmuşes** from Antalya to the village of Serik (every 2hr), a ten-minute drive from the site, and for a couple of euros the driver will usually take you on to Aspendos, a total of 45km southwest of Antalya. If you're here out of season you will have to rely on the buses plying the main coastal highway, which will drop you at the signposted turning just before the humpbacked Selçuk bridge, a few kilometres east of Serik. From here you should be able to get a ride to the site, although it's only a three-kilometre walk. Just before Aspendos, the village of **Belkis** has several eating places. About half a kilometre northeast of the village lie the car park and Aspendos **site entrance** (daily 8am–7pm; 10YTL).

Some history

Aspendos first came to prominence in 469 BC when the Persian wars culminated in a huge and bloody naval battle at the mouth of the nearby Eurymedon river. The Greeks won and went on to defeat the Persians again in a land battle, when, heavily outnumbered, they outwitted their opponents by coming ashore disguised as Persians, using the element of surprise to stage a successful attack.

This wasn't the end of Persian influence in Pamphylia. The locals, particularly the people of Aspendos, weren't any keener on the Greeks, and in 389 BC, they murdered an Athenian general sent to collect tribute, after which control of the area passed to Sparta. The Spartans proved to be ineffective rulers and by 386 BC the Persians were back, staying until the arrival of Alexander the Great in 333 BC. On hearing of Alexander's approach, the rulers of Aspendos agreed to surrender but asked Alexander not to garrison soldiers in the city. Alexander accepted their terms on condition that they paid him a tribute of money and horses, and went off to lay siege to Sillyon. After his departure he was angered to learn that the citizens of Aspendos were busy fortifying the city and he returned demanding a larger tribute and hostages. His demands were met, and Aspendos had to accept a Macedonian governor into the bargain.

After Alexander's death in 323 BC, Aspendos became part of the Seleucid kingdom and was later absorbed into the realm of the kings of Pergamon. In 133 BC, the city became part of the Roman province of Asia. Roman rule consisted mainly of a succession of consuls and governors demanding protection money and carting off the city's treasures. Only with the establishment of the Roman Empire did the city prosper, growing into an important trade centre, its wealth based on salt from a nearby lake.

Aspendos remained important throughout the Byzantine era, although it suffered badly from the Arab raids of the seventh century. During the thirteenth century the Selçuks arrived, followed a couple of hundred years later by the Ottomans, who ruled here until the eighteenth century, when the settlement was abandoned.

The theatre

The Aspendos **theatre** was built in the second century AD by the architect Zeno. He used a Roman design, with an elaborate stage behind which the scenery could be lowered, instead of allowing the natural landscape behind the stage to act as a backdrop, as had been the custom in Hellenistic times.

The stage, auditorium and arcade above are all intact, as is the several-storey-high stage building, and what you see today is pretty much what the spectators saw during the theatre's heyday, a state of preservation due in part to Atatürk, who, after a visit, declared that it should be preserved and used for performances rather than as a museum. A dubious legend relates that the theatre was built after the king of Aspendos announced that he would give the hand of his beautiful daughter to a man who built some great work for the benefit of the city. Two men rose to the challenge, one building the theatre, the other an aqueduct, both finishing work simultaneously, with the result that the king offered to cut his daughter in two, giving a half to each man. The builder of the theatre declared that he would rather renounce his claim than see the princess dismembered and he was, of course, immediately rewarded with the hand of the girl for his unselfishness. Later, the theatre was used as a Selçuk *kervansaray*, and restoration work from that period – plasterwork decorated with red zigzags – is visible over the stage. There's also a small **museum** to the left of the entrance, exhibiting pictures of theatre "entrance tickets" and coins.

The acropolis and aqueduct

To the right of the theatre door, a path leads up to the **acropolis**, built, like the one at Sillyon, on a flat-topped hill. The site is a little overgrown, but a number of substantial buildings are still in place, foremost among them being the **nymphaeum** and **basilica**, both 16m in height, as well as sections of the main street and a drainage system in good condition.

To the north of the acropolis, on the plain below, stretches a Roman **aqueduct**. Originally 15km long, it brought water to Aspendos from the mountains above and incorporates an ingenious siphonic system that allowed the water to cross the plain at low level; you can still (with care) climb the towers. The aqueduct and towers can also be reached by taking a left turn down a dirt track just outside Belkis, skirting around the western side of the hill.

Köprülü Kanyon national park and Selge

Inland of Aspendos, the **Köprülü Kanyon national park** (Köprülü Kanyon Milli Parkı) and its Roman bridges, with the sparse ruins of **Selge** high in the mountains above, make a good full-day outing with a leisurely lunch stop. There is little public transport to Selge (the ruins of which are scattered amongst the modern village of Zerk, also referred to as Altınkaya) or to the national park – one elusive afternoon dolmuş (ostensibly at 3 or 4pm) passes by each day between Serik, on the coastal highway, to Selge/Zerk, returning next morning at 7am. However, many companies operate half-day **rafting trips** down the Köprülü river, allowing time for a stop en route for a swim and lunch. Be warned that in peak season up to 45,000 rafters a day are bussed into this area, making both the road and river very crowded places – serious rafters should look elsewhere. Contact a tour operator in Antalya or Side for bookings.

The national park

The turn-off for both the national park ("Milli Parkı") and Selge (see below) is signposted 48km east of Antalya on Highway 400; past Sağgırınköyü is a left turn over the river, but you should pass this and continue straight on the asphalt road to **Beşkonak**, a straggly village. Five kilometres or so further on, you reach a series of trout restaurants which have sprung up to service hungry rafters. Just above these the road narrows; take the left fork, and inch across the first of two Roman spans, the **Oluk bridge**. You can park here and walk into the canyon via a footpath just after the bridge. From here, it's 13km up to Selge, reached by taking the right fork just after the bridge. Return on the west bank past the **Böğrüm bridge**, which has a huge, popular picnic and swimming area just downstream from it. Past here are a couple more trout restaurants and pensions and the river crossing back to the tarmac. In all honesty the bridges are nothing special, little different from hundreds of others in Turkey, and it's only the setting that makes Köprülü stand out.

Selge

The road up to **Selge** is now paved. As you climb to an eventual altitude of 900m, the panoramas become more sweeping, the thickly wooded countryside more savage, and the 2500-metre Kuyucak range ahead more forbidding. At the scattered hamlet of **ZERK** (also known as Altınkaya), food, tour guides and accommodation can be found at *Şerif's House* (℡0242/765 8091; ❷) near the ancient theatre, but you'll need your own sleeping bag to roll out on the raised wooden verandah of the family's house, or to camp in their field. Expect to pay around €13 for accommodation and three home-cooked meals. Şerif's son, Emrah, has limited English but is very friendly and knows the area intimately. You may also eventually be collared by the site attendant and sold a ticket for the ruins (4YTL).

The theatre that dominates **ancient Selge** is impressive despite the stage building having been pulverized by lightning some decades ago, and the highest tier of seats having sustained rain damage in 1989. Three of the five doors giving access backstage still remain.

Close by are the ancient agora and two hilltop temples. The **agora** will excite amateur archeologists with its part-visible paving, jumbled masonry and chunks of unexcavated inscriptions. The foundations of a **Byzantine church** sit up on a hill to the southeast and enjoy panoramic views down the valley and up to the snow-streaked peak of Bozburun, while the jumbled remains of a temple of Zeus and a large water cistern lie to the northwest along the ridge. From here you can catch views to the ruined temple of Artemis and old city wall to the northwest and to the stoa in the valley below. Returning to the main track via some village farmyards, you'll pass the **stadium**, of which only the western ranks of seats are left; the sporting area itself is now a wheat field. Little is known for certain of the origins of Selge; it only left the realm of mythological ancestry and anecdote to enter history – and the Roman Empire – in the first century AD. The city was famous for its storax gum, made from a local shrub, and was inhabited until early Byzantine times. The site has always been arid – only recently did modern Zerk get a permanent spring – and the ancient town must have been abandoned when the aqueduct supplying it with water collapsed. The overwhelming impression you'll have is of the determination necessary to keep a city of 20,000 thriving in such a godforsaken wilderness.

Side

About 25km east of Aspendos, **SIDE**, one-time trysting place of Antony and Cleopatra, was perhaps the foremost of the Pamphylian cities. The ruins of the ancient port survive, but over the last few years Side has changed almost beyond recognition. These days, the resort has one of the highest tourist densities of any town in Turkey, and local people are beginning to recognize that their home has been ruined by indiscriminate development. However, many improvements have been made recently, and work is currently underway restoring the colonnades of Roman shops that flank the main street leading to the city gate. Despite the effects of package tourism, which have pushed up the prices of accommodation and food, Side remains a very attractive resort, especially if you can avoid the peak months of July and August. The beaches are superb, the ruins evocative and the nightlife lively.

Two days on the St Paul Trail: Oluk bridge to Selge

This section of the St Paul Trail (see box, p.608) includes a dramatic ascent of one wall of the Köprülü canyon, swimming opportunities in the gushing Köprülü river, and takes in beautiful forest, ancient Selge and sections of Roman road. The first day should take around six hours and is steep in parts, the second entails a more demanding hike of eight hours-plus.

To reach the start of the hike, take the afternoon bus from Serik to Selge (3pm), alighting at the Oluk Roman bridge, a couple of kilometres north of the village of Beşkonak. It should be possible to camp on the west bank of the river some 400m downstream of the bridge, where a side stream flows under a second bridge, the Böğrüm, and joins the main river; alternatively, you'll find a couple of pensions and chalets 300m or so south of the bridge, though these are often full with rafting groups. Otherwise, if you arrive early enough, you could push on for another hour and a half to get to the next overnighting option, further along the route (see below), before dark.

The next morning, cross the Oluk bridge and head northeast, using a combination of marked footpath and the main north–south road through the canyon. After a kilometre or so the path turns west and drops to the river's edge, joining a clear path that heads north to a splendidly isolated stone house (1.5hr). Formerly known as *Tevfik's Place*, now the *Taufic Mountain Lodge* (☏0532/779 0416, ⊛ www.travelturkeylodge .com), it offers ten comfortable wooden bungalows, each of which sleeps two (❸), dormitory rooms in the old house (❷ including breakfast), and camping. There are plans to offer a booking service for village houses on the route, and to open an information centre for the national park.

Continue north along the river to a bridge known as the the Yer Köprüsü. Cross it (you can bathe in the shallows to the north) and walk southwest then west towards the seemingly impregnable canyon wall. A series of zigzags lead up to the rock wall, breached by a diagonal path that rises to the summit over a series of steps and ledges (2.5hr).

The path now runs west, through an area of strangely eroded rock pinnacles and terraces, finally emerging near the theatre in ancient Selge (2hr). You can camp in the terraced fields above the theatre, or stay at *Serif's* (see opposite).

The next day follow the marked trail to the left of the theatre, joining a village road for a short while before heading west down a footpath to join a wonderful section of paved Roman road. From here the trail heads up to the top of a hill and joins an unsurfaced road near Oluk village (1.5hr). Continue on a mix of path and unsurfaced road, through some beautiful oak forest, to the village of Delisarnıç. The trail continues, roughly due north, through a similar mix of terrain to the hamlet of **Kestanelik** (Chestnut village), a collection of vine-covered houses (4.5hr). From here it is a further two hours, much of it along a partly paved section of old droving road known as the Sarp Yolu, to **Çaltepe**, a sizable village set in a broad valley. Çaltepe is locally famous for **oregano**, the mainstay of the local economy, ubiquitous in the mountains hereabouts and celebrated with a festival each October. The friendly *Barca* pension (☏0242/771 1038; ❷) provides clean rooms, delicious home-cooked food and cold beer. Just below the village, on a bend in the Köprülü river, is a great pool for swimming.

Some history

Side (meaning "pomegranate" in an ancient Anatolian dialect) was founded in the seventh century BC, its colonists attracted by the defensive potential of the rocky cape. It grew into a rich port with an estimated 60,000 inhabitants during its peak in the second century AD. Initially a significant proportion of Side's wealth rested on the slave trade, with the city authorities allowing pirates to run an illegal slave market inside the city walls, in which thousands of human beings were bought and

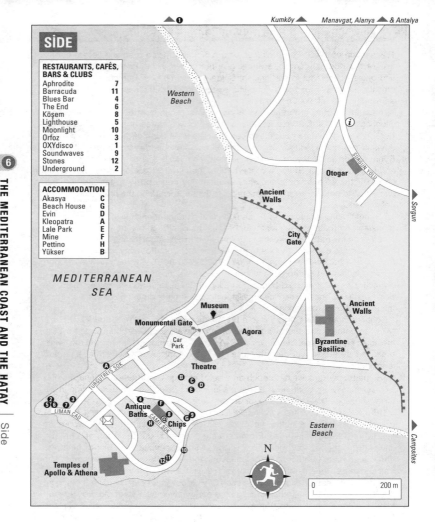

SIDE

RESTAURANTS, CAFÉS, BARS & CLUBS
Aphrodite	7
Barracuda	11
Blues Bar	4
The End	6
Köşem	8
Lighthouse	5
Moonlight	10
Orfoz	3
OXYdisco	1
Soundwaves	9
Stones	12
Underground	2

ACCOMMODATION
Akasya	C
Beach House	G
Evin	D
Kleopatra	A
Lale Park	E
Mine	F
Pettino	H
Yükser	B

Kumköy ▲   Manavgat, Alanya ▲ & Antalya

Western Beach

Otogar

Ancient Walls

City Gate

MEDITERRANEAN SEA

Museum

Monumental Gate

Car Park

Agora

Ancient Walls

Byzantine Basilica

Theatre

Antique Baths

Chips

Eastern Beach

Temples of Apollo & Athena

N

0   200 m

Sorgun

Campsites

sold every day. This trade was later outlawed, and after the collapse of the western Roman Empire, Side survived only until the Arab invasion during the seventh century AD. The Arabs put the place to the torch, driving out the last inhabitants, and Side was abandoned until the beginning of this century, when it was resettled by Muslim fishermen from Crete, who built a village known as Selimiye among the ruins. Despite later attempts by the Turkish government and various archeological agencies to evict them, these villagers stayed, and by the 1980s their descendants were starting to reap the rewards of Side's tourist boom.

Arrival, information and services

Intercity buses drop passengers at the *otogar* in Sorgun, from where there are dolmuşes every twenty minutes to Side's small bus station. From here it's a five-minute walk into town, though in season tractors drag wagons full of tourists to the entrance to town at the top of the main street.

Side is effectively **pedestrianized** and cars can only enter the town between 7am and 10am, 3pm to 6pm, and again after midnight (though if you have your own vehicle and are making your way to your hotel with luggage, the attendants will let you through). The **car park** is just outside the barrier and a modest daily fee is charged – don't make the mistake of parking anywhere along the approach road as towing is vigorously carried out.

Side's **tourist office** (Mon–Fri 8am–5pm, Sat 10am–2pm; ☎0242/753 1265) is on the main road into town, just before the *otogar*, though it won't overburden you with information. **Banks** and a **PTT** can be found on the square at the southern tip of the promontory. **Car rental** places are ubiquitous, with outfits on the road approaching the main town entrance: Europcar (☎0242/753 1764) is next to the car park; Avis is just off the approach road at Fatih Cad 25 (☎0242/753 1348). There are a couple of **Internet** cafés – *Side* and *Chips* – near the *Pettino Otel* on Cami Sokak. **Tours** from Side include outings to Aspendos, Manavgat and, most interesting, rafting on the Köprülü river.

Accommodation

Side's best and most atmospheric **accommodation** lies within the town's ancient city walls, where you are surrounded by ruins, restaurants and bars, and the beach is never more than a few minutes' walk away. Bear in mind, though, that while the western section within the walls affords sunset views, it's noisier and hotter than the east, which is cooled by onshore breezes. Even in the height of the season it is possible to find a room in the village, as some of the package operators are put off using the smaller hotels and pensions within the walls because of airport transfer difficulties.

Akasya Motel Lale Sok 3 ☎0242/753 1776, ⓦ www.akasyaotel.com. Good-value accommodation, with spotless en-suite rooms in a stone-built house tucked away in a pleasant garden. The Irish manageress is very welcoming and helpful. You'll pay extra for either a fan or air conditioning. ❷

Beach House Hotel Barbaros Cad ☎0242/753 1607, ⓦ www.beachhouse-hotel.com. Highly recommended seafront establishment. Most of the twenty comfortable rooms have pretty wooden balconies overlooking the beach, and the charming rear garden boasts the remains of a Byzantine villa, a dovecote and a trampoline. It is immaculately run by a Turkish/Australian couple, and the food is wonderful. Incidentally, this was Side's first hotel, and Simone de Beauvoir stayed here back in the 1960s. ❸

Evin Pansiyon Lale Cad ☎0242/753 074. This budget, family-run establishment has airy, whitewashed rooms, though it is now looking a little dated. Air conditioning costs an extra 10YTL per night. It's reached from the footpath running behind the theatre. ❷

Kleopatra Hotel Turgut Reis Cad ☎0242/753 1033, ⓕ753 3738. Situated on the western seafront, this large hotel, with a funky concrete facade, has comfortable air-conditioned rooms with digital TV and dated but clean furniture. ❸

Lale Park Lale Sok 5 ☎0242/ 753 1131, ⓦ www.hotellalepark.com. A traditional stone-built hotel, set back from the beach though some rooms have sea views. Muted pastel walls and white linen curtains give the rooms a soothing atmosphere. There's a shady garden, a small pool, darts and a pool table. Two apartments have recently been added, one sleeping four, the other five, for €60 and €70 respectively – good value for families. ❸

Mine Motel Gül Sok 8 ☎0242/753 2358. The cheapest option in town, with fourteen rooms painted a cheerful blue, new en-suite, and a pleasant courtyard shaded by orange, plum and pomegranate trees. The friendly Turkish owner only speaks a few words of English. ❷

Pettino Otel Cami Sok 9 ☎0242/753 3608,

@Pettino@superonline.com. Australian–Turkish venture aimed at the backpacker market, the *Pettino* has small but homely rooms with air conditioning, running around an L-shaped balcony above a courtyard. It gets booked up pretty quickly in high season. ②

Yükser Sümbül Sok ☎0242/753 2010, ⓦwww .yukser-pansiyon.com. Small but well-appointed rooms with fans in a very attractive stone building with wooden shutters. The well-tiled bathrooms are spotless. The garden is beautiful, the location very quiet and the owners quietly hospitable. ③

Ancient Side

Ancient Side has been almost overwhelmed by the modern town, but fortunately even the inroads of mass tourism have been unable to smother the grandeur of its buildings and monuments. The road into town actually passes through the **city gate**,

△ Athena temple at Side

although this is in such a bad state of repair you could be forgiven for not noticing it. The **city walls** have fared better; the section running east from the city gate is particularly well preserved, with a number of towers still in place.

The agora and museum

From the city gate, a colonnaded street runs down to the **agora**, the site of Side's second-century slave market, today fringed with the stumps of many of the agora's columns. The circular foundation visible at the centre of the agora is all that remains of a **Temple of Fortuna**, while in the northwest corner, next to the theatre, you can just about make out the outline of a semicircular building that once served as a public latrine, seating 24 people.

Opposite the agora is the site of the former Roman baths, now restored and home to a **museum** (daily 8am–noon & 1–5pm; 5YTL). It retains its original floor plan and contains a cross-section of locally unearthed objects – mainly Roman statuary, reliefs and sarcophagi. Many of the statues are headless, decapitated in an outbreak of religious zeal during the early days of Christianity.

The monumental gate and theatre

Just south of here, the still-intact **monumental gate** now serves as an entrance to the town's modern resort area. To the left of the gateway is an excavated monument to Vespasian, built in 74 AD, which takes the form of a fountain with a couple of water basins in front. Inside the gate is the entrance to Side's stunning 20,000-seat **theatre** (10YTL), the largest in Pamphylia, and different from those at Perge and Aspendos in that it is a freestanding structure supported by massive arched vaults, and not built into a hillside. The two-metre wall surrounding the orchestra was built to protect the audience from the wild animals used during gladiatorial shows.

Other ruins

From the monumental gate, modern Side's main street leads down to the old harbour and turns left toward the **temples of Apollo and Athena**. The Athena temple has been partly re-erected, and its white portico is becoming Side's trademark and a favourite place to take sunset photographs. Both temples were once partially enclosed in a huge Byzantine basilica, parts of which gradually disappeared under the shifting sand; the still-visible section now provides a home to birds and bats.

In the days when Side was an important port, the area to the west of the temples was a harbour. Even in Roman times it was necessary to dredge continuously to clear silt deposited by the Manavgat river, and it soon became clogged up after the city went into decline. Elsewhere, you'll find a number of other buildings, including the city agora, on the eastern side of the peninsula just a stone's throw from the sea, and, a little inland from here, a ruined **Byzantine church** that's gradually disappearing under the dunes. Off Camii Sokak, behind the Nilgin market, are the remains of **antique baths** where Cleopatra is supposed to have bathed, which include several separate rooms, baths, a garden and even a marble seat with a dolphin armrest.

The beaches

Given Side's fine sandy **beaches**, it's not surprising the resort has developed so rapidly. To the west, the ten-kilometre stretch of beach is lined with expensive hotels, beach clubs and watersports-rental outfits. **Sorgun** beach, 3km to the east, is well maintained by the local authority and is quieter and less tacky than Side's beaches. A dolmuş runs there every half-hour from Side.

Ten kilometres from Side, beyond the western beach, is **Kumköy**, with nearly as much in the way of beachside development as Sorgun, but again, its beaches aren't as crowded as Side's. Some of the buses and dolmuşes that run between Antalya and Side now go via Kumköy.

Eating

There are plenty of places to **eat** in Side, with what seems like hundreds of restaurants catering to all tastes. The main problem is trying to walk past one of them without being dragged inside by the smooth-talking hustlers employed for just this purpose. Also watch out for the ten-percent service charge virtually every establishment here levies.

Aphrodite İskele Caddesi. Set back from the harbour, a low wooden building with tables out front. The fish fillets are reasonable value, the speciality Chateaubriand a steep 45YTL for two.

Köşem Yasemin Sok. Almost certainly the cheapest take-out in town, aimed more at the local shopkeepers than at tourists. A tasty flat-bread *döner* costs 1.5YTL.

Moonlight Barbaros Cad 49. A romantic venue, with tables laid out on gravelled terraces overlooking the sea. The food is decent too, with a good range of *mezes* and fish dishes (lambfish kebab is 14YTL). Cheaper and more interesting is *filet papyan*, chicken breast stuffed with cheese and pistachios.

Orfoz Liman Cad 58. Down by the harbour, with tables on a large paved terrace and a small play-area for kids. Steaks are the speciality here, starting from 15YTL, and fish is priced per kilo. Good for watching the sun go down.

Soundwaves Restaurant Küçük Plaj Üstü Köyçi. A very popular place, decked out like a pirate ship with waiters to match, and fine nautical views over the eastern beach. It does a tasty mix of Turkish standards (including *testi kebap*, a casserole of meat and vegetables baked in a sealed clay pot) and European dishes such as garlic mushrooms and spinach pancakes. The wine is good value at 15YTL a bottle.

The End Liman Caddesi. Not bad value for a harbour restaurant, with a wide range of dishes from steak and fish to pizza. Expect to pay around 25YTL for a starter, main and a beer.

Drinking and nightlife

There are plenty of places to while away the evening hours in Side. Turn left at the harbour and you'll pass a line of chic seafront **bars**. From here, walk through the Apollo and Athena temples to the southeast corner of town, where music-led bars, such as the *Stones Bar* (which sometimes puts on "girls'" nights and karaoke) and *Barracuda*, offer **dancing** and fine views out onto the Mediterranean. The *Blues Bar* on Cami Sokak is also worth a look. To save money, you can cruise the staggered happy hours that run in different bars between 6pm and 9pm.

The *Lighthouse*, just west of the harbour, plays a variety of (mainly dance and techno) music, with Russian podium-dancers as a diversion and beers at around 5YTL. The smaller *Underground*, also on the western seafront, plays a wider range of music. Some 3km out of town on the west beach is the popular *OXYDisco* (11.50YTL fee), a huge, 3000-capacity laser-lit rave venue. It has its own pool, more podium dancers and 5YTL beers.

Every September, the town's Roman theatre hosts a two-week programme of classical music, ballet, opera and traditional Turkish music, with tickets at 15YTL per event; for details contact the tourist office (see p.549).

Manavgat and around

Fifteen minutes east of Side by dolmuş, the small town of **MANAVGAT** is not especially alluring, its chief attractions the river-boat tour up to the rather over-rated Şelale or Manavgat waterfalls nearby and the isolated ruins of Seleucia, 20km inland. The eight-kilometre round trip to the **waterfalls** will set you back around €8, boats leaving from a landing upstream of the town bridge. However, a longer trip offered in Side to the falls and Manavgat costs around €25, and is far more interesting.

To reach **Seleucia**, take the dolmuş from the northwest corner of the Manavgat *otogar* (see below) by the bridge to the Oymapınar Baraj. Alight at a left-hand turn signposted for Seleucia, from where it's a walk of 5km to the ruins. You will prob-ably be able to hitch the first 4km to the nearest village, from where it's an uphill walk along a tractor track through pretty farmland. Set on a slope in pine forest, Seleucia, a Macedonian foundation later incorporated into the Roman Empire, is very overgrown. The tractor path leads through a city gate to some baths and an agora, the most obvious surviving structures. In spring, a pretty little waterfall cascades past the baths to a stream in the valley below.

If you have a car, another worthy excursion from Manavgat is to head inland along the signposted Akseki road east of Manavgat, a route that runs through beautiful country between the **Ahmetler canyon** and the **Alara river**. Any left or right turn-off takes you through wooded gorges to villages of antiquated stone houses with cedar balconies and vine-wreathed terraces.

Just under 30km east of Manavgat, a road spears off north to **Alarahan**, with its quirky thirteenth-century Selçuk *kervansaray* built for the benefit of traders oper-ating between the Selçuk city of Konya and the port of Alanya. It was the creation of Sultan Alâeddin Keykubad (who was also responsible for the castle at Alanya). The building has lost some of its character as the interior now houses a number of tacky souvenir shops. Further up the same road, ranged around a pyramidal hill, there are the spectacular ruins of an ancient **castle**, scarcely discernible against the stony backdrop but accessible by way of steep stairs in a tunnel fifteen minutes' walk on from the *kervansaray*.

Dolmuşes and buses shuttle between Manavgat (the dolmuş stop is just west of the bridge in the town centre) and Side every fifteen minutes. It's worth bearing in mind that intercity buses now use the new *otogar* at Sorgun, midway between Man-avgat and Side, with service buses and dolmuşes linking it with Manavgat.

Alanya and around

ALANYA is one of the Mediterranean coast's major resorts, a booming and popu-lar place that in the last twenty years has expanded beyond all recognition along its sandy beaches. In addition to the massive influx of tourists, locals reckon that some thirty percent of the population is made up of expat Germans, whose villas litter the hillsides behind the town. Most visitors enter the town from the west, an approach that shows Alanya at its best, the road passing through verdant banana plantations on the outskirts and suddenly revealing a rocky promontory, topped by a castle, rearing out of the Mediterranean.

Little is known about Alanya's early **history**, although it's thought that the town was founded by Greek colonists who named it Kalonoros, or "beautiful moun-tain". Things were pretty quiet until the second century BC, when Cilician pirates began using the town, known by now as Coracesium, as a base to terrorize the

ALANYA

ACCOMMODATION

Bedesten	F
Best	C
Çınar	D
Hermes	B
Kaptan	G
Temiz	E
Üstün Aile	A

RESTAURANTS, CAFÉS & BARS

Bizim Ocakbaşı	2
The Doors	7
Evimiz	5
Gaziantep Başpınar	4
James Dean	6
Janus	8
Hancı Patisserie	3
Ottoman House	1

West Beach

Alanya Museum

MEDITERRANEAN SEA

Damlataş

Market

Beach of Cleopatra

Casper

Dolmuş Terminal

Old City Walls

East Beach

Fosforlu

Aksebe Türbesi

İç Kale

Süleymaniye Camii

Mint

ALANYA CASTLE

Kızılkule

Monastery

Aşıklar Mağarası

Harbour

Cilyarda Burnu

Tersane

Korsanlar Mağarası

Tophane

N

▲ Dim Mağrası, Dimçay & Anamur

| 0 | 200 m |

Pamphylian coast. Eventually, the Romans decided to put an end to the activities of the pirates and sent in Pompey, who destroyed the pirate fleet in a sea battle off Alanya in 67 BC. In 44 BC, Mark Antony gave the city to Cleopatra as a gift. Romantic as this might sound, there was a practical reason for his choice: the area around the city was an important timber-producing centre, and Cleopatra needed its resources to build up her navy. In 1221, the Byzantine city fell to the Selçuk sultan Alâeddin Keykubad, who gave it its present name and made it his summer residence. It's from this period that most buildings of historical importance date.

Arrival, orientation and information

Most of **old Alanya** is set on the great rocky promontory that juts out into the sea, dominating the **modern town** below it. Apart from the hotels and restaurants, and the Alanya Museum, there's little to see in the modern town.

It's about a twenty-minute walk to the town centre from Alanya's **otogar**, but there are plenty of *servis* minibuses to shuttle bus passengers in. Dolmuşes operating from the central terminal will take you to many of the local beaches. There are hydrofoils to Girne in Turkish Cyprus (see "Listings", p.558, for details).

The **tourist office** is opposite the Alanya Museum on İsmet Balcı Caddesi (April–Oct daily 9am–noon & 1–5.30pm; Nov–March Mon–Fri 9am–noon & 1–5.30pm; ☏0242/513 1240).

Accommodation

Despite the boom in package tourism, rooms are easy to find in Alanya, even in high season, and competition has kept the prices manageable. If you've come primarily for the beach scene, then you might want to choose from one of the hotels on Meteorologi Sokak, near the *otogar*, from where it's an easy walk to the west beach. Keykubat Caddesi, the extension of Atatürk Caddesi, leading off to Mersin and backing the eastern beach, is Alanya's out-of-town resort strip, lined with more upmarket hotels

Around Damlataş Caddesi

Pension Best Alaaddinoğlu Sok 23 ☏0242/513 0446, ✉bestapart@hotmail.com. On the fourth floor of an apartment block, just off Damlataş Cad, the rooms here are kept spotless. Four- and six-person apartments with bathroom, living room and kitchen are also available. Rooms ❷, apartments ❹

Çınar Otel Damlataş Cad ☏0242/512 0063. Near where the street becomes İskele Cad – a real oddity in this tourist mecca, a traditional Turkish town-centre hotel, basic but clean rooms (with fans) and passable bathrooms. The front rooms are a little noisy, the 1950s-style cube-effect tiles in the halls and rooms are fun. Great value and very central. No breakfast. ❷

İskele Caddesi

Hotel Kaptan İskele Cad 70 ☏0242/513 4900, ☏513 2000. Comfortable, central and reasonably classy, with its own pool and two restaurants, one overlooking the harbour. The rooms are blandly done out in white and pastel yellow, but have satellite TV and minibar. The front rooms overlooking the sea are more expensive. ❷

Hotel Temiz İskele Cad ☏0242/513 1016. Lives up to its name (*temiz* means clean) and has a very

impressive reception. Rooms at the back are quiet, the breakfast terrace has a lovely view and guests have use of the nearby sister hotel's pool. ❸

Meteorologi Sokak

Hotel Hermes Meteorologi Sok 2 ☏0242/513 2135, ❂www.hermesotel.com. Closest to the beach, with a small pool and forty appealingly white rooms with new en-suite bathrooms. It's well run, and the manager speaks good English, though the clientele is largely Scandinavian. ❹

Üstün Aile Pansiyon Meteorologi Sok 4 ☏0242/513 2262. Run by a charming retired bank manager – spacious rooms painted a dubious but cheerful mustard yellow, with balconies (some with sea views) and a communal kitchen. ❸

Kale district

Bedesten Kale ☏0242/512 1234, ❂www.bedestenhotel.com. The most interesting hotel in Alanya is a thirteenth-century former *kervansaray* near the Süleymaniye mosque, on the winding road up to the castle. Recently refurbished, most of the well-furnished rooms (once shops and accommodation for merchants) lie around a courtyard, with a couple of suites above, and there's a network of huge underground cisterns and a harem room to explore, as well as a pool. ❼

The Town

Guarding the harbour on the east side of the promontory stands the **Kızılkule** – the "Red Tower" – a 35-metre-high defensive tower of red stone built by Alâeddin Keykubad in 1226 and restored in 1951. Today it houses a pedestrian **ethnographic museum** (Etnografya Müzesi; Tues–Sun 8am–noon & 1.30–5pm; 2YTL), and has a roof terrace that overlooks the town's eastern harbour. Old

△ Alanya castle

wooden houses cling to the slopes above the tower, and you can follow the old coastal defensive wall along the water's edge to the **Tersane**, an Ottoman shipyard, consisting of five workshops linked by an arched roof. Beyond here is a small defensive tower, the **Tophane**.

Alanya castle

It's a long, winding climb up to **Alanya castle**, and takes about an hour – in summer set off early to avoid the heat or, better, late afternoon and catch the sunset from the top. There are lots of restaurants and little cafés to stop off at on the way up. Alternatively, there's an hourly bus (on the hour) from the junction of İskele and Damlataş *caddesi*.

The castle itself is a huge fortification system, with walls snaking right around the upper reaches of the promontory. A huge archway (bearing an inscription in Persian) leads into an area that demarcated the original limits of Alanya back in Selçuk times. In among the foliage off the road is an area known as **Ehmediye**, a small village with a few old Ottoman houses clustered around the dilapidated sixteenth-century **Süleymaniye Camii**, a *kervansaray* and the **Aksebe Türbesi**, a distinctive thirteenth-century tomb.

At the end of the road is the **İç Kale**, or Inner Fortress (daily 9am–8pm; 5YTL), built by Keykubad in 1226. Inside the gates, local women sell tablecloths and lace and the smell of lavender hangs in the air. The fortress is pretty much intact, with the shell of a **Byzantine church**, decorated with fading frescoes, in the centre. Look out for the **cisterns** that supplied the fortress with water and to which it owed much of its apparent impregnability. In the northwestern corner of the fortress, a platform gives fine views of the western beaches and the mountains, though it originally served as a point from which prisoners were thrown to their deaths on the rocks below. These days tour guides assure their wards that it's customary to throw a rock from the platform, attempting to hit the sea rather than the rock below – an impossible feat supposed to have been set for prisoners as a chance to save their necks.

Alanya Museum

On the western side of the promontory, the **Alanya Museum** (Alanya Müzesi; Tues–Sun 8am–noon & 1–5pm; 2YTL) is filled with local archeological and ethnological ephemera, including finds from (and photographs of) several small Pamphylian sites in the region. Most unusual is an inscription in sixth-century BC Phoenician, a sort of halfway house between cuneiform writing and the alphabet as the Greeks developed it. There's also a mock-up Ottoman living room complete with a beautiful carved ceiling, shutters and cupboards, and a model of a village wedding. The best thing about the museum, though, is the garden, a former Ottoman graveyard in which you can take refuge from the heat in summer; re-creations of grape presses and other farm implements share space with a gaggle of peacocks and chickens.

The beaches

Alanya's **beaches** are extensive, stretching from the town centre for a good 3km west and 8km east, and they are the reason most vistors come here. The resort offers a range of **watersports**, and the outlets along the west beach offer jet-ski rental (€25 for 15min), parasailing (€25 for 15min), water-skiing (€19 for 30min) and banana-boat rides (€6). If you fancy some scuba diving, head to Dolphin Dive, by the harbour, the biggest school in town. You can even go bungee-jumping (€60) in the east bay around from the harbour.

The caves and boat tours

Not far away from the museum, accessible from behind the *Damlataş Restaurant*, you'll find the **Damlataş**, or "Cave of Dripping Stones" (daily 10am–sunset; 2YTL), a stalactite- and stalagmite-filled underground cavern with a moist, warm atmosphere said to benefit asthma sufferers. There are other caves, dotted around the waterline at the base of the promontory, and various local entrepreneurs offer **boat trips** around them, charging about €10 per person for a five-hour trip, or €20 for a longer excursion that includes dolphin-watching. Boats leave from the harbour near Kızılkule, usually departing around 10am.

The first stop is usually the **Fosforlu** (Phosphorus Cave), where the water shimmers green; then it's on round the **Cilyarda Burnu**, a long spit of land that is home to a ruined monastery and former mint. It's not actually possible to go ashore, but on the other side of the skinny peninsula is the **Aşıklar Mağarası** (Lovers' Cave), in which, according to a bizarre local story, a German woman and her Turkish boyfriend were stranded for three months in 1965 while the police and army mounted searches for them. A little further round is the **Korsanlar Mağarası**, which, according to more believable stories, is where the pirates of yesteryear used to hide out. You will also be taken to **Cleopatra's Beach**, where the legends claim the queen used to descend to bathe while staying here with Mark Antony.

Eating

There are countless restaurants in Alanya, but most of them are overpriced (and invariably add on a ten-percent service charge), so be prepared for take-outs if you're on a tight budget. The more expensive establishments line the harbour area; cheaper options can be found in the backstreets between Atatürk Caddesi and Gazipaşa Caddesi, and along Damlataş Caddesi. The weekly **market**, with masses of fresh provisions, is held every Friday, next to the dolmuş station, north of İsım Tokuş Bulvarı.

Bizim Ocakbaşı Müftüler Cad, Kalgıdım Sok. Bustling first-floor place on a sidestreet behind the police station. Starters cost a reasonable 2YTL, kebabs a heftier 13YTL and up, beer 3YTL. Well-frequented by locals.

Evimiz Hükümet Cad, Şenli Işhanı 48/D, next to the Yeni Cami, just behind the waterfront. Good for home-style Turkish food, including *dolma* (stuffed

peppers) and *yaprak dolması* (stuffed vine leaves). Some tables are set out on the pavement. A full meal costs around 6YTL, but there's no alcohol served. Run by a friendly group of women, it's a good budget option.

Gaziantep Başpınar Kebap ve Lahmacun Salonu Hükümet Cad, Kapalı Otopark Üstü. The huge green-and-yellow fronted restaurant serves good stews with flat bread, *lahmacun* and kebabs; a filling meal will set you back 5–8YTL.

Janus İskele Cad. Rather flashy waterfront joint, with high prices (expect to pay 19–40YTL for a full meal), but it's been around since 1954 and has a good reputation for fish and steaks. It has an attached bar and disco.

Hancı Patisserie Hasan Akçalıoğlu Cad 12, fronting Atatürk Caddesi. A continental-style patisserie, with decent filter, espresso and cappuccino coffees

for 2.5YTL, and delicious cherry tarts for the same price. There are a few tables set out on the street.

Ottoman House Damlataş Cad 23. A characterful Ottoman-era building, with high wooden ceilings, bare boards, antique kilims and a vine-shaded verandah set back from the street. The food is only average and prices a little high (expect to pay around 25YTL for a full meal with a beer, a little more for fish), but the ambience is good.

Drinking and nightlife

Alanya has a large number of bars, discos and clubs, but they are very much geared towards package tourists, and often centre on the complexes out of the town centre. One long-standing dance establishment is *Auditorium*, out on the west side of town, an open-air disco complete with its own pool. There are a couple of options close to the harbour. If you want to drink expensive beers (7YTL) to a pumping MOR rock soundtrack, head for *The Doors Rock Bar*, a *Hard Rock* derivative just behind the waterfront, with mock palms, a cherry-red 1950s Chevy suspended from the ceiling and a tank of gormless-looking fish behind the bar. The adjacent *James Dean Bar* is equally overpriced, but plays a wider variety of music and has a choice of bars.

Listings

Banks and exchange There are several banks with ATMs on Atatürk Cad and Hükümet Cad.

Bicycle and motorbike rental Bikes cost €5 per day, mopeds €15 and motorbikes €35, available from numerous outlets around town.

Boats Fergün Denizcilik (ⓦwww.fergun.net.) runs hydrofoils to and from Girne in Turkish Cyprus in the summer season only; services leave Mondays and Fridays at noon, returning from Girne on Sundays and Thursdays at 11am (€40 one way; 3.5hr).

Buses Regular buses link Alanya with destinations east and west, including Antalya, Mersin and Adana, as well as north to Ankara, İstanbul and Konya. Most of the buses, however, start their journeys elsewhere, so make sure you book your departure seat well in advance.

Car rental There are numerous operators in Alanya; try several places and bargain hard as prices are higher than Antalya. Main agencies include Avis, Atatürk Cad 53 (ⓣ0242/513 3513), and Europcar, Keykubat Cad 21/A (ⓣ0242/513 1929). Cheaper is Force Rental, Damlataş Cad 68/A

(ⓣ0242/519 6262).

Hospital The State Hospital (Devlet Hastane) is on the bypass, east of the centre.

Internet Casper Internet Café, behind the Yeni Cami on the waterfront.

Post office The PTT, Atatürk Cad, opposite Kültür Cad (daily 8am–midnight), sells phone cards. There are also PTT caravans scattered about the town during the summer.

Shopping Touristy silverware and carpets are on sale in İskele Cad, and there are yet more shops on the sidestreets between Gazipaşa Cad and Hükümet Cad. Genuine and fake designer-label clothes are better purchases, and if you are looking to add to your collection of soccer replica shirts, Alanya is the place to do it.

Tours and travel agents FAM Tour, Damlataş Cad (ⓣ0242/511 1527), Indiana Tour, Keykubat Cad (ⓣ0242 512 4454), and Mem-Tours, Gazipaşa Cad (ⓣ0242/511 4450), all offer trips to Cappadocia, Pamukkale or the Pamphylian cities (from €25), as well as jeep safaris and boat tours; often they'll pick you up at your hotel.

Around Alanya

Alanya's tourist office distinguishes itself by its dearth of information about sites in the region, and even archeological sites are not signposted from the road, so haphazard is tourism development here. Private tour operators are helping to fill the gap, with trips to Alanya's nearby mountain villages and to the Dimçay river, but otherwise you'll need a good map and a car to get the most out of the town's surroundings.

The Dimçay river and the Dim Mağrası

The **Dimçay river**, 6km from the centre of Alanya, has become horribly disfigured by development along its lower reaches, and upward of thirty trout restaurants litter its banks higher up. You can reach the river area by dolmuş (take an hourly "Dimçay" or "Banana" dolmuş out of town from along Keykubut Caddesi to the bridge signposted "Dimçay"), but there are far more beautiful and peaceful valleys in the Toros mountains.

A more rewarding day out from Alanya is the **Dim Mağrası** (daily 9am–6pm; 6YTL), a spectacular cavern set in the mountains high above the river, 11km from the town centre. A 360m-long walkway has been built through the well-lit cavern, with a series of limestone formations providing interest en route to the prime attraction, a lovely crystal-clear pool. There's a small café-cum-restaurant at the entrance, with great views over the heavily wooded mountains.

The cavern is served by the "Kestel" dolmuş from Alanya, which departs (and returns) hourly in season. With your own transport, continue past the Dimçay bridge for a few hundred metres, do a U-turn through a gap in the central reservation, head back to the bridge and take the right turn just before it. Follow this road for 3km before turning right and following a track for a further 5km through increasingly attractive scenery.

Mahmut Seydı

Alanya's principle *yayla* or summer mountain retreat is **MAHMUT SEYDİ**, an attractive village a tortuous 25km out of town. Minibuses aren't designed to meet the needs of tourists, since they arrive in the evening and leave the following morning, and there's no accommodation. To get there by car, take Yayla Caddesi off Atatürk Caddesi and head for the hills.

It's worth renting a car to get to Mahmut Seydı, partly to escape from Alanya's oppressive summertime heat, but also to visit the town's thirteenth-century **mosque**. The exterior of the building is modern, but most of the interior fittings, including the woodwork of the ceilings, doors, cupboards and galleries, are original. Unfortunately, the woodwork was painted in recent restorations, but its former glory can still be appreciated, especially in the fine work of the ceiling. In the courtyard is part of the original fountain and a 650-year-old fir tree. From viewing platforms next to the tree and the mosque, the valley, its surrounding mountains and village houses are visible, as well as the distant beach of İncekum.

Alanya to Adana

The region between Alanya and Adana formed ancient **Cilicia**, and was settled by refugees from Troy at the same time as Pamphylia further west. Its remoteness meant that it was never as developed and, although it had a couple of significant centres, the region seems to have been largely wild and lawless. In ancient times it was divided between Cilicia Tracheia (Rough Cilicia) – Alanya to the western edge of the Çukurova – and Cilicia Campestris (Smooth Cilicia), comprising the dull flatlands of the Ceyhan delta.

Cilicia Tracheia, with its rugged, densely wooded coastline, was a haven for pirates, whose increasingly outrageous exploits finally spurred the Romans into absorbing Cilicia into the empire in the first century BC. Today, it retains a wild appearance, and travel through it involves some frighteningly daring drives along winding mountain roads that hug the craggy coastline, traversing the rocky coves that once served as pirate hangouts. All this is to the good if you're trying to escape the crowds further west, since far fewer people make it along here. There are some decent stretches of beach around **Anamur**, overlooked by an Armenian castle and a partially excavated Greek site, while in the mountains above **Silifke** – the next major town – the abandoned city of **Uzuncaburç** is perhaps the most extensive of the region's ancient remains. After **Kızkalesi**, where two huge castles break up the shoreline, there are more good beaches and weird ruins, running through flatter land into the outskirts of **Mersin**. This marks the beginning of what was Cilicia Campestris, and the end of the area's real touristic interest, with ferries to Northern Cyprus but nothing else to stop for. Similarly, **Tarsus**, a little further on, has little to betray its former historical importance; while **Adana**, Turkey's fourth largest city, contains few remains of any era despite a venerable history, but does have excellent market shopping.

Alanya to Silifke

Heading east from Alanya, the road starts to cut through the mountains, traversing occasional valleys planted with bananas but rarely losing sight of the sea. On the way, you'll pass little wayside restaurants, sheltered but difficult-to-reach sandy bays, and the odd camping ground.

To make the most of this stretch of coastline you really need your own transport, as only the beaches around the tiny resort of **İskele** (Anamur) merit a longer stay, and the few sites are difficult to reach by public transport. **Taşucu**, near to Silifke, is the best place to cross to Northern Cyprus.

Iotape

The first place of interest after leaving Alanya's hotel sprawl behind is **Iotape**, around 45km away. Oddly situated on a rocky promontory between the road and the sea, this ancient site was named after the wife of the Commagenian king Antiochus IV (38–72 AD), and struck its own coins from the reign of Emperor Trajan until that of Emperor Valerian.

The ruins are mainly very tumbledown apart from a fairly impressive triple-arched bath-house, which can be clearly seen from the road. Closer inspection uncovers drainage and heating systems. The acropolis is on the promontory out to sea and a colonnaded street runs east–west along the valley linking the promontory to the mainland. Also visible from the road are statue bases giving information about successful athletes and philanthropists of the city, and there are frescoes to be seen inside the niches of a small, single-aisled church. The **beach** below Iotape is idyllic: if you're lucky you might get it to yourself.

Gazipaşa

The first significant settlement after Alanya is **GAZIPAŞA**, about 50km to the east, an aspiring resort with a yacht harbour still under construction. The *Selinus Hotel*

(℡0242/572 1986, ✉info@selinushotel.com.tr; ❹), 3km southwest of the town centre, is worth considering if you want a few days on a quiet beach. It has bright, spacious rooms, a decent pool, and loungers and umbrellas on the beach; the price is for half-board accommodation. Better value, though, are the bungalows of the *Belediye Dinlenme Tesisleri* (℡0242/572 1631; ❷), also right on the beach, which have a small kitchen with a fridge, a double bedroom and a living room. There is a large swimming pool here, and a couple of places to eat and drink, though the units are often fully booked in July and August by Turkish families. To get here, take a dolmuş from outside Gazipaşa's *Belediye* offices on the main coastal highway. The ruins of ancient **Selinus** sprawl across the hillside east of the beach.

Antioch Ad Cragum

Some 20km east of Gazipaşa, a sign points south off the main road to the site of **Antioch Ad Cragum**, 5km along a road that, for its last 2km, is unsurfaced and very steep and narrow – be warned. The setting of this remote site, founded by the Seleucid king Antiochus IV, is stupendous, perched on a rocky promontory jutting out into a deep-blue sea, edged in white where the waves crash onto the rocks. There's not a lot to be seen in the way of remains, but when you are here you can understand how the Cilician pirates held out against the might of Rome for so long.

Anamur, İskele and around

There's little of interest in **ANAMUR** – 80km east of Gazipaşa – but its small harbour suburb, **İSKELE** (*İskele* means quay), 4km away, is slowly developing as a fully fledged, but unpretentious resort, packed in summer with holidaying Turks. It's reached via an unmarked road south from Anamur's *otogar*, which is at the junction of the main street and the coast road. Dolmuşes run from here to İskele from 7am until midnight in season, until 7pm in winter. İskele's small **museum** (Tues–Sun 8am–noon & 1–5pm; 2TYL), just west of the town centre, contains some fine *Yörük* kilims and saddlebags, and finds from nearby classical sites, best of which is a Hellenistic-era cylindrical pottery burial-cask.

If you arrive in the early hours at Anamur *otogar* try the nearby, friendly *Dedehan Hotel* (℡0324/814 7522; ❷). In İskele itself, the cheapest **accommodation** is the *Meltem Hotel* (℡0324/814 1191; ❷), which has large rooms with air conditioning and TVs, but only passable bathrooms. By far the best budget choice is the ✴ *Eser Pansiyon*, a block back from the sea (℡0324/814 2322, ⓦwww.eserpansiyon.com; ❸), which offers clean air-conditioned rooms, either en-suite or with a bathroom shared between two rooms, a vine-shaded rooftop terrace where decent evening meals are served, a laundry service and Internet access. The owner and his son, Tayfun, both speak very good English, know the local area extremely well, and can help arrange visits to nearby Anemurium and a taxi or dolmuş to Mamure Kalesi (for both see below), or even a jaunt into the mountains. Tayfun also runs the great-value *Bella Hotel* (℡0324/816475, ✉eser@eserpansiyon.com; ❸) just down the road, where the simply decorated but quality rooms all have balconies and multichannel TVs. To the west, on the seafront, the *Yan Hotel* (℡0324 814212; ❸) is built around an atrium, with dark but comfortable rooms and a roof terrace with wonderful sea views; breakfast and dinner are included in the price. The *Ünlüselek* (℡0324/814 1973, ✉unluselk@hotmail.com; ❷), 1.5km west of İskele, has large air-conditioned rooms, its own stretch of beach and a seaside restaurant.

İskele has several simple **restaurants**, all of which seem incredibly cheap after the overpricing so prevalent further west. The *Kap Anamur*, west of the main square, has a good reputation for fish, from 10YTL a serving, and *mezes* are great value at 2YTL.

The interior is a vibrant blue and white, with funky "naïve"-style fish tiles. The *Elele*, right on the beach, dishes up standard Turkish grills and snacks at low prices. It's best at night when tables are laid out on the sand right to the water's edge.

Anemurium

Six kilometres southwest of modern Anamur, but without a local dolmuş service, is the ancient settlement of **Anemurium** (Tues–Sun 8am–8pm; 2YTL), on the eastern side of a headland formed where the Toros mountains jut out into the sea. An access road leads down to the partially excavated site from the main road (look out for the yellow sign). Anemurium was at its peak during the third century AD, and most of what remains dates from this period. As you approach you'll see two parallel **aqueducts** running north to south along the hillside to the right. Below these, a sun-baked **necropolis** contains numerous freestanding tombs whose cool interiors harbour murals of mythological scenes on the walls; however, the most notable tombs have been barred off with locked gates. To the right of the road are the hollow ruins of three **Byzantine churches**, set starkly against the blue backdrop of the Mediterranean.

Further down towards the beach you'll see the crumbling remains of a **bath complex** and a desolate **palaestra** or parade ground. Southwest of here is a ruined but still identifiable **theatre** set into the hillside of the headland. Above the theatre on the slope, between the lower and upper aqueducts, are the remains of a number of houses, some of which have intact vaulted roofs; and east of here is the shell of a building containing sixteen curved rows of seating and a mosaic floor, thought to have been either a **council chamber** or **concert hall** (possibly both). Returning towards the theatre and heading south, you'll come across another **baths complex**, a two-storey vaulted structure with discernible traces of decoration and tile-work on the interior walls.

With time, you might want to clamber up the scrubby slopes of the headland to what was once Anemurium's **acropolis**. There isn't a lot to see here, but the promontory is **Turkey's southernmost point**, and on a clear day gives views of the mountains of Cyprus, 80km to the south.

Mamure Kalesi

In the opposite direction from Anamur, a couple of kilometres east of İskele, is **Mamure Kalesi** (daily 8am–7pm; 2YTL), a forbidding castle built by the rulers of the Cilician kingdom of Armenia on the site of a Byzantine fort. It was later occupied by Crusaders, who had established a short-lived kingdom in Cyprus and used Mamure Kalesi as a kind of bridgehead in Asia. Used by successive rulers of the area to protect the coastal strip, it was most recently garrisoned by the Ottomans, who reinforced it after the British occupied Cyprus in 1878, maintaining a strong presence here during World War I. Constructed directly above the sea, its stark façade of crenellated outer walls and watchtowers are certainly impressive. The interior, of languorously decaying buildings, has formed a backdrop to many Turkish films.

From İskele it is possible to walk the 2.5km along the seashore to the castle, though this requires being ferried across the Dragon River by boat for around 1.5YTL. Alternatively, take a dolmuş from İskele to the BP garage on the main road, then another east along the coastal highway to the castle.

Opposite the castle are a couple of small fish **restaurants** and a few noisy pensions, while a couple of kilometres east there's a good forested **campsite**, the *Pullu Mocamp*, which has a beach and an excellent restaurant.

Taşucu

Moving on, there are a couple of quiet bays with sandy beaches, but most people push straight on to the scruffy port of **TAŞUCU**, from where there are frequent ferry and hydrofoil services to Cyprus. Crossing the next day is the only reason you would choose to stay the night here, though the **Amphora Museum** (daily 9am–6pm; 1YTL), set in a restored *han* behind the quay, has a fascinating collection of amphorae of Hellenistic, Roman and Byzantine origin, mostly from locally salvaged wrecks. Of **accommodation** options, on the east of town near the harbour, try the *Tuğran Pension* (℡0324/741 4493; ②), a single-storey building in a garden set back from the beach. Just down from the *Tuğran*, the German-Turkish-run *Holmi Pansiyon* (℡0324/741 5378; ③) has spotless and cheerful rooms with fans, large en-suites, and a pleasant breakfast area. Best in town is the *Lades Motel*, Atatürk Cad 89 (℡0324/7414008, ⓦwww.ladesmotel.com; ③), west of the centre. Painted in cooling blues and whites, it is heavily booked with birdwatchers in spring and autumn. A retro-style bar houses a collection of 1960s-vintage German-made roulette machines, and it has a swimming pool and fine sea view.

There are several **restaurants** backing the port area. Best is the *Baba*, on Atatürk Caddesi, next to the *Lades*, which offers a good range of *meze*, grilled meats and fish at competitive prices (a meal with beer for around 15YTL)

Ferries and hydrofoils to Cyprus

The cheapest way to the Turkish Republic of North Cyprus (TRNC) is by ferry (Sun–Thurs at midnight; 6hr; €35 one way, €62 for a car) to Girne/Kyrenia, though as these are packed with heavy lorries and their drivers, women travellers may feel uncomfortable. A more pleasant alternative (assuming the sea is calm) is to take the hydrofoil (*denizotobüsü*; daily at midday; 2.5hr; €37.50 one way). **Tickets** for both services are available from Akfer (℡0392/815 1615, ⓦwww .fergun.net.), on the waterfront. At present, EU, US, Canadian and Australasian citizens require only a valid passport, on which your Turkish entry visa has not expired, for entry into the TRNC. It's not possible to enter southern (Greek-speaking) Cyprus from the TRNC.

Silifke

About 10km east of Taşucu, **SILIFKE** was once ancient Seleucia, founded by Seleucus, one of Alexander the Great's generals, in the third century BC. Nowadays, it's a quiet, fairly undistinguished town. Only the occasional tourist, en route to the ruins at Uzuncaburç, passes through.

Silifke Kalesi, a Byzantine castle, dominates the local skyline though it looks a lot less spectacular close up. It's about a twenty-minute walk southwest of town and at the top there's a café and a great view. On the way up you'll pass an old **cistern** – the so-called *tekir ambarı* or "striped depot" – which kept Byzantine Silifke supplied with water. Other sights include the second-century AD **Jupiter Tapınağı** (Temple of Jupiter) on İnönü Caddesi, which comprises little more than a pile of stones and one standing pillar with a stork's nest on top. On the main road to Taşucu and Antalya, about half a kilometre from the turn-off to Silifke, there's an **archeological museum** (Arkeoloji Müzesi; Tues–Sun 8am–noon & 1–5pm; 2YTL) containing the finds from excavations at Meydancıkale, a fourth-century BC temple site in the mountains above the coast. Relics include two enormous caryatids; huge, shapeless stone blocks with human-looking feet carved into the bases; and a horde of 5200 silver coins dating from the reigns of Alexander and his generals in Egypt, Syria and the province of Pergamon.

The Göksu delta

Of Turkey's twelve designated areas of outstanding environmental importance, the **Göksu delta** is one of the largest, its 14,500 hectares comprising most of the flat lands east of the Göksu river and south of Silifke. The southern portion of the delta has been designated as the **Kuşcenneti bird reservation** and boasts a tremendous variety of flora and fauna, most notably millions of water birds who inhabit two natural lagoons enclosed by a huge sand-spit which juts into the sea. Despite Göksu's protected status, the area is under long-term threat by the proposed construction of an upstream dam at Kayraktepe, and the battle between environmentalists and the developers continues.

The best place to start an exploration of the area is **Akgöl**, the westerly lagoon, where viewing platforms and huts are under construction. Bird species on Akgöl include pygmy cormorants, Dalmatian pelicans, marbled and white-headed ducks and even the practically extinct black francolin and purple gallinule, two huge birds that have traditionally been shot for food. The **sand spit** is a nesting ground for loggerhead and green turtles as well as a home to sea daffodils and Audouin's gulls. East of this, reached by an access road halfway between Taşucu and Silifke, are extensive ditches where you'll see kingfishers (including the rare chestnut brown and white Smyrna variety), coots, wagtails, spoonbills, egrets and grey, purple and squacco herons. Marsh harriers circle lazily and, in season, migrating vultures and eagles feed in the lush hunting grounds here, gathering strength for their journey north or south. Still further east, the huge natural fishpond of **Paradeniz lagoon** and the flats beyond it harbour waders, ospreys and terns; more viewing platforms are being installed.

You'll see the highest number of birds during the **nesting and migration seasons**: between February and May in the spring (with a peak between late March and early April), and in October, though the storks will have left by autumn. Information leaflets on the delta are available from the **Özel Çevre Koruma Kurumu** (Special Environmental Areas Protection Agency; ℡ 0324/713 0888), 5km west of Silifke, near the church of Aya Tekla, in the grounds of the DSİ waterworks complex; if you contact them in advance you can also arrange an English-speaking guide for group trips. If you want to go independently, you'll need your own car or a taxi.

Incidentally, it was near Silifke that **Frederick Barbarossa**, the Holy Roman Emperor, met his end: he drowned while fording the Calycadnus (now Göksu) river about 9km north of town, en route to Palestine with the Third Crusade; today a plaque marks the spot. Otherwise, heading 4km west of Silifke and then 1km north takes you to Meyemlik and the early Christian site of **Aya Tekla** (open daily, assuming the warden is around; 2YTL). There's little to see except the underground chapel (bring a torch) used in secret by the early Christians, including Tecla, the first female Christian teacher.

Practicalities

The centre of town is Menderes Caddesi, around fifteen minutes' walk from the **otogar** along İnönü Caddesi. Silifke's helpful **tourist office** is at Veli Gürten Bozbey Cad 6 (Mon–Fri 8am–5pm; ℡ 0324/714 1151), reached by way of the Roman bridge spanning the Göksu river.

Hotel possibilities are limited. The *Arısan Pansiyon* on İnönü Caddesi (℡ 0324/714 3331; ❷) is not far from the *otogar*. Its rooms are bright and come with a fan; you pay a little more for an en-suite bathroom. Best-positioned hotel in town is the *Göksu Hotel*, Atatürk Cad 16 (℡ 0324/712 1021, ℻ 712 1024; ❸), on the north riverbank, with large, well-furnished rooms with air conditioning and TV, and wonderful views over the river, bridge and castle. The two-star *Otel Ayatekla*, opposite the *otogar* (℡0324/714 392; ❸), is comparable to the *Göksu*, with an excellent restaurant and bar.

There are lots of basic places to **eat and drink**, but most close after dark, leaving you with only a few options for an evening meal. Best bet is the *Babu Oğlu*, opposite the *otogar*, which has medium-priced grills but expensive fish. The *Göksu Hotel* serves excellent food and beer in its waterside garden, though you'll need to book in advance, as they cook to order. The *Gözde Lokantası*, on a quiet alley off Menderes Caddesi, a couple of hundred metres from the river, has decent *sulu yemek* and grills for around 5–8YTL for a full meal. For a dessert, cross the river and head for the popular *Özkaymak Pastanesi*, just down from the *Göksu Hotel* on Atatürk Caddesi. The *şübiyet*, a kind of *baklava* with cream, is particularly good; it also does a range of savouries, including decent burgers.

Inland: Uzuncaburç and Alahan

Dolmuşes bound for the ancient city of **Uzuncaburç** leave from outside the tourist office every ninety minutes from 9am to 3.30pm weekdays, from 10.30am weekends (though the last one back departs at 2pm); the ride costs 2YTL each way. The thirty-kilometre ride to Uzuncaburç is spectacular, taking you through a jagged gorge and a couple of villages that time seems to have forgotten. Beyond Uzuncaburç, with your own vehicle, it's possible to loop back to the main highway to Konya, calling in at the Byzantine site of **Alahan** en route.

Demircili

If you are driving, you might care to stop off in the village of **DEMİRCİLİ** 7km north of Silifke, known in ancient times as Imbriogon, where there are six **Greco-Roman tombs** spread out on either side of the road among the olive trees. They are unattended and unrestored – looking more like long-vacated houses than tombs – and it's hard to believe that they have survived the depredations of time and stone plunderers. The first is a simple one-storey affair just to the right of the road; a little further along, there's a larger two-storey structure. To the west of the road is the **Çifte Anıt Mezarları**, or "double mausoleum", consisting of two linked tombs, the right-hand one of which contains three sarcophagi with various decorative features: one with a relief of a lion and another featuring a man's head, the nude figures of two women and the heads of two women.

Uzuncaburç

From Demircili, the road continues uphill and then turns off to the right towards the ruins at **Uzuncaburç**, originally a Hittite settlement that was known to the Greeks as Olba and to the Romans as Diocaesarea. A small, modern village has grown up in haphazard fashion around the ruins, but few concessions have been made to tourism. Uzuncaburç is famous for leather bags and handmade rugs known as *çul*; examples are often sold at makeshift stalls. Local culinary specialities include *kenger kahvesi* (coffee made from acanthus) and *pekmez* (grape molasses).

The main site

The main **site of Uzuncaburç** (always open; 2YTL when the site guardian is around) lacks the size and scale of Perge and Aspendos, but is atmospheric enough in its own way, if only because of its relatively neglected state. Although the area was first settled by the Hittites, they left little behind and the most impressive ruins

△ Uzuncaburç

that survive date from Hellenistic times.

Start your explorations at the overgrown Roman **theatre**, overlooked by a couple of beautiful houses whose walls are chock-a-block with Classical masonry. From here, pass through an enormous five-columned **monumental gateway**, beyond which is a colonnaded street, once the city's main thoroughfare: keep your eyes open for what look like small stone shelves on the columns, which once supported statues and busts. On the northern side of the street is a **nymphaeum**, now dried up, which once formed part of the city's water-supply system. This was part of a large network of pipes and tunnels, built by the Romans nearly two thousand years ago, that still supplies water to the modern village and others around.

To the south, the **Temple of Zeus Olbios** is one of the earliest examples of the Corinthian order, erected during the third century BC by Seleucus I, of which only the fluted columns now remain intact. Look out for the fine sarcophagus carved with three Medusa heads and a sarcophagus lid depicting three reclining figures. At the western end of the colonnaded street is the **Temple of Tyche**, dedicated to the goddess of chance, reckoned to date from the second half of the first century AD. Five marble columns still stand, joined by an architrave bearing an inscription stating that the temple was the gift of a certain Oppius and his wife Kyria. From here a right turn leads to a large three-arched **city gate**, which, according to an inscription, dates from the fifth century AD and is home to nesting owls.

Other ruins

The majority of Uzuncaburç's remaining attractions lie to the north of these ruins. Walk from the drop-off point as far as the *Burç* café and turn right for the **High Tower**, a 22-metre-high, five-storey Hellenistic structure that once formed part of the city wall and which today gives its name to the modern town (Uzuncaburç means "high tower"). An ancient Greek inscription above the entrance gives details of repair work carried out during the third century AD. It is believed that in addition to playing a defensive role this tower was also part of an ancient signalling network, whereby messages were relayed by flashing sunlight off polished shields.

Just outside the modern village, past the *Burç* café as far as the Atatürk bust (heed the signs for the "Antik Mezar" and follow the curve to the right), is a **necropolis** used by Greek, Roman and Byzantine inhabitants of the area. It has three basic types of resting place: sarcophagi, graves carved into the rock and cave-tombs housing whole families. Most of these are clearly visible, and it's even possible to enter some of the cave-tombs, though they have long since been cleaned out by grave robbers.

About 1km south of Uzuncaburç, 500m west of the main road, is another **mausoleum**, this time with an eye-catching pyramid-shaped roof, dating from Hellenistic times. Inside, the tombs were hidden under the floor and, outside, the rim of the roof was lined with statues of the deceased.

Another possible excursion from Uzuncaburç is to the ruins of **Olba** (present-day Ura), 5km to the east, a similar but less impressive ancient city which was the third-century BC capital of a temple state run by a powerful priest-caste. At the village crossroads you will find a nymphaeum, cistern and theatre nestling at the base of an acropolis. Five hundred metres further northeast you can see the aqueduct built to feed the nymphaeum, and the watchtowers built to protect the aqueduct.

Alahan: the road to Konya

Some 110km northwest of Silifke, and reached by a spectacular road cutting through the Toros mountains en route for Konya, lies **Alahan**, a well-preserved monastic complex in a beautiful mountain setting. The site is well signposted, 2km to the east of the main road (Highway 715). Intact buildings at the site include two late fifth- and sixth-century basilicas, one sporting elaborate relief sculptures of the Evangelists and the two archangels, and a baptistery. Alahan is best reached using your own transport, though the buses plying between the coast and Konya will drop you at the turn. Following your explorations you'll have to chance your luck on flagging down a Karaman/Konya bus.

East from Silifke

East of Silifke the coast road winds above the ocean to Kızkalesi, but a rash of development is rapidly despoiling this stretch of coastline. There are some interesting sites, particularly the Roman baths at **Narlıkuyu** and the caves of **Cehennem** and **Cennet**, but you need your own transport to make the most of them. Anyone with a special interest in exploring more ruins off the beaten track should buy Celal Taşkiran's *Silifke and Environs*, an exhaustive guide to all the sites between Anamur and Mersin, best bought at Silifke's tourist office for €10.

Narlıkuyu

Some 20km from Silifke, **NARLİKUYU** lies on the fringes of a rapidly developing bay with several restaurants. There's a small car park in the centre of the village, next to which are the remains of a Roman bath-house, known after its founder as the **Bath of Poimenius** (2YTL). Inside, there's a dusty mosaic depiction of the well-rounded nude forms of the Three Graces, the daughters of Zeus and companions of the Muses. The bath was fed from the limestone caves above by an ancient Roman spring that supplied a celebrated fountain, the waters of which were supposed to confer wisdom on those who drank from them.

Cennet ve Cehennem

From Narlıkuyu, a narrow paved road winds 3km northwards into the hills through groves of olive trees to **Cennet ve Cehennem**, or the "Caves of Heaven and Hell" (open in daylight hours; 2YTL) – some of the most impressive of the many limestone caverns scattered along this coast. At the end of the road there's a car park and a cluster of teashops and souvenir stands.

The site consists of a series of three caves. Immediately adjacent to the parking space, the largest and most impressive is **Cennet Deresi** (Cave of Heaven), actually a seventy-metre-deep gorge formed when the roof of an underground canyon collapsed. You enter via 452 steps cut into the rock on the eastern side of the canyon. On reaching the bottom, head south towards the entrance to the **Tayfun Mağrası** (Cave of Typhon), a bona fide cave of some depth, at the end of which runs a stream of drinkable water from the same source as the spring water in Narlıkuyu. As you go further in, it gets progressively more difficult to breathe and it's best not to hang around too long, a fact recorded by Strabo, the ancient geographer, leading some historians to believe that this cave may have been considered one of the mythical entrances to Hades. According to the legend, Typhon, after whom the cave is named, was an immense hundred-headed fire-breathing lizard, the father of Cerberus – the three-headed dog who guarded the entrance to Hades on the banks of the River Styx, allowing only the souls of the dead to enter and refusing to let them out. At the entrance to the cave is the **chapel of the Virgin Mary**, a well-preserved Byzantine church built over the former temple of Zeus and still containing a few frescoes.

About 100m to the north of "Heaven", the **Cehennem Deresi** (Cave of Hell) is impossible to enter, as its sides are practically vertical. According to legend, Zeus imprisoned Typhon here, before banishing him forever to the depths of the earth or, as one legend goes, trapping him underneath Mount Etna in Sicily. This gorge is supposed to be another of the entrances to Hades, and local people used to tie rags to surrounding trees to placate evil spirits.

About 500m west of "Heaven" is a fourth cave, the **Dilek Mağarası** (Wishing Cave), the opening of which has been specially widened and a spiral staircase provided for ease of access. Down below, solid pathways connect a number of subterranean halls, with a total length of about 200m. The main chamber is filled with stalactites and stalagmites, and the air down below is supposed to be beneficial for asthma sufferers.

Kızkalesi and around

A few kilometres east of Narlıkuyu, and about halfway between Silifke and Mersin, **KIZKALESI** ("Maiden's Castle") is the longest established resort along this stretch of coastline. It has scores of hotels, *pansiyons* and restaurants, and the fine sandy beach slopes gently into the sea, making it ideal for kids (camels provide an alternative to donkey rides). The more active can parasail and jet-ski from the pier in front of the *Albatros Restaurant Café Bar*.

Known as Corycus in ancient times, Kızkalesi changed hands frequently until the arrival of the **Romans** in 72 BC, after which it prospered, becoming one of the most important ports along the coast. Roman-period relics still survive in the area, notably a series of mysterious rock reliefs north of town and the carvings at the chasm at Kanlıdivane to the east. Kızkalesi continued to thrive during the Byzantine era despite occasional Arab attacks – against which the town's defences were strengthened with two **castles** constructed during the twelfth and thirteenth centuries – before falling to the Ottomans in 1482.

Food and drink

Contemporary Turkish cuisine is among the best in the world. In the more sophisticated restaurants and meyhanes (taverns) you'll find a bewildering array of mezes, simply cooked fish or grilled meat dishes with mountains of salad and fresh bread. In fish restaurants in particular, the drink of choice is fiery rakı (known colloquially as "lion's milk"), though reasonable quality wine and good local lagers are widely available. Many basic eating places (usually unlicensed) specialize in kebabs and other grilled meats, others in pide (Turkish pizza). Equally ubiquitous are sulu yemek (steamtray food) joints serving a range of stews, from tender okra to chicken. For pudding, head (like the locals) to a pastahane (sweet shop) for some toothsome baklava.

Fish and seafood

Turkey has an enormous coastline, and fish and seafood have long been an important part of the national cuisine. From the cooler waters of the Black Sea comes the humble *hamsi* (anchovy), which, when fried and served in a hunk of fresh, warm bread, forms a tasty, nourishing street-snack. Served up in a fancy restaurant, accompanied by corn bread and a glass of *rakı*, it is a delicacy in its own right. İstanbul, the bustling metropolis which serves as the nation's historical and cultural (though not actual) capital, sits astride the fish-rich Bosphorus strait (which links the Black Sea and Mediterranean). The country's best fish restaurants and *meyhane*s are to be found here, dishing up specialities such as bluefish (*lüfer*), small bonito (*palamut*) and large (*torik*), this last the source of *lakerda*, marinated white-fleshed slices that are a five-star *meze*. The Aegean and Mediterranean, despite overfishing, still provide tempting fish dishes, notably sea bass (*leverek*) and turbot (*kalkan*). Shrimps and prawns (either marinated

Fish market

in a vinaigrette or served hot with butter) are common fare in most fish restaurants, whilst the humble mussel is sold, Molly Malone style, by street vendors.

Helva

Sweets

Few people return home from their first trip to Turkey without a box of glutinous **Turkish Delight** (actually called *lokum* in Turkey). If the rose-flavoured, sugar-dusted basic variety is too sweet or scented for your taste, try the (more expensive) versions stuffed with walnuts, hazelnuts or pistachios. Less well known to outsiders, but equally ubiquitous, is **helva**. The first recipe for this traditional sweetmeat, consisting mainly of flour, butter, sugar and sometimes milk or starch, was recorded in 1473 and hasn't changed significantly since. An entire domed hall of the imperial kitchens, in use from the fifteenth century until 1924, was devoted exclusively to its preparation. Much of the *helva* made today is basically *tahini* (sesame) paste mixed with sugar, with extra flavour coming from the added nuts or chocolate powder. It makes a great treat when travelling or trekking, as it's a real energy-booster and doesn't melt in the heat.

Sweet or pudding shops (*pastahane*) are a great tradition in Turkey, and even the smallest town will have one. The best serve a huge variety of sweets. Avoid the tempting chocolate- and icing-covered cakes (they are oversweet, cloying and full of artificial cream – and the mainstay of children's parties across the country). The traditional **baklava**-type sweets are far better, different mixtures of syrup-soaked filo pastries stuffed with nuts. Best of these is *fıstık sarması*, a filo-pastry roll chock-full of pistachios. The quality of *baklava* varies enormously – as a general rule the more you pay, the higher the ratio of nuts to pastry and syrup.

Milk-based sweets are also very popular in Turkey, from *tavukgöğsü* (an unusual and delicately flavoured pudding made from strained chicken-breast mixed with semolina and milk), to oven-baked, burnt-topped rice puddings (*sütlaç*).

Coffee vs tea

Not many people are aware that the Ottomans introduced **coffee** – as well as the notion of the coffeehouse – to the west, both reaching England during the seventeenth century via Venice and Vienna. The coffee bean was originally cultivated in Ethiopia and then Yemen, and began spreading to other parts of the Middle East by the fifteenth century. Despite coffee being proscribed by religious authorities as a stimulant (and therefore forbidden by the Koran) in the early years, coffeehouses had become a fixture of İstânbul society by the mid-sixteenth century, after again having been intermittently banned as hotbeds of sedition and vice.

Mezes

Mezes

The Turkish kitchen is famed for the variety and freshness of its appetizers (*mezes*). In the better licensed restaurants and *meyhane* (taverns) diners can choose from thirty or more tasty starters. Some dishes, like stuffed olives and pickled vegetables, are very simple. More unusual is a mixed dish of walnuts and *tulum* (a delicious, strong and dry goat's cheese made by curing the cheese in a goatskin) – best eaten with lashings of the paper-thin bread known as *lavaş*. *Sigara böreği*, cigar-shaped, deep-fried cheese-filled pastries are delicious, and are particularly suitable for main-course-skipping vegetarians as they are served piping hot. Aubergines are a standard of the *meze* table, sometimes mashed with lemon juice, sometimes in a ratatouille-type dish with potatoes and tomato sauce. King of the aubergine dishes is *imam bayaldi* (the imam fainted), a half-aubergine topped with tomato and onion and served cold. *Hibeş* is a dip of whipped sesame paste and olive oil spiced with hot pepper; *fava* (much favoured by *rakı* drinkers in fish restaurants) is a puree of fava beans topped with slices of onion. Add to this list cold beans in olive oil, *mücver* (courgette fritters served cold), stuffed vine leaves and masses of salad dishes – ranging from rocket to yoghurt-drenched purslane (*semizotu*) – and you begin to get some idea why the main course in these restaurants is usually a basic grill of fish or meat accompanied by a light salad.

Turkish coffee

The Ottomans devised a new way of preparing the beverage: finely grinding the roasted beans and then placing the resulting powder, with water and sugar to taste, into a long-handled, tapering small pot called a *cezve*. The brew was – and still is – allowed to rise twice without actually boiling, with the precious resultant froth decanted first into little cups. Turks today drink their coffee unsweetened (*sade*), medium sweet (*orta şekerli*) or very sweet (*bol şekerli*).

Ironically, coffee hasn't played as much of a role in the national psyche during the past century, ever since the empire's Arabian possessions were lost, tea-growing along the eastern Black Sea was encouraged as part of the new republican policy of economic autarky, and crippling import duties put even the meanest brands of instant beyond most people's reach from the 1960s onwards. Black **tea** – as anyone who has strolled through a Turkish bazaar soon learns – is now the ritual hot drink of choice. Served in tiny, tulip-shaped glasses, it's most palatable drunk *açık* (weak), preferably in one of the ubiquitous shady outdoor tea-gardens that grace many town centres, parks and recreation areas. Many Turks will protest otherwise vociferously, but home-grown Turkish tea is inferior to Indian and Sri Lankan varieties, and if steeped too long can be stomach-churning – you have been warned! On the bright side, since the European customs union was concluded, the price of coffee has fallen and its popularity begun to recover in the land that introduced it to the wider world.

For more on Turkish cuisine see p.63.

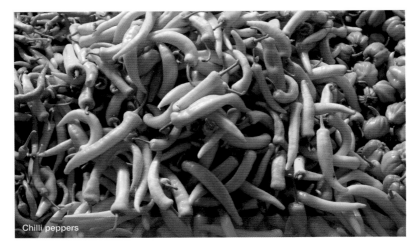
Chilli peppers

The Town

The town's most compelling feature is the thirteenth-century **sea castle**, the *Kızkalesi* or Maiden's Castle (daily dawn–dusk; 2YTL), on an island lying about 300m offshore. The story (examples of which are found all over Turkey) goes that one of the Armenian kings who ruled the region in medieval times had a beautiful daughter. After it was prophesied that she would die as the result of a poisonous snakebite, the king had the castle built and moved the girl out to it, imagining that she would be safe there. One day one of the king's advisers sent a basket of fruit out to the island for her, out of which slid a snake that killed the girl. According to local stories, the snake still lives on the island, and the only people who venture out to it are tourists, for whose benefit boat services operate (3.5YTL return trip) from the western end of the beachfront. The unadorned walls and sturdy towers still stand, but apart from masonry fragments and weeds there's little to see within.

Opposite the sea castle, the overgrown ruins of the mighty **land castle** (*Korkyos Kalesi*) at the eastern end of the beach (2YTL, if there's anyone around to collect it) are easily explored and its battlements make a good venue for some sunset-watching. The main gate, constructed from ancient stones, bears various Greek inscriptions. The western gate was originally a Roman structure, built during the third century AD and later incorporated into the castle.

Immediately northeast of the town, across the main road from the land castle, is a **necropolis**, dating from the fourth century AD and containing hundreds of tombs and sarcophagi, some of them beautifully carved. Many of the epitaphs give the jobs of the occupants – weavers, cobblers, goldsmiths, vintners, olive-oil manufacturers, ship owners and midwives, who all had their last resting places here. Also scattered around this area are the remains of a number of Byzantine churches and cisterns.

Practicalities

Orientation is simple, as **buses** plying the coastal road to and from Mersin will drop you on the main road in the town centre. Nearly all the **accommodation** is found between the main road and the beach to the south. It is possible to find somewhere to stay here, even in the very crowded months of July and August, while out of season you'll be able to negotiate a substantial discount. It's worth noting that all the hotels may be subject to thudding music coming from beach-front bars.

Running from east to west along the beachfront, furthest east is the German package-oriented *Hotel Peyda* (☎0324/523 2607, ✉HotelPeyda@hotmail.com; ❸), with clean, spacious air-conditioned rooms and breakfast tables set out on the path running parallel to the beach. Next one along, the *Hantur* (☎0324/523 2322, ✉hotelhantur@tnnn.net.tr; ❸), stands on its own right on the beach, less noisy than many of its neighbours and with great views across to Maiden's Castle from its spotless, bright-white rooms; guests have use of beach umbrellas and loungers. North of the *Hantur*, set back from the beach, is the *Yaka Hotel* (☎0324/523 2444, ⦿www.yakahotel.com; ❸), where the rooms are comfy, well-proportioned and have tea-making facilities, the garden is delightful, and the helpful owner speaks English, French and German. The westernmost hotel on this strip is the swanky *Club Barbarossa* (☎0324/523 2364, ✉chbarbarbarossa@ttnet.tr; ❺) lying still further west, its lawn sloping down to the beach and littered with classical capitols. The air-conditioned rooms here have satellite TV, and the price is for half-board accommodation.

There are plenty of places to **eat and drink** and, generally speaking, the further away from the beach they are the better the value. The grills, *mezes* and fast-food places offer better value than those serving seafood. There are also a few beach-front bars and a couple of discos.

Around Kızkalesi

Really only practicable with your transport, or by taxi, are three nearby sites: the **Adam Kayalar rock reliefs**, and the ancient cities of **Elaioussa Sebastae** and **Kanytelis**. You could see them all in a day away from the beach.

Adam Kayalar rock reliefs

Most intriguing side-trip from the town is to the series of **rock reliefs** in a valley about 6km to the north (the turning is near the PTT), marked by a sign bearing the legend "Adam Kayalar" (Man's Rocks). Follow the path indicated from here for about a kilometre until it starts to dip down into a valley, where steps cut into the rock lead down to a platform from which you can view a series of Roman men, women and children carved into niches in the wall. There are seventeen human figures and a mountain goat. Unfortunately, extensive damage has been caused to one of the figures by treasure hunters who used dynamite in the hope of finding booty supposedly secreted inside the statue. It's not clear who the figures are, or why they might have been constructed, and the fragmentary inscriptions below most of them offer few clues.

Elaioussa Sebastae

East of Kızkalesi, on both sides of the road, various ancient ruins stretch as far as the village of **Ayaş**, 3km away. This was the site of the settlement of **Elaioussa Sebaste** (currently under excavation), which in the time of Augustus was important enough to coin its own money. Below the village is a theatre, and below that baths, a city gate and possibly a nymphaeum. An aqueduct leads to an underground cistern near the baths, although villagers are still ploughing on top of this area. Above the site is a prominent house-tomb in remarkably good condition, dedicated by a mother to her husband and two sons. On the south side of the road is a Byzantine church, almost on the beach, while scattered around the area are numerous tombs, many of them richly decorated with reliefs.

Kanytelis

About 7km east of Kızkalesi, a signposted turn-off leads 3km north to the village of **Kanlıdıvane**, literally "place of blood". This, the site of the ancient city of **Kanytelis**, is where locals used to believe condemned criminals were executed by being thrown into a huge chasm and devoured by wild animals. A car park and ticket-seller's hut mark the entrance to the **chasm** (daily 8am–7pm; 2YTL), which is certainly large and frightening enough to have given rise to the legends – at 90m long by 70m wide and 60m deep, it forms the core of the ancient city. Visitors descend into it by way of an eroded staircase. On the southern and western sides of the chasm there are a number of carvings in niches, one a portrait of a family of six and one of a Roman soldier. On its southwestern edge near the car park, a seventeen-metre-high Hellenistic tower bears an inscription on the southwestern corner next to a three-pronged triskele, a symbol that links the region to the nearby state of Olba. Near the tower are a number of large Byzantine basilicas in various states of collapse, of which the best preserved is the Papylas church. There's another big cluster of tombs northeast of the chasm, with numerous ancient sarcophagi and a few modern graves.

Mersin

The largest Mediterranean port in Turkey, with a population of 1.5 million, **MERSIN** is the first of the three large cities that gird the Ceyhan delta. It's a modern harbour city that – aside from its regular ferry connections to Cyprus – is almost entirely without interest, despite being inhabited since Hittite times. Until the beginning of the twentieth century the settlement was little more than a squalid fishing hamlet. However, over the last century rapid growth and industrialization, coupled with Mersin's role as an international free-trade zone, have turned it into a model, if soulless, example of contemporary Turkish urban planning.

The only real diversion is the local **museum** on Atatürk Caddesi (Tues–Sun 9am–noon & 1–5pm; 2YTL). Housing a small but well-presented collection of local archeological finds from Neolithic times to the Byzantine era, especially notable are some Roman clay sarcophagi, some with lift-off, and others with sliding, lids. The garden area is also attractive, with some fine stone carvings shaded by palms. Adjacent to the museum is a substantial **Greek Orthodox church**, in a walled compound which is also home to a family of caretakers who, if not too busy, will show you the interior.

Practicalities

The city's **otogar** is some way out of town and you'll need to take a service bus or a dolmuş into the centre. Unfortunately, the dolmuşes don't pass directly in front of the *otogar*, and it's a five-minute walk to the dolmuş stop on Gazi Mustafa Paşa Bulvarı, the major road one block northwest of the *otogar*. The dolmuşes drop off at the eastern end of İstiklâl Caddesi in the city centre. The **train station** (services to and from Adana) is very central and convenient for the listed hotels. The **tourist office** is by the harbour just off İsmet İnönü Bulvarı (Mon–Fri 9am–5pm; ℡0324/238 3271).

On İsmet İnönü Bulvarı, opposite the tourist office, *Olcartur* sells **THY** plane tickets. **Car rental** companies include Avis, at İsmet İnönü Bulvarı, Uysal Apt 100 (℡0324/232 3450).

Accommodation

As an important port, Mersin has plenty of accommodation, but all of it is aimed at business travellers. Most of the hotels are on İstiklâl Caddesi and Soğuksu Caddesi, which run parallel to the seafront. A **budget** choice, on Soğuksu Caddesi, is the *Hotel Hitit* (℡0324/231 6431; ❷). It is reasonable value, though not especially friendly; plain rooms have air conditioning and TV. **Mid-range** possibilities include the *Aktaş Hotel*, İstiklâl Cad 152 (℡0324/233 7007, ℻232 3168; ❹). It has spotless, carpeted rooms with TV, fridge, air conditioning, double glazing and new, "wet" bathrooms. Rooms at the back are much quieter, and there's parking out front. The *Hotel Gökhan*, Soğuksu Cad 20 (℡0324/231 6256, ℻237 4462; ❹), is slightly more expensive but is more atmospheric, with nice touches like fish tanks in the lobby and bar. The rooms are spacious, pastel-hued and air-conditioned, and the bathrooms immaculate. Swisher, and only marginally dearer, is the *Nobel Oteli*, İstiklâl Cad 73 (℡0324/237 7700, ⓦwww.nobelotel.com; ❹), where the foreign-language channels on the satellite TV may attract you more than the ballroom. **Top-of-the-range** business hotels include the *Mersin Hotel*, in the centre of town on Gümrük Meydanı (℡0324/238 1040, ℻231 2625; ❺), and the towering *Mersin Merit* at Hastane Cad 165 (℡0324/336 1010, ℻336 0722; ❼), easily visible to the north, with stunning views of Mersin from the upper floors.

Eating and drinking

There are plenty of places to **eat** in Mersin. One of the best, opposite the *Nobel Oteli* on İstiklâl Caddesi, is the *Hacibaba Et Lokantası* – cheerful, spotlessly clean and with excellent service. As well as the normal grills (kebabs start at 4YTL) it also dishes up southeastern Turkish specialities such as *kuburga* (lamb ribs) and *perde pilaf* (delicately spiced pilau rice, which forms a tasty skin as it is cooked). Diners also get a free mixed salad and miniature *pide* breads. Another fine choice is the *Konak*, in a converted mansion building on Silifke Caddesi on the edge of the **Balık Pazarı** (fish market) and opposite the *Hotel Gökhan*. There's a *şatk köşesi* laid out with cushions and low tables in one room, and all types of grills. The *lahmacun* are large rounds, hotly spiced with red pepper. The only drawback is the incongruous, Western-style, piped pop Muzak.

Ferries to Cyprus

Ferries depart from Mersin to Mağosa (Famagusta) in Northern Cyprus on Mondays, Wednesdays and Fridays at 8pm. Buy tickets from Fergun on İsmet İnönü Bulvarı, Guvec Is Merkez (☎0324/23828810) or Deniz Yolları in the harbour; foot passengers pay €26 one way, cars €56.

In Mersin, the **TRNC consulate** is at Hamidiye Mahalle Karadeniz (☎0324/237 2482). You can also buy tickets in Mersin for the **Taşucuu–Girne ferry and hydrofoil** (see p.589) – a much faster crossing – from Akfer Denizcilik Şirketi, on İsmet İnön Bulvarı (☎0324/238 2881).

Tarsus

About 30km east of Mersin, across the factory-dotted cotton fields of the Çukurova, lies **TARSUS,** birthplace of St Paul and the city where Cleopatra met Mark Antony and turned him into a "strumpet's fool". St Paul was born as Saul in Tarsus about 46 years after the meeting between Cleopatra and Antony. He returned after his conversion on the road to Damascus, fleeing persecution in Palestine. He seems to have been proud of his roots and is described as having told the Roman commandant of Jerusalem: "I am a Jew, a Tarsian from Cilicia, a citizen of no mean city." Nowadays, however, few reminders of the town's illustrious past remain. Indeed, Tarsus is spectacularly ugly, with pot-holed streets, crumbling buildings and a skyline festooned with electricity pylons and telephone cables. Only the very centre, around the Kancık Kapısı, has any charm or order.

Near the main bus drop-off point, the **Kancık Kapısı** ("the gate of the bitch") is a Roman construction, also known as Cleopatra's Gate. Although it doesn't actually have any known connection with the Egyptian queen, she is thought to have come ashore for her first meeting with Mark Antony somewhere in the vicinity (at that time Tarsus was linked to the sea by a lagoon which has since silted up).

From Cleopatra's Gate, go south to a roundabout flowing with fountains and turn right; a hundred metres west, the Cultural Centre (Kültür Merkezi) houses **Tarsus museum** (Tues–Sat 9am–5pm; 2YTL), with an unexplained mummified lower arm of a woman and the odd case of jewellery. Immediately opposite the museum and down a sidestreet is Cumhuriyet Alanı, where the **Antik Şehir** or "old city" has been exposed by excavations. A good section of black-basalt main street and associated stoas and temples lie well beneath present-day ground level.

Make your way through the backstreets to **St Paul's well**; you'll have to ask for "Sen Pol Kuyusu". It may be something of a disappointment, since it's just a borehole in the ground covered by a removable lid. However, as it's said to be on the site of St Paul's house, the steady stream of visitors gladly pay 2YTL for a sip of water from a bucket hauled up from the depths. North of the well, past the Hükümet Konağı (law courts), is a large mosque and local landmark known as **Makam Cami**. Opposite is the **Eski Cami**, a mosque that started life as a church, and, next door, the Roman baths.

From the Eski Cami it's a few minutes by dolmuş to **Şelale**, a waterfall in a park on the banks of the Tarsus Çayı, just within the town limits, with tea gardens and restaurants. On the hill above is a cave, **Eshabi Kehf** (unrestricted access), reputed to be home to seven sleepers, whose hands clutch Byzantine coins to enable them to buy bread when they awake. This legend is associated with St Paul and Mary Magdalene and repeated in Ephesus, her reputed final home. It's a hot trek up the signposted path that leads to the cave and, once there, there's not much to see save the view over town.

Practicalities

Tarsus's **otogar** is near Cleopatra's Gate, right in the town centre. **Accommodation** possibilities are limited, with the best budget option the *Cihan Palas Oteli* (℡0324/624 1623; ❷), 400m to the south, almost opposite the *otogar*; it has been decorated and modernized, and the air-conditioned rooms have fridges. Out of town, the monstrous *Tarsus Mersin Oteli* (℡0324/614 0600; ❺) overlooks the Şelale waterfall. It has its own pool and large air-conditioned rooms, and is often virtually empty, so you may be able to negotiate a substantial discount.

Adana

Forty kilometres east of Tarsus sprawls **ADANA**, Turkey's fourth largest city with 1.5 million inhabitants: a modern place, which has grown rapidly since the 1918–1920 French occupation. Today, as in the past, Adana owes much of its wealth to the surrounding fertile countryside of the Çukurova, with a textiles industry that has grown up on the back of the local cotton fields. It is also an important centre for the trade in gold.

Despite its contemporary, metropolitan feel, Adana has historical roots going back to 1000 BC. The arrival of the Greeks precipitated an on-off power struggle between them and the powerful Persian Empire to the east that was to last for a thousand years, ending only with the arrival of the Romans during the first century BC. Under the Romans the city became an important trading centre, afterwards passing through various hands before falling to the Ottomans during the sixteenth century. Despite all this, Adana has few sites of real interest, but if you are here between buses (it is an important communication hub) there is sufficient to keep you occupied for a few hours.

Arrival and information

Adana's **otogar** is located about 5km west of town on the E5 (referred to by many sources as Cemal Beriker Bulvarı). Frequent dolmuşes run from here to the town centre, and your bus company will probably lay on a *servis* minibus to their office in the centre (see "Listings", p.576). The city's **train station** is at the northern end of Atatürk Caddesi, about twenty minutes' walk north of the town centre, though there are dolmuşes from town. To get into town from the **airport**, 4km from the centre, don't take a cab from outside the door unless you want to pay double; instead, walk another 50m to the street and either catch a dolmuş into the centre

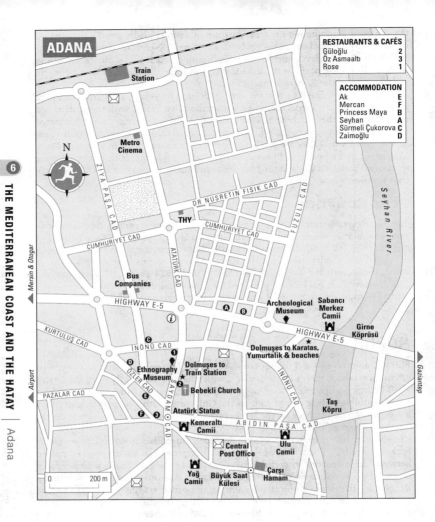

◄ Mersin & Otogar

◄ Airport

Gaziantep ►

or a normal cab. A THY shuttle bus leaves the city-centre THY office an hour and a half before departure, and there is (theoretically) a THY bus awaiting arrivals.

The local **tourist office** is at Atatürk Cad 13, near the roundabout junction with the E5 highway (Mon–Fri 8am–5pm; ☎0322/359 1994).

Accommodation

With a few exceptions, Adana's accommodation is uninspiring and tourists are a rare sight in the city's hotels. On and around Saydam Caddesi and Özler Caddesi, you'll find some cheap hotels, with mid-range places on İnönü Caddesi. The best options are listed below.

Ak Özler Cad 19 ☎0322/351 2603. Very basic rooms, some waterless, and carpets and curtains of dubious cleanliness, but undeniably cheap. ❶

🏃 **Mercan** Melek Girmez Çarşısı ☎0322/351 2603, ⓦwww.otelmercan.com. Very central and recently refurbished to an extremely high standard, soothing decor, air conditioning and pristine en-suite bathrooms. The owner is very affable, speaks good English (learned while at Manchester University) and can help point you in the right direction for places to eat. Highly recommended. ❸

Princess Maya Cemal Beriker Bul 14 ☎0322/459 0966, ⒻＦ459 7710. Only two minutes' walk from the museum, recently renovated, with a Neoclassical facade and rooms with all mod cons; rooms at the rear are much quieter. Will bargain out of season. ❻

Otel Seyhan Cemal Beriker Bul 18 (aka E5) ☎0322/457 5810, ⓦwww.otelseyhan.com.tr. Massive five-star, traditionally furnished rooms with all the facilities you'd expect including a pool, Jacuzzis, gym and a free film channel. ❻

Sürmeli Çukurova Özler Cad ☎0322/352 3600. Comfortable rooms with air conditioning, TV and nice bathrooms in a modern building. Luxuries include a decent sauna and well-stocked bar. ❽

Zaimoğlu Özler Cad 22 ☎0322/363 5353, ⒻＦ363 5363. Large, elegant rooms with air conditioning, TV and minibar. Friendly staff help make it a recommended option. ❻

The City

The city is divided, by the E5 Highway, into the swanky north, with its cinemas and designer malls, and the more traditional bustling south, with the markets, mosques and hotels of the old town. Traffic is uniformly helter-skelter and, as there are no pedestrian bridges or underpasses, you have to jaywalk to reach many of Adana's sights.

Start off with the **Archeological Museum** (Arkeolji Müzesi; Tues–Sun 8.30am–noon & 1–4.30pm; 2YTL) on the north side of the E5 Highway, containing predominantly Hellenistic and Roman statuary, plus some fine sarcophagi and Hittite statues. The **Sabancı Merkez Camii** next door – with a 28,500 capacity and the highest dome in Turkey – is the third largest mosque in the world and a testament to the continued strength of Islam in the southeast. It was built mainly by subscription, but finished with the aid of the Sabancı family, local boys made good and now the second richest family in Turkey.

One hundred metres southeast, the city's most substantial ancient monument is the **Taş Köprü**, an impressive sixteen-arched Roman bridge built by Hadrian to span the Seyhan river and still carrying heavy traffic. Not far from the bridge in the centre, the **Ulu Cami**, on Abidin Paşa Caddesi, was built in the Syrian style out of white and black marble in 1507, the sole legacy of Halil Bey, Emir of the Ramazanoğlu Turks, who ruled Adana before the Ottoman conquest. Inside the mosque, Halil Bey's tomb has some fine tile-work and beautiful mosaics.

South of Ulu Cami, the large clocktower, **Büyük Saat Kulesi**, is at the edge of a bazaar area, where the sound of metalworking echoes through the air. Nearby, **Çarşı Hamam** (see "Listings" overleaf), with a beautiful doorway, is reputed to date back to the time of Piri, son of Emir Halil Bey. Walking west towards the Atatürk statue, you'll see the **Yağ Cami**, accessed across a courtyard; unusually, one bay of the mosque was a church until it was incorporated into the main structure in 1502. A peculiar square building in the courtyard has an interesting domed roof supported by a line of slabs with Selçuk decoration; its original purpose is unknown. Another old building just off İnönü Caddesi, first a church, then a mosque, now houses the **Ethnography Museum** (Etnografya Müzesi; Tues–Sun 8.30am–noon, 1–4.30pm; 3YTL), full of carpets and weaponry, with a nomad tent and its contents as an added attraction.

If you are weary of the heat of the city, about 5km north of Adana is the **Seyhan Barajı**, a huge artificial lake along whose shores bathing (though not at the southern end due to strong currents) and sailing are permitted. It's a popular weekend retreat for overheated city-dwellers, who come here to picnic or enjoy the many fine lakeshore restaurants and bars. The reservoir supplies the area with fresh water, and there's a bird sanctuary immediately to the west. Dolmuşes marked "Baraj" or "Universite" go there from Füzulı Caddesi near the museum.

Eating and drinking

The local speciality is the spicy *Adana kebap* – minced lamb and pepper wrapped around a skewer and grilled – but frankly, you can eat better ones outside Adana. Pavement **food stalls** selling sandwiches and pastries abound, as do hole-in-the-wall *börek* and kebab places near the central PTT. The *Öz Asmaaltı*, on a sidestreet near the *Mercan* hotel, is a basic but clean, friendly kebab-oriented restaurant. The *Güloğlu* on Saydam Caddesi serves up tasty *börek* and *kır pide* at rock-bottom prices. The *Rose* **café**, next to the Ethnographic Museum, is also recommended, with beer and light food served in a friendly, homely atmosphere at reasonable prices.

Listings

Airlines THY, Prof Dr Nuşret Fişik Cad 22 (℡0322/457 0222), for flights to Ankara, İstanbul and İzmir; KTHY, Atatürk Cad (℡0322/363 1224), near the tourist office, has five direct flights to Cyprus per week. For flights to İstanbul and Ankara Onur Air's office is at the airport (℡0322/436 6756), while Atlas Jet's is at Toros Caddesi, Cemal Paşa Mah. Özlem apt 13/A, Seyhan (℡0322/444 0387).

Banks and exchange Most banks are located near the tourist office; Vakıf and Garanti banks have ATM machines. There are also several *döviz* offices around Saydam Cad and Özler Cad.

Buses Most of the major bus-company offices are concentrated on Ziya Paşa Cad, just north of the E5. When you want to leave town, buy a ticket from one of these and a *servis* bus will take you to the *otogar*, from where you can reach virtually every city in the country.

Car rental Avis, Ziyapaşa Bul, Nakipoglu Apt 9/A ℡0322/453 3045; Budget, Gazipaşa Bul 274, Sok

3/19 ℡0322/457 0754; Europcar, at the airport ℡0322/433 2957; and Talay Turizm, Gazipaşa Bul 46/B ℡0322/457 1712.

Cinemas Try the Metro, a couple of blocks south of the *otogar*.

Hamams Çarşı Hamam, Büyük Saat Civarı (daily: women 9.30am–3pm, men 5–11pm; 7–13YTL depending on level of service).

Hospital State Hospital (Adana Devlet Hastane) is on Riza Cad ℡0322/321 5752.

Newspapers and magazines Yolgeçen Kitabevi, 64 Atatürk Cad.

Post office The main PTT office (8.30am–9pm) is on Ulu Cami, the street running parallel to Abdin Paşa Caddesi, sells phone cards and jetons.

Shopping For foodstuffs, clothing and toiletries etc, head for Çetinkaya shopping arcade at the roundabout at the western end of İnönü Cad. Also try the huge Galeria Shopping Mall, nearby on Fuzulı Cad.

East of Adana

Heading east from Adana, towards İskenderun and Antakya (referred to as "Hatay" at the *otogar*), the first town you reach, after 20km, is **YAKAPİNAR** (also known as Misis), just south of the main road. This has a small **mosaic museum** (Tues–Sun 9am–5pm; 2YTL), worth a quick look for its examples of locally unearthed Roman mosaics. Beyond here you'll see an Armenian castle on top of a mountain, 3km to the south of the main road – the **Yılan Kalesi**, or "Snake Castle" (always open; 1YTL). If you're travelling with your own car, you can drive up to the top to admire the view of the meandering Ceyhan river.

About 12km further on is **CEYHAN**, which, despite the colourful-looking old houses in the town centre, doesn't rate more than a cursory look. About 40km east of Ceyhan the main road forks. Due east leads to Gaziantep and beyond, while the southern fork heads towards Antakya. The black basalt castle you can see towering above the road junction is **Toprakkale**, much fought over by the Armenians and Crusaders during medieval times, but abandoned since about 1337. You can visit Toprakkale, but be careful – much of it is very unstable and there are numerous concealed rooms and cisterns waiting for unwary people to fall into them.

Karatepe Arslantaş national park

If you have your own transport you might want to consider a seventy-kilometre detour to the **Karatepe Arslantaş national park** (Karatepe Arslantaş Milli Parkı), with its fine neo-Hittite stone-carvings. The route is via Osmaniye on the main highway, where you turn north, crossing the Ceyhan river and passing the columned Hellenistic ruins of Hierapolis Castabala, before following signs up to the green pines and turquoise waters of the park – the **Arslantaş dam** that surrounds Karatepe's stranded site provides the perfect venue for a picnic or a barbecue. Park your car at the entrance (2YTL) and walk up to the gatehouse where you will be sold a ticket (Tues–Sun 8.30am–noon & 2–5.30pm; 2YTL) and escorted on a tour of the site.

Karatepe is thought to have been a frontier castle or summer palace of the neo-Hittite king Asitawanda, whose capital at Pahri near modern Yakapınar reached its peak around the ninth century BC before finally being sacked by the Assyrians. Little of the building complex remains, but the eloquent stone-carvings arranged around the two entrance gates of the former palace are exquisite. The designs at the first gate depict sacrificial, hunting and feasting scenes, all guarded by sphinxes, horses and lions tattooed in hieroglyphics. The second gate has similar statues of winged sphinxes, one with eyes of ivory, and other fine carvings. Look out for a mini-pantheon of Hittite gods, including Bez the monkey god and a Hittite sun god. There is also a spread of more personal carvings in an almost cartoon style, including one of a woman suckling her child under a date tree.

Dörtyol and Yakacık

South of Toprakkale, the Antakya road is rather nondescript, and the first major town, **DÖRTYOL** ("crossroads"), does little to break the monotony. It was about 10km north of Dörtyol that Alexander the Great defeated the Persian king Darius at the **battle of Issus** in 333 BC. After being outmanoeuvred on the enclosed coastal plain, Alexander's army of about 35,000 took on a Persian force of over 100,000, but despite these unfavourable odds Alexander carried the day by personally leading an attack against Darius and his entourage. Darius panicked and fled, only narrowly avoiding capture (though he was forced to leave his wife and three children behind); Alexander's supply route was saved and the route south was opened up for him and his army. Today, the exact site of the engagement is uncertain, and the task of identifying it from contemporary accounts has been made harder by the fact that, due to earthquakes, the physical appearance of the landscape has changed over the intervening two thousand years.

At **YAKACIK** (Payas) about 10km south of Dörtyol, the little-visited **Sokullu Mehmet Paşa** complex, dating from the early sixteenth century, incorporates a *kervansaray* with kitchens and dining hall, a hamam half-walled in marble, a *medrese* and a mosque surrounding a courtyard where there's a huge gnarled olive tree rumoured to be as old as the mosque. A well-preserved former Genoese **fortress**, with views of the mountains from its battlemented walls, completes the complex.

The Hatay

The **Hatay**, which extends like a stumpy finger into Syria, is an Arab enclave and has closer cultural links with the Arab world than with the Turkish hinterland, and its multiethnic, multifaith identity gives it an extra edge of interest. **Antakya**, the largest town, is set in the valley of the Asi river separating the Nur and Ziyaret mountain ranges. The city, which dates back to Seleucid times, was an important centre under the Romans, and although little has survived from its ancient past, Antakya's cosmopolitan atmosphere, its excellent museum and great food make it worth a day or two on anyone's itinerary. The Hatay's other main centre is **İskenderun**, a heavily industrialized port that has more to offer than might appear at first sight.

The Hatay only became part of modern Turkey in 1939, having been apportioned to the French Protectorate of Syria following the dismemberment of the Ottoman Empire in the aftermath of World War I. Following the brief-lived independent **Hatay Republic** of 1938 it was handed over to Turkey after a plebiscite. This move, calculated to buy Turkish support, or at least neutrality, in the imminent world war, was successful. It was Atatürk, in a move to "Turkify" the region, who dreamt up the name "Hatay", supposedly based on that of a medieval Turkic tribe. The majority of people here speak Arabic as their first language and there's some backing for union with Syria, which in 1983 led to serious unrest in Antakya. For its part, Syria is keen to see the Hatay returned, or at least to use its avowed irredentist policy as a bargaining chip with Turkey. Tensions between the two countries eased considerably in 1998, when the Syrians expelled the PKK leader Abdullah Öcalan from Damascus and ended their covert support for the Kurdish rebels. Cross-border trade is steadily increasing following normalization of relations between the two countries – indeed links are now so good that the Bush administration chastized Turkey in 2006 for supporting a "terrorist"-harbouring nation.

In fact, Arab influence in the Hatay goes back to the seventh century AD, when Arab raiders began hacking at the edges of the collapsing Byzantine Empire. Although they were never able to secure long-lasting political control over the region, the Arabs were able to establish themselves as permanent settlers, remaining even when the Hatay passed into Ottoman hands. Prior to the arrival of the Arabs, the area had been held by the Romans and before that the Seleucids, who prized its position straddling trading routes into Syria.

İskenderun and around

İSKENDERUN was founded by Alexander the Great to commemorate his victory over the Persians at the nearby battle of Issus (see p.577) and, as Alexandria ad Issum, it became a major trade nexus during Roman times. Under the Ottomans, İskenderun became the main port for Halab (Aleppo), now in Syria, from where trade routes fanned out to Persia and the Arabian peninsula. The town was known as Alexandretta during the French-mandate era and is now essentially an industrial, military and commercial centre. Although there is little of historical interest left to see in İskenderun, the town centre is visually appealing, with its broad promenade and the magnificent backdrop of the Amanus mountains. A group of churches provides the main focus of a visit, while a trip to the nearby hill-town of Belen is rewarding for birdwatchers, lying as it does on a major migration route.

The Town

Traces of the town's cosmopolitan Levantine trading past survive amongst the new apartment buildings. The offices of the Catoni shipping line are housed in a crumbling nineteenth-century building just behind the seafront – the upstairs suite once housed the British vice-consulate and, though now abandoned, is still filled with 1930s furniture and a forlorn framed print of a young Queen Elizabeth II. The **Adliye Sarayı** (courtroom) at the junction of Şehit Pamir Caddesi and Atatürk Bulvarı is an imposing French-mandate-era building, neo-Oriental in style but sporting Lyon-made clocks in its twin towers.

İskenderun, like the rest of the Hatay, prides itself on its tolerance, a virtue that can be seen most clearly by visiting the town's churches. Smallest of these is the **Surp Karasun Manuk Ermeni Kilisesi**, situated on a sidestreet off Şehit Pamir Caddesi, more or less opposite the *Açıkalın Hotel*. Built in 1872, but very recently restored, this small, plainly decorated church serves an Armenian community of around eighty families. It's usually locked, though the key is held at an Armenian accounting business whose office is reached via a flight of steps to the right of the church – look for the sign *Serbest Musabeci*. A member of the family will be only too pleased to show you around.

Further away from the seafront, on the opposite side of Şehit Pamir Caddesi, is the pastel-coloured Greek Orthodox church of **St Nicholas**, built in 1876, while a little more difficult to find is the older, but smaller, whitewashed **St George's**, opposite the *jandarma* post on Denizciler Caddesi. This is the most atmospheric of the town's churches, with a walled garden of palm and cypress trees, in which gravestones bear inscriptions in Greek, Arabic and even French. Families live in houses adjoining both the Orthodox churches and they are usually willing to let you look around. The largest of İskenderun's churches is Catholic **St Mary's**, a substantial nineteenth-century building behind the tourist office.

Practicalities

Buses to all major towns, including Adana and Mersin, drop you at the *otogar*, a fifteen-minute walk north of the seafront. **Trains** also run daily to Adana and Mersin and are much safer but slower than the road. The station is 1km east of the town centre, reached by following 5 Temmuz Caddesi and then Bahçeli Sahil Evler Caddesi. Buses to Antakya leave hourly from Karaoğlanoğlu Caddesi, a twenty-minute walk back from the waterfront, following Şehit Pamir Caddesi, and take an hour.

The helpful local **tourist office**, at Atatürk Bul 49/B (Mon–Sat 8am–noon & 1–5pm; ☎0326/614 1620), is on the waterfront, a couple of hundred metres west of the junction of Şehit Pamir Caddesi and Atatürk Bulvarı. The manager speaks good English and will furnish you with a reasonable city guide, including a street plan locating the churches and train station.

Accommodation

Most of the town's cheaper **pansiyons and hotels** are centrally located. The best of the inexpensive places is the *Hotel Açıkalan*, Şehit Pamir Cad 13 (☎0326/617 3732; ❷), with clean and airy rooms including some good-value singles. Practically next door is the *Altındişler Oteli* (☎0326/617 1011; ❷) – slightly more upmarket, with primitive but still functioning air-conditioning in its plain but spacious rooms. The traditional rooms of the *Hotel Cabir* at Ulucami Cad 16 (☎0326/612 3391; ☎612 3393; ❸) are rather worn, but the service is good, the atmosphere friendly, and there's an American-style bar and a disco.

The best **restaurant** is the *Saray*, near the tourist office, with tables set out on the broad pavement. The *mezes* include *cevizli biber* (or *muhammara* in Arabic, a paste of walnuts, chilli peppers and wheat), tender grills for the main course and, of course, cold beer. The *Hasan Baba* at Ulucami Cad 43/E has excellent İskender *kebap* (which originates in Bursa, not here), while round the corner towards the *Hotel Açıkalan*, more *lokanta*s – such as the *Şehir* – serve cheap but tasty meals.

Café Körfez on Şehit Pamir Caddesi is good for **breakfasts**, including *menemen* (scrambled omelette with tomatoes). A hole-in-the-wall juice stand just up from the church of St Nicholas whips up delicious fresh juices; try the *Atom*, a local speciality mix of banana, milk, peach, cherry, apricot and pistachio. Several **patisseries** serve excellent *karışık dondurma* (mixed ice-cream decorated with loads of fruit) at ridiculously low prices. The promenade area is home to several *gazino*s where you can enjoy a beer overlooking the sea.

Belen

The road southeast from İskenderun rises up into the mountains, passing through the small hill-town of **BELEN**, 13km away. From here, the road strains and curves through the **Belen pass** (Belen Geçidi) – of great strategic importance during Roman times, when it was known as the *Pylae Syriae* or "Gates of Syria". For a week or two in early October (if the winds are right), Belen becomes the most important **migration route** on the western Palearctic corridor for birds of prey; an observation post has been recording sightings for the last few years and a photo safari is organized each year. If you want to witness the spectacle, get here early; after midday, all the birds have flown through. Unfortunately, the new motorway currently under construction, set to link the Hatay firmly with the rest of Turkey, will change the character of the pass.

About 5km beyond the Belen pass you'll come to a major road junction, from where a right turn leads towards Antakya. After a few kilometres a sign marks the road to **Bakras Kalesi**, an imposing medieval castle about 4km off the main road and a fifteen-minute climb from the village below. The first castle to be built on this site was erected by the Arabs during the seventh century and destroyed during the First Crusade. Later the Knights Templar built a new fortress, which became an important link in their defensive system, and which forms the basis of the impressive remains you see today. It was much fought over, and in 1156 a bloody battle took place here between the Templars and the soldiers of Thoros, ruler of Cilician Armenia. In 1188 the castle fell to Arabs but possession was fiercely contested until the Ottomans took over during the sixteenth century.

Antakya

ANTAKYA, 45km south of İskenderun, stands on the site of ancient Antioch and, although there's little sense of historical continuity, the city's laid-back pace, cosmopolitan outlook and subtly Arab atmosphere make it unique in Turkey. Flanked by mountains to the north and south, it sits in the bed of a broad river-valley planted with olive trees, providing a welcome visual relief after travelling from the drab flatlands surrounding Adana. Although little survives from the city's Seleucid and Roman past, it has enough attractions to merit at least an overnight stop, including an excellent archeological museum and an unusual cave-church from which St Peter is said to have preached. The food in Antakya is some of the most varied and best in Turkey, thanks to the city's Arab heritage.

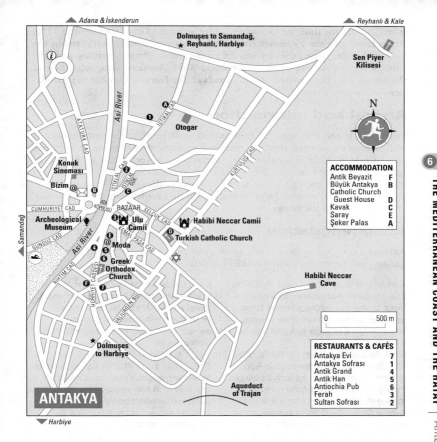

ANTAKYA

Adana & İskenderun

Reyhanlı & Kale

Dolmuşes to Samandağ,
★ Reyhanlı, Harbiye

Sen Piyer
Kilisesi

Asi River

ISTIKLAL CAD

Otogar

ATATÜRK CAD

KURTULUŞ CAD

N

Konak
Sineması

Bizim @

ISTIKLAL CAD

İSTİKLAL SOK

CUMHURIYET CAD

ATA
KÖPRÜSÜ

BAZAAR

SELÇUK CAD

ACCOMMODATION
Antik Beyazit   F
Büyük Antakya   B
Catholic Church
  Guest House   D
Kavak   C
Saray   E
Şeker Palas   A

Samandağ

Archeological
Museum

Asi River

GÜNDÜZ CAD

RIHTIM CAD

Ulu
Camii

KEMAL PAŞA CAD

Habibi Neccar Camii

Turkish Catholic Church

Moda

HÜRRIYET CADDESI

Greek
Orthodox
Church

YAVUZGÜN BUL

Habibi Neccar
Cave

0   500 m

★ Dolmuşes
to Harbiye

Aqueduct
of Trajan

RESTAURANTS & CAFÉS
Antakya Evi   7
Antakya Sofrası   1
Antik Grand   4
Antik Han   5
Antiochia Pub   6
Ferah   3
Sultan Sofrası   2

▼ Harbiye

Some history

The city was founded as Antioch in the fourth century BC by Seleucus Nicator, one of the four generals among whom the empire of Alexander the Great was divided. It soon grew into an important commercial centre and by the second century BC had developed into a multiethnic metropolis of half a million – one of the largest cities in the ancient world, a major staging-post on the newly opened Silk Road trade routes from the Mediterranean to Asia, and a centre of scholarship and learning. It also acquired a reputation as a centre for all kinds of moral excess, causing **St Peter** to choose it as the location of one of the world's first Christian communities in the hope that the new religion would exercise a restraining influence. Indeed, the patriarchy of Antioch became one of the five senior official positions in the early Christian Church's organization.

Despite being razed by a series of earthquakes during the sixth century AD, Antioch was able to maintain its prosperity after the Roman era, and only with the rise of Constantinople did the city begin to decline. In 1098 the Crusader kings Bohemond and Raymond took the city in the name of Christianity after a vicious eight-month siege and a savage massacre of Turks, imposing a Christian rule in Antioch that lasted until the city fell to the Mamluks of Egypt, who sacked it in 1268. By the time the Ottomans, under Selim the Grim, took over in 1516, Antioch had long since vanished from the main stage of world history, and by the turn of the last century the city was little more than a village, squatting amid the ruins of the ancient metropolis. After World War I, Antakya, along with most of the rest of the Hatay, passed into the hands of the French, who laid the foundations of the modern city.

Arrival and information

From the **otogar**, it's a ten- to fifteen-minute walk south to the town centre. As well as domestic services, there are regular daily departures to towns in Syria (see box on p.586), while buses also travel several times a week direct to Amman in Jordan, from where you can get to Israel and Saudi Arabia (though you need a transit visa to pass through Syria). Antakya's **tourist office** (Mon–Fri 8am–noon & 1–5pm; no phone) is rather inconveniently sited on a roundabout fifteen minutes' walk northwest of the bridge.

Accommodation

Antakya has a good range of hotels across every price range, including some uninspiring cheapies on and around İstiklâl Caddesi.

Antik Beyazit Hotel Hükümet Cad 4 ☎0326/216 2900. The town's most appealing hotel is this French colonial-style building, a restored former government building with well-furnished rooms. Unfortunately, it is no longer such good value as it was. ❻

Büyük Antakya Oteli Atatürk Cad 8 ☎0326/213 5860, ℻213 5869. Flashy four-star, with fussy, tastelessly furnished rooms, but worth the splurge if you're looking for an open-buffet breakfast boasting 45 different dishes, a bar or a disco. ❻

Catholic Church Guest House Kurtuluş Caddesi, Kutlu Sok 6 ✉dominicobertogli@hotmail.com. Accommodation for pilgrims with a shared kitchen. The rooms are high-ceilinged, comfortably furnished, and ranged around a shady courtyard. Very good value and peaceful – but you'll be expected to attend mass. The Italian *padre* is very friendly and has written a worthy history of Antakya. Summer ❷, winter ❹

Kavak Otel İstiklâl Cad 16 ☎0326/214 3530, ℻www.kavakotel.com. A good-value mid-range choice, with slightly fussy but immaculately clean rooms. The en-suite bathrooms sport glass-screened showers, and there's satellite TV and air conditioning. ❻

Hotel Saray Hürriyet Cad 3 ☎0326/214 9001, ℻214 9002. The best-value deal in Antakya with spotlessly clean rooms with TV and fans. Good views from the rear rooms over the old quarter and the hillside beyond, and a squawking parrot to keep you company at breakfast. ❸

Şeker Palas Oteli İstiklâl Cad 79 ☎0326/215 1603. A convenient choice just outside the *otogar*. Despite the spartan rooms and basic shared bathrooms, the hotel has a homely feel, with glass cabinets on each floor bursting with kitsch ornaments, and lovely old tiled floors. It is also very clean. Try to bag a rear room as they are much quieter. ❶

The City

Antakya is cut in two by the **Asi river**, known in ancient times as the Orontes. Once a sizable river, it's now a brown and sluggish shadow of its former self, its flow depleted by water backed up in dams and drawn off for irrigation. The eastern bank is home to **old Antakya** – a maze of narrow streets, backed by the rocky cliffs of the Ziyaret Dağı range (ancient Mount Sipylus). It's well worth spending an hour or two wandering around the bazaar and market areas north of Kemal Paşa Caddesi (running from west to east just north of the Ata Köprüsü). The **Kurşunlu Han**, incorporated in the bazaar, offers a shady courtyard for a tea stop. At the edge of the bazaar close to the bridge, the **Ulu Cami** mosque is an early Ottoman construction with a squat minaret. Far more recent is the **Gunduz** building, at the western end of the Ata Köprüsü. Resembling a typical 1930s suburban cinema (and now used as a porn cinema), with its graceful curves, geometric friezes and porthole windows, it was actually the Parliament building of the short-lived **Hatay Republic**. There are plans to turn it into a cultural centre and house the tourist office there.

At the junction of Kemal Paşa Caddesi and Kurtuluş Caddesi is the **Habibi Naccar Camii**, a mosque incorporated into the shell of a former Byzantine church, which was in turn built on the site of an ancient temple. The distinctive pointed minaret was added during the seventeenth century and is not – as you might be tempted to imagine – a former church tower. Over a kilometre to the east of here, in the hillside above the town, is the **Habibi Neccar cave** (Habibi Neccar Mağrası), a minor Muslim holy place that was once home to a solitary prophet. Habibi Naccar was violently done to death by the Christians; his head is said to be entombed under the mosque, his body in the cave.

The Hatay has a long history of tolerance, and some 4000 Christians live in the region, 1500 of them in Antakya itself. The majority are **Greek Orthodox**, and their substantial nineteenth-century church in Antakya is on Hükümet Caddesi, and contains some beautiful Russian icons. The **Catholic church**, just off Kurtuluş Caddesi, is built around a pretty courtyard filled with orange trees and the resident Italian nun is very friendly. Antakya is also home to a **Protestant church**, established by a Korean mission and housed in the imposing former French Consulate building. Links between Turkey and Korea go back to the 1950s, when Turkish troops formed part of the NATO forces ranged against the Communists. Not far from the Catholic church, on Kurtuluş Caddesi, is a small **synagogue** much visited by Israeli tourists, but identifiable only by the Star of David above its inconspicuous doorway.

The Archeological Museum

From the Ata Köprüsü, it's a quick hop across to the western side of the river and the **Archeological Museum** (Arkeoloji Müzesi; Tues–Sun 8.30am–noon & 1.30–5pm; 5YTL), whose collection of locally unearthed Roman mosaics ranks among the best of its kind in the world. Imaginatively lit and well laid out in the first four rooms of the museum, they are in a state of near immaculate preservation – bar the odd bare patch where the *tesserae* have fallen off – and mostly depict scenes from Greco-Roman mythology.

The majority were unearthed at the suburb of Daphne (now Harbiye), which was Antioch's main holiday resort in Roman times, and this is reflected in the sense of leisured decadence that pervades many of the scenes. A good example is the charming **Narcissus and Echo** (room 2, no. 3), which depicts Narcissus gazing admiringly into a pool of water, in love with his own reflection, as an unrequited Echo looks on in sadness. One of the finest in terms of size and scope is the so-called **Buffet Mosaic** (no. 4), a vivid depiction of the rape of Ganymede, abducted by Zeus in the form of an eagle, and a banquet scene showing different courses of fish, ham, eggs and artichokes. Memorable images in room 3 include bouncing baby **Hercules** strangling the serpents sent to kill him by jealous Hera (no. 4), and a fascinating depiction of the **Evil Eye** – a superstition that still has remarkable resonance in modern Turkey – being attacked by a raven, dog, scorpion, snake, centipede, panther, sword and trident as a horned goblin looks away (no. 6). Room 4 continues with an inebriated Dionysos, too drunk to stand (no. 12); Apollo capturing Daphne as her clothes conveniently fall off (no. 14); Orpheus surrounded by animals entranced by the beauty of his music (no. 23); and a fine portrait of **Thetis and Oceanus** (no. 24), the latter recognizable by the lobster claws protruding from his wet hair, one of many water-inspired motifs that decorated the floors of public and private baths.

△ Sen Piyer Kilisesi, Antakya

After the mosaics, the rest of the museum seems a little mundane, with only a couple of first-century AD statues of Venus in the entrance hall, a fine statue of Hades and Cerberus in the penultimate hall, and some Hittite and Assyrian reliefs and idols recovered from funeral mounds on the Amık plain, to write home about. Among the last, look out for the two stone lions, which were used as column pediments during the eighth century BC.

Sen Piyer Kilisesi

At the northeastern edge of Antakya is the **Sen Piyer Kilisesi** (Tues–Sun 8am–noon & 1.30–6pm; 5YTL), the famous cave-church of St Peter, from which it's said that the apostle preached to the Christian population of Antioch. It's reached by following Kurtuluş Caddesi in a northeasterly direction for about 2km until you come to a signposted right turn. Follow the road towards the mountains and after about five minutes' drive you come to the church, set into the hillside just above. It's about a forty-minute walk, or you can catch a dolmuş on Kurtuluş Caddesi, which will take you as far as the turn-off.

Whether St Peter really did preach from the Sen Piyer Kilisesi is – like the exact dates of his stay in the city – open to question. All that theologians seem to be able to agree on is that he spent some time in Antioch between AD 47 and 54, founding one of the world's first Christian communities with Paul and Barnabas. Indeed, the church must have been one of the first ever built and quite possibly the place where the term "Christian" was first heard (in other parts of the Middle East Christians were known as "Nazarenes"). Inside, water drips down the cave walls and the cool atmosphere provides a welcome break from the heat of summer. Beneath your feet you'll be able to discern traces of **mosaic** thought to date from the fifth century AD, while to the right of the altar is a kind of font set in the floor and fed by a spring with reputed curative properties. Left of the altar is a blocked tunnel down which the early Christians could flee in the event of a raid. A special **service** is held here on June 29 to mark the anniversary of St Peter's death, attended by members of Antakya's small Christian community, while Sunday afternoon Mass is held every week at the tiny Catholic church on Kurtuluş Caddesi.

Neatly incorporated into walling around the church are a few **sarcophagi**, and if you follow the new path around to the left of the church for 200m and then clamber up the hillside, you'll find a relief thought by some to be of Charon, ferryman of the River Styx at the entrance to the underworld – though the portrait is more likely the face of a veiled woman, with a tiny man (probably the second-century BC Seleucid emperor Antiochus Epiphanes IV) perched on her shoulder. With your own transport it's possible to drive the 15km – along Kurtuluş Caddesi and around the back of Mount Sipylus – up to the ruined *kale* (castle), from where there are fine views over the city.

Eating and drinking

Antakya's food is wonderful and shows its Arab influence with many **regional specialities.** Starters include *muhammara*, a fiery puree of walnuts, hot pepper and wheat; hummus, usually served topped with melted butter, pine nuts and hot pepper; *Şam oruğu*, an egg-shaped case containing minced meat and walnuts; *içli köfte*, similar but without walnuts; *bakla*, a puree of broad beans, garlic, tahini, olive oil, red pepper, cumin, lemon juice and parsley; and *tarator*, a tasty mix of tahini, walnuts and yoghurt. Main courses include *İspanak Borani*, a soup-like stew of spinach, chick peas, shredded meat, yoghurt and lemon juice; *serimsek börek*, a sort of chicken-filled samosa; and *kağıt kebap*, kebabs cooked in greased-paper packages. Sweets include *künefe*, a shredded wheat and soft, mild cheese concoction, baked in the oven and served soaked in syrup, and *Haleb Burması* (Aleppo roll), a sweet confection stuffed with pistachios, which makes a welcome change from *baklava*. Another dessert is a combination of *kabak tatlısı* (a kind of crystallized, sweet pumpkin), *ceviz reçeli* (sweet pickled walnuts), served drizzled with tahini and topped with ground pistachio and walnut.

Antakya Evi Silahlı Kuvvetler Cad. Antakya's best eating place, its intimate, upstairs rooms of a nineteenth-century townhouse tastefully restored. The food is excellent and a full meal with beer should cost no more than 14YTL/€9. A speciality is the Antioch *kebap*, a *köfte* of minced lamb stuffed with cheese, walnuts and olives.

Antakya Sofrası İstiklâl Cad 6, Ada Çarşısı. Tucked away amongst backstreets specializing in furniture retailing, this is Antakya's best-kept secret. Home-cooked food includes unusual dishes such as *biberli ekmek*, a kind of spicy chapati spread with garlic, chilli and other spices, and *doyme*, a stew of meat and soaked whole grains of wheat spiced with cumin. The stuffed vegetables are delicious, and all meals are served with a (free) heap of mint-strewn salad. A full meal won't set you back more than a bargain 4YTL, but the place closes early evening.

Antik Grand Hürriyet Cad. Smart first-floor place and good value, with hummus and *muhammara* at 2.5YTL a portion, the usual range of kebabs at 5YTL, and pizzas for the same price. Can be soulless when not busy.

Antik Han Hürriyet Cad. The unprepossessing exterior hides a walled garden courtyard and rooftop terrace. This is the place the

locals come to drink *rakı* and beer, so the *mezes* are particularly good (the hummus is a meal in itself, or try the *muhammara*) and the *ızgara* (grills) better than average. Check the cost before ordering, though, as the menu lacks a price list, and there's a ten-percent service charge.

Antiochia Pub Hürriyet Cad. The downstairs bar caters largely to off-duty businessmen and merchants, the upstairs to the well-heeled young. It's a smart place but Efes is reasonably priced at 3YTL, imported beers are a little more.

Ferah Just down from the Ulu Cami. A long-established pudding shop, this is one of the best places to try the ubiquitous *künefe*.

Sultan Sofrası İstiklâl Cad 20. Serves all the regional dishes, including delicious *ıspanaklı katıklı ekmek* (like an Indian paratha) and *asır*, a stew of chickpeas, meat and wheat. Prices are a little higher than the competition (main courses from 5–9YTL), and it's much favoured by tour groups, but the food and service are outstanding.

Zeynel Üstanın Köprübaşı Büfe Alley off Kemal Paşa Caddesi. Tiny place with two items on the menu: hummus at 1.5YTL a portion, and *bakla* (see above) for the same price. A great place for a cheap and authentic Hatay lunch.

Crossing into Syria

A number of bus companies operating out of Antakya offer services to cities in Syria; the best operator is Has, whose buses for Halab (Aleppo) depart from the *otogar* at 9am daily (6YTL) and take three hours, while those for Şam (Damascus) depart at noon (10YTL) and take seven hours. Another reputable company is Güney. Buses cross the border to the east of Antakya at Cilvegözü/Baba al Hawa, and delays can be considerable. Given massively improved relations between Turkey and Syria, far more people are crossing the border, and Turks are beginning to take day-trips from Antakya to Halab. A quicker option to Halab might be to get a dolmuş to Reyhanlı and then make your own way by shared taxi to the border, 5km away, from where you can pick up an onward Syrian microbus. There is also a daily bus to Laskiye (Latakia; 8YTL) on the Syrian coast. It's also possible to take a bus from Antakya's Köy Garajı (village bus-garage) to the customs post 5km beyond Yayladağ (13YTL) and from there cross into Syria.

There are several other border crossings between Turkey and Syria, and the following departure points are all covered in Chapter 11. From Gaziantep, take a dolmuş to Kilis (1hr), from where you can take a shared taxi (€25 for the vehicle) to Halab. It is also possible, in theory, to take a dolmuş from Urfa to Akçakale (1hr), walk across the frontier, and take a taxi to Abiyat, and then onto Halab or Damascus. From Nusaybin (near to Mardin) it is again possible to walk across the border, to Kamışlı, and then on to other Syrian destinations.

For some nationalities it may be possible to obtain the Syrian visa on the border, but you would be well advised to enquire at the Syrian embassy in your home country before departure. Obtaining a visa from the Syrian embassy in Ankara can be time-consuming and expensive. You may also have to name the border you intend to use in advance.

Listings

Banks and exchange There are several banks on İstiklâl and Atatürk cads, and you can change money at the weekends at the *döviz* on Kurtuluş Cad.

Car rental From Titus Turizm, under the *Büyük Antakya Oteli*, Atatürk Cad 8 ☎0326/613 4232.

Cinema Konak Sineması, 100m east of the Ata Köprüsü, behind the PTT, has four screens showing first-run Western movies.

Hospital The Devlet Hastane (State Hospital) is a couple of kilometres southeast of the centre.

Internet Modanet, on Hürriyet Cad, and Bizim,

between the PTT and the Konak Sineması, on the west bank of the river.

Police Selçuk Cad; emergency number for foreigners is ☎0326/213 5953.

Post office The PTT is northwest of the roundabout at the western end of the Ata Köprüs (daily 9am–8pm).

Swimming There's an open-air pool on Gunduz Cad (summer daily 10am–3pm; 2YTL) with lockers where you can leave your gear if you are heading out on an evening bus.

West of Antakya

There are a number of interesting places to visit in the fertile, hilly countryside to the west of Antakya. The **Saint Simeon monastery** is the most renowned destination, while other local sights can be visited from the nearby resort of **Samandağ**. If you want to see all of the places in a day from Antakya, it's worth renting a car or taking a taxi and driver, as public transport is limited.

Saint Simeon monastery

One of the more bizarre aspects of early Christianity was the craze for pillar sitting, which developed in Antioch during the fourth century. The trend was started by Simeon Stylites the Elder, whose basilica still stands at Qala'at Samaan near Halab in Syria, and was perfected by **Simeon Stylites the Younger**, whose **monastery** perches on a high ridge southwest of Antakya, 7km south of the road to Samandağ.

Simeon the Younger first chained himself to a rock in the wilderness in an act of ascetic retreat and then ascended progressively higher pillars before reaching a final height of some thirteen metres. He lived chained to the top of this pillar for 25 years, meditating and making sporadic pronouncements castigating the citizens of Antioch for their moral turpitude. The base of the pillar still remains, surrounded by the complex octagonal layout of the monastery that grew up around Simeon as he began to attract growing numbers of curious pilgrims eager to share in his enlightenment. About 250 followers mounted pillars of their own throughout the Middle East. Just south of the pillar you can still see the steps that pilgrims would climb to gain audience with the holy man. It's possible to climb on top of the diminutive pillar, which is just wide enough to lie down on and reap the same views of the Orontes valley and of Mount Cassius looming out of the Mediterranean that Simeon must have enjoyed over fifteen centuries ago.

To reach the monastery, turn south off the main Antakya–Samandağ road at **Uzunbağ**, just past Karaçay. Continue uphill along a good road for about 4km, before branching off to the right, by a white Muslim shrine, and following a bad dirt track for another couple of kilometres. There is no public transport at all to the monastery, but you should be able to find a taxi in Karaçay willing to take you.

Samandağ

About 25km southwest of Antakya, **SAMANDAĞ** is an Arabic-speaking resort town of about 30,000 people. The town is currently undergoing something of a building boom, financed in part by local boys made good in the Gulf, displaying their newfound wealth with gaudy villas and four-wheel-drive utility vehicles. It is served by regular dolmuşes from Antakya *otogar*, which will deposit you in the town's unprepossessing centre, a couple of kilometres inland. Here you'll find a few shops and restaurants and a couple of banks. To get to the **beach**, take any dolmuş heading for "Deniz" (the sea) – although swimming here is not really recommended because of pollution from İskenderun, 50km or so up the coast.

Vakıflı

The tiny village of **VAKİFLİ**, with its apparently unremarkable mix of dilapidated mudbrick and timber houses and modern concrete villas, is in fact unique. For this is Turkey's sole surviving **Armenian village**, set amidst orange groves on the lush lower slopes of Musa Dağı. Armenian settlement of this region is said to predate that of neighbouring Cilicia. At the heart of the village is the recently restored and extended **Surp Asdvadzadzin Kilisesi**, to which the village *muhtar* (headman) has the key, though the church is not always locked. The congregation is made up of the 32 Armenian families who live here year-round (though the population swells in summer when relatives and friends descend from the Armenian community in İstanbul). During the Turkish deportations and massacres of the Armenians in 1915 the inhabitants of Vakıflı, along with the Armenian population of five nearby villages, held out against the Turkish forces until they were evacuated to Port Said by French and British warships. Most of the villagers returned in 1919 when the

Hatay became part of French-mandated Syria. It wasn't until the Hatay joined the Turkish Republic in 1939 that the Armenians, bar the inhabitants of Vakıflı, decided to leave, most of them ending up in Lebanon's Bekaa valley.

Dolmuşes from Samandağ travelling the six or so kilometres to the village don't tend to leave till mid-afternoon (after the villagers have travelled into Samandağ and completed their shopping and errands), so it is best reached with your own transport or by taxi. If you do choose to visit the village, remember that it is a living community and not a mere curiosity.

Çevlik

A few kilometres north of Samandağ is the village of **ÇEVLIK**, easily reached by dolmuş from Samandağ town centre. In ancient times, Çevlik was the port of **Seleucia ad Piera**, serving Antioch, and it is from here that Paul and Barnabus are thought to have set off on their first evangelical mission to Cyprus. There are still a few ruins scattered around, including the 130-metre-long **Titus ve Vespasiyanus Tüneli** (open dawn–dusk; 2YTL), a huge channel carved out of the hillside to prevent flooding and silting of the harbour. It's usually easy to find someone who will assist you to scramble around the huge gorge-like site (expect to leave a tip); two inscriptions at the upper end give details of its construction. Also scattered around you'll see foundations, sections of ruined wall and Roman tombs. Swimming is probably unwise, although the village beach is popular with local fishermen.

Çevlik has a few *pansiyon*s and a campsite, and you can also camp on the beach, although strictly speaking this is illegal and you might get moved on.

South: Harbiye and the road to Syria

About 10km south of Antakya is **HARBIYE**, the ancient and celebrated suburb of Daphne, a beautiful gorge to which revellers and holiday-makers flocked in Roman times, drawn by shady cypress and laurel groves dotted with waterfalls and pools. Those who could afford to built villas here, while lesser mortals had to content themselves with a day-trip. Today, Antakya's modern citizens follow their example, while Arab tourists have their summer residences in the village. To get there, flag down a dolmuş in Antakya (travelling southwest along Kurtuluş Caddesi), but note that the gorge is really not worth visiting unless the heat in Antakya is absolutely unbearable or you have been invited by the locals to join in a picnic.

The Romans built a temple to Apollo here, since it was generally held to be the setting for the god's pursuit of Daphne. According to the myth, Daphne, when seized by amorous Apollo, prayed for deliverance; in answer to her prayers, Peneus transformed her into a laurel tree. Another legend relates that the resort was the venue of Paris's gift of the golden apple to Aphrodite, indirectly precipitating the Trojan War. Later, and with possibly more basis in fact, Mark Antony and Cleopatra are said to have been married here. Harbiye was also home of the Antioch Games, which were in their day more spectacular than the ancient Olympics, and a haven for escaped slaves and prostitutes, who ran a brisk trade among the laurels. In later years local Christians pulled down the temple of Apollo and used its stone to build their churches. With the departure of the Romans the place went into decline, a process compounded by the destructive attacks of the Persians and Arabs during the sixth and seventh centuries. Now Harbiye is famous for Defne soap, made from the fruit of the laurel tree and doubling as shampoo.

From the dolmuş drop-off point follow a road past modern houses until you come to a waterfall. From here, a litter-strewn path runs down into the gorge, where a number of shady and shabby tea gardens and trout **restaurants** (but not much else) await amid a landscape that has been constantly eroded by the river since Roman times.

About 8km south of Harbiye lies **Qalat az Zaw**, a ruined fortress originally built to defend the southern approaches to Antioch and much fought over by Crusaders, Arabs and Mamluks. Twenty-odd kilometres further on, close to the Syrian border, is the village of **YAYLADAĞI**, a quiet spot that has a pleasant picnic area, set in mountain woods down towards the frontier – a good point for a break if you're en route to the border itself.

Travel details

Trains

Adana to: Ankara (1 daily, overnight; 14hr); Gaziantep (4 weekly; 3hr); İskenderun (3 daily; 2hr 30min); Mersin (6 daily; 1hr 15min).
İskenderun to: Adana (3 daily; 2hr 30min); Mersin (3 daily; 3hr 30min).
Mersin to: Adana (6 daily; 1hr 15min).

Buses and dolmuşes

Adana to: Adıyaman (7 daily; 6hr); Alanya (8 daily; 10hr); Ankara (hourly; 10hr); Antalya (5 daily; 12hr); Diyarbakır (5 daily; 10hr); Gaziantep (8 daily; 4hr); Kahta (2 daily; 7hr); Kayseri (3 daily; 7hr); Konya (hourly; 7hr); Malatya (3 daily; 8hr); Şanlıurfa (4 daily; 6hr); Van (1 daily; 18hr).
Alanya to: Adana (8 daily; 10hr); Ankara (8 daily; 10hr); Antalya (every 30min; 2hr); Diyarbakır (3 daily; 14hr); İstanbul (4 daily; 18hr); Konya (3 daily; 8hr); Mersin (8 daily; 9hr); Samsun (1 daily; 24hr); Silifke via Taşucu (8 daily; 7hr).
Antakya to: Adana (hourly; 3hr); Aleppo, Syria (4 daily; 4hr); Amman, Jordan (3 weekly; 12hr); Ankara (1 daily, 13hr); Antalya (3 daily; 14hr); Damascus, Syria (2 daily; 8hr); Gaziantep (8 daily; 5hr); İskenderun (hourly; 1hr); İstanbul (4 daily; 22hr); Riyadh, Saudi Arabia (3 weekly; 20hr); Samandağ (hourly; 1hr); Şanlıurfa (daily; 8hr).
Antalya *otogar* to: Adana (several daily; 11hr); Afyon (hourly, 5hr); Alanya (hourly; 2hr); Ankara (24hr service; 10hr); Antakya (3 daily; 14hr); Denizli (6 daily; 5hr 30min); Diyarbakır (3 daily; 16hr); Eğirdir (9 daily; 3hr); Fethiye, by inland route (6 daily; 4hr); Isparta (hourly; 2hr 30min); İstanbul (24hr service; 12hr); İzmir (6 daily; 9hr 30min); Konya (8 daily; 5hr 30min).
Antalya (Devlet Hastane roundabout) to all destinations southwest of Antalya: Camyuva (10 daily; 1hr 20min); Fethiye by coastal route (7 daily;

8hr); Finike (9 daily; 2hr); Kalkan (9 daily; 5hr); Kaş (9 daily; 4hr 30min); Kemer/Beldibi/Göynük (every 30min; 1hr); Tekirova/Phaselis (10 daily; 1hr 30min).
İskenderun to: Adana (5 daily; 2hr 30min); Antakya (hourly; 1hr); Antalya (4 daily; 13hr).
Silifke to: Adana (every 15–20min; 2hr); Alanya (8 daily; 7hr); Antalya (8 daily; 9hr); Konya (12 daily; 5hr); Mersin (every 20min; 2hr).

Ferries

Mersin to: Mağosa/Famagusta, North Cyprus (3 weekly; 10hr), with an onward service to Syria during summer. Tickets cost €26 one way for foot passengers, cars €56.
Taşucu to: Girne/Kyrenia, North Cyprus (daily except Fri & Sat; 6hr). One-way tickets cost €35, cars €62.

Hydrofoils

Alanya to: Girne/Kyrenia, North Cyprus (twice weekly; 3hr 30min). €40 one way.
Taşucu to: Girne/Kyrenia, North Cyprus (daily; 2hr 30min). Tickets cost €37.50 one way.

Flights

Turkish Airlines:

Adana to: Ankara (2 daily; 1hr); İstanbul (6 daily; 1hr 15min); İzmir (3 weekly; 1hr 30min); Lefkoşa/Nicosia, North Cyprus (5 weekly; 1hr).
Antalya to: Ankara (2 daily; 1hr); İstanbul (6 daily).

Onur Air

Adana to: İstanbul (3 daily; 1hr 30min).
Antalya to: İstanbul (3 daily; 1hr).

Atlas Jet

Adana to: İstanbul (Mon–Fri 2 daily; 1hr 30min);
İzmir via İstanbul (Mon–Fri 2 daily; 3hr 30min);
Trabzon via İstanbul (MonFri 1 daily; 3hr 40min);
Van via İstanbul (Mon–Fri 1 daily; 4hr 40min).

Antalya to: İstanbul (at least 5 daily; 1hr 10min);
Trabzon via İstanbul (1 daily except Sat; 4hr 5min);
Van via İstanbul (1 daily except Mon & Sat; 4hr
30min).

South Central Anatolia

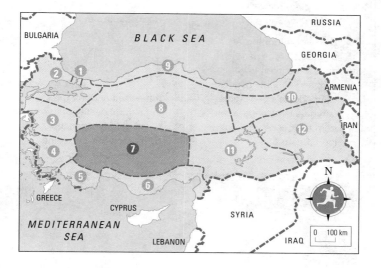

CHAPTER 7

Highlights

✳ **St Paul Trail** Follow in the footsteps of the renowned missionary over the Toros mountains to stunning Lake Eğirdir. See p.608

✳ **Eğirdir** Eat fillets of crisply fried lake-fish as the sun sets over Lake Eğirdir. See p.602

✳ **Whirling dervishes, Konya** Watch the dervishes whirl each December in their spiritual home. See p.618

✳ **Hot-air ballooning** An unforgettable experience – the interplay of light and shadow over Cappadocia's geological fairy-tale landscape, seen from the basket of a balloon. See p.634

✳ **Göreme Open-Air Museum** The frescoes inside Göreme's cave-churches are a vibrant reminder of the region's Christian past. See p.639

✳ **Esbelli Evi** Immaculately run hotel, elegantly fashioned from a series of old village houses located high above the Cappadocian town of Ürgüp. See p.647

✳ **Mustafapaşa** One of Cappadocia's most attractive villages sports a wonderful concentration of old Greek houses. See p.649

✳ **Ihlara valley** Don't miss the natural beauty of this fertile gorge, enhanced by its rock-cut Byzantine churches. See p.658

△ Building in Mustafapaşa

South Central Anatolia

The **central Anatolian plateau** seems at first sight to be an unpromising prospect. A large area around the lake of Tuz Gölü is virtual desert, while much of the central plateau is steppe, suitable only for the grazing of livestock. During summer, water is scarce except in the river valleys and in areas that have been artificially irrigated, and in winter the region is blitzed by cold and heavy snowfall.

Turkey's **Lakeland**, the region south of **Afyon** and west of **Konya**, has been largely ignored by the Turkish tourist industry. Stretches of azure and silver waters stand out against the grey plateau, or appear suddenly between mountains to startling effect. Many of them, like **Çavuşçu Göl** or **Acı Göl**, have a high salt content, which discourages aquatic life and human settlement alike; others are avoided by would-be settlers as their flat shores are liable to flood. But around the main plateau, forest cloaks the slopes of the mountains around the western lakes of **Beyşehir**, **Eğirdir** and **Burdur**. The residents of their namesake towns, and of the small community on the banks of **Akşehir Gölü**, manage to make a tenuous living out of fishing or reed cutting, while Eğirdir's erstwhile fishermen now earn their livelihoods running simple *pansiyon*s for an ever increasing number of visitors.

To the east of the lakes, the plateau rises gradually towards the highlands. **Tuz Gölü** to the north is little more than a vast salt-producing basin, and aridity in the region is increased by the underground dissipation of water. The light forest that once covered this land was destroyed between 5000 and 1000 BC by herds of livestock that grazed the steppe.

Despite the inhospitable nature of this region, it has been populated as long as anywhere in Anatolia. From the early Paleolithic age man was drawn to the lakes, which provided a livelihood for primitive hunters and fishermen, and during the Bronze Age the **Hittites**, a race who once rivalled the Egyptians, chose the plateau as their homeland. By the early historical period, northern Lakeland had been settled by the **Pisidians**, mountain people with a reputation for fierce independence who worked as mercenaries throughout the eastern Mediterranean. Their strategically situated settlements were difficult to subdue, and Xenophon described them as obstinate troublemakers, who managed to keep their towns independent despite the encroachments of the Persian Empire.

Further east, the area between the extinct volcanoes of **Erciyes Dağ** and the Melendiz range is **Cappadocia**, whose legacy of compacted lava-ash soil is

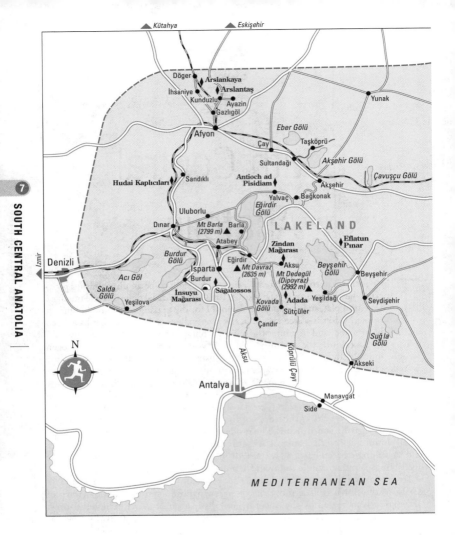

favourable to vine growing and horse breeding. Water and wind have created a land of fantastic forms from the soft rock known as tuff, including forests of cones, table mountains, canyon-like valleys and castle-rocks, all further hewn and shaped by civilizations that have found the region particularly sympathetic to their needs. Rainfall is low, but Cappadocia is nevertheless extremely fertile compared to the rest of South Central Anatolia, and it became an important crossroads and home to a politically autonomous state between the third and first centuries BC. From the seventh to the eleventh centuries AD, it was a place of refuge during Arab and Turkish invasions into the steppe. Today its churches and dwellings carved from the rock, particularly by monastic communities, and its unearthly landscapes make an irresistible tourist draw.

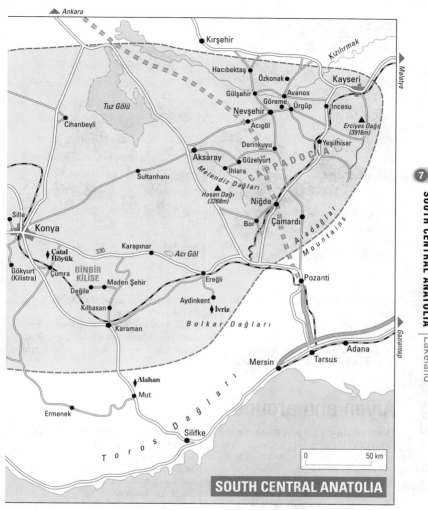

Lakeland

After years of isolation, Turkish **Lakeland** is just beginning to be discovered by plant enthusiasts, birdwatchers, trekkers and winter-sports aficionados. Other tourists, meanwhile, stop off here at **Eğirdir** on the route from Cappadocia and Konya to the south coast around Antalya or Fethiye. At present, facilities are unevenly spread and not luxurious, but the various Lakeland attractions make it ideal for quiet, unhurried holidays away from the seething coastal resorts. As well as the eye-catching **lakes** themselves, there are the remains of Pisidian cities to

△ Lake Eğirdir

see (most impressively at **Sagalassos** and **Antioch ad Pisidiam** near Yalvaç), and largely unspoilt provincial towns, notably **Ayfon**, to explore.

Access to the lakes is from Antalya in the south, over the Taurus range to Isparta; from the plains of Konya in the east, over the Sultan Dağları to Eğirdir; and from Eskişehir or Kütahya in the north via the main north–south road to Afyon and Isparta. All routes are well served by buses.

Afyon and around

Dominated by a tall and imposing rock on which stands a powerful ancient citadel, **AFYON** certainly leaves a vivid impression. The town remains impressive on closer inspection: it is clean and relaxed, retaining much interesting Ottoman architecture as well as a number of attractive mosques. A few reasonably priced hotels make it a good choice for a night's stopover en route to the lakes, and there are several interesting side-trips that can be made from town.

In honour of the fortress, and the 200-metre-high dark rock on which it's built, the city until recently bore the resounding name of Afyon Karahisar, or "**Opium Black Fortress**". The rock is believed to have first been fortified by the Hittite king Mursil II, and remains have also been found dating to the Phrygian era. The Romans and Byzantines – who called the city Akronium or "High Hill" – also occupied the city, the Byzantines building the greater part of the present-day fortress, which was subsequently used as an imperial treasury by both Selçuks and Ottomans.

For three weeks leading up to August 26, 1922, Afyon was Atatürk's headquarters, prior to the last, decisive battle of the independence war, fought against the Greeks at nearby Dumlupınar. The town's statue commemorating the Turkish victory – depicting one naked man towering over another in an attitude of victory – is one of the most moving memorials to Atatürk.

Today, Afyon is a relative backwater, noted for its production of *sucuk* (sausage), *pastırma* (pastrami) and *kaymak* (clotted cream) – and its role as a stronghold of fundamentalists and right-wing nationalists. When Elia Kazan, the noted American film-maker of Anatolian-Greek descent, was looking for a location in western Asia Minor in the mid-1980s to shoot a historical extravaganza, he approached the city fathers for permission to use Afyon's exquisite old town as the setting – and was told in no uncertain terms to go elsewhere.

The Town

The best way of establishing what's where on arrival is to head for the highest point in town: the **fortress** on its 226-metre-high black monolith, which is scaled via some 700 steps on the southern face of the rock (a twenty-minute hike best avoided in the heat of the day). On the way up look out for hoopoes among the varied birdlife, and at the top for votive rags, representing wishes, tied to trees by petitioners. At prayer time, the calls to prayer from as many as eighty minarets resound and echo off the rock to dramatic effect. The fortress itself is thought to stand on the site of the Hittite fortress of Khapanouwa, built around the middle of the second millennium BC. The rock was subsequently fortified by the Phrygians, the Byzantines and the Turks, but all that remain are a few crenellated walls and towers.

Immediately surrounding the fortress rock is the **old town**, a warren of tiny streets. Afyon's domestic **Ottoman architecture** is renowned in Turkey; the half-timbered houses here all support overhanging upper storeys, some even complete with a *kafes*, the wooden latticework on the windows designed to protect the chastity of a household's womenfolk.

There are a number of impressively well-preserved mosques near the citadel, with many more somewhat less distinguished ones in the bazaar proper. Opposite the base of the steps leading up the side of the rock stands Afyon's most ancient mosque, the **Ulu Cami** (outside of prayer time wait for the caretaker to let you in; small donation). This typically square Selçuk construction, built between 1272 and 1277, has been restored, so its originally flat roof is now pitched, but it retains forty original carved wooden columns with stalactite capitals and beams supporting a fine geometric ceiling.

Slightly downhill from the Ulu Cami, the **Mevlevî Camii** is a double-domed mosque noticeable for its pyramid-roofed *son cemaat yeri*, a porch in which late-comers pray – literally the "place of last congregation". The adjoining *semahane*, or ceremonial hall, has a walnut-wood floor on which Mevlevî dervishes once performed their whirling ceremony. This building has now been converted into the **Mevlevî Museum** (Mevlevî Müzesi; open at prayer times or on request to the *imam*), with exhibits of musical instruments and the ceremonial costumes of the dervishes. Afyon became the second largest centre of the Mevlevî order after the branch of Islamic mysticism was introduced to the city from Konya by the son of the Mevlâna, Sultan Veled.

The **Archeological Museum** (Arkeoloji Müzesi; Tues–Sun 8.30am–5.30pm; 2YTL), 1km east of the centre on Kurtuluş Caddesi, warrants a visit. Despite rather dimly lit display cabinets, the objects are attractively set out and the explanatory signboards well written. The most interesting finds are Roman, excavated at nearby Çardalı and Kovalık Höyük, dating from the third and fourth centuries AD. Exhibits from this period include a small marble statue of Diana and a price list from an agora, outside in the covered gallery. A beautifully carved sarcophagus dating from the reign of Septimus Severus is very impressive, as is the collection of miniature sarcophagi. The museum garden is full of impressive (and unlabelled) marble work and statuary from the Roman, Phrygian, Byzantine and

Opium

A town called **"Opium"** (the translation of *Afyon*) could hardly be accused of reticence concerning its most controversial claim to fame. This region produces 25 percent of the world's legal opiates: it used to be almost half, but in 1971 the United States forced Turkey to impose a ban on production because of the extent of illegal drug trafficking. Nowadays, although poppy seeds are sprinkled liberally on bread loaves and the leaves of the plant are used in salads, all of the 20,000 tonnes of capsules processed around Afyon must arrive at the factory intact, and the poppy fields are regularly patrolled by government officials, who check if the seed heads have been illegally "bled" for heroin. If you want to take a look at the crop, in May/June head out of town for around 5km on the Sandıklı road, and the open fields of poppies are clearly visible from the road. Much more grows arund Yalvaç and in the Toros mountains.

While the authorities may be circumspect about touting the city's eponymous enterprise as a tourist attraction, there are still telltale signs of civic pride in the traditional industry: a close look at the fountain in the town square reveals that it is a graceful bronze sculpture of poppy seed-pods.

Ottoman eras. It is unsurprising that there are so many marble remains here, as the region was (and remains) the heart of the marble-quarrying industry in Anatolia.

Also on Kurtuluş Caddesi, but nearer the centre in its own patch of parkland, the **Gedik Ahmet Paşa Külliyesi** was built for one of the viziers of Mehmet the Conqueror in 1477. Adjoining it are a stone *medrese* and a functioning hamam – the original marble floors are in good condition, but it's otherwise in a bad state of repair. The complex's mosque, identified as the **İmaret Camii**, has a fluted minaret dashed with zigzagging blue İznik tiles.

Atatürk's brief stay in Afyon is commemorated in a museum, the **Zafer Müzesi** (daily 9am–5pm; free), next to the tourist office on Milli Egemenlik Caddesi. This is the building in which he planned his victory at Dumlupınar: his office has been preserved, and weapons and other paraphernalia from the war, as well as old photos of Atatürk and Afyon, are on show.

Practicalities

The **train station** is at the far north end of Ordu Bulvarı, about 500m from the centre, while the **otogar** is about the same distance east of town on the *çevre yolu* (ring road). Both terminals are linked with the middle of town by a dolmuş service marked "Sanayi/PTT", though if you arrive by bus there should be a free service to the town centre from the *otogar*. Towards the end of the dolmuş service's run, it passes close by all the city's best hotels, coming to rest at a terminal on Ambaryolu, two blocks behind the main **PTT** (which stands on the main north–south street, Milli Egemenlik Caddesi).

There is a **tourist booth** (Mon–Fri 8am–noon & 1.30–5.30pm; ☎0272/215 6525) in Hükümet Meydani, which dishes out town maps and a brochure to the nascent "Afyon Tourism Route" (see opposite) to the north of the city. The tourism official speaks good English and is very helpful. The major **banks and ATMs** are on Banklar Caddesi.

Accommodation

The cheapest **hotel** is the *Otel Lale* on Banklar Cad 23 (☎0272/215 1580; ❶). The rooms are basic but adequate, with en-suite bathrooms, and it is very central. Also centrally located is the *Hotel Soydan* at Turizm Emeksiz Cad 2 (☎0272/215 6070,

ⓕ 212 2111; ❷), a friendly place with small, prettily furnished rooms with bathrooms and TVs. It has a restaurant serving traditional dishes. The relaxed *Sinada*, at Ambaryolu 25 (ⓣ0272/215 6530, ⓕ213 6165; ❷), has scruffy carpets but otherwise decent rooms, with pastel-hued walls, clean sheets and spotless bathrooms; rooms at the front have a lot of street noise. A considerable step up is the *Grand Özer* at Süleyman Gonçer Cad 2 (ⓣ0272/214 3300, ⓦwww.grandozer.com; ❹) just east of Hükümet Meydanı, with airy rooms, satellite TV, a pool and hamam.

Eating and drinking

Established in 1922, the old-fashioned 🍴 *İkbal Lokantası*, close to Hükümet Meydanı on Uzun Çarşı, is the most famous **restaurant** in town. It exudes a period charm rare in Turkey, with a snaking Art-Deco staircase leading up to the family dining area, a monumental gilt mirror, and white tablecloths with white napkins. It's not cheap (a full meal will set you back up to 15YTL) but the grills are excellent, the stewed okra tender, and the famed puddings, all served with a generous slice of thick Afyon cream, delicious. On Ambaryolu 48, opposite and just up from the *Sinada*, is the *Kuru Fasuliyeci*, an unusual place specializing in dried-bean dishes. Try them plain (in a tomato sauce), with meat or with *pastırma* for 3YTL, best accompanied by a bowl of *cacık*. This small and extremely clean establishment also offers four varieties of soup for breakfast. For a different feel, the *YKM Café* (on the top floor of the YKM department store, off Hükümet Meydanı) dishes up decent pizzas to the town's youth.

Around Afyon

The most interesting side-trip from Afyon is to see a series of sixth-century **Phrygian sites**, notable for their stone-carvings, in the vicinity of İhsanıye. There are also several areas of rock formations here similar to those in Cappadocia, and even some rock-cut churches. This whole area is being promoted by the local tourism authorities, but as yet the *Afyon Turizm Kuşağı* (Afyon Tourism Route) exists largely in a brochure rather than on the ground.

The Afyon region is also well known for its **hot springs**, whose waters bubble up at temperatures between 50 and 80°C and have a high content of fluoride, bromide and calcium salts. Mineral water from this region is bottled and sold all over Turkey.

Ayazın, Kaya and Döğer

The trip to see the **Phrygian sites** is best done with your own transport (make sure you pick up the *Afyon Turizm Kuşağı* brochure from the tourist office) but even then you may find following the village roads tricky, as they are ill-signed and locals completely unused to foreigners. It may be preferable to hire a taxi, which should cost around €80 for a full day. It is possible to see at least some of the sites by public transport: there are three convenient daytime trains from Afyon to **İhsaniye**, as well as dolmuşes that leave from a garage at Ordu Bulvarı 11/A, opposite the tourist office. It's about a forty-minute journey, and beyond İhsanıye it's necessary to rent a dolmuş to take you to Döğer (about 10km north of İhsaniye) or Ayazın (about 15km east of İhsaniye, 30km from Afyon). You can also get a bus straight to the village of Kunduzlu, near Ayazın, from Voyvoda Gazlıgöl Caddesi, opposite the *Belediye* building in Afyon.

Best of the remains are those of a Phrygian town located in the modern-day village of **AYAZİN**, reached via a right turn off the minor Afyon–Eskişehir road at Kunduzlu. **Cave houses** and a well-preserved ninth-century **Byzantine church** are visible across fields of opium poppies on the road to the village. Closer observation reveals lion reliefs and the scars from excavations by locals and archeologists, who have found coins and other objects in the rooms.

The rock-cut tomb of **Arslantaş** (Lion Stone), near the village of **KAYA** (formerly Hayranveli), is flanked by another relief of lions, two enormous beasts snarling at each other with bared teeth. This should not be confused with another Phrygian cult monument called **Arslankaya** (Lion Rock), featuring a high relief of the goddess Cybele flanked by two more enormous lions. Arslankaya is near Lake Emre in the village of **DÖĞER**, where the remains of a fifteenth-century Ottoman *kervansaray* can also be found.

Local spas

Fourteen kilometres north of town on the Kütahya road, is the massive *Termal Resort Oruçoğlu* (☎0272/251 5050, ⓕ251 5060; ⓺), a **thermal hotel** offering half-board accommodation in luxurious rooms with air conditioning and balconies, and thermal water on tap. The price also includes use of the hamam, sauna, indoor and outdoor pools and a jolly water-slide; various massages and treatments are extra. This hotel is one of several in the **Ömer/Gecek Kaplıcaları** hot springs complex, with treatments accessible to less privileged customers, who usually stay in simple chalets. The tourist office should be able to help you find accommodation, and there are several dolmuşes a day from Afyon.

Hudai Kaplıcaları 48km south of Ayfon, beyond Sandıklı off the Denizli road, is worth a visit if only for a wallow in its deep mud baths. Dolmuşes run there every half-hour from Sandıklı. The place is like a large village, with a mass of basic chalets for cure-seekers, and public treatment centres, including mud baths (entry 4YTL). The *Hudai Termal Otel* (☎0272/535 7300, ⓦwww.hudai.sandikli.bel.tr; ⓺ half-board, discounts for longer stays) has comfortable rooms and its own attached treatment centre, with mud baths that range up to 50°C and a small, naturally heated thermal pool. The spring waters of the thermal pools all have their own specific properties, which are used as curatives for a variety of ailments – rheumatism especially, but also kidney stones, neuralgia and chronic period pains. The mud baths are believed to help remedy joint and spine calcification.

Isparta

Set on a flat plain dominated by 2635-metre Mount Davraz to the south, **ISPARTA** is a mostly modern town whose only suggestion of romantic appeal lies in its chief industries: rosewater, distilled here for over a century, and carpets, manufactured in industrial quantities.

Despite a paucity of monuments, Isparta has long been an important city. The Hittites and Lydians were here as, briefly, were the Macedonians. After Selçuk occupation in 1203, Isparta came under the control of the Hamidoğlu emirs in the late thirteenth century, and was capital of a territory delimited by the four great lakes of Beyşehir, Burdur, Akşehir and Eğirdir. Following Ottoman expansion the Hamidoğlu emir cut his losses and sold the kingdom to the Ottoman sultan Murat I in 1381, and thereafter its star waned. Only when Eğirdir lost its importance did Isparta and neighbouring Burdur regain significance as market towns in their respective areas. This process gained impetus towards the end of the twentieth century, when large numbers of Muslim refugees from the Balkans settled in the area, particularly Bulgarians who brought their rosewater-distilling skills with them. The local carpet industry dates from approximately the same era.

The Town

There are several things to see and do in Isparta. On Kaymakkapı Meydanı, the **Ulu (Kutlubey) Cami** dates from 1417, its size and grandeur attesting to the importance of the town in Ottoman times; but the interior is badly restored. Up until the 1923 exchange of populations many **Greeks** lived in Isparta, and their old residential quarter is a fifteen-minute walk from the town centre, near the Devlet Hastanesi (State Hospital). The once handsome lath-and-plaster houses are now crumbling, but there are a couple of restored nineteenth-century churches to admire.

The town's **Archeological Museum** (Arkeoloji Müzesi; Tues–Sun 8.30am–noon & 1–5pm; 2YTL) is on Kenan Evren Caddesi, 500m northeast of the *Belediye* building. It has a reasonable collection of local finds, including some fine Roman grave stelae, plus assorted pithoi, jugs, bowls and idols from a nearby Bronze-Age burial site. The ethnonography section includes a wonderful felt and reed *yurt*, which, along with the fine old carpets and kilims also on show, attests to a nomadic culture once an integral part of this region. Isparta's **market** day is Wednesday, when people come in from the surrounding rural areas to sell agricultural produce and stock up on necessities.

Gölcük is the closest local attraction, 13km to the southwest, a tiny crater lake surrounded by trees, with a picnic area nearby in a clearing. In the summer, buses go from opposite the *Büyük Isparta* hotel, passing through beautiful fields of cultivated roses en route.

Practicalities

The **train station** is at the far north end of Hükümet Caddesi from the town centre, a 500-metre walk, and the *otogar* is 5km west of town on Süleyman Demirel Bulvarı – free service buses run in to the centre and to the **minibus terminal** (known as the *köy garaj*) in the middle of town, about 500m southwest of Valikliği Binası, from where you can take a dolmuş to Burdur, Eğirdir, Ağlasun or Atabey, all around half an hour away. There have been tales of travellers being ticketed to Eğirdir, but then left stranded in Isparta's *otogar*. If this happens to you, head for the *köy garaj* and thence onto Eğirdir by dolmuş, a twenty-minute journey costing 2YTL (last bus at 7.30pm). Note that Isparta Petrol Turizm lays on a service bus into Eğirdir, so try to use this if you can.

Isparta's regional **Directorate of Tourism** is on the third floor of the Valikonağı, or governor's building (Turizm Müdürlüğü; Mon–Fri 8am–noon & 1.30–5pm), next to the main square, the Kaymakkapı Meydanı. There are several **ATMs** on Banklar Caddesi. The **PTT** (Mon–Sat 8.30am–noon & 1.30–5.30pm) is near the Valikonağı on Hükümet Caddesi.

Accommodation-wise, a recommended place, popular with the French, is the *Hotel Artan*, in a quiet sidestreet at Cengiz Topel Cad 12/B (℡0246/232 5700, ℻218 6629; ❸). The well-furnished rooms have central heating and satellite TV, and they serve a good buffet breakfast. The larger *Hotel Bolat*, off Kaymakkapı Meydanı at Süleyman Demirel Bul 67 (℡0246/223 9001, ℻218 5506; ❸), has both air conditioning and heating, a decent top-floor restaurant with great views towards Mount Davraz, and an American-style bar.

Isparta's two best **restaurants** are virtually side by side on Kaymakkapı Meydanı: the *Hacı Benlioğlu* and the *Kebabçı Kadir*. Both serve excellent grills and fine desserts.

Burdur and around

Lying 50km southwest of Isparta, **BURDUR** town is situated some way from its lake. Despite its status as a provincial capital, flat-roofed village houses are in evidence, and the only impressive monument is the **Ulu Cami**, originally a fourteenth-century relic of the Hamidoğlu dynasty, but destroyed by an earthquake in 1914 and completely rebuilt. The only real reason to visit is the excellent **museum** (Burdur Müzesi; 8.30am–noon & 1.30–5.30pm; 4YTL). Housing finds from nearby Sagalassos (see p.609) and Kremna, it is well laid out and informative.

Frequent dolmuşes cover the scenic hour's drive from Isparta to Burdur and it's a twenty-minute walk into town from the *otogar*. If you decide to stay, the *Hotel Özeren*, Gazi Cad 51 (☎0248/234 1600, ⓦwww.ozeren.netteyim.net; ❸), is the best choice, with spotless rooms with newly fitted bathrooms, satellite TV and a buffet breakfast. Failing this, the *Turistic Burdur Oteli*, Gazi Cad 37 (☎0248/233 2245; ❸), is slightly cheaper, but the wood-panelled rooms are a little dowdy and the carpets stained. For **eating**, the *Emniyet Lokantası* at Cümbüzlü Cad 9 is an old-fashioned place with cheerful check tablecloths and reasonable *sulu yemek* at lunchtimes, grills evenings. The *Urfa Sofrası*, also on Gazi Caddesi, churns out standard kebabs for 4YTL and *lahmacun* for 1.5YTL.

The lake, **Burdur Gölü**, is disappointing, with a drab, fly-blown shoreline and unappetizing swimming. If you do want to get up close, it is most easily reached along Highway 330 to Denizli and Acıpayam. A far better excursion from Burdur is to the 600-metre-long cave, **İnsuyu Mağarası**, signposted off the Burdur–Antalya road, 14km from Burdur and easily reached on any Antalya-bound bus. The cave (daily 8.30am–6pm; 2YTL) is well organized with lighting and footpaths, and features a series of seven beautiful underwater lakes, the largest of which, Büyük Göl, measures 150m by 30m and can attain a seasonal depth of 15m. Its mineral-rich water is phosphorescent blue, warm and supposedly therapeutic for diabetics. Be warned that the lakes are prone to dry up, especially in late summer, in which case the cave itself will be much less impressive.

Eğirdir and around

EĞIRDIR is the natural focus of Turkey's Lakeland, boasting an astonishingly beautiful setting, clinging to a strip of flat land between the Toros (Taurus) mountains and Turkey's second largest freshwater lake (488 square kilometres). Lying around 900m above sea level, air temperatures are warm in summer (around 30°C), while the clear waters usually remain swimmable until the end of September (though sudden storms can cool things off at any time of year). In April the lake basin's numerous apple orchards bloom and in August/September the apples are harvested.

The lakeside town tends to suffer from its convenience as a stopover between the coast and Cappadocia, and most travellers stay only a night or two. This is a pity as **Yeşilada**, a tiny island connected to mainland Eğirdir by a kilometre-long causeway, is a wonderfully relaxing place to stay. It has many excellent *pansiyons* and makes a useful base from which to explore the region's natural and historic sights. **Watersports** are in their infancy in Eğirdir, though it is possible to rent small sailing dinghies and windsurfing is beginning to take off. Tandem paragliding is on offer for the more adventurous, but Eğirdir is best suited to its role as the Lakeland's **trekking** centre and major stop on the long-distance walking route, the **St Paul Trail** (see box, p.608).

Some history

Founded by the Hittites, Eğirdir was taken by the Phrygians in 1200 BC, but it was not until Lydian times, when it straddled the so-called King's Way from Ephesus to Babylon, that the town became famous for its recreational and accommodation facilities.

Early in the thirteenth century the town came under the control of the Konya-based Selçuks, who refortified it in its role as a gateway to Pisidia. Shortly thereafter the city reached the height of its fortunes as capital of the **emirate of Felekeddin Dündar**, remaining prominent during the reign of the Hamidoğlu clan. In 1331 the geographer Ibn Battuta could still describe Eğirdir as a rich and powerful city; when the Ottomans took over fifty years later, however, its strategic significance – and opulence – disappeared. The Byzantines knew the place as **Akrotiri** ("promontory" in Greek) after its obvious geographical feature; this name was originally corrupted in Ottoman times to **Eğridir** (meaning "it's bent"), but was changed again in the mid-1980s to **Eğirdir**, meaning "s/he's spinning", which officialdom apparently thought more dignified.

Opposite the town is the island of **Yeşilada**, until 1923 home of a Greek community over a thousand strong. Unfortunately, the Turks missed the opportunity of putting a preservation order on the beautiful stone and timber houses they left behind and, when the causeway was built in the late 1980s, many of them were "redeveloped" as concrete hotels or pensions.

Arrival, information and services

The **otogar** is right in the town centre, opposite the Hızırbey Camii, from where there are eight daily buses (five in low season) to Yeşilada, the last one at 9pm; alternatively it is only a fifteen-minute walk across the causeway – head east, passing the **harbour** (with its fishing boats, day-trip cruisers and dinghies) on your right and the castle on your left.

The **tourist office** at 2 Sahil Yolu 13 (Mon–Fri 8.30am–noon & 1.30–5pm; ℡ 0246/311 4388) by the lakeside, a five-minute walk out of town on the Isparta road. Staff can suggest hotels or *pansiyon*s and give limited advice on trekking. **Getting around** this compact market town is easy on foot as everything lies within five minutes' walk of everything else. There are a couple of **ATMs** in the town centre, and several **banks** where you can change money. Some of the pensions on the Kale and Yesilada have **Internet** access, or you can try the *Klas* next to the *Özcan Pastanesi* on Belidiye Caddesi. Galeri Nomad, opposite the main harbour on the peninsula, rents out good-quality **mountain bikes** (including helmets, spare tubes and a repair kit) for €12 a day, and also kayaks and windsurfers (€8 and €12 respectively per day).

Accommodation

Room prices in Eğirdir are reasonable, partly because of cut-throat competition, partly through *Belediye* control. It's best to stay on **Yeşilada** in order to take full advantage of the lake's charms, though the **Kale** district on the tip of the peninsula is nearer the town proper and has been less developed than the island. It is possible to stay in the town, but the accommodation tends to be charmless, over-priced and noisy.

The Kale

Çetin's Pansiyon ℡ 0246/311 2154, ⊛ www .egirdirnet.com. Small, friendly place, run by a fisherman's family. The five clean rooms, each with either pine floors or ceilings, overlook the lake and Mount Barla. Evening meals on request. ❷

 Lale Pension Kale ℡ 0246/311 2406, ⊛ www.lalehostel.com. The cheapest option in town, with dorms (€5 per person) and en-suite doubles. There's a top-floor terrace restaurant with harbour views and a wide choice of breakfasts including pancakes, plus Internet access, beer and bike rental. İbrahim, the friendly proprietor, rents out bikes and kayaks, and organizes all kinds of trips – from trekking around Kovada lake to night-time beach barbeques and excursions to Sagalassos. ❸

Yeşilada

🏃 **Ali's Pension** Eastern side of the island ☎0246/312 2547, ⓦwww.alispension .com .tr. The most hospitable place in town, located on the sunrise-facing shore. The newly decorated rooms are spotlessly clean, have hot water, central heating and bare wooden floors; the home cooking is wonderful and there are free fishing trips at 7am each morning. It's a thirty-metre stroll to a pleasant stony beach/swimming area, or you can rent a car for €25 a day and go exploring. ❸

Big Fish Western side of the island ☎0246/312 4413. Restaurant-pension facing the sunset, with newly refurbished rooms with small balconies affording lake views. There are a couple of big family rooms on the top floor, which sleep up to nine. ❸

Göl Pension Southern side of the island ☎0246/311 2370, ⓔahmetdavraz@hotmail.com. Serves breakfast beside the lake and has extremely well-kept rooms with balconies; pricier rooms on the terrace offer the best views. ❸

Halley Pension On the south shore ☎0246/311 3625, ⓔhalleypension@hotmail.com. Immaculately clean rooms, redecorated annually. The friendly family will collect you from the *otogar* if you reserve in advance or ring on arrival. The evening meals are of a high standard (the family ran a restaurant for many years), and are eaten on a cosy, vine-shaded verandah. ❸

Paris Pension South side of the island ☎0246/311 5509. The owners of this tiny pension are extremely friendly. Mehmet still works as a fisherman, his wife cooks fine evening meals, and the atmosphere is intimate. The three rooms are a little small but prettily painted and ideal for those seeking a family atmosphere. ❸

Sehsuvar Peace Pension Eastern side of the island ☎0246/311 2433, ⓔsehsuvar-o@hotmail .com. Just behind *Ali's*, with large, clean, simple rooms with white walls and wood floors. The location is peaceful, looking onto the island's mulberry-shaded *meydan*, and the family very friendly. ❷

The Town and Yeşilada

Eğirdir's secular architecture was largely damaged by Byzantine–Selçuk conflict, but the religious edifices survived and have been incorporated in the modern town centre. On a preliminary wander the most obvious remains are of the **Dündar Bey Medresi**, which began life in 1218 as an inn, was converted into a *medrese* by Felekeddin Dündar in 1281 and now serves as a shopping precinct. The adjoining **Hızırbey Camii** has also been nicely restored; the roof is supported by Selçuk wooden pillars and it has an ornately carved door, wooden porch and İznik-tiled *mihrab*. The earliest building in the *medrese* complex is Eğirdir's six-domed **bathhouse** (1202) which retains its sixteen original washing basins. It provides six rooms for men and a large separate room for women (daily 8am–11pm). Nearby, overlooking the approach to the island, are the ramparts of the Byzantine and Selçuk **citadel** (*kale*), on which an imposing cannon is still perched as a reminder of the importance of the trading interests that were once protected.

Across the causeway, **Yeşilada** itself boasts the twelfth-century Byzantine church of **Ayios Stefanos**, now re-roofed but still awaiting internal restoration. The remaining Greek houses are mainly set in the centre of the island in walled gardens dominated by mulberries and grapes, accessed by tiny cobbled lanes. The small pebble **beaches** that border the island are hard on the feet, but the convenience of being able to take a dip from your pension before breakfast compensates.

Back on the mainland the **Belediye Plajı**, 750m from the town centre in the Yazla district, is the least attractive of the town's beaches. Much better is **Altınkum**, out by the train station, a sandy pay-beach (2YTL), great for children because of the shallow waters and offering umbrellas, pedal-boats and camping. However, its charm is diminished by a holiday-camp ambience and the modern housing development that backs it.

Eating and drinking

Not surprisingly, **lake fish** – especially carp (*sazan*), zander and crayfish – figure prominently on local restaurant menus. On the island, many *pansiyon* owners double as fishermen and offer fresh-caught lake fish presented either as batter-fried fillets, grilled or poached in tomato sauce (*bulama soslu*). Most of Eğirdir's restaurants serve alcohol.

Big Apple On the west of the island, with a choice of indoor or outdoor dining, with a wide range of *mezes*. Main courses are substantial, the beer is cheap and there's a good (by local standards) choice of wine. A full meal, excluding alcoholic drinks, should cost no more than 10YTL.

Big Fish Next door to the *Big Apple*, this bright-white building is decked out with house plants and an incongruous Swiss Alpine scene. The food and service are good, with the oven-baked trout both very tender and reasonably priced at 5YTL. Tables are also set out on the lake's edge in summer.

Felakabad Northeastern tip of the island. A good lunchtime choice, with simple meals including delicious *gözleme* and a decent range of desserts.

Kemer Opposite the Hızırbey Camii, a bustling place offering everything from *döner* sandwiches to *sulu yemek* and home-made rice pudding. Good value, but no alcohol.

Melodi Southeastern tip of the island. A deservedly popular establishment serving up better-than-average lake fish and a wide range of *mezes*. Expect to pay around 10YTL for a full meal, but a bottle of wine will set you back the same amount. The tables set out under plane trees right on the foreshore are wonderful on a warm summer's evening.

Özcan Pastanesi Belediye Cad Sok 15. Eğirdir's longest established *pastane* dishes up decent *porça*, *simit* and cakes. It's also the cheapest (though not the smartest) in town.

Poyraz Lokantası A friendly new venture on the north of the island. It specializes in *pide* (2–3YTL depending on the topping), but also does fish dishes and grills. No *mezes* or alcohol.

Excursions from Eğirdir

Many of the *pansiyon*s in Eğirdir offer half- and full-day **boat trips** out on the lake (from about €8 per person) and the fishermen who take you usually know the best swimming and barbecue spots. There's also a range of minibus and taxi **excursions** to points of interest within a few hours' journey of the town. Unless you have a car, it's worth signing up for these, as you'd otherwise never get to many of the places described below. Prices vary between €8 and €15 per person for a typical day-trip, depending on whether it is a taxi or minibus, the distance and the number of people sharing.

Davraz Ski Centre

From December through to the end of March, the northern slopes of 2635-metre Mount Davraz, a thirty-kilometre, half-hour drive from Eğirdir, offer decent downhill skiing and snowboarding – and the views from the slopes down to Lake Eğirdir are superb.

If you have your own transport, the cheapest and best option is to stay in Eğirdir itself. There are, however, a couple of hotels virtually on the slopes at an altitude of 1800m. The *Davraz Kayak Merkezi* (☏0246/267 2020; ❺ weekdays; ❻ weekends) has comfortable, if rather spartan rooms, and the cavernous dining hall offers à la carte lunch and evening meals, with main courses around 10YTL. The much grander *Sirene Davraz* (☏0242/226 2858, ⓦwww.sirendavraz.com; ❼) should be fully operational for the 2007 season.

Snow conditions are fairly reliable, though the limited runs won't satisfy everyone. Ski rental weekdays is 30YTL, snowboards 40YTL, and a weekday lift pass costs 20YTL. Prices for both rental and lift passes rise by fifty percent at weekends.

Atabey and Barla

Midway between Eğirdir and Isparta, the village of **ATABEY** is set on the flat Isparta plain in a lush agricultural landscape. Of most interest to visitors is the **Medrese of Dündar Bey**, built in 1224, and the wooden-porched mosque next to it.

Virtually the only settlement of any size near the lakeshore (other than Eğirdir itself) is the old village of **BARLA**, 25km northwest of Eğirdir, which spills down a hillside about 200m above the water level. It makes an excellent starting point for day-walks, and you can see the roofless remains of the church of **Ayios Georgios** (dated 1805 but perhaps earlier) and a far older rock-cut tomb and cyclopean walls in the valley above the village.

Prior to 1923 Barla had a mixed Greek and Turkish population, but many of those now living here are descendants of Kurdish villagers – moved here in the turbulent years following the proclamation of the republic – from the east of Turkey. Barla was also the home for a short time of the controversial religious figure **Sait Nursi**. The wooden house where he lived and preached is something of a shrine for the *Nurculuk* ("followers of light") who admire his interpretations of the Koran.

Barla can only be reached by public transport via Isparta, a time-consuming process. However, it would make an excellent day's cycle-ride, perhaps combined with a swim at **Bedre** beach, some 13km from Eğirdir en route to Barla. **Camping** is possible at Bedre and there is a seasonal **restaurant** with toilet facilities for campers.

Antioch ad Pisidiam

Almost equidistant (75–80km) from Eğirdir whether you travel via the east shore road past apple orchards, or make the complete circuit of the lake via Barla, the ancient city of **Antioch ad Pisidiam** (Tues–Sun 8.30am–5.30pm; 3YTL) lies about 2km northeast of the modern town of Yalvaç, itself at the head of a valley draining southwest into the lake.

The city was originally a Hellenistic foundation of the late third century BC, later becoming a part of the Roman province of Galatia and eventually, around 25 BC, a Roman *colonia* settled by legionary soldiers from Gaul. Following the creation of the province of Pisidia at the end of the third century AD, Antioch became its capital and remained important well into Byzantine times, finally being abandoned and lost to history in the eleventh century AD. Historically, the city is important as the place where the apostle **St Paul** first attempted to convert pagans to Christianity.

The most unusual extant remains are of the sizable **temple**, at the highest point of the city, built in a semicircular colonnaded precinct in honour of the Emperor Augustus. Situated just below the temple is the toppled three-arched **propylon** (gateway) dedicated to Augustus, where the Tiberius and Augustus squares meet; most of the blocks lie scattered along the line of the road. Even more substantial are the remains of the **baths** fed by an **aqueduct**. There are also surviving sections of flagged Roman **street**, which once linked the various parts of this walled city and was once spanned by a wing of the **theatre**.

At the lower end of the site, a few courses of monumental stone blocks belonging to the fourth-century **Church of St Paul** (on the site of the synagogue) still stand, but little else can be seen except for the ground plan and some small areas of mosaic floor.

If there are insufficient people to warrant a taxi or minibus tour, you can take a **bus** instead to Yalvaç from Eğirdir, departing at 10.30am – the journey takes an hour and a half. There are a couple of reasonable places to **stay**, including the long-etablished and rather cavernous *Antiochia* (☎0246/441 437; ④), on Isparta Yolu, and the newer and better-value *Obo Oteli* (☎0246/441 6544; ③) on Hastane Cad 30/A. Alternatively, buses return to Eğirdir at either 3pm or 5pm. This would give you the opportunity to take a quick look at the small but fine **Yalvaç Museum** (Yalvaç Müzesi; Tues–Sun; 2YTL), which houses finds from the site. From Yalvaç you'll have to walk or, more sensibly given the time constraint, take a taxi the 2km on to the site.

Kasnak forest, Kovada Gölü and the Kral Yolu

Twenty kilometres south of Eğirdir lies **Kasnak forest**, reached by a dirt road through the village of Yukara Gökdere and past the dam above it. The park is famous for the single large specimen of *quercus volcanicus*, the volcanic oak, only found here. The beautiful mixed oak, juniper and cedar forest also contains orchids, iris and the deep red wild peony, *peonia maculata*, which flowers in May. Native birds include three species of woodpecker, as well as many tits, shrikes and nuthatches.

Continuing south, and taking the road on the left marked Sütçüler, the lake, marshland and forests of **Kovada Gölü**, 35km from Eğirdir, form a carefully tended and hardly visited national park. Animals found in the reserve supposedly include wolves and bears, though more certainly there are wild boar and snakes – and swarms of butterflies, which attract aficionados in springtime. The lake itself, teeming with fish, receives the outflow of Eğirdir Gölü. The limestone shore is harsh and the lake itself weedy so it is not particularly good for swimming. However, there's a picnic place with fresh water and seating.

Most tours continue another 30km south on the main road through a gorge towards **Çandır** (signed Yazılı Kanyonu), passing a series of icy but scenic pools and waterfalls, crisscrossed by bridges and best sampled at the height of summer. Here, too, are identifiable, well-preserved stretches of the road locally known as the **Kral Yolu**, or "King's Way", an ancient road that threaded through Pisidia. Just outside the park, and reached by a footbridge, is a **trout restaurant**, the *Baysallar Dinleme Tesisleri*.

Adada and the Zindan Mağarası

Signposted off the Aksu road, 65km from Eğirdir, **Adada** is another ancient town cut from grey stone. Although there is a warden, no admission is charged and, as the site lies along both sides of a minor road, it is permanently open to visitors. It has never been excavated, but was recently surveyed and mapped by Isparta University students. History books are strangely silent on the place, even to the extent of its original name, but judging from coins found in the area, the place was thriving during imperial Roman times. Visible remains include a particularly well-preserved Corinthian temple, plus two other small temples, a forum with unusual seating along one side, a badly preserved theatre, a church, and various Hellenistic buildings. Tumbled statue bases with inscriptions lie along the main road through the site. If you follow the stream-bed between the acropolis hill and the adjacent hill, heading southwest behind the forum, it's possible to trace the original Greco-Roman road from the south; below the city this contours the hillside on an impressive line of enormous slabs. This is almost certainly the original road that St Paul walked on his first missionary journey from Perge to Antioch in Pisidia.

Easily visited on the same tour is the **Zindan Mağarası**, a sizable cave beyond the village of Aksu. It's 27km from Eğirdir – go straight up Cumhuriyet Caddesi in Aksu until you come to the river, crossed by an attractive Roman bridge: the entrance to the cave is in the rock face opposite. At present, workmen are installing electric light and flooring, but you are still free to explore. Inside, the cave has everything from bat colonies and guano stench to stalactites and stalagmites.

Opened in 2004, this rugged trail offers over 500km of trekking in the spectacularly beautiful Toros mountains. Waymarked to internationally recognized standards, using red and white flashes painted on rocks and trees, it allows relatively easy exploration of a remote, unspoilt area of Turkey. A detailed guidebook (which includes a map), written by Kate Clow, accompanies the trail (see p.1041).

The route has twin starting points, the ancient cities of Perge (see p.541) and Aspendos (see p.543), on the Mediterranean coastal plain. It was from Perge that St Paul set out, in AD 46, on his first proselytizing journey, his destination the Roman colonial town Antiochia Ad Pisidiam (see p.606) high on the windswept Anatolian plateau just northeast of Lake Eğirdir, where he first preached Christ's message to non-Jews.

En route from the Mediterranean to the Anatolian plateau the trail crosses tumbling mountain rivers, climbs passes through limestone peaks soaring to near 3000m, dips into deeply scored canyons and weaves beneath shady pine and cedar forest. It even includes a boat ride across the glimmering expanse of Lake Eğirdir. Those with an interest in archeology can discover remote, little-known Roman sites and walk along original sections of Roman road. The irrevocably active can raft the Köprülü river, scale 2635-metre Davraz and 2799-metre Barla (ascents of both appear in the trail guidebook; for more information check @ www.trekkinginturkey.com), or even tackle the mighty Dedegül (2992m).

The trail also affords a unique insight into the lives of the nomadic *Yörük* – descendants of the first Turkic peoples to arrive in Asia Minor from Central Asia – who move their flocks of sheep and goats up the limestone slopes. Their black goat-hair tents dot the mountains in the summer months. As a traveller hereabouts, you will be treated as a *Tanrının misafiri* (or "guest of God") and offered sweet black tea, yoghurt and paper-thin *yufka* bread – the staple diet of a proud but poor people.

Practicalities

Eğirdir (see p.602) makes an ideal base for forays along the trail. The town's pension owners will probably be able to help you sort out the relevant dolmuşes, negotiate car rental or taxi hire and let you store unwanted gear until your return from the hills. The Donatım Ticaret shop near the Dündar Bey Medresi, Belediye Cad 15, Sok 7/A (☎ & ☎0246/311 6080), has a wide range of **outdoor equipment** and may provide maps. **Guides** can be arranged by İbrahim at *Lale Pension* (see p.603). Other accommodation is springing up along the trail, with the *Karacan Pension* (☎0246/351 2411; dorm beds €6) in Sütçüler, an hour's drive south of Eğirdir, an alternative base.

Dedegül

The highest and most extensive of the Lakeland massifs, and the least accessible from Eğirdir, **Dedegül** lies some 10km off the trail. What follows is a brief description of the mountain, but remember that this is a remote area, and even if you manage to source a decent map (try the *Lale Pension*) you should treat it with great respect.

The base camp at Melekler Yaylası (Angels' Pastures) is an hour and a half's drive southeast of Eğirdir across the Toros. Wildflowers carpet the camp ground in May and June, and there are many interesting walks in the pine forests. Pinargözü (Spring Eye), where cool waters from an underground lake spout out of the mountain, is a thirty-minute stroll east down the forest road from Melekler Yaylası.

The summit is a steep five-hour ascent from the *yayla* at 1700m. Head more or less due south from the *yayla* and ascend a dry valley to a ridge, which joins the true summit to the slightly lower Kartal Tepesi (Eagle Hill). Turn right for the summit, left for Kartal Tepesi. The views of Beyşehir lake and Dedegül's steep and stark satellite peaks are impressive. Dedegül means "Grandfather's Rose" and refers to an unusual pink flower that blooms on the peak in summer. The descent to base takes three to four hours.

The Yaka canyon, on the stream below the forest road returning from the *yayla* to Eğirdir, makes a pleasant two or more hours' walk with a wide range of flowers in spring; be prepared to get your feet wet.

When the lighting is finished, the excitement of commando-type adventuring will be eliminated, but at present a lamp and old clothes are essential if you intend to plumb all 2500m of the cave's depths; the first kilometre is the best.

Sagalassos

Although nearer Isparta, the Pisidian site of **Sagalassos** is a popular organized trip from Eğirdir, 55km to the northeast. It's by far the most impressive Pisidian site and is undergoing extensive excavations undertaken by a team that stays on site all summer. Many finds from the site are now on display in Burdur's museum (see p.602). The site is well signposted from Ağlasun, has picnic tables at the entrance and the helpful guardian will probably sell you a map and, if asked, open up the building housing the restored library.

The remote site – 1400m above sea level and tucked onto the two-thousand-metre flank of Akdağı – was found by P. Lucas in 1806; he later translated an inscription, which identified it as the first city in Pisidia. Alexander the Great, of course, stormed the town with a frontal assault in 333 BC. Sagalassos then settled down to life under Macedonian garrison and then as part of Roman Asia Minor. In 25 BC Sagalassos was made a metropolis and free city by Augustus, who also put retired legionaries in it, as a type of *colonia*. Most of the site dates from Roman imperial times. The population of Termessos (see p.538) probably moved to Sagalassos in 244 AD after an earthquake, though the site was abandoned soon after, when the population moved downhill to the present town.

The **site** (daily 7.30am–6pm; 4YTL) is well labelled with illustrations of the buildings in their original state. To the right of the entrance is the 96-metre wide **theatre**, just as the earthquake left it, with seating mostly in place, but the stage building rather more wrecked. Two restored **nymphaea** (fountain-houses) are here: the smaller is a three-sided roofed trough with flat column mouldings, encased in a protective building. The restoration shows both early and Byzantine phases; the floor mosaic is almost intact, as are the alcoves and a major inscription. Walking west you come to the **upper agora**, of which the second, huge nymphaeum formed one side, two ceremonial arches opened off and there was a pagoda-like monument in the centre.

Just above, north of the upper agora, is one of the oldest parts of the site, a Doric **temple** of the second century BC, built of massive blocks still standing on two sides; it was later incorporated into the city walls and you can spot the joins. Walking down from the upper agora you'll see fragments of beautiful Roman friezes laid out like a giant jigsaw. Turn right on the level track through the site for **graves** cut into the rock face; they contained cremations. Below the main track is the **lower agora** with adjacent baths. Earthenware pipes and hypocausts reveal how water was distributed and heated. Beyond this area is a temple with Corinthian columns dedicated to Antonius Pius, now in rubble, but an informative contrast to the Doric one.

Straight ahead down the steps is the **necropolis** containing many graves, and a hill which locals say is the site of an Alexander monument – they believe that a gold statue dedicated to Alexander is waiting to be discovered.

Beyşehir and its lake

Leaving Eğirdir in the direction of Konya the next major lake you come to is Beyşehir Gölü. The town of **BEYŞEHIR** – on its eastern shore – sees a lot of through traffic heading in this direction, and its attractive lakeside position and historical legacy make it a good prospect for at least a day-trip.

Judging by the Neolithic remains found in the region, there has been human settlement here since the sixth or seventh millennium BC. There is also extensive evidence of Hittite settlement around the lake. The town itself was originally Byzantine, known as Karallia, and in Selçuk times was surrounded by walls, as well as acquiring a citadel, mosques and hamams. The local golden age, though, came under the Eşrefoğlu dynasty (1277–1326), and its best building dates from that time.

There are a number of attractive monuments in the town, and a lovely weir-bridge, built by German workers in 1902, across the lake's outlet. From here you can watch locals throwing their nets out for the evening catch of *sazan* (carp) in defiance of the "No Fishing" signs.

The Town

The most important monuments in Beyşehir are situated right on the lakeshore to the northwest of the modern town. Finest of these is the **Eşrefoğlu Camii** (most reliably open at prayer time), built by Eşrefoğlu Seyfeddin Süleyman between 1297 and 1299. This large, flat-roofed stone building surmounted by a typical Selçuk flat-sided cone, is an exceptional example of a medieval wooden *beylik* mosque – the *beylik*s being the minor Turkish principalities that ruled Anatolia before the Ottomans gained supremacy. Restoration carried out in the 1950s explains the ugly concrete blocks at the base of the minaret, but otherwise the mosque is in a remarkable state of preservation. There's an especially beautiful carved main north portal (albeit partly marred by a modern pine porch), typically Selçuk in its geometric ornateness.

The effect inside is incredibly forest-like: not only are the columns and capitals wooden, but also the rafters, the galleries, the furniture and the balustrades. Adding to the sylvan effect, light plays on the columns from a central aperture, now glassed over, and from high-set windows. Below this is a deep pit, which (according to the *imam*) once held ice for preserving food and cooling the mosque. The *mihrab* is decorated in typical Selçuk style, its turquoise, black and white tiles being almost the last surviving of their type, and the *minber* is also a lovely period-piece of woodcarving, echoing the star motif apparent throughout the mosque.

The **Eşrefoğlu Türbesi**, the conically roofed building attached to the east side of the mosque, dates from 1302, and was also built for Eşrefoğlu Seyfeddin Süleyman who died in that year. It's worth asking the *imam* if he'll open it up for a look at its beautifully tiled interior, one of the most ornate surviving examples of its type.

Behind the mosque, to the south, stands a small *medrese* with an almost equally ornate portal. To the north of the mosque there's the late thirteenth-century **Dokumacılar Hanı** (Cloth Hall), also originally built during the Eşrefoğlu period, with six domes recently restored in brick; again, you'll need to ask permission to see it. It's one of the earliest remaining domed bazaars; unlike the Byzantines, and the Ottomans after them, the Selçuks tended to use domes in secular business buildings rather than in their monumental religious architecture. To the northwest of the hall there's a double **hamam**, dating from 1260, usually open, but in poor and dilapidated condition. Outside, at the door, there's a pipe that is said to have supplied milk for bathing purposes.

Practicalities

The **otogar** (regular services from Eğirdir, Konya, Antalya and elsewhere) is 2km out of town, but a regular service bus links it with the centre, dropping you near the weir-bridge.

Beyşehir's only decent central **hotel** is the characterful *Beyaz Park* (☎0332/512 4535,

ⓕ 512 3865; ❸), an imposing stone building overlooking the weir at Atatürk Cad 1. Built in the early twentieth century, it has pleasantly furnished rooms; for period atmosphere and coolness, ask for the old building (as opposed to the modern extension), preferably overlooking the river as the roadside is noisy.

The best **restaurant** in town is at the *Beyaz Park*, with reasonable food (including lake fish) and drinks, served in the riverside garden, weather permitting. The surprisingly homely *Café Yaren*, behind the *Beyaz Park*, is the favoured choice of the town's students, and offers **Internet access** and kitsch wall decorations. Opposite the *Beyaz Park* is a **carpet and antique dealer's** called Ceylanlar Sarraf, which sells a good selection of kilims, copperware, Ottoman handguns and old jewellery.

Around the lake

Religious and civic architecture aside, the most obvious local lure is the shallow, freshwater **Beyşehir Gölü**; although Turkey's largest lake in surface area, its 650 square kilometres average a mere 10m in depth. The number of its islands is a hotly disputed topic among the locals, which may be explained by the fact that smaller ones appear and disappear according to the water level (presently very low), but the named ones – many with ruined Byzantine monasteries upon them – number about twenty. The best beach on the lake is **Karaburnu**, 18km from Beyşehir on the Yeşildağ road, then signposted 500m off to the right. It's possible to rent a boat here and explore the islands and the lakeshore.

You can **circumnavigate the lake** by car (rental can be arranged through Muhitten at the *Beyaz Park* hotel) and the little-visited west shore is beautiful. Alternatively, rent a **boat** from Gedikli Köy, on the northwest shore, and visit the once magnificent Selçuk island palace of **Kubadabad**, whose unique tiles can be seen in the Karatay museum in Konya.

More easily accessible on the main, east-shore road towards Eğirdir is the **Eflatun Pınar** (Violet Spring), a thirteenth-century BC Hittite shrine initially signposted 15km northwest of town, just before a petrol station. Turn right, following a paved side-road for 5km, then bear left for 2km more along a dirt track to the eponymous village.

At the outskirts, a large, walled pond filling a natural depression in the hummocky countryside receives the flow of vigorous springs. At one corner stand huge carved blocks bearing four relief figures with winged sun discs (symbols of royalty) carried by semi-human monsters. To either side at water level are statues of seated divinities. Excavations by the Konya museum have revealed a row of mountain gods with holes in their skirts which once gushed water, and a large stone block with bull reliefs.

Konya

Focus of Sufic mystical practice and teaching for the Middle East, **KONYA** is a place of pilgrimage for the whole of the Muslim world. This sprawling city has overrun the surrounding mud-walled villages and at its heart is the medieval Selçuk capital, which tugs at the hearts of all pious Turks and is often spoken of with more pride than the better-known tourist resorts. This was the adopted home of Celaleddin Rumi, better known as the Mevlâna (Our Master), the Sufic mystic who founded the **whirling dervish** sect, the Mevlevî; his writings helped reshape Islamic thought and modified the popular Islamic culture of Turkey.

In western Turkey, Konya has a reputation as one of the country's most religious and conservative cities, and while the teachings of Sufic mystics like the Mevlâna and

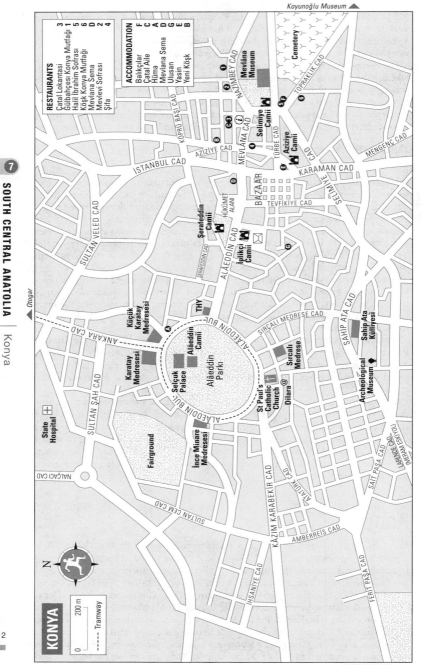

KONYA

0 | 200 m

- - - - Tramway

N

▲ Otogar

▲ Koyunoğlu Museum

Train Station ▲

RESTAURANTS

Çatal Lokantasi	3
Gülbahçesi Konya Mutfağı	1
Halil İbrahim Sofrası	5
Köşk Konya Mutfağı	6
Mevlana Şema	0
Mevlevi Sofrası	2
Şifa	4

ACCOMMODATION

Balıkçılar	F
Çatal Aile	C
Hüma	A
Mevlana Sema	D
Ulusan	G
Yasin	E
Yeni Köşk	B

Cemetery

Mevlâna Museum

Selimiye Camii

Azizîye Camii

BAZAAR

HÜKÜMET ALANI

Şerafeddin Camii

İplikçi Camii

Küçük Karatay Medresesi

THY

Karatay Medresesi

Alâeddin Camii

Selçuk Palace

Alâeddin Parkı

Sırçalı Medrese

St Paul's Catholic Church

Dilara

Archeological Museum

Sahip Ata Külliyesi

İnce Minare Medresesi

Fairground

State Hospital

Streets: NÂZİMBEY CAD, TOPRAKLIK CAD, MENGENÇ CAD, KARAMAN CAD, TÜRBE CAD, MEVLÂNA CAD, AZİZİYE CAD, İSTANBUL CAD, KÖPRÜ BAŞI CAD, TEVFİKİYE CAD, SELİMİYE, SULTAN VELED CAD, ALÂEDDİN CAD, ŞERAFEDDİN CAD, ANKARA CAD, ALÂEDDİN BUL, SIRÇALI MEDRESE CAD, SAHİP ATA CAD, SULTAN ŞAH CAD, NALÇACI CAD, SULTAN CEM CAD, İHSANİYE CAD, KÂZIM KARABEKİR CAD, ATATÜRK CAD, LARENDE CAD (MERAM ESKİYOL), SAİT PAŞA CAD, AMBERREİS CAD, FERİT PAŞA CAD

of Hacı Bektaş are still important in Konya, it is also a stronghold of Islamic fundamentalists, suggesting a strong current of mainstream Islamic thought. An episode
stuck in the minds of western Turks is that of a local severely beaten for smoking in
the street during Ramadan during the 1980s; foreigners, however, are treated with
more forbearance. In their defence, the citizens of Konya point out that while the
place may appear underdeveloped, with poorly equipped schools and people more
dour and less sophisticated than those nearer the Aegean, this is partly because they
are not allocated their fair share of resources by Ankara. Even the city's obligatory
Atatürk statue faces north – towards Ankara and away from the city centre – which
locals claim is symbolic of the fact that they have been ignored since the establishment
of the Turkish Republic.

The "backwardness" in fact goes some way to creating what for many visitors
is Konya's charm. This may be Turkey's eighth largest city but there are relatively
few private cars on the road and bikes have a higher profile than in İstanbul and
Ankara. Konya is surrounded by some of Turkey's most fertile countryside (the
region is known locally as "the breadbasket of Turkey"), and its parks add a splash
of greenery to the ubiquitous light-coloured stone. However, the city can seem
bleak in winter and sun-bleached in summer, and you'll find this contrast the rule
rather than the exception for Turkish inland towns.

Some history

Konya boasts a history as long and spectacular as that of any Turkish city. The earliest remains discovered date from the seventh millennium BC, and the acropolis
was inhabited successively by Hittites, Phrygians, Romans and Greeks. **St Paul**
and **St Barnabas** both delivered sermons here after they had been expelled from
Antioch and, in 235 AD, one of the earliest Church councils was convened in the
city – known then, under the Byzantines, as Iconium.

It also took a central role during the era of the western Selçuks, becoming the
seat of the **Sultanate of Rum**. After they had defeated the Byzantine army at
the battle of Manzikert in 1071, the Selçuks attempted to set up a court in İznik,
just across the Sea of Marmara from İstanbul. They were expelled from there by
the combined Byzantine and Crusader armies, but still ruled most of eastern and
central Asia Minor until the early fourteenth century.

While the concept of a fixed capital was initially somewhat alien to the Selçuks,
Konya became the home of their sultans from the time of Süleyman Ibn Kutul-
muz, successor to Alparslan, the victor at Manzikert. **Alâeddin Keykubad**, the
most distinguished of all Selçuk sultans, established a court of artists and scholars
in Konya early in the thirteenth century, and his patronage was highly beneficial
to the development of the arts and philosophy during the Selçuk dynasty. Many
of the buildings constructed at this time are still standing, and examples of their
highly distinctive tilework, woodcarving, carpet making and masonry are on display in Konya's museums. All of these art forms later served as the basis for their
Ottoman counterparts.

Arrival, orientation and information

Konya's **otogar** is a very inconvenient 15km north of the city centre. Take a tram
marked "Alâeddin" to Alâeddin Parkı. From here you can walk or take a dolmuş
to the main street, Mevlâna Caddesi. The **train station** is slightly closer, at the far
end of Ferit Paşa Caddesi, connected to the centre by dolmuş or by taxi (around
3.5YTL). A THY shuttle bus links the city centre with Konya's **airport**.

Konya has its share of carpet-shop hustlers and self-styled guides, many having
only a hazy idea of the location and history of Konya's monuments. Ignore them

if you can, as finding your own way around in the compact city-centre is not difficult. The town centre consists of a large roundabout – encircling the hillock of **Alâeddin Parkı** – and one main street, first called **Alâeddin Caddesi** and, later, **Mevlâna Caddesi**, leading southeast from the hill to the Mevlâna museum. The city's preferred hotels and restaurants are all situated in this central area, and all of the monuments and other attractions are within walking distance.

The **tourist office** (Mon–Fri 8am–5.30pm; plus discretionary weekend hours May–Sept; ☏0332/351 1074) is at Mevlâna Cad 21. This handles bookings for the December **dervish festival** (see box on p.618), for which you should contact them well in advance, as seats for the ceremonies always sell out.

Accommodation

Most of Konya's **hotels** are located on or just off Alâeddin/Mevlâna Caddesi. Finding a room shouldn't be a problem, except during the December festival, when Konya fills up, room prices rise substantially, and an advance booking is an absolute necessity.

Balıkçılar Mevlâna Karşısı ☏0332/350 9470, ℉351 3259. If money's no object and you want an excellent location, try this flashy three-star hotel opposite the Mevlâna complex, with air conditioning, satellite TV, and balconies with views over the museum. ❼

Çatal Aile Naci Fikret Sok, off Mevlâna Cad ☏0332/351 4981, ℉351 4981. The friendly management makes it popular with both Turks and backpackers; small, plain rooms and a roof terrace, and very centrally located down an alley off Mevlâna Caddesi. No breakfast. ❸

Hüma Alâeddin Bul 8 ☏0332/350 6618, ℉351 0244. This low-rise balconied neo-Selçuk building, very handy for transport and the sights of Alâeddin Parkı, has tasteful, air-conditioned rooms, a relaxing dining room and bar, and a disco for night owls. ❹

Mevlâna Sema Mevlâna Cad ☏0332/350 4623, ℉352 3521. Centrally heated, with air conditioning and minibar – the smallish rooms have been tastelessly refurbished, with garish bedspreads and wallpaper, but are at least comfortable. ❹

Ulusan Çarşısı PTT Arkası ☏0332/351 5004, ⓦwww.ulushotel.sitemynet.com. A cosy, spotless hotel behind the post office. The shared bathrooms, which serve the rooms on the first floor, are immaculate and the fittings brand new. Second-floor rooms are en-suite, prettily decorated and have TV and fans. Extremely good value, but breakfast is not included. ❷

Yasin Aziziye Cad Sok 25 ☏0322/3511 624. Situated in a quiet alley near the Aziziye Camii, the *Yasin* has large, clean rooms with tiled floors and TV, though some of the en-suite bathrooms have peeling walls. The friendly management speak English, and the downstairs breakfast room is very pleasant. Good value. ❷

Yeni Köşk Esra Kadalar Sok 28, off Aziziye Cad ☏0332/352 0671, ⓦwww.yenikoskoteli.com. Small, quiet and well-maintained, receiving uniformly positive reviews for its clean, air-conditioned rooms with TVs and bright-blue-tiled bathrooms. The breakfast room is cheerful, and the management very welcoming. ❹

The Mevlâna Museum

A visit to the **Mevlâna Museum** (Mevlâna Müzesi; May–Oct Mon 10am–6pm, Tues–Sun 9am–6pm; Nov–April Tues–Sun 9am–5.30pm; tickets sold until 20min before closing time; 4YTL) is among Turkey's most rewarding experiences. It's housed in a former *tekke*, the first lodge of the Mevlevî dervish sect, at the eastern end of Mevlâna Caddesi, and can most easily be found by locating the distinctive fluted turquoise dome that rises directly above Celaleddin Rumi's tomb.

The site of the *tekke* is thought to have been presented as a gift to the Mevlâna's father, Bahaeddin Veled, by the Selçuk sultans. Bahaeddin Veled was certainly buried here in 1232, and his tomb stands upended beside that of his son. According to popular myth, Veled's tomb rose until it stood upright when the Mevlâna was buried alongside in 1273, a measure of the unusual respect held by the father

△ Mevlâna Museum, Konya

The life and teachings of the Mevlâna

Celaleddin Rumi, later known as the **Mevlâna**, was born in Balkh, a central Asian city, in 1207. Various prodigies attended his infancy and a wandering dervish prophesied that the boy was destined for greatness. At the age of 20, vouchsafed a warning vision, the young man convinced his father to flee Balkh with him for western Asia, which they did just in time to avoid being massacred with the rest of the town by marauding Mongols.

They settled in Konya, where the reigning sultan Alâeddin Keykubad received them cordially. Poised on the marches between Byzantium and the young Turkish principalities, the city had a cosmopolitan population, whose beliefs were not lost on the young man; it was almost inevitable that he should emerge as a leading heterodox mystic or Sufi. In 1244 came a fateful meeting with **Shams-i-Tabriz**, a wandering dervish from Iran, whom Rumi immediately recognized as a spiritual mentor. For several years the two men kept near-constant company until some of Rumi's followers, jealous of the interloper's hold on their teacher, plotted to have Shams murdered.

Until the 1250s Rumi remained inconsolable, and apparently only reconciled himself to his companion's death in the process of composing a masterpiece of Persian devotional poetry, the **Mathnawi**. A massive work covering several volumes (see p.1043 for a recommended translation of excerpts), it concerns the soul's separation from God – characterized as the Friend – as a consequence of earthly existence, and the power of a mutual yearning to bring about a reunion, either before or after bodily death. The Mevlâna – as Rumi was by now widely known – himself died on December 17, 1273, a date subsequently referred to by his followers as the Wedding Night.

On a practical level, the Mevlâna instructed his disciples to pursue all manifestations of truth and beauty, while avoiding ostentation, and to practise infinite tolerance, love and charity. He condemned slavery, and advocated monogamy and a higher prominence for women in religious and public life. The Mevlâna did not advocate complete monastic seclusion – the Mevlevîs held jobs in normal society and could marry – but believed that the contemplative and mystical practices of the dervish would free them from worldly anxieties.

The teachings of the Mevlâna were an exciting departure from Islamic orthodoxy, and they're still one of the most attractive aspects of the religion to Westerners and liberal Muslims alike. Although his ideas have never been fully accepted as Islamic orthodoxy, it's reassuring that a man who was expressly opposed to religious bigotry, while advocating song, dance and humility as a means to divine union, should still have a dedicated following among devout Muslims.

towards his son. (Conversely, the custom of a son rising to his feet when his father enters a room is still prevalent in Turkey.)

The structures adjacent to the tomb were subsequently enlarged by the *çelebi*s (literally "nobility"), the disciples of the Mevlâna who took over leadership of the order after his death. They served as a place of mystical teaching, meditation and ceremonial dance (*sema*), from shortly after Rumi's death in 1273 until 1925, when Atatürk banned all Sufic orders. Over the centuries the various dervish orders had become highly influential in political life and thus could pose a threat to his secular reforms.

Most of the **buildings** in the compound, including the *tekke* and *semahane*, were built late in the fifteenth and early in the sixteenth centuries by the sultans Beyazit II and Selim I. Opposite the entrance a *şadırvan*, or fountain for ritual ablutions, still plays. Along the south and east sides of the courtyard are the **cells** where the dervishes prayed and meditated, today containing waxwork figures dressed in the costume worn during the whirling ceremony. Before they were allowed the privilege of seclusion in the cells, the novices had to spend a period of a thousand

and one days in manual labour in the **soup kitchens**, which are also open to the public. After the novitiate they could return to the community and take jobs, even marry, while retaining membership of the order. Next to the quarters of the şeyh (head of the dervish order), now the museum office, is a **library** of five thousand volumes on the Mevlevî and Sufic mysticism.

Across the courtyard in the main building of the museum is the **mausoleum** containing the tombs of the Mevlâna, his father and other notables of the order. You should leave your shoes at the door and shuffle along in a queue of pilgrims, for whom this is the primary purpose of their visit. Women must cover their heads, and if you're wearing shorts you'll be given a skirt-like affair to cover your legs, regardless of sex. The measure of devotion still felt toward the Mevlâna is evident in the weeping and impassioned prayer that takes place in front of his tomb, but non-Muslim visitors are treated with respect and even welcomed. This is in strict accordance with Rumi's own dictates on religious tolerance:

Come, come whoever you are, whether you be fire-worshippers, idolaters or pagans. Ours is not the dwelling-place of despair. All who enter will receive a welcome here.

If you're a lone *gavur* (infidel) in a centre of Islamic pilgrimage this sentiment is surely one to be cherished.

The semahane

The adjoining room is the original **semahane** (the circular hall in which the *sema* was performed), considered the finest in Turkey. Exhibits include some of the musical instruments of the original dervishes, including the *ney* (reed flute). Novice dervish-musicians did not, and still do not, buy a *ney*, but are given one by their *murşid* or spiritual (and music) teacher, who fashions it for them. The reeds for these flutes are still grown throughout southeastern Turkey; it is said that the sound they make is a cry for their nursery reed-bed. An analogous but more esoteric explanation in the *Mathnawi* describes it as the lament of the human soul for reunion with the Friend, the dervish epithet for the Godhead. The instrument indeed has the same range as a human voice, and in the hands of a virtuoso the sound is extremely poignant. A tape of dervish music plays continually in the museum, and the "voice" of the *ney* is clearly distinct above the other instruments.

Other exhibits include the original illuminated *Mathnawi* – the long devotional poem of the Mevlâna now translated into twelve languages – and silk and woollen carpets, some of which form part of the great body of gifts received by Celaleddin Rumi from sultans and princes. One 500-year-old silk carpet from Selçuk Persia is supposed to be the finest ever woven, with 144 knots to the square centimetre; it took five years to complete. The Selçuk rugs on display here give credence to the theory that their skills were adopted by the Ottomans, since many of the patterns and motifs, previously unique to Selçuk works, recur in subsequent carpetwork throughout Asia Minor, and some of the same knots are used in Selçuk, and later, Ottoman examples.

The latticed gallery above the *semahane* was for women spectators, a modification introduced by the followers of the Mevlâna after his death. The heavy chain suspended from the ceiling and the concentric balls hanging from it have been carved from a single piece of marble. In the adjoining room, a casket containing hairs from the beard of the Prophet Mohammed is displayed alongside some finely illuminated medieval Korans.

The dervish festival and ceremony

Since Konya is the spiritual and temporal home of the whirling dervishes, the city plays host to the annual **dervish festival** every December 10–17, during the week prior to the anniversary of the Mevlâna's death. Unfortunately this is not the best place or season to witness a dervish rite: with sub-zero temperatures, doubled hotel rates and shops full of whirling dervish lamp-stands and other kitsch, Konya is probably at its worst.

Moreover, the troupe that performs the ritual in a new, purpose-built hall does not profess to live as Mevlevîs; before you fork out for the ticket it's worth remembering that the best place to witness a ceremony is probably in the restored *semahane* in İstanbul, the Galata Mevlevîhane (see p.173). The group there has official recognition as a dance troupe, but its members are also practising dervishes who have undergone the novitiate and live according to the teachings of the Mevlâna on a daily basis. Alternatively, in July and August, there are official *sema* performances in the Cultural Hall next to the Mevlâna complex, priced at €15.

Contrary to the main body of Islamic belief, the Mevlâna extolled the virtues of music and dance, and the **whirling ceremony** – more properly the *sema* – for which the Mevlevî dervishes are renowned is a means of freedom from earthly bondage and abandonment to God's love. Its ultimate purpose is to effect a union with God.

The **clothes** worn by the Mevlevîs during the observance have symbolic significance. The camel-hair hat represents a tombstone, the black cloak is the tomb itself, and the white skirt the funerary shroud. During the ceremony the cloak is cast aside, denoting that the dervishes have escaped from their tombs and from all other earthly ties. The **music** reproduces that of the spheres, and the turning dervishes represent the heavenly bodies themselves. Every movement and sound made during the ceremony has an additional significance, and is strictly regulated by detailed and specific directions. As an example, the right arms of the dancers are extended up to heaven and the left are pointing to the floor, denoting that grace is received from God and distributed to humanity, without anything being retained by the dervishes themselves.

The **three stages of the dance** are: knowledge of God, awareness of God's presence and union with God. As the dancers turn they repeat a *zikir*, or "chant of remembrance", under their breath, while the musicians sing a hymn expressing the desire for mystic union. In the final part of the ceremony, the *şeyh*, or current head of the order, the incarnation of the Mevlâna, joins the dancers and whirls with them.

The rest of the city

The modern city radiates out from the **Alâeddin Parkı**, at the opposite end of Mevlâna/Alâeddin Caddesi from the Mevlâna Museum. As traffic islands go, it's a lovely, wooded place for a stroll; there are also many outdoor cafés to sit at. The site of the original acropolis, the *tepe*, has yielded finds dating back to 7000 BC as well as evidence of Hittite, Phrygian, Roman and Greek settlers, most of which are now in the museum in Ankara. At the foot of the hill to the north are the scant remains of a **Selçuk palace**: two pieces of stone wall, incongruously surmounted by an ugly concrete canopy.

The only other surviving building to bear witness to any of the long history of this mound is the imposing **Alâeddin Camii** (daily 9.30am–5pm; donation requested), begun by Sultan Mesut I in 1130 and completed by Alâeddin Keykubad in 1221. Masonry on the northeast facade survives from an earlier, unidentified, Classical construction and comprises a row of marble columns whose varying sizes have been cleverly compensated for in the surrounding stonework and whose diminishing heights echo the slope of the hill. The original building probably consisted of the fan-shaped hall, whose flat mud roof is supported on six more rows of Roman columns.

Its typical plain Selçuk interior contains 42 ancient columns with Roman capitals supporting a flat roof, with a small domed area over the *mihrab*. The beautiful carved ebony *mimber*, dated 1155, is the oldest inscribed and dated Selçuk work of art in existence. A hoard of Selçuk carpets, discovered when the mosque was renovated, has been relocated to the Mevlâna Müzesi, but the remains of eight Selçuk sultans, including the warrior Alparslan and Alâeddin Keykubad, are still in a **tomb** located in a separate hall of the mosque interior.

The Karatay Medresesi

The nearby **Karatay Medresesi** on Ankara Caddesi (Mon–Sat 8.30am–noon & 1.30–5.30pm; 2YTL) is another important Selçuk monument. Built in 1251, the *medrese*, or school of Islamic studies, now houses a museum of ceramics, but the building itself provides greater interest. The main **portal** is a fine example of Islamic art at its most decorative, combining elements such as Arabic striped stonework and Greek Corinthian columns with a structure that is distinctly Selçuk: a tall doorway surmounted by a pointed, stalactite arch, reminiscent of the entrance of a tent. The features that distinguish Konya's two important Selçuk portals – this and the even more decorative example at the entrance of the İnce Minare Medresesi – from other examples of Selçuk masonry are the use of Koranic script and interlacing, geometric patterns in the decoration.

Inside the *medrese* the most attractive exhibit is again part of the building itself. The symmetrical tiling of the famed **dome of stars** is a stylized representation of the heavens in gold, blue and black monochrome tiles. Painted Ottoman tiles from İznik and Kütahya appear clumsy in contrast with those of this delicate mosaic. Selçuk **ceramics** on display in the galleries bear witness to the fact that pious concerns were overruled by secular taste – not to mention the contributions of conquered Christian and pagan subjects – even in medieval times. The striking images of birds, animals and even angels would have been strictly forbidden in more orthodox Islamic societies.

The İnce Minare Medresesi

Behind its fine Selçuk portal the **İnce Minare Medresesi**, or "Academy of the Slender Minaret" (Tues–Sun 9am–noon & 1.30–5.30pm; 2YTL), on the west side of Alâeddin Parkı by the tramway stop, is now being used as a lapidary (gem) and woodcarving museum. The minaret from which it takes its name was severely truncated by lightning in 1901; today the most exquisite feature is the **portal**, even more ornate than that at the Karatay Medresesi.

Most of the exhibits in the museum, like the ceramics in the Karatay Medresesi, came from the ruined Selçuk palace across the way. The finest individual items on display are Selçuk stone reliefs, explicitly showing the influence of Byzantium. Most prominent are winged angels, bestiary pediments and a two-headed eagle relief, said to be from the vanished walls of the medieval city and now the official logo of the modern town.

The Sırcalı Medrese and the archeological museum

A short walk southeast of Alâeddin Parkı along Ressam Sami Sokak, the thirteenth-century **Sırcalı Medrese** (Mon–Fri 8.30am–5.30pm; 2YTL) now houses government offices. Highlights of the building, mostly restored in harsh brick, are the fine blue-glazed tilework in the rear porch, all that remains of what was once a completely ornamented interior, and the handsome portal – all visible even if the gate is locked.

Continuing in the same direction, you'll reach the **Archeological Museum** (Arkeoloji Müzesi; Tues–Sun 9am–noon & 1.30–5.30pm; 2YTL), containing the only pre-Selçuk remains in the city. These include the few Hittite artefacts from the nearby site of Çatal Höyük (see p.622) that have not been relocated to Ankara, and three well-preserved Roman sarcophagi from Pamphylia, one of which depicts Hercules at his twelve labours. Just northeast of the museum, the thirteenth-century **Sahip Ata Külliyesi** is semi-ruined but retains its beautiful brick and stone entrance portal, plus a tiled *mihrab*.

Around the bazaar

On Hükümet Alanı, the north edge of Konya's workaday **bazaar** is marked by the brick **İplikçi Camii**, Konya's oldest (1202) mosque to survive intact and still be in use; legend claims that the Mevlâna preached and meditated here. It is also worth looking out for the **Aziziye Camii** in the bazaar, an Ottoman mosque easily recognized by its unusual (for Turkey) Moghul-style minarets. The bazaar, like the city itself, is very traditional and surprisingly relaxed. Look out for the alternative healing remedies on sale, from daisy water to leeches.

The Koyunoğlu Museum

Around 1.5km away, on the southeast side of the centre, the **Koyunoğlu Museum**, at Kerimdede Cad 25 (Koyunoğlu Müzesi; Mon–Sat 8am–5.30pm; 2YTL), is an eclectic private collection donated to the city by the Koyunoğlu family. Downstairs are black-and-white pictures of old Konya, but the museum is mainly interesting for its ethnographic section upstairs, which consists of a rich collection of embroidered textiles, some Selçuk and Ottoman ceramics and objects from everyday nineteenth-century life, such as bath clogs and musical instruments. There's also a fine collection of antique carpets, which enthusiasts shouldn't miss, including examples from Niğde, Konya and Karaman. Adjoining it is the restored period **house** of the donor family (same hours as museum; free), containing original woodwork and furnishings.

Eating and drinking

Konya's innate religious conservatism has hampered the development of a real "eating out" culture and, although this has begun to change recently, **restaurants** serving alcohol are few and far between, while decor and service are usually strictly functional. The better restaurants are listed below, but if you are after **fast food** check out the numerous places on Atatürk Bulvarı.

Çatal Lokantasi Naci Fikret Sokak, off Mevlâna Cad. Small, homely restaurant that serves a decent, tender version of the local speciality, *fırın kebap* (a small portion of lamb or mutton oven-roasted in a clay dish) for around 3YTL.

Gülbahçesi Konya Mutfağı Nazimbey Cad. Built around the small courtyard of a period house and, like the nearby Mevlevî Sofrası, featuring a roof terrace with uninterrupted views of the Mevlâna complex and *sofra* tables where you sit cross-legged on cushions, but somehow lacks the atmosphere of the *Mevlevî Sofrası* (see below).

Halil İbrahim Sofrası Opposite the Mevlâna complex. Housed in an old building to the right of the *Balıkçılar Hotel*, and recommended by locals for tender kebabs and crispy *pide*.

Köşk Konya Mutfağı Topraklık Cad 66. A five-minute stroll south of the Mevlâna complex, this unusual restaurant serves a wide range of kebabs and grills, and specializes in a variety of *börek* dishes – at around 4YTL per portion. In summer tables are set out along a verandah fronted by a pretty garden/allotment area, while in winter a converted 1930s mansion houses the dining room.

Mevlâna Sema Mevlâna Cad. Rooftop terrace-restaurant of the hotel, offering a standard range of grills and kebabs, but also a delicious green-bean stew. A full meal with beer should cost around 12YTL.

Mevlevî Sofrası Nazimbey Cad; north side of the Mevlâna complex. Perhaps the best place to eat in town – a restaurant contained within a series of beautifully restored houses, where prices for a wide range of well-prepared

Turkish *mezes*, grills and kebabs are reasonable, around 10YTL a head. More unusual dishes include okra soup and the local semolina-based sweet, *hoşmeriim*.

Şifa Mevlâna Cad, opposite the *Şifa Otel*. Convenient and well patronized, with a wide variety of hot and cold *mezes*, plus the standard grills and a *pide* oven.

Listings

Airport THY office, Alâeddin Cad 9 ☎0332/351/2000; airport buses leave 45min before flights.
Banks and exchange There are several *döviz* offices and ATMs on Hükümet Alanı.
Car rental Available from Avis, Nalçacı Caddesi, Acentacılar Sitesi, B-Blok 87 (☎0332/237 3750); Rüya Turizm, Alâeddin Cad (☎0332/352 7228); and Selen, Aziziye Cad (☎0332/353 6745).
Hamam Behind Şerafeddin Camii on Hükümet Alanı. It's everything you could ask of a Turkish bath: white stone and marble with traditional tiny round skylights striping the steam with rays of sun-

light. It has separate wings for men and women, and the masseurs are skilled and thorough. 16YTL for a scrub and massage.
Internet access Dilara, opposite the front entrance of the Catholic church, just off Alâeddin Bul, and another couple of Internet cafés near *McDonald's* on Alâeddin Bul.
Police Ferit Paşa Caddesi ☎0332/322 2816.
Post office PTT on Hükümet Alanı (daily 8.30am–midnight).
Tours Selen, Aziziye Cad (☎0332/353 6745), offers city tours, and trekking and hunting trips around Beyşehir.

Around Konya

There's little to see in the immediate environs of Konya, save the tumbledown village of **Sılle**, though enthusiasts might be persuaded to spend a day or so touring the area's more remote archeological and historical remnants – namely **Çatal Höyük**, possibly Anatolia's earliest settlement; the church of **Kilistra**, with its St Paul connections; and the ruined Byzantine churches and monasteries of the **Binbir Kilise** region.

Everything else to see from Konya is firmly **en route to Cappadocia**, a couple of hundred kilometres to the east. Depending on your available time, and your inclination, the journey can either take in the **Sultanhanı Kervansaray** (on the most direct route east) or, much more roundabout, the crater lake of **Acı Göl** and the isolated ancient site of **İvriz**.

Apart from Sılle and (less easily) Çatal Höyük, which can both be visited by public transport, it goes without saying that you'll need your own transport to tour any of the sites scattered across the flat, fertile and relentless Konya plain.

Sılle

Hidden in a canyon 8km northwest of Konya, **SİLLE** is accessible by the #64 city bus from the small bus garage on the ring road near the market. With your own vehicle, thread through the village, following the canal spanned by a series of tiny old bridges, until arriving at the bus's final stop, labelled "Son Durak". It's best to show up while school is in session – otherwise the village children can be particularly annoying.

A **Byzantine church** (Tues–Sun 9am–4pm; free), more impressive than handsome, stands visible just to the southwest. The brickwork of the drum dome surmounting the vast, boxy structure is obviously medieval. Inside, however, the naive nineteenth-century decor, collapsed icon screen and fairly well-preserved ceiling murals show that the church was in use until 1923. In the surrounding cliffs you can glimpse some hermitages.

Gökyurt and Kilistra

GÖKYURT, left off the Seydişehir road, 42km southwest of Konya, is a spec-tacularly situated traditional farming village, with views over a green valley reminiscent of the Ihlara gorge. The village overlies **Kilistra** (unlocked; free), a church that has a claim to fame in a visit from St Paul (although it's nearby Lystra, which has less visible remains, that is the place quoted in the texts). On the hill is a charmingly complete rock-cut church of cruciform plan, of the early Byzantine/Christian era, and below it some troglodyte dwellings. It's worth walking down the hill from the village to see the humpback bridge carrying a cobbled road that St Paul may have trodden.

Çatal Höyük

Excavations of prehistoric tumuli at the important Neolithic site of **Çatal Höyük** continue under an international team resident on site during the summer. This is the best time to visit, bearing in mind that there's little to see so you need a lively imagination. There are dolmuşes from Konya to the town of **Çumra**, 48km southeast, from where you will need to take a taxi to the site itself, 10km north of Çumra. With your own transport, leave Konya on the Karaman/Silifke road, Highway 715, and take a left to Çumra 2km before İçeri Çumra. The road to the site is marked in the town.

Discovered by the British archeologist James Mellaart in 1958, **the site** (open daylight hours; free) consists of twin, flattened hills that are supposed to resemble the shape of a fork, hence the name Çatal Höyük, or "Fork Tumulus". A number of exciting discoveries made here gave significant clues about one of the world's oldest civilizations. Thirteen strata have been identified, the earliest dating from 6800 BC, the latest from 5500 BC. Evidence pointed to entire complexes of houses, crammed together without streets to separate them, and entered through holes in the roof. Also found were murals of men being eaten by vultures, ani-mal-head trophies stuffed with squeezed clay, and human bones wrapped in straw matting and placed under the seats in a burial chamber. There is also the world's first landscape painting, a mural depicting the eruption of a volcano, presumably nearby Hasan Dağa.

Most famous of all the discoveries are statuettes of the **mother goddess**, sup-posed to be related to the Phrygian goddess Cybele and her successor Artemis. The baked earthenware or stone figures are 5–10cm tall and show a large-breasted, broad-hipped woman crouching to give birth. The most interesting pieces are now in Ankara's Museum of Anatolian Civilizations (see p.685), though a small **museum** near the site entrance houses some of the less fascinating finds.

Binbir Kilise

Binbir Kilise, or "A Thousand and One Churches", is the name given to a remote region directly north of Karaman, itself 107km southeast of Konya. Scattered across the base of the extinct volcano Kara Dağ are indeed close to that number of ruined churches and monasteries, mostly dating from the ninth to the eleventh centuries, when the region was a refuge for persecuted Christians.

To get there, travel on the paved road 21km north from Karaman via Kılbasan, and then turn left (northwest) on a rougher dirt track for 10km more towards the village of **MADEN ŞEHIR**, in the middle of one of the main concentrations of basalt-built chapels. These, many in good condition, are all that's left of a substan-tial, unidentified town that flourished from Hellenistic to Byzantine times. If you're intrigued, and have a tough car, there's another abandoned town to see, with a cluster of churches, at the hamlet known variously as **DEĞİLE** or **DEĞLER**, about 8km to the west. Villagers at Maden Şehir may well offer guiding services, and it's probably a good idea to take them up on it.

Sultanhanı Kervansaray

The **Sultanhanı Kervansaray** (daily 7am–7pm; 2YTL), 108km of dull driving from Konya on the Aksaray road, was one of the many public inns built by the Selçuks during the reign of Alâeddin Keykubad, testifying to the importance placed on trade and social welfare by this highly cultured society. The buildings date from 1229, but have been substantially restored, first by Mehmet the Conqueror, evidence of the continued importance of this east–west trading route in the Ottoman period, and more recently by Turkish Radio and Television, which used the *kervansaray* as the location for a historical drama.

The emphasis placed on security is clear from the high walls surrounding the compound, and from the size of the **portal**, truly massive and impressively ornate. Inside, the most prominent building is the small **mosque**, which takes a central position raised high above the courtyard on four pillars, away from the dangers of stray pack animals.

Animals were stabled opposite the entrance, in the enormous hall with five cradle-vaulted naves divided by huge pillars. The height of this room suggests accommodation for elephants rather than camels and mules, but it was meant to convey an impression of might and vigour to the foreign merchants who would stay here for up to three days completely free of charge. To either side of the entrance were private rooms and dormitories for servants, a hamam, workshops, a smithy and storerooms.

Practicalities

The best of the two **pension/campgrounds** in Sultanhanı village, a kilometre or so southeast, is the *Kervan* (☎0382/242 2325, ✉kervancamping@mynet.com; ❷), run by a friendly, welcoming family; it has comfortable rooms, plus attractive camping facilities on the lawn (a tent and two people will set you back €2) and mother cooks a good evening meal, often eaten out in the garden. Much nearer the *kervansaray*, the unimaginatively named *Kervansaray* (☎0382/242 2429; ❷) is a little cheaper but not such good value. Both places cater more to groups and RV travellers than to independent travellers, though you'll be made welcome enough.

Acı Göl and İvriz

Ninety kilometres east of Konya, just off Highway 330, there's a very beautiful crater lake, **Acı Göl**. It lies just east of Karapınar, hidden from the road – the turn-off is a narrow, unsignposted, white-dirt track a little way east of a *Türkpetrol* truckstop on a knoll, about 11km after the Karapınar turn-off. You can camp, and perhaps even swim here, as you're far enough from the road to ensure some privacy, but as the name (Bitter Lake) implies, the water is undrinkable.

Keep to the highway as far as Ereğli for access to **İvriz**, a remote Assyro-Hittite site in the foothills of the Bolkar Dağları Toros range. Highway junction signs are misleading inasmuch as a 21-kilometre drive south of Ereğli only brings you to Aydınkent, the village closest to İvriz. From there a road continues up a spectacular canyon to a couple of neo-Hittite **rock-reliefs.** To reach the best preserved of the two, turn right immediately after the bridge, and head through the gate. The relief, almost at eye-level with the viewer, shows the deity Tarhunzas presenting a bunch of grapes and an ear of corn to the ruler of the nearby Hittite kingdom of Tuvanuva (near present-day Niğde). Like many such Hittite cliff shrines, it seems intended to bestow fertility on the river floodplain below the gorge – still heavily cultivated today.

Without your own transport, a visit would be best timed for a summer weekend, when local families head out from Aydınkent to picnic in the gorge, and may well offer you a ride.

Cappadocia

A land created by the complex interaction of natural and human forces over vast spans of time, **Cappadocia** is a unique environment and should be visited and revisited. Its complexities cannot be understood in the time it takes a tour party to polish off a few frescoes on a photo-stop between hotel and carpet shop.

Initially, the great expanses of eroded, carved and shaped volcanic matter can be disturbing. The still dryness and omnipresent dust give an impression of barrenness, and the light changes with dramatic effect to further startle and alienate the observer. Only with time comes the realization that the volcanic tuff that forms the land is exceedingly fertile, and that these weird formations of soft, dusty rock have been adapted over millennia by many varying cultures and for many ways of

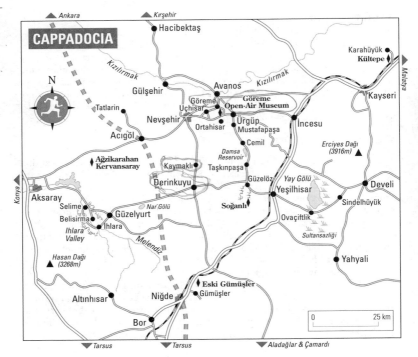

The geological formation of Cappadocia

The peaks of three volcanoes – **Erciyes**, **Hasan** and **Melendiz Dağları** – dominate Cappadocia. It was their eruptions some thirty million years ago, covering the former plateau of Ürgüp in ash and mud, that provided the region's raw material: **tuff**. This soft stone, formed by compressed volcanic ash, has been worked on ever since, by processes of erosion, to form the valleys and curious **fairy chimney** rock formations for which the region is so famous.

The original eruptions created a vast erosion basin, dipping slightly towards the Kızılırmak river, which marks an abrupt division between the fantasy landscape of rocky Cappadocia and the green farmland around Kayseri. In the south especially, the plateau is formed of a very pure, homogenous tuff and rivers have carved out a number of straight-sided valleys. Elsewhere, where the tuff is mixed with rock, the erosion process has resulted in various formations. The stages in the creation of these extraordinary scenes can be clearly seen in many places: a block of hard rock that resists erosion, usually basalt, is left standing alone as the tuff around is worn away, until it stands at the top of a large cone. Eventually the underpart is eaten away to such an extent that it can no longer hold its capital: the whole thing collapses and the process starts again.

In the Cemil valley, near Mustafapaşa, the cones give way to tabular formations – **table mountains** – caused by the deep grooves made by rivers in the harder geological layers. The area is characterized by increased amounts of water and high cliff-banks surmounted by vertical rocks.

Another important region lies to the northwest of the Melendiz mountain range, the valley of the Melendiz Suyu, or **Ihlara** valley. The most individual feature of this region is the red canyon through which the river flows, probably the most beautiful of all the Cappadocian landscapes.

life. While the invading armies of great empires have generally disregarded Cappadocia, indigenous peoples have always exploited the region's potential, living in conditions of comparative cultural and material wealth. The most fascinating aspect of a visit to the area is the impression of continuity: **rock caves** are still inhabited; the fields are still fertilized with guano collected in rock-cut pigeon-houses; and pottery is still made from the clay of the main river, the Kızılırmak. **Wine** is produced locally as it has been since Hittite times, and the **horses** from which the region takes its name (Cappadocia translates from the Hittite as "land of well-bred horses") are still widely used in the region, along with mules and donkeys, in transport and agriculture.

The increase in the number of tour companies that pass through the area may have given rise to some large and ugly hotels, as well as to the omnipresent carpet mafiosi and to seasonally packed museums, but the crowds are confined to a few designated areas and tour guides ensure they don't stray too far. The essential Cappadocia is still there, waiting to be explored by travellers with time to appreciate changing forms and light, and to learn a little about how such an environment has been affected by – and has affected – the peoples who have settled there.

The best-known sites of Cappadocia, and those most frequented by tour groups, are located within the triangle delineated by the roads connecting Nevşehir, Avanos and Ürgüp. Within this region are the greater part of the valleys of **fairy chimneys**, the **rock-cut churches** of the Göreme Open-Air Museum, with their beautiful frescoes, and the **Zelve monastery**, a fascinating warren of troglodyte dwellings and churches. **Nevşehir**, largest of the towns, is dull, but is an important centre for travel in the region, while **Ürgüp** and its neighbouring villages, **Göreme**, **Çavuşin**, **Üçhisar** and **Ortahisar**, all make attractive bases from which to tour the surrounding valleys, but aren't well served by public transport. **Avanos**, beautifully situated on the Kızılırmak river, is a centre of the local pottery industry.

Outside the triangle heading south, but still fairly well frequented by tour groups, are the underground cities of **Derinkuyu** and **Kaymaklı**, fascinating warrens attesting to the ingenuity of the ancient inhabitants. Less well-known sites are located further to the south, to the east and west. The **Ihlara** valley near **Aksaray**, a red canyon riddled with churches cut into its sides, is the most spectacular sight yet to feel the full force of tourism. **Kayseri** has long been a quiet provincial capital, recommended for its Selçuk architecture and bazaars, and side-trips out to the ski resort on Erciyes Dağı and the Sultansazlığı bird sanctuary. To the south, attractions around the town of **Niğde** include the **Eski Gümüşler** monastery, whose frescoes rival the more famous examples in Göreme.

Some history

The earliest known settlers in the Cappadocia region were the **Hatti**, whose capital, Hattuşaş, was located to the north of Nevşehir. The growth of the Hattic civilization was interrupted by the arrival of large groups of Indo-European immigrants from Western Europe, the **Hittites**. By 2000 BC these immigrants had imposed their rule on the region, mixing their own language and culture with that of the Hatti. The result was a rich and varied culture, and a body of laws that was remarkably humane for its time. The torture and mutilation of political prisoners, common contemporary practices, were unknown to the Hittites, incest was forbidden by law, and the Hittite king was "first among equals" rather than an absolutist monarch. In the Hittite laws it was written concerning the power of the monarch: "Whoever commits evil against his brothers and sisters answers for it with the royal head. Call the assembly, and if the things come to a decision he shall pay with his head."

After the **fall of the Hittite Empire** around 1200 BC, the region was controlled to varying degrees and at different times by its neighbouring kingdoms, Lydia and Phrygia in the west, and Urartu in the east. This situation continued until the middle of the sixth century BC, when the Lydian king Croesus was defeated by the **Persians** under Cyrus the Great.

Cappadocia was saved from Persian rule by the arrival of **Alexander the Great** in 333 BC, and subsequently enjoyed independence for 350 years, until it became a Roman province with Kayseri (Caesarea) as its capital. Despite this nominal annexation, effective **independence** was ensured in the following centuries by the relative disinterest of the Roman and Byzantine rulers, whose only real concerns were to control the roads (and thereby keep open eastern trading routes), to make the best use of the local manpower for their armies and to extort tributes of local produce. Meanwhile the locals existed in much the same way as they do now, living in rock-hewn dwellings or building houses out of local stone, and relying on agriculture, viniculture and livestock breeding.

This neglect, combined with the influence of an important east–west trading route, meant that a number of faiths, creeds and philosophies were allowed to flourish here. One of these was **Christianity**, introduced in the first century by St Paul. Taking refuge from increasingly frequent attacks by Arab raiders, the new Christian communities took to the hills, and there they literally carved out dwelling places, churches and monasteries for entire communities.

In the eleventh century the **Selçuk Turks** arrived, quickly establishing good relations with the local communities. They, too, were interested primarily in trading routes and their energies went into improving road systems and building the *kervansaray*s that are strung along these roads to this day. In the middle of the thirteenth century the Selçuk Empire was defeated by the **Mongols** and Cappadocia was controlled by the Karaman dynasty, based in Konya, before being incorporated into the Ottoman Empire in the fourteenth century. The last of the Christian Greeks left the area in the 1920s during the exchange of populations by the Greek and Turkish governments.

Nevşehir and around

Said to be home to Turkey's richest community, **NEVŞEHIR**, at the very heart of Cappadocia, can hardly be accused of an ostentatious display of wealth: the town consists of a couple of scruffy streets, with no real centre or monumental architecture. However, Nevşehir is an important transport node and arriving buses stop here and distribute their passengers to their final destinations on smaller buses. If you do stay, you'll find that it's easy to make side-trips by dolmuş to the monastic complex at Açıksaray.

Arrival, information and services

From the **otogar** it's a short dolmuş ride or a fifteen-minute walk to the town centre. Orientation is a simple matter: the **kale** (castle), which stands at the heart of the old city – to the southwest of the modern centre – is a constant landmark. The new city below is divided by two main streets: **Atatürk Bulvarı**, on which are situated most of the hotels and restaurants, and **Lale Caddesi**, turning into Gülşehir Caddesi to the north.

The **tourist office** is on Atatürk Bulvarı (daily 8am–6pm; ☎0384/213 3659), on the right as you head downhill towards Ürgüp. There are several **döviz offices** and banks with **ATMs** close to the tourist office. The **PTT** is on Yeni Kayseri Caddesi, on the way out to the museum.

△ Priests in Cappadocia

Accommodation

Accommodation in Nevşehir tends to be less good value than elsewhere in Cappadocia, and the nearby towns are so much more attractive that an overnight stop here is by necessity only.

Lowest rates are at the comfortable and friendly *Hotel Şems* (℡0384/213 3597; ❷), on Atatürk Bulvarı above the *Aspava Restaurant*. Rooms have en-suite bathrooms and guaranteed hot water, but are dingily furnished; the main problem, however, is traffic noise, so ask for a room at the back, where the views are better, too. The pleasant *Şekeryapan*, Gülşehir Cad 8 (℡0384/213 4253; ❷), is much better furnished, with its own hamam and sauna, and is conveniently placed on the road to the *otogar*.

The Town

The long walk up to the remains of the Ottoman **kale** is pleasant enough, but once you get there, there's little left apart from a few crenellated walls.

To the southeast of the *kale* is the small shantytown of **Muşkara**, a village of eighty houses and some three hundred people. It was lucky enough to produce a Dick Whittington–type figure who left home and went to seek his fortune in İstanbul. He found work in the Topkapı Palace, married a daughter of the sultan and eventually became grand vizier **Damat İbrahim Paşa**, who profoundly affected the reign of Ahmet III, particularly in terms of its architecture. Like all good heroes he never forgot his roots, and he returned to Muşkara to found a "new town" (the meaning of Nevşehir), based around his own mosque complex. The town was planned with wide, Western-style boulevards – for which the buildings are nowhere near grand enough – and with a long, broad piazza between the market and the mosque.

The **Damat İbrahim Paşa Camii** (1726) is still the most imposing building in Nevşehir, situated on the side of the citadel hill with its *medrese* and library above it and a tea garden directly below. It is set in a large precinct made all the more impressive by the cramped streets of the surrounding residential centre. The stone of the building is a pleasant, unadorned yellow, and its internal painting, especially under the sultan's loge and around the casements, is lovely. The cool, dark interior is further enhanced by small details such as the fan-shaped decoration on the marble capitals, and the original carved wooden *kafes*, the screens that separated the women's balcony from the main hall.

Nevşehir Museum, on Yeni Kayseri Caddesi (Nevşehir Müzesi; Tues–Sun 8am–noon & 1–5pm; 2YTL), is well worth the fifteen-minute walk out from the tourist office. Its comprehensively labelled exhibits include three terracotta sarcophagi, dating from the third to fourth century AD, which resemble abstract mummy cases with little doors inserted at face and knee level. Finds from the Phrygian and Byzantine periods include mirrors, pins, spoons, terracotta pots and the like; upstairs is an exhibition of Turkish carpets and kilims and the looms on which they were made, as well as lovely, old, heavy silver Ottoman jewellery.

Eating and drinking

The *Aspava Restaurant*, at Atatürk Cad 100, serves well-prepared, cheap *lokanta* food and kebabs. Just down from it the *Pınar Pastanesi* doles out wonderful *baklava*, best eaten with a helping of ice cream, for 2.5YTL.

Nevşehir's **market** is important to the region and consequently runs from Sunday morning to Monday night, taking over a large area below Eski Sanayı Meydanı.

Açıksaray

About 19km north of Nevşehir, the **Açıksaray** – reached by half-hourly Gülşehir dolmuşes from Nevşehir's *otogar* – is a sixth- to seventh-century monastic complex, carved out of fairy chimneys and tuff cliffs. Two kilometres further on the same road towards Gülşehir is the far more rewarding **church of St John** (daily 8.30am–5.30pm; 5YTL). The Gülşehir dolmuşes, which depart half-hourly from near the Şekerpayam hotel in Nevşehir, will drop you on the main road. From here it's a five-minute walk to the church, signposted Karşı Kilise/St Jean Church. The **frescoes**, rescued from beneath the soot in 1995, are amongst the most vibrant in Cappadocia. As it is so rarely visited, you have time and space to appreciate the poignant biblical scenes, including the *Last Supper* and the *Betrayal by Judas*.

Hacıbektaş

The small town of **HACIBEKTAŞ**, about 50km north of Nevşehir, was chosen by one of the greatest medieval Sufic philosophers, Hacı Bektaş Veli, as the location of a centre of scientific study. The town was renamed in his honour after his death. The tomb of Hacı Bektaş Veli is located within the monastery complex, but the main part of the complex dates from the Ottoman period, when it was the headquarters of a large community of Bektaşi dervishes. The teachings of Hacı Bektaş Veli (see box on p.630) had reverberations throughout the Muslim world, and different sects, including the Bektaşi, the Alevî and the Tahtacı, still follow traditions that originated in his doctrines. These sects are now the main counterbalancing force to Islamic fundamentalism in Turkey.

Four daily Ankara-bound **buses** from Nevşehir run to the town (1hr), and there are frequent dolmuşes from Gülşehir, 20km north of Nevşehir, itself linked to Nevşehir by regular dolmuşes. The town of Hacıbektaş is also well known for its **onyx**, which is by far the cheapest in the region – the shops are found in the street leading up to the Hacıbektaş monastery complex.

The monastery complex

Construction of the **monastery complex** was begun during the reign of Sultan Orhan in the fourteenth century, and it was opened to the public as a **museum** (Tues–Sun 8am–noon & 1–5pm; 3YTL) in 1964, after extensive restoration. It comprises three courtyards, the second of which contains the attractive Aslanlı Çeşmesi, the **lion fountain**, named after a lion statue that was brought from Egypt in 1853. The sacred *karakazan* or **black kettle** (actually a cauldron) can be seen in the kitchen to the right of the courtyard. Important to both the Bektaşi sect and the janissaries, the black kettle originally symbolized communality, with possible reference to the Last Supper of the Christian faith. Subsequently, as the janissaries gained power, the symbolic significance of the kettle changed: by overturning it, the janissaries showed their displeasure with the sultan, and this could end in his deposition, as was the case when Selim III tried to replace the corps with his New Model Army.

To the left of the courtyard is the **Meydan Evi**, bearing the earliest inscription in the complex, dated 1367. The timber roof of the Meydan Evi – where formal initiation ceremonies and acts of confession took place – has been beautifully restored, showing an ancient construction technique still in use in rural houses in central and eastern Anatolia. It's now an exhibition hall containing objects of significance to the order, including musical instruments and a late portrait of Hacı Bektaş, apparently deep in mystical reverie, with a hart in his lap and a lion by his side.

The life and teachings of Hacı Bektaş Veli

Little is known about **the life of Hacı Bektaş Veli**, but he is believed to have lived from 1208 to 1270. Like other Turkish intellectuals of the time he was educated in Khorasan, where he became well versed in religion and mysticism. After journeying with his brother, who was later killed in battle, he returned to Anatolia and lived in Kayseri, Kırşehir and Sivas. Eventually he settled in a hamlet of seven houses, Suluca Karahöyük, the present location of the monastery.

As a religious leader and ethical teacher Hacı Bektaş prepared the way for the Ottoman Empire in Asia Minor: he was the recognized spiritual leader of soldiers and peasants, promoting the Turkish language and literature among them and helping to popularize the Islamic faith in pre-Ottoman Turkey. The **Bektaşi sect** grew rapidly in Anatolia after the founder's death, largely because of the demoralization and impoverishment of monastic foundations and the similarity of many of the Bektaşi rites to Christian ones, including sprinkling a congregation with water in a ceremony resembling the baptism. The Bektaşi sect was closely linked to the janissary corps, known as the sons of Hacı Bektaş, and the two were abolished at the same time though the Bektaşis were allowed to re-emerge in 1863.

While the life of Hacı Bektaş Veli may be a subject for speculation, his **teachings** are well known, especially his great work, the **Makalat**, which gives a valuable account of his mystical thought and philosophy.

According to Hacı Bektaş, the way to enlightenment has four stages, which he called "the Four Doors". The first is the ability to judge between clean and dirty, right and wrong, as taught by the laws of religion. Second is the duty of the dervish to pray night and day, and to call on God's name – a striving towards a future life. The third stage he called *Marifet*, or "enlightenment", claiming that enlightened mystics are like water, making other things clean, and that they are beloved of God. The last stage, *Hakikat* or "reality", is achieved by those who practise modesty, resignation and submission: those who have effaced themselves in the presence of God and attained a level of constant contemplation and prayer.

The faults that grieved Hacı Bektaş most were those of ostentation, hypocrisy and inconsistency: "It is of no avail to be clean outside if there is evil within your soul." This could be the origin of the unorthodox customs of later followers of the Bektaşi sect, which included drinking wine, smoking hashish, eating during Ramadan and – for women – uncovering the head outside the home. Hacı Bektaş's own dictum on women was unequivocal, and it is one of the most popularly quoted of all his sayings: "A nation which does not educate its women cannot progress."

The third courtyard is the location of a **rose garden** and a well-kept **graveyard**, where the tombs bear the distinctive headware of the Bektaşi order. The **tomb of the sage** is also located in the third courtyard, entered through the Akkapı, a white-marble entranceway decorated with typical Selçuk motifs including a double-headed eagle. Off the corridor leading to the tomb is a small room that is said to have been the cell of Hacı Bektaş himself.

Derinkuyu and Kaymaklı

Among the most extraordinary phenomena of the Cappadocia region are the remains of **underground settlements**, some of them large enough to have accommodated up to thirty thousand people. A total of forty such settlements, from villages to vast cities, have been discovered, but only a few have so far been opened to the public. The best known are **Derinkuyu** and **Kaymaklı**, on the road

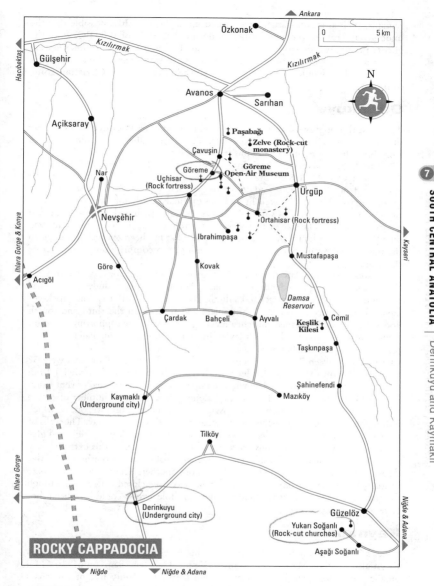

from Nevşehir to Niğde. There are no fairy chimneys here (see box on p.625), but the ground consists of the same volcanic tuff, out of which the beleaguered, ever-resourceful Cappadocians created vast cities that are almost completely unnoticeable from ground level.

In origin, the cities are thought to date back to **Hittite** times at least (1900–1200 BC). Hittite-style seals have been found during excavations and other Hittite remains, such as a lion statue, have turned up in the area. It is possible that the underground rooms were used as shelters during the attacks of 1200 BC, when the Hittite Empire was destroyed by invaders from Thrace. Later the complexes were enlarged by other civilizations, and the presence of missionary schools, churches and wine cellars would seem to indicate that they were used by **Christian communities**.

Derinkuyu

The most thoroughly excavated of the underground cities is located in the village of Derinkuyu, 29km south of Nevşehir. There are half-hourly dolmuşes here from Nevşehir *otogar*, and a daily bus from Aksaray.

The underground city of **Derinkuyu** (daily: May & June 8am–6pm; July–Sept 8am–7pm; Oct–April 8am–5pm; 10YTL) is signposted off to the left as you approach from Nevşehir. It's advisable to get there before 11am, when the tour groups arrive. The city is well lit and the original ventilation system still functions remarkably well, but some of the passages are small and cramped, and can get overcrowded. The size of this rock-cut warren is difficult to comprehend even on a thorough exploration, since only part of what has been excavated is open to the public, and even the excavated part is thought to comprise only a quarter of the original city.

The area cleared to date occupies 1500 square metres and consists of a total of eight floors reaching to a depth of 55 metres. What you'll see includes: on the first two floors, stables, wine presses and a dining hall or school with two long, rock-cut tables; living quarters, churches, armouries and tunnels on the third and fourth floors; and a crucifix-shaped church, a meeting hall with three supporting columns, a dungeon and a grave on the lower levels. In a room off the meeting hall is a circular passageway, which is believed to have been a confessional.

Dropping between 70 and 85 metres to far below the lowest floor level were 52 large **ventilation shafts** and the **deep wells** (Derinkuyu means "deep well"), from which the city takes its name. The whole complex is riddled with smaller ventilation ducts – fifteen thousand on the first level alone. There are also a number of escape routes from one floor to another, and passages leading beyond the city, one of which is thought to have gone all the way to Kaymaklı (see below), 9km away. The walls of the rooms are completely undecorated, but chisel marks are clearly visible and give some idea of the work that must have gone into the creation of this extraordinary place. Most evocative of the lifestyle of former inhabitants are the huge **circular doors** that could be used to seal one level from another. The doors, which were virtually impregnable from the outside, would have been closed with a pole through the circular hole in their centre, and through this hole arrows could have been shot once the door was secure.

Kaymaklı

Nine kilometres north of Derinkuyu, the Nevşehir–Niğde highway passes **Kaymaklı** (daily: March–Sept 8am–7.30pm; Oct–Feb 8am–5pm; 10YTL). Smaller and consequently less popular than Derinkuyu, only five of this city's levels have been excavated to date. The layout is very similar: networks of streets with small living spaces leading off them open into underground plazas with various functions, the more obvious of which are stables, smoke-blackened kitchens, storage space and wine presses.

Üçhisar

ÜÇHISAR, 7km east of Nevşehir on the Nevşehir–Ürgüp and Nevşehir–Göreme dolmuş runs, is the first truly Cappadocian village en route to the centre of the region from Nevşehir. It's an attractive place, with some of the best accommodation options in the region, dominated by a central, sixty-metre-high **rock/castle** (daily 8am–8.30pm; 2YTL) riddled with caves and tunnels which once housed the entire village, but are now abandoned. The best time for a visit is at sunset, when the views of the surrounding countryside, including Erciyes Dağı to the east and Melendiz and Hasan Dağları to the southwest, are particularly alluring. It's an excellent place to get a first impression of Cappadocia's extraordinary geology.

Practicalities

Dolmuşes from Nevşehir drop you just west of the centre of the upper village. The **PTT** is just east of the main square, but there are no banks here so you'll have to drop into Göreme if you run short of cash.

Accommodation

Much quieter than neighbouring Göreme, Üçhisar is extremely popular with French visitors, and for such a small place, has a remarkable range of **accommodation**, much of it in the middle and top end. The most atmospheric places are in the old village on the hillside below the rock, many of which are at least partially carved into the hillside.

Garden of 1001 Nights On the new Göreme road as you leave the village ☏0384/219 2293, ☏219 2505. Occupying a series of caves cut into fairy chimneys, some with en-suite bathrooms and with magnificent views from its balconies, this place combines the quirkiness of a rock-cut *pansiyon* with the facilities of a hotel. ❹

Kaya Pansiyon Below the rock/castle ☏0384/219 2441, ⓦwww.kayapension.com. The pleasant terrace restaurant affords fantastic views, an excellent buffet-style breakfast is included in the price and evening meals are a reasonable 12YTL. Standard rooms ❷, cave rooms ❸

Lale Saray Tekelli Mah ☏0384/219 2333, ⓦwww.lalesaray.com. In the old town under the rock/castle, a very attractive pale-stone building, with bands of carved black stonework framing doors and windows. Rooms are a mix of barrel-vaulted cellars and caves, all fitted with the usual mod cons, and immaculate bathrooms with hydro-massage baths or showers. ❺–❼

Les Maisons de Cappadoce Belediye Meydanı ☏0384/219 2782, ⓦwww.cappadoce.com. A group of self-catering stone houses lovingly and stylishly restored by a French architect. Breakfast is delivered by basket to your door, otherwise you're left to your own devices. The fanciest room costs €250 a night. ❻–❽

Les Terrasses D'Üçhisar ☏0384/219 2792, ⓦwww.terrassespension.com. Run by a charmingly extrovert French family, with well-furnished cave rooms, great views and excellent food. Marco, the owner, leads visitors on free local walks. ❸

Mediterranee Belediye Meydanı ☏0384/219 2210, ⓦwww.medpension.com. Just off the main square, it is not the most characterful place, but has home cooking, clean and simple rooms, and fine views from the rear. ❸

Museum Hotel Tekhelli Mah ☏0384/219 2220, ⓦwww.museum-hotel.com. In the lower village, a warren of expensively restored cave- and vaulted cellar-rooms, many with superb views. Rooms are individually furnished with fine antiques, and have digital TV, tea/coffee machines and Internet connections. Three luxury suites have been newly added; the most expensive will set you back over €600. ❺–❽

Eating

Unsurprisingly, given the village's popularity with the French, Üçhisar has several good **restaurants**. *Les Terrasses D'Üçhisar* is open to non-residents, and serves fine French food for around 15YTL a head. The smart *Elai*, below the castle (the owner will collect you from your hotel in Göreme or Ürgüp: ☏0384/219 3181), is recommended for its magnificent views, both from the roof terrace and the window end of the high-ceilinged dining room. Service is attentive and the French-oriented cuisine (the owner spent many years as a chef for *Club Med*) superb. Specialities include shoulder of lamb served in a pepper and garlic sauce and a shrimp-filled *pilaf* roll. Portions are not huge, and dinner with wine will set you back around 32YTL, but it's well worth it for a treat. *Üçhisar 96*, just off the village square, is more basic and serves up good-value *güveç* for a reasonable 6YTL. The open-air *Centre*, on the village square, serves good-quality traditional Turkish *mezes* and grills.

Göreme

The large village of **GÖREME** – just 3km northeast of Üçhisar – is of central importance to Cappadocian tourism, partly because of its open-air museum, located a couple of kilometres away on the Ürgüp road, but mostly because it is the most famous of the few remaining Cappadocian settlements whose rock-cut houses and fairy chimneys are still inhabited. However, tourist development has

Outdoor and adventure tourism in Cappadocia

Cappadocia's rugged terrain lends itself to outdoor and adventure tourism, from the relative effortlessness of hot-air ballooning to arduous ascents of towering volcanic peaks. Development has been poorly planned but inexorable, responding to the desire of many visitors to escape the standard minibus excursions and actively experience the unique landscape.

The region's canyons and fairy chimneys take on a whole new aspect when viewed from above, and **hot-air-balloon** trips are now incredibly popular. The original operator, well into its second decade, is **Kapadokya Balloons** (℡0384/271 2442, ⓦwww .kapadokyaballoons.com), based in Göreme. Its highly professional European pilots ensure clients get the most out of their flight by manoeuvring the balloon between treetops and fairy chimneys. "Classic" flights (1hr 45min) usually begin around dawn, when the conditions are best, and cost €230 per person, including transfers, insurance and a champagne breakfast. A cheaper, 45-minute flight costs €140, with beer rather than champagne on touchdown. If you can afford it, the longer flight really is worth the extra. Other reliable companies offering similar deals are **Göreme Balloons** (℡0384/341 5662, ⓦwww.goremeballoons.com) and **Ez-Air** of Çavuşin, (℡0384/341 7096 or 532 7045).

Whitewater rafting on the spectacular, foaming Zamanti Cayı in the Aladağlar mountains (see p.656) makes for a thrilling highlight to a Cappadocia holiday. A one-day trip takes you down 12km of exciting grade 1–4 rapids, and as bonus you get to see the Kapuzbaşı falls, which, fed by a series of snow-filled caves, gush straight out of a mountainside. The guides are mostly tough, unflappable Israelis, who cover the safety angles well. Nevşehir-based **Medraft** (℡0384/213 3948, ⓦwww.medraft .com) charges €95 for one-day's rafting, including a substantial barbecue meal. The only drawback to the day-trip is the two-and-a-half-hour drive to the start-point, but Medraft also offer two-, three- and four-day trips (€195, €325 and €445 respectively).

Cappadocia is tailor-made for **mountain biking**, with a network of dirt tracks connecting villages to each other and to their fields, hilly terrain and plunging valleys. The annual **Cappadocia Mountain Bike Festival** (ⓦwww.cappadociamtbfestival.com) attracts top bikers from around the world. The first local agency on the mountain-biking scene was Ürgüp-based **Argeus** (℡0384/341 4688, ⓦwww.argeus.com.tr) which offer one- to irrevocably changed Göreme's character. It has become an institution on the Turkish backpacker circuit (though it receives plenty of well-heeled visitors as well) and its main street is given over almost entirely to servicing tourists – there are carpet shops, *pansiyons*, tour companies and restaurants everywhere, and you can now wander straight out of your cave room and connect to the Internet.

Whilst the influx of visitors has enabled the local economy to boom, the fragile environment is being put under increasing pressure. Already scarce water resources are dwindling as hotel owners compete with each other to install hydro-massage showers, Jacuzzis and swimming pools, and illegal building is scarcely controlled by inadequately resourced and corruptible local authorities.

However, despite the commercialization, the place has managed to hold onto a degree of authentic charm, and a short stroll will still take you up into tuff landscapes, vineyards that the locals cultivate for the production of *pekmez* (grape molasses), and the occasional rock-cut church, unknown to the hordes who frequent the nearby museum.

Local public transport around the region is adequate, bicycle, motorbike and car rental outlets are plentiful, and daily tours are competitively priced, so it's not a bad base from which to make your explorations.

ten-day guided tours. Trips are entirely off-road, and prices depend largely on whether clients wish to camp, use simple pensions or luxury hotels. Argeus has seven of its own bikes, but riders usually bring their own. Another good bike-trip operator is Kirkit Voyage of Avanos (see below). Both companies, and many other outlets in Göreme and Ürgüp, rent out bikes for half- and full days.

With its wide-open spaces, big skies, canyons and mesas, Cappadocia is reminiscent of the American West, and **horse riding** is a natural way to explore. There are several ranches in the region. **Kirkit Voyage** (℡0384/511 3259, ⓦwww.kirkit.com; see p.652) has a well-regarded stable in Avanos, with 45 well-groomed horses. An all-day tour costs €40, while a nine-day, all-inclusive camping expedition is €600. Also at Avanos, with similar standards and prices, is the **Akhal-Teke** (℡0384/511 5171, ⓦwww.akhal-tekehorsecenter.com). The **Rainbow Ranch** (℡0384/271 2413) just outside Göreme offers three-hour sunset rides for €19 as well as longer tours, but does not provide helmets or boots.

Walking is an ideal way to explore the valleys, though so far only basic sketch maps are available, and signposts nonexistent. The trail from Göreme to Üçhisar through Pigeon Valley (see p.638), and the Ihlara Gorge are just two routes popular with independent walkers, though there are many more. **"Walking Mehmet"** (℡0532/382 2069), based in Göreme, knows the area inside out, and leads groups of up to four people for €40 per day (see p.638 for more). More serious hiking possibilities include the two-day climb of 3916-metre Erciyes Dağı, the glaciated extinct volcano on the eastern horizon, recommended for experienced walkers. The volcano to the southwest, 3268-metre Hasan Dağı, is an easier climb (also two days). One of the best companies to take you is **Middle Earth Travel** (℡0384/271 2528, ⓦwww .middleearthtravel.com), of Göreme, which charges €30 for a one-day walk, €40 for the Ihlara valley, €150 to climb Erciyes or Hasan Dağı, and around €400 for a one-week trek. It also offers abseiling from rock pinnacles in Ortahisar for €40.

From Christmas to early March, winter snows give the Cappadocian landscape an ethereal, hauntingly beautiful appearance, and **snowshoeing** is growing in popularity. Kirkit (see above) rents out equipment for €30 per day, and one-week guide-tours around Hasan Dağı cost €300 all-in. For downhill skiing the resort on the flank of Erciyes Dağı (see p.666) has reliable snow and reasonable facilities. Both Kirkit and Argeus can help organize **ski-touring/mountaineering** in the region.

Arrival, information and services

Orientation is quite straightforward in Göreme, as the **otogar** is right in the centre of the town. An unofficial **tourist office** is also here, while right next to it is a Vakıf Bank **ATM**. The **PTT** is a five-minute walk away – head northeast on the main road to Avanos and turn left more or less opposite the right turn signposted "Göreme Open-Air Museum". Most pensions have **Internet** access, but the *Sedef* restaurant on the main road is a good fall-back. It's a small town and the locals are more than happy to point you in the direction of your target accommodation, which may be necessary if it is one of those tucked away in the narrow back-streets.

Local tours

Reputable **tour companies** include Zemi Tours (☎0384/271 2576) and Neşe (☎0384/271 2525), both on the main street, and Ötüken Voyage (☎0384/271 2588, ⓦwww.otukentravel.8m.com) on Üzündere Caddesi on the road out to Pigeon Valley. All three offer a variety of daily tours of the region for around 50YTL per person (standard itineraries include Ihlara and the underground cities, and Mustafapaşa and Soğanlı). Make sure you check out what, if any, shopping stops are included before signing up. The more costly Matiana (☎0384/271 2902) usually sticks to the sites, hence the higher tour prices as there is no commission to be made.

If you want to do it yourself, the three companies just mentioned offer **car rental**, as does Öz Cappadocia (☎0384/271 2159), near the *otogar*: cars from 70YTL per day, mountain bikes (25YTL a day) and 100cc mopeds (35YTL a day) available. Several other companies around the *otogar* also rent out cars, mountain bikes and scooters. Look around for the best deal, but make sure you check for any dents or scratches, as some agencies have been known to charge for damage caused by previous customers.

Accommodation

Göreme's *pansiyon*s have long been a favourite with young travellers looking for cheap lodgings with a relaxed, easy-going atmosphere, and despite the occasional hassle most visitors are not disappointed. A small office at the bus station has information about most of the town's *pansiyon*s, including photographs, prices and so on. There are a number of more expensive establishments in the village, and these too are generally good value. Many of the hotels and *pansiyon*s are now run by Turkish–European/Australian partnerships, and those that aren't will have fluent English-speakers at hand.

Pansiyons and hotels

Cappadocia Cave Suites Unlu Sok 19 ☎0384/271 2800, ⓦwww.ccscappadoci-acavesuites.com. The most luxurious hotel in Göreme (though a little lacking in character), a beautifully restored series of cave and vaulted cel-lar rooms with digital TV and Jacuzzis. ❽

Flintstones Cave Karşıbucak Cad ☎0384/271 2555, ⓦwww.hostelworld.com. A mix of cave and vaulted cellar rooms, and spotless en-suites. The bed linen is a little tasteless, but the real draw here is the decent-sized pool, and the bar with free use of the pool table, ADSL Internet connection and English-language films. Dorm rooms are €6 including breakfast. ❷

Göreme House Eselli Mah 47 ☎0384/271 2668, ⓦwww.goremehouse.com. A good example of how traditional stonecutting skills have survived; natural woodwork and local soft furnishings re-create an elegant period-style mansion. Immaculately run by a Turkish/Australian partnership, all thirteen rooms are good value. ❹–❻

Holy Caves Müdür Sok 3 ☎0384/271 2584, ⓦwww.holycaves.com. Very central, the down-stairs barrel-vaulted cellar rooms are especially appealing and better furnished than the plainer upstairs rooms. There's a kilim-strewn cave-bar downstairs, and a roof terrace with fabulous views over the village. Dorm beds are €4, rooms €15. ②

Kelebek Aydınlı Mah Yavuz Sok 1 ☏0384/271 2531, ⓦwww.kelebekhotel .com. Deservedly popular place above the town, essentially two separate establishments – one a pension, the other a hotel – with a range of rooms and suites all finished to a very high standard and furnished with locally sought antiques. The owners have also just opened a couple of luxurious new suite-hotels nearby – check ⓦwww.sultan-cavesuites.com and ⓦwww.cappadociataskonak .com for details. ②–❼

Kookaburra Konak Sok 10 ☏0384/271 2549, ⒺKookagoreme@hotmail.com. Nicely furnished rooms in an old Ottoman house with great views from the terraces – some rooms en-suite, others waterless, plus dormitory accommodation (€6 excluding breakfast). English-language films shown, plus satellite TV and a pleasant terrace bar. With a free beer or glass of wine thrown in on arrival, it's great value. ②

Köşe ☏0384/271 2294, ⒺDawn@kosepension .com. Travellers' favourite just off the Avanos road, offering a pleasant garden with an excellent swimming pool, and a choice of dormitory beds (€4), doubles with and without bathrooms, and simple singles. The food is well regarded, too, mixing local fare with backpacker staples. ❸

Local Cevizler Sok 11 ☏0384/271 2171, ⓦwww .localcavehouse.com. Well-restored cave and cellar rooms with central heating and air conditioning, set around a courtyard with a tempting pool, antique furniture and kilims. Recommended. ❹

Paradise Müze Cad ☏0384/271 2248, ⓦwww.paradisepension.com. Popular among backpackers and well deserving of its reputation for hospitality, friendliness and excellent cooking (Ramazan was chef at the *Sedef* restaurant for many years). You can stay in a centrally heated cave with en-suite bathroom. Satellite TV and free Internet access. ②

Ufuk Müze Cad ☏0384/271 2157, ⓦwww.ufuk-pension.com.tr. Smoothly and professionally run, with both cave and normal rooms, funky bed linen, gleaming bathrooms, and spacious terraces with views of the chimneys. ❸

Walnut House Zeybek Sok ☏0384/271 2564, ⓦwww.walnuthouse.cjb.net. Right in the village centre, long established, with luxuriously furnished rooms in Ottoman style; excellent value, and with a pleasant lounge-restaurant area. ❸

Campsites

Berlin Camping Ürgüp road, opposite *Flintstones Cave Bar* ☏0384/271 2249. Good facilities and lots of shade.

Kaya Camping Ortahisar road, 2.5km out ☏0384/343 3100, Ⓕ343 3984. Excellent views over Göreme, Zelve and Çavuşin, with shade provided by apricot and cherry trees, and a pool.

Panorama Üçhisar road, 1km out ☏0384/271 2352. Hot water and good facilities, plus panoramic views of the fairy chimneys, but it's a bit exposed to the road and has no trees to speak of.

The Village

The village's long history and the variety of its cultures are clear from the fact that Göreme is the fourth known name bestowed upon it. The Byzantines called it Matiana, the Armenian Christians Macan, and the Turks originally called it Avcılar, only giving it the name Göreme ("unseen") much later, in honour of its valley of churches of the same name.

After you've drunk your quota of apple tea you may be pleased to escape to the more rarefied climes of the tuff hills above Göreme, where people perpetuate the traditions of centuries despite the recent changes in the village below. Pigeon droppings are still collected and used to fertilize the crops, the main form of transport is the donkey and fields are irrigated with water stored in nearby caves.

There are two churches located in these hills, both off Uzundere Caddesi near the prominent *Ataman Hotel*, and signposted from the road. The **Kadir Durmuş Kilisesi** (named after the man who owns the neighbouring fields) has a cave house with rock-cut steps next door to it, clearly visible from the path across a vineyard. It's not painted, but it has an impressive and unusual upstairs gallery, and cradle-shaped tombs outside. Thought to date from the seventh century, it could have been a parish church. The second church, the eleventh-century **Yusuf Koç Kilisesi**, is also known as "the church with five pillars"; its sixth was never carved. There are two domes, one of which has been damaged in the past to accommodate a pigeon coop, and frescoes in very good condition. Among them are the Annunciation, to the left; SS George and Theodore slaying the dragon, to the right; and Helena and Constantine depicted with the True Cross beside the door. In the dome above the altar are the Madonna and Child, and below, beside the altar, are the four Evangelists, the only paintings in the church to have suffered substantial damage.

The wealth enjoyed by Göreme in Ottoman times is reflected in the structures surviving from that period, including the **Konak Türk Evi** (behind the *Phoenix* pension), also known as the Mehmet Paşa House, after its original owner, an Ottoman dignitary. The palatial building has been restored and is notable for the frescoes in the two main rooms, the *haremlik* and the *selamlık*, originally painted by the artist of the Ahmet III dining room in Topkapı Palace.

The walk to Üçhisar

The best-known, most rewarding walk in the Göreme region is to Üçhisar (12km; 4hr), along a path starting from just above the *Ataman Hotel*, through the Uzundere valley, passing through rock-cut tunnels into the heart of the Cappadocian countryside. Good shoes are a necessity, and the final descent into Üçhisar is precipitous, with fairly narrow stretches of path. It's better to go in a group from a *pansiyon* (the *Köşe* owner knows the route well), or with a local guide. "Walking Mehmet" (T 0532/382 2069) knows the area intimately. He charges €40 per walk, quite reasonable for a small group. He's often to be found outside Kapadokya Balloons office (see box on pp.674–635).

Eating

Despite the large numbers of travellers, the quality, variety and price of **restaurant** food is surprisingly good. It's still possible to find plenty of places serving traditional Turkish food, while local attempts at "backpacker" dishes, such as burgers, French fries, pizza and spaghetti are, on the whole, very successful.

Alaturca Müze Cad. Probably the best in town, and with very generous portions. Try sharing the mixed *meze* dish for 10YTL. For vegetarians, the delicately spiced, stuffed potatoes (8YTL) make a good choice. Unusual meat dishes such as Ottoman chicken and Paşa's beef are 12YTL. The dining terrace is atmospheric, service excellent and the local wines well chosen. Overstuffed cushions on the downstairs lawn will keep the kids happy, especially when combined with a triple-thick chocolate milkshake.

Café Turca Bilal Eroğlu Cad 1. Aiming at the same market as the *Alaturca*, this upmarket addition to the local scene succeeds pretty well. The views from the terrace are great, and there are some unusual dishes on offer, including lamb shank served on a bed of puréed potatoes, and beef stuffed with cheese. It's not cheap, though – a meal with wine costs around 40YTL.

Dibek Hakkı Paşa Meydanı. A good lunchtime choice: sit at *sofra* tables in a cool, vaulted cellar room and eat delicious home-cooked food including *gözleme*, *mantı* and *güveç* at bargain prices. No alcohol.

Local Müze Caddesi, before the *Flintstones Cave Bar*. Restaurant noted for its "Ottoman Special" – chicken served in a tasty cheese sauce. It also does good burgers and freshly squeezed orange juice.

Mercan Bilal Eroğlu Caddesi. Boasts an atmospheric terrace and good-value food. The hummus, served with flat *lavaş* bread, is tasty, and the *pirzola* (lamb chops) are tender.

Orient Restaurant Adnan Menderes Caddesi. Excellent *menemen* (Turkish-style scrambled egg) breakfasts, and a varied, reasonably priced daytime and evening menu, including a tasty rack of lamb, served in a pleasant garden. A full meal will set you back around 16.5YTL.

Sedef Bilal Eroğlu Caddesi, opposite the *otogar*. Reasonably priced *crêpes* for breakfast, and decent *pide*, kebabs and grills – expect to pay 6.5–9.5YTL.

Drinking and nightlife

There is a very lively **bar scene**, particularly on Fridays and Saturdays, when the locals descend in force, mixing with the backpackers and expats down from Ankara for the weekend.

Flintstones Cave Bar In front of *Paradise Pansiyon*. Offers films, music, a disco and local beers at 3YTL a pop.

Pacha Bar Müze Caddesi, near the *otogar*. Has the town's biggest dance-floor and is more disco than bar, usually heaving at the weekend. There's an electronic dart-board and a billiard table for quieter week nights, and beers are a reasonable 3YTL, accompanied by a free dish of salted nuts.

Red Wine House Müze Caddesi. Lovely old barrel-vaulted cellar bar, with a wide range of Cappadocian wines. It also serves beer and you can have a puff at a *nargile* while watching one of the free films (get there early and choose your own).

Sedef Bilal Eroğlu Caddesi, opposite the *otogar*. An Internet café under the restaurant of the same name, with a cool cellar sporting *sofra* tables, kilim cushions, cheap beer and free ADSL Internet use. It has become one of the prime hang-outs for both long-stay visitors and travellers.

Göreme Open-Air Museum

The **Göreme Open-Air Museum** (daily 8.30am–5.30pm; winter closes 5pm; 12YTL) – easily reached by walking the 2km from the village, up a steep hill on the road to Ürgüp – is the best known and most visited of all the monastic settlements in the Cappadocia region. It's also the largest of the religious complexes, and its **churches**, of which there are over thirty, contain some of the most fascinating of all the frescoes in Cappadocia. Virtually all date from the period after the Iconoclastic controversy, and mainly from the second half of the ninth to the end of the eleventh century.

The best preserved and most fascinating of all the churches is the **Tokalı Kilise** ("Church with the Buckle"), located away from the others on the opposite side of the road, about 50m back towards the village. The church is different in plan to others in the area, having a transverse nave and an atrium hewn out of an earlier church, known as the "Old Church". Most striking as you enter is the bright blue colour used in the background to the paintings. The frescoes of the **Old Church**, dating from the second decade of the tenth century, depict various scenes from the life of Christ. They are classic examples of the archaic period of Cappadocian painting, which was characterized by a return to the forms of the best work of the fourth to sixth centuries: the style is linear, but like the mosaics of Aya Sofya in İstanbul, the faces are modelled by the use of different intensities of colour and by the depiction of shadow. The paintings in the **New Church** are some of the finest examples of tenth-century Byzantine art. Again they represent a return to archaic models, depicting a series of tall and elegant figures, the niches in the walls of the nave serving to give a sense of depth and substance to the paintings. The pictures represent more scenes from the life of Christ and reflect an interpretation of the apse as the sepulchre of Christ and the altar as his tomb. The crucifix is in the conch of the apse, and the semicircular wall is used for the four scenes of the Passion and Resurrection: the Descent from the Cross, the Entombment, the Holy Women at the Sepulchre and the Resurrection.

The best known of the churches in the main complex of Göreme are the three columned churches: the **Elmalı Kilise** ("Church of the Apple"), the **Karanlık Kilise** ("Dark Church", restored but with a separate entrance fee of 5YTL) and the **Çarıklı Kilise** ("Church of the Sandals"). These eleventh-century churches were heavily influenced by Byzantine forms: constructed to an inscribed cross plan, the central dome, supported on columns, contains the Pantocrator above head-and-shoulders depictions of the archangels and seraphim. The painting of the churches, particularly of Elmalı Kilise, is notable for the skill with which the

Christianity in Cappadocia

For many centuries Anatolia was the most vital centre of Christianity in the Mediterranean region. The great ecumenical councils, which established the elemental doctrines of the faith, were all held in Anatolia and the region was home to some of the greatest early ecclesiastical writers. These included the fourth-century **Cappadocian Fathers**: Basil the Great, Gregory of Nazianzen and Gregory of Nyssa. The religious authority of the capital of Cappadocia, Caesarea (present-day Kayseri) extended over the whole of southeast Anatolia, and it was where Gregory the Illuminator, the evangelizer of Armenia, was raised. The creative art forms in the region are attributable to a long and complex history. Before becoming a Roman province in 18 AD the kingdom had enjoyed 300 years of independence, during which time small states, centred on a sanctuary and controlled by priests, had been the predominant units of power. Cappadocia's religion until the arrival of Christianity had been Semitic- and Iranian-influenced, and its own language didn't die out until the fourth century. Caesarea came under the Patriarchate of Constantinople in 381 AD, and from then on was influenced more and more by religious ideas from the capital.

Turbulent years

Most disruptive was the **Iconoclastic controversy** of 726–843, which had a profound effect on the creative life of Cappadocia. By the beginning of the eighth century, the cult of images had become extravagant, particularly noticeable in contrast to Muslim and Jewish hostility to the worship of images. In addition, the political power of the monks, whose numbers had increased considerably during the seventh century, began to cause concern. The Iconoclastic movement led to the closure of monasteries and confiscation of their property. The worst period of repressive activity occurred during the reign of Constantine V, marked by the **Iconoclastic Council** of 754. All sacred images, except the cross, were forbidden, but at the same time the destruction of any religious building and its furnishings, whether or not they were decorated with idolatrous images, was prohibited.

form and movement of the figures correspond to the surfaces they cover. They are clad in drapery, which closely follows the contours of their bodies, and their features are smoothly modelled, with carefully outlined eyes. The facade of the Karanlık Kilise is intricately carved to give more of an impression of a freestanding building than elsewhere in Göreme. The expensive blue colour obtained from the mineral azurite is everywhere in the church, whereas in the Elmalı Kilise grey is the predominant tone.

A number of other late eleventh-century single-aisle churches in the museum are covered in much cruder geometric patterns and linear pictures, painted straight onto the rock (unlike the frescoes of the three columned churches, which were preceded by a layer of plaster). In the Tokalı Kilise, this kind of painting can be seen appearing from beneath the plaster, but in churches where it was not plastered over, the painting is extensive. The predominant colour of this style was red ochre and the ubiquitous symbol was the cross, which indicated that the church had been consecrated.

In this style is the **Barbara Kilise** (Church of St Barbara), named after a depiction of the saint on the north wall. Christ is represented on a throne in the apse. The strange insect-figure for which the church is also known must have had a symbolic or magical significance that is now lost.

The **Yılanlı Kilise** ("Church of the Snake"), also in this group, is most famous for the depiction of St Onophrius on the west wall of the nave. St Onophrius was a hermit who lived in the Egyptian desert in the fourth and fifth centuries, eating only dates, with a foliage loincloth for cover. According to Cappadocian guides and

From the mid-sixth century the region had also been suffering a 300-year period of turbulence as the battleground of the Byzantines and the Arabs, and was subjected to continual **Arab raids**, characterized by widespread plunder and destruction. The inhabitants responded with ingenuity: in the plains they went to ground, creating underground cities (or extended existing complexes); and in rocky Cappadocia they took to the hills, carving monastery complexes at precarious heights in the tuff cliff-faces.

After the restoration of the cult of images in 843, there was a renewed vigour in the religious activity of Cappadocia. During this period, the wealth of the Church increased to such an extent that in 964 monastery building was prohibited, an edict only withdrawn in 1003. Meanwhile, the religious communities were brought to heel, controlled to a greater extent by the ecclesiastical hierarchy. Even though Cappadocia continued to be a centre of religious activity well into the Ottoman period, it had lost the artistic momentum that had produced the most extraordinary works of earlier centuries.

Remaining churches

Today, the number of churches in the Cappadocia region is estimated at more than 1000, dating from the earliest days of Christianity to the thirteenth century. About 150 of these are decorated. Religious complexes are scattered all over Cappadocia, and despite the damage caused by time and man, some of them are exceptionally well preserved. The technique of excavation, still used today, is evident in the fresh-looking pick marks on walls and ceilings. Most of the architecture is barely discernible from the outside, apart from a few small holes serving as doors, windows or air and light shafts. Inside the churches re-create many of the features of Byzantine buildings. Later churches have domes, barrel-vaulted ceilings and inscribed cross plans supported by pillars, capitals and pendentives that have no structural significance.

literature, the saint was originally a woman, and a bit of a temptress at that. When eventually she repented her wicked ways and asked to be delivered from the desires of men, she was granted her wish, and received a beard, like that of the figure in the fresco. The story probably derives from the emphasized breasts of the figure in the picture, and from the desert foliage, which the saint uses as a loincloth.

Opposite St Onophrius, Constantine the Great and his mother St Helena are depicted holding the True Cross. After a vision in which she saw the True Cross, St Helena travelled to Jerusalem at the age of 80 to find it. She unearthed three crosses and to test which of them was genuine she laid them in turn on the coffin of a dead youth, who revived at the appropriate moment. Next to this painting, two of the "Soldier Saints", George and Theodore, are seen trampling a serpent. St Theodore was a Roman soldier who refused to enter into pagan worship and set fire to the temple of the mother goddess in Amasea (Amasya), Pontus; as a result he was tortured and thrown into a furnace. Between the Yılanlı and the Karanlık churches is a **refectory** with a rock-cut table designed to take about fifty diners.

There are a couple of churches worth visiting on the road back to Göreme village from the open-air museum. The **El Nazar Kilise** or "Evil Eye Church" (daily 8.30am–5pm; 5YTL), carved from a tuff pinnacle, has been over-restored but contains some fine frescoes. The **Saklı Kilise** ("Hidden Church"), about halfway between the museum and the village, uses Cappadocian landscapes complete with fairy chimneys as a background for biblical scenes. It lives up to its name, and you're advised to ask the church's keyholder (who's also the proprietor of the shop Hikmet's Place, which is where you'll find him) to show you the way.

Çavuşin

Six kilometres from Göreme, off the road to Avanos, **ÇAVUŞIN** is a small village with a good hotel and a few nice *pansiyons*, as well as a really beautiful church located in the hills nearby. The best approach to the village is to **walk from Göreme** – through fabulous tuff landscapes – on a path beginning just beside *Kaya Camping*, 2.5km from Göreme, on the road to Ürgüp/Ortahisar. Follow the path for about half an hour, and where it takes a helter-skelter bend through a tuff tunnel to the left, follow the precipitous path to the right, heading down into the Kızılçukur valley: this will lead you to Çavuşin in another half-hour or so. Alternatively, the Avanos dolmuş will drop you at the village.

The villagers have gradually moved out of their cave dwellings as a result of rock falls, but the old **caves**, in the hills above the village, can be explored if some care is taken; it's best to take a guide from the *Panoram Café* in Çavuşin. In their midst is the **church of St John the Baptist** (always open; free), a large basilica thought to have been a centre of pilgrimage. Its position up on the cliff-face, combined with the imposing aspect of its colonnaded and moulded facade, gives it prominence over the whole valley. The church, most probably constructed in the fifth century, contains a votive pit, the only one in Cappadocia, that is thought to have contained the hand of St Hieron, a local saint born a few kilometres away. The walls are covered with paintings ranging in date from the sixth to the eighth century, probably *ex votos* from grateful pilgrims.

A short distance away, located in a tower of rock in the same valley, the church known as the **"Pigeon House"** has frescoes commemorating the passage of Nicephoras Phocas through Cappadocia in 964–965, during his military campaign in Cilicia. The frescoes probably commemorate a pilgrimage to the church of St John the Baptist by the Byzantine emperor, who is known to have hankered after the monastic life and dreamed of retiring to Mount Athos with his spiritual father.

Practicalities

For **accommodation** in the village itself, there's the İn (☎0384/532 7070; ❸), on the left as you descend to the main road, a simple but comfortable *pansiyon* with a shared bathroom. Set back from the road, just out of town, *Panorama Pansiyon* (☎0384/532 7002; ❷) has slightly better facilities, a pleasant attached restaurant with *saç tava* (lamb, tomatoes and onions cooked in a wok) on the menu, and a sunken Ottoman-style seating-area-cum-bar. Behind the *Panorama*, the *Turbel Pansiyon* (☎0384/532 7084, ⓕ532 7083; ❷) has well-furnished rooms with superb views over the dramatic rock containing the Pigeon House church. A recent upmarket addition is *The Village Cave Hotel* (☎0384/532 7197, ⓦwww.thevillagecave.com; ❺), nestling beneath a cliff at the head of a small valley, and with wonderful views across to the cliff church and abandoned houses. The hotel complex has been in the owner's family for generations and has newly reopened after a seven-year restoration programme; it offers a range of tasteful vaulted cellar and cave rooms, delicious home-cooked food and a very warm welcome.

Zelve

The deserted **monastery complex** spread across the three valleys of **Zelve** (daily 8.30am–5.30pm; 5YTL), 3km off the Avanos–Çavuşin road, is one of the most fascinating remnants of Cappadocia's troglodyte past. It's accessible by the hourly circular dolmuşes, which run between Avanos, Göreme and Ürgüp, and drop at Zelve on request. The churches in Zelve date back to the pre-Iconoclastic age (that is before the ninth century) but the valley was inhabited by Turkish Muslims until 1952, when rock falls, which still occur, made the area too dangerous to inhabit.

For the most part, the structure of the complex is dictated by the form of the tuff rock-faces into which it is carved: the inhabitants simply hacked out their dwellings, making few attempts – apart from the odd dividing wall – to diversify the structure with architectural features. On the left-hand side of the first valley (now accessed via the middle valley because of a rock fall that has cut off the entrance), are the remains of a small Ottoman mosque, the prayer hall and *mihrab* of which are partly hewn from the rock, showing a continuance of this ancient architectural tradition.

An exploration of the complex really requires a torch and old clothes, along with a considerable sense of adventure. At the top of the right-hand valley, on the right as you go up, a honeycomb of rooms is approached up metal staircases. Once you're up on the rock-face the problems start: some of the rooms are entered by means of precarious steps, others by swinging up through large holes in their floors (look out for ancient hand and foot holes); on occasions, massive leaps to a lower floor are required. Another daunting challenge is the walk through the tunnel that leads between the two valleys on the right (as you face them from the car park) – impossible without a torch and nerves of steel. None of this is recommended for the infirm or claustrophobic, but it's good fun if you're reasonably energetic and have a head for heights.

A large number of chapels and medieval oratories are scattered up and down the valleys, many of them decorated with carved **crosses**. This preponderance of crosses, combined with the relatively small number of frescoes in the valleys, is thought to demonstrate a pre-Iconoclastic opposition to the cult of images. The few **painted images** found in Zelve are in the churches of the third valley, on the far right. The twin-aisled **Üzümlü Kilise** has pre-Iconoclastic grapevines painted in red and green on the walls, and a cross carved into the ceiling.

The most picturesque of all the Cappadocian valleys, **Paşabağı**, located 2km north of the Zelve turn-off on the Avanos road, is possibly also the most photographed. Previously the area was known as "Valley of the Monks", because it was a favourite place of retreat for stylite hermits who lodged in the fairy chimneys – which, with their black basalt caps, are double- or even triple-coned here. In one of the triple-coned chimneys is a **chapel** dedicated to St Simeon Stylites, hollowed out at three levels, with a monk's cell at the top. A hundred metres east of the chapel is a **cell**, bearing the inscription "Receive me, O grave, as you received the Stylite."

Ortahisar and around

A friendly little village located a little off the road between Göreme and Ürgüp, **ORTAHISAR** sees none of the hordes that are affecting Göreme village so profoundly. Despite being surrounded by the storehouses of Turkey's lemon mafiosi (the rock-cut caves in the region are particularly congenial to the storage of the fruit), the village itself has retained a degree of charm and innocence. After a few hours here you feel as if you know the whole population – and they will certainly know you.

One of the chief attractions of Ortahisar is the fortress-like, 86-metre-high **rock** (daily 7.30am–8.30pm; 2YTL) that, as at Üçhisar, once housed the entire village.

△ Ortahisar

It can now be explored and climbed for excellent views of the surrounding valleys. The only other sight in town is the **Culture Museum**, in an atmospheric, restored *konak* building on Cumhuriyet Meydanı in the town centre (daily 9am–9pm; 2YTL). It comprises a series of rooms with tableaux depicting Cappadocian life as it was lived until very recently (and indeed still is in remoter areas).

The village itself is clustered around two squares, the first of them dominated by the **bus station**, the second, Cumhuriyet Meydanı, crouched beneath the village rock. Regular *Belediye* buses run from Nevşehir direct to the village, otherwise board an Avanos–Ürgüp **dolmuş**, which will drop you on the main Nevşehir–Kayseri road, from where it's a fifteen-minute walk down the hill.

There's plenty to explore in the valleys around Ortahisar, so if you don't have your own transport and you want to spend time in the area it makes sense to **stay** the night. The *Hotel Gümüş* (☎0384/343 3127; ❷), next to the PTT on the road into town, has plain but comfortable rooms with bathrooms, and fabulous views from the terrace, at the back of which there are more attic-style rooms with sloping roofs. Just down from the *Gumuş*, the *Mersin Oteli* (☎0384/343 2220; ❷) is better than it looks from the outside, and has basic but clean en-suite rooms, some with great views. A more intriguing budget option is the *Pigeon Pension* (☎0384/343 3748) tucked away below the rock next to steps leading down into the valley. At the moment it's basically dormitory-type accommodation, with guests sleeping in large, kilim- and cushion-bedecked cellar rooms (€20 per bed), though the friendly owner, Nazim, is working on private rooms. There's home-cooked food and Nazim will drop/collect you at the start/end of local walks (which he knows intimately). A real addition to the accommodation here is the ⚲ *Alkabris* (☎0384/343 3433, ⓦwww.alkabris.com; ❻–❼) on Ali Reis Sok 23, signposted from the main road into town. It's actually tucked away in a peaceful warren of old dwellings behind the village rock, and has incomparable views of both it and distant Mount Erciyes. It has to rank as one of the most tasteful restorations in Cappadocia: from the soft cream goat-hair blankets which serve as bedspreads through to the immaculately white en-suites, it is a model of stylish, yet comfortable, restraint. The only drawback is the limited English of the friendly and knowledgeable Turkish owners.

The best **restaurant** is attached to the Culture Museum on Cumhuriyet Meydanı in the town centre, with excellent-value set menus (6–25 YTL) and attentive service. The *Park* on Cumhuriyet Meydanı has a shady garden area much frequented by the locals, serving soup, *pide*, *sulu yemek*, *izgara* and cold beer.

There are also a few good **antique shops**, at the foot of the rock, selling old light fittings, door knockers, silver- and copperware. Much of the larger architectural salvage comes from Armenian houses being demolished in nearby Kayseri and more distant Tokat.

Churches around Ortahisar

The village **guide** is a deaf mute, Ercan, who seems to know the area better than anyone. Enquire in Hisar Onyx: it would be almost impossible to find some of the churches in the surrounding valleys without him.

Taking the road marked "Pancarlık Kilise" off the second square, you'll come to the valley of the Üzenge Çay, the opposite side of which is covered in pigeon coops. If you walked down this valley to the left for a little over 2km you'd arrive in Ürgüp, but straight ahead a rough track leads across the valley to the **Pancarlık church and monastery complex** (2YTL), 3km from Ortahisar. Hardly visited because of the difficulty of access, the church has some excellent frescoes in good condition – even their faces are intact. They include the Baptism of Christ and the Annunciation, and to the left of the altar is the Nativity.

Heading the other way out of Ortahisar, down Hüseyin Bey Camii Sokak and into the Ortahisar ravine, there's a group of churches that includes the **Balkanlar Kilise**, said to contain some of the oldest frescoes in Cappadocia, and the **Sarıca Kilise**, which has a dome and two freestanding pillars, as well as frescoes of the Annunciation and, on the pendentives, angels. Another church in this valley has a carving typical of the symbolism of the Early Christian period: it shows a palm, representing the Tree of Paradise, above a cross enclosed within a crown.

Another interesting rock-cut complex, hardly known to the public, is the **Hallaç Hospital Monastery**, once thought to have been an infirmary. To reach it, take a right from the Ürgüp road, a couple of hundred metres past the main Ortahisar turn. The site is half a kilometre down a dusty track, signed off to the right. The complex is carved and painted inside and out, the facade decorated with mock doors, windows and pillars, painted in green, black and red.

Ürgüp

ÜRGÜP is a tourist-friendly town, with a very different atmosphere than backpacker-oriented Göreme: if you're looking for good facilities, nightlife and shopping in a pleasant environment, then Ürgüp was made for you. But unlike many resorts of this size, the place has also had the resilience and composure to accommodate its visitors without too many compromises. Before the exchange of populations in 1923, Ürgüp had a largely Greek population and there are still many distinctive and beautiful houses of Greek (and Ottoman) origin scattered around the town. The tuff cliffs above the town are riddled with man-made cave dwellings, now put to use as storage space and stabling for the donkeys whose braying takes the place of a dawn chorus all over Cappadocia. Viticulture and apple farming along the banks of the Damsa river provide an income for some, but tourism is the mainstay of the economy, and the younger generation has moved out of the family caves, and opened shops, hotels and other tourist-related businesses in the town below.

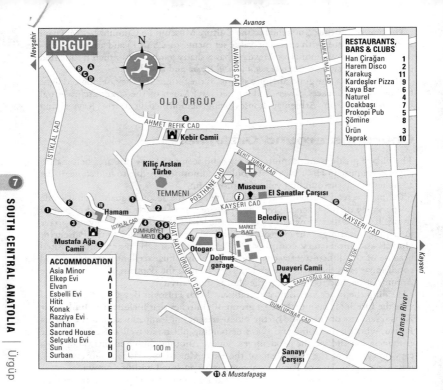

RESTAURANTS, BARS & CLUBS

Han Çirağan	1
Harem Disco	2
Karakuş	11
Kardeşler Pizza	9
Kaya Bar	6
Naturel	4
Ocakbaşı	7
Prokopi Pub	5
Şömine	8
Ürün	3
Yaprak	10

ACCOMMODATION

Asia Minor	J
Elkep Evi	A
Elvan	I
Esbelli Evi	B
Hitit	F
Konak	E
Razziya Evi	L
Sarıhan	K
Sacred House	G
Selçuklu Evi	C
Sun	H
Surban	D

Arrival and information

The **otogar** is right in the centre of town, from where it's possible to get dolmuşes and *Belediye* buses to nearby villages such as Mustafapaşa, Göreme and Avanos, as well as more distant cities. The tourist office, PTT, museum, shops and banks are all close by. The best hotels are, at most, a cheap taxi-ride away.

Kayseri Caddesi, the street leading downhill to the tourist office and museum, is also the main shopping street. The **tourist office** (daily: May–Sept 8.30am–8pm; Oct–April 8.30am–noon & 1.30–5.30pm; ℡ 0384/341 4059) is at Kayseri Cad 37, located next to the museum in a park complete with tea garden, where you can peruse their maps and hotel price-list.

Accommodation

Ürgüp has a wide range of hotels. Those on the outskirts cater largely to tour groups, but there are plenty of good-value pensions and wonderfully restored old houses (now serving as upmarket "boutique" hotels) in the town centre and the Esbelli district.

Asia Minor İstiklâl Cad ℡ 0384/341 4645, ⓦwww.cappadociahotel.com. A range of newly renovated rooms in one of Ürgüp's oldest and loveliest buildings, with an attractive garden

courtyard. ④

Elkep Evi 1 & 2 Eski Turban Oteli Arkası ℡ 0384/341 6000, ⓦwww.elkepevi.com. A handsomely restored pair of cave houses, with extremely comfortable cave or cellar rooms decorated with local handicrafts and antiques. ❹

🏃 **Elvan** Barbaros Hayrettin Sok 11 ☎0384/341 4191, ⓦwww.hotelelvan@ superonline.com. A highly recommended mid-range choice, this old house is set around two characterful courtyards. The proprietors, Fatma and Ahmet, are extremely friendly and keep the place spotless. Some rooms have vaulted stone ceilings, and there's a cool, semi-underground lounge area. ❸

✓ 🏃 **Esbelli Evi** Esbelli Mah 8 ☎0384/341 3395, ⓦwww.esbelli.com. The original features of this collection of village houses have been retained, and the rock-cut rooms are tastefully furnished with period furniture. The owner, Suha Ersöz, has the knack of making his guests feel like his friends and you're invited to help yourself from the fridge in the kitchen, cook a meal and sit in a communal sitting room, listening to CDs. Breakfast is excellent and the views from the rooftop terrace delightful. ❻

Hitit İstiklâl Cad ☎0384/341 4481, ⓦwww .hitithotel.com. A 600-year-old house owned by a charming family. The rooms, looking onto a pleasant courtyard, have attractive vaulted ceilings, Kayseri rugs, minibars and TVs, but otherwise furniture and fittings, which include central heating, are everyday and practical. ❺

Konak Esbelli Mah ☎0384/341 3222. Balconied rooms with large windows afford views of rock-cut houses and pigeon coops opposite, but the rooms are quite basic (marley-tiled floors) and musty. It's an OK option if your budget is tight. ❷

Razziya Evi Cingilli Sok 24 ☎0384/341 5089, ⓦwww.razziyaevi.com. A wonderful, restrained restoration of an old house. The barrel-vaulted cellar rooms are elegantly furnished, the en-suites gleaming. There's no view, but the verdant walled garden more than compensates. Excellent value for money. ❹

Sacred House Barbaros Hayrettin Sok 25 ☎0384/341 7102, ⓦwww.sacred-house.com. Seven individually furnished rooms in a beautifully restored mansion. Genuine antiques mix well with reproduction pieces; dinners are candlelit, as are the Jacuzzi-focused bathrooms. The rooms may be a little dark and fussy for some tastes, but they've been done with flair and certainly promote relaxation. ❼

Sarıhan Güllüce Cad ☎0334/341 2264, ☏341 5820. Plain, simple and very clean rooms in a modern stone-built block backed by a mass of poplar and fruit trees. A family-run place in a quiet part of town. ❺

Selçuklu Evi Yunak Mah ☎0384/341 7460, ⓦwww.selcukluevi.com. A new venture that promises to be well run, this restored house-complex has a series of antique-furnished double and suite-rooms with opulent bathrooms. ❻–❽

Sun Dead-end street leading off the western edge of the main square ☎0384/341 4493, ☏341 4774. Ramshackle affair with a pleasant terrace and a welcoming owner; some rooms are caves, and others have en-suite bathrooms. It's looking a little tired now, with dull brown blankets on the beds and basic bathrooms, and is slightly dearer than the *Konak*. ❸

Surban Yunak Mah ☎0384/341 4761, ⓦwww .hotelsurban.com. Well-decorated, modern and comfortable, with neat bathrooms. The rooms all have arched ceilings, and there's a satellite TV room. Reasonable value. ❹

The Town

Despite its rather incongruous modern central square, Ürgüp retains some of its rural village charm. Men and women in traditional working clothes, leading horse-drawn vehicles and donkeys out to the surrounding vineyards, orchards and vegetable gardens, are not an unusual early-morning sight. This is the time to explore the **old village**, whose buildings appear to be slowly emerging from the rocky hills into which they have been carved. Some feature stylish pillared and decorated facades of the same stone, others are simple caves with doors and windows cut into the cliffs themselves.

The walk up to the Temmeni "wishpoint" begins with a flight of steps opposite the thirteenth-century **Kebir Camii** and includes a 700-metre-long tunnel, which leads through the hill to a door and "balcony" on the other side, furnishing panoramic views of the town and surrounding countryside. Continuing uphill, past the former troglodyte town dwellings (now mainly used for storage or abandoned altogether), brings you to a park known as **Temmeni** ("Hill of Wishes"; daily 8.30am–6pm; 1YTL), where a Selçuk tomb, the **Kılıç Arslan Türbe**, dating from 1268, is open to visitors. A small renovated *medrese* from the same period is now used as a café.

The town's **museum** (Tues–Sun 8am–5.30pm; 2YTL) on Kayseri Caddesi is tiny and not particularly well labelled, but the helpful staff are prepared to explain the exhibits. These include a selection of prehistoric ceramics, figurines, lamps, stelae, statues and ornaments found during excavations in the area.

Wine tasting is possible at any of Ürgüp's six wineries, but the best local wines are widely acknowledged to be those produced by the Turasan house in Esbelli, a kilometre northwest of the town centre, and by the welcoming and cheap Taskobirlik co-operative in a former *kervansaray* (also out of town, though they have a town-centre shop). It's worth remembering that white Cappadocian wines are much better than red; the reds are mixed with wines from other regions, and dyes are added. A comprehensive collection of local wine is available from Mahzen Şarap Evi on Cumhuriyet Meydanı.

Eating, drinking and nightlife

There's a decent selection of **restaurants**, from simple places serving traditional dishes to more tasteful places suitable for a night out. For snacks, there are several decent *pastane*s around Cumhuriyet Meydanı. Ürgüp's **nightlife** is also excellent when you consider that this is central Anatolia and there's not a beach in sight.

Restaurants

Han Çirağan Cumhuriyet Meyd. Atmospheric old house with a vine-shaded garden. Serves simple regional food, such as *düğün çorbası* (wedding soup), *saç tava* (lamb, tomatoes and onions cooked and served on a wok) and *mantı* (Turkish ravioli). A full meal costs around 11–16YTL.

Karakuş Entertainment Centre Pancarlık valley, south of town on Mustafapaşa Cad ☎0384/341 5353. An elaborate underground restaurant-floor-show complex hewn out of soft rock. The €25 entrance fee gets you a substantial meal, unlimited wine, whirling dervishes, folk dancing and a disco.

Kardeşler Pizza Restaurant Dumlupınar Cad 9. Serves excellent crusty *pide* and beer, at around 8YTL for two people. Its sister *Kardeşler* restaurant on Cumhuriyet Meydan is famous for *guveç*, a stew cooked in a clay pot sealed with bread (5YTL).

Naturel Cumhuriyet Meyd. Small patisserie with tables set out on the central square, with decent coffee and excellent *baklava*.

Ocakbaşı Near the market place. Unpromisingly located up a flight of steps, serves traditional Turkish kebabs cooked over charcoal, and is very popular with the locals for its quality food and rea-

sonable prices (allow 5YTL for a substantial meal).

Şömine Cumhuriyet Meyd ☎0384/341 8442. Ürgüp's best restaurant, recently revamped, and situated on the main square. The service is friendly and the well-prepared food good value (allow 11–23YTL for a complete meal). Local specialities include *osbar* (haricot beans with pastrami) and *testi kebap* (a lamb and vegetable stew cooked slowly in the oven).

Yaprak Opposite the *otogar*. Cheap and cheerful restaurant serving *lahmacun*, kebabs and soups.

Bars

Kaya Bar Cumhuriyet Meyd. Almost next door to the *Prokopi*, up a flight of stairs and with a pleasant terrace overlooking the square. Internet and *nargile* (hookah) service, and beers for 3.5YTL.

Prokopi Pub Cumhuriyet Meyd. Using the old Greek name for the town, it has a nice courtyard and cosy cellar bar, though it's rather pricey with beers at 5YTL.

Ürün İstiklâl Cad. Arty *meyhane* cum café in the cellar of an old Greek house. Serves wine, beer and traditional food cooked in a *tandır* oven.

Listings

Banks and exchange Vakıf Bank (summer daily 8.30am–noon & 1.30–9.30pm; normal banking hours in winter), Kayseri Cad 38, opposite the tourist office, has an ATM. The central Ziraat Bankası has a 24hr currency exchange machine.

Bike rental Alpin, on Dağıstanlı Sok for scooters (€15 a day). Argeus (see "Tours", below) is good for mountain bikes.

Car rental Avis, İstiklâl Cad, Belediye Pasajı ☎0384/341 2177; Europcar, İstiklâl Cad 10 ☎0384/341 8855.

Hamam İstiklâl Cad, for men and women (daily 9am–8pm, 13YTL including massage).

Hospital Posthane Cad ☎0384/341 4031.

Internet Kaya Bar on Cumhuriyet Meyd.

Pharmacy Hulya Eczanesi, Açıkpazar Yeri 41,

behind the *otogar*, is friendly, with some English spoken.

Police Opposite the PTT, in the centre.

Post office The PTT is on Posthane Cad (daily 8.30am–11pm for phone tokens and cards, 9am–5pm for ordinary business).

Tours Argeus, İstiklâl Cad 7 (☎0384/341 4688,

www.argeus.com.tr), is the best local agent, and has comprehensive tours to the Ihlara valley and Soğanlı (€65), plus trips to the Kaçkar mountains and winter skiing tours to Erciyes – all its guides speak English. The all-inclusive tours use the best restaurants, and shopping stops are by request only.

Mustafapaşa and around

The small village of **MUSTAFAPAŞA**, 6km south of Ürgüp, makes for a pleasant excursion. The charm of the place lies in the concentration of attractive carved house-facades dating back a century or so, when it was known as Sinasos and home to a thriving Greek community; it is also central to a cluster of little-visited churches. Unfortunately, a paucity of public transport makes Mustafapaşa an awkward base unless you have own transport.

The church of **Ayios Vasilios** is located to the north of the village, beyond the *Hotel Pacha*; pick up the key from the makeshift **tourist office** (opening hours variable), next to the Kervansaray carpet shop, before setting out. The church has well-preserved frescoes, although the faces are damaged, and four rock-cut pillars. Another church, below Ayios Vasilios in the Üzengı Dere ravine, is the **Holy Cross**, partly rock-cut and partly masonry-built, with pre-Iconoclastic and tenth-century paintings including a most attractive Christ of the Second Coming.

On the other side of the village, passing through streets of houses cut by former Greek occupants into the tuff cliffs, is a monastery complex including the churches of **Aya Nicolas** and **Aya Stefanos**.

Practicalities

There are several good **places to stay** in Mustafapaşa. Under restoration at the time of writing, the *Monastery* (☎0384/353 5005, ✉monasterypension@yahoo.com; ❸) has a lovely, vine-shaded courtyard and twelve smallish rooms, with wooden floors and spotless bathrooms. Medium-priced options include the *Lamia Hotel* (☎0384/353 5413, www.lamiapension.com.tr; ❹), with five homely rooms around a flowery courtyard, perched high above town at the end of a steep cobbled street with fine views. You'll share the garden with a dalmatian, several cats, three tortoises and an aviary full of canaries and budgies. Close by is the *Ukabeyn* (☎0384/353 5533, www.cappadociapension.com; ❹), a small but atmospheric place with six well-restored rooms and delightful terraces for relaxing. A real plus is the small pool, situated on the lip of a cliff overhanging the valley below. A slightly more expensive option is the wonderfully preserved *Old Greek House* (☎0384/353 5306, www.oldgreek.house.com; ❹). More than 200 years old, it was until 1923 the residence of the Greek mayor; several of the rooms have original murals and painted ceilings, and a tiny old chapel off the shady courtyard is now a Turkish bath. The hotel also has its own highly recommended **restaurant** serving Turkish specialities for around 16YTL a head, eaten whilst sprawled on cushions around *sofra* tables.

South of Mustafapaşa

Along the Soğanlı road south from Mustafapaşa – there's no public transport – the fairy chimneys give way to a table-mountain formation that is no less fantastic and surreal than preceding landscapes: the red canyon ridge that the road follows could be a backdrop for *Roadrunner*.

About 3km from Mustafapaşa, a precipitous dirt-track marked *Alabalık tesisleri* leads to a tiny fish-farm and **restaurant** serving oven-baked trout. To the right of the Soğanlı road, 5km from Mustafapaşa, lies the **Damsa Reservoir**, where it is possible to bathe from a small, sometimes crowded pay-beach.

The next village along is **CEMİL**, a picturesque hamlet of tuff houses piled up against the cliffside. One and a half kilometres beyond the village, just off the road, lies the **Keşlik Kilesi monastery complex** – three churches, a wine press and a refectory. This is believed to be one of the earliest communal monastic establishments in the region. The watchman, who speaks some English, gives a worthwhile tour of the frescoes in the churches: the first, named after a prominent picture of the archangel Gabriel, includes depictions of the Last Supper, the Annunciation and the Flight to Egypt, all badly damaged and soot-blackened (a torch is essential); the church of St Michael has a wine cellar downstairs; while the church of St Stephen (seventh or eighth century) is the most beautiful of all, elaborately and unusually decorated. Non-figurative ornament includes stylized foliage and interlaced patterns reminiscent of Turkish kilims, and figurative designs include depictions of various fruits and animals, and three peacocks eating grapes.

Four kilometres further along the same road is the village of **TAŞKINPAŞA**. Here a fourteenth-century Selçuk mosque, the **Taşkınpaşa Camii**, is flanked by two hexagonal *türbe* (tombs). The original marble pillars and their disparate capitals are still in place, supporting the twin domes of the mosque, and the old Selçuk minaret can be reached by a set of steps, but the intricately carved *mihrab* and *mimber* for which the building was originally famed have now been removed to Ankara. Just beyond the village, to the left, you can see the remains of another Selçuk building believed to have been a **medrese**, with an attractively carved stone portal.

Ayvalı

Turning right just before Mustafapaşa, coming from Ürgüp, a little-used road leads 10km to the charming village of **AYVALI**, where you can gain some idea of what Göreme and Ürgüp were like before tourism hit. Built in a narrow valley, it consists of cave houses, a rock-cut Byzantine church and an arched bridge of the same period. The *Gamirasu Hotel* (☎0384/354 5815, ⓦwww.gamirasu.com; ❺–❻), a combination of cave dwellings and old village houses down in the gorge, is the only place to stay. It's of a very high standard, with an emphasis on organic foods.

The Soğanlı valleys

One of the most spectacular sights this side of Ürgüp are the **Soğanlı valleys** (daily 8am–5/6pm; 2YTL), 5km off the road from Taşkınpaşa to Yeşilhisar, and less than 20km from either. **SOĞANLI** itself is an attractive village in two parts, Yukarı (upper) and Aşağı (lower) Soğanlı, set into the side of a table-top mountain. Part of the place's charm derives from its inaccessibility; it's off the tour route of all but small local companies. There are just a couple of simple **restaurants**, a few stalls selling the village-made rag dolls, and one **hotel**: the tiny, basic and friendly *Emek Pansiyon* (☎0352/653 1029; ❶), with one double and one five-bed dormitory room, both fashioned from caves. There's no public transport to the village, and in winter it is often completely cut off by snowdrifts.

The Soğanlı valleys were continuously occupied from early Byzantine times to the thirteenth century, and are remarkable for the architecture of their churches and the beauty of the ninth- to thirteenth-century frescoes they contain. The name is supposed to derive from the Turkish *sona kaldı* (meaning "left to the end"), rather than "with onion", the literal meaning of *soğanlı*. This could be a reference to the fact that this was the last village to be taken during the Arab invasion of Cappadocia led by Battal Gazi in the sixth century.

The most interesting of the churches and monasteries are located in the right-hand valley (as you face Yukarı Soğanlı). To reach the two-storeyed **Kubbeli Kilise** ("Church with the Dome"), follow the footpath across a streambed from the village square, and proceed uphill through the village and along the side of the valley. This has perhaps the most interesting exterior of all the Cappadocian rock-churches, its form – a conical dome that is the tip of a fairy chimney resting on a circular drum – being an imitation of a masonry structure. The **Saklı** (Hidden) **Kilise**, with frescoes of the apostles, is 100m before the Kubbeli Kilise, its door facing into the valley.

Descend to the road and then head up the other side of the valley to reach the **Meryem Ana Kilisesi** ("Church of the Virgin"), which has four apsidal chapels with frescoes and Iconoclastic decoration. The **Yılanlı Kilise** ("Church of the Snake") is best seen using a torch, as it is blackened and damaged by Greek and Armenian graffiti. It derives its name from an eleventh-century painting of St George slaying the dragon, to the left of the entrance. Returning towards the village, the **Karabaş Kilise** ("Church of the Black Head") has two adjoining apsidal chapels, the first of which has well-preserved tenth- and eleventh-century frescoes depicting scenes from the life of Christ.

In the second Soğanlı valley, reached by passing the restaurants of Yukarı Soğanlı, the **Geyikli Kilise** ("Church with the Deer") has two aisles that were decorated in the eleventh century, and derives its name from a damaged depiction of St Eustace with a poorly defined deer. Further up the valley the **Barbara Kilise**, a single-aisled basilica divided in two by a transverse arch, has an inscription dating it to the early tenth century.

Avanos and around

The old city of **AVANOS** clambers up hills overlooking the longest river in Turkey, the Kızılırmak. A magnificently "Red River" with a temper to match, the Kızılırmak appears after a good rainfall to be on the verge of bursting its banks. Avanos itself is a town of some character, separated from the rest of Cappadocia by the river and distinguished from all other towns in Turkey by the distinctive earthenware pottery made here. The same red clay that colours the river has been worked for many centuries, and techniques dating right back to Hittite times are still in use. Strolling through the cobbled backstreets of the old town you'll find superb views out across the river – only slightly marred by the new housing development all too evident on the south bank. Exploration of the fields and hills around the town reveals further attractions: calcium pools and thermal springs, a tiny *kervansaray*, and even an underground city, 14km away at Özkonak.

Arrival, information and tours

Transportation to Avanos is good, with half-hourly **dolmuşes** from Ürgüp, Göreme and Nevşehir. From the **otogar**, cross the bridge into town and the **tourist office** (summer Mon–Fri 8am–noon & 1.30–7.30pm; winter Mon–Fri 8am–noon & 1.30 5pm; ℡0384/511 4360) is more or less immediately on your right. The **PTT** is located just beyond the pottery monument on the main street, Atatürk Caddesi, next to the public toilets. Uğur Mumcu Caddesi runs parallel to the river.

Kirkit Voyage, Atatürk Cad 50 (☎0384/511 3259, ⓦwww.kirkit.com), is an excellent **tour operator** that runs horseback trips, as well as bike and snowshoe tours all over Cappadocia (see box on p.634).

Accommodation

It's easy enough to find **accommodation**, with a selection of hotels and *pansiyon*s catering to most tastes and requirements. The *Venessa Pansiyon*, Atatürk Bul, Hafızağı Sok 20 (☎0384/511 3840, ⓦwww.katpatuka.org/venessa.com; ❹), is a rambling building with a bohemian atmosphere and wonderful views over the town and river. *Kirkit Pension*, off Atatürk Caddesi (☎0384/511 3148, ⓦwww.kirkit .com; ❸), belonging to the tour company of the same name, is a series of beautifully converted sandstone houses, decorated with kilims; rooms have either full bathrooms or just a shower. The *Sofa Hotel* (☎0384/511 3840, ⓦwww.sofa-hotel. com; ❹) is just next to the Haci Nuri Bey Konağı (an imposing neo-Ottoman mansion highly visible as you cross the bridge). The hotel has been put together from twenty redesigned Ottoman houses, with immaculate rooms, a garden courtyard and a restaurant. The friendly owner has a fine collection of old radios, keys and scissors, and is in the process of opening an art gallery in the premises. More upmarket, the *Tokmak Konak Evi* (☎0384/511 4587, ⓦwww.tokmak-guesthouse .com; ❺–❻) on Camii Sokak slightly above the main square, is run by a friendly local family recently returned from Germany. The restored rooms, some with old wooden ceilings, others vaulted, are luxuriously equipped and all en-suites have a bath. Breakfast can be taken with the family, who produce their own jams and *pekmez* (grape syrup). If you want to **camp**, head to *Ada Camping* (☎0384/511 2429), on the south bank of the Kızılırmak, which has its own pool.

The Town

Though the quaint, cobbled backstreets and rustic, tumbledown Ottoman, Armenian and Greek buildings are enjoyable, Avanos's real tourist attraction is **pottery**. The monument on the main street – a clay sculpture depicting a potter and, beneath it, a mother and daughter working a loom – is the town's celebration of its art (and of the other local craft of weaving), while the potters' square and the streets that surround it contain numerous tiny workshops where the Cappadocian potters' techniques can still be observed or even attempted. To reach this quarter, carry on walking past the monument for a few minutes, then turn right into the quarter at the *Şanso-Panso* restaurant.

Perhaps the most famous of all the Avanos potteries is **Chez Galip** (☎0384/511 4240, ☏511 4543), belonging to master potter Galip. A tour of the workshop reveals a cellar where some fifty to sixty tonnes of local red earth, collected from dried-up beds of the Kızılırmak, is stored awaiting the water that will transform it into malleable clay. The clay is worked on a wheel, turned by the foot of the potter, in natural light from the open doorway. Afterwards, the polished finish on the pots is achieved by a laborious process using the rounded end of a piece of metal, a technique thought to date back to Hittite times. The pots dry slowly in a storeroom upstairs, above the workshop, and later more quickly out in the open air. They are then fired in a wood-fired furnace at 950–1200°C for ten hours, and sometimes the firing is repeated to produce the distinctive blackened colour of some of the pots. Before you leave, check out the potter's bizarre collection of **hair**, collected from female visitors over the years and displayed in a museum-like cave in one of the back rooms. Female visitors today will be asked to contribute.

Chez Güray, opposite Alâeddin Camii and the Atatürk statue, and **Chez Ömurlü**, adjacent to Chez Galip, have a mixture of avant-garde and traditional pottery, though the best – such as waist-high water coolers – are too difficult to take home.

Eating, drinking and nightlife

Sofra, on the main street near the PTT, is a reasonably priced **restaurant**, serving *döner* and steamtray food in a friendly atmosphere. The *Tafana Pide Salonu*, on Atatürk Caddesi, is also cheap, and serves a local speciality called *kiremit kebap* (lamb cooked on a pottery dish), as well as excellent *pide*, but the pavement tables can be noisy. *Bizim Ev* just behind the *Sofa Hotel*, is the pick of the local restaurants, located in an atmospheric, well-restored Greek house, with specialities including *Bostan kebap*, a mix of aubergines, lamb and cheese cooked in a clay pot; it is reasonably priced, with a full meal costing around 8YTL. *Dayının Yeri* on Atatürk Caddesi has a garish green and yellow exterior, but is good value for all the standard kebabs and grills.

The *Kervanhan Disco-Bar* off the main square has nightly *saz* and *özgün* music and attracts the younger residents and visitors. The *Duygu Bar* on Atatürk Bulvarı plays good *halk* music and is popular with the locals, with beers around 3YTL. The nearby *Keyf-i-Sefe* is more of a daytime hang-out, where you can toke on a *nargile* or sip herbal teas. The *Labirent*, set in the crumbling old houses above the town, occasionally sees sets from Erkin Koray, one of Turkey's most famous guitarists.

Around Avanos

There are several worthwhile trips to be made from Avanos. The most interesting is to **Özkonak** (daily: summer 8am–7pm; winter 8am–5pm; 5TL), 14km north of Avanos off the Kayseri road, is one of the least-known and least-excavated underground cities in the Cappadocia region. Dolmuşes from Avanos leave hourly from beside the PTT.

In its present state it's not as interesting as Derinkuyu or Kaymaklı, but by the same token it's not as crowded. The city was discovered in 1972 by a muezzin, Latif Acar, who was trying to find out where the water disappeared to when he watered his crops. He discovered an underground room, which, later excavation revealed, belonged to a city with a capacity for sixty thousand people to exist underground for three months. Ten floors descend to a depth of 40m, though at present only four floors are open (to 15m), but throughout the village can be seen parts of rooms belonging to the first and second levels. These first two levels were used for food storage and wine fermentation, and a press and reservoir are labelled, as are mangers for stabled animals. Another typical feature is the stone doors, moved by wooden levers; above them was a small hole, through which boiling oil would have been poured on an enemy trying to break the soft sandstone door.

Six kilometres east of Avanos, on the new Kayseri road, the Selçuk-era **Saruhan Kervansary** (daily 9am–6pm; 2YTL) is well worth a visit. It is beautifully restored, and now offers evocative evening performances by a troupe of **whirling dervishes**, usually at 9pm. The show is prominently advertised in Avanos and Göreme, and the price of €25 includes admission and food. It's best booked ahead through one of the local agencies or your hotel/pension.

Best reached with your own wheels, the **Hacı Bayram Kapılıca**, 22km from Avanos off the old Kayseri road, is a small, informal thermal-resort set in an unspoilt village surrounded by vineyards. One of the most welcoming springs is **Yalı Camping** (admission 5YTL), which has a decent-sized pool filled by constantly running 45°C spring water. Surrounded by a brick wall and concrete changing rooms, it's hardly Baden-Baden, but an evening swim in the warm waters, with the stars twinkling overhead, is a real treat.

Southern Cappadocia

The majority of Cappadocia's visitors never get beyond the well-worn Nevşehir–Avanos–Ürgüp triangle, leaving **southern Cappadocia** far less charted and trampled. Although there's a consequent feeling of excitement about explorations made in this area, there's also less to be explored. The two major towns, **Aksaray** and **Niğde**, leave a lot to be desired as tourist centres, and the scenery is generally scrubby, barren steppe, more prone to cause depression than to recharge your holiday spirits.

The area does have its peculiarities and fascinations, however, and these are worth a degree of discomfort to experience. On the way to Niğde you can stop off at the underground cities of Derinkuyu and Kaymaklı (see p.632), located in a rain-washed basin between the central Anatolian plateau and the valleys of cones. Southwest of here is the **Ihlara valley**, where the Melendiz river, running between Aksaray and Niğde alongside the Melendiz mountain range, has created perhaps the most beautiful of all Cappadocian landscapes, a narrow ravine with almost vertical walls being cut ever deeper by the river that runs through it. Also easily accessible from Niğde is a small enclave of beautifully painted rock-cut churches belonging to the **Eski Gümüşler** monastery. South and east of Niğde the spectacular limestone spires of the **Aladağlar mountains** rear up from the plateau, affording excellent trekking and climbing.

Niğde and around

Despite a long history spent guarding the important mountain pass from Cappadocia to Cilicia, the small provincial town of **NIĞDE** has few remaining monuments of any great interest. Apart from a Selçuk fortress perched above the main street on a hill of tuff, and a couple of medieval mosques, the town looks as if it has been thrown together by people who were more interested in nomadic wandering than town planning. Nearby, however, is the Eski Gümüşler monastery complex, with its impressive, well-preserved frescoes – the only real reason for coming to Niğde unless you are en route to the Aladağlar mountains.

Niğde's **history** really began in the tenth century, when Tyana, the town that formerly controlled the pass between the Melendiz mountains to the west and the Toros mountains to the east, was ruined by Arab incursions. From then on Niğde – mentioned as early as Hittite times by the name of Nakida – took on the defensive role. Conquered by the Selçuks towards the end of the eleventh century, it was endowed with some attractive buildings during the reign of Alâeddin Keykubad. When the Arabian geographer Ibn Battuta visited the town in 1333, it was in ruins, probably as a result of the wars between the Mongols and the Karamanoğlu, the great rivals of the Ottoman dynasty. The Ottomans finally moved in in 1467, since when the town has been little more than a landmark on the Kayseri–Adana road.

The Town

The **citadel** was originally founded by the Selçuk sultan Alâeddin at the end of the eleventh century, but was restored by Işak Paşa in 1470, and the keep, all that remains today, probably dates from that time. On a mound to the south of the castle stands the **Alâeddin Camii**, dating from 1203 and later restored by Sultan Alâeddin. The facade is striped grey and yellow and there is a beautiful portal to the east, richly decorated with arabesques and sculpted designs. Below the mosque is the eighty-metre-long **bedesten**, a covered market street dating from the sixteenth and seventeenth centuries, and opposite this, on Nalbantlar Önüat at the foot of the citadel hill, is the fourteenth-century **Sungur Bey Camii**. Its portal is framed by geometrical mould-ings, and above the door to the east of the prayer hall a rose window gives the mosque a Gothic look. At the other end of this street, approaching Vali Konağı Caddesi, is the **Akmedrese**, built in the Selçuk open-courtyard style with a white-marble portal. It currently houses a research wing of Niğde University, and is intermittently open to the public. **Niğde Museum** (Niğde Müzesi; Tues–Sun 8am–noon & 1–5pm; 2YTL) is well laid out and user friendly. The Chalcolithic-era finds from nearby mounds are very interesting – look out for the stone idols from Köşk and the reconstruction of domestic quarters from the same site. Other exhibits of note include Hittite stelae, Phrygian pottery, and finds from Roman Tyana. The mummified remains of a Byz-antine nun, flanked by the mummies of four small children, are rather poignant in a grotesque kind of way.

Practicalities

The **otogar** is 1km from the centre, off the Nevşehir–Adana highway, on Emin Eşirgil Caddesi, and there are frequent dolmuşes from here into town. The **train station** is right on the highway, within sight of the citadel's clocktower, a con-venient marker for the centre. To get into town from here, cross the highway and take İstasyon Caddesi into the centre, a walk of ten minutes or so. The **tourist office** (Mon–Sat 8.30am–noon & 1.30–5.30pm; ☎0388/232 3393) is at Atatürk Meydanı 16, right in the town centre. To book a **trek in the Aladağlar moun-tains** (see p.656) go to Sobek Travel on İstasyon Caddesi (☎0388/213 2117, Ⓔsobek@kaynet.net), a well-established, reputable company, mainly dealing with package groups, so pre-booking would be sensible.

Niğde's choice of **hotels** is uninspiring. An absolute rock-bottom option is the *Star Oteli*, İstasyon Caddesi (☎0388/213 1645), with a droll proprietress. The three- and five-bed rooms go for 5YTL a bed. The shared bathrooms at either end of the dingy corridors are passable, the SpongeBob SquarePants motifs on some of the bedding and the chimes from the clocktower opposite less so. The *Yeni Otel Evim* on Hükümet Meydanı (☎0388/232 3536, Ⓕ232 1526; ❹) has reasonable rooms with showers, and offers substantial discounts if you're prepared to bargain. A welcome addition to the accommodation scene is the *Grand Hotel Niğde* on Hükümet Meydanı (☎0388/232 7000, Ⓦwww.grandhotelnigde.com; ❼) with soothingly decorated and furnished rooms, immaculate bathrooms, satellite TV, and a rooftop restaurant/terrace with fabulous views over the Melendiz mountains.

Niğde's **restaurants** are mainly very basic, concentrating on kebabs, *pide* and soups. Best of a bad bunch is the *Saruhan* on Bor Caddesi, a five-minute walk south of the central square, Hükümet Meydanı. Located inside a restored *han*, the kebabs are reliable. A passable place for a cheap beer for male travellers (or brave couples) is the *Yuba Birahanesi*, pleasantly done out in rough timber and kilims. If you're hungry they'll send out for kebabs, and the prostitutes soon lose interest once you've made your intentions clear.

Eski Gümüşler monastery

The **Eski Gümüşler monastery** (daily: summer 9am–noon & 1.30–6.30pm; win-ter 8am–12.30pm & 1.30–5.30pm; 2YTL) lies 6km east of town, off the Kayseri road. To get there, take the white *Belediye* bus that leaves the Niğde *otogar* every 45 minutes for the village of Gümüşler. Gümüşler itself is attractively set in a valley surrounded by cherry orchards, but for the monastery you stay on the bus past it.

The monastery, rediscovered in 1963, has a deserved reputation for the excellent state of preservation of its paintings, which seem to have escaped Iconoclastic and other vandalism through the ages. Even the faces are intact, providing some of the finest examples of Byzantine painting yet to be discovered in Cappadocia.

The **main church**, with its tall, elegant pillars, is entered through an almost circular arched doorway opposite the entrance to the courtyard. Decorated with black-and-white geometric designs, the church contains beautiful frescoes in the most delicate greens, browns and blues. They include a Nativity scene complete with tiny animal heads peering in at the swaddled Jesus and the Magi, off to the left, and a tall, serene Madonna, framed in a rock-cut niche. The linear stylization of the figures is marked, the features are drawn boldly and simply, and the light and shade of draperies is reduced to monochrome.

The upstairs **sleeping quarters** were formerly reached by means of niches cut into the side of a shaft; now a metal ladder has been provided. The walls of the bedroom, which is complete with rock-cut beds, are decorated with a wolf, a deer, a lion, and a flamingo, being hunted by men with bows and arrows; there's also a depiction of a Roman soldier.

Connected to the church is a **wine press**, complete with metre-wide wine vats, and outside in the central courtyard there's a skeleton in its grave, protected under glass. Next to the graves are round holes in which precious belongings would have been buried. Other rooms excavated to date include a kitchen and underground baths reached down a set of steps, while below ground level are various chambers and a water reservoir.

The Aladağlar mountains

The **Aladağlar mountains** are part of the Toros range at the point where it swings north of the Mesopotamian plain. Occupying a north–south rectangle 35km by 20km, they are accessed by a minor road from Niğde to Pozantı via Çamardı; on the west they drop away to the Ceyhan river, but there is no access road from this side. Approached in the afternoon, the mountains form a spectacular pink skyline above the poplars of the valley. The six main summits are Büyük and Küçük Demirkazık (3756m and 3490m respectively), Emler (3723m), Kızılkaya (3725m) and Kaldı (3736m) in a north–south line, and Vay-vay (3600m), set back to the east.

The isolated gorges and lakes of the Aladağlar are a birdwatchers' paradise, best during the autumn migration – when the snow has melted and access is (relatively) easy – day-trips can be arranged via the *Şafak Pansiyon* (see below). *Yayla*s (mountain pastures) are used after snowmelt by nomad families and their flocks; black tents dot the upper valleys from June to September. The *Yörük* here are used to tourists and less welcoming than elsewhere in the Toros; you may, however, be able to buy yoghurt and cheese.

Practicalities

Access is by **minibus from Niğde** to Çamardı; there are four daily services from the *otogar* in summer, taking about an hour. Ask for the Demirkazık road or the driver will automatically put you off at the *Şafak Pansiyon*. If you have your own transport you could drive from Adana via Pozantı – look for the turning marked to Kamızlı. Otherwise, take one of the occasional dolmuşes that run from Pozantı to Çamardı. The best **trekking season** is May to June followed by September, when the weather is at its most dependable.

Accommodation close to the trailhead, just off the Niğde road, is provided by *Şafak Pansiyon* (℡0388/724 7039; ❷), in the hamlet of Çukurbağ, 4km east of Çamardı, which provides half-board in small rooms without bathrooms and with unreliable hot water but with excellent cooking. It's also possible to camp here. The state-owned *Demirkazık Dağ Evi* (℡0388/724 7200; ❹), a ski lodge at Demirkazık, is a few kilometres nearer the mountains (ask the dolmuş to drop you at the signed turn, from where it's a 3km walk) and provides large, en-suite double rooms, and a camping area (€8). Coastal football clubs use it for high-altitude training, so it can be fully booked, especially just before the season starts.

As soon as you have stocked up with food (preferably in Niğde – there's a Migros supermarket on Istasiyon Caddesi) you can head off into the hills and camp near any suitable spring. Note that the Aladağlar mountains form a national park, and you will be charged an **entrance fee** (0.5YTL per person, plus 0.80YTL per tent) if you enter on one of the major tracks when there is a warden about. It is better to pay up as the authorities are then more likely to be able to find you should you fail to emerge.

By far the most popular way up to the peaks is via the **Emler valley**, where, in season, there are permanent base camps run by Sobek Travel (see "Niğde: Practicalities" on p.655). From here you can take day-walks up many of the peaks, and also cross into the **Kokorot valley** on the east, or walk the north–south section of the range, emerging on the **Acıman plateau**. At the end of both these routes you have to hitchhike or catch a rare dolmuş to Adana.

For walking alone, the tourist office in Niğde has some acceptable **maps**, while a technical **guide** (see Contexts, p.1041) in English and Turkish is published by Redhouse and available from Redhouse Books in Turkey. Ali Şafak, owner of the *Şafak Pansiyon*, can arrange guided **one-day walks** or transport by tractor for groups of birdwatchers, but people have reported being massively overcharged for the trip.

Aksaray

Huddled in an oasis on the Melendiz river, on the far side of the Melendiz mountain-range from Niğde, **AKSARAY** is a market town with no real interest except as a base for reaching the Ihlara valley. Aksaray probably occupies the site of the Byzantine town Archelais, and was subsequently occupied by the Selçuks, the Mongols and, in the fourteenth century, the Karamanoğlu. After the fall of Constantinople in 1453, part of the population of Aksaray was transferred to the capital. The displaced people named the district of İstanbul in which they settled after their hometown, a name which that lively suburb still retains.

Of marginal interest are the thirteenth-century **Eğri Minare**, the **Ulu Camii** on Banklar Caddesi, and the main square, with its Atatürk statue and restored public buildings. **Aksaray Museum** (Aksaray Müzesi; daily 9am–5.30pm; free) is housed in an architecturally interesting fourteenth-century *medrese*.

Practicalities

Aksaray is linked by regular bus with Niğde, 110km southeast (2hr), and Nevşehir, 85km north (1hr 30min). The **otogar** is some 6km west of the town centre, linked by service bus or the blue *Belediye* bus. If you arrive late, you may have to take a taxi into town. The **tourist office** (Mon–Sat 8am–noon & 1.30–5.30pm; ☎0382/213 2474), at Kadioğlu Sok 1, is in a nicely restored Ottoman building a couple of minutes' signed walk from the main square.

Accommodation is limited, but you might need to stay over before making the onward trip to Ihlara. Best bet is the *Otel Yuvam* (☎0382/212 0024; ❸) which occupies a renovated old townhouse next to the Kurşunlu Camii at Eski Sanayı Caddesi; rooms are attractively furnished and clean, with modern bathrooms. A little cheaper, the *Otel Erdem* (☎0382/214 1500; ❷) on Banklar Caddesi, is a useful fall-back. There is nowhere exciting to eat in Aksaray; try the basic **kebab places** around Hükümet Meydanı.

The Ihlara valley

A fertile gorge cut by a deep green river between red cliffs, the **Ihlara valley** is as beautiful a place as you could conceive. If you add some of the most attractive and interesting churches and rock-carved villages in the Cappadocia region, it's easy to see why the valley is an increasingly popular destination. Most come only as part of a day-excursion from Ürgüp or Göreme, but to appreciate the valley at its best (early morning and early evening) try to spend a night in either Selime or Ihlara villages.

Minibuses to Ihlara village leave from Aksaray *otogar* three times daily, passing Selime and the turn-off to Belisırma, and returning the same day. A **taxi** from Aksaray to Ihlara costs €15 (round trip €25) – you can also arrange to be picked up in Belisırma or Selime after you have completed your walk. In addition, there are six dolmuşes daily from Aksaray to Güzelyurt, and frequent dolmuş connections between Güzelyurt and Ihlara. A large enough group could rent a whole minibus either from the drivers in Aksaray *otogar* or from Ürgüp (you'll need about ten people to make it viable). There are three **entry points to the valley**, at Ihlara village, Belisırma and Selime (each open daily 8am–6pm; 5YTL). It's possible to gain entry outside these times, in which case you should pay on exit.

If you have time, it's satisfying to do the trip **independently**. The six-kilometre walk from Selime to Belisırma takes around three hours, and a further three hours to complete the ten-kilometre walk to Ihlara village. There are places to eat en route, in Belisırma, and one or two river-pools to swim in if it's hot. Of course it is perfectly possible to do the walk in reverse, and there is accommodation in both Selime and, more plentifully, in Ihlara.

Selime

One of the most beautiful parts of the whole valley, the troglodyte village of **SELIME** has previously been passed over in favour of the better-known, more frequented Ihlara village area. It's the first village you pass on the way to Ihlara or to the official entry to the valley, and it's worth at least a couple of hours' visit, if not a stopover in one of the valley's best **hotels**. The *Piri Motel and Camping* (T0382/454 5114; ❷) offers spotless, comfortable rooms, and its owner Mustafa is willing to act as a guide to the surrounding churches. The less conveniently located *Çatlak Pension* (T0382/454 5065; ❷) has reasonable rooms and offers **camping**, but is a long walk from Selime's attractions.

A number of massive, rather squat **fairy chimneys** dot the valley at Selime, many of them containing churches, and there's even a rock-cut cathedral, divided into three aisles by irregularly shaped pillars. The village takes its name from a Selçuk **mausoleum** in the village cemetery, with a pyramidal roof inscribed "Selime Sultan", a dedication of unknown origin.

Belisırma

The troglodyte village of **BELISİRMA** blends in with the tawny rock-face from which it was carved to such an extent that in a bad light it can all but disappear from view. Its tranquil riverside location provides the opportunity to rest at a table in the water at one of the simple tree-shaded restaurants on the west bank.

The most rewarding way to reach Belisırma is to **walk along the valley**, either from Selime (3hr) or from Ihlara village (3hr) – from the latter, you can take in the majority of the valley churches.

Belisırma village is home to three primitive **campsites**: *Valley Anatolia* has tents for rent and an excellent **restaurant** where you can eat trout or *saç kavurma* very cheaply, while the *Aslan* (T0382/213 3780) also has a riverside restaurant. The *Tandırcı* (T0382/457 3110) is also a restaurant/camping ground, and has a good reputation.

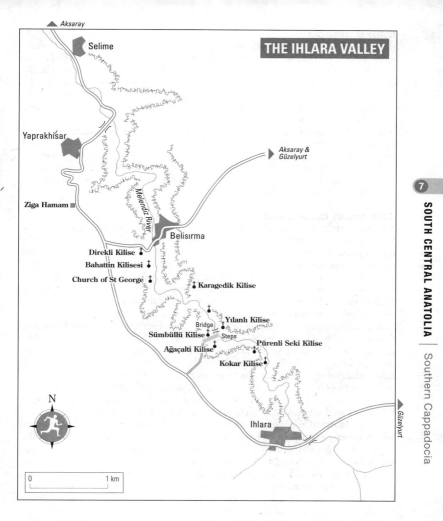

Around Belisırma, the eleventh-century **Direkli Kilise** ("Church with the Columns") has fine examples of Byzantine frescoes, including a beautiful long-fingered Madonna and Child on one of the columns from which the church takes its name, and a picture of St George fighting a three-headed dragon.

The **church of St George**, 50m up the cliffside, a half-kilometre south of Belisırma and 3km from the stairs at the main entrance, was dedicated to the saint by a thirteenth-century Christian emir, Basil Giagoupes, who was in the army of Mesut II. It bears an inscription expressing Christian gratitude for the religious tolerance of the Selçuk Turks. St George is depicted in armour and cloak, holding a triangular shield and flanked by the donor and his wife Tamara, who is handing a model of the church to the saint. To the right of this oblation scene, St George can be seen in action, killing a three-headed serpent, with an inscription above that reads "Cleanse my soul of sins."

Ihlara village

Best known of the quaint villages in the valley bottom, **IHLARA** is slightly more developed than its rivals. Set by the river in the centre of the village, the *Star* (☎0382/453 7676; ❷) is overpriced for its clean, but waterless, rooms. To compensate, its location is the best in Ihlara. Above the old village, set on the lip of the valley, are four more **pensions**. The modern, well-built *Akar Pansiyon* (☎0382/453 7018, ☏453 7511; ❷), just off the road to the main valley entrance, is the best – clean and quiet, with comfortable doubles and a basic restaurant attached. The owner speaks good English and will arrange for you to be picked up from the Selime exit of the valley for a reasonable €6. Nearer to the valley entrance, the friendly *Anatolia Pansiyon* (☎0382/453 7440, ☏453 7439; ❷) also makes a comfortable base. Both these *pansiyon*s offer **camping** in their gardens.

The **hamam** (daily 10am–10pm; 1YTL), reached down a set of steps behind the mosque on the road out of the village, is served by natural hot springs.

The main churches

The monastic occupation of the Ihlara valley, or **Peristrema** as it was originally known, seems to have been continuous from early medieval times until the fourteenth century, a long period of use reflected in the numerous adaptations and restorations of the churches. It would seem from the decoration of the churches, whose development can be traced through pre- and post-Iconoclastic periods, that the valley was little affected by the religious disputes of the period. Paintings show both eastern and western influence, so that some figures wear Arab striped robes, whereas others resemble those in Byzantine frescoes in Europe.

Descending from the **main entrance**, midway between Ihlara and Belisırma, down several hundred **steps** to the valley floor 150m below, is precipitous, but manageable. The most interesting of the churches are located near the small wooden **bridge** at the bottom of the flight of steps. It's also possible to walk from Ihlara village along the southwest bank of the river to the bridge, or from Belisırma to the northwest keeping to the same side of the river. Walking from either village to this point takes about an hour and a half, a fairly straightforward hike that's well worthwhile for the tremendous sense of solitude.

At the bottom of the steps is a plan showing all the accessible churches, most of which are easy enough to find. To the right of the bridge, on the same side as the steps, is the **Ağaçaltı Kilise** ("Church under the Tree"). Cross-shaped with a central dome, the church originally had three levels, but two of them have collapsed, as has the entrance hall. The most impressive of the well-preserved frescoes inside depict the Magi presenting gifts at the Nativity, Daniel with the lions (opposite the entrance in the west arm) and, in the central dome, the Ascension. The colours are red, blue and grey, and the pictures, naive in their execution, suggest influence from Sassanid Iran, particularly in the frieze of winged griffins. Unfortunately, in recent years these frescoes have suffered serious damage.

The **Pürenli Seki Kilise** lies 500m beyond this, also on the south bank, and can be seen clearly from the river, 30m up the cliffside. The badly damaged frescoes here mainly depict scenes from the life of Christ. Another 50m towards Ihlara, the **Kokar Kilise** is relatively easy to reach up a set of steps. Scenes from the Bible in the main hall include the Annunciation, the Nativity, the Flight into Egypt and the Last Supper. In the centre of the dome, a picture of a hand represents the Trinity and the sanctification.

One of the most fascinating of all the churches in the valley is located across the wooden footbridge, about 100m from the stairs. The **Yılanlı Kilise** ("Church of the Snakes") contains strikingly unusual depictions of sinners suffering in hell. Four female sinners are being bitten by snakes: one of them on the nipples as a punishment for not breast-feeding her young; another is covered in eight snakes; and the other two are being punished for slander and for not heeding good advice. At the centre of the scene a three-headed snake is positioned behind one of the few Cappadocian depictions of Satan; in each of the snake's mouths is a soul destined for hell.

Another church worth exploring is **Sümbüllü Kilise** ("Church of the Hyacinths"), just 200m from the entrance steps. The church shows Greek influence in its badly damaged frescoes and has an attractive facade decorated with blind horseshoe niches.

Güzelyurt

GÜZELYURT, the nearest small town to the Ihlara valley, 13km northeast of Ihlara village, provides an opportunity to catch a glimpse of the old, untouched Cappadocia, and to stay in the best hotel in the region. If that isn't enough incentive, there are good dolmuş connections with Aksaray and Ihlara, and plenty of sites worth visiting in the town and within easy walking distance.

The beautiful *Karballa* **hotel** on the main square (℡0382/451 2103, Ⓦwww .kirkit.com; ④) occupies a nineteenth-century Greek monastery. The monks' cells are now bedrooms, with central heating and individual bathrooms now added, the refectory has become an excellent **restaurant**, with superb evening meals for 11YTL, and there's a small pool. The *Hotel Karvallı* (℡0382/451 2736, Ⓔkhl-tur-izm@superonline.com; ④), on the southern outskirts of the town, has comfortable rooms in a new, but traditionally styled, building that has stunning views over a small lake, Yüksek Kilise (see below) and Hasan Dağı. Near the *jandarma* post in the town *Halil's Family Pension* (℡0382/451 2707; ③) has a couple of spotless rooms in a genuine Turkish home, where you eat from a *sofra* table with the welcoming family. It's great value as the price includes breakfast and an evening meal.

The important religious community of Güzelyurt was established by St Gregory of Nazianzen in the fourth century, and a church dedicated to him, called **Cami Kilise** by locals, is located a short walk from the main street, past the PTT and mosque, on Kör Sokak. Renovated several times by the town's Greek community, the church is now in line for further work, with plans to turn it into a museum. A golden bell given to the church by a Russian Orthodox community in Odessa is now in Afyon museum, but other items of interior decor, such as a carved wooden iconostasis and chair, gifts from Tsar Nicholas I in the eighteenth century, can still be seen *in situ*. In place of the bell-tower now stands a brick minaret, dating from the church's conversion to a mosque after the departure of the Greeks in 1923. Elsewhere on Kör Sokak and in the **old town** around it are still-inhabited troglodyte dwellings and old Greek houses with beautifully carved facades.

The most impressive sight in the Güzelyurt area, however, has to be "**Monastery Valley**", below the town to the northeast, approached by taking a right turn out of the village after the Cami Kilise. The valley is riddled with over fifty rock-cut churches and monastery complexes – some dating from the Byzantine era – of which the most attractive is the nineteenth-century **Yüksek Kilise** ("High Church"), dramatically located on a high rock. A walk up the entire 4.5-kilometre-long valley takes about two and a half hours, and brings you to the village of **Sivrihisar**. From there, a signposted fifteen-minute walk south leads to a freestanding church of note, the sixth- or seventh-century **Kızıl Kilise** ("Red Church"), one of the few remaining churches containing masonry in the whole of Cappadocia.

Kayseri and around

Green fields, wooded hills and a snow-capped volcano surround the modern-looking concrete that is today's **KAYSERI**, encircling an old Selçuk settlement of black volcanic stone. The city has a reputation for religious conservatism and ultranationalism; it's the heartland of the Milli Hareket Partisi, the nearest thing there is to a fascist party in the country. In spite of this, there's a gentle acceptance of the waywardness of foreigners. It's also a thriving business centre, where traditional commerce, particularly raw textiles and carpets, still flourishes in the medieval *hans*. The long history and strategic importance of the town have left it with a littering of impressive monuments, while two nearby attractions are Sultansazlığı bird sanctuary and Mount Erciyes, ideal for picnics in summer and skiing in winter.

Some history

Ancient civilization in the region dates back to the fourth millennium BC and a Chalcolithic site at **Kültepe**, 21km from Kayseri on the road to Sivas. During the early Hittite period the site was composed of two settlements: **Kanesh**, the capital of the kingdom of the same name, probably the most powerful in Anatolia in its time; and **Karum**, which was established by Assyrian merchants as a bazaar, one of the oldest in the world.

The site of present-day Kayseri was originally called Mazaka. Its origins are unknown, but the city gained importance under the rule of the Phrygians. In 17–18 AD it was named **Caesarea** in honour of Emperor Tiberius, and at the same time it became the capital of the Roman province of Cappadocia. Captured by the Persians after the battle of Edessa (Urfa), it was quickly regained by the Romans. As part of the Byzantine Empire, Caesarea was relocated 2km to the north of the ancient acropolis, allegedly around a church and monastery that had been built by St Basil, the founder of eastern monasticism and a bishop of Caesarea in the fourth century. The position was strategic in terms of both trade and defence, and it soon became a leading cultural and artistic centre, though always vulnerable to attack from the east. The Arab invasions of the seventh and eighth centuries were particularly threatening, and in 1067 it finally fell to the great Selçuk leader Kılıç Arslan II. The town became capital of a powerful Danişmend emirate, which included Cappadocia, Sivas and Amasya. In 1097 the Crusaders were in brief possession and it was ruled equally briefly by the Mongols in 1243. Passing through the hands of various Turkish chiefs, it came into the possession of Beyazit I in 1397, but when he was defeated by Tamerlane at the battle of Angora the city was occupied by the Karamanoğlu and then the Mamluks before finally becoming part of the Ottoman Empire in 1515, under Selim the Grim.

The City

Part of the delight of Kayseri is that its beautiful old buildings still play an important part in the everyday life of the place, their very existence witness to the social conscience of the Selçuks. Koranic teaching forbade excessive concern with private houses, so public figures poured money into buildings for public welfare and communal activities.

Other buildings still integral to Kayseri's life are the covered markets; there are three in the town centre, all dating from different periods. The **Bedesten**, built in 1497, was originally used by cloth-sellers but is now a carpet market; the **Vezir Hanı**, built by Damat İbrahim Paşa in 1727, is where raw cotton, wool and Kayseri carpets are sold, and leather is prepared for wholesale; while the recently restored **covered bazaar** in the same area, built in 1859, has five hundred individual shops.

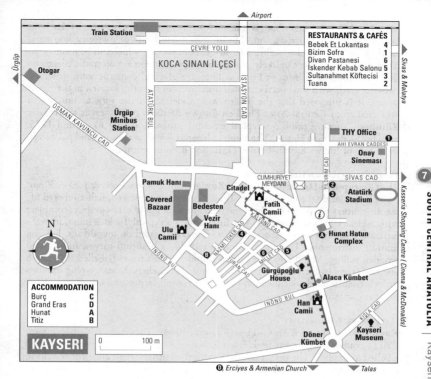

▲ Airport

Train Station

ÇEVRE YOLU

KOCA SINAN İLÇESİ

Otogar

OSMAN KAVUNCU CAD

İSTASYON CAD

ATATÜRK BUL

Ürgüp
Minibus
Station

◀ Ürgüp

▶ Sivas & Malatya

RESTAURANTS & CAFÉS
Bebek Et Lokantası   4
Bizim Sofra   1
Divan Pastanesi   6
İskender Kebab Salonu   5
Sultanahmet Köftecisi   3
Tuana   2

THY Office

AHİ EVRAN CADDESİ

Onay
Sineması

CUMHURİYET
MEYDANI

SİVAS CAD

YILDIRIM CAD

Pamuk Hanı

Citadel

Covered
Bazaar

Bedesten

Vezir
Hanı

Ulu
Camii

Fatih
Camii

Atatürk
Stadium

KALE ÖNÜ CAD

NAZMİ TOKER CAD

TURAN CAD

İNÖNÜ BUL

MİLLET CAD

Hunat Hatun
Complex

Gürgüpoğlu
House

Alaca Kümbet

İNÖNÜ BUL

Han
Camii

KISLA CAD

Döner
Kümbet

Kayseri
Museum

N

ACCOMMODATION
Burç   **C**
Grand Eras   **D**
Hunat   **A**
Titiz   **B**

KAYSERI

0   100 m

▼ Erciyes & Armenian Church   ▼ Talas

Kasseria Shopping Centre (Cinema & McDonalds)

Bargain hard: stories can be heard all over Turkey about how hard-nosed the businessmen of Kayseri can be. (The one about a Kayseri man stealing a donkey, painting it and selling it back to its owner has become even more hostile in recent years: the man now abducts his mother, paints her up and sells her back to his father.)

The towering crenellated walls of the **citadel**, built from black volcanic rock, are a good place to start exploring, since the life of the town seems to centre on this point. A sixth-century fortress erected in the reign of the emperor Justinian once stood here, but the citadel you see was built in 1224 by the Selçuk Sultan Keykubad, and has been much restored since, particularly by Mehmet II, who also built the **Fatih Camii**, the small mosque near the southwest gate.

Near the citadel, **Hunat Hatun** *külliye* was the first mosque complex to be built by the Selçuks in Anatolia (construction began in 1239). It consists of a thirteenth-century mosque and *medrese*, the latter one of the most beautiful examples of Selçuk architecture in Turkey. This former theological college has an open courtyard and two *eyvan*s (vaulted chambers open at the front). A wooden box containing a hair reputed to be from the Prophet Mohammed is to be found near the beautifully decorated *mihrab*.

Beyond the market area is the first of several ancient mosques in the city, the **Ulu Cami**, or Great Mosque. Constructed under the Danişmend Turkish emirs in the first half of the thirteenth century, the mosque, which can be entered from three sides, is still in remarkably good condition. Its roof is supported by four rows of stone pillars with varied marble capitals, and it retains its original carved wooden *mimber*, although the central dome is modern.

Kayseri has been described as the **city of mausoleums** because of its large number of tombs: curious, squat, beautifully carved bits of masonry known as *kümbets*, dating from the twelfth to fourteenth centuries, which can be found scattered about in the most unlikely places – a couple of them are on traffic islands on the main highway to Mount Erciyes. They are graceful constructions, generally two-storeyed, with the burial chamber and sumptuous coffin located in the upper storey. It is supposed that the design was modelled on the *yurt*, a conical tent imported from Central Asia. The best known of them in Kayseri is the **Döner Kümbet**, "turning tomb", a typical example probably dating to around 1275, built for Shah Cihan Hatun. The tomb is decorated with arabesques and palmettes, and a tree of life with twin-headed eagles and lions beneath.

The Gürgüpoğlu House

The **Gürgüpoğlu House** (Gürgüpoğlu Konağı; daily 8.30am–noon & 1.30–5.30pm; 2YTL), just inside the city walls off Turan Caddesi, is a restored, half-timbered fifteenth-century Ottoman family home used as a museum of ethnography, complete with tableaux of wax dummies. The first room is a typical Turkish salon, its walls intricately painted using natural dyes, with models seated on low divans, holding musical instruments. The guest room upstairs has a beautiful carved and painted wooden ceiling. You'll also be escorted round a bride's room (labelled in Turkish but the scene is fairly self-explanatory) and the kitchen. Ethnographic exhibits include beautiful Selçuk tiles from the Hunat Hatun, carpets and kilims and a *topak ev*, or nomad's tent.

Kayseri Museum

Kayseri Museum on Kışla Caddesi (Kayseri Müzesi; Tues–Sun 8.30am–5.30pm; 2YTL) contains important finds from Kültepe (see p.667) and is extremely well labelled in English. The first room deals with the Hittites, their cuneiform writing and hieroglyphics, and includes a fascinating Hittite rock-relief from Develi and the head of a sphinx. Items from Kültepe include early Bronze-Age depictions of the mother goddess, Assyrian bowls and jugs in the shape of animals, dating from the second millennium BC, and a collection of clay tablets in their clay envelopes – essentially small cheques – from the same period.

In the second room are finds from around Kayseri itself, including Hellenistic and Roman jewellery, and grave gifts from a Roman tumulus, among them highly worked pieces in gold and silver. In the garden is a pair of lovely seventh-century BC Hittite lions, with all their own teeth, from Göllüdağ near Niğde.

Surp Krikor Lusuvoriç

The substantial Armenian church of **Surp Krikor Lusuvoriç**, a half-hour walk out of town on the Hacılar/Erciyes road (ask the tourist office for directions), is the last architectural reminder of just how important Kayseri was in the Byzantine Christian world. Dating from around 700 AD, it is said to be Turkey's largest consecrated church, and can hold a congregation of a thousand, though at present services are held just twice a year, on March 16 and June 16. The worshippers are largely diaspora Armenians from İstanbul and elsewhere (only around fifty Armenians still live in Kayseri), who hold this church in high regard as Surp Krikor (St Gregory), the first bishop and official founder of the Armenian Church, spent much of his early life here. The church is easily recognizable by its large dome and cross, though the old Greek and Armenian houses that surround it are being bulldozed for new apartment buildings and a road. To gain entry, ring the bell and the caretakers, a friendly Armenian family from İstanbul, will be happy to let you look around.

Practicalities

To get into town from the **otogar**, take the "Terminal" dolmuş from the opposite side of Osman Kavuncu Caddesi. Minibuses to and from Ürgüp use the minbus station instead, a few hundred metres down the road towards town. The **train station** is 1km out of town at the end of Atatürk Bulvarı: "Terminal" dolmuşes into town – and to the *otogar* in the other direction – pass frequently. THY (Turkish Airlines) has an office at Yıldırım Cad 1 (℡0352/222 3858). An Argeus tour agency minibus (see "Ürgüp: Listings", p.649) also meets Turkish Airlines flights if requested and will deposit you in the village of your choice in Cappadocia. This costs 10YTL per person to Ürgüp, for example. Neşe (see p.636) performs the same service for Onur Air flights, whose office is on Ahmetpaşa Caddesi (℡0352/231 5551). Thanks to the local taxi mafia, there is currently no shuttle bus between the airport and Kayseri.

The central **tourist office** (daily: summer 8.30am–noon & 1–5.30pm; winter 8am–noon & 1–5pm; ℡0452/222 3903) is next to the Hunat Hatun complex. It has train, plane and bus timetables, hotel and restaurant lists, and the latest on the Mount Erciyes ski resort. The **banks**, **ATMs** and *döviz* are mainly found on Nazmi Toker (Bankalar) Caddesi, though İş Bankası has an ATM on Sivas Caddesi. For **Internet** access, try the Hollywood Internet Café on Sivas Cad 15.

Accommodation

The *Hunat Otel*, behind the Hunat Hatun complex (℡0352/232 4319; ❷), is the best budget option. Quiet, convenient and clean, its en-suite rooms have pleasant views of the mosque and the management is very friendly. The good-value *Hotel Titiz*, Maarif Cad 7 (℡0352/222 5040, ℉222 5542; ❸), has small but nicely furnished rooms, with TVs, fridges and tiny bathrooms. Alternatively, the *Hotel Burç*, on Çevik Sokak (℡0532/2224364, ✉Burcotel@ttnet.net.tr; ❸), has clean, comfortable rooms and is very central.

A decent choice, a little way out of the town centre en route to the Armenian church, is the *Grand Eras Hotel* (℡0532/330 5111, ⓦwww.granderashotel.com; ❺), with all the four-star facilities you'd expect, if rather more glitz than perhaps you'd want.

Eating, drinking and entertainment

Although more famous for its spicy, garlicky *pastırma* (cured meat), *sucuk* (a kind of sausage-like salami) and *mantı* (perhaps the original ravioli) than for its actual **restaurants**, Kayseri does have some decent eateries.

First stop should be the 🍴 *Bizim Sofra* on Ahı Evran Caddesi, opposite the Onay Sinemasi (from Sivas Caddesi, turn left opposite the Atatürk stadium and cut down an alley past the Melikgazi Hastanesi). Unusually for anywhere in Turkey, never mind conservative Kayseri, you'll be cooked for, and served by, women. The *Kayseri mantı* with yoghurt and garlic is delicious (eat it sprinkled liberally with *sumac*, mint and crushed chilli); *yaprak sarması* (grape leaves stuffed with spicy rice, served in a rich tomato sauce) is another speciality, and you won't spend more than 5YTL. The immaculately clean, air-conditioned *Tuana Restaurant* near the PTT on Sivas Caddesi, serves reasonably priced kebabs, fresh fish, *mantı* and desserts, and has good views across to Mount Erciyes. The *Bebek Et Lokantası*, Nazmi Töker (Bankalar) Cad 9, is a more upmarket option, very popular with the locals and offering the widest variety of dishes in town. The *günün yemeği* (speciality of the day) is reasonable value at 2.5YTL, but portions are small. Otherwise an old favourite is the *İskender Kebap Salonu* at Millet Cad 5, across from the Hunat Hatun complex, with main grills around 6.5YTL. Near the *Tuana*, *Sultanahmet Köftecisi* is good for *köfte*, kebabs and burgers, while the air-conditioned *Divan Pastanesi* on Millet Caddesi is the place to eat ice cream and cakes.

A fifteen-minute walk out of town along Sivas Caddesi (or a two-minute bus ride) will bring you to the gleaming **Kasseria shopping centre**. Here, films (usually the latest Hollywood fare, in English) are shown at the four-screen **Kasseria Sinemaları** (performances start at around 11.30am, with last showings at about 9pm).

Erciyes Dağı

Erciyes Dağı, the 3916-metre-high extinct volcano dominating the city to the southwest, is one of the greatest pleasures the area offers. If you have transport, take a packed lunch and head for the foothills of Erciyes, a twenty-minute drive out of town. Otherwise, the Develi-bound dolmuş, which you can catch from near the Han Camii on Talas Caddesi, will take you to Tekir Yaylası, at an altitude of 2150m. Here you'll find *Kayak Evi*, a **ski lodge** run by Kayseri council (☎0352/342 2032; €10 per person in summer, including breakfast; €15 during ski season). The *Dedeman* chain also has an expensive hotel on the mountain (☎0352/342 2115, ℱ342 2117; ◐) with an indoor swimming pool, kids' area, live music bar and its own ski school. The **ski season** runs from December to May, and there are five lifts and some 12km of piste; **ski rental** is around €12 per day (ski clothes also available). It's a little barren, but snow conditions are often very good.

Once you get beyond the foothills, Erciyes is a harsh mountain, with little vegetation to soften its contours. For potential climbers, the two most reasonable routes start at the *Kayak Evi*, but even in summer Erciyes can be difficult and dangerous, with snow frozen solid in the early hours but mush by mid-morning, and stonefall from the loose volcanic rock common. Crampons, ice axe and helmet are essential and a guide is advisable – either *Kayak Evi* or the tourist office in town should be able to find you one. More worrying than the natural dangers of the mountain, early in August each year the vast upland meadow of Tekir Yaylası becomes a tent city of up to 50,000 flag-waving ultranationalist supporters of the Milli Hareket Partisi.

Sultansazlığı

Beyond Erciyes Dağı the countryside around the Kayseri–Niğde road becomes flat, dull steppe, which you might well assume was as barren of bird or plant life as the fairy chimneys of Cappadocia. Consequently, the oasis of the **Sultansazlığı** bird sanctuary is easy to miss in the small back-lanes that wind around the tiny lakes in the region, but it's worth the effort of hunting out.

The complex of wetlands at the bottom of a closed basin comprises two main lakes – **Yay Gölü** and the smaller **Çöl Gölü** – and about two thousand hectares of surrounding marshes, covered in reed and cane. The lakes are saline, while the marshland is entirely fresh water, and this particular combination of lakes, marshland, mudflats and steppe makes for an enormous variety of ecosystems. This, allied with the fact that the area is positioned right at the crossroads of two large bird migration routes, make Sultansazlığı an extremely important wetland for breeding migrant and wintering birds.

Although no really detailed ornithological research has so far been carried out, at least 250 **species** have been recorded here, 69 of which breed in the area. Most excitingly for the lay birdwatcher, visiting species include flamingos (particularly in the Yay Gölü region), pelicans, storks, golden eagles from the surrounding steppes, herons, spoonbills and cranes.

There's a **watchtower** in the hamlet of Ovaçiftlik, which can provide very good viewing as long as the water isn't too low (as it may well be in the height of summer), and a little thatched **museum** exhibiting stuffed examples of the feathered species found in the region. There are also various good birdwatching opportunities to the northeast of Ovaçiftlik, near the small village of Soysallı.

Practicalities

The marshes, also known as Kuş Cenneti (Bird Paradise), are easily accessible **from Kayseri**: take the Yahyalı bus (8 daily until 5pm from the *otogar*) and get off at Ovaçiftlik (1hr), from where it's a one-kilometre walk to the water.

The best time to **birdwatch** is at dawn, so it's worth staying in one of Ovaçiftlik's two **pansiyons** with camping facilities. *Sultan Pansiyon and Camping Restaurant* (☎0352/658 5549, ⓦwww.sultanpansionbirding.com; ❷) has fourteen en-suite rooms, and plates of *saç tava* (wok-fried lamb). It runs expensive **boat trips** in a flat-bottomed punt (be prepared to haggle) and organizes tours around Yay Gölü. *Atilla Pansiyon* next door (☎0352/658 5576; ❷) has similar accommodation and a boat for rent.

Kültepe

Twenty-two kilometres northeast of Kayseri the important archeological site at what is now known as **Kültepe** (Tues–Sun 8.30am–5.30pm; 2YTL), was, before excavation, the largest artificial mound in Turkey. The site's importance, however, derives from the fact that the earliest written documents of Anatolia were found here, in an ancient city called Kanesh. Nearby is the **Karum of Kanesh**, a sort of chamber of commerce, where a colony of Assyrian traders lived and worked controlling commerce between Assyria and Anatolia. To get there by **public transport** you'll have to take a bus, from Sivas Caddesi in Kayseri, along the main eastern highway headed for Bünyan. After some 20km the site is signposted, near a petrol station, but it's a 2km hike from the bus drop-off.

Some 15,000 clay tablets and a well-preserved selection of household furnishings, including human and animal statuettes, were discovered here – the best of which are housed in Kayseri and Ankara museums. The site itself has been well excavated and gives some idea of building plans and street layouts, as well as construction techniques that are still prevalent in Anatolia.

Some history

The walled city of Kanesh was inhabited continuously from the fourth millennium BC to the Roman era, but its golden age was in the second millennium BC. At that time, the Karum of Kanesh – the most important of nine Assyrian *karum*s (trade centres) in Anatolia, importing tin, fine garments and other textiles in exchange for cattle, silver, copper and skins – was inhabited by the Assyrian trading colony and the lower classes, while Kanesh itself was reserved for royalty of Anatolian stock. The thin layer of ash covering the site (the origin of the name Kültepe, "ash hill") dates from two massive conflagrations, the first in around 1850 BC, when the *karum* was also destroyed, and the second between 1200 and 1180 BC. After the first, the *karum* was rebuilt and continued to trade until 1780 BC, when, it would appear, the traders departed in a hurry, leaving behind numerous personal belongings, including large quantities of earthenware vessels, many with graceful or comical animal forms. The city lost its importance during the Hittite age, but was still settled during the Hellenistic and Roman periods.

The sites

Excavations labelled "level II", from the second millennium BC, dominate the upper site of Kanesh, especially the Large Palace, which covered an area of 3000 square metres and included a paved central courtyard, and the **Palace of Warsana**, king of Kanesh. Walls were generally of large mud bricks with stone foundations, though the Large Palace had long storage rooms with stone walls.

The **Karum** is a five-minute walk further down the country lane that leads past the entrance to Kanesh. Here, excavations have revealed the foundations of shops, offices, archives and storerooms, all packed closely together inside a defensive wall. Houses from this period had one or two storeys built of mud bricks resting on stone foundations. The dead were buried together with precious gifts under the floors of their own houses in stone cist graves, some of which can be seen on site. Upstairs were the living quarters, while downstairs were workrooms, stores and, in some houses, ovens for baking tiny **clay tablets**, the records of all business transactions at Kanesh. In one archive alone, 1500 of these tablets were stored, recording the import of lead, cloth and garments, and the export of metals, mainly copper, to Assyria. The tablets also reveal that the Assyrians and Anatolians had friendly relations, and even intermarried.

Travel details

Trains

Afyon to: Denizli (2 daily; 5hr); Gaziantep (3 weekly; 19hr); Isparta (2 daily; 5hr); İstanbul (4–5 daily; 8hr 30min); Konya (4–5 daily; 5–6hr).

Isparta to: Afyon (2 daily; 5hr); Denizli (1 daily; 5hr); İstanbul (1 daily; 13hr); Konya (3 daily; 1hr 10min).

Kayseri to: Adana (2 daily; 7hr); Ankara (1 hourly; 8hr 30min); Diyarbakır (4 weekly; 20hr); İstanbul (2 daily; 12hr); Malatya (1 daily; 6hr); Kars (1 daily; 24hr); Van (3 weekly; 22hr).

Konya to: Adana (3 weekly; 8hr); Afyon (4–5 daily; 5–6hr); Gaziantep (3 weekly; 13hr); Isparta (3 daily; 1hr 10min); İstanbul (2 daily; 14hr).

Niğde to: Adana (2 daily, 4hr); Kayseri (2 daily; 3hr).

Buses

Afyon to: Adana (3 daily; 10hr); Alanya (5 daily; 6hr 30min); Ankara (6 daily; 4hr); Antalya (6 daily; 5hr); Aydın (4 daily; 5hr); Bursa (3 daily; 5hr); Fethiye (2 daily; 7hr); Isparta (3 daily; 2hr); İstanbul (6 daily; 8hr); İzmir (4 daily; 6hr); Konya (3 daily; 3hr); Kuşadası (2 daily; 7hr); Kütahya (5 daily; 1hr 30min); Marmaris (1 daily; 9hr).

Aksaray to: Ankara (5 daily; 4hr 30min); Konya (6 daily; 2hr 30min); Niğde (6 daily; 2hr).

Avanos to: Göreme (half-hourly; 30min); Nevşehir

(half-hourly; 40min); Özkonak (half-hourly; 30min);
Ürgüp (half-hourly; 30min).

Beyşehir to: Alanya (6 daily; 4hr); Ankara (5 daily;
5hr); Antalya (5 daily; 4hr); Eğirdir (6 daily; 1hr
30min); Isparta (6 daily; 2hr 30min); İstanbul (3
daily; 10hr); İzmir (5 daily; 8hr); Konya (hourly; 1hr
15min).

Eğirdir to: Ankara (5 daily; 7hr); Antalya (9 daily;
3hr); Beyşehir (6 daily; 1hr 30min); Denizli (8 daily;
3hr); Göreme (2 daily; 8hr); İstanbul (1 daily; 10hr);
Konya (8 daily; 4hr).

Göreme to: Alanya (2 daily; 12hr); Ankara (5 daily;
4hr); Antalya (2 daily; 10hr); Denizli (2 daily; 10hr);
Eğirdir (3 daily; 8hr); İstanbul (3 daily; 11hr); İzmir
(1 daily; 11hr 30min); Kayseri (hourly; 1hr 30min);
Konya (3 daily; 3hr); Marmaris (2 daily; 15hr);
Nevşehir (half-hourly; 30min); Ürgüp (every 20min;
30min).

Isparta to: Afyon (3 daily; 2hr); Beyşehir (6 daily;
2hr 30min); Kayseri (3 daily; 9hr); Konya (2 daily;
4hr).

Kayseri to: Adana (10 daily; 5hr); Adiyaman (1
daily; 8hr); Afyon (6 daily; 9hr); Ankara (hourly;
4hr 30min); Antalya (5 daily; 11hr); Bursa (4 daily;
11hr); Isparta (3 daily; 9hr); İstanbul (9 daily; 12hr);
İzmir (3 daily; 12hr); Konya (8 daily; 4hr); Niğde
(hourly; 1hr 30min); Ürgüp (8 daily; 1hr 30min).

Konya to: Afyon (3 daily; 3hr); Ankara (hourly; 3hr);
Antalya (8 daily; 5hr); Beyşehir (every 30min; 1hr
15min); Bursa (2 daily; 10hr); Göreme (3 daily;

3hr); Isparta (2 daily; 4hr); Kayseri (8 daily; 4hr);
Silifke (5 daily; 4hr).

Nevşehir to: Adana (1 daily; 5hr); Ankara (4 daily;
4hr); Antalya (2 daily; 11hr); Fethiye (1 daily;
12hr); Göreme (every 30min; 30min); İstanbul (3
daily; 10hr); Kayseri (8 daily; 2hr); Konya (4 daily;
3hr); Mersin (2 daily; 5hr); Ürgüp (every 30min;
30min).

Niğde to: Aksaray (7 daily; 1hr 30min); Alanya (1
daily; 12hr); Ankara (8 daily; 4hr 30min); Antalya
(2 daily; 10–12hr); Çamardı (summer 4 daily; 1hr);
Derinkuyu (hourly; 45min); İstanbul (3 daily; 12hr);
Kayseri (12 daily; 1hr 30min); Konya (5 daily; 3hr
30min); Mersin (5 daily; 4hr); Nevşehir (hourly; 1hr
30min); Samsun (1 daily; 8hr); Sivas (2 daily; 6hr).

Ürgüp to: Adana (1 daily; 5hr); Ankara (6 daily;
5hr); Antalya (2 daily; 10hr); Denizli (2 daily; 12hr);
Göreme (half-hourly; 20min); İstanbul (1 daily;
13hr); Kayseri (hourly; 1.5hr); Konya (6 daily; 3hr);
Marmaris (2 daily; 15hr); Mersin (3 daily; 5hr);
Nevşehir (half-hourly; 30min); Side (2 daily; 13hr).

Flights

Kayseri to: İstanbul (4 daily; 1hr 20min); Trabzon
via İstanbul (3 daily; 3hr 45min); Van via İstanbul (1
daily; 5hr 20min).

Konya to: İstanbul (at least 1 daily; 1hr 15min);
Van via İstanbul (1 daily; 4hr 5min).

North Central Anatolia

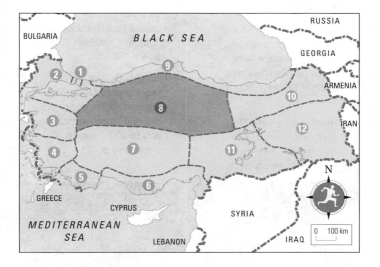

CHAPTER 8

Highlights

* **Museum of Anatolian Civilizations, Ankara** A treasure-hoard of artefacts contained in one of the most prestigious museums in Turkey. See p.685

* **Safranbolu** Ancient pastel-coloured timber houses in a town where the old way of life has stayed remarkably intact. See p.708

* **Hattuşa** Enclosed by six-kilometre-long walls, the Hittite capital was an immense city and its scale is still awe-inspiring today. See p.715

* **Yazılıkaya reliefs** The thirteenth-century BC rock-hewn reliefs pay homage to nearly a hundred Hittite gods. See p.720

* **Rock tombs of Amasya** Massive rock tombs of the Pontic kings carved into a cliff-face and lit up at night to great effect. See p.727

* **Ottoman hotels, Amasya** Sleep in low-slung Ottoman beds in stunningly restored Ottoman houses with creaky floorboards and authentic antiques. See p.725

* **Sivas's Selçuk monuments** Mongol-inspired architecture with highly decorative facades and beautiful mosaic work. See p.733

△ Hittite capital at Hattuşa

North Central Anatolia

When the first Turkish nomads arrived in Anatolia during the tenth and eleventh centuries, the landscape must have been strongly reminiscent of their Central Asian homeland. However, the terrain that so pleased the tent-dwelling herdsmen of a thousand years ago has few attractions for modern visitors. There are monotonous, rolling vistas of stone-strewn grassland, dotted with rocky outcrops and hospitable only to sheep. In winter it can be numbingly cold, while in summer temperatures rise to almost unbearable levels.

It seems appropriate that the heart of original Turkish settlement should be home to **Ankara**, the political and social centre of modern Turkey. This European-style capital rises out of a stark landscape, a symbol of Atatürk's dream of a secular Turkish republic. Though it's a far less exciting city than İstanbul, Ankara does make a good starting point for travels through Anatolia. And even if it's a city more important for its social and political status than for any pronounced architectural or aesthetic merit, it does have great moments. A visit to the **Museum of Anatolian Civilizations** is an essential way of gaining some impression of how Anatolia has developed since it was first settled during Neolithic times.

North Central Anatolia also boasts the remains of **Hattuşa**, one of the earliest known cities in Turkey. Located near the village of **Boğazkale**, Hattuşa was once the capital of the Hittite Empire. East of here, several later cultures and civilizations have left their successive marks: at **Amasya**, the rock-cut tombs of the pre-Roman Pontic kings tower over a haphazard riverside settlement of Ottoman wooden houses; **Tokat** has a fine Selçuk seminary; while **Sivas** displays some of the finest Selçuk architecture found in Turkey. Hidden away in the mountains to the north of Ankara you'll find **Safranbolu**, an almost completely intact Ottoman town, whose wooden houses are tucked into a narrow gorge. North of Ankara and east of Safranbolu is **Kastamonu**, home to a couple of interesting mosques, which fall under the shadow of the town's huge citadel.

Attractions in the less accessible west of the region are sparse. High points are the remains of the Phrygian capital of **Gordion** and the Roman temple site of **Aezani**. Situated between these two, the sacred site at **Midaş Şehri** is worth visiting if you have your own transport. En route you'll invariably pass through **Seyitgazi**, with its dervish monastery built around the tomb of a legendary Arab warrior. **Eskişehir** is the largest city hereabouts, but has little of intrinsic interest. It functions principally as a staging post on the way to Bursa, Bandırma and the Sea of Marmara, or to **Kütahya**, from where there's access to Aezani.

All the region's towns, set within the forbidding northern Anatolian landscape, bear witness to nearly ten thousand turbulent years of human settlement, punctuated by the complexities of war and waves of conquest. Anatolia was the Roman front line against the Persians, and in a sense it's still an arena where the conflicting

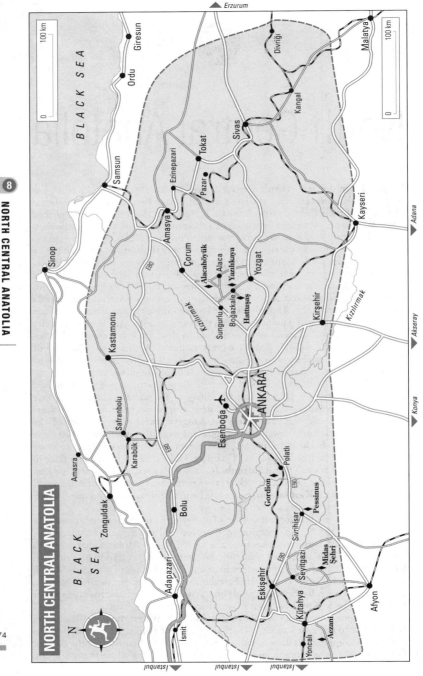

NORTH CENTRAL ANATOLIA

N

B L A C K   S E A

Erzurum

B L A C K   S E A

Giresun

Ordu

Samsun

Sinop

Amasra

Zonguldak

Kastamonu

Safranbolu

Karabük

Bolu

Adapazarı

İsmit

Ezinepazarı

Tokat

Amasya

Çorum

Alacahöyük

Sungurlu

Boğazkale

Alaca

Yazılıkaya

Hattuşaş

Pazar

Sivas

Divriği

Kangal

Malatya

Yozgat

Kayseri

Kırşehir

Kızılırmak

Kızılırmak

Kızılırmak

Esenboğa

ANKARA

Polatlı

Gordion

Pessinus

Sivrihisar

Midas Şehri

Seyitgazi

Eskişehir

Kütahya

Yoncalı

Aezani

Afyon

Erzurum

Adana

Akseray

Konya

İstanbul

İstanbul

İstanbul

100 km

0

100 km

0

E80

E80

E90

E90

E90

currents in Turkish society are played off against each other. The clash of the traditional and the new is immediately apparent in cities such as Ankara, where radically different ways of life are set side by side. Here sizable European-oriented middle-class populations coexist with people from the countryside who, only a decade or two ago, adhered to a centuries-old peasant existence.

Ankara

ANKARA is really two cities, each of which seems to exist as a distinct entity with its own separate time-zone. The double identity is a result of the breakneck pace at which Ankara has developed since its declaration as the capital of the Turkish Republic in 1923. Until then Ankara (formerly known as Angora) had been a small provincial city, almost lost in the midst of the steppelands and known chiefly for its production of angora, soft goats' wool. This older city still exists in and around the citadel, which was the site of the original settlement. The other Ankara is the modern metropolis, Atatürk's capital, which has grown up around the original city, surrounding and almost swamping it – a carefully planned attempt to create a seat of government worthy of a modern, Westernized state.

For visitors, Ankara is never going to be as attractive a destination as İstanbul, and the couple of excellent museums and handful of other sights that it can offer are unlikely to detain you for more than a day or two. Even so it's worth the trip just to find somewhere as refreshingly forward-looking as Turkey's administrative and diplomatic centre.

Some history

It was the **Hittites** who founded Ankara around 1200 BC, naming it Ankuwash. Under them the town prospered due to its position on the royal road running from Sardis to their capital at Hattuşa. The Hittites were succeeded by the **Phrygians**, who called the city Ankyra (and left a significant reminder of their presence in the shape of a huge necropolis uncovered near the train station in 1925), and they, in turn, by the **Lydians** and the **Persians**. Alexander the Great passed through on his way east, while in the third century BC invading **Galatians** (Gauls) held sway for a while, renaming the city Galatia.

By the beginning of the first century BC the **Romans** had made substantial inroads into Asia Minor, and in 74 BC their fourteen-year campaign against the kingdom of Pontus culminated in the defeat of Mithridates the Great by the Roman general Pompey. This event opened up central Anatolia to Roman control and in 24 BC Ankara was officially absorbed into the Empire under Augustus and renamed Sebaste (Greek for Augustus). Ankara thrived under the Romans, thanks to its location astride major trade routes, and by the third century AD it had developed into a flourishing city of 200,000 inhabitants. The later Byzantine era ushered in a period of decline and sporadic attack at the hands of whoever happened to be waging war in the area. Arabs, Persians, Crusaders and Mongols stormed the city en route to greater prizes, but only the **Selçuks** were to settle, taking control of the city in 1071.

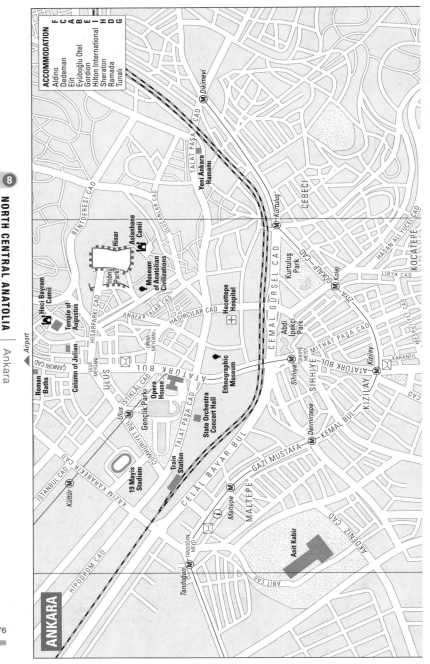

ANKARA

ACCOMMODATION
Aldino	F
Dedeman	C
Elit	A
Eyüboğlu Otel	B
Gordion	E
Hilton International	I
Sheraton	H
Ramada	D
Tunali	G

▲ *Airport*

ISTANBUL CAD

ⓂKülltür

KAZIM KARABEKİR CAD

CUMHURİYET BUL

HIPODROM CAD

ÇANKIRI CAD

BENTDERESİ CAD

HISARPARKİ CAD

UÇANLAR CAD

Roman Baths

Column of Julian

Temple of Augustus

Haci Bayram Camii

İnönü Parkı

Hisar

Aslanhane Camii

Museum of Anatolian Civilizations

ULUS MEYDANI

Ⓜ Ulus

ANAFARTALAR CAD

HASIRCILAR CAD

İSTIKLAL CAD

OPERA MEYDANI

Opera House

Gençlik Parkı

19 Mayis Stadium

Train Station

TALAT PAŞA CAD

State Orchestra Concert Hall

ATATÜRK BUL

Ethnographic Museum

Hacettepe Hospital

CEMAL GÜRSEL CAD

TALAT PAŞA CAD

Ⓜ Dikimevi

Yeni Ankara Hamamı

Ⓜ Kurtuluş

Kurtuluş Park

CEBECİ

GÖKALP CAD

HASAN ALI YÜCEL CAD

KOCATEPE

Ⓜ Kolej

LIBYA CAD

ZİYA

MITHAT PAŞA CAD

Abdi İpekçi Park

Ⓜ Sıhhiye

SIHHIYE MEYD.

SIHHIYE

KIZILAY

Ⓜ Kızılay

ATATÜRK BUL

MESRUTIYET CAD

KARANFIL

KARANFIL CAD

CELAL BAYAR BUL

Ⓜ Demirtepe

KEMAL BUL

GAZİ MUSTAFA

MALTEPE

Ⓜ Maltepe

ⓂTandoğan

TANDOĞAN MEYD.

ℹ

AKDENİZ CAD

ANIT CAD

Anıt Kabir

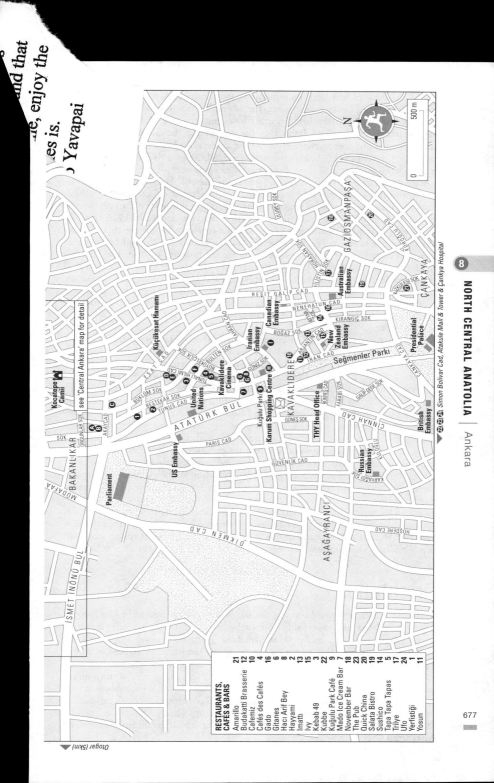

RESTAURANTS,
CAFÉS & BARS
Amarillo   21
Budakatti Brasserie   12
Cafemiz   10
Cafés des Cafés   4
Gado   16
Gitanes   6
Hacı Arif Bey   8
Hayyami   2
Imatti   13
Ivy   15
Kebab 49   3
Kubbe   22
Kuğulu Park Café   9
Mado Ice Cream Bar   7
November Bar   18
The Pub   23
Quick China   20
Salata Bistro   19
Sushico   14
Tapa Tapa Tapas   5
Trilye   17
Ufo   24
Yerfıstığı   1
Yosun   11

By 1361 Ankara had been incorporated into the burgeoning **Ottoman state**, briefly occupying centre stage when the Mongol ruler Tamerlane defeated the army of Beyazit Yıldırım 30km north of the modern city in 1402. The defeat precipitated several years of dynastic in-fighting among the Ottomans as Beyazit's sons fought it out among themselves for the succession. With the eventual restoration of Ottoman rule, Ankara went into something of a decline, with only its famous wool to prevent it from disappearing altogether.

After Atatürk's final victory, Ankara was made the official **capital of the Turkish Republic**, a decision that was ratified by parliament on October 13, 1923. Atatürk chose Ankara for its strategic central location during the Turkish War of Independence, and out of personal preference (between 1919 and 1927 he never set foot in İstanbul). However, at this time the city was little more than a backward provincial centre. The majority of its population lived in mud-brick buildings, and electricity or running water were almost unheard-of luxuries. Turkey's vociferous pro-İstanbul lobby was dismayed by the choice of Ankara as capital and many foreign governments also baulked at the idea of establishing embassies here. Gradually, however, the lure of free land for the building of embassies and a softening of opposition to Atatürk's republic lured in the diplomatic corps, with the British, who had been vocal denigrators of the new capital, snapping up one of the best sites.

The government recruited German and Austrian town planners to transform the city. New streets, public buildings and parks were established – matching Atatürk's vision of a modern, Westward-looking capital – while tens of thousands of people were soon drawn to Ankara from the Anatolian countryside in search of work and a higher standard of living. The planners reckoned on the city's **population** swelling from 30,000 to about 800,000, but the influx far exceeded their expectations and the total number of inhabitants now stands at well over four times that figure. Incomers took advantage of an old Ottoman law, stating that anyone who could build a house in a single night on an unused plot had the right to legal ownership. *Gecekondu* **squatter settlements** now ring the city as, over the decades, what were originally shantytowns have become established as legitimate communities.

The city authorities are working hard at expanding Ankara's infrastructure and there have been concerted efforts to woo foreign investment. Since the terrorist attacks on the United States and elsewhere, the **diplomatic corps** in Ankara has increased its presence dramatically, as Turkey is a key ally in the "war against terrorism". The likes of the Ankara *Hilton* and *Sheraton* have benefited from the new influx of foreign political and military visitors, while upmarket restaurants, bars and Western-style shops are starting to feature heavily in the wealthier suburbs.

Orientation

The city is neatly bisected along its north–south axis by the five-kilometre **Atatürk Bulvarı**, and everything you need is in easy reach of this broad and busy street. At the northern end is **Ulus Meydanı** – usually known simply as **Ulus** ("Nation") – a large square and an important traffic intersection, marked by a huge equestrian Atatürk statue. The square has lent its name to the surrounding area: not a particularly attractive one, dominated by the sprawling PTT sorting offices and run-down shopping centres, but the point to which you'll probably gravitate on arrival as it's the home of cheap hotels and well positioned for both sightseeing and city transportation. About 1km east of here, up Hisarparkı Caddesi, stands the **Hisar**, Ankara's old fortress and citadel, not far from the famous **Museum of Anatolian Civilizations**.

Heading south down Atatürk Bulvarı from Ulus brings you to the main west–east rail line, beyond which lies **Sıhhıye Meydanı**, an important junction marking the beginning of **Yenişehir** ("New City"). A ten-minute walk south of Sıhhıye brings you to **Kızılay**, the busy square that is the main transport hub of the modern city, and shares its name with the surrounding shopping and restaurant district. Keep going south and you'll pass the **Parliament** building on the right, thereafter moving into the **Kavaklıdere** district, home of several major embassies and upmarket hotels. At the bottom of Atatürk Bulvarı is **Çankaya**, Ankara's most exclusive suburb and location of the **Presidential Palace**.

Arrival and information

Ankara's **Esenboğa airport** (general enquiries and flight information ☎0312/398 0100) is 33km north of the city. Green-yellow-and-white Havaş buses from the airport into the centre (3YTL) tend to depart about half an hour after flights land. These will drop you off at the Havaş bus stop by the train station (see below). A taxi into the centre of Ankara from the airport will set you back about 33YTL (double this between midnight and 6am).

If you **arrive** at the **city otogar**, Aşti, in the western suburbs, there will be a free *servis* minibus into the centre from the car park out front. These run through to the plush hotels in Kavaklıdere, but for Ulus the drop-off point is on the corner of Cumhuriyet Caddesi and İstiklâl Caddesi, from where it is a short five-minute walk or taxi ride to the hotels around Ulus Meydanı. Alternatively, catch the Ankaray (LRT light railway) from Aşti station at the *otogar* to Kızılay, where there is a metro connection to Ulus and buses to Kavaklıdere.

The **train station** (☎0312/311 0602) is close to the heart of things at the bottom of Cumhuriyet Bulvarı, with frequent buses from outside the main entrance to Ulus and Kızılay – check the signs on the front of the bus. Or you can walk through the tunnel under the railway line to Maltepe Ankaray (LRT) station, close to the tourist office.

Information

Ankara has two tourist offices: at Esenboğa **airport** (daily 9.30am–6pm, sometimes later depending on the time of flight arrivals; ☎0312/398 0348) and in **Maltepe** at Gazi Mustafa Kemal Bul 121 (summer Mon–Fri 9am–6.30pm, Sat & Sun 10am–5pm; winter Mon–Fri 9am–5pm, Sat 10am–5pm; ☎0312/231 5572). The latter is generally more helpful, is easy to get to from the train station via an underground tunnel, and is close to the Maltepe Ankaray (LRT) station. Both offices will provide you with a city plan.

City transport

Buses run the length of Atatürk Bulvarı from Ulus to Kızılay, and then either branch off to Maltepe under a tunnel or continue to Çankaya via Kavaklıdere. Check the destinations on the front of the bus – most useful is the #391, which runs the length of Atatürk Bulvarı from Ulus Meydanı to the Atakule Mall and Tower in Çankaya. The bulk of buses are blue-and-white EGO municipality buses, though a substantial number are privately run. For all municipality buses you'll need to buy an EGO **ticket** in advance, which you then deposit in the green machine next to the driver on boarding the bus. EGOs are sold at ticket kiosks next to main bus or metro stops and at some *büfe*s (newsagent's stands). Sometimes you may board a privately run bus (usually older and shabbier looking, and often blue) where you pay the conductor – seated to the left of the front entrance – in cash. Routes overlap with those of the municipal services and prices are the same (a flat fare of 1.25YTL a journey).

There are two city **metro lines** with modern stations and efficient trains running at regular intervals throughout the day until around 10.30pm. One line is called the **Ankaray** or LRT (light railway), which runs between the *otogar* at Aşti and Dikimevi in the eastern suburbs. It joins the second line – simply called the **metro** – at Kızılay, where there is a huge underground station under Güven Parkı. The metro runs north from Kızılay to Sıhhıye, Ulus, and then through the northwest suburbs to Batikent. EGO **tickets** for both lines (1.25YTL) are available at booths at the stations, which are then deposited into turnstiles. You can also buy a computer-generated **EGO card** for 12YTL, accredited with ten standard fares, which can be used on the two metro lines as well as the buses.

To get out to the **Aşti** *otogar*, take one of the buses marked "Yeni Garaj", "Yeni Otogar", "Terminal" or "Aşti" which leave from the minibus terminal 300m southwest of Ulus Meydanı; the "Ankaray" (LRT) runs directly to Aşti from Kızılay. **Taxis** are plentiful and can be flagged down just about anywhere, with 1YTL (double between midnight and 6am) as the minimum fare. A trip such as Ulus to Kavaklıdere works out at about 7YTL.

Accommodation

Accommodation covers the full price and quality spectrum, and finding a room is rarely a problem, given the relative absence of tourists. There are plenty of decent possibilities offering doubles for under €20.

Most of the cheaper hotels are in **Ulus**, centred on the streets east of Atatürk Bulvarı **between Ulus Meydanı and Opera Meydanı**, around the main PTT and close to the Museum of Anatolian Civilizations and the castle. Most are presentable but pretty featureless options where the most you can expect is a bed in a plain room with or without plumbing. It's also worth bearing in mind that lone women may not feel so comfortable here. More expensive two- and three-star options can be found around **Çankırı Caddesi**, north of Ulus Meydanı, but the traffic is horrendous on this road so ask for rooms at the back. Moving down into **Sıhhıye** and **Kızılay** will take you up another notch or two, and then prices and standards steadily increase as you move further south and into **Kavaklıdere**, home to top-of-the-range places such as the *Hilton* and *Sheraton*. In the highly unlikely event that you draw a blank in these areas head for **Maltepe** where Gazi Mustafa Kemal Bulvarı (running northwest from Kızılay) and the surrounding streets offer everything from fleapits to classy comfort.

A little **haggling** can go a long way, even at the more expensive establishments (though perhaps not the *Hilton*), particularly out of season. At the very least you can try to get the seventeen-percent **KDV** (local sales tax) knocked off your bill if you offer to pay cash.

Hotels in Ulus (between Ulus Meydanı and Opera Meydanı, and around Çankırı Caddesi), and in Sıhhıye and Maltepe, are marked on our "Central Ankara" map (see pp.682–683), those in Kızılay and Kavaklıdere on our main "Ankara" map (see pp.676–677).

Between Ulus Meydanı and Opera Meydanı

Otel Akman Opera Meyd, Tavus Sok 6 ☎0312/324 4140, @akmanotel@ttnet.net.tr. Clean and bright rooms with spacious wall-to-ceiling tiled bathrooms and a convenient and inexpensive *pide* restaurant attached. Breakfast €2 extra. ❸

Otel Buhara Sanayi Cad 13 ☎0312/310 7999, ⓕ324 3327. Centrally located, renovated hotel, whose immaculate rooms have satellite TV. A good mid-range choice with friendly English-speaking service – one of the few places to provide parking in the area. ❸

Otel Devran Opera Meyd, Tavus Sok 8 ☎0312/311 0485. Well-run, cheap and friendly, with small but decent en-suites; you'll get a bathtub if you're lucky. Breakfast €2 extra. ❷

Farabi Oteli Denizciler Cad 46 ☎0312/310 0777. One of Denizciler Cad's better choices, with helpful staff and a spread of plain singles and doubles with shower. Good value for lone travellers. ❶

Otel Fuar Opera Meyd, Kosova Sok 11 ☎0312/312 3289. Bare but quiet rooms with washbasins only. Breakfast not available, and showers cost an additional €2. ❶

Hisar Oteli Hisarparkı Cad 6 ☎0312/310 8128. A popular budget option with presentably clean rooms with washbasins only, and a couple of en-suites for €6 more. There's a men-only hamam in the basement where for an extra €5 you can get a head-to-toe bath. ❶

Otel Sipahı Opera Meyd, Kosova Sok 1 ☎0312/324 0235. Clean rooms adorned with some great tourism posters from the 1960s, and reliable hot water. One of the better budget choices on this street. ❷

Around Çankırı Caddesi

Capital Hotel Çankırı Cad 21 ☎0312/310 4575. Spotless, business-class three-star with satellite TV and all mod cons. ❺

Otel Çevikoğlu Çankırı Cad, Orta Sok 2 ☎0312/310 4535, ⓕ311 1940. Clean two-star in a quiet backstreet just north of Ulus. Simple white-washed rooms have TV and minibar. ❹

Hotel Selvi Çankırı Cad 16 ☎0312/310 3500, @selvihotel@yahoo.com. Presentable possibility with a large ornate lobby with barbershop. Some attempt has been made at updating the old-fashioned rooms, and extras include air conditioning, a phone in the bathroom and hair dryer. Rooms at the front can get noisy, though there is a swimming pool, so all in all, not bad value. ❹

Turist Hotel Çankırı Cad 37 ☎0312/310 3980, ⓦwww.turisthotel.com.tr. On the main road, but with double-glazed front windows to keep out the noise. The grand lobby aside, the rooms are in need of modernizing, but have TV, minibar and balcony. Other conveniences include hairdresser, Turkish bath, gym, room service and indoor parking. ❻

Maltepe

Otel Örnek Gülseren Sok 4 ☎0312/231 8170, ⓦwww.ornekhotel.com. Friendly, intimate hotel in a boxy bright-blue building down a sidestreet off Gazi Mustafa Kemal Bul, close to the tourist office. Neat rooms with TV, hairdryers, minibars and 24hr room service. ❻

Sıhhıye

Büyük Sürmeli Hotel Cihan Sok 6 ☎0312/231 7660, ⓦwww.surmelihotels.com. The works, as you'd expect for around €128 a double, including a lovely outdoor pool surrounded by sun loungers, a fabulous kidney-shaped indoor pool, gym, Turkish bath and assortment of restaurants and bars. The huge rooms are modern, if somewhat frilly, with cable TV and minibar. ❽

Kızılay

Elit Otel Olgunlar Sok 10 ☎0312/417 4695, @elitotel@superonline.com. Nicely decorated with bright duvets and curtains, and equipped with heating and air conditioning, minibar and TV. There's a simple restaurant/bar in the lobby and it even has a garden out back – a rare find. ❹

Eyüboğlu Otel Karanfil Sok 73 ☎0312/417 6400, ⓦwww.eyubogluhotel.com. At the quieter end of this busy street, whilst still being close to the cinemas and bars. The rooms are nothing special but are adequate and modern – a regular venue for Turkish coach parties. ❹

Kavaklıdere

Otel Aldino Tunalı Hilmi Cad, Bülten Sok 22 ☎0312/468 6510, ⓦwww.hotelaldino.com. Prime location for dedicated shoppers, with a Turkish bath, two restaurant/bars, and garage parking. Air-conditioned rooms are bright and spacious with satellite TV, minibars and hairdryers. Friendly for a high-end place and rates are negotiable. ❻

Hotel Dedeman Büklüm Sok 1 ☎0312/417 6200, ⓕ417 6214. A luxury place in a residential area, with pool, babysitting service, beauty salon and gym. Modern functional rooms go from €120, but when there are no businessmen around you may be able to negotiate a worthwhile discount. ❼

Gordion Hotel Büklüm Sok 59 ☎0312/427 8080, ⓦwww.gordionhotel.com. Very expensive, and rather exclusive new hotel with large, comfortable rooms all done in a tasteful, classical style. There's also a pool, and candelit massages on offer in the

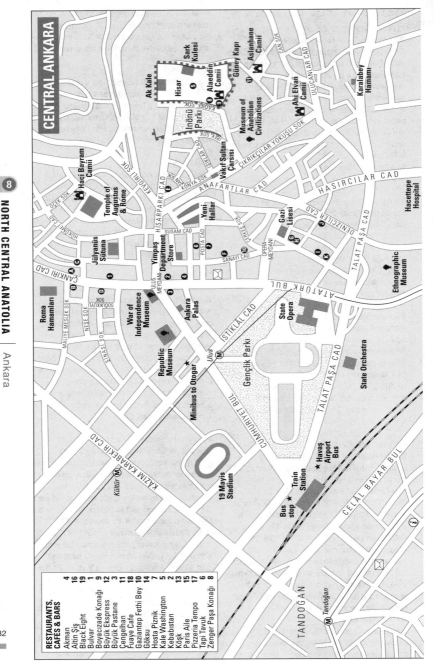

CENTRAL ANKARA

Roma Hamamları

War of Independence Museum

Republic Museum

Ankara Palas

Minibus to Otogar

Ulus

19 Mayıs Stadium

Gençlik Parkı

State Opera

State Orchestra

Bus stop

Train Station

Havaş Airport Bus

TANDOĞAN

Tandoğan

CELÂL BAYAR BUL

KAZIM KARABEKIR CAD

Kültür

MALIYE MESLEK SOK

NEŞE SOK

SINASI SOK

ÇANKIRI CAD

HÜKÜME CAD

İPEK SOK

SÖĞÜKKUYU SOK

Roma Hamamları

Jülyanüs Sütunu

Temple of Augustus & Rome

Haci Bayram Camii

KEYİFLİ SOK

HİSARPARKI CAD

KONYA SOK

KOÇ SOK

SUSAM CAD

POSTA CAD

SANAYİ CAD

OPERA MEYDANI

Yimpaş Department Store

Yeni Hallar

Vakıf Sultan Çarşısı

ANAFARTLAR CAD

Gazi Lisesi

DENİZCİLER CAD

EREFES SOK

SIKLAR CAD

İPEK SOK

KADİFE SOK

İnönü Parkı

Ak Kale

Hisar

Sark Kulesi

Güney Kapı

Alaeddin Camii

Aslanhane Camii

CAN SOK

ULUCANLAR CAD

Museum of Anatolian Civilizations

Ahi Elvan Camii

ÇIKRIKÇILAR YOKUŞU SOK

HASIRCILAR CAD

Karalabey Hamamı

Hacettepe Hospital

TALAT PAŞA CAD

ATATÜRK BUL

İSTİKLAL CAD

CUMHURİYET BUL

TALAT PAŞA CAD

Ethnographic Museum

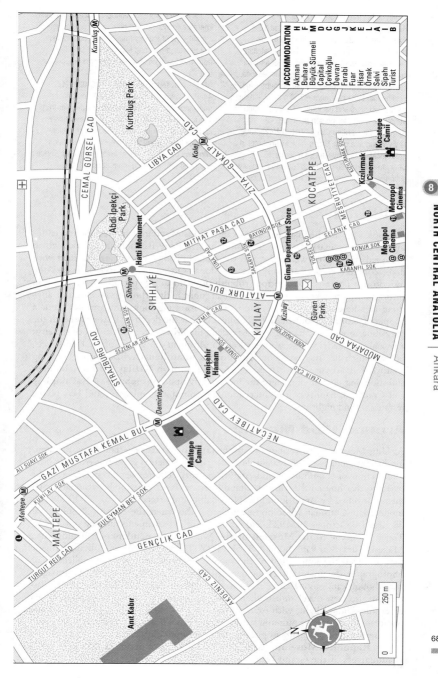

ACCOMMODATION

Akman	H
Buhara	F
Büyük Sürmeli	M
Capital	D
Çevikoğlu	C
Devran	G
Farabi	J
Fuar	K
Hisar	E
Örnek	L
Selvi	A
Sipahi	I
Turist	B

Kurtuluş

Kurtuluş Park

CEMAL GÜRSEL CAD

Abdi İpekçi Park

LIBYA CAD

Kolej

ZIYA GÖKALP CAD

GÖKALP CAD

Hatti Monument

Sıhhiye

SIHHIYE

MITHAT PAŞA CAD

BAYINDIR SOK

SAKARYA SOK

TUNA CAD

Gina Department Store

KOCATEPE

MEŞRUTIYET CAD

Kızılırmak Cinema

KIZILIRMAK SOK

Kocatepe Camii

SELANIK CAD

Metropol Cinema

YÜKSEL CAD

KONUR SOK

Megapol Cinema

KARANFIL SOK

ATATÜRK BUL

Kızılay

KIZILAY

Güven Parkı

Kızılay

İZMIR CAD

CINAH SOK

SEZENLAR SOK

STRAZBURG CAD

Demirtepe

Yenişehir Hamam

SÜMER SOK

ADEM YAVUZ SOK

İZMIR CAD

NECATIBEY CAD

MUDAFAA CAD

Maltepe

Maltepe Camii

ALI SUAVI SOK

GAZI MUSTAFA KEMAL BUL

KUBILAY SOK

MALTEPE

SÜLEYMAN BEY SOK

GENÇLIK CAD

TURGUT REIS CAD

AKDENIZ CAD

Anıt Kabir

N

0   250 m

health club. From €150 per room. **8**
Hilton International Hotel Tahran Cad 12
℡0312/468 2888, ⓦwww.hilton.com. Luxury
rooms on sixteen floors, decorated in Anatolian
stone and lots of plants, with individual air-condi-
tioning/heating systems and laptop connections.
For those on a generous expense account – the
presidential suite is a mere €780 a night – though
discounted weekend packages (Fri–Sun) weigh in
at around €120 per person per night. **7**
Ramada Tunalı Hilmi Cad 66 ℡0312/428 2000,
ⓦwww.ramada.com. Brand-new luxury hotel in a
great location for Kavaklıdere nightlife. **7**
Sheraton Noktalı Sok ℡0312/468 5454, ⓦwww.
sheraton.com/ankara. Enjoy a pampered existence

in this newly restored, cylindrical concrete monolith.
There's a friendly atmosphere for a five-star hotel,
a great view of the city from the top, plus various
restaurants, a pool and two cinemas. Doubles
from €220 and no shortage of people prepared to
pay. **8**
Otel Tunalı Tunalı Hilmi Cad 119 ℡0312/467
4440, ⓦwww.hoteltunali.com.tr. A good upper-
mid-range option run by the same family for thirty
years, cheaper than most places in Kavaklıdere
and close to all the nightlife. Rooms are ordinary
but functional with fridge, satellite TV and huge
windows overlooking busy Tunalı Hilmi Cad. Coffee
shop and formal dining room attached. **6**

The City

For most visitors, the first taste of Ankara is **Ulus Meydanı** and it's none too enticing. Ulus once marked the westernmost limits of pre-Republican Ankara, which
occupied the area between here and the citadel. Today, the streets are lined with
drab, concrete stacks and only the occasional Ottoman-era survivor breaks the
monotony. There is also a serious rubbish problem in this part of town, which in
turn attracts street kids and hawkers late at night raking through in search of anything to take home or sell. Despite these unpromising looks, the area does hide a
couple of **Roman monuments**, offering a hint at the depth of history beneath the
prevailing modernity. East of Ulus Meydanı, the **Hisar** is the oldest part of the city:
a Byzantine citadel whose walls enclose an Ottoman-era village of cobbled streets,
below which lies the excellent **Museum of Anatolian Civilizations**. The long
Atatürk Bulvarı runs south from Ulus down through **Kızılay**, Ankara's business
and shopping district, and on to the increasingly upmarket suburbs of **Kavaklıdere**
and **Çankaya**, haunts of the international community, embassies, and best of the
restaurants and nightlife.

Around Ulus Meydanı

At Ulus Meydanı, a towering equestrian **statue of Atatürk** – flanked by threatening bronze soldiers in German-style coal-scuttle helmets – gazes out over the busy
intersection of Cumhuriyet and Atatürk *bulvarı*. The former president faces the
building that housed the Turkish Grand National Assembly, the provisional parliament convened by Atatürk and his Nationalist supporters on April 23, 1920. This
modest, late-Ottoman schoolhouse building is also where the Turkish Republic was
declared on October 29, 1923, and it served as the parliament building until 1925.
Today it's home to the **Museum of the War of Independence** (Kürtülüş Savaş
Müzesi; Tues–Sun 9am–noon & 1–5pm; 2YTL), devoted to the military struggle
that preceded the foundation of the modern republic. An extensive collection of
photographs, documents and ephemera covers every detail of the various campaigns
and, though captions are all in Turkish, much of the material speaks for itself. Visitors can also view the chamber where delegates sat in small school desks, illuminated
by candle- and oil-light, with Atatürk overseeing from the vantage point of a raised
platform. Opposite the museum stands Ankara's first hotel, the **Ankara Palas**, once
again serving as a government guesthouse for visiting dignitaries.

The **Republic Museum** (Cumhuriyet Müzesi), housed in the post-1925
headquarters of the Grand National Assembly on Cumhuriyet Meydanı, which

concentrates on the achievements of the Turkish Republic, was closed for restoration at the time of writing, and it is unclear when it will reopen.

From Ulus, Hisarparkı Caddesi leads east to the Hisar. On the way, make a quick diversion south down Susam Caddesi, followed by a fork to the left, to reach the **Yeni Hallar**, the city's premier fruit and veg market. Just behind here on Konya Sok is the **Vakıf Sultan Çarşısı**, a restored *han*, now home to multitudes of cheap clothing shops.

Roman Ankara

What's left of Roman Ankara lies just north of Hisarparkı Caddesi. Following Hükümet Caddesi and taking the first right fork leads to the remains of the **Temple of Augustus and Rome**, Ankara's most important ancient monument. Built in honour of Augustus between 25 and 20 BC, after Ankara was made the provincial capital of Galatia, its main claim to fame is an inscription on the outer wall. Detailing the *Res Gestae Divi Augusti* (Deeds of the Divine Augustus), this was the emperor's political testament, which was carved on every temple of Augustus in the Roman world after his death. The Ankara version is the only one that survives in its entirety. The temple, whose walls alone have endured, was converted into a Christian church around the fifth century AD, and during the fifteenth century it became the *medrese* of the **Hacı Bayram Camii**, named after Bayram Veli, founder of the Bayrami order of dervishes and Ankara's most celebrated Muslim saint. His body is buried in the tomb in front of the building.

A couple of hundred metres to the southwest on Hükümet Meydanı is the **Jülyanüs Sütunu** (Column of Julian), commemorating a visit to Ankara by the Byzantine emperor Julian the Apostate, chiefly remembered for his short-lived attempt to revive worship of the old Roman gods in the fourth century. The column's stonework is characterized by a strange, layered effect rather like a long, cylindrical kebab. Once memories of the Byzantine Empire had faded, the locals took to calling the column Belkis Minaresi, "the Queen of Sheba's Minaret".

Ankara's other main Roman remains, the **Roma Hamamları**, or Roman Baths (daily 8.30am–12.30pm & 1.30–5.30pm; 2YTL), are about ten minutes' walk north of here on the western side of Çankırı Caddesi. The baths are set in a large *palaestra* (exercise field) scattered with overgrown truncated columns and fragments of cracked masonry. Of the baths themselves, which date back to the third century AD, only the brick pillars that supported the floors – and allowed warm air to circulate and heat the rooms above – survive.

Museum of Anatolian Civilizations

From İnönü Parkı, at the eastern end of Hisarparkı Caddesi, a sharp right turn leads to the **Museum of Anatolian Civilizations** (Anadolu Medeniyetleri Müzesi; daily 8.30am–5.15pm; 10YTL), an outstanding archeological collection documenting the peoples and cultures of Anatolia from the late Stone Age through to Classical times. When you see a replica artefact at an archeological site elsewhere in Turkey, you can bet the original is here. Housed in a restored fifteenth-century *bedesten*, this unmissable museum is, for most visitors, the highpoint of a visit to Ankara.

Its vast cache of artefacts is laid out in chronological order, clockwise from the entrance, with large stone reliefs dating from the Hittite and Phrygian periods in the central chamber. Most exhibits are clearly labelled in English and German. As you enter, you may be approached by an **official guide** offering to accompany you on your tour. If you have 40YTL or so to spare, and like the look of whoever approaches you, this can be worth doing – many of the guides are moonlighting academics and correspondingly well informed.

The collection concludes with a look at finds from the most **recent excavations**, and then spills Greek and Roman statuary over into the **café** and outdoor garden. The museum **bookshop** offers a fine catalogue, postcards and some useful, if pricey, introductory history books.

Paleolithic (Old Stone Age) section

An assortment of bone fragments and primitive stone tools and weapons from a cave-site at Karain, 30km northwest of Antalya, bear witness to the two-million-year period of hunter-gatherer development that ended about ten thousand years ago. Later finds from Karain include more sophisticated bone awls, needles and ornaments that are a foretaste of the more complex artefacts found in the following sections.

Neolithic (7000–5500 BC) and Chalcolithic (5400–3000 BC) sections

Objects found at Çatal Höyük, a settlement of New Stone Age mud-brick houses 52km north of Konya, have yielded significant evidence about the Neolithic period. It was then that settled agriculture began, accompanied by a refinement of tool-making techniques and the appearance of handmade pottery. One of the most interesting features here is the re-creation of a room from a Çatal Höyük dwelling, complete with characteristic bull's-head emblem and wall paintings. The importance of agriculture in this era may account for the abundance of fertility goddess figures – represented by baked-clay female forms of ample proportions – that reappear in various forms throughout the museum. Later evidence of a more sophisticated lifestyle emerges in finds dating back to 5700–5600 BC from a settlement at Hacılar in southwest Anatolia. Vessels in the shape of animals, and a red cup in a stylized female form, reveal improvements in pottery-making methods. Other objects on display include simple bead jewellery, and tools and weapons made from obsidian and flint.

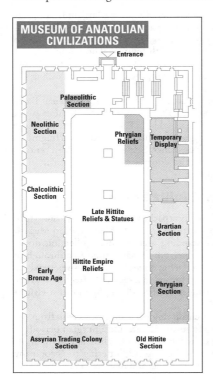

Further finds from Hacılar are displayed in the Chalcolithic section, including simple copper implements, the first use of metal in Anatolia. The pottery is decorated with geometric designs that become more complex as the centuries go by. Stone seals suggesting formal property ownership bear witness to an increasingly well-organized society.

Bronze Age section (3000–2000 BC)

Hammering and casting techniques were greatly refined during this period, with the methods used to work not only bronze but also gold, silver and electron (an alloy of gold and silver). This era was characterized by large settlements of mud-brick houses built on stone foundations and surrounded by defensive walls. Most of the objects here come from Alacahöyük; among the most striking exhibits are the pieces of gold jewellery unearthed in the royal tombs. Other memorable objects are cult symbols featuring stags, bulls and the sun. The pottery is plainer than that of the preceding Chalcolithic period but better made, with obvious spouts and handles. This was a time when Anatolia reached an advanced level of civilization, with well-established trade links between the various settlements. One symbol of continuity, the mother goddess figure, was now slimmed down or transformed into a distinctive violin shape.

Assyrian Trading Colony section (1950–1750 BC)
Included here are some well-preserved examples of the earliest written records in Anatolia in the shape of cuneiform tablets produced by the Assyrians. Also striking are the libation vases in the form of birds and animals, and vases made of obsidian and rock crystal. This period saw Assyrian traders from northern Mesopotamia establishing a trading network that covered most of Anatolia, importing tin, goat-hair felt, cloth, garments, ornaments and perfumes, and establishing markets called *karum*s outside their cities. The central one was at Kaniş (Kanesh), outside Kültepe, and it's from this *karum* that most of the objects on display in this section are drawn.

Old Hittite section (1700–1450 BC)
The Hittites left behind spectacular sites at Boğazkale and nearby Yazılıkaya, east of Ankara; most of the objects on display are from Boğazkale and Alacahöyük. Hittite pottery is similar to that found in the Assyrian Trading Colony period, the most sophisticated example here being a vase with a relief depicting a lively wedding procession. There's also some well-executed metalwork, including statues of gods and goddesses in bronze. Also included are a number of stelae carved with hieroglyphics that have proved a valuable source of information about the Old Hittite kingdom.

Hittite Empire (1450–1200 BC) and Late Hittite section (1200–700 BC)
This period of expansionism and warfare, particularly against the Egyptians, represents the zenith of Hittite power. The large and elaborate reliefs from Alacahöyük in the central hall indicate the sophistication of Hittite culture during this time. Most depict religious themes: a king and queen offering libations to a bull, and an elaborate festival scene with a juggler, acrobat and musician stand out in particular. If you're planning to visit Hattuşa, look out for the lion and sphinx figures from the city gates and the bearded, hook-nosed figure of the weather-god Teshuba. The originals are here, replaced with replicas at the site itself.

The main Late Hittite sites were at Kargamiş, Karatepe and Malatya-Aslantepe. A number of well-preserved and detailed reliefs from this period are in the central hall. One of the most vivid is a battle scene depicting a chariot carrying an archer running over a dead man. Others show the children of the Hittite king Araras at play, a procession of three women in mourning and the Hittite mother-goddess Kubaba in various poses.

Phrygian section (1200–700 BC)
Most of these objects were recovered from the royal tumulus at Gordion, capital of Phrygian Anatolia after the fall of the Hittites. The timber-framed chamber

at the heart of the tumulus has been re-created and objects from it are on display nearby. Most impressive are a wooden table of intricate design and skilfully wrought bronze vessels. Other exhibits attest to cultural sophistication: pottery with stylized animal reliefs and a translucent glass bowl, one of the earliest known examples of glasswork.

Urartian section (1200–700 BC)

Main rivals of the Phrygians and descendants of the Hurrians, the Urartians established a vast empire centred on Van and extending from Sivas and Erzincan to Iran, held together by a series of fortified citadels. Most of what is known about the Urartians derives from clay tablets listing military successes. On the evidence of those artefacts on display here their culture was less sophisticated than that of the Phrygians, though the large bronze cauldron resting on a tripod with cloven bronze feet is austerely beautiful.

The citadel and old town

A pathway leads steeply up through İnönü Parkı between the inner and outer walls of the **Hisar**, the Byzantine citadel whose walls enclose the oldest part of the city. It's an Ottoman-era village of cobbled streets and ramshackle wooden houses that of all Ankara's districts most fully rewards a relaxed and aimless stroll. Most of the area is defiantly unrestored, not to say verging on the squalid, and at times the old-world atmosphere is pungently authentic with the stench of rotting rubbish and bad drains hanging heavy in the air. All this is changing, though, and a number of grand Ottoman mansions have been renovated, decked out with carpets and antiques, and transformed into restaurants or carpet shops geared towards the tourist trade. Some succeed in recapturing the atmosphere of times past, while others are just hopelessly kitsch.

Ankara's **city walls** were probably first constructed by the Hittites over three thousand years ago when they recognized the defensive potential of the citadel outcrop. The walls that are seen today are much more recent, built on the orders of the Byzantine emperor Michael III (remembered as "Michael the Sot") in 859, who updated defences built by the Roman emperor Heraclius (who in turn had used earlier Galatian fortifications as a foundation).

At the northern end of the citadel is the **Ak Kale** (White Fortress), presenting tremendous views of Ankara. The northeastern edge of the city, just about visible from here, is the approximate site of the battlefield where Pompey defeated the Pontic king Mithridates the Great in 74 BC. **Şark Kulesi**, a ruined tower rising out of the eastern walls, also has a panoramic outlook, as well as being a favourite kite-flying spot for local children. It's from here that you can best appreciate the impact of the squatter settlements that have grown up around modern Ankara.

At the southern end of the citadel is the **Güney Kapı** (South Gate), with two vast towers flanking a twin portal. Embedded in the wall connecting the towers are various fragments of Roman masonry, including altars supported by recumbent statues of Priapus. Just inside the gate is the **Alâeddin Camii**, a twelfth-century mosque, much restored in later years, whose unexceptional exterior conceals a painstakingly carved Selçuk *mimber*.

An unadulterated example of Selçuk architecture can be found a few streets to the southeast in the shape of the **Aslanhane Camii** (Lion-House Mosque), Ankara's oldest and most impressive mosque. The Aslanhane Camii is a "forest mosque", so called because of the 24 wooden columns (arranged in four rows of six) that support the intricately carved wooden ceiling. The astonishingly detailed walnut *mimber* dates back to 1209 and is one of the last examples of Selçuk decorative carving. It's well complemented by the stucco and tile *mihrab*, another outstanding piece of work. Ahi Zerafattin, the founder of the Aslanhane Camii, is buried opposite the mosque in Ankara's sole surviving Selçuk **tomb**, with its distinctive octagonal plan and pointed roof.

There's another forest mosque, the **Ahi Elvan Camii**, a few minutes' walk southwest of here. It's an Ottoman example of the style, dating from the late thirteenth century and, though not as impressive as the Aslanhane Camii, still worth a look. This particular mosque was founded by the Ahi brotherhood, a medieval guild associated with the dervish orders. The carved *mimber*, though overshadowed by the example up the road is, nonetheless, a fine piece of work.

Between these two mosques, off At Pazarı Sok and Can Sok is the **Pirinç Han**, built beneath the walls of the citadel in the eighteenth century as an inn for travellers to provide protection from bandits. It was the first inn in Ankara, constructed with a wooden frame filled in with sun-dried bricks, and was used as such until the War of Independence in 1921, when it was taken over by the military and, because of its strategic position on top of the hill, served as a command post. It's been fully restored since as a shopping centre, with forty shops selling an assortment of carpets, paintings, antiques, spirit lamps, glass, copper and silverware. You can stop by for a glass of tea in the cool courtyard, where you'll hear the gentle sound of craftsmen tapping hammers on copper drifting from the inner rooms. A little further to the east, in front of the Museum of Anatolian Civilizations, the old shops on **Çıkrıkçılar Yokuşu Sok** are also worth a browse for copper, carpets, antiques, costumes and embroidery.

South to Kızılay

It's roughly a two-kilometre walk south from Ulus Meydanı to the centre of Kızılay, or fifteen minutes on the bus (though heavy traffic makes progress by bus slow). Immediately south of Ulus you pass Ankara's main PTT, on the east side of Atatürk Bulvarı, and thereafter comes a succession of banks. Look out for the entrance to **Gençlik Parkı** (Youth Park) on the right after the roundabout. The park was built on the orders of Atatürk to provide a worthy recreational spot for the hard-toiling citizens of his model metropolis. The park's strangely named Monument to a Secure and Confident Future bears his words: "Be proud, hardworking, and believe in yourself". On most summer evenings, the park is packed with families strolling around the artificial lake and enjoying the numerous teahouses. Occasional outdoor concerts are held here and there's also a Luna Park funfair full of antiquated rides. The **State Opera House** (Devlet Opera), looking like a dark pink, Art-Deco underground station, stands near the entrance and was built at Atatürk's behest – he developed a taste for opera while serving as military attaché in Sofia in 1905.

Heading on down Atatürk Bulvarı you pass the **Ethnographic Museum** on Talat Paşa Cad (Etnografya Müzesi; Tues–Sun 9am–noon & 1–5pm; 2YTL), a grandiose white-marble building that was the original resting place of Atatürk before the construction of the Anıt Kabir mausoleum (see p.693) – hence the equestrian statue of Atatürk out front. The museum contains an extensive collection of folk costumes and artefacts from Selçuk times onwards, and is packed with carpets, furniture and domestic utensils, alongside a number of re-created Ottoman household interiors. There are also some fine examples of Selçuk woodcarving, including a *mihrab* from a village mosque near Ürgüp that must represent thousands of hours of carving.

A little way further south of the museum, beyond the rail and road bridges and past the Abdi ıpekçi Parkı, **Sıhhiye Meydanı** announces the beginning of modern Ankara. Here the road branches in three directions, while at the centre of the square stands the **Hatti Anıt** (Hatti Monument), with a statue based on the Bronze-Age Anatolian stag symbol. Staying with Atatürk Bulvarı leads you into **Kızılay**, the centre of the modern city, which turns out to be yet another immense traffic junction with a small park, **Güven Parkı**, and a mighty Atatürk statue. It's a useful orientation point: the Gima department store on the eastern side of Atatürk Bulvarı, with a restaurant and café society in the parallel pedestrian precincts; and numerous fancy clothes shops along Atatürk Bulvarı to the south.

Kocatepe, Kavaklıdere and Çankaya

Real-estate values increase exponentially as you move south of Kızılay towards Çankaya. A few blocks east of the main thoroughfare, the minarets of the massive **Kocatepe Camii** tower above the surrounding streets. This neo-Ottoman structure, finished in 1987 after twenty years of building, and complete with shopping centre and car park underneath, is Ankara's largest mosque and, indeed, one of the biggest in the world.

Half a kilometre or so beyond Kızılay is the Grand National Assembly, Turkey's functional modern **Parliament** building. It's the prelude to a strip of well-appointed embassy buildings and glossy hotels that stretches all the way to the Presidential Palace. About halfway along is the innocuous little **Kuğulu Parkı**, so packed with trysting couples that you'll feel like a voyeur as you stroll through it. At the eastern side of the park is the gleaming **Karum shopping centre**, which, with its air conditioning and mall kids, comes as something of a culture shock after the crowded streets of Ulus and Kızılay. The area hereabouts is **Kavaklıdere**, one of the capital's smartest suburbs and also one of the liveliest. It is the place to come for Western-style nightlife and designer stores, both of which you'll find in abundance along **Tunalı Hilmi Caddesi**, running north from the Kuğulu Parkı roundabout.

△ Kocatepe Camii, Ankara

Modern Turkey is largely the creation of one man, **Mustafa Kemal Atatürk**. A complex and often contradictory figure, driven by fervent patriotism and blinding ambition, he salvaged the Turkish state from the wreckage of the Ottoman Empire and defined it as a modern, secular nation. The omnipresent public statues and portraits are not merely symbols of the personality cult that has been built up around him; they also reflect the widely held conviction that without him Turkey in its present form simply would not exist.

Born in 1881 in Salonica (Thessaloníki), on the fringes of the declining Ottoman Empire, Atatürk set his sights on a military career from an early age. After the death of his father, a minor civil servant and unsuccessful businessman, he persuaded his reluctant mother to let him attend military school where he proved to be an excellent pupil.

Early career

In 1902 his military education took him to the Staff College in İstanbul. By now, popular feeling thought that it was time to replace the decay of the old regime with a democratic structure. Atatürk was soon involved in anti-government political activities, which continued after his commission into the regular army. In 1906 he helped form a revolutionary patriotic society called *Vatan* (Fatherland), which in the following year became part of the **Committee of Union and Progress** (CUP), a radical political organization set up by supporters of the Young Turk revolutionary movement.

In April 1909, Atatürk played a key role in the CUP **coup** that deposed Sultan Abdülhamid, leading the "Army of Liberation" into İstanbul and securing the city for the revolutionaries. Despite his prominent role in these events, political and personal differences with the increasingly authoritarian CUP leadership led to his political sidelining (and a couple of unsuccessful assassination attempts). Appointments in distant parts of the empire, followed by a posting to Sofia as military attaché, served to keep him out of the way until the outbreak of World War I.

Gallipoli victory

In February 1915, Atatürk was sent to **Gallipoli**, where an Allied landing was imminent. It was to prove a highly significant posting in terms of both Atatürk's own career and the Turkish war effort. When the Allied assault came in April he organized a daring counter-attack, preventing the Allies from breaking out of the Arıburnu (Anzac Cove) bridgehead. His skill as a commander, coupled with his willingness to put his own life at risk, galvanized the Turkish troops into fierce and heroic defence, and he was rewarded with promotion to colonel and given command of the army corps controlling the strategically vital Anafarta ridge. In this role he was successful at repulsing a second major attack in August, in which he was wounded. Atatürk's key role in the defence of Gallipoli established his military reputation and, more significantly, brought him a nationwide respect that he would put to good use after the 1918 armistice.

As a result of his Gallipoli successes, Atatürk was promoted to general. There was little he could do to turn the wider tide of defeat about to engulf the Ottoman Empire and he spent the remainder of the war taking part in rearguard actions on the southern fringes of the empire. When the armistice was signed on October 30, 1918, he began the task of trying to preserve the demoralized army, knowing there were further battles to come.

Battle for independence

Recognizing that the victorious World War I Allies were about to carve up the empire, and that Sultan Mehmet VI's government wasn't going to do anything about it, Atatürk decided to organize **Turkish resistance** from Anatolia, where Nationalist guerilla

[continued overleaf]

bands were already active. In May 1919 he secured a posting to Samsun, ostensibly to restore order in the region. His arrival there can be seen as the beginning of the Turkish struggle for independence. In the words of Atatürk's biographer, Patrick Kinross, he had "set up his standard of liberation on the shores of the Black Sea".

He came out into the open on June 21 in the town of Amasya, delivering a speech that called for national resistance to outside attempts at dismembering Turkey, which as the recent Greek occupation of İzmir had shown, were now well under way. Thus Atatürk and his followers became embroiled in open rebellion against the government. He went on to preside over Nationalist congresses at Erzurum and Sivas, which launched a political manifesto known as the **National Pact**, calling for the preservation of Turkey's existing frontiers and the establishment of a provisional government.

With growing support for the Nationalists, the Allies occupied İstanbul and, a month later, the sultan suspended parliament. The time was right for Atatürk to realize his plan to create an alternative Anatolian-based government and, on April 23, 1920, the first session of the **Grand National Assembly** opened with him as president. A month later the sultan's goverment condemned Atatürk and some of his followers to death. Turkey was now split in two and Atatürk was the undisputed figurehead of the Nationalist cause.

Birth of the Republic

In his role of Nationalist leader, Atatürk oversaw a series of complex political and military manoeuvrings, most significant of which was the repulsion of the Greek invasion of Anatolia in 1921. This culminated in the epic **Battle of Sakarya**, which took place 100km west of Ankara between August 23 and September 13. Atatürk took personal command in the field, smashing the Greek advance, and the following summer he directed a lightning offensive that drove the Greeks from Anatolia, culminating in the sacking and burning of İzmir. On October 11, 1922, an armistice agreement was signed with the Allies and on November 1 the Nationalists abolished the sultanate.

The following year saw the consolidation of Atatürk's gains. The Treaty of Lausanne, signed on July 24, 1923, established Turkey's borders and in October the Allies withdrew from İstanbul, allowing the Nationalist troops to occupy the city. In the same month Ankara was officially made capital, and on October 29, Turkey was declared a **Republic** with Atatürk as its president.

At the end of Atatürk Bulvarı is Çankaya Caddesi, beyond which lies the **Presidential Palace** (Çankaya Köşkü; open Sun and national holidays only 1.30–5pm; free), Atatürk's Ankara residence, to which he moved in 1921. A visit here is something of a reverential pilgrimage for Turks, but if you want to go you must arrange a visit in advance with the tourist office, which will fax ahead a day or two beforehand – on arrival, check in at the guardhouse and surrender your passport before joining a group tour. The house itself is a reasonably modest affair, a largish two-storey villa set in formal grounds, but by no means a palace. The ground floor is furnished in the Ottoman Baroque style, with much heavily carved and inlaid dark-wood furniture in evidence. Upstairs in Atatürk's living quarters the decor is a little more relaxed, with personal touches, such as a billiard table, on display.

Back on Çankaya Caddesi, at the junction with Atatürk Bulvarı is the unmissable **Atakule Mall and Tower**, a vast mushroom of a tower in reinforced concrete and mirror glass, with another smart shopping centre at its foot. It's worth shelling out 2YTL for the lift ride (daily 10am–10pm) up the 125-metre-high structure to enjoy an unbeatable view of the city and an expensive drink in the revolving bar (see p.697).

Reforms

Having achieved his wider political and military objectives, Atatürk turned his attention towards **internal reform**. His main aim was to transform Turkey into a modern, Western-oriented society, and between 1923 and 1934 he introduced dramatic reforms that touched upon every aspect of Turkish life. Among the most significant of these were the separation of religion and state with the abolition of the caliphate in 1924, the adoption of Latin script in 1928 and the establishment of full suffrage for women in 1934. In the same year, it was decreed that all Turks should adopt surnames. Atatürk's own name, meaning "**Father Turk**" dates from then – previously he had been known only as Mustafa Kemal.

Despite a reformist strategy, Atatürk's style of rule is best described as **benign despotism**. For example, he used a Kurdish revolt in 1925 as a pretext to ban Turkey's sole opposition party and institute censorship of the press. The revolt itself was suppressed with mass hangings of the ringleaders in Diyarbakır. The following year an amateurish plot against Atatürk's life was uncovered, an event that was blown up into a full-scale conspiracy and provided a convenient excuse for hanging several members of the former CUP leadership who had been vocal opponents of Atatürk. The 1926 purge succeeded in muting the opposition and was not repeated.

Atatürk and his associates pursued a policy designed to create a self-sufficient industrial base for Turkey, along the lines of fascist Italy. It proved a failure, as massive subsidies crippled the rest of the economy. Atatürk's foreign-policy dealings met with greater success, and his resolute noninterventionism kept Turkey out of the impending European conflict.

By the mid-1930s, it was clear that Atatürk's greatest achievements were behind him and his **final years** present a sad picture of decline. Bad health accelerated by heavy drinking made him increasingly unpredictable and irascible. By the winter of 1937 it was evident that he was seriously ill. He survived long enough to oversee the first stages of the transfer of the Hatay from France to Turkey, the last political action in which he took a personal hand. He died of cirrhosis at İstanbul's Dolmabahçe Palace on November 10, 1938, and was succeeded the next day by İsmet İnönü.

Anıt Kabir

Anıt Kabir (Mon 1.30–5pm, Tues–Sat 9am–5pm; winter closes 4pm; free), Atatürk's mausoleum, is a national shrine to the memory of the man who shaped modern Turkey. The main entrance to the mausoleum is reached by travelling up Anıt Caddesi from Tandoğan Meydanı (at the northwestern end of Gazi Mustafa Kemal Bulvarı), and it's this approach that reveals the place at its most impressive (though you can also enter the grounds of the mausoleum from a rear entrance on Akdeniz Caddesi). Bus #265 runs from Ulus Meydanı, dropping you at Tandoğan Meydanı, or alternatively catch an Ankaray (LRT) train to Tandoğan.

A flight of steps at the main entrance leads up to a colonnade, guarded by Hittite-style stone lions, which in turn leads to the central courtyard of the mausoleum. The entrance to the colonnade is flanked by two towers: the **Independence Tower** on the left and the **Freedom Tower** on the right. Inside the towers you'll find a scale model of the Anıt Kabir complex, a selection of before-and-after aerial shots of its construction from 1944 to 1953, and some intriguing runner-up designs that never quite made it off the page.

At the head of the central courtyard lies the **mausoleum** itself, a squared-off Neoclassical temple with huge bronze doors. Visitors wearing hats must remove them as they enter and soldiers stand guard to ensure that everyone evinces the appropriate degree of respect. The mausoleum interior is almost completely bare – the only decoration is some discreet mosaic work – so that all attention is focused on the plain sarcophagus. Atatürk's body was brought here in 1953 from its original resting place in what is now the Ethnographic Museum.

On the opposite side of the courtyard is the **tomb of İsmet İnönü** (1884–1973), Atatürk's old comrade and long-time supporter, who served as first prime minister of the Turkish Republic and became president after Atatürk's death. Three large halls are positioned around the courtyard. The largest of these, on the southern side, houses the **Atatürk Museum** in which you'll find everything from Atatürk's evening dress to the rowing machine he used for exercise. Among the most eye-catching exhibits are a gun disguised as a walking stick, of which Ian Fleming would have been proud, and the gifts of a diamond-encrusted sword from the shah of Iran and an elegant toilet set from the king of Afghanistan. An adjacent hall contains Atatürk's cars, namely a couple of Lincoln limousines used for official business and an imposing black Cadillac (reputedly still in working order) for personal use. In the nearby information centre there's not much in the way of information, but fans of esoteric **souvenirs** will appreciate the selection of Atatürk key rings, ashtrays and wall-clocks that propel the Atatürk personality cult into the same league as those of Lenin and Chairman Mao.

Eating

Although there's no shortage of standard kebab and *pide* places in Ankara, and an abundance of good sweet and cake shops, on first appearance there seems to be very little else. In fact there are decent **restaurants** in Ankara, they just take a little finding, and the good ones are tucked up backstreets in the leafy suburbs, catering to the diplomatic corps and embassy staff. As with hotels, the further south you move the more expensive places tend to become. Ankara also has a better range of non-Turkish restaurants than anywhere else in the country and with a little exploration you'll find excellent and authentic Chinese, Japanese, Mexican and Italian food.

Ulus is your best bet for cheap eats, **Kızılay** has most of the mid-range places (particularly on and around Karanfil and Selanik *sokaks*), and the classier restaurants can be found in **Kavaklıdere** and **Çankaya**. The exceptions to this general rule are the restaurants that have opened up in restored Ottoman houses in the **Hisar** (citadel) over the last few years.

Workers' cafés and *lokantas*, particularly in the commercial district of Ulus, tend to open early at 6am, closing at around 4pm (and all day Sunday). Other cafés generally **open every day** between 9am and 9pm; restaurants open for lunch and dinner, with last orders at 10/11pm, though the more popular restaurants and bars in Kavaklıdere stay open until the early hours.

Hisar, Ulus and Kızılay restaurants are marked on our Central Ankara map (pp.682–683), those in Kavaklıdere and Çankaya on the Ankara map (pp.676–677).

Hisar

Boyacızade Konağı aka *Kale Restaurant*, Berrak Sok 9. Spread across several floors of a rambling mansion-house, decorated with carpets and bric-a-brac, and specializing in traditional cuisine. There's a good wine list and prices are surprisingly reasonable, from around 25YTL a head. The separate fish restaurant on the second floor lacks atmosphere, though the dishes are tasty.

Çengelhan Museum Sutepe Mahallesi, Depo

Sok 1. Classy restaurant set in the courtyard of a restored sixteenth-century *kervansaray*. Ideal for a coffee stop or a full-blown meal. There's an interesting museum arranged around the courtyard, charting the history of trade in Ankara.

Kale Washington Kale Sok 1. Atmospheric restaurant with a view-laden terrace perched on top of the old city walls. A good place for a cool beer, or for a dinner of the usual Turkish staples or something a little different, such as beef stroganoff or chicken Kiev.

Zenger Paşa Konağı Doyran Sok 13. Restored mansion offering traditional Anatolian fare and packed with Ottoman-era ephemera. *Kuzu kapama* (a spicy lamb dish) and *gözleme* (filled pancake) are recommended, as is the enormously long *pide*, all at reasonable prices with fabulous views over the city. Expect to pay 16YTL a head.

Ulus

Akman Boza ve Pasta Salonu Atatürk Bul 3. In a shopping plaza just south of the Atatürk statue and underneath *Kebabıstan*. Serves light meals, pastries and *boza* (a refreshing millet-based drink) – the open-air seating makes this a popular breakfast spot.

Bulvar Işkembecisi ve Lokantası Çankırı Cad 11. Excellent *İskender kebap*, *fırın sutlaç* (baked rice pudding) and other trusty favourites in a round-the-clock dining operation. It's next to the *Hotel Selvi*.

Büyük Pastane Atatürk Bul. In the shopping centre opposite the Museum of the War of Independence. Milk puddings, *baklava* and chocolate pastries served in a shady courtyard adorned with potplants and a fountain.

Gaziantep Fethi Bey Sanayi Cad 31. Simple, cheap workers' canteen, with soups soaked up with plenty of bread, meat and vegetable stews and *baklava* to follow. The cooking's not great but you can't beat the prices.

Hosta Piznik Posta Cad 10. Ulus branch of the fast-food chain, with *doner* and *ayran* for 2YTL and a busy *sandviç* trade at lunchtimes. There's another branch in Kızılay, at the corner of Sakarya and Selanik soks.

Kebabıstan Atatürk Bul 3. Very popular family-run joint, in a shopping plaza above the *Akman Boza*, for hearty lunchtime portions of *kebap* and *pide*. It attracts nearby bank workers so come early for a better choice of dishes, each costing little more than 3YTL. Closed Sun.

Tapi Tavuk Posta Cad 7. Good-value canteen-style cafeteria where what you see is what you get. A wide selection of vegetable side-dishes combine well for a filling meal. Closed Sun.

Kızılay

Altın Şiş Karanfil Sok 17. Reasonably priced kebab place with good puddings; a favourite with local office workers.

Göksu Bayındır Sok 22 ☎ 0312/431 2219. Upmarket Turkish dishes in authentic surroundings. There's a huge menu of excellent kebabs, grills and fish (including salmon, trout and sea bass), with main courses from 10YTL.

Köşk Tuna Cad, İnkılap Sok 2. The best *İskender kebap* and *inegöl köfte* in Ankara, and despite its well-earned reputation prices are still low – 6YTL for a plate of succulent *köfte*. Eat on the lovely terrace from crisp white tablecloths, or inside the spotless two-storey restaurant decorated with chandeliers, gleaming brass and even ornate cages of songbirds.

Paris Aile Salonu Selanik Cad 32. A surreal Wild West–style gaming den packed to the gills with old men arguing about politics, or playing cards, dominoes, pool, chess or backgammon. There are snacks available, open-air seating and primitive Internet access upstairs. Women are seated separately on the mezzanine level at the back, from where they keep a close eye on their husbands below.

Pizzeria Tempo Corner of Meşrütiyet Cad and Karanfil Sok. Very popular pizza-and-pasta place, with a reasonably authentic Italian atmosphere and moderate prices. Pizzas are generally a safer bet than the pasta dishes, which can miss the mark slightly, but service is quick and lone travellers – particularly women – will feel comfortable here.

Kavaklıdere

Budakatti Brasserie Budak Sok 6. Pleasant bar-café with garden tables, serving an excellent Sunday brunch of omelettes, toast, ham and cheese (alas no bacon) between 10am and 2pm. There's another branch on the sixth floor of the Beymen clothes shop on Tunalı Hilmi Cad, where Ankara's wealthy shoppers meet to drink tea.

Gado Filistin Cad 4. Vaguely bizarre Dalí-inspired restaurant, done out in an Indonesian style but with dishes from all over the world on its excellent and varied menu. Meals are prepared in the open kitchen at the back, and you should make an effort to visit the outrageous toilets.

Hacı Arif Bey Güneş Sok 48. One of the oldest and most established eateries in town, for succulent kebabs in *bona fide* restaurant surroundings (rather than the usual canteen ambience). Expect to pay in the region of 25–30YTL per head and to battle it out with occasional mass invasions by Turkish families here for weddings or birthdays.

Hayyami Bestekar Sok 82. Cosy, laid-back wine-bar-cum-restaurant. Tasty local dishes and an enormous wine list to choose from, all served to a background of cool jazzy sounds. You'll pay around 25YTL per head.

Imattı Arjantin Cad 34. Good-value Italian place with home-made pasta, pastries, pizza and authentic Italian coffee. This is where to come for a late-night *latte* and to watch Ankara's bright young things attempt to negotiate their BMWs into the tight parking spaces outside.

Kebab 49 Bestekar Sok 13/A. Kebabs and table-cloths under the same roof in a fashionable part of town. It's a popular spot for family dinners.

Sushico Arjantin Cad 10. Fast and fabulous sushi spot with outdoor dining and a wide-ranging menu, featuring Japanese, Chinese and Thai dishes. Meals cost around 35YTL per head, although there are occasionally some cheaper lunch deals.

Tapa Tapa Tapas Tunalı Hilmi Cad 87. Large, popular tapas restaurant, complete with well-stocked horseshoe bar. Live music on Tuesdays, and frequent salsa nights held on the dance floor at the back.

Trilye Reşit Galip Cad, Hafta Sok 11 ☎0312/447 1200. Superb fish restaurant set in a lovely garden lit by twinkly lights and candles. Treat yourself to lobster thermidor – though the chef's special of oven-baked seafood comes in much cheaper at 12YTL.

Yosun Iran Cad 27 ☎0312/467 5464. Customers return again and again for an authentic Turkish night out – start with *meze*s, then move on to fish (red mullet, sea bass or bream), while Tolon, the aged owner, provides the entertainment by singing and playing the piano and accordion. Expect to pay around 25YTL with a half-bottle of wine or *rakı* thrown in.

Çankaya

Kubbe Atakule Tower ☎0312/440 7412. Highly romantic revolving restaurant right at the top of the tower complete with star-studded ceiling, live music and fantastic views.

Quick China Uğur Mumcu Sok 64 ☎0312/437 0303. Excellent, swanky restaurant, serving up a varied menu of Cantonese and Thai dishes, as well as a good choice of sushi, for around 25–30YTL per head.

Drinking and nightlife

For drinking you'll have to head south from Ulus; it's a commercial district and apart from the odd hotel-bar and kebab restaurant, shuts up at night after the shops and banks close. The *meyhane*s (taverns) on and around Bayındır, Karanfil and Selanik *sokak*s in **Kızılay** make a good starting point, and although these are largely male-dominated haunts, female visitors shouldn't attract too much unwelcome attention. For something more trendy head for the bars of **Kavaklıdere**, particularly on Tunalı Hilmi Caddesi or the swisher Arjantin Caddesi, near the *Sheraton*, which is the city's main see-and-be-seen strip.

Bars and cafés

Most **cafés** open during the day to offer food, tea, and obligatory backgammon boards, some serving alcohol as the evening progresses. Not many of Ankara's **bars** feature live music, but those that do attract a cover charge when a band is on and generally go on a bit later than most, until 1 or 2am. The Kızılay cafés and bars are marked on the Central Ankara map (pp.682–683), the Kavaklıdere and Çankaya ones on the Ankara map (pp.676–677).

Kızılay

Black Eight Selanik Cad 76. Just at the entrance of the Metropol cinema. Fat sofas, stripped-wood floors and doors combined with hi-tech furniture, beer on tap and live music at weekends.

Büyük Ekspress Bayındır Sok 11. Expat and student haunt that looks a bit rough and ready but is a good place for a beer. Greasy burgers and kebabs complement the serious drinking.

Fuaye Café Selanik Cad 69. Atmospheric live-music bar belting out a mix of Western pop and traditional songs. It's one of several places near the Metropol cinema that makes a good venue for an after-film drink.

Kavaklıdere

Cafemiz Arjantin Cad 19. Frilly, flowery café that's a place to be seen in, with a good range of sandwiches, light meals and cocktails which you can also enjoy in the conservatory out back.

Cafés des Cafés Tunalı Hilmi Cad 81. Although the bar serves food this joint primarily provides an ideal resting place for a caffeine and nicotine fix. Despite looking like a pub, there's no alcohol.

Gitanes Tunalı Hilmi Cad, Bilir Sok 4/3. An intimate candlelit bar with regular live-music performances – often attracting the better-known Turkish jazz bands. As good a starting point as any for your in-depth exploration of the Tunalı Hilmi scene.

Ivy Arjantin. Large, very chic brasserie with a tempting though expensive food and drink menu; order a frozen margarita, accompanied perhaps by something from the vast home-made cheesecake menu. It's a perfect spot for a sundowner, and there's a good selection of English-language magazines.

Kuğulu Park Café Kuğulu Parkı. Pleasant open-air retreat from the traffic, serving pastries, snacks and nonalcoholic drinks by the fountain until around 10pm.

Mado Ice Cream Bar Tunalı Hilmi Cad, Kuğulu Parkı. Swanky modern place full of young people on first dates sampling every flavour of ice cream under the sun.

November Bar Çevre Sok. Pleasant, laid-back bar, faintly reminiscent of your grandmother's sitting room. Good place for a late-night drink, although it won't come cheap.

Salata Bistro Reşit Galip Cad 57, Gaziosmanpaşa. Café-bar popular with the student crowd, serving snacks. There's outside seating in the garden during summer, and in winter they warm things up inside with a log fire.

Yerfistiği Bestekar Sok 88. Strange concept-bar serving monkey nuts (hence the name), the shells of which smother the floor. Good selection of beers and drinks, and the music pulls a large crowd at weekends. Not a place for those with nut allergies.

Çankaya

Amarillo Kizkulesi Sok 20. Funky country'n'western-style bar, with fake cacti and saloon doors to boot. Live music throughout the week, including popular Monday swing nights. It also does a good line in huge burgers, t-bone steaks, ostrich, and pork sausages.

The Pub Ahmet Efendi Sok 4. Beery, verging on studenty pub, with draught beer, good bar snacks and crêpes, a large screen for sporting events, an open-air terrace with nice views of the city, and the occasional darts night.

Ufo Atakule Tower (see p.692). Fantastic bar just below the restaurant at the top of the Atakule Tower, with fabulous views over Ankara. Good for pricey cocktails, or tasty cakes and coffee, and open daily until 3am.

Clubs

Nightlife in Ankara is limited and the only places that stay open late are a series of seedy *gazino*-type joints along Gazi Mustafa Kemal Bulvarı in Maltepe, and a few tacky clubs in Kavaklıdere and Kızılay. Foreigners are more likely to feel at home in the couple of upmarket venues where the music is influenced by the current MTV playlist, but they don't come cheap. There are some studenty late-night venues hidden away in the backstreets of the university district, Cebeci, but you really need to find a local to guide you to them. Listed below are the best of an untempting bunch.

Arpej Selanik Cad 28, Kızılay. Dingy basement dance-hall frequented by Turkish university students on binge nights, when drinking here takes on an illicit feel. Daily 1pm–3am.

Copper Club *Sheraton Hotel*, Noktali Sok, Kavaklıdere. Newly renovated super-club frequented by expats and diplomats. One of the few places in Ankara where you can successfully order a gin & tonic, but except to pay through the nose for it. Live music nightly from 10pm to 2am, closed Sun.

My Way Corner of Selanik Sok and Ziya Gökalp Cad, Kızılay. Average fish restaurant on a balcony with *fasıl* music and plenty of *rakı*, with a downstairs disco playing Turkish pop daily until 4am, attracting die-hard clubbers still hanging around Kızılay after other places have closed.

Opera Konur Sok 6, Kızılay. Café-bar during the day, Turkish dance music on a tiny overcrowded dance floor at night. Open until 2am, closed Sun.

The arts and entertainment

With Ankara's designation as capital of the new republic, the city then had the responsibility of becoming the cultural capital of Turkey, supported by the opera-loving Atatürk. While İstanbul is Turkey's more culturally diverse city, Ankara holds its own as home of the prestigious **State Opera and Ballet** and **Presidential Symphony Orchestra**, as well as hosting a large number of state theatres that feature the work of Turkish playwrights. Concerts, and in particular the opera, are well worth attending here if you can. The atmosphere is refreshingly informal and as concerts are subsidized by the government, tickets are cheap. Otherwise, there are plenty of **cinemas** (*sinemasi*) found all over Ankara.

Classical music and opera

A visit to Ankara's Opera House is a unique experience if you are in town at the right time of year. Otherwise, there are classical music performances by the State Orchestra at the State Concert Hall and at various venues across the city. The main season starts in earnest in October and runs through to March, and monthly programmes are listed in the Sunday edition of the *Turkish Daily News*. The city hosts the **International Ankara Music Festival** during May (information on Ⓦwww .ankarafestival.com).

State Opera (Devlet Opera). Atatürk Bul, just south of the entrance to Gençlik Parkı ☎0312/324 2210. Performances of classics such as *Tosca*, *La Bohème* and *Madame Butterfly*, as well as occasional piano recitals and classical concerts. Tickets (10–20YTL) are available from the box office in season (9.30am–5.30pm, 8pm on performance days), up to a month in advance and from the Dost bookshop in Kızılay (see "Listings", below).

State Orchestra (Devlet Orkestrasi). Talat Paşa Cad 38, just south of the Opera House and Gençlik Parkı ☎0312/309 1343. The Presidential Symphony Orchestra performs here twice weekly at 8pm on Fri, and 11am on Sat during season, showcasing classical music by Turkish and foreign composers. Tickets (5–8YTL) are available from the State Opera box office (see above).

Film

Recent international releases are usually in the original language with Turkish subtitles, and tickets cost around 5YTL, with discounts before 6pm and for students. The tourist office can supply details of Ankara's **film festivals** – the International Film Festival in March, and the International Cartoon Film Festival in May.

Kavaklıdere Tunalı Hilmi Cad 105, Kavaklıdere ☎0312/468 7193. Several screens showing up-to-date Hollywood films, popular with students and situated amongst several cafés.
Kızılırmak Kızılırmak Sok 21, Kocatepe ☎0312/425 5393. Small and intimate three-screen theatre with frequently changing new releases.
Megapol Konur Sok 33, Kızılay ☎0312/419 4493. More arty than the Metropol, which it backs onto, screening anything from Japanese to Eastern European films. Look out for the occasional English-speaking classic.
Metropol Selanik Cad 76, Kızılay ☎0312/425 7479. Hugely popular multi-screen cinema showing new releases and special screenings of classic movies and foreign films. There's a coffee shop inside, a beer garden outside and any number of cafés and bars along this street.
Sheraton Cinema Noktalı Sok, Kavaklıdere ☎0312/468 5454. Two small, cosy cinemas, open to nonresidents, with some of the comfiest seats you could find. 16YTL per screening.

Listings

Airlines Most airline offices are in Kavaklıdere or Çankaya. THY (ⓦ www.turkishairlines.com) has offices at the airport ☎0312/398 0100; at Atatürk Bul 154, Kızılay ☎0312/428 0200; and Atatürk Bul 231, Kavaklıdere ☎0312/468 7300. Others include: Aeroflot ☎0312/440 9874; Air France ☎0312/467 4400; Atlasjet, airport only ☎0312/398 0201; Austrian Airlines ☎0312/433 2533; Delta ☎0312/468 7805; Lufthansa ☎0312/398 0374; Singapore Airlines ☎0312/468 4670; and Swiss ☎0312/468 1144.

Airport Esenboğa airport, general enquiries and flight information ☎0312/398 0100. Havaş buses for the airport (every 30min; daily 4am–11pm; 5YTL) leave from the Havaş bus stop next to the train station.

Banks and exchange Banks and ATMs are all over the city, especially south of Ulus along Atatürk Bul. Outside banking hours you can exchange cash (not travellers' cheques) at PTT branches (see "Post office", below). For travellers' cheques, try the number of *döviz* offices along the Kızılay section of Atatürk Bul, or the cashiers at the big hotels, though they are often reluctant to cash cheques for nonresidents. The airport also has several places to change money.

Books Tuhran, corner of Konur Sok and Yüksel Cad, Kızılay, has a good selection of books in English, French and German, plus contemporary books on Turkey, and guide- and phrase-books. Dost, Karanfil Sok 11, Kızılay, has English novels and a good selection of pricier coffee-table books.

Bus Aşti (☎0312/224 1000), the main bus station, houses over 150 bus companies. If you don't already have your ticket, you'll need to locate the correct company and booth for your destination. Ask at the helpful information desk by the main doors, or consult the departure board above, which provides a list of destinations and ticket-desk numbers.

Car rental Atak, Cinnah Cad 42, Çankaya ☎0312/441 9000; Avis, airport ☎0312/398 0315, and Tunus Cad 68, Kavaklıdere ☎0312/467 2313; Best, Büklüm Sok 89/9, Kavaklıdere ☎0312/467 0008; Budget, Tunus Cad 39, Kavaklıdere ☎0312/417 5952; Europcar, airport ☎0312/395 0506, and Koza Sok 154, Gaziosmanpaşa ☎0312/398 0503; Hertz, airport ☎0312/398 0535, and Atatürk Bul 138, Kavaklıdere ☎0312/468 1029; National Car Rental, Tunus Cad 73, Kavaklıdere ☎0312/427 6453.

Embassies Australia, Nenehatun Cad 83, Gaziosmanpaşa ☎0312/459 9500; Canada, Cinnah Cad 58 ☎0312/409 2712; Iran, Tehran Cad 10, Kavaklıdere ☎0312/468 2820; New Zealand, Iran Cad 13, Kavaklıdere ☎0312/467 9054; Russian Federation, Karyağdı Sok 5, Çankaya ☎0312/439 2122; USA, Atatürk Bul 110, Kavaklıdere ☎0312/455 5555; UK, Şehit Ersan Cad 46/A, Çankaya ☎0312/455 3344.

Emergencies Ambulance ☎112; Fire ☎110; Police ☎155.

Hamams Karacabey Hamamı, Talat Paşa Cad 101, Ulus, is the oldest in town, built in 1445 (daily 10am–10pm; bath 12YTL, massage 5YTL). Otherwise, there's the Küçükesat Hamamı, Esat Cad 81/A, Kavaklıdere (daily: women 8am–2pm; men 6pm–10pm; 7YTL). More tourist friendly are the baths at the *Büyük Sürmeli Hotel*, Cihan Sok 6, Sıhhıye ☎0312/231 7660 (daily 10am–10pm), where a bath with massage will set you back around 13YTL.

Hospitals Hacettepe Hastanesi, just west of Hasırcılar Cad in Sıhhıye (☎0312/466 5858 or 5859), should have an English-speaking doctor available at all times. You may be treated more quickly at one of Ankara's private hospitals: Çankaya, Bülten Sok 44, Çankaya (☎0312/426 1450), is the most central.

Internet Most of the numerous Internet cafés are concentrated in Kızılay, though you will find a couple in Ulus on Çankiri Caddesi too.

Laundry All but the cheapest of hotels offer a reasonably priced laundry service, but if you get stuck try the Yimpaş department store on Sanayı Cad in Ulus – on the second floor is a laundry and dry cleaners.

Left luggage At the train station (daily 7.30am–10pm; 2.50–5YTL depending on the declared value of your bag).

Pharmacies In each neighbourhood pharmacies take turn in providing a 24hr service called *Nöbetçi*, the information posted on the window of the other pharmacy shops. Most central is Ülkü, Meşrütiyet Cad 23, Kızılay.

Police The tourist police (☎0312/384 0606) are located in Ankara's main police station (Emniyet Sarayı) in the district of Akköprü, a short walk south of the Akköprü metro station, two stops northeast of Ulus. If you need to file a complaint, the tourist office will provide an interpreter.

Post office Ankara's main PTT is on Atatürk Bul in Ulus (open 24hr) for international calls and to buy stamps, phonecards, *jetons* etc. You can also place transfer-charge calls here. There's also a PTT at the train station (7am–11pm), and one on Gazi Mustafa

Kemal Bul (8.30am–7pm) near the tourist office. **Shopping** Antikite, Cinnah Cad 32, Çankaya, has general antiques and bric-a-brac, marginally cheaper than you might expect to find at home. The old shops in Çıkrıkçılar Yokuşu are worth a browse for copper, carpets, antiques, costumes and embroidery, as is the Pirinç Han at the citadel.

There are shopping centres at Atakule, Cinnah Cad/Çankaya Cad, Çankaya; Beğenik, Kocatepe (beneath Kocatepe Camii); and Karum, Aran Cad, Kavaklıdere. Western and Turkish cassettes and CDs are available from the Supersonic Music Centre, Tunalı Hilim Cad, Kavaklıdere, and from Dost, Karanfil Sok 11, Kızılay, and adjacent shops.

West of Ankara

Attractions west of Ankara are few and far between and, with one exception, probably best treated as stop-off points on the way to or from the Aegean coast. The exception is the Phrygian capital of **Gordion**, which lies 90km or so west of the capital, making it a feasible day-trip destination. Even further off the beaten track, towards Eskişehir in the west of the region, are the small town of **Seyitgazi**, with its atmospheric dervish monastery, and the important Phrygian centre of **Midas Şehri** – but you're only really going to be able to visit either if you're driving yourself across country. **Eskişehir** itself is on main train and bus routes but is primarily an industrial centre with little to offer other than meerschaum souvenirs. It's a better bet to press on in the direction of **Kütahya**, a relaxed city famed for its ceramic tiles and a good base for excursions to the eerie temple ruins at the Roman site of **Aezani**.

Gordion

After the collapse of the Hittite Empire the Phrygians briefly dominated Anatolia, and their capital, **Gordion**, is one of western Anatolia's most important archeological sites. It's a name of much resonance, associated not only with the eponymous knot, but also with King Midas and his golden touch. The first things you'll see as you approach are the immense royal tumuli scattered across the drab, steppe-like landscape. Inside these, archeologists found a wealth of stunning artefacts indicating the sophisticated nature of Phrygian culture. Nearby, the foundations of the Gordion acropolis have been uncovered.

There are **buses** every half-hour from Ankara's *otogar* to the town of **Polatlı**, 18km southwest of Gordion. From Polatlı *otogar*, take a *servis* minibus into town and seek out one of the dolmuşes (every couple of hours depending on demand) to the village of **Yassıhüyük**, just short of the site itself. A taxi to and from the site from Polatlı will cost around 30YTL.

Some history

The original settlement at Gordion dates back to the Bronze Age and the site was certainly occupied during the Hittite period. The Phrygians probably took up residence during the middle of the ninth century BC and a hundred years later the settlement became capital of the empire founded by the Phrygian king **Gordios**. The history of Gordion under the Phrygians mirrors the history of the Phrygian

The name Midas is inextricably associated with Gordion. A number of Phrygian kings bore this name, and over the centuries a kind of composite mythical figure has emerged around whom a number of legends have grown up. The best known of these is that of **Midas and the golden touch**. According to the story Midas captured the water demon, Silenus, after making him drunk by pouring wine into his spring. In ransom for Silenus, Midas demanded of Dionysos the ability to turn all he touched into gold. Dionysos granted this wish but Midas was dismayed to find he had been taken quite literally, and his food and even his own daughter were transformed. He begged Dionysos for release from the curse and was ordered to wash his hands in the River Pactolus. The cure worked and thereafter the river ran with gold.

Another tale tells of how Midas was called upon to judge a musical contest between Apollo and the satyr Marsyas. Midas decided in favour of Marsyas and in revenge Apollo caused him to grow the ears of an ass (Marsyas came off even worse – the god skinned him alive). To hide his new appendages, Midas wore a special hat, revealing them only to his barber who was sworn to secrecy on pain of death. Desperate to tell someone the king's secret, the barber passed it on to the reeds of the river who ever after whispered, "Midas has ass's ears."

Another story may have some basis in reality. It tells how, during the reign of Gordios, an oracle foretold that a poor man who would enter Gordion by ox-cart would, one day, rule over the Phrygians. As the king and nobles were discussing this prediction, a farmer named Midas arrived at the city in his cart. Gordios, who had no heirs, saw this as the fulfilment of the prophecy and named Midas his successor. Subsequently, Midas had his cart placed in the temple of Cybele on the Gordion acropolis, where it was to stand for half a millennium. Somehow the belief arose that whoever untied the knot that fixed the cart to its yoke would become master of Asia. During his stay in the city Alexander the Great took it upon himself to undo the **Gordian Knot**, severing it with his sword.

Empire itself – a brief flowering followed by destruction and protracted decline. There's little left in the records, save for the myths and legends associated with the empire (see box, above), though some concrete information survives about the final king of the Phrygian Empire. He is referred to in Assyrian records as Mitas (Midas) of Mushki, who paid tribute to the Assyrians after being defeated in battle by them. He is thought to have reigned from 725 BC to 696 BC, and the Greek historian Herodotus describes how he dedicated his throne at the Delphic shrine of Apollo and married the daughter of one of the Ionian kings.

Phrygian prosperity stemmed from the abundant natural resources of the region and the fact that their empire straddled major east–west trade routes. Ironically it was another set of invaders, the **Cimmerians**, who laid waste to the Phrygian Empire, destroying Gordion, and though the Phrygians made a comeback and rebuilt their capital, their power had been irreversibly reduced. In 650 BC the city was occupied by the **Lydians** and then it fell in turn to the **Persians** just over a century later. In 333 BC, **Alexander the Great** wintered here during his great march east, managing to sever the Gordian Knot during his stay. The arrival of the **Galatians** (Gauls) in Asia Minor in 278 BC was the final chapter in the long decline of Gordion, precipitating the flight of the city's population.

The acropolis

From the dolmuş drop-off point in Yassıhüyük village it makes sense to head first for the eighth-century BC **acropolis**. This raised area was the heart of the city, location of the royal palace, temples and administrative buildings, the foundations of which have been revealed by excavations. Substantial remains of the huge Phrygian-era **town gate** survive on the southeastern side of the acropolis. This must have been a formidable structure in its day: even in its present truncated state it's over ten metres high, making it one of the largest surviving pre-Classical buildings in Anatolia. The outer portal was flanked by twin towers, from which defenders would have been able to inflict heavy casualties on attackers in front of the gate. The foundations of what are thought to have been storage rooms stand on either side of the inner portals – the remains of *pithoi*, or stone storage jars, were found in the right-hand one when it was excavated.

The **palace** at the heart of the acropolis consisted of four *megara*, or large halls with vestibules. The second of these is the most impressive, with the remains of red, white and blue mosaics forming geometrical patterns still visible on the floor. When it was excavated, charred fragments of wooden furniture inlaid with ivory were found in the rubble, suggesting that this could have been the central hall of the palace. The fourth *megaron* was probably a temple to Cybele, the Phrygian incarnation of the mother goddess. If this is the case, then it's here that Alexander the Great **cut the Gordian Knot** (see box above). Behind the palace are the foundations of eight more large *megara*, thought to have been the quarters of palace servants.

Just southeast of the acropolis is the **Köçük Höyük**, a clay mound that's actually higher than the citadel itself. Originally a fortified suburb of Gordion, it was destroyed when the Persian army of Cyrus marched through the region en route to Sardis, and was later turned into a tomb for the defeated ruler of Gordion.

The royal tombs and museum

The main concentration of the huge and inscrutable tumulus tombs of the Phrygian kings is at the eastern end of Yassıhüyük, but only the **Midas Tümülüsü** (Royal Tomb) near the museum (Tues–Sun 8am–noon & 1.30–5pm; combined ticket with museum 5YTL) is likely to attract your attention. At 300m in diameter and over 50m high (reduced by erosion from its original height of around 80m), the Royal Tomb dominates the vicinity, and with these dimensions it's easy to see why it was originally thought to house the remains of either Gordios or Midas. However, material found in the burial chamber dates the tomb to somewhere between 750 and 725 BC, too late for Gordios or his successor and too early for the last King Midas. It is thought instead to be that of a Phrygian king, his identity unknown, curiously buried without weapons or ornaments – though the burial chamber itself, made of gabled pine logs, is reputed to be the oldest wooden structure in Anatolia. The tumulus was excavated during the early 1950s, when American archeologists bored a sixty-metre excavation tunnel through to its centre and discovered the intact wooden chamber. Inside they found the skeleton of a man in his 60s on a wooden couch surrounded by grave objects. Among these were three exquisitely crafted wooden tables, inlaid wooden screens, large numbers of bronze clasps for garments and 178 bronze vessels of various sizes, including three large cauldrons.

Across the road, the worthwhile **museum** (hours and price as above) contains some of the items recovered from the tombs and some attractive mosaics, though inevitably the best of the finds are in Ankara's Museum of Anatolian Civilizations.

Seyitgazi

SEYITGAZI sits in a fertile valley set incongruously amid the rolling Anatolian steppe 200km southwest of Ankara. It's little more than a sprawling village, and your arrival may take the tractor-driving farmers by surprise.

Seyitgazi takes its name from Şehit Battal Gazi, the commander of one of the Arab armies that forayed into Anatolia during the eighth century, around whom an unlikely legend has grown up. The story has it that he was killed during the siege of Afyon and buried with a Byzantine princess who had pined away through love for him. The site of their resting place was revealed to the mother of the Selçuk sultan Alâeddin Keykubad, who promptly built a *türbe* (tomb) for the *gazi*. It became a popular place of pilgrimage and during the thirteenth century Hacı Bektaş Veli, founder of the Bektaşi dervish order, established a *tekke*, or monastery, here. During the sixteenth century, the complex was thoroughly restored on the orders of Selim I, a ruler who numbered among his other contributions to religious life in Anatolia the massacre of 40,000 Shi'ites.

The **türbe-tekke complex**, on the slopes of the valley above the town, seems nothing more than an agglomeration of sandy walls topped by grey-white domes when seen from the distance. The ground plan is roughly horseshoe-shaped, open towards the valley slope with a Byzantine church and a Selçuk mosque by the entrance. The former is a reminder that a Christian convent originally stood on the site, while the latter contains the outsize sarcophagus of Şehit Battal, which measures just under seven metres in length. Next to it is the more modest sarcophagus of his princess. To the rear of the complex is an Ottoman mosque dating from Selim's restoration, with adjacent dormitories and ancillary buildings for the monastery.

Midas Şehri

The major Phrygian site of **Midas Şehri** lies about 30km due south of Seyitgazi. To reach it, head in the direction of Afyon and take the first left turn towards the village of Yazılıkaya. The unmetalled road is pretty abysmal but the landscape, with its eerie rock formations, makes up for the discomfort. This whole area is dotted with Phrygian tombs, temples and fortifications, but those at Midas Şehri are by far the most accessible and substantial.

The **site** itself (always open; free) comprises the sketchy ruins of a Phrygian city set on top of a thirty-metre-high plateau whose steep rock sides have been carved with elaborate decorative facades. Despite the fact that Midas Şehri means "City of Midas" in Turkish, there's no specific Midas connection, though for a while it was supposed that one of the Phrygian kings of that name was buried here.

The carved facade on the northwestern face of the plateau has come to be known as the **Midas tomb**. From a distance this huge expanse of tufa, measuring about 15m by 17m, resembles the interior wall of a house that has had a large fireplace cut into it a few metres above ground level. Closer up you can see the rectilinear bands in raised relief that crisscross the facade, topped by a decorative pediment. An early Western visitor to the site in 1800, William Martin Leake, concluded that the "fireplace" niche had to let onto a concealed entrance to a tomb. Attempting to decipher the Phrygian inscription on the monument, he mistranslated one word to read Midas and assumed it was a royal tomb. It's now known that the word Leake took to mean Midas actually reads "Mida", another name for Cybele, and it's probable that the niche housed a cult statue of the goddess. Following the plateau sides round to the west from here leads to more niches carved in the rock, a number of rock tombs and an incomplete relief.

Access to the upper part of the plateau and the remains of the Phrygian **citadel** is via a flight of steps on the eastern side. Near the top of the steps are a number of altars and tombs, some of which bear inscriptions and decorative reliefs. In the southwestern part of the citadel is a **rock throne**, a kind of stepped altar on which the figure of a deity would have been placed. The upper part of this throne has a clear **inscription** and crude decorative scratchings. Elsewhere a few fragments of the citadel's defensive wall survive.

Eskişehir

ESKIŞEHIR – 233km west of Ankara – is a modern industrial city, primarily given over to the construction of railway locomotives and fighter aircraft, but also a hub for the textile industry, cement manufacture and even chocolate production – approaching from the east you might get a welcome whiff from the vast chocolate factory. Out of town to the west, on the E90, is a park with some fifteen to twenty retired light aircraft and fighter jets.

Most visitors, however, come because of the **meerschaum** (literally "sea foam" in German), a porous white stone, large deposits of which are mined in the surrounding villages. While wet, the soft stone is carved into all manner of ornaments, but it's the smoke-cooling properties of a meerschaum pipe that make it the most highly prized item. The mineral is worked in a number of shops around town and with a little haggling it should be possible to pick up some bargains. The largest concentration of **pipe shops** is located under the *Büyük Otel* on İnönü Caddesi.

Despite appearances, Eskişehir has a long history, the modern town having been grafted onto an ancient settlement. Its origins go back at least to Greek times, when it was known as Dorylaeum. Some relics of this old city can be seen in the local **archeological museum** (Arkeoloji Müzesi) on Yunus Emre Caddesi which is rumoured to be reopening in 2006. For a taste of the more recent past head for the old quarter in the northwestern corner of town, centred on an unremarkable Selçuk **castle**. On the opposite, eastern, edge of the city stands the sixteenth-century **Kurşunlu Camii**, attributed to Sinan.

△ Meerschaum pipes

Practicalities

Eskişehir's sights do not amount to a great deal, and it's not a place you'd want to hang around in for more than a few hours. Fortunately, there are good road and rail connections, with trains running to Ankara, İzmir and İstanbul, and frequent buses and dolmuşes on the same routes.

The **train station** is on the northwestern edge of the city centre, while the **otogar**, southeast of town, is linked to the centre by a brand-new tram line (tickets bought from the booth next to the stop). There's a **tourist office** in the *Valilik* building at İki Eylül Cad 175 (Mon–Fri 8am–noon & 1–5pm; ☏ 0222/230 1752), although this will only be of use if the English-speaking member of staff is in. **Hotels** tend to be expensive, catering mostly to business travellers; the best option by far is the *Sale Oteli*, by the tram stop at İnönü Cad 9 (☏ 0222/220 7320, ⓦ www.salehotel.com; ④), or you could try the *Soyiç Oteli*, Yunus Emre Cad 101 (☏ 0222/230 7190, ⓕ 230 5120; ④).

If you have some time to spare, you might want to sample **nuga helvasi**, the nougat-like local delicacy available at every self-respecting *pastane* in town, or stroll past the swish clothes-shops on İnönü Cad to **Haller**, an old market transformed into a collection of cafés and boutique shops where locals gather in the evenings to listen to live music. Failing that, the excellent **thermal baths** at the corner of Hamamyolu Caddesi and Sairtekin Sok are highly recommended.

Kütahya and around

Dominated by an Ottoman fortress, **KÜTAHYA** is famous above all for its fine tiles, which are used throughout Turkey, especially in restoration work on Ottoman mosques, replacing the İznik originals (just as Kütahya has replaced İznik as the country's leading tile-producing centre). Many modern local buildings, including the *otogar*, are entirely covered in tiles; and there are ceramic shops on virtually every street, selling tiles, dinner services and vases – not to mention toilets, of which Kütahya is the nation's largest producer.

Kütahya's earliest recorded inhabitants were the Phrygians and thereafter the city endured the usual Anatolian round of conquest and occupation, coming to the fore briefly when Alexander the Great established his headquarters here en route to Gordion. The town was occupied by the Selçuks after the battle of Manzikert in 1071, but then lost to the army of the First Crusade. The Selçuks returned in 1182 and a century or so later the city became capital of the Germiyanid, a Kurdo–Turkish tribe who had been brought into the area from the east. They were ousted by the Ottomans, only to make a brief comeback after Beyazit Yıldırım's defeat at the hands of the Mongol ruler Tamerlane. The Germiyanid emirate survived until 1428, when Kütahya fell permanently into Ottoman hands.

It was under the Ottomans that Kütahya enjoyed its golden age as a **tile-making centre**. Sultan Selim I forcibly resettled tile-workers from Tabriz here after defeating the Persians at Çaldıran in 1514. He dispatched some of their colleagues to İznik, instigating a two-hundred-year rivalry between the two cities that only ended when the İznik industry was transferred to İstanbul. Contemporary Kütahya tiles look a little garish and crude in comparison with Ottoman-era examples – the secret of the pigment blends that gave the original Kütahya tiles their subtle and delicate lustre has been lost with the centuries.

During the War of Independence, the Greek army occupied the city during its advance on Ankara. The invaders were defeated twice in battles at the defile of İnönü, northeast of Kütahya, in January and April 1921. They managed to break out in the summer of the same year, capturing Eskişehir and Afyon and launching an offensive that took them to within striking distance of Ankara. The following year the Turkish offensive that was to throw the Greeks out of Anatolia once and for all began at Dumlupınar, midway between Kütahya and Afyon.

The Town

A number of well-preserved Ottoman-era houses in the immediate vicinity of the main square, **Belediye Meydanı**, set the tone for Kütahya. The rest of the city's attractions, however, lie at the end of Cumhuriyet Bulvarı, which runs west from Belediye Meydanı. After about 500m, at the point where the road splits off in several directions, you'll find the **Ulu Cami**, an attractive but unexceptional fifteenth-century mosque that stands in the midst of Kütahya's lively **bazaar** area, which extends over several streets in the vicinity.

Just next to the Ulu Cami is the town **museum** (Tues–Sun 8.30am–noon & 1–5.30pm; 2YTL), with a collection of archeological finds from the area, including a beautiful sarcophogus found at Aezani (see opposite) depicting a heroic battle between the Greeks and Amazons. The contents of the museum are considerably less interesting than the building that houses them, the **Vacidiye Medresesi**, a fourteenth-century *medrese* built by the Germiyanid Emir Bey Bin Savcı as an astronomical observatory and school of science and mathematics. The high point of the interior is the central marble pool beneath a dome with glass skylights.

Beyond the Ulu Cami and museum, signs point out the way to the **Kossuth Evi** (Tues–Sun 8.30am–noon & 1.30–5.30pm; 2YTL), a few minutes' walk to the west. This was home to Lajos Kossuth (1802–1894), the Hungarian patriot who fled to Turkey after the failure of the 1848 uprising against Habsburg rule. The immaculate house has been preserved much as it must have been when he lived there in 1850–51, although it's the nineteenth-century Ottoman ambience of the rooms, rather than the Kossuth connection, which will be of interest to most visitors.

Kütahya's **kale** towers above the Kossuth house and signposts point you in the right direction should you wish to wander up to the summit, from where there are predictably impressive views of the city below. The fortress was originally built by the Byzantines and extended by their successors, but these days only the western walls survive in anything like their original state.

Practicalities

If you're arriving by bus you'll be dropped off at Kütahya's **otogar** (known as Çinigar, or "Tile Station") on Atatürk Bulvarı, just to the northeast of the centre. Turn right out of the *otogar* and it's a short walk up the main road, Atatürk Bulvarı, to reach Belediye Meydanı, the town's main square, distinguished by a fountain with a huge ceramic vase as its centrepiece. There's a **tourist information** booth (May–Nov Tues–Sun 8am–5.30pm; ☎0274/223 6213) right on the main square. Emails can be sent from any one of a string of **Internet** joints along Atatürk Bulvarı en route to the *otogar*.

Accommodation

Pick of the budget hotel options is the *Hotel Yüksel*, Belediye Meyd 1 (☎0274/212 0111, ⓔotelyuksel@hotmail.com; ❷), which is plain but clean and about as central as you could hope for. The *Otel Kösk 1*, Lise Cad 1, just north of the square towards the bazaar district (☎0274/216 2024, ⓔotelkosk1@hotmail.com; ❷), has spacious doubles, though is not as clean as the *Yüksel* (if arriving from the bus station, ignore signs off the main street to *Kösk 2* – a less than salubrious hotel).

For considerably more you can enjoy the tiled comfort of the *Hotel Gül Palas*, on Belediye Meydanı (☎0274/216 1233, ℱ216 2135; ●), or the *Hotel Erbaylar*, Afyon Cad 14 (☎0274/223 6960, ℰerbaylar@superonline.com; ●); the latter, although faded, has a pleasant terrace-bar and restaurant, just off the main square.

Eating and drinking

For eating and drinking try *Cınar Köfte*, Lise Cad 7, where you'll get a couple of courses for next to nothing. At the top of Atatürk Bulvarı *Kervan* serves a good range of cheap food, whilst *Candaro Gullari*, on the other side of the square at Cumhuriyet Cad 14, is a good spot for *pide*. Afterwards, you could sample the chocolate cake at the *Inci Pastanesi* just off the square at Atatürk Bul 11, and then cross the road for a beer at one of the trendy bars. There are several sprawling **teahouses** on the main square, where Kütahya's youth go to keep a watchful eye on each other.

Yoncalı

There are several thermal resorts near Kütahya, the closest and largest being **YONCALİ**, 18km west on the Balikesir road. Yoncalı is a simple village dominated by the plush four-star *Yancalı Tütav Termal Otel* (☎0274/249 4212, ⓦwww .tutavtermal.com; ●), which taps into the hot springs and channels them into a variety of outdoor and indoor pools and steaming hot baths. The water is rich in magnesium and calcium and is exaggeratedly claimed to be beneficial for a whole series of complaints, from insomnia to backache. Come by dolmuş from Kütahya (hourly; 20min) and it's possible to use the facilities as a day-visitor for around €10. There are also a couple of cheaper **pansiyons** in the village.

Aezani

Easily reachable, 60km or so southwest of Kütahya, is the site of Roman **Aezani** (always open; free), famed for its atmospheric Temple of Zeus, one of Anatolia's best-preserved Roman buildings. To get there, take a Gediz-, Samav- or Emet-bound **bus** from Kütahya *otogar* or, more conveniently, from the ticket office on Afyon Caddesi, and ask to be let out at **Çavdarhisar** (journey time approximately 1hr) – the site lies just 1km north of this tranquil village. The most convenient buses leave Kütahya at 9.30am and return at 1pm.

The site

The **Temple of Zeus**, built by Hadrian in 125 AD, occupies a commanding position on top of a large, rectangular terrace. To reach it walk up the side road that leads from the main road in Çavdarhisar in the direction of Emet, and cross the Koca Çay over the Roman bridge, with its marble frieze commemorating the successful sea passage of its sponsor, Marcus Eurykles. On the north and west sides of the main temple building, double rows of columns topped by a pediment survive, but elsewhere the columns have largely collapsed and their broken fragments are scattered on the ground nearby; three on the eastern side were repositioned after falling in the Gediz earthquake of 1970.

At the heart of the temple is the **inner sanctum**, once dominated by a magnificent statue of Zeus. Its walls, made of rectangular stone blocks, are largely intact, but the roof has long since caved in. Beneath there's a subterranean **sanctuary** dedicated to Cybele, which the affable site attendant will open up on request. Back outside just northeast of the building, a fallen but well-preserved bust of Cybele – not, as locals will tell you, Medusa – surveys the landscape.

From the temple, you can walk north past the baths to the remains of the uniquely combined **stadium–theatre**. Paths lead up from the fine inscriptions of the southern gate between ruined stadium seats to the backdrop wall of the theatre and the fallen remains of its marble facade. East of the temple stand the arches of the ruined **agora**, and from here the old ceremonial road leads south over a second Roman bridge to the enigmatic **macellum** (marketplace), whose walls carry a fourth-century decree from Emperor Diocletian fixing market prices in an attempt to stop rampant inflation. Complete your circular tour by heading back to the first Roman bridge and ask the site guardian to open up the nearby second set of **baths**, with their satyr mosaic and statue of Hygeia, goddess of the baths.

North of Ankara

The mountain ranges that lie between Ankara and the Black Sea are rugged and pine-clad, forming a landscape that at times becomes almost alpine in flavour. They are undeniably appealing yet, scenery aside, there is little to attract the traveller. Only **Safranbolu**, with its Ottoman mansions of timber construction, set in a steep-sided gorge, rates a visit on its own merits. Other places in this direction – notably **Kastamonu** – are no more than potential stopovers en route to different destinations.

Safranbolu

SAFRANBOLU is a stunning town of half-timbered houses some 220km north of Ankara, approached via the transport hub of Karabük, which is overshadowed by a vast steelworks and perpetually shrouded in a film of industrial grime. From here the road continues on to **Kıranköy**, the modern section of Safranbolu. The road descends into a steep-sided valley, snakes up the other side and finally drops again into the ravine, where you'll find **Eski Safranbolu** (also known as Çarşı), a town far removed in time from its modern counterpart.

Some buses from Ankara make Karabük their final stop, in which case you'll have to take a dolmuş from here into Safranbolu itself. Fortunately, though, most companies now go all the way to **Kıranköy**, and most offer a *servis* bus into the village. Failing that, you'll need to catch the half-hourly dolmuş, or hop in a taxi (6YTL) from the *otogar*.

Eski Safranbolu

Ancient houses line the slopes of the ravine on the descent into town, presenting a smudge of dirty pastel-coloured timber and red-tiled roofs. Although tourism is established in Safranbolu – it's a summer coach-trip destination for Turks – the old way of life stays remarkably intact. Apart from a bazaar of souvenir shops, few concessions have been made to the twenty-first century: come here out of season

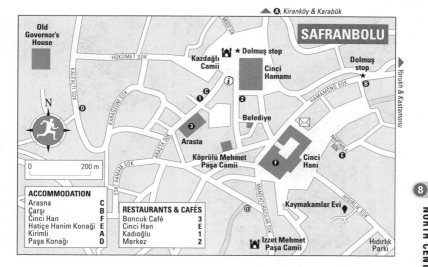

Old
Governor's
House

HÜKÜMET SOK

KALEALTI SOK

KARAÜZÜM SOK

Kazdağlı
Camii

★ Dolmuş stop

Cinci
Hamamı

Dolmuş
stop
★

HAMAMÖNÜ SOK

NAİPLERA SOK

Ⓘ

Ⓒ

Ⓓ

N

Belediye

0   200 m

Ⓖ

Ⓔ

Ⓐ

Ⓑ

❷

Ⓕ

Ⓐ

Arasta

Köprülü Mehmet
Paşa Camii

Cinci
Hani

❸

ESKİ HAMAM SOK

ARASTA SOK

MANİFATURACILAR SOK

Kaymakamlar Evi

HIDIRLIK SOK

@

ACCOMMODATION	
Arasna	C
Çarşı	B
Cinci Han	F
Hatiçe Hanim Konaği	E
Kirimli	A
Paşa Konaği	D

RESTAURANTS & CAFÉS	
Boncuk Café	3
Cinci Han	E
Kadıoğlu	1
Merkez	2

Ⓜ İzzet Mehmet
Paşa Camii

Hıdırlık
Parki

and you might well be the only visitor. Various restoration projects are underway, but most of the town remains slightly run-down and it is all the better for it.

Adjoining the town square, the seventeenth-century Ottoman baths of the **Cinci Hamamı** (separate men's and women's sections; daily 6am–11pm; 8YTL) have been fully restored so that you can relax in comfort surrounded by their marble splendour. Past the hamam, old streets lead towards the restored **Cinci Han**, a huge seventeenth-century *kervansaray*, now hotel and restaurant (see below), dominating the town centre.

Roughly northwest of the Cinci Han is the unexceptional seventeenth-century **Köprülü Mehmet Paşa Camii**, whose courtyard leads to its restored **arasta** (bazaar). This is where the day-trippers are brought to browse at the well-stocked souvenir and antique shops. The bazaar is completely covered by a magnificent vine with bunches of grapes hanging so close above your head you will be tempted to pick them – there are notices telling you not to. South of the *arasta* lies the old bazaar district, where traditional stalls of blacksmiths, cobblers, leatherworkers, tanners and saddlemakers still work away, much as they would have when they serviced the needs of Black-Sea traders, and beyond which lies the **İzzet Mehmet Paşa Camii**, an elaborate, late eighteenth-century mosque. Past here, the town slides into dilapidation, with a ravine now used as a household dump and, further downstream, women washing clothes in the stream. If you walk down here, though, there's a stunning view back towards the mosque, whose domes and minarets seem to hover above the surrounding houses.

Back in town, immediately beneath the southeastern walls of the Cinci Han, there's an open-air market, from where a narrow street to the immediate left of the Ziraat Bankası leads up the side of the valley to the **Kaymakamlar Evi**, the "Lieutenant Colonel's House". It's an Ottoman mansion, or *konak*, typical of many around the town, built in 1727. A traditional conservatism dominates the *konak* design: the ground floor, devoid of external windows, would have been used as a stable, while on the upper floors the *selamlık* (male guest-rooms), overlooking the street, would have been divided from harem quarters, with a separate entrance and lattice windows looking onto interior courtyards. Each room has a distinctively

△ Half-timbered house, Safranbolu

carved wooden ceiling and furniture would have been sparse, with personal items stored in decorative wall-niches, and bedding in cupboards doubling as bathrooms.

If you make your way from here to the hilltop **Hıdırlık Parkı**, vantage points let you look down over the whole town, which appears at its best in the late afternoon light. The palatial-looking edifice above the town, on the opposite side of the ravine, is the old Governor's House, currently undergoing restoration to transform it into a museum and cultural centre.

Practicalities

The **dolmuş** drop-off point in Eski Safranbolu is on the sloping square next to the Kazdağlı Camii. The helpful **tourist office** (daily 9am–5pm; ☎0372/712 3863) is close by, in the main square between the *arasta* and Cinci Hamamı. It hands out brochures and maps, and can provide you with bus times, although tickets must be bought at the *otogar*. Note that if you're travelling on towards Kastamonu, you'll need to buy your tickets at Doğuş Turizm in the centre of Kıranköy instead.

On the main square you'll also find the Grand on Tour **travel agency** (☎0370/725 4001, ⦿www.safranbolutour.com), which can arrange excursions to the nearby village of Yörük, as well as trekking trips and visits to local caves.

Accommodation

Arasna Otel Arasta Sok ☎0370/712 4170, ℱ712 4811. Small, atmospheric hotel right on the main square, boasting a pleasing, if dark, hodgepodge of sloping rooms, though the creaky floorboards struggle to screen out the noise from the bar below. ❸

Çarşı Pansiyon Bozkurt Sok ☎0370/725 1079. Safranbolu's best budget option, with clean, modern doubles, some sharing a bathroom. Great location right near the centre, although the road can get noisy at night, so it's best to get a room at the back. ❷

Cinci Han Hotel ☎0370/712 0680, ⦿www.cincihan.com. Superb hotel housed in a seventeenth-century *kervansaray* in the heart of the town, with lovingly restored rooms arranged around an open courtyard and some fantastic suites on the top floor. ❺

Hatiçe Hanim Konaği Naiptarla Sok 4, ☎0870/712 7545, ⦿www.hotelhaticehanim.com. Large, authentic Ottoman house with rooms named after their traditional functions. Comes complete with creaking floorboards and closet bathrooms. ❺

Kirimli Otel Sağlık Sok ☎0372/725 2485, ⦿www .kirimliotel.com. Cool, clean rooms in a family house at the top of the hill before the road descends towards Eski Safranbolu. A good alternative if you really can't find rooms in the town itself. ❸

Paşa Konağı Kalealtı Sok ☎0370/712 8153, ℱ712 5596. Charming old house on a quiet backstreet, with nice views of the town, and authentic touches such as bathrooms hidden in cupboards. ❸

Eating and drinking

There are a few cheap *lokanta* places on the main drag in the new town, though the nicest places to **eat and drink** are all found in the old town. The pleasant *Boncuk Café* in the *arasta* does tea, coffee, soft drinks and snacks, including burgers, while the *Merkez Lokantası*, next door to the Cinci Hamamı, offers basic dishes. The *Kadıoğlu Şehzade Sofrası* by the *Arasna Otel* is classy, yet inexpensive, and has a garden area, while the restaurant at *Cinci Han Hotel* is one of the most atmospheric (and most expensive) choices in town.

The **bar** in the *Arasna Otel* is among the best places to grab a beer. Safranbolu is famous for its *lokum* and *helva* **sweets**, which you can sample in Eski Safranbolu's *arasta* or at *pastane*s dotted around the town.

Kastamonu

It was in **KASTAMONU** – 245km northeast of Ankara – that Atatürk made his first speech attacking the fez in 1925, during his campaign against traditional religious headgear. Little has happened here since, and it's quite a conservative town, though a couple of venerable mosques, some fine Ottoman houses and a crumbling castle make the place worth a half-day visit on the way to the Black Sea coast.

The Town

On the town's main square you'll find the **Nasrullah Kadi Camii**, Kastamonu's largest and most distinguished mosque, built in 1509 and sporting six domes. The attractive undercover fountain at the front draws the townfolk for a gossip. At the western end of the square, the **Asirefendi Han** is still used for commercial purposes, while a street runs south up to the **Yavapağa Camii**, a modern building screened by the ruins of a larger, much older, mosque complex. The same street curves off up to the west, in the direction of the *kale*, and along the way you'll pass the **Atabey Camii**, a rectangular stone building with a very low interior, built in 1273 but much repaired and restored since.

Just above is the **kale**, unsignposted but hard to miss. It was built under Tamerlane, a ruler more famous for destruction than construction, and time hasn't been kind to it. Only the massive walls and main gateway are wholly intact, but its grassy grounds are a favourite trysting spot. The other town landmark is the **İsmailbey Camii**, a fine twin-domed medieval mosque set atop a plug of rock, adjacent to a small park. It's near the *otogar*, on the western side of the river. The town **museum** (Kastamonu Müzesi; Tues–Sun 8.30am–4.30pm; 2YTL), meanwhile, site of Atatürk's anti-fez speech, is about ten minutes' walk south of the *Ruganci Otel*, with the usual collection of local miscellanea.

Practicalities

The **otogar** is a fifteen-minute walk north of the town centre (if your bus is coming from the south, ask to be let out in the centre), on the eastern bank of the stream that cuts the town in two from north to south. From the *otogar*, turn left onto Kastamonu's main street, Cumhuriyet Caddesi, and follow it south to the main square. There are a couple of bus ticket offices around the main square – a more convenient pick-up point. Check where the bus leaves from as some services heading west pick up on the main road out of town and not at the *otogar*, although companies usually provide a *servis*. Next to the Nasrullah Kadi Camii, at Havaalanı Yanı 15, is the **tourist office** (erratic opening hours; ☏0366/244 3598).

There are quite a few **hotels** around town, but standards are not particularly high. Still, you might have to spend the night if you're travelling by public transport as Safranbolu – the nearest nice town – is another three hours away. At the budget end of the market, the *Otel Ilgaz*, Belediye Cad 4 (☏0366/214 1170; ❶), off Cumhuriyet Caddesi just south of the square, has basic but crummy, waterless rooms. The nearby *Otel Selvi*, Banka Sok 10 (☏0366/214 1763, ⓦwww.selviotel.com; ❷), is a far more comfortable option, though plumping for en-suite facilities and breakfast pushes it up a price category. Nearby, the two-star *Otel Mütevelli*, Cumhuriyet Cad 10 (☏0366/212 2018, ⓦwww.mutevelli.com.tr; ❹) offers clean rooms with excellent showers, although the building suffers from damp. For something a bit more authentic, *Osmanlı Sarayı*, Belediye Cad 81 (☏0366/214 8408, Ⓔ ottoman37@excite.com; ❺), has some grand old rooms in an Ottoman mansion on the main road up towards the *kale*.

There aren't too many places to **eat and drink** in town after dark, and your best bet is the *Uludağ Pide ve Kebap Salonu* at the corner of Belediye and Cumhuriyet *caddesi*s, a white-tablecloth establishment that does excellent *pide*. For dangerously addictive chocolate mousse, simply move next door to the *Segün*. If you're desperate for a **beer**, head for the couple of seedy male-dominated *bira salonu* on the other side of the stream from the *Otel Mütevelli*.

East of Ankara

East of Ankara, prospects improve considerably, with numerous places worth going out of your way for. Just three hours from Ankara lies the ancient Hittite capital of **Hattuşa**, near the modern village of **Boğazkale**. The sheer size of the place is perhaps more astonishing than the ruins themselves, but there's no mistaking the importance of Hattuşa or the surrounding sites of **Yazılıkaya** and **Alacahöyük**.

Northeast of the Hittite capital is the ancient and atmospheric city of **Amasya**, with its spectacular Pontic rock tombs and riverside quarter of Ottoman houses. This easily warrants a day or two of exploration. Southeast of Amasya, **Tokat** has a couple of interesting buildings, including the striking Gök Medrese, and **Sivas**, further southeast, has a profusion of fine Selçuk architecture, though neither of these places invites a long stay.

Sungurlu, Boğazkale and the Hittite sites

The **Hittite sites** centred on the village of **Boğazkale** are the most impressive and significant in the whole of Anatolia. This area was once the heart of the Hittite Empire and Hattuşa, spread over several square kilometres to the south of the modern village, was its capital. A few kilometres to the east is the temple site of Yazılıkaya, while Alacahöyük, a smaller Hittite settlement dating back to 4000 BC, 25km north of Boğazkale, is further off the beaten track, but worth the trip if you have your own transport. Excavation here began in earnest in 1905 and many of the objects unearthed are now housed at the Museum of Anatolian Civilizations in the capital. If you've already seen the museum, a visit to the original excavations is doubly interesting; if not, a quick visit to the new archeological museum in nearby Çorum is definitely worthwhile.

Visiting the sites

Access to Boğazkale and the sites is via the small town of **Sungurlu**, lying just off the main Ankara–Samsun road. Hattuşa and Yazılıkaya can be covered on foot **from Boğazkale** if you're reasonably fit, though it gets very hot here in summer and there are some steep hills to be climbed. You might therefore want to **tour the sites by taxi**: various characters in Boğazkale will offer all-in deals (€20, but haggle), and in the unlikely event that they don't seek you out you'll probably be able to find them at the *Aşıkoğlu Motel* (see "Boğazkale", below). A good compromise is to take a taxi to Yazılıkaya and then on to the Aslanlıkapı (Lion Gate) at Hattuşa, from where you can walk around the site and back to Boğazkale, taking in the ruins at your leisure.

If you don't want to spend the night in either Boğazkale or Sungurlu, then it's also possible to get a **taxi from Sungurlu** around all three sites in a few hours, arriving back in time for an onward bus. This will set you back about €30, though all prices are negotiable.

Sungurlu

You have to pass through **SUNGURLU** when you're heading for the Hittite sites, but there's no other reason to stop here. Sungurlu-bound buses depart roughly every hour from Ankara's *otogar* on a three-hour journey across the rolling, treeless landscape of central Anatolia.

Sungurlu does have a tiny *otogar* but through buses will probably drop you off on the main road at one of two service stations, one kilometre west and east of town respectively, where most of the buses coming from Ankara stop for a break at the adjoining restaurants. Direct services will take you into the town centre, a five-minute walk north of the highway. The departure point for **Boğazkale-bound dolmuşes** is the main square in Sungurlu, though you should be able to pick one up from one of the service stations – particularly from *Mavi Ocak* to the east, which is only one kilometre from the Boğazkale turn-off (there is also a good restaurant here). The **journey to Boğazkale** (29km) takes about thirty minutes, with the last departure at 5pm (last return from Boğazkale to Sungurlu is roughly 5.30pm). Taxi drivers usually hang around the square in Sungurlu, and at the bus drop-off point, looking for tourists (and will probably tell you there is no dolmuş running). They'll ask for €20 to take you to Boğazkale, although you should be able to beat them down to about half that.

If you miss the last Boğazkale-bound dolmuş you might need to stay overnight in Sungurlu. The cheapest of the three friendly **hotels** here is the very basic, waterless *Ferhat*, Kahraman Sok 2 (☏0364/311 8067; ●), 100m east of the clocktower. More expensive (but still good value) is the immaculate *Hotel Fatih*, Cengiztopel Cad V.D. Karşişi 23 (☏0364/311 3488; ●), which is run from a shop next door to the hotel. Otherwise, try the *Hittit Motel* (☏0364/311 8409, ℱ311 3873; ●) on the main road through town, 1km west of the *otogar*, which claims to have put Prince Charles up while he was on a private visit here many years ago.

Boğazkale

BOĞAZKALE, 5km east and then 24km south of Sungurlu, is at the end of a surfaced road cutting across rough pastureland. It's a modern village, with the ancient Hittite capital of Hattuşa fanning out from its southern rim. Finding your way around is fairly straightforward, as it basically consists of one street, running up a hill to the main square. The only attraction in the village itself is a small **museum** (daily 8am–5pm but ask around if it looks closed; 2YTL) on the left-hand side of the street on the way up to the village square. It has a small collection of objects (mainly cuneiform tablets and pottery) from the Hattuşa site, some useful books for sale and a large-scale map that sets the scene for what's to come.

Practicalities

Dolmuşes from Sungurlu drop you in the village square, from where the ticket office and entrance to Hattuşa is just ten minutes' walk to the southeast. There are four **hotels**, often block-booked by tour groups, so it's worth making an advance reservation. Two lie out of the village, on the road leading from Boğazkale to Yazılıkaya, there's one at the entrance to the village, and another right on the village square. The hotels are also the only options in the village for **eating and drinking**. If you're here in winter, note that heating and hot water is far from reliable in the village, so come prepared.

Aşıkoğlu Motel At the entrance to the village ☎0364/452 2004, ⊛www.hattusas.com. Slightly overpriced modern rooms but with immaculate bathrooms and superb buffet breakfast. A cheaper extension has smaller rooms with older bathrooms (priced a category lower), and there's a rarely used campsite at the back (it's better to go to the *Başkent*). The busy restaurant (sometimes swamped with tour groups) has tables in an Ottoman salon, and the food is excellent. Closed Nov–Feb. ❹

Başkent Tourist Motel ve Camping Yazılıkaya Yolu Üzeri ☎0364/452 2037, ⊛www.baskenthattusa.com. The better of the two options perched on a hill on the outskirts, with large sunny rooms overlooking tractor-laden fields, new plumbing in the bathrooms, and a serene campsite for €4 per person per night. The restaurant, although lacking in atmosphere, has a view of the ruins of the Great Temple, and is good value. ❸

🏃 **Hattuşaş Pension & Hotel Baykal** Next to the PTT on the village square ☎0364/452 2013, ⊛www.hattusha.com. Ahmed and Mustafa Baykal,

friendly English-speaking brothers, offer two types of accommodation. Pension rooms are clean and spacious, mostly with showers (discounts for those without), and with kilim-strewn common rooms on each floor. There are also comfortable double/triple rooms in the hotel at the back, with cool granite floors and smart bathrooms. The downstairs restaurant serves up tasty and economical dishes of the day. Breakfast €2 extra. Pension ❶, hotel ❸

Kale Otel Yazılıkaya Yolu Üzeri ☎0364/452 3126, ⊛www.bogazkoyhattusa.com. Family-run hotel in a pretty location, with simple whitewashed rooms and adequate bathrooms, but lacking atmosphere. There's no real restaurant – though you may get a meal if the hotel is already catering for a tour group – otherwise walk down the hill to the *Başkent*. Closed Nov–March. ❸

Hattuşa

Enclosed by six-kilometre-long walls, **Hattuşa** was, by the standards of the time, an immense city, and its scale is still awe-inspiring today. The site was originally occupied by the Hatti, who established a settlement here around 2500 BC. The Hittites moved in after their conquest of central Anatolia, making it their capital from about 1375 BC onwards, during the period when their empire reached its greatest extent. By 1200 BC the influence of the Sea Peoples had put an end to Hittite dominance of the region. Hattuşa was destroyed and later the Phrygians built a large city on the site.

The Hittite city was unearthed by archeologists during the first half of the nineteenth century. It

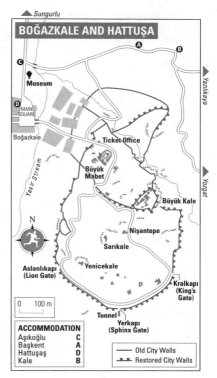

BOĞAZKALE AND HATTUŞA

▲ Sungurlu

Museum
MAIN SQUARE
Boğazkale
Ticket Office
Büyük Mabet
Büyük Kale
Nişantepe
Sarıkale
Aslanlıkapı (Lion Gate)
Yenicekale
Kralkapı (King's Gate)
Tunnel
Yerkapı (Sphinx Gate)

▶ Yazılıkaya
▶ Yozgat

Yazir Stream

N

0   100 m

ACCOMMODATION
Aşıkoğlu   C
Başkent   A
Hattuşaş   D
Kale   B

——— Old City Walls
┈┅┈ Restored City Walls

The Hittites

The **Hittites** appear to have been an Indo-European people who moved into Anatolia around 2000 BC. Where exactly they came from remains unclear, though the Caucasus and the Balkans have been suggested. They entered the territories of the Hatti, an indigenous people, and though no records survive of how the Hittite rise to dominance came about, archeologists have found layers of burned material in most Hatti settlements that can be dated to around 2000 BC, indicating that there was at least some degree of violence involved. However, the fact that the Hittites also absorbed important elements of Hatti culture suggests that a more complex interaction may have taken place.

Initially the Hittites set up a number of **city-states**. These were drawn together during the mid-eighteenth century BC under King Anitta. According to cuneiform tablets found at Hattuşa, he transferred his capital from the city of Kushara (possibly modern Alişar) to Nesha (Kültepe), and destroyed Hattuşa, cursing any Hittite king who might attempt to rebuild the place. A century or so later his successor Labarna returned to Hattuşa and did just that. The Hittites came to regard Labarna and his wife Tawannanna as founders of the Hittite kingdom and their names were adopted as titles by subsequent monarchs. Labarna's son, Labarna II, took the name Hattuşaş and launched a number of military campaigns against his neighbours, extending Hittite territory into modern-day Syria and western Anatolia.

Hittite expansion was not a uniform process and over the centuries the boundaries of their territories ebbed and flowed across Anatolia. In 1595 BC, Mursili I succeeded in capturing distant Babylon, but his successor Hantili (who gained power by assassinating Mursili) lost many previous gains. This early period, known to historians as the **Old Hittite Kingdom**, ended with a descent into succession-related strife. Stability was restored under Tudhaliyas II around 1430 BC, and he re-established the Hittite state as an empire. An important period of expansion followed under King Suppiluliuma (1380–1315 BC), who secured the northern borders of the empire and conquered the Hurrian kingdom of Mitanni, which had exerted an important cultural influence on the Hittites. This achievement raised the Hittites to superpower status, equal with Egypt, Assyria and Babylon. The Egyptians even asked Suppiluliuma to send one of his sons to marry the widow of Tutankhamun (the union never took place as the boy was murdered en route). After Suppiluliuma's death, Hittite expansion continued and in 1286 BC, during the reign of Muwatalli II, a Hittite army defeated

occupies a steeply sloping expanse dotted with rocky outcrops, to the southwest of modern Boğazkale. Of the numerous buildings once scattered over a wide area, only the limestone foundation blocks survive. The vulnerable upper parts, originally consisting of timber frames supporting clay brick walls, have long since vanished. The main points of interest, all conveniently linked by a metalled road, are the Büyük Mabet (Great Temple), just outside the modern village, the section of wall with three gateways at the southern extremity of the site and the Büyük Kale (Great Fortress).

Approaching the site from the village square takes you past a freshly reconstructed section of the old city wall (paid for with Japanese money) and leads to a **ticket office** (daily 8am–5pm, 7pm in summer; 3YTL joint ticket for Hattuşa and Yazılıkaya, 3YTL per car).

The Büyük Mabet

Beyond the ticket office is the **Büyük Mabet**, or "Great Temple", also known as Temple I, one of an original seventy on the site. The largest and best-preserved Hittite temple in existence, it was built around the fourteenth or thirteenth century BC and dedicated to the storm god Teshuba and the sun goddess Hebut. It the Egyptians at the battle of Kadesh, an empire-shaking event that was carved into the columns of Luxor.

Following the conflict, peace between the two empires was established, cemented by the marriage of one of the daughters of Ramses II to Hattuşiliş III. However, the Hittite Empire had less than a century left. The arrival of the Sea Peoples in Anatolia ushered in a period of instability that was to erode Hittite power, culminating in the **destruction of Hattuşa** around 1200 BC, roughly the same time as the fall of Troy. The Phrygians replaced the Hittites as the dominant power in central Anatolia, taking over the ruins of Hattuşa and other Hittite cities.

Hittite culture survived in a number of small successor kingdoms established in southeastern Anatolia and northern Syria, most notably around Carcemish (Kargamiş), Malatya and Karatepe. These Neo-Hittites are mentioned in the Bible, in conjunction with Abraham and David, and endured until around 700 BC when they were finished off by Assyrians, after which the Hittites disappeared from history completely until their rediscovery this century.

Hittite civilization was highly advanced with a complex **social system**. The Hittite kings were absolute rulers, but there was an assembly called the *panku*, which at times appears to have wielded considerable influence. The major division in Hittite society was between free citizens and slaves: the former included farmers, artisans and bureaucrats, while the latter, although they could be bought and sold, probably had the right to own property and marry. Society was regulated by a legal code of two hundred laws under which defiance of the state, rape and bestiality were all punishable by death. Murder and assault, on the other hand, were punished by fines that varied according to whether the victim was free or a slave. For property offences there was a compensatory system of fines.

Hittite **religion** seems to have been adopted from the Hatti, with the weather god Teshuba and the sun goddess Hebut as the two most important deities. Up to a thousand lesser gods also played a role in the beliefs of the Hittites, who were in the habit of incorporating the gods of conquered peoples into their own pantheon. Evidence for all this comes from large numbers of cuneiform tablets found by archeologists. These were kept in chambers maintained specifically for that purpose and subsequently unearthed at various sites.

consisted of a central temple building surrounded by 78 storage rooms laid out in an irregular plan.

As you enter the site through the main gate, you'll be assailed by local men masquerading unconvincingly as archeologists. They will offer to guide you through the ruins and try to sell you little Hittite-style figures carved from local stone, some of which are surprisingly attractive. Such locals are pretty persistent and you may well meet them again later because of their tendency to pursue tour groups around the rest of Hattuşa by motorbike. Note that the local hoteliers have been issued with passes identifying them as free guides, and you can happily ask them for help as they are not permitted to request money in exchange.

After running the gauntlet of would-be guides, you pass between two large stone blocks, remnants of the **ceremonial gateway** that let on to the temple precincts. Nearby is a stone lion that originally formed part of a cistern and, a little further on, a large, green cubic stone, which was reputedly a wedding present from Ramses II of Egypt. In Hittite times the king and queen, in their roles as high priest and priestess, would have led processions through here on holy days. Today most visitors end up following the route they took, along a clearly defined processional way of uneven slabs. The thoroughfare is flanked by the foundations of many storerooms and after about 30m swings round to the right, opening up on the temple proper.

The **temple** consisted of about twelve small chambers around a central court-yard, with the rooms that would have contained the cult statues of Teshuba and Hebut at the northeastern end – the god on the left and the goddess on the right. In the latter room is a small stone slab, which may well have supported the statue of Hebut. In some of the storerooms adjacent to the temple you can see *pithoi*, or earthenware storage vessels, that have been exposed. Some are complete, pieced together by archeologists, with distinctive zigzag markings running round them. In other cases only the jagged shards remain, sticking out of the ground. Just below the Büyük Mabet, archeologists have identified an early Assyrian **merchant quarter**, which held the Hittite equivalent of the Rosetta Stone, a parallel Hittite hieroglyphic and Akkadian inscription instrumental in the final cracking of the hieroglyphic code.

The Yenicekale and the Aslanlıkapı

About 350m beyond the Great Temple, on the site of the original Hattic city, the road forks. Taking the right-hand branch leads you up a steep hill. After about 800m (this is the worst foot-slogging section), the **Yenicekale**, a ruined fortress, is visible about 50m to the left of the road. Although little remains, its construc-tion was clearly a considerable achievement as Hittite engineers had to create an artificial platform out of the uneven and rocky terrain before they could even start building.

A little higher up is the **Aslanlıkapı** or "Lion Gate", one of the three gateways that studded the southern section of the city wall. The Aslanlıkapı takes its name from the two stone lions that flank the outer entrance, symbolically guarding Hattuşa from attackers and evil spirits. The Aslanlıkapı marks the beginning of the surviving section of dry-stone **city wall**, which runs along the top of a massive sloping embankment ten metres in height and surfaced with irregular limestone slabs. Rectangular towers were placed along it at regular intervals and the founda-tions of some of these are still visible.

The Yerkapı

The road follows the embankment to the **Yerkapı**, or "Earth Gate", more popu-larly known as the Sphinx Gate after the two huge sphinxes that once guarded its inner portal, but which now live in museums in İstanbul and Berlin. The most striking feature of the Sphinx Gate is the seventy-metre **tunnel** that cuts through from the city side of the walls to the exterior. The tunnel was built using the corbel arch technique, a series of flat stones leaning towards each other creating its trian-gular profile. One theory about its purpose is that it served to let the defenders of the city make surprise attacks on besieging enemies. However, its obvious visibility from the outside and the presence of two sets of monumental steps leading up the embankment on either side of the outer portal cast doubt on this, and a more cere-monial function has been suggested.

It's possible to walk through the tunnel to the outer side of the city walls. From here you can scramble up the embankment to examine the scant remains of the Sphinx Gate and also enjoy the view of the rest of Hattuşa. The sphinxes that stood on the inner side of the gate were found in fragments, but archeologists pieced them back together to reveal imposing leonine figures complete with wings. The outer side of the gate was also flanked by sphinxes – one survives, but prolonged erosion by the elements has made it virtually unrecognizable. The scat-tered foundations visible on the far side of the road immediately to the north of the Sphinx Gate are the remains of seven large temples.

The Kralkapı, the Nişantepe and the Sarıkale

Following the road east from the Sphinx Gate leads to the **Kralkapı**, or "King's Gate", named after the regal-looking figure carved in relief on the left-hand pillar of the inner gateway. This actually represents the god Teshuba and shows him sporting a conical hat while raising his left fist in the air as though holding an invisible sword. What you see is a copy – the original is in Ankara's Museum of Anatolian Civilizations.

Further down the hill lies the **Nişantepe**, a rocky outcrop with a ten-line Hittite inscription carved into its eastern face. The thirty-centimetre hieroglyphs are badly weathered but enough has been deciphered to suggest that it's a memorial to Suppiluliuma II, last of the Hittite kings. To the immediate southwest of the Nişantepe is the **Sarıkale**, the foundations of a Phrygian fort built on the site of an earlier Hittite structure.

The Büyük Kale

From the Nişantepe the road leads down to the **Büyük Kale**, or "Great Fortress", which served the Hittite monarchs as a fortified palace during the fourteenth and thirteenth centuries BC. The palace consisted of three courtyards, each higher than the previous one, meaning that any attacker would have had to capture it piecemeal. The lower and middle courtyards are thought to have been given over to servants and aides of the royal family, while the upper courtyard was the palace proper. It's easy to see why they chose to reside at this wild and windswept location on the very eastern edge of Hattuşa. In effect, it was a citadel within the city, protected on all flanks by steep drops. On the outer side to the east these are natural, but the inner side was originally a man-made construction with a series of terraces supported by retaining walls made of vast limestone blocks.

Access today is via a flight of steps leading up to what was the southeastern gate of the palace. On the site of a building near this entrance archeologists found three thousand **cuneiform tablets**, which, when deciphered, yielded important clues about the nature of Hittite society. Among them was the Treaty of Kadesh, signed in around 1270 BC by the Hittite king Hattuşiliş II and Ramses II of Egypt, the earliest surviving written treaty between two nations. The lower parts of walls and some masonry fragments are all that survive of the Büyük Kale, offering few clues as to the original layout. But it's worth coming up here to wander among the weather-battered remnants and take in the stunning view of the Great Temple. The eastern end of the site, where the ground falls away sharply into a ravine below, is particularly atmospheric.

Yazılıkaya

From the Hattuşa ticket office, signs point to the temple site of **Yazılıkaya** with its famous reliefs, about 3km (or under an hour's walk) to the east. The route there, which more or less follows the Hittite processional course from city to temple, dips down into a river valley then up towards the *Başkent Turist Motel*, from where further signs point the way onwards and then left (the road right continues to Yozgat). When you arrive you'll have to fight your way through the inevitable crowd of would-be guides and souvenir-sellers to reach the **ticket kiosk** (normally unmanned as joint tickets are now sold at Hattuşa).

Archeological evidence suggests that a temple of some sort existed on the site as early as 1500 BC, but it wasn't until the thirteenth century BC that the two small ravines cutting into a rocky outcrop at the rear of the site were decorated with reliefs (hence Yazılıkaya, Turkish for "inscribed rock"). At roughly the same time a **gateway** and the **temple buildings** were constructed. Today, a few sketchy foundations are all that remain of these ancient structures and attention is focused on the two "galleries" of reliefs depicting nearly a hundred figures, mostly gods from the vast array of Hittite deities.

The reliefs

The entrance to the **larger ravine** of the two is on the left behind the temple foundations. The left-hand wall is lined with images of gods moving from left to right, and the right-hand one with images of goddesses wearing identical long, pleated dresses and conical headgear. A number of the figures on the male side of the ravine stand out, in particular the group of twelve war gods bringing up the rear of the procession. Further along are two figures with human bodies and bulls' heads. The deities seem to rise in rank as the procession progresses, and towards the front are the conspicuous figures of the moon god Kusuh, with a crescent moon, and the sun god, seemingly balancing a winged sun symbol on his head.

The two lines of deities meet on the far wall of the ravine. The scene carved here depicts Teshuba astride a couple of mountain peaks facing Hebut, who is standing on a panther. Behind her is their son Sharruma, also standing on a panther, with two lesser goddesses nearby. All are identified by hieroglyphs written above an uplifted hand. Just behind the procession of goddesses near the ravine entrance is a well-preserved image of a male figure. This represents Tudhaliyas IV (1250–1220 BC), who is thought to have built the temple. He is holding a standard in his left hand and a winged sun-disc in his right. Hittite accounts of religious rituals seem to suggest that this gallery was used for new-year celebrations, which probably coincided with the beginning of spring.

The **smaller ravine** lies over to the right and can be reached via the short flight of steps that leads up to a cleft in the rock. The entrance to the ravine is guarded by two sphinx reliefs, which can be hard to spot, while a group of twelve figures armed with swords lines the left-hand wall. These are similar to the warrior-god figures seen in the first ravine but are much better preserved. Opposite this group are two separate reliefs. One shows an unusual figure that has come to be known as the "Sword God", a blade with a human torso and head where the handle should

△ Hittite reliefs at Yazılıkaya

be. To add to the already strange effect, lions' heads, instead of arms, sprout from the torso shoulders. This vaguely disturbing image is thought to represent Neargal, the Hittite god of the underworld. Next to it is a relief depicting the god Sharruma embracing Tudhaliyas IV. The god is shown as a giant figure in a conical headdress with a protective arm around the slightly built king. The discovery of the remnants of cremations in niches in the rock, next to the gods armed with swords, suggests that this part of the temple may have been used for the funerals of Hittite kings.

Alacahöyük

After Hattuşa, **Alacahöyük** 25km north of Boğazkale, is the most important Hittite site in existence. Originally a major Hattic settlement, it was taken over by the Hittites during the early stages of the second millennium BC and, as at Hattuşa, the Phrygians seem to have taken over the site for a while after the demise of the Hittites. The ruins that remain are mainly Hittite, but a number of extensive archeological digs have unearthed a vast array of Hattic artefacts, including standards featuring stags, bulls, sun-discs and statues of the earth goddess, from a number of tombs on the site.

From Boğazkale head back in the direction of Sungurlu and turn right at the road signposted for Alacahöyük. After about 11km take a signposted left turn for the remaining 12km to the site. By public transport, you should be able to pick up a **dolmuş** from Boğazkale or Sungurlu to the village of Alaca, about 10km southeast of the site, but from there you'll have to hitch. The only other alternative is to take a **taxi from Boğazkale or Sungurlu**, which will set you back at least 33YTL.

The hamlet of **HÖYÜK** next to the site is small, but it does have a basic shop and a PTT. In theory there's also a *pansiyon* with a restaurant, the *Kaplan Restaurant ve Hotel* (no phone; ❶), but don't bank on it being open.

The site

Next to the **site** (daily 8am–noon & 1.30–5.30pm; 3YTL) is a small **museum** (same hours, but closed Mon), which, for once, is well worth investigating, as it includes some striking Hattic standards and pottery with elegant designs. There's a less-inspiring ethnographic section downstairs devoted mostly to farm implements.

The site is entered via the southern **Sphinx Gate**, named after the large sphinxes that guard it. These eerily impressive figures, stained ochre by lichen, have blunted faces with empty eye sockets, and sweeping headdresses. There's a double-headed eagle at the right-hand base of the gate, a symbol that appears on seals found at the Assyrian trading colony at Kültepe. Either side of the gate are **reliefs** (copies of originals now in Ankara), depicting religious ceremonies. The left-hand section is the more lively of the two, showing a procession moving towards the god Teshuba – shown here as a slightly comical-looking bull with outsized sex organs. Approaching him are a king and queen, followed by sacrificial animals and priests, with a group of what look like acrobats bringing up the rear.

The Sphinx Gate opens onto a pathway with excavated areas on either side, all well signposted in English. Immediately behind the gate are vast irregular blocks, the remnants of the city walls, followed by the foundations of storage buildings. Beyond the storage areas, a few metres below ground level to the left of the path, are thirteen **tombs**. These date from the Hattic period and yielded much of the vast hoard of archeological treasure now in the Bronze Age section of the Museum of Anatolian Civilizations in Ankara. Judging by the opulence of the grave goods found in them, these were the tombs of Hatti monarchs. The two largest tombs are set on raised platforms and the timber cladding that covered them has been re-created.

To the right of the pathway are the foundations of what may have been palace buildings, while the tumble of ruins at the head of the pathway was almost certainly a temple. Beyond the tombs are a series of irregular mounds identified only as "Hittite building levels". The foundations of the west gate of the settlement entrance survive, as do the beginnings of a tunnel system, similar to the one under the Sphinx Gate at Hattuşa.

Çorum

The only real reason to visit **ÇORUM**, about 100km northeast of Boğazkale, is to see its newly renovated **Archeological Museum** (Tues–Sun 8am–5pm; 2YTL), which has gathered together some of the better finds from nearby Hittite sites and smaller museums, as well as later archeological discoveries from across the region. It's just a ten-minute walk from the town's *otogar* – head past the *Anitta Otel* (see below) towards the roundabout and follow the signs.

There are excellent bus connections to almost everywhere in Turkey from Çorum, and it makes a good stop-off point if you're heading east from Sungurlu (reached from the latter by hourly dolmuş). It's not really the kind of place you'd want to **stay**, but if you get stuck *Otel Aygün* on the main İnönü Caddesi (☏0364/213 3364; ❷) has good clean rooms near the *otogar*, as does the rather classy *Anitta Otel* opposite (☏0364/213 8515, ☻www.anittahotel.com; ❻).

Amasya

The journey to **AMASYA** does little to prepare you for the charm of the place. Along the E80 highway (the main approach road if you're coming in from points west), the landscape is thoroughly uninspiring until just a few kilometres before the town itself, when you suddenly find yourself amid the lush farmland and orchards of the Yeşilırmak valley. Once you've made the dolmuş trip into town from the *otogar*, however, Amasya turns out to be one of the high points of North Central Anatolia. It occupies a point in the river valley so narrow that it's almost a gorge, and is blessed with a super-abundant historical legacy. Most people come here to see the rock tombs hewn into the cliffs above the town by the kings of Pontus over 2000 years ago, but Amasya also harbours some truly beautiful Selçuk and Ottoman architecture, and a multitude of colourful, restored nineteenth-century wooden houses.

Some history

According to some accounts, including that of the locally born geographer and historian **Strabo** (64 BC–25 AD), Amasya was founded by the Amazon queen Amasis. In reality it's more likely that the town began life as a Hittite settlement, later falling to Alexander the Great. The decades of upheaval that engulfed Anatolia after the death of Alexander resulted in the creation of a number of small kingdoms. One of these was **Pontus**, established by Mithridates, a refugee-adventurer from Cius (a Greek city-state on the shores of the Sea of Marmara), who fled east after his city fell to Antigonus. Mithridates arrived in Amaseia (as the town was then known) in 302 BC, setting himself up in the local castle and in time establishing a kingdom. Pontus survived for two hundred years and, at its height, occupied a mountainous region roughly bounded by the Kızılırmak and

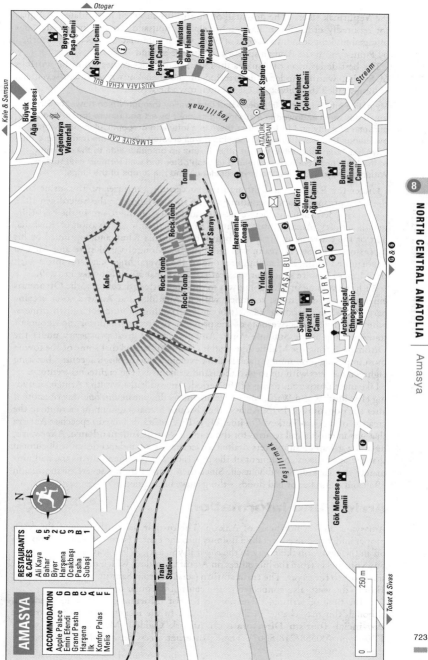

AMASYA

ACCOMMODATION
Apple Palace — G
Emin Efendi — D
Grand Pasha — B
Harşena — C
İlk — E
Konfor Palas — A
Melis — F

RESTAURANTS & CAFES
Ali Kaya — 6
Bahar — 4, 5
Biyer — 2
Harşena — C
Ocakbaşı — 3
Pasha — B
Subaşı — 1

N

▲ Otogar

◀ Kale & Samsun

Beyazit Paşa Camii

Şıranlı Camii

Mehmet Paşa Camii

Sinhı Mustafa Bey Hamamı

Birmahane Medresesi

Gümüşlü Camii

Büyük Ağa Medresesi

Leğenkaya Waterfall

MUSTAFA KEHAL BUL.

Yeşilırmak

Atatürk Statue

ELMASIYE CAD.

Pir Mehmet Çelebi Camii

Stream

ATATÜRK MEYDANI

Taş Han

Kileri Süleyman Ağa Camii

Burmalı Minare Camii

Kale

Rock Tomb

Rock Tomb

Rock Tomb

Rock Tomb

Tomb

Kızlar Sarayı

Hazeranlar Konağı

ZİYA PAŞA BUL.

Yıldız Hamamı

ATATÜRK CAD.

Sultan Beyazit II Camii

Archeological/ Ethnographic Museum

Yeşilırmak

Train Station

Gök Medrese Camii

▼ Tokat & Sivas

250 m

0

the Yeşılırmak rivers. The downfall of Pontus began when Mithridates VI Eupator reputedly ordered the massacre of eighty thousand Romans in one day and plunged his kingdom into a series of wars, which culminated in its being absorbed by Pompey into the Roman sphere of influence around 70 BC.

The best description of Amasya during ancient times comes from the writings of Strabo, who compiled a description of the then-known world in seventeen volumes called the *Oikomene*. Of his own town he wrote:

My native city is located in a deep and large valley through which flows the River Iris. It has been endowed in a surprising manner by art and nature for serving the purpose of a city and fortress. For there is a lofty and perpendicular rock, which overhangs the river, having on one side a wall erected close to the bank where the town has been built, while on the other it runs up on either side to the summits of the hill. These two are connected to each other and well fortified with towers. Within this enclosure are the royal residence and the tombs of the kings.

Under the Romans, and through the succeeding centuries of Byzantine rule, the town prospered, and it continued to do so after falling to the **Selçuks** in 1071 – who later left their distinctive architectural mark on the town. In the mid-thirteenth century, Amasya was caught up in the first Mongol invasion of Anatolia, part of the catastrophic irruption begun by **Genghis Khan** and continued by his successors. The Selçuk realm was reduced to a Mongol vassal-state and Amasya apportioned to the Il-khan Empire, one of the several huge khanates into which the Mongol Empire split after the death of the Great Khan Möngke in 1259.

With the waning of Mongol power in the late thirteenth century, the **Ottomans** emerged as a force to be reckoned with in Anatolia, and Amasya soon became part of their burgeoning state. It became a training ground for crown princes, who would serve as governors of the province to prepare them for the rigours of statesmanship at the Sublime Porte. Amasya enjoyed great prosperity under the Ottomans during the Middle Ages and it's from this period that some of the town's most imposing monuments date. It also developed as a theological centre, boasting eighteen *medreses* with up to two thousand students by the eighteenth century.

Like most prosperous towns of the period, Amasya had a wealthy Armenian trading class until World War I. Most of its members disappeared in one way or another after the **pogroms** of 1915. Amasya then became a vital staging post en route to the creation of modern Turkey. On June 21, 1919, Atatürk delivered a speech at Amasya that was in effect a call to arms for the coming **War of Independence**. Afterwards, he and a group of supporters drafted a Declaration of Independence, a document that presaged the establishment of the provisional government in Ankara, and ultimately the Turkish Republic itself. Since then – apart from a severe earthquake in 1939 and a number of bad floods – things have been quiet.

Arrival and information

Amasya is 306km northeast of Ankara. The **otogar** lies to the east of the town proper and you'll need to take a dolmuş into the centre (some buses will drop you off in the centre on their way to the *otogar* if you ask). When leaving town you can buy your ticket from the bus offices on Atatürk Caddesi, which might well provide transport to the *otogar*. The **train station** (services from Samsun and Sivas) is about 1km to the west, also connected to the centre by regular dolmuşes.

At the time of writing, there was no **tourist information office** in operation, although this may change in the near future. In the meantime you could try the **Provincial Tourism Directorate** on Atatürk Caddesi (Mon–Fri 9am–noon & 1.30–4pm; ☎0358/218 5002). There's **Internet** access on Ziya Paşa Bulvarı, near the road junction.

Accommodation

Recently a clutch of antique-decorated, kilim-strewn *pansiyon*s has opened in the restored Ottoman houses, with more doubtless to follow, making Amasya an essential overnight stop. At the time of writing, rates were more than reasonable but this is bound to change. Otherwise, Amasya's budget options are fairly unprepossessing.

Apple Palace Hotel 3km south of town ☎0358/219 0019. Amasya's newest hotel, perched right at the top of the southern hill – you'll have to take a taxi. It's three-star standard, with modern rooms, aimed at tour groups; there are plans for a pool, nightclub and Internet café. Its undisputed advantage is the spectacular view from the front balconies and the vast restaurant terrace overlooking the Amasya valley. ❹

Emin Efendi Pansiyon Hazeranlar Sok 73 ☎0358/212 0852, ⓕ212 2552. Friendly *pansiyon* with a few simple rooms, some overlooking the river, and with bathrooms in cupboards in the corridor. There's also an attractive vine-shaded courtyard where, if you're lucky, you may be treated to a little evening music. ❸

Grand Pasha Otel Across the Alçak footbridge ☎0385/212 4158, ⓦwww.grandpashaotel.com. Beautiful Ottoman house on the river, arranged around a leafy courtyard. Small, with only eight vast, traditionally decorated rooms with cabinet bathrooms and river views. ❹

Harşena Otel Across the Alçak footbridge ☎0358/218 3979, ⓦwww.harsena.com. Stunning former Ottoman residence with creaky floorboards and rooms furnished with period antiques, lace and linen curtains, and low-slung Ottoman beds. Some overlook the river, where you can breakfast on the balcony, but the best rooms are at the back under the floodlit rock tombs where you can sleep to the sounds of gentle guitar music from the garden below. ❹

İlk Pansiyon Hittit Sok 1 ☎0358/218 1689, ⓔilkpansion@hotmail.com. Faultlessly restored eighteenth-century Armenian mansion, retaining much of the original decor and period antiques. Reservations advisable as there are just six rooms, some of which are priced a category higher. ❸

Konfor Palas Oteli Ziyapşa Bul 2 ☎0358/218 1260, ⓕ218 0558. The only decent budget option in Amasya. Large, impersonal hotel in a nice location near the river, although the bustling square below can get a little noisy. All rooms are en suite, with TV but no breakfast, and it may be worth haggling. ❷

Melis Hotel Yeniyol Cad 135 ☎0358/212 3650, ⓦwww.melishotel.net. A modern building in a backstreet on the south side of town, stuffed full of antiques and interesting bric-a-brac. Rooms are bright and pleasant, if slightly overpriced, with satellite TV and central heating, and there's a rooftop bar and Internet access. ❹

The Town

At the centre of Amasya, the riverfront Atatürk Meydanı commemorates Atatürk's 1919 visit with an equestrian statue of the hero surrounded by admirers. At the eastern end of the square, the creamy yellow **Gümüşlü Cami**, or "Silvery Mosque", was originally built in 1326 but has been reconstructed at various intervals since. Its almost pavilion-like oriental exterior and carved wooden porch overlook the river, and there's an unusual tall brick minaret.

There's another architectural oddity on the south side of the square in the shape of the **Pir Mehmet Çelebi Camii**, which dates from 1507. It's an extremely small *mescit*, or mosque without a minaret, the Islamic equivalent of a Christian chapel. The carved facade of this particular example has been decorated with ochre paint, and it's improbably tiny, almost as though it were a play mosque built for children.

West to the Gök Medrese Camii

West of the square, Atatürk Caddesi runs off through the town. Two hundred metres or so along, on the southern side, is the **Kileri Süleyman Ağa Camii**, an imposing but conventionally designed Ottoman mosque, built in 1489. Behind it lies the eighteenth-century **Taş Han**, a crumbling old brick and stone structure that is now home to a metal workshop. To the rear of the Taş Han is the **Burmalı Minare Camii** (Twisted Minaret Mosque), named after the spiral effect of the stonework of its minaret. The compact building was erected in 1242 but heavily restored in the eighteenth century following a fire.

Back on Atatürk Caddesi, a twin-domed **bedesten** in grey stone stands opposite the Kileri Süleyman Ağa Camii, still home to various shops and businesses. Continuing west brings you to the **Sultan Beyazit II Camii**, set in a spacious rose garden on the northern side of the street. Built in 1486, this is Amasya's largest mosque, laid out on a symmetrical plan with two large central domes flanked by four smaller cupolas and two slightly mismatched minarets. Though some of Amasya's other mosques beat it for sheer whimsicality, none of them can quite match it for structural harmony. The front of the mosque faces the river, flanked by two plane trees thought to be as old as the mosque itself, and it's from this side that the whole is best appreciated. The five-domed porch runs along the facade protecting a minutely carved entrance portal. Either side of this are two marble columns, which though they appear to be fixed are in fact free to rotate in their housings. Any shift in their position (after an earthquake for example) gives warning about the mosque's structural state. Adjoining the mosque are a multi-domed *medrese* and a library housing some fifty thousand volumes, including three thousand ancient manuscript copies of the Koran.

Continue west along Atatürk Caddesi, past the museum (see below), and it's a five-minute walk to the **Gök Medrese Camii**, the thirteenth-century Selçuk "Mosque of the Blue Seminary", with a particularly intricate carved doorway (the actual door is in the museum). This doorway was once covered in blue tiles – hence the name – but time seems to have taken its toll and today there's little trace of them. The **türbe** beside the mosque, with traces of turquoise tiles on its octagonal turret, is that of Emir Torumtay, a Selçuk governor of the town. The tomb is reputed to be haunted by the ghost of the Selçuk sultan, Kiliç Aslan, who appears on horseback holding a sword that drips blood.

Archeological and ethnographic museum

Amasya's **Archeological/Ethnographic Museum** (Arkeoloji/Etnografya Müzesi; Tues–Sun 8.30am–noon & 1.30–5.30pm; 2YTL) is a gem among Turkish municipal museums, well worth an hour or so of your time. Archeological finds dating back as far as the Bronze Age are represented by some practical-looking pottery and a caseful of rather unwieldy tools. Hittite relics include beak-spouted jugs, some with what look like built-in filters, and there's also a bronze statue of the storm god Teshuba – though this tends to get loaned out to other European museums. From here things jump forward to ornate Roman glassware and coins recovered from burial sites complete with clay containers.

Centre of attraction, however, is the door of the Selçuk Gök Medrese Camii, on the second floor, a riot of arabesque geometrical patterns enclosing lattice-reliefs. The rest of the floor is devoted to Ottoman times, with a comprehensive selection of costumes, weapons, astronomical instruments and mother-of-pearl inlaid wooden items, including some fetching hamam clogs. There are some excellent carpets (a vivid nineteenth-century prayer rug from Avanos stands out), and a number of studded wooden cupboard doors from Ottoman-era homes. Along one wall is a line of Anatolian handicraft scenes, where dummies toil over antique looms, ploughs, saddles and blacksmith's anvils. A morbid curiosity is the tomb in the museum grounds labelled "Mummies", containing eight desiccated human husks that were found underneath the Burmalı Minare Camii. These are identified as the remains of two Mongol governors, a "concubine" and the children of a Selçuk family.

North of Atatürk Meydanı

The **Bırmahane Medresesi** was built by the Mongols in 1308 as a lunatic asylum. The popular image of the Mongols as a brutal, destructive people makes the presence of this abiding monument to their occupation of Amasya something of a surprise. But the heirs of Genghis Khan were more settled than their forebears, and the Bırmahane Medresesi is a typical example of the way in which they adapted the architectural styles of their subjects, with heavy Selçuk influences in its design. The Mongols used music therapy to pacify the lunatics in the asylum and throughout the centuries the *medrese* has been used as a music school. Today it's a conservatory with a kilim-covered stage against the far wall and a manager who is a famous *fasıl* musician. Students here study original written sheets of *sema* (religious) and *sanat* (classic) scores and learn to play traditional instruments, notably the *darbuka* (goblet drum), *klarnet* (clarinet) and *ud* (lute). There's a lovely atmosphere in the courtyard and it's well worth asking if you can step inside – you may be offered tea – to listen to the impromptu practice sessions. Around the walls are framed pages from a book on rudimentary medical instruments, written by Şerateddin Sabmicioğlu in Amasya in the mid-nineteenth century. As the formidable doctor used graphic, naked illustrations in order to explain how to use the instruments – as you will see from the pictures – the head *imam* at the time banned it, though the book was in use elsewhere in Europe in the late nineteenth century.

Further on is the **Sıhhı Mustafa Bey Hamamı** (daily: men 7–10am & 5–11pm; women 10am–5pm; 5YTL for bath, 5YTL extra for massage), very old but very much in use, as the wreaths of vapour emerging from its chimneys testify. Next comes the **Mehmet Paşa Camii**, constructed in 1486 by Mehmet Paşa, who was the tutor of Prince Ahmet, son of Sultan Beyazit. It's a sizable place, with a guesthouse, soup kitchen and *medrese*, and boasts a finely decorated marble pulpit.

A little further along is the **Şıranlı Camii**, built a little over a hundred years ago though it looks far older. According to a sign outside, it was constructed using money that had been raised by Azeri Turks, although it's not at all clear why they should have paid to build a mosque in Amasya. The final mosque of any importance is the early fifteenth-century **Beyazit Paşa Camii**, whose leafy riverbank location enhances the quiet beauty of its architecture.

From here a bridge crosses the Yeşilırmak river to the **Büyük Ağa Medresesi**, a seminary/university founded in 1488 by the Chief White Eunuch of Beyazit II. This roughly octagonal structure of stone and brick is nowadays a Koran school. Although it's not officially open to the public, no one seems to mind if you take a look inside the courtyard where the boys who study here play football between lessons.

Across from the *medrese*, on the right-hand side of Elmasiye Caddesi, is a tiny garden at the bottom of a sheer cliff. On the cliff-face is an **Arabian inscription** that mentions a field, a mosque and a caravan stop, thought to have been inscribed by Amasya's Hittite founders. To the left of this is the man-made **Leğenkaya waterfall**, a modern addition to Amasya's attractions, where water is pumped down the rock face between 3pm and 10pm each day and lit up very effectively after dark.

The rock tombs

The massive **rock tombs** (daily 8am–5pm; 2YTL) of the Pontic kings are carved into the cliff-face on the northern bank of the Yeşilırmak. There are two main clusters of tombs, and bearing right from the Kızlar Sarayı will bring you to the most accessible group, as well as to a café and toilet. You may want to clamber up inside some of the tombs through the raised stone doorways, but if you find the doorways padlocked you will need to rouse the site guardian to open them. Passages cut out of the rock run behind two of the tombs and you can only marvel at the work that must have been involved in excavating them. Bearing left will bring you to two larger tombs; beside the entrance to one of them is the mouth of a tunnel, thought to lead to the river. More tombs can be found with a bit of effort – there are a total of eighteen throughout the valley – but none is as impressive as these. At night, the rock tombs are lit up to give the city a spectacular backdrop.

Ottoman houses

Below the rock tombs, on the narrow strip of land between the railway line and river, is Amasya's other big attraction, the half-timbered **Ottoman houses** that contribute so much to the atmosphere of the town. While there are still a few dilapidated structures with preservation orders pasted on what is left of their doors, almost all the houses here have been superbly restored with funding from the Ministry of Culture (and free wood from the Ministry of Forestry). Since the buildings have been put to some use again, there's now a wonderful atmosphere in this old quarter, with many of the houses opening as authentic and atmospheric antique shops, *pansiyons* and restaurants, in keeping with the general Ottoman theme.

A good starting point for explorations is the nineteenth-century **Hazeranlar Konağı** (Tues–Sun 9am–noon & 1.30–5pm; 2YTL), an imposing mansion at the river's edge. The heavily restored interior has been turned into a convincing re-creation of a nineteenth-century family home, liberally decked out with carpets (shoes are removed at the door), period furniture and domestic artefacts. It incorporates typical features of the time: wall niches for oil lamps, bathrooms secreted away behind cupboard doors, and *sedirs* or divan seating running along the walls, all of which reflect the nomadic distaste for cumbersome furniture. In the basement of the house, accessed by a separate entrance, there's a small **art gallery** (same hours as above; free). Paintings by local artists are displayed and it's often possible to watch artists at work.

Follow the street west from the Hazeranlar Konağı to the **Yildiz Hamami** (daily: men 7–10am & 5–11pm; women 10am–5pm; 5YTL for bath, 5YTL extra for massage), built in 1270, making it the oldest in town, though it's been thoroughly restored. Continue westwards as far as the footbridge leading across to the Sultan Beyazit Camii and it'll take you through the heart of the old house district.

The kale

In the crags high above the rock tombs is Amasya's sprawling citadel, or **kale**, a structure that dates back to Pontic times, though the surviving ruins are of Ottoman vintage. The *kale* is difficult to reach, but well worth the effort for the stupendous views of the town below. The most straightforward way to get there is to follow the Samsun road out of town from near the Büyük Ağa Medresesi until you spot the "Kale" sign hidden in a backstreet to the left. From here a steep dirt road winds its way up to the summit for about 2km. It's quite a climb on foot (reckon on an hour or two), so if you're not up to the trek, consider taking a taxi – 8YTL for the journey there and back.

At the top, the outer walls of the *kale* have been rebuilt in bright, modern stone, but beyond you'll find the crumbling remains of the Ottoman-era fortress. Nothing is signposted and there are no clear paths through the ruins, so much of the time you'll find yourself scrambling over rocks and rubble and through undergrowth. At the southeastern extremity of the ruins, you'll find a rough breezeblock shed containing an old cannon that's discharged to thunderous effect at sundown during Ramadan. Beware of a large unfenced hole hidden in the undergrowth nearby. The best views are to be had from the western end of the *kale*, where the Turkish flag flies.

Eating and drinking

With a riverside setting and the rock tombs above lit up at night, dining out in Amasya provides unbeatable ambience. Classical music is a feature here, too, with many of the **cafés** catering to the students from the town's music *medresesi* who meet to practise their instruments. Cheap eats can be found at a number of *lokanta*-style joints around Atatürk Caddesi on the south side of the river, or for 13–17YTL you can enjoy a traditional meal in one of the Ottoman-house **restaurants** on the north side.

Ali Kaya On the hill on the south side of town; look up and you'll see the sign. Owned by the same people and with a similar menu as the *Bahar*, though more expensive. Magnificent views, attentive service and tables under shady pine trees. You might want to get a taxi there and back.

Bahar Sadikesan Sok 3 & 6. Sister restaurants, popular with locals; one located below a block of residential flats (no alcohol), the other (licensed) across the street. Both supply large portions of kebabs, grills, roast chicken and good vegetarian options.

Biyer Ziyapaşa Bul. Great studenty place, entered through a small door at street level, playing rock music, and serving cheap and cheerful Turkish and Western fare from around 3YTL per meal. Aim for one of the tables on the small balcony overlooking the river.

Harşena Otel Across the Alçak footbridge. The café-bar here is a fine Ottoman restoration overlooking the Roman bridge, offering cold beer on tap, *nargiles* and backgammon boards to while

away hours in the kilim-covered booths. More of Amasya's formidable musicians play in the garden every evening.

Ocakbaşı Restaurant Ziya Paşa Bul 5. Popular place with outdoor seating area but surly waiters. Inexpensive and piping hot selection of stews, soups, *pides*, and more Westernized dishes such as pizzas and lamb burgers.

Pasha Across the bridge from the main square ℡0358/218 6269. Stylish venue with bare wooden floors, rustic furniture, exquisite antiques and kilims, a pretty walled garden with wishing well, and a riverside balcony. À la carte menu is typically Turkish, and there's an atmospheric basement bar, with tiny wooden tables and cushions set into stone walls, that stays open until 5am if the demand is there.

Subaşi Café Across the bridge from the main square. Ottoman-inspired teahouse with stone floors, wooden beams and a terrace over the river, attracting earnest-looking university students. No alcohol.

Tokat

TOKAT clusters at the foot of a jagged crag with a ruined Pontic fortress on top. Despite its undeniably dramatic setting, it comes as something of an anticlimax after Amasya, with none of the soothing riverside atmosphere and much less to see – the local claim to fame is the Gök Medrese, another Selçuk "Blue Seminary", now used as a museum. Nonetheless, Tokat makes a good stop-off when travelling between Amasya and Sivas.

The journey from Amasya, 103km away, takes about an hour and a half, with a couple of ruined *kervansarays* en route. The first – after about half an hour – is at **Ezinepazarı**; in the days of the great caravans, this was a day's ride by camel from Amasya. The second is at the signposted village of Pazar, about 26km short of Tokat, where you'll find the well-preserved Selçuk **Hatun Hanı**.

Some history

Tokat first came to prominence as a **staging post** on the Persian trans-Anatolian royal road, running from Sardis to Persepolis. Later it fell to Alexander the Great and then to Mithridates and his successors. In 47 BC, **Julius Caesar** defeated Pharnaces, son of the Pontic king Mithridates VI earlier Eupator, who had taken advantage of a period of civil war in Rome to attempt to re-establish the Pontic kingdom as an independent state. Caesar's victory in a five-hour battle at Zile, just outside Tokat, prompted his immortal line *"Veni, vidi, vici"* (I came, I saw, I conquered).

Under **Byzantine rule**, Tokat became a frontline city in perpetual danger of Arab attack, a state of affairs that continued until the Danişmend Turks took control of the city after the battle of Manzikert in 1071. Less than one hundred years later the İlhanid Mongols arrived, ushering in a period of war and uncertainty that finally ended in 1392 when the citizens of Tokat, tired of the endless strife, petitioned Sultan Beyazit Yıldırım to be admitted to the Ottoman Empire. Their request was granted and peace returned until the arrival of the second great Mongol wave under **Tamerlane**. On this occasion the town was sacked, but the castle survived a lengthy siege.

With the departure of the Mongols and return of the **Ottomans**, life returned to normal and a period of prosperity ensued. In time, though, trade patterns shifted, the east–west routes to Persia lost their importance and Tokat became the backwater it remains today.

The Town

The real reason to stop is to visit the **Gök Medrese** on the main Gazi Osman Paşa Bulvarı, a squat, rectangular building with a portal whose recessed arch resembles a picturesque cluster of stalactites. Built in 1275 by the Selçuk emir Mu'in al-Din Süleyman (also known as Pervane, or "butterfly", an epithet given to advisers of the Selçuk sultans), the *medrese* was named for the turquoise tiles that once covered its entire exterior. Most of these have unfortunately vanished, but a few still tenaciously grip the walls of the inner courtyard.

Today the Gök Medrese is home to the town's **museum** (Tues–Sun 8.30am–noon & 1–5pm; 2YTL), a repository for local archeological finds and various unusual relics collected from the churches that served the town's sizable Greek and Armenian communities before World War I. Typical of these is a wax effigy of Christina, a Christian martyred during the rule of the Roman emperor Diocletian. The ethnographic section features examples of local *yazma*-making – printing on cloth by means of wooden blocks to produce colourful patterned handkerchiefs, scarves and tablecloths.

Keep walking down Gazi Osman Paşa Bulvarı towards the main square and you'll come to the **Taş Han**, originally called the Voyvoda Han, built in 1631 by Armenian merchants. A large, rectangular building of two storeys, it houses a collection of shabby shops centred on a weed-infested courtyard. On the other side of the street is a market area, and on the street behind is the **Hatuniye Camii**, an impressive Ottoman mosque with an adjoining *medrese*, built in 1485 during the reign of Sultan Beyazit II.

A number of Ottoman-era half-timbered houses survive in the sidestreets of Tokat, but most are in states of advanced decrepitude. One exception is the **Latifoğlu Konağı** (Tues–Sun 9am–noon & 1.30–5pm; 2YTL) on Gazi Osman Paşa Bulvarı, a couple of hundred metres past Cumhuriyet Alanı. Heavily restored, it stands out a mile from the surrounding modern buildings with its plain white walls, brown-stained woodwork and low-pitched roof. The interior is opulent almost to the point of tastelessness, but gives a good impression of how a wealthy nineteenth-century family would have lived. High points are the Paşa's Room upstairs, with its exquisitely carved ceiling and elaborately decorated fireplace, and the Women's Room with garish floral motifs on the walls and windows that incorporate Star of David designs. The pleasant *Konak Café* in the garden is a good place for a break.

Tokat's **kale** dominates the town from its jagged eminence northwest of Cumhuriyet Alanı. Originally a Pontic fortress (although its exact construction date is unknown), it was later used by the Selçuks and Ottomans who added to the existing defences. You might be able to find a way up to the top if you are keen to view the town from on high, but the surviving walls enclose only rubble.

Practicalities

Tokat's **otogar** is a little way outside town on the main road. It takes about fifteen minutes to walk to the centre – head for the roundabout near a bridge flanked by cannons and turn left down Gazi Osman Paşa Bulvarı. Pressing on straight down the main street eventually brings you to busy **Cumhuriyet Alanı**, the town's central square, location of the **PTT** and an underground shopping mall.

Tourist information is available from the office on Gazi Osman Paşa Bulvarı, in Taş Han (daily 8am–6pm), but you'll need a phrase book to extract any information and there are no maps or leaflets to collect.

Finding a **place to stay** should present few problems. The best budget option is the friendly, modern and clean ⌁ *Hotel Çağrı*, Gazi Osman Paşa Bul 92 (⊤0356/212 1028; ❷), which offers a spread of clean en-suites. A little further along, the *Yeni Çinar Otel* at no.167 (⊤0356/214 0066, ⓕ213 1927; ❹) has business-like en-suites and a good buffet breakfast, whilst across the road at no. 168, the *Çavuşoğlu Otel* (⊤0356/212 2829, ⓕ212 8568; ❹) is a brand-new boutique-style establishment, with colourful, individually decorated rooms. A further jump up in quality is the semi-luxurious *Büyük Tokat Oteli* (⊤0356/228 1661, ⓕ228 1660; ❻), a couple of kilometres northwest of the town centre. The magnificent reception hides rather less impressive rooms, but a swimming pool goes some way to compensate.

There are cheap **restaurants** on virtually every street in town. If the weather's good, head for the tea garden in the Dudayev Parkı, next to the Vilayet building on Cumhuriyet Alanı. To sample the local speciality, *Tokat kebap*, a mouthwatering and very filling combination of roast lamb, potatoes, aubergine, tomato and peppers, head for the *Sofra Restaurant* at Gazi Osman Paşa Bul 8 (just south of Cumhuriyet Alanı); portions tend to be gargantuan. If you're driving and don't want to stop in town, try the rooftop restaurant of the *Yimpaş* department store, on the approach road from Amasya, which serves up good *Tokat kebap* for around 5YTL.

Sivas

As much as any other city in Turkey, **SIVAS** has been a battleground for the successive empires struggling to rule central Anatolia. Now this well-planned city of 200,000 people wouldn't figure on anybody's itinerary were it not for a concentration of Selçuk buildings – among the finest in Turkey – conveniently located in a town-centre park. The 113km journey southeast from Tokat is uninspiring, over barren hills that rise to 1600m metres, with the presence of snow poles giving some indication of what this region looks like in winter.

Sivas has been settled since Hittite times and according to local sources was later a key centre of the Sivas Frig Empire (1200 BC), which seems to have been consigned to historical oblivion. Under the Romans Sivas was known as Megalopolis and then Sebastaea, which in later years was corrupted to Sivas. The town's real flowering came during **Selçuk** times, after the battle of Manzikert (1071), and Sivas intermittently served as the Selçuk capital during the Sultanate of Rum in the mid-twelfth century, before passing into the hands of İlhanid Mongols during

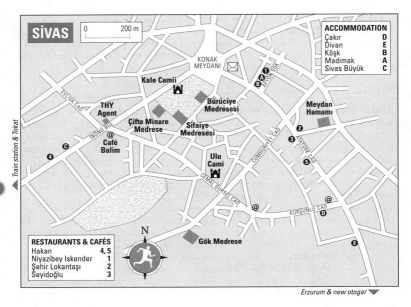

Erzurum & new otogar ▼

the late thirteenth century. The Ottomans took over in 1396 only to be ousted by the Mongols four years later under Tamerlane, who razed much of the city after an eighteen-day siege and put its Christian inhabitants to the sword. The Ottomans returned in 1408 and Sivas pretty much faded out of history until the twentieth century.

On September 4, 1919, the **Congress of Sivas** was convened here when Atatürk arrived from Amasya, on his mission to rally resistance against Allied attempts to carve up the Ottoman Empire. Delegates from all over the country came to Sivas, and the congress was a milestone on the way to establishing modern Republican Turkey.

Arrival, information and services

Buses from Ankara and beyond arrive at the **otogar**, 1.5km south of town at the junction with the main Erzurum road. From here *servis* buses run to the centre of town, along İnönü Bulvarı. The **train station** is 2.5km west of town, but municipal buses and dolmuşes run down İstasiyon Caddesi (later İnönü Bulvarı) to Konak Meydanı.

The centre of Sivas is Konak Meydanı, location of the main municipal buildings and **PTT**. You can **rent a car** from the THY agent, Sivas Turizm Seyahat, at İnönü Bul 50 (☎0346/221 1147). **Emails** can be sent from any of the vast number of Internet cafés that line Kurşunlu Caddesi, including the extravagantly castle-like *Café Balim*. Just past the Yimpaş department store on Atatürk Caddesi is a line of small **shops** selling traditional instruments and *nargile*s – if you want to take a hubble-bubble pipe home as a souvenir you are likely to get one here at a realistic price.

Accommodation

The hotels in Sivas have improved over the years, and it's unlikely that you'll have trouble finding a decent room for the night.

Otel Çakır Kurşunlu Cad 20 ☎ 0346/2222 4526, ✉ cakirotel@hotmail.com. Ageing, but acceptable, budget choice with dark en-suites with TV and shower. **②**

Otel Divan Atatürk Cad ☎ 0346/221 7878, ✆ 221 1407. Best budget option in Sivas. Friendly, newly renovated hotel with spotless rooms and reliable hot water. You'll also get a large buffet breakfast thrown in. **②**

Hotel Köşk Atatürk Cad 7 ☎ 0346/255 1724, ⓦ www.kostotel.com. Beautifully decked-out contemporary hotel, complete with fitness centre. All rooms are spacious and spotless, with excellent showers, and breakfast is included in the price. **⑤**

Otel Madimak Eski Belıdiye Sok 2 ☎ 0346/221 8027, ✉ madimakotel@yahoo.com. Large, comfortable, if slightly dated two-star in a great central location. Breakfast included. There's a ten-percent reduction if you pay in cash. **④**

Sivas Büyük Oteli İstasyon Cad ☎ 0346/225 4762, ✉ buyukotel-sivas@yahoo.com. Monolith of a hotel with slowly fading rooms which still tries to cling onto its class. Large, soulless rooms, but it's useful to know that the dining room is one of the few places in town that serves alcohol. **⑥**

The Town

Most of Sivas's Selçuk monuments were built during the Sultanate of Rum and in the period of Mongol sovereignty that followed under the İlhanids. With their highly decorative facades and elaborately carved portals, the buildings epitomize Selçuk architectural styles, and nearly all are conveniently grouped together in and around a small park just off **Konak Meydanı**.

Closest to the *meydan* is the **Bürüciye Medresesi**, founded in 1271 by the İlhanid emir Muzaffer Bürücirdi. The building consists of a series of square rooms laid out to a symmetrical ground plan around a central courtyard. As you pass through the entrance, the *türbe* of the emir and his children is to the left. The *medrese* ostensibly houses an archeological collection, which in fact consists of three lonely pieces of stonework; more worthy of attention are the carpet-sellers, who hang their wares from the walls, a small bookshop, and a café that spills out into the open. Nearby is the **Kale Camii**, an oddity in this area as it's a straightforward Ottoman mosque, built in 1580 at the behest of Mahmut Paşa, a grand vizier of Sultan Murat III.

South of here is the stunning **Çifte Minare Medrese** (Twin Minaret Seminary), also built in 1271. The facade alone survives, adorned with tightly curled relief filigrees, topped by two brick minarets, which are adorned here and there with pale blue tiles. Behind, only the well-defined foundations of student cells and lecture halls survive. Directly opposite is the **Şifaiye Medresesi** (1217), a hospital and medical school built on the orders of the Selçuk sultan Keykavus I. Inside are a bazaar, selling everything from kilims to hats, and a delightful tea-garden bedecked in traditional rugs and kilims. Easily overlooked amid all the commercial activity is the **tomb of Keykavus** to the right of the entrance. A number of glazed tiles with eight-pointed star motifs cling to the brickwork and the sarcophagi within are also tiled. In its heyday, the Zifaiye Medresesi was a centre for the treatment of psychological disorders and apparently music therapy and hypnosis were among the healing techniques employed.

The rest of the town's Selçuk monuments lie outside the park. If you turn on to Cemal Gürsel Caddesi (just south of the park), you'll find the **Ulu Cami**, the oldest mosque in Sivas, built in 1197. This is an unattractive building, topped by an ugly corrugated-iron roof punctuated with equally displeasing chimneys; but if you step inside the northern entrance you will enter the subterranean cool of a hypostyle mosque, supported by fifty wooden pillars. The peaceful silence is broken only by the murmur of boys reading from the Koran.

A right turn from Cemal Gürsel Caddesi will take you onto Cumhuriyet Caddesi where, on the left after a couple of hundred metres, you'll find the **Gök Medrese**, with its ornate tile-studded minarets. This could well be the most attractive "Blue Seminary" you've yet seen, particularly if you catch it during the afternoon, when the absence of shadows reveals the best of the brickwork, carving (tree-of-life and

△ Çifte Minare Medrese

star symbols are recurring motifs) and tiles that embellish its stunning facade. It was built in 1271 by the Selçuk grand vizier Sahip Ata Fahrettin Ali, who was also responsible for buildings in Kayseri and Konya.

Eating, drinking and entertainment

There are a number of cheap **kebab places** lining the road behind the PTT, and some **teahouses** in the park serving up snacks. The *Şehir Lokantaşı*, just around the corner from the Meydan Camii, and the plusher *Niyazibey İskender* next to the *Hotel Madimak* do tasty, cheap *pide*s and kebabs.

Sivas also has plenty of sweet and **pastry shops**, including the *Seyidoğlu Baklava ve Pasta Salonu* on Atatürk Caddesi, opposite the Meydan Camii. Alternatively, you could try one of the two branches of *Hakan*, on Atatürk Cad 22 and İnönü 16, which serves tasty savoury dishes as well as some of the best *baklava* and desserts in town.

It's more or less impossible to find any alcohol in Sivas, so you could amuse yourself by seeing a **movie** at the Klas Sinemalari, further up at İnönü Bulvarı 6, opposite the park. Otherwise, up a sidestreet leading off Atatürk Caddesi, stands the **Meydan Hamamı** (daily 7am–10.30pm; 5YTL for bath, 5YTL extra for massage), which has been hissing and steaming for over four centuries and is still going strong.

Divriği

Stuck in the middle of a mountainous nowhere, on a hill overlooking a tributary of the young Euphrates, 162km southeast of Sivas, **DIVRIĞI** merits a visit for the sake of a single monument, the whimsical and unique Ulu Cami and its dependency, the Darüşşifa (Sanitorium). These date from early in the thirteenth century, when the town was the seat of the tiny Mengüçeh emirate; the Mengüçehs were evicted by the Mongols in 1252, who demolished the castle here but left the religious foundations alone, and the place was not incorporated into the Ottoman Empire until 1516.

Divriği is most easily reached by dolmuş from Sivas; four daily make the four-hour run from the *otogar*, returning to Sivas at 5am, 9am, 12.30pm and 5pm. There is also one daily train here from Erzurum.

The Town

Sleepy Divriği lives off the nearby iron and steel works, but retains a ramshackle bazaar crisscrossed by cobbled lanes and grapevines. Architecturally the town sports distinctive wooden **minarets** and old houses with inverted-keyhole windows, neither of which are seen elsewhere in Anatolia.

The conspicuous mosque and sanitorium, joined in one complex at the top of a slope 250m east of town, command a fine view. The **Ulu Cami**, dedicated in 1228 by a certain Ahmet Şah, is remarkable for its outrageous external **portals**, most un-Islamic with their wealth of floral and faunal detail. Rather far-fetched comparisons have been made to Indian Moghul art, but a simpler, more likely explanation is that Armenian or Selçuk craftsmen had a hand in the decoration. The north door, festooned with vegetal designs, is the most celebrated, although the northwestern one is more intricately worked – note the pair of double-headed eagles, not necessarily copied from the Byzantines since it's a very old Anatolian motif. Inside, sixteen columns and the ceiling they support are more suggestive of a Gothic cloister or a Byzantine cistern. There's rope-vaulting in one dome, while the northeastern one sports a peanut-brittle surface, in terms of both the relief work and variegated colouring; the central dome has been rather tastelessly restored. The *mihrab* is plain, flanked by an extravagant, carved wooden *mimber*.

The adjoining **Darüşşifa** was also begun in 1228 by Adaletli Melike Turan Melek, Ahmet Şah's wife. Its portal is restrained in comparison to the mosque's, but still bears medallions lifted almost free from their background. The sanitorium complex is theoretically open daily 8.30am to 5pm, but in these lean tourist times the gate is usually locked, so you must find the caretaker to gain admission – easiest just after prayers next door. A small donation is requested after signing the guest register at the conclusion of the tour.

The caretaker proudly points out some of the more arcane features of the interior, which is asymmetrical in both ground plan and ornamentation, and even more eclectic than the mosque. Of four dissimilar columns surrounding a **fountain**, two are embossed; the eight-sided pool has a curlicue drain-hole as well as two more conventional feeder-spouts. Overhead, the dome has collapsed and been crudely replaced in the same manner as the mosque's, but four-pointed **vaulting** graces the entry hall, with even more elaborate ribbing over a raised platform in the *eyvan*, or domed side-chamber, at the rear of the nave. The fan-reliefs on the wall behind this once formed an elaborate **sundial**, catching rays through the second-floor window of the facade; the caretaker claims that the suspended carved cylinder in front of this opening once revolved, though it's unclear how this helped the sundial function – perhaps there was a prism mounted in it. Musicians may once have played on the raised platform to entertain the patients, whose rather poky bedrooms on both ground and upper storeys you're allowed to visit. One of the side-rooms contains the **tombs** of Ahmet Şah and his father Süleyman Şah.

Practicalities

The **train station** is down by the river, a twenty-minute walk from the bazaar; taxis meet most arrivals and don't cost more than a couple of dollars. The **otogar**, essentially a dirt car-park, is 400m south of town on the road to Elazığ.

Accommodation in Divriği is pretty poor, so it's best to avoid staying the night if you can. There are only two basic **hotels**, the vastly preferable being the government-run *Belediye Hotel* (☎0346/418 1825; ❶), a little out of the centre towards the station. Here the rooms are large, passably clean, and come with showers (though the solar hot-water supply means you only stand a chance of a warm shower in the middle of the day); stay on an upper floor to avoid the noise from the downstairs restaurant. **Eating** options are a little better, with a *kebap salonu* and an oven-food place near the hotels, the *Üçler Pide Salonu* in the bazaar and the licensed *Belediye Restaurant* on the main square, below the Mengüçeh monuments.

Travel details

Buses and dolmuşes

Amasya to: Ankara (hourly; 6hr); İstanbul (12 daily; 12hr); Kayseri (3 daily; 8hr); Malatya (5 daily; 9hr); Samsun (10 daily; 3hr); Sivas (6 daily; 3hr 30min); Tokat (10 daily; 1hr 30min).

Ankara to: Adana (12 daily; 8hr); Adıyaman (hourly; 13hr); Amasya (10 daily; 6hr); Antalya (12 daily; 9hr); Bodrum (10 daily; 10hr); Bursa (hourly; 6hr); Çorum (hourly; 3hr); Diyarbakır (6 daily; 14hr); Erzurum (4 daily; 15hr); Eskişehir (5 daily; 5hr); Gaziantep (12 daily; 12hr); İstanbul (every 30min; 7hr); İzmir (hourly; 8hr); Karabük (6 daily; 4hr); Kastamonu (9 daily; 4hr); Kayseri (14 daily;

5hr); Konya (14 daily; 3hr 30min); Kütahya (5 daily; 7hr); Mardin (3 daily; 16hr); Nevşehir (12 daily; 4hr 30min); Polatlı (every 30min; 1hr); Safranbolu (9 daily; 4hr); Samsun (10 daily; 8hr); Sivas (hourly; 8hr); Sungurlu (hourly; 3hr); Şanlıurfa (4 daily; 12hr); Trabzon (5 daily; 12hr).

Eskişehir to: Ankara (4 daily; 5hr); Bursa (6 daily; 1hr); İstanbul (4 daily; 4hr); Kütahya (12 daily; 1hr).

Kastamonu to: Ankara (9 daily; 4hr); İnebolu (6 daily; 2hr); Safranbolu (hourly; 3hr); Samsun (3 daily; 6hr).

Kütahya to: Afyon (14 daily; 1hr 45min); Antalya (5 daily; 5hr); Balıkeşir (4 daily; 5hr); Bursa (12 daily; 3hr); Eskişehir (10 daily; 1hr); İstanbul (14 daily; 6hr); İzmir (12 daily; 6hr); Uşak (5 daily; 1hr 15min); Yoncalı (hourly; 20min).

Sivas to: Amasya (10 daily; 4hr); Ankara (12 daily; 8hr); Divriği (4 daily; 3hr); Diyarbakır (12 daily; 10hr); Erzurum (12 daily; 9hr); Kayseri (10 daily; 3hr); Malatya (12 daily; 5hr); Tokat (10 daily; 2hr).

Tokat to: Amasya (12 daily; 2hr); Ankara (12 daily; 8hr); Erzincan (1 daily; 8hr); Erzurum (2 daily; 11hr); Sivas (10 daily; 2hr).

Trains

Ankara to: Adana (1 daily; 11hr 50min); İstanbul

(6 daily; 8–9hr 30min); İzmir (1 daily; 15hr); Sivas, Erzurum & Kars (1 daily; 8hr); Sivas, Malatya & Diyarbakır (Mon, Wed, Fri & Sat; 6hr 30min); Zongulak (1 daily; 12hr 15min).

Divriği to: Erzurum (1 daily; 8hr); Sivas (2 daily; 4–5hr).

Sivas to: Divriği (1 daily); Diyarbakır (1 daily); Erzurum (1 daily); Samsun (1 daily).

Flights

Ankara to: Adana (at least 5 daily; 1hr); Ağri (2 weekly; 1hr 40min); Antalya (8 daily; 1hr); Batman (1 daily; 1hr 30min); Bodrum (at least 4 daily; 3hr); Dalaman via İstanbul (3 daily; 3hr); Denizli via İstanbul (5 weekly; 3hr); Diyarbakır (at least 2 daily; 1hr 20min); Elazığ (1 daily; 1hr 45min); Erzincan (2 weekly; 1hr 25min); Erzurum (1 daily; 1hr 25min); Gaziantep (3 daily; 1hr 20min); İstanbul (at least 12 daily; 1hr); İzmir (8 daily; 1hr 20min); Kars (1 daily; 1hr 40min); Kayseri via İstanbul (3 daily; 3hr 30min); Malatya (2 daily; 1hr); Mardin (5 weekly; 1hr 30min); Muş (4 weekly; 1hr 30min); Şanlıurfa (5 weekly; 1hr 30min); Trabzon (2 daily; 1hr 15min); Van (2 daily; 1hr 40min).

9

The Black Sea coast

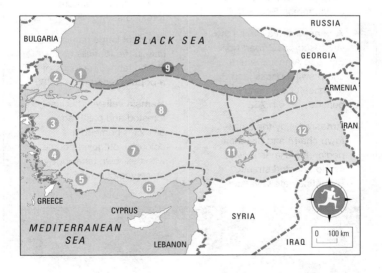

CHAPTER 9 # Highlights

* **Tea** Learn the skills of making the nation's favourite drink and watch the leaves being picked from the hillsides surrounding Rize. See p.777

* **Tatlıca valley** Take a ramble through the valley near Sinop, where twenty-eight waterfalls tumble down hillsides covered in beech forest. See p.752

* **A coastal drive** Cruise the little-used coast road from Sinop to Amasra, where sharp switchbacks lead to peaceful bays and long beaches. See p.752

* **Amasra** Enjoy the small-town charm and historical pedigree of Amasra, with its old cobbled streets, Byzantine gateways and Genoese castle walls. See p.754

* **Aya Sofya** Thirteenth-century frescoes in this Byzantine monastery at the edge of Trabzon are among the most vivid sacred art in Anatolia. See p.766

* **Sumela** Cliff-clinging thirteenth-century monastery in a superb forested setting. See p.772

* **Uzungöl** Large natural lake in the foothills of the Pontic range, the focus of a popular resort. See p.780

* **Hemşin valleys** This lushly forested and pastured district is home to a colourful, outgoing people with their own tenaciously preserved culture. See p.781

△ Byzantine mosaic, Aya Sofya, Trabzon

The Black Sea coast

xtending from just east of İstanbul to the frontier with Georgia, the **Black Sea** region is an anomaly, guaranteed to smash any stereotypes held about Turkey. The combined action of damp northerly and westerly winds, and an almost uninterrupted wall of mountains south of the shore, has created a relentlessly rainy and riotously green realm. It's not unlike North America's, or Spain's, northwest coast. The peaks force the clouds to disgorge themselves on the seaward side of the watershed, leaving central Anatolia beyond the passes in a permanent rain shadow.

The short summer season means there is little foreign tourism and no UK package operators currently serve the area (though Trabzon airport gets a few summer charters from Germany). However, in those months when the semi-tropical heat is on (July and August), you'll certainly want to swim. The sea here has its own peculiarities, just like the weather. It is fed huge volumes of fresh water by the Don, Dnieper and Danube rivers to the north, and diminished not by evaporation but by strong currents through the Bosphorus and the Dardanelles. The resulting upper layer is of such low salinity that you could almost drink it, were it not for the pollution of recent decades – much of which has been carried down the Danube from as far afield as Germany and Austria. Each year around fifty thousand tonnes of oil and huge quantities of phosphates are discharged into the Black Sea's waters. All of this has had a predictably devastating effect on aquatic life. Attempts to formulate an effective environmental policy for the region have been hampered by the sheer number of countries involved, and chaotic conditions in Russia and the recently independent Caucasian republics.

The coastal ranges begin as mere humps north of Ankara but attain world-class grandeur by the time the Georgian border is reached. Until recently they made land access all but impossible, and provided redoubts for a complex quilt of tribes and ethnic subgroups. Many of these are still there, making the Black Sea one of Turkey's most anthropologically interesting regions. Even so, travelling around largely consists of soaking up the atmosphere. You rarely need worry about missing important sights, as there really aren't many.

The region divides neatly into western and eastern halves, with the former comparatively lacking in character. Everything between the coal-mining town of **Zonguldak** and İstanbul is essentially a beach suburb of the latter. Between Zonguldak and **Samsun**, the largest and most featureless city of the region, only the Byzantine/Genoese harbour of **Amasra** and the historic, evocatively located town of **Sinop** deserve a special trip. The **beaches** between Amasra and Sinop are generally quiet and magnificent, but the road on this stretch will probably remain substandard for some years yet, with the infrequency of bus and dolmuş links sheltering the area from mass tourism. Travelling by car, or even cycle touring (as long as you have the stamina), is likely to be more rewarding than taking the bus.

East of Samsun, beach tourism has clearly taken a back seat to infrastructure development, as the new four-lane highway from the Georgian border to Sinop (and soon possibly beyond) irrevocably cuts off towns from their shore. Under the onslaught of ambitious tunnelling, sea walls and revetments, many formerly popular beaches have shrunk or simply disappeared; the coast is further disfigured by enormous T-shaped breakwaters built with small craft, rather than bathers, in mind. Surviving decent swimming opportunities along this entire stretch can be just about counted on one hand, fortunately at or near potentially pleasant stopovers in the old mercantile towns of **Ünye** and **Giresun**. Beyond **Trabzon** (Trebizond) – along with the nearby **monastery of Sumela**, the only established tourist destination on the Black Sea – beaches diminish as the scenery inland becomes more imposing. Other than the **Hemşin valleys** and the **Kaçkar mountains** themselves, though, there are few specific destinations to point to.

Some history

With much trepidation, the ancient Greeks ventured onto the Pontos Euxine (as they called the Black Sea) at the start of the first millennium BC. They tilted with the local "barbarians" and occasionally, as in the semi-legendary tale of Jason and the Argonauts, got the better of them. Between the seventh and fourth centuries BC numerous colonies of the Aegean cities were founded at the seaward ends of the trade routes through the Pontic mountains. These became the ancestors of virtually every modern Black Sea town, whose name more often as not is a Turkification of the ancient moniker. The region had its first brief appearance on the world stage when one of the local Pontic kings, **Mithridates IV Eupator**, came close to expelling the Romans from Anatolia. Even after the suppression of the several Mithridatic rebellions, the Romans concentrated on the western section of the Black Sea and its hinterland, leaving the portion from Trabzon eastwards in the hands of vassals. This, and the climate's heavy toll on all but the stoutest structures, accounts in part for the near-total absence of ancient ruins here.

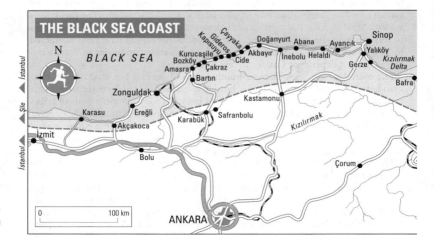

With the arrival of Christianity, relations between natives and imperial overlords hardly changed at all. Only the Byzantine urban centres by the sea became thoroughly Hellenized, while subjects with grievances embroiled the Byzantine Empire in continual wars by appealing for aid to the neighbouring Armenian and Persian empires. The Byzantine defeat at Manzikert in 1071 initially meant little to the Black Sea, safe behind its wall of mountains; the fall of Constantinople to the Fourth Crusade in 1204 had far greater immediate effects, prompting the Black Sea's second spell of historical prominence. The empire-in-exile of the Komnenos dynasty centred on **Trebizond** (today's Trabzon) exercised influence grossly disproportionate to its size for two and a half cultured (and ultimately decadent) centuries.

After Manzikert, Turkish chieftains had begun to encroach on the coast, especially at the gap in the barrier ranges near Sinop and Samsun; the Trapezuntine dynasty even concluded alliances with them, doubtless to act as a counter to the power of the Genoese and Venetians who also set up shop hereabouts. Most of this factionalism was brought to an end under the **Ottomans**, though even they entrusted semi-autonomous administration of the Pontic foothills to feudal *derebey*s (literally "valley lords") until the early nineteenth century. This delegation of authority, and the fact that the usual replacement of Christian populations by Muslims took place only in the vicinity of Trabzon, meant that the region remained remarkably poor in Ottoman monuments and that until early this century many towns were almost half Greek or Armenian.

The equilibrium was upset when the Black Sea area entered the history books for the third time as a theatre of war between imperial Turkey and **Russia**. These two clashed four times between 1828 and 1915, with the Tsarist regime giving active aid and comfort to various separatist movements in the region after 1877. Between 1918 and 1922, Greeks attempting to create a Pontic state fought with guerillas loyal to Atatürk's Nationalists. Following the victory of the **Republic**, the Greek merchant class was expelled along with the rest of Turkey's Greek Orthodox population, and the Black Sea experienced temporary economic disarray, verging on famine during the 1930s.

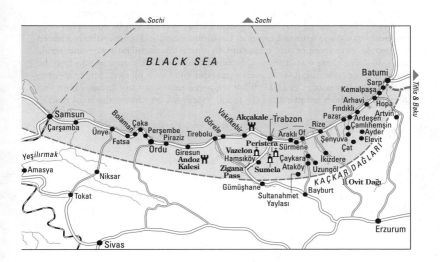

Black Sea trade

Since the opening of Turkey's eastern border, large numbers of Caucasians and Russians regularly visit the region. Every town of any size has its *Rus Pazar* or *Avrasya Pazar* (Russian Bazaar/Eurasian Bazaar), where **traders** sell everything from cigarettes to car parts and ceramics, raising hard currency to buy clothing and leather goods for later resale back home. Convoys of battered buses and arthritic cars stream along Black Sea roads heading to and from these symbols of long-severed trade routes in revival. Markets in larger cities are well-organized affairs overseen by the *Belediye Zabitası*, or market police, but in smaller towns they resemble roadside car-boot sales.

An equally important aspect of cross-border economic activity has been a boom in **prostitution** with so-called *natashas* (also sometimes called *madam*) plying their trade in many local hotels. Considered exotic by their Turkish clients, Western-looking women from Russia and elsewhere in the former Eastern Bloc are much in demand and have become an underclass in much of northeastern Turkey. This can cause problems for women travellers in the region, as local men tend to assume all foreign women are here on "business". Brothels are notoriously hard to spot: one general guideline when looking for accommodation is that the presence of a *mescid* (prayer room) or a few words of Arabic script above the door tend to indicate a pious management with a strict "*madam yok!*" policy. To minimize the likelihood of hassle try to check out which hotels are currently OK with local tourist offices, though many might deny a problem exists in their town. In recent years, however, with Turkey's current economic woes the extra disposable income to indulge in such extracurricular activities has all but dried up for most locals, and prostitution is much less prevalent along the coast than it was during the 1990s.

Most of the credit for the recent **recovery** must go to the *hamsi*s, as the locals are nicknamed (after the Black Sea anchovy formerly caught here in large numbers during winter). Enterprising, voluble and occasionally scandalous, they have set up mafias in the shipping, property and construction industries throughout the country, much of which is funded by remittances from industrious *hamsi*s overseas.

All of the above goes some way towards explaining why most Black Sea towns are so hideous. In the old days the shore was the province of Christian businessmen, who were largely responsible for the little attractive architecture that has survived. The scattered dwellings of inland villages tended to be connected only tenuously to a single store and mosque; the idiosyncratic and independently minded hill people were freed of any constraint to cluster by abundant water and arable fields. In short, there was little indigenous tradition of town planning, so when the boom hit, concrete blight set in as everyone did what they pleased. The reopening of the Georgian border since 1990 has triggered new spasms of urbanization and lorry traffic, which has provided the main pretext for improving the coast road.

The western Black Sea

The coast from Samsun west to Amasra is perhaps the least visited part of the entire Turkish shoreline. This neglect is a joint result of poor communications and the relative lack of tourist facilities and specific attractions. **Samsun** makes a dreary and discouraging gateway to the region, but matters improve as you head northwest to **Sinop**, a more interesting place than any other Black Sea town except Trabzon. Beyond Sinop the coast road west is tortuous and slow, but spectacular scenery, scattered, unspoiled beaches and small ports do something to compensate. The only place that gets much custom is **Amasra**, an old medieval stronghold at the western end of this beautiful stretch.

As a rule, the **beaches** are cleaner and the weather drier along this section of the Black Sea than further east. Figs and olives attest to the mild climate, and if you just want to laze on the sand without any other stimulation, then you'll find plenty of opportunity. Sparse **bus** and **dolmuş** schedules are the only drawbacks; check frequencies to avoid getting stranded.

9

Samsun

Despite its long and turbulent history **SAMSUN** has absolutely no remaining historical or scenic attractions. This thoroughly modern city of 330,000 people, laid out on a grid plan, with seemingly endless unruly suburbs stretching some 30km along the east–west coast road, is the centre of Turkey's tobacco industry. Most of the locals work directly or indirectly for the Tekel (state monopoly) cigarette factory. It's also a busy port and centre for the processing of local agricultural produce. Any spare time you have is likely to weigh heavy on your hands – though it has a fair amount to offer in terms of food and lodgings.

For the record, Samsun – like several of its neighbours – began life as a colony of Miletus in the seventh century BC. Because of its strategic location, the place changed hands frequently over the centuries; besieged, captured (and usually sacked) by the Pontic kings, Romans, Byzantines and several tribes of Turks. The final insult came in 1425, when the Genoese – who had a major trading station here – torched the town rather than hand it over to Ottoman control.

With the advent of the railway, which facilitated the transport of tobacco to Ankara and beyond, Samsun's flagging fortunes revived and by 1910 it was a thriving city of 40,000 inhabitants. Atatürk's arrival here on May 19, 1919, after fleeing İstanbul, further boosted the town's prominence, and can be said to have marked the start of the War of Independence. Rather than disbanding the groups of Turkish guerillas who had been attacking Greeks in the area, as he had been ordered to do, he began organizing them into a cohesive, national resistance army.

Arrival information and accommodation

The **otogar** lies 2km east of the city centre on the main Trabzon road, but just about all the bus companies have ticket offices on the east side of Cumhuriyet Meydanı on 19 Mayıs Bulvarı, from where service buses run to and from the *otogar*. The **train station** is halfway towards the centre; buses #2 and #10, as well as dolmuşes marked "Garaj", link both with Cumhuriyet Meydanı, the town's hub. Tourists unable to get seats to Trabzon often fly in to Samsun instead; the **airport**

▲ *Bafra, Sinop & Amasya*

Ferry Terminal

RIHTIM
CAD

NECIPBEY CAD

100 YIL BUL

BELEDIYE
MEYD

SAAT KÜLESI
MEYD

KÂTIPPASA CAD

THY
Office

i

Atatürk Museum

Archeological Museum

CUMHURIYET
MEYDANI

Gazi Museum

İSTIKLAL CAD

19 MAYIS BUL

GAZI CAD

GAZI GEÇIDI

OSMANIYE CAD

AĞABALI CAD

BAĞDAT CAD

MESRUTIYET SOK

TALIMHANE CAD

ATATÜRK BUL

100 YIL BUL

LISE CAD

İSTIKLAL CAD

CUMHURIYET CAD

**Akyol
Lunar Park**

**Train
Station**

BLACK SEA

N

Doğu
Parkı

ÇARSAMBA CAD

Mert River

Otogar

SAMSUN

RESTAURANTS, CAFÉS & BARS	
Cumhuriyet Restaurant	1
C Bar	3
Oskar Restaurant	2
Odam Şark	4

ACCOMMODATION	
Anakent Sosyal Tesisleri	F
Büyük Samsun Oteli	B
Cem Otel	A
Otel Necmi	C
Vidinli Hotel	D
Otel Yafeya	E

0 ———— 500 m

Airport (19 km), Ordu, Giresun & Trabzon ▼

is 19km out of town on the coastal road to Trabzon and linked to the town centre by a service bus.

Samsun's **tourist office** (daily 8am–noon & 1–5pm; ☎0362/431 1228) is in a kiosk on Atatürk Bulvarı next to the Archeological Museum. The helpful English-speaking staff dispense a range of maps and booklets.

The number of **hotels** is a result of the tobacco trade rather than either tourism or prostitution. Samsun's hoteliers go to some lengths to keep their town "respectable", so single women may be asked of their intentions and couples shouldn't be surprised if they're grilled on their marital status before being given a room key. You're advised to book ahead in July, when Samsun hosts an international trade fair lasting the whole month, and possibly during the national folk-dance festival in the last week of March.

Hotels

Anakent Sosyal Tesisleri Atatürk Bul, Doğu Parkı ☎ & ☎0362/228 1470. Good-value upmarket hotel, with quiet and comfortable rooms with balconies, most overlooking the sea, plus a restaurant and tennis courts. Drivers should go past the *otogar* as if heading out of town and at the first roundabout turn back towards the centre along a

small unmarked road on the shoreside of the main road. ⑤

Büyük Samsun Oteli Atatürk Bul ☎0362/432 4999, ☎431 0740. Samsun's four-star offering, overlooking the harbour, with an outdoor pool, 24hr restaurant and "American" bar, though relatively mediocre rooms. ⑦

Cem Otel Neciphey Cad 33 ☎0362/431 1588.

Well-equipped clean and tidy business hotel with a/c and TVs in all rooms. The lobby promises more than the impersonal rooms can deliver, but good value nevertheless. ❹

![icon] **Otel Necmi** Kale Mah 6, Bedesten Sok ☎0362/432 7164. Functional and clean single, double and triple rooms with TVs, shared bathrooms and helpful, friendly staff. The lobby walls are adorned with old prints of Samsun. It's in the Tarihi Bedestan Çarşışı (Cloth Bazaar). Excellent-value budget option. ❷

Vidinli Hotel Corner of Cumhuriyet Meyd and Kazımpaşa Cad ☎0362/431 6050, ⓦwww .otelvidinli.com.tr. Three-star option with satellite TV, restaurant and terrace-bar, though charges the same for singles and doubles. ❺

Otel Yafeya Cumhuriyet Meyd ☎0362/435 1131. Best-value central three-star option, housed in an imposing building on the corner of the square. Large, comfortable rooms, bar and restaurant, and spacious air-conditioned lobby popular with businessmen conducting earnest meetings. ❹

The City

The main coastal road separates Samsun's museums from its hotels and shops. In the city centre, **Cumhuriyet Meydanı** boasts a statue of Atatürk on horseback and some wilting foliage, beneath which you'll find an uninspiring underground shopping arcade. **İstiklâl Caddesi** runs parallel with the main highway and is the heart of the new and young city, in marked contrast to the profusion of narrow and twisting sidestreets to be found clustered around the **Saat Külesi Meydanı**. The rest of the city is largely concrete, though there are a couple of unremarkable fourteenth-century mosques, Hacı Hatun Camii and Pazar Camii.

Well labelled in English, the **Archeological Museum** (Arkeoloji Müzesi; Tues–Sun 8.30am–noon & 1.30–5.30pm; 2YTL), off Atatürk Bulvarı, is probably the best place to fill time. The main exhibit is a Roman mosaic found in Karasamsun, site of the ancient acropolis (now a military area), jutting out to sea 3km to the west of Samsun. Thought to have been repaired by the Byzantines, the mosaic is almost complete, and depicts the Four Seasons and a struggle between Triton and nereids. Next door, the **Atatürk Museum** (Atatürk Müzesi; Tues–Sun 8.30am–noon & 1.30–5.30pm; 2YTL) has a large collection of weapons, clothes and photographs of Turkey's most famous citizen. The **Gazi Museum** on İstiklâl Caddesi (Gazi Müzesi; Tues–Sun 9am–5pm; 2YTL) is the former *Mintika Hotel*, where Atatürk stayed on his visit to the city in May 1919. It's now a second museum to Atatürk's memory, with his bedroom, study and the hotel's conference room all preserved as he left them.

Eating and drinking

For food and drink head for the area around Saat Külesi Meydanı, the clocktower square, where there are reasonably priced possibilities. Otherwise you can take your pick from the *kebap* joints and *pastanes* along İstiklâl Caddesi.

C Bar Corner of İstiklâl and Dr Kanil Caddesi. Despite the rather brothel-like exterior, this pub tries hard to look and feel like a traditional pub on the inside, and comes approved by the tourist board. **Cumhuriyet Restaurant** Şeyhhamza Sok 3, off Belediye Meyd. A very good local reputation for fish, *mezes* and every imaginable grilled item. A big portion of *İskender kebap* and *lahmacun* will set you back about 10YTL.

Odam Şark off İstiklâl Caddesi at Umraniye Sok 50. Small student bar/café where 20-somethings read papers by day and chill out over drinks by night.

![icon] **Oskar Restaurant** Şeyhhamza Sok 3, off Belediye Meyd. Downstairs and through a different entrance to the *Cumhuriyet*. Highly recommended for its surroundings, service and food, offering *mezes* (2.5YTL), a variety of meat and fish dishes (5YTL), and sweets to follow.

West to Gerze

Head west out of Samsun along the coast road and it soon cuts inland through extensive tobacco fields to the market town of **BAFRA**, an ugly, grimy town of around 80,000 who mostly work in the tobacco industry. There's no reason to stop, though the surrounding countryside encompasses the **Kızılırmak delta**, also called Bafra Balık Gölleri ("Bafra fish lakes"), a 56,000-hectare region of wetlands, lakes, flooded forests, reedbeds and sand dunes formed by the Kızılırmak river as it falls into the Black Sea. In the delta plain, located to the north of the Samsun–Sinop highway, over 310 bird species have been recorded (there are only 420 throughout Turkey), including pelicans, herons, storks, eagles and falcons. Over 100,000 birds spend their winters here. There is no visitor centre as yet, but there is a road that follows the course of the Kızılırmak river directly north for about 10km from Bafra right to where the mouth of the Kızılırmak river hits the sea. When driving out of Bafra, look for signs for the villages of Koşu, Karıncak and Karpuzle.

Continuing west from Bafra, the road returns to the sea, passing some stunning sandy beaches and pastoral scenery a few kilometres before **GERZE**, a pretty village with many handsome old buildings in a reasonable state of repair. Its handful of hotels – the pick of which is the *Ermiş* (no phone; ❷) overlooking the harbour – and restaurants are flanked by stony, not too crowded beaches. In the third week of July, the **Gerze Festival of Culture and Arts** is a mass circumcision of local boys, who are distracted by international folk groups, the nomination of a local beauty queen and round-the-clock revelry. Outside festival time most people will press straight on to Sinop, 26km further west, though there is a bizarre petrol station on the coast road as it runs past Gerze with over two hundred small "petting" animals – for those that may have an overpowering desire to hug a bunny.

Sinop and around

Blessed with the finest natural harbour on the Black Sea, **SINOP** straddles an isthmus at the foot of an exposed, eastward-jutting headland. The town does some justice to its fine setting, with a clutch of monuments bestowing a real authority on the place. However, it's a sleepy town, where development has not caught up with its potential as a holiday resort, despite the best efforts of the local tourist office to promote it. The port, long outstripped by those of Samsun, Trabzon and Zonguldak, is now dominated by fishing, which along with tourism provides most of the local income for the 30,000 inhabitants. This also used to be the location of a NATO listening post: the Sinop peninsula is just about the northernmost point of Anatolia, less than two hundred nautical miles from the Crimea, and this formerly US-run base played a front-line role in the Cold War.

Sinop takes its name from the mythical **Sinope**, an Amazon queen and daughter of a minor river-god. She attracted the attention of Zeus, who promised her anything she desired in return for her favours. Her request was for eternal virginity; Zeus played the gentleman and complied.

The site's natural endowments prompted Bronze Age settlement long before the city was founded as an Ionian colony during the eighth century BC. The first famous native son was **Diogenes the Cynic**: Alexander the Great is said to have visited the barrel in which he lived and been sufficiently impressed to claim, "If I were not Alexander, I would rather be Diogenes." (He had earlier asked if there was anything he could do for Diogenes, to which the cynic replied, "Yes, stand aside, you're blocking my light.")

In 183 BC the indigenous Pontic kings made Sinop one of their main cities, and later that century Mithridates Eupator, the future terror of the Roman republic, was born here. After making the city his capital, he adorned it with splendid monuments, but of these, and of the Roman structures built after the general Lucullus captured the place in 63 BC, virtually no trace remains.

Sinop declined during the Byzantine period, and sixth- and seventh-century attempts to revive the town's fortunes were thwarted by Persian and Arab raids. The Selçuks took the town in October 1214, converting a number of churches into mosques and erecting a *medrese*, but after the Mongols smashed the short-lived Selçuk state, Sinop passed into the hands of the İsfendiyaroğlu emirs of Kastamonu until Ottoman annexation in 1458. Thereafter the town was rarely heard of, except on November 30, 1853, when the Russians destroyed both Sinop and an Ottoman fleet anchored here, thus triggering the Crimean War, and again on May 18, 1919, when Atatürk passed through en route to Samsun.

Arrival, information and services

Sinop's **otogar** is adjacent to the prison, at the beginning of Cumhuriyet Cad, on the western edge of the town centre. It's either a short walk to the centre, or you can take the "Karakum" dolmuş and get off at the stop behind the *Hotel Melia ve Kasım*. Next door, just to the north of the hotel, you'll find the friendly **tourist office** (June–Aug daily 9am–11pm; ☏0368/261 5298) where, for 1.7YTL, you can buy a whole information pack on Sinop, a useful investment if you are going to stay for more than a day or two.

There are two **PTTs** in town: one on Atatürk Caddesi near the harbour, the other on Kurtuluş Caddesi (both open daily 8am–11pm for phone calls, 8.30am–5pm for full counter services).

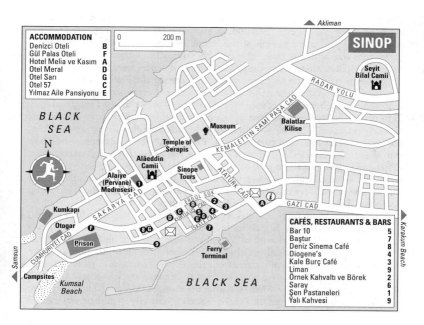

Accommodation

Sinop has a reasonable selection of town-centre **hotels**, mostly in the streets behind the harbour, but they tend to fill up in summer. In recent years many small *pansiyon*s have sprung up at Karakum beach near the large *Holiday Village*, a couple of kilometres east of the centre, though these are mostly private homes offering their spare bedroom to rent for the night and you will have to look carefully for the signs. About five minutes' walk from the *otogar* at Kumsal beach, you'll find a couple of **campsites** – *Öztürkler Kamping* (no phone; €7) and the nearby *Yuvam Dinlenme Tesisleri* (☎0368/261 7414; €6), which has a basic restaurant.

Otel 57 Kurtuluş Cad 29 ☎0368/261 5462, @otel57@hotmail.com. Another good-value place with very comfortable air-conditioned rooms with balconies. ❸

Denizci Otel Kurtuluş Cad 13 ☎0368/260 5934. One of the plushest and best-value options in town with modern tastefully decorated doubles with stylish en-suites and satellite TV. ❸

Gül Palas Oteli Cumhuriyet Cad 13 ☎0368/261 1737. Clean and presentable, monastic doubles with shared bathrooms in this quirky ramshackle old house with garden and a cheap restaurant. ❶

Hotel Melia ve Kasım Gazi Cad 49 ☎0368/261 4210, @261 1625. Old, shabby rooms in this faded palatial hotel, some with en-suite baths and TV, but suffering from the noise of the tacky *gazino* (night-club) downstairs. All have great views overlooking the sea and harbour. ❹

Otel Meral Kurtuluş Cad 1 ☎0368/261 3100. Bare but functional rooms, with or without plumbing, plus great harbour views from the smaller front rooms. Twenty-percent student discounts offered. ❷

Otel Sarı Kadir Derinboğazağzı 22 ☎0368/260 1544. Small basic doubles with standard trimmings and en suites with good views over the quieter western end of the harbour. ❸

Yılmaz Aile Pansiyonu Tersane Çarşısı 11 ☎0368/261 5752. The best-value budget option close to the water's edge with small but clean doubles with TV, basic shared bathrooms, and a kitchen for guest use. ❶

The Town

The first thing you'll notice on entering the town is a small **prison** out near the *otogar* on Sakarya Caddesi. The building was put to this use in 1882; before that it was a dockyard and a bastion of the citadel. Sinop's **city walls** are still highly prominent and, although time has inevitably taken its toll, they remain by far the most atmospheric thing about the town. The first defences were built by the original colonists back in the seventh century BC; during the Pontic kingdom more fortifications straddling the isthmus were added, and every subsequent occupier enlarged, strengthened and adapted the whole, until they reached a length of over 2km under the Byzantines. Most of the present structure dates from Byzantine/Genoese times, with Selçuk modifications. Considerable chunks are now missing, but much is still intact, in particular the **Kumkapı**, which juts out bastion-like into the sea on the northern shore. Down near the harbour, a hefty square tower offers good views out to sea (and of the development swarming up onto the headland), and you can stroll along nearby sections of wall. Watch out, though, for the vicious ravens who seem to regard this as their personal territory: they can swoop down and deliver a swift peck on the back of the head to unwary visitors.

Heading east from Kumkapı, Sakarya Caddesi leads to the **Alâeddin Camii**, a mid-thirteenth-century Selçuk mosque that's the oldest in town. Entry is via the tree-shaded courtyard with a central *şadırvan*, where a blue-painted porch lets onto a plain interior enlivened by a fine *mimber*. Behind the mosque is the **Alaiye Medresesi**, which also dates from the 1260s. The most notable feature is a marble-decorated entrance portal, relatively restrained by Selçuk standards. It's also known as the Pervane Medresesi after its founder, Mu'in al-Din Süleyman. The Selçuk sultans conferred the title of *Pervane* ("butterfly") on their viziers, and this particular chief minister became so powerful that he did away with his sovereign in 1264, ruling as the virtual autocrat of this area until dispatched in turn by the Mongols in 1278.

Heading north down one of the sidestreets at the end of Sakarya Caddesi leads to Sinop's **museum**, which has an array of objects from the Bronze Age onwards. Many of its oldest exhibits were unearthed at Kocagöz, an archeological site a few kilometres southwest of Sinop. Even though the museum is currently closed for refurbishment, some of its exhibits, including Roman amphorae and a small mosaic are perfectly visible over the small picket fence to the museum's rear. They are a reminder of the days when Sinop was an important trading centre, with ships unloading and loading wine and olive oil. Also in the museum grounds are the sparse remains of the Hellenistic **Temple of Serapis**, excavated in 1951.

Following Kemalettin Sami Paşa Caddesi onto the headland will bring you to the forlorn **Balatlar Kilise**, a ruined seventh-century Byzantine church with scant traces of frescoes inside. There are a few mosques out here, too, flanked by tombs, though only the hilltop **Seyit Bilal Camii**, with its decorative tiles, is worth seeking out.

The town beaches

Sinop's main beaches are **Kumsal**, under a kilometre southwest of the bus station, and a pay beach at **Karakum** (meaning "black sand", which is a fairly honest description). They are connected with each other, via the *otogar* and the town centre, by twice-hourly dolmuşes. Kumsal beach is smaller, and backed by untidy campsites, but the sand is lighter and the sea rather more enticing than at Karakum. The best beach on the northern side of the peninsula is **Akliman**, a twenty-minute *dolmuş* ride from town, where a fine stretch of white sand is backed by pine forests and picnic areas, but it's less frequented than the other beaches, as unpredictable currents make swimming here dangerous.

△ Sinop

Eating and drinking

For food and drink, there are plenty of options down by the harbour on İskele Caddesi. The picturesque wooden *Yalı Kahvesi* and the *Liman*, in a restored stone house next door, are the most popular of the many **teahouses**, with chairs on the waterfront and a fine view of the boats in the harbour. Further along there are several fish **restaurants** in a tightly packed row: the 🌟 *Saray* is the most popular with fresh *palamut* or salmon for 10YTL served out on little floating piers. Moored in front of the line of restaurants is the *Baştur*, a fish restaurant on a converted boat with live music most evenings. *Örnek Kahvaltı ve Börek*, at İskele Cad 1/A, serves light and delicious breakfast pastries for 1.7YTL, while the *Şen Pastaneleri* at Sakarya Cad 34 sells a wide variety of gooey desserts in air-conditioned comfort.

For a taste of local **bar** life, head for the popular but badly signposted *Diogene's Disco-Bar* next to the Ayhan boat shop off İskele Caddesi, or to the *Kale Burç Café* on top of the massive stone tower by the waterfront, which plays folk music well into the night. Another option for live music is the small and smoky *Bar 10* at Kucuklar Sok 24. Alternatively, if you're in the mood for a drink and evening **film**, check out the arty *Deniz Sinema Café* (shows at 6.30pm and 9.30pm), up a side-street north off Kurtulus Caddesi near the *Otel Meral*.

Around Sinop

If you have your own wheels, the pretty **Hamsilos bay**, 11km up the headland to the west, is worth the drive out for a swim. The bay's entrance is so narrow, it's almost a fjord. A little further west, 24km from Sinop is the **most northerly point in Turkey**. There's nothing to see except the functioning Inceburun lighthouse marking the spot, but birdwatchers may appreciate the two-kilometre-long **Sarıkum lake**, which attracts pelicans, herons and storks. The lake is separated from the sea by a ribbon of land, where (supposedly) a herd of wild horses resides.

Forty-two kilometres south of Sinop, and 14km south of the village of Efelek, lie the **Tatlıca waterfalls**. Here, twenty-eight large and small waterfalls tumble down a narrow two-kilometre valley, flanked by an attractive beech forest. Whilst some are quite dramatic, most are little more than mountain streams, but it's a lovely area and worth making a trip out for a couple of hours if you fancy a hike. The site has only just opened to tourists and has been designated a national park – though plans to develop campsites and picnic grounds here will doubtless lead to despoilation. Go while Tatlıca is still a rare untouched corner of Turkish countryside. Without any signposting the falls are almost impossible to find on your own, so the best way to visit is with the English-speaking Sinope Tours, Kibris Caddesi 3 (☏0368/261 7900), which offers a **day-trip** from Sinop, including a picnic lunch and plenty of time for rambling, for 25YTL per person.

West of Sinop: the coast to Amasra

Most public transport from Sinop heads either east towards Samsun or inland to Kastamonu. There are dolmuşes plying the little-travelled coast **west to Amasra**, but none provides a direct service. Expect to travel from village to village and change frequently. Because of this the nine hours' total driving time will probably have to be spread over two days due to infrequent departures. However, with your own vehicle the recently resurfaced roads enable you to explore the coastline's empty coves and sleepy villages at your leisure. Low mountains hedge the sea and force the road to wind around their knees. The region has always been a backwater, home in ancient times to the "barbarian" Paphlagonians and only lightly gar-risoned by the Romans. It's still thinly populated, with many residents working overseas for ten months of the year.

The coast road and the scenic but narrow inland route converge just south of Ayancık, reaching the coast again only at **HELALDI**, a pleasant fishing port with a decent beach and a couple of *pansiyons*. **ABANA**, a small resort 40km to the west, is the next place you might consider breaking the journey – a somnolent town with a decent, albeit shingly, beach.

Most, however, will press on to nearby **İNEBOLU**, the biggest place between Sinop and Amasra, but still a sleepy resort mustering only nine thousand inhabit-ants. A few isolated Ottoman houses grace the web of narrow streets, which is bisected by a river and wedged between the hills and the sea, with a long, empty shingle beach. Between the coast road and the sea, on the western approach to the centre via İsmet Paşa Caddesi, are a couple of recommended **resorts**, both with rambling beachside tea gardens where women holiday-makers sit and knit while their husbands throw pebbles into the sea: the *Huzur Motel* (☎0366 811 4502; ❷) is better value than its neighbour, *Yakamoz Tatil Köyü* (☎0366 811 4305, ℉811 3100; ❹). As for **eating and drinking**, start with a beer at the *Samata Bar* on the front next to the *Huzur Motel*, and then head to the *Liman*, a pale blue harbour building just east of town, where fish, salad and a beer will still leave you with change from 20YTL. *Root Internet Café* is a few doors along at Hacinuman Cad 38, back towards the seafront.

West of İnebolu, the cliff-top road winds its way through a succession of sleepy little havens, including Doğanyurt, İlyasbey (with two *pansiyons*), Akbayır and Çayyaka, where you might want to break your journey for an hour or so. **DOĞANYURT**, in particular, just north of the road, is well off the beaten track and worth a look for precisely that reason; it also boasts a friendly restaurant.

The constant curves mean that it takes a good two hours to drive to **CIDE**, whose town centre is actually a couple of kilometres inland: it's basically a small grid of shops with a PTT, a range of banks, an Internet café and tiny *otogar*, served by one daily direct bus to İstanbul. Most arrivals take the "Sahil" bus from the *otogar* to the harbour at the east of the shorefront esplanade and **stay** at the *Yalı Hotel* (☎0366/866 2087, ⓦwww.yaliotel.com), where there's a choice between standard en-suite rooms (❷) and better-furnished accommodation with fridges, TVs and balconies (❸); a basic restaurant downstairs serves alcohol and good *köfte*, and overlooks the quiet little harbour. The **beach** near here is pebbly but extends for nearly ten uncrowded kilometres to the west of the harbour.

GİDEROS, 15km west of Cide, is a small cluster of houses surrounded by green cliffs and makes a serene, beautiful spot to take a break. A friendly harbourside fish restaurant serves fried red mullet (*barbunya*) and can offer lodgings for the night if you get stranded. Swimming is possible from rocks next to the pretty natural har-bour, overlooked by a ruined medieval castle.

The road continues up a few steep grades and through a number of small villages with boatyards. The next popular stop is **KAPISUYU**, an idyllic village where a mountain stream enters the Black Sea. The river's bank is shaded by trees and, at its mouth, a fine stretch of sand has accumulated. It's a quiet place with just a single small *pansiyon* and restaurant, but many people camp along the beach.

Just a few kilometres ahead lies **KURUCAŞİLE**, long renowned as a boat-build-ing centre. After centuries of turning out oak-timbered fishing and cargo boats, craftsmen can still be seen hard at work on the eastbound road, making pleasure boats for customers from all over Turkey and northern Europe. The town's *Kalyon Hotel*, at İskele Cad 18, is pleasantly located on the harbour (☎ & ℉0378/518 1463; ❶), with adequately furnished rooms.

A final, slow series of switchbacks brings you to **ÇAKRAZ**, whose good beaches and scattering of *pansiyons* do little to disturb a splendid torpor. The best local strand is at **BOZKÖY**, nestled at the bottom of cliffs out of sight of the road, a couple of kilometres west. It can get crowded at holiday time, when infrequent dolmuşes on the Kurucaşile–Amasra run are jammed to sardine-can density.

Amasra

AMASRA brazenly flaunts its charms to new arrivals. Approached from any direction, the town suddenly appears below you, swarming up onto a rocky headland sheltering two bays. Amasra's historical pedigree and colourful atmosphere make it worth at least an overnight stop. During the day it is a quiet place, full of shady corners to sit and contemplate; by night it's much livelier and the old walls are lit up rather attractively, though it doesn't lose its small-town charm.

Originally called Sesamus – mentioned in Homer's *Iliad* – it was colonized by Miletus in the sixth century BC. The name Amasra derived from Queen Amastris, a lady of the court of Alexander the Great, who, after the death of her husband, acted as regent for her young son, only to be repaid with murder at his hands. The city then passed rapidly through the grip of a succession of rulers, until avid letter-writer Pliny the Younger was appointed Rome's special commissioner of the region in 110 AD. From the ninth century, after a barbarian attack, the town declined in importance, though the Byzantines maintained a garrison here. The Genoese took over when Byzantine strength began to decline, and held the city until the Ottomans assumed control in 1460.

The Town

The modern town occupies a headland; a narrow stone bridge links the main town to the island of Boztepe further out. The headland shelters the west-facing Küçük Liman (Little Harbour) on one side and the east-facing Büyük Liman (Big Harbour) on the other. Both the main town and island are scattered with stretches of ancient fortifications from two Byzantine/Genoese **castles** near the tip of the peninsula. One of these is situated in the modern town above Büyük Liman, and a short walk in this area, above the *Amasra Oteli*, reveals old cobbled streets straddled by Byzantine gateways. The other castle is reached by following Küçük Liman Caddesi across the bridge to **Boztepe**, where a ruined watchtower on a piece of land jutting out into the harbour is still visible. Boztepe's heavy-duty walls, pierced by several gates, are still largely intact. The **inner citadel** is studded with towers and the Genoese coat of arms; of the two **Byzantine churches** that you can hunt down in the maze of alleys on Boztepe, the larger was converted to a mosque after the Ottoman conquest, while the ruined smaller one was in use until 1923.

Amasra also boasts a good **museum**, located at the inland extremity of Küçük Liman (Tues–Sun 8.30am–5.30pm; 2YTL). It contains locally unearthed archeological finds, mainly from the Roman period. Pride of place is given to the torso of an emperor, with Romulus and Remus carved on his tunic, discovered in the citadel area in 1995. Eighteenth- and nineteenth-century woodcarvings demonstrate a quality of craftsmanship sorely lacking nowadays; throughout town, you'll come across the hopelessly kitsch objects – goblets, ashtrays and back-scratchers, as well as more useful kitchen utensils – which local workshops churn out by the thousand for the tourist market.

Küçük Liman across the isthmus, near the watchtower, is the most likely spot for a quick **swim** (if the jellyfish aren't too numerous). Elsewhere, the water is seriously polluted, particularly at the deceptively attractive town beach fronting the eastern fishing port, and it's best to regard Amasra as a base for forays to better beaches further east.

Practicalities

The **dolmuş and bus terminal** is near the **PTT** on the small Atatürk Meydanı, near the middle of the main part of the headland. From here everything is in easy reach, including a small **tourist information kiosk**, near the *Belediye* council building, which is open whenever they can find someone to staff it.

Accommodation

The cheapest **accommodation** is found overlooking the eastern beach on the Büyük Liman side of town, reached from Atatürk Meydanı by taking Büyük Liman Caddesi. The *Huzur Aile Pansiyon*, İskele Cad 8 (℡0378/315 1082; ❷), is a delightfully friendly, accommodating and homely place with variously sized rooms and shared bathrooms; its owner has English-speaking daughters. One block back from the eastern beach, the *Amasra Oteli* at Büyük Liman, İskele Cad 59 (℡0378/315 1007, ℻315 1722; ❹), has sea views, while the nearby *Otel Timur*, Çekiciler Cad 57 (℡0378/315 2589, ✉oteltimur@ttnet.net.tr; ❹), is deservedly popular on account of its comfortable – though dated – rooms and professional management. Just to the northeast of the main square, the bright pink *Hotel Türkili*, Özdemirhan Sok 6 (℡0378/315 3750, ✉turkilihotel@ttnet.net.tr; ❹), is plush with modern air-conditioned comfort but no views. On Cumhuriyet Meydanı, the brand new *Amastris Otel* (℡0378/315 2465, ✉amastrisotel@amasra.net; ❻) is the most opulent option in town with 21 variously sized luxury doubles, buffet breakfast, à la carte dinner menu and an enormous swimming pool. In addition, there are numerous small *pansiyon*s among the alleyways between the fortresses: pick of the bunch is the lovely *Emek* (℡0378/315 3548; ❷), practically built into the city walls on Topyanı Sokak above Büyük Liman, where you'll get clean sheets, hot water and a spectacular cliff-top view, though your early evening may be marred by the music emanating from the disco down below on the harbour. In summer you can **camp** on the harbour front, near the Bartın road, but be prepared for traffic noise.

Eating, drinking and entertainment

The *Mustafa Amca'nin Lokantasi* is easily Amasra's most colourful establishment, a 60-year-old fish **restaurant** with terraces on the water side of Küçük Liman Caddesi, with booze and *ıstavrit* (Black Sea mackerel) dished up for around 22YTL. Drop in at the *Han Bar* a few doors north for more drinking (and probably some singing) or make your way to the *Karadeniz Pide Salonu*, Hamam Sok 9, which serves up hot *pide* for 4YTL. On the eastern beach, near Büyük Liman, there are two excellent restaurants: the *Çeşmi Cihan*, a three-storey affair at the harbour entrance with wraparound balconies and commanding views (around 16YTL for fish, salad and a beer); and the smartest place in town, the *Liman Restaurant*, right on the harbour with a rooftop terrace, and an impressively long fish menu (around 12YTL per dish) including salmon (*saumon*), turbot (*kalkan*) and crayfish (*ıstakoz*), plus a bar stocked with champagne and Scotch whisky.

After dark the town takes to the streets along both harbour fronts. Büyük Liman boasts the tacky *Bedenaltı* music café near the excellent **waterside food-stalls**, while the *Nür Taverna*, a family affair, is the big draw across the headland on Küçük Liman, with traditional **music** and lots of *rakı*-induced dancing. *Bofe Bar* near the *Amastris Otel*, is the trendiest spot in town with hard house, UV lights and video screens.

Beyond Amasra

Southwest of Amasra, Highway 010 leaves the coast, dipping inland to **BARTİN**, a large town of Ottoman wooden houses (most of which are sorely in need of restoration), with superior bus connections to Safranbolu and Ankara. If you want to continue along the coast, or demand sleeper-train comfort for travelling to Ankara, you'll have to make for the provincial capital of **ZONGULDAK**, nearly 100km away. Bang in the heart of Turkey's main coal district, its high levels of air pollution make it an unappealing stopover choice.

AKÇAKOCA, well on the way to İstanbul, is a glitzy Mediterranean-style resort, with a lively promenade. It has a Genoese fortress, a seven-kilometre-long sandy beach and hotels jammed with clients from the nearby metropolis. A thirty-kilometre drive west through hazelnut groves brings you to **KOCAALİ**, with more sandy strands but no shade. Beyond Kocaalı, there's so much sand on the stretch of road to **KARASU** that the fields bordering the dunes are desert-like, and used as campsites by groups of nomads. West of Karasu, it's best to ignore Kandira in favour of Ağva or Şile, both attractive resorts with a number of accommodation possibilities.

The eastern Black Sea

The eastern coast of the Black Sea sees far more visitors than the western half, partly because there's more of interest here, partly because it's easier to get to. **Trabzon**, with its romantic associations and medieval monuments, is very much the main event and, with good plane and bus services, it makes a logical introduction to the region. It's also the usual base for visits to **Sumela monastery**, the only place in this chapter that you could describe as overwhelmed by tourists. Other forays inland, however, are just as rewarding – particularly the superlatively scenic **Hemşin valleys**, home to a welcoming, unusual people, and the northern gateway to the lofty Kaçkar Dağları, covered fully in Chapter 10.

Other than Trabzon, the coast itself between the Georgian frontier and Samsun offers little apart from fine scenery and increasingly restricted swimming opportunities – **Perşembe**, **Giresun** and **Ünye** being the most attractive and feasible bases for exploration. All this is best appreciated with your own transport, but even without this you'll face few problems. The towns are close together, served by seemingly endless relays of dolmuşes, and as just about every journey is covered, you can safely ask to be set down at an isolated beach in the near certainty that another minibus will be along to pick you up when necessary.

East of Samsun: the coast to Trabzon

Just east of Samsun, the Black Sea coastal plain, watered by the **Yeşilırmak delta**, widens to its broadest extent. The area was once thought to be the land of the **Amazons**, a mythical tribe of men-hating women who cauterized their right breasts to facilitate spear-throwing and arrow-shooting, and who only coupled with men – their neighbours the Gagarians – during two months of the year, sending male babies to the Gagarians to rear. Nowadays the delta is home to rather more conventional Black Sea Muslims, who are welcoming enough to members of either sex.

The road, slightly elevated to avoid flooding, heads well inland, across one of the most fertile patches along the coast. South of the highway, tobacco is the main crop. North of the asphalt the landscape becomes a morass of channels, copses and lagoons, teeming with wildlife pursued by the local fishermen and hunters; if you're interested in exploring, a canoe might be of more use than a car or local bus.

Ünye and around

ÜNYE, the ancient Oinaion, is a small, friendly place just over 100km east of Samsun that makes for a thoroughly pleasant overnight stay. Inland from the busy shore highway, the town has a few grand buildings dating from Byzantine times and its eighteenth-century heyday as a regional port, including a former Byzantine church that now serves as a hamam (men-only most days, women Sat) on the main square, Cumhuriyet Meydanı. The Black Sea "renovation" craze has not yet hit Ünye; its fine buildings, many of them on Kadılar Yokusu, leading uphill from just behind the church-hamam, are rotting, and most are occupied by squatters. It's worth coinciding with the burgeoning **Wednesday market**, where you'll see gold-toothed farm women selling hazelnuts (harvested in August) and unusual edible plants (described under the catch-all term of *salata*), alongside churns full of farm-produced milk and cheese.

Ünye also profits from its status as a **beach resort**. You see the best strands approaching from the west, where the highway is lined by ranks of motels and *pansiyon*s of a concentration not seen since the Aegean or the Marmara regions. The luckier of these give onto aptly named **Uzunkum** (Long Sand) beach, though signs warn you not to bathe when the sea is rough, and there's no consistent life-guard presence.

The only specific local sights are each well inland from town, reached by different roads. The medieval **fortress of Çaleoğlu**, badly signposted as "Ünye Kalesi", lies just off the minor 850 road to Niksar and Tokat. Just over 5km from the coast, turn left (south), following signs for the *Kaledibi* streamside teahouse/grill; 1.2km along, turn right at a junction and proceed 1.3km more to track's end at the base of a natural pinnacle crowned by the fortifications. The Byzantine ramparts around the south-facing gateway have been restored, but the adjacent rock-cut tomb, of Roman or Pontic-kingdom vintage, suggests that one or the other originally fortified the site. Beyond the gate little remains intact, though you can follow a slippery, usually damp path to the summit, with the final approach by steps cut into the rock and – at the last moment – a rickety ladder to scramble up. Your reward is the view south over an exceptionally lush valley, and north to the Ünye coast.

For the rock-cut **tomb of Tozkoparan**, head east out of Ünye and, just over 4km from the centre, turn south onto a minor road signposted "Tozkoparan Mezarı". Pass the giant cement plant, which employs a good many locals, and, 1.5km along, where a two-tap fountain stands by the roadside, bear right up a dead-end cement drive leading to a group of three houses. The rock-tomb stands in private land, in a low cliff at the top of the hazelnut grove behind the leftmost house; the owners are happy to point the way.

Practicalities

Ünye's minuscule **otogar** is at the eastern edge of town, by the road to Niksar; there's a separate stop for minibuses to Tokat. The usually enthusiastic **tourist** office (June–Aug daily 8am–6pm; Sept–May Mon–Fri 8am–noon & 1–5pm; ☎0452/323 4952) is housed in the ground floor of the *kaymakamlık* (county administrative offices) building at the rear of central Cumhuriyet Meydanı, though offerings are limited to a single Turkish-text leaflet with a useful sketch map.

For central **accommodation**, one of the best options is the *Hotel Grand Kuşçalı*, at Şehir Merkezi 42 (☎0452/324 5200; ❺), with modern en-suite bathrooms, an on-site *hamam* and tasty traditional meals from 8.5YTL. For beachside accommodation, continue 2km further west to Uzunkum, where the three-star *Park Hotel* (☎0452/323 2738, ℱ 323 7032; ❻) has well-equipped en-suite rooms with TVs, a pool table in the bar, and breakfast on the lawn garden. **Campers** should head for the well-equipped *Uzunkum Restaurant Plaj and Camping* (☎0452/323 2022; €6), sheltering in the pines west of the *Belediye Çamlık Motel*.

The hotels mentioned above and the campsite have **restaurants** of some sort, though you're well advised to check seafood prices beforehand at the barn-like *Belediye Çamlık*. Even in the town itself, there aren't many proper *lokanta*s or *meyhane*s: *Sofra Osmanlı Mutfağı* on the main road just before the Tokat turn-off, is worth a try, though it doesn't have sea views. Further along, the moderately-priced *Park* has a popular summer roof-terrace with a fairly limited menu of seafood, *meze*s and grills, and is the only "family" restaurant serving alcohol.

East to Ordu

At **BOLAMAN**, the ancient Polemon, 10km east on the same bay, the so-called "castle" of the Haznedaroğlu clan overlooks the harbour. The clan, de facto rulers of the area during the eighteenth and nineteenth centuries, called themselves the governors of Trabzon, in defiance of the Ottomans. A wood superstructure, whose restoration is indefinitely stalled, perches atop a Byzantine/Genoese fortress. Tiny Bolaman merits a stop if you're in your own vehicle: alongside the castle, the pretty harbour is fringed by Ottoman houses, the beach is set back from the busy road, and there are a couple of restaurants and a tea garden.

The coast highway winds on northeastwards past more sandy coves to an inconspicuous sign at Yalıköy pointing towards **Yason**, a cape where mariners once sacrificed at a temple of Jason (the Argonaut) before venturing further on the temperamental waters of the Black Sea. The temple was replaced in due course by a medieval church, 500m off the road, still well preserved except for a chunk missing out of the dome.

Once past Yason, the scenery regains the drama of the stretch between Sinop and Amasra, as the hills tumble down directly into the water. **ÇAKA** has one of the eastern Black Sea's prettiest white-sand, forested beaches – **Beyzakum** – but there's no place to sleep overnight indoors, only Turkish-style *kamping*s next to restaurants hiding under the mulberry trees.

Just the other side of Çam Burnu sprawls **PERŞEMBE**, a pretty fishing port where the two-star *Hotel Vona* (☎0452/517 1755; ❹) fronts a small beach just east of town. With fair-sized, well-furnished rooms, all with balconies and sea views, and its own pool and playground, it's a surprisingly upmarket establishment for such a small town.

Ordu

Called Kotorya by the ancients, **ORDU** is now an undistinguished city of 117,000, with just a few older houses scaling the green slopes of Boztepe to the west, above the recently restored nineteenth-century Greek Orthodox cathedral. The only other historic remnants are in the **museum** in the Paşaoğlu Konağı (daily 8am–5pm; 2YTL), signposted off Hükümet Caddesi, past the main PTT. Once home to a leader of the Muslim immigrants fleeing the Caucasus in 1877–1878, this typical example of nineteenth-century Black Sea architecture is well worth a look if you have the time. Downstairs there's a fairly dull museum of ethnography, but upstairs the two bedrooms and their original furnishings have been beautifully restored. Ordu is best known, however, for its hazelnut-in-chocolate products: there's a whole shop full of the stuff, called **Sağra Nuthouse**, at Süleyman Felek Cad 95, the road that runs parallel to Atatürk Bulvarı and perpendicular to Hükümet Caddesi.

The **otogar** is 2km east of the centre on the Trabzon-bound highway, while the **tourist office** (summer Mon–Sat 8.30am–noon & 1–5.30pm; winter Mon–Frii 8.30am–noon & 1–5.30pm; ☎0452/223 2593) is located in the *Belediye* building a little to the east of the Atatürk statue, also on the main highway (called Atatürk Bulvarı while threading through the town centre).

There are few really appealing or decent-value **hotels** in or around Ordu. The outstanding exception, just uphill from the Greek cathedral, is the *Karlıbel İkizevler Hotel* (☎0452/225 0081, ℱ223 2483; ❺), occupying two surviving old mansions. Both the smaller doubles and larger suites (sleeping three) offer wooden floors and good bathrooms with shower cubicles. A cheaper, passably comfortable alternative is the basic two-star *Turist Otel*, Atatürk Bul 134 (☎0452/225 3140, ℱ214 1950; ❹), some of whose rooms have balconies and sea views.

Stopping for **lunch** is probably more rewarding than staying the night. Dead central, at Atatürk Bul 1, opposite the great man's monument, stands *Ayışığı*, a combined restaurant and events centre; local dishes, based for example on chard and beets, are served, while events include an annual Volkswagen-bug rally.

Giresun

A nautical mile or so off the coast of **GIRESUN**, the second-century BC foundation of the Pontic king Pharnaces, lies **Giresun Adası**, the only major island in the Black Sea. In pre-Christian times it was called Aretias, and was sacred to the Amazons who dedicated a temple to the war god Ares on it. Jason and his Argonauts supposedly stopped here to offer sacrifice, but were attacked by vicious birds. The islet is still the venue for fertility rites on May 20, dating back four thousand years to the celebration of Priapus and Cybele, respectively the phallic god and Anatolian mother goddess, and described in one 1990s tourist-office handout as a festival of "abundance and male pro-creative power". Any village woman who doesn't have babies yet is ritually passed through a trivet (a hoop-like affair on legs); this is followed by a boat tour of the island for a large part of the population of Giresun, and then pebbles (representing troubles and misfortunes) are cast into the sea. Finally, upon return to the mainland, general inebriation ensues.

East to Trabzon

Curled above a bay enclosed by two headlands 41km east of Giresun, **TİREBOLU** is an attractive spot. A Greek Orthodox community until 1923, it's virtually unique hereabouts in not having been entirely overrun by concrete atrocities. On the easterly promontory stands the intact **castle of St John**, built for a fourteenth-century Genoese garrison: your only chance to see the fort's interior is by visiting the nocturnal tea-garden that operates on the lawn inside the castle – pleasant except for the blaring pop music. As well as Tirebolu's central *Belediye* **beach**, there's a much larger if more exposed sandy stretch to the east, plus more decent beaches around Espıye, 12km west.

Tirebolu lies at the heart of the *fındık*- or **hazelnut-growing** area, which extends roughly from Samsun east to the Georgian frontier. During late July and August you'll see vast mats of them, still in their husks, raked out to dry. Impatient locals perversely insist on eating them slightly green, when the taste resembles that of acorns.

East of Tırebolu you'll see more of the numerous **castles** built, mostly by the Genoese but occasionally by the Byzantines, during the thirteenth and fourteenth centuries to protect the sea approaches to Trabzon. One well-preserved stronghold lurks 15km inland, up the Harşit Çayıat Bedrama; this river, just east of Tırebolu, marks the furthest line of advance by the Tsarist army in 1916.

Nearby **GÖRELE** boasts a fine collection of Black Sea houses, though it's only really worth the effort for buffs of vernacular architecture with their own cars. The town's name is an obvious corruption of nearby Coralla citadel, just before Eynesil.

Another Byzantine castle at **AKÇAKALE**, close to the road, is the best preserved between Tırebolu and Trabzon; the fortress on **Fener Burnu** is less obvious. In addition to fortresses, there's a final flurry of wide beaches – especially between Vakfıkebir and Fener Burnu – but they're generally unshaded and functional at best.

Trabzon

No other Turkish city except İstanbul has exercised such a hold on the Western imagination as **TRABZON** (ancient Trebizond). Travel-writers from Marco Polo to Rose Macaulay have been enthralled by the fabulous image of this quasi-mythical metropolis, long synonymous with intrigue, luxury, exotic customs and fairy-tale architecture. Today the celebrated gilded roofs and cosmopolitan texture of Trebizond are long gone, replaced by the blunt reality of an initially disappointing Turkish provincial capital of over 200,000 people. But a little poking around the cobbled alleyways will still turn up tangible evidence of its former splendour – not least the monastic church of **Aya Sofya**, home to some of the most outstanding Byzantine frescoes in Anatolia.

Some history

The city was founded during the eighth century BC by colonists from Sinope and Miletus, who settled on the easily defensible bluff isolated by today's Kuzgun and Tabakhane ravines. From the promontory's flat summit – *trapeza* or "table" in ancient Greek – came the new town's original name, Trapezus, and all subsequent variations. Under the Romans and Byzantines the city continued to prosper, thanks to extensive patronage by Hadrian and Justinian, and its location at the northeast end of a branch of the Silk Route.

Trabzon's romantic allure is derived almost totally from a brief, though resplendent, **Golden Age** during the thirteenth and fourteenth centuries. A scion of the royal Komnenos line, Alexios, managed to escape the Crusaders' sacking of Constantinople in 1204; shortly after, he landed at Trebizond in command of a Georgian army and proclaimed himself the legitimate Byzantine emperor. Despite the fact that there were two other pretenders, one in Epirus and the other at Nicaea (it was the latter's descendants who eventually retook Constantinople), it was the pint-sized Trapezuntine Empire that was arguably the most successful.

The empire owed its unlikely longevity to a number of factors. Mongol raiders of the mid-thirteenth century swept across the Middle East, accentuating the city's importance by forcing the main Silk Route to divert northward through Tabriz, Erzurum and ultimately Trebizond. The empire's diplomats, hampered by few scruples and with the survival of the state as their only aim, arranged short- and long-term alliances with assorted Turcoman and Mongol chieftains manoeuvring at the borders. In this they were aided by the preternatural beauty of the Komneni princesses, who were given in marriage to any expedient suitor, Christian or Muslim. Accordingly, garbled tales of Christian princesses languishing in the grasp of the infidel reached Western Europe and, among other literature, apparently inspired Don Quixote's quest for Dulcinea.

Someone had to transport all the goods accumulated at Trebizond's docks and this turned out to be the **Genoese**, followed soon after by the Venetians as well. Each demanded and got the same maritime trading privileges from the Trapezuntine Empire as they did from the re-established empire at Constantinople. Western ideas and personalities arrived continually with the Latins' boats, making Trebizond an unexpected island of art and erudition in a sea of Turkish nomadism, and a cultural rival to the Italian Renaissance city-states of the same era.

Unfortunately, the empire's factional politicking was excessive even by the standards of the age. In this respect they managed to outdo even the Medicis, lending extreme meaning to the disparaging adjective "Byzantine". The native aristocracy fought frequent pitched battles with transplanted courtiers from Constantinople, and the Italian contingents rarely hesitated to make it a three- or even four-sided fray. One such civil war in 1341 completely destroyed the city and sent the empire into its final decline.

It was Mehmet the Conqueror, in a campaign along the Black Sea shore, who finally put paid to the self-styled empire; in 1461 the last emperor, David, true to Trapezuntine form, negotiated a more or less bloodless surrender to the sultan. Under the Ottomans the city became an important training ground for future rulers: Selim the Grim, while still a prince, served as the provincial governor between 1490 and 1512, and his son Süleyman the Magnificent was born and reared here until his accession in 1520. Given these early imperial associations and the sultans' vigorous local Turkification programme, Trabzon, as it was renamed, was and still is a relatively devout place.

In late Ottoman times the city's Christian element enjoyed a resurgence of both population and influence. The presence of a rich merchant class justified the foundation of numerous European consulates in Trabzon and a spate of sumptuous civic and domestic building. But it was a mere echo of a distant past, soon ended by a decade of world and civil war and the foundation of the Republic. Shipping dwindled after the construction of the railway between Ankara and Erzurum and roads beyond into Iran.

Today the outlook is still uncertain: though there was a brief boom during the Iran–Iraq war, both port and town have been overtaken by Samsun to the west. Trabzon now makes much of its living as a transshipment point for lorries taking goods to the recently independent Caucasian republics.

Arrival, orientation and information

Trabzon's **airport** is 7km away at the eastern edge of town, connected by frequent dolmuşes to a town-centre stop near the *Horon Oteli*; the **otogar** is closer, 3km out, near the junction of Highway 010 with Route E97/885 (heading towards Sumela and Erzurum) and served by dolumşes marked "Meydanı". All services, whether long-distance coaches or short-hop minibuses, use this terminal now that the old mid-town minibus stand has been abolished. **Parking** is a trial anywhere in congested Trabzon – the closest legal car park to the centre is near the İskender Paşa Camii.

All roads converge on **Atatürk Alanı**, usually called "Meydanı" or "Parkı". This tree-shaded square is the hub of both Trabzon's social life, most of the hotel

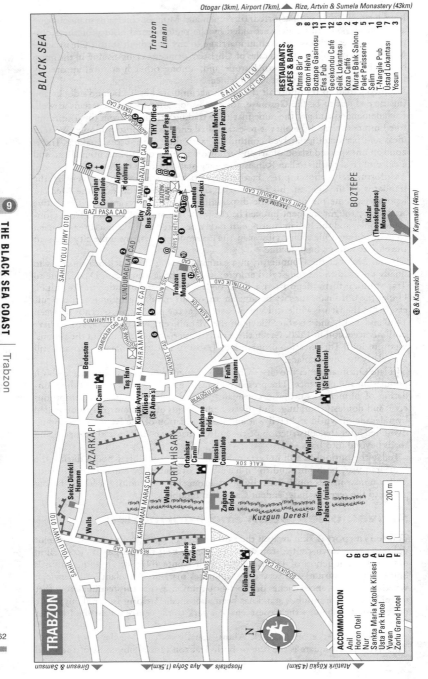

Otogar (3km), Airport (7km), ▲ Rize, Artvin & Sumela Monastery (43km)

TRABZON

BLACK SEA

Trabzon Limani

RESTAURANTS, CAFES & BARS

Altmıs Bir'a	9
Beton Helva	8
Boztepe Gasinosu	13
Efes Pub	11
Gecekondu Café	12
Gelik Lokantası	6
Koza Caffé	2
Murat Balık Salonu	4
Palet Patisserie	5
Selim	1
T-Nargile Pub	10
Üstad Lokantası	7
Yosun	3

SAHİL YOLU

ÇÖMLEKÇİ CAD

İSKELE CAD

HALKEVİ CAD

HYV Office

İskender Paşa Camii

Russian Market (Avrasya Pazarı)

Georgian Consulate

Airport dolmuş

SIRAMAGAZALAR CAD

ATATÜRK ALANI

Sumela dolmuş-taxi

GAZİ PAŞA CAD

City Bus Stop

ŞEHİT SANİ AKBULUT CAD

TAKSİM CAD

BOZTEPE

Kızlar (Theoskepastos) Monastery

Kaymaklı (4km)

SAHİL YOLU (HWY 010)

KUNDURACILAR CAD

KIBRIS ŞEHİTLERİ CAD

UZUN SOK

KAHRAMAN MARAŞ CAD

Trabzon Museum

KAZIM SOK

ZEYTİNLİK CAD

ORDU CAD

& Kaymaklı

CUMHURİYET CAD

SEMERCİLER CAD

SUME CAD

HÜKÜMET CAD

Bedesten

Taş Han

Çarşı Camii

Küçük Ayvasıl Kilisesi (St Anne's)

Fatih Hamamı

Yeni Cuma Camii (St Eugenius)

PAZARKAPI

Sekiz Direkli Hamam

Walls

Walls

KAHRAMAN MARAŞ CAD

BILALOĞLU SOK

Ortahisar Camii

Tabakhane Bridge

Russian Consulate

ORTAHİSAR

Walls

KALE SOK

Walls

Byzantine Palace (ruins)

Zağnos Bridge

Kuzgun Deresi

200 m

0

SAHİL YOLU (HWY 010)

REŞADİYE CAD

Zağnos Tower

ZAĞNOS CAD

Gülbahar Hatun Camii

SÖĞÜKSU CAD

N

ACCOMMODATION

Anıl	C
Horon Oteli	B
Nur	G
Sankta Maria Katolik Kilisesi	A
Usta Park Hotel	E
Yuvan	D
Zorlu Grand Hotel	F

choices plus endless dolmuş, bus and taxi traffic. Major bus-company ticket-offices also congregate at the corners of the square. Most of Trabzon's sights are within walking distance of Atatürk Alanı, though you'll need a dolmuş (here often a saloon car rather than a minibus) to get to Aya Sofya, and a bus or taxi to reach the Kaymaklı monastery behind Boztepe.

From Atatürk Alanı, İskele Caddesi winds down to the port, while the city's two major longitudinal avenues lead west towards the old town. **Kıbrıs Şehitler Caddesi**, becoming **Uzun Sokak**, the pre-Republican high street, cobbled and narrow, heads off from the southwest corner, **Kahraman Maraş Caddesi** (shortened in addresses to Maraş Caddesi), the modern boulevard carrying most traffic, from the northwest corner. **Taksim Caddesi** (also known as Şehit Sani Akbulut Caddesi) leads from the southeast angle up toward **Boztepe**, the hill dominating Trabzon.

Information

The **tourist office** (March–Aug daily 8am–7pm; Sept–Feb Mon–Fri 8am–5pm; ☏0462/326 0748) is located on a sidestreet just east of Atatürk Alanı, opposite the İskender Paşa Camii. The staff here are friendly, helpful and English speaking. They keep a broad range of fairly useful brochures to hand, are eager to suggest excursions into the mountains (particularly *yayla*-based tourism) and, crucially, can advise if any of the city's hotels have slid down the slippery slope to brotheldom.

Accommodation

Given Trabzon's status as the first major stopoff after the ex-Soviet border, many of the city's hotels spent the 1990s doubling as brothels. This activity has been relatively subdued of late, but could revive in the future. The traditional red-light district lies along İskele Caddesi and the streets immediately off it, right down to the port; Güzelhisar Caddesi just west is more wholesome. **Hotels** on the latter street that we've mentioned below are reputable, though single women may want to choose a hotel in a more salubrious area.

Trabzon is a big, gritty, bustling city, with many new arrivals initially repulsed by the traffic, noise and subtropical mugginess. Atatürk Alanı is the heart of the city, home to many of its hotels, nightclubs, restaurants and tourist sights, as well as being the main transport hub for attractions further afield such as Sumela; staying near here will help make Trabzon a surprisingly straightforward and hassle-free base. That said, if you have transport, you might consider more peaceful stopovers on the way to Sumela, at Uzungöl or between Maçka and the Zigana Pass. And in midsummer, you may have to stay elsewhere, as the more comfortable lodgings in Trabzon are often block-booked by tour groups.

Anil Güzelhisar Cad 12 ☏0462/326 7282. Best of the cheapies with clean, small, plain rooms with TV. Sea breeze (and coast-road noise) in lieu of air conditioning. Attractive ground-floor breakfast salon, and help with arranging excursions. **3**

Horon Oteli Sıramağazalar Cad 125 ☏0462/326 6455, ⓦwww.otelhoron.com. Don't be scared off by the plush lobby and rack rates aimed at business customers – staff readily offer big reductions, even in summer. Rooms are furnished in style, with superior new bathrooms, air conditioning and double glazing. Also a large if rather spartan rooftop sea-view bar/restaurant, relatively easy street

parking, and nearby car-parks. **5**

Nur Cami Sok 15 ☏0462/323 0445, ⓕ323 0447. Small, well-worn but decently equipped rooms with fridge, TV and double glazing. Good-natured management, used to foreign guests. **4**

Sankta Maria Katolik Kilisesi Sümer Sok 28 ☏0462/321 2192. The most characterful and cheapest place to stay in Trabzon is this French Capuchin church and monastery, built around two courtyards just north of Atatürk Alanı. The welcoming voluntary staff offer spacious double rooms and hot showers down the hall to guests of any religion in return for a reasonable donation (say 15–30YTL) at the end of a visit; kitchen, washing machine and garden are all available, free of charge.

Usta Park Hotel İskenderpaşa Mah 3 ℡0462/326 5700, ℻326 5700. Large, modern, plush hotel with impressive plasma-screened lobby and 120 luxury en-suite rooms with all the trimmings you'd expect. Pricey (rooms start at €115), but discounts of up to 25 percent are easily negotiable. ❸

Yuvan Güzelhisar Cad 10B ℡0462/326 6823. A plain, if clean and apparently *natasha*-free, en-suite cheapie, probably as basic as you'll want to

be in Trabzon. ❷

Zorlu Grand Hotel Maraş Cad 9 ℡0462/326 8400, ⊛www.zorlugrand.com. Rooms are plush, with marble-clad bathrooms, but you're really paying for the facilities – especially the grand, opulent atrium, two restaurants, "English pub", nightclub, gym and indoor pool. Rack rates (€143 a room) are massively overpriced, but advance booking/ bargaining may produce discounts. Nonresidents can breakfast in the atrium for €11. ❽

The City

Trabzon straggles along the coast and penetrates inland for several kilometres, presenting you with the choice of short rides or substantial walks to get to many points of interest – a characteristic aggravated by the modern city centre being a full kilometre from the ancient and medieval focus of settlement. On foot, you can see most of the in-town sights in a day; the suburban monuments require both extra time and use of public transport for access. If time is limited, concentrate on the two remote monasteries of Aya Sofya and Kaymaklı.

Around Atatürk Alanı and Uzun Sokak

An east-to-west walk along the seaward portion of town begins unpromisingly: the Genoese bastion straddling the coast highway tunnel, approached along Güzel-hisar Caddesi, is an officers' club, off-limits to the public; detour slightly left instead, to the flyover taking you to a tea garden and small park on the west flank of the castle. This seems to be Trabzon's sole acknowledgement of its seaside location, since – apart from the Russian market – the shoreline in general is amazingly dead, with the city introverted up on its plateau. The **Catholic church of Sankta Maria** (Tues–Sun 2–3pm), a few alleys west of the ramparts, is the last surviving reminder of the western powers' former pivotal role here.

If you visit one **Russian market** on the Black Sea it should be that of Trabzon, which – labelled "Avrasya Pazar" – occupies a long covered area at the foot of the cliff occupied by the İskender Paşa Camii. The nominal entrance fee will be waived if they realize you're not Turkish: hard currency is always welcome. Stalls display a wide variety of Eastern European memorabilia, from interesting *matryushka* dolls, balalaika maestros immortalized on vinyl to the more prosaic pirate DVDs (sadly, the sale of vodka is forbidden in the Russian markets).

Shifting northwest of Atatürk Alanı, pedestrianized **Kunduracılar Caddesi** (Shoemakers' Street) is the usual entry to Trabzon's **bazaar**. Ironically just about everything *except* shoes can be found on this avenue, with a special emphasis first on pharmacies and doctors, then gold jewellery. Once past Cumhuriyet Cad-desi, Kunduracılar veers right to become **Semerciler Caddesi** (Saddlers' Street), devoted to a mix of factory-made clothing and the vibrantly coloured, striped *keşans* (shawls) and *peştemals* (waistbands) that are standard issue for so many Trabzon-province women. Copper merchants and tin-platers cluster on and just off Alacahan Sokak, which leads downhill from Semerciler to the water.

Sooner or later you'll stumble upon the monumental heart of the bazaar, and the **Çarşı Camii**, Trabzon's largest mosque, with a handsome exterior, but garish late-Ottoman interior. Just behind it, the sixteenth-century **Taş Han** is a rather stand-ard tradesmen's hall, still the location of retail outlets and (inside the courtyard) tailors' workshops. The **Bedesten**, below the mosque, was built by the Genoese in the fourteenth century, and revamped by the Ottomans. Although it looks square from the outside, the interior is actually octagonal, but the four pillars were evidently insufficient to support the dome, which has long since fallen in. After decades of dereliction, and use as a lumber mill, the *bedesten* has been restored as a somewhat touristy crafts bazaar, with a small café-restaurant on the top floor.

Leave the bazaar going uphill, cross Kahraman Maraş Caddesi, and you can't miss the ninth-century Byzantine **Küçük Ayvasil Kilisesi** just the other side. Also known as St Anne's, the diminutive shrine is permanently locked – little matter as its frescoes have been obliterated since 1923. A stroll along Uzun Sokak, lying to the southeast and dotted with imposing *belle époque* mansions, may be more satisfying. There's no real concentration of old houses in Trabzon; the appeal of leisurely strolling lies partly in the unexpected confrontation with a creaking masterpiece on an otherwise unremarkable block.

One of the best examples of this is the Italian-designed Kostaki Theophylaktos Konağı, just south of Uzun Sokak on Zeytinlik Caddesi, now housing the **Trabzon Museum** (Trabzon Müzesi; Tues–Sun 9.30am–noon & 1–5.30pm; 2YTL). The ground-floor rooms, with their parquet floors, painted ceilings, fancy drapes and plush armchairs give a good idea of life amongst the *belle époque* Ottoman bourgeoisie. There's a rather perfunctory ethnographic collection upstairs, while the basement is devoted to the archeological collection, where pride of place is given to a complete but slightly crushed bronze, life-sized statue of Hermes. This was found during excavations in 1997, smashed into several pieces by a fallen column on the grounds of his presumed temple in the Tabakhane district, and meticulously reassembled.

The old town

Following Uzun Sokak further west soon brings you to the **Tabakhane Deresi** (Tannery Ravine) and the namesake bridge spanning it. On the other side sprawls the fortified old town on its "table", but before crossing you should make a detour left along the east bank of the ravine, being careful to bear onto **Bilaloğlu Sokak** (from the bridge, follow the hamam sign and then take a sharp right at the first turning – there is a street sign but it's hard to spot), away from markers pointing to the Fatih Hamamı. After about 350m you'll come to the thirteenth-century **Yeni Cuma Camii**, formerly the church of St Eugenius, patron saint of Trabzon. There may have been a shrine of sorts here as early as the third century, when Eugenius disrupted the cult of Mithra at Boztepe and was martyred by Diocletian for his pains. As so often happened in these cases, his skull was found on the spot within a few years of the arrival of a new ruler, Alexios Komnenos, and the present church was erected to house the holy relic. The saint's intervention supposedly spared the city from the Selçuks in 1222, but he let the side down in 1461; Mehmet the Conqueror offered up his first Friday prayers here after capturing Trabzon, and immediately reconsecrated the church and added its minaret. You'll need to time your visit to the plain but relatively undisturbed interior around the daily cycle of prayers.

Crossing the Tabakhane bridge you arrive in the **Ortahisar** (Middle Castle) district of the old town; further upstream, at the steepest point of the gullies flanking it, is the upper citadel, while below, tumbling off the tableland, sprawls the less defensible lower town, huddled behind a third circuit of walls that reach the sea. The walls are in variable condition but at their crenellated and vine-shrouded best give some idea of Trabzon's skyline in its heyday.

The highlight of Ortahisar is the former church of Panayia Khrysokefalos, now the **Ortahisar Camii** (usually open) and also referred to as the Fatih Camii. As in the case of the Yeni Cuma Camii, there was almost certainly a church on this site from the third century, but the present building dates mostly from the thirteenth, with massive renovation after a fire during the 1341 civil war. This was the main cathedral of the Trapezuntine Empire, and most royal weddings, funerals and coronations took place here; the epithet *Khrysokefalos* or "Golden-Headed" recalls the zenith of the dynasty, when the Komneni could afford to plate the dome with gold. This is, of course, long vanished and the Byzantine frescoes inside, smothered under layers of Islamic whitewash, and a thirteenth-century mosaic floor, cemented over during the 1980s, are equally unavailable for viewing, though some fine Byzantine *opus sectile* stonework remains visible in the apse. Today it's the volume of the soaring basilica, with its massive interior columns, that impresses.

From the apse end of the former church you can bear south, uphill, about 400m along Kale Sokağı, through a gateway astride the street, to enter the upper citadel. Of the glittering Komnenos **Byzantine palace**, in the southwest corner of the highest terrace overlooking the Kuzgun Deresi (Raven Canyon), nothing is left but battered masonry. From the eastern ramparts, dominating the Tabakhane Deresi, there's a fine view across to the Yeni Cuma Camii. Some careful navigating could get you through the maze of shacks and market gardens in the ravine bottom and up the other side.

Heading west from Ortahisar Camii, the **Zağnos bridge**, built by a Greek convert who was one of Mehmet the Conqueror's chief generals, leaves Ortahisar over the Kuzgun ravine where dilapidated Greek mansions are steadily losing ground to contemporary tenements. On the far side, the **Zağnos tower**, the southernmost dungeon in the outer boundary walls, sports the ornate, late-Ottoman, Abdullah Paşa fountain at its base.

Across a busy boulevard and a swathe of parkland from the tower squats the **Gülbahar Hatun Camii**, the most important Ottoman monument in Trabzon. However, its background is more fascinating than the run-of-the-mill mosque you see now. The mother of Selim I and wife of Beyazit II – known in later life as *Gülbahar* or "Spring Rose" – was originally a Komneni princess famous for her piety and good works among Christians and Muslims alike. She died in 1512, the first year of Selim's reign, and he completed the mosque and her adjoining tomb by 1514.

From just in front of the Gülbahar Hatun complex, Soğuksu Caddesi heads up toward the finest surviving example of the palatial bourgeois follies that sprouted locally at the end of the nineteenth century.

The Atatürk Köşkü

Set in immaculately maintained gardens, the **Atatürk Köşkü**, or Atatürk Villa (daily 8am–5pm; 2YTL), began life in 1903 as the property of the Greek banker Karayannidhis, who was obliged to abandon it two decades later. Atatürk stayed here on the first of three occasions in 1924, and the city formally presented it to him a year before his death. As another example of patrician Black Sea architecture, the mansion is more compelling than the contents – which include a bevy of photos of Atatürk, plus a map bearing his strategic scribbles during the Kurdish Dersim revolt of 1937.

Both dolmuşes to the "Köşk" stop and red-and-white city buses marked "Park-Köşk" serve the villa – which is 6.5km southwest of Atatürk Alanı. You can also catch the bus as it passes Gülbahar Hatun.

Aya Sofya

Alone on a park-like bluff overlooking the Black Sea west of the city, the monastery **church of Aya Sofya** (Haghia Sophia) is one of the most romantic set of Byzantine remains, and even the fact that Trabzon's suburbs have long since overtaken it does little to detract from the appeal. It seems certain that there was a pagan temple here, and then an early Byzantine chapel, long before Manuel I Komnenos commissioned the present structure between 1238 and 1263. The ground plan and overall conception were revolutionary at the time, successfully assimilating most of the architectural trends, Christian and Muslim, prevalent in contemporary Anatolia. Aya Sofya's role as a model for many later Byzantine churches will be evident if you've already seen St Saviour in Hora (Kariye Camii) or the Pammakaristos church (Fethiye Camii) in İstanbul. Converted to a mosque after 1461, Aya Sofya subsequently endured some even leaner and more ignominious times as an ammunition store and then as a hospital. Between 1957 and 1964, technicians working under the supervision of David Talbot Rice and David Winfield rescued the building from certain oblivion, in particular restoring dozens of frescoes to their former glory. Well lit and accurately labelled in English, these are compulsory viewing even if you've only a passing interest in religious art.

From Atatürk Alanı numerous **dolmuşes** labelled "BLK Sigorta/Aya Sofya" cover most of the 3km to the monument, dropping you 300m south of Aya Sofya, with the way onwards fairly well signed.

The site

The **church** (April–Oct daily 9am–6pm; Nov–Feb Tues–Sun 8am–4pm; March Tues–Sun 8am–5pm; 2YTL) is laid out along a greatly modified cross-in-square scheme, with a dome supported by four columns and three apses at the east end of the triple nave. At the west end of the building a narthex extends across the full width of the nave; barrel-vaulted porticoes adorn the north, west and south sides of the exterior. Before rushing inside to view the famous frescoes, take a moment to study the finely sculpted, albeit weatherworn, **frieze** illustrating *Adam and Eve in the Garden of Eden*, which surrounds the south portal, the only one of the three not tampered with by the Ottomans when they reconsecrated the church.

△ Aya Sofya, Trabzon

This relief work is the most obvious evidence of the strong Armenian, Georgian and even Assyrian influence on the craftsmen – who left, in lieu of signature, the single-headed eagle of the Komnenos dynasty over the biblical work of art.

In their fluidity, warmth and expressiveness, Aya Sofya's **frescoes** represented a drastic break with the rigidity of prior painting, and compare well with the best work of their century, and the next, in Serbia and Macedonia as well as in Constantinople itself. The most important compositions are in the apse and the narthex, as well as in the north porch – which many people miss.

In the central **apse** a serene *Ascension* hovers over *The Virgin Enthroned* between the two Archangels; on the north wall of the same apse appears *The Miraculous Draught of Fishes*. The southeast apse is thought to have once been the location of Manuel I's tomb. The Pantocrator in the **dome** was unhappily beyond repair, but a host of angels swirls around him, just above the Apostles.

The **narthex**, whose ceiling is divided into three sections by stone ribs, is almost wholly devoted to scenes from the life of Christ. The central zone exploits its complicated quadruple vaulting by depicting each of the Tetramorphs, symbols of the Evangelists, accompanied by seraphim. Alongside, such miraculous episodes as *The Wedding at Cana*, a decidedly adolescent *Child Jesus Teaching in the Temple*, *Healing the Blind Man at Siloam* and *Healing the Canaanite's Daughter* (complete with vomited demon) fill the south vault, while *Feeding the Five Thousand* and *Calming the Storm on the Lake of Galilee* grace the north vault. The north portico is taken up mostly by Old Testament scenes, including *The Sufferings of Job* and *Jacob's Dream*.

Just north of the church an ensemble of sunken masonry was once the baptismal font; the square belfry to the west is a 1443 afterthought, indicative of the strong Italianate flavour of the waning empire. If the tower is open – a rare event – you'll find that the frescoes within are not nearly of the same quality as those in the church proper.

In the garden opposite the ticket office is a small **museum** (same days and hours as Aya Sofya; separate 2YTL admission), consisting of a village house built and furnished in typical Black Sea style, and a 1920s-vintage *serender* or grain crib on stilts, with wooden disks at the top of the stilts, to prevent mice attacking the stored grain. A pleasant adjacent café offers light snacks and drinks.

Boztepe

Boztepe, the hill dominating Trabzon to the southeast, has always been held in religious esteem. In the past it was the site of the amalgamated cults of the Persian sun-god Mithra and the Hellenic deity Apollo, an ironic dedication when you consider how little unfiltered sun this coast receives. This reverence persisted into Christian times, when the hill was studded with churches and monasteries. Two of the latter still stand – after a fashion – and one at least is well worth the effort to visit.

Theoskepastos Convent

The ruined former **Convent of the Panayia Theoskepastos** or "God-protected Virgin" (in Turkish, Kızlar Manastırı) backs into the rocky slope 1.5km from Atatürk Alanı, reached by following Taksim Caddesi south and then bearing left when you see the shell of the building on the hillside. Dolmuşes marked "Boztepe" leave from Atatürk Alanı.

Though founded in the fourteenth century, and in continuous use by the Greek Orthodox Church until 1923, few internal frescoes or other artistic details remain, and in any case the place has been securely locked since the early 1990s while the Ministry of Culture deliberates how or whether to restore it. Just above the convent an appealing picnickers' park, a tea garden and a single restaurant (see "Eating" below) share the view over the city with a military base and the locked **mosque and tomb of Ahi Evren Dede**, a target of pilgrimage for Trabzon's faithful.

Kaymaklı monastery

The former Armenian **Kaymaklı monastery** (dedicated to the Saviour), reached by a 900m side-track 3.5km beyond the turn-off for Theoskepastos, is in an altogether different league, containing as it does the finest frescoes in the region after those of Aya Sofya and Sumela. It's too far to walk, so take a taxi, or a bus marked "Çukurçayır" from Atatürk Alanı. The bus will drop you at the Mısırlı Cami, out by the local prison on the flat summit of Boztepe; 100m past the mosque, turn left (east) and down onto an unsigned but paved lane. Bear right at a fork 250m along, then keep right again a similar distance along, soon reaching concrete's end next to an ugly green-and-cream house with a garage underneath. When the ground is dry you can continue by vehicle another 150m along dirt track to the proper "car park" in the centre of a farmyard.

What's left of Kaymaklı studs a green plateau overlooking the highway to Erzurum; today the monastery grounds are a farm, and the resident family is used to showing visitors around. Much of the place dates from the mid-fifteenth century, though more recent tenants have wedged a concrete dwelling into the former cells on the east edge of the courtyard. The subsidiary chapel or baptistry is bare, but the main *katholikon* is a marvel, its interior protected until the early 1990s by its use as a hay barn. Today, a sturdy, steel roof protects the frescoes from the elements.

The **west wall** bears a Bosch-like conception of *The Last Judgement*, complete with a *Four-Headed Cerberus*, *The Whore of Babylon Riding the Beast of the Apocalypse* and *The River of Fire* draining into Hell; adjacent hagiographies and admiring angels are less lurid, especially the stoning of a haloed, unidentifiable saint on the **north wall**. In the badly damaged **apse**, you can still make out a *Dormition* and *The Entry of Christ into Jerusalem*, with the Saviour riding a horse rather than an ass. None of the frescoes dates from earlier than the seventeenth century, but they are far more sophisticated in concept and execution than you'd expect for such comparatively recent work.

Eating

There are plenty of places to eat in central Trabzon, most are good value but few of them are really outstanding. Apart from the establishments listed, booze in this conservative town is hard to come by, as is – surprisingly for a port – fish. The almost uninterrupted line of **restaurants** on the north side of Atatürk Alanı gets most of the tourist custom, though not all the places here deserve to. Most restaurants offer at least some **desserts** – the confectioners of Hemşin (see box on p.782) aren't far away – but some exclusively sweet-dedicated venues are worth seeking out.

Restaurants

Boztepe Gasinosu İran Cad 14, Boztepe, 4km from centre. Two *meze* plates, a beer, trout, service charge and "*garsoniye*" (mandatory tip) work out at around 17YTL – expensive for Trabzon – but the food's not at all bad and the setting, on a sloping lawn with sweeping views of town, idyllic.
Gelik Lokantası Uzun Sok 84/B, by the police sta-

tion. The city's best all-rounder; unusual vegetarian *mezes* such as mushroom salad, corn and other novelty breads, assorted meat-based steamtray dishes, *döner* and sweets, served on two floors.
Koza Caffé Kunduracılar Caddesi, Sanat Sok 1. First-floor café serving a surprising array of coffees and teas from around the globe. Despite the ersatz castle interior it's a warm and welcoming place to

while away a few hours.

Murat Balık Salonu Atatürk Meyd, north side. Tiny hole-in-the-wall joint doing inexpensive grilled *hamsi* (anchovy) in winter, otherwise *mezgit* or *uskumru* (mackerel), accompanied by salad and soft drinks. Closes 9.30pm.

Üstad Lokantası Atatürk Alanı 18. Busy lunchtime restaurant with a good selection of the Turkish dinnertime usual suspects from 2YTL per dish.

Yosun Kunduracılar Cad 14. An upstairs restaurant with Art Deco windows, Black Sea specialities from 7YTL and live music. Try to get a table on one the outside balconies.

Sweets and desserts

Beton Helva Uzun Sok. Huge blocks of *helva* on display – thus the somewhat off-putting name, "Concrete Helva" – but also good *dondurma* (ice cream) and *sıra* (half-fermented grape must), in wonderfully retro-1950s surroundings, next to Seyitoğlu Lahmacun.

Palet Patisserie Cumhuriyet Cad 2/C, corner of Uzun Sok. The most popular of three in a row here; famous for its *dondurma* and *profiterol*. Stiff competition for a table in summer.

Selim Gazipaşa Cad 11/A. A wide range of *dondurma*, milk-based sweets, pastry and *boza* (a millet-based drink), served in airy surroundings; open from 7am until nearly midnight.

Drinking and entertainment

Apart from the **bars and clubs** of the three most upmarket hotels, women will have some difficulty finding anywhere to drink comfortably in the evening (see *Efes Pub* below). The *birahane*s on and off İskele Caddesi are predictably late-night pick-up joints for prostitutes and their clients, and probably best left to the imagination if signs seen in the area ("Entry with Loaded Weapons Forbidden") are anything to go by – indeed, the area's nickname is "Guns and Noses". The *Saray Sineması*, about 400m west of Atatürk Alanı, then south of Uzun Sokak, on Kasımoğlu Çıkmazı, shows slightly dated Hollywood **films**, often with the original soundtrack.

Altmış Bir'a Atatürk Meyd, south side. Large, male-dominated beer hall where football is taken seriously. Named after the car license-plate number for Trabzon – 61.

Efes Pub Maraş Cad 5. A surprisingly accurate rendition of an English pub where music takes a backseat to conversation and the eponymous beer can be had for 2.5YTL. The right-hand room is for couples and women only.

Gecekondu Café Eskikız Sanat Lisesi 5. The closest this town gets to a dance club – though no alcohol! Three floors, each controlled by a laptop-wielding DJ playing to a young student crowd.

T-Nargile Pub Uzun Sok. Up a tiny sidestreet, this restored Ottoman house serves beer and *nargile* on huge comfy sofas. An atmospheric choice for a quiet chat.

Listings

Airlines Atlas Jet, Atatürk Cad 1 ☎0462/444 0387; Azerbaijan Airlines, Sıramağazalar Cad, opposite Ustatour Travel agency ☎0462/326 2497; Fly Air, Atatürk Alanı 30/2 ☎0462/326 9015; Onur Air, Gazipaş Cad 18 ☎0462/326 9545; THY, in front of the *Usta Park Hotel* ☎0462/321 1680.

Airport There are frequent dolmuşes marked "Havalimanı" from a small plaza one block north of Atatürk Alanı, just off Sıramağazalar Cad near the *Horon Oteli*.

Banks and exchange For after-hours encashment of travellers' cheques, try the *Usta Park Hotel*, Teleğrafhane Sok 3; the PTT and Akbank may also oblige. There are *döviz* offices all over the centre, particularly on Atatürk Alanı, Kahraman Maraş Cad, and Kunduracılar Cad. All banks have ATMs taking

the usual range of plastic.

Camping gas Small cartridges for French-made Bleuet stoves can usually be found at Milangas, Gazipaşa Cad 21.

Car rental In summer, when Trabzon swarms with locals returned from northern Europe, getting any kind of vehicle can be nearly impossible; you'll need to start your search weeks in advance and contact all the multiple numbers given to find anyone responsible (English is not widely spoken). Companies with both in-town offices and airport booths include: Avis, Gazipaşa Cad 20/A ☎0462/322 3740, ℻326 3520; Cande, Atatürk Alanı, southwest corner ☎0462/321 6289 or 0532/745 2135; Ceyhun, Atatürk Alanı, southwest corner ☎0462/326 8014 or 0542/396 8484,

⑨321 7507; and Decar/Thrifty, airport ☎0462/321 6289.

Consulates Georgia, Gazipaşa Cad 20, 3rd Floor ☎0462/323 1343; Russia, opposite Ortahisar Camii, Refik Cesur Cad 6 ☎0462/326 2600.

Ferries Apolloniya Tur (☎0462/326 4484), Karden Tur (☎0462/321 3479) and Gürgen Tur (☎0462/321 4439), all along İskele Cad; see "Travel details" at the end of the chapter for schedules and ticket prices to Russia.

Hamams Much the best on offer is Sekiz Direkli Hamam, Pazarkapı 8, Direkli Hamam Sok 1 (daily 7am–11pm; women-only on Thurs, men-only all other days; 7.5YTL). Second choices include Fatih Hamamı, three blocks south of Uzun Sok, a little to the east of the Tabakhane bridge (daily 8am–10pm; women on Wed; 9YTL); and the Meydan, located just off Atatürk Alanı on Kahraman Maraş Cad (men and women daily 6am–10pm; 9YTL).

Hospitals The Özel Karadeniz (private), Reşadiye Cad (☎0462/229 7070), and SSK (Social Security), Trabzonspr Bul (☎0462/230 2285), are both out near Aya Sofya. However the biggest hospital in the region is the KTÜ's medical-school teaching hospital, or Tıp Fakültesi Hastanesi (☎0462/325 3011) – buses and dolmuşes marked "KTÜ" run from the centre.

Internet access The most central of a half-dozen or so are *World*, above *McDonald's* on the south side of Atatürk Alanı, and *Pruva* and *Cağm* nearby, on the eastside of the square. All offer fast access for around 2YTL per hour.

Laundry Pak Çiti, Zeytinlik Cad 18/B, off Kıbrıs Şehitler (daily 8.30am–9.30pm). Dry cleaning at Galip, Uzun Sok 30.

Newspapers and magazines Very limited foreign-language selection (no books) at Aksakal, opposite the THY building at the corner of Uzun Sokak and Atatürk Alanı.

Police Tourism Police, at the harbour customs-zone gate, and on the east side of Atatürk Alanı (daily 9am–7pm; ☎0462/326 3077).

Post office PTT at Posthane Sok, corner of Kahraman Maraş Cad (post and exchange daily 8am–7pm); also a booth at southeast corner of Atatürk Alanı. Payphones and card sales on the south side of Atatürk Alanı.

Travel agencies Two reputable agencies are Afacan, İskele Cad 40/C (☎0462/321 5804) and Ustatour, İskele Cad 3–4 (☎0462/326 1870). Both offer day-tours to Sumela, Ayder, assorted caves in the mountains, and Uzungöl, while Ustatour also sells air tickets and rents cars.

Crossing to Russia, Georgia and Azerbaijan

At present, all non-Turkish travellers need to buy a **visa for Russia** in their country of nationality in order to go from Turkey into Russia. Changing circumstances may permit the granting of visas in İstanbul or Ankara, but it's best not to count on this. Travellers from the European Union no longer require **visas for Georgia** for stays of 90 days or under; otherwise contact the Georgian consulate, Gazi Paşa Cad 20, in Trabzon ☎0462/323 1343 (Mon–Fri 9am–5pm).

In the wake of severe economic conditions affecting all countries concerned, **trans-Black-Sea services** to both Russia (Sochi) and Georgia (Poti) have been severely reduced; see "Travel details" at the end of this chapter for specimen frequencies/prices, and contact one of the ferry agencies in Trabzon (see "Listings" above) for the most current information. Azerbaijan Airlines may still offer twice-weekly **flights to Baku** in Azerbaijan.

Overland **bus services** have been less affected; the main operator out of Trabzon is Göktaş Ardhan Tur (☎0462/325 0411), with offices in Çömlekçi Mahallesi, under the *Kardelen Oteli*. They run daily services in the afternoon and evening to Georgia and (indirectly) Armenia and Azerbaijan (again see "Travel details" on p.788), but some buses originate in Samsun and can arrive at Trabzon's *otogar* full. The **Georgian frontier** is crossed either at Sarp, or (for onward connections to Armenia and Azerbaijan) Posof, which only opened in 2001 for non-local traffic. It's easy enough to do the trip to Georgia in smaller chunks, taking a dolmuş or taxi from Sarp to the border and then arranging local transport on to Batumi on the Georgian side.

The monastery of Sumela

At the beginning of the Byzantine era a large number of monasteries sprang up in the mountains behind Trabzon; this tendency was reinforced during the life of the Trapezuntine Empire, when many of them also played a military role near the tiny realm's southern frontier. The most important and prestigious monastery – and today the best preserved – was **Sumela** (increasingly signposted as Sümela), clinging to a cliff-face nearly a thousand feet above the Altındere valley, the sort of setting that has always appealed to Greek Orthodox monasticism. Despite the habitual crowds, often rainy or misty weather – and rather battered condition of the frescoes – Sumela still rates as one of the mandatory excursions along the Black Sea.

The name *Sumela* is a Pontic Greek shortening and corruption of *Panayia tou Melas* or "Virgin of the Black (Rock)", though some translate it – taking a few more grammatical liberties – as "of the Black Virgin". She has been venerated on this site since at least the year 385, when the Athenian monk Barnabas, acting on a revelation from the Mother of God, discovered an **icon** here said to have been painted by St Luke. He and his nephew Sophronios found the holy relic on a site that matched the one in his vision – a cave on a narrow ledge part of the way up the nearly sheer palisade – and installed the icon in a shrine inside.

A **monastery** supposedly grew around the image as early as the sixth century, but most of what's visible today dates from the thirteenth and fourteenth centuries, when Sumela was intimately linked with Trebizond's Komnenos dynasty, several of whose rulers conducted their coronations at Sumela rather than in the imperial capital. Over the centuries the icon was held responsible for numerous miracles, and the institution housing it shared its reputation, prompting even Turkish sultans to make pilgrimages and leave offerings.

Sumela was hastily evacuated in 1923 along with all other Greek Orthodox foundations in the Pontus; six years later it was gutted by fire, possibly set by careless squatters. In 1931 one of the monks returned secretly and exhumed a number of treasures, including the revered icon, from their hiding place. The Virgin's icon is now housed in the new monastery of Sumela, in northern Greece; unfortunately, when the other reliquaries were opened on arrival in Greece, precious illuminated manuscripts from the Byzantine era were found to have rotted away during their damp eight years underground.

Since 1996, the monastery of Sumela has been undergoing **restoration**. The aim has been to shore up what was left standing and rebuild the rest; by the standards of often brutalist Turkish public renovations, the work done thus far is in reasonable taste, even extending to proper ceramic canal-tiles for the roof. Most important of all, the surviving frescoes have been consolidated and cleaned.

The buildings

However you arrive, all paths converge at the **ticket booth** by the monastery gate (daily: June–Sept 9am–6pm; Nov–Feb 9am–4pm; March–May & Oct 9am–5pm; 5YTL).

Sumela actually occupies a far smaller patch of level ground than its five-storeyed facade would suggest. A climb up the original entry stairs, and an equal drop on the far side of the gate, deposits you in the central courtyard, with the monks' cells and guest hostel on your right overlooking the brink, and the chapel and cave sanctuary to the left. Reconstruction of most of the former living areas is complete, though there are still a number of off-limits areas and unsightly scaffolding. The degree of vandalism and decay is appalling: sophisticated art thieves were

9

△ Sumela monastery

caught levering away large slabs of the famous frescoes in 1983, and any within arm's reach have been obliterated by graffiti-scrawlers – much of the graffiti is pre-1923 vintage Greek, with some even as old as 1875, but Turkish, European and North American visitors have also left their marks.

The main grotto-shrine is closed off on the courtyard side by a wall, from which protrudes the apse of a smaller chapel. A myriad of **frescoes** in varying styles cover every surface, the earliest and best ones dating from the fourteenth or fifteenth century, with progressively less worthwhile additions and retouchings done in 1710, 1740 and 1860. The highest cave paintings are in good condition – ceilings being harder to vandalize – though the irregular surface makes for some odd departures from Orthodox iconographic conventions. The Pantocrator, the Mother of God and various apostles seem to float overhead in space; on the south (left) wall is an archangel and various scenes from the Virgin's life (culminating in *The Virgin Enthroned*), while *Jonah in the Whale* can be seen at the top right.

Outside on the divider wall, most of the scenes from the life of Christ are hopelessly scarred. Among the more distinct is a fine *Transfiguration* about ten feet up on the right; just above sits *Christ in Glory*, with two versions of the *Ascension* nearby. At the top left is *Christ Redeeming Adam and Eve*. On the apse of the tiny chapel the *Raising of Lazarus* is the most intact image. Next to it is the *Entry into Jerusalem*, with the *Deposition from the Cross* just right of this. On the natural rock-face north of all this appears the *Communion of Saints in Paradise*. When craning your neck to ogle the surviving art gets too tiring, there is (mist permitting) always the spectacular view over the valley – and the process of imagining what monastic life, or a stay in the wayfarers' quarters, must have been like here in Sumela's prime.

Practicalities

Without your own transport, you have three ways of getting to Sumela from Trabzon: **taxis** from a rank signposted "Sumela Manastırı'na" on the south side of Atatürk Alanı, which charge 80YTL return for a carload of four people; a **minibus** to Sumela, from next to the taxi rank, for 25YTL per person return; or an **organized tour**, run at 10am daily by the Afacan and Usta travel agencies in Trabzon (see "Listings", p.771) and costing 20YTL per person for a return minibus seat (you pay the admission fee), with a stop for tea thrown in en route. However you arrive, you should make it clear that you're interested in a very full half-day out, since the distance, frequent road blockages from landslips and the final walk in dictates two hours thirty minutes for the return trip, and you'll want nearly as much time at the ruins.

Driving, it's 43km in all from the coastal junction of highways 010 and E97/885, 3.5km east of central Trabzon, to the main parking lot for Sumela; after 26km you turn off Highway E97/885 at Maçka to follow the Altındere valley upstream. This side road provides a stunning approach to the monastery; as you climb, the habitual cloud ceiling of these parts drifts down from the equally dense fir forest to meet you. In exceptional circumstances you may catch an advance glimpse of the monastery's faded, whitewashed flank soaring above the trees at the top of the valley, at an altitude of 1200m.

The monastery proper is linked to the valley bottom by the most commonly used, often slippery woodland **trail** (30min). Those with their own car may prefer to use the steep, initially paved track (no buses) that lurches up the valley for 3.5km to a point about level with the monastery; park where you can before a shed used by the restoration crew and cover the last ten minutes on foot. There's a third approach, less busy than either of these two options; about 1km along the cement drive, keep an eye out for a wood bridge over the stream – this path, going via an abandoned chapel, joins the more usual trail just below the monastery.

Accommodation and eating

By far the best local **accommodation** option, an attractive alternative to staying in Trabzon, is the *Kayalar Turistik Dinleme Tesisleri* (☎0462/531 1057, ℱ531 1054; ❸), about 3km before the admission booth (see opposite). All rooms in this charming, rambling, wood-floored building have balconies and en-suite plumbing (some with bathtubs), plus there are a few family suites – and the inevitable trout farm/restaurant on site.

The environs of Sumela have been designated a national park (admission 6YTL per private car), which means a picnic area, a **snack bar** (the *Çardak*) and a full-on **restaurant** (the *Sümela Sosyal Tesisleri*), which, though not brilliant (chaotic service, bumped-up prices and mandatory ten-percent service charge), does have a lovely setting and a token nod towards regional cooking, with such dishes as *lahana sarması* (stuffed baby-cabbage leaves). Also on the Altındere valley floor are some basic but attractive **bungalows** (reserve on ☎0462/230 2179 or 531 1061) that can be rented for €15 per person. Further downstream, the valley teems with **trout farms** of variable quality – *Sumela Çiftlik Restaurant*, 2km beyond Maçka, comes recommended for good *meze* as well as fish.

Vazelon and Peristera monasteries

So many monasteries are crumbling away in the Pontic foothills that some may never be documented before they disappear forever. Two of the more famous ones, relatively close to Sumela, are best visited with your own transport – but in all honesty they will appeal only to committed enthusiasts.

To reach the cloister of **Vazelon**, dedicated to St John the Baptist, proceed 7.5km south of Maçka on the road to Erzurum, until a black-on-yellow sign reading "Vazelon Manastırı, 3" points to a track up and right (the "3" may be defaced to a "7"). Some 1.5km along this reasonable track, bear left at a junction; the track worsens before reaching, just over 3km along, a trout farm (rarely open) and car park. It's prudent to leave non-4WD vehicles here and continue on foot for half an hour up the even rougher track heading east. Make a hairpin right (west) at the fork; any vehicle must halt at a massive washout over a concrete culvert some 2km beyond the trout farm. The monastery will be visible from here, like a mini-Sumela on the cliff-face ahead, but the final path approach is not obvious – it starts inconspicuously on the uphill side of the track about 150m past the culvert.

In fact Vazelon once ranked second to Sumela in wealth and ecclesiastical clout, but its deterioration since the mid-1980s has accelerated alarmingly. Frescoes exclaimed over in the past have vanished under the ministrations of rain, campfire smoke and vandals, and within a few more years all will have disintegrated. For the moment, the side chapel outside the walls contains a *Dormition*, a *Raising of Lazarus* and a *Baptism*, each dating from the sixteenth century and in fair-to-poor condition. A rockfall from the palisade above smashed the roof at some point during the 1990s, so these images are doomed to disappear within a decade or two. The *katholikon*, or main sanctuary, reached by much crawling through rubble and nettles, has collapsed; only the northern exterior wall bears bits of a naive, eighteenth- or nineteenth-century *Last Judgement*.

There is good, *yayla*-based **accommodation** in the hills just northwest of Vazelon; take the signposted dirt track, heading west of Highway 885 between Maçka and the Vazelon turning, to the *Lişer Yaylası Dinleme Tesisleri* (☏0456/553 1104; ❸), a fourteen-bed inn serving meals. The monastery of **Peristera** (in Turkish, Hızır İlyas Manastırı) is somewhat easier to reach but in no better condition. From Km 22 of Highway 885 bound for Maçka, bear left (southeast) onto a minor road signposted as "Şahinkaya" and proceed 14km on poor surface to the village of Şimşirli, formerly Kuştul. More nettles await the intrepid scaler of the nearby crag on which perch the monastery walls. No art remains here; the view is the main thing, especially the view to the monastery from across the valley – most people don't actually bother with the climb up.

The Zigana Pass and environs

Highway E97 continues southwest towards the Trabzon provincial border at the fabled (but rather anticlimactic) **Zigana Pass** (2025m), 60km from the coast, though the modern highway now goes 200m under the pass via a 1990s-built tunnel and the 883 bypass road. First-time visitors might prefer to use the old 885 highway, which winds through the dispersed village of **HAMSİKÖY**, famous for its ultra-rich *sütlaç* (rice pudding) sold by the roadside. This old route carries on over the pass proper, from where, in 339 BC, the remains of Xenophon's army, retreating from a disastrous campaign in Persia, first caught sight of the Black Sea, raising the legendary cry of relief "**Thalassa, thalassa!**" (The sea, the sea!) – though the ancient Greek would probably have been pronounced *thalatha*, and the sea is not actually visible from any point of either existing road.

Between the pass and "downtown" Hamsiköy, at Bekçiler, awaits the most ambitious and luxurious of the area's *yayla* **accommodation**, the *Zigana Yayla Tatil Köyü* (☏0462/542 6115 or 326 5815; ❺), a wooden bungalow complex (two- and four-person units) at the edge of the forest, complete with enormous restaurant. It's open all year, with heating and a small cross-country ski centre nearby during winter. At just 50km from the airport, the holiday village could make an excellent and relatively convenient alternative to staying in Trabzon.

East of Trabzon

The shore **east of Trabzon** gets progressively more extreme as you approach the Georgian border – if the Black Sea coast as a whole is wet, here it's positively soggy. The mountains increasingly impinge on the sea and soar ever more steeply upward, and the people match the landscape in their larger-than-life qualities. Natives of this area have long exercised a disproportionate influence in national politics, the best current example being Rize province's Mesut Yilmaz, once foreign- and prime minister, whose 1990s patronage of local prestige projects has done as much to raise the area's profile as the important local tea industry (see box opposite).

Civics and commerce aside, however, the coast route has remarkably little to offer travellers. Visually, the only colour is lent by the uniformly red, black and white-striped **keşans** (shawls), **dolaylıks** (vertically striped skirts) and multicoloured **peştemals** (waistbands) worn by women between Tirebolu and Çayeli. Another exotic touch is lent by occasional roadside signs in Georgian and Russian, aimed at visitors from the former Soviet Union – 1990 marked the first time either language appeared publicly in print in Turkey since 1923. If you happen upon a summertime knees-up, the **music** will be that of the *kemençe*, the Pontic (and rather monotonous-sounding) three-string spike fiddle, and less often the *tulum*, the slightly more versatile local goatskin bagpipe.

Arakli to Çamburnu

For a swim and a half-day out from Trabzon, the first decent, unpolluted beaches are found between **ARAKLI** and **SÜRMENE**. The towns themselves are nothing to write home about, and the only point of cultural interest hereabouts is the late eighteenth-century mansion of the Yakupoğlu clan, the *derebeys*, or feudal overlords, of these parts. Otherwise known as the **Kastel**, or the Memişağa Konağı, this squats above the west bank of the Kastel Çayı, 4km east of Sürmene, opposite a seashore teahouse, the *Kastel Restaurant*. Abandoned in 1978 by the Yakupoğlus – whose ranks once included one of the richest men in the country, Cevher Özden, and for contrast Zeki Baştımar, former head of the Turkish Communist Party – it's locked and beginning to decay, but is still impressive. Four stone bulwarks guard the tapered centre of the ground plan; the lightness of the wood and stucco-work on the upper storey, and the whimsical toadstool roof, seem incongruously wedded to the forbidding lower level.

It would only really be worth stopping at these places if you had your own car, and the same goes for the boatyards with their colourful, top-heavy *taka* fishing boats at **ÇAMBURNU**, 3km east. A much-touted pay beach is tucked at the base of the cliff just beyond the port, but equally good or better free beaches line the road to Of.

Rize

A modern Turkish city of over 70,000 in a grand setting, **RIZE**'s name at least will be familiar to every traveller who's bought a souvenir box of "Rize Turist Çay". Of its ancient history as Rhizos nothing survives, and of its role as the easternmost outpost of the Trapezuntine Empire hardly more than a tiny, eighth-century castle. If you do pause it would be to visit the **Tea Institute** (Mon–Fri 7am–noon; ☎0464/213 0241), a combined think-tank, botanical garden, tasting (9am–10pm) and sales outlet on a hill overlooking the town; follow the signs to the "Çay Araştırma Enstitüsü".

There are two main streets, Atatürk Caddesi (inland) and Cumhuriyet Caddesi

East of Trabzon, thanks to a climate ideal for its cultivation, **tea** is king. The tightly trimmed bushes are planted everywhere between sea level and about 600m, to the exclusion of almost all other crops. Picking the tender leaves is considered women's work, and during the six warmer months of the year they can be seen humping enormous loads of leaves in back-strap baskets to the nearest consolidation station. The tea, nearly a million raw tonnes of it annually, is sent more or less immediately to the cutting, fermenting and drying plants whose stacks are recurring landmarks in the region.

Oddly, tea is a very recent introduction to the Black Sea, the pet project of one Asim Zihni Derin, who imported the first plants just before World War II to a region badly depressed in the wake of the departure of its substantial Christian population in 1923. Within a decade or so tea became the mainstay of the local economy, overseen by Çaykur, the state tea monopoly. Despite the emergence of private competitors since 1985, and the Chernobyl accident, which caused condemnation of the 1986 crop, Çaykur is still the major player in the domestic market. Export, however, seems unlikely since supply can barely keep pace with domestic demand.

which runs parallel to the sea; the town square, **Belediye Parkı**, lies between them. The PTT here has been smartened up with wooden trimmings, complementing the two nineteenth-century restored **wooden houses** and the barn on stilts that are visible on the hill behind. East of the square lies Rize's major **tea garden**, which, not surprisingly, is the focus of the town's social whirl. Surrounding shops sell Rize tea in every conceivable packaging, plus the unlikely spin-off product of tea cologne.

Practicalities

The **otogar** is 800m to the west of town, with service buses bringing you into the centre. However, minibuses heading east and west also leave from the main highway, the shore road. The main **long-distance coach** company operating from Rize is Ulusoy, which has offices on Cumhuriyet Caddesi off the northwest corner of the square. International **buses to Georgia** are dealt with by Aybakı Tourism on Tophane Karakolu Yanı (℡0464/217 3763) in the Rus Pazar: walk five minutes east of the square along Cumhuriyet Caddesi and turn right at the roundabout and you'll find the office 100m along on the left. There's at least one bus daily to Batumi and Tbilisi (Georgian visas obtainable in Trabzon; see p.771).

On the north side of the park, near the mosque, there's a helpful summer-only **tourist office** usually staffed by eager local English students (daily 9am–5pm; ℡0464/213 1716). Ayala Tur, at Fevzi Çakmak Cad 6 (℡0464/213 1716), organizes **tours** into Georgia and the Kaçkar mountains, while the *Rize Dedeman* hotel (see below) is the local outlet for Decar/Thrifty **car rental**.

Most **hotels** stand on or near Atatürk Caddesi and Cumhuriyet Caddesi running east of Belediye Parkı. Many double as brothels, though a good exception is the *Otel Efes* at Atatürk Caddesi, 100m east of the square (℡0464/214 1111; ❸): it's a friendly wood-panelled place, bedecked with kilims, but slightly let down by its bathrooms. The two-star *Otel Keleş*, off Cumhuriyet Caddesi at Palandöken Cad 2 (℡0464/217 4612, ℻217 1895; ❸), has better bathrooms and comfortable, though faded, rooms with fridges and TVs. The better value of Rize's two three-star establishments is the newish *Asnur* at Cumhuriyet Cad 165 (℡0464/214 1751; ❹), with all mod cons in the rooms, plus a sauna, gym and bar. For the full works, head for the luxurious, four-star *Rize Dedeman* (℡0464/223 4444, ⓦwww.dedemanhotel.com; ❼) on Alipaşa Koyu, at the western outskirts of town; it's pricey, though bartering can often bring the rack rate down.

For **food**, there are several simple but hearty *pide ve kebap salonları* along Cumhuriyet Caddesi: the large *Bekiroğlu*, at no. 161, is clean and cheap with friendly service and wide-ranging menus of soups, fish (including grilled trout), kebabs and excellent *pide* starting at around 5YTL. The *Lale Restaurant*, on the east side of the central square, is an *"aile"* (boozeless), multi-levelled institution famous for its *etli kurufasulye* (white haricot bean stew with chunks of lamb). The *Müze Kafeteriya*, a restored Ottoman house behind the PTT, is a little more atmospheric and features regional dishes such as *muhlama* (similar to fondue). The centrally located *Merkez Bar*, Deniz Cad 26, is the best of the limited **drinking** options in town, with downstairs being the better of the two floors. For slow but cheap (1YTL per hour) **Internet** access, head for the *Park Internet Café*, Belediye Parkı Karsısı, 3rd floor.

Hopa

HOPA, which used to be the end of the road until the nearby frontier was opened and the route to it was militarily declassified, is a grim industrial port, devoted to shipment of the copper mined slightly inland. The **otogar** is just on the east bank of the Sundura Çayı, which laps the west side of Hopa.

Lazland

Thirty to forty kilometres beyond Rize you pass the invisible former eastern limit of the Trapezuntine Empire and enter the territory of the **Laz**, the Black Sea's most celebrated minority group – though other Turks have an annoying habit of stereotypically classing anyone from east of Samsun as "Laz". Strictly speaking, the Laz are a Caucasian people speaking a language related to Georgian, 150,000 of whom inhabit Pazar, Ardeşen, Fındıklı, Arhavi and Hopa, plus certain inland enclaves. The men, with their aquiline features and often reddish hair, particularly stand out; they also distinguish themselves by an extroversion unusual even for the Black Sea, a bent for jokes – practical and verbal – and an extraordinary business acumen that's the source of envy and of so much of the Laz-baiting and misidentification further west. A fair chunk of Turkey's shipping is owned and operated by Laz, who recruit crews from improbably small villages. The wealth so generated makes them relatively progressive in outlook; the women are out and about in Western garb from Fındıklı east, and the men, too, seem better dressed in the latest styles, though "progress" has also been translated into making the five municipalities listed some of the ugliest on the Black Sea – which is saying a lot.

From Ardeşen east the coast has absolutely no plain. Instead, the imposing mountains, shaggy with tea and a few lingering hazelnut trees, drop directly into the sea. These natural defences have helped the Laz maintain a semblance of independence throughout their **history**. It seems most likely that they're descendants of the ancient Colchians (from whom Jason supposedly stole the Golden Fleece). The Laz accepted Christianity in the sixth century and almost immediately got embroiled in a series of protracted wars with the Byzantines, whose governors had managed to offend them. No power managed fully to subdue them until the Ottomans induced conversion to Islam in the early sixteenth century. Like their neighbours the Hemşinli (see box, p.782), they don't lose too much sleep over their religious affiliation, though with their peripatetic habits and far-flung enterprises the Laz are now well integrated into the national fabric.

Perhaps too well integrated – **Lazuri**, the spoken language, is under threat, as until recently no systematic transcription system existed. The Turkish authorities have strongly discouraged any attempts, declaring persona non grata one Wolfgang Feurstein, a German linguist studying the language *in situ*. Working abroad thereafter, Feurstein finally compiled the first Turkish–Lazuri dictionary, complete with specially devised alphabet, in 1999.

If you have to stay here – and this would only happen if you were en route to Georgia and arrived too late to get an onward connection – head for one of several reasonable, relatively *natasha*-free **hotels** within walking distance of the *otogar*, almost all of them on the coast road, Ortahopa Caddesi. Just on the far side of what passes for the central *meydan* and tiny adjacent park stands the helpful, clean one-star *Cihan* (℡0466/351 2333, ℱ351 4898; ❸), though despite the presence of fridges and TVs, the baths are more contemporary than the rooms; there's also an on-site restaurant and a small car park in front. Top billing, however, goes to the 2001-built *Otel Peronti*, Turgay Ciner Cad 78 (℡0466/351 7663, ⓦwww .peronti-otel.com; ❹). It has almost no balconies, but some of the modern rooms have air conditioning and small tubs in the baths; there's off-street parking and a slightly gloomy breakfast salon.

There's only one **restaurant** in town not affiliated to a hotel – the large *Beslen Lokanta*, between the *meydan* and the coastal highway by the park – but fortunately it's pretty good: generous portions of *sulu yemek*, *pide*, *döner* and desserts in salubrious surroundings, though no fish or booze – three courses cost about 10YTL.

On to the Georgian border

Ten cliff-hemmed, twisty kilometres northeast of Hopa, **KEMALPAŞA** is the next-to-last Turkish village on the Black Sea, with a huge pebble beach, still known by its pre-1923 name of **Makriyalı**, on the seaward side of the four-lane blacktop. The highway has done for most of the makeshift Turkish "*kampings*" that used to be here, and there's no other accommodation, but you won't starve thanks to a handful of restaurants.

Minibuses cover the 20km from Hopa to the **Turkish–Georgian frontier**, set by the Turkish and Soviet revolutionary governments in 1921 at the stream dividing the previously insignificant village of **SARP** (rather than more logically at the Çoruh river by Batumi). The crossing was virtually inactive between 1935 and 1988, a casualty of Stalinist, then Cold War, paranoia, but since the gates have opened, Turkish Sarp has become a busy 24-hour way-station. Convoys of Georgians and Russians head through here for the markets of Turkey's Black Sea cities and towns. If you intend to do more than just ogle the colourful spectacle, bring your passport (see p.771 for via requirements); minibuses to Batumi in Georgia leave early evenings from Sarp.

Inland: the foothills from Trabzon to Rize

While Sumela is a hard act to follow, there are a number of other possible destinations in the hills southeast of Trabzon. The valleys leading to and past them are also useful alternative routes toward Erzurum, avoiding some or all of the often congested E97/885 Highway.

Of, Çaykara and around

The coastal starting point for excursions up the valley of the Solaklı Çayı is **OF** (pronounced "oaf", the ancient Ophis). Both Of and **ÇAYKARA**, around 7km south, the unexciting main town of the lower valley, are renowned for their devoutness, with the highest ratio of *kuran kursu*s (Koran schools for children) per capita in the country, and phalanxes of bearded and skull-capped *hoca*s and *hacı*s striding about in the shadow of huge, ever-multiplying mosques. A further

❾

peculiarity is that anyone over 50 speaks the Pontic dialect of Greek as their first language. It seems probable that the tribes of this valley were Hellenized (along with others such as those around Maçka) at some point during Byzantine rule, though they never lost their reputation as fierce brigands. Upon conversion to Islam at the end of the seventeenth century, their ferocity was transmuted into piety; as the saying goes, when the devil grows old he becomes a monk. It should come as no surprise, then, that you haven't a prayer of anything stronger than a fruit juice between Of and Uzungöl.

Sixteen kilometres inland stands the covered wooden bridge of **Hapsiyaş** (Kiremitli), photogenic despite its prosaic setting. The present structure dates from only 1935, and was badly damaged to the point of collapse by floods in 1998, but it seems likely there's been a span here for several centuries.

The right-hand turning above Çaykara leads after 3.5km to **ATAKÖY**, formerly one of the better preserved of the Black Sea foothill villages. Don't expect a museum piece like Safranbolu, but there are still scattered clusters of half-timbered farmsteads above the main street. The municipality runs its own occasional bus between here and Of. With your own 4WD vehicle the 70km from here to Bayburt, via the 2330-metre **Soğanlı pass** at the head of the Solaklı valley, makes for a very scenic and challenging drive – the road was opened by the Russians in 1916, hasn't been much improved since, and features 22 switchbacks to get up a 700-metre cliff.

Uzungöl

From Çaykara, it's 45km on a paved road up to **Uzungöl** (Long Lake), the main attraction of this area. After Sumela, it's the second most popular excursion out of Trabzon, and especially at weekends the place is a bit too popular for its own good. Frequent dolmuşes make the hour and a half trip up from Of, and tours (about 13YTL a head, transport only) are laid on daily according to demand by Trabzon travel agencies (see p.771). The lake, at just under 1100m, is only averagely scenic, with a bazaar district around its outlet; the remaining wooden houses of the namesake village, clustered on the slope above, are more picturesque, though again outnumbered by modern concrete and brick structures.

Uzungöl makes an ideal base for rambles southeast up to the nearby peaks of **Ziyaret** (3111m) and **Halizden** (3376m), with a chain of glacier lakes at the base of the latter. It's a very long day's hike there and back – though you can go part way by car to save time – so take a tent and food for two days if at all possible.

Practicalities

In line with its mushrooming popularity as a destination, **accommodation** here is plentiful, with five licensed "motels" and a handful of *pansiyon*s; it's a popular overnight stop for foreign travellers en route to or from Trabzon airport. The *İnan Kardeşler Tesisleri* (☎0462/656 6021, ⓦwww.inankardesler.com.tr; ⑤), at the high south end of the lake, where most minibuses end their run, is the oldest hotel in town, a combination trout farm/restaurant/wood-bungalow complex whose menu consists of reasonable trout, salad and pudding, but no alcohol. Opposite, the *Ensar Motel* (☎0462/656 6321, ⓦwww.ensarmotel.com; ③) has a welcoming feel, friendly management and good traditional cuisine, with wooden cabins and en-suite doubles arranged around small gurgling fountains. On the other side of the lake around the base of a large waterfall, the *Aygün Motel* (☎0462/656 6042; ⑤) has wood-panelled doubles with satellite TV and landscaped gardens. For a more homely and friendly option, the *Huzur Pansiyon* (☎0462/656 6095; ②) is downstream from the village on the hillside. At weekends, when Uzungöl gets particularly busy, you might well be better off at **Sultanmurat Yaylası**, reached by a different road 45km southwest of Çaykara, where the well-regarded *Taşkın Hotel* (℡05336322746; ❹) is typical of the new wave of lodging that has sprouted at formerly primitive pastoral communities.

The İkizdere Valley

The next major valley east of Uzungöl, the **İkizdere Valley**, holds no special attraction to stop for, but the scenery along the way is memorable and the road eventually winds up to the highest drivable pass in the Pontic ranges – one of the three loftiest in all Turkey. The place is mostly worth knowing about as an alternative route to Erzurum, or as an approach to the Kaçkar range (see Chapter 10).

İKIZDERE, with frequent minibuses from Rize, is the main town; just before the town, the *Hanci'nin yeri* **restaurant** has tables set next to the raging river and serves *köfte* cooked over hazelnut shells. İkizdere is also the transfer point for the 27-kilometre trip up the Yetimhoca valley to Başköy, the westernmost trailhead for the Kaçkar Dağları. Watch out though: there are at least three other Başköys or Başyaylas in a thirty-kilometre radius, so don't let yourself or your driver get confused. A better alternative, if possible, is to arrange transfer to Saler, the highest village in the valley with road access.

Beyond İkizdere, the main road soon finds itself between jagged peaks and the *yayla*s gathered at the 2640-metre **Ovitdağı pass** (only negotiable May–Oct), marking the edge of Rize province and far more alpine than the overrated Zigana Pass to the west. On the way up you'll pass various grill and trout **restaurants**, and the large, incongruously placed concrete-block **hotel** in the middle of nowhere, the *Genesis* (℡0462/476 8090; ❸).

The Hemşin valleys

The most scenic and interesting of the foothill regions east of Trabzon are the valleys of the **Fırtına Çayı** and its tributaries, which tumble off the steepest slopes of the Pontic ranges, here known as the Kaçkar Dağları. Between the mountains and the sea lie a few hundred square kilometres of rugged, isolated territory that have been imperfectly controlled at best by the prevailing imperial, or regional, powers of every era.

The area is known simply as **Hemşin**, a word whose etymology encapsulates local history: "-*eşen*" is a local dialect suffix, derived from Armenian, meaning "population" or "settlement", as in "Hamameşen" or "the settlement around the baths" (the hot springs at today's Ayder). Over time this was abbreviated to Hemşin, and came to describe the triangular zone with its base against the mountains and its apex at Pazar, and by extension the people in it.

Çamlıhemşin

ÇAMLIHEMŞIN, 21km upstream from the mouth of the Fırtına Çayi, is still too low at 300m to give you a real feel for the Hemşin country, but offers a hint of what's to come. It's the last proper town before the mountains, utilitarian and busy, with a constant chaos of minibuses (mid-June to mid-Sept hourly from Pazar until 7pm) and shoppers clogging its single high street.

There's a **bank** with an ATM, a **PTT**, stores for last-minute hiking supplies, and a recommended **travel agency** at no. 47 on the main street, Türkü Tourism (℡0464/651 7230, ⓦwww.turkutour.com). Proprietor Mehmet Demirci is among the most genial and knowledgeable of local mountain guides, and offers a variety of five- to seven-day treks (early June to late Oct), starting at €300 per person, either tent-based (camping equipment provided) or *pansiyon*-based.

To either side of Çamlıhemşin, along both the main stream and the tributary flowing down from Ayder, you begin to see some of the two dozen or so graceful **bridges** that are a regional speciality. Their age and attribution are both subject to debate, but many have been dated to the eighteenth century (one, controversially, to 1696) and credited to Armenian craftsmen. Just before one of these bridges, at Yolkıyı Köyü, is the rambling, somewhat institutional *Otel Doğa*, 4.5km uphill on the way to Şenyuva (T0464/651 7455; **4**, half-board only), offering one-, two- and three-bed rooms, plus family suites, mostly with baths and river-view balconies. Owner İdris Duman speaks English and French, and is a mine of information about the area.

Şenyuva

One of the most gravity-defying bridges, the **Taş Kemer**, spans the Fırtına Çayı at **ŞENYUVA** (Şinçiva in Hemşinli; 450m), a typically dispersed community of occasionally impressive farmstead dwellings 6–8km above Çamlıhemşin. These date principally from the late nineteenth and early twentieth centuries, the result of locals working in Russia and upon returning building these mansions as a gesture of wealth. Many of these farms have no road access, but are still served by *teleferikler* (motorized pulleys), which winch supplies – and occasionally people – up the rankly vegetated slopes.

> ### The Hemşinlis and their yaylas
>
> The **Hemşinlis** are, according to competing theories, either ethnic Armenians who arrived here at or before the time of the Georgian kingdoms, or natives descended from the Heptacomete tribesmen of old, who, through contact with "true" Armenians, adopted a dialect of Armenian and were nominally Christian or pagan until the early nineteenth century. In any event, religious affiliation did not much trouble these people; there is no evidence of either church or mosque in these hills before the twentieth century. Curiously, there also exists a group of Islamic Armenian-speakers south of Hopa who call their dialect Hemşince and claim origins in Hemşin proper.
>
> Certainly the main body of Hemşinlis – strong-featured and fair-complexioned women and Caucasian-looking men – appear anything but mainstream Turkish, and these outgoing, merry, occasionally outrageous people are diametrically opposite in behaviour to the more serious central Anatolians. This has a lot to do with wearing their Islam lightly; there's none of the overt piety of the Çaykara valley, and you're unlikely to be blasted out of bed at dawn by a muezzin for the simple reason that most communities are too small to support a mosque. Despite stern little signs in local shops warning that "alcohol is the mother of all ills", the men in fact are prodigious drinkers, a tendency aggravated by the **environment**. This is by far the dampest and mistiest part of Turkey, with the sun in hiding two days out of three and up to 500cm annually of rain in some spots. It doesn't take a genius to predict cloud-forest vegetation, with everything from moss-fringed fir and alders down to marsh species and creeping vines clinging to the slopes, as well as moods swinging wildly between moroseness and euphoria among the inhabitants.
>
> Like the nearby Laz, whom they dislike being mistaken for (the feeling is mutual), the Hemşinlis are intrepid and independent. They also have a special genius for the profession of **pastry chef and pudding-maker** (*pastanes*) of major Turkish cities are usually owned and/or staffed by natives of these valleys. The number of Hemşinlis living in diaspora, a process begun under Russian rule last century, far exceeds the 10,000 permanently inhabiting this rather compact domain.
>
> You know you've left the Laz coastal zone when, a little way inland from Pazar or Ardeşen, you begin to see the brilliant yellow, black and red **scarves** (called *puşi* or

Currently the only **accommodation** in Şenyuva is at the *Fırtına Pansiyon* (T & P 0464/653 3111 or 0532/783 2708, W www.firtinavadisi.com), opened in 2000 and housed in the former schoolhouse. It's basic – one shower and one small hamam make up the bathing facilities – and a bit pricey for what's on offer, but is friendly and very trek-savvy, with route knowledge and an excellent sketch map to consult (also shown on their website). Sleeping facilities consist of three conventional rooms in the rear building, a free-standing chalet sleeping six at a pinch, and a five-person dormitory (€6.50 per person). Rooms and chalets are charged on a half-board basis (❺).

A short trek: Pokut and Amlakit

If your level of commitment isn't up to multi-day treks involving camping out in the high mountains, consider the track that heads southeast from Şenyuva via Sal to Pokut *yayla*. **POKUT**, three hours' walk from Şenyuva, is fairly representative of the more substantial Black Sea *yayla*s, with handsome woodwork capped by mixed tin-and-timber roofs rising from stone foundations. For the first night's **lodging**, Pokut has the cheap but very basic *Demirci Pansiyon* (T 0464/651 7495; ❷ half-board), offering half-board accommodation.

The following day you hike east to **Hazindag** (Hazıntak), a handsomely clustered settlement just above the tree-line, and then briefly follow a majestic river canyon

poşi) of the Hemşin women, skilfully worn as turbans and contrasting with the drabness of the men's garb. Curiously, the scarves are not local but imported from India, perhaps a relic of the days when Trabzon was a terminus of the Silk Route.

As in attire, so in **housing**, the mix of vernacular and borrowed styles and materials reflecting wealth earned outside the area. Some positively baronial residences preside over tea terraces and cornfields at lower elevations (Hemşin, incidentally, is one of the few places in Turkey where corn is made into food for human consumption rather than fed to animals). But to fully understand the Hemşin mentality you need to visit at least one *yayla*, or summer pastoral hamlet.

Yaylas are found throughout Turkey in the uplands, but in the Kaçkar in general – and especially Hemşin – they are at their best. Tightly bunched groups of dwellings, usually stone-built to waist height and chalet-style in timber thereafter (but with metal roofs), they begin just at tree-line and recur at intervals up to 2700m. They're inhabited only between late May and early September, when the snow recedes and their tenants come from as far away as Holland or Germany to renew attachments to what they consider their true spiritual homeland. At the more primitive, roadless *yayla*s, sanitary mod cons are rare – shrouded in acrid smoke, awash in mud and nettles, these seem more part of, say, Nepal than a country with EU candidacy – but provision of a road usually brings electrical power, satellite dishes, sundecks with parasols sporting "Coca-Cola" and "Tamek" logos and even the odd phone hook-up in its wake.

Traditional **summertime activities** include the making of yoghurt, butter and cheese (though much less so now that flocks are diminished), and (increasingly) catering to trekkers' needs – which has inevitably put a commercialized tinge to the formerly spontaneous provision of hospitality to wayfarers.

There is wide variation in the spelling of **Hemşinli place names**, especially the *yayla*s, as this Armenian-derived language isn't yet written, doesn't observe vowel harmony and thus isn't particularly amenable to attempts at Turkified standardized spelling. Thus you will see Apevanak or Apıvanak, Palovit or Polovit, Hazindag or Hazıntak, Tirovit or Tirevit or even Trovit, and so on. In this book, we have opted for the more regional rendering, as used by local trekking maps.

on a corniche route south before veering up and southeast to the primitive rock-and-sod cottages of **Samistal**. From the ridge above Samistal, weather permitting, you'll have spectacular views of the main Kaçkar summit ridge. You then double back west to **AMLAKIT**, with its *Amlakit Pansiyon* (book through Türkü Tourism in Çamlıhemşin, see above; ❷), or drop in stiff zigzags from Samistal to Aşağı Kavron and minibus service down to Ayder (see p.786).

If you stay in Amlakit, a final day of walking would see you use a direct trail north to Hazindag and thence back to Pokut and Sal (a steep path northeast through cloud forest direct to Ayder exists, but it's presently in bad condition). Alternatively, keener trekkers can carry on south from Amlakit for 45 minutes on a rough road to Palovit (2300m), and thence to Apevanak Yayla (2500m) en route to the true alpine zone. For details on the rest of the Kaçkar, refer to Chapter 10.

The upper Fırtına valley

Above Şenyuva, along the main branch of the Fırtına Çayı, the road steadily worsens while the scenery just as relentlessly becomes more spectacular. Below, the water roils in chasms and whirlpools that are irresistible to the lunatic fringe of the rubber-rafting fraternity – as well as the central government which, in the face of local opposition, plans to divert most of the river's flow into assorted hydroelectric projects.

Some 12.5km from Çamlıhemşin, the single-towered castle of **Zilkale**, improbably sited by either the Byzantines or the Genoese to control a decidedly minor trade route, appears at a bend in the track. The tree-tufted ruin, more often than not garnished with wisps of mist, today dominates nothing more than one of the most evocative settings in the Pontus. No such lonely castle would be complete without its resident ghosts, and the locals claim that after dark it's haunted by the shades of its former garrison and their horses – so don't get left behind if your minibus pauses to let you snap a picture. Under your own power, you can conduct a more leisurely survey of the various castle bastions (free, may be locked after dark) dating from the thirteenth to fifteenth centuries.

Çat and around

After another 15 or 16km of violent abuse to your vehicle's undercarriage – rental sedans will lose their mud flaps at the very least – you'll arrive at **ÇAT**, 1250m up. Despite the horrid road in, there is now a fairly regular – at least daily – dolmuş service from Çamlıhemşin, but it's more comfortable to use your own transport, whether mountain bike or 4WD. This is another classic base for rambles in the western Kaçkar, though there's not much to the village beyond a few scattered buildings and a final, exquisite bridge leading seemingly nowhere, just upstream.

The most conspicuous building is a surprisingly good combination **hotel/restaurant** (and general store/souvenir shop), the 🍴 *Cancık* (☎0464/654 4120; ❹ half-board), with six clean wood-trim rooms upstairs, and a hot shower on demand down the hall. Meals of trout, salad, *muhlama* (a fondue-like dish) and a meat dish of the day are served in a gazebo by the stream (4.2YTL for nonresidents). If the *Cancık* is full, your fallback is the concrete *Toşi Pension*, 1km downstream (☎0464/654 4002 or 0535/621 5215; ❺ half-board), again with a riverside terrace, though the double, triple and quad rooms can get packed out by organized trek groups.

At Çat the upper reaches of the Fırtına divide. A road running parallel to the main fork heads 30km due south to Ortayayla or Başhemşin, passing Zilkale's sister fort of **Varoş** (Kale-i-Bala) at Kaleköy, where yet another side-road winds up to an alternative trailhead for the western Kaçkar mountains at Kale Yayla.

△ Hemşinli women in Ayder

Don't try to walk any more of these tracks than you have to – between Kale Yayla and Çat, for example, you've a very boring three-to-four-hour slog in either direction – but wait for the one daily minibus at the junction in Çat.

The other turning above Çat bears almost due east, still on a poor surface; minibuses ply the 7km up to **ELEVIT** (1800m), a surprisingly substantial place with summer villas multiplying where there were only pastoral huts until the road was opened in 1989. This is as far as ordinary cars will prudently go – the road, braved by a few jeeps, daily minibuses and reckless non-4WD vehicles, continues east to Karunç, Tirovit and Palovit, but it's hardly worth the risk to your suspension. Elevit, like its nearest neighbour Tirovit, an hour and a half's walk east, is a Laz *yayla*, an enclave of sorts in Hemşin territory. It's also high enough to be a good trek-from-your-doorstep base, though the only **accommodation** is the exceedingly basic *Otel Kartal* (no phone, no sign – look for the eagle statue; ❸ half-board), and a slightly seedy independent **restaurant**, *Aruçoğlu/Naci'nin Yeri*.

For the lightly equipped, there are several possible day-hikes from Tirovit, most rewardingly the three-hour walk up to **Yıldızlı Göl** (Starry Lake) at the top of the vale opening to the south of Elevit. You won't appreciate the name unless you camp overnight there, for just after sunrise little scintillating points of light flash briefly – for perhaps twenty minutes – on the surface of the water.

The properly outfitted can continue along a superb **three-day traverse** southwest across the western Kaçkar, taking in Başyayla, Çiçekliyayla, the 2800-metre-high lakes at the base of Tatos and Verçenik peaks – all potential campsites – and finishing at Başhemşin at the head of the Fırtına valley. If necessary you can "bail out" at Çiçekliyayla, which has a road in.

Ayder

The busiest, most trout-farm-laden road above Çamlıhemşin ends after 17km at **AYDER**, the highest permanently inhabited settlement in the Hemşin valley system. (At Km13, all cars pay a toll of 6YTL.)

Ayder has long since given up the struggle to be a genuine village or *yayla* and now revels in its role as a spa resort and showcase for Hemşinli culture (see box on p.782). Commercialized it may be, but the displays of ethnic pride during August – spontaneous outbreaks of *horon* (dancing) on the central meadow; the skirling of *tulum*s until late from most of the restaurants; and Hemşinli women normally resident in İstanbul or Rotterdam striding about in full regalia – seem genuine. For some years concrete tattiness threatened to overwhelm the indigenous stone-and-wood structures, but this cellblock architecture has happily been checked by municipal edict and all new building must be in traditional style, with stone foundations and olde-worlde wood higher up. That said, the surrounding scenery – a narrow, sharply inclined valley with waterfalls pouring off the sides – has always been the main attraction, but with roads being pushed ever higher, Ayder can no longer rate as a genuine trekking trailhead. Every walk necessitates a minibus transfer: the two notables are the day-jaunt to the Çengovit lakes above the Laz *yayla* of Yukarı Avusor, and the three lakes above Kavron.

Arrival, orientation and services

In season (mid-June to mid-Sept), hourly **minibuses** depart from Pazar (between 10am and 6pm) for the one-hour-plus trip to Ayder; you may have to change vehicles in Çamlıhemşin, and out of season you may have to stump up 50YTL or so for a taxi beyond. Back down to the coast from Ayder, there are hourly departures to Pazar, three daily to Rize and one to Trabzon. You can descend from Ayder to pick up the single daily minibus going up the Fırtına valley toward Çat and Elevit without having to return all the way to Pazar, but you'll need to be in Çamlıhemşin by noon or so.

Ayder is divided into two *mahalles* or districts: **Birinci** (Lower) Ayder at about 1250m, and İkinici (Upper), better known as **Yukarı Ambarlık**, at about 1350m elevation. Birinci has the spas, **dolmuş stop** and most of the considerable high-season noise and congestion; Yukarı Ambarlık is loads calmer and has most (but not all) of the more desirable accommodation. An ancient bus has been converted into a **PTT** booth in Birinci Ayder, but there are no banking facilities, so get any money you need in Pazar or Çamlıhemşin. There is slow, unreliable **Internet** access from the café near the minibus stop.

Accommodation

Most establishments are open April to October only, though a bare few trade all year round; showing up on an August weekend without a reservation is not recommended. Owing to the proximity of the spas, the local hotels used to be decidedly basic, though now most have en-suite facilities.

Birinci Ayder

Fora Pansiyon First, highest building on left hillside as you enter town ☎0464/657 2153; or book through Türkü Tourism in Çamlıhemşin. Excellent choice for its trek-friendly atmosphere, with on-site sauna, *teleferik* to hoist up your packs and a lovely terrace for grilled suppers prepared by welcoming hosts Mehmet and Kader Demirci. Mostly double en-suite rooms (though a few triples); the Demircis also manage a four-person chalet, the *Sincina*, near Çamlıhemşin, plus the *pansiyon* in Amlakit. ❸ half-board

🎿 **Haşimoğlu Otel** ☎0464/657 2037, ⓦwww.ayderhasimogluotel.com. Large, well-run, luxurious hotel with cosy communal areas with fireplaces. All the wood-lined double rooms are en suite with TV. ❻ half-board

Otel Yeşilvadı Just below the road ☎0464/657 2050. Tidy, efficient and salubrious modern structure. Breakfast served at the adjacent affiliated restaurant. ❸

Yukarı Ambarlık

Ahşap Pansiyon North hillside, path-only access ☎0464/657 2162, ⓦwww.ahsappansiyon.com. All-wood (*ahşap* in Turkish) outfit, built in 2000, with smallish en-suite rooms, a couple of large self-catering apartments and good meals (8.5YTL) – sometimes even running to fried *hamsi* – at the terrace restaurant with views. Advance booking advisable, as it's popular with tour groups. ❸

Koru Oteli On the through road between *Ahşap* and *Kuşpuni* ☎0464/657 2083, ⓕ657 2010. A bit dowdy, but the en-suite rooms are 2000-vintage with TV. ❹

Kuşpuni Downhill from *Koru* ☎0464/657 2052, ⓕ657 2151. The highest-standard establishment, open all year, popular with city professionals and expat Turks. Centrally heated rooms vary from doubles to family suites. The regional food – inevitably trout, plus salads, *muhlama* at breakfast and home-made desserts – is abundant and deftly executed. ❼ half-board

Serender Pansiyon Near top of Yukarı Ambarlık ☎0464/657 2201. Decent wood-trim rooms (with wooden cubicle bathrooms) in varying formats: it's in a peaceful location, with lots of common sitting areas and a self-catering kitchen. ❸

Eating and drinking

Most people arrange half-board with their *pansiyon*s and local **cuisine** tends to be limited and repetitive, based largely on farmed trout, salad and *muhlama* (a fondue-like dish of cheese, butter and corn flour), the last scooped up with corn bread.

The best placed **restaurant**, and one of the few licensed ones, is the *Ayder Sofrası* between Birinci and Yukarı Ambarlık, with outdoor seating overlooking the river. Up in Yukarı Ambarlık, the only option is the *Huzur Ocakbaşı* near the *Kuşpuni* and *Koru*, with a strong line in grilled meat. One of the better eateries in Birinci Ayder is the prosaically set *Nazlı Çiçek*, with a steady clientele and thus a healthy turnover in food such as grilled chicken and trout (no alcohol available). It's also one of the more reliable venues to witness the *horon* outside of August; supposedly the dancers' limb-movements, the rhythm set by the *tulum*, imitate those of the Black Sea waves, boats and *hamsi* fish.

The spas

Ayder once had two old *kaplıcalar* or sulphurous **hot springs**, one on each bank of the stream. Those on the far (south) side – incidentally marking where the muddy, slippery, little-used path descends from Hazindag – shut down in the mid-1990s. The north-bank premises (daily 5am–10pm; men dawn & evenings, women all day; 2.5YTL), just downhill from Birinci's main mosque, carry on the tradition of a stone-and-concrete lined communal *havuz* (pool) fed by scalding water (close to 60°C) spurting from an overhead pipe; a shower on entry is mandatory before joining the venerable townsfolk, lounging like Roman senators. The huge, modern

upper bath complex built in the early 1990s (separate sections for men and women; daily 7am–7pm; 5YTL) is predictably sterile, with even hotter water filling rectangular, tiled group pools. More expensive private tub-rooms are available as well as safe-boxes for your valuables.

Travel details

Trains

Samsun to: Amasya (1 daily; 4hr 30min); Kayseri (4 weekly; 19hr); Sivas (1 daily; 12hr).
Zonguldak to: Ankara (1 daily, overnight; 9hr 10min).

Buses and dolmuşes

Amasra to: Bartın (every 30min; 25min); Sinop (6 daily; 6hr); Zonguldak (3 daily; 1hr 45min).
Ayder to Pazar (hourly; 1hr); Rize (3 daily; 2hr).
Bartın to: Ankara (5 daily; 5hr); Safranbolu (8 daily; 1hr 30min); Zonguldak (hourly; 1hr 20min).
Giresun to: Ordu (every 30min; 1hr); Tirebolu (every 45min; 45min); Trabzon (hourly; 2hr 15min).
Hopa to: Artvin (hourly 7am–5pm; 1hr 30min); Rize (hourly; 1hr 45min).
İnebolu to: Kastamonu (10 daily; 1hr 45min).
Ordu to: Giresun (every 30min; 1hr); Perşembe (every 30min; 20min); Samsun (hourly; 2hr 45min); Ünye (hourly; 1hr 20min).
Rize to: Ankara (4 daily; 14hr); Ayder (3 daily; 2hr); Bursa (2 daily; 18hr); Erzurum via İspir (4–5 daily; 7hr); Hopa (hourly; 1hr 40min); İkizdere (hourly; 1hr); İspir (5 daily; 4hr); İstanbul (4 daily; 18hr); Samsun (every 30min; 8hr); Trabzon (every 30min; 1hr).
Samsun to: Afyon (4 daily; 10hr); Amasya (10 daily; 2hr 30min); Ankara (6 daily; 7hr); Artvin (4 daily; 10hr); Balıkesir (1 daily; 14hr); Erzurum (2 daily; 10hr); Giresun (4 daily; 3hr 30min); İstanbul (10 daily; 11hr); Rize (every 30min; 8hr); Sinop (every 30min; 3hr); Sivas (3 daily; 6hr 30min); Trabzon (hourly; 7hr); Van (2 daily; 23hr).
Sinop to: Ankara (5 daily; 9hr); İstanbul (5 daily; 10hr 30min); Kastamonu (9 daily; 2hr 30min); Samsun (every 30min; 3hr).

Trabzon to: Ankara (7 daily; 12hr); Artvin (5 daily, may have to change at Hopa; 5hr); Bayburt (5 daily; 4hr 30min); Erzurum (6 daily; 6hr); Giresun (hourly; 2hr 15min); Hopa (every 30min; 3hr); İstanbul (10 daily; 18hr); İzmir (3 daily; 22hr); Kars (2 daily with change at Erzurum or Artvin; 12hr); Of (every 30min; 1hr); Rize (every 30min; 1hr); Samsun (hourly; 7hr).
Zonguldak to: Ankara (hourly; 5hr 30min); İstanbul (6 daily; 6hr).

International buses

Rize to: Batumi, Georgia (1 daily; 3hr 30min); Tbilisi, Georgia (1 daily; 14hr); Erevan, Armenia (1 daily; 14hr).
Samsun to: Tbilisi, Georgia (1 daily; 21hr).
Trabzon to: Baku, Azerbaijan (1 daily via Georgia; 25hr; €50); Batumi, Georgia (1 daily; 4hr 30min; €12); Erevan, Armenia (15hr; €45); Posof, Georgian border (daily at 7.30pm; 7hr; €16); Tbilisi, Georgia (1 daily at 1pm; 13hr; €30).

International ferries/catamarans

Samsun to: Sochi, Russia (twice-weekly catamarans; 7hr). Around €75 one way.
Trabzon to: Sochi, Russia (twice-weekly ferries; 15hr; departures typically around 6pm; €60 one way for a cabin berth).

Flights

Samsun to: İstanbul (2 daily; 1hr 20min).
Trabzon to: Adana (2–3 daily via İstanbul or Ankara; 3hr 30min–4hr); Ankara (1–2 daily; 1hr 30min); İstanbul (3 daily; 1hr 50min); İzmir (3 daily via İstanbul; 3hr 30min–4hr).

Northeastern Anatolia

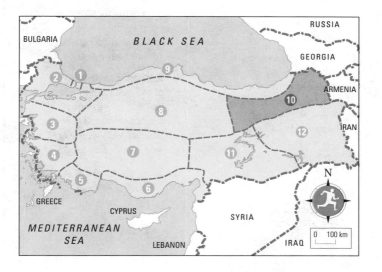

CHAPTER 10

Highlights

❋ **Erzurum** The twelfth- to fourteenth-century monuments of the Saltuk, Selçuk and İlhanid emirs at Erzurum comprise the finest collection of Islamic architecture in the northeast. See p.795

❋ **Ani** Don't miss the ruined medieval capital at Ani, site of the region's densest concentration of Armenian churches and castles. See p.807

❋ **Georgian churches** The early medieval Georgian churches in the river valleys between Erzurum, Artvin and Ardahan spawned the Romanesque churches of Western Europe and retain

superb relief decoration. See p.820

❋ **Whitewater rafting on the Çoruh river** Yusufeli is the base for a sport that draws hundreds of enthusiasts during May and June. See p.826

❋ **Kaçkar Dağları** The glacially sculpted, wildflower-carpeted Kaçkar mountains rank as the most versatile and popular alpine trekking area of Turkey. See p.830

❋ **Kafkasör festival** One of the most authentic folkloric expressions in the country can be witnessed every June outside Artvin. See p.836

△ Ezurum Gallery

Northeastern Anatolia

Bleak, rugged and melancholy, **northeastern Anatolia** is Turkey's version of Siberia or the Australian Outback. Much of it is a high, windswept plateau segmented by ranks of eroded mountains that seem barely higher, despite impressive altitudes on the map. Four great rivers – the Çoruh, Kura, Aras (Ahuryan in Armenia) and Euphrates (Fırat in Turkish) – rise here, beginning courses that take them to scattered ends in the Black, Caspian and Persian seas. Their sources almost meet at the forbidding roof of the steppe near Erzurum, but as the rivers descend through warmer canyons and valleys at the edge of the uplands, oases and towns appear, lending much of the interest and attraction of the region.

A great deal of governmental attention, both military and civilian, has been lavished on the provinces of Kars, Artvin and Erzurum, which form the heart of the region. But despite ambitious development projects, most of the terrain will never be suited to anything except cultivating grain, hay and sugar beets (between May and September), or the grazing of livestock. The area and its farms remain stubbornly poor, with horse-drawn harrows and hand tools still just outnumbering combine harvesters and tractors. Huge flocks of sheep are tended by men, while the herding of gaggles of geese in every village is considered women's work. Given the treeless landscape, the making and stacking of cow-dung patties (*tezek* in Turkish) for fuel becomes a conspicuous necessity for villagers unable to buy coal, the dung vying in height with the equally ubiquitous haystacks. The harsh, seven-month winters dictate a troglodytic architecture of semi-subterranean burrow-houses – and a stoic, self-contained character to go with it. Only the relatively prosperous and forested valleys around Yusufeli and Artvin have a lighter atmosphere and quasi-Mediterranean climate, as a tangible Caucasian influence begins to be felt.

As a traveller, you will probably have the place largely to yourself, except for the mountainous areas bordering on the Black Sea. Tourism, never exactly booming elsewhere in the region, was hobbled by the long-running Kurdish troubles in the adjacent southeast. Although these have now abated, the aftermath of a Georgian civil war to the north and an Azeri–Armenian war nearby in Nagorno-Karabakh – the latter closing until further notice the land frontier between Turkey and Armenia – have combined to choke off any subsequent recovery.

However you approach – from central Anatolia, the extreme southeast of Turkey, or the Black Sea – your first stop is likely to be **Erzurum**, long a goal of armies and merchants and the only real urban centre. Today it's the main jumping-off point to just about anywhere else in the region, with a clutch of post-Selçuk Turkish monuments to distract you. To the northeast, **Kars**, the last major town before the Armenian frontier, serves as the base for visits to the

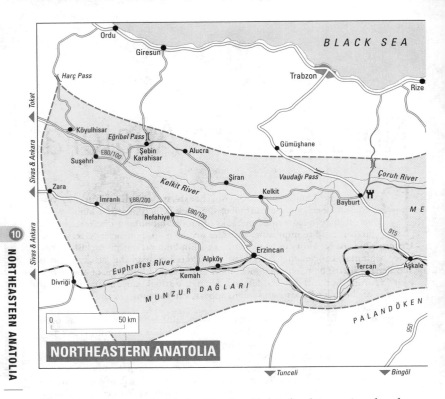

former Armenian capital of **Ani** and less heralded, isolated **Armenian churches and castles** in the province, together comprising the biggest tourist attraction in the region. North of Erzurum, the southernmost **valleys of early medieval Georgia**, now part of Turkey, hide nearly a dozen churches and almost as many castles – enchantingly set, little visited and arguably the most rewarding targets in this area. The provincial capital of **Artvin** and the pleasant town of **Yusufeli** are the logical overnight stops while in search of Georgian monuments, and Yusufeli also sits astride the most popular southern approach to the magnificent **Kaçkar Dağları**, a trekkers' paradise that separates northeast Anatolia from the Black Sea.

Some history

Perhaps because of the discouraging climate and meagre resources, this corner of the country was thinly settled until the second millennium BC. The **Urartians** had their northernmost city at today's Altıntepe, near Erzincan, between the ninth and sixth centuries, but the next real imperial power to make an appearance was the **Roman** Empire, succeeded by the Byzantines and **Armenians**. The eleventh-century undermining of the Armenian state and the Byzantine defeat at Manzikert marked the start of a pattern of invasion and counterattack, which was to continue until 1920. The **Selçuks**, their minor successor emirates and the newly ascendant **Georgian** kingdom jockeyed for position in the territory until swept aside by **Mongol** raids in the early thirteenth century and Tamerlane's juggernaut

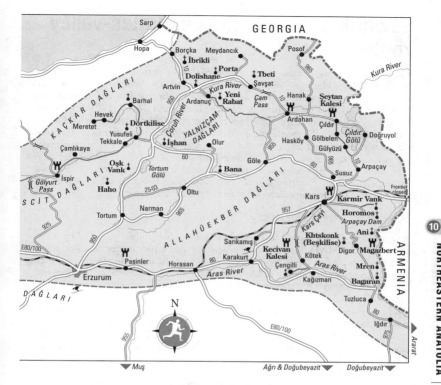

in the early 1400s; the **Ottomans** finally reasserted some semblance of centralized control early in the sixteenth century.

Just as the northeast had been a remote frontier of the Byzantines, so it became the border of this new Anatolian empire, confronting an expansionist Tsarist Russia, which effectively ended what remained of Georgia's autonomy in 1783. As the Ottomans declined, **Russia** grew bolder, advancing out of its Caucasian fortresses to lop off slices of the region on several occasions during the nineteenth century, though they got to keep their conquests only in 1829 and 1878. Until 1914 nearly half of the sites described in this chapter were under Russian rule, with additional conquests up to 1917 nullified by the Bolshevik Revolution and the collapse of the Caucasian front. Between 1915 and 1921 the area was the scene of almost uninterrupted **warfare** between White Russian, Armenian Dashnakist and Turkish Nationalist armies, and of massacres among the mixed civilian population that had historically been over a third Armenian and Georgian-Christian.

By 1923 the northeast was all but prostrate, with ninety percent of its former population dead or dispersed. The present international boundaries between Turkey and Georgia or Armenia are the result of treaties between Atatürk and the **Soviet Union** in March and October 1921, and don't necessarily reflect historical divisions (indeed as late as 1945 Stalin was still demanding that Kars and Ardahan be returned to the "Russian motherland").

Towards Erzurum: the Euphrates-valley route

Coming from the west, many travellers cover the lonely, potholed stretch of Highway 200/E88–100/E80 between Sivas and Erzurum in one day. With more time at your disposal, a leisurely approach via the valleys of the **Euphrates river** and its tributaries is preferable. Most of the countryside between Kangal and Kemah is all but trackless, the railway still the most dependable link to the rest of Turkey; during daylight hours a **train trip** through the spectacular, ruddy river-gorges flecked with oases is certainly the most enjoyable and scenic introduction to northeastern Turkey. The river itself, green and opaque, is warm enough above the giant Keban Dam to support carp – an anomaly in a region famed for trout. In addition to the long-distance expresses between Ankara and Erzurum, a local "milk run" train sets out most days early in the morning **from Divriği** in central Anatolia to Erzincan and Erzurum.

Kemah and Alpköy

If you don't mind the risk of being stranded for half a day, you could get off the train at **KEMAH**, a historic town perched over a picturesque reach of river. There's a complex of tombs from different eras perched above the river, and a huge Byzantine/Selçuk castle with cellars to explore. The place is fairly small, however, and can muster just a few tiny shops and one unmarked, rudimentary hotel. Except at weekends, dolmuşes along the paved 50km to Erzincan are fairly regular.

Kemah is theoretically a major trailhead for treks across the **Munzur Dağları**, which tower snow-streaked above the Euphrates' south bank, but there have been sporadic Kurdish-related troubles since the 1930s – which may or may not have subsided since the capture and imprisonment of PKK leader Abdullah Öcalan. If you inform the *jandarma* post of your intention to go mountaineering you may still be prevented from doing so. **ALPKÖY**, twenty minutes further east along the tracks, is a better place to start – nobody will stop you here, and a giant canyon leading straight up to the heart of the mountains opens out very close to the station.

Erzincan

ERZINCAN – once one of the most elegant cities in Turkey, with several Armenian monuments on the outskirts and dozens of mosques and *medrese*s in the town – was devastated by earthquakes in 1939 and again in 1983. There's no reason to linger longer than the time it takes to change buses (the *otogar* is at the far eastern end of town) or trains (train station at the southwestern edge) – connections on to Erzurum are frequent, but transport to Divriği only gets going in the afternoon.

Tercan

Exactly halfway between Erzincan and Erzurum, near the head of the Euphrates valley, you should try and break the journey at **TERCAN** (not so easy on public transport), graced by a *türbe*, *kervansaray* and bridge erected by the Saltuk emirs of Erzurum at the beginning of the thirteenth century. The **Mama Hatun Türbesi** in particular is bizarre, built to a design found elsewhere only in Central Asian Turkestan and signposted pessimistically as "1km" northeast from the through highway (it's more like 500m). The west–southwest portal, with its stalactite vaulting, Kufic inscriptions and flanking false columns with intricate relief (including an interlocking five-pointed star motif on the false capitals), runs a close second to the Divriği monuments for extravagance. The tomb itself, inside the circular outer enclosure elaborated into a dozen *eyvan*s, has eight lobes (in which are interred other members of the Saltuk dynasty) and a conical "witch's-hat" roof. The complex is unfortunately locked while its environs are being rather desultorily groomed and landscaped; the **kervansaray** just opposite was also locked at the time of writing.

Retracing your steps through the lively contemporary bazaar with its simple **restaurants** to the main highway junction, you'll find a single basic **hotel**, the *Kervansaray*, available in the *Belediye* building (℡0446/441 2588; ❶), for emergency use if you get stranded.

Erzurum

Nearly 2000m up, its horizons defined by mountains a further 1000m above, and rocked by frequent earthquakes, **ERZURUM** is Turkey's highest and most exposed city, and one of its most devout; some women wear gunny-sack-like *çarşaf*s (full-length robes with hoods and veils) tinted the same dun colour as the surrounding steppe, whilst others wear the black *chador*, a cultural import from nearby Iran. Because of a strategic location astride the main trade routes to Persia, the Caucausus and western Anatolia, its sovereignty has always been contested, and today it's still a major garrison town of over 400,000 people. All told, the combination of history, climate and earthquakes has resulted in a bleak, much-rebuilt place where sunlight can seem wan even in midsummer, and where the landscaped, broad modern boulevards often end abruptly in literally the middle of nowhere.

While it spent the 1960s and 1970s as a transit stop for overlanders on the way to Iran, Afghanistan and India, Erzurum never really made the transition to mass tourism, though it gets some trade in winter thanks to the excellent skiing facilities at **Palandöken** just to the south (see p.799). During summer, the city serves as an occasional base and staging point for mountaineering and rafting expeditions bound for the Kaçkar Dağları, but it also deserves a full day in itself to see a compact group of very early Turkish monuments.

Some history

Although the site had been occupied for centuries before, a city only rose to prominence here towards the end of the fourth century AD, when the Byzantine emperor Theodosius II fortified the place and renamed it **Theodosiopolis**. Over the next five hundred years the town changed hands frequently between Constantinople and assorted Arab dynasties, with a short period of Armenian rule.

After the decisive battle of Manzikert in 1071, Erzurum – a corruption of Arzer-Rum, or "Domain of the Byzantines" in Arabic – fell into the hands of first the Selçuks and then the Saltuk clan of Turks. These were in turn displaced by the İlhanid Mongols during the fourteenth century, forerunners of Tamerlane himself, who used the city as a springboard for his brief blitzkrieg into western Anatolia.

Erzurum was incorporated into the Ottoman Empire by Selim I in 1515, where it remained securely until 1828, after which the Russians occupied it on three occasions. With the memory of the last Russian tenure (1916–1917) still fresh in their minds, and the city held by renegade General Kâzım Karabekir, supporters of the Nationalists convened a congress here in July 1919, at which the present borders of the Turkish Republic were put forth as the minimum acceptable.

Arrival, transport and information

Erzurum has two main bus terminals: the long-distance **otogar**, located almost 3km northwest of the city centre (taxis into the centre won't exceed 8YTL), and

ERZURUM

Artvin & Yusefeli

Elâzığ, Bingöl & Palandöken ⬥⬥⬥⬥ Palandöken, Iranian Consulate & Research Hospital

ACCOMMODATION

Akçay Hotel	E
Dedeman Palandöken	G
Dilaver Hotel	C
Kardelen Oteli	H
Kral Otel	F
Oral Otel	D
Palan Otel	J
Polat Otel	B
Polat Renaissance	I
Sefer Hotel	A

RESTAURANTS

Erzurum Evleri	7
Güzelyurt	4
İstanbul Self Service	1
Kılıçoğlu Sütiş	3
Salon Asya	2
Salon Çağın	6
Serender	5

the **Gölbaşı Semt Garajı**, for Yusufeli and Artvin, much more conveniently situated just over 1km northeast of downtown. Many, though by no means all, long-distance buses stop at both of these stations – when it's time to move on from Erzurum, make sure you know exactly which one your vehicle starts from; there are ticket offices scattered around town, as well as at the terminals.

The **train station** is over 1km north of the centre, close to a concentration of inexpensive accommodation. If you fly into the newly renovated **airport**, 10km northwest of town at the end of the same road serving the *otogar*, try and catch the THY bus (3YTL) into town – a taxi will set you back 13YTL.

Aside from walking, **taxis** are really the way to get around Erzurum. There are municipal **buses** – particularly useful is the #2, which links the *otogar* with Cumhuriyet Caddesi, the main east–west thoroughfare – but it's tedious to hunt down ticket sales-points, and taxi ranks are everywhere. The **tourist office**, at Ömer Nasuhi Bilmen (ex-Cemal Gürsel) Cad 9, 500m west of the centre, may be able to hand out a town map, but will only be of further use if you're lucky and catch one of the volunteer English students who sometimes work there.

Accommodation

The supply of **accommodation** in Erzurum usually exceeds demand, and you should have no trouble finding a decent room to suit any budget without resorting to the city's surviving fleapits, although finding a hotel not used by prostitutes can be a little trickier. If you're on a long haul overland, it's wise to break the journey here, since there's nowhere else as good to overnight for hundreds of kilometres. With your own vehicle, it makes most sense to stay south of town at the base of **Palandöken** ski resort, where four hotels (three open all year) offer unregulated parking, comfort and quiet at affordable rates.

City centre

Akçay Hotel Kâmil Ağa Sok, off Cumhuriyet Cad 2 ☎0442/235 3264. Fairly quiet spot, with off-street parking, but about as basic as you'll want to be in Erzurum: 1970s-decorated rooms that vary in plumbing arrangements, but all tend to be dank, with lurid hospital-green walls and muddy-coloured carpets. ❷

Dilaver Hotel Pelit Meyd, Aşağı Mumçu Mah ☎0442/235 0068, ⓦwww.dilaverhotel.com.tr. Despite a rooftop-view restaurant, tubs in the bathrooms and BBC/CNN on the telly, this three-star has one star too many. Breakfast served in the mezzanine bar. Ignore the ridiculous rack-rates of €65; they'll generally part with rooms for €40. ❻

Kral Otel Erzincankapı 18, near southwest corner of the central park ☎0442/234 6400, ⓔkralhotel@gmail.com. Don't let the dire exterior fool you – this was almost completely overhauled in 2001 and now offers the best value in town. Each floor boasts a different theme – the most striking rooms feature mock İlhanid-Mongol decor in their mosaic-tiled baths – even the tubs – and marble sink-surrounds, paired with double glazing and carpets. Multi-person suites also available. ❹

Oral Otel Terminal Cad 3 ☎0442/235 2500, Ⓕ235 2600. On a quiet, almost leafy (for Erzurum) street, this worthy three-star is a 1970s period piece (albeit a well-kept one), from the lobby with its white-leather armchairs to the individual room decor, most charitably described as "eclectic", though bathrooms have been updated and fridges added. Decent on-site restaurant, money exchange at near-bank rates. ❷

Polat Otel Kâzım Karabekir Cad 2 ☎0442/235 0364, Ⓕ234 4598. Renovated in 2000 (and now two-star), but most of the money was spent on modernizing the half-tub bathrooms, and fitting double glazing and heating, rather than upgrad-ing the rather plain rooms themselves (some with balconies). ❷

Sefer Hotel İstasyon Cad ☎0442/235 0818, Ⓕ235 0831. Old warhorse one-star, with musty 1970s-vintage rooms and fake doubleglazing. Passable, however, and a little more comfortable than the *Akçay*. ❷

Palandöken

Dedeman Palandöken 8.5km from Erzurum ☎0442/316 2414, Ⓕ316 3607. Four-star hotel in an alpine bowl at 2450m, pitched at doorstep ski-ers who want to be right at the heart of the action. Large, if spartan, rooms and wooden mock-chalet common areas. Closed mid-May to Nov. ❼

Kardelen Oteli 5km from Erzurum ☎0442/316 6851, Ⓕ316 6070. Definitely the runt of the litter of the Palandöken hotels, this three-star is the least expensive up here but fairly basic, barely function-ing in summer and with a management somewhat suspicious of foreigners. ❹

Palan Otel 6.5km from town ☎0442/317 0707, ⓦwww.palanotel.com. Second-best all-year choice here, at about 2250m; rooms – try not to get one facing the often noisy car park – are on the large side, decorated in shades of beige, with tubs in the baths. Breakfasts are disappointing for a four-star, but there's an indoor pool, gym and sauna. Winter ❼, summer ❻

Polat Renaissance Erzurum Oteli 5km from Erzurum ☎0442/232 0010, ⓦwww.polatrenaissance.com. Turkey's most comfortable hotel east of Cappadocia, built in 2000, this five-star at 2200m is a bit remote from most of the ski slopes – a private chairlift bridges the gap – but compensates with cheerful, fair-sized rooms with cable TV and Internet access. Palatial common areas include a pleasant indoor pool, hamam and gym. Discounted packages available during ski season. Winter ❼, summer ❻

The City

All features of interest in Erzurum lie along – or just off – Cumhuriyet Caddesi, and a leisurely tour shouldn't take much more than half a day. Start at what is the de facto city centre – the Yakutiye Parkı – a landscaped area with benches and a tea garden around the Yakutiye Medresesi.

Yakutiye Medresesi and around

The **Yakutiye Medresesi** was begun in 1310 by Cemaleddin Hoca Yakut, a local governor of the İlhanid Mongols, and with its intricately worked portal, and truncated minaret featuring a knotted lattice of tile-work, it's easily the most fanciful building in town. The minaret in particular seems displaced from somewhere in Central Asia or Persia – not such a far-fetched notion when you learn that the İlhanids had their seat in Tabriz. The beautiful interior of the *medrese* – note especially the stone stalactite carvings of the central dome – now holds an excellent **Museum of Islamic and Turkish Arts** (Türk-İslam Eserleri ve Etnografya Müzesi; Tues, Thurs, Fri & Sat 8am–noon & 1.30–5.15pm; 2YTL), nicely arranged around the students' cells. Exhibits include displays of local *oltu taşı* jewellery (see opposite), various dervish accessories, *ehram* (woven waistcoats for pilgrims to Mecca) and a selection of interesting old prints of Erzurum, among them a fine photograph taken from the roof of the old British consulate (Britain had a commercial agent in Erzurum as early as 1690). A **türbe** at the east end of the *medrese* was intended for Yakut but never used. Just behind the tomb squats the uninspiring, mid-sixteenth-century **Lala Mustafa Paşa Camii**; it was supposedly designed by the famous architect Sinan, but you'd never guess it.

Ulu Cami, Çifte Minareli Medrese and Üç Kümbetler

Continuing east about 300m along Cumhuriyet Caddesi, past an obscure *türbe* jostled by the surrounding shops, you pass the **Ulu Cami**, erected in 1179 by Nasirüddin Muhammed, third in the line of Saltuk emirs. Like most mosques of that age, it's a big square hall, with dozens of columns supporting bare vaults; the one note of fancy is a wedding cake of stalactite vaulting culminating in the central skylight. At the *mihrab* the orderly rows of columns – seven aisles of six each – break up around an odd wooden dome built of overlapping timbers and pierced by two round windows.

Immediately adjacent stands the **Çifte Minareli Medrese**, the purported main tourist attraction in Erzurum (interior closed for repair at the time of writing). The name – meaning "double-minareted" – derives from the most conspicuous feature of the seminary, two thirty-metre-high towers curiously devoid of a balcony for the muezzin to sound the call to prayer. There is some dispute about the structure's vintage, but the majority opinion holds that Hüdavend Hatun, daughter of the Selçuk sultan Alâeddin Keykubad II, commissioned it in 1253, making it a contemporary of the similar Gök Medrese in Sivas. In conception the Çifte Minareli was the boldest and largest theological academy of its time, but was never finished. The stalactite portal, whose carved dragons and double-headed eagle designs hark somewhat un-Islamically back to an earlier nomadic animism, gives onto a vast, bare courtyard, with stairways at the front corners leading to an upper storey of cells (alas, rarely open). At the back looms an unusual cylindrical or *kümbet*-style tomb, thought to be that of the foundress; the sarcophagus, which may in fact be empty, lies in a separate subterranean chamber below the dome.

A cluster of less enigmatic mausoleums, the **Üç Kümbetler**, graces another small park about 250m directly south. The oldest of the three tombs, and the most interesting, is probably that of the first Saltuk emir and dates from the early twelfth century, its octagonal base of alternating light and dark stone breached by half-oval windows demonstrating the mutual influence of Georgian, Armenian and early Turkish architecture. The other two *kümbet*s in the ensemble date from at least a century later and aren't nearly as compelling.

The citadel and Rüstem Paşa Bedesteni

On the opposite side of Cumhuriyet Caddesi from the Çifte Minareli Medrese, a narrow lane leads past some of the oldest houses in town and a handful of carpet/antique shops to the **citadel** or *kale* (daily 8am–5.30; 2YTL), whose vast rectangular bulk was originally laid out by Emperor Theodosius II. The interior is bare except for a shoebox-like *mescit*, or small mosque, capped by an afterthought of a *kümbet*-style dome. The adjacent freestanding **Tepsi Minare** now doubles as a clocktower; like the mosque it's mostly twelfth century, though the super-structure (which can be climbed) was added by the Russians during one of their occupations. Stairs on the east side lead up to the ramparts, and while the citadel is no longer the highest point in town since Erzurum began to spread to its rim of hills, it still lends the best view over the city – and the great, intimidating vastness of the plateau beyond.

Just northwest of the castle, but easiest reached by retracing your steps along Cumhuriyet Caddesi to descend Menderes Caddesi, stands the **Rüstem Paşa Bedesteni**, the covered bazaar, endowed by Süleyman the Magnificent's mid-sixteenth-century grand vizier. Erzurum owed much of its wealth to transconti-nental trade routes and even in the nineteenth century some forty thousand laden camels were passing through the city every year. Today trade is almost totally monopolized by **oltu taşı**, an obsidian-like material mined near Oltu, 150km northeast, and most frequently made into *tespih* (prayer beads), *kolye* (necklaces) and *küpe* (earrings). Prices start at about €8 for a tiny, ten-centimetre *tespih*; silver clasps cost €3–4 extra. Earrings go for anything between €3.50 and €11, depend-ing on the size and number of stones, but most importantly whether the setting is gold or silver; a longish necklace with a silver chain will run about €15.

The Archeological Museum

Erzurum's least compelling sight is the **Archeological Museum** (Arkeoloji Müzesi; Tues–Sun 8am–noon & 1–5pm; 2YTL), 400m south of Havuzbaşı roundabout. The ground floor has assorted Urartian and Caucasian pottery, plus some Roman and Hellenistic glassware and jewellery. There is also a rather unedifying "massacre room", containing items removed during the 1980s from two mass graves in the province – the property, it is claimed, of Turks and Kurds slaughtered by Arme-nians between 1915 and 1918.

Palandöken: skiing

Palandöken, stretching 5–6.5km south of town, offers far and away the best skiing in Turkey, more than adequate compensation for being stuck in Erzurum during its habitually arctic winters. With largely north-facing slopes ranging from 2300m near the *Palan Hotel* up to Point 3125 on Mount Ejder, excellent conditions (essentially nice dry powder on a two-metre base) are just about guaranteed. Pistes total 35km at present, with 10km more (and the lifts to serve them) projected; currently seven chairlifts, two drag-lifts and a telecabin give access to eight easy, six intermediate and two advanced runs, as well as four recognized off-piste routes.

Eating and drinking

Restaurants in Erzurum tend to offer good value, with a concentration of sorts on or around Cumhuriyet Caddesi and the central park; thanks in part to the local student contingent, they're also open later than you'd expect for the Anatolian interior, serving until 11.30pm or midnight in most cases. Not surprisingly in this devout town, licensed places are rare.

Restaurants

🏃 **Erzurum Evleri** Yüzbaşı Sok 18, south of Cumhuriyet Cad. Eight old dwellings knocked together to make an institution that's equal parts funhouse maze, folklore museum and restaurant. Antique displays comprise everything from Ottoman houseware to 1950s portable gramophones. The food's only just better than average, from a very limited menu, but the seating, shoeless on cushions around low tables occupying various alcoves with fireplaces and skylights, is highly atmospheric. Around 20YTL per head.

Güzelyurt Restaurant Cumhuriyet Cad 54/C. One of the oldest (founded 1928) restaurants in town, and one of the few licensed ones, where women can dine comfortably with friends or significant others. Erzurum's *beau monde* retire behind curtained windows for a nip of *rakı* (in small-measure pitchers), wine or beer to accompany good vegetable *meze*s and less-exalted grilled mains. Budget 25YTL depending on how much booze you have; price includes *garsoniye* charge for obsequious service and muzak covers of greatest (Western) classical hits.

🏃 **İstanbul Self Service** Mumcu Cad. Excellent, and popular, studenty place with wide range of traditional dishes served canteen-style. A two-course meal will set you back 3YTL.

Kılıçoğlu Sütiş Cumhuriyet Cad 20. The main branch of three in town for this premier pudding-shop and nemesis of dieters: two dozen flavours of *dondurma*, all other milk sweets, plus profiteroles, biscuits and every imaginable sort of oriental sticky cake.

Salon Asya Cumhuriyet Cad 27. Ace for kebabs and a full soup menu, with willing service, dazzling (read migraine-inducing) lighting and contemporary decor; you can fill up for under 8YTL.

Salon Çağın Cumhuriyet Cad 18/C. Fusty subterranean environment with contrastingly good food, including *mantı* (Asian ravioli) on Sunday and trout daily in summer; a big meal will set you back 8YTL.

Serender Pastanesi Cumhuriyet Cad 32. Cheaper but less varied offering than *Kılıçoğlu*; open until after midnight.

Listings

Airport bus Departs 2hr before flight time from in front of the THY office, Cumhuriyet Cad, Eren İş Merkezi 88/3 ☎0442/218 1904.

Banks and exchange The Türk Ticaret Bankası branch situated near the Gürcü Kapı roundabout up at the top of İstasyon Cad and the Garanti Bankası near THY accept travellers' cheques. You're better off using the three İş Bankası ATMs opposite the Yakutiye Parkı or the scattering of *döviz* stalls, such as Cihan Döviz, on the west side of Çaykara Cad, or Erzerum Döviz next to the *Salon Asya* on Cumhuriyet Cad.

Camping gas Small 190ml cartridges are usually available at İpragaz, İstasyon Cad 12/A.

Car rental Avis, Terminal Cad, Mavi Site, Birinci Blok ☎0442/233 8088; Evis, Terminal Cad 13/A ☎0442/234 4400, airport ☎0442/327 1377; Decar/Thrifty, airport only ☎0442/233 3560.

Cirit This is a sort of cross between polo and a jousting tournament, with the players on horseback eliminating opponents from the field by thrusts of a blunted javelin. Ask at the tourist office during spring and summer if a match is scheduled nearby.

Consulate Iran, Ülçer Apartments, Atatürk Bul, Yeni Şehir Girişi, on the minor road to Palandöken ☎0442/316 2285, ℗315 9983 – and read the box on p.921 for details on crossing into Iran before you leave Erzurum.

Hamam Most historic and salubrious is probably the Boyahane Hamamı, in the warren of lanes west of the Rüstem Paşa Bedesteni.

Hospitals One is north of Havuzbaşı on Hastaneler Cad, another south of Havuzbaşı on Yenişehir Cad, and still another (probably the best), the research and teaching hospital, south of the Ağrı- and Kars-bound highway in Yenişehir itself.

Internet cafés There are a number of them along Cumhuriyet Cad.

Supermarket Migros, by the train station, for "European-packaged" goods, especially trek-suitable fare.

Northwest of Erzurum: Çoruh-river citadels

As you head west out of Erzurum on the way to the Black Sea, you'll follow either of two roads away from the lorry route to Ankara. One follows the old Silk Route northwest down to Trabzon via **Bayburt**; the other leads north to Rize via **İspir**. After scaling the first range of peaks beyond Erzurum, both routes drop dizzyingly from 2300-metre passes to the **Çoruh river**, which flows through a deep trench that lies well below the level of the Anatolian plateau. This remote valley, reminiscent of deeper Central Asia or the American Southwest, was the ancestral homeland of the Bagratid clan (see box on p.820), who went on to furnish early medieval Armenia and Georgia with so many of their rulers.

Bayburt

BAYBURT is dwarfed by the largest **fortress** in Turkey, its history virtually synonymous with the town. Thought to have been erected in the sixth century during Byzantine emperor Justinian's skirmishes with the Laz tribe from the Black Sea, it was later appropriated by the Bagratids, until being taken and renovated by the Saltuk Turks early in the thirteenth century. The citadel was a much-coveted prize in the Russo-Turkish wars of the nineteenth and twentieth centuries, so it's something of a miracle that the perimeter walls are in such good condition – though this isn't true of the interior, where there's not much to see apart from the view.

Little else redeems Bayburt other than its position astride the young Çoruh river, best enjoyed at one of several riverside **restaurants** or **cafés** with wonderful views of the castle. There are thirteenth- and fourteenth-century **mosques** founded by Saltuk Turks and the İlhanid Mongol governor Cemaleddin Hoca Yakut – he of the *medrese* in Erzurum – but these fall squarely in the category of time-filling exercises, and the main reason to pause here is to break a journey between Trabzon and Erzurum. Otherwise content yourself with a glance at the fort while in transit.

Practicalities

Bayburt's small **otogar** is 500m south of the centre on the main highway, but buses to and from Erzurum often begin and end in the bazaar. If you need to stay, your best bets are two **hotels** on Cumhuriyet Caddesi, the main drag aiming right for the castle. The budget *Saracoğlu* at no. 13 (☎0458/211 7217; ②) has rooms overlooking the river, en-suite showers but toilets down the hall; across the road, a little way towards the *otogar*, the two-star *Hotel Adıbeş* (☎0458/211 5813; ③) is clean and comfortable, with large doubles and an attached restaurant.

For **eating out**, the enclosed *Yeni Zafer*, next to the central vehicle bridge over the Çoruh, is more appealing in winter, but the *Çoruh Lokantası* upstream, with riverbank seating under willow trees, has the edge during the warm months.

İspir

İSPIR, the Byzantine Hyspiratis, once rivalled Bayburt in importance, but has precipitously declined. The setting, overlooking a bend of the Çoruh, with a monument-crowned acropolis, promises much but disappoints up close. There's not even a proper gate left to the Bagratid **castle**, which hardly rewards a climb through the town's shanties; inside there's a squat, little-used mosque from the Saltuk era, and a badly ruined Byzantine church. The town itself is shabby, the only foreigners passing through those en route to the scenic Salaçur mountains just to the north. The two or three **hotels** and **restaurants** are among the most loathsome in Turkey, so it's a very good idea to avoid getting stuck here.

If you've arrived by **bus** from Rize on the way to Erzurum, or vice versa, you can get an onward bus the same day as long as you've made an early start. The last ones can be as late as 2.30pm, but it's safest to get a through service. If you deliberately alight here, one of the most interesting things to do is to cover the rough but scenic 91km of partly paved Highway 50 to Yusufeli, sometimes by public transport (dolmuşes run almost halfway, as far as Çamlıkaya) but more often than not by thumb.

Northeast of Erzurum: the road to Kars

Convoys of lorries often clog the heavily travelled Highway E80/100 beyond Erzurum, bound for Iran and (in peaceful times) Georgia. Once past Pasinler, the road follows the increasingly scenic valley of the infant Aras river, an excellent backdrop should the hard-pressed Turkish cinema industry ever crank out a string of "*pilav* Westerns".

Pasinler and around

PASINLER, 41km along, is distinguished only by the crumbled citadel of **Hasankale**, an originally Bagratid stronghold taken over by the Akkoyun Turcomans during the fifteenth century, and by its famous hot springs and mud baths. However, the town itself is shabby and the bath-building sterile and regimented, while the spa-side "two-star" *Kale Hotel* (℡0442/661 4994; ❶) has been awarded two stars too many, though it makes a feasible emergency overnight stop.

Twenty kilometres east, just past Köprüköy, the graceful thirteenth-century **Çobandede bridge**, the finest medieval bridge in Turkey, spans the Aras river in six arches near the beginning of its course, a particularly bewitching sight in late-afternoon light. The road, railway and river stick together until **Horasan**, where the E80/100 to Iran – via Ağrı and Doğubeyazit – peels off to the southeast, and the train tracks and Highway 80 meander north.

Sarıkamış

At Karakurt junction the river forsakes Kars-bound Highway 957, and starts a sharp descent toward the Caspian Sea. The next place of any consequence, nestled 6km off the main road amidst an unexpected forest of conifers, is **SARIKAMIŞ**, subject to the coldest climate in the country (and reachable by most Kars-bound buses). The winter of 1914–15 proved lethal here for the Ottoman Third Army under the command of the megalomaniac Enver Paşa, when – in one of the worst Turkish defeats of World War I – 75,000 men froze to death, died of typhus or were killed attempting to halt a Tsarist force of roughly equal size; in the wake of the debacle the Russians advanced to Erzurum and beyond, and you can still see their vast barracks, built to garrison troops at the then-frontier from 1878 until 1917.

Today the thick seasonal snow supports the very good **Cibiltepe ski resort**, 3km back east towards the main highway. Thus far, facilities comprise just two chairlifts from 2150m up to 2700m, serving two advanced runs, two intermediate ones and one novice piste threading the trees. At the foot of the lifts, the ostensibly three-star *Çamkar Sarıkamış "Motel"* (℡0474/413 5259, ✉camkar@domi.com.tr; ❹ half-board) offers medium-sized standard units with small, dated, shower-only bathrooms in a chalet-style structure with a sauna and licensed restaurant. The newer *Toprak Hotel* (℡0474/413 4111, ✉salessarikamishotel@toprak.com.tr; ❺), nearby, is a deal more comfortable.

If you intend to ski here, the budget alternative would be to arrange rental of equipment, lift passes and instruction at the lift offices and stay instead at the *Sarıkamış Turistik Otel* at Halk Cad 64 in the town centre (☎0474/413 4176; ❷), with its funky rustic-style lobby and spacious rooms. Other **hotels** on the same street are fleapits, and there's only one proper **restaurant**, *Dönerci Canbaba*, one block over at Belediye Cad 245; happily it's excellent and inexpensive, with a broad selection of kebabs, *pide*, soups and baked puddings.

The Kümbet Kilise

North of Sarıkamış, the scenery becomes humdrum again as the mountains level out onto the high, grassy steppe that surrounds Kars. About 9km before Kars, 200m northwest of the road near the village of Kümbetli and a smoking beet-sugar refinery, you'll glimpse the ruined, tenth-century Armenian church known as the **Kümbet Kilise**, the first of various such monuments in the province. The church was reported destroyed as long ago as 1830, and its original name forgotten. Far more interesting inside than its battered exterior suggests, this four-apsed, octagonal rotunda is essentially a miniature of the Holy Apostles church in Kars proper (see below). In the fan-top niches between the column capitals are four little relief gargoyles representing the Evangelists: the man of Matthew (southeast), the eagle of John (northeast), and the lion of Mark and bull of Luke (northwest/southwest), so badly worn as to be indistinguishable.

Kars

Hidden in a natural basin on the banks of the Kars Çayı, **KARS** is an oddly attractive town, unusual in Turkey with its incongruous terraces of Russian *belle époque* buildings. Although a couple of hundred metres lower than Erzurum, the climate is even more severe; the potholed streets never quite recover from the fierce winters and when it rains, which it often does, the outskirts become a treacherous swamp. There are a few sites in town worth dallying for, but most visitors have made the long trek out here for the sole purpose of visiting the former Armenian capital of Ani (see p.807).

Kars has improved beyond all recognition since the early 1990s. Central streets are well signposted, and/or repaved in cobbles or bricks, with even a designated pedestrian zone or two. There is a large Global Heritage Fund project underway (due to finish in 2007) which is seeing the area around the *kale* being revamped, Ottoman houses rebuilt, and ruined *hamam*s and churches restored. Also, something approximating a local middle-class, and the establishment of the Kafkas Üniversitesi, have prompted the emergence of better lodging, eating, drinking and shopping options.

Some history

Originally founded by the Armenians who knew it as Kari, Kars became the capital of their Bagratid dynasty early in the tenth century when the citadel, which still dominates the town, was substantially improved. Later in that century the main seat of Armenian rule was transferred to nearby Ani, and Kars lost some of its importance. The Selçuks took it along with almost everything else in the area during the mid-eleventh century, but devastating Mongol raids made a mockery of any plans the new overlords had for Kars. In 1205 the Georgians, profiting from the wane of both Selçuk and Byzantine power in the area, seized the town and held it for three centuries until displaced by the Ottomans.

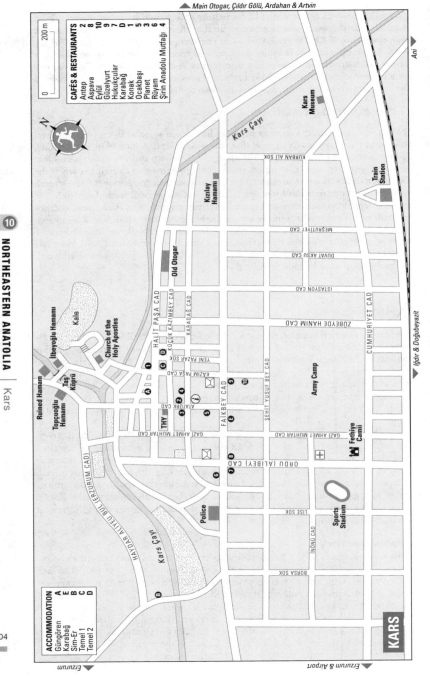

Main Otogar, Çıldır Gölü, Ardahan & Artvin

Ani

İğdır & Doğubeyazıt

Erzurum & Airport

Erzurum

KARS

CAFÉS & RESTAURANTS	
Antep	2
Aspava	8
Evtül	10
Güzelyurt	9
Hukukçular	7
Karabağ	D
Konak	1
Ocakbaşı	5
Planet	3
Rüyam	6
Şirin Anadolu Mutfağı	4

ACCOMMODATION	
Güngören	A
Karabağ	E
Sim-Er	B
Temel 1	C
Temel 2	D

Kars Museum

Kars Çayı

Kızılay Hamamı

Kurban Ali Sok

Train Station

Mesrutiyet Cad

Duvar Aksu Cad

İstasyon Cad

Zübeyde Hanım Cad

Cumhuriyet Cad

Old Otogar

Halit Paşa Cad

Karadağ Cad

Küçük Kazımbey Cad

Yeni Pazar Sok

Kazım Paşa Cad

Atatürk Cad

THY

Falkbey Cad

Gazi Ahmet Muhtar Cad

Şehit Yusuf Bey Cad

Army Camp

Gazi Ahmet Muhtar Cad

Fethiye Camii

Ordu (Alibey) Cad

Police

Kars Çayı

Haydar Aliyev Bul (Erzurum Cadi)

Sports Stadium

Lise Sok

İnönü Cad

Borsa Sok

Ruined Hamam

Topçuoğlu Hamam

İlbeyoğlu Hamam

Taş Köprü

Kale

Church of the Holy Apostles

0   200 m

N

Kars defends the approaches to Erzurum just as the latter is the key to the rest of Anatolia; the Russians tried repeatedly during the nineteenth century to capture the place. Sieges in 1828 and 1855 were successful – the latter during the Crimean War, when a British and Turkish garrison was starved out of the citadel after five months – but on both occasions Kars reverted to Turkey by terms of peace treaties. Not so in 1878, when, after a bloody eight-month war between the two powers, Kars was finally awarded to the Tsar. It remained in Russian or Armenian hands until 1920, a period that bequeathed both the unusual grid layout of the city centre and the incongruous *belle époque* buildings found here. Today Kars is, not surprisingly, still a major forward military position, swarming with soldiers who supplement its native population of 90,000.

Arrival and information

In the northeast of the town and within walking distance of most points of interest, the **old otogar**, on Küçük Kâzımbey Caddesi, now houses only dolmuşes to nearby Yusufeli, Ardahan, Posof (for Georgia) and Iğdır (change there for Doğubeyazit). For major towns such as Erzurum and beyond, you'll need the **long-distance otogar**, 5km east of the town centre – *servis* buses link it with bus company ticket offices in the town centre. Daily flights from Ankara land at the **airport**, 6km south of town beyond the bypass highway; a shuttle-bus service runs you into the centre, stopping at the THY office (see "Listings" on p.807). The **train station** lies 1km southeast of the centre, off Cumhuriyet Caddesi, on the way to the museum.

The **tourist office**, on the corner of Atatürk and Karadağ *caddesi*s (daily 8.30am–5.30pm; ☏0474/212 6817) issues maps of Ani, but tend to be unhelpful about anything else; they almost certainly won't be able to help you with information about the province's assorted churches and castles (see below). They may, however, refer you to the local English-speaking "fixer" and knowledgeable **guide** Celil Ersözoğlu (☏0532/226 3966, Ⓔcelilani@hotmail.com), who arranges reliable group taxi and minibus tours to Ani and remoter monuments – though he will probably find you first.

Accommodation

Accommodation options in Kars have improved immeasurably through the years, although some cheaper establishments remain beyond the pale (we've had a report of theft from a room at an unlisted dosshouse).

Güngören Oteli Millet Sok 4, just off Halitpaşa Cad ☏0474/212 5630, Ⓕ223 4821. Large rooms with shocking colour schemes but modernized baths, plus decent ground-floor restaurant and a hamam. ❸
Hotel Karabağ Faikbey Cad 142 ☏0474/212 3480, Ⓦwww.hotel-karabag.com. A 1994-built, overpriced three-star whose decor and furnishings are already ageing. Rear rooms are the largest and quietest, with tubs in large bathrooms, and there's heating throughout. There's a naff bar-with-disco-ball just off the lobby, itself the smoky meeting place of local worthies at all hours, but the mez-zanine breakfast salon/restaurant (see "Eating and drinking", overleaf) is OK. ❺
Sim-Er Hotel West edge of town on the old

Erzurum road, Haydar Aliyev Bul ☏0474/212 7241, Ⓦwww.simerhotel.com. An externally grim high-rise, built in 1999 as a four-star, with most effort devoted to the common areas. The sharply overpriced, pastel-coloured rooms have poor bath-rooms, though the four-person suites are worth the extra outlay. Rooms ❺, suites ❼
Temel 1 & 2 Yeni Pazar Cad, just off Halitpaşa Cad ☏0474/223 1376, Ⓕ223 1323. The best choices in Kars; *Temel 1* had a thorough year-2000 refit, making it a cosy, clean place to stay, whilst 100m down the same street, the brand-new *Temel 2* offers even better value. The friendly management also arranges minibus excursions (20YTL per person) to Ani. *Temel 1* ❸, *Temel 2* ❷

The Town

The **Church of the Holy Apostles**, just the other side of the Kars Çayı on the way to the castle, was erected between 930 and 937 by the Armenian king Abbas I. Crude reliefs of the twelve apostles adorn the twelve arches of the dome, but otherwise it's a squat, functional bulk of dark basalt; the belfry and portico are relatively recent additions. A church when Christians held Kars, a mosque when Muslims ruled, it briefly housed the town museum before being reconsecrated in 1998 as the Kümbet Camii. Just before or after prayer times, you can slip inside to view the elaborately carved altar-screen.

Before climbing the short distance to the *kale*, or castle, detour slightly up the tributary of the Kars Çayı to see the **Taş Köprü**, or "Stone Bridge", made of the same volcanic rock as the nearby church and restored during the 1580s by order of Murat III. A few **hamams**, none dating from before the eighteenth century, huddle nearby: **İlbeyoğlu**, the **Mazlutağa** and **Topçuoğlu**, the latter scheduled for imminent restoration.

There has been a fortress of some kind on the hill overlooking the river confluence for well on two millennia. The Armeno-Byzantine structure was maintained by the Selçuks but levelled by the Mongols; the Ottomans rebuilt it as part of their late sixteenth-century urban overhaul, only to have the Russians blast it to bits, then put it back together again during the nineteenth century. On October 30, 1920, an Armenian Dashnakist army besieged in the castle surrendered to Turkish general Halitpaşa (he of the street), and with that went any hopes of an Armenian state straddling both banks of the Ahuryan river.

After decades as an off-limits military reserve, **Kars Kalesi** as it's officially known (daily 9am–7pm; free), is now open as a park. Locals come to pay their respects at the tomb of Celal Baba, a holy man of the fourteenth century, and to enjoy the panorama over Kars, but there's little else to see other than the black-masoned military engineering.

At the time of writing, the only other compelling attraction in Kars is the excellent **Kars Museum** (Kars Müzesi; daily 8.30am–5.30pm; 2YTL), a fifteen-minute walk out to the east end of town, whose ethnographic section includes such curiosities as a ceramic *yayık* (butter churn) and a cradle, as well as jewellery, leatherwork and extensive exhibits on local carpets and kilims. Downstairs is given over to ancient pottery, and ecclesiastical artefacts of the departed Russians and Armenians, particularly a huge church bell inscribed "This Tolls for the Love of God", and a pair of wooden doors, which graced one of the cathedrals before 1920. On the way back pay a visit to the **Fethiye Camii**, a converted nineteenth-century Russian Orthodox church.

Eating and drinking

Fortunately the **restaurant** scene in Kars is a bit more promising and fairly priced than the hotel prospects. It's also easier than in Erzurum to get alcohol with your meal, though be aware that the after-hours *müzikhols* ("music-halls") along Halitpaşa Caddesi are haunted by a certain *natasha*-influenced, vodka-soaked sleaziness – and often knots of police cars parked in readiness outside. The limited number of youth-oriented **bars** are better bets for a night out, especially for women; doyen of these is the *Planet* at Atatürk Cad 108, which has occasional live music at weekends as well as pastries, fast food and a full range of hard drinks (about 4YTL each).

Antep Pide ve Lahmacun Atatürk Cad. The most varied and best-executed *pide* and *lahmacun* in the city. Unlicensed.

Aspava Lokantası Faikbey Cad 74, corner Ordu Cad. Never mind the lurid lighting and kitsch decor, this is the best of a handful of

24-hour soup and *sulu yemek* kitchens in town – a godsend if you've arrived on a late bus; chunky, reviving *İşkembe* a speciality. The name, incidentally, is an anagram of the popular prayer *Allah Sıhhat Para Afiyet Versin Amin* (God Grant Truth, Money and Health, Amen).

Eylül Kâzımpaşa Cad, just south of Faikbey Cad. The most appealing and quietly set of a handful of *pastanes*, with milk-based sweets, wood-panelled decor and an upstairs gallery. Try the famous local honey (*bal*) with a continental breakfast.

Güzelyurt Lokantası Faikbey Cad, corner Kâzımpaşa Cad. Large, basic cheapie, surprisingly enough licensed, featuring soups in the morning and wraparound windows for you to watch the world (and vice versa).

Hukukçular Ordu Cad 218, corner Faikbey Cad. Upstairs *meyhane* that's better (and friendlier) than it looks from outside. Full booze list but the menu is limited to a half-dozen vegetarian *mezes* of the day, and a range of grills. Budget 6YTL for a meal with beer.

Karabağ *Karabağ Hotel*, 1st floor, Faikbey Cad 142. This is the spot for white-tablecloth service and a full wine list, though the food (only *mezes* and grills after the few ready dishes run out) doesn't really rate the prices asked – 14YTL or so each with a modest intake of drink.

Ocakbaşı Atatürk Cad 176. Not to be confused with a namesake two doors down, this unlicensed outfit gets a brisk trade for the sake of its good kebabs and *pide* (if not the often shambolic service) in a mock-troglodytic/Flinstones environment.

Rüyam Pizza Faikbey Cad 19. Excellent, cheap pizza-place which also serves burgers, kebabs and *pide*. Plan on spending 5YTL for a good meal.

Şirin Anadolu Mutfağı Karadağ Cad 5. Despite the name ("Amiable Anatolian Cuisine"), this merely offers standard *pide* and *kebap* – but very well done. It's in the heart of Kars's first pedestrian zone, opposite the fountains, with ground-floor seating in a contemporary environment and a pleasant, nocturnal café-only section upstairs for dessert and nonalcoholic drinks.

Listings

Airport bus Shuttle bus (3YTL), departing 1hr 45min before flight time from the THY agent, which is Sınır Turizm, Atatürk Cad 86 (℡0474/212 3838), or from Atlas Jet on Faikbey Cad 66 (℡0474/212 4747), also 1hr 45min before take-off.

Banks and exchange There are several ATMs dotted around the town centre. Otherwise use several efficient *döviz* on Kazımpaşa Cad.

Hamams The *Güngören Hotel* has an attached hamam for men only. The newer Kızılay Hamamı (men 6.30am–11pm; women noon–5pm) is about 500m northeast of the town centre on Faikbey Cad.

Hospital Near army camp and sports stadium on İnönü Cad.

Internet access Try the *Marmara*, also with pool tables, directly above the listed *Ocakbaşı* restaurant.

Post office Main PTT branch (open late into evenings) is a bit out of the way on Ordu Cad; there's also a useful çarşı branch on Kâzımpaşa Cad.

Ani

Once the capital of Bagratid Armenia, **ANI** is today a melancholy, almost vacant triangular plateau, divided from Armenia by the stunning Arpa Çayı (Ahuryan river) gorge and very nearly separated from the rest of Turkey by two deep tributaries. The site is mainly an expanse of rubble, but from it rise some of the finest examples of ecclesiastical and military architecture of its time. The Armenians were master stoneworkers, and the fortifications that defend the northern, exposed side of the plateau, and the handful of churches behind, are exquisite compositions in a blend of ruddy sandstone and darker volcanic rock. These, and the cliffs fringing the river, are the only vertical features here, dwarfed by an evocative but relentlessly horizontal landscape. It is inconceivable that you'd venture east of Erzurum or Artvin without fitting Ani into your plans.

Some history

There was a settlement here before Christian times, centred on the citadel near the southern tip of the upland; the name Ani is perhaps a corruption of "Anahit", a Persian water-goddess who was one of the chief deities of the pagan Armenians. The city first came to prominence after the local instalment of the Armenian Gam-sarkan clan during the fifth century. Situated astride a major east–west caravan route, Ani prospered, receiving fresh impetus when Ashot III, fifth in the line of the Bagratid kings of Armenia, transferred his capital here from Kars in 961. For three generations the kingdom and its capital, under the successive rule of Ashot, Smbat II and Gagik I, enjoyed a golden age. Beautified and strengthened militarily, with a population exceeding a hundred thousand, Ani rivalled Baghdad and Constantinople themselves.

By the middle of the eleventh century, however, wars of succession and the religiously motivated enmity of the Byzantines (the Armenian Apostolic Church was deemed heretical) took their toll. The Byzantine Empire, having neutralized Bagratid power, annexed the city in 1045, but in the process dissolved an effective bulwark against the approaching Selçuks, who took Ani with little resistance in 1064. After the collapse of the Selçuks, the Armenians returned in less than a century, this time with the assistance of the powerful Georgian kingdom. The Pahlavuni and Zakhariad clans ruled over a reduced but still semi-independent Armenia for two more centuries, continuing to endow Ani with churches and monasteries. The Mongol raids of the thirteenth century, a devasting earthquake in 1319 and realigned trade routes proved mortal blows to both Ani and its hinterland; thereafter the city was gradually abandoned, and forgotten until noticed by European travellers of the nineteenth century.

Visiting the site

Ani lies 45km southeast of Kars, just beyond the village of Ocaklı. Without your own transport, the most common way of getting there is to take a **taxi tour** for about €40 a vehicle. Solo travellers typically band together at the tourist office; the taxis hold four passengers, and minibuses carrying up to nine customers (€12 each) are also available. The ruins are scattered, and many monuments are absorbing, so allow a good two and a half to three hours at Ani, plus two hours for going there and back – make sure your driver agrees to a **five-hour** stint. Midsummer is usually very **hot**, so you're advised to bring a hat, sun cream and water to tour the site – as well as some snack food.

Although **restrictions** for visiting Ani were recently lifted, and you no longer require a permit, the site still nudges up against the highly sensitive Armenian border, and whole areas remain out of bounds. The *jandarma*, who patrol the site continuously, will let you know which areas these are.

The site

The vast **boundary walls** of Ani, dating from the late tenth century and studded with countless towers, are visible from several kilometres as you approach past villages teeming with sheep, buffalo, horses, donkeys and geese. The **ticket office** (daily 7am–8pm; 5YTL) is at the **Aslan Kapısı**, so named because of a sculpted Selçuk lion on the wall just inside, and sole survivor of the four original gates.

Once beyond the inner wall you're confronted with the sight of the vast forlorn, weed-tufted plateau, dotted with only the sturdiest bits of masonry that have outlasted the ages. A system of **signposted paths**, many of them remnants of the former main streets of Ani, lead to or past all of the principal remains.

Church of the Redeemer

Bear slightly left and head first about 500m southeast to the **Church of the Redeemer** (Prkitch), built between 1034 and 1036. In 1957, half of the building was sheared away by lightning, so that the remainder, seen from the side, looks uncannily like a stage set, albeit one with the carved filigree crosses and Armenian inscriptions. Three metres up on the exterior wall you can see a frieze

△ Church of the Redeemer, Ani

of a cross on an ornate rectangular background; this is a fine example of the typically Armenian *khatchkar* (literally "cross-stone") carvings that gave their name to the Kaçkar mountains. Adjacent are the labelled remains of an "**oil press**" – more likely a wine press, as even a millennium ago the climate here would not have been mild enough to support olive cultivation.

Church of St Gregory and Convent of the Virgins

Some 200m east, tucked down a stair-path by a course of wall overlooking the Arpa Çayı, the charming monastic **Church of St Gregory the Illuminator** (Tigran Honents) is the best preserved of Ani's monuments, and somewhat confusingly one of three dedicated to the saint who brought Christianity to Armenia at the start of the fourth century. The pious foundation of a merchant nobleman in 1215, it's unusually laid out in a rectangle divided width-wise into three (though a colonnaded narthex and small baptistry have mostly collapsed). The ground plan reflects the prominent Georgian influence in thirteenth-century Ani, and the fact that the Orthodox, not the Armenian Apostolic, rite was celebrated here. The church still sports delicate exterior relief-work, including extensive avian designs.

But Tigran Honents is most rewarding for its **frescoes**, the only ones surviving at Ani, which cover most of the interior and spill out around the current entrance onto what was once the narthex wall, giving the church its Turkish name *Resimli Kilise* or "Painted Church". They are remarkable both for their high degree of realism and fluidity – especially compared to the static iconography of the contemporaneous Byzantines – and for the subject matter, depicting episodes in early Armenian Christianity as well as the doings of ordinary people. As you enter the first of the two nave compartments, you'll see in the lower two rows of images on your right *The Trial of St Gregory by King Trdat III*, *The Martyrdom of Hrpsime* (an early female convert) and *The Torture of St Gregory*. All these events took place before Trdat's repentance and conversion, the earliest sovereign to do so; to the left are secular vignettes from the life of King Trdat. The transept is taken up by scenes from the life of Christ: on the south wall are *The Annunciation*, *The Nativity*, *The Entry into Jerusalem* and *The Dormition of the Virgin*; to the north is *The Raising of Lazarus*, with *The Apostles* ringing the drum of the dome. On the upper level of the apse is shown *The Communion of the Apostles*, depicting Christ dispensing the Host. All images have had eyes and faces vandalized by pious Muslims.

From Tigran Honents, a narrow trail leads past the Selçuk baths and skims the tops of the cliffs above the Arpa Çayı before finding a steep way down to the thirteenth-century **Convent of the Virgins** (Kusanats), perched on a ledge even closer to the river. A minuscule, rocket-like rotunda church, contemporary with Tigran Honents, is flanked by a smaller chapel or baptistry, and the whole enclosed by a perimeter wall. Just downstream are the evocative stubs of the ruined medieval **bridge** over the Arpa, though it's unwise (if not actually forbidden) to approach it – the Turkish bank of the river is stoutly fenced and probably mined as well.

The cathedral and around

Rejoining the main plateau trail heading west from Tigran Honents, you reach the elegantly proportioned **cathedral**, completed between 989 and 1010. The architect, one Trdat Mendet, could present rather impressive credentials, having very recently completed restoration of the earthquake-damaged dome of Aya Sofya in Constantinople. However, this is a surprisingly plain, rectangular building, with just the generic blind arcades of Armenian churches and no external apse; the dome, once supported by four massive pillars, has long since vanished. The main entrance was – unusually – not to the west, opposite the apse, but on the side of the nave, through the south wall. A **replica** of this church was in the early stages of being built at the time of writing – across on the Armenian side of the river, and clearly visible (and audible) from Ani itself.

A little to the west, within sight of the cathedral, is an excavated area, apparently a medieval **street lined with shops**. Just beyond stands what's known as the **Menüçehir Camii**, billed as the earliest Selçuk mosque in Anatolia, though its lack of *mihrab*, its alternating red and black stonework and its inlaid mosaic ceiling, invite suspicions of mixed antecedents. Certainly the view from the ornate gallery over the frontier river fits more with use as a small palace. The truncated minaret was briefly off-limits for a while after a tourist committed suicide by leaping off, though the daring may now clamber up the eroded steps for an unrivalled aerial view of the site. Slightly southwest, the foundations of a purportedly verified "**palace**" have been exposed.

At this point, you'll probably meet the friendly *jandarma*, who will prevent you from wandering any further, and, presumably, from climbing up the minaret.

At the southern tip of the triangular site lies the inner **citadel** or İç Kale, which has long languished in a forbidden zone and is likely to remain so. Beyond the fortress at the far south end of the city, also off-limits but visible from many points of the riverbank escarpment, perches the fairy-tale monastery of **Kız Kilisesi**, spectacularly sited above a sharp curve in the river gorge, and originally accessed by a tunnel carved into the rock that has long since eroded. Should you be allowed out here by lenient *jandarma* personnel, the view back towards the main site gives an insight into the defence of the city, with steep gorges protecting the east and west flanks of the city, and high walls linking the two sides.

The northerly churches

North of the Menüçehir Camii stands the second **Church of St Gregory** (Abighamrets), begun in 1040 by the same individual responsible for the Church of the Redeemer. This rotunda is like no other at Ani – instead of just merely blind arcades in a flat surface, the twelve-sided exterior is pierced by functional recessed vaults, which alternate with the six rounded interior niches to lend extra structural stability. The east side of the building is slowly but surely losing its dressed stone.

The nearby, so-called "Kervansaray" began life as the eleventh-century **Church of the Holy Apostles** (Arak Elots), and despite ruinous first impressions proves a rewarding hybrid Selçuk–Christian monument. At first the church seems to have an odd south-to-north orientation, with a rounded apse at the north end – then you realize that this is the *kervansaray* bit added at a later date, and that the western half of the church nave is three-quarters crumbled but still discernible. Copious Armenian inscriptions confirm the building's original use, while overhead in the nave, superb four-way ribbing arcs cross an intricate ceiling in a two-colour mosaic pattern, culminating in a stalactite-vaulted dome.

The main circuit continues north to the sparse ruins of a third **Church of St Gregory of Gagik**, begun in 998 by Trdat, architect of the cathedral. Intact, it would have been one of the largest rotundas in medieval Armenia proper, but the design, based on the three-storey, seventh-century rotunda at Zvartnots in Armenia, collapsed almost immediately, so that today only man-high outer walls, bases of the dome piers and giant column-stumps remain.

Before completing your tour at the Aslan Kapısı, you can stop in at the **Selçuk Palace**, the only indisputably Islamic item at Ani, tucked into the northwest extremity of the ramparts. Since 1988, this has been meticulously rebuilt – the only structure to receive any degree of archeological investigation and maintenance, and a striking example of ultranationalist archeology in action.

Other churches and castles around Kars

The present-day province of Kars formed an important part of the Bagratid kingdom between the sixth and the eleventh centuries, and of the Zakhariad clan's holdings during the thirteenth century, so it's not surprising that there are numerous local **churches and castles**, mostly Armenian, besides those at Ani. The Armenians had a particular flair for poising their churches on sheer rock-faces overlooking river canyons, and many of the remains detailed below adhere to this pattern; even in their ruinous state they are still among the most impressive sights in northeastern Turkey.

Visiting them is not always straightforward, however: some are in bad condition, others accessible only by atrocious, poorly marked roads or on foot, or else they lie in military security zones – sometimes all three. You'll really need your own transport or a cooperative taxi-driver, enough Turkish to ask directions from villagers, and one of the two most detailed **maps** available – the 1:800,000 GeoCenter/RV *Turkey East*, or the Reinhard Ryborsch 1:500,000 Karayolları Haritası no. 6, *Rize-Kars-Erzurum-Muş-Diyarbakır-Van* – though even these are full of serious, potentially time-wasting errors.

The only useful **public transport** in the area described below are the daily minibuses from Kars to Iğdır and from Kağızman to Çengilli, and the more regular Kars–Digor and Kağızman–Tuzluca minibuses.

Access, restrictions and information

The **border region** abutting Armenia is generally subject to strict army or *jandarma* control in a zone varying in width from a few paces (as at Ani) to several hundred metres; if you actually approach the Arpa (Ahuryan) stream, which forms

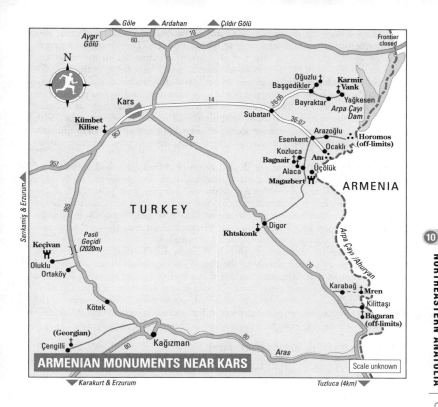

the frontier until its union with the Aras river, you may well spark off an international incident. At times in the past, the entire region between the Digor–Tuzluca highway and the frontier was a no-go area after dark – even the villagers were not allowed to move about. The main road between Digor and Tuzluca still has at least two *jandarma* **checkpoints**, but upon presentation of ID foreigners are waved straight through.

At the time of writing, only two of the monumental zones described below – Horomos and Bagaran – remain absolutely **off-limits**, though Magazbert fortress will require a parley (and thus a local taxi-driver's assistance) with the *jandarma* detachment stationed nearby. To visit Horomos or Bagaran, contact the central military command in Ankara several weeks in advance, presenting yourself as a high-level university student of medieval art or architecture, with supporting documents; permission is more often denied than granted, and in practice most tourists simply don't have the time. Don't just head off hoping for the best; you'll certainly be detected by the military and turned back, and should you somehow slip through, be aware that the area around Horomos in particular is known to be mined.

For many years the tourist-information authorities in Kars were markedly disinclined to help visitors find these monuments; this becomes more understandable once you accept that the past treatment of these churches is as sensitive a topic as the alleged mistreatment of the Armenians themselves in 1895 and 1915. Officially

Armenians don't exist historically, and any archeological evidence of their past rule is either ignored or misattributed to Islamic builders. The continued presence of recognizable churches in this part of Turkey constituted a major inconvenience to most post-1923 Turkish governments, which saw them as the basis for potential Armenian territorial claims and demands for reparations. Certain entities would rather that outsiders did not see the churches, and would probably be relieved if they disappeared altogether. Several sources claim that army demolition units have helped the process along with dynamite or bulldozers since the 1950s – compounding extensive damage done between 1914 and 1923 – and while this is debatable, it's certainly true that nothing is being done to preserve these monuments.

Since the late 1990s, however, Kars tourism honchos have had a change of heart, correctly reckoning that tourists would stay an extra night or two in town if they had a good reason besides Ani to do so. There are now pictures of all the monuments noted below prominently posted in the tourist office as well as the museum, and civilian authorities have made some slow progress in allowing visits to Ani without permits. Matters can only improve as some of the local bitterness engendered by the long Armenian–Azeri war abates.

Once you show up at a remote church or castle, **local villagers** are generally only too happy to point the way to the ruins. They have no ethnic axe to grind and are honoured that someone should bother to visit what for them is a barn – or a quarry for building stone. Incidentally, some degree of attention from outsiders is often enough to stop any ongoing vandalism, not so much in anticipation of the monetary benefit of increased tourist traffic, but because the village elders consider that they lose face if a "cultural" institution on their patch deteriorates.

Monuments around Ani

A number of churches and castles in the immediate vicinity of Ani are easily visited with your own transport or a cooperative taxi; they will enjoyably fill a day already half-spent at the more extensive ruins. Be warned that there are absolutely no formal tourist facilities near any of those remote sites – bring picnic fare or trust in village hospitality (often forthcoming, in conjunction with a lot of curious attention from the locals).

Oğuzlu, Karmir Vank and Horomos

Just before Subatan, itself 27km from Kars, head northeast 11km along the minor 36-06 road to Başgedikler, then bear left at the T-junction, for 2km more to **Oğuzlu**. The massive, tenth-century hilltop church here is visible from some distance, but proves disappointing up close; roofless and half-collapsed, it's devoid of ornament other than some blind niches on the exterior, flanking the apse. The original name and dedication are unknown.

Much more intact and interesting is the thirteenth-century **church of Karmir Vank** (in Turkish *Kızıl Kilise* – both mean "Red Monastery"), reached by returning to the junction at Başgedikler and proceeding 4.5km east on a now-dirt road to the hamlet of **Bayraktar**, looping around on its right, forking left (northeast) just above the village and continuing for 3.2km more to the westernmost *mahalle* of **Yağkesen**. The church is helpfully visible on the final stretch, often protruding vertically from the flat Kars steppe; it's a beauty, despite being currently used as a barn, with hay and *tezek* patties stacked to one side and the land sloping gently down to a stream on the other. This compact, cross-in-square-plan building of 1228 was well restored in 1887 and still retains its dome and checkerboard-patterned cladding stone. The apsidal end is flat; ornamentation is confined to *khatchkar*s and inscriptions on the west facade, simple carvings over the windows, and blind niches on the north and south walls.

About 5km northeast and upstream from Ani via the village of Arazoğlu, just below the Arpa Çayı dam, the intriguing monastic complex of **Horomos** (sometimes Köşe Vank) huddles on a secluded terrace above the river; it's currently off-limits to tourists. Founded in the tenth century, Horomos comprises a church (complete with a delicate lantern over the dome), a *zhamatoun* or chapter house, and various Selçuk and Armenian mausoleums in a walled enclosure at the brink of the Arpa Çayı. Because of its tucked-away location, Horomos never got much press from nineteenth-century travellers compared to Ani, but locals who were able to visit before the checkpoints and mines went in say it runs a close second in interest to its neighbour – and is worth pestering the authorities over, to see if the no-access policy has changed.

Bagnair and Magazbert

These two monuments are both south of the 36-07 provincial road linking Kars with Ani. Just 6km before the ruins, there's a right-angle intersection at the edge of Esenkent village; go south onto the side road and after 6km more turn right (west) towards the village of **Kozluca**, 2km further on. The two churches of Bagnair should be in plain sight. Incidentally, disregard all maps which show Bagnair by the village of Bulanık, about 15km northwest. Fork right at Kozluca's lowest buildings to proceed directly to the smaller church; the other track leads to the larger structure, though it's easy enough to walk the 200m between them.

The larger monastic church at **Bagnair** (or Bagnayr) was founded between 1010 and 1012 by the Armenian prince Smbat, supplanting the smaller church, which had already existed here for some decades. The latter continued as a dependency of the new monastery, which vanished from history after the 1200s, though travellers reported the buildings largely intact until early in the twentieth century. Today the main *katholikon*, consisting of a shrine to the Mother of God abutting a *zhamatoun*, is two-thirds vanished; the *zhamatoun* retains a dome, fine stalactite vaulting in the ceiling, and several massive columns, and still dwarfs the church abutting it, of which only the west nave remains. Across the ravine, the **smaller church**, like its neighbour used as a hay-barn, has fared much better; its twelve-sided dome-drum crowns a hexagonal structure, with five internal apses and a west portal (difficult to reach through all the hay) in lieu of a sixth.

To reach the Armeno-Byzantine fortress of **Magazbert** (aliases Mağazbert, Magarsbert), return to the side road from Kozluca and drive 3km south to the turning east for the village of **Üçölük** – and in all probability a detachment of *jandarma* at the junction, who will quiz you as to what you're up to (a local escort is helpful here) and consult by walkie-talkie with their HQ. Assuming you get permission, head 1.3km towards the village – don't actually go to the central "roundabout" unless you want a guide – and find another track heading south from near the *jandarma* post; non-4WD cars must be left at a huge, suspension-destroying rut. The track descends into a mostly dry ravine draining to the Arpa Çayı, crossing to the far bank and giving a good view of Cappadocian-style fairy chimneys on the north flank on its progress (35min on foot) to the base of the fortress.

What impresses on approach are the three western bastions, like elephant's toes, fronting a long, narrow, internally desolate **castle** dominating a sharp S-bend in the frontier river – be sure to come in the late afternoon as they catch the sun's last rays. Originally erected during the late tenth or early eleventh century, the fortress was taken in 1579 by the Ottomans, who made some modifications around the gateway (commemorated by an inscription), but abandoned it within a few decades as part of a truce with the Persians.

From the *jandarma*-manned junction it's possible to continue about 20km more, via Âlem, to Digor.

Monuments around Digor

The two currently visitable churches covered below are even more architecturally and historically significant than those around Ani, but require fairly long walks to reach and together will occupy nearly a full day in themselves, even with your own transport. **Digor** (Tekor in Armenian), 40km southeast of Kars, is the closest large village but has few amenities other than fairly frequent dolmuşes to and from Kars.

Khtskonk

The closest monument to Digor is a dramatically set church at **Khtskonk** (Beşkilise), a few kilometres upstream along the Digor Çayı; ignore all maps, which erroneously show a "Chtskonk" northeast of the highway. If you don't want to walk a fairly taxing hour up the gorge from the village, have the bus set you down, or drive, 4.5km north of town along Highway 70, near the top of the pass. Leave the vehicle here and turn onto a rough dirt track veering southwest from the asphalt, heading some 600m towards the gorge of the Digor Çayı. Walk behind the white-pumice quarry and uphill, west-northwest, for 200m and then turn left down a dry ravine. The path follows the right-hand bank downhill and then curves northwest to enter the gorge. Continue along the path, midway between the valley floor and clifftop above, for twenty minutes to reach the church (a total of 35–40min from your start point).

There were originally five churches (*beşkilise* in Turkish) perched at the Khtskonk monastic complex on the rim of the narrow canyon, but the rotunda of **St Sergius** (Sargis), founded in 1029, is the sole survivor. All five were restored in 1878, but at some time between 1920 and 1965 the other four were destroyed either by rolling boulders onto them or with explosives. St Sergius's side-walls are rent by fissures, but the dome is still intact and the west wall is covered in intricate Armenian inscriptions, making it the equal of any single monument at Ani.

Mren and Bagaran

From Digor, Highway 70 continues just under 45km to the intersection with Highway 80, passing the side roads for two important Armenian monuments. The only one currently accessible is the seventh-century Cathedral of Mren, a unique specimen even in a region rich in such art and well worth the long trip out.

Some 21km southeast of Digor, keep an eye peeled for a dirt road heading east, rustily signposted for the village of **Karabağ**; if you overshoot the turn-off, you'll know it, as the cathedral also shows clearly to the east from the main road, after about 10km further on. After 2km along the proper detour, Mren appears on the horizon beyond the village. Keeping the church in sight, drive through Karabağ, adopting the onward track between a sheet-roofed mosque and the livestock wallow-pond; about 700m beyond these – roughly 5km in total from the highway – non-4WD vehicles must be left at track-side, on a slope above the Digor Çayı. From here it's fifty minutes' walk east-southeast at an average pace to the church, which is bigger (and further away, at 4.5km) than it looks. The track first descends to the stream, which has both a jeep ford and narrow pedestrian bridge, and then curls up the far bank of the valley before dwindling on the far side as it crosses a volcanic plateau within sight of two military watch-points (whose occupants, if any, make no attempt to stop passers-by).

Once the focus of a fair-sized town, **Mren** (Mirini) stands atop a very slight rise on this desolate plateau, near the confluence of the Digor and Arpa streams, which both flow out of sight. The town was abandoned at some point in the fourteenth century amidst İlhanid Mongol raids, but its rubble still litters the immediate surroundings. The cathedral itself was completed in 639–640 by David Saharuni, Prince of Armenia, and as one of the earliest examples of Armenian architecture it exhibits a marked Byzantine influence with its elongated cross-in-square, three-aisled ground plan and octagonal dome supported by four pillars. The structure, built of alternating red and dark basalt blocks, weathered the centuries remarkably well before 1920 – the dome still retains most of its tiles – though the southwest corner and south transept vault have collapsed since then. A fissure is threatening to detach the north wall and the floor has been completely dug up by treasure-hunters.

The most outstanding **decorative features** include numerous, extravagant *khatchkar*s on the inner and outer south wall; the outer apse and north wall are by contrast featureless except for a somewhat defaced lintel relief over the north door, showing the *Restoration of the Cross* at Jerusalem in 630, following its removal by the Persians in 614. The Byzantine empereror Heraklios, on the left, walks from his horse towards a young man steadying the Holy Rood, while to the right stands Modestos, Bishop of Jerusalem, and a Tree of Life. Much clearer is the relief over the west door: here two angels hover above Christ (centre), St Peter and St Paul, in turn flanked by the donors of the church – Sarahuni and the bishop Theophilos (right), and the clean-shaven princeling Nerses Kamsarakan (left). This kind of relief ornamentation continued to be used in the Caucausus long after it passed from favour in Byzantium.

The ninth-century Bagratid citadel-town of **Bagaran** (or Pakran) incorporates an earlier seventh-century square four-apsed cathedral, but unless Armeno-Turkish relations improve dramatically, the site will remain off-limits. The adjacent modern village is Kilittaşı, to which an unmarked side-turning 5.5km south of the Karabağ access road leads after a like distance to a roadblock manned by *jandarma* – who will curtly send you back the way you came, so don't bother trying.

Çengilli and Keçivan Kalesi

Just south of the confluence of the Aras and Arpa rivers, right on the Armenian border, Highway 70 joins Highway 80 – the latter leading south to Tuzluca and Iğdır (see below), or west to Kağızman. Just below Kağızman – which is 4km uphill off the main highway – a bridge over the Aras carries Highway 965 north back towards Kars. Some 800m past this bridge, the first dirt road to the left (west) follows a rutted, jeep-only 25-kilometre route up into the mountains, through three timeless villages, to finally arrive at **ÇENGILLI**, home to an anomalous thirteenth-century **Georgian monastery**. Not only was the contemporary population of the area largely Armenian, but the architecture apes the tenth- and eleventh-century styles of Georgian specimens further north – specifically Tbeti (see p.839). Unlike Tbeti, the enormous church here has survived fairly intact to this day. Public transport from Kağızman is limited to a single daily minibus, departing from the main square at about 3.45pm – enforcing an overnight stay in primitive Çengilli.

From the Kağızman bridge, Highway 80 scenically follows the Aras west and upstream as far as Karakurt on the Erzurum–Kars road. It's a colourful journey in an often otherwise drab area, where the green and blonde of hay fields and apricot orchards contrast with the tones of the volcanic rock comprising the valley flank. In the relatively tidy riverside villages, satellite dishes jab the skyline along with poplars and pyramids of hay or dung.

Returning north from the Kağızman bridge towards Kars via Kötek, after about 20km a choice of side roads lead west towards **Keçivan Kalesı** (Geçvan in Armenian). Access is either via Ortaköy, 3.5km off the asphalt, with a subsequent hour and a half's walk, or by a rough twelve-kilometre drive, the first 5km to Oluklu and then 7km southwest from there. The castle's western ramparts and gates are in fair condition, though little else remains of the third-century Armenian fortified town sacked by the Persians after a year's siege. Back on the main road, the route back to Kars crosses the **Paslı pass** (2020m) and the ensuing plateau, before dropping back into the valley of the Kars Çayı.

Tuzluca to Iğdır

Frequent buses from Kars to Iğdır follow the Digor–Tuzluca–Iğdır route, with the Digor Çayı or the Aras River for company much of the way; at Iğdır you must change vehicles to reach Doğubeyazit.

TUZLUCA itself, 8km south of the Highway 80/70 junction, is a pretty dire place, notable only for some salt-bearing caves in the bluff immediately east; apparently the stuff is still mined, and you can see white streaks where it's leaching out of the rock. If you've visited Mren cathedral you might schedule a lunch-stop here, but neither of the main-drag **restaurants** (the *Turistik* and the *Hayat*) is particularly recommendable, and you'll do much better in Iğdır.

Beyond Tuzluca, the road skirts the Armenian frontier (if not quite so closely as near Bagaran), with watchtowers plainly visible to the north, before dropping sharply into a basin only 850m in elevation. The more temperate climate here permits the cultivation of rice, cotton and grapes; the inhabitants are mostly **Azeri Shi'ites**, resettled here during the nineteenth century. They used to – and may still – indulge in a bizarre rite during the first ten days of the Islamic holy month of Muharrem, in which frenzied worshippers flagellated themselves to bloodiness.

Should you need to break the journey to Doğubeyazit, **IĞDIR** – a pleasant though unremarkable provincial capital at the southern corner of the valley – would be the place to do so. There are a handful of decent **hotels**, including the two-star *Azer* off Atatürk Caddesi at Cırcır Mevkii 13/15 (℡0476/227 7190, ℱ227 9753; ❷), with an attached restaurant, and the slightly more comfortable two-star *Parlar*, İrfan Cad 14, Söğütlü Mahallesi (℡0476/227 7199, ℱ227 6451; ❷). The best **eating** in the area is at the western edge of town, at the *Ağırkaya Petrol Dinleme Tesisleri* – filling stations in eastern Turkey aren't generally the best source of *haute cuisine*, but this one whips up patently fresh, traditional fare, served in a lush orchard-garden.

North from Kars: Çıldır Gölü and Ardahan

From Kars most travellers will want to move northwest towards Artvin without making the lengthy detour through Erzurum. There are basically three routes to consider: first via **Çıldır Gölü** and Şeytan Kalesi to Ardahan and then Şavşat; second via Susuz to Ardahan and Şavşat; third via Göle to Ardahan and onwards. The first, most northeasterly route is the scenically superior but it's difficult without your own vehicle. Two **dolmuşes** a day run from Kars to Çıldır town, but only one morning minibus connects Çıldır to **Ardahan**, 47km further west.

Çıldır Gölü

The slate-like expanse of **Çıldır Gölü**, nearly 2000m up, is the primary source of the Arpa Çayı/Ahuryan river, and the highest sizable lake in Turkey; only during the summer – when hay and grain are growing by the shore – is there a hint of colour. Men on horseback, wielding scythes, rakes and other farming implements, canter splendidly across the steppe against the backdrop of 3197-metre Kısır Dağı, but their families live like moles, with houses burrowed even deeper than the norm for this province. The shallow lake itself is frozen over for six months of the year, but it's an important **bird habitat** during the warmer months, when handsome falcons and hawks swoop over your vehicle, while migrating waterfowl include pelicans and more mundane gulls.

This region was an extension of medieval Georgia rather than Armenia, and most of the decidedly minor local monuments are of recent vintage compared to those at Ani. At **DOĞRUYOL** (Djala in Georgian), the only substantial town on the lake's eastern shore, the thirteenth-century hilltop church masqueraded until recently as a mosque; there are other eleventh-to-thirteenth-century churches on the lake's south-west shore at the villages of **GÜLYÜZÜ** (Pekreşin; badly ruined) and **GÖLBELEN** (Urta; in a better state, still used as a mosque).

A few kilometres beyond Doğruyol, the islet of **Akçekale** (Argenkale) is criss-crossed by crumbled walls and linked to the semi-fortified village opposite by a causeway. There is also a fragmentary eleventh-to-fourteenth-century chapel on the far end of the islet, above the football pitch and last streetlights, with only the northwest walls and part of the apse surviving; of uncertain date is the crudely built fortification tower on the point to the south, opposite some islets. With its birds, fishing boats and changeable weather the lake here bears an uncanny resemblance to a Scottish-highland loch.

The town of **ÇILDIR** is an unprepossessing place north of the lake, out of sight of the water; the single commercial street is hard-pressed to muster a proper restaurant, and the only grubby "hotel" is best left unpatronized. Çıldır serves as the theoretical jumping-off point for **Şeytan Kalesi** (Satan's Castle), but local taxis are pricey and it's more usually visited on a group tour from Kars, which takes in the lake as well. Perched on a precipitous bend of the Başköy gorge, the castle lies a thirty-minute walk downstream from Yıldırımtepe village, itself 3.5km north-west of Çıldır: 2km on the highway, then 1.5km north on an unmarked but obvious dirt road. A path winds into the gorge from just above the village and leads up to the brooding medieval keep and watchtower.

Ardahan

From Çıldır town you've a fairly bleak stretch west to **ARDAHAN**, one of the smallest Turkish provincial capitals, faintly reminiscent of Kars with its Russian grid-plan and *fin-de-siècle* architecture – and a pervasive military presence. There's nothing in particular to see in Ardahan, except a fine old **bridge** over the Kura river, just opposite the massive **citadel**, originally Georgian but restored by Selim the Grim early in the sixteenth century. It's still an army camp, so no photography is allowed.

Ardahan isn't somewhere you'd want to stay for long, and its hotels are less than inviting, many of them occupied by prostitutes. If you need to **stay**, try the *Kera Oteli*, Atatürk Cad 21 (T 0478/211 3458; ❹). Moving on is pretty simple: from town, regular buses run to Erzurum and Yusufeli, departing from the **otogar** near the citadel; for Kars, Artvin or Çıldır you'll have to seek out the **dolmuş depot** in the centre. The route northwest out of Ardahan leads through a vast plateau of hay fields and huge mossy boulders, as you begin the climb up to the **Çam pass** (*Çamlıbel* in Turkish; 2640m), northeastern gateway to the Georgian valleys.

North from Erzurum: the southern Georgian valleys

Highway 950 heads north out of Erzurum across the steppe, aiming for a nearly imperceptible gap, too trivial to call a pass, in the surrounding mountains.

The Georgians

Georgians have lived in the valleys of the Çoruh, Tortum, Kura and Berta rivers, now in Turkey, since the Bronze Age. Like the neighbouring Armenians, they were among the first Near Eastern nations to be evangelized, and were converted rapidly to Christianity by St Nino of Cappadocia in the mid-fourth century. Unlike the Armenians, they never broke with the Orthodox Patriarchate in Constantinople, and maintained good relations with Byzantium.

The Georgian kingdoms

An effective Georgian state only entered the local stage early in the ninth century, under the auspices of the **Bagratid** dynasty. This clan contributed rulers to both the Georgian and Armenian lines, and hence the medieval history of both kingdoms overlapped to some extent. They claimed direct descent from David and Bathsheba, which explains a preponderance of kings named David, a coat of arms laden with Old Testament symbols and curiously Judaic stars of David embossed on many of the churches they built.

Feudal Bagratid lords initially emerged in the nominally Byzantine-ruled districts of Tao (centred around today's İspir, Yusufeli and Oltu) and Klarjeti (Ardanuç and Ardahan), from where **Ashot I Kuropalates** began the first stages of territorial aggrandizement at the expense of Byzantium and the Arab Caliphate – and the initial wave of church-building in the area, under the guidance of the monk **Gregory Khantzeli**. Ashot's descendants included **David Magistros ("the Great")** of Oltu, a late tenth-century ruler responsible for several of the churches described on these pages, and Bagrat III, who in 1008 succeeded in unifying the various Georgian principalities into one kingdom with a capital at Kutaisi.

A decade or so later the Byzantines compelled Bagrat's successor, Georgi I, to evacuate Tao and Klarjeti, making it an easy matter for the Selçuks to step in during 1064. They ravaged Georgia and all of eastern Anatolia, but as soon as they turned to confront the Crusaders a Bagratid revival began. **David the Restorer** not only managed by 1125 to expel the Selçuks, but moved the Bagratid court to newly captured Tbilisi, and reunited the various feuding principalities ruled by minor Bagratid warlords.

Under the rule of David's great-granddaughter **Tamara**, medieval Georgia acquired its greatest extent and prestige, controlling most of modern Georgia, Armenia and Azerbaijan from the Black Sea to the Caspian, as well as the ancestral Georgian valleys. The queen was not only a formidable military strategist and shrewd diplomat, but displayed a humanity and tolerance in her domestic administration unusual for the era. Many churches and monasteries were repaired or re-endowed by Tamara, and despite being a woman and a non-Muslim, her name still elicits respectful compliments and even a proprietary pride in the now-Turkish valleys of southern Georgia.

Following Tamara's death the Georgian kingdom began a slow but steady decline, precipitated by Mongol and Persian raids in the mid-thirteenth century but most of all by Tamerlane's apocalypse early in the 1400s. Tamara's Georgia was effectively partitioned between the Ottoman and Persian empires, and although Bagratids

Almost without noticing it you're across the watershed, and as you begin a slow descent the landscape becomes more interesting, with the Tortum Çayı alongside and trees appearing for the first time in a long while. Most buses bypass the nondescript town of Tortum, 57km from Erzurum; 15km beyond here, a pair of **castles** to left and right, crumbling away atop well-nigh inaccessible pinnacles, announce more effectively than any signpost that you've now reached the southern limits of **medieval Georgia** (see box, below).

continued to occupy thrones in Tblisi, they were essentially puppets. The rise of imperial Russia was a mixed blessing: while it prevented further Muslim encroachment, it signalled the end of any viable Georgian state, and the last semi-independent king effectively surrendered what was left of his autonomy to Catherine the Great in 1783.

Georgian monuments

Tangible evidence of the Georgian heyday is still abundant in the northeastern parts of Turkey, not least in the common prefix "Ar-" (as in Ardahan, Artvin, Ardanuç and so forth), equivalent to "-ville" or to "-burg".

The Bagratids were a prolific bunch, and their princelings stuck **castles** on just about every height; generally a passing glance is what you'll have to be satisfied with, since access to many of these eyries has long been impossible except for technical climbers. Most remarkable, however, are the early Bagratid monastic **churches**, all dating from before the move northeast to the Caucasus proper, and most sited amid oases at the heads of remote valleys. As a rule, the core conventions of Armenian religious architecture – domes supported on four freestanding columns, a cruciform east–west ground plan with prominent transepts, blind exterior arcades and intricate relief work – were borrowed wholesale, and it takes a trained eye to distinguish the two styles, though in general the Georgians rarely attempted the rotundas or multi-lobed domed squares beloved of the Armenians. Georgian building has, however, been pinpointed as one of the major vehicles by which church architecture was transported to Russia, and together with Armenian structures directly spawned the Romanesque and early Gothic churches of western Europe.

There's not been nearly the degree of official stonewalling about Georgian Christians as there is concerning Armenians, and the churches have become recognized as tourist attractions. We've only detailed the most intact examples; there are numerous unsung others, slowly collapsing in isolated settings, that villagers will be happy to show you. Virtually every church has suffered some damage from dynamite- and pickaxe-wielding **treasure-hunters**: the locals have an unshakeable conviction that all of the Christians who left the area in 1923 or before secreted precious items in or under their churches before departure in the mistaken belief that they'd eventually be able to return.

You'll need your own vehicle, or a lot of time for walking and hitching, to visit most of the sites. There's usually a small village nearby, or even surrounding the monument, but invariably **bus services**, where they exist, arrive in the afternoon and depart for the nearest town in the morning – exactly the opposite of tourist schedules. Some of the roads are bad, but if you can assemble a group and find a **taxi** driver willing to risk his undercarriage, this can end up being far cheaper than renting a vehicle in Erzurum or Trabzon. Even with a car or taxi **three days** will be required to see all of the monuments detailed in this text; for example, a loop south out of Artvin, taking in Öşk Vank, Haho, Bana and İşhan is only really possible with an early start during the long days of May to July, and judicious use of the short-cutting Highway 25-03 from Highway 950 to Oltu.

Bağbaşı and the church of Haho

Twenty-six kilometres north of Tortum, turn off to the west over the Taş Köprü humpback bridge, obeying signposting for "Taş Camii, Meryemana Kilisesi", keep left in the first large village you come to, then take another left towards İspir, a few minutes later by a modern mosque. Finally, take a right at the next, well-marked junction; it's 8km in total from Highway 950 to the main square of **BAĞBAŞİ**, a large community dispersed in a fertile valley. Two minibuses a day make the trip from the Gölbaşı Semt Garajı in Erzurum out to the village, but that's a lot of to-ing and fro-ing just to see Bağbaşı's only sight. Beyond the streamside square – really just a handful of minibuses loitering by a widening in the road, with shops, teahouses and the *Belediye* opposite – bear left 200m past the football pitch, and after another 500m you will find, hidden behind some ablution toilets to the right, the dome of the late tenth-century **church of Haho** (Khakhuli).

This is the first of several institutions that were constructed by David Magistros (the Great), ruler of Tao between 961 and 100. For once, most of the monastery complex – the boundary wall and gate, and three satellite chapels – is in good condition, the effect spoiled only by aluminium corrugated sheets on the roof, though the conical-topped dome is still covered in multicoloured tiles. Over the south transept windows, a vigilant stone eagle grasps a doe in his claws, before a fan of alternating light and dark masonry.

An arcaded, barrel-vaulted narthex on the west side of the nave still exists (you gain entry by crawling in a window), but the doors to the nave have been blocked off. Entry to the church proper is now through a gallery on the south, a skilful addition of the thirteenth century that appears at first glance to be part of the original building. On either side of the old south entrance, now inside the **gallery**, there's a lion and a chimera in relief; on the right a whale that looks suspiciously like a dog devours Jonah, while below struts a cock (presumably the one of obstinate Pride, such as Jonah's). Inside, a small but well-executed swathe of frescoed angels and apostles set on a blue background hovers over what was once the apse.

Haho's excellent state of repair is owed to its continual use as a mosque since the eighteenth century. Entry is only possible on Friday around prayer time, or by tracking down the key-keeper in the village. After your visit, sign the "guest register" and make a donation.

Öşk Vank

Downstream from the Haho turning, the Tortum valley widens appreciably. The side road to the monastery church of **Öşk Vank** (Oshkhi), 15.4km from the Haho turning and just before Tortum lake, is prominently marked with a white-on-brown archeological-site sign. It's an easy, mostly paved 7.2km straight run up to **Çamlıyamaç** village, but the church, with houses built up to the very walls, seems initially the least evocative of all in the area. Given the good road in, this is also the one Georgian monument that's the target of coach tours – though a small teahouse near the south door sees little trade in these depressed times.

None of this should deter you, since Öşk Vank is the most elaborate example of Georgian Gothic in these valleys. Another late tenth-century foundation of David Magistros, it represents the culmination of Tao Georgian culture before the Bagratid dynasty's move northeast and the start of the Georgian "Golden Age" after 1125.

A protruding porch shelters the main entry through the **facade** of the south transept; blind arcades, topped by scallop-shell carving, flank it, with reliefs of the archangels hovering high overhead. Alternatively, you are able to enter from the southwest corner of the building, through a triple-arched **narthex** with an

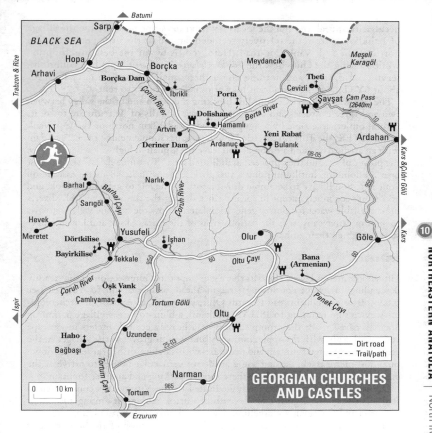

engaging zigzag roofline. The interior colonnade – with no two columns alike – exudes a European Gothic feel with its barrel-vaulted, coffered ceiling; the most westerly column-capital sports sculpted angels. The roof over the nave, elongated to the west, has fallen in, leaving the dome stranded atop four essential **pillars**, two of which have their massive bases intricately worked in sinuous geometric designs. Halfway up the south transept wall, the vanished wooden floor of the mosque that once occupied the premises acted as protection for a stretch of **frescoes**, the best preserved in any of the Turkish Georgian churches. Bracketing half a dozen ethereal saints in hieratic poses are a vivid scene to the north, possibly from the life of Christ, and on the south a model of the church, with its presumed congregation assembled outside.

Tortum Gölü and falls

A little way past the turn-off for Öşk Vank lies the inlet end of **Tortum Gölü**, a substantial body of water roughly 10km long by 1km wide, that forces the road up onto a corniche bypass above the western shore. The water is by turns muddy green, milky beige and dull slate even on a bright day, so a swim doesn't necessarily appeal, though the locals try from the stone beach below the village of Balıklkı, or from the relatively secluded far end of the little peninsula 8km north of the Öşk Vank side-road. Here, too, is by far the best **lunch** option while touring the churches: the *İskele Alabalık Tesisleri*, simple but salubrious, serving salad, trout and nothing else – three small fish make a tasty meal for about 6YTL, and the restaurant may also have rowboats to rent.

The lake was formed by a landslide blocking the north end of the valley between two and three centuries ago. The famous *şelale* or **falls of Tortum** are today its natural outlet, accessible by a signposted side road 12km north of the Öşk Vank turning. TEK, the Turkish Electric Foundation, has supplemented the natural dam with an artifical one and a turbine; you leave the asphalted highway where you see the power plant, and then proceed as indicated by a "Tortum Şelalesi" sign for just over a kilometre, until glimpsing a vast rock ledge with its 48-metre cascade on your left. You'll have to scramble down a path to the left to get a good look, and you won't see much except in spring, since during the summer the TEK diverts most available water for power generation later. Below the falls the valley narrows to an impressive canyon as the various arms of the Kara, Aksek and Dutlu ranges start to tighten their embrace.

İşhan

Fifteen kilometres below the falls there's an important intersection in the steadily descending highway; continuing straight ahead will lead you to Yusufeli (see p.826). Bearing right instead towards Olur, you reach, after 6km, an archeological-service sign pointing to **İŞHAN** (Ishkani), a bluff-top oasis village 5.7km up a partly paved road; the crumpled hills of a heavily eroded, lifeless moonscape contrast sharply with the apple, mulberry and walnut groves in the village. At the central two-spouted fountain and teahouse-with-satellite-dish, bear left and down on a 300-metre track, passing some attractive vernacular houses to arrive at the environs of the sanctuary, where there's ample parking and another fountain.

The imposing **church**, originally dedicated to the Virgin, was constructed in stages between the eighth and eleventh centuries, ranking it among the oldest extant sacred Georgian architecture. The semicircular colonnade lining the apse, with superb carved capitals, is the earliest surviving portion of the building, and was modelled consciously after the church at Bana (see opposite); great chunks of the roof are now missing, meaning that the 42-metre-high dome, built in a similar fashion to Öşk Vank's, rests in isolation on four columns. The acoustics, however, remain superb, as you can hear for yourself if you stand directly beneath the dome. There are some patches of fresco to be seen high up on the surviving walls of the south transept, portraying portions of the *Vision of Zacharias*, and in the cupola, there's an abstract cross from the Iconoclastic era. The external eleventh-century **relief work** is far more interesting, though, particularly on the small baptistry with its bestiary and semicircular inscription commemorating King Bagrat III (ruled 1000–1014), opposite a bricked-up southern portal where a lion and snake are locked in combat above an upper window to the right. Sadly, however, the church in general was much tampered with as part of its conversion during its decades as a mosque, particularly on the northwest corner – defaced with ill-advised masonry – and in the nave, completely blocked by a modern wall.

Oltu and Bana

A detour from Tortum via Narman and Oltu on Highway 965 is time well spent, especially if you have your own vehicle. Invariably dismissed in other sources, this alternate approach to İşhan and Yusufeli compares well to similar landscapes in

Turkey's
religious architectural heritage

The two great religions of Islam and Christianity have left indelible architectural marks on Turkey. From the mighty fifteenth- and sixteenth-century Ottoman mosques at Edirne in the west, to the poignant tenth- and eleventh-century Armenian churches at Ani in the distant east – and at every point in between – there's a wealth of Islamic and Christian monuments for the curious traveller to explore, and fascinating architectural links to discover.

The birth of Christianity and the earliest churches

Sen Piyer Kilisesi

The apostle Paul (himself a native of Tarsus in present-day Turkey) first preached Christ's message to non-Jews in the mid-first century AD, making Anatolia the **birthplace of Christianity**. Early followers, subject to intermittent persecution, worshipped either in each other's homes or, less frequently, in caves. Not surprisingly, then, early Christian places of worship were humble. The small cave-church of **Sen Piyer Kilisesi** (the Church of St Peter; see p.584), situated at the foot of a cliff just outside the fascinating and cosmopolitan city of Antakya (ancient Antioch), not far from the Syrian border, is a good example of this. Architecturally it is insignificant, the interior barely more than damp cave walls, and the plain facade dating largely from the nineteenth century. But one of the world's first Christian communities took root in Antioch, led by SS Peter, Paul and Barnabas between AD 47 and AD 54, and it is probable that the term "Christian" (as opposed to "Nazarene") was first used here.

Armenian churches

Separated from the mainstream church of Byzantium by geography, race and a contrary view of the nature of Christ, Armenian ecclesiastical architecture developed its own distinctive style. The most obvious feature of most Armenian churches of the ninth to eleventh centuries (when Christian Armenia's prestige and power were at their height) is a centrally located polygonal drum, surmounted by a pyramidal roof. Constructed during the reign of the Armenian king Gagik Atruzuni between 915 and 921, the church of **Akdamar Kilisesi** (the Church of the Holy Cross; see p.911) is the highlight of any trip to southeastern Turkey. Set on an islet in the incredibly blue waters of Turkey's largest lake, Van, with a panorama of lake and snow-capped mountains all around, it must rank as one of the world's most spectacularly sited churches. Akdamar Kilisesi itself is tiny (just 12m by 15m), but its graceful proportions and profuse relief carvings of biblical scenes (notably David squaring up to Goliath, and Jonah under attack from a whale) give it an aesthetic merit belying its size. Akdamar, along with other notable churches at **Ani** (see p.807) and elsewhere in the remote highlands of eastern Turkey, stand as silent witness to the Armenians who populated this region until the early twentieth century.

Akdamar Kilisesi

The rise and fall of Christian architecture

Architecturally, everything changed in the fourth century when Christianity, embraced by the emperor Constantine, became the official religion of the Roman (later Byzantine) Empire. Then the wealth and expertise of a powerful empire could be put into the glorification of the holy trinity, and the building of specific places of worship – ie **churches** – began, reaching its zenith in the sixth century.

One of the major features of the classic Byzantine church was the **dome**, rising above a square or rectangular nave. The apogee of this style, the mighty domed church of **Aya Sofya** (the Church of the Divine Wisdom; see p.127) dominated the Byzantine capital of Constantinople (now İstanbul) for nearly a millennium. Inaugurated by the emperor Justinian in 537, it symbolized the strength, wealth and holiness of Byzantine society until the capture of the city by the Turks in 1453, when it was transformed into a mosque. It was built on a scale previously (and subsequently) unknown to the Byzantines,

Aya Sofya

and the interior of its massive thirty-metre dome, seemingly hovering above the worshippers far below, was designed to imitate the heavenly vault. Aya Sofya is also justly famed for the wonderful mosaics adorning its interior.

Christianity's Anatolian heyday effectively ended with the invasion of the Selçuk Turks in the eleventh century. Although both they and the Ottoman Turks, who captured Constantinople in the fifteenth century, tolerated Christianity, virtually no new churches were built until the nineteenth century, when there was a brief Christian renaissance – cut short by the advent of twentieth-century secular Turkish nationalism.

The development of Islamic architecture

Following the defeat of the Byzantine army at Manzikert in 1071 by the **Selçuk Turks**, Anatolia began to see the construction of **mosques** on a grand scale. Like the Arabs before them, the Selçuks were not adverse to converting churches into mosques, or building on their sites (and invariably pilfering them for columns and the like). Sometimes the two faiths shared the same building, as in the eleventh-century **Ulu Cami in Diyarbakır** (the first great Selçuk mosque in Anatolia – see p.877), built on the site of the fifth-century Church of St Thomas. Most early Selçuk mosques in Anatolia were based on the Arab, hypostyle (columned) mosque, with its flat-roofed prayer hall and colonnaded courtyard. In later examples the courtyard was incorporated into the main structure by providing it with a domed roof.

Notable Selçuk mosques include the thirteenth-century **Ulu Cami at Divriği** (see p.735), with the most intricately carved, un-Islamic portals in Anatolia, and the **Eşrefoğlu Camii at Beyşehir** (see p.610), built in the twilight of Selçuk power and the most outstanding specimen of the so-called "forest" type of mosque, where multiple wooden (a specifically Selçuk innovation) columns stake out an almost basilica-like interior; examples are also found at Birgi (p.348) and Eğirdir (p.604).

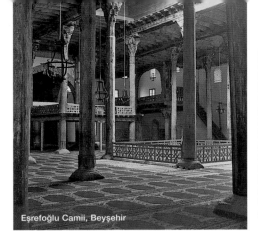

Eşrefoğlu Camii, Beyşehir

The **Ottomans**, who gradually gained control of Anatolia between the thirteenth and fifteenth centuries, and then dominated it until the early twentieth century, perfected the **domed mosque** (clearly inspired by the domed churches of the Byzantine world). Having defined the style, the Ottomans went on to produce some of the world's finest religious architecture – including the magnificent Selimiye Camii (see box). Most Westerners' image of the mosque is based on the classic Ottoman design, with its domes and slender, cylindrical minarets.

The ultimate Ottoman mosque – the Selimiye Camii

The epitome of the Ottoman, domed mosque, completed in 1575 by the greatest Ottoman architect, Mimar Sinan, the **Selimiye Camii at Edirne** (see p.232) commands both the town and the Thracian plain from its hilltop position. Unlike many other imperial mosques in both Edirne and İstanbul, the Selimiye has few auxiliary buildings such as *imaret*s or academies to distract from the effect of the massed turrets and semi-domes culminating in the main dome, largest in Turkey, whose diameter (as Sinan expressly intended, and boasted of in his memoirs) exceeds that of Aya Sofya in İstanbul by just 25cm. This calligraphically decorated vault is supported by eight surprisingly unobtrusive columns, rather than the massive piers used in Byzantine churches. Like other Edirne mosques, however, there is a fine courtyard with a sixteen-sided *şadırvan* or ablutions fountain.

Selimiye Camii

Afghanistan and the American Southwest. Stands of poplars and green fields are juxtaposed against a cobalt sky and reddish bluffs, often crowned with crumbling Georgian castles. If you're travelling on a day-circuit out of Artvin, similar scenery (and 22km less driving) can be enjoyed on Highway 25-03, linking Sevenyurt with Oltu and far better than depicted on touring maps.

Oltu

Beside the river at **OLTU** stands the first of the citadels – well restored by the Ottomans and again in 2002. A further 18km north brings you to the junction with Highway 80; continue left for 4km to the confluence of valleys as the Penek Çayı joins the Narman Suyu to become the Black Sea–bound Oltu Çayı. Here on either side of the strategic Y-fork rise two castles – one backed into the cliff, the other freestanding and flanked by a small church. Continuing towards İşhan takes you past yet another redoubt, atop a rock spur by the minor road to Olur.

Bana

Bearing right (east) instead onto Highway 80 leads towards Göle and Kars; 28km beyond Oltu (or 37km southwest of Göle) you'll see, just before the river valley narrows drastically, the seventh-century Armenian **church of Bana** on the north bank of the Penek (Irlağaç) Çayı. Its original name is "Banak", which lives on in the Turkified village name of Penek. To actually get to Bana, carry on 4km further east from your first glimpse of it – 14.5km in total from the junction – to take the side track that hairpins off left just before the gorge, just past where the main road crosses the river. Continue through the village of **Penek**, branching left after 2.8km to approach the church – in sight much of the way – from the northeast; depending on ruts and mud an ordinary car can drive with care almost up to Bana.

Perched on a knoll surveying water meadows, and dominated in turn by tawny crags, the church enjoys a commanding position. A century after local Christians abandoned it, the Ottomans accordingly fortified Bana during the Crimean War, adding the crude bulwark still visible on the south side. The Russians blasted the upper levels off during the 1877–1878 war, and later carted away much of the masonry to build a turn-of-the-nineteenth-century church in Oltu.

What remains – the first floor of an originally three-storeyed, vast rotunda half-submerged in its own ruins – is still impressive. The original plan was identical to (and of the same vintage as) the massive rotunda at Zvartnots in eastern Armenia – hardly surprising, since the two had the same builder, the Katholikos (Bishop) Narses I, who built this church during a six-year (653–658) local exile. The east apse retains a colonnade virtually identical to the later one at İşhan, with an equally generous ambulatory behind, though only one column survives with its carved capital.

The western Georgian valleys

The area around the confluence of the **Barhal and Çoruh rivers** is scenically and climatically one of the most favoured corners of the northeast. During the balmy summers, every sort of fruit ripens and you're treated to the incongruous spectacle of rice paddies (and further downstream, olive groves) by the Çoruh, within sight of parched cliffs overhead. Functional **Yusufeli** is gateway to these river valleys, which in their lower reaches can offer **Georgian churches** near **Tekkale** and **Barhal**, plus trekkers' trailheads higher up at **Hevek** and **Meretet**, as well as Barhal.

The rivers themselves are a magnet for visitors, making Yusufeli a popular base for **whitewater rafters** finishing the challenging runs from İspir or Barhal upstream. Highest water is between early May and late June, when the overseas adventure companies (listed in the "Getting there" section of Basics) run their trips, but there is always at least one local outfitter arranging days out on the spot from May to September.

General tourism has never really taken off in the area, and the stark simplicity of local facilities will appeal mostly to the hardier breed of traveller. Even if you're not an outdoor-sports enthusiast, you'll need a steady hand at the wheel – or a strong stomach if you're a minibus passenger – for the often bumpy, steep rides out to the local Georgian churches.

Yusufeli

Straddling the Barhal Çayı just above its junction with the Çoruh, **YUSUFELI** is a gritty, rather time-warped town living under a death sentence; if funds ever permit construction, it will disappear under the waters of the highest Çoruh dam, and accordingly nothing new has been built here since the 1970s. Yusufeli constitutes a fairly conservative and devout anomaly in the secular, relatively progressive, province of Artvin, a situation partly explained by the fact that a high proportion of the inhabitants are descended from Bulgarian Muslim settlers of the 1890s. Traveller opinion on the place is sharply divided: some can't wait to see the back of it, hitching out at dusk to avoid staying the night, while others, en route to or from the Kaçkar mountains, end up spending a few nights here and making a day-trip up one of the nearby river valleys.

Arrival, onward transport, and services

If you're unable to get a direct **bus** service to Yusufeli from Erzurum, ask to be set down at Su Kavuşumu junction, 10km below the town centre. The last Artvin–Yusufeli bus doesn't roll past the turn-off until about 4pm, but if you've missed it, or your heart is set on being in Barhal that evening (see below for onward schedules), **taxi** shuttles up to Yusufeli from the junction are available for about 10YTL per car. Heading in the other direction, the junction is also a good place to pick up transport to Ardahan and Kars, and the aforementioned sights along the way.

Yusufeli marks the start of **dolmuş routes** to various villages further upriver, including Barhal and Hevek. Service to these two high settlements is available daily all year, since both are inhabited in winter, but adheres to a somewhat informal schedule. The Barhal vehicles leave Yusufeli from the **otogar** or the main road outside the *Çiçek Palas Oteli* between 2 and 5pm, the first and last departures going all the way to Hevek. In theory all are linked to the arrival of afternoon buses from Artvin. If there is a group of you, and you want to guarantee your connection into the mountains, try calling local guide and dolmuş owner Osman (☎0466/826 2026), who will ferry you up to Barhal.

The most active **rafting** outlet is run by Cumhur Bayrak (☎0466/811 2393, ✉denizgolu22@yahoo.com), from offices underneath the *Çiçek Palas*. He runs four-hour outings, involving about three hours on the river, for around €25 per person. Note that in May and June the river runs a lot faster, meaning that the trips take considerably less time.

Three **banks** (with ATMs), a **PTT** and **shops** with basic trekking staples round out the list of essential services. For trekking in the Kaçkar mountains (see p.831), local **guide** Sirali Aydın (☎0466/811 3893, ✉sirraft@hotmail.com) rents equipment and arranges expeditions; failing that, ask at the rafting centre under the *Çiçek Palas*.

Accommodation

The rather basic style of **accommodation** does nothing to encourage lingering, and few can be recommended with much enthusiasm; hot water, for instance, is rarely reliable anywhere in Yusufeli. **Hotels** are all grouped within 200m of each other, and when business is slack – generally the case except during May and June – it may be possible to get a three- or four-bed room for the same price as a double. Best of the lot is probably the *Barhal Hotel* (☏ 0466/811 3151; ❷), near the pedestrian suspension bridge, with small, cleanish, en-suite rooms, though attempted overcharging here is common. Alternatively, try the *Çiçek Palas Oteli* (☏ 0466/811 2102; ❷) at Halitpaşa Cad 8/A, with shared showers.

Of the two **campsites** about 700m upstream from the foot bridge, on the far side of the river, the leafier, remoter *Greenpeace* (☏ 0466 8112271; 3YTL per person) is to be preferred, having double rooms (❶) and an attached restaurant with riverside seating.

Eating and drinking

The *Çınar Restoran* under the *Barhal Hotel*, with a terrace overhanging the river, offers the highest-drawer **eating** in town – strictly *mezes* and grills; three can eat well with a beer apiece for 15YTL. Runner-up is the *Mavi Köşk*, just off İnönü Caddesi (the main drag), opposite Halkbank. During springtime most places are likely to be packed out by rowdy, carousing rafters unless you arrive early in the evening.

Tekkale and its churches

Sleepy **TEKKALE** lies 7km southwest of Yusufeli on the same bank of the Çoruh, connected by dolmuşes heading to either Kılıçkaya or the remoter Köprügören, 27km further upriver and the last point served by public transport. The road to Tekkale passes two ruined chapels (one perched above the Çoruh in Yusufeli town, the second on the far side of the river 2km upstream) and a vertiginous castle guarding the valley road, before curving the last 2km into the village.

The only **accommodation** is at Cemil Albayrak's *Dört Kilise Resting Camp*, aka *Cemil's Pansiyon* (☏ 0466/811 2908, ℻ 811 2105; ❶ half-board), with a choice of simple doubles downstairs or sleeping-bag space on the wooden terrace; there's a single communal hot shower, pitches for tents, and a tank full of trout. Unlike many other backpacker havens it's fairly pleasant, without being a "scene", attracting a widely varied clientele. Cemil may play his *saz* for you after nightfall, and also offers useful sketch maps and guiding services for an unusual trekking approach to the Kaçkars (see p.831).

Dörtkilise and Bayırkilise

From Tekkale, just a few paces upstream from *Cemil's Pansiyon*, a dirt side-road heading uphill and away from the Çoruh allows you to walk or drive the 6.3km further to **Dörtkilise** (Otkhta Eklesia; the road sign says "7"). En route, ignore the first two bridges spanning the stream to the right, and find the church a bit uphill to the left on a grassy hillside at 1140m, just beyond the third bridge over a tributary. Despite the name – meaning "Four Churches" – only one is found intact, but it's very fine and unlike most other Georgian places of worship. Domeless, with a steep gabled roof and relatively plain exterior, Dörtkilise is a twin of the church at nearby Barhal, though built several decades earlier and later renovated by David Magistros. Since the closest *yayla* is about 3km away, Dörtkilise was never reconsecrated as a mosque, and is now home only to bats, swallows and occasionally livestock. Inside, a double line of four columns supports the barrel ceiling hiding under the pitched roof; some traces of fresco persist in the apse, while an unusual choir takes up much of the west end. The large half-ruined building to the north-east, arcaded and double-vaulted, was the monastery refectory, joined to the main body of the church by an equally decrepit gallery that served as a narthex.

The adventurous – equipped with anti-bug juice – can continue west on foot to the remote chapel of **Bayırkilise** (elevation 1680m); it's a tough ascent, with a proper path for only about two-thirds of the way. The route begins at a jeep "ramp" and culvert by a power pylon, 150m north of Dörtkilise; an initially broad path dwindles as it climbs, changing banks of the adjacent stream and fizzling out completely about 45 minutes along, just after recrossing the stream. Thereafter you face an increasingly steep, trackless half-hour scramble on unstable surface, though the church – outrageously perched on a seemingly inaccessible pinnacle rearing above the canyon – is in distant view just long enough to give you bearings. In fair-to-middling condition, Bayırkilise has a gabled roof like its lower neighbour, with a single barrel vault and traces of frescoes inside; the views, and the sense of accomplishment in arriving, are the main rewards. The downhill return takes just under an hour, for a two-hour-plus round trip; Cemil's sketch map traces the route more or less correctly.

Barhal

The most popular route out of Yusufeli follows the valley of the Barhal Çayı north through a landscape straight out of a Romantic engraving, complete with ruined Georgian castles on assorted crags overlooking the raging river. After 18km of one-lane asphalt, the road surfaces changes to dirt at river-straddling Sarıgöl; **BARHAL** (1300m), officially renamed Altıparmak after the mountains behind, is reached 11km beyond, an hour and a half's drive in total from Yusufeli.

With its scattered wooden buildings peeking out from lush pre-alpine vegetation, Barhal conforms well to most people's notions of a mountain village. There are several **accommodation** options, for which advance booking is strongly advisable in July or August. Mehmet Karahan's *Karahan Pansiyon* (☎0446/826 2071, ⓦwww .karahanpension.com; ❸ half-board), 1.2km out of the centre on the Altıparmak-

△ Villagers' social gathering, Barhal

bound turning and then uphill, is the most characterful: choose between treehouse-type double chalets or mattresses on the airy terrace-dorm. The roadside *Barhal Pansiyon* (☎0466/826 2031; ❶) at the entrance to Barhal is an acceptable alternative. Right next door are the clean double/triple/quad rooms (sharing bathrooms) of Ahmet Pehlivan's three-storey 🌲 *Marsis Village House* (☎0466/826 2026, ⓦwww .marsisotel.com; ❸ half-board). A *teleferik* winch hoists your bags up the slope from the roadside; suppers are large and strictly vegetarian, with beer available. You'll wake early here, as every footfall reverberates from the upper floors to the lower ones. Village facilities are completed by a **bakery**, a few well-stocked **shops**, a restaurant and a well-attended **teahouse**.

Barhal church

The tenth-century **church of Barhal** (Parkhali), the final legacy of David Magistros, is a twenty-minute walk up the secondary track toward the Altıparmak mountains (not the main one headed towards Hevek and the central Kaçkar); follow signs for the path to the *Karahan Pansiyon*, which climbs a lushly vegetated slope. Set in a hillside pasture next to the *mahalle*'s school, it's virtually identical to Dörtkilise, except for being somewhat smaller – and in near-perfect condition owing to long use as the village mosque. It's now only used for Friday prayers, but it's worth securing admission (try the school next door for keys) to appreciate the sense of soaring height in the barrel-vaulted nave – and the debt European Gothic owed to Georgian and Armenian architects. The interior is now bare and whitewashed, but frescoes may be hiding underneath; painted grafitti in Georgian along the exterior roofline dates only from the nineteenth century and supposedly contains an admiring reference to the local mountains.

Hevek

HEVEK (Yaylalar) lies another hour and a half's drive from Barhal along a scenic 21-kilometre dirt road. At over 2000m, this fairly substantial if remote village has a choice of places to stay – all run by the same owner (☎0466/832 2001, ⓦwww .kackar3937.com). The 25-bed *Altunay Pansiyon* (€9 per person) is the cheapest option, whilst across the road, the brand-new *Çamyuva Pansiyon* (❹ half-board) is a deluxe version with an open kitchen and a sitting room. There are also some four-person chalets to rent (€30 per chalet) which work out pretty reasonably. Genial manager İsmail also runs a large food shop and the village **bakery** downstairs, hires out mules for €30 per day and generally arranges **trekking expeditions**. Architecturally the village varies from new concrete to century-old houses, though the only specific sight is an Ottoman **bridge** just downstream at the mouth of the Körahmet valley. If you're leaving by dolmuş, rather than on foot, there's usually one departure a day at dawn for the spectacular ride to Yusufeli.

Meretet

MERETET (officially Olgunlar), currently road's end and the highest trailhead for the Kaçkar at 2200m, is a three-kilometre hike southwest of Hevek, though private cars regularly make the journey in dry conditions, and the dolmuş calls once daily in summer. The spartan but clean *Deniz Gölü Pansiyon* (☎0466/832 2105; ❷) with its communal balcony, self-catering kitchen and reliable hot water provides an even more scenic alternative to a night in Hevek. Backing onto this is the newer *Kaçkar Pansiyon* (☎0466/832 2047, ⓦwww.kackar.net; ❹ half-board, ❶ bed only) with large en-suite rooms, a communal TV area, and shared kitchen. You can rent trekking equipment here, including tents, for around €8 per day, and friendly owner İsmail is able to help you with your trekking plans.

The Kaçkar Dağları

A formidable barrier between the northeastern Anatolian plateau and the Black Sea, the **Kaçkar Dağları** are the high end of the Pontic coastal ranges – and Turkey's most rewarding and popular trekking area. Occupying a rough rectangle some 70km by 20km, the Kaçkars extend from the Rize–İspir road to the Hopa–Artvin highway, with the more abrupt southeast flank lapped by the Çoruh river, and the gentler northwest folds dropping more gradually to misty foothills. At 3972m, their summit ranks only fourth highest in Turkey after Ararat, Gelyaşin peak in the Cilo mountains and Süphan Dağı, but in scenic and human interest they fully earn their aliases "the Little Caucasus" and "the Pontic Alps".

"Kaçkar" is the Turkish spelling of *khatchkar*, sculpted Armenian votive crosses or gravestones once abundant in eastern Turkey – perhaps a reference to the complicated and tortured outline of the range, with multiple hanging valleys and secondary spurs. In addition to the principal summit area, several other major massifs are recognized: the Altıparmak and Marsis groups of about 3300m, at the north end of the Bulut ridge, which links them with Point 3932; and the adjacent Tatos and Verçenik systems of about 3700m, at the extreme southwest of the chain. Exceptionally for Turkey, the Kaçkars are a young granite-diorite range instead of the usual karst, and were much transformed by the last Ice Age; there are still remnants of glaciers on the north slope of the highest peak, and hundreds of lakes spangle the alpine zone above 2600m.

Partly because of intensive human habitation, the high Kaçkars support relatively few large **mammals**; bear and boar prefer the forested mid-altitude zones, while wolves and ibex are ruthlessly hunted in the treeless heights. **Birds** of prey and snow cocks are more easily seen and heard, while the summer months witness an explosion of **wildflowers**, butterflies – and vicious deer flies. Between May and September, migration from the nearby lowlands to the *yayla*s, or summer pastoral settlements is the norm: the lower, more substantial ones are occupied first, the higher ones once the snow recedes.

Given the ethnic variety here, it's no surprise that local **place names** are similarly tangled – a discerning glance at the map will turn up plenty of Georgian and Armenian words, plus Turkified versions of same. Thus Pişkankara (the original form) has become Pişenkaya (Turkish for "the cooking rock"), while other more provocatively foreign ones such as Sevcov lake are camouflaged outright as Deniz Gölü. The recurring suffix "-evit" is an Armenian dialect particle meaning "*yayla*".

Practicalities

The six most popular **trailhead villages** are – on the Black Sea slopes – Çat and Ayder (see Chapter 9), and on the Çoruh side Barhal, Hevek, Meretet and Tekkale (see "The western Georgian valleys" starting on p.825). The approach from the Black Sea hills is gentler, with clearer trails, but the paths and villages can be crowded, and the almost daily mist rising up to 2900m is a problem. Hiking grades are tougher on the Çoruh flank, but the weather is more dependable. The main **season** is June to September, with the mists less of a hazard as autumn approaches; if you show up earlier than late July, you may need crampons and an ice axe to negotiate some of the higher passes. If you're hardy, it gets warm enough in midsummer for a quick swim in most of the lakes.

In terms of **itineraries**, the Kaçkars are infinitely versatile. The manic and the pressed-for-time cross from Hevek to Ayder via certain passes in two gruelling days, but there's little pleasure in this, and a more reasonable minimum time to

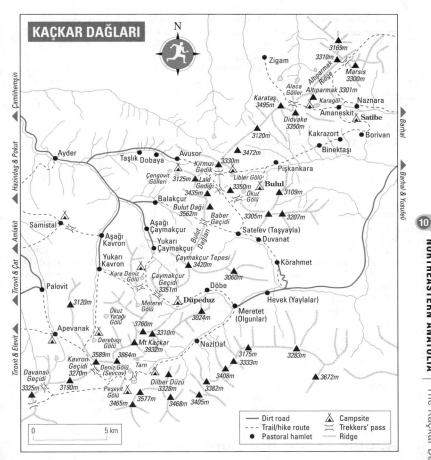

switch sides of the mountains would be three or four days, and most people are happy to spend a week or even ten days trekking around. The Kaçkars are lately enjoying a vogue amongst Turkish and Israeli trekkers, with just a token presence of British, Dutch, German and Spanish hikers in most years. Total numbers are in fact slightly down from the early-to-mid 1990s, but you wouldn't know that from the abundant rubbish at over-subscribed campsites such as Dilber Düzü and (to a lesser extent) Kara Deniz Gölü. Purists and misanthropes may prefer less frequented routes in the far southwest, or the southerly approach from Tekkale.

Guides and treks

If you'd rather go with a **guide**, there are a number of helpful individuals in Ayder and Şenyuva, as well as in Yusufeli, Hevek and Meretet. Otherwise most of the adventure travel companies listed in the Basics section of this book run some sort of Kaçkar group itinerary, almost always subcontracted to a Turkey-based

expedition outfitter. With advance notice from within the country, two of these are particularly worth contacting for fully outfitted treks: Ogzala Turizm, İstiklâl Caddesi, Bekar Sok 16/4, Beyoğlu, İstanbul (☎0212/293 9195, ⓦwww.ogzala .com), and Bukla Seyahat, Yeniçarşi Cad, Gür Han 28/1–2, Galatasaray, İstanbul (☎0212/245 0635, ⓦwww.bukla.com). Both companies offer regular one-week trips from June to September under the supervision of keen mountaineers who often grew up in the area; English-language guiding cannot be guaranteed, but you'll be trekking with sophisticated city Turks, and land-only prices are pitched at the local economy.

Equipment, local conditions and hazards

You'll need a **full trekking kit** appropriate to similar conditions in the Scottish Highlands, the Pacific Northwest or the Pyrenees: quick-draining, non-rotting, heavy-duty boots, wool socks, waterproof trousers or gaiters, a backpack cover and/or cagoule, and a proper, free-standing tent. A camp stove and ample back-packing food are also essential – and you should bring ten to twenty percent more **supplies** than you think you'll need for the projected length of the trek, to allow for being stuck for an extra day by thick mist. Pure **water**, available everywhere from springs, is never scarce.

The lack of good-quality, large-scale **maps** is a major drawback, but some thorough route descriptions are available in mountaineering books (see p.1041) – though they don't offer cartography much better than the sketch map in this book. Even though no compatible maps exist, a GPS device is still very use-ful: the integral altimeter function will be a godsend in the typically unstable weather conditions where conventional barometric altimeters are useless.

Paths are not waymarked or signposted, but cairns may be present at ambiguous points. Otherwise, there are few specific **dangers**, besides the absolute necessity of crossing all tricky passes early in the day – certainly by noon – before they're shrouded in mist or storm cloud. Territorial domestic bulls are also a nuisance, far more likely to charge a tent than any wild beast. It's useful to know that the ubiq-uitous Pontic azalea, from whose blossoms the notorious hallucinogenic *deli bal* is made (the "mad" honey that gave Xenophon's soldiers chronic diarrhoea), contains sufficient flammable resin to ignite even in damp conditions. The mountain people consider it a pest and uproot it with little compunction.

Routes in the northern Kaçkar

Starting from **Barhal** (1300m), most trekkers head west to the top of the valley walled off by the Altıparmak chain, finishing a tough first day either near **Karagöl** (2800m) or the nearby **Satibe** meadow (2450m). The following day usually involves a drop down to the Kışla/Önbolat valley just south, threading through the *yayla*s of Borivan, Binektaşı and Pişkankara before making camp higher up. If you pitch tent at **Libler Gölü** (2700m), near the top of the main valley, the next day will see you over the tricky Kırmızı Gedik saddle for an easy descent to **Avu-sor**, end of the road up from Ayder.

Alternatively, you can bear south from Pişkankara up to a camp in the Bulul val-ley, at the head of which is the wonderful **Öküz Gölü** (Ox Lake; 2800m) and an initially easy – but later steep – pass giving on to the **Körahmet valley**, still on the Çoruh side of the range. From an overnight next to **Satelev** *yayla*, you can choose between crossing the Bulul ridge via the Baber pass, dropping down to **Balakçur** just above Ayder; or rolling down-valley to **Hevek** via Körahmet (now served by a dirt road), with the option of ending your hike or stocking up to continue through the central Kaçkar.

Routes in the central Kaçkar

Above Hevek, two more valleys lead up to the base of the highest Kaçkar peaks; at **Meretet** (2200m) the split occurs. Bearing right (northwest) takes you within three and a half hours to camping spots near spectacular wildflowers high up in the Düpedüz valley, just below the **Çaymakcur pass** (3230m), the easiest in the entire Kaçkar range. You should leave for the pass (1hr 30min further) early the following morning, when you'd camp at **Kara Deniz Gölü** an hour beyond, with plenty of time for a day-hike south up to a group of three lakes at the top of the Cennakçur valley (see opposite) – and from a nearby overlook, your first, spectacular nose-to-nose view of Point 3932's north face. From Kara Deniz Gölü you can reach **Ayder** in another long walking day north, via the upper and lower **Çaymakcur** *yayla*s, which may have minibus service.

The path through the other valley follows the Büyük Çay southwest and upstream to the apparent cul-de-sac of the meadows at **Dilber Düzü** (3050m; 3hr from Meretet), a popular (and oversubscribed) camping venue at the formidable base of Point 3932 itself. Despite appearances there is a way up and out: first to the lake of **Sevcov** (Deniz Gölü; 3400m; 1hr 45min more), with just two or three cramped sites for tents, and then over the low crest just south to **Peşevit** (Soğanlı; 3377m; 2hr 15min from Dilber Düzü) lake with much better camping. Try to get an early enough start out of Meretet to make one of the lakes before dark, in preference to Dilber Düzü. Sevcov, where ice floes last into August during many summers, is the veering-off point for the moderately difficult, five-to-six-hour return climb north to the **summit**, where the climbers' register is hidden underneath a rubble cairn.

From Peşevit lake you've a pathless scree-scramble west up to a false pass, then an even more miserable scree descent, another climb and a final drop to some water meadows near the top of the **Davali valley**, where a faint cairned path takes you up to the **Kavron pass** (3310m; 2hr 45min from Peşevit). Because of the rough terrain, no organized expeditions or pack animals come this way, and you'll need some sort of self-arrest device to save your knees – and yourself from a nasty fall.

Once on the Black Sea side of the pass, the most popular choice involves following the distinct path north an hour to another col (3200m) overlooking the **Kavron valley** – and allowing superb afternoon views of Point 3932's west flank. The trail, fainter now, drops within 45 minutes to **Derebaşı lake** (2885m) where you'll prudently camp. There are limited sites at the inflow, and a few better ones by the lake's exit, where you scout around for the easiest cross-country route down to the floor of the U-shaped, glacial Kavron Deresi. After two hours, the latter half of this on a clear, right-bank trail, you'll reach a roadhead at the busy, electrified *yayla* of **YUKARI KAVRON** (2350m), a quite substantial place with daily minibus service down to Ayder, a central teahouse where you can get basic supplies and the more trekker-friendly *Şahin Pansiyon/Kamping/Kafeterya* (no phone; ❶) at the outskirts, with double chalets.

From just past the *Şahin Pansiyon* on the access road, a sporadically cairned route leads west-southwest up the **Çennakcur valley** to the lakes at its head (2hr 30min; ca. 2900m). There are at least three lakes here – **Kavron Gölü**, right by the path with emergency camping, and **Büyük Deniz** and **Meterel** off to one side – Meterel is the highest and, in summer, often the driest. Another hour over a saddle behind Kavron Gölü will take you to Kara Deniz Gölü, and usually a lot of company. From here it's simple enough to reverse the directions given above for traversing the Düpedüz valley and Çaymakcur pass from Meretet, and complete a three-day, three-night circuit around Point 3932 – an excellent plan if you've left a vehicle or stored extra gear in Meretet or Hevek.

Another possibility from the ridge above Derebaşı lake is to veer west, initially cross-country, to Apevanak *yayla*, which is linked by path or track to the *yayla*s of Palovit and Tirovit; the latter gives access to the western Kaçkar.

Routes in the western Kaçkar

Elevit *yayla* (see p.785) is roughly midway between Tirovit and Çat, and is the starting point for the march up to **Yıldızlı Gölü** (Star Lake; good camping), just across the top of the valley from Haçevanag *yayla*. The nearby, gentle Capug pass allows access to the headwaters of the Fırtına Çayı, though the onward route is briefly confused by the maze of bulldozer tracks around Başyayla (2600m) and Kaleyayla. At the latter, bear south up toward campsites by a lake at the foot of Tatos peak; the following day you'd cross a saddle to another lake, Adalı, at the base of 3711-metre Verçenik.

From this point you'd either descend to Çat via Ortaköy and Varoş, using a morning bus if possible part of the way, or continue walking west for another day, past other lakes just below the ridge joining Verçenik to Germaniman peak. A final 3100-metre pass just north of Germaniman leads to the valley containing Saler and Başköy *yayla*s, linked by daily bus to **İkizdere**.

Routes in the southern Kaçkar

Starting from Tekkale, the same dirt road that serves Dörtkilise continues another 3km to Bölükbaşı *yayla* and the start of a two-to-three-day traverse finishing in the Hevek valley. The weather is more reliable (and also hotter) than elsewhere in the Kaçkar, but this route is thus far relatively unspoilt; sketch map and arrangements are available from Cemil at his *pansiyon* in Tekkale (see p.827).

From **Bölükbaşı** (1400m), a path heads west via the *yayla*s of **Kusana** (1630m) and **Salent** (2400m), before reaching a pair of **lakes** (imaginatively dubbed Küçük – "little" – and Büyük – "big"), below a 3300-metre pass. You'd prudently overnight east of the pass, possibly beside **Büyük Gölü** (2900m), before descending a valley northwest to **Modut** *yayla* (2300m) and then **Mikeles** (1700m), on the side of the Hevek Deresi, about 5km downstream from Hevek itself.

Artvin province: the northern Georgian valleys

The northerly Georgian valleys form the heart of the **province of Artvin**, lying within a fifty-kilometre radius of the town of the same name. Nowhere else in Turkey, except for the Kaçkars, do you feel so close to the Caucasu: ornate wooden domestic and religious architecture, with lushly green slopes or naked crags for a backdrop, clinch the impression of exoticism. Here, too, you may actually encounter native **Georgian-speakers**, though they're mostly confined to the remote valleys around the towns of Camili, Meydancık and Posof, and the immediate surroundings of Şavşat. Whatever their antecedents, the people here are remarkable for their high literacy rate and left-of-centre polling practices – and their seasonal presence. Disgusted by the lack of local opportunities, many have emigrated internally to work ten months of the year at the factories around Bursa and İzmir, to the extent that there are now more *Artvinli*s out west than in the province itself. This situation may or may not change upon completion of the ambitious local hydroelectric schemes (see box, below).

△ The Kaçkar Dağları

The region, with its wet, alpine climate on the heights, formerly had potential as a winter-sports playground, but global warming – and the fact that, in Turkey's current economic straits, existing ski resorts can barely cope – scotched such hopes. For the moment most tourists come in summer to see the local **Georgian churches**; individually these are not as impressive as their southern relatives, but their situations are almost always more picturesque.

The Çoruh-river hydroelectric schemes

The Çoruh, hitherto one of Turkey's few remaining wild rivers, became the target during the late 1990s of the country's most ambitious **hydroelectric schemes** – far less publicized than the controversial İlisu Dam on the Tigris. Two of the biggest dams, one at the Georgian border, and the other just above Borçka, have already been completed, whilst the mammoth, 210-metre-high dam for the **Deriner Reservoir**, being built by a Swiss–Russian consortium just south of Artvin, has proven more problematic, but should be ready by 2010. By inundating a critical stretch of Highway 10, the Deriner project has added 22 very steep kilometres to the journey into Artvin from all points south or east; no commercial maps as yet show the new route correctly.

French contractors are contemplating two further dams: one in the canyon narrows at Narlık, roughly halfway between Artvin and Yusufeli, and another just below Yusufeli itself, which will drown that town as well as Tekkale. While the lower three projects were in regions where the riverbank was largely uninhabited and non-arable, the mooted upper two would entail expensive compulsory purchase of real estate at a time when the country is effectively broke. Though the main pretext for the projects – the constant shortfall in power to supply Turkey's heavy industry – has evaporated with the parlous state of said industry, ongoing works are being justified by the proposed sale of surplus electricity to the neighbouring Caucasian republics and even Russia. What remains to be seen is whether the proceeds of such sales would be ploughed back into the impoverished northeast, or spent elsewhere by the central govenment.

Artvin

As your vehicle winds up several kilometres' worth of zigzags from the Çoruh river, you begin to wonder just where **ARTVIN** is, especially if you've approached from the Black Sea, without the benefit of the broadside views from the new southerly highway. Suddenly the town reveals itself, arrayed in sweeping tiers across a steep, east-facing slope, seeming much higher than its actual 500–600m of elevation. Unusually, the medieval **Livane Kalesi**, now occupied by the army, is down low by the river; the only other buildings with a patina of history are houses from the Russian era, tucked here and there on the hill above the centre, but falling increasingly victim to the wrecker's ball. Certainly it has the least flat ground of any Turkish provincial capital, and – within the city limits at least – perhaps the fewest specific attractions. But Artvin is pleasant enough for a night or two, and becomes a destination in its own right for several days over the third or fourth weekend in June, when the **Kafkasör festival** takes place at a *yayla* above town. Highlight of this has traditionally been the pitting of bulls in rut against each other, but since the opening of the nearby frontier the event has taken on a genuinely international character, with wrestlers, vendors, jugglers, musicians and dancers from both Turkey and Georgia appearing among crowds of over 50,000. It's one of the last genuine folk fairs in the country, unlikely to be mucked about with by tourism officials, so be there if you can.

Arrival and services

The **otogar** is just down the hill from the main street; all the bus companies have ticket offices along **İnönü Caddesi**, the single high street running past the Hükümet Konağı (Government Hall), where you'll also find the **PTT**, various **banks** with ATMs, and a handful of **Internet cafés**.

Accommodation

Things have improved slightly since the 1990s when nearly every **hotel** featured hot and cold running *natasha*s as standard and Artvin ranked as the hooker capital of Turkey. Even so, there's still only one passably comfortable place, the two-star *Karahan* at İnönü Cad 16 (☎0466/212 1800; ❺ during Kafkasör, otherwise ❹). Access from İnönü Caddesi is up a concrete stairwell in a grim shopping centre just downhill from the hotel sign; if you're driving, swing around behind to the tiny, controlled-access parking lot. The rooms, mostly en suite, are clean and comfortable, with air conditioning and satellite TV.

The best budget alternative is the *Otel Kaçkar*, Hamam Sok 5 (☎0466/212 9909, ℻212 8315; ❷), which has a sign visible from İnönü Caddesi but is in an alley parallel and downhill from the main road. Fair-sized rooms, with a variety of views and bed formats, were redone as cheerful en-suites with TV and central heating in 1999. Most of the other "hotels" in Artvin remain little more than brothels and are best given a wide berth.

During the festival it may be more convenient to stay at the municipally run *Kafkasör Tatil Köyü Dağ Evleri* (☎0466/212 5013; ❷), which offers en-suite bungalow rooms up on the Kafkasör meadow, 10km out of town – though you must book months in advance to secure a vacancy.

Eating and drinking

The **restaurant** of the *Hotel Karahan* is one of just three licensed places in town, acceptable and not too overpriced. At the very base of İnönü Caddesi, where the curvy access road straightens out, the *Nazar Restorant* plugs its "million dollar view", but the *meyhane*-format food's not bad or expensive either, running to

4YTL for a couple of *mezes*, a *bir buçuk* portion of chicken and a couple of drinks. Among **unlicensed eateries**, the *Dostlar Sofrası*, upstairs at İnönü Cad 36 near the *meydan* and government buildings, has all the usual *hazır yemek* dishes in a cheerfully contemporary environment. *Bakıroğlu Kebap Salonu* opposite has a stronger stress on grills, served on an outdoor terrace. Breakfast-time *börek* and the usual range of **puddings** are on offer at the competing cake-shops *Köşk* and *Sedir*, more or less opposite each other near the top of İnönü Caddesi.

Borçka and İbrikli

Some 30km downstream from Artvin on Highway 10 en route to Hopa, **BORÇKA** is a nondescript market town of interest only for its riverside setting – and a decent, three-star **hotel**, the *Demirkol* (☎0466/415 3660; ❷), overlooking the Çoruh river. Room furnishings are a bit well-worn, and disco noise can reach everywhere except the fourth floor, but all units have balconies and tubs in the bathrooms, and there's nothing else between Artvin and Hopa. Independent **restaurant** options around Cumhuriyet Meydanı, the main square with a taxi rank, are limited – the *Sofram* is better than the poorish *Gizem Pide/Lahmacun Salonu*.

Borçka is, however, the reference point for visits to **İbrikli**, the only frescoed medieval church in Artvin province, completely absent from most archeological surveys or manuals. It is in fact "Greek" in origin rather than Georgian, as there were always small Greek Orthodox communities inhabiting the northern and western Caucausus until well into the twentieth century.

On Highway 10, 6.3km southeast of Borçka, head up an unsigned, appalling dirt track on the inland (northeast) side of the highway, away from the reservoir. Ignore hairpin turns to the left at 200m and 1.5km along; after 5.2km, you'll reach the village of İbriklı, whose use of ceramic roof-tiles lends it a Mediterranean feel. Bear left and up at the first possible junction, away from the mosque, then 200m later ignore another track right towards the mosque and village centre, then 300m further along do go right and down onto an even steeper descending side-track. You may have to park at a cluster of houses 300m from this last junction. The quickest path to the church – whose dome can be glimpsed in the pastures and hazelnut groves below – begins 200m uphill, at a sharp curve where you may also be able to leave a vehicle.

This access trail goes straight down past, but not to, the **church** – after 200m hop the field boundary fence to approach the utterly crumbled exterior, overgrown with wild fig and bracken. Crudely built to a cross-and-square plan with a brick dome, this diminutive country chapel – for it was never more than this – retains the most complete cycle of **frescoes** this side of Ani, but they're predictably badly damaged. Greek lettering makes identification of some scenes just possible, and they would seem to date from the fourteenth century at the earliest.

Ardanuç and Yeni Rabat

The river valleys east of Artvin are no less spectacular than their counterparts around Yusufeli. The approach to **ARDANUÇ**, once the capital of Klarjeti Georgia, is through the spectacular, high-walled gorge of the Köprüler Çayı, defended by the **Ferhatlı Kale**, 5km along. **Dolmuşes** from Artvin do the 45-minute trip all morning, starting at 8am, with the last one back at 5pm. The dwindling, slightly shabby old quarter of Ardanuç, 10.5km from the main highway, crouches at the foot of a giant wedding-cake of crumbling orange rock, on top of which sits the giant Bagratid **castle of Gevhernik**. With an early start to beat the heat, you can climb it on foot or (part way) by car, but to do that and see the church up the valley in one day you'll need your own transport.

The newer bazaar cantonment, a kilometre or so further, is arrayed around a pleasant, plane-tree-studded "village green" – a legacy of the Russian occupation – with teahouse tables in the middle and a few *döner/pide salonları* at which to stop for a **snack**. All hotels here – which were never up to much – have closed down, so don't get stranded.

Yeni Rabat

The 08-05 road east of Ardanuç is being widened and paved, eventually all the way to its junction with the 955 above Ardahan; beyond some messy and ambitious tunnel works, the scenery is idyllic and gets ever more so as the dirt road worsens. Just under 26km from the main highway, a sign points left (north) towards "Yeni Rabat Kilisesi 6" and the village of "Bulankık/Lengetev" (in a burst of ethnic pride, Georgian place-names are now commonly indicated in this region). Despite the horrid surface, one daily Ardanuç-based dolmuş lurches along, bound for Bulanık and Tosunlu, across the valley.

From the *meydan* in "downtown" **Bulanık**, 1km along and distinguished by fine vernacular log cabins, an onward dirt track leads off slightly down and left (east-northeast) for the remaining 2.5km (best done in a 4WD) to the tenth-century monastery church of **Yeni Rabat** (Shatberdi), nestled in the vegetable gardens of its four-house hamlet, with an idyllic setting up the slopes of one of the loveliest Georgian valleys. The long-vanished monastery, founded a century earlier by Gregory Khantzeli, was renowned as a school for manuscript illuminators. The dome, nave and transept are still virtually intact, with extensive relief carving on the south and east facade, but the exterior has been stripped of most of its dressed stone.

The lower Berta valley: Dolishane and Porta

From the Ardanuç area, retrace your steps to the junction with Highway 10 linking Artvin and Şavşat, which parallels the Berta river (Imerhevi in Georgian). Exactly 300m upstream from the Ardanuç turning, a fine stone **bridge** leaps over the water, and directly opposite this the new bypass highway begins its tortuous journey to Artvin.

Dolishane

Some 3.5km above the stone bridge (or 2.5km from Köprübaşı at Artvin), a badly marked dirt road (there may be some hand-painted signs reading "Dolishane Kilisesi" up on the rock face) leads within 2.5km more to the village of Hamalı. The dome of the tenth-century church of **Dolishane** peeks above the lush vegetation of this oasis village; most ordinary cars will have to stop at the base of the final grade up. The church has not fared well since it ceased serving as the village mosque (when the new adjacent one was built in the mid-1990s); the interior is now being used as an agricultural tool shed. The exterior is more rewarding, the south facade window surrounded by such reliefs as the Bagratid builder-king Smbat I (954–958) offering the church to Christ, a Star of David and an archangel.

Porta

Twelve kilometres above the turning for Artvin, or 26km downstream from Söğütlü Kale (see below), an easily missed yellow metal sign – posted by the management of the *Otel Karahan* – points to the start of the direct path up to **Porta**, modern name for the ninth-century monastery of Khantza, home to the architect-monk Gregory Khantzeli. It's an enjoyable but steep 45-minute climb up to the

Bağcılar district of Pırnallı village, though you'll need stout, treaded shoes and preferably a self-arrest device, since the trail is very slippery; for the same reason reckon on the same amount of time down. Some ten minutes up the hill, you need to go up and left very briefly where a newer bulldozer track disrupts the path. The seasonally inhabited hamlet, an oasis tucked into a side ravine of the main canyon running up to Pırnallı, is built higgledy-piggledy around and up against the dilapidated monuments; it's an excellent example of the rural "chalet-style" architecture of these valleys, wooden upper floors on stone-built ground floors, garlanded here with utility wires and the odd satellite dish.

The main tenth-century **church**, still impressive despite gaping holes in the dome and walls, is similar in plan to the one at Haho, with low-ceilinged, arcaded aisles flanking the nave. To the west stands a separate, smaller sixteen-sided **cupola**, once part of a belfry or (less likely) a baptistry. A Georgian inscription is chiselled across its two-toned masonry, still in good condition. Of the monastery quarters themselves, oriented west to east, only the southeastern corner remains. Beside the path in, the eastern wall of an isolated chapel shelters an **ayazma**, or sacred spring, which supports the local walnut groves – a contrast to the endemic scrub oak (*pırnal*) that gives the main village its name.

The upper Berta valley: Tbeti, Meşeli Karagöl and Şavşat

Georgian vernacular architecture reaches its apotheosis along the upper reaches of the Berta stream and its tributaries, most notably in the intricately carved chestnut-wood balustrades of the houses' wraparound balconies. The saturated greens of the lower hillsides rival those around Bulanık, while higher up dense forest cover evokes the alps of central Europe.

Tbeti

The last local Georgian church lies 10.5km off the Artvin–Şavşat road, starting from the compact fortress of **Söğütlü Kale**. Turn up the paved but one-lane sideroad marked for Veliköy, and follow the Kaleboyu stream valley for 7km to the village of Ciritdüzü. Bear left here by a "mini-market", following signs for Cevizli village and "Tibet (sic) Kilisesi"; just over 9km from the highway, by the Cevizli "city limits" sign, bear right with the asphalt, then left beside the school for the final short distance to the church.

The remains of the tenth-century monastic **church of Tbeti**, peeking out of the trees at the head of a beautiful valley, are visible at a distance to the sharp-eyed, though up close the building – extensively damaged by local treasure-hunters a few decades ago – is heartbreaking. Tbeti was unique in its non-elongated cross-in-square ground plan, with only the church in far-off Çengilli (see p.817) approximating it. Now, only the south transept and east apsidal facade retain any relief work, with particularly fine carved windows and medallions at the base of the capitals of false columns on the south facade. According to tradition the great medieval Georgian poet, Shota Rustaveli, studied here for a time; he is said to have fallen hopelessly in love with Queen Tamara while serving as one of her ministers and, being briskly rejected, ended his days in a Jerusalem monastery.

Meşeli Karagöl

The only tourist facility in the area is found at **Meşeli Karagöl**, 20km beyond Ciritdüzü via Veliköy and Meşeli villages, and so qualified to distinguish it from the five thousand others called "Karagöl" (Black Lake) in Turkey. The last 4km of road beyond Meşeli are atrocious, but your reward is the slightly reedy lake, set in dense spruce forest on the lower slopes of Cin Dağı – and the simple but salubrious, four-room *Karagöl Pansiyon* (☎0466/537 2137 or 537 2300; ❷), an ex–Forest Service **lodge** now run privately by Atanur "Babo" Şahin, one of the characters of the district. It's popular in summer, so reservations are suggested unless you don't mind camping – though note that bears, wild boar and deer roam hereabouts at night.

Şavşat and beyond

Back on Highway 10, Söğütlü castle, just west of the town-limits sign, heralds your arrival in **ŞAVŞAT** (Shavsheti in Georgian), but there's little to stop for in this thoroughly modern, grubby town; the local carpet-weaving tradition has died out and prostitution is prominent at most local **accommodation**, though the *Gökçe Pansiyon* at Yeni Cad 13 (☎0466/517 2126; ❷) may be an exception.

The road east from here to Ardahan proves wonderfully scenic if steep. Just 4km east of Şavşat, the idyllic hay meadows of **Yavuzköy** look like they've escaped from the cover of a Swiss chocolate box, but the first facility – and more appealing than any eatery in Şavşat, Ardanuç or Ardahan – is a licensed **meat-and-trout grill**, above a curve in the road some 10km east of Şavşat. A mixed coniferous forest persists until about 2350m elevation, while sinuous switchbacks lead up to a final picturesque *yayla* of log cabins and sheet-metal roofs, just below the **Çamlıbel pass**, at the border between Artvin and Ardahan provinces.

Travel details

Trains

Erzurum to: Ankara/İstanbul (daily at noon & 8pm; 24hr/35hr); Divriği (1 daily; 7hr); Kars (daily at 7.30am & 5.20pm; 5hr).
Kars to: Erzurum (daily at 7.10am; 5hr).

Buses and dolmuşes

Artvin to: Ardahan via Şavşat (10 daily; 3hr); Ardanuç (6 daily until 4pm; 45min); Erzurum (4 daily; 4hr 30min); Hopa (hourly until 3pm; 1hr 30min); Kars (1 daily at noon; 6hr); Rize (hourly until 3pm; 2hr 15min); Şavşat (7 daily; 2hr); Trabzon (5 daily; 4hr); Yusufeli (4 daily; 1hr 45min).
Erzurum to: Ankara (6 daily; 13hr); Artvin (5 daily; 4hr 15min); Bayburt (hourly; 2hr); Doğubeyazit (4 daily; 4hr); İspir (3 daily; 2hr); Kars (6 daily; 3hr); Rize (2 direct daily; 6hr); Sivas (5 daily; 7hr 30min); Trabzon (3 daily; 5hr); Van (1–2 daily; 6hr); Yusufeli (3 direct daily; 3hr).
Kars to: Ardahan (hourly; 1hr 30min); Artvin via Göle (1 daily at 8.30am; 5hr); Çıldır (2 daily at 11am & noon; 1hr 30min); Digor (hourly; 45min); Erzurum (6 daily; 3hr); Iğdır (hourly; 3hr); Trabzon (1 daily at 8.30am; 7hr).

Yusufeli to: Artvin (5 daily; 1hr 45min); Barhal (4 daily; 1hr 30min); Erzurum (2 daily in the morning before 1pm; 3hr); Hevek (2 daily; 3hr); Tekkale (1–3 daily; 15min).

Flights

Erzincan to: Ankara (3 weekly; 1hr 20min).
Erzurum to: Ankara (1 daily; 1hr 30min); İstanbul (2 daily; 2hr).
Kars to: Ankara (1 daily; 1hr 50min); İstanbul (2 daily; 3hr 30min).

Travel to Armenia

The Turkish–Armenian border at Doğukapı east of Kars has been closed since 1994, due to diplomatic wranglings and historical enmity between the two nations. Through trains, as well as vehicle transit, from Kars to Gyumri (ex-Leninakan), the first major Armenian city, is thus suspended until further notice. Oddly, it is still possible to fly from İstanbul to the Armenian capital of Erevan – currently the only way to travel between the two countries.

11

The Euphrates and Tigris basin

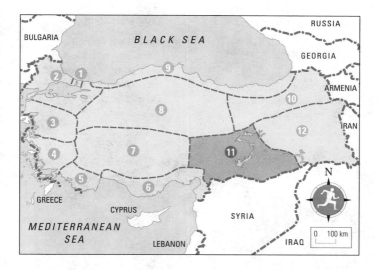

CHAPTER 11

Highlights

* **Gaziantep Archeology Museum** A magnificent collection of Roman-era mosaics, rescued from the drowned site of Zeugma and displayed in a state-of-the-art museum. See p.848

* **Şanlıurfa's "pizza"** Home of the spicy dish, *lahmacun*, best eaten amidst the hustle and bustle of one of Turkey's best bazaars. See p.856

* **Nemrut Dağı** The massive stone heads of Hellenistic deities glare out from a remote mountain-top. See p.864

* **Diyarbakır** Walk around the mighty basalt walls of this predominately Kurdish city, high above medieval alleys teeming with street kids. See p.871

* **Mardin** A hilltop town of beautiful Arab-style houses interspersed with graceful mosques and solid churches. See p.880

* **Syrian Orthodox Church** Catch a service in Diyarbakır, Mardin or Midyat, and experience a liturgy that has remained virtually unchanged for 1500 years. See p.884

* **Hasankeyf** A once grand city, spectacularly situated on a soaring cliff overlooking the green Tigris. See p.888

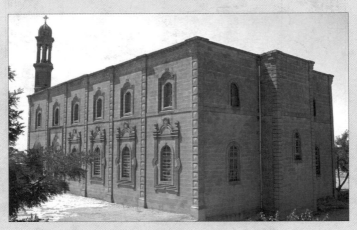

△ Syrian church, Midyat

The Euphrates and Tigris basin

E ast of the Mediterranean coast, you leave the tourist hordes behind and the going gets rougher: there are no full-scale resorts, few travelling companions and only minor conventional attractions. Yet for many, the **basin of the Euphrates and Tigris rivers**, a broad, fan-shaped flood plain ringed on three sides by the mountains containing their headwaters, is the most exotic part of Turkey, offering a number of compelling ancient sites and some fascinating, isolated towns.

Historically, this has always been a border zone where opposing empires and civilizations have met and often clashed. Settlements on the Euphrates formed the eastern boundary of the Roman Empire against the Parthians, and subsequently the Byzantines pushed their frontier further southeast against the Persian heartlands. With the birth of the new religion, Islam, in 632 AD, Byzantine authority began to crumble under pressure from the Arabs to the east and south. Thereafter, almost everybody of any import in Middle Eastern affairs seems to have passed through at one time or another: Arabs, Crusaders, Armenians, Selçuks, Turcomans, Mongols and finally the French, who invaded southeastern Turkey as part of a wider attempt by the victorious World War I Allies to break up the defeated Ottoman Empire.

Today a frontier atmosphere persists and you'll notice that ethnic Turks are in the minority in most places. Close to the Syrian border, Arab influence is strong, but the further east or north you go, particularly into the remoter valleys of the Tigris and its tributaries, you'll find an ever-increasing proportion of the population is made up of Kurds. The potential volatility of this racial mix has been exacerbated by the fundamentalist or separatist sympathies of some of the population, sometimes aggravated by the heavy-handed tactics of the Turkish authorities. Traditionally, smallholding farmers and herdsmen have barely scratched a living from the rocky and unrewarding land, and the new dams of the Southeastern Anatolian Project (see box on p.845) have only improved farming in the west of the area, where water finds its way to the fields via huge irrigation tunnels. Outside this area, high pastures are being abandoned due to drought and low farm prices, and, in spite of the decline in PKK activities, population drift to the big cities continues.

Coming from the west, most visitors pass first through Gaziantep, the last outpost of Europeanized Turkey and a cheerful, booming city benefiting from

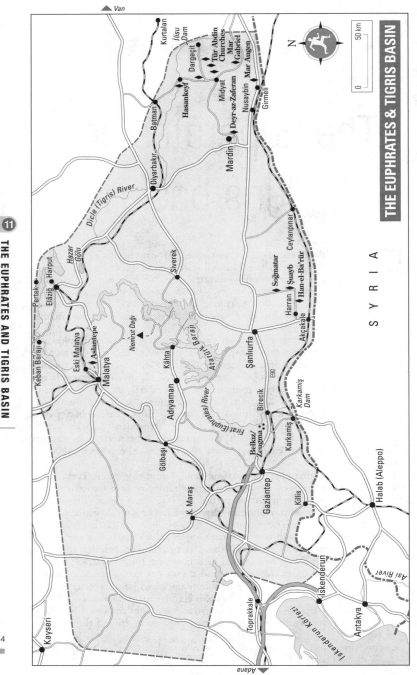

its newfound industrial wealth. From Gaziantep a narrower road leads across the Euphrates to **Şanlıurfa**, mentioned in the Bible as the birthplace of Abraham and one of the region's most rewarding destinations.

The Southeastern Anatolian Project

The *Güneydoğu Anadolu Projesi* (GAP), or **Southeastern Anatolian Project**, was begun in 1974 with the construction of the Keban Dam across the upper Euphrates near Elazığ. Upon completion (originally scheduled for 1997, and now well underway) the scheme will total no fewer than 22 **dams** in the ring of foothills around the joint Euphrates–Tigris basin. A series of large-bore tunnels leading to areas as far-flung as Harran and Ceylanpınar near the Syrian border have begun to irrigate 1.6 million hectares of what was previously partial wasteland. Moreover, seventeen of the dams will generate **electric power**, for a total hourly capacity of 26 billion kilowatts – a third of this from the massive **Atatürk Dam**, fourth largest in the world at 80m high and 800m broad at the base, tapering gradually to 20m at the top. As evident from the mind-boggling numbers, the GAP is an undertaking of pharaonic confidence and ambition, intended to be a panacea for most of the southeast's economic and social ills, although Syria, Turkey's southern neighbour, has complained bitterly that its share of water from the Euphrates has been halved since the completion of the Atatürk Dam.

In conjunction with tax incentives offered by the government to companies who move their operations here, hydroelectrification has also triggered some rapid **industrialization** to the west of the basin. Proprietors of textile mills in western Turkey have even gone so far as to dismantle loss-making plants and machinery and ship them for reassembly in the GAP area, where the cheap power and huge pool of inexpensive labour will allow them to run at a profit. Promoters of the scheme plan to send any excess power to western Turkey, though the inefficiency of Turkey's national grid makes this difficult at present.

In terms of the local benefits of GAP, the improvement to agriculture is apparent from the main road. Eastwards from Gaziantep, the area has greened – new pistachio and olive plantations flourish, cotton is being grown around Harran, and many fruits and vegetables are under seasonal cultivation. A new university was founded at Şanlıurfa to investigate the application of new agricultural methods and provide trained experts. However, only **large landlords** are able to qualify for credits from the state bank to purchase the fertilizer and machinery necessary to engage in large-scale agribusiness. Smaller farmers are being forced off the land as small fertile riverside plots are submerged under the rising waters. Many of these smallholders have migrated to the cities to seek work in factories, which has contributed to the creation of *gecekondu*, or **slum areas**, populated by a permanent urban underclass of unskilled or semi-skilled labourers.

Rural depopulation aside, the other major effects of GAP have been on the region's archeological and natural heritage. Immense efforts have ensured that artefacts from many sites in the Euphrates have been saved, with the finds taking pride of place at local museums (especially Gaziantep; see p.848). However, major settlements such as Samsat, occupied since pre-Roman times, proved too big a challenge to the overworked international teams and have vanished forever beneath the waters. The dam on the Euphrates at **Birecik**, as well as drowning part of the Roman frontier town of Zeugma, has caused severe environmental disruption as endemic populations of animals, birds and plants have seen their habitat disappear. The lower dam at **Karkamış** also threatens an important archeological site. Despite an international outcry, the **İlisu** project, the first of a series of dams planned on the Tigris, is scheduled for completion in 2012.

In the mountains to the north of Gaziantep, the spectacular temple and tomb of **Nemrut Dağı** fully justifies a pilgrimage. **Kahta**, the closest village, is a scruffy development that concentrates on servicing the Nemrut Dağı tourism trade. The two nearest towns, **Adıyaman** to the south and **Malatya** to the north, are not particularly enticing either, although the former has an interesting old quarter and the latter offers easy access to the nearby attractions of **Eski Malatya** and **Aslantepe**.

From either Şanlıurfa or Malatya, it's a journey of half a day or less to **Diyarbakır**, a teeming city built on the banks of the River Tigris. South of Diyarbakır, the other major destination for travellers in the Tigris region is **Mardin**, with its atmospheric collection of beautiful vernacular houses set on a crag overlooking the Syrian plain. To the east of Mardin, the isolated **Tür Abdin** plateau is home to most of the remaining Syrian Orthodox Christian population of Turkey and to a scattering of monasteries and churches. At its heart lies **Midyat**, a town of elegant mansions, once the equal of those in Mardin but now crumbling into almost irredeemable abandonment. Finally, following a different route back to Diyarbakır, the village of **Hasankeyf**, breathtakingly sited on the Tigris, is slated to disappear beneath the waters of the İlisu Dam by 2012.

Travelling around is easy, with good bus links between all the major towns. The once pot-holed roads in the eastern part of the region have been patched up and are generally in excellent shape. Hotel facilities have improved steadily, and only in the small towns, such as Midyat, will you have trouble finding a reasonable hotel. In summer, the harsh terrain bakes in an intense heat, though the lack of humidity does something to mitigate the fierce temperatures. To enjoy the region at its best, try to visit during spring or autumn.

It's worth bearing in mind that the main jumping-off point for **crossing to Syria** is not, in fact, in this region, but Antakya in the Hatay (see p.586).

The Euphrates basin

As you approach from Adana, the **flood plain of the Euphrates** opens out to the east and northeast, reaching the southern fringes of the Anatolian plateau, from which the Euphrates river itself (Fırat in Turkish) winds its turbid way into Syria. The broad alluvial plain has been inhabited for several millennia and was once a lush, fertile region; indeed, remains of some of the world's oldest known human settlements have been discovered here. Unfortunately, the thirteenth-century Mongol destruction of ancient irrigation canals and the depredations of herds of goats have resulted in a dusty steppe-land.

Approaching from the west, the first major centre is **Gaziantep**, where the narrow lanes of the old quarter make a sharp contrast to the modern, shop-lined boulevards. East of Gaziantep, the road shoots across the plain of the Euphrates, crossing the river at bleached, sandy **Birecik** before cutting through rocky uplands to the venerable town of **Şanlıurfa** – or Urfa, as it's commonly known – well worth a couple of days' sightseeing and also a good base for exploring **Harran**, a village of mud-brick beehive houses continuously inhabited for over 6000 years.

Arguably the region's main attraction, though, is the Commagene mountain-top temple of **Nemrut Dağı**, Eastern Turkey's most photographed and publicized site. It's easily approached from Urfa, or from **Adıyaman** to the south or from the north via **Malatya**, a civilized, rather bland town set in the middle of the rolling, gorge-cut plateau that divides İç Anadolu (Inner Anatolia) from Doğu Anadolu (Eastern Anatolia). From Malatya, it's also a fairly easy matter to make your way to **Elazığ**, an ugly, modern place notable only for its archeological museum and the presence of the ruined city of **Harput** just outside town.

Gaziantep

Gaziantep, a booming modern city, is the largest in the region, with a population in excess of a million. It's one of the main beneficiaries of the GAP dams project and has a prosperous air. Progressive local government has overseen the construction of an industrial quarter separated from the city by a belt of forest and the various town-planning strategies and investment incentives have been a palpable success. Gaziantep looks set to become a major tourist destination with the revitalization of its **archeological museum**, which now houses more than 800 square metres of mosaic rescued from the dam waters which flooded nearby Zeugma. The city boasts some fine domestic architecture in the Christian/Jewish quarter, as well as several mosques and a ruined castle, and is also famed for its incredible **pistachio nuts** – properly *şam fıstığı* but often referred to as *Antep fıstığı* – some of the best you'll taste anywhere in Turkey. Geographically, it's a handy staging post on a journey to more exotic destinations to the north or further east.

The city is known by local people (and, significantly for visitors, by most bus companies) as "Antep", a corruption of the Arab *ayn teb* ("good spring"); the prefix "Gazi" ("warrior for Islam") was only added in 1920 after Nationalist forces defending the city withstood a ten-month siege by the French, who had advanced up from their Syrian protectorate in an attempt to seize a portion of defeated Turkey.

Arrival, information and services

Gaziantep's old quarter is built on a hill; from here, Hürriyet Caddesi/İstasyon Caddesi runs 1.5km down through a large park surrounding the river to the museum and stadium. Atatürk Caddesi/Suburu Caddesi crosses this main artery just north of the old city and the Sinema Merkez complex, the latter a local landmark.

The **otogar** lies 5km northwest of the centre, so you'll need to take a service bus or dolmuş into town. Get off at Hükümet Konağı (the Sinema Merkez complex), near the junction of Suburcu and Hürriyet *caddesi*s, where you'll find most of the city's hotels and restaurants. The **train station** stands at the north end of İstasyon Caddesi, 2km from downtown; dolmuşes shuttle up the hill into town. There are daily flights from Ankara and İstanbul to **Sazgan airport**, 10km southeast; Havaş buses (5YTL) meet arrivals and will shuttle you to the **THY terminal** at Atatürk Bul 30/B (☎0342/230 1565), west of Sinema Merkez. Onur Air has a ticket office in İncirli Pınar Mah, Kazaz İş Merkezi 26 (☎0342/221 0304).

Gaziantep's helpful **tourist office** occupies a pink and cream colonial-style building in Yüzüncü Yıl Park (Mon–Fri 9am–noon & 1–5pm; ☎0342/230 5969) a kilometre northwest of the junction of Suburcu and Hürriyet *caddesi*s. Staff can provide printed maps of the town and lists of accommodation, but speak only basic English. The main **PTT** is 100m south of the Sinema Merkez complex, and there's **Internet** access at the *Metpas Internet Café* on Atatürk Bulvarı. Finally, there are a number of **car rental** outfits in town: Met-Kar, Atatürk Bul 90/A (☎0342/232 0021), and Al-

Ser, Gazı Paşa Bul 19/B (☎0342/234 3084), are likely to be cheaper than Avis, Ordu Cad 15/A (☎0342/336 1194), and Hertz, Ordu Cad 92/C (☎0342/336 7718).

Accommodation

The city has a wealth of hotels, though most are business oriented. The best budget choice is the *Evin*, on Kayacak Sok 11, 50m southwest of Sinema Merkez (☎0342/231 3492; ❷). Newly renovated, it's very homely and friendly, with small but well-appointed en-suite rooms, and it's handily situated between the modern centre and the old quarter.

In the medium range, a good choice for both rooms and location is the comfortable and (except on match days) quiet *Katan*, 100m from the archeological museum at İstasyon Cad 58 (☎0342/230 6969, ☞220 8454; ❸). The prominent, good-value *Belkiz*, on a sidestreet off Suburcu Caddesi 300m east of the Sinema Merkez (☎0342/220 2020, ☞234 2675; ❸), has rather dowdy but quiet and comfortable air-conditioned rooms, and is convenient for the bazaar and castle. Gaziantep now has a couple of very impressive boutique hotels, both with English-speaking owners. Best value is the ★ *Belkis Han*, centrally located on Kayacık Ara Sok 16, near Sinema Merkez (☎0342/231 1084, ⊛www.belkishan.com; ❺). A carefully restored old townhouse built around a courtyard, it offers individually decorated and furnished rooms, and wonderful breakfasts. The *Anadolu Evleri* on Köroğlu Sok 6 near the bazaar (☎0342/220 9525, ⊛www.anadoluevleri.com; ❼) has a magnificent tiled courtyard, and comfortable high-ceilinged rooms with ornately tiled floors and decorated ceilings.

The City

Gaziantep, like so many places in this part of Turkey, has been occupied by the Hittites, Assyrians, Persians, Alexandrines, Romans, Selçuks, Crusaders, Byzantines and Arabs. Industrialization based on textile mills has brought prosperity to the city, but also an influx of country people looking for a better standard of living. They tenant the maze of multi-storey buildings and slums, which spread up the surrounding hills.

Gaziantep's prize asset is its **archeological museum** on İstasyon Caddesi (Arkeoloji Müzesi; Tues–Sun 8.30am–noon & 1–5pm; 2YTL), south of the park and opposite the football stadium. The museum has a massive new wing, opened in 2005, and displays a superb collection of some 800 square metres of mosaic recently rescued from the once-luxurious Roman border-city of Zeugma (see p.850), now virtually submerged by the Birecik dam on the Euphrates. Particularly impressive are the (partial) re-creations of Roman peristyle villas, complete with their original mosaic flooring. Also on show are some fine frescoes, salvaged from Zeugma by archeological rescue teams, and a magnificent bronze statue of the god of war, Mars. The original part of the museum also houses a collection of draft Hittite reliefs from Yesenek, 100km west of Gaziantep, once one of the main open-air stone-carving centres of the entire Hittite empire.

The most prominent survivor from Gaziantep's past is the **kale**, which dominates the town from the eastern hill – an artificial mound formed by layers of accumulated debris from thousands of years of human occupation. The castle dates back to late Roman times, but the present structure, with its 36 towers, owes more to the Selçuks. To reach it, take any road running east from İstasyon Caddesi; bear right at the square and you'll come to a ramp that leads up to the main doors. Inside are the remains of an excavated baths, with a hypocaust floor and a domed roof.

From the *kale*, Gümrük Caddesi takes you through the surrounding **bazaar quarter**, where several *han*s are today used for metalwork. You might find craftsmen manufacturing the local speciality: furniture inlaid with *sedef* (mother-of-pearl), although lately it's just as likely to be plastic. To the southwest of Sinema Merkez is the former **Christian/Jewish quarter**, unfortunately still undergoing "redevelopment" (ie demolition of the old houses). Here the remaining inward-looking houses, with their black-and-white arched gates, were each once a family fortress. In readiness against successive invaders, each had its own well, food cellars and stabling, as can be seen at the well-signed **Hasan Süzer Ethnography Museum** (Hasan Süzer Etnografi Müzesi; daily 8am–noon & 1–5pm; 2YTL). The museum freeze-frames the life of an upper-class Antep family in the 1930s, with a series of traditionally laid out rooms only slightly let down by the incongruous mannequins. Under the courtyard is a basement used originally for food storage, some thirty degrees cooler than the surroundings. Perched on the nearby hill is the monumental **Kurtuluş Camii** (Independence Mosque). Built in 1892 as an Armenian cathedral, it served as a prison during the War of Independence and after, and then stood empty until its conversion to a mosque. The facade, with black and white stone trim and restrained carvings around the windows, would do credit to a French city square, and it's set in a pleasant courtyard shaded by plum, mulberry, walnut and fig trees. Inside, Corinthian columns support the porch, while the main space is covered by a huge, cleverly constructed dome.

The same architect built the **Alauddevle Camii**, on the north side of Eski Saray Caddesi, which runs east from Sinema Merkez. Another nineteenth-century church, the Catholic **Kendirli Kilisesi**, on Atatürk Bulvarı, is now a theatre/exhibition hall, but its imposing black and white banded exterior still bears bullet and shrapnel scars from the War of Independence. Nearby is the **Martyrs Memorial and Museum**, remembering the 6317 Turks who lost their lives between April 1920 and February 1921, defending their city against a vastly superior French force.

Eating and drinking

Gaziantep is noted for spicy dishes such as *çiğ* (raw) *köfte*, made from cracked wheat, flavoured with pepper and tomato, and served with lettuce and lemon juice. The city is also unrivalled in Turkey for sweets, particularly pistachio-based pastries like *fıstık sarma*.

One of the city's best **restaurants** is the unlicensed, faux-Ottoman ⚘ İncilipinar Antep Sofrası, a fifteen-minute walk east of the centre at 100 Yıl Atatürk Parkı İçi, where standard Turkish dishes and local specialities (5–6YTL for a main course) are served at tables set on the edge of a pleasant park. Try the tiny, sour *köfte* or the tender mushroom kebabs. Closer to the city centre, on Atatürk Bul, Çınarlı Sok 6, is the cheerful *Çınarlı*, an upstairs room done out, like İncilipinar Antep Sofrası, in mock-Ottoman style. Of its many local dishes (mains around 5YTL), try the delicately spiced *tavuk dolma* (chicken thighs stuffed with pistachio, almond, potato, carrot, rice and yoghurt sauce) or *mercimek aşı*, a pilaf made from *bulgur*, black lentils, onion, garlic, tomatoes and spices. Though there's no alcohol, there is regular live Turkish music.

Another characterful place is the *Ekim 29 Lokantası*, in an old Armenian house on Gaziler Cad, Çekemoğlu Çıkmazı, a cul-de-sac off the main street in the pedestrian area, which sometimes has live Kurdish music. Best at lunchtimes (when it's thronging with local shopkeepers, craftsmen and shoppers) is the long-established *İmam Çağdaş*, on Kale Cıvarı Uzun Çarşı 14, in the bazaar. The *lahmacun* are huge and delicious (1.5YTL) and the *ayran* is served up in a tinned copper bowl. As for **drinking**, the *Berivane*, a few minutes' walk from the Sinema Merkez on Atatürk Caddesi, is a Kurdish drinking den with cheap beer (3YTL). They'll send out for decent kebabs if you're peckish.

East of Gaziantep: towards Şanlıurfa

Travelling east of Gaziantep is hellishly hot in summer, with temperatures edging into the mid-forties centigrade. When buying a bus ticket, try and make sure you get a seat on the shady side. En route to **Birecik**, there are a couple of moderately interesting archeological sites, Hittite **Karkamış** and Roman **Zeugma**.

Karkamış

About 30km from Gaziantep, just before the Euphrates bridge at Birecik, amid a landscape of pistachio and olive groves stippled with hilltop villages, there's a turning for **Karkamış**, the ancient Hittite city of Carchemish. It's 25km south of the highway, situated just south of the railway bridge at the junction of the Euphrates and a tributary. A number of important reliefs (including scenes from the Assyrian epic of Gilgamesh) were unearthed here by British archeologist Leonard Woolley with T.E. Lawrence during excavations financed by the British Museum between 1910 and 1915, and again in 1920.

Many of the finds have been removed to the Museum of Anatolian Civilizations in Ankara. The **site** itself, in principle always freely open, is subject to dam construction and military restrictions, as it lies just a few kilometres north of the border with Syria and adjacent to the new Karkamış dam. It's difficult to reach except by car, though an adventurous alternative is the one daily train from Gaziantep (leaves 7am, returns 2pm), to Barak, a kilometre from the site. Ask at Gaziantep tourist office for the latest information.

Zeugma

From Nizip, on the same highway, it's 9km to the waterside excavations at **Zeugma**, just northwest of Birecik. The once-rich city of Zeugma, originally Seleucia, was strategically founded on a major crossing point of the Euphrates by Seleucius Nicator, one of Alexander the Great's generals. The Scythian legion and other troops guarded the Roman frontier crossing, and the town merchants, enriched by border trade, built sumptuous villas below the town. Zeugma was devastated, first by Sassanid raids in 252 AD, then by an earthquake, but partly resettled in the Byzantine and Abbasid eras.

The waters of the Birecik dam have now submerged most of the wealthy villas, and part of the town. The massive but late international archeological rescue mission of 2000 recovered many mosaics, now superbly displayed in Gaziantep museum (see p.848), but many frescoed walls were drowned. Currently, although the site is set to become an open-air museum, little is visible except the ongoing excavations of the Dionysus villa. Until further excavations have been completed, it is only worth coming here if you want to see the location of the ancient city. Otherwise, visit Ⓦ www.zeugmaweb.com, which although slightly out of date does have some photos of the mosaics in situ, prior to their salvage.

Birecik

The highway crosses the Euphrates river and the provincial border at the shabby town of **BIRECIK**, around 40km from Gaziantep, where all Urfa-bound buses stop. The town is of interest mainly to ornithologists as one of the few places in the world where you can see the **bald ibis**, a relative of the stork, that once nested wild on the castle walls but is now confined to a **breeding station** (April–Oct daily during daylight hours; 1YTL), 1km north of town on the east river-bank.

Excess birds are released into the wild every year, but so far none has migrated back. **Storks** themselves are far more in evidence and here (as elsewhere in both the Euphrates and Tigris basins) large numbers can be seen occupying their untidy nests in the spring and summer months. The Birecik environs are also home to several other bird species; you might see eagle owls and Bruce's Scops owls (the latter a regular visitor to the *Belediye* tea garden on the east river-bank in town), yellow-throated and pale rock sparrows, menetries warblers, see-see partridges and sand grouse.

Birecik's ruined **castle** was founded during the eleventh century as a frontier outpost for the Crusader state of Edessa, but isn't worth going out of your way to inspect closely, though its entourage of old houses backed into the cliff-face are appealing from a distance. If you want to stay in the area, there's the bland but clean *Mirkelam Tesisleri Motel* (☎0414/652 1178, ⓕ652 3047; ❷), set amongst the last petrol stations before the bridge over the Euphrates. In Birecik itself, the *Deniz Restaurant*, north of the bridge on the east bank, serves excellent, reasonably priced food, including river fish and a good range of *mezes*.

Şanlıurfa

The name of **ŞANLIURFA**, or "Glorious Urfa" (most of the locals just say Urfa), commemorates resistance to the French invasion and occupation of 1918–1920. It's a place of pilgrimage for many religions; you could easily spend a day taking in the local monuments, which include the reputed birthplace of the prophet Abraham and a mosque complex of some beauty, reflected in the limpid waters of the town's famous lakes.

Just as compelling is Urfa's Middle Eastern atmosphere. A significant proportion of the population is Kurdish: women are veiled and often tattooed with henna, and men wear baggy trousers and traditional headdresses. Amongst the Arab population, women tend towards brightly coloured clothes and rich fabrics, while visiting pilgrims are often fully veiled and clad in black from top to toe. For visitors coming from western Turkey, the traditional dress of women in Urfa's bazaars make this seem like the place where "the Orient" really begins, but to the north, around the university, students are smartly dressed in Western fashions. In Turkey this so-called "city of the prophets" has gained a reputation as a focus for Islamic fundamentalism; alcohol has almost disappeared from restaurants and the good citizens retire early to bed. Despite the supposed wealth generated by the GAP project, the poorest inhabitants can still be seen queuing at the east end of the Şurkav Çarşısı for cooked rice and bread distributed by the local governor.

Some history

Even by Turkish standards, Urfa is an old city. According to both Jewish and Muslim sources, it was while living in Urfa that Abraham received his summons from God to take himself and his family to Canaan. Other stories record that the prophet Job was a resident for a while, though claims that the Garden of Eden was somewhere around here are probably based more on wishful thinking.

Whatever the factual basis of these legends, it's certain that people have been living on the site for thousands of years. The first settlers were the Hurri, members of one of Anatolia's earliest civilizations, who built a fortress on the site of the present citadel around 3500 BC and controlled much of the surrounding area. The Hurri, who probably named the place Orhoi – corrupted in modern times to Urfa – were followed by the Hittites and Assyrians, the latter remaining in control until

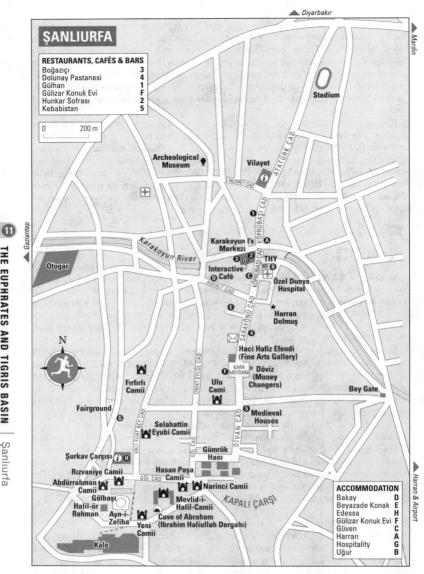

ŞANLIURFA

RESTAURANTS, CAFÉS & BARS

Boğazıçı	3
Dolunay Pastanesi	4
Gülhan	1
Gülizar Konuk Evi	F
Hunkar Sofrası	2
Kebabistan	5

0   200 m

Diyarbakır

Mardin

Gaziantep

Stadium

Archeological Museum

Vilayet

S. NUSRET CAD

ATATÜRK CAD

KÖPRÜBAŞI CAD

Karakoyun River

Otogar

Karakoyun İs Merkezi

THY

Özel Dunya Hospital

Interactive Café

ASFALT CAD

KÖPRÜBAŞI CAD

SARAYÖNÜ CAD

Harran Dolmuş

Haci Hafiz Efendi (Fine Arts Gallery)

KARA MEYDANI

Döviz (Money Changers)

Bey Gate

ONİKİ EYLÜL CAD

Fırfırlı Camii

Ulu Camii

Fairground

VALİ FUAT BEY CAD

Medieval Houses

DİVAN CAD

Selahattin Eyubi Camii

Şurkav Çarşısı

Rızvaniye Camii

Abdürrahman Camii

Gölbaşı

Halil-ür Rahman

Ayn-i-Zeliha

Gümrük Hanı

GÖL CAD

Hasan Paşa Camii

Narinci Camii

KAPALI ÇARŞI

Mevlid-i-Halil-Camii

Cave of Abraham (Ibrahim Haliullah Dergahı)

Yeni Camii

Kale

Harran & Airport

ACCOMMODATION

Bakay	D
Beyazade Konak	E
Edessa	H
Gülizar Konuk Evi	F
Güven	C
Harran	A
Hospitality	G
Uğur	B

Alexander the Great swept through after his victory at Issus. Renamed Edessa, after the Macedonian town, the place was an important eastern outpost for the Romans against the Persians.

From the second century AD, Edessa was a thriving centre of Christianity, particularly the Nestorian variant. The city changed hands between Byzantine and Arab several times; according to Syriac legend it was once ransomed for the

△ Sheep on the street in Şanlıurfa

"mandalyon" (see box on Syrian Orthodox Church, p.884). When Byzantine power finally collapsed, the Arabs moved in permanently, staying until the eleventh century, when, during the First Crusade, a French count, Baldwin of Boulogne, stopped off en route to Tripoli and the Holy Land to establish the county of Edessa, a short-lived Christian state. In 1144 the Arabs recaptured Edessa, giving the rulers of Europe a pretext to launch the Second Crusade, although the city was soon forgotten and never wrested back from the Arabs. In 1260 it was put to the sword by the Mongols and never really recovered, declining into obscurity before being absorbed (as Urfa) into the Ottoman Empire in 1637.

Arrival and information

Şanlıurfa's **otogar** is more than a kilometre west of the centre, so take a dolmuş into town (or bargain for a taxi if arriving late at night – you shouldn't pay more than 8YTL). Head for the *Hotel Harran* on Köprübaşı Caddesi, which makes a good orientation point, as most of the hotels and other tourist facilities are found around here. The **airport** is about 6km south of town, on the road to Harran, with a THY bus to take you into the centre; the **THY office** is at Sarayönü Cad 74/A (☎0414/215 3344).

The **tourist office** is now inconveniently located in the *Vilayet* building (Provincial Governor's headquarters), way out of town on Atatürk Caddesi, and is next to useless.

Accommodation

Urfa's popularity as a prime destination for Middle Eastern tourists on religious quests means that accommodation at the cheap end of the market is plentiful. Mid-range options are less abundant, and the group-oriented top-end hotels tend to be exorbitant for independent travellers.

Bakay Hotel Asfalt Yol Cad 24 ☎0414/215 8975, ℱ215 1156. Excellent value, with clean and cheerful air-conditioned rooms with TVs. Friendly management and a relatively quiet location (ask for a rear room) make this a good choice. ❷

Beyazade Konak Sarayönü Caddesi, Yusufpaşa Camii Yanı ☎0414/216 3535, ⓦwww.beyazadekonak.com. Despite the disappointingly furnished rooms (though they are equipped with air conditioning and TVs), this authentic old mansion building is excellent value, with real character. Particularly impressive are the downstairs rooms, with their vaulted ceilings, now used as a dining room and *sira gecesi* (traditional-music night) room. ❹

Hotel Edessa Göl Cad ☎0414/215 9911, ⓔhotel-edessa@superonline.com. The *Edessa* promises far more than it delivers, with its superb location overlooking the Gölbaşı complex and elegant stone exterior in no way compensating for the bland, dated rooms and outrageous prices. ❼

Gülizar Konuk Evi A beautiful old Armenian courtyard mansion that tries to be all things to all people, housing a hotel that also doubles as a restaurant-cum-live-music venue. The delightful but waterless upstairs rooms serve as *sofra*-style banqueting halls – but once the meal is over the tables are cleared, bedding is unrolled and you can get some sleep. ❹

Hotel Güven Köprübaşı Cad ☎0414/215 1700. You'll have to endure the alternately offhand and belligerent management to enjoy the power showers, fluffy towels and air conditioning of the obsessively clean rooms. ❸

Harran Atatürk Cad ☎0414/313 2860, ℱ313 4918. Popular with tour groups, the *Harran* is equipped with its own swimming pool, hamam and top-floor bar, sometimes with a floor show patronized by local businessmen. The rooms are comfortable and bathrooms spotless – only the noisy main-road location lets it down. ❻

Hospitality Pension Kızılkoyun Sok 29 ☎0535/373 8926. This very basic pension, set to become a backpackers' favourite and run by a friendly Kurdish couple, has three spotless but waterless doubles set around a pleasant courtyard. Aziz, the owner, speaks English and will pick you up from the *otogar* free of charge. The home cooking is both authentic and delicious (and you can get a beer with it). In summer you can sleep on the roof for a nominal sum. ❷

Otel Uğur Köprübaşı Cad 3 ☎0414/313 1340. Behind the Özel Dünya Hospital, the *Uğur* is much favoured by backpackers, with clean air-conditioned rooms and comfy beds. The few waterless rooms are even cheaper. The helpful owner can arrange Harran/Nemrut tours. ❷

Old Urfa

At the extreme south end of Sarayönü Caddesi is the restored **Hacı Hafız Efendi** house, which is now a fine arts gallery; take a look at its current exhibition and enjoy the cool courtyard and pretty architecture. Adjacent is the **Kara Meydanı**, boasting a venerable-looking nineteenth-century mosque, the Yusuf Paşa Camii. Past Kara Meydanı, Sarayönü Caddesi becomes Divan Caddesi, where you'll find the twelfth-century **Ulu Cami**, with a design based on that of the Grand Mosque in Halab (Aleppo) in Syria. You can take a look around the courtyard with its octagonal minaret (originally the belfry of an earlier Byzantine church) and graves, though the interior is unexceptional.

East of Divan Caddesi lies an extensive warren of bustling narrow streets boasting examples of Urfa's rather plain, pale limestone **medieval houses**, whose distinctive features include lattice-windowed overhangs supported on ornate corbels. At the end of Divan Caddesi sprawls the **Gümrük Hanı**, a late sixteenth-century *kervansaray*, whose shady courtyard is taken up by the tables of teahouses and watch repairers. This is surrounded by the **Kapalı Çarşı**, or covered bazaar, a maze-like commercial area spilling out into the narrow streets nearby. There are stalls and hole-in-the-wall shops selling everything imaginable, from spices to guns. Traders sell green Diyarbakır tobacco by the kilo out of plastic sacks, and domestic appliances are occasionally auctioned off the back of horse-drawn carts, while the pungent stink of skins from freshly slaughtered sheep vies with the more pleasant odour of various powdered herbs. Exotic fabrics, including velvets in glowing colours and beaded or sequined cloth, are an excellent buy.

Turning right out of the Gümrük Hanı brings you to the *bedesten* next door, beyond which lies the **Hacı Kamil Hanı** and the coppersmiths' bazaar. Further west lie the **Sipahi** and **Hüseyniye** bazaars, both left over from the time when camel caravans moved regularly between Urfa and Aleppo, Palmyra, Mari and Baghdad.

İbrahim Halilullah Dergahı

From the bazaars, make your way west along Göl Caddesi to the Mevlid-i Halil Camii and so into the gardens of the **Hızır İbrahim Halilullah**, a colonnaded mosque and *medrese* complex named after the "Prophet Abraham and Friend of God", which has grown up to serve the large numbers of pilgrims – as have stalls selling religious tracts. The **İbrahim Halilullah Dergahı** or "Cave of Abraham" (daily 8am–5.30pm; donations welcomed) is set in the wall of the far courtyard. According to local legend, the prophet Abraham was born here, spending the first ten years of his life in hiding because a local Assyrian tyrant, Nemrut (Nimrod), had decreed that all newborn children be killed.

As Abraham is recognized as a prophet by Muslims, his birth-cave remains a place of worship, the majority of visitors being pilgrims from all over Turkey and the Muslim world rather than tourists. Although there isn't actually much to see inside, the atmosphere is very reverential; there are separate entrances for men and women, dress must be respectful and shoes removed. There is another holy cave nearby, reputed to hold a hair plucked from Mohammed's head, and a recently constructed mosque, the Yeni Cami.

Gölbaşı and the kale

It's a short walk from the cave to **Gölbaşı** – literally "at the lakeside" – where you'll find a shady park, a pair of mosques and two pools filled with fat carp. According to a continuation of the local legend, Abraham, after he emerged from his cave, became an implacable opponent of King Nemrut and tried to smash the idols in the local temple.

The tyrant was displeased and had Abraham hurled from the citadel battlements into a fire below. Abraham was saved when, on a command from God, the flames turned into water and the firewood into carp. The carp have long been considered sacred, and it's said that anyone who eats them will go blind.

Beside the first pool, the **Ayn-i-Zeliha** (named after the daughter of Nimrod), are teahouses and restaurants where you can sit in the shade after feeding the carp with bait bought from poolside vendors; you can even take a small rowing boat out onto the water. The elongated **Halil-ür Rahman** or Balıklı Göl is the pool that saved Abraham from a fiery end; it's surrounded by stone arches, its banks usually swarming with pilgrims and the water seething with fish.

The far western end of Balıklı Göl is closed off by the seventeenth-century **Abdürrahman Camii**, which you are free to look around. The present mosque replaced an older twelfth-century building whose distinctive square minaret has survived. The entire north side of the pool is flanked by the **Rizvaniye Camii**, built by an Ottoman governor in 1716, with some intricately carved wooden doors giving onto its peaceful courtyard.

Above Gölbaşı, and reachable via a signed path between the new mosque and the first pool, is Urfa's **kale** (Tues–Sun 9am–6pm; 1YTL), a massive citadel whose construction is claimed by everybody who ever occupied the city. Much of the castle's surviving structure is thought to date from the time of the twelfth-century Frankish Crusader state. The fortifications are completely ruined now, but it's worth climbing up there for the view of the mosques and pools down below. At the top are a couple of massive, lone Corinthian columns, thought to be the remains of a third-century Christian chapel. They are referred to as the Throne of Nemrut, and local people will tell you that this is the spot from which Nemrut cast Abraham down into the flames.

North to the archeological museum

If you head north from Gölbaşı up Vali Fuat Bey Caddesi, you'll come to the **Selahattin Eyubi Camii**, built in 1860 as the Armenian church of St John and only recently converted into a mosque. Head north again for a glimpse of the former Armenian church of the Twelve Apostles, now converted to **Fırfırlı Camii**. Echoes of former worship can be seen in the star and moon carvings on the old clocktower, which now serves as the mosque's minaret. Continue north to the **Karakoyun river**, the traditional northern boundary of the old town, and if you have time, check out the Byzantine aqueduct, built in 525 and now squeezed between two Ottoman bridges. Some of the ruined old houses above the river still bear pockmarks made by French rifle bullets during the assault on the city in 1920.

The city's excellent **archeological museum** (Arkeoloji Müzesi; Tues–Sun 8.30am–noon & 1.30–5pm; 2YTL) is just north of the town centre. Inside, there's jewellery and pottery from funerary tumuli on the Euphrates flood-plain, and from the sites of ancient Harran and Lidar. An ethnographic section includes statuary from the province's vanished Christian communities, plus magnificent carved doors from demolished mansions. The outdoor collection of reliefs, with inscriptions ranging from Hittite to Armenian, is particularly fascinating, thanks to the sharpness and clarity of the carvings.

Eating and drinking

This is the home of the **Urfa kebap** (spiced minced meat on a skewer) and of **lahmacun** (a thin, chapati-like bread topped with spicy lamb). Stalls in Urfa bazaar sell it hotter, spicier and cheaper than anywhere else. There are numerous simple eateries offering other local specialities based on bulgur (cracked wheat), notably *çiğ köfte*) and *dolmalı köfte* (stuffed meatballs). **Desserts** such as *dondurma*, *kadife* (shredded wheat with cream cheese and honey) and *baklava* are best sampled from shops or cafés along Sarayönü Caddesi.

Dotted along a terrace opposite and at right angles to the *Harran* hotel on Atatürk Caddesi, a line of **bars** serves alcohol (beer or *rakı*) and snacks such as fruit, yoghurt and nuts, but will also send out for kebabs if you want to eat. The only alternatives for alcoholic drinks are the upmarket bars at the *Harran* and the

Edessa hotels.

Boğaziçi Off Atatürk Cad. Set in an old stone building with a vaulted ceiling, it's the best of the bars on this strip, recommended for its attentive service and cheap beer (2.5YTL).

Dolunay Pastanesi Sarayönü Cad PTT Karşısı 2. A flashy patisserie serving delicious chocolate puddings, *baklava* and ice cream.

Gülhan Atatürk Bulvarı Akbank Bitişiği. Highly recommended, particularly for the lunchtime *sulu yemek* (3YTL) and the evening grills (6YTL for a delicious kebab). Well frequented by the locals, its bustling nature ensures a fast turnover and fresh food.

Gülizar Konuk Evi Karameydan Camii Yanı 22. Probably the most atmospheric place to eat in town, with its superb setting in a courtyard mansion, but a little pricey (around 12YTL for a full meal including *mezes* and kebabs). It also hosts *sıra gecesi* (music/entertainment evenings) which are great if you are in the mood for partying with coachloads of elderly İstanbul Turks, but otherwise should be avoided.

Hunkar Sofrası Karakoyun ış Merkezi. Just off Köprübaşı Caddesi, this rooftop restaurant is spotlessly clean and very good value, with tender kebabs at 5YTL, and passable pizzas at the same price. No alcohol.

Kebabistan Yıldız Meydanı 23. Very popular with locals (the upstairs *aile salonu* has *sofra* tables and kilim cushions, and is usually packed with families and headscarved women with children). The kebabs are good and the *lahmacun* large, hot and spicy. Cool, creamy *ayran* comes in bowls with ladles.

Listings

Airport The Turkish Airlines ticketing office is in Kaliru Turizm, on the ground floor of the Özel Dünya hospital on Sarayönü Caddesi. Airport shuttles depart from here (3YTL).

Banks and exchange There are a couple of convenient *döviz* offices and many ATMs on Sarayönü Cad.

Buses The usual eastern bus companies have offices all around town, especially on Sarayönü Cad, and provide service buses to the *otogar*. Harran Nemrut Tur (see "Tours", below) and some hotels will also book tickets for you. Local companies include Urfa Cesur ("Urfa the Brave"), which runs right through to Ankara and İstanbul.

Car rental Harran Nemrut Tur, and one or two other places, rent cars for €30 daily upwards.

Hospital Özel Dünya Hastanesi (Dünya private hospital), Köprübaşı Cad ☎0414/216 3616/215 4348; Devlet Hastane ve Polikliniği (State Hospital), Hastane Cad ☎0414/313 1928/313 1220.

Internet Interactive Café, opposite the Boğaziçi, just off Atatürk Cad. There are others in the student quarter near the stadium.

Police Police station is on Sarayönü Cad.

Post office The PTT is on Sarayönü Cad (Mon–Sat 9am–noon & 1–5pm for money exchange and mail; 24hr for telephones).

Tours Harran Nemrut Tur (☎0414/215 1575), just behind the Özel Dünya hospital, runs half- and full-day trips to Harran (€10 half-day, €25 full-day including Şuayb and Soğmatar), as well as to Nemrut Dağı (€35), Mardin and Deyr-az-Zaferan monastery (€20 depending on group size). For €45 per person (minimum four people), Harran can also arrange a two-day monastery tour that includes a night in Midyat and visits to several monasteries on the Tür Abdin plateau as well as Hasankeyf and Diyarbakır.

Harran and around

Some 45km southeast of Urfa, the beehive-style houses in the village of **HAR-RAN** (also known as Altınbaşak) have become an established tourist attraction. It's the last surviving such community, the bleak plain around being dotted with the ruins of other mud-built villages in this Syrian-influenced style. The village has strong biblical links: in Genesis 11:31 and 12:4, the patriarch Abraham is described as having dwelt here for a while on his way from Ur to Canaan.

Harran is thought to have been continuously inhabited for at least 6000 years, which makes it one of the oldest settlements on earth. It first came to prominence under the Assyrians, who turned it into a prosperous trading town, as well as a centre for the worship of Sin, god of the moon; there was a large temple here, later also used by the Sabian cult (see "Soğmatar" on p.859), on the site now occupied by the ruins of a Crusader fortress. In 53 BC the Roman general Crassus's advance east was halted here, where he was defeated, crucified and had molten gold poured into his mouth by the Parthians. Despite this, the Romans were later able to convert Harran into an important centre of learning, a role it continued to play under the Byzantines and subsequently the Arabs, who founded a university in the town. However, the arrival of the Mongols during the thirteenth century meant devastation. Today, the village overlays the scattered ruins; the beehive houses are mainly between the more extensive sections of the walls (east) and the fenced remains of the mosque and university (northwest).

Getting there

The Harran Nemrut Tur company in Şanlıurfa (see "Listings" on p.857) runs four-hour **excursions** to Harran departing early or late in the afternoon during summer to avoid the horrific heat. **Dolmuşes** to Harran (2.5YTL) also run hourly from Şanlıurfa *otogar*; the last return dolmuş is at 7pm. Alternatively, you'll pay the fixed price of €20 to hire a taxi for the two-way trip with waiting time; in slower periods, you should be able to get a cheaper rate.

If you have your own transport, take the road south from Urfa towards Akçakale for 35km, following irrigation canals that bring water from the Atatürk Dam, until you reach a yellow-signposted turning; Harran is about 10km east of here.

Old Harran

These days, semi-nomadic Arabs and a few Kurds live amid the ruins of old **Harran**, surviving by farming the newly irrigated fields and smuggling sheep (in exchange for instant coffee, Ceylon tea and other foreign luxury goods) across the Syrian border 10km to the south. It is they who have built – and to some extent still live in – the mud-brick beehive-shaped buildings that dot the area, the distinctive shape of which is owed to the fact that no wood is used as support. However, if you're expecting a homogenous community of gumdrop houses, you'll be disappointed, as they're interspersed with conventional cottages and increasingly used for storage or animal – not human – habitation.

If possible try to visit out of season when the heat won't be quite so intense. Soft drinks are available from cafés to the east and west of the main site, and in the dark, cool communal house used as a point of sale for local handcrafts. The *Bazda Motel* (☎0414/441 2001; ❹) on the village bypass road offers clean, en-suite but overpriced **accommodation** in a mock beehive-style concrete building. It is also possible to stay in the more atmospheric *Harran Kültür Evi* (☎0414/441 2477; €15 per person half-board), a complex of restored beehive dwellings on site. You'll sleep on mattresses on the floor, but the place is scrupulously clean and the food good.

The site

The enigmatic ruins of old Harran have a kind of tragic grandeur, dwarfing the beehive dwellings, and it's not difficult to picture the town as it must have been before the arrival of the Mongols. Near the *jandarma* is an artificial tumulus thought to mark the site of the original settlement. Just north of here, and surrounded by broken fencing, stands the most impressive of the ruins, the **Ulu Cami**, with its graceful square tower, built by an Arab caliph during the eighth century and mistaken for a cathedral belfry by T.E. Lawrence when he passed through in 1909. Scattered around are broken pillars, a central water pool with carved seats and remnants of the Arab university, which, judging from the surviving fragments, must have been an exceptionally beautiful complex.

While wandering around, you'll be accosted by village kids begging for *para* (money) and *stilo* (pens). If you take pictures of the little girls in traditional costume they'll demand presents, and throw tantrums if you don't cough up. One or two may attach themselves to you as guides; some are gifted linguists with good twenty-word vocabularies in English, German and French; in addition, they all speak Arabic (their first language), Turkish (learned in school) and often Kurdish.

The eleventh-century **Crusader fortress** is built on the site of the ancient moon temple at the eastern end of the village. There are plenty of ruins to scramble around, although much of the structure looks in a dangerous state of near-collapse. Watch out for the distinctive ten-sided tower; part of its ramparts once ringed the city, and a few sections are still visible to the south. A lion relief is on the **Aslan Kapısı** (Lion Gate) at the northeast edge of the ancient town.

Around Harran

Northeast of Harran are the **Tek Tek Dağı**, a range of dusty hills dotted with ruins and remains; the most accessible and interesting are included in the Harran Nemrut Tur tours (see "Listings" p.857). You could visit with your own vehicle, but the unmarked junctions make navigation frustrating.

Twenty-five kilometres east of the uninspiring twelfth-century *kervansaray* of **Han-el-Ba'rür**, itself 23km from Harran, you'll reach **ŞUAYB**, an ancient, partially subterranean village founded in Roman times and inhabited until the Mongol raids. Various lintels and archways above ground mark still-occupied caves and chambers below.

From Şuayb, continue north 17km to the site of ancient **Soğmatar** (Sumatar on some maps), about 65km from Harran or Urfa. The Sabians, inheritors and elaborators of the local moon cult at Harran, worshipped here from early Christian times onwards. Though nominally believing in a single god called Marilaha, the sect in fact revered all the planetary bodies in ancient Chaldean astrology, and accounts describe lurid orgies and acts of human sacrifice made in the course of their worship of the stars and planets. Soğmatar's position on the frontier enabled the Sabians to elude Christian Byzantine authorities until the Arabs, disgusted by their rites, gave them the choice of death or conversion to Islam.

Ringing the village are seven circular hilltop ruins with ancient Syriac inscriptions on the walls. These are the Sabians' principal observatory and temple complex. In a cave near the centre of the village are carved statues and lunar signs. Local boys in this desperately poor Arab settlement will show you round for a tip.

Adıyaman

ADIYAMAN, 60km northeast of Gaziantep, is the least used base for the trip to Nemrut Dağı, but there are a few things worth exploring here, including the **copper bazaar**, south of the bus station at the far end of town, and, behind it, a *kervansaray*, used for tethering animals. Between the main traffic lights and the bus station, the **museum** (Tues–Sun 8am–noon & 2–5pm; 2YTL) houses artefacts from local tumuli, which were excavated prior to submersion under the Atatürk Dam waters. There is also a small **Syrian/Armenian church** in a green garden in the old quarter.

Practicalities

The **bus station**, where Nemrut tours are booked, is east of the main traffic lights on Atatürk Bulvarı, and less than 100m north of Harıkcı Caddesi. Adıyaman has a rather sleepy **tourist office** next to the PTT at Atatürk Bul 41 (Mon–Fri 9am–noon & 1–5pm; ℡0416/216 1008).

A reasonably cheap **hotel** is the *Otel Yoluç*, Harıkçı Cad 26 (℡0416/213 5226; ❷), with functional rooms and close to the restaurants and shops. To the east, past the bus station, the comfortable and quiet *Motel Beyaz Saray*, Atatürk Bul 136 (℡0416/216 4907; ❸), has the unexpected luxury of a garden swimming pool. Adıyaman's lushest and largest hotel is also on Atatürk Bulvarı, the

---

Excursions to Nemrut Dağı

Organized **minibus trips** to Nemrut Dağı run in the summer season (May–Oct) from Kahta, Adıyaman, Malatya, Şanlıurfa and Cappadocia and, given the distances involved, these are about the only way of getting there unless you have your own transport. Note that the summit road is only open from April 15 until the first snowfall of winter, but outside the peak summer months (July and August) there may well be insufficient demand to make up groups each day. For more on the best time of day to visit the site, see p.864.

From Kahta

Kahta (p.861) is the closest and therefore most convenient base, despite its drab concrete buildings and dusty streets. It has several reputable operators as well as a few sharks. Don't be bludgeoned into booking a tour before you have checked various options. In season, there are sunrise or sunset tours (sunset trips leave at 1pm and return at 9pm; sunrise tours leave at 3am, returning at 10am). The trips cost about 50YTL per person and should include the subsidiary sites of the Karakuş tumulus, Cendere bridge and the ancient Commagene capital of Arsameia.

From Adıyaman

Adıyaman (p.860) has more facilities than Kahta; the only disadvantage is the additional half-hour journey time. Adıyaman Unal bus company, based in the *otogar*, runs daily daytime tours (8–9hr, early-morning departures) for a minimum of three people for around 25YTL per person; prices are lower for larger groups. Tours take in the subsidiary sites – Karakuş tumulus, Cendere bridge and Arsameia – and the Pirinç prehistoric caves.

From Malatya

Tours from Malatya (p.866), on the north side of the range, may look more expensive, but if you count in the night's stay at the *Guneş Hotel* virtually at the summit, the difference is negligible. The main disadvantage is that you miss out on Nemrut's subsidiary sites (though see below), but on the other hand you view both sets of heads

comfortable but dull *Bozdoğan Hotel* (℡0416/216 3999, ℻216 3630; ❹), also with a swimming pool.

Kahta

From Adıyaman, regular dolmuşes make the half-hour journey to drab, dusty **KAHTA**, 25km to the east. It is only about a kilometre from the waters of the Atatürk Baraji, though you can't see the lake from the town.

The obvious budget **accommodation** choice is the *Hotel Kommagene* (℡0416/725 9726, ⓔkommagenem@hotmail.com; ❷), at the junction of the town's main street with the road up to Nemrut, which attracts (or even grabs) backpackers and relieves them of their money; it also has rudimentary camping facilities. Rooms with air-conditioning will put it into a higher price bracket. However, the best of Kahta's inexpensive hotels is the laid-back, refurbished *Mezopotamya* (℡0416/725 5112; ❷) at the west edge of town: rooms have private bathrooms and air-conditioning, and there's a decent restaurant. At the top end of the scale is the overpriced *Hotel Hans Bardakçı* (℡0416/725 8060, ℻725 5385; ❺), whose large rooms all have TVs, while Kahta's most luxurious hotel is the new *Zeus Hotel* (℡0416/725 5694, ⓦwww. zeushotel.net. ❺), with pleasantly landscaped swimming pool, bar-restaurant, and rooms with air-conditioning and foreign-language TV.

at sunrise and sunset, and you get to stay at the welcoming stone-built *Guneş Hotel*, a well-built hotel with clean and cheerful en-suite rooms and good food. A Kurdish *yayla* (summer tent encampment) lies but a few minutes' walk away.

Bookings are best made the day before at the tourist office. Departures are usually at noon (though can be later), reaching the summit in good time for sunset; the return trip starts at about 7am, having given you time to admire the sunrise, reaching Malatya at about 11am. Assuming a fifteen-person minibus chartered from the tourist office, the cost is a good-value 50YTL per person for transport, lodging and two meals; the entrance fee is extra. If it suits your onward travel plans, you could walk over to the south side of Nemrut and find a lift to Kahta. This way, you get to see the subsidiary sites – the Malatya operator gives a small discount for this arrangement. Cheapest way to visit from Malatya is to take a public dolmuş from Malatya dolmuş garage on the ring road to Büyüköz; for an extra fee, the driver will take you right to the *Guneş Hotel*, where you can camp, or sleep in the hotel's mock nomad tent.

From Şanlıurfa

Visiting Nemrut from Şanlıurfa (p.851) has the advantage of cutting out Adıyaman and Kahta, and can include a trip to see the Atatürk Dam, but the 420-kilometre (14-hour) round trip takes in lots of uninteresting scenery. Harran Nemrut Tur currently offers these gruelling day-trips: sunrise tours depart Urfa at midnight, sunset tours at 8am, both costing 50YTL per person (minimum of three) people and including the subsidiary sites.

From Cappadocia

Many operators in Urgup, Göreme and other Cappadocian towns offer tours to Nemrut Dağı, usually spanning three days and two nights and including Urfa. It's a long and tiring journey, but all the hassles are removed and, if you're not planning any further eastern travel, they make sense. The all-inclusive price is around €150 per person.

There are a few cheap and basic **restaurants** on Kahta's broad main street, though the only one worth specifically recommending, for its leafy setting, is the *Yayla Çay Bahçesi ve İzgara*, south of and well below the main boulevard. A couple of kilometres east of town, overlooking the Atatürk lake is the *Neşetin Yeri* **fish restaurant** which serves excellent-value lake fish and grills on terraces with a view of the mountain and lake, but you really need your own transport or a taxi to reach it.

The road to Nemrut Dağı

The 75-kilometre road from Kahta up the mountain to Nemrut Dağı is mostly paved but potholed and therefore slow going; only the last few kilometres pose any danger to your vehicle's suspension. A road also connects Karakuş to Narince but misses out many of the interesting subsidiary sights on the way. The trip is easily done in your own transport, but make sure you fill up with fuel in Kahta.

Karakuş tumulus and Cendere Köprüsü

The first attraction is about 9km north of Kahta, where a huge mound suddenly rises up by the roadside, just past a small oil-drilling field. This is the **Karakuş tumulus**, said to be the funeral mound of Antiochus's wife. It's surrounded by pillars bearing animal motifs, the best of which is an intact eagle that gives the site its name – "black bird". From the top, you can see the waters trapped behind the Atatürk Baraji, and catch views of Nemrut Dağı to the northeast.

Another 9km along, the **Cendere Köprüsü** is a Roman bridge built between 193 and 211 AD during the reign of Emperor Septimius Severus, and still in use after repairs. It's a graceful, single-arched, humpback structure with tremendous views all around – especially up the adjacent Cendere canyon. Three of the original four columns at each end are still in place.

Eskı Kahta and Arsameia

After another 6km or so you come to the turning for **ESKI KAHTA**, a traditional village layered onto the hills behind and dominated by the **Mamluk Yeni Kale**. The castle's fine keep and watchtower are ripe for exploration and give access to several hundred steps chiselled out of the sheer rock-face that once led into the thundering gorge below – however, they are now too dangerous to use. Just past the Eski Kahta turning, an alternative road goes over a Selçuk bridge, from where you can get down into the scenic river-canyon below for a dip. From Eski Kahta, the direct road runs some 20km northeast to Nemrut Dağı.

Arsameia

Signposts a kilometre or two beyond the Selçuk bridge point the way east to the ancient site of **Arsameia** (7YTL including access to the summit site), the capital of the ancient Commagene kingdom, which lies nearly another 2km away at the end of an unsurfaced track. This was excavated by German archeologists during the 1950s and is worth a quick detour for the chance to admire the mountainous local scenery as well as the site itself.

From a rudimentary parking-space a path leads along the hillside, where steps detour to a truncated relief-stele of the god Mithras, before the trail forks left past two fingers of rock (one inscribed) to a cave with a tunnel running to a cistern. Just below the cave is another damaged stele, this one showing Mithridates I Callinicus,

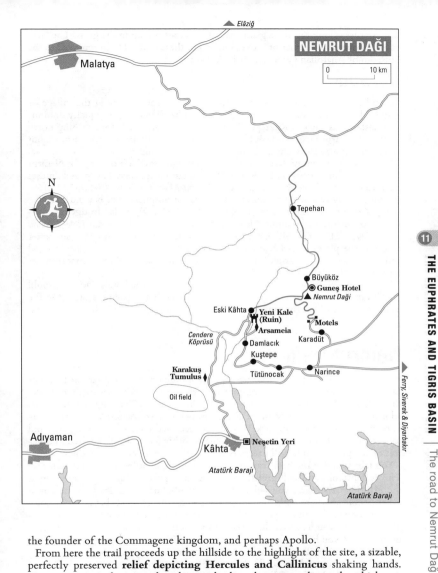

the founder of the Commagene kingdom, and perhaps Apollo.

From here the trail proceeds up the hillside to the highlight of the site, a sizable, perfectly preserved **relief depicting Hercules and Callinicus** shaking hands. Next to it is another tunnel with steps leading down into the earth, which terminates in a cave-in after about 150m. It's steep and roughly surfaced inside, and you'll need a torch if you want to take more than a cursory look. Above the tunnel entrance a huge, 25-line inscription tells you that Mithridates I Callinicus, father of Antiochus (founder of the complex at Nemrut Dağı), is buried in the vicinity, and that the site is consecrated to him.

Just above the relief depicting Hercules and Mithridates sprawls a plateau with some sketchy foundations – so sketchy that it's difficult to determine what they once were. Also scattered around are fragments of what must have been quite large statues – look out for a giant, sandal-clad foot hiding in the grass. The Germans uncovered a number of mosaics here, but these have all been removed to the Museum of Anatolian Civilizations in Ankara.

Karadüt

Beyond the Arsameia turn-off, the road heads due south, passing the village of Damlacık after a couple of kilometres and then heading east past equally diminutive settlements such as Kuztepe, Tütünocak and Narince, before turning north again for Nemrut Dağı. You could come this way directly from Kahta instead, but you'd miss out on the Cendere bridge and Arsameia ruins.

Nine kilometres out of Narince, there's a well-signposted left turning for Nemrut Dağı, while 3km further on **KARADÜT** is the last village served by local dolmuşes from Kahta. Just above the village is the *Karadüt Motel Pansiyon* (☎0416/737 2169; ❶) with newly renovated rooms and a friendly atmosphere and, beyond that, the similar *Çeşme* restaurant and *pansiyon* (☎0416/737 2032, ❶); the last **budget accommodation** before the summit. Nearer Nemrut Dağı; you'll pass the *Hotel Euphrat* (☎0416/737 2175; ❺), with a pool and reasonable rooms, though a cheaper, better choice is the pleasant *Otel Kervansaray Nemrut* (☎0416/737 2190; ❹), with good bathrooms and a shady pool. Both rates include half-board and offer opportunities for high-level walks and exploration.

Allow three hours at least to walk to the summit from the hotels. Drivers should watch out for sharp-edged, tyre-shredding, broken basalt paving stones. On the descent beware of overheating brakes.

Nemrut Dağı

A day's journey northeast of Gaziantep, the mountain-top sanctuary at **Nemrut Dağı** is an unforgettable place, remote and grandiose, drawing visitors who make the long journey up the mountainside by minibus and car. The mighty stone heads adorning the temple and tomb of King Antiochus have become one of the best-known images of Eastern Turkey. They are recycled endlessly on postcards and souvenirs, and if you find yourself anywhere within a couple of hundred kilometres of the place, people will naturally assume that you're here to see them.

You'll be told that the **best time to visit** is at dawn, in order to watch the sunrise. This is debatable, and will probably involve setting out at 2am; upon arriving at the 2150-metre summit you will almost inevitably find that at least several dozen other people are there with the same idea. You might also find that it's quite cold, so come prepared, while if you're visiting out of season check up on weather conditions before you leave, as there's often snow on the ground from late October until May. If you have a choice, it is better to visit at sunset, when it is less chilly and the setting sun illuminates the western terrace in a warm glow.

Finally, if you are here in the last week in June, you can witness the **Commagene Festival**, when folk dancing and music performances take place on the mountain. See posters in Kahta for details.

Some history

The result of one man's delusions of grandeur, the great tomb and temple complex of Nemrut Dağı was built by **Antiochus I Epiphanes** (64–38 BC), son of Mithridates I Callinicus, the founder of the Commagene kingdom. The Commagene dynasty was a breakaway from the Seleucid Empire, covering only a small territory from modern Adıyaman to Gaziantep, and it wouldn't rate much more than a passing mention in histories of the region were it not for the fact that Antiochus chose to build this temple as a colossal monument to himself. Despite having shown early promise as a statesman by concluding a non-aggression treaty with the Romans, Antiochus later decided he was divine in nature, or at the very least an equal of the gods, declaring: "I, the great King Antiochus have ordered the construction of these temples . . . on a foundation which will never be demolished . . . to prove my faith in the gods. At the conclusion of my life I will enter my eternal repose here, and my spirit will ascend to join that of Zeus in heaven."

Antiochus's vanity knew no bounds – he claimed descent from Darius the Great of Persia and Alexander the Great – but eventually he went too far, siding with the Parthians against Rome, and was deposed. This was effectively the end of the Commagene kingdom, which afterwards passed into Roman hands, leaving only Antiochus's massive funeral-folly as a reminder of its brief existence.

Even this was forgotten by the outside world until the late nineteenth century, when Karl Puchstein, a German engineer, came across the site while making a survey in 1881. In 1883 he returned with Karl Humann (the man who removed the Pergamon altar to Berlin) to carry out a more thorough investigation, but it wasn't until 1953 that a comprehensive archeological survey of the site began, under the direction of an American team. Since then Nemrut Dağı, hitherto only reached after an arduous journey of several days, has been put back on the map.

The summit

You may well find yourself travelling the last few kilometres in a convoy of minibuses and, at first sight, **the summit** of Nemrut Dağı often seems to be no more than a parking area full of milling crowds. Just adjacent are a small café, souvenir shop and toilet facilities. The café provides tea, soft drinks and low-alcohol beer, and usually breakfast for groups, but sometimes only has dry biscuits, so it makes sense to bring your own food. They rent out **dormitory beds** here too (10YTL), but you'd be well advised to bring your own sleeping bag. Far better suited to those ascending from Malatya is **accommodation** at the comfortable *Guneş Hotel* (no phone; ❷), a half-hour walk below the summit site and reachable from the south only on foot. If you are determined, it is possible to visit the site from the Kahta side, then walk down to the *Guneş* to spend the night, and thence onto Malatya.

The site

Behind the car-park buildings is the entrance to the **site** (7.5YTL), beyond which is a fifty-metre-high tumulus of small rocks (rated by the *Guinness Book of Records* as the world's largest man-made mound, some 59.8m high and covering an area of 7.5 acres), thought to cover the tomb of Antiochus; signs tell you that it's forbidden to climb the mound. In any case you don't need to be at the very top to enjoy the awesome views for hundreds of kilometres around. Antiochus selected virtually the highest peak in his kingdom to give free rein to his megalomania.

A paved path leads along the south side of the tumulus, coming to a terrace area after ten to fifteen minutes' walk, on which stands the **eastern temple** with six decapitated seated statues, each several metres in height. From left to right they represent: Apollo, Fortuna (symbol of the Commagene kingdom), Zeus, Antiochus and Hercules plus an unidentified figure. Scattered in front of these truncated figures are the much-photographed **detached heads**, each measuring a couple of metres in height – just three in the case of the eastern terrace, with Fortuna squeezed behind the bodies, and perhaps a little disappointing after all the hype, but remarkably intact bar the odd missing nose or two.

They were meant to incorporate several similar deities drawn from different cultures, according to the principle of syncretism, which Alexander the Great had promoted to try and foster a sense of unity among the disparate peoples of his empire. On the date of Antiochus's birthday and the anniversary of his coronation, the Commagene people would file up to the mountain-top to witness the dawn sacrifice and make offerings, carried out in strict accordance with the Greek inscriptions carved onto the back of the royal statues. The sacrificial altar still stands in front of the statues, in a space now used as a helipad for VIP visitors.

The **altar** makes a good vantage point from which to admire the statues and wonder at the immense effort that must have gone into their construction. Scattered around about are fragments of a massive stone eagle and a lion, symbolic temple guardians that once stood like bookends at either end of the royal line-up.

A path leads around the northern base of the tumulus to the **western terrace**, lined by slabs once decorated with reliefs. None of the western statues is even partially intact, although the dispersed **heads** here are much less weathered than those on the other side of the tumulus, and there are more statues – a complete set of five, plus two eagle-heads to flank them – which argues in favour of a sunset visit. The line-up is the same, although it's harder to work out who's who. Look out for Fortuna, with a garland of leaves and vines in her hair, and Apollo, claimed by some to be a dead ringer for Elvis Presley.

A number of **reliefs** have, however, survived adjacent to the statuary debris – three depict Antiochus shaking hands with Apollo, Zeus and Hercules. Another shows a lion with the planets of Jupiter, Mars and Mercury and a moon representing the Commagene kingdom draped around his neck; it's thought to be an astrological chart referring to the date of Antiochus's conception.

Malatya and around

MALATYA, 120km north of Nemrut Dağı, is a lively, cosmopolitan city of around 600,000 people, where smart shops line tree-shaded boulevards. There's little to see within the city limits, but it's a pleasant enough place for an overnight stop before tackling Nemrut Dağı, and there are possible excursions out to the old town of Eski Malatya and the nearby site of ancient Aslantepe.

Malatya has always been a political town and is the home of two former presidents of the Republic, General İsmet İnönü (who gets a statue in his honour) and part-Kurdish Turgut Özal (who has a road named after him). There's a university and a huge army base. It's also the centre of a fertile fruit-growing region, particularly famed for apricot production.

Arrival, information and services

Whilst Malatya is large, the centre is compact and most of the hotels and restaurants are within walking distance of each other.

The **otogar** and **train station** (both served by bus #11 from opposite the *Vilayet*) are 7km and 2km respectively west of the centre on the Çevre Yolu (ring road). Service buses run into town from the *otogar*, dropping you at the Çevre Yolu junction closest to the centre. If you are heading east to Elazığ, the Doğu Garajı dolmuş terminal is on Sivas Caddesi, twenty minutes' walk northeast of the centre. From Malatya's **airport**, 28km northwest of the city, a shuttle bus meets THY flights and ferries passengers to Sivas Caddesi, a ten-minute walk northeast of the town centre. The THY office is on Kanal Boyu Cad 10 (☎0422/324 8001), while Onur Air's is on İnönü Cad 17 (☎0422/325 6060).

There's a helpful **tourist office** (Mon–Sat 9am–noon & 1–5pm; ☎0422/323 3025) in the *Vilayet* (governor's office) building, behind the statue of İnönü in the main square, İnönü Meydanı. The office's main function is to sign you up for a **trip to Nemrut Dağı** (see box on p.860), though the ever helpful English-speaking Bülent doles out all kinds of useful information, and an accurate city plan. At weekends, the Vilayet Parkı behind the *Vilayet* building hosts an informal tourist office for intended visitors to Nemrut. The **PTT** is near the square at the very start of İnönü Caddesi. You'll find **Internet cafés** along and at the south end of Fusili Caddesi near the museum; **banks and exchange facilities** are in the same area.

It's worth noting that the plan of the city handed out by the tourist office doesn't make it clear that the main boulevard is called **İnönü Caddesi** west of the *Vilayet* building, but becomes **Atatürk Caddesi** east of it – and the whole thing is referred to as **İstasyon Caddesi** by some sources.

Accommodation

Malatya's hotels are spread between the ring road and the İnönü statue in the city centre. A reasonable **budget** option is the spotlessly clean *Otel Park*, Atatürk Cad 17 (☎0422/321 1691; ❷), which offers clean, pastel-hued en-suite rooms, but no breakfast; be warned that as it backs onto a mosque and fronts a major road, it's noisy. The quieter *Otel Kantar*, Atatürk Cad 21 (☎0422/321 1510, ℻321 3125; ❷), seems to have cornered the backpacker trade and has clean rooms, some with showers though all sharing toilets in the corridor, and includes breakfast. A recommended option is the friendly ⚘ *Hotel Aygün*, PTT Cad 7 (☎0422/325 5657, ⓦwww.aygunlar.ltdsti.tc; ❷), which dates back to the 1940s; its newly renovated rooms are small but tidy, with TVs and central heating, and there are great mountain views from its terrace. A good **mid-range** option is the two-star *Malatya Büyük Hotel*, Yeni Cami Karşısı (☎0422/321 1400, ℻321 5367; ❸), which has a good view of the pretty, early twentieth-century Yeni Camii, is very friendly and serves up an excellent buffet breakfast. Moving **upmarket**, the *Altın Kayısı*, İstasyon Caddesi (☎0422/211 4444, ℻238 0083; ❺), is inconveniently located out of town near the train station, but is equipped with a mouthwatering array of top-notch facilities, including smart restaurant, gardens and a pool.

The City

The **Şire Pazarı**, in the centre between Atatürk Bulvarı and the ring road, is devoted to local agricultural produce, namely cherries, mulberries, apples, walnuts and, especially, apricots. Indeed, the best time to visit town is during the apricot harvest in July, when there's an **apricot festival** (July 15–22) at Mişmiş Parkı, 5km east of the town.

Next to the Şire bazaar is Malatya's **copper bazaar**, giving you an opportunity to watch the craftsmen hammering away or tin-plating surfaces intended for use with food. A bit of scrabbling on the dirty shelves of stalls will reveal old pieces with Armenian inscriptions – antique copper is cheaper and more likely to be genuine here than anywhere else.

On the south side of Malatya, at the end of Fuzuli Caddesi, are attractive landscaped **gardens** set alongside a stream. Close by is the excellent **Malatya museum** (Malatya Müzesi; Tues–Sun 9am–noon & 1–5pm; 2YTL). Small but extremely well laid-out, it concentrates on finds from nearby, Hittite, Aslantepe (see p.868). The room to the left as you enter has fine examples of pottery and copper swords, plus reconstructions of graves from Aslantepe. Upstairs is a glass case devoted to decorative seals (used to guarantee the integrity of goods in containers), the most common motifs in evidence being deer and antelope.

Northwest of the town beyond the ring road is a neglected **Armenian church** of impressive size, currently closed to visitors.

Eating and drinking

There are plenty of **cafés and restaurants** in Malatya, but few are outstanding; around the bazaars you can eat well for 8YTL. The *Kışla Restaurant* on Atatürk Caddesi near the *Otel Park* is a basic grill redeemed mostly by its nice *sütlaç* (rice pudding) and the fact it's open 24 hours a day. Opposite the *Kışla* and good for *porça*, cakes and Maraş ice cream is the *Sevinç Pastanesi*. Further east on Atatürk Caddesi is the *Beyaz Sarayi*, good value for *pide*, kebabs and soups – it also serves comb honey and creamy yoghurt for breakfast. The monumental *Kombe İskender Yemek Salonu* on PTT Cad 9 offers a set meal of *döner* or İskender kebab with *pilav*, salad and a soft drink for a bargain 2.5YTL.

For a little more in the way of entertainment (but still no alcohol) try the funky *Eftelya Nargile and Café* on Atatürk Caddesi. Decked out with kilims, cushions, *sofra* tables, old radios, fish tanks and kitsch alpine and tropical scenes, this youth-oriented café has live Turkish folk music most evenings, and serves snack meals such as *köfte* and *gözleme*. For beer, the *Çardak Birahane*, ten minutes' walk northeast of the centre and just off Sivas Caddesi, is passable.

Eski Malatya

About 12km north of the modern city, **ESKI MALATYA**, or "Old Malatya", a ruined Roman/Byzantine town, is served half-hourly by blue city buses marked "Batalgazi"; catch them from the northwest side of the traffic lights on the Çevre Yolu, a few hundred metres due east of the city centre. You can return to Malatya via the red *Belediye* bus, which takes longer but makes a scenic tour around local villages.

The old town walls are still visible but much of the original settlement, which boasted 53 churches and a couple of dozen monasteries, has been built over. The local angle on the creation of "Old" and "New" Malatya has it that when the Ottoman army was billeted inside the walls in 1838–39 BC, the citizens, in order to keep their wives and daughters away from the rough soldiery, moved to their summer houses further up the hill at present-day Malatya; most never moved back.

Buses arrive at the main square, from where it's a 200-metre walk southwest to a partially restored seventeenth-century *kervansaray*, and a further couple of hundred metres south to the Selçuk **Ulu Cami**. This huge mosque complex was commissioned by the powerful Selçuk sultan, Alâeddin Keykubad. It was built by Yakub bin Ebubekir around a central *eyvan* and consists of summer and winter mosques. The latter is of plain stonework with massive pillars in the usual Selçuk style, but the former consists of a central bay with a soaring domed roof flanked by two wings, the whole surrounding the *eyvan*. The brickwork of the dome reveals complicated herringbone patterning and inset blue-glazed tiles that sparkle like stars. The *mimber* is of intricately carved wood topped by turban-shaped finials. The arches onto the *eyvan* – decorated with intricate turquoise and black tile-work – are still in reasonable condition, although modern glass doors have been installed in them. Just south of the mosque is a ruined *medrese* and the stranded **Melik Sunullah minaret** (1394) with traces of tile-work still clinging to it.

Aslantepe

One of the most actively excavated ancient sites in central Anatolia, Hittite **Aslantepe** lies just over 4km from the northeastern edge of Malatya; city bus #36 from the Çevre Yolu stop, labelled "Orduzu", passes within 800m of the site, or take a bus marked "Bahçebaşı" from opposite the *Vilayet* building.

Like many similar settlements in Turkey, the mound here is largely artificial, raised up a convenient distance from a river in the midst of what has always been an oasis; from up top there's a view over well-watered apricot groves. The name – "Lion Hill" – derives from the stone lions found guarding the north gate of the Hittite city, now in Ankara's Anatolian Civilizations Museum. They, and many other Hittite treasures, were uncovered by French scholars in the 1930s using the now-discredited technique of deep, rapidly cut, exploratory trenches. Since 1962 Aslantepe has been more meticulously uncovered by Italian archeologists, in residence each August to October – the prime time for a **visit to the site** (daily 8.30am–5pm), since at other times tarpaulins shroud much of the area. Members of the team speak good English and will escort you around, making sense of a dig that is otherwise still very much of specialist interest.

The most exciting discovery to date is a vast **palace complex**, the earliest known, built of mud bricks on a stone foundation and dating from the end of the fourth millennium BC. Also unusual are a pair of eerie **wall-paintings** from approximately 3200 BC. The room with the painted wall is flanked by storehouses in which were found pots and clay seals for accounting and administration of food-stuffs, since writing was as yet unknown.

Adjoining the palace to the west is a **temple** to an unknown deity, with concentric oval decorations stamped into its walls. On the northwest of the tumulus, some Neolithic remains predate the palace, while the northeast slope, now overgrown, was the location of the Hittite town and its spectacular finds.

Elazığ and Harput

One hundred kilometres northeast of Malatya, and easily accessible by dolmuş, **Elazığ** is not really on any kind of a normal tourist route. With a population of 300,000, it's a friendly but uneasy mix of Kurd and Turk, Alevî and Sunni, founded in 1862 by Sultan Abdülaziz to house the overspill population from the old settlement of **Harput**, wracked by earthquakes and now largely abandoned. It's an important grape-producing town, the centre of an area where *okuzgözü* (ox-eye) grapes, used to produce the red Buzbağ wine, are harvested.

Elazığ

ELAZİĞ, virtually destroyed by an earthquake in the 1950s, is modern and soulless, but it does have a decent **archeological museum** (Tues–Sun 8.30am–noon & 1.30–5pm; 2YTL), displaying objects from various local ancient sites, most notably a remarkable collection of Urartian jewellery. Buy a bus ticket from a little pavement kiosk behind the bus stand, then take a *Universite* bus from opposite the *Polis Evi* (Police House) on the main square and alight at the university gates; enquire here for the museum.

If you want to stay overnight, the best-value **accommodation** is at the *Turistik Otel* (℡0424/218 1772; ❷), Hürriyet Cad 41 in the town centre, just east of the main square. It's modern, clean and friendly, and rooms here even have a (noisy) balcony. Opposite the *Turistik* is the *Hotel Çinar* (℡0424/218 1811; ❷), also up to date but with better-quality furnishings, TV in the rooms and secure parking.

Elazığ has a number of simple **lokantas**: the *Hacioğulları* on Hürriyet Caddesi is bright and cheerful, and serves excellent *lahmacun* on wooden platters. Head for the *aile salonu* upstairs, with its low, kilim-covered benches and relaxed atmosphere.

The main *otogar* is 2km east of the centre – service buses run there from the many bus offices on Hürriyet Caddesi. The dolmuş terminal for Malatya-bound buses is a five-minute walk southwest of the centre.

Harput

The all-but-abandoned town of **HARPUT** lies a five-kilometre ride to the north of Elazığ, at the end of a road lined by military installations guarding the Keban dam. From Elazığ, take red city bus #19 or a dolmuş. Harput was a thriving commercial centre of many thousands until the late nineteenth century, when a series of disastrous earthquakes led to mass emigration to Elazığ.

Today, the sleepy town is studded with yellow signs pointing to numerous **mosques**, **hamams** and **tombs** of much-venerated saints. A tiny **museum** stands at the town entrance; its most interesting exhibit is a black-and-white photograph showing Harput in the late nineteenth century, dominated by the massive bulk of the American/French missionary school, now totally destroyed.

At the northeast edge of the site, the originally Byzantine **castle** is now a shell, except for its fine restored gateway and a small church inside. Despite apparent impregnability on top of a rocky outcrop, it was captured by Tamerlane during the second Mongol wave and again by Sultan Selim I in 1515. The view from the top of the citadel is pleasant, with the blue waters of the Keban dam glinting below the rolling mountains.

Back in the centre of Harput, the still-functioning **Meydan Camii** and its attached hamam are the remaining focus of life in the town. Nearby is the **Arap Baba Türbesi**, housing the body of a local holy man. The town's oldest mosque is the box-like twelfth-century **Ulu Cami**, with its brick minaret leaning at a crazy angle.

In the blissfully peaceful leafy park adjoining the simple Kurşunlu Cami, you can get *ayran*, **tea and snacks** including *Harput köfte*, the local meatball dish.

The Tigris basin

Approaching the **valley of the River Tigris** (Dicle in Turkish) from the northwest, from Malatya, the road threads through an Asiatic canyon-riddled landscape. Hazar Gölü, the only natural lake in a land of reservoirs, is marred by a rash of holiday homes around its shores. Travelling from the east, from Urfa to Mardin or Diyarbakır, you leave the lush green of newly irrigated plantations behind and enter a barren but austerely beautiful landscape that provides a fitting introduction to the underdeveloped provinces of the southeast.

Most points of interest lie on the southwestern banks of the River Tigris. The natural gateway is **Diyarbakır**, a rapidly expanding, predominantly Kurdish city, with a unique cultural mix and character that makes a memorable impact on most visitors. The main road to Iraq from Şanlıurfa heads due east to the stunning architecture and narrow lanes of **Mardin**, a town isolated on a limestone bluff above the Syrian plain and preserving a way of life apparently frozen in the past. Mardin has never been hit by the poverty of Diyarbakır, perhaps because its proximity to the border has allowed the black economy to thrive. East of here, **Midyat** and its hinterland is the traditional home of Turkey's Syrian Orthodox Christian community, who split with the rest of Christendom 1600 years ago. There are now only six Christian villages on the **Tür Abdin plateau** that extends to the east of Midyat, dotted with churches and monasteries (many now under restoration). Some churches still function on a rotational basis, but it is the monastery of **Mar Gabriel**, supported largely by émigrés, that keeps the faith alive. Further north, on the Tigris, are the spectacular medieval ruins of **Hasankeyf**, again under threat from the planned İlisu dam.

Diyarbakır

Superbly positioned at the edge of the Tigris flood-plain, the old city of **DIYARBAKIR** shelters behind massive, ancient walls of black basalt, which enclose a maze of cobbled streets and alleys peppered with beautiful mosques, imposing *han*s, stately mansions and intriguing churches. Inside the Mardin gate, some of the *gecekondu* (shantytown) dwellings have now been pulled down, creating a pleasant strip of parkland. There's a lively, energetic atmosphere to the place, and on the whole, the residents – who number two million – are generally open, helpful and self-confident. From the west, though, the first sight of Diyarbakır is uninspiring: the modern town has long since burst out of the confining walls, and the soulless multi-storey apartment buildings of the new quarters hide the old city. Despite the friendly atmosphere, Diyarbakır has something of a bad reputation in other parts of Turkey. Long a hotbed of separatist activity, violent street demonstrations in the spring of 2006 have done nothing to improve its image, but as long as you avoid these it's no more dangerous than any other large Turkish city (several of which have also witnessed violent demonstrations). A

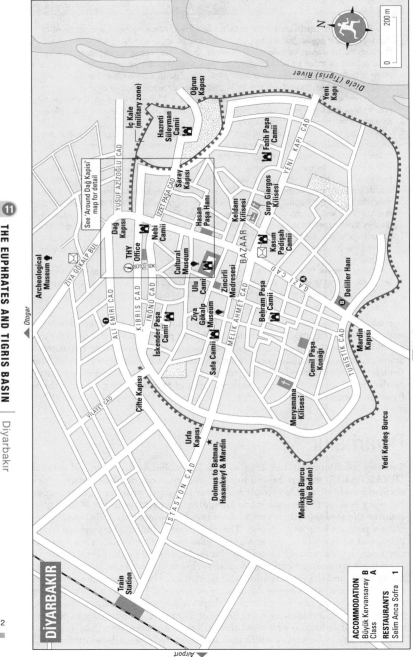

DIYARBAKIR

N

0   200 m

Dicle (Tigris) River

▲ Otogar

Archeological Museum

Train Station

ZIYA GÖKALP BUL

ALI EMIRI CAD

KIBRIS CAD

INÖNÜ CAD

VILAYET CAD

ISTASYON CAD

Çifte Kapısı

Urfa Kapısı

Dolmuş to Batman, Hasankeyf & Mardin

Meliksah Burcu (Ulu Badan)

Yedi Kardeş Burcu

Mardin Kapısı

TÜRISTIK CAD

Meryamana Kilisesi

Cemil Paşa Konağı

Behram Paşa Camii

MELIK AHMET CAD

GAZI CAD

Safa Camii

Iskender Paşa Camii

Ziya Gökalp Museum

Ulu Camii

Zincirli Medresesi

Cultural Museum

THY Office

SÜTÇÜ SOK

Nebi Camii

Dağ Kapısı

YUSUF AZIZOĞLU CAD

IZZET PAŞA CAD

See 'Around Dağ Kapısı' map for detail

İç Kale (military zone)

Hazreti Süleyman Camii

Oğrun Kapısı

Saray Kapısı

Hasan Paşa Hanı

Keldani Kilisesi

BAZAAR

Surp Giargos Kilisesi

YENI KAPI CAD

Fatih Paşa Camii

Yeni Kapı

Kasım Padişah Camii

Deliller Hanı

▼ Mardin

▲ Airport

ACCOMMODATION
Büyük Kervansaray   B
Class   A

RESTAURANTS
Selim Anca Sofra   1

△ Children in Diyarbakır

far more common nuisance are the hordes of noisy children in the slum areas (some of whom indulge in stone throwing) and the general bustle in the streets.

To avoid the attentions of hustlers and street kids (of whom there are some 20,000 according to recent figures), try to hook up with one of the many students keen to practise their English, who will give you a guided tour of the town. Talking to these students is a good way to learn about Diyarbakır and pick up a basic Kurdish vocabulary – *sipas* (pronounced "spaas" – thank you) and *rojbaş* (pronounced "rojebosh" – good day) are good words for starters. They will point out the finer points of Kurdish dress, the predominance of Kurdish cassettes for sale and the nuances of the local dialects, Zaza and Kurmancı. This concrete evidence of **Kurdish identity** makes you realize why Diyarbakır has long been a focus of discontent.

Moreover, the rapid population influx over the last fifteen years has done nothing to alleviate Diyarbakır's already precarious **economic situation**: eight-to-ten-child families are the norm, some of the sidestreets are frankly squalid, and beggars are not an uncommon sight. Class sizes in the poorest schools can approach a hundred, and many children starting school speak only Kurdish – not very helpful when the entire curriculum is in Turkish. Children are taught in shifts and the kid that sells you a *simit* at 10am may well not be starting his school day until 5pm. The effect of the legislation permitting education in Kurdish is unlikely to have much effect as it only applies to private, fee-paying schools. Unemployment approaches forty percent, with no real industry to speak of; the only significant product is watermelons, grown on the banks of the Tigris with pigeon droppings as fertilizer. Fifty-kilo monsters are the result, but it's claimed that in the old days Diyarbakır melons weighed as much as 100kg and had to be transported by camel and cut with a sword.

Some history

Diyarbakır is not only the capital of the upper Tigris valley, but has some claim to being one of the oldest settlements on earth. Certainly the city existed at the time of the Hurrian Empire, some 5000 years ago, and it subsequently saw successive periods of Urartian, Assyrian and Persian hegemony, before falling to Alexander the Great and his successors, the Seleucids.

The Romans appeared on the scene in 115 AD and over the next few centuries they and their successors, the Byzantines, struggled violently over the town with the Sassanid Persians. The Romans, who knew Diyarbakır as **Amida**, built the first substantial walls around the city in 297 – the ones you see today were initially Roman, rebuilt by the early Byzantines and finished off by Arab rulers. The threatening, basalt bulwarks gave the place its popular ancient name – Amid the Black – still used in the Kurdish languages. The modern name comes from the Arabs: in 638 the Bakr tribe of Arabs arrived and renamed the city Diyar Bakr or "Place of the Bakr". With the decline of Arab influence in the region, Diyarbakır became a Selçuk, then a Turcoman, and finally an Ottoman stronghold.

In 1925, after the new Republican government had dashed Kurdish hopes of autonomy, a rebellion erupted in the area around Diyarbakır. The city was besieged and Turkish troops were rushed in by train through French-occupied territory. The siege was soon lifted and hundreds of rebels were hanged on the spot, though the bloodshed didn't end there. Over the next few years the lives of between forty thousand and quarter of a million Kurdish villagers are thought to have been taken in reprisals.

Arrival, orientation and information

Most of what you need in Diyarbakır is in the old city, within the great walls. The **train station** lies a kilometre west of town at the end of İstasyon Caddesi, the **otogar** 2km northwest at the top of Ziya Gökalp Bulvarı. A new *otogar* is currently under construction further out of town. Dolmuşes are on hand to ferry new arrivals into the centre from either terminal; don't believe any taxi drivers who tell you that there aren't any. You'll be dropped off at **Dağ Kapısı** (formerly known as Harput Kapası), a tower which was once one of several gigantic city-gateways. **Dolmuşes from Mardin** arrive at a dolmuş terminal just outside **Urfa Kapısı**. Kaplaner **airport** is 3km southwest of town, and a taxi to the centre will set you back around 10YTL. The **THY office** is at İnönü Cad 8 (℡0412/228 8401), with **Onur Air** nearby at number 28/B (℡0412/223 5312).

The local **tourist office** (Mon–Sat 9am–5pm; ℡0412/221 2173), in the tower at Dağ Kapısı, will dole out city plans, and staff are eager to chat in limited English. Finding your way around Diyarbakır is straightforward enough if you keep to the main roads. From Dağ Kapısı, **Gazı Caddesi**, running south to the Mardin Kapısı, bisects the city from north to south, and **Melik Ahmet Caddesi**, later becoming **Yeni Kapı Caddesi**, does the same from west to east. The backstreets, however, are a maze of narrow alleys, where it's easy to lose your bearings.

Accommodation

Most of the desirable accommodation in Diyarbakır lies within a short walk of the Dağ Kapısı – the further away from here, the quieter it's likely to be. Accommodation is marked on the "Around Dağ Kapısı" map, except for a couple of places towards Mardin Kapısı and outside the walls, which are shown on the main Diyarbakır map.

West of Dağ Kapısı

Balkar Hotel Kıbrıs Cad 38 ℡0412/228 1233, ℻224 6936. Beautifully fitted out with nice textiles and paintwork, with a terrace res-

taurant for breakfast. Homelier than average and highly recommended. ❸

Dicle Oteli Kıbrıs Cad 3 ℡0412/223 5326. Large, airy place with air-conditioned rooms, but it's

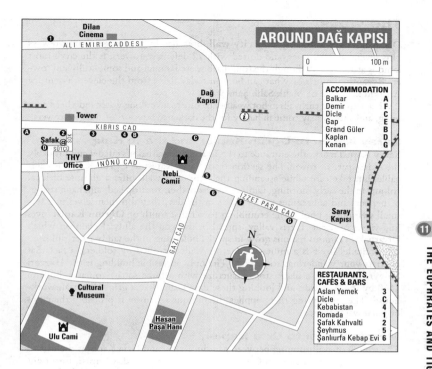

0   100 m

ACCOMMODATION

Balkar	A
Demir	F
Dicle	C
Gap	E
Grand Güler	B
Kaplan	D
Kenan	G

RESTAURANTS, CAFÉS & BARS

Aslan Yemek	3
Dicle	C
Kebabistan	4
Romada	1
Şafak Kahvalti	2
Şeyhmus	5
Şanlıurfa Kebap Evi	6

become rather seedy. A last resort if the other budget hotels are full. No breakfast. ❷

Hotel Gap İnönü Cad 3, Çıkmaz 3 ☎0412/221 1218. Basic but colourful yellow-painted rooms with iron bedsteads, some with ceiling fan, some with air conditioning (extra), set around a cool courtyard where the garrulous Kurdish owner serves breakfast. Good budget choice. ❶

Hotel Grand Güler Kıbrıs Cad 13 ☎0412/229 2221, ℰ224 4509. Although now a bit dated, this business-oriented hotel has well-fitted air-conditioned rooms, an open buffet breakfast and secure parking. Good value. ❸

Hotel Kaplan Sütçü Sok 14 ☎0412/224 9606, ℰ224 0187. Friendly and in a quiet location on a sidestreet to the north of İnönü Cad. All rooms have a TV, fridge and air conditioning, but not such good value since the advent of home-grown package tourism. ❸

Southeast of Dağ Kapısı

Demir Otel İzzet Paşa Cad 8 ☎0412/228 8800, ⓌWww.demirhotel.com. Not much charm, but the rooms are well furnished and there's a flashy mir-

rored lobby, restaurant and swimming pool. ❹

Hotel Kenan İzzet Paşa Cad 20/B ☎0412/221 6614. Clean, spacious rooms with cheery, blue-tiled floors and yellow walls, set around a central courtyard well. It has an attached hamam, but no breakfast. ❷

Towards Mardin Kapısı

Büyük Kervansaray Gazı Cad, Deliller Hanı ☎0412/228 9606, ℰkervansarayas @superonline.com. Smallish air-conditioned rooms, nicely decorated and with new bathrooms, set in a converted *kervansaray* with a large swimming pool and hamam. The central courtyard is an oasis of peace, and wonderful for a relaxing breakfast or evening meal. It's much frequented by UN personnel, and non-guests are welcome to drink and/or dine here. ❼

Class Hotel Gazı Cad 101 ☎0412/229 5000, Ⓦwww.diyarbakirclasshotel.com. A modern hotel, with good facilities and value-for-money prices. Behind the flashy facade is the restored courtyard of a medieval mansion, now with swimming pool, bar and restaurant. ❼

The walls

Diyarbakır's six-kilometre-long **city wall**, breached by four huge main gateways plus several smaller ones, and dotted with 72 defensive towers, is the city's most famous attraction. Although the foundations are Roman and some walls and towers Byzantine, much of what can be seen today dates from the eleventh-century Artukid kingdom of Malık Salih Şah.

When exploring the walls in hot weather be sure to take along water and a head covering, and a torch may come in handy for the darkened interiors of the gate-towers.

Saray Kapısı to Oğrun Kapısı and the İç Kale

Saray Kapısı marks the entrance to the **İç Kale**, Diyarbakır's citadel and probably the oldest part of town. The section from Saray Kapısı to Oğrun Kapısı is navigable, but take care while ascending the steps. The walls offer a glimpse of local colour: in the early morning, families rise from their rooftop beds and hang strings of peppers and aubergines to dry; later in the day, they dip themselves in a few small swimming pools. The crumbling tower just south of **Oğrum Kapısı** gives fine views over the Tigris valley, spread below you the alluvial plain on which Diyarbakır's famous melons grow in special holes dug in the sandy riverbanks.

The citadel itself is a military zone, its walls patrolled by soldiers, a fact that restricts your wanderings somewhat. The only accessible building is the **Hazreti Süleyman Camii**, a black stone structure with a huge square minaret, built in 1160 by the Artukids, and looking these days rather like a grim Victorian workhouse. The cool spring that supplies the mosque's *şadırvan* is probably the city's original water source.

Mardin Kapısı to Urfa Kapısı

The stretch of wall running between Mardin Kapısı and Urfa Kapısı is the best to walk. Head south down Gazi Caddesi until you reach **Mardin Kapısı**, turn right and follow the inside of the wall for some four hundred metres, at which point some newly restored steps lead up to the battlement walkway. Turn left and head back to Mardin Kapısı, threading through a vaulted passageway en route to an excellent view-point, then retrace your steps and head west along the ramparts. The first point of interest is the **Yedi Kardeş Burcu** (Seven Brothers Tower), a huge circular bastion decorated with Selçuk lions and a double-headed eagle, and beyond this is the **Melikşah Burcu** (also known as the Ulu Badan), which is again decorated with Selçuk motifs.

The views from the walls and towers over the Tigris are superb, and the rooftop life of the locals whose houses abut the exterior of the ramparts fascinating. Although the walkway is some two metres wide, you should take care as it is frequently uneven and gravelly underfoot – and there is no handrail. Allow around thirty minutes to reach **Urfa Kapısı**. Follow the steps down into the gate-tower (hold your nose as there is a pungent stench of human excrement) and take care as finding the next set of steps down to street level is not easy in the semi-darkness.

The City

You may not be able to climb up to the walls there, but **Dağ Kapısı** makes a good starting point for an exploration of the city proper. Give yourself the best part of two days to do justice to the city sights and monuments.

Nebi Camii and Hasan Paşa Hanı

Immediately to the south of the gateway, at the intersection of Gazi Caddesi and İnönü Caddesi, stands the **Nebi Camii**, or Mosque of the Prophet, a late fifteenth-century foundation of the Akkoyun Turcomans. The mosque's most distinctive feature is the alternating bands of black basalt and white sandstone used in its construction, especially effective in the minaret. You'll come across this striped effect frequently in Diyarbakır, as both stones are quarried locally and their combination is considerably less threatening than the unrelenting black of the walls.

Continuing down Gazı Caddesi will bring you to the **Hasan Paşa Hanı** on the eastern side of the street, and more bands of black and white stone. The *han* dates from the late sixteenth century and is still in commercial use, mainly for carpet and jewellery shops, while the city's **main bazaar** area occupies the narrow, twisting streets all around.

The Ulu Cami and around

Opposite the *han* stands the gatehouse of the **Ulu Cami**, Diyarbakır's most important mosque. The first of Anatolia's great Selçuk mosques, it was probably extended in 1091 by Melik Şah, the Selçuk conqueror of the city, though legend claims that it was built on the site of, and with masonry from, the Byzantine church of St Thomas at the time of the Arab conquest in 639, giving rise to the assertion that this is the oldest mosque in Anatolia. It was gutted by fire in 1155 and extensively refurbished, but has been little altered since. In support of the later foundation date, many have noted that the Ulu Cami closely resembles the Umayyad mosque in Damascus.

On passing through the entrance portal, decorated with bull and lion motifs, you find yourself in a large **courtyard**, perhaps the most impressive part of the building. Two *şadırvan*s occupy the centre of this courtyard, with its two-storeyed facades at the eastern and western ends. The north and south sides sport true arcades, constructed using pillars salvaged from earlier Roman and Byzantine buildings; on some of the columns and capitals are visible fragments of Greek inscription. The wing to the east and above the arch, with storks nesting on its roof, is actually a library, incorporating a much earlier stoa beneath it. At the northeast corner of the courtyard is the locked entrance to the **Mesudiye Medresesi**. Built in 1198 by the Artukids, this became the first university of Anatolia and is still in use as a Koran school.

The mosque itself is entered via a doorway in the centre of the southern side of the courtyard; a carved white *mimber* graces the cavernous interior. The central bay is of much earlier origin, supporting the theory that the Ulu Cami was converted from what was originally a church, and has a superbly decorated roof in the porch area. The minaret is tall and angular, like many such structures in Diyarbakır.

If you leave the mosque courtyard via a door in the southwestern corner you enter a narrow alleyway. Turn left into the clothes bazaar and then right, and you will eventually come to the **Ziya Gökalp museum** (seldom open; 1YTL), former home of the architect of Turkish nationalism, which houses sections devoted to the man's life and work and an unexceptional ethnographic collection. Another restored mansion, opposite the Surp Giragos church, is the **Esma Ocak Diyarbakır Evi**, a typical black-and-white stone construction around a courtyard. The rooms have been refurbished as they would have appeared in 1899, and there are photographs of the original owners on the walls. The caretaker will open up for you and let you look around in return for a small tip.

Diyarbakır's other mosques

Heading west from the Ziya Gökalp museum brings you to the stunning fifteenth-century **Safa Camii**, a mosque of notably graceful design and construction. Its tall, cylindrical minaret, a departure from the city norm, still bears traces of blue tile-work on its white, relief-worked surface. Archway masonry in the courtyard alternates between black and white in the local fashion, while the interior ceiling is accented by blue and green tile-work.

Some way southeast across Melik Ahmet Caddesi stands the **Behram Paşa Camii**, Diyarbakır's largest mosque, built in 1572 by Behram Paşa, the governor, but currently closed for extensive renovation.

Also worth seeking out, east of Gazi Caddesi on Yenikapı Caddesi in the Balıkçılarbaşı bazaar, is the early sixteenth-century **Kasım Padişah Camii**, virtually the last Akkoyun monument built before the Ottomans took over. Its tall, square detached minaret, set on four two-metre basalt pillars, is known colloquially as the *Dört Ayaklı Minare* ("Four-Legged Minaret"). According to legend, if you walk around the minaret seven times and make a wish, it will be granted.

Diyarbakır's churches

To reach the **Keldani Kilisesi**, walk past the Kasım Padişah Camii and turn left down an alley, then immediately right. The church is about 100m down the alley on the right; ring the bell for entry. The church and bell tower date from 1602; the spacious, arched interior contains a rather garish altar with a crucifix and icons. It's a Chaldean foundation (a Catholic schism of the Nestorian church), used by the thirty surviving Chaldean families, who worship here every second Sunday of the month.

Continuing past the Chaldean church the alley takes a sharp left. Follow it round, and in the wall on the right is a door marked "4". Knock and the friendly family who live here will probably let you through their courtyard into the grounds of the **Surp Giragos Kilisesi**, a once-thriving church in the days when the population of Diyarbakır was one-quarter Armenian. Regrettably, the roof fell down in 1992, but the huge shell still contains the gold-painted woodwork of the altar and the building has supposedly been scheduled for restoration.

There's also a Syrian Orthodox compound, the **Meryamana Kilisesi** (Church of the Virgin Mary), southwest of the Behram Paşa Camii; to get there, use the prominent bell-tower as a guide. A small door leads on to a paved courtyard surrounded by buildings that were once part of a seventh-century monastery. The church itself dates from the third century (though the site was a temple to the god of the sun in pre-Christian times, and four marble tablets in the church date from this period), making it one of the oldest in the world. It was reconstructed after a fire a couple of centuries ago, and has been much renovated recently, the funding coming from the sizable Syrian Orthodox diaspora. Visitors are welcome to attend the services, which are conducted in either Syriac (a form of Aramaic) or Turkish at 8am each Sunday morning, and you're also free to look around at other times. A contribution should be made to the caretakers and the Syriac priest, who is striving to keep his small community (some 45 families remain) together and is putting himself out especially for you.

The archeological museum

Diyarbakır's **archeological museum** (Arkeoloji Müzesi; Tues–Sun 8.30am–noon & 1.30–5.30pm; 2YTL) lies just outside the old city, near the main PTT. To reach it, head out along Ziya Gökalp Caddesi: you'll see a fairground on the northeastern (right) side of the road, and the typical black-on-brown sign in the vicinity will lead you down a sidestreet to the museum. As well as early historic carvings, it contains extensive local Roman remains, some from the Akkoyun and Karakoyun Turcoman dynasties that ruled much of eastern Anatolia and western Persia in medieval times, and Korans and ceremonial items from Derviş Tekkes (monasteries).

Eating and drinking

The **local speciality** is lamb *kuburga* (ribs stuffed with rice), available at various restaurants in town. A particular Diyarbakır institution is the pavement liver-heart-and-offal **grill stalls** that set up shop on summer evenings along Gazı Caddesi and Kıbrıs Caddesi. The meat bits are skewered and grilled as you watch, then served up hot and savoury with a raw vegetable garnish. Portions are generous and you can eat well for a couple of dollars, but don't go overboard the first time or you'll regret it the next day. There are several more **grill restaurants** outside the Urfa Kapısı, set in shady gardens under the walls.

Aslan Yemek Salonu Kıbrıs Cad. Welcoming air-conditioned restaurant – try the *yufkalı incik*, lamb on the bone with peas, pepper and tomato, wrapped in pastry.

Büyük Kervansaray Gazı Cad, Delililer Hanı (see map, p.872). The courtyard of the hotel hosts the closest thing in the city centre to a nightclub; dinner is served around the pool, and there's live music and dancing most nights. Expect to pay around 13YTL for a meal.

Dicle Oteli Kıbrıs Cad 3. The cheapest licensed restaurant (and one of the most atmospheric) is attached to the hotel, where tasty, generous portions of kebabs and other grills are served on a rooftop terrace in the summer.

Kebabistan Kıbrıs Cad 19. A fine choice for *sulu yemek*, this clean and cheerful establishment dishes up excellent *guveç* and *kuru fasulye* for 4YTL a throw.

Romada Ali Emiri Cad. One of many slightly seedy beer, grill and live-music joints in this area, where a kebab and a small beer will set you back 10YTL. It is not recommended for unaccompanied women,

particularly as the steps to the restaurant lead past a porn cinema. Male travellers may well be offered female company.

Şafak Kahvaltı Salonu Sütçü Sok. A good choice, serving comb honey with butter and fresh bread for breakfast as well as the usual soups or Turkish breakfasts; they also dish up *pide*, *lahmacun* and kebabs later in the day.

Selim Amca Sofra Salonu Ali Emiri Cad. A Diyarbakır institution, a 5min walk west of Dağ Kapısı, serving both chicken and lamb *kuburga* mains, *içli köfte* starters and *İrmik helvası* desserts. A fixed menu will set you back 20YTL, good value considering the opulence of the surroundings and the quality of the food, but there's no alcohol.

Şeyhmus Pastanesi Junction of İzzet Paşa Cad and Gazı Cad. Sweets and pastries to take away or eat in with Turkish coffee or tea.

Şanlıurfa Kebap Evi İzzet Paşa Cad 4. Very popular with the locals for its fast service, tasty food and bargain prices (it's hard to spend more than 5YTL).

Listings

Airlines The THY office is at İnönü Cad 8 (☏0412/228 8401). The Onur Air office is at İnönü Cad 28/B (☏0412/223 5312).

Banks and exchange Most of the banks and *döviz* offices are on Gazı Cad; Akbank takes most credit cards and travellers' cheques.

Buses The usual eastern bus companies have booths near Dağ Kapısı on Kıbrıs Cad, and service buses run from here to the *otogar*. The Batman/Hasankeyf/Mardin dolmuşes run from the dolmuş terminal outside Urfa Kapısı.

Car rental Class, next to the *Class Hotel* on Gazı Cad 101 (☏0535/921 5572), or Avis, İnönü Cad (☏0412/229 0275).

Hospital The Devlet Hastanesi (State Hospital) is north of Dağ Kapısı.

Internet Try the *Şafak* on Sütçü Sokak, off Kıbrıs Caddesi.

Police Police station on Gazı Cad, just north of the main crossroads.

Post office There is a small PTT on Yeni Kapı Cad, near the junction with Gazı Cad (Mon–Sat 9am–noon and 1–5pm for mail; 24hr for telephones). For money exchange, go to the larger PTT on Ziya Gökalp Bul, 300m north of Dağ Kapısı (same hours).

Trains The *Güney Ekspresi* departs for İstanbul every Monday, Wednesday, Friday and Sunday. Tickets from the station at the end of İstasyon Cad.

Travel agencies Diyarbakır has several reputable agencies, best of them being Bianca Seyahat, İnönü Cad 42 (☏0412/223 14250).

11

THE EUPHRATES AND TIGRIS BASIN | Diyarbakır

Mardin

Seen from the south at a distance, **MARDIN** looks spectacular, its tiered layers of houses, mansions, mosques and churches clinging to a huge citadel-topped rock which rises out of the endless level plain. The town itself affords breathtaking views, especially at sunset, over the Syrian plain. Mardin's position has always made it a strategic military outpost – the higher of the two castellated bluffs today sports golf-ball radar domes. Mardin's population is a mix of Kurds, Arabs, Turks and Syrian Christians, and, like Diyarbakır, the town has had to cope with an influx of people from surrounding villages fleeing the burnt-out shells of their homes. The political situation is more stable than it was, and Mardin is starting to receive its fair share of visitors, though the budget-hotel situation is dire.

Some history

Mardin's probable Roman origins are lost in the welter of war and conquest that forms this region's historical backdrop, while the town's later history is tied up with the development of early Christianity. The first Christians to settle here were Syrian Orthodox, who arrived during the third century AD. The Christians survived the period of Arab occupation from 640 to 1104, and were left alone by the Selçuk and Turcoman rulers. Today, eleven churches are hidden away in the backstreets, of which eight still serve the dwindling community on a rotation basis.

From the twelfth to the fourteenth centuries, the citadel was the capital of the Artukid Turcoman tribe. They were able to beat off Arab attacks and endure an eight-month siege during the first Mongol onslaught, falling only to the second Mongol wave under Tamerlane in 1394. The Mongols doled out death and misery in equal measures to Christian and Muslim alike, before, in 1408, handing Mardin over to the Karakoyun Turcoman tribe, who built the (now ruined) palace and mosque inside the citadel walls. In 1517, the Ottomans under Selim I took the town and governed it quietly until a Kurdish rebellion in 1832, when a number of public buildings were blown up. There was a brief Egyptian occupation in 1839–1840, after which the town sank back into somnolence until World War I.

Before and during Turkey's War of Independence, Mardin's Christian population was drastically reduced by massacre and emigration. There were renewed emigrations in the early 1990s and today only a few hundred practising Syrian Orthodox and Catholic and Armenian Christians remain – roughly one percent of the town's population. Local émigrés made good in Europe and the USA are now pouring money into the local Syrian Orthodox communities in Mardin and the Tür Abdin.

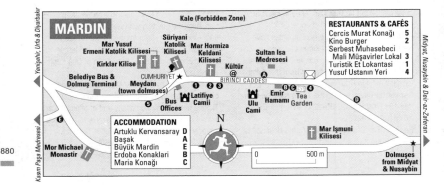

Arrival, orientation and information

It's not difficult to find your way around old Mardin. The citadel bluff is skirted by one road on the north, leading to Midyat, and another on the southern edge, which heads off to the southeast and the Syrian border. The old town itself lies on the steep southern slopes below the citadel. The principal street, **Birinci Caddesi**, branches off the main road at the western end of town, and rejoins it at the eastern end.

There's no *otogar* as such. Buses for Diyarbakır and other destinations usually depart from the **Belediye bus terminal** at the western end of Birinci Caddesi. For some far-flung destinations, *servis* buses from the couple of coach companies located at the western end of Birinci Caddesi will take you down into Yenşehir (New City) to board the bus. There is a **dolmuş terminal** at the eastern end of town on the main Syria-bound road, with services to Midyat and Nusaybin. City dolmuşes go from Cumhuriyet Meydanı in the city centre to either of these terminals.

Mardin's **tourist office** is in the Valilik Binası, in Yenisehir, 2km from the old city, and the detour there is a waste of time. The *Kultur* **Internet café**, just off Birinci Caddesi, is the most reliable in town.

Accommodation

Recent years have seen an explosion of pricy boutique hotels, but for budget travellers the situation is still fairly grim. The central *Otel Başak*, on Birinci Caddesi (☎0482/212 6246; ❷), is friendly but the carpets are grubby, the rooms dingy and the shared bathrooms grimy and often lacking hot water.

The cheapest boutique hotel is the *Maria Konağı* (☎0482/213 6552; ❹) just off Birinci Caddesi. The integrity of the old rooms has been spoiled by the en-suite bathrooms, but they are undeniably comfortable and have air conditioning and satellite TV. The *Erdoba Konakları Hotel* (☎0482/212 7677, ⓦwww.erdoba .com.tr; ❻) has a main building in Birinci Caddesi, with air-conditioned rooms equipped with fridge and TV, built in "period style" around a courtyard at the rear; there's an upmarket restaurant attached. There's also a separate, associated building with a few more rooms lower down the hill (accessible only on foot), in a converted merchant's mansion that has retained much of its character. The *Artuklu Kervansaray* at Birinci Cad 70 (☎0482/213 7353, ⓦwww.artuklu.com; ❺) looks set to challenge the *Erdoba*, with characterful, comfortable rooms in a restored mansion dating back to the thirteenth century. A plaque outside commemorates a visit by Prince Charles, who came to see the restoration work in progress. On Yeni Yol Caddesi, at the foot of the old town, and aimed squarely at the coach-tour trade is the monumental *Büyük Mardin Oteli* (☎0482/213 1047, ⓦwww.dunyain-sanlarininevi.com; ❻), which offers attractively furnished rooms (with kilims for curtains) boasting air conditioning and satellite TV.

The Town

Mardin boasts some superb **Islamic buildings**, including some of the old Arab-style houses. Following the main street, Birinci Caddesi, east from Cumhuriyet Meydanı leads you to a famous example – a beautiful stone facade with three arches, on the north side of the street. This is one of the finest private houses in town, and now serves as home to an extended family.

Several hundred metres beyond the house, the easterly of two sets of stone steps lead up to the **Sultan İsa Medresesi** (daily 9am–6pm; free) built in 1385, a striking, albeit crumbling, white structure with a magnificent Selçuk doorway, from which you can look out across the town towards Syria. Friendly tourist-police

will show you the semi-translucent volcanic stones used in the *mihrab*, which glow when illuminated with a torch. You can also climb onto the roof to enjoy the view and a detailed look at the fluted dome of the **Ulu Cami**, an eleventh-century Selçuk mosque east of Cumhuriyet Meydanı blown up during the 1832 rebellion and much restored since.

Above the Sultan İsa Medresesi is the **kale**, or citadel, originally built by the Romans and extended by the Byzantines. You may be able to enjoy the views from the terrace, but the castle interior and the golf-ball-crowned summit are a strictly off-limits military zone. From the terrace you can see the **Hediye Minare**, though not its twin staircases, built so that those ascending do not catch a glimpse of those descending.

To the south of Cumhuriyet Meydanı is the **Latifiye Camii**, dating from the fourteenth century. It has a carved Selçuk-style portal, and a courtyard with a shady garden – just the place to escape the blinding summer heat. Around here lies a maze of streets, forming part of the **bazaar**. At the western end of town, south of the main road (you'll have to ask directions), is the fifteenth-century **Kasım Paşa Medresesi**, similar in design to the Sultan İsa Medresesi.

Mardin has a vibrant **Christian heritage**, and many of its churches have survived the vicissitudes of history. This may well be because the Muslims and Christians here have always lived side by side; there were never separate quarters for the different faiths. The Syrian Orthodox **Kirklar Kilise** (Arbin Söhad in Syriac) or Church of the Forty Martyrs, is the most welcoming to visitors and dates back, in part, to the sixth century. The door is usually open, and the priest, Father Gabriel, speaks excellent English and may tell you something of the ancient history of the once-powerful church. Next door to the Kirklar Kilise is **Mar Yusuf** (St Joseph's), which now serves the town's tiny Armenian Catholic population. Lacking a priest, it's usually locked, and the congregation attends services at the Kirklar Kilise. To the east, adjoining the museum (see below), is the town's largest church, the **Süriyani Katolik Kilisesi** (Church of the Virgin Mary), used by five families of Syrian Catholics. If you can gain admission (the door is often locked) to the damp-damaged but handsomely vaulted interior (donations invited), you'll be shown many portraits of saints and an icon of the Virgin. On Birinci Caddesi, opposite *Kino Burger*, is the tiny **Mar Homizd Keldani Kilisesi**, a Chaldean church. A family still lives there, but it is difficult to gain access, though the bell tower is visible from the street. Currently under restoration, and with a typical Syrian Orthodox walled courtyard, is the **Mar İşmuni Kilisesi** at the bottom of the hill in the southeastern part of the old town.

Immediately above the two car parks at Cumhuriyet Meydanı is Mardin's **museum** (Tues–Sun 8.30am–4.30pm; 2YTL), housed in a restored mansion, with a small café and gift shop. It contains finds from the Sumerian, Assyrian and Urartian periods, as well as the usual Greek and Roman statuary and coins.

Eating and drinking

There are a few places to eat along Birinci Caddesi, of which the best is *Yusuf Ustanın Yeri*, opposite the PTT, an *ocakbaşı* (charcoal grill) garden **restaurant** serving excellent kebabs but no alcohol. The *Turistik Et Lokantası*, at the Meydan end of Birinci Caddesi, serves a wider range of food (including the local speciality, *sembusak*, a kind of folded-over *lahmacun*) but its setting, beneath the now-defunct *Bayraktar Hotel* is less atmospheric, and it no longer serves beer. *Kino Burger* on Birinci Caddesi, midway between the Meydan and the PTT, is favoured by the local youth, and is good for burgers and *köfte*. The *Serbest Muhasebeci Mali Müşavirler Lokal*, halfway along Birinci Caddesi on the south side, is a restaurant/club for local accountants. This makes it sound very dull, but it's friendly, and the best place in town for a beer, also serving kebabs and *mezes*. There is a pleasant dining area or a terrace with superb views over the Syrian plain. For upmarket dining, the ⚔ *Cercis Murat Konağı* to the west of the Meydan on Birinci Caddesi, is the best choice. Set in a restored Süriyani house, with great views from the terrace, it specializes in local dishes such as *incassıye*, lamb flavoured with sweet *pekmez*, plums, chilli and tomato. It serves alcohol too, but on the downside is expensive (expect to pay around 10YTL for a main and 6YTL for a beer) and is often full of Turkish tour groups.

Opposite the PTT is a small and leafy terrace **tea garden**, where you can watch the sun set over Syria.

Deyr-az-Zaferan

Six kilometres southeast of Mardin, **Deyr-az-Zaferan** (also known as Deyrül-zafran, or the "Saffron Monastery", so named for the yellowish rock from which it's built) is the most accessible of the area's surviving Syrian Orthodox religious communities. Founded in 493 AD, it was, from 1160 until the 1920s, the seat of the Syrian Orthodox patriarch – though he has since relocated to Damascus. A surprisingly large rectangular building of three storeys, set on a low bluff overlooking an approach road, it wouldn't look out of place in southern Italy or Spain and, judging by the different styles of stonework, was built in stages, with frequent pauses for restoration. Now only two monks remain, running a school for about 25 orphans with the assistance of a few lay helpers.

Visiting Deyr-az-Zaferan is easy enough. You can walk to it in an hour and a half from Mardin, following the brown signs leading southeast: first take the Nusaybin road, then turn left following a little brown sign, passing through the village of Eskikale. Eventually you'll come to another signposted turning leading you to the monastery. Failing that, pick up a taxi from Mardin's Cumhuriyet Meydanı or the dolmuş terminal; reckon on paying 16YTL for a return trip with waiting time.

Syrian Orthodox priests believe that the **Syrian Church** was established in this area during the lifetime of Jesus, when he himself was invited by King Abgar I of Edessa (modern Şanlıurfa) to move his ministry to the area. He refused, but a handkerchief – the *mandalyon* – bearing an imprint, or possibly a painting, of his face was despatched as a gift. This, together with a letter from Jesus, became the most holy relic possessed by the Church until it was lost to Arab conquerors, who passed it on to the Byzantines as ransom for the city of Urfa. According to legend, it ended up in Constantinople, where it was lost in the sack of 1204.

The area around Mardin has been a stronghold of the Syrian Orthodox or Jacobite Church since 543 AD, when one Yakoub Al-Bardai (better known in the West as Jacobus Baradaeus), was appointed bishop of Edessa (Şanlıurfa) and revived the persecuted and faltering Church. A native of Mesopotamia, Baradaeus was – like most of the Christians in the eastern and southern reaches of the Byzantine Empire – a Monophysite, subscribing to an anathemized doctrine locked in a century-old theological dispute with the patriarchate in Constantinople about the divine nature of Christ. According to the ecclesiastical Council of Chalcedon, convened in 451 AD, Christ had both a human and a divine nature, but dissenting bishops throughout the Middle East held that Christ had only a divine nature – a creed known as **Monophysitism**, whose adherents risked condemnation as heretics and excommunication.

Present-day Syrian Orthodox Christians deny explicit Monophysite leanings, calling themselves "non-Chalcedonian Orthodox". In fact, the core and uniqueness of Syrian Orthodox observance, which has enabled the Church to endure over time, is its liturgy in the **Syriac language**. Written from right to left in its own script, this had already evolved from ancient Aramaic – the mother tongue of Jesus – by the second century, when the first recognizable Syriac New Testament translations appeared. Between 541 and 578 AD, Baradaeus served as an energetic and peripatetic proselytizer throughout what is now the Hatay and Syria, helping to revive his Church as it suffered determined attack by the agents of Constantinopolitan orthodoxy. From the advent of local Arab dominion in the seventh century, Syrian Orthodox Christians enjoyed considerable religious freedom and, by the time of the First Crusade at the end of the eleventh century, the Tür Abdin in particular encompassed four bishoprics and eighty monasteries, the ruins of which are dotted across the plateau. Ironically, it was Christian Crusaders from Edessa and Antioch (Antakya) who unleashed a major, determined attack against what they regarded as a heretical Church, forcing abandonment of the traditional Syrian patriarchal seat in Antioch. They were followed by the Mongols whose motives had little to do with religion – they massacred and pillaged everybody regardless of race, colour or creed.

Under the Ottoman Empire, order was restored, and the Christian community once again enjoyed a long period of tolerance and stability. Unfortunately, during World War I, they were tainted by association with Allied plans to dismember the Ottoman Empire and suffered widespread persecution and massacre, a fate they shared with the Armenian and Greek minorities. Today the number of Syrian Christians worldwide totals nearly three million, though this figure may include members of the breakaway **Syrian Catholic (Uniate) Church**, which acknowledges the authority of the Pope. The largest surviving national community is, perhaps surprisingly, in Kerala, India; in Turkey there remain just the bishoprics of Tür Abdin, Mardin (currently vacant) and İstanbul, where many thousands of beleaguered Tür Abdin residents have fled. The seat of the Patriarchy is in Damascus.

From the hills, ancient but still intact rock channels bring water to the monastery, whose **entrance portal** bears an inscription in Syriac. After being greeted and perhaps offered a glass of tea, visitors are usually entrusted to one of the older orphans or visiting students and taken on a guided tour.

First stop is an **underground vault**, said to have been used as a temple by sun worshippers as long ago as 2000 BC. A now-blocked window at the eastern end enabled them to watch the sunrise, while a niche on the southern wall served as an altar (possibly sacrificial). The vault is topped by a stone ceiling constructed without mortar. The room above, entered via huge 300-year-old walnut doors, is a **mausoleum**, whose walls contain the grave niches of seven Syrian Orthodox patriarchs and metropolitans (the equivalent of bishops).

Tours move on from here to the **chapel**, with fine relief-decorated arches and a carved stone altar (replacing a wooden one destroyed by fire fifty years ago), and the patriarch's or metropolitan's throne, on which are carved the names of all the patriarchs since 792 AD. Services in the chapel are held in Syriac, and if you can manage to be here at around 6pm you may be able to attend one of them.

Beyond are a couple of rooms containing sedan chairs once used to transport the patriarchs; you'll also be shown a carved walnut altar, made without using nails, and an ancient mosaic said to come from the grotto of Sen Piyer in Antakya.

Upstairs, across the peaceful courtyard, you may also be shown the monastery's **guest rooms** (it is possible to stay overnight, but bear in mind that the quarters are intended for people visiting for religious reasons) and a more personalized suite intended for the use of the Patriarch on his rare visits from Damascus. Lastly, you'll be taken out onto the roof terrace for fine views south into Syria, and the orphans will point out surrounding abandoned cave hermitages and two ruined monastic churches: Mar Yakoub and Miryam Anna.

Nusaybin and Mar Augen

About 50km southeast of Mardin is **NUSAYBIN**, on the frontier with Syria. The last 33km of the journey runs parallel to the border, along the main D400 to Iraq. Nusaybin was the site of the **Roman town of Nisibis** and has a triumphal arch. More interesting is a sporadically functioning Syrian Orthodox church, **Mar Yakoub** (officially open only on Sundays), which has a crypt containing the bones of St Jacob. From here it's a fifty-metre walk southeast to the border-crossing point with Syria. The town's ornate **train station**, built by the Germans just before World War I and the last stop in Turkey on the Berlin–Baghdad railway lies out to the east, as does the stone and iron railway bridge, the Alman Köprüsü (German Bridge). There are currently no international services, and just one slow local train daily at dawn to Gaziantep.

The monastery of **Mar Augen** is the most evocatively set and most poignant of all the abandoned monasteries in the area, though only the bare fifth-century monastery church is intact, with all traces of decoration long since erased. With your own car, drive 25km towards Cizre and turn left to the village of Girmeli, 1km away; just past the village take a right turn and follow it 3km to the foot of the cliffs below the monastery. You'll need good ground clearance as the track is boulder strewn. From a parking point it's a twenty-minute climb up to the monastery. In the absence of your own transport, it is best reached by taxi from Nusaybin (around 40YTL). On the main road to the monastery from Nusaybin, just before the Girmeli turn, is the *Nezirhan Motel* (T 0482/446 341, W www.nezirhan.com; ❷). The modern concrete equivalent of a *kervansaray*, it is something of an institution on this godforsaken border-road, and has comfortable if dated rooms with air conditioning and an Olympic-sized pool out back

11

The Tür Abdin plateau

Less than 100km east of Mardin spreads the undulating plateau of the **Tür Abdin**, a traditional homeland of the Syrian Orthodox Church – whose independence from the Greek Orthodox Church was formalized by theological disputes of the fifth century (see box on p.884). The Tür Abdin is still home to a few Christians, who coexist uneasily with the local Kurds. Aside from a traditional livelihood of grape growing, the rocky, parched plateau is a poor region even by the standards of eastern Turkey, but the Christian villages are partly supported by émigrés.

Midyat is the western gateway to the Tür Abdin proper, which still has six villages wholly, and two partly, inhabited by Syrian Orthodox Christians, plus 46 **monasteries and churches**, some recently restored. To reach them, because of the distances and lack of public transport, you'll really need your own transport, or a taxi arranged in Midyat. The positions of several are shown more or less correctly on the GeoCenter/RV map of eastern Turkey.

Midyat

From Mardin, **MIDYAT** is an uneventful journey of just under an hour. It's actually a double town: the westerly portion is the unremarkable, Kurd-inhabited business district of **Estel**, where the *Demir Dağ* (☎0482/462 5630; ❸) on Mardin Caddesi is a reasonable hotel, with clean and comfortable doubles. Two kilometres east is the originally Christian portion of half-abandoned medieval mansions, known as **Eski** (Old) **Midyat**. Tourism is beginning to take off in the town, though facilities are still limited. The *Metro* hotel, on the fringes of old Midyat (☎0482/464 2317; ❶), just northeast of the central roundabout on the Hasankeyf–Batman road, offers waterless rooms with metal-framed beds but is friendly enough and reasonably clean. An alternative, on a hill top in the centre of the old quarter, is the *Konak Evi*, a beautiful old mansion-house which at the time of writing was being converted into a boutique hotel, with rooms for a bargain 50YTL. The house is also open to visitors (1YTL) and its rooftop gives wonderful views over the entire town and surroundings, especially appealing towards sunset. Midyat now boasts an exellent restaurant, the ⅔ *Cihan Lokantası*, just south of the junction roundabout on the Mar Gabriel road. Spotlessly clean, it is packed at lunchtimes for the superb *sulu yemek*, which includes tender *kaburga* (rib of lamb) and *perde pilaf* (delicately spiced rice with shredded chicken). The creamy *ayran* comes in copper bowls and is drunk from a ladle.

There is no *otogar* in old Midyat; **dolmuşes** stop at a roundabout (signed to Cizre, İdil and Mar Gabriel in the southeast, and to Batman to the north) at the foot of the old town. Buses for Mardin, Hasankeyf/Batman and Nusaybin run more or less hourly from 7.30am to 6pm. Above a small **bazaar** the residential quarter climbs up a slight hill, all cracked streets with open drains and mysterious gateways opening onto the courtyards of imposing mansions, inhabited by extended families of Kurds, Syrian Orthodox Christians and a very few Armenians.

As recently as 1974 there were nearly 5000 Syrian Orthodox Christians in residence here, the men mostly engaged in gold- or silver-smithing, but following PKK extortion of money from the merchants and death threats by Muslim bigots during the PKK war, the population has dwindled to eighty families and one priest. However, because of the changed political climate, the exodus has halted and conditions improved, though the renewed PKK activity reported in 2006 could jeopardize this.

The town's **churches** are easily spotted by virtue of their graceful belfries and can all be reached on foot. The two at the top of the hill are Syrian Orthodox **Mor**

Sharbel and the now-defunct Protestant **Mar Mariam**. South of these is **Mor Shmuni**, dating back to the eleventh century. The resident caretaker will show you around the simple whitewashed interior with its hand-painted altar curtains and illuminated Syriac missals that are between 300 and 1000 years old. A group of schoolchildren meets after school in the courtyard schoolroom to have Bible lessons, so if you time it right you may be able to listen to them chanting the liturgy in the language reputedly used by Christ. **Mor Barsaumo**, to the west, was built as early as the fifth century, destroyed in 1793 and rebuilt in 1910.

Mar Gabriel

Southeast of Midyat, the monastery of **Mar Gabriel** (Deyrulumur) is the geographical and spiritual centre of the plateau. To get there with your own transport, leave Midyat on the Cizre-bound road; after 20km turn northeast onto a signed tarmac road that leads to the monastery gate in just over 2km. A **taxi** to the monastery gates and back will cost $20, including waiting time. Using **public transport** from Midyat, walk down the Cizre road for about 100m from the roundabout to a dolmuş stop. The Cizre and İdil dolmuş will drop you at the signed Mar Gabriel junction, a half-hour journey, from where you will have to walk the final two kilometres.

Founded in 397 AD, Mar Gabriel is not only the oldest surviving Syrian Orthodox monastery, but the most vital in Turkey, with nineteen resident nuns and monks occupying separate wings, as well as a fluctuating number of local lay workers, guests and students sent by Syrian Orthodox emigrants to learn the Syriac language and retie hazy cultural connections. It is also the seat of the metropolitan bishop of Tür Abdin, who speaks good English, and with whom you may be granted an audience.

Compared with the showcase of Deyr-az-Zaferan, Mar Gabriel is a working community, set among gardens and orchards, and somewhat disfigured by a 1960s-vintage hostelry. The monastery's primary purpose is to keep Syrian Orthodox Christianity alive in the land of its birth by providing schooling, ordination of native-born monks, and – if necessary – physical protection to the faithful. You visit for the opportunity to gain some insight into the Church through a **guided tour** – visiting hours are 9am to 4.30pm. A lay person will take you around; the teacher of the Syriac language also speaks excellent English and can answer your questions. At noon you are welcome to attend the liturgy conducted in the subterranean church underneath the belfry, a heady mix of Syriac chants, swirling incense and prostration.

Restoration and new building work is in progress and there's a tangible aura of prosperity, a sign that secure times have returned again to the Tür Abdin. The heavy steel gates to the monastery are now locked to protect the gardens from the depradations of goats, rather than protecting the inhabitants from danger.

Village churches

In the opposite direction from Midyat – travelling north 4km towards Hasankeyf, then east along the secondary road to Dargeçit – lie the rest of the Tür Abdin's historic churches.

Finest, though also the most remote, is the monastic church of **Meryemanna** (İndath Aloho in Syriac). To reach it follow the Hasankeyf road for 3km, then turn right for Dargeçit. After 17km turn right (signed Meryemanna/Hah) and follow the road for 6km to Hesterek village, turn left here for Anıtlı, a further 7km away. The recently restored (and very beautiful) church is on your right as you enter the village. Regarded by the local Süriyanis as the jewel in the Tür Abdin crown, this fifth-century foundation sports a two-storey wedding-cake turret with blind arches atop a pyramidal roof; the archways and lintels are also heavily ornamented. The village itself is fascinating. Once the centre of a community of several thousand, with over 44 churches in the vicinity, there are now just sixteen families remaining. At the centre of the village, atop a small rise, are a group of fortified houses where some five thousand Christians held out for months against a vastly superior Ottoman force in 1915 – with no Christian lives lost. Downhill from here are the remains of the church of **Mor Bacchus**, dating back to the second century, and en route back to Meryemanna is the sixth-century church of **Mor Sovo**, destroyed by Tamurlane.

Closer in, 10km along the Dargeçit road and then 3km north on a dirt track, the **Mar Yakoub** monastic church in Kurdish Baraztepe (Salah) village is substantial, but lacks the grace of Meryemanna. It is currently under restoration, and is cared for by three monks and two nuns, though the village itself is entirely Muslim. Returning to the Dargeçit road, continuing east for 2km and then turning south for a further couple of kilometres, you reach the slightly later church of **Mar Kyriakos**, with its small courtyard, in the mixed Christian/Kurdish village of Bağlarbaşı (Arnas). Its architect also built the **Mar Azazael** church on a knoll at the edge of Altıntaş (Keferzeh) village, about 7km east of Mar Kyriakos.

Hasankeyf

The spectacular ruined settlement of **HASANKEYF**, built on and around a rocky spur on the banks of the Tigris, contains remarkable medieval remains of Selçuk, Arabic and Kurdish origin. The original settlement was founded by the Romans as an eastern bastion of Asia Minor, and later became the Byzantine bishopric of Cephe. In 640, the conquering Arabs changed the town's name to Hisn Kayfa. During the twelfth century the Artukid Turcoman tribe made it the capital of their realm, which it remained until the Mongols arrived in 1260. Hasankeyf then served as the stronghold of the Ayyubids, a clan of Kurdish chieftains supplanted by the Ottomans early in the fifteenth century.

Hasankeyf is once again under threat from the proposed construction of the **İlisu dam** across the Tigris. Slated for 2012, it will drown the village, bridge and lower part of the site as well as impeding water-flow to Syria for a number of years. The locals (having suffered from planning blight for years) are currently trying to make as much as possible from the increasing number of tourists, both foreign and Turkish, as evinced by the burgeoning number of souvenir stalls and temporary restaurants lining the road to the cliff-top site.

The Town

The modern town trails along for several hundred metres, overshadowed by the ruined Artukid city to the southwest, which covers two square kilometres of a cliff-top above the right bank of the Tigris river. The **site** (always open; 2YTL) is reached by turning west down a narrow paved street just west of the modern Tigris bridge. After a kilometre look out for a ruined gateway halfway up the right side of the gorge, beyond which a stone pathway, currently being restored, leads uphill to the twelfth-century **palace of the Artukid kings**, perched high above the Tigris. From here there is a fine view of the river, a sheer drop of several hundred metres below, while behind you stretches the rest of the city. Although they look like standard-issue ruins from the road, many of its skeletal houses contain intricate decorative features. Particularly impressive are the well-preserved **mosque** and a couple of domed **tombs**.

To get a closer look at the Tigris, head back towards town and turn left by a gorgeous carved minaret (that of the El Rizk Camii, a fourteenth-century Ayyubid construction) to drop down to the river bank, where families come to paddle, wash their cars and eat at the summer-season fish and grill restaurants. The several hundred steps carved into the sheer cliff-face, which give secret access to the Artukid palace above, have been closed on grounds of safety. Just downstream are the four pillars of an old **Artukid bridge** that in its day was apparently one of the finest in Anatolia.

The fifteenth-century **Zeyn El-Abdin Türbesi**, a sizable, onion-domed cylindrical building clad in glazed turquoise tiles and red brick, is conspicuously isolated in a walled orchard on the north bank. Possibly the most Timurid-influenced monument in Turkey, it is easily reached on foot, starting opposite a filling station on the main road towards Batman, or via the north bank of the Tigris from the bridge.

Practicalities

The journey north from Midyat to Hasankeyf involves a gradual, scenic descent towards the river and provides an excellent return route to Diyarbakır, without having to backtrack to Mardin. Regular dolmuşes run from Hasankeyf to Batman (1hr, 2YTL), where you change buses for the final leg of the journey to Diyarbakır (1.5hr, 4TL) along an attractive green gorge of the Tigris, but these local buses stop running at about 6pm.

Hasankeyf has basic **accommodation**, and an overnight stay is recommended especially for photographers, as the morning and evening lighting effects are spectacular. The *Oğretmen Evi* on the south side of the bridge is only open to tourists in June, July and August (the rest of the year it houses teachers working in the local villages). This provides basic waterless rooms with bunk beds for €3 and has a shady courtyard where tea and soft drinks are served. Just below and opposite the *Oğretmen Evi* is the *Hasankeyf Motel* (❷), with dirty carpets, no hot water and no en-suite rooms, but great views over the river. The *Antik Kent Et Lokantası* on the main street is good for soup, grills and *lahmacun*, as is the nearby *Fırınlı Et Lokantası*. Further up is the Kardeşler **Internet café** on the east of the main road, and a small PTT on the west. There's an ATM back towards the river.

Travel details

Buses and dolmuşes

Adıyaman to: Adana (4 daily; 6hr); Ankara (5 daily; 13hr); Diyarbakır (1 daily; 3hr 30min); Kahta (hourly; 45min); Kayseri (1 daily; 8hr); Malatya (6 daily; 3hr); Şanlıurfa (8 daily; 2hr 30min).
Batman to: Hasankeyf (6 daily; 1hr); Diyarbakır (10 daily; 1hr 30min).
Diyarbakır to: Adana (6 daily; 8hr); Ankara (6 daily; 13hr); Batman (hourly; 1hr 30min); Bitlis (5 daily; 3hr 30min); Gaziantep (5 daily; 5hr); Malatya (6 daily; 4hr 30min); Mardin (6 daily; 1hr 45min); Şanlıurfa (8 daily; 3hr); Siirt (hourly, 3hr); Siverek (hourly; 2hr); Sivas (4 daily; 10hr); Tatvan (4 daily; 4hr); Van (4 daily; 7hr).
Gaziantep to: Adana via Mersin (10 daily; 3hr 30min); Ankara (12 daily; 10hr); Antakya (8 daily; 4hr); Diyarbakır (5 daily; 5hr); Malatya (3 daily; 4hr); Mardin (5 daily; 5hr); Şanlıurfa (10 daily; 2hr).
Hasankeyf to: Batman (6 daily; 45min); Midyat (6 daily; 45min); Van (1 daily; 7hr); Cizre (1 daily; 2hr).
Kahta to: Adıyaman (hourly; 45min), Karadüt (1 daily in season; 3 hrs); Siverek (several daily; 2hr).
Malatya to: Adana (5 daily; 7hr 30min); Adıyaman (5 daily; 2hr 30min); Ankara (8 daily; 10hr); Diyarbakır (6 daily; 4hr); Elazığ (hourly; 1hr 40min); Erzurum (1 daily; 7hr); Gaziantep (3 daily; 4hr).
Mardin to: Cizre via Nusaybin (3 daily; 3hr); Diyarbakır (6 daily; 1hr 45min); Midyat (frequently on demand; 1hr); Şanlıurfa (5 daily; 3hr).
Midyat to: Hasankeyf (4 daily; 45min); Batman (6 daily; 1hr).
Şanlıurfa to: Adana (6 daily; 6hr); Adıyaman (6 daily; 2hr 30min); Ankara (5 daily; 13hr); Diyarbakır (7 daily; 3hr); Gaziantep (8 daily; 2hr); Harran (hourly 7am–7pm; 1hr); Mardin (5 daily; 3hr).

Trains

Diyarbakır to: Ankara (4 weekly; 26hr 15min); Kayseri (4 weekly; 18hr); Sivas (4 weekly; 13hr).
Gaziantep to: İstanbul (3 weekly; 29hr); Konya (3 weekly; 16hr); Nusaybin via Karkamiş (1 daily; 6hr).
Malatya to: Adana (daily; 8hr 30min); Ankara (daily; 20hr); Diyarbakır (3 weekly; 6hr 30min); Tatvan (3 weekly; 10hr 30min).

Flights

Turkish Airlines
Diyarbakır to: Ankara (2 daily; 1hr 30min); İstanbul (5 daily; 1hr 55min).
Elazığ to: Ankara (1 daily; 1hr 15min); İstanbul (1 daily; 1hr 45min).
Gaziantep to: Ankara (4 weekly; 1hr 20min); İstanbul (6 daily; 1hr 50min).
Malatya to: Ankara (5 weekly; 1hr 10min); İstanbul (2 daily; 1hr 40min).
Şanlıurfa to: Ankara (5 weekly; 1hr 30min); İstanbul (5 weekly; 2hr).
Onur Air
Diyarbakır to: İstanbul (2 daily; 1hr 45min).
Gaziantep to: İstanbul (1 daily; 1hr 45min).
Malatya to: İstanbul (1 daily; 1hr 45min).
Atlas Jet
Malatya to: Antalya via İstanbul (6 weekly June–Oct; 3hr 50min).

Lake Van and the southeast

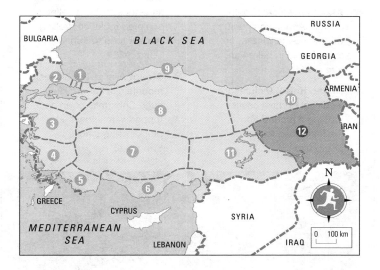

CHAPTER 12

Highlights

* **Nemrut Dağı** This unique mountain habitat shelters migrating birds in May and September, and in between offers the possibility of a dip in the crater lakes. See p.898

* **Van Kalesi** The "Rock of Van" was fortified by ancient Urartians, whose cuneiform inscriptions are inscribed on the cliff-side. See p.905

* **Akdamar Kilisesi** Tenth-century Armenian church with stone-cut friezes, on a tiny island in Lake Van. See p.911

* **Hoşap Kalesi** Picturesque medieval Kurdish castle topping a mound above the main road to Hakkari. See p.913

* **Hakkari** Join in the dancing to fiddle, pipe and drums at a traditional Kurdish wedding. See p.916

* **Muradiye waterfalls** The gushing falls near Van boast a twenty-metre drop and a wonderful early-summer display of wildflowers. See p.920

* **İshak Paşa Sarayı** An architectural folly of golden limestone, set in a valley of sculpted rocks controlling the silk road to Iran. See p.922

* **Mount Ararat** The highest mountain in Turkey, like a huge Christmas pudding, topped with snow and a puff of rising smoke. See p.923

△ Detail of carving from Akdamar Kilisesi

Lake Van and the southeast

he **southeast** of Turkey is the least developed and most ethnically distinct part of the country. It is a high, rugged, sparsely populated area with a natural beauty on which people seem to have made little impression (other than deforestation) over the ages. At the heart of it all lies **Lake Van**, a vast inland sea trapped by laval deposits from the dormant or extinct volcanoes that soar over the undulating steppeland of central Anatolia. The volcanoes culminate in the peak of 5137-metre Ağrı Dağ – better known as **Mount Ararat** – while extensions to the Toros range loop around the south and east of Lake Van. The climate is as severe as the terrain, with torrid summers (from June onwards) giving way to freezing winters starting in early November.

Main roads have been improved significantly, often due to military require-ments during the PKK troubles (see box on p.871), but towns are often far apart. Restaurant food is plain and most hotels basic, but the region contains sights and monuments which are some of the most diverse and impressive in Turkey.

You might consider flying into the regional capital, **Van** (1642km from İstanbul), with its ruined ancient citadel and atmospheric skeleton of an old town. This rapidly expanding city lies a few kilometres inland from the lake, and is a remarkably civilized and welcoming centre for exploration. Overland, the con-ventional approach is by bus from Diyarbakır (see Chapter 11), via the old trade route through the stark hill-town of **Bitlis** and dreary **Tatvan**, itself a base for seeing the northwestern parts of Lake Van. Alternatively, from Erzurum (Chapter 11), travellers can head due east to **Doğubeyazıt** and its fanciful palace below the dominating bulk of Mount Ararat. The more adventurous, coming from the southeast, can approach via Şırnak and the border road to **Hakkari**.

Siirt and around

East of Diyarbakır, en route to Tatvan, the first reasonable diversion is provided by the isolated town of **SIIRT** (900m), which lies 40km south of the main highway (99) between Diyarbakır and Van. It's about a three-hour drive from Diyarbakır, with little to stop off for on the way, save the **Malabadi Köprüsü**, 20km east of Silvan, a beauti-ful stone bridge with an enormous single arch, constructed in 1146 by the Artukids.

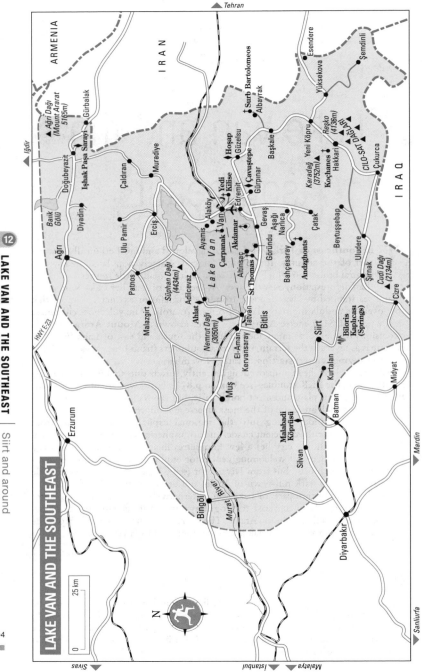

LAKE VAN AND THE SOUTHEAST

0 25 km

N

ARMENIA

Tehran

IRAN

Igdir

Ağrı Dağı
(Mount Ararat
5165m)

Gürbulak

Doğubeyazit

Işhak Paşa Sarayi

Baiik
Gölü

Diyadin

Muradiye

Çaldiran

Ulu Pamir

Erciş

Ağrı

HWY E23

Patnos

Malazgirt

Süphan Dağı
(4434m)

Adilcevaz

Ahlat

Nemrut Dağı
(3050m)

Tatvan

El-Aman
Kervansaray

Muş

Bingöl

Murat River

Erzurum

Lake Van

Ayanis

Çarpanak † Van

Altinsaç

St Thomas

Bitlis

Siirt

Alaköy

† Yedi
Kilise

Akdamar

Göründü

Bahçesaray

Andzghonts

Edremit

Gevaş

Aşağı
Narlıca

Çatak

Biloris
Kaplıcası
(Springs)

Kurtalan

Batman

Malabadi
Köprüsü

Silvan

Diyarbakır

Surb Bartolomeos

Albayrak

Esendere

Şemdinli

Yüksekova

Reşko
(4136m)

CILO-SAT DAĞLARI

Çukurca

Hoşap

Güzelsu

Çavuştepe

Başkale

Gürpinar

Karadağ
(3752m)

Koçhanes †

Hakkari

Beytüşşebap

Uludere

Şirnak

Cudi Dağı
(2134m)

Cizre

IRAQ

Midyat

Mardin

Şanlıurfa

Sivas

İstanbul

Malatya

From 1992 to 1994, the kidnappings of foreign tourists by Kurdish-separatist PKK operatives made headlines overseas for the Van region. The Turkish military's response to the insurgency, culminating in the capture of the rebel leader Abdullah Öcalan in February 1999, resulted in the PKK declaring a unilateral ceasefire on September 1, 1999. The authorities reciprocated by lifting emergency rule in the region. At the time of writing, the PKK has resumed attacks on the Turkish military, police and village guards. Whilst no foreigners have been involved, the renewed tension means that travellers who stray off the beaten track – especially into the mountains south of Lake Van – may be viewed with some suspicion by the authorities.

Another problem in the area is the **smuggling** of people (illegal immigrants) and goods (petrol and heroin). This is unlikely to affect tourists, although it has made the military reluctant to grant access to Ararat and other mountainous areas close to the borders.

For the average traveller visiting major towns and sites, apart from the odd checkpoint, travel is no different from other areas of Turkey. However, circumstances can change at any time, so keep your ear to the ground. The southeast has been unstable for so long that both locals and officialdom are understandably suspicious of all outsiders, but once you gain the trust of the locals most are extremely friendly and helpful. If you intend to hike in the mountains, birdwatch or botanize, or visit remote rural sites and villages, it's worth heeding the following.

Transport

Most local **dolmuş** services stop running in mid-afternoon; start your journey early in the day to ensure you reach your destination before nightfall. **Car rental** is expensive; by renting a minibus or taxi instead, you have the advantage of a **driver** who knows local conditions and can often get you with minimum delay to your chosen destination.

Travel permission

If you intend making forays into the mountains south of Van (excepting the main road to Hakkari, which presents no problem), it should be possible (though you need either decent Turkish or a translator) to get initial clearance at the **Jandarma Hareket Merkezi** (Movement Centre) at the large barracks on the Hakkari road, about 3km outside Van. Leave your name and your intended purpose and destination, as any patrol that subsequently stops you will have to report to the centre for instructions.

Trekking advice

Forays into some of the mountains are becoming possible again, although we recommend taking a local guide. **Permits** for Mount Ararat are now available for foreigners (see p.924) and Mount Süphan is unrestricted. The mountains south of Van, including the Cilo-Sat mountains of Hakkari (the real treasure of the region) remain to all intents and purposes off-limits because of renewed PKK activity. Take **up-to-date advice** from the website ⓦ www.mountainsofturkey.com, or other genuine mountaineering sources, rather than tourist offices.

Originally settled by the Babylonians, Siirt's heyday was during the period of Arab rule preceding the arrival of the Selçuks. It was the Selçuks, though, who left a lasting impression on the town. Siirt's main attraction, the twelfth-century **Ulu Cami**, is behind the market area, uphill from the roundabout on the Bitlis road, well hidden amongst mud-brick houses. Its tall, square, brick minaret is adorned with geometrically patterned tiling. Also worth seeing are the thirteenth-century **Cumhuriyet Camii** and the Selçuk-built **Kavvan Hamam**; otherwise there's not much to detain you.

Practicalities

Siirt has very little experience of tourism and the **local police** might take an interest in your presence. You may be asked to show your passport and explain what you are doing there (not easy unless you speak Turkish), or even accompany the police to the station where they will photocopy your passport before sending you on your way.

Minibuses leave daily in all directions from the garage at the roundabout end of Aydınlar Caddesi; there are also a few long-distance bus-company offices on the roundabout. There is at least one daily **dolmuş to Van**, which leaves at around 9am and takes three to four hours; otherwise, dolmuşes run north on demand to Ziyaret, at the junction with the main highway, where you change for Tatvan and Van. The main **otogar** is 2km west of town, with services to Diyarbakır, Hasankeyf and Batman. Buses also head south to the small town of **Şırnak** (springboard for the time-consuming but spectacular trip along the Iraqi border to Hakkari) on empty roads, via green and pleasant valleys with occasionally interesting rock strata and formations. Four mornings a week, currently Monday, Wednesday, Friday and Sunday, **trains** leave Kurtalan (dolmuşes from Aydınlar Caddesi), 30km west of Siirt, for the long trip to Kayseri and Ankara via Diyarbakır; trains may not run to time.

The town has limited **accommodation**. The *Vatan Hotel* (no phone; ❶) on Aydınlar Caddesi, opposite the dolmuş garage, offers only semi-clean doubles with temperamental hot water. Better but dearer is the *Otel Erdef* (☎0484/223 1081; ❹) on Cumhuriyet Caddesi (downhill from the roundabout), with huge, spotless, air-conditioned en-suite doubles, a dainty white-frilled breakfast room-cum-restaurant, comfortable lobby-bar and gardens.

The *Metro* **Internet café** is next to the *Vatan Hotel*, and there's a **currency exchange** office opposite. Good, cheap food is served cheerfully in a busy, noisy hole-in-the-wall **restaurant** next to the dolmuş garage, and there are kebab houses and fruit stalls in the **market** area north of Aydınlar Caddesi.

Bitlis

From the Siirt highway turn-off, it's 44km to **BITLIS**, along an attractive winding gorge dotted with *han*s and old bridges.

A strange and atmospheric town, impoverished Bitlis (1545m altitude) is set in a steep-sided valley and famous for its tobacco. It once controlled the pass from Syria to the Van region and Persia and Armenia beyond. Nowadays the population is predominantly Kurdish, often unemployed and passing their time in the teahouses, but before World War I about half the inhabitants were Armenian.

The Town

Modern Bitlis is essentially a one-street place, threading its way along the banks of a river that's torrential in winter but dries to little more than a sluggish trickle in summer. Its dark stone houses and steep valley setting give it the feel of an isolated nineteenth-century English mill-town. The most notable monument is the sixteenth-century **Şerefiye Camii**, with a fine carved portal, echoing the Selçuk style, on the northern bank of the stream. Also of interest are the **Ulu Cami**, an unusual-looking mosque built in 1126 by the Artukids, and the **Saraf Han** *kervansaray*.

Reached by the steps above the Tatvan dolmuş stop on the main street is a walled complex containing the **Küfrevi Türbesi**, dating from 1316, and a much more modern *türbe* built by Greek craftsmen under the orders of Sultan Abdülhamid in 1898. Together they house the tombs of six Sunni saints, who draw pilgrims from all over the Muslim world. Ring for entry; Mustafa, the caretaker, whose family have lived here for generations, speaks some English and, in the Bitlis trading tradition, he buys tea in Sri Lanka and sells it all over Europe.

A huge **citadel** built on a rock outcrop looms over the north side of the town. You can walk up to it by following a road that snakes around its base to the far side, from where a dirt path continues to the summit, with great views over the town.

Practicalities

The main **dolmuş stop** is to the south of the centre, but some Tatvan dolmuşes depart from the foot of the steps below the Küfrevi Türbesi, on the main road 400m northeast of the *Hanedan* hotel. The first dolmuş to Tatvan leaves at 8am and they run regularly through the day. Van buses heading west to Diyarbakır pass through Bitlis, but may be full.

The town's parlous economic state is reflected in the fact that there is only one shabby **hotel** remaining – the *Hanedan* (no phone; ❶) – which is less grim than the slog up several flights of stairs through the apparently abandoned Social Security building would suggest.

Bitlis's **food** is equally uninspiring; the local speciality is *buryan kebap*, leg of goat steamed in a *tandır* oven for four hours and served on the bone, but better examples are available in Tatvan. Reasonable *lahmacun* is served at a hole-in-the-wall **café** near the Şerefiye Camii, and excellent *su böreği* (savoury cheese or mincemeat pastries) and *porça* (savoury breakfast rolls) can be found at the **bakery** opposite the Tatvan dolmuş stop.

The El-Aman Kervansaray

Between Bitlis and Tatvan, on the right as the road reaches the plain, just after the turning to Muş, is the **El-Aman Kervansaray**. A classical Ottoman *kervansaray* built of volcanic black stone by Hüşref Paşa in 1502, it is one of the largest of the period, 90m long and with 160 rooms.

The interior is based on the pointed arch, reaching great spans in the hall to the right of the entrance. Passing through the main building, the rear extension is now unroofed, but once consisted of more cell-like rooms. A small mosque and bath-house adjoined the entrance courtyard. The gently deteriorating building is a reminder of the volume of trade through the Bitlis gap; it's well worth a visit and afterwards you can hail a passing dolmuş to continue your journey to Tatvan, half an hour away.

Tatvan and around

Some 20km northeast of Bitlis, **TATVAN** squats between Lake Van and the surrounding hills, an unattractive place with limited facilities that nonetheless makes a good base for exploring the surrounding sights. To the north is the massif of **Nemrut Dağı** with its crater lakes; northeast are the impressive Selçuk remains at Ahlat (p.900); while to the south are the hills around Hızan, well-watered, forested with oak and hiding remote farming villages and the ruins of several Armenian churches.

Practicalities

Tatvan's streets follow the grid layout common in new developments in Turkey with the main street, **Cumhuriyet Caddesi**, running east to west 100m south of the lake.

The town's **otogar** is 1km along the Bitlis road, but buses invariably drop passengers near the PTT on Cumhuriyet Caddesi. You can pick up onward **dolmuşes** from in front of the various companies' ticket offices around here. The dolmuş to Van costs 5YTL and takes around three hours, following the main road along the beautiful south shore of the lake; Ahlat dolmuşes leave approximately every 45 minutes from the corner of the PTT, near Cumhuriyet Caddesi, and run along the north shore of the lake, taking some 45 minutes.

The **train service** (Van Gölü Express) between İstanbul and Tatvan/Van has now resumed; trains for İstanbul depart on Tuesday and Thursday at 7am. All services run from the station 1km northwest of the town centre on the Ahlat road and are subject to hours of delay. Trains are shipped **across the lake to Van** on antiquated ferries, and theoretically there are daily crossings, one morning and one early evening. It's a great way to arrive in Van (and cheap too, at 3YTL for a foot passenger) – but timings are very unpredictable.

The **tourist office** is inconveniently located in the new Kültür Merkezi, 1km out of town on the Bitlis road. Bang in the middle of Cumhuriyet Caddesi is the **PTT**. The best **Internet café** is the *Sena Internet Café* (one street south of Cumhuriyet Caddesi from the *Alize* hotel).

Accommodation

Opposite the PTT, Belediye Yanı leads south to the town's top-rated **accommodation**, the large *Hotel Kardelen* (☎0434/827 9500, ✉otelkardelen@turkei .net; ➏), with a restaurant, bar, sauna and spacious but dowdy rooms with satellite TV. It's outrageously overpriced, but they may bargain. The *Alize Hotel*, Cumhuriyet Cad 160 (☎0434/828 0020, ⊕828 0022; ➍), is better value, offering clean and comfortable accommodation with nicely fitted bathrooms. Even better is the *Hotel Dilek*, on Yeni Çarşı just east of the main street (☎0434/827 1516; ➋), with compact but spotless rooms, tidy bathrooms (though some are starting to peel) and a breakfast room with stunning views over the lake and Mount Nemrut. Best cheapie option is the shabby but clean *Üstün Otel*, Hal Cad 23 (☎0434/827 9014; ➋), a couple of blocks east of Cumhuriyet Caddesi, catering mainly for the less-prosperous male business-traveller, with shared bathrooms and no breakfast. A more atmospheric choice is the *King Hotel* (☎0434/827 7111; ➌), set right on the lake shore 1km out of town on the Van road. You can camp here for a modest fee.

Eating and drinking

On Cumhuriyet Caddesi are a number of **breakfast** places serving fresh bread with comb honey, butter and cheese. The *Koşem* restaurant, just east of the *Alize Hotel*, serves excellent soup and kebabs and has a big eating-salon upstairs. Nearby, the *Şimşek* offers a similar range of food, for around 5YTL a head. A block behind the *Alize* is the *Eyvan*, a basic but clean restaurant serving up tasty *pide* (2.5–4YTL) and *menemen*, a delicious egg, vegetable and cheese concoction served up sizzling hot in a small wok-style pan.

Nemrut Dağı

Immediately north of Tatvan, the extinct volcano of **Nemrut Dağı** (no relation to the mountain with the statues), rises to 3050m. Six thousand years ago Nemrut

Lake Van, virtually an inland sea of almost 4000 square kilometres, at an elevation of 1750m, is one of the most unusual features of eastern Turkey. Along with Lake Sevan in Armenia and Lake Urumiya in Iran, it is one of a trio of huge upland lakes without outlets in the region. Surrounded on all sides by a narrow but fertile plain, and then mountains, the lake – nearly 200m deep in spots – occupies what was once a lowland basin that was later dammed by lava flowing from Nemrut Dağı. Owing to rapid evaporation in this desert climate, the lake water is highly **alkaline**, rendering it slightly soapy and slimy to the touch; local people can sometimes be seen washing clothes in it.

Yet **pollution**, plus the summer mosquito population, particularly around Van, has meant that swimming is not recommended close to the major towns. You can **swim** from the stony beaches on and opposite Akdamar Island, and around Edremit, or along the more sparsely populated stretches of shoreline, especially on the north side. Even non-swimmers will float – the water's specific gravity is greater than the sea. Two species of **fish** – one called *dareka*, attaining forearm size – live in the lake, though only near mouths of the streams feeding it, where they are caught for food during spring. The shore remains largely unexploited, and apart from around Edremit, there's a notable scarcity of boat-rental or watersports facilities.

The lake is on the main **bird migration route** to Africa, so is seasonally filled with migrants. You may see a few pelicans, gulls, flamingos and cormorants, and there are lesser kestrel and night heron colonies on Akdamar. Two other forms of local animal life are worth noting. First, there's the famous **Van cat**, a fluffy white beast endowed naturally with one blue and one gold eye, and an affectionate disposition; its pure strain is disappearing from careless interbreeding with ordinary cats, but a few specimens are still kept at local hotels and carpet shops as tourist bait. Less commonly seen is the **Lake Van monster**, or Van Gölü Canevarı – this two-metre-long beast was supposedly first spotted in the 1960s and has been growing ever since, but recent reported sightings are of a dinosaur-like monster about the size of a bus . . .

is believed to have been 4450m high; as a result of a huge volcanic explosion, the whole upper section of the peak was deposited in the Van basin, thus blocking the natural outlet and creating the lake. The present-day volcanic cone contains two crater lakes, one of which is pleasantly warm.

After snowmelt in May/June, the crater lakes are accessible by car or dolmuş. The tourist office in Tatvan can organize full-day **dolmuş excursions** for groups at €35 per group, including waiting time. This will probably be under the auspices of Mehmet Selinci (☏0542/832 4228), a local guide who speaks reasonable English and who also arranges trips to local villages, *zoma* (the Kurdish for summer pastures) and remote churches. If you're travelling under your own steam, either take the Bitlis road out of Tatvan and almost immediately turn right for Şentepe, or head for Ahlat and look for the signpost. Either way, it's about 15km to the crater rim.

From the rim, an asphalt road drops down and right towards the warm lake; bear left on dirt track to the cold crater lake. The **crater**, 7km in diameter, seems to have its own microclimate and the lush vegetation (beech, aspen and juniper) contrasts sharply with the bare landscape outside. Water birds that stop off here include gulls, stilts, herons and ducks, notably the rare, black velvet scoter; the crater is also noted for its snowmelt vegetation. The only other inhabitants are transhumant Kurds whose flocks graze the slopes during the summer months. The crescent-shaped **Soğukgöl** (cold lake) occupies the western half of the crater and lives up to its reputation all year round, but there are some hot springs on the east shore that are good for a swim, as well as cold, potable ones. Better still, take a dip in the smaller **Sıcakgöl** (warm lake,) connected to its partner by a narrow path leading east or a left branch off the asphalt road.

Ahlat and the northern shore

The lake's northern shore is well worth exploring, although it takes three hours longer to reach Van by this route. A somewhat forbidding and bleak volcanic landscape is relieved intermittently by charming pastoral valleys and a lush foreshore, not to mention the forbidding bulk of Süphan Dağı. First point of interest, 42km from Tatvan, is the shabby town of **AHLAT**, known chiefly for its Selçuk cemetery, with hundreds of medieval stone graves, and for its monumental tombs. The journey from Tatvan takes in some lovely views of Nemrut Dağı and the lake.

First an Urartian, then Armenian settlement, Ahlat fell to the Arabs during the seventh century, was retaken by the Byzantines two hundred years later, and passed to the Selçuks after the nearby battle of Manzikert in 1071. The Mongols arrived in 1244, succeeded by the İlhanids from Persia a century later; by the 1400s Ahlat was the main base of the Akkoyun Turcomans. Even after the local Ottoman conquest of 1548, real power in this remote region remained in the hands of the Kurdish emirs of Bitlis. Ahlat was a populous, polyglot city until World War I.

Today Ahlat's famous *kümbet* **tombs** are scattered about some 2km southwest of the modern settlement's centre. In a typical local *kümbet* (which accommodated one to four persons), the deceased was interred in an underground chamber, beneath a prayer room reached by steps from the outside. It's thought that the traditional nomadic tent inspired the distinctive conical design, executed in deep brown basalt, often by Armenian stonemasons.

You'll see the first (and largest) of them, the two-storey **Ulu Kümbet** (Great Tomb), in a field just south of the main road as you approach the town. This simple tomb of a late thirteenth-century Mongol chieftain is the largest in the Van region (there are a few more at Gevaş, on the opposite shore of the lake). On the other side of the road, next to one of the entrances to the cemetery, is a small **museum** (Tues–Sat 8am–noon & 1–5pm; 2YTL) with stone animals and other monuments standing outside, including an undated stone portraying reliefs of the tombs. Inside, you'll find some Urartian bronze pieces and jewellery, and miscellany from other eras.

The **Selçuk cemetery** covers almost two square kilometres, crammed with tilted, lichen-encrusted headstones dating from the eleventh to the sixteenth centuries. The headstones appear in all shapes and sizes, most covered with floral, geometric and calligraphic decorations. The language of most inscriptions is not Turkish but – like the town's predominant linguistic profile until the fourteenth century – Persian and Arabic.

Set back outside the wall on the north of the cemetery stands the **Çifte Kümbet** (Twin Tomb), similar to the Ulu Kümbet in age and design (only double) and also a Mongol mausoleum, in this case for two couples. Nearby is the **Bayındır Türbesi**, most impressive of all the tombs hereabouts with its colonnaded upper storey and distinctive *mescit* (prayer room); it was built in 1492 to house the remains of the Turcoman chief Bayındır.

The **fortress** to the northeast of town was built during the sixteenth century by sultans Süleyman the Magnificent and his son Selim. Once grand, it is now a crumbling ruin with good views of the lake.

Practicalities

Dolmuşes from Tatvan take 45 minutes. Ahlat's transport hub is near the *Belediye* in the middle of town with something – be it bus or dolmuş – going in either direction (to Tatvan or Erciş/Van/Doğubeyazıt) every hour or two.

Regarding **accommodation**, avoid the monumental *Selçuklu* on Zübeyde Hanım Caddesi (℡ 0434/412 5697, ℻ 412 5699; ❸), which, despite its superb position right on the lake at the extreme east end of town is overpriced, dirty, and doubles as the town brothel. Far better is the modest *Göktaş* (℡ 0434/412 5050; ❶), a little further east on the inland side of the main road, a very basic but spotlessly clean hotel above a more than passable restaurant.

Around Ahlat

Continuing 25km northeast from Ahlat will bring you to the attractive modern village of **ADILCEVAZ**, huddled in a fertile valley surrounded by poplars, walnut and apricot trees. It is dominated by a mighty Selçuk fortress, which is in turn overshadowed by the 4434m volcanic peak of **Süphan Dağı**. The mountain, Turkey's second highest, is not technically difficult to climb, but it is remote, with an unreliable water supply and semi-wild sheepdogs on the loose. It has become popular with ski-mountaineers, who brave temperatures which can drop to -50°C in winter. Below Adilcevaz, look out for the **Tuğrul Bey Camii**, a distinctive thirteenth-century mosque near the shore, constructed using the dark brown volcanic stone typical of the area. The lakefront near here now has an attractive promenade area and a pleasant café.

For a wonderful half-day **walk**, head north-northwest out of the town, to a small dam. High on the bare mountainside above, the remains of the **Armenian monastery church of Skantselorgivank** can be seen on a ridge. Head down into a dip, then follow a dirt road for a short while before heading off to the left on a prominent path. A rocky trail leads to the church, which boasts a startlingly evocative shattered shell, with bands of red and black stonework, *khatckar*s (stones inscribed with crosses) and a black basalt font. To return, retrace your steps initially, but keep to the west of the dam and town, following the line of a concrete irrigation channel which contours the hillside. This will eventually bring you close to the top of the Selçuk citadel. After admiring the superb views, scramble down to the lakeshore café for a well-earned drink (allow 3–4 hours for the round trip).

Beyond the church are the remains of the Urartian citadel of **Kefkalesi**, separated from the church by a steep, scree-strewn valley which the locals say can only be negotiated with difficulty. To reach Kefkalesi from Adilcevaz, therefore, it's probably better to take a taxi direct to the Urartian citadel (around 20YTL) and walk back to town. In the grounds of the citadel archeologists have unearthed the foundations of an Urartian palace.

Adilcevaz is a charming place (especially in comparison to either Tatvan or Ahlat) and it is well worth stopping the night. The obvious choice of **hotel** is the rambling *Otel Park* (℡ 0434/311 4150; ❶), with big, cheerful en-suite rooms and a restaurant, though it lacks atmosphere and is a bit grubby. Far cheaper and better, at the northeast end of town beyond the square, is the *Otel Kent* (no phone; ❶) with waterless but immaculately clean rooms (you have to take off your shoes before entering your room; slippers are provided), spotless shared bathrooms, and fruit trees out back. Just south of the main square is a most unexpected and welcoming *birahane*, serving beer and delicious salads and grills at bargain prices. There is an Internet café just down from the *Otel Kent*.

Ulu Pamir

From Adilcevaz, it's worth making the two-hour bus journey to Ercis, east along the lake, an uninspiring place in itself but with a daily dolmuş service to the remarkable Kirghiz village of **Ulu Pamir**, 30km north, a settlement for refugees from the Pamir region of Afghanistan since the early 1980s.

Forced to leave their homeland in 1979, these Central Asian villagers, ethnic kin of the Turks, set up home first in Pakistan before the Turkish authorities airlifted them and their flocks to Turkey in 1982. After a couple of false starts, the Kirghiz refugees ended up in this remote but beautiful green upland valley north of Van, where they still live. Like so many people in exile, they have clung tenaciously to their language, culture and dress. The older men sport *kalpak* hats and distinctive, heelless leather boots, whilst the women wear pillbox-style hats surmounted by flowing scarves. Families have erected felt *yurts* in the yards of the houses provided for them by the Turkish government, and the horse is the favoured method of transport.

Life is hard for these displaced people, who make a living from selling cheese and yoghurt from their herds in Ercis, but every June the place comes to life with a **festival** that includes horse-riding competitions, falconry and folk dancing. Without your own transport it is difficult to visit Ulu Pamir as the daily dolmuş from Ercis does not leave till the late afternoon, and there is no accommodation. If you are prepared to chance it, you could camp near the river, or the village *muktar* may offer to put you up. A dolmuş returns to Ercis at 6am, from where there are good connections onto either Van or Doğubeyazıt.

Van

Capital of the region, sited on the eastern side of the lake, **VAN** is initially disappointing but grows on you with acquaintance. Devastated during World War I, an earthquake in the 1950s destroyed what remained of the town's Ottoman architectural heritage, and enabled the modern concrete construction and grid layout which accommodates 600,000 people. The town is set 4km back from the lake against a mountain backdrop, but ancient **Van Kalesi**, the so-called Rock of

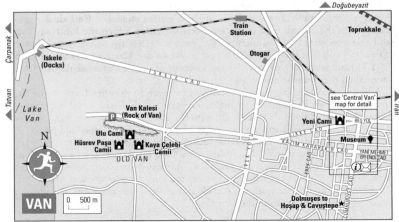

Edremit, Merit Hotel, Airport, Akdamar, Tatvan, Bitlis & Diyarbakır ▼   ▼ Hoşap & Hakkari

Van, is spectacularly situated by the lake. Van is also the base for exploring the surrounding area, notably the Armenian island church of Akdamar.

Arriving in Van by the Tatvan boat, which berths near the Rock, is the most dazzling approach, though as the boats are highly unreliable it's far more likely that you will arrive by the scenic **southern-shore route** from Tatvan. This initially follows a pretty willow-fringed valley to the pass of Kuskunkıran, with spectacular views over the eastern lake basin, then a descent through a checkpoint and along the lake shore with vistas of Akdamar and Süphan Dağı reflected in the still waters. The road then turns north through the lake-shore town of Edremit, now a virtual suburb of sprawling Van.

Arrival, information and services

The **airport** is 6km south of town, linked to the centre by shuttle bus and taxis. The **otogar** is a little way northwest of the centre: dolmuşes and *servis* buses run from here to the busy junction of **Beş Yol**, at the northern end of Cumhuriyet Caddesi. **Trains** arrive at the station 3km northwest of the centre, where you can find a dolmuş or taxi into town. If you arrive by **ferry**, a dolmuş runs the 5km into town. The brand-new **tourist office** at Cumhuriyet Cad 127 (☎0432/216 2018) has little to offer apart from a sightseeing brochure worth picking up for its photos of some obscure sights. If you're thinking of moving east, note that there's no **Iranian consulate**.

Accommodation

Van has plenty of **hotels,** in all price ranges; and for women travelling alone staying in Van is more comfortable and safer than other towns in the area.

Otel Ağansoy Hastane Cad 23/C ☎0432/216 1686, ☎212 0551. A brightly painted building in a quiet cul-de-sac, with a clientele of Turkish student groups; the small, clean en-suite rooms have TVs. ❷

Akdamar Hotel Kazım Karabekir Cad 56 ☎0432/214 9923, ⓦwww.akdamarotel.com. Very friendly, efficient place with restaurant, barber's shop, bar and comfortable lounge. The rooms are looking a little jaded and the public areas can be smoky, but it's good value nonetheless. ❸

Hotel Aslan Cumhuriyet Cad, Sok 3 ☎0432/216 2469. Slightly more expensive than the neighbouring *İpek*, but better for solo women. Newly decorated, with basins in all the smallish rooms and a shower on each floor. Try to avoid a room overlooking the noisy dancehall opposite. No breakfast. ❷

Büyük Asur Hotel Cumhuriyet Cad, Turizm Sok 5 ☎0432/216 8792, ℮rb_asuroteli@hotmail.com. Overpriced (but spotless) accommodation. The management speaks good English and offers daytrips taking in Hoşap, Çavuştepe and Akdamar from €30 per person, not including boat tickets. ❸

Büyük Urartu Oteli Hastane Cad 60 ☎0432/212

0660, ☎212 1610. Best of the plush town-centre hotels, with rather old-fashioned, though comfortable rooms, plus swimming pool and sauna. ❻

Otel İpek Cumhuriyet Cad, Sok 3 ☎0432/216 3033. Clean, simple, but jail-like rooms with high-level windows, with or without attached shower; some include washbasins at no extra cost. No breakfast. ❷

Merit Edremit Yolu ☎0432/312 3060, ⓦwww .merithotels.com. Situated on the lake shore, this is undoubtedly Van's best hotel. The large rooms are tastefully decorated and the en-suites all have large baths. Photographs of the surrounding attractions brighten up the public spaces, and the buffet breakfast is excellent. The drawbacks are that it is primarily aimed at the coach-tour market and it's 12km from town. ❻

Hotel Şahin İrfan Baştuğ Cad ☎0432/216 3062, ⓦwww.otelsahin.com. Newly renovated, with all-new beds and furniture, but the back rooms are claustrophobically close to the next building. Front rooms are spacious and, together with the rooftop breakfast room, have great views over Toprakkale. ❷

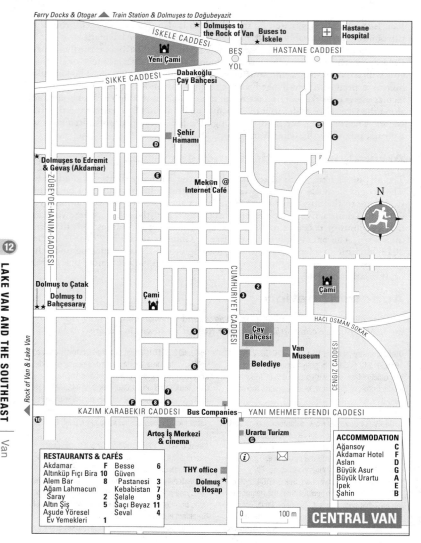

Ferry Docks & Otogar ▲ Train Station & Dolmuşes to Doğubeyazit

İSKELE CADDESİ

★ Dolmuşes to
the Rock of Van

Buses to
★ İskele

Hastane
Hospital

BEŞ
YOL

HASTANE CADDESİ

Yeni Çami

SIKKE CADDESİ

Dabakoğlu
Çay Bahçesi

Ⓐ

Ⓞ

Ⓑ

Şehir
Hamamı

Ⓒ

Ⓓ

★ Dolmuşes to Edremit
& Gevaş (Akdamar)

ZÜBEYDE HANIM CADDESİ

Ⓔ

Mek@n
Internet Café

@

Dolmuş to Çatak

Dolmuş to
★★ Bahçesaray

Çami

N

Ⓩ

Ⓒⁿᵈ

CUMHURİYET CADDESİ

Çami

Ⓐ

Çay
Bahçesi

HACI OSMAN SOKAK

Ⓑ

Ⓒ

Van
Museum

CENGİZ CADDESİ

Belediye

Ⓕ

Ⓔ⑧⑨

⑦

KAZIM KARABEKİR CADDESİ

Bus Companies

YANI MEHMET EFENDİ CADDESİ

⑩

⑪

Artoş İş Merkezi
& cinema

Urartu Turizm
Ⓖ

ACCOMMODATION

ⓘ   ✉

Ağansoy   C
Akdamar Hotel F
Aslan   D
Büyük Asur   G
Büyük Urartu A
İpek   E
Şahin   B

RESTAURANTS & CAFÉS

Akdamar   F
Altınküp Fıçı Bira 10
Alem Bar   8
Ağam Lahmacun
  Saray   2
Altın Şiş   5
Aşude Yöresel
  Ev Yemekleri   1

Besse   6
Güven
Pastanesi   3
Kebabistan   7
Şelale   9
Saçı Beyaz   11
Seval   4

THY office

Dolmuş ★
to Hoşap

0   100 m

CENTRAL VAN

Rock of Van & Lake Van ◀

⑫ LAKE VAN AND THE SOUTHEAST | Van

The City

Following liberalizing parliamentary legislation on Kurdish education and the winding down (if not ending) of the war with the PKK, the locals are beginning to wear their **Kurdish identity** on their sleeves. Many of the villagers who arrived in the 1990s as refugees from the troubled mountain areas appear to have been absorbed by the urban culture, while others have now returned to their former homes, either through homesickness or the lack of economic prospects in the city.

Van is the commercial centre of the area, with colourful market streets, livestock sales and general lack of tourist rip-offs. If you decide to buy Kurdish rugs here, one place to look is the **Türkiye Eğitim Hizmet Çalışma Vakfı**, on Barış Caddesi, Onur Sokak, Bostaniçi Mah (℡0432/215 1513), 8km from the city centre. This is a charitable trust set up to aid poor village women by giving them a decent wage and good working conditions, with profits going to improving village health services. The kilims are woven to traditional regional designs using natural dyed wool and time-honoured methods, and cost around 130YTL a square metre (no credit cards). **Galeri Van Gölü** at the Kartal Işhanı Altı 25, on Cumhuriyet Caddesi, is a more conventional outlet with a wide range of carpets and kilims at decent prices.

Van museum

Van museum (Van Müzesi; Tues–Sun 8am–noon & 1.30–5.30pm; 2YTL) lies just east of Cumhuriyet Caddesi on Cengiz Caddesi. The exhibits are undoubtedly impressive, but are unimaginatively displayed, despite some recent attempts at re-labelling.

The room to the left of the ticket office displays **Urartian** gold jewellery, bronze work and terracotta figures unearthed at Çavuştepe, plus some intricately decorated bronze belts and jewelled breastplates. Adjacent to this gallery is a small conservatory, containing various **rock carvings** from Mesolithic times (9000–8000 BC) through to the Bronze Age. Some of these are very primitive representations of stags, which could almost be prototypes of the stag carvings in the Museum of Anatolian Civilizations in Ankara, while others are more sophisticated animal figures. Also on display are children's sarcophagi from the fourteenth century BC and a number of cuneiform inscriptions.

Upstairs there's an **ethnographic** section displaying some fine kilims from Van and Hakkari provinces, as well as a **Genocide Section**, devoted to atrocities committed against Muslims in the area during World War I. The display includes books debunking foreign allegations of an officially sponsored massacre and mass expulsion of the Armenian population (see box on p.908). The exhibits in the garden outside include some interesting Armenian gravestones, huge Urartian statues with inscriptions, and many medieval stone sheep.

Toprakkale

Van's only other significant site, **Toprakkale**, is situated in a military zone and has been off-limits for many years. Toprakkale is a largish rock outcrop just north of town, the location of an eighth-century BC Urartian citadel, which has been identified as the town of Rusahinili, founded by Rusas I in 733 as a counter to Assyrian aggression.

Van Kalesi: the Rock of Van

From the Beş Yol junction in town frequent dolmuşes (0.5YTL) run 3km west to **Van Kalesi**, a narrow outcrop 1.5km long, over 100m tall and perhaps 300m wide at the base; equipped with its own spring, it was once an eminently suitable Urartian stronghold. Visit in the afternoon and you'll be treated to a magnificent sunset over the lake. Entry is from the car park and **ticket booth** (2YTL) on the north side.

The dolmuş will drop you at the eastern end of the Rock, from where you follow the road for 500m towards the lake to a car park and teahouse with a pretty stone bridge and willows. Passing the northern face, you will note a small modern mosque and a *türbe* (tomb) that attract many pilgrims. Above these is a terrace, the site of an **Urartian temple**, of which only a couple of arched niches remain.

△ Inscriptions on Van Kalesi

Cuneiform inscriptions on a statue base in one of the niches document the life and works of Menua, an important Urartian king. In the tea gardens is a large stone rectangle with an inscription of Sarduri I, originally an **Urartian jetty**, though the water is now a kilometre away.

The ticket booth leads to a steep path followed by stairways and landings leading to the citadel at the top. As you climb you'll find that the views are increasingly spectacular, sometimes vertiginous. The low-lying site of Old Van lies immediately south of the Rock of Van (see below); beware of the sheer drops.

What follows is an attempt to guide you through the more salient features, but it's difficult to precisely locate features. In general, the Cyclopean well-cut stone blocks are Urartian; the later poor-quality workmanship is Armenian or Ottoman.

On the north face you can walk along what's left of the stone **battlements**. At one point a flight of stairs cut into the rock leads down to a cliff-side terrace from where you can reach the vast rock **tomb of Sarduri II** (762–733 BC), where three chambers lead off from the central one.

Continuing upwards, you pass through an arch onto a ramp, leading up to the **kale** precinct. In Ottoman times the citadel was garrisoned by three thousand janissaries as well as by conventional troops. Today the most prominent building is a **ruined mosque** with a minaret, whose partially intact steps can be climbed; the arched-roofed building is a *medrese* while nearby are barracks. On a large stone block an Urartian cuneiform **inscription** in suitably self-glorifying language credits Sarduri I (840–825 BC) with the construction of the first walls.

Past the *kale*, from the terraces overlooking the old town, steps cut into the strata lead down to the rock-hewn **tomb of King Argishti** (786–762 BC), successor of Menua. Nearby, on another terrace overlooking Old Van, are two more **rock tombs**, those of kings Ishpuini (825–810 BC) and Menua (810–786 BC); the latter was the builder of the 65-kilometre aqueduct, portions of which are still used, supplying the Rock with water. A little more accessible than that of Argishti, these tombs are reached via a winding path that snakes down from the summit. Each consists of a large central chamber with three smaller chambers branching off. The southern edge of the terrace is marked by the remains of mud battlements.

The huge and famous inscription on the southern face of the Rock is only visible from below; it was first recorded in 1827 by the traveller/archeologist Schulz (who was later murdered by Kurdish tribesmen), dangling on a rope from the summit. The fifth-century BC **cuneiform inscription** in Persian, Medean and Babylonian celebrates the Persian king Xerxes.

Old Van

The destruction of **Old Van** in 1915 (see box on p.908) was so thorough that today only three mosques and fragments of an Armenian church remain. The rest is a sea of overgrown, rubble-strewn mounds. These days, the locals come here to pasture their cattle or picnic on the grassy knolls and appreciate the view of the Rock of Van, the silhouette of which has been likened to that of a kneeling camel. You may also see Kurdish women washing their carpets and kilims in the nearby stream, which loses itself in marshes towards the lake. In these marshes, one of Turkey's rarest birds, the citrine wagtail, flourishes, alongside the far more common feldegg yellow wagtail, which is a conspicuous egg-yolk yellow.

It's possible, but hair-raising, to scramble down to ground level at the southeastern edge of the Rock and walk across the dead town, but far easier to circle the Rock on the lakeside. Huddled right under the Rock at its southeastern corner are the remains of an Armenian church, still bearing traces of frescoes; behind it are some *khatchkar*s inscribed onto the rock-face. The closest mosque to the Rock is the ruined thirteenth-century **Ulu Cami**, with a squat brick minaret.

The southern limits of the old town are bounded by a road, near to which stands a pair of sixteenth-century mosques. The easterly one is the **Kaya Çelebi Camii**, a sealed-up shell whose white stone *mihrab* has unaccountably survived; the western mosque, rather more intact, with attractive banded stonework and an attached tomb, is the **Hüsrev Paşa Camii**. The only other significant remnants are some stretches of the medieval wall that once girded the town, a couple of tombs and a ruined hamam.

These ruins represent a once-attractive settlement, with stone and wood houses inhabited by some 80,000 people. Within the walls lay a thriving bazaar, several churches, the government offices and even some foreign consulates. A few nearby orchards give an indication of the once-extensive "garden suburbs" where the bulk of the population lived.

Eating and drinking

The **restaurant** scene in Van is fairly standard: the regional favourite *Kürt köfte* – a doughy ball of herb-flavoured wheat – only features in home cooking, while *otlu peynir*, a sharp, dry, spiced cheese, is best sampled at one of Van's famous **breakfast salons**. Most of these are on Cumhuriyet Caddesi and serve a selection of cheeses, olives, honey and cream (*kaymak*) with fresh hot bread and gallons of tea.

The **bars** of the big hotels make reliable if sterile drinking venues; the *Akdamar* is popular with wealthier locals. Alternatively the *Altınküp Fıçı Bira* on Kazım Karabekir Caddesi is a typical *birahane*, and not suitable for lone females. To sample Van's nascent rock scene try the *Alem Bar* on Sanat Sokağı Devamı Bilal Sokak. A smoky, gloomy, graffitied cellar bar, it serves Van's students (there's a campus 12km out of town educating some 6000 young Turks) and has live music most nights. The atmosphere's friendly and the beer cheap (3YTL).

For the modern Turkish state, the history of Van and its province is sensitive, being inextricably bound up with that of eastern Turkey's now-vanished Armenian population.

Ancient precursors: the Hurrians and Urartians

The earliest inhabitants of the Van region were the **Hurrians**, who established a kingdom stretching as far south as modern Syria around 1900 BC. Their territorial ambitions brought them into conflict with the Hittites, who defeated them around 1400 BC.

The fragmented Hurrian kingdom later re-emerged as the **Urartian Empire** during the ninth century BC; Van, now known as **Tushpa**, was its capital. Under King Argishti I (786–762 BC), it encompassed most of the territory described in this chapter, plus parts of present-day Iran, Iraq and Syria.

Around a dozen Urartian citadels have been unearthed in southeastern Turkey and modern Armenia. They were also skilled jewellers, with fine examples of their gold-working visible in Van Museum, and have even been credited with the discovery of wine-making. Eventually centuries of fighting with the Assyrians and later the Scythians took their toll, and the Urartian Empire went into decline at the start of the seventh century.

The coming of the Armenians

The **Persian** Scythians and Medes annexed the weakened Urartian state around 612 BC. Concurrently, **Armenian** settlers drifted into the Van basin, intermarrying with the indigenous population. It's thought that the Armenians originally came from the Caucasus, although Herodotus refers to them as Phrygians, and Strabo suggested Babylonian or Syrian ancestry. Whatever their provenance, during the reign of the Persian king Darius I (521–486 BC), the Armenians were established enough to count as a vassal principality.

In 331 BC, **Alexander the Great** defeated the Persians and became the new ruler, starting a series of changes of overlord which became a theme of Armenian history. After his death, Armenia became part of the Seleucid Empire before passing into Parthian and **Roman** hands. Between 95 and 55 BC, Armenia, under King Tigranes II, ("the Great"), wrested short-lived independence from the Romans, in alliance with his father-in-law Mithridates of Pontus. After protracted campaigns against both, the Romans effectively re-absorbed the region.

The advent of Christianity

Under the Romans and Byzantines, Armenia played an important role in the growth of **Christianity**. Towards the end of the third century, during the reign of King Trdat III, it became the first nation to officially adopt Christianity, thanks to the efforts of St Gregory, known henceforth as "the Illuminator". Following the Edict of Milan in 313, Christianity became tolerated throughout the Byzantine Empire, enabling the Armenian church to consolidate and establish its own identity. By 404 the monk Mesrop Mashtots had devised the **Armenian alphabet**, surviving virtually unchanged to the present day.

The **Armenian Apostolic Church**, as it's technically known, refused to accept the ruling of the Byzantine ecclesiastical Council of Chalcedon (451), which declared that Christ had two equal and co-existent natures. The Armenians, like the Coptic and Syrian Orthodox Christians, retained their monophysite doctrine, maintaining that the human nature of Christ was absorbed in the divine.

The ninth and tenth centuries saw the greatest flowering of Armenian culture, particularly in the Van basin under the **Atzruni dynasty**. But the long-running religious antipathy between the Byzantine capital at Constantinople and outlying provinces such as Armenia fatally weakened the empire. The Selçuks took Van in 1064, even before the crucial battle in 1071 at nearby Manzikert. Fleeing Armenians formed the short-lived kingdom of Cilicia, ruled by a rival dynasty. Armenia proper, now vassal of the Georgians, revived during the twelfth and thirteenth centuries, but suffered from repeated raids by the Turcomans, and the disastrous Mongol and Persian onslaughts of the thirteenth and fourteenth centuries.

Ottoman rule

The **Ottomans** finally took control of Armenia during the fifteenth and sixteenth centuries, snatching Van from the Persians in 1548. Ottoman rule benefited the Armenians who, like the other non-Muslim minorities, were conceded substantial control over education and family law, and even earned for themselves the epithet of *sadık millet* (loyal nation). In the nineteenth century, as the "sick man of Europe" declined, Christian subjects of the Ottoman Empire developed nationalist aspirations. Armenian nationalists were encouraged to acts of violence by the Russians, who were intent on fragmenting the Ottoman Empire. With the outbreak of **World War I**, individual Armenians were forced to choose sides, but by 1918 there were very few Armenians left in the Van area, or indeed anywhere else in Turkey except İstanbul.

The events of 1915–1918

Though thousands of Armenians served in the Ottoman army from 1912 until 1915, many others in eastern Anatolia saw the global conflict as a chance to found an **independent Armenian state** centred on its traditional territories, and went over to the Russian side.

Local Turks and Kurds attacked Van's Armenian civilians, who barricaded themselves in the old town. The Turkish garrison up on the Rock responded by pulverizing the walled quarter from above with heavy artillery. The bloodshed ceased temporarily when the Russians took the town in May 1915, and when the Ottomans counterattacked, the remaining Armenian townspeople fled with the Russian army.

The Russians, accompanied by some Armenian regiments, returned to Van and elsewhere in the east that August, remaining until the Tsarist collapse in late 1917. During these occupation years the Armenians and their nominal allies, the Russians, retaliated for the events of 1915 by forcing the Muslim population out of potentially Armenian sovereign territory. Turkish sources estimate that up to **600,000 Turks and Kurds** were killed – it is these victims who are highlighted by the "Genocide Sections" of the Van and Erzurum museums.

Meanwhile the Turkish authorities moved against the Armenian population within Turkish control. It seems that the CUP (Young Turks), at the instigation of Interior Minister Talaat Paşa, ordered the **deportation** of all Anatolian Armenians – not just potential combatants – to Syria. Numerous eyewitness accounts describe the rounding up in major towns of Armenian women, children and elderly for transportation to Syria, and the summary execution of any men of fighting age or in positions of authority. It appears that between **700,000 and one million Armenian civilians** were dispatched in various ways between 1915 and 1920.

When the first census of the Turkish Republic was conducted in 1927, Van town had a population of just a few thousand, as against 80,000 before the war. The annihilation of Old Van had been so complete that it was never rebuilt. Instead modern Van was founded 4km inland, beyond the "garden suburb" of the vanished Armenian merchants.

Ağam Lahmacun Saray Ordu Cad 8. Just east of Cumhuriyet Caddesi, this bustling place dishes up tasty and cheap *cevizli* (walnut) and *isot* (hot pepper) *lahmacun* (1YTL), kebabs (3.5YTL) and *pide* (4YTL).

Altın Şiş Salonu Cumhuriyet Cad. Serves excellent vegetarian *kaşarlı pide*, which comes on a round base dripping with cheese (4YTL); the kebabs are good value, too.

Aşude Yöresel Ev Yemekleri Van Devlet Hastanesi Karşısı, Bayramoğlu Apt 3. Occupying the upstairs floor of a detached 1940s villa, with wooden floors, swish glass-topped tables and draped windows, it's homely in a modern fashion. The food is excellent value, with *içli köfte*, *mantı* and *cığ köfte* among the home-cooked dishes.

Besse Melek İş Merkezi, Sanat Sokak. Already an institution with Van's middle-classes, the *Besse* ("enough" in Kurdish) boasts plush decor, subdued lighting and excellent food. There's a fixed menu which includes lentil soup, salad, *cacık*, a main grill and fruit to follow. Try the

fıstıklı kebap (with pistachios) or ask for any kebab "*bol kaşarlı*" (dripping with cheese). A full meal should set you back around 8–10YTL. No alcohol.

Güven Pastanesi Cumhuriyet Cad. A central cake-shop with a cavernous interior and good-quality cakes, *baklava* and coffee.

Kebabistan Off Kazım Karabekir Cad. A three-storey affair specializing in large, hearty kebabs (around 5YTL) and catering for groups.

Saçı Beyaz King of Van's patisseries, occupying a prime place at the junction of Cumhuriyet and Kazım Karabekir *caddesi*. It's the place to be seen tucking into delicious *baklava*, gateaux or ice cream.

Şelale Off Kazım Karabekir Cad. Around the corner from *Kebabistan*, on the new pedestrian precinct, is this third-floor restaurant serving kebabs and other dishes.

Seval İş Bank Arkası, PTT Cad. A down-to-earth breakfast salon, serving up hearty quantities of comb honey, clotted cream, herb cheese, olives, yoghurt and boiled eggs.

Listings

Airlines Turkish Airlines, Cumhuriyet Cad 196 ☎0432/215 5354; Atlas Jet, Cumhuriyet Cad Belediye Sarayi Altı 1 ☎0432/4440 387.

Airport bus A shuttle (2YTL) from THY office on Cumhuriyet Cad 196 (☎0432/2155 354), ninety minutes prior to flight departure.

Banks and exchange Cumhuriyet Cad is home to several banks with ATMs.

Buses The major companies have offices clustered around the junction of Cumhuriyet/Kazım Karabekir/Fevzi Çakmak *caddesi*.

Car rental Hertz's local agency is Akdamar Oto Kıralama, Cumhuriyet Cad, Ornek İş Merkezi 1 (☎0432/215 8990 or 0532/596 0144); Avis works with Erek Turizm Şeyahat, Hastane Cad, behind

the *Büyük Urartu* hotel (☎0432/214 6375 or 214 4333).

Hamam The Şehir on Zübeyde Hanım Cad is modern, clean and friendly; it's 5YTL for the standard works.

Hospital The Devlet Hastanesi is on Hastane Cad, just east of Beş Yol (☎0432/216 4740).

Internet The *Mek@n*, upstairs in the Saraçoglu İş Merkezi on Cumhuriyet Cad, has fast ADSL connections and comfy chairs.

Police West of town on İpek Yolu.

Post office Currently behind the tourist office, though a new one is set to open on Cumhuriyet Cad.

Around Van

The area to the south of Van is the most physically impressive in Turkey, featuring rugged mountains dotted with isolated settlements and stretching all the way to the Iraqi and Iranian borders. The Armenian churches on the islands of **Akdamar and Çarpanak**, the less-visited church of **St Thomas**, the ancient Urartian royal palace at **Çavuştepe** and **Hoşap** castle all make excellent day-trips from Van. In the rocky foothills east of Van, there are more church remains at **Yedi Kilise**, and to the north is the Urartian **Ayanış castle**.

Akdamar Kilisesi

On an island just off Lake Van's southern shore stands the justly famous tenth-century Armenian **Akdamar Kilisesi** (open daily dawn–dusk), an incredible example of Armenian architecture, set amid stunning scenery.

The church was built as the cathedral of the royal court between 915 and 921 AD by Gagik Atzruni, ruler of the Armenian kingdom of Vaspurakan. The palace and monastery he also had built here have not survived, but the church is intact, a small four-apsed building some 15m by 12m, with a central cupola over 20m high, and an exterior profusely decorated with well-preserved **reliefs** depicting biblical scenes. Three reliefs on the south side describe the story of Jonah and the Whale, one of them showing Jonah being swallowed by a chimeric creature with ears and teeth. Also well represented are episodes demonstrating the rewards of faith: along the southern wall you'll find Abraham and Isaac, and David and Goliath. The most famous panel is on the north wall showing Adam and Eve (inexcusably vandalized) and next to it, a very butch Delilah is cutting off Samson's hair. The west wall is adorned by Gagik the builder-king presenting a model of the church to the clergy, and incorporates some fine **khatchkars** – the Celtic-looking, obsessively detailed carved crosses that the Armenians used both as celebratory or commemorative offerings and as grave markers. Mythical and real animals (at one point being named by Adam, elsewhere placed purely for whimsy, or to illustrate virtues or vices) and inscriptions in the hook-like Armenian alphabet also abound. You'll find more *khatchkar*s beside the church, to the northeast, where a group of handsome specimens date from the thirteenth to seventeenth centuries.

Stretching all around the church exterior, starting from the west wall, is a breath-taking vine-leaf trellis that runs above the reliefs: in the first scene, a prelapsarian woman embraces a beast, while towards the end there's hunting and animals feeding on the vine itself. Unfortunately, the **interior** is more or less gutted, its faded murals daubed with graffiti. The famous golden bell and the illuminated Bible that feature in the reliefs have long since been whisked away to the Moscow museum.

Practicalities

Dolmuşes (3YTL) run from a yard in Van one minute's walk up Zübeyde Hanım Caddesi, near the junction of Sikke Caddesi, from 6am to 7pm in summer. Out of season (before May and after September) the dolmuş may only run as far as the town of Gevaş, 5km short. From the **quay** by the roadside, the boatmen charge 30YTL per boat for the round trip, or 2.5YTL per person if there are twelve or more passengers. There's a further charge of 2YTL for admission to the island. Near the quay stands *Akdamar Camping Restaurant* (☎0432/216 1515), where you can camp free providing you eat at the (reasonable) restaurant.

The church of St Thomas

The monastic **church of St Thomas** (Kamrak Vank), situated on an isolated promontory in the lake and visible from the island of Akdamar, can be reached with your own vehicle or by taxi; it's about thirty minutes' drive from the main road and two hours from Van, followed by an hour's walk. The church overlooks the bay of Varış from a plateau 5km from the modern village of Altınsaç (formerly Ganjak); alternatively, a zigzag path (2hr) starts from Göründü village, which is quite close to the main road. It's also possible to visit **by boat from Akdamar** (3hr), though you would have to make arrangements at the Akdamar quay (see above) at an off-peak time of the day/week.

A monastery existed here as early as the tenth- and eleventh-century Vaspurakan heyday, when it was built to house supposed relics of the apostle to India, and was

occupied until the communal troubles of 1895. Most of the compound, enclosed in rectangular walls, is in ruins, though the church itself is still in good condition. Built to a cruciform plan, its sparsely decorated walls uphold a twelve-sided, capped drum; on the west is the building's glory, an extensive covered courtyard added late in the seventeenth century.

Edremit

On the road between Van and Gevaş, 15km southwest of Van, is the would-be resort of **EDREMIT**, a straggling lake-shore town with a few hotels and waterside tea gardens, much favoured by Van's barbecue fraternity at weekends. Dolmuşes run here hourly. It's possible to swim from Edremit's mixed sand and pebble **beaches** below the tea gardens.

Çavuştepe

The village of **ÇAVUŞTEPE**, 28km from Van on the Hakkari road and accessible by the Hakkari or Güzelsu dolmuş or bus, is the site of an **Urartian royal palace**, built between 764 and 735 BC by King Sardur II. To the right of the road is a long hill, on top of which the palace buildings once stood; a brown sign leads you up a single-track road to what remains of the ancient citadel.

The former warden is one of the few people in the world who can read, write and speak Urartian, and now lectures in the language at Van University. His son, the current warden, has mastered the basics of this dead language. If he is in attendance you should pay him an entrance fee (2YTL) plus a tip; he also has a few souvenirs and drinks for sale. He will lead you past some sunken grain-storage jars to a temple with a number of black basalt blocks covered with remarkably well-preserved cuneiform, which he can read and interpret impressively. There's also a sacrificial altar, several cisterns and even an ancient loo. Beyond here is the palace itself, but extensive excavations have failed to reveal anything much of its structure.

Hoşap Kalesi

Continuing along the Hakkari road from Çavuştepe, and 45km from Van, you pass the lake of Zernek Baraj, where the road winds just above water level. Over a small pass, and around 55km from Van, you arrive at the impressive medieval Kurdish fortress of **Hoşap Kalesi** (daily 8.30am–noon & 1.30–5pm; 2YTL), which towers above the squat modern village of Güzelsu (a Turkish translation of *Hoşap*, which is Kurdish for "beautiful water"). Dolmuşes heading for Güzelsu depart from the Sevimli office in the bazaar in Van, behind İş Bankası.

The fortress, an extraordinary, now half-ruined, flight of fancy, was constructed at the behest of Sarı Süleyman Mahmudı, a local Kurdish strongman, in the 1640s. According to legend, he was so pleased with the result when the castle was completed that he had the architect's hands lopped off, to ensure that he would never build another to rival it.

To reach the fortress, cross the river either by a bridge with alternate light and dark stone courses and a major inscription, dating from 1671, or a road bridge 100m further on, and follow a dirt track winding around to the far side of the hill. This will bring you to the **main entrance**, set in an immense round tower. If the caretaker is on hand he will let you in and relieve you of the entrance fee; if not, he will send his son running up from the village below. The entrance, above which are lion **reliefs**, a symbolic chain of power and a Persian inscription, opens into a tunnel leading to the interior of the fortress. Little is left of the original structures, which included a couple of mosques, three hamams and a *medrese*. The best-preserved part is the **keep** – reached by a path from the outer fortress. There is a cooling system built into the walls of the castle, and drainage pipes in the hamam below. Looking east from the fortress you can see the line of mud defensive-walls that once encircled the village: aeons of erosion have turned these battlements into a row of rounded plates, reminiscent of a line of browsing stegosauruses.

Yedi Kilise

About 10km east-southeast of Van, in the village of Yukarı Bakraşlı, are the remains of the once-grand monastery of the Holy Cross, founded in the seventh century and beautifully situated in the foothills of Erek Dağı. The locals know the village as **YEDI KILISE** (Seven Churches), or "Varaga Vank" in Armenian, as seven Armenian churches and the monastery once stood here. Unfortunately, most of the structures have been destroyed by earthquakes and vandals, but one remains behind the new village mosque; it has now been locked and you will be charged a small fee for access. This is the once-domed **church of St George**, conforming to a cruciform ground-plan, built or perhaps rebuilt during the thirteenth century. The porch is enlivened by intricate stone-carvings, and an arched stone portal with an Armenian inscription leads to the interior, which has retained traces of seventeenth-century frescoes and crosses carved into the walls. A trip here will also give you a glimpse of contemporary Kurdish village life.

The best way to reach Yedi Kilise is by **taxi from Van**. The taxi drivers outside the *Akdamar* hotel will take you there, find the key to the locked church, wait and bring you back, for around 24YTL.

Çarpanak

The well-preserved remains of the **monastery church of St John** are curiously set on the long, narrow island of **Çarpanak** (Ktuts in Armenian), 1.5km offshore from a promontory some 25km northwest of Van. You can rent a boat for the hour-and-a-half trip there from Van İskelesi (docks), but you need a Turkish speaker to bargain

– expect to pay 125YTL. Alternatively, you could chance your luck at Van İskelesi on a Sunday morning, when locals cross by boat to picnic. There is a huge gull colony on the island, so peace and quiet is not assured.

A monastery grew up here around a twelfth-century church at least as early as 1414, but a disaster befell it during the next century and the present church was heavily restored during the early 1700s. Despite this late date it's a handsome, rectangular compound, with a shallow dome sporting a pyramidal roof, though graffiti mars some of the walls.

Ayanış castle

Ayanış castle is a recently excavated Urartian fortification set on a typical hill-top site right above the lakeside north of Çarpanak. The only access is by private car; drive 20km north of Van on the main road, turn left at the signpost and, some 8km further on, turn right in the village of **Alaköy**; from here the unsurfaced road rises over hills and approaches the lake, veering right through a small settlement to the obvious hill-top site.

A trek to the hill-top is rewarded with views of **excavations** of the perimeter walls and an impressive central **temple** compound. The temple doorway bears a long cuneiform inscription in excellent condition on both sides of the main entrance.

Bahçesaray

The rural town of **BAHÇESARAY**, 106km southwest of Van, rates at least one TV mention every year, on the occasion of the reopening of the road over the Karabel Geçiti that links it to the outside world. At 2985m, this is the highest (unsurfaced) road-pass in Turkey and usually the last to open after the winter snow (May/June). Bahçesaray was once far more important than its present-day size would suggest, with a population of 12,000 over a century ago (three times today's size), and if you have two days to spare, the long (six-hour) bumpy journey here from Van is better than the trip to Hakkari (see p.916) for the variety of scenery, vegetation and birdlife on display, both up on the pass and in the nearly deserted countryside beyond. On the east slopes of the pass are seasonally scattered **encampments** (*zoma*) of Kurdish transhumant shepherds and their flocks, forming a colourful complement to the spectacular mountain scenery. The descent west from the pass plunges you down steep slopes towards villages hidden under canopies of walnuts and stands of poplars.

Entering the town, you pass attractive tea-gardens at the start of the single main street, which ends at a mosque and welcoming restaurant by the stream. Bahçesaray, still known to most of the locals by the Armenian name of Müküs, has the remains of a small Armenian church, called **Andzghonts**, lying on the eastern slopes above the town. Much damaged by fire in 1805, it still has *khatckars* (stones inscribed with crosses) visible in the exterior walls. Other pleasant diversions are an upstream walk to the underground source of the **Botan Çay**, a tributary of the Tigris and, a few kilometres downstream, a single-arched brick Selçuk bridge, the **Kızıl Köprü**. However, the Armenian monastery of **Aparank**, in the hills west of the Botan Çay, is impossible to find without a guide (and military permission).

Practicalities

A daily **dolmuş** (8YTL; bag the front seats) from Van leaves any time after 9am from the *Bahçesaray Çay Evi*, a small teahouse off Zübeyde Hanım Caddesi.

It's possible to stay the night in Bahçesaray at the local council **visitors' house** (*misafir evi*), which contains a couple of rooms with beds and blankets, and a small washroom; enquire at the **restaurant** by the stream, which – if you're interested – will also find a vehicle to take you to the Selçuk bridge.

If you are rash enough to wish to **drive to Bahçesaray**, enquire first at the Jandarma Hareket Merkezi outside Van (see p.895), fill up with petrol and, after Edremit, turn left and then right onto the Çatak road, then right to Aşağı and Yukarı Narlıça. At the time of writing there is a major **checkpoint** and barracks at Yukarı Narlıça; you may be asked to visit the commanding officer to explain yourself, and he has authority to turn you back.

Çatak

If you can't spare the two days needed to visit Bahçesaray, the large mountain village of **ÇATAK**, 40km south of Van, is a good alternative. Dolmuşes (4YTL) depart from a garage just below the Bahçesaray teahouse, hourly from 8am, and take one and a half hours; the last one back to Van departs at 5pm. The road from Van heads south into the mountains, passing the village of **Emlacı** with the remains of the Armenian church of Surb Tikin, and (5km short of Çatak), the popular picnic spot of **Kanispi**, where a cascade of white water spurts out of the mountainside. There's not much to see in the village bar the remnants of the once sizable Armenian church of St John the Baptist (the roofless interior now serves as a "walled" garden for local villagers) and the gushing headwaters of the Botan Çayı. There are no checkpoints on this road until you reach the village, but be careful not to stray off up the valley sides as this may incur the suspicion of the local military/police.

The route to Hakkari

The three- to four-hour bus or dolmuş trip to **Hakkari**, along the gorge of the Zab river, has spectacular mountain scenery, especially beyond the town of **Başkale**. Both the Çavuştepe and Hoşap Kalesi excursions from Van are off the Hakkari road and, with your own transport, could be visited en route.

Head south of Van on the Hakkari-signposted road, not the Gevaş shore road. After a few kilometres it starts to climb and, at an altitude of about 2260m, you traverse the Kurubaş pass. Some 5km beyond here the road forks: a right turn will point you towards the southern shore of Lake Van, while left continues towards Hakkari.

Başkale and around

Past the plains around Çavuştepe and the lake at Zernep, 45km southeast of Güzelsu, and lying at 2500m, **BAŞKALE** is the highest town in Turkey. South of here the **Zab gorge** is at its most spectacular and photogenic, but mainly inhabited by sheep and shepherds: look out for the quaint plank and wire bridges that enable the flocks to cross the river. Here and there tracks lead off to medieval-looking settlements, and you may well spot the odd transhumant encampment.

On the way to Başkale, 14km before town, a road leads northeast to the village of Albayrak, where you'll find the old Armenian **church of Surb Bartolomeos**. Once the focus of a monastery, it's now half-ruined, the roof and cupola collapsed, but retaining fine reliefs on what's left of the facade. The huge number of trucks operating on this road are smuggling petrol in from Iran, apparently tolerated by the authorities, provided no more than 500 litres are carried per trip. This area may still be restricted; enquire at Van's Jandarma Hareket Merkezi (see p.895) before you attempt to drive there.

Yüksekova and the Iranian border

Some 60km south of Başkale is **Yeni Köprü**; at the time of writing there is a major checkpoint where the road forks: right is to Hakkari, while a left turn in the direction of the yellow sign marked "İran" takes you 35km to **YÜKSEKOVA**. Before the insurrection, this was the favoured base for climbing in the 3794-metre **Sat** range and for **Reşko** (4135m), Turkey's third highest peak, in the Cilo range. From there, a side road continues to Dağlıca, base for trekking in the Sat mountains, where there is a ruined Armenian church.

From Yüksekova it is respectively 40km and 50km to Esendere and Şemdinli, and several kilometres beyond them to the **Iranian border-crossing points**. Foreigners require Iranian visas in order to cross (available in Ankara, İstanbul or before leaving home). Taxis are available at the border crossings, and the attitude to foreigners is now said to be quite friendly.

Hakkari and around

HAKKARI, 196km south of Van, is sited right in the Kurdish heartland, where the mountain ranges start to sweep down to the northern Iraqi plain. It's a sprawling building-site of a place, due to the influx of villagers forcibly evacuated from their outlying villages during the unrest. Trekking in the mountains – the main reason to come so far off the beaten track – remains off-limits for the foreseeable future.

Hakkari itself is dull. The only historic monument is the small square **Meydan Medresesi** in the lower town, just south of the petrol stations. This contains a collection of primitively carved prehistoric statues found in the locality, but to visit you'll have to get a key from the tourist office (see below).

Various points in town give striking views of Sumbul Dağı and, looming behind it, the 4135-metre Cilo range.

Practicalities

Buses and dolmuşes arrive outside the bus offices on the main street. Hakkari's **tourist office** (Mon–Fri 9am–noon & 1–5.30pm; ☎0544/ 211 6509) is opposite the Turk Telecom building in the sidestreet adjacent to the bus-company offices. The **PTT** is in another sidestreet, opposite the Atatürk statue.

For **accommodation**, the overpriced *Ümit Otel* (☎0438/ 211 2469; ❷) on Altay Caddesi, has a restaurant (though no breakfast) and clean rooms with patched-up bathrooms – get one with views of the mountains. On Bulvar Caddesi is the more expensive *Şenler Hotel* (☎0544/211 5512 or 5515, ☞211 3808; ❸), a three-star place with large rooms opening off rambling, marble corridors. The rooms and bathrooms are almost luxurious but breakfast does not live up to the promise of the decor. Below is a complex with hamam, sauna and hairdresser.

If you're looking for somewhere to **eat and drink**, try the *Derya Kebap Salonu*, where you'll find the usual lamb kebabs, beans and bread; the *Diyar 21 Ocakbaşı* near the tourist office also seems promising. The *Damla Pastanesi* does a wonderful breakfast and has an upstairs tearoom that serves ice cream as well as *baklava* and other sweets. There are several (smoky and slow) Internet cafés on the main drag.

Around Hakkari

Some 20km north of Hakkari is **Koçhanes** (Quodshanes on some maps), once the patriarchal seat of the Nestorian Christians (see box on p.918). Small and plain, save for some inscribed geometric designs around the doorway, the church is beautifully situated on a grassy spur high above the Zab valley. The church is best found with the help of a taxi driver from Hakkari, though he may not want to risk his car the whole way on the increasingly bad dirt-road, in which case you'll have to walk the last few kilometres. You would also be wise to get official clearance before setting out. The village around the church is in ruins (the roofs of the houses were destroyed by the army) but a couple of elderly watchmen and former residents tend vegetable plots here in the summer.

There are many other Nestorian churches scattered through the surrounding mountains, including one at Diz, in the Zab valley below Hakkari, and at Kursin, a tiny hamlet en route to the glacier at the foot of Reşko (4135m), the highest peak in the Cilo range. How many other Nestorian churches have survived the burning and levelling of the mountain hamlets by the security forces during the troubles remains to be seen.

Above Koçhanes lies **Berçelan** *zoma*, a huge, lush summer pasture. The area was briefly "reopened", but at the time of writing the *zoma* was once again off-limits due to renewed PKK activity, though a nearby village has been resettled. With

Nestorian Christians

The history of the **Nestorian Church** parallels that of the Syrian Orthodox Church in many ways, although their respective theological positions are completely opposed. **Nestorius**, bishop of Constantinople from 428 to 431, formulated a doctrine that held Christ to be predominantly human in nature and refused to recognize the term "Mother of God" as appropriate for the Virgin Mary. In 431, however, the Council of Ephesus declared his positions to be heretical. The works of Nestorius were burnt and he was deported to the Egyptian desert after suffering hideous tortures.

Despite his fate, Edessa (Şanlıurfa), Antioch (Antakya) and Nusaybin near Mardin became important Nestorian centres, though later the focus of the faith moved to Persia, where the Sassanid emperors officially encouraged it along with Zoroastrianism. After the Mongol attacks the Nestorians relocated again to the inaccessible Zagros mountains of western Iran, and to the equally remote area around present-day Hakkari in southeast Turkey. Isolated in the inaccessible mountains, the Nestorians developed their own ethnic as well as religious identity, with half the population organized into tribes little different from their Kurdish neighbours.

During the nineteenth century, however, serious rivalries developed between the Nestorians and the Kurds. This was due in no small part to the British and American missionaries who had infiltrated the region in search of easy converts. The missions aroused the distrust of the local Kurdish leaders, leading to the massacre of Nestorian men around Hakkari and the selling of the women and children into slavery. Their fate was sealed in 1915 when the Nestorian patriarch came out in support of the World War I Allies. When the Russians withdrew from the region in 1918, the Nestorians deemed it wise not to linger as targets for reprisal, but more than half their number perished anyway in the flight to Iran and Iraq. A short-lived attempt to resettle their mountain fastnesses was crushed by Atatürk in the early years of the Turkish Republic.

Today just a few tens of thousands survive in Iraq, Iran and Syria, with the patriarchate now in Chicago. There is also a small Nestorian church in Hanwell, West London. In modern times adherents of this sect are confusingly referred to as Assyrians, because – like the Syrian Orthodox – most surviving believers speak Syriac.

luck it, along with the other high-altitude pastures in these highlands, will soon be studded with black goat-hair tents from late spring (end of May) through to September. Close to the pastures is a small glacial lake and the 3752m peak of **Karadağ**, suitable for a day-hike and giving superb views across the Zab valley to the spectacular **Cilo-Sat** range of mountains. The Cilo-Sat are one of the last remaining strongholds of the *fritillaria imperialis* (misnamed in Turkish as *ters lale*, or upside-down tulip), a tall fritillary with a stunning head of hanging orange-red bell-like flowers. Bunches of them may be for sale in the street market in June.

West from Hakkari to Şırnak and Cizre

South and west of Hakkari, a **border road** runs between the Çukurca road and Şırnak, mainly just south of the mountainous massif. As this road is parallel to the Kurdish enclave in northern Iraq (and was built in order to police this volatile border) expect a heavy military presence. One **bus** from Hakkari runs every other day at some time after 8.30am, and takes about six hours (13YTL). A separate dolmuş runs at 8.30am on dirt roads for **Beytüşşebap**, an isolated village five hours away on the River Habur, but since there are no hotels or other facilities here, and no regular dolmuş service on to Uludere, there seems no real reason to go. It's also possible to get off the Şırnak bus at the Uludere junction and hitch the 7–8km into **Uludere** village, which has some shops, a teahouse and a bank or two, but again there is nowhere to stay and the police may encourage you to leave.

The border road runs parallel to the rapid-strewn Zab river for about 50km; at a major checkpoint the bus turns right instead of continuing to Çukurca, down on the border with Iraqi Kurdistan. From here, it rises over the Konaklı mountains to a beautiful pass at 2350m, and descends to a junction with the Beytüşşebap road in a gorge. The climate is noticeably warmer here than around Hakkari, with walnuts, poplars and even rice paddies in the valleys. The Egyptian vulture abounds, as do rolls of discarded razor-wire in the bushes.

Şırnak

An hour past Uludere is **ŞIRNAK**, perched on a hillside with views over Cudi Dağı. The town has two **hotels**; the primitive *Otel Menteşe* (no phone; ❶) has tiny rooms with bathroom and, if you can force the balcony door, views as far as Syria. Uphill, on Cumhuriyet Caddesi, the road into the town centre, is the slightly better *Hotel İlkar* (℡0486/216 6464, ℻216 4444; ❷), a modern building with large but already seedy rooms with TV, and a rooftop restaurant/breakfast terrace.

Around Cumhuriyet Caddesi are various **restaurants**, including the cheerful, clean *Merkez* and *Merkez II pide* and kebab joints, doing a lively trade. Nearer to the *Otel Menteşe* is the small, cheap *Dost Lahmacun* restaurant, with fresh salads and friendly service; do not make the mistake of eating at the *Menteşe*'s restaurant. The *Atatürk Park* **tea garden** in the town centre has extensive views of the vast cemetery and its blue irises, which dominates the southern slopes of the town. From the corner opposite the tea garden, **buses** leave to Siirt at 8.30am and to Cizre every hour until mid-afternoon. The Hakkari bus leaves from the Uludere road at 8.30am.

Cizre

In Kurdish tradition, the resting place of Noah's Ark is **Cudi Dağ**, a modest 2134m peak above the River Tigris and the town of **CIZRE**, near the point where the modern Turkish, Syrian and Iraqi frontiers meet. The only other reason to go to Cizre is to catch a bus to westward destinations such as Mardin and Diyarbakır. The town is a major truck-stop on the route to Iraq, so is well equipped with hotels, but foreigners are not normally permitted to cross the Habur border-gate into the Kurdish enclave in northern Iraq.

The road to Doğubeyazıt

Heading **northeast from Van**, the road skirts the lake until it branches north where the encircling mountains open out to a wide valley, which rises gradually from the lake towards the Iranian border. At the north end is the pass over the laval flows from the eruption of Mount Tendurek, with the first spectacular views of Mount Ararat. Between these two volcanoes on a major pass from Iran, is Doğubeyazıt (see below), starting point for any exploration of the Mount Ararat area.

It's three hours from Van to Doğubeyazıt by direct public transport, but it is possible to break your journey at the roadside waterfalls at **Muradiye**. Dolmuşes depart hourly from a sidestreet leading north off İskele Caddesi, 500m west of Beş Yol in Van, and from the northbound side of the main road in Tatvan. As long as

△ The Muradiye waterfalls

you don't tarry until late afternoon, it's pretty easy to pick up another northbound dolmuş to resume your journey; there are regular services between Muradiye and Çaldıran, a major bus garage, 26km further northeast and from Çaldıran to Doğubeyazıt.

If driving yourself, take the road signed "Ağrı" (D975) out of Van and turn right at the major junction north of the lake.

Muradiye waterfalls

The **Muradiye waterfalls** are signed on the west side of the main Doğubeyazıt road, some 20km north of the junction with the road from Tatvan and past the village of Muradiye, and are entered via a car park with ticket booth (1YTL). A wooden bridge gives good views of the frothing twenty-metre falls, and leads to a large café and kebab house on the far bank. From here there are **riverside walks** along the stream and through cool poplar woods. One kilometre south of the falls is an old bridge known as **Şeytan Köprüsü** (Devil's Bridge), spanning the deep gorge. The valley channels birds migrating north from Lake Van and hundreds of species, some rare, can be observed during a short period in May. In May/June, the fields around also contain two stunning examples of the region's **flora** – a huge chocolate-and-white coloured iris and a brilliant red *phelepya*.

Doğubeyazıt

Lying 185km northeast of Van, and with Iran just half an hour away, the dusty streets of **DOĞUBEYAZIT** are full of cross-border traders and even a few overland travellers en route to India. The rapidly modernizing town is the base for ascents of Mount Ararat and for visits to the fine old fortress of İshak Paşa Sarayı, set on a hill above. Thanks to its border position and largely Kurdish population, Doğubeyazıt is heavily militarized, with a huge army base just outside town on the road to İshak Paşa Sarayı.

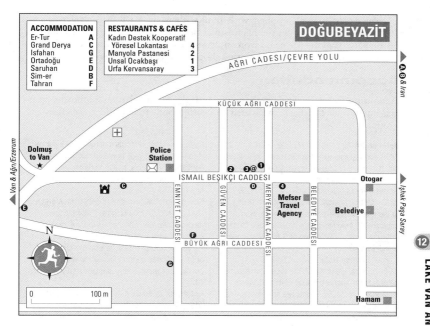

Arrival, information, services and tours

Dolmuşes drop you on the eastern side of town on Küçük Ağrı Caddesi (this road, with its southern extension, Büyük Ağrı Caddesi, is also known as the Çevre Yolu, or ring road); buses stop at the **otogar**, on the western side of the town centre.

There is no official tourist office, but the various **travel agents** and **bus companies** – mainly on Belediye Caddesi (south of the Atatürk statue) – will be able to tell you about transportation. Mefser Travel Agency on Belediye Caddesi (℡0472/312 6772) offers half- and full-day **tours** from €25, combining visits to the Iranian border, a meteor crater and a Kurdish village. It also arranges ascents of Ararat (see p.923).

On to Iran

Most people **enter Iran** on a week-long **transit visa** (issued to non-US citizens at major Iranian consulates on proof of a Pakistani visa), which most travellers then extend for up to a month upon arrival in a major Iranian town (Tabriz is a good choice, Tehran and Isfahan can be more problematic). It is generally better to get this visa in your home country as the Iranian consulates in İstanbul, Ankara and especially Erzurum have a reputation for being obstructive – eg, requiring a letter of invitation from Tehran, which can take two weeks to arrive and be processed. If your plans change at the last minute, the Mefser Travel Agency in Doğubeyazıt (see p.921) may be able to obtain the visa for you.

The **Iranian border** is at Gürbulak, 34km out southeast of Doğubeyazıt, accessible by a dolmuş from Ağrı Caddesi. You can obtain Iranian Riyals at the border; from there, take a taxi to Maku and then an onward Iranian bus to **Tabriz**. Travellers (especially women) should be aware of Iranian dress codes.

Doğubeyazıt is well supplied with **banks**, there's a **PTT** (Mon–Sat 8.30am–12.30pm & 1–5.30pm) on the main İsmail Beşikçi (Çarşı) Caddesi, and a **hamam** off Belediye Caddesi (men and women; from 6YTL). The best **Internet café** is the *Omega* on the second floor of a clothes shop opposite the *Hotel Saruhan*.

Accommodation

Accommodation in Doğubeyazıt is plentiful, catering largely to border traders, but several hotels are well used to hosting both independent travellers and groups.

Hotel Er-Tur Ağrı Cad ☏0472/312 7866, ⓕ312 7868. Clean place, with modern rooms with showers; the restaurant serves breakfast (included) and there's a good set-meal for 5YTL. ②

Grand Derya Çarşı Cad ☏0472/312 7531, ⓕ312 7833. Central, friendly place, almost next door to the mosque (so expect an early awakening), popular with trekking groups. Rooms are a little tatty, but there's a TV lounge with English-language broadcasts. ②

Isfahan Hotel Emniyet Cad 26 ☏0472/312 4363. The most atmospheric hotel in town, largely because of its dark wood, alpine-style bar/lobby. Rooms are spacious and the bed firm. Good value. ②

Hotel Ortadoğu Büyük Ağrı Cad 105 ☏0472/312 4225, ⓕ312 7702. Large, well-equipped and clean rooms with TV and fridge; some have views of Ararat. Very friendly management. ②

Hotel Saruhan Çarşı Cad ☏0472/311 3097. Best option at the budget end of the scale, with clean, basic but carpeted rooms (charged at €2 per bed if you share) and a 24-hr electric shower; breakfast not included. Owners, Nesim Saruhan and his brother Fetuh, speak English and organize local day-tours. ①

Sim-er Hotel 5km east of Doğubeyazıt, Ararat road ☏0472 /312 4842, ⓕ312 4843. A low, modern hotel with attached restaurant, much used by tour groups. For those with their own transport, it's very tempting – gardens with morning views of Mount Ararat, comfortable rooms with TV and gushing hot water, and generous buffet breakfasts. ③

Hotel Tahran Büyük Ağrı Cad124 ☏0472/312 0195, ⓦwww.eastturkey.com. Despite the cramped toilets, scruffy carpets and absence of breakfast, this is a good-value budget option, with friendly management, free Internet access and comfortable beds. Some rooms have Ararat views. ①

Eating and drinking

For **breakfasts and desserts**, try the *Manyola Pastanesi*, Dr İsmail Beşikçi Cad 78, with a large selection of sweets and savouries, and a swish *aile salonu* upstairs. For the most part Doğubeyazıt has run-of-the-mill **restaurants** without a great deal of variety, but the *Unsal Ocakbaşı*, Meryemanna Cad 18, is recommended as the best place to celebrate an ascent of Ağrı, with huge "cook your own" grills costing 6.5YTL a head. The *Urfa Kervan Sarayı* at Dr İsmail Beşikçi Cad 64, dishes up decent *sulu yemek* at lunchtimes for 2.5TL a portion, and kebabs for 5YTL; if the weather's good, head for the pleasant rooftop terrace, with partial views of Ararat. For home cooking, try the *Kadın Destek Kooperatif Yöresel Lokantası*, above a shop on Dr İsmail Beşikçi Caddesi; a women's co-operative, it's ideal for solo women and serves delicious *pide* and *köfte* for a bargain 3YTL.

İshak Paşa Sarayı

Six kilometres southeast of Doğubeyazıt, the **İshak Paşa Sarayı** (Tues–Sun 8am–5pm; 5YTL), is a half-ruined seventeenth-century palace set on a 2000-metre-high plateau overlooking the town. The designer seems to have taken elements from every architectural style extant in Anatolia and incorporated them into the palace's construction: Selçuk, Ottoman, Armenian, Georgian and Persian influences are all clearly evident.

A fortress was constructed here in Urartian times, later the Selçuks and Ottomans built castles to control east–west traffic on the Silk Route. The palace itself, more Xanadu pleasure-dome than military stronghold, was begun in 1785 by Çolak Abdı Paşa, a local chieftain of uncertain (Kurdish, Armenian or Georgian) background, and completed by his son, İshak Paşa, in the nineteenth century. According to legend, the Armenian architect had his hands amputated once he'd completed the work to prevent him from building anything else as magnificent. Another legend asserts that the palace originally had 366 rooms, one for every day of a leap year. By 1877 the complex was already in decline, being used by the Turkish army as a barracks; subsequent periods of Russian occupation set the seal on its decay.

In recent years the complex has been overrestored by the Culture Ministry, and has lost some of its charm.

The palace

You enter via a grandiose **gateway**, which once boasted gold-plated doors: the Russians removed these in 1917 during their retreat from Anatolia, and they're now on show at the Hermitage Museum in St Petersburg. From the outer courtyard, an ornately carved portal leads to a smaller, inner courtyard. Straight ahead of you is the harem entrance, while to the right is the entrance to the *selamlık* or men's quarters. The **tombs** of İshak Paşa and his favourite wife stand in a *türbe* in one corner of the inner court.

The **harem** contains fourteen fireplace-equipped bedrooms (in which four hundred soldiers were quartered in 1877) overlooking the valley below, a kitchen and two circular bathrooms. At its centre is a colonnaded dining hall.

The *selamlık* also contains a library, bedrooms and a fine **mosque**, retaining much of its original relief decoration and ceiling painting. You can reach the roof of the chambers adjoining the mosque, giving fine views of the domes and points of the skyline. Across the valley is a mosque dating from the reign of Selim I, who defeated the Persians at the battle of Çaldıran (70km south of Doğubeyazıt) in 1514, and a much older fortress dating from Urartian times. The visible remains, however – excepting an Assyrian relief – are more recent. The foundations on the plain below are all that's left of Eski Beyazıt (Old Beyazıt), a city founded by the Urartians. It was inhabited until 1930, when – in the wake of an unsuccessful local Kurdish rebellion – the place was forcibly depopulated and the new Doğu (East) Beyazıt founded in its present location.

Practicalities

To reach the İshak Paşa Sarayı take a **taxi** from Doğubeyazıt's Atatürk statue for about 10YTL return (this includes waiting time). If you're visiting out of season, ask your hotel or a travel agency to confirm opening times, as these can sometimes be a little erratic. There's a teahouse/snack bar above the entrance gate and a basic **campsite** (*Murat Camping*) on the road below the palace, charging about €2 a tent, with a **restaurant** and washing facilities.

Mount Ararat

Few mountains west of the Himalayas have as compelling a hold on Western imagination as **Mount Ararat** (Ağrı Dağı in Turkish). And for once this huge volcano

– where Noah's Ark supposedly came to rest – manages to deliver that promise in reality. There are two peaks; the larger, 5165m one, is known as **Büyük Ağrı** and the lesser cone, measuring 3925m, is **Küçük Ağrı**. Traditionally, Armenian monks considered Mount Ararat holy and nobody was allowed to climb it, so it was not until 1829 that Dr Johann Jacob Parrot, a German academic, conquered the peak. Numerous other ascents have followed, but even today some villagers believe that it's not possible to climb the mountain, and Turkish officials did not allow it until the 1950s.

Despite the efforts of American astronaut James Irwin and others, no reliable trace of Noah's Ark has so far been found – not too surprisingly given the centuries-long effects of lava and glaciers on wood. Locals however insist that the oval mound of earth spotted by a Turkish airforce pilot on a routine flight over the region is the real thing, and the "Ark", complete with visitors centre, is routinely included in tours of the area. Ararat of course may simply be the wrong place to look. The passage in Genesis 8:4, which reported the Ark coming to rest on the "mountains of Ararat" is prone to misinterpretation; Ararat was the Assyrian rendition of Urartu, an ancient empire – and by extension, geographical area – extending quite far south of Lake Van as well as north. Mount Ararat is still sacred to the Armenians, who must be content to gaze at it on rare clear days from their capital, Erevan.

Access to Mount Ararat

Unfortunately, the mountain lies in a sensitive military zone, adjoining both the Armenian and Iranian frontiers, and was also a focal point for PKK insurgency. The mountain was out of bounds for several years; it is now open, though on a strict permit-only basis.

Many local touts and companies will advise you that they can **obtain a permit** immediately; this is not true and you risk the loss of your deposit at best and, at worst, arrest, if you take their advice. Conditions of granting a permit include the provision of a recognized guide, so you need to apply at least two months in advance through a registered tourism **agency** offering treks. Permits are processed by the Tourism Ministry and, through them, by the local military and civil authorities and it is not possible to shortcut the process. The Mefser agency in Doğubeyazıt (see p.921) charges around €400 per person for the trip. The main **climbing season** is from June to September, so if you intend to be in the area during this time and would like to join a climbing group, then you should start to plan several months in advance. See ⓦ www.mountainsofturkey.org, for current information.

Necessary **equipment** includes good winter-trekking gear (snow goggles, hat, gloves, down jacket, winter boots, gaiters, crampons and ice axe, plus four-season sleeping bag and mat); you are hardly likely to have this lot with you on a normal holiday and although it may be possible to rent some of it from your trekking firm, you definitely need your own boots. The major problem on the trek is dehydration – caused by altitude and lack of fresh water supplies, not altitude sickness; make sure your company has adequate means to supply you with several litres per day.

The ascent

Currently, ascents are only permitted from the **southwest side** of the mountain; the other faces are sensitively close to Armenia and Iran. **Treks** are normally of five to six days' duration, allowing for acclimatization and two attempts at the summit, and are supported up to Camp 2 by mules. The usual starting point is **Eli**, a village on the southern slopes of Büyük Ağrı, a little over 10km north of Doğubeyazıt.

From here you head up to **Camp 1** (3200m) at the base of the mountain proper; reckon on an afternoon start to reach this camp by nightfall.

After this **Camp 2**, at 4200m, is a strenuous half-day's march above, so it's wisest to halt the rest of the day there and avoid the risk of altitude sickness. From Camp 2, a dawn start is needed to reach the summit before cloud cover becomes too thick. At around 4900m the stones give way to permanent snowpack and then glacier, where crampons are necessary. Winds can be strong here and your company should have means of roping you together. In the past, most climbers have reached the main summit four hours or so after leaving Camp 2, and the views on a clear day are stupendous, compensating for the hard slog of the ascent.

A ski resort is under construction on the **north side** of the mountain, accessed by a right turn on the road to Iğdır about 15km north of Doğubeyazıt. This may in future provide another starting point for the ascent. Finally, if you ever have the opportunity, ascend from the **northeast flank** of the mountain, using the town of Aralık as a jump-off point – this way at least you may see some ruined Armenian monuments, dramatic evidence of the last (1840) eruption, and a lake, Köp Gölü.

Travel details

Trains

Kurtalan (Siirt) to: Diyarbakır (daily; 2hr 30min); İstanbul (4 weekly at 8.15am; 39hr) via Malatya (10hr), Kayseri (22hr) and Ankara (32hr).
Tatvan to: İstanbul (Tues & Thurs at 7am; 40hr); Tehran (Wed at 10am; 28hr).
Van to: Tehran (Wed at 2pm; 24hr).

Buses and dolmuşes

Doğubeyazıt to: Ağrı (every 30min; 2hr); Ankara (1 daily at 1pm; 16hr); Erzurum (10 daily; 4hr 30min); Iğdır (every 30min; 45min); Kars via Iğdır (every 30min; 4hr); Van (4 daily; 3hr).
Hakkari to: Beytüşşebap (1 daily; 5hr); Şırnak (1 every other day; 8hr); Van (3 daily; 3–4hr); Yuksekova (15 daily, 1hr).
Siirt to: Kurtalan (1hr before train; 30min); Batman (1 daily; 2hr); Diyarbakır (1 daily; 5hr); Van (1 daily; 4hr).
Şırnak to: Hakkari (1 every other day; 8hr); Siirt (4 daily; 3hr 30min); Cizre (hourly; 30min).

Tatvan to: Ahlat (every 45min; 30min); Bitlis (hourly; 30min); Ercis (2 daily; 2hr), Diyarbakır (5 daily; 4hr); Van (5 daily; 3hr).
Van to: Ağrı (every 30min; 5hr); Ankara (12 daily; 22hr); Diyarbakır (6 daily; 7hr); Doğubeyazıt (3 daily; 3hr); Erzurum (4 daily; 7hr); Hakkari (hourly in daylight hours; 3–4hr); Şanlıurfa (6 daily; 9hr); Tatvan (5 daily; 3hr); Trabzon (2 daily; 15hr).

Ferries

Tatvan to: Van and vice versa (2 daily; 4hr).

Flights
Turkish Airlines
Ağrı to: Ankara (3 weekly; 1hr 35min).
Van to: Ankara (1 daily; 1hr 35min); İstanbul (2 daily; 2hr 10min).
Atlas Jet
Van to: Antalya via İstanbul (6 weekly; 6hr 10min); İstanbul (6 weekly; 2hr 10min); İzmir via İstanbul (6 weekly; 3hr 30min).

Contexts

Contexts

The historical framework

S o many cultures and states have held sway on the Anatolian peninsula that a thorough unravelling of its past would demand scholars of comparative religion, linguistics and archeology as well as historians. The present-day Turkish Republic is just the core remnant of a vast, late-medieval empire, which at its zenith extended from the Indian Ocean almost to the Atlantic – and all of these realms contributed personalities and events. What follows is only the barest outline of a complex subject.

The earliest cultures

Discoveries in the heart of modern Turkey – the region known historically as Anatolia or Asia Minor – suggest that there has been settled habitation since the eighth millennium BC, among the oldest on earth. The **earliest finds**, including cave deposits in the region of Antalya, and surface finds from the Ankara and Hatay regions, prove that Anatolia was inhabited in the Paleolithic Age. More extensive discoveries from the **Neolithic** period include entire farming communities, of which the best known is **Çatal Höyük** near Konya (c.6500–5650 BC), demonstrating that early settlers lived in sizable villages surrounded by defensive walls. Their tools were made from local obsidian and flint; pottery was beautifully burnished, and included stylized figures representing the Mother Goddess.

Oriental influence brought southeast Anatolia into the **Chalcolithic Age**. The commercial and technical interaction of cultures is particularly noticeable in pottery types and the use of metal tools; shared features are found from Upper Mesopotamia and northern Syria. Sites of this period were more like fortified towns, and frequent evidence of violent destruction suggests that they regularly waged war with each other or with new arrivals. In central Anatolia and the west Anatolian lakeland there was less influence from the east; cultures that developed here are characterized by bright, burnished pottery and idols of local deities.

The third-millennium BC **Bronze Age** witnessed the rise of local dynasties, and the organization of land resources by communities inhabiting fortified settlements. The sophisticated metal equipment found in the royal cemetery of **Alacahöyük** suggests metallurgy was one of the principal reasons for the rise of the early Anatolian kings. Religious art included standards crowned with highly stylized deer and bulls; hoards of gold jewellery as well as musical instruments were prominent among the finds. It is thought that the Alaca dynasty originated in northeast Anatolia, since their culture shares features of those in the Caucasian and Pontic zones.

Meanwhile, on the south and west **coasts**, trade was becoming increasingly important. On the Aegean, **Troy** was in trading contact with the Aegean islands and mainland Greece, and with other Anatolian rulers in the southeast, around present-day Tarsus and Mersin. Anatolian metals, jewellery, weapons and tableware were exported in exchange for exotic goods such as lapis lazuli, rock crystal and ivory. The material advantages of a coastal situation, which provided maritime contacts with the Aegean and the Orient (particularly Syrian trading ports), are obvious from the comparative wealth amassed by the rulers of cities like Troy, for example the so-called "Treasure of Priam", a third-millennium hoard of jewellery and tableware discovered in the late nineteenth century.

The **Middle and Late Bronze Ages**, during the second millennium BC, began with a period of violent destruction and turbulence, out of which a race of people known as the **Hatti** emerged in central Anatolia, whose culture was later to be assimilated by the Hittites. This was an age of highly systematic commerce along fixed trading routes, and many Anatolian cities were annexed by colonies of Assyrian business agents. Their meticulous records have been discovered in many places, including the most famous of all these trade centres, Karum near Kanesh (modern Kültepe) in south central Anatolia. Textiles and tin were the main imports, and the principal export was copper; ornamental pottery for local use was skilfully crafted.

The Hittites

The first truly major civilization to emerge in Anatolia was that of the **Hittites**. Moving into Hatti territory, they seem to have first appeared around 2000 BC, but their so-called "Old Kingdom" is reckoned to have been founded by King Labarnas between 1700 and 1600 BC. The capital at Hattuşaş was created by his son and successor, Hattusilis I, remaining a power to be reckoned with until 1200 BC.

Hattuşaş was a huge city for its time, the kings residing in a citadel located on a rock overlooking a gorge; within were domestic quarters, administrative buildings, storage units and archives. The Hittite artistic style was a direct outgrowth of Anatolian predecessors and, unlike Syrian art, was never overwhelmed by Mesopotamian and Egyptian conventions. The principal examples are enormous rock-cut reliefs, including warrior gods and stylized sphinx-like beings, adapted from the Egyptian tradition.

While the warlike, imperialist nature of the Hittite rulers left an enduring impression on a previously non-aggressive Anatolia, the Hittites are also known for the humanity of their constitution and religion, and for a highly developed sense of ethics. Diplomacy was preferred to warfare, and often cemented by royal marriages. Libraries, archives and bureaucracy all had their place in Hittite society, and rulers were not despotic but tied to a constitution like their subjects. The Old Kingdom dynasty lasted several generations before being riven, apparently by succession struggles; after a confused interlude, the state was re-established as the Hittite Empire by Tudhaliyas II, in about 1430 BC. By this time a rival power had arisen in Upper Mesopotamia. The Mitanni, ruled by an Indo-European dynasty, were basically East Anatolian Hurrians. They exerted an important cultural influence on the Hittite Empire before being defeated in battle by the Hittite ruler Suppiluliumas (1385–1345 BC).

Under Muwatallis, the Hittites confirmed their military strength at the battle of Kadesh (1290 BC), where they defeated the Egyptians under Ramses II. After the battle, friendship between the two dynasties was cemented by the division of Syria and by the marriage of Ramses II to a daughter of another Hittite ruler, Hattusilis III, in 1250 BC. The real threat to both, however, lay with the arrival of the **"Sea Peoples"**, early Iron Age merchants from the Greek archipelagos and mainland, which was to have widespread repercussions.

The land-bound Hittite Empire was surrounded by **smaller states**. The southern and western coasts were inhabited by tribes of Indo-European stock, with their own kings, languages and feuds, and a major interest in sea-borne trade. In the southeast Mediterranean, the land later known as Cilicia was taken from the Hittites by Hurrians, and referred to as Kizzuwadna. They remained closely related to the Hittites, however, with regular intermarriage between the respective ruling families.

On the west coast, a greater degree of independence on the part of local dynasties meant that their activities were not well documented in Hittite records, but excavations at the site of Troy show that, simultaneous with the apogee of Hittite power, Troy was being rebuilt by a new dynasty, and great supplies were amassed inside the large citadel. The second-millennium Trojans were serious rivals to the Greeks in the Aegean, and Troy was ultimately sacked by the Greeks around 1200 BC in the **Trojan War**, at about the same time that the Hittite Empire finally collapsed.

The post-Hittite era

Identical factors can ultimately account for the demise of both civilizations: migrations, invasions and sudden increased pressures from all sides. New tribes, of Indo-European origin, poured into Anatolia from east and west. The Hittite capital and other centres of Hittite rule were attacked and burnt as Anatolia entered a long cultural Dark Age.

Small city-states were founded in the southeast by the surviving Hittites and their Anatolian allies, and these **Neo–Hittite** centres, for instance at Malatya, Sakça Gözü and Karatepe, managed to salvage something of the old culture. Neo-Hittite culture was important as a bridge between the Bronze and Iron Ages, rescuing Hittite traditions and at the same time creating lively trading centres for the Greek **Iron Age** merchants. Thus early Greek art was confronted by Hittite reliefs and statuary, and knowledge of oriental mythology and religion was also transmitted to Greece via the Neo-Hittites. The Neo-Hittite city-states were finally conquered and destroyed by the Arameans and the Assyrians in the eighth century BC.

To the east, in the region which was later to be known as Armenia, the kingdom of **Urartu** was founded by a people thought to be descendants of the native Anatolian Hurrian race. Their cities, including the capital at Tushpa near Lake Van, were well engineered, with walled citadels and elaborate tunnel systems for escape or survival under attack. The Urartians extended their power into central Anatolia and northern Syria, before they were curbed, in the second half of the eighth century BC, by the Assyrians. The Urartians specialized in metalwork, and their bronzeware was traded as far away as Greece.

To the west, a new tribe of immigrants who attained some prominence in the eighth century BC, especially under their most famous king, Midas, were the **Phrygians**. Their capital was at Gordion, on a strategic east–west trading route, by the River Sangarius (today the Sakarya). **King Midas**, according to Greek tradition, had a Greek wife and dedicated a throne at the sanctuary of Delphi. His kingdom reached its height during his rule, around 725 BC, but when Cimmerian horsemen looted and burned Gordion, he is said to have committed suicide in despair, and the Phrygian kingdom came to an abrupt end.

The southwest coast was inhabited during the Iron Age by the **Lycians**, probably the survivors of a nation of sailors and pirates referred to as the "Lukka" in Bronze Age records. Their language and culture had a local pedigree, suggesting that they were descendants of native Anatolian Luvians. Their architecture – timber forms copied in stone – was strikingly unique. Greek influence on the Lycians is attested to in the Bronze Age by the legend of Bellerophon and the Chimera, and by the later importance of the cult of Apollo, Artemis and their mother Leto.

The country of the **Lydians** was an inland district of western Anatolia, its capital at Sardis in the Hermus valley. The Lydians survived the Bronze Age with a language of Anatolian derivation, emerging from the turmoil of the eighth century BC to dominate western Anatolia, including areas that had previously been Phrygian. Lydian ivories, textiles, perfumes and jewellery were exported to Greece and the East, and their refined and elegant art forms influenced those of Greek Ionia and even Persia.

The Persians and Alexander

Lydian power lasted until 546 BC, when their last king, **Croesus**, was defeated by the newly ascendant **Persian Empire** under **Cyrus**. Over the next half-century, the Persians subdued the Greek coastal trading colonies as well as the entire interior, ending the last vestiges of Anatolian self-rule. **Satraps** (compliant local puppets) were installed in various seats of power and obliged to pay tribute to the self-styled "Great King" of the Persians; even more rankling was the fact that Persian allies, such as the Phoenicians, were favoured at the expense of the Greek Anatolian cities in their role as commercial intermediaries with the West. In 499 BC, western Anatolia, under the leadership of Miletus, **revolted** against Persian rule, but in the absence of massive aid from mainland Greece, the rebellion was doomed to fail.

Enraged by even the token support of the Athenians for the rebels, **Darius I** and his successor **Xerxes** crossed into Greece proper and were soundly defeated at the famous land battles of Marathon and Plataea, and the sea engagements of Salamis and Mykale, the latter in the straits between Samos and Anatolia. This blunting of Persian strength initially availed the cities of Asia Minor little, though as time went on they were able to exploit the growing rivalry between Athens and Sparta to negotiate a bit more autonomy. Indeed, by the middle of the fourth century BC, some virtually independent dynasties had arisen in western Anatolia, the most notable being the **Hecatomnid** clan at Halicarnassus, whose more illustrious rulers included the Hellenizing **Mausolus** (377–353 BC), and his wife and successor **Artemisia II**.

In spring 334 BC, a new power swept out of Macedonia and across Asia Minor: **Alexander**, later "the Great", possessed of little other than a guiding vision and some Corinthian volunteers to supplement his small Macedonian army. Having crossed the Dardanelles near present-day Çanakkale, he quickly defeated the Persians and proceeded down the west coast via all of the major cities, treating them with lenience or harshness depending on whether or not they rallied to his standard. Having wintered in Lycia, Alexander and his juggernaut rolled on across Pamphylia, inland to Gordion where he cut the eponymous knot with his sword, then crossed the Toros range into coastal Cilicia, intent on attacking the Persian heartland beyond Syria. **Darius III** awaited Alexander at **Issus** (modern Dörtyol), but was soundly defeated by the Macedonians, despite outnumbering them two to one. This conquest of Anatolia in less than a year was indicative as much of rottenness at the core of Persian rule as it was of Alexander's military genius.

The prodigy swept on through Persia proper as far as the Indus valley, but died of a fever – or possibly poisoning – at Babylon on the return trip, in 323 BC. Following his death, Alexander's generals divided the vast Anatolian empire between them: **Lysimachus** took the west, while **Seleucus** – succeeded by **Antiochus** – received most of the southeast of the peninsula; much of the centre and north remained independent. Lysimachus's most important successor was **Philetarus**,

who contrived to keep the treasure of Pergamon intact and made it the greatest Hellenistic city of Asia Minor. By the end of the second century BC, however, his heir **Attalus III** virtually invited the Romans into Anatolia by dying without issue, having willed the kingdom of Pergamon to them.

Roman rule

Almost immediately Roman power in Asia Minor was challenged by **Mithridates of Pontus** (ruled 110–63 BC), a brilliant, resourceful polymath and unscrupulous opponent. From 89 BC on, his rebellious campaigns kept an assortment of Roman generals occupied, most notably Sulla, Lucullus and Pompey. In 72 BC, at a low point in his fortunes, Mithridates sought refuge at the court of Tigranes the Great of **Armenia**, whose kingdom had enjoyed three decades of regional power and prosperity; this now came to an end as the Romans invaded Armenian territory in response to Tigranes' cooperation with Mithridates. It suited the Romans to maintain Armenia as a buffer principality between themselves and the **Parthians** on the east, successors to the Persian Empire. The accession of the first emperor Augustus marked the start of fairly durable peace in Anatolia proper, though the eastern frontier would always be problematic.

In general, Anatolia prospered under Roman imperial rule, as witness the vast quantity of ruined cities dating from this period, especially those endowed during the reign of **Hadrian** (117–138 AD). Politically, however, it always remained a backwater, with only the ethnographic and geographic comments of such writers as Strabo and Pliny to flesh out life here – as well as the first-century AD biblical writings of **St Paul** during his various evangelical tours of Asia Minor.

In 284 AD, the emperor **Diocletian** attempted a solution to pressing imperial problems by dividing the empire into two administrative units, each ruled by an emperor (or *Augustus*) acting in concert with a designated successor (or *Caesar*), together comprising the so-called tetrarchy. Early in the fourth century, however, this system collapsed into civil war. The victor, **Constantine**, moved the headquarters of the eastern portion from Salonica to the minor, but strategically located, ancient Greek town of **Byzantium**, on the western shores of the Bosphorus straits linking the Black Sea and the Sea of Marmara. This new capital was consciously rebuilt in imitation of Rome and presently renamed **Constantinople** in the emperor's honour. Soon afterwards Constantine announced his sympathy with Christianity, which by the end of the century became the state religion of an empire that had long persecuted Christians.

The unity of the empire, too unwieldy to be governed from a single centre, did not survive much beyond the forceful rule of Constantine. **Theodosius the Great**, during whose 379–395 reign paganism was officially proscribed, was the last sovereign of a united empire, which upon his death was formally **divided** into two realms: the western one Latin-speaking and Rome-based, the eastern part Greek-speaking and focused on Constantinople.

The Byzantine Empire

The western provinces had always been financially dependent on the east, and ineffective rule in the west meant that it could not easily survive the loss of this revenue – or the invasions of "barbarian" tribes from the north. The wealthier, more densely populated **Byzantine Empire** – as the east came to be known – had abler rulers and more defensible frontiers. But internal **religious disputes** would contribute heavily to weakening this empire. Rule from Constantinople was resented in the southern and eastern border provinces of Egypt, Palestine, Syria and Armenia, not only because the indigenous cultures were so different from Classical Greece and Rome, but also because the churches in these areas embraced the **Monophysite doctrine**, which maintained that Christ had a single divine nature. Until the thirteenth century clerics in the capital would persecute the "heretics" on the periphery, at the same time resenting claims to papal supremacy in Rome and quarrelling over points of belief with the west. All this would ultimately culminate in the formal separation of the eastern **Orthodox** and western **Roman Catholic** churches in 1054.

Byzantium's response to the collapse of the west, brought on by the "barbarian" raids of the fifth and sixth centuries, was vehement and expansionist – or more accurately, nostalgic. The energetic emperor **Justinian** (527–565) and his empress Theodora attempted to recapture the glory and territory of ancient Rome in a series of military campaigns throughout the Mediterranean basin. The imperial generals Belisarius and Narses reabsorbed Italy, North Africa and southern Spain into the empire, though the Byzantines were unable to stem the flow of Slavs into the Balkans, and were forced to adopt an uneasy truce with the Persian Empire after a long and inconclusive war.

After the quelling of the **Nika revolt** in 532, Justinian was also able to carry out an ambitious domestic agenda. He inaugurated a widespread programme of construction and public works, particularly in Constantinople, which resulted in such masterpieces as the church of **Aya Sofya** in the capital and San Vitale in Ravenna. Justinian's streamlining and codification of the huge and often contradictory body of old Roman **law** was perhaps his most enduring achievement: the new code became the basis for the medieval legal systems of France, Germany and Italy.

Justinian's reign marked the definitive emergence of a strictly Byzantine, as opposed to Roman, identity, with institutions that were to sustain the empire for the rest of its life. Having widened its boundaries to their maximum extent and established the theocratic nature of Byzantium, he can be reckoned one of the greatest of Byzantine emperors. In the long run, though, many of his achievements proved ephemeral, and so exhausted the empire's resources that it had difficulty withstanding subsequent outside attacks.

Later Byzantium and decline

In the two centuries following Justinian's death the character of the empire changed radically. All of his peripheral conquests were lost: the western realms to the Lombards and Goths, the southeastern provinces in the seventh century to the Persians and Arab raiders. By 711, the Byzantine Empire consisted only of the Balkan coasts, parts of Italy, and **Anatolia**, which would henceforth be the most important part of the empire. Equally significant, the empire had acquired a strongly Greek character, both linguistically and philosophically, and Latin influence faded as relations with Rome worsened.

It was only from 867 onward that the empire regained any of its old resilience. The so-called **Macedonian** dynasty, founded by **Basil I**, a former stable-boy who rendered Justinian's law code into Greek, reversed Byzantium's fortunes. Under **Basil II** (976–1025), nicknamed "Bulgar-Slayer" for his ruthless campaigns against the Slavs, the empire again swelled its frontiers well into present-day eastern Turkey and up the Balkan peninsula, while Constantinople itself enjoyed unparalleled prosperity at the crossroads of the new Eurasian trade routes. Literature and the arts flourished, and missionaries converted many Balkan Slavs to the Orthodox Church.

After the reign of the second Basil, however, the empire began its **final decline**, slow but relentless over the course of four centuries. For the first six decades of the new millennium, Anatolia was in a state of virtual **civil war**, with the clique of civilian bureaucrats in Constantinople pitted against the caste of landed generals out in the countryside. Each promoted their own candidates for the throne, resulting in a succession of nonentities as emperors, amenable to manipulation by either faction, and utterly unequal to the outside threats the empire would soon face. Simultaneously the Orthodox patriarchate renewed its **vendetta against the Monophysite churches**, whose members were concentrated in the critical eastern borderlands. The warlords reduced the free peasantry to serfdom, eliminating the main source of revenue and military recruitment; the bureaucrats, usually in control at Constantinople, matched their own extravagance with stinginess toward the army – increasingly staffed by unreliable mercenaries.

The first major threats came from the west. The **Normans**, their greed excited by the reputation of Byzantine craftsmanship and splendour, invaded the Balkans late in the eleventh century, and were only repulsed with help from the **Venetians**, who in return demanded extensive trading concessions within the empire – as did the **Genoese**. Government tolls and taxes plummeted as imperial monopolies were broken by the new Latin maritime powers, and western covetousness – which would culminate in the sacking of Constantinople by the Fourth Crusade in 1204 – knew no bounds. Though able emperors did emerge from the twelfth-century **Komnenos** dynasty and the later **Paleologos** line, without consistent western aid the Byzantines were doomed to fight a long, rearguard action against enemies from the east and north. The imperial twilight was distinguished by a final flourishing of sacred art and architecture, as Anatolia and the Balkans were adorned with numerous beautiful **churches,** which were this period's main contribution to posterity.

The arrival of the Turks

Early in the eleventh century a new people began raiding Byzantine territory from the east. They had originally emerged in Mongolia during the seventh or eighth century, a shamanistic, nomadic bunch whom the Chinese called "Tu-kueh" or *Dürkö* – **Turks** to the West. Driven by drought and population pressure to seek new pastures, the Turkish tribes began migrating westward, encountering the Arabs by the ninth century. The latter, recognizing their martial virtues, recruited them as auxiliaries and began converting them to Islam, a process mostly completed by the tenth century.

One branch of the Turkish tribes, followers of the chieftain **Selçuk**, adopted a settled life and **Sunni** Islam, setting down roots in Baghdad. The majority, however, referred to by the catch-all label of "Turcoman", remained nomadic and heterodox in belief, drawing on the **Shi'ite and pagan** heritages, and rarely amenable to control by any state. The Selçuk rulers took advantage of their warrior zeal by diverting them from their own realms into those of the Byzantines.

The raiders penetrated as an advance guard deep into Byzantine Armenia, and it was as much to restrain them as to confront the Byzantines that the Selçuk ruler Alparslan marched north from Baghdad in **1071**. Meeting, almost accidentally, the motley, demoralized armies of Byzantine emperor Romanus IV Diogenes, he defeated them easily at **Manzikert**. The Selçuks didn't follow up this victory, but it did leave the way open to redoubled rampages by the Turcomans across all of Anatolia. The Byzantines, alternately menaced and assisted by Latin crusaders, managed to reoccupy the western third of Anatolia, plus the Black Sea and Mediterranean coasts, as of the mid-twelfth century, by which time the Selçuks had established a state in the area devastated by the unruly Turcomans. This was the **Sultanate of Rum**, with its capital at Konya (Iconium). After winning the battle of **Myriokephalo**, nearby, in 1176, the new Selçuk state came to terms with the Byzantines.

After the occupation of Constantinople by the **Fourth Crusade** in 1204, the Selçuks continued their good relations with the provisional Byzantine Empire based at Nicaea; with peace assured, the Sultanate of Rum evolved into a highly cultured mini-empire at the heart of Anatolia, reaching its zenith in the first half of the thirteenth century. Their territories were endowed with a system of imposing *kervansarays*, *medreses*, bridges and other public monuments, with the encouragement of trade being paramount. On a smaller scale, the Selçuks excelled in tile- and relief-work, and in the spiritual field the sultanate, despite its Sunni orientation, provided a refuge for many heterodox religious figures, including Celaleddin Rumi, founder of the Mevlevî dervish order.

Before long, however, a new scourge appeared in the form of the **Mongols**; they crushed the Selçuk armies at the battle of **Köse Dağ** in 1243, and although the sultanate lingered on until the turn of the century, the Turcoman tribes, never fully pacified, took the opportunity to swarm over the lands of both the Selçuks and the Byzantines, who had virtually abandoned Asia Minor after returning to Constantinople in 1261. There was to be a two-century gap in which there was no single political authority on the Anatolian peninsula, but during which time the process of Turkification and Islamization, begun in 1071, continued gradually nonetheless.

The rise of the Ottomans

In the turmoil following the collapse of the Selçuk state, Anatolia fragmented into numerous petty, mostly Turcoman **emirates**. That centred on Söğüt, near Eskişehir, settled on lands granted to the chieftain Ertuğrul by Selçuk ruler Alâeddin, was not initially an important one. Ertuğrul was a typical *gazi*, a recent convert to Islam patrolling the frontier marches between Selçuk and Byzantine territory, carrying the faith ever westward in the face of infidel opposition. His son **Osman**, however, head of the clan from the 1290s onwards, was to give his name to a dynasty: *Osmanlı* in Turkish, "**Ottoman**" to the West. Spurred by proximity to Constantinople, the emirate began to expand under Osman's son **Orhan**, who had taken the important Byzantine centres of Bursa and İznik by the 1330s.

Anatolian culture had for some time been a hybrid one, with frequent intermarriage between Muslims and Christians, and many descendants or converts bilingual in Greek and Turkish. Certain dervish orders – particularly the Bektaşi – effected a synthesis between Islam and numerically declining Christianity. As Byzantine authority in a given area diminished, the assets and facilities of Christian monasteries were often appropriated by the **vakıfs**, or Islamic pious foundations, which sponsored various public-welfare projects; the demoralized Christian priesthood and population often converted to Islam simultaneously.

Complementing these processes was the **devşirme**, a custom that arose in the fourteenth century, whereby a certain percentage of boys from conquered Christian districts were levied by the Ottomans to serve as an elite force, the **janissaries**. They became slaves of the sultan, were admitted to the more eclectic Bektaşi branch of Islam, and were given the best training available with an eye to their becoming not only warriors but Ottoman administrators. Free-born Muslims were expressly ineligible for elevation to the corps, and promotion was strictly through merit, so that (until abuses crept in) the Ottoman state, up to and including the office of grand vizier, was run by converts from Christianity. The only chance for advancement for those born Muslim was within the **ulema**, the body of Koranic sages who decreed on religious matters, or as a member of the **defterdar**, or "accountant" class – a huge bureaucracy overseeing the empire's various sources of revenue.

Though the janissaries formed a powerful praetorian guard, they were supplemented by a standing army, whose members were paid indirectly by assignment of a **timar**, or land grant. All conquered territory remained the property of the sultan, who dispensed such grants with the understanding that the man's "salary" was the proceeds of the estate – and that he remained liable for armed service whenever his ruler summoned him. Initially *timar*s reverted to the crown upon the holder's death, with his sons having to re-earn their portion by service. This system, based heavily on Byzantine practice, was not genuinely feudal, and resulted in a stability of rule that often prompted immigration of Christian peasantry from maladministered neighbouring territory.

Despite religious tolerance shown to Christians of whatever rank, Ottoman society was **hierarchical**, with distinctions between Muslims and infidels – known as *raya*, or "cattle" – preserved in every particular from dress code to unequal status before the law. Christians were not conscripted for campaigns, and hence could not qualify for land grants; instead they paid a tax in lieu of military service, and tended to congregate in towns and cities as tradesmen.

To continue the system of *timar*s, more land had to be made available for awarding, and the *gazi* ethos continued. By the mid-fourteenth century the Ottomans had crossed the Sea of Marmara to Thrace, and in 1362 **Sultan Murat I** took Adrianopolis (henceforth Edirne). Constantinople was virtually surrounded by Turkish territory, and indeed the almost-vanished Byzantine Empire existed on Ottoman sufferance. With Latin and Orthodox Christians at each other's throats, Ottoman ascendancy was virtually assured, and Murat further isolated Constantinople with new acquisitions in the lower Balkans, routing a Serbian-led coalition at **Kosovo** in 1389. Murdered on the battlefield by a Serbian infiltrator, he was succeeded by his elder son **Beyazit I**, who established an unfortunate precedent by promptly strangling his brother Yakub to assure his own succession. Beyazit, nicknamed **Yıldırım**, or "Lightning", for his swift deployments in battle, bested a huge Hungarian/Crusader army at Bulgarian Nicopolis in 1396, and the fall of Constantinople seemed imminent.

However, in expanding eastwards into Anatolia, Beyazit – more impulsive and less methodical than his father – had both overextended himself and antagonized the great Mongol warrior **Tamerlane**. Tamerlane routed Beyazit's armies at the **Battle of Ankara** in 1402, trundling the captive sultan about in a cage for a year before his demise, and proceeded to lay waste much of Anatolia. Even though the Mongols soon vanished, the remnant of the Byzantine Empire was granted a fifty-year reprieve, and for a decade the fate of the Ottoman line hung in the balance as Beyazit's four sons fought a civil war. The victor, Mehmet I, and his successor the mystically inclined Murat II, restored Ottoman fortunes, the latter deflecting one last half-hearted Latin crusade in 1444.

But the greatest prize – **Constantinople** – still eluded the Ottomans. Both symbolically, as the seat of two prior empires, and practically – as a naval base controlling passage between the Black Sea and the Mediterranean – its capture was imperative. **Mehmet II**, who ascended the throne in 1451, immediately began preparations for the deed, studding the sea approaches to the now half-depopulated capital with fortresses, engaging ballistics and artillery experts from Europe with an eye to breaching the city walls, and for the first time outfitting a substantial Ottoman fleet. The final siege of Constantinople, in the spring of 1453, lasted seven weeks, ending on **May 29** when the sultan's armies finally succeeded in entering the city while the last Byzantine emperor died unnoticed in the melee.

Mehmet's epithet was henceforth *Fatih*, "the Conqueror", and there was no longer any room for doubt that the Ottoman Empire was the legitimate successor of the Roman and Byzantine ones. The imitation of Roman and Byzantine models in Ottoman imperial practice, begun in the preceding century and a half, increased.

Mehmet the Conqueror to Süleyman the Magnificent

Mehmet immediately set about refurbishing the city, now renamed İstanbul, as a worthy capital of the empire, repopulating it with both Muslims and Christians from rural areas, establishing markets and public-welfare institutions and constructing a fine palace at Topkapı. The non-Muslim communities were organized into **millets**, or "nations", headed by a patriarch or rabbi, answerable for his flock's good behaviour (and tax remittances) and under whom Greek or Slavic Orthodox, Armenian and Jew were governed by their own communal laws. This system, which tended to minimize sectarian disorder and guaranteed more freedom of worship than prevalent in contemporary Europe, persisted until 1926.

Overseas, defeats along the Danube were followed by easier mop-up campaigns during 1458–60 in the Peloponnese and along the Black Sea, eliminating satellite Byzantine states and their Genoese cohorts. Persisting in the pre-1453 pattern of alternating Euro-

▲ Süleyman the Magnificent

pean and Asian campaigns, Mehmet returned to the Balkans, adding Wallachia, most of present-day Greece, Bosnia-Herzegovina and part of Albania to his domains, while simultaneously building up his navy to counter his main rivals, the Venetians.

Mehmet was succeeded in 1481 by his son **Beyazit II**, "the Pious", who despite a retiring disposition presided over the final relegation of Venice to secondary naval-power status – often by the enlistment of pirates into the Ottoman navy – and realized his father's ambition of revitalizing the core territory of the Byzantine Empire. The skills of Greek renegade statesmen and Italian mercenaries were supplemented in 1493 by the scientific knowledge of **Iberian Jews**, the ancestors of most contemporary Turkish Jewry, fetched by "mercy ships" sent by the sultan upon their expulsion from Spain and Portugal.

In 1512 Beyazit was forced to abdicate by his son **Selim I**, a vigorous personality in the mould of his grandfather, but with an added streak of wanton cruelty and bigotry, hence his epithet *Yavuz* ("the Fierce" – known as "the Grim" to the West). Both of Selim's predecessors had privately toyed with Sufic and heterodox Persian doctrines, but now religious orthodoxy was seen as vital within the Ottoman realm, since neighbour and rival Shah İsmail of Persia was starting to promote **Shi'ism** both within and without his frontiers. Selim massacred forty thousand Shi'ites in Anatolia, and went on to defeat the Shah at east Anatolian **Çaldıran** in 1514. Rather than press on into Persia, however, Selim turned his armies south against the Mamluks, overrunning Mesopotamia, Syria and Egypt by 1516 and occupying at one fell swoop most of the **holy cities** of Islam. By capturing the caliph resident in Cairo and transporting him back to İstanbul, Selim essentially proved his claim to be the Defender of the (Sunni) Faith – and the **caliphate** effectively became identical with the Ottoman sultanate.

Though the empire would reach its greatest physical extent after his death, it was **Süleyman the Magnificent** who laid the foundations for this expansion during a 46-year reign, which began in 1520. In his first few years on the throne, the strongholds of the Knights of St John at Rhodes and Bodrum – from where they controlled the sea lanes to Egypt – were taken, as was Belgrade, leaving the way further up the Danube valley unguarded. By 1526 Budapest, with most of Hungary, was in Ottoman hands, with the Habsburgs compelled to pay tribute for retaining a small portion. Campaigns in Persia and the Arabian peninsula were successful, but the first siege of Vienna in 1529 was not – and nor was an attempt to drive the Portuguese out of the Indian Ocean. The Ottomans were better able to control the Mediterranean, with such admirals as Greek-born Barbaros Hayrettin (**Barbarossa**) and his protégé Turgut Reis besting Venetian/Habsburg fleets. But in 1565 the siege of Malta, where the Knights of St John had retreated, failed, marking the end of the Mediterranean as an Ottoman lake. Nonetheless, the Ottoman Empire, however unwieldy, heterogenous and difficult to defend, was arguably the leading world power of the sixteenth century.

It was, not surprisingly, regarded with a mixture of terror and fascination by the states of Europe; only the **French**, under Francis I, saw the possibility of alliance and manipulation, concluding a treaty with the Ottomans in 1536. In addition to granting France trading advantages in the empire, the treaty's commercial clauses set forth various privileges for French nationals which came to be known as the **Capitulations**: exemption from most Ottoman taxes and the right to be judged by their own consuls under foreign law. What began as an inducement to increased trade became, as time passed, a pernicious erosion of Turkish sovereignty, as many European nations and overseas companies secured such "capitulations" for themselves, extending rights of immunity to local employees (usually Christian) provided with appropriate passports.

Domestically Süleyman distinguished himself as an administrator, legislator, builder and patron of the arts, and indeed in Turkey he is known as *Kanunî*, "the Lawgiver". In his personal life, however, his judgement was to have enduringly harmful consequences for the Ottoman state. He became so enamoured of his favourite concubine **Roxelana** that he broke with Ottoman precedent and actually married her. Scheming and ambitious, she used her influence over the sultan to turn him against his capable son and heir (by a previous liaison), **Mustafa**, inciting Süleyman to murder him and later her own son Beyazit – as well as his first grand vizier, İbrahim. Perhaps a bad conscience over these deeds heightened Süleyman's basic moroseness and introversion, and he died a lonely man on his last campaign on the Danube in 1566. With his two ablest sons gone, there were no obstacles to the succession of Roxelana's first-born son, the useless Selim.

Centuries of Ottoman decline

While it's impossible to assign an exact date to the beginning of the Ottoman Empire's decline, the reign of the ineffectual **Selim II** (Selim "the Sot" to the West) is as good a start as any. He was followed by sixteen other, generally mediocre sultans, of whom only the bloodthirsty but resolute **Murat IV**, and the peace-loving aesthete **Ahmet II**, did much to prevent the gradual deterioration.

It is far easier to catalogue the causes of the decline. From Roxelana's time onwards the **harem** was moved onto the grounds of the Topkapı palace itself, so that the intrigues of its tenants impinged directly on day-to-day government. At the start of the seventeenth century the previous grisly custom of fratricide upon the enthronement of a new sultan was abandoned in favour of the confinement of the other heirs-apparent, sequestered in the so-called *Kafes*, or **Cage**. Few sultans campaigned overseas any longer, or presided personally over the *divan* (council of state), instead delegating most authority to their **grand viziers**.

When these viziers were able and honest, the downward slide of the empire was halted or reversed, but on the whole nepotism and **corruption** flourished in the decadent palace atmosphere. The early Ottoman principle of meritocracy was replaced by a **hereditary aristocracy**; the *devşirme* or levy of Christian boys was all but abandoned by the end of the seventeenth century, and the janissary corps was no longer celibate or religiously exclusive. Sinecure passed from father to son, and the corps expanded further as free Muslims rushed to enrol. Many – in direct contradiction of the institution's purpose – were artisans whose only martial act was to show up to collect pay, desire for more of which often prompted the inefficient, swollen corps to rebel, extorting money from hapless villagers and sultans alike, and on several occasions to depose and murder the sovereign. Similarly, land grants to the *sipahı* (cavalry) tended to become hereditary, and the holders evolved into a class of local warlord (the *derebeys*, or "lords of the valley"). Revolts of these and other idle, underpaid troops devastated Anatolia, already wracked by population pressure and land shortage; thus began a steady rural depopulation which continues today.

Much of the impetus for decline came, however, from outside the empire. The influx into the Mediterranean of gold and silver from the Spanish conquests in the New World set off a spiral of inflation and debased coinage. The Age of Exploration saw new sea routes forged around Africa to the East Indies, reducing the importance of overland caravan routes through Ottoman territories. Most importantly, Europe underwent the **Renaissance** and **industrialization**, while the Ottomans remained stagnant under the influence of the conservative *ulema*. The Turks had become used to easily despatching the ragtag armies of assorted principalities during the fifteenth and sixteenth centuries, and failed to grasp the reasons for their frequent defeats thereafter. New, highly centralized nation-states in the West had established rigorously trained standing armies and navies, availing themselves of the benefits of new armaments, ships and navigation, direct outgrowths of the Renaissance's spur to scientific enquiry. To these manifestations of European superiority the Ottomans – especially the reactionary janissaries – generally reacted disdainfully, seeing no reason to learn from the infidels, given the perfection of Islam.

External **evidence** of the rot took nearly a century to show: although the defeat of an Ottoman fleet at **Lepanto** (today Greek Náfpaktos) in 1571 shattered the myth of Turkish invincibility, that victory was essentially neutralized by the capture of Cyprus from Venice the same year, and the reconquest of North Africa by 1578. The 1600s proceeded well, with the successful siege of Crete and seizure of parts of Poland, but already the Ottomans were compelled to draw up treaties with their adversaries as **equals** – a far cry from the days when victorious sultans condescended to suppliant Christian kings. Worse was to follow during the second half of the seventeenth century, when the most notorious of several defeats at the hands of the Austrians and allies was the bungled **second siege of Vienna** in 1683, where an entire Turkish army was wiped out. Most of Hungary and other east European territory were lost as well before the **treaties of Carlowitz** (1699) and **Passarowitz** (1718) stabilized the Balkan frontier for nearly two centuries.

During the eighteenth century most of the territorial attrition at the Turks' expense was courtesy of the **Russian Empire**, newly consolidated under Peter the Great. Russo-Turkish enmity was to be a constant in Turkish history thereafter until the mid-twentieth century. Russia went on under Catherine the Great to thoroughly humiliate the Turks, presenting them with the **treaties of Küçük Kaynarca** (1774) and **Jassy** (1792), which ceded extensive territory to the tsarina and gave Russia long-coveted access to the Black Sea and the straits guarding İstanbul – as well as the right to interfere, anywhere in the Ottoman Empire, to protect the interests of Orthodox Christian subjects.

The start of the reform era

Selim III's accession to the throne in 1789 coincided with the advent of revolutionary regimes in France and the US; thus the name of his proposed reforms, the **Nizam-i-Cedid**, or "New Order", was a deliberate tip of the hat to them. With the Napoleonic wars as a background and warning, he enlisted foreign experts to set up an army, trained, equipped and attired along Western lines. This aroused the hostility of the janissary corps and their allies among the *ulema*, and Selim was deposed, then murdered, in 1808, after he had dissolved his new army as a futile sop to the conservatives.

The new sultan, **Mahmut II**, was more tactful, moving gradually towards innovation. He managed to outlast both Russian and French designs on his realm only to be confronted by the major crisis of his reign: **full-scale rebellion in Greece**, which broke out in 1821. This proved impossible to crush, even after the Westernized army of **Mehmet Ali**, semi-autonomous ruler of Egypt, was despatched to the scene. The destruction of an Ottoman fleet at Navarino by French, Russian and English ships in 1827, an overland attack by Russia on İstanbul in 1829 and a treaty in 1830 guaranteed the emergence of an **independent Greece** – the first substantial loss of Turkish territory in the south Balkans. The French simultaneously invaded Algeria, and Mehmet Ali chose this moment for an attack on Anatolia, which went unchecked until the Russians, this time as allies of Mahmut, landed on the Bosphorus. In consideration for services rendered they extracted the **Treaty of Hunkâr İskelesi** from the sultanate, which effectively gave the tsar exclusive unimpeded access to the straits.

Despite this disastrous record abroad, Mahmut II had notably more success at home. In 1826 the janissaries had mutinied once again, but the sultan liquidated them with loyal forces in what came to be known as the "**Auspicious Incident**". The Bektaşi sect, the "house religion" of the janissaries, was simultaneously suppressed until the 1860s, and a Western-style army created. During the 1830s Prussian and Austrian advisers came to train it, beginning a tradition of Teutonic involvement in Turkey's military, which was to endure for nearly a century. A military academy and medical school were established, with French the language of instruction.

A formal **foreign service** and a **civil service** were also created, and the *ulema* was brought to heel by subordination to the secular bureaucracy. An approximation of Western dress for all except clerics became mandatory – including the replacement of the turban by the more "progressive" **fez**. The entire programme represented a quantum increase in **centralization** – and unintentionally widened the gap between the Ottoman masses and the new elite.

The Tanzimat and the Young Ottomans

Mahmut's strenuous efforts bore more fruit posthumously when his son Sultan Abdülmecid and minister Mustafa Reşid proclaimed the **Tanzimat**, or "Reorganization", in 1839, essentially an Ottoman Magna Carta which delegated some of the sultan's law-making authority to advisers, promised an end to taxation irregularities, and stipulated equal treatment of Muslim and non-Muslim before the law. Although the climate engendered by such noble sentiments permitted the founding of newspapers and private, secular schools in the ensuing decades, the proposal of infidel equality deeply offended most of the population.

Foreign economic penetration of the Ottoman Empire increased suddenly, with growing commercial activity in all coastal cities, and massive imports of European products; in the process the Greek, Armenian and foreign-Christian merchant class of the ports benefited in a disproportionate manner. Simultaneously, inland centres and traditional bazaar crafts went into precipitous decline, unable to compete with the products of the industrial revolution.

By mid-century the empire had become thoroughly enmeshed in the **power struggles of Europe** – a far cry from the smug aloofness of 250 years before, and a consequence of the fact that England and France had determined that, for better or worse, the Ottomans must be propped up as a counter to Russian expansionism. Thus the empire found itself on the winning side of the 1853–56 **Crimean War**, which began as a dispute between Russia and France over the protection to be extended by each to, respectively, the Orthodox and Catholic churches in Ottoman Palestine. The war ended with little significant territorial adjustment, but did bring a twenty-year interval of peace for the Ottomans.

Abdülmecid had been a well-meaning but weak and extravagant ruler, and was succeeded in 1861 by his brother **Abdülaziz**, who combined all of his predecessor's defects with a despotic manner. There sprung up in reaction, from the ranks of the first graduates of the empire's secular schools, the **Society of Young Ottomans**, which strove for the evolution of a constitutional monarchy along British lines. Its most enduring figure was the poet and essayist **Namık Kemal**, and it made extensive use of the newly admitted media of the press, drama and literature to get its points across. Predictably the group aroused the ire of the sultan, who exiled the boldest; undeterred, the Young Ottomans overseas mounted a barrage of written material, much of it smuggled back into the empire to good effect.

Faced with Abdülaziz's flagrant financial irresponsibility in the period preceding the crash of 1873–75, and his growing mental instability, together with new Russian mischief in İstanbul and brutally suppressed revolts in the Balkans, the Young Ottomans among the bureaucratic elite – particularly **Mithat Paşa** – deposed him on **May 30, 1876**. The sultanate was passed to his promising nephew Murat, but he shortly suffered a nervous breakdown, was declared unfit to rule and in turn placed in seclusion. The next heir-apparent was his younger brother **Abdülhamid**, an unknown quantity, who was offered the throne on condition that he accept various Young Ottomans as advisers and rule under a constitution.

Abdülhamid and the Young Turk revolution

The new sultan did in fact promulgate the **constitution** drafted by the Young Ottomans, presided over the opening of the first Ottoman parliament and retained – for a time – his hapless brother's advisers, including Mithat. But Abdülhamid soon moved to forestall a government by ministers, exiling Mithat (and later having him murdered).

As so often in late Ottoman history, the implementation of liberal reforms was interpreted by the Great Powers as a sign of weakness. Accordingly Russia attacked on two fronts in **1877**, in the Caucasus and in the Balkans, with an explicitly pan-Slavic agenda. The war went badly for the Ottomans, with extensive territorial losses confirmed by the harsh peace treaty of San Stefano (at the ceasefire line just a stone's throw from İstanbul), later modified, under British pressure, at the 1878 **Conference of Berlin**. The final settlement provided for the independence of Romania, Montenegro and Serbia; an autonomous if truncated Bulgaria; the cession of Thessaly to Greece, and Kars and Ardahan districts to Russia; and the occupation of Bosnia and Herzegovina by Austria. **Nationalism** had been unleashed – and rewarded – in the Balkans, and would be a theme for the next forty years, and indeed to this day. Britain, in compensation for fending off further Russian advances, was given the right to "administer" – and garrison – **Cyprus**.

Throughout all this the new **parliament** displayed altogether too much independence for the sultan's taste, criticizing war policy and summoning certain government ministers to answer for their conduct. In early 1878, between the San Stefano and Berlin negotiation sessions, Abdülhamid finally dropped all pretence of consultative government and dissolved the Chamber of Deputies; it was not to meet again for thirty years.

With any restraining influence out of the way, Abdülhamid chose to rule despotically and directly. A **police state** emerged, attended by huge numbers of spies and rigorous press censorship; the introduction of a **telegraph network** provided a tremendous boost to the surveillance system. The only clause of the constitution still honoured was the repeatedly invoked one that entitled the sultan to exile troublemakers.

After the disastrous wars marking the start of his reign, Abdülhamid's **foreign policy** was xenophobic and Asia-oriented, espousing Islam as a unifying force and, for the first time in centuries, emphasizing the sultan's second role as **caliph**. This ideology didn't, however, prevent the loss of Tunis and Egypt, and had as a corollary the steadily worsening treatment of the **Armenians** of eastern Anatolia, who began to show the same nationalist sentiments as the Christians of the Balkans. The abuses culminated in the organized pogroms of **1895–96**, in which nearly 150,000 Armenians died, provoking (albeit short-lived) outrage abroad. In 1897, war with Greece and a revolt on Crete coincided; even though the Prussian-trained army defeated the Greeks in the field, the Ottomans were forced to grant the island autonomy.

Despite his political obscurantism, Abdülhamid presided over widespread **technological Westernization**; carefully cultivated ties with Germany resulted in much-needed development projects – most famously the German-built **rail system** across Anatolia. Important investment credits were also extended, and a **Public Debt Administration** was created, which gathered revenues of the various state monopolies to service the enormous debt run up earlier in the century. At the same time, secular schooling and technical training were encouraged, as long as they didn't directly challenge the sultan's rule – but the creation of an educated elite inevitably resulted in change.

In 1889 the Ottoman Society for Union and Progress – later the **Committee for Union and Progress** (CUP) – arose, mainly among army medical staff but also drawing on the talents of the huge European exile community. Soon it took strongest root in **Macedonia**, the worst-administered and most polyglot of the Ottoman provinces, and completely infiltrated the officer ranks of the Third Army at Salonica (Thessaloníki), a city where the sultan's repression was less, and where Westernizing Jews, Dönme sect members and Masons were influential. Threats of further intervention by the great powers in Macedonia – where disorderly Greek, Bulgarian and other nationalist guerilla bands were rampant – coincided with failure to pay the army, providing the spark for the revolt of the "**Young Turks**", as the CUP plotters were nicknamed. In July 1908, the Macedonian army units demanded by telegraph that Abdülhamid restore the 1876 constitution, or face unpleasant consequences. Abdülhamid's spies had either been oblivious to the threat, or he had chosen not to believe them, and on **July 24**, the sultan assented. There was widespread rejoicing on the streets of the major imperial cities, as *mullahs* fraternized with bishops, and Bulgarians walked arm in arm with Greeks. With the sultan's despotism over, surely a peaceable kingdom was imminent.

After the revolution – the Balkan wars

The euphoria prompted by the reactivation of the 1876 constitution soon subsided as the **revolutionary government** fumbled for a coherent policy. The coup itself had had as immediate goals the curbing of Abdülhamid's powers and the physical preservation of the empire – but even these limited aims proved beyond it. By October 1908 Bulgaria had declared full independence and absorbed eastern Rumelia, and Austria had formally annexed Bosnia and Herzegovina, occupied since 1878. **Elections** for the reconvened parliament were reasonably fair, and the "Young Turks", their CUP newly organized as a political party, gained a majority. Opposition to the Westernization and autocracy represented by the CUP simmered, however, and in spring 1909 a joint **revolt** of low-ranking soldiers, anti-CUP politicians and religious elements ousted the new government and took control of İstanbul. Abdülhamid, overestimating the rebels' strength, unwisely came out in their support. The CUP fought back from its base in Salonica, sending Third Army general Mahmut Şevket to crush the insurrection, and topped this off by **deposing the sultan**, banishing him to house arrest in Salonica. His younger brother ascended the throne as Mehmet V, promising to respect the "will of the nation".

The revolution had been saved, but there was still no agreement on a programme. Three main ideas vied for consideration. **Ottomanism** asserted that a Eurasian empire, federal in stucture, in which all ethnic and religious minorities had equal rights – and who in turn were loyal to the central government – was both viable and desirable. The adherents of **Pan-Islamism**, the pet creed of Abdülhamid, stressed the Islamic nature of the Ottoman Empire and the ties between Muslim Albanians, Caucasians, Kurds, Arabs and Turks. **Pan-Turanism** was more blatantly racial, dwelling on the affinities between all Turkic peoples between central Asia and the Balkans, disproportionately promoted by Caucasian Muslims exiled by the Russians during the 1870s; as time went on it was modified to a more realistic **Turkism**, or the promotion of the interests of the Turkish-speaking Muslims of Anatolia, and it was this notion which would eventually carry the day.

Discussion of these alternatives – and cultural life in general – flourished uninhibitedly for a while. Between 1908 and 1912 the CUP, beset by internal disputes, was by no means monolithic, and parliamentary opposition was not completely quelled until 1912.

The growing **authoritarianism** of CUP rule coincided with renewed **external threats** to the empire. Italy invaded Tripolitania (today's Libya) in 1911, and the next year took all of the Dodecanese islands. In late 1912, the Balkan states of Bulgaria, Serbia, Montenegro and Greece united for the first and last time in history, driving Turkey out of Europe in the **First Balkan War** and indeed approaching within a few miles of İstanbul by the beginning of 1913. Enraged at attempts to limit the army's, and the CUP's, involvement in government, and the unfavourable terms of a pending peace treaty, key CUP officers staged a coup, murdering the minister of war and continuing on the battlefield; when the new grand vizier Mahmut Şevket was assassinated in retaliation soon after, the CUP used it as an excuse to suppress all dissent and establish a **military junta**.

The unlikely Balkan alliance soon fell apart, with Bulgaria turning on Serbia and Greece in the **Second Balkan War**, and the Ottomans taking the opportunity to regain eastern Thrace up to Edirne. This action made temporary heroes of the junta, which by now was in effect a triumvirate: **Enver Paşa**, an officer of humble origins, dashing, courageous, abstemious, as well as vain, ambitious and megalomaniac; **Talat Paşa**, a brutal Thracian civilian who would eventually be responsible for ordering the 1915 deportation of the Armenians; and **Cemal Paşa**, a ruthless but competent professional soldier from an old family.

World War I

The CUP's ideology was now resolutely Turkish-nationalist, secular and technocratic, as well as anti-democratic – and increasingly pro-German. Public opinion, and the more level-headed CUP members, hoped that the Ottoman Empire would remain neutral in the obviously impending conflict, but Germanophile Enver had signed a secret agreement with the Kaiser on August 2, 1914. By coincidence Britain committed a major blunder the same day, impounding two half-built battleships, which had already been paid for by public subscription in Turkey. The German government pulled off a major public-relations coup by sailing two **replacement ships** through the Allied Mediterranean blockade to İstanbul in October, presenting them to the Turkish navy – whose German commander promptly forced Turkey's hand by sending them off to bombard Russian Black-Sea ports. By November Turkey was officially **at war** with the Allies, though various CUP ministers resigned in protest. "This will be our ruin," said one prophetically, "even if we win."

Despite appearances, the CUP did not become puppets of the Germans, nor Turkey a complete satellite; although men and weaponry were diverted to the European eastern front and Anatolia used as a granary by the Central Powers, the Capitulations were unilaterally abolished over German protests (they affected the French and English more anyway), and monetary policy was determined without outside interference for the first time in sixty years. These measures counted on military successes to reinforce them, though, and the **Turkish war effort**, carried out on five fronts simultaneously, was an almost unmitigated disaster. Over the four-year duration, the empire lost all of its Middle Eastern domains, as the Arabs threw in their lot with the British on the promise of subsequent autonomy, thus proving pan-Islamism as dead as Ottomanism. Enver Paşa demonstrated his incompetence by losing an entire army on the Russian front during the winter of 1914–15; the subsequent Tsarist advance deep into Anatolia was only reversed after the Bolshevik revolution.

The two bright spots from the Turkish point of view were the defeat of a British army at the bloody campaign of Mesopotamian Kut, and the successful defence of the **Gallipoli peninsula**, guarding the Dardanelles and thus the sea approaches to İstanbul. Credit for the successful Turkish resistance for seven months from April 24, 1915, belonged largely to a hitherto unknown colonel named **Mustafa Kemal**, later Atatürk, ranking Turkish officer in the operations. He had come of age in the midst of the pre-1908 Young Turk agitation, and like many other junior officers had been sent into internal exile for "disloyal" activities. Though an early member of the CUP, he had opposed its autocratic tendencies and entry into the war on Germany's side. The Turkish public craved a hero at this point, but upon Kemal's return to İstanbul the jealous Enver deprived them of this satisfaction, shuttling Kemal between various backwoods commands, until war's end saw him overseeing a strategic retreat to the hills on the Syrian border.

For the Ottoman Empire's **Armenians**, April 24, 1915, was also a fateful day, on which the CUP authorities ordered the disarming of all Armenians serving in the Turkish army, and the roundup of Armenian civilians from Anatolian cities, towns and villages; only those living in İstanbul and İzmir were exempted, for economic and public-relations reasons. Over the next ten months of deportations, the men were usually shot immediately by gendarmes, Kurdish irregulars or bands of thugs recruited for the purpose, while women and children were forced to march, under conditions that guaranteed their abuse and death, hundreds of kilometres towards concentration camps in the Mesopotamian desert. Estimating **total casualties** is difficult and controversial, but Ottoman and foreign censuses at the turn of the century showed nearly 1.5 million Armenians living in Anatolia. Allowing for the roughly half-million refugees who managed to hide in Turkey or escape abroad by 1923, most of the one-million difference can be assumed to have perished, making it the first deliberate, large-scale genocide of the twentieth century.

The above scenario is hotly disputed by recent Turkish governments, which deny that any officially sanctioned, systematic expulsion or killing took place, and admit a maximum of 300,000 Armenian fatalities from unspecified causes – but implying that most of these were combatants in treasonous alliance with Russia or France. While it is true that many Armenians, particularly in Van, Kars and Adana provinces, sided with those two powers in the hopes of securing a postwar state for themselves, this happened *after* the deportation and massacre orders were issued, and could be construed as legitimate self-defence. In any event, the issue is still very much alive, with relatively clumsy Turkish propaganda developed since the 1980s to counter vigorous, and increasingly successful, Armenian lobbying for international recognition of the tragedy.

On **October 30, 1918**, Turkish and British officers signed an armistice on the Greek island of Límnos. Two weeks later an Allied fleet sailed into İstanbul, and strategic points around the Sea of Marmara were occupied by the victors, though Turkish civil administration was allowed to continue on condition that no "disturbances" took place. In the interim the CUP triumvirate had fled on German ships, and all met violent deaths in the following years: Talat killed in revenge by an orphaned Armenian in Berlin; Cemal assassinated in Caucasian Georgia; and Enver – dying as flamboyantly as he had lived – as a self-styled emir fighting the Bolsheviks in central Asia.

The struggle for independence

The Allies were now in a position to carry out their long-deferred **designs on the Ottoman heartland**, as per secret wartime protocols. By early 1919 French troops were in occupation of parts of southeast Anatolia near the present Syrian and Iraqi frontiers, the Italians landed on the coast between Bodrum and Antalya, and the Greeks disembarked at İzmir, where Greek Orthodox civilians formed a large part of the population. The British concentrated their strength in İstanbul and Thrace, and along with the other victors garrisoned in the capital effectively dictated policy to the defeated Ottoman regime. The new sultan **Mehmet VI** was interested only in retaining his throne, and prepared to make any necessary territorial or administrative concessions to that end – including the dissolution of the last wartime parliament.

İstanbul, under de facto occupation, was a poor seedbed for a war of independence. In Thrace and Anatolia, however, various **Committees for the Defence of (Turkish) Rights** – patriotic Turkish guerilla bands – had sprung up, and a substantial remnant of the Ottoman armies survived at Erzurum, under the control of **Kâzım Karabekir**. Together these would form the nucleus of the liberation forces. All that was lacking was visionary leadership, and further provocations from the Allies; neither was long in coming.

Mustafa Kemal, the hero of Gallipoli and the Syrian front, was the only undefeated Ottoman general at war's end; was not compromised by close association with the CUP leadership; and could hardly be accused of being pro-German. Popular and outspoken, he was considered too dangerous by the Allies to be kept idle in the capital. For his part, Kemal itched to cross over to Anatolia and begin organizing some sort of resistance to the pending imperialist schemes, but dared not do so without a suitable pretext. This was provided in the spring of 1919, when Kemal managed to wangle from the collaborationist war ministry a commission as a military inspector for all Anatolia, empowered to halt the activities of the various Committees for the Defence of Rights and seize their arms. His first stop was to be the Black Sea, where Turkish guerrillas had been fighting it out with

Greeks bent on setting up a Pontic republic. On **May 19, 1919**, Mustafa Kemal landed at Samsun, four days after Greek operations began at İzmir – the last straw for many hitherto apathetic Turks. Contrary to his brief, Kemal promptly began organizing and strengthening the Turkish guerillas. The puppet government in İstanbul, realizing too late what he was up to, attempted to recall him, then summarily relieved him of duties, and finally ordered his arrest; he returned the compliment by resigning his commission. Kemal and Karabekir, along with **Rauf**, **Ali Fuad** and **Refet** – three high-ranking officers of old Ottoman families – drew up a provisional plan for resistance, with the strong support of the Anatolian religious authorities. Two **ideological congresses** were scheduled, one at Erzurum in July, and another in Sivas in September. Both gatherings elected Kemal as chairman, and both ratified the so-called **National Pact**, which demanded viable Turkish borders approximating those of today, an end to the Capitulations and a guarantee of rights to all minorities. At the same time the pact reaffirmed its loyalty to the institution of the caliphate, if not the sultan himself, who was deemed a prisoner of the Allies. It was still far too early in the game to antagonize the religious elements, and indeed secularization was probably still a gleam in Kemal's eye.

Throughout these manoeuvres the **Nationalists**, as they came to be called, made good use of the **telegraph lines** installed by Abdülhamid, often conducting convoluted arguments with the İstanbul regime over the wires. By the autumn of 1919, they forced the resignation of the grand vizier and the announcement of elections for a new parliament. These, in early 1920, returned a large Nationalist majority, which openly proclaimed the National Pact – and created a climate where thefts from Allied arms depots, often with the connivance of the French and Italians who opposed Greek aims in Anatolia, became a routine occurrence. At the instigation of the outraged Ottoman court, the British placed İstanbul under formal military occupation on **March 16, 1920**, raiding parliament and bundling a few score deputies into exile on Malta. Luckier MPs escaped to Ankara, where Kemal and others had prudently remained, and on **April 23** opened the first **Grand National Assembly**, in direct defiance of the sundry Allied encroachments. Turkey's first Ankara-based parliament met in a Wild-West atmosphere, lit by oil lamps for several years, while its members tethered their horses to wooden railings out front.

The sultanate reacted vehemently to all this, securing a **fetva** (ruling) from the Islamic authorities sanctioning a holy war against the "rebels" and condemning the Nationalist leadership to death in absentia. Kemal and friends secured a counter-*fetva* from sympathetic religious figures in Ankara, and soon afterwards the head of the Bektaşi dervish order publicly commanded his followers to help the Nationalists.

Such moral support was vital to the beleaguered guerillas, who were now fighting for their lives in a **multiple-front war**: against the French in the southeast, the Italians in the southwest, Armenians in the northeast, irregular bands supporting the sultan in various locations and – most dangerously – the Greeks in western Anatolia. The only consistent aid came from the newborn Soviet Union, which sent gold and weapons, then partitioned the short-lived Armenian Dashnakist republic between itself and Turkey, thus closing that theatre of war by late 1920.

The Allied governments, oblivious of the new reality on the ground in Turkey, attempted to legitimize their claims to Turkish territory by presenting the humiliating **Treaty of Sèvres** to the Ottoman government in May 1920. By its terms, partly motivated by the Wilsonian Fourteen Points, but more by unalloyed greed, an independent Armenia and an autonomous Kurdistan were created; the straits of the Sea of Marmara and İstanbul were placed under international control; Thrace plus İzmir and its hinterland were given to Greece; France and Italy were assigned spheres of influence in those portions of Anatolia remaining to the Ottomans; and Turkish finances were placed under Allied supervision, with a revival of the Capitulations. By signing this document, the demoralized sultanate sacrificed its last shred of credibility, convinced any remaining waverers of the necessity of the Nationalist movement – and sparked a predictable Greek response.

The **Greek expeditionary armies**, acting with the authorization of British prime minister Lloyd George, not only pressed inland from İzmir but captured Edirne, İzmit and Bursa, seeking to revive notions of a "Greater Greece" straddling both shores of the Aegean. Only French and Italian objections caused them to halt just short of the strategic Afyon–Eskişehir railway. In early 1921 the Greeks were on the move again, but Nationalist general İsmet Paşa stopped them twice, in January and April, at the defile of **İnönü**, from which he would later take his surname. Both sides had undergone subtle changes: since the fall of the republican Venizelos government in Greece, and the return of the royalists, the Greek Anatolian armies had become progressively more corrupt, incompetently led and brutal in their treatment of Muslim civilians. Kemal's forces, on the other hand, had become more cohesive and professional, with irregular bands either defeated or absorbed.

But when the Greeks advanced east once more in July 1921, they swiftly captured Afyon, Eskişehir and the vital railway that linked them; the Nationalists strategically retreated east of the Sakarya river, less than 100km from Ankara, to buy time and extend the enemy's supply lines. Panic and gloom reigned in Ankara, with calls for Kemal to be instated as commander-in-chief at the head of the defending army, to share its fate. This was done, and soon the Greeks went for the bait, sniffing an easy chance to finish off the Nationalists. But in the ferocious, three-week **battle of the Sakarya** beginning on August 13, they failed to make further headway towards Ankara. Although most of the Greek army survived, anything less than its capture of the Nationalist headquarters was a decisive defeat. The jubilant Grand National Assembly conferred on Kemal the title *Gazi*, or "Warrior for the Faith".

The victory at Sakarya greatly enhanced the Nationalists' international position: both the **French and Italians** soon concluded peace treaties, withdrawing from southern Anatolia, and contributions from various Asian Muslim countries poured in to finance the "holy war". With remaining support for the Greek adventure evaporating, the British tried unsuccessfully to arrange an armistice between Greece and the Nationalists. Both camps dug in and waited until, on **August 26, 1922**, Kemal launched his final offensive at **Dumlupınar** near Afyon, designed to drive the Greeks out of Anatolia. The Greek lines crumbled and those not taken prisoner or killed, fled down-valley in a disorderly rout towards waiting boats in İzmir, committing atrocities against the Turkish population, destroying the harvest and abandoning Greek civilians to the inevitable Turkish reprisals. The latter included the **sacking and burning of İzmir** within four days of the triumphant entry of the Nationalists.

Despite this resounding triumph, the war was not yet over, and indeed the threat of a prolonged conflict loomed. A large Greek army remained intact in **Thrace**, disposed to fight on, and British contingents guarding the strategically vital **Dardanelles** faced off against the Nationalist army sent north to cross the straits. Some of Kemal's associates even urged him to retake western Thrace and Greek Macedonia, a sure invitation to renewed world war. Cooler heads prevailed at the last minute, however, and at Mudanya on **October 11, 1922**, an armistice was signed, obliging the last Greek troops to depart from eastern Thrace. A week later British premier Lloyd George, his pro-Greek policy utterly discredited, was forced to resign.

There remained just one obstacle to full Nationalist control of Turkey: Sultan Mehmet VI still presided over a diminished realm, consisting of İstanbul alone. Few in Ankara had a good word to say about the man himself, but many expressed reluctance to abolish his office, favouring a constitutional monarchy with royalty exercising a stabilizing influence as in Britain. The Allies themselves helped decide the matter by extending a clumsy double invitation to a final peace conference at Lausanne – one addressed to the sultanate, the other to the Grand National Assembly. The outrage thus provoked in the latter quarters made it an easy matter for Kemal to persuade the deputies to **abolish the sultanate** on November 1, effective retroactively as from March 16, 1920, the date of British direct rule in İstanbul. Within two weeks Mehmet VI, last of the House of Osman, sneaked ignominiously out of the old imperial capital on a British warship, bound for exile in Italy; his cousin Abdülmecid was sworn in as caliph, but with no temporal powers whatsoever.

The **peace conference** at Lausanne was convened immediately, with İsmet Paşa as the sole Turkish representative. If the Allies were hoping to dictate terms as at Versailles and Sèvres, they were quickly disappointed; İsmet soon proved as dogged at the negotiating table as on the battlefield, reducing seasoned diplomats to despair by feigning deafness and repetitive insistence on the tenets of the Erzurum–Sivas National Pact. The conference was suspended for two months in early 1923, the Allies doubtless hoping to wear İsmet down, but in the end it was they who gave in. The **Treaty of Lausanne**, signed on July 24, recognized the frontiers won in the recent war of independence; abolished the Capitulations; demilitarized the Dardanelles and the islands at its mouth; and postponed a decision on the status of the oil-rich Mesopotamian district of Mosul (now in Iraq).

More drastically, Greece and Turkey agreed to an **exchange of minority populations** to eliminate future outbreaks of communal conflict. Nearly half a million Muslims in Greece were sent to Turkey, and the remaining 1.3 million Greek Orthodox Christians in Turkey were officially despatched to Greece (most had already fled there). The only exceptions were the Turkish minority in western Thrace, and Greeks with Ottoman citizenship resident in İstanbul and on Imvros and Tenedos islands at the mouth of the Dardanelles. The sole criterion was religious affiliation; incalculable suffering was caused, especially among Turkish-speaking Christians and Greek-speaking Muslims who suddenly found themselves in a wholly alien linguistic environment.

The pact marked the true end of World War I, and saw Turkey, alone of the defeated nations, emerge in dignity, with defendable territory and modest demands made of her. Compared to the old empire, it was a compact state – 97 percent Anatolian and Muslim. A new political party, the **Republican People's Party** (RPP), incorporating the resources and personnel of the various Committees for the Defence of Rights, and the precepts of the National Pact, was formed, and a new parliament was swiftly created, its members drawn from the ranks of the new entity.

The young republic and Kemal Atatürk's reforms

The Nationalists may have won the military battle for political sovereignty in Anatolia, but after ten years of constant warfare the country was physically devastated and economically a shambles. Export agriculture and urban commerce had largely

△ Atatürk teaching the new alphabet

been in the hands of the Greek and Armenian minorities. With their departure or demise, and that of the foreigners who had benefited from the Capitulations, the Turks were obliged to start from zero agriculturally and commercially, which they failed to do for many years.

Kemal had little patience for or understanding of intricate economics, and preferred to emphasize sweeping social change by fiat. In October 1923 the Grand National Assembly officially moved the capital to **Ankara** and proclaimed the **Republic**, to which there was no practical obstacle since the last sultan had absconded. Kemal was designated head of state and İsmet İnönü was named prime minister. Though the sultan was gone, the caliph Abdülmecid was still around and very much a public personality – an intolerable situation for Kemal and the other Westernizers; since the war had been won they no longer felt the need for the legitimizing function of Islam. In March 1924 the caliphate was abolished and all members of the House of Osman exiled, the *medrese*s and religious courts closed, and the assets of the *vakıf*s supervised by a new Ministry of Religious Affairs.

Even some of Kemal's longtime supporters were dismayed by his increasingly autocratic ways, and a few – including military men Ali Fuad, Rauf Orbay and Kâzım Karabekir – resigned from the RPP in October 1924 to form an opposition, the **Progressive Republican Party** (PRP). At first Kemal tolerated the new party as a means of blowing off steam, even replacing the unpopular İsmet as prime minister to placate them, but the RPP became alarmed when PRP speakers attracted large crowds and elements of the less supervised İstanbul press began siding with them.

Events soon provided Kemal with a basis for more action. In February 1925 the first of several twentieth-century **Kurdish revolts** erupted at Palu, near Elazığ, under the leadership of a Nakşibendi (Naqshbandi) dervish leader. The revolt was both fundamentalist Muslim and separatist-nationalist in ideology, and it took the central government two months to suppress. Kemal, demanding unity in a time of crisis, secured the abolition of the PRP and established a series of sanguinary **Independence Tribunals** invested with summary powers; not only the leaders of the revolt but a few minor members of the PRP found themselves on the wrong end of a rope, and freedom of the press was quickly curtailed. By autumn 1925 all the **dervish orders** had been made illegal throughout Turkey (though they were never completely suppressed), and the veneration of Sufi saints at their tombs was forbidden. Simultaneously, Kemal embarked on a campaign against **traditional headgear**, in particular women's veils, the turban and the fez. Although the caliphate had been dissolved with hardly a murmur, the sartorial laws outlawing the turban and fez, and requiring the donning of the hated European hat, were met with stiff resistance; dress for the Ottomans had always served as a vital indicator of rank. Not a few offenders were hanged from lampposts by the reactivated Independence Tribunals, but the secularists have never to this day succeeded in eliminating the cloaking of women in the rural areas, and there is still no law against it.

More drastic measures followed at a dizzying pace. By 1926, the **Gregorian calendar** had replaced the Muslim lunar one for official use, and the *şeriat*, or Islamic **law code**, was replaced by adaptations of the Western European versions. The same year, the Jewish, Armenian and Greek minorities relinquished the last vestiges of their communal laws; henceforth all citizens of the Republic were to be judged by a uniform legal system. Parallel with the introduction of a secular law code came the relative **emancipation of women**: marriage and divorce became civil rather than religious or customary, polygamy was abolished, and within four years women were voting in local elections.

Not surprisingly all this inflamed the existing opposition to Kemal, and in mid-1926 a **plot** to assassinate him was uncovered. Those involved were mostly disgruntled minor deputies and ex-CUP men, but Kemal took the opportunity to charge and try most of the former Progressive Republican Party's leadership, including war hero Karabekir. Several, including all the surviving CUP leadership, were hanged, and even those acquitted were effectively barred from public life in the future. This was the last mass purge, however, and soon after, the feared Independence Tribunals were disbanded, having served their purpose. There was to be no more public opposition to Kemal during his lifetime, except for a period in 1930 when a second short-lived opposition party was again judged to be a "premature experiment".

Kemal now felt secure enough to press on with his agenda, and chose as his next field **alphabet reform**. A special commission prepared a Roman script within six weeks in 1928, and by the end of the year its universal use was law, with the *Gazi* himself touring the country to give lessons in public parks. Reform was extended to the entire language over the next few years, with the founding of a language commission charged with the duty of purging Turkish of its Arabic and Persian accretions and reviving old Turkish words, coining new ones or adopting French words to underline the break with the Islamic past. Nowadays most observers admit that the process was carried too far, with the language soon as top-heavy with borrowed Western words as it had been with Eastern ones, but together with the script change the measures resulted in a substantial increase in literacy and comprehension. (A deliberate side-effect of the language reform was to isolate many Turks from their own history; unable to read Ottoman Turkish, they became estranged from the imperial past.)

Less successful, and ultimately embarrassing, were programmes intending to rewrite history, in which it was variously asserted that all other languages derived from Turkish; that the Turks were an Aryan race (and other racial nonsense uncomfortably close to Nazi theories), or that they were the descendants of the Hittites or Sumerians. Such hypotheses, springing from a mix of inferiority feelings and a need for political legitimacy, lingered on in Turkish schoolbooks into the 1970s. A more constructive move, in 1934, was full **suffrage for women** in national elections and the mandatory adoption of **surnames** by the entire population; previously this had been discretionary. Kemal chose for himself the unique **Atatürk**, "Father-Turk", dropping his first name Mustafa.

Belatedly Atatürk and his associates had turned their attention to the **economic** sphere, where Turkey's weaknesses had been accentuated by the crash of 1929. Despite public discontent at deprivation and stagnation, **Kemalism**, as Atatürk's ideology was named, continued to stress industrial self-sufficiency through state investment in heavy industry with a goal of complete import substitution (except for factory equipment). Development banks had been set up in 1925, and subsequently the strategically important rail network was extended, and mining, steel, cement and paper works heavily subsidized on a pattern modelled on Italian fascism. This paternalistic programme was, however, grossly inefficient, and proceeded at the expense of the agricultural sector, which remained in abject condition until the 1950s. The east of the country was effectively condemned to a subsistence existence – aggravating Kurdish feelings of punitive neglect – a situation unchanged until the massive, controversial irrigation and hydroelectric projects of the 1970s and 1980s.

Turkey's **foreign policy** during the post-independence years was rooted in noninterventionism and isolationism, though the country did join the League of Nations in 1934, and opposed appeasement of the fascist regimes in Europe. Atatürk's slogan "Peace at home, peace in the world" may have had an unfortunate resemblance to Neville Chamberlain's utterances after Munich, but in practice secured for Turkey years of badly needed calm. Though the RPP may have imitated aspects of contemporary European totalitarian systems, Turkey had no wish to follow Germany, Italy and the USSR into an abyss. Atatürk removed a remaining irritant to Anglo-Turkish relations by consenting to the cession of the Mosul region to Iraq, but began in 1936 an ultimately successful campaign to annex the Hatay, part of the French protectorate of Syria with a large Turkish population. Alliances of the 1930s, with Greece, Yugoslavia and Romania to the west, and with Iraq, Iran and Afghanistan to the east, were opportunistic and short-lived, nowhere near as durable as a Treaty of Friendship promulgated with the Soviet Union.

Fortunately for Turkey, Atatürk had accomplished the bulk of his intended life's work by **1938**, for his health, after a lifetime of heavy drinking, was steadily worsening. He died from complications caused by cirrhosis of the liver in İstanbul's Dolmabahçe palace at 9.05am on November 10, 1938. Thousands of mourners bearing torches lined the route of his funeral cortege-train between

İstanbul and Ankara. Fifteen years later he was interred in a mausoleum, the Anıt Kabir – designed by an Italian and a German, and loyal to the monumental fascist aesthetic of the 1930s.

Atatürk's **legacy** is a considerable one: unlike the totalitarian rulers of his day, he refrained from expansionist designs and overt racial/ethnic hatred, leaving behind a stable, defensible state and a guiding ideology, however uneven, expressly intended to outlive him. Personally he was a complex, even tragic figure: his charisma, energy and quick grasp of situations and people were unparalleled, but he had little inclination for methodical planning or systematic study. While respected, even revered, he was not loved by his associates or particularly loveable – despite his sponsorship of the advancement of women, he was himself a callous, compulsive womanizer, with one brief spell of unhappy marriage. In his fundamental loneliness, he nursed grudges and suspicions, which often had deadly consequences for those who, as partners, might have been able to extricate Turkey from later awkward situations. By his stature and temperament Atatürk, like a tree allowing nothing to grow underneath, deprived Turkey of a succeeding generation of leadership. The cult of his personality, obvious from the silhouettes and signs on every hillside, is in some ways symptomatic of an inability to conceive of alternatives in ideology or heroes, though since 1983 reverence for the economic principles of Kemalism has fallen completely by the wayside.

World War II and the rise of multiparty politics

Atatürk was succeeded as president by his longtime general and prime minister **İsmet İnönü**, and his policy concerning the **Hatay** was posthumously vindicated in 1939, when annexation of the nominally independent Hatay republic was ratified. France, eager for Turkish support in the impending war, acquiesced, and was apparently rewarded by the Turkish signing of a deliberately vaguely worded treaty of alliance with France and Britain in 1939.

In the event the treaty turned out to be a dead letter: France was swiftly defeated, and German propaganda convinced the Turkish government that Britain was probably doomed as well, and that the Axis would also dispatch Russia, the hereditary Turkish enemy. Accordingly a "Treaty of Friendship" was signed with Nazi Germany in 1941, guaranteeing at least Turkish non-belligerence. Entry into the war on either side had in fact been doubtful from the start, since Turkey's armed forces had become desperately antiquated. Memories of the Ottoman Empire's humiliation at the hands of the World War I Entente powers were strong too. Turkey instead remained **neutral**, selling strategically vital chromium ore to both Germany and Britain. Despite this fence-sitting, the country was essentially on a war footing, with all its able-bodied men mobilized, and the economy subject to the stresses of shortages, black markets, profiteering and huge government budget deficits.

All these, and the partial infiltration of Nazi ideology, provoked the institution in 1942 of the so-called **Varlık Vergisi**, or "Wealth Levy", a confiscatory tax applied in a discriminatory manner against businessmen of Armenian, Greek, Jewish and Dönme (nominal Muslims, ex-disciples of a false Jewish messiah) descent. Defaulters had their property confiscated and/or were deported to labour camps in the interior, where many died. The measure, having in fact raised very little money, was rescinded in 1944, but not before urban commerce had been set back a decade, and the Republic's credibility with its non-Muslim minorities severely damaged.

Even after the collapse of the Italians, Turkey still declined to enter the war, despite assurances of Allied support. Turkey only declared war on Germany in early 1945 to qualify for membership of the UN, not soon enough to prevent the USSR from renewing demands for the return of the Kars and Ardahan districts, and joint control of the straits at each end of the Sea of Marmara. Though these were summarily rejected, Turkey badly needed a protective ally in the international arena, and found it in the **United States**. The arrival in İstanbul of the American warship USS *Missouri* in 1946 was greeted with such euphoria that the city fathers, in a famous instance of Turkish hospitality later worked into popular literature, ordered the local bordellos thrown open for free to the sailors.

The eventual results of the mutual wooing were, first, Turkey's participation in the Korean War, and subsequent admission to **NATO** after an initial application had been rejected. This new pro-Western stance had several further consequences: the expulsion from Warsaw Pact Bulgaria into Turkey of vast numbers of ethnic Turks, a harbinger of an identical act four decades later; consistently bad relations with neighbouring Arab states, particularly after Turkey's recognition of Israel and the overthrow of the Iraqi monarchy by the Ba'ath Party; and a short-lived alliance with Greece and Yugoslavia, effectively dissolved by the first Cyprus crisis of the mid-1950s.

On the home front, discontent with one-party rule, secularization and the stiflingly centralized economy came to a head when four politicians – including Celal Bayar and Adnan Menderes – having been expelled from the RPP, formed the **Democrat Party** in early 1946. Despite prematurely scheduled elections of that summer and widespread balloting irregularities, the new opposition managed to gain nearly fifteen percent of the parliamentary seats. The fact that this gain was not reversed by force or chicanery was due as much to the climate of Turkish public opinion, demanding a change, as to any subtle pressure exerted by the Americans, whose **economic aid** was now pouring into the country.

A showdown could not be long postponed, however, and campaigning for the **elections of May 14, 1950**, was strenuous and unimpeded. The Democrat Party's platform promised an end to anti-business strictures for the embryonic middle-class, freer religious observance for the devout, and attention to the badly neglected agricultural sector. Though it was a safe bet that the Democrats would win, the scale of their victory – 55 percent of the vote, and, by a winner-take-all system similar to the UK's, over eighty percent of parliamentary seats – caught everyone by surprise. Bayar replaced İnönü as president, and **Menderes** took office as prime minister.

Populist governments

Virtually the first act of the new government was to permit, after a seventeen-year gap, the recitation of the call to prayer in Arabic – neatly coinciding with the start of Ramadan. Simultaneously, rashes of fez- or turban-wearing, polygamy and use of the Arabic script erupted in the provinces (where Atatürk's reforms had never really penetrated). There followed far-reaching programmes of rural loans and public works, an end to various government monopolies and restrictions on investment by foreigners, plus massive imports of luxury goods and farm machinery, based on the assumption that Turkey's allies would quietly subsidize all this.

While many of the projects were controversial, in retrospect Menderes can be credited with opening up a country where for three decades very little in the way of people, ideas, capital or goods had moved in or out. Despite lip service paid to private enterprise, however, much of this development was unplanned, uncoordinated investment in state enterprises, and most of it took the form of expensive rewards to supporters. Menderes himself, a largely self-taught farmer/lawyer, had his colossal vanity aggravated by the adulation of the peasants, who not only sacrificed livestock in his honour at his public appearances, but went so far as to name boy children after him.

The honeymoon with the electorate continued through the first years of the 1950s, aided by bumper harvests, though by 1954 clouds loomed on the horizon: the **national debt** and trade deficit were enormous, and the black-market value of the Turkish lira was one-fourth the official exchange rate. But the increasingly sensitive Democrats would not tolerate even mutterings of criticism: in 1953 assets and institutions of the ousted RPP had been expropriated and abolished, and the right-wing/religious National Party, with its handful of seats in parliament, was proscribed. The first of a series of **repressive press laws** was passed in early 1954, further poisoning the atmosphere just before the May elections. These the Democrats won even more easily than four years previously, but instead of imbuing them with confidence, they took the result as a mandate to clamp down harder on dissent and to run the country ever more shamelessly for the benefit of their clientele. The economy continued to worsen, with the first bouts of rampant **inflation,** thereafter to be a constant feature of Turkish life. During 1955 the government, looking for a distraction from, and scapegoats for, domestic problems, found both in the form of the Cyprus issue and minorities – especially İstanbul Greeks. DP-orchestrated street demonstrations got out of hand, ending in destructive **riots** aimed at foreigners and the wealthy in all three major cities.

In the wake of all this, support for the government tumbled, but probably not enough for it to have lost honestly contested elections in 1957. These, however, were heavily rigged, and the results – trimming the Democrats' strength to just over two-thirds of total – were never officially announced. Turkey thus approached the end of the decade in a parlous state, with a huge, dangerous gulf between the rural, largely pro-DP population and the intellectual/commercial elite in the towns – and, more dangerously, an alienated, antagonized military.

The first military intervention and the 1960s

Nowhere had dismay over the intentions and policies of the Democrat government been felt more keenly than in the military, who considered themselves the guardians of Atatürk's heritage. The officer corps, debarred from voting and watching the value of their fixed salaries eroded by inflation, felt betrayed as the new middle-class and Democrat apparatchiks surpassed them economically and socially. Cliques of officers had begun to formulate plans for action as far back as 1954, but it was not until May 27, 1960, that middle-ranking officers, enlisting a few commanders as figureheads, staged a **coup** – announced on the radio by a certain Colonel Alpaslan Türkeş (see p.959).

The putsch was bloodless, swift and complete. Democrat Party MPs and ministers were jailed, and there was rejoicing on the streets of the larger cities. For the next sixteen months, a **National Unity Committee** (NUC) ruled the country, and oversaw the preparation of a new, extremely liberal constitution to supersede that of 1924. The ruling committee, however, was an uneasy marriage of convenience, incorporating not only idealistic top-brass hoping for a speedy return to civilian rule, but junior officers who wished for an indefinite period of authoritarian military government, and who in fact embarked on disruptive purges of university faculties and the officer corps themselves. Committee chief and acting head of state **Cemal Gürsel** adroitly outflanked this element, exiling their representatives overseas to minor posts and lifting the ban on political activity early in 1961. The new constitution, which provided for a bicameral legislature, proportional representation in the lower house and a constitutional court, was submitted to public referendum in July, with elections scheduled for October.

The **referendum**, which was essentially a vote of confidence in the NUC, showed just 62 percent in favour of the new constitution. This was hardly gratifying to the junta, who panicked at the display of lingering support for the Democrat Party. Since the coup, several hundred leading DP members, including Menderes and Bayar, had been imprisoned and on trial at bleak Yassıada in the Sea of Marmara, on charges of undermining the 1924 constitution, corruption and complicity in the riots of 1955. Upon the return of guilty verdicts and fifteen death sentences, the NUC hastily ratified three of these – against Menderes, foreign minister Zorlu and finance minister Polatkan – while commuting the others, including that of Bayar, to life imprisonment. The three hangings, carried out a month before the elections, backfired badly, making Menderes a martyr and ensuring a long electoral life for the Justice Party (JP), the new incarnation of the now-banned Democrat Party.

The inconclusive **parliamentary elections** proved a further disappointment to the NUC; neither the Justice Party nor a refurbished RPP gained a majority, with the balance of power held by splinter groups. Under threat of another coup, the two major parties were induced to enter into a coalition, with Cemal Gürsel as president and İnönü again prime minister for the first time since 1938. These compromises rankled with certain disaffected junior officers who had hoped to be rid of the Democrats once and for all, and they resolved to clean up the "mess" with two subsequent coup attempts, one in February 1962 and another fourteen months later. The latter, involving veterans of May 27, was quelled and its leader executed. There would be no more putsches from below.

Civilian political life settled into a semblance of **normality**, with more unstable coalitions until 1965. In terms of standards of living, the promised economic reforms of the NUC had not borne fruit; the import-substitution policies of the old RPP, whereby industrial self-sufficiency – however uneconomic – was subsidized, were quietly revived, while land reform and rural development were again deferred. The first wave of **emigration** to Germany and other Western European countries acted as a social safety-valve, and the "guest workers" would return at holiday time with cars, consumer durables and – to a limited extent – European notions and wives. For the first time, independent labour unions began organizing and recruiting inside Turkey, with the right to strike finally confirmed in 1963. The growing urban proletariat found a political voice in the newly formed Turkish Workers' Party (TWP), whose very existence nudged the RPP, now led by future prime minister **Bülent Ecevit**, leftward into a social-democratic mould. **Süleyman Demirel**, who was to emerge as one of the most enduring political figures over the next three decades, became leader in 1964 of the JP, which was obliged to come out strongly for free enterprise and foreign investment. In October 1965, Demirel's Justice Party gained a majority of votes in national elections, with the RPP and TWP together tallying less than a third.

International events began to assume increasing importance in the Turkish domestic scene. Neighbouring **Cyprus** had gained independence in 1960 by terms of a treaty between the new Cypriot republic and its guarantors Britain, Greece and Turkey. Incorporated in the Treaty of Guarantee and the Cypriot constitution were extensive concessions to the Turkish Cypriot minority, who constituted roughly one-fifth of the island's population. By 1963 Cypriot president Makarios declared these clauses unworkable, and sought to limit the veto power of the Turkish community. Members of EOKA, the right-wing paramilitary force of the Greek population, took this as a cue to commence attacks on Turkish Cypriots, who replied in kind. Virtual civil war beset the island through much of 1964, with the ranks of both sides swelled by illegal, smuggled-in Greek and Turkish troops. A full-scale Greco–Turkish war was only narrowly avoided by US pressure on both countries. The Turkish government had to confine its response to retaliations against the Greek population of their two Aegean islands and İstanbul (including the expulsion of 12,000 resident Greek nationals), while communal violence recurred sporadically across Cyprus, despite the imposition of a UN-supervised truce, for the rest of the decade.

Turkey was also not immune from the spirit of May 1968, which here took the form of increased **anti-Americanism** and leftist sentiments, particularly on and around university campuses. Many Turks felt betrayed by the US's lack of support on the Cyprus issue, having studiously followed the American lead on foreign-policy issues since the end of World War II. Even the ruling establishment found the obviousness of American tutelage offensive to sentiments of national independence, and soon most of the half-dozen US military installations were quietly given over either to Turkish sovereign control or alternatively that of NATO. At the same time, relations with the Soviet Union improved dramatically. Ironically perhaps, the most lasting American legacy to Turkey would be swarms of classic automobiles and 110-volt household appliances, provided as part of Marshall Plan assistance during the 1950s or sold off by departing diplomatic and military personnel throughout the 1960s.

Demirel was returned in **1969** for a second term as prime minister, but his majority and authority were soon eroded by the defection of sixteen percent of the JP to legally reform the Democrat Party. More ominous was the upsurge in **political violence** in the streets and the universities, which was to be a pervasive feature of Turkish life until 1980. Extreme left-wing groups such as Dev Sol (Revolutionary Youth) fought it out with right-wing and/or Islamist activists such as the notorious Grey Wolves, who had set up paramilitary training camps under the tutelage of **Alpaslan Türkeş**, spokesman of the 1960 coup and founder of the fascist Nationalist Action Party (NAP).

The second military intervention and the 1970s

Against this backdrop of domestic unrest, lingering corruption and continued nonproductive parliamentary manoeuvres, the generals acted again. On March 12, 1971, they issued a proclamation forcing Demirel and his cabinet to resign in favour of an "above-party" government of reformist technocrats. This **"coup by memorandum"** allowed parliament to continue functioning, while stealing the wind from the sails of numerous restive NCOs who had hoped for a full-scale military regime. Martial law was, however, imposed on the major cities and the ever-troublesome southeast, and thousands from the university community, the press and broadcasting were arrested and tried, mostly on charges of inciting violence or class conflict. In September amendments were promulgated to limit the freedoms granted by the 1961 constitution, but soon the "above-party" regime, effectively stymied by JP operatives in the Grand National Assembly, was forced to resign. Despite, or because of, the threat of another putsch, acting premier Nihat Erim managed to cobble together a merry-go-round of successively less radical and more acceptable cabinets, and preserved a semblance of civilian rule for two more years. The army, mindful of the hash that the colonels' junta had made of neighbouring Greece since 1967, decided to let the politicians take the blame for any adverse outcome in Turkey.

The surprise winners of the **October 1973 elections** were Bülent Ecevit and his RPP, though they were soon forced into uneasy alliance with Islamist **Necmettin Erbakan**'s National Salvation Party (NSP), which gained control of several ministries. During Ecevit's short but momentous period of office, the economy was savaged by OPEC's oil-price hike, which preceded the Turkish **military intervention in Cyprus**.

The military junta then ruling Greece had ousted Cypriot president Makarios in July 1974 and replaced him with EOKA extremists supporting union with Greece. Ecevit's pro forma appeal to Britain to intervene in accordance with the Treaty of Guarantee went unheeded, so he gave the order for Turkish troops to invade the island on July 20. The EOKA regime fell three days later, after the Turks had secured a bridgehead around Kyrenia. A ceasefire was declared while furious negotiations between the Greek, Turkish and British foreign ministers continued over several weeks; on August 14, after the Greek Cypriots refused an ultimatum from Turkey, its army advanced further to occupy the northern third of the island. Over the next three decades, the situation scarcely changed: the **ceasefire** (hostilities never formally ended) was policed by UN peace-keeping patrols along the "Attila Line" between the Greek Cypriot–controlled south and the self-proclaimed Turkish Republic of Northern Cyprus. Back on the domestic front, Ecevit – riding a "victory"-induced tide of popularity – resigned in September to seek early elections and hopefully a workable parliamentary majority. This proved a major blunder, for opposition foot-dragging ensured that polling was delayed until April 1975, when Süleyman Demirel was able to assemble a coalition government along with the Islamist National Salvation Party and the fascist Nationalist Action Party, and hung on to power after inconclusive elections two years later.

All this served only to further polarize the country, which from 1976 onwards was subject to steadily increasing political **violence** by extremists at each end of the political spectrum. Annual death tolls escalated from about three hundred during 1976–77 to over three thousand during 1980, with the number of wounded and bomb explosions during this period well into five figures. While the perpetrators initially confined their activities to each other, a steady deterioration of parliamentary decorum and the politicization of trade unions and the civil service meant that incidents were soon widespread. Tit-for-tat murders in İstanbul reached twenty per day at one point, with various neighbourhoods run by particular factions – entry to these with the wrong newspaper in hand, or the wrong attire and moustache (each faction had a "dress code") guaranteed a beating or worse.

Ecevit regained power for about eighteen months from the close of 1977, and attempted to address the **dire economic situation** aggravated by successive governments' profligate public spending, trade deficits and other inflationary policies. International assistance was secured, but on condition that the budget was balanced, protectionism reduced and the lira devalued; none of this materialized. In December 1978, street battles in the southern city of Maraş between right-wing, fundamentalist Sunni gunmen and left-wing Alevîs claimed more than a hundred lives within a week; Türkeş's NAP orchestrated most of the clashes. Martial law was declared with some reluctance by Ecevit in many provinces, but this failed to prevent the establishment of an Alevî commune in the Black Sea town of Fatsa, where the army eventually sent tanks through street barricades. Against such a background of events, Demirel assumed office again in October 1979, but he too failed to halt the slide into **civil and economic chaos**.

The 1980 coup and its aftermath

The armed forces soon decided that the Republic was facing its gravest crisis yet. A planning group for a military takeover apparently existed as early as 1978, but public rumblings first surfaced in the form of a warning letter to the two major political parties at New Year 1980. By this time **martial law** was in force in all of the major cities as well as the southeast, and an economist and engineer named **Turgut Özal** had been appointed head of the State Planning Organization, in which capacity he jettisoned the import-substitution policies prevalent since the founding of the Republic in favour of an **export-oriented economy**.

Now international events intervened. Turkey's strategic importance to the West had been emphasized by the Iranian revolution and Soviet invasion of Afghanistan, and the Americans in particular were anxious to secure a stable base in the Middle East. After five years of cool relations, prompted by an embargo of arms to Turkey in the wake of the Cyprus action, rapprochement feelers were put forth. By the time the Iran–Iraq war began in April 1980, these began to include signals of tacit approval for a coup. Some sources have also alleged that, given the existing martial-law controls, the continued escalation of domestic violence was inconceivable without the military's toleration of it – even to the extent of using *agents provocateurs* to guarantee a solid pretext for a full-scale takeover.

This occurred bloodlessly on **September 12, 1980**, to the initial relief of a vast majority of the population. The frenzied killings ceased; Demirel, Ecevit, Erbakan and Türkeş were detained; all political parties were disbanded shortly after; and all trade unions and associations were closed down. Turgut Özal was, however, left in charge of the economy, since his reforms were seen as both effective and essential to Western support.

It soon became apparent that this coup was drastically different from the previous two. A junta of generals, not junior officers – the **National Security Council** (NSC) – were firmly in control from the start, and return to civilian rule would be long delayed, and within a new framework. Meanwhile, bannings, indictments and purges punctuated the early 1980s, and while the radical Right was by no means immune from prosecution, it became clear that the Left would bear the brunt of the crackdown. Nationalist right-wing beliefs, if not explicitly violent or fascist, were compatible with the generals' agenda – as was an encouragement of mildly Islamic views as an antidote to secular Marxism, as long as the fundamentalists stayed out of the military itself.

The new rulers' principal **targets**, which had been relatively untouched in prior putsches, were labour syndicates, internationalist or separatist groups and the left-leaning intelligentsia. DİSK, the far-left trade-union confederation, had 1477 of its members put on trial after its dissolution; 264 were convicted, despite lack of evidence of advocacy of violence, though the proceedings dragged on for so long – until 1990 – that many defendants qualified for immediate release on the basis of time served on remand. Even more controversial was the six-year court case against the Turkish Peace Association, with twelve defendants, including a former ambassador, sentenced. An example of the relatively lenient treatment of the Islamists was the acquittal, on appeal, of fundamentalist National Salvation Party leader Necmettin Erbakan, on charges of attempting to create an Islamic state. The Nationalist Action Party was, however, decimated, with eight capital verdicts and dozens of longer prison-terms for its members – though Türkeş himself was acquitted.

The military attacked the **universities** and their hotbeds of radicalism less directly, purging 1475 academic staff by outright dismissal, placement on nonrenewed short-term contracts or transfer to less desirable positions. All campuses were put under the control of a new body, the Higher Education Council (YÖK), subject to the direct authority of the acting head of state.

A 160-strong Consultative Committee of carefully vetted applicants was convened, which promulgated a new, highly **restrictive constitution** in 1982, expressly reversing most clauses of its 1960 predecessor. This was ratified by ninety percent of the electorate in a controversially coercive referendum, which was also an election for the presidency. No campaigning against was allowed; the only candidate was **General Kenan Evren**, head of the NSC, and it was presented as an all-or-nothing package.

Return to civilian rule and the rise of ANAP

Civilian politics was tentatively reintroduced in the **general elections of November 1983**, although severe controls were placed on parties and candidates. Precoup parties and their leaders remained excluded from politics, and only three of the fourteen newly formed parties were allowed to campaign, the rest being deemed transparent proxies for banned organizations. Nonetheless, the centrist slate backed by the generals came last, and Turgut Özal's centre-right Motherland Party (initials ANAP in Turkish) won just under half the votes and just over fifty percent of the parliamentary seats.

ANAP was a party of uneasy alliance, incorporating a wide range of opinion from economic liberals to Islamists. Özal embodied these contradictions in his person: though a devout Muslim, ex-member of the NSP and adherent of the still-clandestine but progressively bolder Nakşibendi dervish order, he had strong appetites for booze, tobacco, food and *arabesk* tunes, while his colourful and charismatic speaking-manner belied his Texan training in engineering. As party leader and prime minister, he managed the almost impossible task of balancing the opposing technocratic and traditionalist forces in the new party; simultaneously he set a scorching pace of **economic reform** during his first term, with exports reaching record levels and growth rates averaging more than six percent during the period 1983–88. Inflation, however, continued to soar, as public budgets were reflated to buy support, especially among the farmers and civil servants; by 1986 foreign indebtedness and spiralling prices were again critical issues.

In retrospect, ANAP (and Özal) during their heyday can be credited with sweeping economic and legal **reforms** bringing Turkey more into line with the international economy – and at the same time blamed for the **debasement** of public culture. Under ANAP, money and its ostentatious display assumed paramount importance, with the exact means of earning it secondary – creating an ethical climate conducive to sharp practice and the growing wave of public scandals. A provincial elite, matching Özal's small-town, lower-middle-class background, rode on his coat-tails, earning an initial reputation of being able to "get things done", in contrast to the fumbling of the 1970s. Though trained abroad (mostly in the US), they hadn't necessarily absorbed Western values, and when they had, their cue was taken from Texas rather than Europe. English became the preferred language of this *nouveau riche* class, and of the best universities, which in the wake of the National Security Council's efforts during the early Eighties had become little more than apolitical polytechnics geared to cranking out technicians. Thatcher-Reaganism was the order of the day, unlike the *noblesse oblige* of the RPP elite: **large conglomerates** and holding companies were expressly favoured, and many small businesses were forced to the wall. Along with the export earnings – and mass tourism can be included in this – came a flood of luxury goods that contrasted with the 1970s shortages: just about anything became available, for a price, flaunted by the new consuming classes. This of course aggravated the ballooning trade deficit, since Turkish manufactured products – despite improvements since the 1970s – were still not competitive on most markets.

In the 1984 and 1986 local elections, opposition parties gained some ground, particularly Erdal (son of İsmet) İnönü's Social Democrat Party (SHP in Turkish), and the True Path (DYP) and Democratic Left (DSP) parties, fronts respectively for the activities of still-proscribed Demirel and Ecevit. Another banned politician to return undercover to the hustings was Necmettin Erbakan, whose old Islamist apparatus regrouped itself as the Welfare Party (*Refah Partisi* in Turkish). Popular pressure grew for a **lifting of the ban** on pre-coup politicians, which was narrowly rescinded in mid-1987. Parliamentary elections in November showed just 36 percent support for ANAP but, because of the skewed system put into effect especially for the occasion, they took nearly two-thirds of the seats in the Grand National Assembly. The SHP emerged as the main opposition, with nearly a quarter of the seats, though they were impeded by public perception of **Erdal İnönü**, a university professor turned politician, as a nice but ineffectual individual whom the unkind nicknamed "ET" after his resemblance to Spielberg's hero.

The DYP did badly; Ecevit, his DSP party failing to poll the ten-percent nationwide figure required for parliamentary representation, tearfully announced his (very temporary) retirement from politics.

The late 1980s: trends and problems

Özal's two prime-ministerial terms were marked, not surprisingly in view of his background, by a dramatic increase in **Islamic activity**. The Department of Religious Affairs received extra staffing and funding, and the mandatory teaching hours devoted to Muslim issues in schools rose. Much of this could be attributed to a conscious effort to offset or channel the influence of Iranian-style fundamentalism, but there was also a deliberate policy of promoting moderate Islamic sentiment as a safeguard against the resurgence of communist ideology. Outside of the government apparatus, the *vakıfs*, or pious endowments, also grew spectacularly, mostly through donations from Saudi Arabia. Educational and welfare programmes run by the *vakıfs* offered, and continue to offer, some hope and relief to those trapped in the burgeoning *gecekondus* of the principal cities, where life is most precarious, but the assistance also encouraged fanatical and intolerant elements. On the other hand, the military periodically conducted purges of Islamists who managed to infiltrate the ranks.

Kurdish separatism, an intermittent issue since 1925, resurfaced in a violent form in the southeastern provinces through the actions of the Kurdish Workers' Party (PKK). Its guerilla war of attrition against the Turkish government did not initially win it widespread support, but its position was undoubtedly strengthened by the frequent over-zealous reactions of the Turkish authorities. (For a complete discussion, see p.988.)

Ties with Greece were strained not only by the Cyprus issue but by ongoing disputes over airspace, sea-bed exploitation rights and territorial waters in the Aegean, and by the Greek government's denial of full civil rights to the Turkish minority in Greek Thrace. **Bulgarian–Turkish relations** made international headlines throughout the summer of 1989, as the Communist Bulgarian regime's policy of forced Slavification of the Bulgarian Turkish minority resulted in dozens of deaths and ultimately escalated into the largest European mass emigration since World War II. Between May and August, over three hundred thousand ethnic Turks fled Bulgaria for Turkey, which initially welcomed them (the government had in fact invited them as part of a war of words with Bulgaria) and attempted to capitalize politically on the exodus. The reality of the number of refugees to be settled soon hit home, however, the border was closed, and by 1990 the new post-communist government in Sofia had formally renounced the heavy-handed assimilationist campaign of its predecessor, while most of the new arrivals eventually decided to return to Bulgaria or emigrate to Western Europe.

In direct contrast to the Turkish government's concern for the rights of Turkish minorities abroad, there was an ongoing pattern of **human-rights violations** at home. This consisted principally of inhumane conditions in prisons but more importantly torture of suspects by law-enforcement agencies, and continual harassment of the press. At various times government spokesmen admitted that torture was practised during the 1980–83 period of military rule, when hundreds of thousands of individuals were arrested, but declined comment on – or denied – allegations of continuing incidents. Several cases of official torture during the subsequent period of civilian rule were belatedly admitted, and some token prosecutions of those responsible conducted, but the guilty were often quietly promoted out of harm's way rather than being jailed.

Abuses continued into the 1990s and Amnesty International claimed that **torture** remained systematic; other monitoring organizations maintained that, while still widespread, it was no longer officially condoned. However, only after the 1991 national elections was there an official proclamation forbidding maltreatment of nonpolitical suspects prior to formal charging, to be done within 24 hours.

Restrictions on the press showed no signs of abating, with a record number of prosecutions of journalists, editors and publishers after 1984, a result of the media's boldness in testing the limits of censorship. An unsettling echo of the Menderes years was the increasing sensitivity of Özal to even the mildest criticism in print, with dozens of libel and slander suits filed by government prosecutors.

Meanwhile, in not entirely unrelated developments, Turkey's Europe-oriented **foreign policy** suffered various setbacks towards the end of the decade. Turkey had been an associate member of the EC since 1964, but its 1987 application for full membership was shelved indefinitely by the Community, ostensibly because of the need to concentrate on increased integration of the existing Twelve.

At the same time substantial PR efforts were devoted to beating back repeated proposals in the United States Congress, sponsored by the American-**Armenian lobby**, to designate April 24 as a day of "national remembrance" for the alleged genocide perpetrated against the Armenian community in 1915. This marked an increase in the sophistication of the more extreme Armenian advocates, who abandoned the policy of terrorist attacks on Turkish diplomats and installations which characterized the years 1973–82.

Finally, the dramatic changes in Eastern Europe further marginalized the country, as Soviet influence in the region diminished and doubts were cast on the strategic importance of a post-Cold War Turkey.

The presidency and death of Özal

ANAP's influence was waning by early 1989, when municipal elections showed strong support for the opposition SHP and DYP. This was due to continuing high domestic inflation, blatant nepotism benefiting Özal's cronies and extended family – including his flamboyant, cigar-smoking, whisky-drinking wife Semra – and the inevitable corruption. Under the circumstances, most observers found Özal's self-nomination for the **presidency** – and election to it in November 1989 by a parliament half-empty owing to an opposition boycott – extremely presumptuous.

As only the second civilian president in Turkish history, Özal strategically distanced himself from the nationalist/religious wing of ANAP in favour of the liberal one. Despite his official description as "above-party", Özal was still perceived as the real leader of ANAP. He effectively chose the next prime minister, **Yıldırım Akbulut**, a lacklustre yes-man unable to command much respect either within the party or among the public, where jokes at his expense became a favourite pastime. Akbulut's position was repeatedly undermined by Özal himself, who – in contravention of the constitution – assumed many of the executive functions of the prime minister. Özal's continued **interference** – including quotable, foot-in-mouth utterances that were the despair of cabinet ministers – prompted several of their resignations.

Iraq's **invasion of Kuwait** in August 1990 reinforced Özal's position, and also reminded NATO and the US of Turkey's continuing strategic position. Özal, not the prime minister, contacted other heads of state and was central in defining

△ Turgut Özal

Turkey's stance as an enthusiastic adherent of the UN sanctions, in anticipation of tangible rewards from the West for such support. He enthusiastically provided the US with landing facilities at İncirlik and Diyarbakır air bases, despite the risk of Iraqi attack, and incurred considerable financial loss by complying with UN sanctions, closing the pipeline which shipped Iraqi oil out through Turkish territory. Later in 1991 he permitted the stationing of coalition troops near the Kurdish "safe haven" across the Iraqi border.

Özal perhaps entertained hopes that Turkey would be rewarded after the war by the return of the oil-rich province of Mosul. All he tangibly got for Turkey's cooperation was President Bush the Elder's undertaking that an independent Kurdistan would not be set up by dismembering Iraq. In the end the coalition treated Turkey shabbily, failing to compensate it adequately for its losses – or for its reluctant hosting of hundreds of thousands of terrified Iraqi Kurdish refugees. Turkey's participation in the anti-Iraq alliance sparked fundamentalist and leftist **attacks** on local American and foreign property and personnel throughout early 1991, and sporadic street demonstrations against the war. A police crackdown ensured a calm environment for President Bush's visit in July, the first of an American leader to Turkey in several decades and growing evidence of Turkey's importance for the US as a regional ally.

Moreover, a nationwide **political vacuum** in terms of maturity and substance was yawning both before and after the war. ANAP, beset by resignations, defections and factions, had lost its original energy and direction, but the opposition was not yet able to capitalize on this. The SHP, rent by an internal power struggle in which chairman İnönü ousted general secretary Deniz Baykal, accordingly slipped from its 1989 electoral standing, while Bülent Ecevit's DSP rebounded from the dead by doing extremely well at the SHP's and DYP's expense in August 1990 municipal elections. İnönü renewed his call for a merger of the two left-of-centre parties but was rebuffed by Ecevit.

Overall the electorate was uninspired by personality politics and almost complete lack of coherent party agendas or manifestos. The only consensus that developed was the posthumous **rehabilitation of Menderes** and his cronies, an act of contrition that took the form of naming streets and public facilities after Menderes, and – on the thirtieth anniversary of the hangings of the three ministers – their solemn reburial in a special mausoleum in İstanbul.

The new ANAP premier and party leader **Mesut Yılmaz** decided to go to the polls considerably earlier than the November 1992 limit stipulated: with the economy worsening, he preferred earlier to later, while some of Özal's aura might still rub off on ANAP.

But the **October 1991 elections**, considered the fairest since 1983, produced a surprise result: the DYP was top finisher, with ANAP a strong second, and İnönü's SHP third. The biggest surprise, however, was Erbakan's Welfare Party's unprecedented seventeen percent of the vote. But since no party secured an absolute majority, a **coalition** was inevitable – between DYP and SHP, forged after several weeks of negotiations. Demirel was designated prime minister, İnönü deputy prime minister, with the various lower ministries divided between their two parties.

The coalition began with considerable optimism and goodwill (or at least forbearance) on all sides, even from the excluded ANAP; both parties pledged to pull together in tackling the country's pressing economic problems. Rapid privatization of state firms was envisioned, along with a better deal for labour, and tax reform to make the wealthy pay their fair share after the freewheeling ANAP years. The unenviable task of tackling inflation was assigned to **Tansu Çiller**, state minister for economy and the sole woman cabinet-member.

There were also promises to make Turkey a *konuşan* (talking) society, where opinions were freely aired without fear of retribution, in contrast to the intimidated silence of the past. This intention ran into an immediate snag, however, when some of the 22 parliamentary deputies of **HEP** (considered a PKK front; see p.990) – legally compelled to run on the SHP ticket but winning a quarter of the party's seats – caused an uproar when they refused to recite the standard loyalty oath upon being sworn in. **Deniz Baykal** further destabilized the SHP by repeatedly challenging İnönü for its top post, with the latter defending his position by predicting the demise of the coalition should Baykal replace him.

Legislation **un-banning pre-1980 parties** saw the Republican People's Party revived, setting off a scramble as to who would assume its leadership: 1979 chief Ecevit, İnönü (envisioning its incorporation into the coalition) or his persistent adversary Deniz Baykal. Baykal won, and as defections to his standard from DSP and SHP mounted, coupled with resignations of HEP deputies from SHP, the coalition's governing majority dwindled to three.

Throughout 1992 **Özal** played an increasingly negative, spoiling role, much of it a function of the personal antipathy between him and Demirel, who openly sought a way to have him impeached. Özal also sparred with ANAP leader Yılmaz for influence in a party which as president he ostensibly no longer led, attempting to unseat his old protégé. In his capacity as president, Özal delayed the signing of many bills, prompting serious discussion of having him removed from office, a drawn-out procedure requiring a two-thirds majority in parliament. In the event, this proved unnecessary; Özal **died suddenly** of a heart attack on April 17, 1993.

It was impossible for anyone to remain indifferent to Özal, despite his many faults the most eloquent and influential head of state since Atatürk. Respected by many for his energy, courage and vision, despised by an equal number for his overbearing manner and shameless self-aggrandizement, he remains an ambiguous figure who sometimes did the right thing (for example his advocacy of concessions to the Kurds) for opportunistic reasons.

After Özal

Demirel eventually emerged as president, while **Tansu Çiller** – not Demirel's top choice – became **prime minister** in June 1993. Like Özal and Demirel on the centre-right of Turkish politics, she was a US-educated academic-technocrat recruited by Demirel in 1989 as part of an effort to modernize his party's image. With her assertive style and telegenic manner, she attracted considerable popular support, and her rise to power was initially viewed with optimism.

Hopes, however, were soon dashed as the new prime minister proved woefully inadequate to the tasks at hand. Expectations of a fresh look at the **Kurdish problem** vanished as Çiller relegated all initiative to military hardliners. Despite repeated assurances that the PKK was all but defeated, the death toll in the undeclared civil war in east Anatolia continued to mount. Expulsion of villagers from affected areas resulted in a tide of internal refugees, while efforts to foster a political solution foundered when the latest pro-Kurdish Democracy Party (DEP) was proscribed and most of its MPs prosecuted.

The government's **economic policy** was characterized by hasty improvisation. Inflation shot up from 66 percent in 1993 to a staggering 120 percent during 1994 – when the Turkish lira lost half its value in one month – hovering around 80 percent in subsequent years. A bold programme of privatizations and tax reform failed to materialize since, given the complete lack of unemployment or early retirement benefits, or retraining schemes, such moves would have caused enormous social distress and threatened social stability. A spate of industrial disasters with large loss of life made headlines despite a commitment to a better deal for labour, while massive strikes by public-sector workers won them only paltry wage increases. In late November 1994, a privatization bill was finally passed, eleven years after being first discussed.

In **foreign relations**, hesitation replaced Özal's active (if at times bumbling) intervention in Balkan, Central Asian and Middle Eastern affairs. Seven foreign ministers in thirty months prevented the emergence of consistent policies. Russian displeasure resulted in the toning down of noisy public support for the Chechen rebels. Equally vociferous Turkish sympathy for the Muslim cause in Bosnia failed to translate into a coherent policy initiative. Tensions with Greece flared periodically into crises aggravated by demagogic posturing by political leaders in both countries; in February 1996 the two countries nearly went to war over the sovereignty of the Kardak/İmia archipelago, a pair of uninhabited rocky islets in the Aegean Sea. While there had long been considerable unity of opinion on the Cyprus issue, in that the status quo was seen as the only viable option, from the mid-1990s on, economically strapped Turkey began withdrawing some troops from Cyprus and hinting to the intransigent and sometimes ungrateful Turkish-Cypriot leadership that some accommodation with the South would end the international isolation of the North – and on this issue, of Turkey as well, in forums like the UN and the EU.

Uncivil liberties: human rights in Turkey

Turkey's **human-rights record** has been a perennial irritant in relations with the EU. Despite Demirel's 1991 election pledge that police stations would have "walls of glass", international human-rights monitoring organizations reported little substantive change in subsequent years, with torture and suspicious deaths in custody routine occurrences. Despite 1995 modification of many objectionable clauses of the 1982 constitution, and of the notorious Article 8 of the 1991 Anti-Terrorism Law, Turkish prisons still contained over a hundred nonviolent political prisoners well into the millennium. The civilian government habitually deferred to chiefs of the internal security forces, which, together with elements of the State Security Tribunals (finally abolished in 2002), the police and the gendarmerie, form a virtual para-state – the "deep state" in dissident parlance – accountable to no one.

Between 1990 and 2000 a sharp rise in urban terrorism occurred, with literally scores of **political assassinations** perpetrated by Islamic fundamentalists, far-leftists and possibly rogue civilian operatives of the Special Warfare Department, the common feature being the inability of police to identify or apprehend any suspects. Targets have included American personnel during and after the Gulf War; officers in the army and security forces; secularist professors, including the head of the national bar society; and (after a two-decade respite) members of Turkey's Jewish community.

But it was the demise of **Uğur Mumcu** in an Ankara car-bombing of January 1993 which caused the most widespread revulsion. His funeral, attended by hundreds of thousands (including the National Security Council), was the occasion for mass demonstrations of support for his ideals of secularism and pluralistic democracy. As ever, nobody significant was apprehended in the case, with his relatives alleging a cover-up amidst wider murmurings of involvement by radical fundamentalists, in connivance with elements of the "deep state". Meanwhile, police devoted most of their energies to crushing the Marxist terrorist group Dev Sol with a series of spectacular shoot-ups of alleged safe houses in İstanbul and elsewhere. Another feature of the Çiller era was the huge upsurge in the number of **"disappeared" persons** – usually left-wing or Kurdish activists who vanished after being detained by police or by

The only significant – if controversial – foreign-policy success of the Çiller-led coalition was the conclusion in March 1995 of a **customs–union** agreement with the EU. Overseas, there was considerable opposition in view of Turkey's poor human-rights record; within the country, opponents pointed out that billions of dollars in annual import duties were being forfeited, while Turks would still not have freedom of movement to and within Europe. Though falling considerably short of full EU membership for Turkey, the agreement, which would take effect incrementally between 1996 and 2000, was still trumpeted as a triumph by the increasingly beleaguered government.

Perhaps the most important civic issue facing Çiller's government was its handling of major **corruption scandals** which erupted almost weekly. As in Italy, no political party was immune from guilt, as all had governed since the 1960s. Most scandals concerned public entities such as the PTT, the Health Ministry and the Social Security Administration, whose officials allegedly took kickbacks for awarding contracts to private companies. In the most spectacular case, Özal's widow and daughter were accused of contracting a mafia hit-team to shoot Engin Civan, chairman of a state bank, who allegedly received a $5 million bribe to fix a credit deal but failed to deliver the goods. Another who figured prominently was the prime minister's husband, Özer Çiller, a businessman who amassed $50 million worth of real estate (partly in the US) during his wife's term in office. An Associated Press feature in September 1996 listed Tansu Çiller among the world's ten most corrupt politicians, so it was hardly surprising that she did little to combat

unidentified civilians. From 1995 to 2001, female relatives of "disappeared" persons rallied regularly at İstanbul's Galatasaray Square each Saturday, defying police harassment and occasional mass arrests.

Early 1996 saw the conclusion of year-long court proceedings against internationally acclaimed novelist **Yaşar Kemal**. He had been charged with promulgating "separatist propaganda" and fomenting "hatred between races", following his January 1995 article in *Der Spiegel* describing the Turkish state as a "system of unbearable repression and atrocity" and claiming that the Kurdish rebellion was a justifiable response to seventy years of official repression (an English version appeared in the special "File on Turkey" of *Index on Censorship*, Vol. 24 1/1995). With the eyes of the world on Turkey so soon after the customs-union ratification, he was given a suspended twenty-month sentence in March, but not before 99 other prosecutions under Article 8 had been brought against artists and intellectuals who had rallied to his support.

The need for genuine action was again underlined in May 1998, with the assassination attempt by ultra-nationalist extremists on Akın Birdal, head of the İHD (Turkey's Human Rights Association), who was facing twenty different court cases trying to link him to the outlawed PKK (Kurdish Workers' Party). Despite being confined to a wheelchair after the shooting, Birdal was sentenced to one year in jail for "inciting racial hatred" (ie acknowledging that there is a Kurdish minority in Turkey).

Similar court cases and violent incidents continued into the new millennium, until just before the unprecedented liberalization laws passed by the Turkish parliament during summer 2002. But there was another upsurge in late 2005, occasioned by Orhan Pamuk's comments to a Swiss newspaper about the killing of Armenians and Kurds (see p.982), and the fallout from a September conference in İstanbul on the fate of Armenians under the Ottomans, with five journalists facing charges for merely reporting that the gathering had taken place. Abundant human-rights guarantees have always existed in Turkey on paper since late Ottoman times – the EU will only be impressed in the coming years by the practical application of the latest versions.

this endemic feature of Turkish political culture. Even before June 1993, there had been widespread disillusionment with the coalition, and Çiller's inadequacies soon also fuelled discontent within government. Old DYP bosses led internal opposition to Çiller with the tacit backing of President Demirel, whose dislike of his former protégée was apparent. The anti-Çiller front found a ready ally in ANAP leader **Mesut Yılmaz**, whose opposition also seemed motivated principally by intense personal hatred of "that woman".

The junior coalition partner fared no better. Former Ankara mayor Murat Karayalçın, who had replaced retiring Erdal İnönü as SHP leader in September 1993, proved unable to quell feuding within the party or to subordinate his rivalry with CHP leader Deniz Baykal in the interests of the long-mooted merger. By late 1994, saddled also with the dismal performance of SHP-led municipalities and rent by increased radicalism within the traditionally leftist Alevî community, the SHP was disintegrating. In February 1995, the party formally dissolved and the remnants merged with the CHP; former foreign minister **Hikmet Çetin** was designated interim leader of the unified party, and thus Çiller's newest deputy prime minister. But in September, Deniz Baykal returned as head of the neo-CHP, and after falling out with Çiller, announced the end of the electoral pact. Elections were set for December, with the tattered coalition as interim caretaker government.

The 1995 elections and the rise of Refah

The **election results** provided a rude shock for established parties of both right and left. DYP did poorly with 19.2 percent of the vote, down eight points from 1991; the European Parliament's ratification of the customs-union agreement just the week before had no effect. ANAP under lacklustre Mesut Yılmaz tied for second place with an almost identical vote share, down five points from 1991. The CHP, with 10.8 percent, came within a whisker of not passing the statutory ten-percent nationwide minimum for parliamentary representation; Ecevit's DSP did only slightly better at fourteen percent. HADEP, the latest Kurdish-interest party, failed to gain seats at 4.8 percent, though it scored a majority in several southeastern provinces; Turkeş's quasi-fascist MHP also missed the barrier at 8.7 percent. The only clear winner in the election was **Refah** with 21.3 percent of votes cast, taking 197 out of 550 seats in the recently enlarged parliament.

The result was hardly surprising, as political Islam had been making impressive gains since the 1980s, when Özal and the NSC had given its milder expressions their blessing. Refah established itself as the most active grassroots party; alone among political groups, it harnessed the energies of women (however conservatively attired) and employed door-to-door canvassing techniques, relying on campaign material that addressed – in however skewed a manner – social issues such as prostitution and income inequality, rather than stressing personalities and platitudes. In the burgeoning *gecekondu*s, it alone seemed to represent the values and aspirations of the newly urbanized underclass, attracting it with populist rhetoric. To the lower-middle-class bazaar craftsman most at risk from the trappings of liberal capitalism, Refah promised protection in the form of a sharply renegotiated customs union. In the conservative east, its Islamic ecumenicism seemed to provide a reasonable alternative to many Kurds alienated by the more usual forms of Turkish nationalism. Last but not least, many voters threw in their lot with Refah simply in protest at the corruption and inertia of the discredited mainstream parties.

In 1994 **municipal elections**, Refah carried a plurality of cities across the country, including both metropolitan İstanbul and Ankara (by contrast, it did poorly in rural areas and small towns). In İstanbul, initial fears of puritanism run amok – alcohol-free pubs, gender-segregated buses, *Swan Lake* in harem pants – were quickly dispelled as the administration of Mayor Recep Tayyip Erdoğan proved pragmatic, efficient and remarkably honest by Turkish standards. Pollution was substantively addressed, extra buses laid on, the rubbish collected regularly and disabled facilities provided. Cynics said the rabbits would stop coming out of the Refah skullcap as soon as clandestine donations from the Saudis dried up; others pointed out that Refah's success was earned both by their opponents' moral bankruptcy and by their own organizational skill. Relative Refah competence in Turkey's largest city helped convert many voters in time for the national elections, and seemed to establish young Erdoğan as heir apparent to the party's septuagenarian leader Erbakan, nicknamed "the Hoca".

The **Islamic revivalism** which had gripped increasingly broader segments of Turkish society since Özal's time can just be seen as the latest in successive cycles of reaction against the Atatürkist secular republic. In post-1923 Turkey, "secularism" and "laicism" had always meant subordinating the clergy to a Ministry of Religious Affairs, simultaneously keeping it out of politics, suppressing the public expression of Islam and deeming it strictly a matter of private conscience – quite different from its Western interpretation as freedom of belief and equal treatment for all religions. The long-standing official ban on **traditional Islamic dress** at state functions meant in practice that many young people of conservative social background could never expect to enter a public career, or even be admitted to university. A December 1989 decree empowering individual universities to allow, at their discretion, attendance by women wearing headscarves was viewed by secularists as the thin edge of a wedge of increased religiosity. For them, such garb is not akin to a Sikh train-driver in Britain wearing a turban, but a red flag before the bull of official atheism. But by the mid-1990s, wearers of the scarf or the prophetic beard had grown from an initial radical fringe to include some of the brightest members of the academic community.

The prohibition of **dervish orders** had also begun to grate, as the various mystical brotherhoods emerged from underground and gained renewed popularity in the 1980s. For a majority of the population, Islam remained a much stronger cultural presence than the assertive Westernizing of the elites, and a more homespun expression of the national spirit than the quasi-colonial arrogance often associated with the Atatürkist establishment. On a wider level there was a general **distrust of the West**, regarded as the wellspring of Christian prejudice and capitalist exploitation, sworn enemy of the Muslim world and betrayer of the Bosnians, Chechens, Azeris and Palestinians. From this posture it was not too far a leap to overt anti-Semitism and hostility towards Israel; opposition to a series of military cooperation agreements signed between Turkey and Israel during the final months of the DYP–CHP coalition formed a key plank in Refah's campaign.

Refah takes power

The political establishment reacted to the December election results with a jerryrigged **DYP–ANAP coalition** of second-bests, expressly designed to keep Refah from assuming power. But they could only muster 267 seats out of the 276 needed for a working majority, and overtures to both left-of-centre parties, in order to form a three-way, right–left coalition, failed as Mesut Yılmaz presided over an unstable minority government, characterized by intensified mutual loathing between himself and Çiller, and constant sniping from Refah – which felt cheated of its electoral spoils – and from the rest of parliament, which rang down the curtain in June 1996 with a motion of no confidence.

The annual spring offensive against the PKK and the highly visible Yaşar Kemal case indicated the pervasive influence of the ex-security service chiefs who had infiltrated Çiller's entourage at her express invitation, giving the DYP the nickname of "Police Academy". But they were unable to protect her against impending investigations into corruption, in particular allegations that she'd helped herself to $6.5 million from the central bank to finance the recent elections. To save her skin, in mid-July she negotiated a **DYP coalition with Refah**, something she'd sworn she would never do, with Erbakan as prime minister and herself as foreign minister and deputy prime minister; her price was the dropping of all proceedings against her, which Erbakan had encouraged. Secularist, professional women, who had believed her claim to be their last line of defence against the *hoca*s, faxed their resentment in plenitude to DYP headquarters; feelings ran equally high in parliament, where punch-ups flared and handguns were drawn as the coalition was approved by a narrow vote of 278 to 265. Lurid press headlines predicted coup and disaster as Erbakan embarked on a series of controversial trips to Iran and Libya, sent emissaries to Iraq and generally made friendly noises towards various global pariahs.

The courtly, soft-voiced Erbakan, with a taste for expensive shoes and ties plus 25 pilgrimages to Mecca under his Gucci belt, initially proved nimbler than his detractors. While secularists conjured spectres of turbaned *kadi*s (Islamic judges) and obligatorily veiled women, Refah moved quickly to divest itself, in public at least, of its threatening image. Within weeks of taking office, after a discreet word from the military's US minders, the government meekly signed a new military treaty with Israel, making mockery of its campaign promise to tear up such documents. Authorization for the use by NATO aircraft of two airbases in the southeast was quietly extended, despite prior characterization of NATO as a "formal occupation". An IMF negotiating team, in Ankara to sort through the morass of Turkish finances (its foreign debt ranked among the top ten worldwide), was pleasantly surprised to hear nothing further about either zero-interest banking or a proposed "Islamic currency". A September party conference jettisoned much of the radical vocabulary that the Islamists had accumulated over 23 years in opposition, and Refah trod softly in the cities which it controlled. Non-veiled wives of Refah MPs began making the social rounds, and soon Erbakan himself was spotted committing the ultimate Islamist sacrilege: laying the customary wreath at Atatürk's tomb. Critics alleged that Refah was merely practising **taqiya** – the temporary concealment of one's true aims in the interest of Islam – and that given a clear electoral majority, a radical fundamentalist programme would in fact be implemented. Certainly the party contained, in addition to technocrat renegades from ANAP, a radical fringe eager to embrace Iran-style rule – and ominously, sales of shotguns burgeoned in Refah-dominated neighbourhoods.

In terms of day-to-day administration, the performance of the new government disappointed. There were no imaginative initiatives against hyperinflation and the mayhem in the east, only a proposal for an "M-8" of developing Muslim nations to parley with the Group of Seven. And worst of all, in November 1996, a high-speed **car crash at Susurluk** near Ankara virtually proved the long-muttered assertions of a link between right-wing-nationalist assassins, top police chiefs, the anti-PKK Kurdish drug mafia, and certain elements of the DYP. A representative member of each faction was found dead or dying in the wreckage, along with a fair quantity of weaponry and drugs, and DYP Interior Minister **Mehmet Ağar** was compelled to resign when his close ties to the group were demonstrated. The assassin, Abdullah Çatlı, long wanted by Interpol for participation in the 1981 attempt to murder Pope John Paul II, was given a state funeral, and even though a desultory investigation sputtered along for two years, Susurluk – characterized as "equal to 100 Watergates" – became a byword for cover-ups, the corruption of politicians and the strength of the "deep state".

Islam under fire

The military's growing unease with Refah surfaced at a marathon meeting of the **National Security Council** on February 28, 1997. The NSC, consisting of Turkey's five top military commanders, plus the president, the prime minister and three leading ministers, meets monthly and is acknowledged by most Turkey observers as the country's final arbiter of power. It stipulated **twenty measures** designed to safeguard secularism and curb the growth of private weapons purchases, Islamic schools, religious brotherhoods and the Islamic media. With European relations at an all-time low and with US support certain in the face of any perceived Islamic threat, the military had little to lose by baring their teeth. Tanks duly rolled through the streets of an Ankara suburb when its Refah mayor and the Iranian ambassador made speeches advocating the introduction of *sharia* law. Yet even in its beleaguered condition Refah managed to secure closure of the country's 79 **casinos**, their billion-dollar annual turnover having acted as a honeypot for Turkish, Russian and Israeli mafiosi.

Pressure on Refah increased, with attention focused on the right of female civil servants to wear "Islamic" headscarves at work, and plans to build a series of giant mosques in central Ankara and İstanbul. Two DYP cabinet ministers resigned, calling for fresh elections and another DYP-ANAP coalition to exclude Refah. In late June 1997 the inevitable happened when, under duress, **Erbakan stepped down** and judicial proceedings were instigated against Refah. This "silent coup" left President Demirel free to invite ANAP's Yılmaz to form a new government of "national reconciliation" along with Bülent Ecevit and his DSP, bolstered by defections from the DYP.

One of the new coalition government's first moves to combat the Islamists was cunning legislation raising the **compulsory secular education** span from five to eight years (from ages 7–12 to ages 7–15). This denied parents the opportunity to send their children to the religious **imam hatip okulları** (religious oratory schools) until they were 15 rather than 12, fatally reducing the religious schools' enrolment and income in the process. Legislators claimed that they had acted in the best educational interests of Turkey's youth, while many parents and children (particularly from poor areas) rued the demise of these academically very successful schools, which had burgeoned with official tolerance since 1980, and where only a few weekly hours were devoted to Arabic and the Koran.

The secularist establishment scored another victory over the Islamists in January 1998, when **Refah's forcible dissolution** was ordered by the Constitutional Court (for "acting against the principles of the secular Republic"), with Erbakan banned again from politics for five years. International condemnation of these moves came from both the EU, which had just rejected Turkey's renewed application to join, and the US. The Islamists were far from beaten, however, and a new successor party, **Fazilet (Virtue)**, was established immediately. Many former Refah deputies flocked to it, and Fazilet held the largest number of seats in parliament. Led by former Erbakan aide **Recai Kutan**, Fazilet sought to present a more moderate image than its precursor, with an ostensibly pro-EU and pro-human-rights manifesto.

In September 1998 the popular Fazilet mayor of İstanbul, **Recep Tayyip Erdoğan**, was jailed for four months for a speech the prosecution claimed "incited armed fundamentalist rebellion"; he had in fact quoted some admittedly provoca-tive lines ("The mosques are our barracks, the minarets our bayonets, the domes our helmets, and the believers our soldiers...") from a poem by Ziya Gökalp, a hard-line Republican nationalist and one of Atatürk's intellectual godfathers. Erdoğan was widely respected for both literally and metaphorically cleaning up İstanbul, and his brief imprisonment – which attracted queues of visiting well-wishers – was widely regarded as a hollow victory by a suspect secular establish-ment over an honest (albeit "Islamist") politician. Prime Minister Yılmaz – who had returned to power on an anti-corruption platform – ironically found himself implicated in a financial scandal revealed by the ongoing investigations of the Susurluk incident. A vote of "no confidence" instigated by the main opposition party, Deniz Baykal's CHP, brought down the coalition in November 1998.

The return and retreat of the Grey Wolves

President Demirel was now obliged to ask his perennial political foe, Ecevit, to form an interim government. The nominally left-wing Ecevit was unsurpris-ingly reluctant to ask Fazilet to join him; the CHP was similarly cold-shoul-dered; but **elections** were actually held on schedule in **April 1999**. Ecevit's DSP, bolstered by the public euphoria surrounding PKK supremo Abdullah Öcalan's capture (see p.992), won the largest number of votes (22 percent) and 136 parliamentary seats. The biggest surprise, however, was the meteoric return of the National Action Party (MHP in Turkish), who finished second with 18.2 percent of the vote (compared to 8.7 percent in 1995), which translated into 129 seats. Notorious founder Alpaslan Türkeş had recently died, succeeded by **Devlet Bahçeli**, who made valiant attempts to portray the MHP in a more moderate light, while glossing over the party's history of political violence and lurid symbolism of a howling wolf (in ultranationalist mythology, a grey wolf had led the first Turkic tribes west out of central Asia). The MHP capital-ized on public anger over the seemingly endless war with the PKK and equally futile attempts by Turkey to be accepted for EU candidacy. Fazilet saw its vote-share drop to 15 percent (against 21.3 percent polled for Refah in 1995), hardly surprising given the military and secular establishment's vendetta against Islamists. They did, however, manage to retain control of İstanbul and Ankara in the simultaneous municipal elections. The second electoral shock was to find Atatürk's old party, the CHP, with no seats in the new parliament as it had failed to clear the ten-percent barrier. ANAP finished fourth, just over the ten-percent barrier for 86 seats, and together with the two front-running parties formed yet **another coalition** to exclude the Islamists.

The pact between leftist but nationalist Ecevit – wary of the EU, hardline on the Cyprus issue – and the rightist MHP initially proved surprisingly stable, as MHP leader Bahçeli was willing to compromise on his followers' hot-button issues. As the world watched what it would do with the imprisoned Öcalan, the government declined to ratify the death sentence handed down in July 1999 and allowed Öcalan's appeal to the European Court of Justice to take its course. Action against the Islamists continued, however, and the country's chief prosecutor opened a case in the Constitutional Court aimed at **closing down Fazilet**.

Economic fragility resulting from the worst touristic year in a decade was compounded by the **catastrophic earthquake** which struck northwestern Turkey on August 17, 1999. Registering 7.4 on the Richter scale, it devastated property in Turkey's most industrialized and heavily populated region, and killed nearly twenty thousand. Survivors were outraged by needless deaths in collapsed apartments built on unsuitable sites and/or with substandard materials. Public anger was directed at local authorities for winking at violations of the zoning and building codes, and at the shambolic response of the emergency services; foreign aid teams were equally appalled, idly waiting for directions while trapped victims perished. Even the army, usually either too respected or too feared to be criticized by ordinary Turks, came under fire for saving its own first and failing to help the public. This scapegoat-hunting, in which the housing minister himself was implicated, ignored universal complicity in decades of shoddy building; blocks of flats were often priced unrealistically cheaply, making them fatally attractive to rural migrants who bought them no questions asked – and got, structurally, what they paid for.

Ironically, the earthquake had some lasting **positive consequences**. An outpouring of material aid and sympathy from arch-rival Greece – whose aid teams were first on the scene – heralded a sustained thaw in bilateral relations. In December 1999, after foreign minister İsmail Cem had presented Turkey's case and negotiated several compromises over long-standing problems, Greece dropped its objections and Turkey became an official candidate for **eventual EU membership**; Greece has since in fact become Turkey's major EU sponsor, a not entirely altruistic stance since admission would shift the Union's eastern frontier – and the arduous policing duties that go with it – to Turkey.

Early in 2000, nationwide police raids uncovered an alarming network of "safe houses" set up by **Turkish Hizbullah**, an extreme Islamic fundamentalist organization. Found at several of the group's hideouts were the dismembered remains of the group's victims, most of them businessmen of Kurdish origin or members of rival Islamic organizations. Recai Kutan, leader of the beleaguered Fazilet party, dared to voice what many privately believed – that the state itself had been turning a blind eye to Hizbullah's actions, seeing them as a useful counter to the Marxist PKK, Hizbullah's sworn enemies. Kutan was roundly criticized by the Turkish military, and pressure on moderate Islamists continued; in March, former prime minister Erbakan was given a one-year suspended prison sentence and a permanent ban from politics for a speech made in 1994.

In May a constitutional crisis was avoided by the appointment of **Ahmet Necdet Sezer** to the presidency. PM Ecevit had wanted his old rival Demirel to continue in office, but the constitution forbade more than one seven-year term as president, and attempts to amend the office to two five-year terms failed. A last-minute compromise candidate and a Constitutional Court judge (rather than a politician or general like all of Turkey's previous presidents), Sezer has since acted as an advocate of freedom of expression and a stickler for adherence to the law, as well as proving influential in pushing forward reforms necessary to begin the process of EU accession. However, in July the state prosecutor renewed his call for the closure of Fazilet on the grounds that it was a continuation of the banned Refah. The embattled Islamists got a brief reprieve in July when Sezer, in a principled stand, proved less maleable than anticipated by refusing to sign a government decree sacking hundreds of pro-Islamic civil servants; he has since vetoed other measures which in his opinion violate democratic principles.

Late in 2000, the authorities attempted to introduce so-called "F-type" jails with one-to-three-person "white" cells replacing dormitory accommodation in the nation's overcrowded **prisons**. While an ostensibly humane move, the real motive was to dissolve the dorms, which allegedly served as "universities for indoctrination" by jailed "terrorists" who effectively ran many of the prisons, and make it easier to isolate alleged troublemakers for torture in the privacy of solitary confinement. The prisoners, many of them members of the proscribed Marxist-Leninist Revolutionary Party, responded with **hunger strikes** and barricades. December assaults by elite troops on prisons nationwide led to the deaths of at least thirty inmates and two soldiers and the mass transfer of the survivors to the F-type jails. This harsh strategy backfired as the number of fasters increased, some of them released MLRP members fasting at home in solidarity. In May 2001, an amendment to the Anti-Terror Law allowed F-cell inmates to mix with others in recreational areas, and civic committees were set up to monitor prisons, but by autumn 2002, over fifty of the several hundred hunger strikers had died, with neither the fasters nor the authorities inclined to back down. The issue of the "white" cells remains live to this day.

In the international arena, the controversy surrounding Turkey's **treatment of Armenians between 1895 and 1915** stubbornly refused to go away. During autumn 2000, the Turkish government reacted with anger and a threat to cancel defence contracts worth billions of dollars when the United States House Foreign Relations Committee actually approved a resolution deeming as "genocide" the slaughter of the Armenians in 1915. Outgoing President Clinton, deciding that US–Turkish relations hung in the balance, ensured that the bill never had a floor vote. By contrast **France**, at the instigation of an MP of Armenian descent, officially recognized the massacres by a parliamentary resolution of January 2001, joining Russia and just ahead of Canada (2002) in doing so. Following the recall of the Turkish ambassador to France, mobs attacked the French Embassy and business leaders called for a boycott of French goods. In further retaliation, Turkey cancelled bridge-building and satellite deals with French companies, and refused to accept French tenders for military contracts. On a lighter note, Prime Minister Ecevit, who had given up his Renault in protest, was forced to use it again when his Hyundai broke down.

Economic and political meltdown

After a deceptively smooth economic ride for Turkey since the 1999 elections, private **banks** began to fail in late 2000; by the end of this initial crisis, a half-dozen were wound up or put into receivership of the state-run **Savings Deposit Insurance Fund**, which compensated account-holders who'd lost their savings. The last and most spectacular crash occurred in November, when Demirbank found itself without liquidity after making the classic mistake of borrowing short-term at high rates while lending long; it ended up being rescued by HSBC, which now owns it.

A new **crash of late February 2001** was the final straw, sending share prices reeling and another half-dozen unsteady banks into the arms of the SDIF. After a snap decision by foreign capital to quit the country, compounded by insider trading, the Turkish lira – which had been artificially tied to the dollar in an IMF-backed plan to reduce chronic inflation – was free-floated. The exchange rate rocketed as everyone rushed to buy dollars, whose price nearly doubled by April.

Inflation, at 21 percent in February, rose to nearly fifty percent by May. Stoical Turks saw the value of their savings, investments and wages slashed overnight.

As damage limitation, **Kemal Derviş**, an experienced, Washington-based World Bank vice president, was appointed Minister of the Economy as an independent, though with his extraordinary powers he functioned in effect as a "fourth party" of the coalition. Viewed as an economic messiah, Derviş persuaded the IMF to release billions in aid far earlier than planned. Among his stringent reforms was the overdue decoupling of politics and economics by the privatization or liquidation of the four state-owned banks, which had hitherto acted as conduits for ruling parties to funnel dubious loans to supporters. The only silver lining to the cloud was the cancellation of a $19.5 billion spending spree by the military, at the same time as neighbouring Greece was cutting back on military expenditure.

In June, the Fazilet party was finally **banned** by the Constitutional Court for "anti-secular activities", specifically for inciting protests against the prohibition of headscarf-donning by women in education and government employment, and for backing MP Merve Kavakçı's bid to swear an oath of office wearing said scarf. The futility of banning Fazilet was immediately demonstrated by the rapid formation of the AK (*Adalet ve Kalkınma*, Justice and Development) party, under former Fazilet mayor of İstanbul **Recep Tayyip Erdoğan**; a rival party (*Saadet* or "Contentment") attracted the old Islamist guard, again under Recai Kutan.

Summer 2001 saw parliament working desultorily on a draft package of **constitutional amendments** to bolster Turkey's EU bid, including guarantees for greater freedom of thought, expression and association, and the easing of restrictions on public use of the Kurdish, Laz and Circassian languages. The three coalition partners bickered endlessly, with ANAP ostensibly pro-European and MHP slyly scuppering plans without looking as though they were responsible; one of the nationalists' loopier counter-proposals was to officially replace all "foreign" (ie Greek- or Kurdish-based) place names in Anatolia with purely Turkish ones.

Domestic politics were temporarily overshadowed by the **September 11 terrorist strikes**, which boosted secularist Turks, as worldwide condemnation of Islamic extremism seemed to justify their own persecution of political Islam. Turkey instantly became the "blue-eyed boy" of the US, as the country's role as the major American ally (along with Israel) in the Middle East was highlighted. Tired of European criticism over human rights, Cyprus and economic mismanagement, Turkey briefly basked in the praise (and promises of aid) of a US congressional delegation visiting Ankara. Another piece of good news was an unexpected **thaw in the Cyprus stand-off**, with Greek Cypriot leader Glafkos Clerides and Turkish Cypriot leader Rauf Denktaş renewing negotiations in December after a four-year gap in communication.

The by-now thoroughly unpopular PM Ecevit was hospitalized in May 2002, and didn't reappear at work for two months. By July, the coalition government began to totter as the coalition partners challenged Ecevit's premiership, amid ongoing revelations of corruption scandals and an eight-percent contraction in the GDP, with consequent massive unemployment and layoffs. Loans from the IMF since late 2000 now totalled $31 billion, making Turkey the organization's biggest single debtor. Eventually 63 DSP MPs, including seven ministers, **resigned** from the party, leaving it a distant second in the coalition behind the MHP. Among the defectors was highly respected Foreign Secretary İsmail Cem, who formed the *Yeni Türkiye* (New Turkey) party; everyone expected Economy Minister Kemal Derviş to join him. The MHP began calling for early elections and, surprisingly, Parliament obliged late in the month by setting a date of November 3. Despite the chaos of this parliamentary twilight, legislators **passed the required EU reforms** just before the summer recess. The death penalty was abolished (saving Öcalan from the gallows), education and broadcasting in several minority languages were now theoretically permissible, indigenous Christian religious foundations were allowed freedoms undreamed of earlier, and even the once-sacred could now be criticized in print.

Autumn was dominated by the possibility of a new war in Iraq and the run-up to the November elections. The Turkish military remained terrified that a de facto Kurdish state would emerge in northern Iraq if Saddam Hussein were toppled, leading to Turkey's own Kurds seeking independence or union with Iraqi Kurdistan: a nightmare notion in a state whose "territorial integrity" has been a cornerstone of every constitution. MHP Defence Minister Sabahattin Çakmakoğlu threatened military action if Iraqi Kurds made moves towards independence, and went so far as to describe oil-rich Kirkuk (part of Kurdistan, though it lies outside the protected Kurdish zone) as "Turkish soil". For the first time, the Turkish army admitted what everyone already knew – that they maintained a permanent presence in northern Iraq, ostensibly to control the remnants of the PKK based there. It now seemed clear that the army's true aim was (and remains) preventing the emergence of an independent Kurdistan.

After weeks of press speculation and secret negotiations, Kemal Derviş eventually signed on with Deniz Baykal's CHP, seen by most secular Turks as the one group capable of challenging the pro-Islamic AK party. President Sezer did his best to prevent a showdown between the AK party and the military by obtaining guarantees from the incoming chief of staff, Hilmi Özkök, that he would respect the peoples' choice. However, the secular judiciary fought a rearguard action to fend off the so-called Islamists, and in August AK party leader Erdoğan was formally re-banned from holding political office (as was pro-Kurdish HADEP leader Murat Bozlak) because of his previous conviction for "inciting religious hatred".

The UN had been attempting to **broker a Cyprus settlement** between Clerides and Denktaş for most of 2002, but progress proved elusive and negotiations stalled as Denktaş underwent heart surgery in New York. On both sides of the island, popular feeling in favour of a settlement rose as the year progressed. On October 9, the EU recommended May 2004 admission of ten new member states, pointedly including Cyprus (reunified or otherwise), but deeming Turkey still unready for membership despite "significant progress".

The AK era

Against a background of EU procrastination and continuing economic crisis, it was no surprise that **AK swept to power** on November 3, 2002, garnering 34 percent of the vote and claiming 363 of the 550 parliamentary seats. For the first time in fifteen years Turkey had a majority government, and if AK failed in the tasks ahead it would not be able to blame coalition infighting. The only other party to surpass the required ten-percent barrier was the CHP, who had been excluded in the 1999 election but who now, unsmeared by the sticky mud of the economic crisis, polled twenty percent for 177 seats. The rump of Ecevit's DSP was humiliated, crashing from 22 percent to just over one percent. The ultranationalist MHP also fell short of the *baraj* as it's termed locally, with only eight percent as against a former nineteen percent. ANAP, the third coalition partner, scored well below the minimum, while DYP also polled only nine percent. Smaller, personality-centred splinter groups like İsmail Cem's New Turkey party were utterly buried. DEHAP (a reincarnation of pro-Kurdish HADEP, which had voluntarily closed itself to avoid being banned) increased its share, but still failed to gain any parliamentary seats, although it had come first in thirteen of the Kurdish-dominated provinces of the southeast.

In all, only nine million of the registered electorate of well over thirty million voted for the AK party; abstentions and spoiled papers reached record levels, and – due to the *baraj* system – nearly 46 percent of voters were unrepresented in the new parliament. By European standards, the **ten-percent minimum** for party parliamentary representation seems excessively high – it was promulgated in the 1982 constitution to, among other things, exclude "regional" or "minority" (ie Kurdish) parties; the cut-off point in neighbouring Greece, for example, is five percent. But curiously it doesn't bother most Turks, and none of the defeated parties of November 2002, having benefited handsomely from this system in the past, were in a position to cry foul.

Since de facto AK party-leader Erdoğan was prohibited from serving as an MP and thus assuming the office of prime minister, President Sezer had to choose an alternate. The position fell temporarily to deputy leader **Abdullah Gül**, an English-speaking former economics professor regarded as a moderate. In late December the AK party, with the required two-thirds parliamentary majority, amended the constitution to permit Ergoğan to run in any by-election and thus formally become prime minister once an MP; this happened in February 2003, when Gül stepped down to become Foreign Minister. AK hastened to reassure all concerned that they would pursue a moderate programme with the maximum of consultation on all issues, and immediately invited Baykal to join Erdoğan on his victory tour of European capitals – taking the opportunity to press Turkey's case for a favourable decision on a date for commencement of EU accession negotiations.

Soon the TL exchange rate reversed its habitual inflationary spiral, the local stock market commenced a steady rise, and the World Bank, business community and political opposition expressed their confidence. The new government's programme contained a package of 36 measures designed to meet the so-called "Copenhagen criteria" of acceptable civic practice stipulated by the European Union; Erdoğan made the right noises about zero tolerance of torture, but was simultaneously embarrassed by a domestic TV station filming a boy being beaten up by police officers during a demonstration in Ankara.

Erdoğan was bold enough to make the linkage, denied by most Turkish politicians for years, between Turkey's **eventual accession to the European Union** and an internationally accepted Cyprus settlement. UN Secretary Annan's November 28 deadline for an agreement to his proposals came and went with Denktaş having a relapse. However, the new Turkish foreign minister visited Denktaş in his New York hospital to try to extract a promise to agree to Kofi Annan's terms. In mid-December 2002, the **EU summit** in Copenhagen announced in a statement that "Turkey is a candidate state destined to join the union"; this text fell rather short of the Turks' desire for a fixed date to begin accession negotiations, and PM-in-waiting Erdoğan accused the EU of double standards compared to its treatment of central European states who were to be whisked through the door after a mere decade as candidates. The US and Great Britain, stalwart international supporters of Turkey and anxious not to alienate their crucial Middle Eastern ally in the build-up to a possible war against Iraq, were unable to overcome a Franco–German axis resistant to setting a firm date.

The early months of 2003 were dominated by the imminent **American invasion of Iraq**. The local conspiracy-theorist view that the 2002 election victory for the AK party had been engineered by the US to ensure cooperation over Iraq proved to be spectacularly ill-founded. Despite backing by Erdoğan, a resolution to allow the US to use Turkey as a springboard for access from the north was rejected, and a free parliamentary vote on March 1 ensured that US requests to allow 62,000 troops, 255 jets and 65 helicopters to enter Turkey were turned down. There were various reasons for Turkey refusing to follow its traditional pro-US line (aside from the invasion, lacking a UN mandate, being illegal under international law). The economy was only just recovering from its 2000–01 meltdown, and the 1991 Gulf War had had disastrous consequences for Turkey's finances. Even more important were enduring Turkish fears that, following the widely feared disintegration of post-Saddam Iraq, an independent Kurdish state would emerge from the Kurdish semi-autonomous zone in northern Iraq. Rumour credited the National Security Council with contemplating Turkish troops occupying the Kurdish safe-haven should the US attack. There were also fears in the post-September 11 world that Turkey would suffer an Islamic terrorist "backlash" should it support the US against an Arab state. Add to this Turkey's first pro-Islamic government, and public opinion firmly against any cooperation, and it is easy to see why the Turks took the brave but risky stance they did.

Under heavy pressure from Washington, the Turkish Büyük Meclis (Parliament) voted on March 20 (the same day the "allies" invaded) to allow US planes to fly over Turkish airspace. It was too little, too late to assuage US feelings, and Turko–American relations plunged towards an all-time low. Rock-bottom was reached in July, when Turkish soldiers operating clandestinely in northern Iraq were captured by US troops. Turkish humiliation at seeing their men bound and hooded by the soldiers of a so-called ally knew no bounds (and in 2005 was to provide the impetus for Turkey's biggest-budget-ever film, *Kurtlar Vadisi – Irak* (Valley of the Wolves – Iraq) in which an all-Turkish hero exacts a fictional but bloody revenge on the treacherous Yanks).

In April 2003 the **headscarf** issue again caused headlines when the staunchly secularist president, generals and opposition CHP MPs all boycotted a parliamentary reception because the AK Speaker of Parliament's wife, thought to be attending, wore a headscarf. The party went some way to address secularist concerns in May, when Foreign Minister Abdullah Gül stressed the need for Muslim nations to increase democracy and pay more attention to women's and human rights at an address to the Islamic Conference organization in Iran.

The country suffered its worst-ever **terrorist atrocities** that autumn. On November 15 car bombs outside two İstanbul synagogues exploded, killing 25 and injuring 300. Five days later, on November 20, suicide car-bombers targeted Britain, America's ally in Iraq. Thirty were killed and 450 injured in the blasts, which hit the British consulate and the London-based HSBC bank. The vast majority of casualties were Turks, whose fears of becoming a target of İslamic extremists appeared vindicated, despite the extremely limited support they were offering to the occupation of Iraq. Al-Qaeda were initially blamed for the attacks, but the perpetrators (although linked to al-Qaeda) proved to be ethnic Kurds hailing from the impoverished eastern Turkish town of Bingöl. The spectre of Turkey's "deep state" once again reared its head, as the suicide bombers appeared to be members of Turkish Hizbullah, an Islamic militant group believed by many to have been clandestinely encouraged by the authorities to oppose the nominally communist PKK during the 1990s. Apart from the psychological trauma caused, the attacks (especially in tandem with the ongoing turmoil in Iraq) caused major ripples in Turkey's crucial tourism sector.

Many people, both Turks and foreigners, were well aware of the irony of Turkey's EU membership quest being pushed more competently and fervently by an "Islamic" party than by any of the country's previous, secular, governments. This irony was underlined in March 2004, when the Turkish Land Forces Command directed all military headquarters and local civilian governors to collect information on groups or individuals engaged in "divisive or subversive activities". Along with the "usual suspects" (ethnic minorities, Freemasons, religious groups) were "known supporters of the EU and US". Such xenophobia from the supposedly pro-Western **military** did not go unnoticed, not least by the Turkish press who had leaked the circular. The affair posed the question of whether the military was merely interested in hanging onto power for its own sake, or eventually submitting to civilian control as is the norm in all longstanding EU member states. The military suffered a further setback in May when the government slashed a planned modernization budget for the armed forces from €9 billion to €4 billion, in the wake of a constitutional amendment which made the military accountable for its budget for the first time.

The long-running **Cyprus problem** continued to occupy the foreground of foreign affairs, as the aspirations of the long-isolated Turkish Cypriots suffered a major setback on April 24, 2004. Despite a solid majority (65 percent) of Turkish Cypriots voting in favour of the UN-devised reunification scheme, defying Denktaş's long-standing opposition to it, the plan was scuttled by the Greek Cypriots, three-quarters of whom voted to reject the Annan plan. To add insult to injury, both Northern Cyprus and mainland Turkey (which had quietly supported the plan) had to stand by and watch as southern (Greek) Cyprus was permitted to join the EU a week later as representative of the whole island. Gunter Verheugen, EU Commissioner for Enlargement, claimed he had been misled by the Greek Cypriot government, who had assured him of their support of the UN plan but then campaigned actively against it. Turkish hawks felt vindicated in their mistrust of the "duplicitous" Greeks, but at least the Turks had – for the first time since the island's partition in 1974 – gained the moral high ground. In practical terms, though, Greek Cyprus's accession meant that they could, theoretically at least, block Turkey's entry to the EU. Turkish Cypriots maintained their own initiative to end their international isolation, helped considerably by the fact that the southern Republic of Cyprus's EU accession entitled native-born Cypriots on both sides of the island to Republic of Cyprus passports and hence EU citizenship. In February 2005 the north-Cypriot Republican Turkish Party (CTP), whose major platform plank was reunification, won local elections, garnering some 45 percent of the vote, something which would have been unthinkable up to 2002. The Attila Line across the island had – since spring 2003 in fact – become effectively permeable, with people crossing the border in each direction to work, trade, be tourists and meet old friends.

The ever-controversial and emotive **headscarf** issue resurfaced during summer 2004. PM Erdoğan had been forced to send his two daughters – who like his wife wear head-covering – to university in the US rather than at home where the garb remained taboo, and along with many others he hoped that the headscarf ban could be overturned by the EU Court of Human Rights, to which Turkish litigants now had access. However, the Court actually rejected a claim by two Turkish students that their freedom of religion had been violated by exclusion from Turkish university for wearing their headscarves.

Normally positive relations between the government and the EU were strained that autumn when Erdoğan, possibly as a sop to his more conservative supporters, briefly backed an AK-promulgated bill proposing to criminalize adultery. A mini-crisis ensued, as the EU accession talks threatened to go off the rails, the stock-market plummeted and the value of the YTL fell. The proposed bill was dropped (Erdoğan proving to be nothing if not pragmatic), and soon an EU progress report – made public on December 12 – stipulated that access negotiations could begin in October 2005. A mixture of jubilation and apprehension gripped the country: at last it seemed that Europe was willing to accept the Turks, but the massive reforms needed to meet the EU's Copenhagen criteria would undoubtedly have untold consequences on Turkey's political and social life.

Summer 2005 saw Turkey launch a nationwide campaign to tackle **private gun-ownership** and usage, in particular celebratory firing at weddings and after important football matches – at which it emerged that seven hundred bystanders were killed annually by stray bullets. Equally worrying were statistics showing that one in four households owned a firearm, and a 35 percent increase in crime, particularly in İstanbul.

Although Turkey's treatment of its ethnic Kurdish minority had long dominated attention overseas, in September the nation's treatment of another minority, the Armenians, came to the fore. After two attempts by local and overseas Turkish academics to **organize a conference** on "Ottoman Armenians during the Decline of the Empire" (ie was there a genocide between 1915 and 1918?) were blocked by court orders forbidding the use of public universities as venues, the event finally went forward late that month at private Bilgi University in İstanbul. Despite picketing and heckling by ultranationalists, the baying of the right-wing press (and a half-dozen subsequent prosecutions of attending journalists and some of the organizers), the last taboo in Turkish civic life – including the mooting of the g-word – had been broken. The government, mindful of the EU looking over its shoulder, in fact gave the conference its guarded blessing.

But during the same September, Turkey's leading contemporary author Orhan Pamuk was charged under a stealthily introduced new law with "denigrating Turkishness" for saying (in a 2004 interview with a Swiss newspaper) that a million **Armenians** were killed in Anatolia and only he was prepared to speak out about it. International opinion was outraged, and although the case against Pamuk dragged on until January, it was eventually dropped. Hrant Drink, editor of *Agos*, an İstanbul-based, bilingual Armenian/Turkish newspaper, was not so lucky (probably because he was not a prominent international author), and got a six-month suspended sentence following his conviction for insulting Turkey's national identity, based on his remarks that he was a Turk of Armenian ethnicity and that the national anthem was discriminatory. Freedom of expression, it seemed, remained an elusive goal.

Amidst all this, the EU accession talks formally began on October 3, but the EU enlargement commission noted in November that there were still Turkish deficiencies in the areas of freedom of expression, religious rights of non-Muslim minorities, relations between the military and civil authorities (ie the NSC), the failure of the government to deal decisively with poverty and continued unrest in the southeast. The same report more positively declared that "Turkey can be regarded as a functioning market economy." The AK government, by strictly adhering to IMF guidelines, had proven a competent manager of the economy, and inflation, which had fallen to single figures for the first time in decades, continued on a stable course. Other medium-term snags in the lengthy accession process all revolved around Cyprus. Turkey remained in violation of the EU Customs Union by refusing to accept Greek-Cypriot shipping and aircraft in its ports – let alone the question of actually recognizing the Cypriot government. In December the European Court of Human Rights found in favour of Greek-Cypriot plaintiffs who have been denied the usifruct of their property in northern Cyprus since 1974, and it now seems certain that the Turkish-Cypriot authorities – or more likely mainland Turkey – face a huge bill for compensation in this case and hundreds of other similar ones.

The year 2006 got off to a difficult start, with global attention focused on remote Doğubeyazıt, an ethnically Kurdish town not far from the Iranian border. A bleak, snowy January saw an outbreak of the deadly H5N1 strain of **avian flu**, killing five children from poor families. Infected birds were then found in various locations across Turkey, millions of birds were culled and poultry sales dipped by seventy percent as panic gripped the country. Although the virus was soon carried to several European locales by migratory birds, the outbreak had a savage effect on Turkey's tourism industry, with the news breaking just when many Europeans were planning their Mediterranean summer holidays.

In the spring, against a backdrop of renewed PKK attacks on military targets, violent street demonstrations in the southeast (which the authorities claimed were largely instigated by the pro-PKK Roj TV station broadcasting from Denmark), the government prepared a new anti-terror bill which, amongst other things, would make parents criminally responsible if their children took part in demonstrations. Turkish liberals saw the proposed bill as a return to the bad old days, and their fears were heightened when security forces raided the offices of the pro-Kurdish DTP (Democratic Society Party) and detained many of its members.

Trends for the future

The probability of a successful Taliban-style **Islamic regime** in Turkey has never been high, despite AK's electoral victory – and irresponsible reporting thereof in the Western media. Mainstream Sunni Islam in Turkey has long been tempered by "heterodox" dervish sects under the leadership of charismatic *şeyh*s, which presided over the peaceful fusing of the original Anatolian Christian population with the Turkish settlers. The Christian minority has dwindled to a few thousand Greek Orthodox, Armenian Apostolic and Syrian Orthodox adherents, though Alevî (Shi'ite) numbers are variously estimated at between one in seven and one in five of the population, a joint legacy of Turcoman nomadism, medieval Iranian influence and the Bektaşi dervish order. Since 1923, society's upper crust – the so-called "White Turks" – comprising academia, the army, the civil service and (more recently) big business and the media – have ruled the republic under the ideology of secular Kemalism, and can still be counted on to oppose Gulf-style Islam.

Another military **coup** would have neither public nor overseas support, since it would scupper Turkey's chances of entering the European Union. Equally important, coups are demonstrably ineffective in the long term; the period since 1987 has witnessed the gradual yet total reversal of the 1980–83 regime's agenda. Everything and everyone that the generals sought to eradicate has returned either briefly or permanently – including DİSK, which has helped the workforce regain the right to strike. Cynics observe that the army discreetly does as it pleases through the NSC, having grown progressively more sophisticated in using civilian politicians as window-dressing for foreign consumption. But President Sezer is an experienced and adroit constitutional jurist, and under his aegis civilian politicians and the military have for the most part consulted and respected each other's views without allowing dangerous rifts to develop.

The AK **majority government** has brought much-needed stability to Turkey at a time when consistent performance is vital to keep on course for EU membership and to return hope to ordinary Turks, whose standard of living has plunged dramatically since 1991. Prior regimes lamentably mismanaged the economy, which opened the way for AK's landslide victory. The AK party, most of whose members were until recently devoutly opposed to joining a "Christian" organization, now view EU entry as the best way to raise their voters' standard of living, thus assuring re-election. Political debate in Turkey is now not about secularism versus Islam, but pro- and anti-EU (the latter banner carried by a ragtag alliance of elements in the military, the far right and the ultra-left) and pro- or anti-globalization. The Turkish business sector, having submitted to the customs union and the consequent challenge to their domestic monopolies, is impatient to reap the full benefits of inward infrastructure investment and subsidies which would accompany membership.

To EU or not to EU?

Many Turkish intellectuals long considered **EU membership** a reward for past services rendered to NATO, or imagined that Turkey would thus be passively insured against further rule by its military or other undemocratic elements. European parliamentarians, however, periodically pointed out that three EU members – Spain, Portugal and Greece – with a history of authoritarian regimes had disposed of them and most of their legacy well in advance of joining, and that more proactive remedial measures on Turkey's part are expected. Since October 2005 the pace of **reforms** in preparation for membership has been stepped up. Most conspicuously, a **new "European-style" constitution** is to replace the 1982 army-drafted model. A new constitution will hopefully deny MPs the immunity from criminal prosecution for nonviolent offences (ie corruption) that they currently enjoy. Enhanced police training is also being introduced, and anyone summoned to a police station will now be read their rights before being interviewed.

But a substantial body of **European opinion** still sees Turkey as a Third World country inherently unsuitable for membership in a "white, Christian" club which would be overwhelmed by Turkey's geographically lopsided development. The EU accession process is envisioned to take at least fifteen years, and both France and Austria (which opposed the start of Turkish accession talks until Croatia had also been given a green light) intend to hold referendums where a "no" vote would veto Turkish membership. A new, Muslim member state second in population only to Germany is clearly a threatening prospect, with concomitant demands for influence in the inner councils of EU power. While three-fourths of **Turkish public opinion** in principle favoured EU membership in late 2004, this is now down to about sixty percent; even the "pro" camp remains sceptical, expecting Turkey – despite "associate membership" since 1964, and customs-union membership since the millennium – to fall at the last hurdle. And as all the implications of full membership sink in, with the EU set to poke its nose into every aspect of the country's existence, a backlash is growing amidst the "anti" community of strange bedfellows: nationalists who loathe the prospect of increased minority rights, old-style leftists who see the EU as an imperialist plot, members of the "deep state" who dread the prospect of transparency and police practice according to European norms.

It's the economy, stupid

One **economic reform** already implemented has been a sharp reduction in agricultural subsidies. The government purchase-prices of staple crops has thus dropped, and farmers forced to amalgamate into larger units or quit the land. This, coupled with steadily diminishing water supplies to upland farms, has accelerated urban drift and the growth of a vast underclass of uneducated unemployed. An industrial bright-spot is the probability that Turkey may soon become one of the world's leading auto manufacturers, as overseas names set up plants to take advantage of cheap labour; the country already has a presence in the European household-appliances market with its Beko brand. Enhanced social-security and unemployment benefits should also materialize, but will cost vast sums to fund – most readily done by bringing large numbers of tax-avoiding individuals into the revenue net with new income-tax legislation. There will also be a slimming down of the swollen, inefficient and life-tenured civil service, estimated at one in five of the workforce; privatization of Turkish Airlines, Türk Telekom and the last few state-owned banks will almost certainly be an EU requirement.

The results of the old junta's, and ANAP's, 1980s policies are now almost irreversible, institutionalized as a yawning **disparity in incomes** between the top and bottom of the heap, second globally only to Brazil. This economic landscape has worked to the advantage of speculators and wheeler-dealers, and to the detriment of farmers, tradesmen and wage earners; the rich, ensconced in comfortable suburbs of İstanbul, grow richer as they dabble in government contracts, speculate on the stock exchange or live off their *rentier* incomes. Such inequalities – strongly correlated with inflation historically fuelled by the world's largest arms-import programme – will continue to provide grist for demagogues exploiting social discontent. Meanwhile, economic recovery, though impressive at five-percent growth per annum, is shadowed by a huge debt burden (110 percent of GNP), the result of five effective national bankruptcies since 1950. Turkey's continued reliance on the goodwill of international lending agencies leaves the country vulnerable to any global economic slowdown and US political manipulation.

No more politics as usual?

The 2002 election results and EU-prompted reforms might finally halt the chronic and fundamental **immaturity of civilian politics**, long dominated by a coterie of ageing dinosaurs who had been around since the 1960s. For years there were few young, outstanding politicians about; everyone knew that ultimately the military called the tune, so ambitious, capable graduates went into business rather than politics. At the same time, there were always far too many parties (32 were officially registered in 1998, and 23 contested the 2002 poll), mostly rump factions of older parties formed by defecting MPs and their cronies, long on personality cults and short on issues.

The traditional parties currently excluded from parliament all demanded their leaders' heads as the price of failure; Çiller and Yılmaz in particular, both threatened with renewed criminal investigations, are considering prolonged self-exile in countries having no extradition treaty with Turkey. ANAP is now shattered, with many of its former ministers likely to be tried for corruption, still a debilitating constant in Turkish life. The DYP has become the haunt of out-and-out gangsters, and it may eventually merge with ANAP, now that their two ex-leaders joined in mutual loathing have retired. Only the old and frail Ecevit still heads the ruins of the DSP, poised to die with him; the equally demolished MHP has retreated to its grass roots and is unlikely to contest the next election, set for 2007, which AK is likely to again win handily.

The other potentially important political players are the **Kurds**, but only if AK consents to reduce the minimum nationwide vote percentage from ten to five percent, and also of course if their interest party – currently the DTP – is not banned outright or has its members prosecuted individually. It is still illegal to form an overtly ethnically based party, and historically such parties-in-disguise fool nobody and rarely do well outside of the southeast.

Relations with the Middle East

Turkey seems poised to become a major **regional power**, a role not actively played since World War I. Three-plus decades after their somewhat dubious enterprise in Cyprus, Turkey's armed forces have garnered international respectability by participating as disciplined "policing" contingents in Kosovo and Kabul. The **European Defence Force** issue has now been resolved with a compromise allowing Turkey some veto rights over the use of the force. Strategic realities make it unlikely that Turkey will ever leave NATO; Russia remains an unknown quantity, while relations with Iran and Syria always proceed on a rollercoaster basis. Although the US (until 2003 anyway) supplied over \$2 billion annually in weapons-procurement funding, the military knows that overzealous cooperation with the US is viewed with disfavour by the EU, and their natural inclination is to participate in the European Defence Force as a way to enhance their prestige at home and abroad prior to EU membership.

As post-occupation Iraq lurches towards probable disintegration, Turkey will have to decide how to deal with an all-but-independent Kurdish entity on its southeastern frontier. This could leave Kurds in control of the Mosul and Kirkuk oilfields which were wrested from the defeated Ottomans by the British after World War I – an irredentist issue, now awakened from an almost ninety-year slumber and disguised in exaggerated concern for the local Turcoman minority, which still rankles in oil-poor Turkey. Any overt intervention in the area, however, will obviously nullify Turkey's chances of EU membership, but the military and nationalists may decide that securing something like petroleum self-sufficiency would be worth the consequences.

Turkey has forged a close **relationship with Israel** – especially militarily, with joint naval exercises and the Israeli air force training Turkish pilots while using Turkish airspace for its own training. Turkey is one of the few Muslim countries that Israelis can visit, and many do (though less so since the casinos closed). These ties have of course done nothing to improve **Turkish–Arab relations**. These have also been seriously clouded by the highly controversial **İlisu dam** project on the Tigris river, which – along with the massive Atatürk dam on the Euphrates – would have deprived downstream states Syria, Iraq and Jordan of even more water in an already drought-prone region. International lending agencies dropped İlisu after concluding that it would be politically destabilizing and environmentally disastrous, forcing the UK government to withdraw its financial support. Turkey's current shaky financial position should enforce a medium-term moratorium on large new projects, and reverse the policy of **dam building** as strategic weapon against neighbouring states (though such projects in the northeast, on the border with Georgia, are designed with cross-frontier power sales in mind).

Relations with other countries

If the EU accession process runs aground, Turkey's century-long commitment to the West will face its most serious challenge since Atatürk's time. His restrictive ideology, if not the cult of his personality, has long been given merely lip service, and since 1983 the main question has always been what the change in national direction will be, not whether there will be one. Following the precipitate collapse of the Soviet Union, and the ongoing realignment of the Balkans, wider **regionalist options** have come to the fore as some familiar dynamics of Turkish history reassert themselves.

The independent, ex-Soviet republics of **Central Asia and the Caucasus** were, throughout the 1990s, assiduously courted in mildly **pan-Turkic** terms, and Erdoğan has continued to foster these ties. Such overtures, competing with those of fundamentalist Shia Iran, have been quietly encouraged by the US, which seeks a mildly Sunni counterbalance in the region. After a meagre start in the early 1990s, Turkish business investment in Kazakhstan, Uzbekistan, Turkmenistan and Kyrghizia topped \$6.5 billion by 1995, with civil engineering projects at the forefront.

Oil pipelines from these regions are the most frequently proposed works: to supply oil-deprived Turkey, to banish messy and dangerous tanker traffic from the Bosphorus, and to enable the country to act as a toll-collecting conduit for petroleum products to the West. Thus far the only project completed (in May 2005) is the **Baku–Ceyhan line**, moving oil from Azerbaijan and Kazakhstan to İskendurun on the Mediterranean. A much shorter (and cheaper) pipeline through Iran to the Gulf had originally been mooted, but under US and Israeli pressure, Turkey was chosen as host country instead. This was good news for the Turkish economy, though locals were less enamoured by the giant project, as they were turfed off their land with scant compensation to allow the pipeline to be built (and then secured from "terrorism"). **Natural-gas supply** agreements are more evolved: besides Russian gas being pumped under the Black Sea to Samsun, Turkey is receiving natural gas from Azerbaijan and Iran, despite US pressure to shun a member of the "axis of evil"; trade with Iran, both official and unofficial, is lively and growing.

In the Caucausus, **Azerbaijan** – the most closely linked to Turkey by language, history and (via Nakichevan) a common border – has seen the greatest direct political involvement by Turkey. Successive Turkish governments have ridden out swells of public opinion calling for active official military assistance to the Azeris in their long-running struggle with the Armenians, mindful since Cyprus of the dire consequences of such an intervention – though "freelance" Turkish volunteers and weaponry have found their way to the theatre of war. Since the late 1990s there has been a slight thaw in Turkish relations with **Armenia**, pending a negotiated settlement of the Nagorno-Karabagh issue; however Turkey's refusal to accept responsibility for the 1895 and 1915 massacres and deportations means that contacts are unlikely to develop further, and this denial gives Turkey's overseas opponents a constant source of ammunition. Should Turko–Armenian relations stay chilly, a direct rail line from Kars to the Georgian capial of Tblisi is planned to bypass the currently disused indirect line through Armenian territory.

Hand in hand with pan-Turkism, there has been a whiff of old-fashioned Ottomanism, as Turkey has taken an increased interest in its former Balkan possessions, from which the forefathers of many contemporary Turks emigrated and which retain some Muslim population. Turkey sent officers to retrain the army of predominantly Muslim **Albania**, as well as civilian economic aid and advisers. Relations with **Bulgaria** are vastly improved since the ethnic-Turkish-dominated DPS party serves as a perennial partner in ruling coalitions there. Turkey was among the first countries to recognize the republic of **Macedonia** under that name, much to the outrage of Greece, and the very first to send an ambassador. But perhaps the biggest surprise is rapidly growing trade and cultural links with **Greece**: Turkey is the eighth largest market for Greek exporting firms; the Greek banking industry has a firm toehold in Turkey; and hundreds of thousands of Greeks vacation annually in the country.

The Kurdish question

T he majority of people in the Tigris valley, the Lake Van region and in the mountains between Erzurum, Erzincan and Diyarbakır are Kurds, an originally nomadic people speaking an Indo-European language related to Farsi. They have been here for millennia, though their exact origins are obscure.

Some authorities consider them descended from, or identical to, the "Karduchi" who gave Xenophon's Ten Thousand so much trouble; others have described the nursery of the Kurds as either the Hakkari mountains in present-day Turkey, or the Zagros range in western Iran. Their traditional nomadic **culture**, which focused on horse breeding and pastoralism, brought the Kurds into perennial conflict with farmers and town-dwellers; today the vast majority have adopted a settled lifestyle.

The Kurds have never been united as a nation-state, owing partly to their traditional organization in **clans**, further grouped into tribes headed by all-powerful hereditary *ağa*s, or chieftains. There exist four mutually unintelligible **dialects** of the Kurdish tongue, two of them (Kurmanji and Zaza) spoken in Turkey. Kurds are further subdivided by **religious affiliation**, being both Sunni and Shi'ite Muslim – proportions varying by region – or members of two small heterodox sects, the Yezidis and the Ahl-i-Haqqi. In Turkey, Shi'ite (Alevî) Kurds are concentrated near Erzincan and Tunceli, while in the southeast the Naqshbandi (Nakşibendi) and Qadiri (Kadiri) dervish orders have historically claimed many Kurdish adherents.

The **number** of Kurds in Turkey is a contentious subject, but sober estimates reckon over twelve million (and rising rapidly) out of a population of nearly seventy million, the largest Kurdish population in the Middle East. In neighbouring Iraq, Kurds constitute more (23 percent) of the population, but number only four million – a much smaller absolute number. Until recently Turkish governments have denied Kurds a distinct ethnic and linguistic identity, describing them in official propaganda as "mountain Turks" who have forgotten their racial origins.

The Kurds in pre-Republican Turkey

Under the Ottomans, the majority **Sunni Kurds** were regarded in the same way as other Muslim but non-Turkic subjects, such as the Arabs or Circassians, enjoying no special *millet* (nation) status like the Christian and Jewish religious minorities. The sultans found their warlike qualities useful, often using them as a mobile, irregular raiding force on the frontiers with Russia and Persia. Under Sultan Abdülhamid, they were also allowed to terrorize both Alevî Kurds and the Armenians, their settled neighbours and hereditary enemies across much of eastern Anatolia.

After the Ottoman collapse in 1918, the victorious Allies, in response to pleas from certain Kurdish nationalists, briefly mooted the establishment of a Kurdish state straddling the current borders of Iraq, Turkey and Iran. Most Kurds, however, continued in their martial tradition, standing by the Kemalists in their struggle against the Armenians in the east and the Greeks in the west, the two greatest threats to a Muslim-dominated Anatolian state. But following the Turkish Nationalist victory in 1922, the Kurds found themselves poorly rewarded for their loyalty, as any special privileges for them were explicitly withdrawn.

The first modern rebellions

At the same time as the abolition of the caliphate in 1924, all Kurdish-interest societies were banned. **Resistance** to these reforms was initially Islamic fundamentalist, rather than Kurdish nationalist, in character. In 1925, a Nakşibendi *şeyh* (dervish leader) north of Diyarbakır mounted a rebellion which took two months for the government to crush; at its conclusion all dervish orders were suppressed nationwide. Shortly after another, more overtly nationalist/secular insurrection broke out near Mount Ararat, and lasted until 1929. In 1936 a revolt by the Alevî Kurds of Dersim (now Tunceli), took the Turkish army two years to quell. The Turkish government responded harshly to each rebellion with executions and deportations of villagers to the west, as well as suppression of any local Kurdish cultural manifestations. Most of the east was designated as a **military zone** in order to give the army a free hand against the Kurds, long before sour relations with the Soviet Union provided another pretext for this.

Thereafter Kurds could participate in Turkish public life only if they were willing to be **assimilated**. Kurdish concerns had to be addressed under the vaguer rubric of "development of the east" and – after 1960 – as members of nationwide, left-wing parties where Kurds could have a voice. Sunni Kurdish society had historically been essentially semi-feudal, subject to the *ağa*s who would deliver their charges' vote in return for minimal benefits from Ankara. Alevî Kurds in particular, however, have since the Sixties tended to espouse left-wing beliefs, making them the target of pogroms by Muslim fundamentalist and/or rightist activists, most notably at Kahraman Maraş in 1978. The military interventions of 1971 and 1980 were notably hard on leftist parties in general and anything specifically smacking of Kurdish sectarianism, providing fertile ground for the rise of the PKK (*Partia Karkaris Kurdistan*, the "Kurdistan Workers' Party"). This group therefore represented a continuation, albeit an ideologically extreme one, of Kurdish rejection of forced assimilation or marginalization.

The PKK: beginnings

The **PKK** (pronounced "peh kah kah" in Turkish) was founded in November 1978 by **Abdullah Öcalan**, a political-science student in Ankara, with the express intent of establishing a Marxist, Kurdish-run state in southeastern Turkey. While other Kurdish-separatist manifestos of the 1970s were better articulated, the PKK appealed to poor, badly educated Kurdish youths, without prospects in the underdeveloped southeast, with the possibility of direct guerilla action. After the 1980 military intervention, "**Apo**" – as Öcalan came to be known – fled to Syria and established training camps with the assistance of the Syrian government and the PLO; more camps were opened later in Lebanon's Beq'aa valley. In 1984 the PKK began a **guerilla campaign** in southeastern Turkey, initially targeting isolated *jandarma* posts; the Turkish government declared **martial law** in the affected provinces, and sealed the border with Syria.

The PKK soon widened its attacks to include civilians it branded as accomplices of the Turkish state and representatives of the old "feudal" order, namely large landowners and conservative tribal chiefs. In 1986 the central government effectively augmented this class by creating the **village guards**, Kurds paid (handsomely by local standards) to protect their "pro-government" villages from the PKK. The better-armed PKK often massacred both guards and their entire families. **Schools**, seen by the PKK as centres for government indoctrination and Turkification, were routinely destroyed, and teachers killed, increasing the already high local illiteracy rate. Village life became unbearable, with populations divided into pro- and anti-PKK factions – often merely covers for pursuing old feuds. The rural population was threatened by each side with dire consequences for cooperating with the other, and both the government and the PKK used coercive techniques for recruiting fighters. In 1988, the regular **army** replaced the gendarmerie in the suppression of the PKK, which by now had forged a provisional alliance with urban terrorist groups, allowing it to commit outrages in the larger western cities.

The PKK in politics and battle

Between late 1989 and early 1991, the Kurdish question began to dominate both Turkish public opinion and perceptions of Turkey abroad. PKK actions succeeded indirectly in splitting successive governments between those favouring the adoption of a more conciliatory approach to the Kurds and those advocating a continuation of the iron fist.

In October 1989 the **HEP** (Popular Labour Party) was formed by seven dissident SHP members who had attended an international conference on Kurdish affairs, and were expelled upon their return to Turkey for "weakening national feeling by appealing to narrow class or ethnic interests". For the first time Turkey had a distinct pro-Kurdish party, though under Turkish law such a party could not – and still cannot – be identified as ethnically based. In June 1993 the HEP was forcibly disbanded, only to quickly reform as the **DEP** (Democracy Party), with essentially the same personnel and aims. DEP in turn was shut down in June 1994, to be succeeded by the **HADEP** (People's Democratic Party). By year's end, ten former HEP deputies and six DEP MPs, stripped of parliamentary immunity, had been tried by state security courts and sentenced to prison for up to fifteen years for "separatist activities" (ie clandestine PKK membership) – verdicts widely condemned by American and European parliamentarians. Numerous lower-ranking PKK activists or fellow travellers who were also jailed could expect miserable treatment even by the appalling standards of Turkish prisons.

In the eastern hills, a **yearly pattern** became established: the government would announce sweeping measures to crush the rebels over the winter and early spring, when they were at their most vulnerable, with specially trained commando units. The PKK in turn would usually "celebrate" **Nawroz**, the Kurdish New Year, by some particularly bloody atrocity, inaugurating the summer season of incidents. The conflict became ever more brutal as the 1990s progressed, with the army struggling to contain the insurrection despite increasingly sophisticated weaponry. By 1995 the PKK could muster an estimated 15,000 guerillas or *peshmergas*, plus perhaps 75,000 "part-time" militants. Village guards, inadequately protected by the state, began to resign en masse, no longer wishing to risk their lives for an administration that did not arm them adequately. By early 1997 **over two thousand villages** in both the southeast and Tunceli had been either bombed or forcibly evacuated by the government, and then razed, on suspicion of cooperating with the PKK, or merely for not enrolling in the village-guard scheme. Up to **one million internal refugees**, who filled shantytowns around Diyarbakır and western cities, were thus created.

Since the first Iraq war, the PKK had established bases in the US-proclaimed safe-haven zone in Northern Iraq to launch attacks into Turkey. The Turkish military, supported by the two main Iraqi Kurdish factions – hostile to the PKK for various reasons – responded by crossing the border in "hot-pursuit" raids; the biggest incursion took place in late March 1995, when 35,000 Turkish troops plus supporting air cover and artillery crossed the frontier in a bid to definitively wipe out PKK training camps in the area. After four months Turkish forces pulled out, mission unaccomplished but having created a permanent "zone of influence" and marked out a "line of control" well inside the Iraqi frontier.

The PKK began to use **civil unrest** as a tactic, mobilizing large street demonstrations, staging ostentatious funerals of slain HEP, DEP, HADEP or PKK personnel and inspiring shopkeeper strikes in large southeastern towns. The government played into its hands with a string of decrees muzzling press coverage of events and authorizing the deportations of troublemakers.

Those funerals were evidence of an ominous trend, parallel to a general one in Turkish society at large: the regular **assassination** or **"disappearance"** of nonviolent activists and politicians (HEP/DEP/HADEP in these cases), by "unknown assailants", never apprehended or charged, but widely believed to be shadowy, organized groups of Kurdish Hizbullah fundamentalists or far-right Turkish nationalists operating with the indulgence of the army and gendarmerie. Such killings continued unabated through the 1990s, averaging several individuals per month, with corpses often found mutilated by the roadside or buried in rubbish tips.

The PKK further **diversified tactics** between 1992 and 1996, with demonstrations and attacks on Turkish property and diplomatic missions **overseas**, as well as the abduction of foreigners in the southeast. The PKK then announced the targeting of Turkey's **tourist industry**, one of the country's main foreign-exchange earners, with warnings that the battle would be carried to the resorts. Thus numerous bombings in İstanbul, Fethiye, Marmaris, Antalya and Kuşadası were carried out during 1993 and 1994, with 26 fatalities and many more wounded, accompanied by a brief dip in tourist numbers.

The PKK's **inner command circle** was by most accounts a very unpleasant bunch, steeped in Stalinist cant (and methodology) of the 1950s and 1960s, allegedly financing their operations by opium smuggling in the Van area (as did progovernment Kurds) now that conventional Eastern Bloc support had dried up, and valuing the lives of their ever-younger and more inexperienced recruits as little as those of their victims. Despite all this, Europeans were apt to romanticize the PKK, thanks partly to its vigorous "public relations" efforts overseas.

Beginning in the mid-1990s, there was a mixed but increasingly hostile reaction by various European governments to the PKK. While the Netherlands – to the considerable ire of Turkey – tolerated the convening of a self-styled "Kurdish Parliament in Exile" in April 1995, and the Greeks provided consistent, surreptitious support for PKK activities, the German and French governments shut down PKK offices in their countries later that year at Turkish diplomatic instigation, and the Belgians, in mid-1996, raided the Brussels-based satellite station **MED TV**, which had been broadcasting in the various Kurdish dialects. MED promptly resurfaced in London, licensed by the Independent Television Commission (ITC), where it gained an audience even amongst non-Kurdish Turks for its incisive coverage, despite being jammed by the Turkish authorities.

The war winds down

By 1998, the PKK insurrection had lost impetus, as the Turkish army's increasingly superior weaponry and tactics took their toll; Öcalan's call for a unilateral ceasefire in late summer was summarily dismissed by the Turkish military and government. In late October 1998 Öcalan was **expelled** from Damascus following Turkish threats to invade Syria, the PKK's main backer. After brief stays in Iran and Moscow, he was arrested in Rome in mid-November, but the Italians refused to extradite Öcalan because Turkey retained the death penalty. The Italian embassy in Ankara and consulate in İstanbul were attacked by angry mobs of outraged locals, and an economic embargo was placed on Italian goods. Eventually the Italians, in an untenable situation, obliged Öcalan to leave. After further unsuccessful asylum quests in Greece and Russia, he turned up in mid-February 1999 at the Greek embassy in Nairobi, where he was **captured** in a secret operation by MIT (Turkish intelligence service) operatives. Both the Israeli secret service, Mossad, and the CIA were thought to have assisted Turkey with tip-offs as to his whereabouts.

Following Öcalan's arrest, more than three hundred **incidents** linked to the PKK and Kurdish sympathizers took place, most seriously the bombing of a shopping centre in İstanbul that caused thirteen deaths. Kurds and their supporters protested, sometimes violently, both within Turkey and in many European cities. After six months on probation by the UK's ITC, MED TV was taken off the air in March 1999 for carrying interview quotes urging violence in Turkey in revenge for Öcalan's capture, and for "breaching the impartiality and incitement sections of the programming code".

In the April 1999 Turkish **general elections**, HADEP polled only 4.6 percent of the vote, falling well short of the ten percent needed to send deputies to parliament. HADEP did, however, gain Turkey's most important Kurdish city, Diyarbakır, in the municipal elections. More surprisingly, HADEP almost won Mersin, a Mediterranean city in a predominantly Turkish area. This amply demonstrated just how many Kurds had been forced westward by the war in the southeast.

Turkish public opinion demanded Öcalan's execution, but the more pragmatic realized that this could scupper Turkey's chance of joining the EU. After a June **show trial** on the heavily guarded prison-islet of İmralı, in which Öcalan cravenly recanted his violent campaign and pleaded to be allowed to live as a force of reconciliation, he was found **guilty** of both murder and treason, both capital crimes according to law and the constitution. The Turkish parliament, however, had to ratify the **death sentence**, and with 47 prisoners ahead of Öcalan on Death Row, it seemed unlikely that Öcalan would hang. In what Turkish cynics denounced as a further attempt to save his neck, Öcalan appealed in August for all armed PKK guerillas to leave Turkey for Iraq and Iran; the government dismissed this virtual surrender and beefed up border security.

The end of the armed struggle

Despite objections from the ultranationalist MHP, and relatives of soldiers killed in battle with the PKK, in January 2000 the Turkish parliament bowed to EU pressure and agreed to delay implementation of Öcalan's death sentence until the European Court of Human Rights had given its verdict on the case. In February the PKK formally **renounced their armed struggle**, but this did not prevent the authorities clamping down on more moderate Kurds, and later the same month the HADEP mayors of three southeastern cites were arrested and charged with aiding "separatists", ie the PKK.

In May, Turkish forces launched a major incursion into the Kurdish enclave of northern Iraq, where the majority of the PKK's remaining forces were based; over fifty guerillas were killed. Students of Kurdish history were not surprised to find the Kurds once again indulging in internecine warfare, with KDP (Kurdish Democratic Party) *peshmerga* aiding the Turkish operation. Whether the moderate, pro-Western, but essentially tribal, KDP leader Masud Barzani was motivated by ideological opposition to the Marxist PKK, or pragmatism – because he realized that a strong PKK presence in northern Iraq would invite more Turkish army incursions – remains uncertain, but this uneasy alliance further weakened the PKK in their last "safe haven".

In June the Turkish military finally appeared to acknowledge what most moderate Turks had known all along – that military muscle may have sufficed to crush the PKK but was not enough to solve the "southeastern problem" – and pressured Prime Minister Ecevit into announcing an **aid and redevelopment package** for the economically depressed southeastern provinces. Simultaneously, persecution of HADEP continued, with the arrest of 23 party members for protesting against the death penalty. Later in the year, against the background of proposed reforms allowing broadcasting and education in Kurdish, police closed a theatre in İstanbul which was staging a Kurdish-language play.

The year 2001 opened with another major Turkish-army operation in Iraqi Kurdistan. On this occasion both Barzani's KDP and Jalal Talabani's PUK (Patriotic Union of Kurdistan) helped the Turks, leaving the beleaguered PKK with nowhere to hide. In Turkey itself the authorities followed up the military's successes against the PKK with further moves against HADEP, long suspected of having links with the PKK. In February police detained sixteen HADEP party members in the town of Batman for staging a protest against the disappearance of two activists – last seen in the hands of the authorities – and in March a state prosecutor sought a four-year jail sentence for the director of a publishing house that had printed a book about Öcalan.

Following the effective **collapse of the PKK** as a viable fighting force on Turkish soil, 2002 saw Turkey's attention centred firmly on worrying developments in northern Iraq. With the increasing likelihood of a US attack on Iraq, the Turkish government became increasingly concerned that the collapse of Saddam Hussein's regime would lead to the disintegration of Iraq and the emergence of a de jure independent Kurdish state in Iraq's "safe haven", rather than merely the de facto autonomous zone that had existed up until then. Anything which would indicate that Kurds – any Kurds – were capable of governing themselves was anathema to the Turkish state, and it became clear that the continuing Turkish military presence in the Kurdish enclave was as much about preventing a truly independent Kurdistan emerging as it was about blocking PKK cross-border raids. In September, the Turkish Defence Minister appeared to revive irredentist Turkish claims to parts of Iraqi Kurdistan, asserting that the Iraqi cities of Mosul and Kirkuk were "Turkish soil". This met with robust responses from both Barzani and Talabani, who decried the continued Turkish presence in the north but also denied that their groups were aiming for de jure independence.

Domestically, a positive development for Turkish Kurds was legislation passed in August abolishing the death penalty, thus sparing Öcalan, and guaranteeing the right of several minorities (including Kurds) to broadcast and educate in their own language. Until quite recently, such **reforms** – part of a judicial reform package aimed at EU accession – would have been unthinkable in a state that had strenuously denied the existence of the Kurds as a separate ethnic group, and demonstrated to the Kurds (among others) Turkey's apparently sincere desire to join the EU. Later the same month, one of the country's most respected musicians, Sezen Aksu (an ethnic Turk), gave a concert in İzmir in which she sang in Kurdish (as well as Greek, Armenian and Judeo-Spanish). Although she was predictably criticized by elements in the military and by ultranationalist politicians, the majority of the mainstream press, the Culture Minister and many ordinary Turks applauded her attempt to heal the wounds of ethnic intolerance, exacerbated by the bitter insurrection in the southeast.

With less than ten percent of the nationwide vote in the November 2002 elections, the pro-Kurdish **DEHAP** party, the new successor to HADEP (which had dissolved itself in order to avoid the worse fate of being banned), again failed to claim any parliamentary seats (despite the expected solid support in the southeastern provinces), suggesting that many Kurds elsewhere in Turkey viewed the moderate Islamists of the triumphant AK party as more effective representatives.

Change under the AK government

In March 2003 the long-awaited **US invasion of Iraq** commenced, a worst-case scenario for the Turks. Having refused to allow the US to use Turkey as a launch pad (and thus bringing Turkish–American relations to an all-time nadir), Turkey now had little influence over events in Iraq – specifically in the Kurdish enclave bordering its own ethnically Kurdish southeast. Turkey's nightmare, that the removal of Saddam Hussein would lead to the break-up of Iraq along ethnic lines, and thus allow an independent Kurdish state to emerge, appeared imminent. Viewing with concern the American reliance on the Iraqi Kurds, the Turks increased their support of the significant Turcoman population in northern Iraq. In July US troops arrested eleven Turkish soldiers operating clandestinely in Süleymaniye, a major city in the Kurdish zone. Accused of arming Turcoman militants and/or trying to assassinate a Kurdish official, the Turkish soldiers were detained and questioned for sixty hours before being released. The Turkish public were outraged at TV pictures showing "their boys" hooded and bundled into custody by their supposed American allies.

In July 2003 the Turkish military offered an **amnesty** to PKK (or Kongra-Gel – People's Congress of Kurdistan – as the group now called itself) members who had not taken part in any armed attacks; PKK fighters who turned in their weapons and recanted their views were placed in a supervised programme of community service in western Turkey. With a self-declared unilateral PKK ceasefire still in place, it seemed that, cross-frontier events aside, some headway was being made. June 2004, though, saw the end of the PKK/Kongra-Gel ceasefire (which the Turkish government and military had ignored anyway). More positively, with the Turks heavily engaged in reforms to meet EU criteria, later the same month Leyla Zana and three other prominent Kurdish politicians from DEHAP were **released from prison**, having served lengthy sentences for disseminating separatist (ie pro-PKK) propaganda. Zana in particular had become something of a *cause célèbre* in the west, and viewed as a prisoner of conscience, leading to her nomination for the Nobel Peace Prize. The first broadcast in Kurdish of an official TV channel took place on the prisoners' release date – a sign of the radical transformation Turkey was undergoing. Further indication of this came in November, when police and special forces gunned down a lorry driver and his 13-year-old son in Kızıltepe, near Mardin. Previously, such a brutal attack on two innocent individuals would have been swept under the carpet. Several Turkish papers carried outraged stories about the incident, and the local police chief and three officers were suspended while a major investigation was launched.

The year 2005 saw some setbacks in the gradually improving relations between the Turkish state and its Kurdish citizens, as some Kurds, eager to test the limits of their freedoms, exceeded what sections of the Turkish public and officialdom were prepared to tolerate. During March 21 Nawroz celebrations, two ethnic Kurdish teenagers caught burning a Turkish flag were nearly lynched, and the event catalyzed an impromptu nationwide flag-waving campaign. More seriously, Kongra-Gel attacks on Turkish military and police targets increased in the southeast, with a number of Turkish fatalities, mainly caused by the terrorists' use of remotely controlled mines. During a June visit to Washington, DC, Turkish Prime Minister Erdoğan blamed the US for refusing to do anything about PKK/Kongra-Gel camps in northern Iraq. Bomb attacks on tourist targets in western Turkey in the spring by a group naming itself the Kurdistan Freedom Falcons resulted in foreign fatalities and briefly threatened Turkey's lucrative tourist trade.

During an August 2005 speech in Diyarbakır, PM Erdoğan in two words broke with the decades-old official line that there were no Kurds in Turkey by referring to the "Kurdish problem". Many were predictably outraged, but it was a courageous remark providing real hope for reconciliation. Further positive news came with a statement from Leyla Zana, now leader of the largest pro-Kurdish party, calling for the PKK/Kongra-Gel to end its armed struggle. Unfortunately, a protest against Öcalan's incarceration conditions at the port of Gemlik, harbour for his prison-island of İmralı, led to riots in several major cities and heavy-handed police tactics. To exacerbate matters, Turkish Land Forces Commander Yaşar Büyükanıt accused Zana of organizing an intifada-style protest against Turkey.

Another crisis erupted during November in remote Şemdinli, where an explosion at a bookshop belonging to a convicted PKK member was initially blamed on the PKK itself. Impartial, thorough police investigations, however (in themselves a positive step) implicated paramilitary state officials in the bombings. Was this an attempt by rogue (or not-so-rogue) state employees to keep the conflict in the southeast ticking over to serve their own ends? Or proof of the "deep state" again acting outside the norms of governance? Riots followed in nearby towns, resulting in three people being shot by police. Erdoğan himself was brave enough to visit the region, three members of the security forces were arrested and a parliamentary enquiry was set up. In March 2006, an indictment was filed by Van Province Prosecutor Ferhat Sarıkaya against Land Forces Commander Büyükanıt, accusing the general of complicity in the bombing (strenuously denied by an outraged military establishment and, indeed, by most Turks). During April further rioting in several southeastern cities and İstanbul (sparked by a clash between demonstrators accompanying a funeral procession for slain PKK fighters and security forces) resulted in several fatalities – sadly the latest in nearly **50,000 deaths** on all sides of the conflict, military and civilian, since 1984.

Prospects for the future

Turkey has substantially transformed itself following the election of the AK party in 2002, and the government's commitment to Europe. EU accession talks began in October 2005, and judicial reforms have begun to reduce **human rights abuses**, with the pervasive, long-running detainment, torture and extra-judicial killing of Kurds largely ended. Now that the PKK is no longer a real threat to the territorial integrity of the nation, Turkey has begun to accept the legitimacy of Kurdish-interest political parties like the DTP (Democratic Society Party – successor to the now-defunct DEHAP), and is continuing to pass legislation enshrining freedom of thought and expression. That Kurds can now broadcast and educate in their own language is a hopeful sign that **cultural repression** of Turkish Kurds is over.

The real problem now is economic. Although there are other deprived areas in Turkey, every single ethnically Kurdish-dominated area is **poverty-stricken**. Unemployment, high in the country overall, is endemic in the Kurdish southeast. The infrastructure of poorer quarters of cities such as Diyarbakır has virtually collapsed under the weight of migrants from the denuded countryside, and social problems have burgeoned as formerly tight-knit families crack under the strain. The Bağlar district of Diyarbakır, for example, with a population of nearly 400,000, has grown so quickly that it isn't even on official cadastral plans. This means building taxes – one of the main municipal income sources – can't be collected, and public services can't be improved. Despite government propaganda about rural regeneration, the organization Human Rights Watch claims that only ten percent of the Kurds displaced (estimates vary between 380,000 and one million) during the two-decade conflict have returned to their villages. Few have been compensated for property loss, not surprising given that the same body which supervised the villagers' evacuation is responsible for dealing with compensation claims. Many people sold off their livestock, following bans on access to summer pastures, and now have no funds to renew their herds. Without **economic aid** to the Kurdish southeast (and assurance that it goes into the hands of the deserving poor rather than local drug-dealers or smugglers) there is always a risk that dispossessed and alienated Kurds will drift once again into extremist Islamic parties or militant Kurdish-nationalist organizations such as a resurgent PKK.

It seems unlikely that events **over the border** in the Iraqi Kurdish entity will dramatically affect Turkey's Kurds. Even if the Turks' worst fears become reality and an independent Kurdish state emerges there, the effect on Turkey's Kurdish population is likely to be minimal. With an estimated fifty percent of Turkish Kurds living outside their traditional homeland – in western Turkey or Europe – and the prospect of Turkey becoming part of a wider Europe within a decade or so, the idea of a landlocked Kurdish nation will only appeal to the most radical nationalists and economically disenfranchised. Moreover, a Kurdish voice is likely to be increasingly heard in Turkey, not only because of growing civil freedoms but also because, by some estimates, the rapidly growing ethnic Kurdish population will become the largest single group in the country after 2025. As Turkey moves towards EU membership, there's a real possibility of the nation's Kurds finally being accepted as ethnically distinct from, yet socially and politically an integral part of, an inclusive Turkish state conforming to European democratic norms.

Music

Outside Turkey, Turkish music used to be largely associated with belly dancing, while recently the Mevlevî ("Whirling") Dervishes have gained wide popularity in world music circles. Yet there's much more to it, as exemplified by great Turkish musical influence across the eastern Mediterranean and Balkans, and a loyal following amongst the Turkish and Kurdish diaspora in northern Europe. Belying the stereotypes, there's an enticing variety, from refined classical forms to commercially camp *arabesk* by way of rural bards and fiery Gypsy ensembles. Turkish music today is a multilayered, multifaceted object: at its best representing the heritage of the many civilizations that flourished in the Anatolian area for thousands of years, at its worst globally-marketed pop music with a bit of exotic colour thrown in. Not surprisingly, it's this orientalist strain which finally won the hearts of the Eurovision juries in 2003 with the conservatory-trained soprano Sertab Erener wiggling seductively in an odalisque costume.

Music in the Republic

As with language and ethnicity in Turkey, music has been a major cultural battlefield since the 1923 establishment of the Republic. The new state devoted considerable effort to constructing a unitary national culture; Atatürk and others emphasized the ancestry of the "true" Turks in central Asia, and conversely the supposed cultural distance of contemporary Turks from neighbouring Middle Easterners. This exercise involved some implausible flights of historical imagination, and the deliberate overlooking or denigration of non-Turkish ethnic groups who had always lived in Anatolia.

Although privately aficionados of the various Ottoman urban musical traditions, Atatürk and his cohorts deemed them too tainted by Arab civilization and minority contributions to be an exemplar of **Turkish national culture**. "The capacity of

△ Man playing saz

a country to change is demonstrated by its ability to change its music," he declared, and his cadres set about doing exactly that by banning music sung in minority languages from the state-run radio, prohibiting the broadcast of Ottoman classical music for fifteen months in 1928–29, and (briefly, in 1938) prohibiting the distribution of Arabic-language musical films emanating from Egypt. "Genuine" folk and Western classical music were decreed to be the oddly twinned musical destinies of the nation. Accordingly, officially funded musicologists fanned out across Anatolia from the late 1920s onwards, charged with collecting, archiving and recording the folk repertoire. This proved to be a two-edged sword; whilst an enormous amount of valuable material was rescued for posterity, as in neighbouring Greece and Bulgaria distortions born of ideology and the inherent limitations of the collecting process crept in. Melodies were standardized, ensemble playing was preferred, and improvisation or non-Turkish lyrics were frowned on, on the state-run radio as well as in the field.

There is, however, a **revisionist version** of these events which asserts that Atatürk himself – who famously loved the heterogenous folk songs and dances of his native Salonica in Macedonia, frequently invited musicians and singers to his table, and travelled with a gramophone and 78s in his private railway carriage – never intended matters to be carried this far, and that zealots in his ideological retinue had misinterpreted his utterances, or concocted explicit instructions when none were forthcoming. Musicologist and *saz* player Sadi Yaver Ataman has written a first-hand account (*Atatürk ve Türk Muzikisi*, 1991) about Atatürk's attitudes towards music, and apparently the prohibitions on state-run radio resulted from a misunderstanding. During a private evening listening to Ottoman music, Atatürk said: "What they have sung just now is such a nice composition, which I and you too listened to with pleasure. But is it possible for such singing to give the same pleasure to a European? What I wanted to say was 'Let's find a way to have them [ie Westerners] enjoy those Turkish compositions that we love so much, whatever it takes, be it playing them with their technique, their music theory, their instruments, their orchestras. Let's make Turkish music an international art.' I did *not* say that we should throw away Turkish melodies, take ready-prepared Western music and make it our own, and listen to that music only. They [the state radio policy-makers] misunderstood, but they made such a fuss about it that I could not mention it anymore."

Whatever the truth, the result was a generation of musicians trained in special state schools to propagate orally transmitted folk music in a largely orchestral setting with written scores and massed voices, duly broadcast over the radio and later television; composer-researcher **Muzaffer Sarısözen**, responsible for establishing the folk ensemble of Radio Ankara, and singer **Neriman Altındağ**, who became the first female chief of the choir, were at the heart of this effort. Their direct disciples served as the senior musical policy-makers on state radio and television (TRT) until well into the 1980s, remaining faithful to the secularist vision of a hybrid Western and Anatolian-based culture.

Among those playing in the TRT Orchestras and teaching in the state conservatories were such master solo practitioners as Niyazi Sayın and Akagündüz Kutbay on *ney*, Necdet Yaşar on *tanbur*, İhsan Özgen on *kemençe* and Hurşit Üngay on *küdüm*; during the early 1960s they recorded some superb sessions of improvisational Ottoman classical music, but like Atatürk's private dinner-table entertainments these were essentially "after-hours" basement tapes, not intended for public broadcast. The tradition of discipleship on which this type of music depends was put under severe strain, to say the least.

Such official restrictive policies eventually ran aground. The art-music genre known as *sanat* or *klasik* (see p.1007), associated mainly with the cosmopolitan

Ottoman cities of İstanbul, İzmir and Bursa, underwent a slow process of recuperation, culminating in the foundation of a **dedicated conservatory** in İstanbul in 1976. Here Turkish classical musicians were given the same quality of training as the previously privileged folk musicians, classical ensembles gained an increasing share of radio and television airplay, and the performers cited above were able to teach openly without hindrance.

A decade later, then–Prime Minister Özal began **deregulating the media** as part of his stealthy dismantling of Atatürkist values. Pop, rock and *arabesk* (see p.1010 for definition, despised by the intelligentsia) began to fill the private FM radio stations, plus the satellite and cable TV channels which burgeoned semi-legally until regularized in 1994. Faced with competition, TRT updated its large orchestral formats, while still managing to retain and attract charismatic and talented performers. More startlingly, folk music with minority-language lyrics could be heard either live in trendy İstanbul cafés or purchased on recordings.

So too could religious and Sufi music. Following the forcible suppression of all dervish orders in 1925 – in response to a bloody rebellion incited by a Nakşibendi Sufi *şeyh* near Diyarbakır – a widespread base of dynamical classical music was driven deep underground with the loss of its natural environment, the Mevlevî *tekke*s. Members of the Mevlevî order had been great patrons of music across the Ottoman Empire, but until the 1980s, the Mevlevî *âyin* (musical ritual) was performed in public only as a tourist attraction in Konya, the historical home of the order – but where no living Mevlevî tradition now existed. The Mevlevîs were principal beneficiaries of the reforms of Özal, who encouraged a public face for Islam; the order performs to a new generation of tourists and interested Turks in the restored Mevlevî lodge in Galata, as well as at other locations. Archival and contemporary recordings of such music are easily available in shops, though this is as much or more a reflection of Western interest in Sufi and Ottoman high culture as of any popular religious expression in Turkey.

Folk music

Folk music is, despite (or because of) massive rural migration to the cities in the last six decades, currently the most popular genre in Turkey. It is still performed as part of daily life in its traditional, orally transmitted form; it has become a commercial phenomenon through a new wave of young singers interpreting traditional material in new orchestrations; and it has come of age as top performers have brought the music from its informal village origins to the most prestigious concert halls. Throughout, the mystical current of the Alevî *aşık* tradition (see p.1003) is powerful and influential.

Turkish folk music is dominated by the **saz**, a long-necked fretted lute with a changeable number of strings, and its variant the *bağlama*. Played in a variety of styles as a solo instrument accompanying the voice, the *saz* in particular has an intricate, silvery tone, providing not just notes and rhythmic patterns, but an ambience; it's a partner in a complex dialogue with the singer. Listen to Ali Ekber Çicek's *Haydar Haydar*, a complex and dramatic creation largely of his own inspiration, but anchored in the expressive techniques of the *aşık* and Alevî mysticism (see below). It's hard to say whether the instrument is accompanying the voice, or vice versa. Then listen, for contrast, to Talip Özkan's intricate and idiosyncratic solo style, embracing a variety of Anatolian tunings and plectrum techniques, but with each musical phrase embellished and nuanced to the utmost degree. There

Percussion

Bendir or **bendil** Frame drums of assorted sizes.

Davul or **ramazan davul** A large double-sided drum. One side is covered with goatskin, the other with sheepskin, struck with different-sized sticks to create a bass-and-snare-drum-like effect. During Ramazan the *davul* signals the beginning of fast in the morning before sunrise.

Darbuka, **deblek**, **dümbelek** (*demblik* in Kurdish). A goblet-shaped drum made of pottery, wood or metal and played with special techniques in order to alternate high and low pitches (on the rim, snapping the fingers on the skin, or on the centre).

Def or **tef** Tambourine: a frame drum with added cymbals or metal rings inside the frame.

Erbane Kurdish tambourine with metal rings fixed in the inner frame.

Kaşık A set of wooden or metal spoons, often brightly painted, that are manipulated by placing the handles of the spoons between the fingers.

Küdüm Small kettledrums usually played in pairs, with sticks, providing the rhythm signature (*usul*) of Ottoman classical or Mevlevî music. When used in secular music or *mehter* (military) music, they are called *nakkare*.

Nagara (*koltuk davulu*). A longer, thinner drum placed under the arm and beaten with hands.

Zil Cymbals, especially the pair of small cymbals used by belly dancers and singers.

Wind/reed instruments

Çifte or **arghul** A double instrument sounding similar to the clarinet, with two mouth-pieces and two sets of finger-holes on a pair of reed pipes. Often one set is without pitch-holes and used as a continuous drone (*dem*). The *arghul* is found only in a small area near the Syrian border, and is related to the *arghoul* played in Egypt and Syria. The *çifte* is particular to the environs of Ereğli on the western Black Sea.

Kaval An end-blown flute made of wood, with seven finger-holes in the front and one thumb-hole at the back, and sometimes another at the side. A favourite instrument of Turkish shepherds, it can be 80cm long. The Kurdish version is called *blur*. Almost extinct is the *çığırtma*, made from eagle- or crane-wing bone.

Klarnet The Western valved clarinet, especially in the longish, G-tuned form in metal or wood, using the old Albert system, favoured by the Gypsies and introduced by military bands during the 1870s.

Mey and **duduk** Small instrument with a very large double reed and a much sweeter tone than the *zurna*. Called *mey* in most of Turkey, *duduk* in the northeast and in neighbouring Caucasian republics, *balaban* in Azerbaijan.

Ney An end-blown flute requiring enormous skill to play. It is made from calamus reed or hardwood, with six finger-holes in front and a thumb-hole at the back. The sound is provided by the flow of air blown on the rim.

Sipsi Flute made from bone, wood or more commonly reed. The mouthpiece is completely taken into the mouth while playing. Most widely used in the Aegean region.

Tulum Bagpipe found in the Black Sea provinces. It generally has two pipes, each with five finger-holes, inserted into a goatskin bag which the player inflates before he begins. In Turkish Thrace, a nearly identical instrument is called a *gayda*.

Zurna (*zirne* in Kurdish). A very loud double-reed instrument with seven finger-holes, made of wood with a short conical body ending in a large open "bell". Varies in length between 30 and 60cm and changes accordingly its name from *cura zurna* (the smallest) to *kaba zurna*, by way of *orta*. It has also three tiny holes called "devil's (or genius') holes" whose function is unexplained; an instrument without them would, however, be considered unlucky. It's usually played with continuous breathing technique.

String instruments

Bağlama The most commonly used string folk instrument in Turkey, with seven strings (three doublets and a single). It takes different names according to the regions and according to its size: *bağlama*, *bozuk*, *çögür*, *kopuz*, *cura*, *tambura*. Its body is more bulbous than the *saz*, and the neck shorter.

Cümbüş A fretless banjo-type lute invented in the first decades of the twentieth century which substitutes for the *ud* when playing with louder instruments. It has a large resonating metal bowl covered with skin or plastic.

Çeng An open, angular harp used in ancient court music, long disappeared but now resurrected for "original instruments" ensembles.

Kabak kemane A bowed string instrument, called *ıklığ*, *rabab* or *rubaba* in south-eastern Turkey, *kemança* in Azerbaijan, *gicak* or *gijek* among the central Asian Turkic populations. A thin wooden or metal rod underneath the body is placed on the knee and enables the instrument to rotate while being bowed. The bow is made of horsetail hairs.

Kanun A trapezoidal plucked zither with between forty and a hundred strings, and a system of levers (*mandal*) for tuning to different scales quickly. The hammered version, known as *santur*, was also once used in Turkish music but has now almost disappeared.

Keman Originally a round-bodied version of the *kemençe*; now the name refers to a Western violin, preferred for its tone.

Kemençe or **kemançe** There are two forms of this fiddle with three strings, one typical of the Black Sea coast music, with an oblong wooden body and a short neck. In classical and Mevlevî dervish music a pear-shaped relative is used. The *kemençe* is held vertically and Black Sea musicians hold it by the neck without resting it, playing usually two strings at the same time in fourths; classical *kemençe* strings are stopped with nails, and not with the tip of the finger, giving it its peculiar vocal tone.

Saz A long-necked fretted lute, usually with seven strings (two pairs, and one set of three) played with a very thin plectrum or with the fingers. The *cura saz*, with six strings, is the smaller and highest pitched; next in size is the *tambura*, then the *divan sazı*, with eight strings, pitched one octave below *tambura*; the rarely used *meydan sazı* is the biggest.

Tanbur or **tambur** A very long-necked (up to more than 1m) lute with three strings and a large, semi-spherical body, noted for its very deep tone and because its frets on the neck visually represent the Turkish musical system. It is played with a long tortoiseshell plectrum, whose differently shaped tips can be used for different effects. It is at present used only in Turkey. Tamburi Cemil Bey introduced the bow to *tambur*, thus creating the popular *yaylı tanbur*, with a cello-like sound.

Tar A plucked stringed instrument especially popular in the Kars region as well as in Azerbaijan. "Tar" means "string" in Persian, and the most ancient form of the instrument is called *dutar* ("two strings") from which the word "guitar" is probably derived. Carved from a block of mulberry wood, it has a deep, curved body with two bulges shaped like a figure 8. The upper surface is shaped like two hearts of different sizes, joined at the points and traditionally covered with skin from a buffalo's heart. There are three double courses of melodic strings and a variable number of resonating strings.

Ud A fretless lute with eleven strings (five pairs and one single), nearly identical to the *oud* found throughout the Arab world but differently tuned.

are those who favour playing with a plectrum and those who play without (*şelpe*), plus many regional styles (*tavır* – literally, "attitudes") of playing and tuning (*düzen* – literally, "order"). Some players strive to maintain the regional *tavır*, others support a national style.

Regions and ethnicity

Many varieties of folk music flourish in Turkey today, recognizable by their associated instruments and dances. Outside the large cities in western Turkey, or in their squatter suburbs, one can hear the quintessential **rural Turkish ceremonial music** combination, the *zurna* and *davul* (the shawm-and-drum duo found from the Balkans to as far east as China), at almost any wedding or circumcision celebration. Often played by Gypsies, their enormous and unamplified volume indicates that something important is taking place – inevitably involving **folk dancing**. In the east this will most usually be the stately line-dance known as *halay* (arms linked or on shoulders); on the Aegean coast the macho *zeybek*; and more or less everywhere the *çiftetelli* and *karşılama*, both couples' dances. Among Black Sea Turks or Laz people you'll hear a small upright fiddle (*kemençe*), bagpipe (*tulum*) or smaller versions of the *zurna* and *davul* accompanying the *horon*, whose quick movements are said to imitate the wriggling of *hamsi* – the anchovies that feature conspicuously in their diet. Most of the rural population know, at least passively, these regional dances and their music. The *saz* has become an amplified instrument modelled on the electric guitar, and electronic keyboards and other techno-gadgets are now almost universally used. In provincial cities, the *elektrosaz* and the *darbuka* (goblet drum) constitute the main proletarian musical fare for ceremonial occasions often held in *düğünsalonları* or wedding salons for hire.

Contemporary musicians across the country are updating and reinventing local styles, sometimes creating universally accessible music. A good example is Laz *kemençe* and *tulum* player **Birol Topaloğlu** from the Black Sea coast, who has collected and arranged regional songs in some striking albums. From the same area, popular singer-songwriters **Fuat Saka** and **Volkan Konak** propose their own updated versions of traditional songs. The current popularity of folk music is evidenced by *türkü* bars (*türkü* being a type of folk song) which have sprung up around İstiklâl Caddesi in İstanbul and Kızılay district in Ankara, where young musicians like **Grup Çığ** play traditional songs with pop instrumentation. Actor-singer **Yavuz Bingöl** constitutes the strongest link between "pure" folk and the popular-music scene, his warm personality evident in an intimate solo style often self-accompanied by *saz*.

Bozlak is a free-rhythm, semi-improvised declamation of scorching emotional intensity, somewhat akin to flamenco, associated with the Abdal groups of western Anatolia. The singer sings, literally, at the top of his voice, and the *saz* is tuned in open fifths, allowing for dramatic melodic flourishes and a sparse, astringent sound. Perhaps the greatest exponent in recent years was **Neşet Ertaş**, from Kırşehir, a person of cultic veneration amongst enthusiasts in Turkey, and son of **Muharrem Ertaş**, another *bozlak* singer of mythic reputation. **Ekrem Çelebi**, an extraordinary virtuoso, is perhaps the best known of the younger generation. Traditionally a male preserve, nowadays *bozlak* is being attempted successfully by more and more female singers.

Turkey's population includes around twelve million people speaking several distinct **Kurdish** dialects, a fact only reluctantly acknowledged of late by the government; during the above-cited 1920s and 1930s musicological expeditions, collectors compulsorily labelled Kurdish music and dance as "Turkish". Traditionally, Kurdish folklore and cultural identity have been preserved through the help of the *dengbey* (bard), the *stranbey* (popular singer) and the *cirokbey* (storyteller). A *dengbey* is a singer with an exceptional memory, effectively the guardian of the Kurdish heritage, since he must know hundreds of songs existing only in oral tradition. *Dengbey*s chronicle Kurdish myths and legends, the struggle for freedom and the successive rulers and occupiers of their land, as well as interpreting love songs and lighter entertainment. Owing to periodic strife in the Kurdish-populated areas of the southeast (see pp.988–996 for full coverage), some of the best Kurdish *dengbeys*, like **Şivan Perwer** and **Temo**, live exiled in northern Europe, as did the Kurdish left-wing militant **Ahmet Kaya** (died 2000 in Paris) whose first album *Ağlama Bebeğim* was also the first recording to be banned by the Turkish Supreme Court in the 1980s. Since the late 1990s, however, optional Kurdish-language schooling, and Kurdish-language radio/TV broadcasting, have begun, and there has been an incremental relaxation of the ban on public Kurdish musical events and recording sales; such CDs are now available, with songs reinterpreted by younger artists such as **Aynur** (with two CDs on Kalan label) or **Kardeş Türküler** who season their repertory with Kurdish-lyrics songs. The main instruments used in Kurdish music are reed instruments such as the *blur* and the *duduk* – found in the mountainous regions where the echo from the hills is taken advantage of – and string instruments, such as the *tembur* and the *saz*, used in the towns of the plains.

The aşıks

Aşıks are the folk troubadours who emerged from the **Alevî tradition**. Originally heterodox Muslim communities of inner Anatolia, especially the provinces of Sivas, Tunceli, Çorum and Erzincan, Alevîs are now settled across the country: supposedly they number nearly twenty million (out of a total population of about seventy million). *Aşık*s are considered to have fallen into a trance in which gifts of musical and spiritual knowledge are imparted by the prophet İlyas (Elijah), and henceforth wander the countryside in search of the Beloved. Literally "the ones in love", they sing a repertoire of songs of mystical quest, interspersed with invocation to the various Alevî saints, and to Mohammed's brother-in-law Ali, whom they regard as the rightful heir to the Prophet's spiritual tradition. This makes them Shi'a Muslims, although with different practices than Arab or Iranian Shi'ites; the Alevî faith, and its offshoot the **Bektaşi** dervish order, stresses intersectarian tolerance, the teachings of its saints and bards, and equality between men and women. *Aşık*s play an honoured role in the regular Alevî religious ceremony (*cem*) which includes prayers, recitations, singing and the culminating circle-dance, the *sema*. Alevî music (and their entire culture) is more rural and folk-based than the classical, high-art Mevlevî ritual (see p.1008). It's possible to attend a *cem* at the Şahkulu Sultan (Merdivenköy) *tekke* or the Karaca Ahmet Sultan (Üsküdar) mosque in İstanbul on Sundays and Alevî holidays. The **solo saz** is virtually a sacred object to the Alevî, rich in spiritual significance as a material representation of the İmam Ali: the resonator represents his body, the neck his sword Zulfikar, and the frets the twelve imams. The Alevî *saz* has a special tuning, resulting in a particularly sombre, intense sound, with complex chord patterns emerging from the shifting drones.

Many of the songs have words by or about **Pir Sultan Abdal**, an *aşık* martyr of the sixteenth century, executed for his associations with a rebellion against the Ottoman authorities; his birthplace, the village of Banaz near Sivas, remains a place of pilgrimage. Alevîs in general and many *aşık*s in particular have been the subject of mistrust and contempt from orthodox Sunni Muslims, often officially condoned. Most blatantly, a Sivas hotel hosting a leftist/Alevî conference was attacked and set alight on July 2, 1993, by a fundamentalist mob; 37 poets and *aşık*s died, and the 128 prosecuted over the incident were either released or given risibly light sentences at their 1994 trial.

The most celebrated of these bards was **Aşık Veysel** (1894–1973), born in Sivrialan, Sivas province. He had lost his sight at the age of 7 during a smallpox epidemic which killed his two brothers. Contrary to prevalent *aşık* tradition he did not have a revelatory vision, but was taught by local master *saz* players. His most famous songs, such as "Dostlar Beni Hatırlasın" (May My Friends Remember Me), "Kara Toprak" (Black Earth) and "Uzun İnce Bir Yoldayım" (I'm on a Long Difficult Journey), mystical contemplations on the human condition, are still sung all over Turkey. Like many Alevî he strongly endorsed the secularist stance of the young republic, which seemed to promise the social change Alevîs had always favoured, and lent his talents to official efforts to explain the new regime to Anatolian villages. This assistance was rewarded by honours and a token official pension in 1965, though he died in his hometown in reduced circumstances.

An *aşık* revival was encouraged in the early 1970s by opera singer and *saz* player **Ruhi Su**. Though not an Alevî, he was uncompromisingly left-wing and lost his job at the state opera as a result. While mainstream performers had to compromise, the sacking freed him artistically – his albums sold, and still sell, in large numbers. **Musa Eroğlu** began singing traditional songs of his hometown Mersin, and now his voice is considered by many the purest contemporary incarnation of the *aşık* tradition. **Arif Sağ**, **Eroğlu**, **Yavuz Top**, and the late **Muhlis Akarsu** (killed in the Sivas fire) have made excellent recordings both as a group, **Muhabbet**, and individually. Unfortunately Muhabbet's best productions remain available on cassette only. The best *aşık* music has always had a latent political-protest content. **Ali İzzet** and **Mahsuni Şerif** made this evident in songs ranging from passionate denunciations of social and political injustice to gentle satires on Turkish football. Celebrated by the urban Turkish left in the late 1960s, their songs have been kept alive by the new generation of folk singers. **Feyzullah Çınar** from Ankara is a more recent but very impressive representative of this tradition, "discovered" at the annual gathering of *aşık* at the mausoleum of Hacı Bektaş Veli, founder of the Bektaşi order.

The tradition assumes another distinct form where the *aşık*s make their living as entertainers and storytellers in cafés, particularly in the northeastern districts of Kars and Erzincan, where audiences enjoy the ritualized exchange of insults between two rival performers, which follows a pre-ordained rhyme and musical scheme. No detail of appearance or character trait is spared, and the contest concludes when one musician fails to come up with a witty riposte. Even given the language barrier, it's worth attending such events just to enjoy the sense of occasion, and the tears of laughter rolling down the cheeks of the listeners. **Aşık Şeref Taşlıova** and **Murat Çobanoğlu** are still recognized as the masters of such events, which can be heard occasionally at Çobanoğlu's own café in the town of Kars.

Aşık music is generally easy to identify upon hearing, even to those unfamiliar with Turkish music, as it is one of the few genres featuring solo voice and *saz*. But there have been several orchestral experiments, notably **Arif Sağ's** "Concerto for Bağlama" with two other instrumentalists who currently represent *saz*-playing at its best with their complementary approach: **Erdal Erzincan**, rooted in the tradition, and **Erol Parlak**, a virtuoso who has created a *saz* quintet with a chamber-music sound.

Belkis Akkale was tremendously successful in the wider market from the mid-1980s with recordings directed by **Arif Sağ**, featuring large, buzzing *saz* orchestras, driving rhythms and her deep, soulful voice singing a **türkü** (folk song). A talented younger generation includes **Gülay, Kubat**, and **Sabahat Akkiraz**, steeped in the Alevî culture but capable of taking part in contemporary music projects.

Kardeş Türküler's repertoire is a well-researched choice of Alevî, Kurdish, Armenian, Greek, traditional and contemporary Turkish tunes in new arrangements, adding to excellent *saz-* and *zurna*-playing the sound of electric bass, classic guitar, violin and accordion. Their CDs *Doğu* and *Hemavaz* (Kalan) come highly recommended, as does Kalan's first-ever music DVD, devoted to them.

Greek and Jewish traditions

Collaboration between Turkish and Greek musicians occurs regularly, as do Turkish covers of Greek songs. Even during the worst periods of tensions between the two countries – now eased, but always prone to resurgence – this shared ground was never lost, but the once-flourishing ethnic Greek community of İstanbul, famous for its lively Tatavla (today's Kurtuluş) carnivals, has dwindled to just a few thousand. **Yeni Türkü** (see p.1022) pioneered this recipirocity, while currently other groups focus on different aspects of this shared heritage, from raunchy *rebétika* to classical composition. Accordion player **Muammer Ketencioğlu**'s group Kumpanya features the unique voice of **Ivi Dermancı**, a native-born İstanbul Greek; in a rare instance of voluntary emigration to (rather than from) İstanbul, Greek cantor **Nikiforos Metaxas** (of Kefallonian extraction) created his **Bosphorous** ensemble of Turkish musicians, whose recent hook-up with Greek group **Mode Plagal** exceeds the sum of the parts. Turkish singer **Melihat Gülses** favours melodies dedicated to İstanbul and Athens, while the CD *Letter from Istanbul* (Golden Horn) by *kemençe* virtuosos **Derya Türkan** and **Sokratis Sinopoulos** is a delicate, acoustic dialogue.

The Jewish presence in İstanbul goes back at least to 1493, when thousands of Sephardic Jews expelled from Spain were welcomed by Sultan Beyazit II, who apocryphally remarked, "How can a sovereign (ie the King of Spain) be reckoned wise who drives such productive and enterprising folk to my realms!" They brought with them their language (Ladino or more properly Judeo-Spanish) and their culture, with secular songs (*romanzas*) and liturgical music. Over time they adapted the Ottoman classical style to their own heritage, and many became important composers and performers. The most important current exponents of secular songs are **Janet and Jak Esim**, whose original sessions have just been re-released on Kalan CDs, while the transitory **Maftirim** project – a group of Jewish cantors performing with accompaniment of *ney* and *kanun* – focused on the connections between Jewish and Turkish sacred musics. Israeli researcher and singer **Hadass–Pal Yarden**, long resident in İstanbul, has released *Yahudice* (Kalan), a wide-ranging and fascinating exploration of eastern Mediterranean music.

Classical traditions

Classical Ottoman music has a tradition as long as Western European classical music. Based partly on the theoretical treatises of the ancient Greeks and their Arab successors, a notational system was introduced to the Ottoman court early in the fifteenth century by composer and theoretician **Abdülkadir Merağı** (died 1435). Over the next two centuries or so, the style evolved in cosmopolitan İstanbul under such composers as **Hafız Post** (died 1690), **Buhurizade Mustafa İtri** (1640-1712), the Romanian prince **Dimitri Cantemir** (1673–1727) and other personalities of Greek, Armenian, Jewish, Crimean and Azeri origin. Ottoman urban music continued to flourish under **Sultan Selim III** (1789–1807), himself a composer, and the towering figure of **Hamamizade İsmail Dede Efendi** (1778–

1846). There were even women composers such as eighteeenth-century harem inmate **Dilhayat Hanım**, whose piece in *makam evcara* is still played.

Turkish urban music divides into three broad genres: **religious** (*sema*), **classic** (*klasik* or *sanat*) and **nightclub** (*fasıl*), which all share the compositional rules known as **makam**. The *makam* are musical modes or scales (with associated rules governing melodic flow and prominent notes) in which the musicians compose their songs and instrumental pieces, and, more importantly, weave their improvisations (*taksim*), which are central to classical music performance. The *taksim* improvisation usually precedes, but also punctuates, suites of vocal compositions (*kâr*, later *şarkı*) framed by instrumental pieces (*peşrev* and *saz semaisi*). Most *şarkı* sung today date from the late nineteenth century, the era of one of the great songwriters, **Hacı Arif Bey**.

These classical genres are essentially chamber genres, where the instruments play as a loose collection of soloists, each taking turns at improvising, and each elaborating the melodic and rhythmic line as they see fit. Typical **instruments** are the *ud* (lute), the *ney* (end-blown flute), the *tanbur* (long-necked fretted lute), the *kanun* (zither) and *klarnet* (valved clarinet). Rhythm (*usul*) is provided by the *def* (a frame drum) or the *darbuka* (the omnipresent goblet drum). Some of these instruments, in particular the *darbuka* and *klarnet*, are restricted to secular contexts; others are effectively synonymous with spiritual music, in particular the *ney* and *küdüm* drums. Performers themselves were often extremely versatile, so the stylistic distinctions made below and in the discography following are not rigid; *sanat* and *fasıl* practitioners overlapped considerably, and classical musicians would even perform *türkü*s (folk songs) on demand.

Many famous virtuosi composers are associated with their playing of particular instruments, and still listened to as role models within their archival recordings: **Tanburi Cemil Bey** (1871–1916) and **Necdet Yaşar** (born 1930) on the *tanbur*, **Yorgo Bacanos** (1900–77), **Marko Melkon Alemsherian** and **Udi Hrant Kenkulian** (1901–78) on the *ud*, **Cüneyd Orhon** on *kemençe*, **Tatyos Efendi** (1863–1913), **Kemani Haydar Tatlıyay** and **Kemani Nubar Çömlekçiyan** on violin, **Şükrü Tunar** (1907–62) on the *klarnet*, **Ahmet Meter** (alias Halil Karaduman**, born 1959) on the *kanun*.

Many Ottoman and Republican players and composers inhabited the world of professional, secular music-making, whose profane associations with drink and dance made it the preserve of İstanbul's and İzmir's Armenian, Greek and Jewish minorities, and others, notably Gypsies, who fell outside bourgeois Muslim respectability. Ottoman urban music was zealously attacked by Republican ideologues, who considered it thoroughly decadent because of its reliance on Arabic, Byzantine and Persian forms, not to mention its cosmopolitan (read non-"Turkish") and religious influences. The pertinent section of the State Conservatory was wound up late in the 1920s, but after 1930 a classical group reformed at the İstanbul municipal conservatory, and there were other, semi-officially tolerated Turkish-classical music societies which provided musicians as needed for the state radio.

Despite a lack of public encouragement, these genres flourished in the **private** sector, as proved by abundant reissued recordings made between the 1920s and 1950s. Non-Muslim musicians, who continued to dominate urban music until mid-century, were fêted by no less than Atatürk himself, and an Armenian *kanun* player, Artaki Candan-Terzian, was head of the Sahibinin Sesi (HMV-Turkey) recording studios from 1925 until 1948.

The contemporary scene focuses on a group of top-quality instrumentalists who keep the classical tradition alive as well as producing their own compositions. *Kemençe* player and conservatory teacher **İhsan Özgen** has led his own ensemble,

Anatolia, in a series of brilliant recordings and nurtured a new generation of musicians, including his daughters **Neva** and **Yelda**; in the same group are *kanun* players **Göksel Baktağir** and **Ruhi Ayangil**, *ney* players **Süleyman Erguner** and **Sadrettin Özçimi**, and *ud* player **Yurdal Tokcan**. Two other groups make extremely listenable music exploring a wide range of Turkish styles, with their CDs or concerts featuring special guests: **Yansımalar** (guitarist and *tanbur* player **Birol Yayla** with *ney* player **Aziz Şenol Filiz**), whose repertoire is based on original melodic invention reminiscent of Ottoman music; while guitarist Çengiz Özdemir's acoustic group **İnce Saz** plays an elegant version of the more Western-influenced repertoire of golden-age İstanbul.

Sanat vocal artists

The voice lies at the heart of all classical genres, all influenced by Koranic recitation as well as the *ezan* or prayer heard from all mosques. The late **Kani Karaca**'s recording of different calls to prayer, some *sura*s from the Koran as well as traditional *ilahi*s (hymns) are collected in the double CD *Aşk İle/With Love*, the best acoustic snapshot of sacred music from İstanbul. *Gazel*, or the art of vocal improvisation, has a place both in classical and religious styles, and was popularized by singers like **Hafız Burhan Sesiyılmaz**, **Abdullah Yüce** and again **Karaca**, who displayed in their singing a fascinating variety of voice colours.

Münir Nurettin Selçuk (1901–81) is a key performer, beginning to record in the early 1920s, and later becoming conductor of the ensemble of the İstanbul Conservatory. Selçuk pioneered a more straightforward vocal delivery, less influenced by Koranic recitation and its guttural trills. His unrivalled knowledge of the classical Ottoman musical repertoire and the innovative quality of his delivery gave him in vocal music the same status as Tanburi Cemil Bey in instrumental music. A dashing figure, among the first to stand at centre-front stage and acquire the trappings of a "star", he was equally at home with Western-influenced bel canto and with intense, brooding *gazel*.

Zeki Müren (1931–96), perhaps the highest rated vocalist in the latter half of the twentieth century, studied with Refik Fersan and Şerif Içli, and later worked extensively with the composer **Muzaffer Özpınar**. Müren first made his name through classical broadcasts during the 1950s, then with versions of Egyptian and Lebanese musicals, but came to prominence with his perfect and passionate performances of classical vocal pieces accompanied by TRT musicians during the 1960s, and frequented İstanbul's burgeoning *gazino* clubs during the 1970s. He performed his own compositions as well as specially composed pieces, and his diction is considered to be of the utmost refinement. Müren flirted with all popular genres – tango, chanson and *arabesk* – but throughout his career produced austerely classical recordings. During the 1960s and 1970s, increasingly camp stage decor and personal costuming (he was a gay transvestite) overshadowed musical values, though the 1980s saw such tendencies reined in – and little discernible drop in performance quality. He died dramatically onstage of heart failure while receiving an award in İzmir.

Female singers like **Safiye Ayla** (Atatürk's favourite), **Hamiyet Yüceses** and **Müzeyyen Senar** (born 1918) also attained considerable popularity and are still very much listened to. Their direct heir seems to be **Umut Akyürek**, who debuted in 2004 with a highly successful album, *O Dudaklar Bülbüllesiyor* (BMG). **Bülent Ersoy** studied with Senar, and started her career as a male singer in Turkish classical music; in 1980 she had a sex-change operation, but continues to produce songs in a restrained classical idiom, and supposedly knows more classical songs than any other active singer. Her recordings on Orkide label are particularly fine examples,

CONTEXTS | Music

as is her striking reinterpretation of the turn-of-the-century repertoire, *Alaturka 95*. This outraged devout Muslims by its inclusion of an *ezan* on the opening track (sung by Bülent herself) – the association of religion with this controversial figure was too much for some, and indeed a right-wing nationalist fired a shot at her during one concert. Following her gender reassignment, Ersoy had been forbidden from performing publicly on moral grounds, but she successfully lobbied then-President Özal (a big fan) to lift the ban, and now her artistry is widely celebrated on national TV.

The Mevlevî dervish âyin

Classical religious music is based on the traditions of the **Mevlevî ("Whirling") dervishes**. Mevlevî performances consist of long **âyin**, complex yet delicate compositions, unified by the same, specifically identified *makam*, eg "Ferahfeza Ayini" or "Saba Ayini". They are preceded and followed by instrumental and vocal pieces with words from the thirteenth-century Sufi poet **Celaleddin Rumi (Mevlâna)**, the order's founder, interspersed with *taksims*, particularly on the *ney*, *tambur*, *kanun*, *küdüm* and *rebab*. The best-known Mevlevî composers are **Köçek Derviş Mustafa Dede** (17th century), **Dede Efendi** (18th–19th century) and **Rauf Yekta** (19th–20th century).

Public performances of *âyin* are put on, as indeed they were in Ottoman times, for foreign observers at various venues, but versions of the Mevlevî repertory can also be heard at the lodges of the Halveti-Cerrahi sect, with a heavier emphasis on the practice of *zikr*, a trance-inducing repetition of various of the 99 names of God, and the collective singing of *ilahi* (hymns). Such practices, while freed from the overt suppression of prior decades, are still somewhat clandestine, though one of the greatest Halveti-Cerrahi *şeyh*s (leaders), **Muzaffer Özak**, made a superb recording of Mevlevî *âyin* with **Kudsi Erguner** in the late 1970s.

The Erguner family tradition of ney playing started with **Süleyman** the elder, born into a religious family in 1902 and raised in a mystical environment (the Özbek *tekke* in Üsküdar); his son **Ulvi**, who became director of Radio Istanbul; and his grandsons Kudsi and Süleyman. Since settling in Paris in 1975, **Kudsi** has become one of the most visible exponents of Turkish music abroad, working as a musicologist, publishing his own field recordings, and undertaking ad hoc projects as well as performing. He has composed film soundtracks and recorded albums with jazz performers, appearing regularly in Turkey where his concerts in İstanbul's Aya Irini church are major, message-laden events, for example the 2004 evening with an orchestra and two choirs: one of muezzins and one of Greek Orthodox monks. His labels Equinox and Imaj issue new CDs and re-release old recordings, usually of very high calibre. **Süleyman** the younger chose to stay in İstanbul, where he is one of the foremost local *ney* soloists, as well as an instructor at the İstanbul Conservatory. Lately he is enjoying an even higher public profile as founder and leader of the İstanbul Mevlevî Ensemble, which performs regularly in Turkey and abroad; his recordings are also more readily available since the foundation of his own Erguner label.

Western-style art music

The last years of the Ottoman Empire saw the creation of Western-style bands and orchestras, with Giuseppe Donizetti – Gaetano's brother – leading the new palace ensembles and writing celebratory marches. Musicologist **Emre Aracı** and pianist **Aydın Karlibel** have devoted their research to this repertoire, performing forgotten works on several charming CDs. Later, the republic supported the creation of a national school of Western-style art music. Its leading figures were **Cemal Reşit Bey**, **Ulvi Cemal Erkin** and **Hasan Ferit Alnar**; schooled in Paris, Germany or Austria, these musicians variously tried to combine colours, themes and rhythms of Turkish music with European orchestration, polyphony and harmonies, inspired by Bartok, Hindemith and the Russian school of national composers. CDs with their compositions are surprisingly hard to find, with their music only recently gaining some popularity thanks to a new generation of soloists. Violinist **Cihat Aşkın** has released a series of successful CDs focusing on the chamber music repertory, and interspersing it with arrangements of traditional tunes; on piano, **Seher Tanrıyar** and **Vedat Kosal** recorded **Cemal Reşit Bey**'s transcription of folk songs; while **Hande Dalkiliç** released *Yurt Renkleri/The Colours of Our Country*, a lively, rhythmically strong collection of **Muammer Sun**'s studies on folk dances and melodies.

Gypsies and fasıl music

As so often in the Balkans, Gypsies (*Roman* or *Çingene* in Turkish) have an important local musical presence, particularly in the semi-classical, urban-nightclub style referred to as **fasıl**. This is essentially a vocal suite interspersed with light orchestral ensemble pieces and solo *taksim*s, or improvisations; every short rest (*fasıl* means "interval") is filled with flourishes and improvisations from the stars of the orchestra, frowned upon in strictly classical circles. Like *sanat*, this style was also officially unrecognized, though privately enjoyed, by Atatürk and his retinue.

Fasıl has continued to suffer somewhat from its association with sleazy *gazino* **nightclubs** (also called *pavyon*), and **belly dancing** for tourists, but it's also performed in more respectable restaurants. Downmarket *gazino*s still abound, particularly around Laleli or Aksaray in İstanbul; the music incorporates recent songs, and sticks less assiduously to classical formula – this is, after all, music to drink and dance to. Currently the best place to hear Gypsy musicians around İstiklâl Caddesi is the *Badehane* bar in Tünel.

Although much of the nightclub repertory overlaps with what you might hear on a radio concert, or in a conservatory, *fasıl* is a very different kind of music. The classical values of precision and dutiful respect to tradition are replaced by demonstrative, present-tense music. The *klarnet* and *darbuka* dominate the instrumental ensemble, and many if not all of the most noted performers are Gypsies, playing with great skill and passion. Tunes are tossed around with breathless, exhilarating ease, long notes are held on the *klarnet* for extended yet exquisitely poised moments during improvisation, *kanun* and violin decorate and interrupt; noise and gestural energy flow across the stage like a torrent, carrying all before it. Violinists spike pieces with lightning-fast glissandos, and clarinetists favour the low G-clarinet for the throaty sound that gives *fasıl* its special character.

The most famous of all the clarinetists is **Mustafa Kandırali** (born 1930), who has worked for the TRT and toured and recorded widely. Other celebrated *fasıl* musicians, both living and deceased, include *kanun* player **Ahmet Yatman**, *oud*-ist **Kadri Şençalar**, violinist **Kemani Cemal**, the **Erköse** brothers (clarinettist Barbaros is still performing) and clarinettist **Deli Selim**. Another younger player (born 1957) featuring on several recordings is clarinettist **Selim Sesler**, who began his career as an İstanbul *fasıl* musician but has since distinguished himself as an interpreter of wedding and dance tunes from his native Thrace and beyond. He also appears in an excellent 2005 musical documentary, *Crossing the Bridge: The Sound of Istanbul*, along with octogenarian Müzeyyen Senar.

Burhan Öçal, from Kırklareli in Thrace, is a virtuoso *darbuka* player who graduated from the state conservatory. While he's not from a Gypsy family, he's familiar with the music from his native town and went on to create a combination of classical Turkish and Gypsy musics with his Oriental Ensemble; later he fused classical and Gypsy traditions with ethno-jazz and even drum'n'bass. **Laço Tayfa** was a band drawing on the Gypsy music of Bergama, originally led by clarinet player **Hüsnü Şenlendirici**, son of trumpet player Ergün who played in the early ethno-jazz experiments by Okay Temiz; its infectious music included groovy electric bass and rock drumming as well as guests like the versatile singer **Kibariye**. Other vocalists worth looking out for on recordings include **Perihan Altındağ**, **Mahmut Celalettin**, ethnic Greek **Deniz Kızı Eftalya** and **Kemal Gürses**, a singer whose knowledge of the repertoire was legendary and who became the best leader of *fasıl* recordings during the 1970s.

Arabesk: "oriyental" roots

Arabesk is essentially derived from the folk, classical and *fasıl* traditions, though the name alludes to its predominantly Arabic rather than Turkish melodies. For most locals during the 1980s and early 1990s *arabesk* was the dominant Turkish music, a working-class and, to an extent, outsiders' sound which addressed the everyday realities and problems of the *gariban*, the poor and oppressed. Also known as *minibüs müziği*, after its blaring from such vehicles taking workers into the cities from surrounding slums, *arabesk* was as much a stance towards life – complete with windscreen ornaments, tacky postcards, dayglo stickers and associated melodramatic films – as a music.

Arabesk has its roots in Egyptian "oriental dance" music – **raks şarkı** or **oriyental** – which has long been popular in Turkey. Numerous classical Turkish musicians worked across the Middle East during the early twentieth century, either as film composers, instrumentalists or singers. Violinist **Haydar Tatlıyay** (1890–1963), after returning to Turkey from Egypt in 1947, set up a large dance orchestra as used in Egyptian films. Turkey's nascent recording and film industry subsequently produced versions of Middle-Eastern hits, particularly those associated with Mohammed Abd el-Wahaab and Umm Kulthum, and the Lebanese star Farid al-Attrache. *Sanat* singers Zeki Müren and Münir Nurettin Selçuk actually made their names as film stars during the 1940s and 1950s, singing, in front of large string-based orchestras, abstract but dramatically intense lyrics of unrequited love. But from the late 1940s onwards what would soon become known as *arabesk* per se began to address specifically Turkish problems such as rural–urban migration. **Diyarbakırlı Celal Güzelses** and **Malatyalı Fahri Kayahan** were amongst the earliest to record popularized folk-based forms for an urban audience, drawing on the musical styles and repertoires of southeastern Turkey. **Ahmet Sezgin** took this one step further, bringing urban and rural styles into a creative mix during the mid-1960s; by the 1970s the instrumental heart of *arabesk* consisted of electrified strings (including an obligatory solo *saz*), keyboards and percussion.

The heyday of arabesk

The first major *arabesk* star was **Orhan Gencebay**, born in 1944 on the Black Sea coast, who began his career with Ahmet Sezgin after studying a variety of genres in private lessons, in the military and at TRT. His debut solo recording, *Bir Teselli Ver* (1969), was based on classical forms, but the sobbing intensity of the voice owed much to *gazel*, and the frank lyrics addressed the plight of the lonely lover. A more eclectic set of references, particularly rock and flamenco, was displayed in his 1975 album *Batsın Bu Dünyayı* (A Curse on This World), and this creative and playful eclecticism continues to be found on almost any of his albums. Gencebay is appreciated as much for his virtuoso *saz*-playing and his film-acting skills as for his voice or lyrics.

It is indeed the voice which defines *arabesk* aesthetics, and those of İbrahim Tatlıses, Müslüm Gürses and Ferdi Tayfur (all film actors too) are the most significant. Their songs, thinly disguised autobiographies, tell of self-pity and humiliation in the big city – *Kulak veren yok garibin sesine* ("Nobody listens to the voice of the poor man"), as Gürses once sung – experiences close to the hearts of Turkey's numerous internal migrants. Of mixed Kurdish/Arab background, **İbrahim Tatlıses** himself migrated from the southeastern town of Urfa, central in Turkish musical traditions. He has been a dominant figure since the late 1970s, with a series of albums featuring well-drilled orchestras, danceable tunes and his electrifying voice (plus occasional Kurdish lyrics); now he not only has his own television show, but a chain of restaurants as well as other lucrative enterprises. **Ferdi Tayfur**'s voice also has strong resonances with southeastern vocal styles, and his reputation, like that of Tatlıses', rests heavily on his portrayal of a poor villager made good in the big city. Adana-born **Müslüm Gürses** is still adored by his fans for his older hits: mournful, fate-obsessed numbers inviting the listener to light another cigarette ("Bir Sigara Yak") or to curse the world ("Yeter Allahım"). His audiences were once notorious for their unruly behaviour at concerts, slicing themselves with razor blades during his performances to demonstrate how the songs were expressing their deep pain and suffering. Lately Gürses has stretched to interpreting Dylan and Björk tunes, while his performance in the movie *Neredesin Firuze*, an exhilarating look at the world of Turkish commercial music, as a kind of Turkish Serge Gainsbourg, took many by surprise and won him a new generation of admirers.

Despite (or because of) being a music with a chequered history and dubious (for Turkish nationalists at least) origins, *arabesk* acquired some powerful advocates and defenders during the 1980s, as part of the general "revision" of republican cultural mores. The late President Özal even used an *arabesk* song as the theme for his 1988 election campaign. Establishment apparatchiks were duly horrified; the tragic lyrics were claimed to encourage the retrograde oriental vices of despair, fatalism and even suicide. Accordingly industrial-strength *arabesk* was banned from the airwaves in 1989, and the acting minister of culture attempted to promote a sanitized, inherently contradictory alternative, *acısız arabesk* (painless *arabesk*); it flopped spectacularly, and the prohibition was soon rescinded.

Arabesk stars were quick to take advantage of their new legitimacy and more particularly of Özal's deregulation of electronic media. Private FM radio and TV have given the music a new lease of life, and younger stars have begun acting in TV soap operas, the genre that has largely replaced the *arabesk* movie. **Mahsun Kırmızıgül**'s CD *Sarı Sarı* was the market sensation of 2005, though his style evolved in a more pop-influenced direction; others like **Özcan Deniz** turned to a folkish style. Deniz acted in the hugely successful soap opera *Asmalı Konak*, and in the movie *Neredesin Firuze* (see above).

Rock and özgün

Rock has a surprisingly long history in Turkey – and in the Turkish diaspora, where brothers Ahmet and Nesui Ertegün founded the enormously influential

Atlantic jazz, rock and blues label in New York. But this is just one aspect of the well-established practice of producing local versions – *aranjmanlar* – of fashionable international genres. Tango was enormously popular in Turkey (as in Greece) from the 1930s until the 1950s; French *chanson* had its Turkish exponents such as blonde bombshell Ajda Pekkan; and Elvis Presley spawned a wave of local imitators in the late 1950s, most notably Erol Büyükburç. Subsequently a number of musicians began to try reconciling Anatolian folk with Western rock genres. Most had matriculated the fairly exclusive foreign-language schools in İstanbul, many were members of the city's non-Muslim minorities, and a few had the means to travel across Europe in the 1960s. During the 1970s an **Anadolu (Anatolian) Rock** movement gathered steam; the new bands' growing identification with the international Left movement was reflected in increasingly politicized lyrics, and many groups disintegrated when the generals took over in 1980.

Cem Karaca, who had worked with nearly every significant Anadolu Rock band (Apaşlar, Kardaşlar, Moğollar, Dervişan), fled to Germany just before the coup, returning only in 1987. His is the most interesting voice of the genre, combining rock histrionics with a cultivated bel canto. His songs combined a taste for highbrow literature with social realism; Dervişan's *Safinaz*, recorded in 1979, was a kind of rock opera about a poor girl's struggle with honour and blood feuds. He also superbly recorded the poetry of Nazım Hikmet and Orhan Veli Kanık (the two most influential Turkish poets of the twentieth century) before passing away in 2004. For some observers, Karaca's political integrity was undermined by his craven reconciliation with Özal's government, but his music's jagged intensity and literary intelligence is now celebrated by a new generation of singers. **Moğollar**, under Cahit Berkay, has re-formed; politically edged lyrics are still very much to the fore, while the chamber-ensemble lyricism and complexity of their earlier work has been replaced with an up-tempo stadium-rock style. Perhaps the most successful of their recent recordings is *Dört Renk* (1996), with catchy tunes, punchy lyrics, and something of the old psychedelia to the keyboard and *saz* sound. Other leading figures are **Erkin Koray**, **MFÖ**, **Edip Akbayram** and the late **Barış Manço.**

A few bands maintained the impetus of the earlier countercultural movement into the mid-1980s. **Bulutsuzluk Özlemi** (Longing for Unclouded Skies), one of the most radical, is still active, while the ambitious **Mozaik** group gave way to Ayşe Tütüncü's personal brand of jazz (see below). **Yeni Türkü**, inspired by the Latin American "New Song" movement, was one of the first groups to use traditional Turkish acoustic instruments played in good arrangements, and enjoyed great popularity amongst the intelligentsia from the late 1980s on for their versions of old İstanbul songs and Greek *rebétika* numbers, as well as original lyrics with a liberal-to-left stance on topical issues.

An intimate, mellow vocal style, combining rural melodic forms with guitar- or *saz*-based harmonies, was dubbed **özgün** (original) music. The austere figure of composer and *saz*-player **Zülfü Livaneli** – best known for his work with Greek composer Mikis Theodorakis and singer Maria Farandouri, and for the film music to Yılmaz Güney's film *Yol* – dominated the genre during the 1980s. Born in the eastern Black Sea region, as a leftist intellectual he spent several years during the early 1970s exiled in Sweden, where he first hooked up with like-minded Theodorakis. Singer **Tülay German**, one-time collaborator of electronic master **İlhan Mimaroğlu**, lived in Paris and brought this style to the international stage.

Drawing inspiration from groups like Inti-Illimani and sharing their resolute militant vision, **Grup Yorum** formed during the mid-1980s, but their political commitment was always combined with serious, grass-roots folk research; they remain active and over two decades were widely influential, their singers like **Ayşegül**, **Gülbahar** and **İlkay Akkaya** regularly going for successful solo careers.

Current bands drawing on indigenous styles and instruments as well as technological bric-a-brac and avant-garde inspirations include **Zen**, **Replikas** and **Baba Zula**. Popular mainstream rock acts with Turkish lyrics are **Mavi Sakal**, **Mor ve Ötesi** (Turkish grunge), **Duman**, **Athena** (essentially Turkish Ska) and **Cargo**. Turkish hip-hop, kick-started in Germany with **Cartel**, is today reaching a mass audience with **Ceza**, **Karargah**, and the Circassian rapper **Sultana** whose hit "Kuşu Kalkmaz/Bird Can't Fly", with its explicit lyrics, proved very controversial.

Pop, ethno-jazz and electronica

At the heart of **Turkish pop** stands **Sezen Aksu**: trained as an art-music singer in her native İzmir, her prominence owes much to her early partnership with the late **Onno Tunç**, an Armenian musician who embraced soul and jazz during the 1960s, and who oversaw Turkey's Eurovision Song Contest entries during the 1980s. Aksu's soulful voice, updating traditional Turkish urban musical aesthetics, and Tunç's eliptical arrangements and keyboard-based harmonic style, made for a winning combination. Although Sezen Aksu is still very popular mainly for her love songs, she has also been a canny political figure, embracing concerns and campaigns: Bosnia, feminism, ecology and human rights. Her CDs, some twenty in total since 1975, often anticipate the political zeitgeist, and each one's release has been an event. When *Işık Doğudan Yükselir/*"The Light Rises from the East" came out in 1995, evoking the cultural mosaic of Anatolia in gentle feminist terms, at a time of intercommunal religious rioting in İstanbul and the worsening crisis in the southeast of the country, the album's release was the first item on the state television's evening news programme. Her 1997 *Düğün ve Cenaze/*"Wedding and Funeral" was a collaboration with Bosnian-Serb musician Goran Bregoviç, reworking a number of popular tunes currently circulating widely around the Balkans – and had considerable resonance in a Turkey contemplating the ruins of Yugoslavia, ancestral home to many modern Turks, and the ethnic cleansing of Muslim populations. After the premature death of Onno Tunç it was his brother Arto, a well-known percussionist on the global jazz scene, who took charge as Aksu's arranger. He recruited the members of Night Ark – Ara Dinkjan and Marc Johnson – to create the challenging musical background for her *Deli Veren* album.

Among the singers emerging from Sezen's "conservatory" during the late 1980s and early 1990s was **Levent Yüksel**, a multi-talented instrumentalist and singer, who produced carefully crafted CDs (in particular *Med Cezir*) connecting explicitly with indigenous Turkish traditions and literature; 2003 Eurovision winner **Sertab Erener**; **Yıldız Tilbe**, who also released a vapid CD of *türkü*; teen idol **Tarkan** who crossed the border into the world market – like Sezen's "Şımarık" who became popular in Europe as "Kiss Kiss" with English words; and the powerful **Işın Karaca**. **Candan Erçetin** has done the most to continue the Aksu tradition, drawing on a wide range of Anatolian, Balkan and Mediterranean influences, literary lyrics and good studio engineers. Her French *chanson* leanings are none too exciting, but her recent acoustic CD *Aman Doctor*, sung in Greek and Turkish, proved a major success. Later in the 1990s, a newer genre of pop came to the fore, with lyrics, driving rhythms and melodic style pitched at youthful, cosmopolitan city-dwellers looking for a hedonistic and extroverted music. **Serdar Ortaç** and **Mustafa Sandal** produce energetic and danceable sounds in this idiom.

Turkish percussionist **Okay Temiz** was one of the first exponents of "ethno-jazz", exploring the potential fusion between jazz and Turkish music with his

Oriental Wind group, and then creating a series of ad hoc ensembles for specific projects dedicated to Black-Sea music, *zurnas, mehter* music, and so forth. After living for many years in northern Europe, he's back in İstanbul and his concerts are always interesting events. Lately a strain of electronic music flavoured with ethnic elements has developed in Turkey, harking back to Sufi music; the most popular musician in this field is **Mercan Dede**, whose CDs feature soloists from different genres of Turkish music, recorded over a rich electronic base. **Orient Expressions** is a group of DJs-turned-producers mixing folk music with electronic tracks; **Sabahat Akkiraz** has performed with both. Guitar player **Erkan Oğur** is currently more celebrated as a folk performer, but his jazz experiments on fretless electric guitar in extended improvisations with the trio Telvin are among the best of their kind. Pianist and arranger **Ayşe Tütüncü** is an idiosyncratic stylist drawing inspiration from folk music as well as from the traditional Turkish fascination with tango.

Selected discography

In Turkey the leading label for folk and classical recordings is Kalan (ⓦwww .kalan.com), who release an unrivalled range of archive recordings of classical instrumentalists, contemporary folk, popular singers and the music of minority groups. Their English website page allows you to order from their backlist as well as new releases at Turkish high-street prices. Doublemoon specialize in contemporary (often forgettable) fusion projects, while Ada's catalogue features a wide range of different music, from fringe rock to ethno-jazz and folk. Outside Turkey, Traditional Crossroads (☎1-800/422-6282 in the USA or ⓦwww.rootsworld .com/crossroads/) has an excellent catalogue of archival and contemporary recordings. Golden Horn Records (ⓦwww.goldenhorn.com) also has carefully selected productions covering many different genres in Turkish music. Pressings from American, German or French labels such as Rounder, Music of the World, Ocora, Network or Auvidis can be obtained, often by special order, from major UK/US retail chains, or more easily through Amazon. Turkish-label pressings are available only in Turkey, or overseas in speciality music shops catering to Turkish emigrant communities. Good shops in İstanbul include Lale Plak, Tünel, Galipdede Cad 1, Beyoğlu (☎0212/293 7739); and the Municipal Bookstore, also on İstiklâl Caddesi, which tends to have the best prices, especially for classic and *fasıl*. In Britain, there's an excellent Turkish-label CD/cassette shop with a good stock, ten-day special-order service and reasonable mark-up: Melodi Müzik, 121 Green Lanes, London N16 (☎020/7359 0038; ask for Salih, who speaks perfect English). All titles below are available on CD, and issued by Turkish labels, unless specified otherwise.

General compilations

Made in Turkey (2 CDs; Soulstar, Germany). Compiled by Turkish DJ and Açık Radyo programmer Gülbahar Kültür, this 2005 production is a very intriguing and eminently enjoyable collection featuring a varied choice of Turkish performers, and a good representation of what the cur-

rent music scene in İstanbul perceives as relevant: classical and folk music, Anatolian rock, pop, rap, dance and electronica.

🏃 **Masters of Turkish Music, Volumes 1–3** (Rounder, US). Still the best single starting-point for Turkish music are these three compilations produced by Münir Nurettin Beken, Dick Spottswood and Karl Signell. Based on carefully restored vintage recordings, they feature most of the important genres and artists like Tamburi Cemil Bey, Münir Nurettin Selçuk, Safiye Ayla and Şükrü Tunar, from the beginning of the recording industry to the 1960s. The focus is on early recorded *sanat*, *gazel*, *şarkı* and instrumental solos, with folk music not so well represented.

Folk and aşik: compilations

Ashiklar: Those Who Are In Love (Golden Horn, US). Aşık Mahsuni Serif, Musa Eroğlu, Aşık Bahattin Kader, Aşık Nuri Kiliç, Aşık Ali. Recorded at the Hacı Bektaş festival and the houses of leading *aşık*s during the production of a 1994 documentary, this is a vibrant compilation with a varied repertoire and plenty of lyrics by Pir Sultan Abdal.
Music and Throat Playing of the Yörük in Anatolia (Kalan). This covers the music of the pastoral *yörük*s in the Toros mountains. Beautiful strings and flutes, songs to the animals and throat-vocals (a custom peculiar in Turkey to the *yörük*) using the fingers to change the note while singing.

🏃 **Salkım Söğüt 1 and 2** (Metropol). Good contemporary acoustic-folk samplers with younger artists such as İlkay Akkaya, Arzu Görücü, Birol Topaloğlu and Alaaddin Us. The first two-named (women) performers make the disc, and invite further exploration of their solo titles. The sequel features a reprise by Görücü, singing in Laz by Kazım Koyuncu, and central Anatolian pieces interpreted by Mustafa Özarslan and Hakan Yeşilyurt.

Saz (Kalan). Traces examples of the various *saz* types from Central Asia to Turkey and beyond to Greece: Uzbek *dutar*, Tadjik *tambur*, Kyrgyz *komuz*, Kazakh *dombra*, Iranian *tanbur*, Azeri *saz* and various Turkish varieties, including Ali Ekber Çiçek playing "Haydar, Haydar" on the big *divan saz*. A comprehensive survey, with photos and a few notes in English by leading musicologist Melih Duygulu.
Turquie Aşık: Chants d'Amour et de Sagesse d'Anatolie (Inedit/Auvidis, France). Probably the best introduction to *aşık* music, overseen and annotated by Kudsi Erguner; well balanced between the artistry of Nuray Hafiftaş, Ali Ekber Çiçek and Turan Engin, all from northeastern Turkey, plus a spectacular *saz* solo by Arif Sağ.
Turquie: Musiques des Yayla (Ocora, France). Haunting melodies and songs from settled *yörük* communities near Acıpayam in the southwestern mountains of Turkey. Various types of *saz* and violin predominate, though there's also a sample of the *sipsi* (pine-twig oboe); excellent sound quality and sleeve notes.

Folk and aşik: individual artists

🏃 **Belkis Akkale** *Türkü Türkü Türkiyem* (Sembol Plak). One of the greatest female *türkü* singers at her earthiest, carried along by driving *saz* rhythms – plus almost all of the traditional instruments of Turkey. A second goodie from this TRT stalwart is *Güvercin* (Raks), which epitomizes

her poised, grave and passionate renditions of the popularized Alevî repertory. Includes the Azeri "Bu Gala Daşlı Gala", with its characteristic 6/8 rhythm.
Ali Ekber Çiçek *Folk Lute from Anatolia* (Anadolu). Double CD with recent studio recordings in an orchestral

setting, including a video documentary; confusingly, it has the same title as a previous (but not identical) Canadian disc.

Neşet Ertaş *Zülüf Dökülmüş Yüze* (Kalan). The enormous output of Neşet Ertaş, son of Muharrem, has been organized into a complete, authorized series currently numbering about fifteen CDs. This first volume contains several popular songs, superb examples of his vocal improvisations in the genres of *uzun hava* and *bozlak*, and some astonishing saz-playing. Kalan has also released two excellent DVDs: *In Concert*, with a live concert in İstanbul, including exciting, early bonus footage of his father Muharrem; and *Garip*, a successful documentary by Turkish director Can Dündar.

Erdal Erzincan *Anadolu* (Güvercin). With Arif Sağ again on percussion, this is an excursion through Anatolian folk, with intoxicating *bağlama* playing in both finger-picking and plectrum techniques.

Latife (Ada). Debut CD of a singer from Radio Ankara, this is a well-balanced, warm mixture of the traditional repertory with carefully crafted modern arrangements. The presence of Erkan Oğur and Musa Eroğlu carries the endorsement of the older generation.

Talip Özkan *L'art vivant de Talip Özkan* (Ocora, France). Eight superb tracks encompassing various regional styles and instruments from the large *divan saz* to the small *cura*; if you like this, then go for *L'art du Tanbur* (Ocora), a wonderfully meditative foray into classical *tanbur*, varied by folk melodies and unexpectedly delicate singing. Özkan is a TRT-trained player now resident in France.

Erol Parlak *Bağlama Beslisi* (Akkiraz). Taking Sağ's approach a step further, elegant and complex chamber music for different-sized *bağlamas*.

Arif Sağ Given his status, recordings by Sağ are surprisingly hard to find. His first CD *Gürbeti Ben Mi Yarattım* (Türküola) is specifically *saz*-based,

featuring some choral backings and arrangements by other *aşıks*, including Pir Sultan Abdal, Aşık Veysel and Aşık Davut Suları. *Concerto for Bağlama and Orchestra* (Güvercin) is a landmark recording, combining original compositions with Western classical orchestrations and jazz backing. *Davullar Çalınırken* (Iber) is a striking 2005 album with Sağ on percussion, stressing rhythms from different regions of Anatolia, including *zeybek*, *çiftetelli* and *horon*.

Fuat Saka *Lazutlar II* (Kalan). A dynamic session of Black-Sea folk-rock, with extensive participation by both Georgian (two songs in that language) and Greek Thessalonian musicians (Thessaloníki in northern Greece is home to a huge Pontic refugee community, whose music has changed little since they left the Pontus – Black-Sea region – in 1923).

Ruhi Su *Zeybekler/Ezgili Yürek* (Nepa-İmece Müzik). This label has reissued most of Ruhi's output on a dozen or so CDs; these, numbers 11/13 in the series, are packaged together rather fortuitously but the 1981 *Zeybekler* – traditional West-Anatolian folk epics delivered in Ruhi Su's unmistakeable, dramatically deep voice – ranks among his most famous recordings.

Bayram Bilge Toker *Bayram: Turkish Folk Songs and Sufi Melodies* (Music of the World, US). A riveting collection of folk songs, dances, improvisations and Sufi ritual music sung and played on *saz* by this native of Yozgat.

Birol Topaloğlu *Heyamo* (Kalan). Very listenable album of vocalists from the Black-Sea Laz population, with Topaloğlu on *kemençe* and *tulum*, and musicians from Grup Yorum. The Bulgarian-sounding title track is a well-known work song. His double CD, *Lazeburi*, contains more field recordings but also makes compelling listening.

Aşık Veysel *Aşık Veysel* (Kalan). The "definitive" Veysel collection, a superb 2-CD set with the best available versions of his most-loved songs on 78 or vinyl, fully annotated

in English. "Kara Toprak" exempli-
fies his lyrics, fully rooted in village
life but carrying a universal message:
"I embraced so many, thinking them

as friends/My true love is the black
earth/in vain I wandered, exhausted
myself for naught/My true love is the
black earth."

Classical and devotional music: compilations

The Bektashi Breathes (Cemre).
Bektaşi musical rituals and dances feature hymns called *nefes*, or "breaths".
An extraordinarily powerful disc
which exudes ritual solemnity; melodies sigh and droop expressively, with
an ensemble of *ney*, *kemençe*, *kanun*, *ud*,
cello and percussion.

🏃 **İstanbul 1925** (Traditional
Crossroads, US). Excellent
anthology of the music played by
Turkish, Armenian and Greek musicians in the city during the first decades of the Republic, varied by the
odd urban *türkü* song and *fasıl* instrumental. Highly recommended, with
award-winning notes.
Masters of Turkish Music: Ney

(Kalan). Part of a series dedicated
to instrumental music, reissuing
rare records or previously unissued
tapes from concerts or radio; English
liner notes. The inclusion of various
great *ney* masters allows the listener
to appreciate the diversity of their
approach. Other extremely enjoyable
yet scholarly rigorous collections feature *kemençe* and *ud*.
Women of Istanbul (Traditional
Crossroads, US). An all-singing
companion to *İstanbul 1925*; as usual
with this label, excellent remastering,
intelligent notes and lovingly rescued
archival photos. All the great female
vocalists of cabaret-nightclub style,
mostly recorded in the mid-1930s.

Classic and devotional music: individual artists/ groups

🏃 **Boğaziçi** *Türk Müziğinde Rum
Bestekârlar* (Columbia). A mixture of Greek and Turkish musicians
playing music of the Byzantine, Ottoman and Mevlevî traditions. Beautiful,
landmark 1987 recording of courtly
classical and sacred music.
Tanburi Cemil Bey (Traditional
Crossroads, US/Kalan). Pieces performed on various stringed instruments (including cello) by this
composer-virtuoso, a late Ottoman
genius, recorded between 1910 and
1914 with fairly primitive acoustic
technology. *Tanburi Cemil Bey, Vol. 2 &
3* (double CD; Traditional Crossroads)
is more of the same – a very spare,
elegant style which valiant remastering
has just about made accessible.

🏃 **Mesut Cemil** *Early Recordings
(Volume 1) and *Instrumental and
Vocal Recordings* (*Volumes 2–3*) (Golden

Horn Records, US). Mesut Cemil
was Tanburi Cemil Bey's son, perhaps
the only musician in Turkey to surpass his father as an instrumentalist.
He ran the classical music section of
TRT-İstanbul for decades, creating
its distinctively ethereal ensemble
style. These recordings contain material from the Cairo music congress
of 1932, at which Mesut Cemil was
one of the Turkish representatives;
an extremely rare recording of him
singing; and TRT archival material
interpreted by choirs and ensembles, as
well as some definitive *taksim* improvisations by the master himself – and
a superb two-*tanbur* recording of
Cemil's famous *Nihavent Saz Semaisi*.
Kudsi Erguner *Dervisches Tourneurs
de Turquie* (Arion, France). Leading
ney master Erguner is closely associated with the music of the Mevlevî

dervishes. This disc, featuring a late *şeyh* of the Halveti order, Muzaffer Özak, on vocals, covers the entire ceremony, including parts other recordings miss out, like the opening Naat-i Mevlâna recitation and the recitation of the Koran. *L'Héritage Ottoman* (Institute du Monde Arabe, France) features some of the best young Turkish classical-music soloists performing both Erguner's original compositions and selected classical instrumental pieces. *Les Passions d'Istanbul* (Imaj) is an original Erguner suite by a larger ensemble, including vocal soloists from different traditions, focused on the multinational, multiethnic character of the city. *Tatyos Efendi: Vocal Masterpieces* (Traditional Crossroads, US) is one of the best discs of overtly secular classical Ottoman music, composed by Armenian violinist to the sultan, Kemani Tatyos Efendi (1863–1913). An Erguner-directed ensemble of *ney*, violin, *kanun*, *klarnet*, *ud*, *tanbur* and *def* accompanies Tatyos' *şarkıs*, interpreted by Melihat Gülses, interspersed amongst instrumental passages.

Süleyman Erguner/İhsan Özgen *Tende Canım* (Sera). From the opening notes of Erguner's *ney*, weaving its *taksim* in tandem with Özgen's *kemençe*, this establishes itself as an extraordinary live recording of compositions from the classical and religious traditions. The polished but soulful voice of Koray Safkan provides vocals. Excellent English notes by Erguner, whose previous CD *Şah Ney* (Mega Muzik) is a unique opportunity to hear the lower-register version of the *ney*.

Bülent Ersoy *Alaturka 1995* (Raks). Interpretation of the popular classics from the 1880s to the 1960s, conceived as a tribute to her mentor, Muzaffer Özpınar. Ersoy's best recording in recent years, this recording contains some *gazels* of scorching intensity. *Seçmeler* (Raks) is a collection of all-time greatest hits from her prolific *arabesk* output, including "Biz Ayrılamayız", "Geceler", and "Sevgi İstiyorum".

The Golden Horn Ensemble *Sultan Bestekarlar: Turkish Classical Music Composed by Ottoman Sultans* (Kalan). The Ottoman nobility were all taught a fine art or craft as a discipline and "finishing". Those who took up music included Sultan Beyazit II (1447–1512), Selim III (1761–1808) and deposed Princess Gevheri Osmanoğlu (died 1980); their work is the basis for this extraordinary double-CD covering the entire history of Turkish classical music, accompanied by an illustrated booklet with informative, scholarly articles. Vocal music and instrumentals are interspersed with solo *taksims* – some disconcertingly over-miked – blending formal precision with passion, brought to life in brisk though rather conservative performances.

Udi Hrant Kenkuliyan *Udi Hrant* (Traditional Crossroads, US/Kalan). The great blind *oudist* sings on many of these wonderful tracks from a 1950s tour of the US. *The Early Recordings, Vols. 1 & 2* (also Traditional Crossroads, US), made in Turkey during the 1920s, are equally good, with heart-rending vocals chronicling unrequited love, many of his famous *taksims* and affecting ensemble work with violin, clarinet and piano. As ever, exemplary remastering, liner notes and lyrics translations.

Mevlâna: Dede Efendi *Saba Âyini* (Kalan). A benchmark recording of a complete Mevlevî suite (*âyin*) in *makam saba*, composed by Dede Efendi. The performers read like a who's who of Turkish *sanat* music of the first half of the past century, with Mesut Cemil on cello, Akagündüz Kutbay, Ulvi Erguner and Niyazi Sayın on *ney*, Cüneyd Orhon on *kemençe* and Saadettin Heper on *küdüm*.

Zeki Müren *Kahir Mektubu* (Türküola). Originally recorded in 1979, this was composed by Zeki's longtime associate Muzaffer Özpınar, and heavily influenced by Egyptian star Umm Kulthum's later, monumental style. Simultaneously vast in scope and intimate in style, it was a landmark in *arabesk* history. Remastered from the old HMV catalogue, *Türk Sanat Müziği Konseri* (Coşkun Plak) is a near-perfect example of Zeki's elegant mastery of the classical genre.

🏃 **İbrahim Özgür** *Tangolar: The Bel Ami of Turkish Tango* (Oriente Musik, Germany). After returning from a seven-year tour of Asia, saxophonist and singer Özgür (died 1959) became a fixture on the İstanbul nightclub circuit during the late 1930s. These superb tracks, from the decade after his return in 1938, are a snapshot of cosmopolitan İstanbul. The lyrics speak of longing and the agonies of separation; the music – familiar melodies with a haunting, Middle-Eastern nuance – is restrained.

Münir Nurettin Selçuk *Bir Özlemdir* (Coşkun Plak). One of a series of reissues of the old HMV backlist, this contains some enduring classics: "Aziz İstanbul", "Kalamış", "Endülüste Raks" ("Andalusian Rhythm", a Turkish take on flamenco) and an electrifying *gazel*, "Aheste Çek Kürekleri".

🏃 **Şükrü Tunar** *Şükrü Tunar* (Kalan). Great Gypsy clarinettist from the İzmir region, who served as one of Zeki Müren's first accompanists, and whose repertoire encompassed everything from *zeybek*, *sirtos* and *uzun hava* to *taksims* and *fasıl* songs. In the US, get an identically titled CD compiled by the late Dino Pappas (American Recording Productions).

Vosporos *Zontani Ihografisi sto Irodheio* (MBI, Greece). Vosporos is the Greek name of the identical group Boğaziçi, co-ordinated between 1987 and 1993 by Nikiforos Metaxas in İstanbul; this documents a 1990 concert in Athens. It features Greek composers of Ottoman music and songs of the Alevî *aşıks*, with Kani Karaca, Melda Kurt and Sibel Sezal on vocals.

Hamiyet Yüceses *Makber* (İstanbul). This outstanding collection includes her magnificent recordings of "Bakmıyor Çeşm-i Siyah Feryade", a classic piece by Hacı Arif Bey to which in 1946 she added a long improvised *gazel* section, and "Her Yer Karanlık", an intense 1956 interpretation of the famous Hafız Burhan composition.

Fasıl/Gypsy music

Barbaros Erköse Ensemble *Lingo Lingo* (Golden Horn Records, US). The Erköse brothers – Barbaros, Ali and Selahattin – at one time "were" Gypsy music in Turkey. Since he retired from the TRT, clarinet-player Barbaros has been pursuing a solo career, involving collaborations with Peter Pannke, Anouar Brahem and Craig Harris, among others. *Lingo Lingo* is urban folklore at its best, and a superb demonstration of the art of *meyan* (improvisation over a rhythmic background). Useful liner notes by Sonia Seeman, an authority on Turkish *Rom* music.

Istanbul Oriental Ensemble *Gypsy Rum* (Network, Germany). Led by percussionist Burhan Öçal, this ensemble (traditional line-up of clarinet, violin, *ud*, *kanun* and *darbuka*) delivers fourteen tracks of tight instrumental playing. Emotional twists and lightning virtuosity will have your shoulders shaking; listen for the screaming shrieks from Fethi Tekyaygil's violin. If you like this, try also their follow-up album, *The Sultan's Secret Door* (Network).

Mustafa Kandıralı *Caz Roman* (Network, Germany). Kandıralı's performances have a quiet iconoclasm in their melodic invention. This disc is the epitome of instrumental *fasıl*, including such masters as Ahmet Meter (*kanun*), Metin Bükey (*ud*) and Ahmet Kulık (*darbuka*). The final section of dance tunes is a concert recording from 1984.

🏃 **Karşılama** *Karşılama* (Green Goat, Canada/Kalan). İstanbul Gypsy musicians led by Selim Sesler on G-clarinet, with locally trained Canadian vocalist Brenna MacCrimmon, interpret *Rom* music from western Turkey and the Balkans. Played with real panache, and good to have some of the vocal repertoire – gleaned from archival recordings and manuscripts – expertly showcased.

Kemani Cemal Çınarlı *Sulukule: Rom Music of Istanbul* (Traditional Crossroads, US). Instrumental numbers and chorus-vocals evoking the earthy character of urban Gypsy music. Centre stage are the soaring violin solos of Kemani Cemal (born 1928), a native of Thrace and long a fixture on the İstanbul club scene. On-site recording and uneven miking, however, means occasional strange reverb and absolutely thunderous *darbuka*.

🏃 **The Road to Keşan: Turkish Rom and Regional Music of Thrace** (Traditional Crossroads, US/Kalan). Gypsy music breaks out of its nightclub ghetto and gets a full, thunderously percussive hearing in its native village setting in this superb production overseen and authoritatively annotated by Sonia Seeman. The clarinettist is again Selim Sesler, but all the musicians – including Bülent Sesler on *kanun* and Nüsret Şüte on violin – are excellent. This being Thrace, it's irresistibly danceable, with plenty of influences (and the occasional melody) from Greece, in particular its Pomak communities.

Hüsnü Şenlendirici and Laço Tayfa *Çiftetelli* (Traditional Crossroads, US), also released as *Bergama Gaydası* (Doublemoon). Mildly electrified Gypsy jazz funk, the Turkish equivalent of Cuba's Irakere; the musicianship of Şenlendirici – from a clan of hereditary musicians in Bergama – and the Laço Tayfa band ultimately carries the day. When the percussion, keyboard and bass guitar aren't purring along as an undercurrent, there are some wonderful long clarinet solos by Hüsnü on "Harmandalı" and "İzmir'in Kavakları". Regrettably, the band never repeated this success and had effectively disintegrated by 2005, when leader Hüsnü released an utterly forgettable solo CD.

Arabesk

Orhan Gencebay *Yalnız Değilsin* (Kervan). This recording demonstrates Gencebay's unflagging musical curiosity, taking in Middle Eastern, European and American popular and classical genres in one magisterial sweep. His own virtuoso *saz* playing, as ever, dominates, from the thunderous belly-dance number ("Gencebay Oriyentali") to a mock-Baroque overture ("Nihavent Üvertür").

Müslüm Gürses *Senden Vazgeçmem* (Elenor Plak). A lush orchestra combining violins, a *bağlama* section, and full "classical" instrumentation backs Müslüm "Baba" singing popular songs of his repertoire, their despairing lyrics delivered with the characteristically intense vocal style full of melisma. Discernible European classical and even country-and-western influences, while the tunes include an Azeri folk song and a special rendition of "Haydar, Haydar" with composer Ali Ekber Çiçek himself on *bağlama*. ("Haydar" is an epithet of Ali, meaning the "Lion of Allah".)

🏃 **İbrahim Tatlıses** *Fosforlu Cevriyem* (Emre). This live recording is a rare chance to hear what *arabesk* sounds like in the flesh, and gives a sense of Tatlıses' phenomenal vocal presence. Includes some of his all-time favourites ("Beyaz Gül, Kırmızı Gül", "Fosforlu Cevriyem", "Beyoğlu", "Yeşil Yeşil"), plus superb *uzun hava* semi-improvisations.

Rock, pop, özgün and fusion

Sezen Aksu *Işık Doğudan Yükselir/The Light Rises in the East* (Foneks). An intriguing CD, from the overblown orchestral opening to the intimate sparseness of later tracks which characterizes much of her recent work. Some songs are self-consciously authentic in spirit ("Ben Annemi Isterim", and "Rakkas", based on Black Sea and urban dance styles respectively), others in a more abstract, allusive style ("Halımımı Yaktılar", based on traditional women's laments). Aksu's arguably best disc is 🎵 *Deli Veren* (Balet): from the quiet intensity of "Hoş Geldin" to "Gidiyorum bu Şehirden", it shows her ability to forge productive partnerships with musicians from elsewhere in the Aegean region, here with Haris Alexiou. "Kahpe Kader" and "Yalancı Dunya" suggest an intriguing rapprochement with *arabesk*, and indeed subsequently in the album *Şarkı Söylemek Lazim* she provided the definitive rendition of Müslüm Gürses's own "Tanrı İstemezse"; the nostalgic "İstanbul Olalı" became an instant classic, and "Dansöz Dünya" features fiery percussion work. Her voice continues developing in subtlety, range and lyric control, the songwriting by turns playful and experimental but increasingly her own, her stage presence radiating the unmistakeable magnetism of the greatest songsters.

Cartel *Cartel* (Mercury, Germany). The first (1995) recording by the Turkish-German rap and hip-hop collective. A witty and humorous commentary about life on the Turkish-German street, with high-voltage sampling of Turkish folk music sounds. The paradigm for almost everything that followed, both in Germany and in Turkey.

Kudsi Erguner *Islam Blues* (Act, Germany). The vocals of Yunus Balcıoğlu, Derya Türkan's *kemençe* and Hakan Güngör's *kanun* blend effectively with a jazz group, creating a unique spiritual intensity in this affecting jazz/Middle Eastern crossover, occasionally reminiscent of Coltrane, but often sui generis.

Cem Karaca *Cemaz ül-Evvel* (Kalan). A retrospective of Karaca's major work with his early groups, particularly Apaşlar and Kardaşlar; traces his experiments with a variety of Western pop and rock genres, plus his emerging political radicalism. Essentially the whole story of Turkish highbrow rock, on one recording.

🎵 **Ahmet Kaya** *An Gelir* (Taç). Plangent *saz*, and up-tempo *halay* dance numbers, deep, melancholy vocals; radical in gesture, but social-realist pessimistic in content. The title song is based on a poem by Attila İlhan. Nothing that Kaya, the "Kurdish Jacques Brel", subsequently did lived up to the enormous vitality and lyricism of his fourth album, arranged by Osman İşmen.

Zülfü Livaneli *Maria Farandouri Söylüyor* (Raks). This was a landmark collaboration from the early 1980s between historical enemies: Greek star Maria Farandouri singing Livaneli compositions in both Greek and Turkish. Beautiful, often dark, melodies, exquisitely rendered in fine arrangements.

Erkan Oğur *Gülün Kokusu Vardı* (Kalan). A delicate, ascetic disc of traditional songs from all over Turkey. Exquisite instrumentals and innovative voice stylings in tandem with İsmail Hakkı Demircioğlu. *Hiç* (Kalan) offers instrumental-only versions of classic folk songs, focusing on the musical values rather than words, especially attractive for non-Turkish-speakers. *Telvin* (Kalan) has Oğur's jazz trio on fretless guitar, bass and drums in wide-ranging improvisations.

Burhan Öçal *Groove alla Turca* (Doublemoon). Öçal joins forces with ex-Ornette Coleman electric bassist Jamaladeen Tacuma and trumpet supremo Jack Walrath, for an excitingly jazzy mix. Natasha Atlas guests on some tracks.

Sivan Perwer *Chants du Kurdistan* (Auvidis/Ethnic, France) is a good introduction to this Kurdish bard's earlier, mostly traditional songs, self-accompanied on *saz*. *Kirive, Vol. 1 & 2* (SES Plak) are among nearly twenty "Best Of..." Perwer CDs on this label (Şivan himself is now based in Sweden) with *duduk*, *bloor*, *ud* and *kanun* in addition to *saz*.

Tarkan *Karma* (İstanbul Plak). Tarkan assembles an exotic team of musicians (including Hossam Ramzy's ensemble, Ruben Harutunian on Armenian *duduk*, Jean-Louis Solon on *didj*, *sitar* and *sarod*) who promptly disappear into a dance-oriented mix, dominated by Tarkan's voice, which nicely combines rock heroics and Middle-Eastern sophistry.

Okay Temiz *Zikir* (Ada). Internationally renowned percussionist Temiz deploys not only Turkish drums and gongs but his own electrified version of the Brazilian *berimbau*. Successful jazz/Turkish fusion by an international group which includes Akagündüz Kutbay on *ney*, D.D. Gouirand on soprano sax, Onno Tunç on bass, and Tuna Ötenel on piano.

Yeni Türkü *Her Dem Yeni/New Every Time* (BMG, Turkey). A "greatest hits" album with twenty of their songs, drawing on their various excellent BMG releases. Excellent listening even if you don't speak a word of Turkish.

Original version by Martin Stokes and Marc Dubin
Updated and revised by Francesco Martinelli

Cinema

The films of Yılmaz Güney aside, Turkish cinema has until recently been little known outside Turkey, a result perhaps of its historic preoccupations with what foreign critics have perceived as strictly local issues such as rural-to-urban population drift and the dislocation of traditional lifestyles. Yet wider recognition is now growing, following recent international success from directors such as Nuri Bilgi Ceylan and Fatih Akın.

Although cinema as an art form has only emerged in Turkey over the last four decades, the local film industry has been churning out low-budget melodramas for the better part of 75 years, and indeed continues to do so. All forms of film making have been handicapped by a relative lack of finance and technical resources, and until recently directors and writers wishing to address social or political issues also had to contend with state censorship in varying degrees over the years, which gave rise to a tendency to portray everyday life lyrically or through allegory. In recent years, however, a number of previously taboo subjects, such as Kurdish rights, homosexuality and state corruption have got past the censors, signalling a greater openness.

The growth of the industry

The history of public cinema in Turkey began in 1897 when **Sigmund Weinberg**, a Romanian-Jewish café-owner in the Pera district of İstanbul, staged the city's first film show. It was not until World War I, however, that the government, realizing the propaganda value of film, set up several **army film units**. These units put together a number of documentaries, although the first film ever produced under Turkish government auspices (recording the demolition of a Russian monument in İstanbul) was shot under the direction of an Austrian military crew. A Turkish projectionist, **Fuat Uzkınay**, took the largely symbolic role of holding the camera, under close Austrian supervision.

By the end of the world war, Turkish military film-makers had mastered their trade sufficiently to go on and make documentaries on the War of Independence. With the end of hostilities a number of **production companies** were set up, including one owned jointly by Sigmund Weinberg and Fuat Uzkınay, and Turkey's feature-film industry came into existence.

During the 1920s a trend for ham-fisted adaptations of works by seventeenth-century French playwrights like Molière was established, a field that was dominated by two companies, İpek Film and Kemal Film. The leading director of the period was **Muhsin Ertuğrul**, who made 29 films between 1922 and 1953. His "backlist" includes a couple of features based on the War of Independence: *Ateş'ten Gömlek* (Shirt of Fire; 1923) and *Bir Millet Uyanıyor* (The Awakening of a Nation; 1932). These films did refer to actual events, but they never sought to challenge the official line of Kemalist Turkey, nor did they break any new ground artistically.

Any attempts to do either would probably have foundered against the government's rigorous **censorship laws**, codified in 1932. All films faced a three-tiered process; first, scripts were censored before filming began, then the police controlled sequences as they were shot, and finally government censors inspected the finished work, excising contentious material. Governmental stifling of creativity was exacerbated by chronic lack of cash and equipment, with the result that by World

War II the staple fare of Turkish picture-houses was Hollywood productions and risible B-movies churned out in Egypt by a Turkish producer, **V.O. Bengü**.

In quantitative terms the output of the Turkish film industry picked up significantly in the 1950s with the establishment of a genre of mass-entertainment **melodrama** that continues to this day, lapped up by rural and small-town audiences. These films had a very basic premise that was to prove successful time and again: rural boy meets rural girl, the world tries to keep them apart (in more sophisticated variants, one is temporarily blind to the virtues of the other) but, ultimately, they triumph over tragedy and live happily ever after, having achieved fame and fortune along the way.

One positive effect of this increased cinematic activity was that it enabled a **new generation** of young film-makers to master the skills of cinematography, among them Yılmaz Güney and others who, in the 1960s and 1970s, would go on to develop a home-grown Turkish cinematic identity.

The new wave and Yılmaz Güney

During the 1960s, the first attempts were made to produce films that moved away from melodrama into the realm of social criticism. A leading director of the period was **Lüfti Ö. Akad** who, having cut his teeth on melodramas and a few derivative gangster pictures during the 1940s and 1950s, went on to direct *Tanrı'nın Bağışı Orman* (The Forest, God's Gift) in 1964, a documentary study of the feudal hierarchy in Anatolia. In 1966 he made *Hudutların Kanunu* (The Law of the Frontier), a dramatic treatment of similar issues, dealing with the stranglehold of wealthy landlords on the rural population in the southeast. He later directed *Kızılırmak-Karakoyun* (Red River, Black Sheep), based on a play by poet Nazım Hikmet. Between 1973 and 1975 Akad produced an important trilogy, exploring the drift of population from rural Anatolia to the cities, and the conflict between traditional lifestyles and modern, Westernized city life: *Gelin* (The Bride), *Düğün* (The Wedding) and *Diyet* (Retribution).

During the 1970s **Yılmaz Güney** took over as Turkey's leading serious director and became, in the process, the first Turkish director to gain real recognition outside his native land. After serving his apprenticeship on the melodramas of the 1950s, Güney had scripted *Hudutların Kanunu* for Akad and took the lead acting role in *Kızılırmak-Karakoyun*. The first major film he directed, in 1970, was *Umut* (Hope), the story of a taxi driver who loses his house and stakes his remaining money on a mad treasure-hunting venture. Though not an outstanding film, it is indicative of the thematic direction that Güney's later works were to take, and certain scenes, notably the final one where the maddened hero circles a hole in the ground blindfolded, are echoed in later films.

Umut was followed in 1971 by *Ağıt* (Lament), in which a man is forced to resort to smuggling by economic circumstance, and *Acık* (Sorrow), a film about lost love and revenge. Güney was imprisoned after the 1971 coup, remaining in jail until 1974. Upon his release he made the film *Arkadaş* (The Friend), which, like the earlier *Umutsuzlar* (Those Without Hope) and *Baba* (The Father), dealt with the lot of Turkey's urban poor, an area in which Güney was less confident as a director. In the same year Güney was imprisoned again, accused of murdering a judge. He began directing films from his cell, writing scripts and passing on instructions to fellow directors; paradoxically, some of his finest work was produced in this period.

In 1979 *Sürü* (The Herd), written by Güney with **Zeki Ökten** directing, was released; like Güney's earlier films its theme is rural dislocation. Life among feuding nomadic families in the south is the starting point; with their traditional grazing lands threatened by development, a Kurdish family decide to take their sheep to the markets of Ankara. Visually the film is dominated by the road and rail journey of the shepherds and their flocks, and this is used to highlight the dichotomy between their lifestyle and city ways. The political turmoil that surrounds them, but which they are barely aware of, is suggested by characteristic Güney touches: almost impressionistic sequences of manacled prisoners and a youth being shot for distributing pamphlets.

Güney also worked on his most famous film, **Yol** (The Road), from the confines of his prison cell, with the outside directorial assistance of **Şerif Gören**. It's an extraordinary film, taking an allegorical look at the state of the nation by following the fortunes of five prisoners who have been allowed a week's parole. Even when temporarily released they are unable to make their own way through a society that seems unreal to them, and their behaviour is determined by social conditions over which they have no control. One prisoner, Ömer, returns to his Kurdish village and is faced with a choice between returning to prison or taking to the hills. He eventually opts for the latter but there is a strong sense that the decision is forced on him. The film focuses, though, on Seyit Ali, who returns to his village to find that his wife, who has become a prostitute, is being held by his brothers, who expect him to kill her. He refuses to do so outright, but abandons her in the snow – after a change of heart he returns to save her, only to find that she's dead. Güney, having escaped from jail, was able to edit this film in exile in France, and the final result, released in 1982, is permeated by a strong sense of longing for his homeland. *Yol* shared the Cannes Film Festival's Palme d'Or for that year with Costa-Gavras's *Missing*, greatly elevating Turkish cinema's international standing. Banned in Turkey itself, it was not until 1999 that *Yol* finally made it onto the country's cinema screens, where it played to packed houses.

△ A still from Yılmaz Güney's film *Yol*

Güney's last film was *Duvar* (The Wall), made during his French exile and released in 1983. Unrelentingly brutal, it's a composite portrait of Turkish prison life, focusing on the experiences of a group of young detainees, hardly older than children. The prison of the film becomes a microcosm of Turkish society as seen through the eyes of its inmates. The prison hierarchy, with the director of prisons at the top, is shown as unmerciful and inflexible; complaints are responded to with violence and the prisoners have no chance of redress for the wrongs done to them. This is graphically demonstrated by the fate of Şabah, one of the young inmates; he is sexually assaulted by one of the guards and, encouraged by his fellow inmates, decides to report the incident to the prison doctor. At the last moment his nerve fails him. His friends ostracize him, and in despair he attempts to escape, and is killed. Güney died of cancer, aged 46, the year after *Duvar*'s release.

An important contemporary of Güney was **Ömer Kavur**, whose first film, *Emine*, was released in 1974. Set in a small provincial town at the turn of the century, the film looked at the role of women in traditional society. In 1979 Ömer directed *Yusuf İle Kenan* (Yusuf and Kenan), the story of two young boys forced to leave their village after their father is killed in a blood feud. An increasingly important element of modern Turkish life, the experience of the migrant worker, was explored in *Otobüs* (The Bus) by **Tunç Okan**. This 1977 film examines the dislocating effect of having to leave the homeland in search of work through the eyes of a group of Turks who, having come to Sweden in search of work, find themselves abandoned in Stockholm, ripped off by a fellow countryman.

The 1980s

Turkish film output actually peaked numerically in 1972 with 299 films, but as the decade progressed there was a steady decline amidst the political turmoil and violence preceding the 1980 coup. In that year, however, **Ali Özgentürk** released *Hazal*, a dramatic depiction of life in a spectacularly isolated, semi-feudal village, where a young woman attempts to escape from an arranged marriage to a 10-year-old boy in order to be with her lover, but suffers swift, harsh retribution. In the wake of the 1980 coup, however, the work of many directors was banned, and the Turkish film industry was effectively driven into exile.

The early to mid-1980s saw something of a revival. In 1982 Ali Özgentürk made *At* (The Horse), a co-production with West German colleagues, which has been aptly described as a bleaker reworking of *Bicycle Thieves*. The film tells the story of a peasant and his son who arrive in İstanbul in search of a better life. The father hopes to be able to earn enough as a street trader to put his son through school, but is inevitably overwhelmed by the big city.

In 1983 *Hakkâri'de Bir Mevsim* (A Season in Hakkâri), directed by **Erdan Kıral** in another German-funded co-production, was released. Arguably the best Turkish film of the 1980s, and certainly the one that won most international acclaim, this visually stunning film examines the experiences of a young teacher sent to a distant Kurdish village to staff the local school. He is shocked by the poverty and isolated from the locals by vast linguistic and cultural gaps. Gradually, however, through his relationship with two local orphans, the girl Zazi and her brother Halit (a smuggler, also excluded from village life), he comes to identify with his surroundings, a process helped when the locals call on his aid during an epidemic. When he receives notice from the authorities that he can leave the village he is reluctant to go, having found a stability previously absent from his rootless existence.

Although many Turkish films of the decade were notably subdued, focusing on themes of individual struggle to skirt direct political comment, a few made after the middle of the decade addressed issues such as social hypocrisy, or the position of women in Turkish society. *Bir Yudum Sevgi* (A Sip of Love), directed by **Atif Yılmaz** in 1984, looks at one woman's struggle to win her personal independence. Related themes emerge in *Asiye*, an unusual musical adapted from a stage play, lambasting the notion of the woman as male property through the tale of a peasant woman who becomes a prostitute and later brothel madam.

The director **Başar Sabuncu** chalked up a number of noteworthy films during the later 1980s. *Çıplak Vatandaş* (The Naked Citizen) is a fairly light-hearted 1986 satire, following the fortunes of a man who, while temporarily deranged by economic misfortune and confrontation with bureaucracy, runs almost naked through his home town, only to be subsequently exploited by an advertising firm who use him in a TV ad for bath salts. *Kupa Kızı* (Queen of Hearts), released the following year, is an acidic reworking of *Belle de Jour*, telling of a woman who turns part-time prostitute and uses sex as a means of revenge. In *Asılacak Kadın* (A Woman to be Hanged), a young woman becomes a judicial scapegoat for the murder of an old man who has sexually abused her. The film fell foul of the censors and its release resulted in the banning of the novel that inspired it, for "offending national morality". Sabuncu's next film, in 1988, was *Zengin Mutfağı* (Kitchen of the Rich), an adaption of a stage play set among the servants in the kitchen of a wealthy family, intended as an allegory of the situation immediately before the 1971 military coup.

Other Eighties films worthy of mention include **Nesli Çölgecen**'s 1986 effort *Ağa* (The Landlord) and Ömer Kavur's 1986 return to the director's chair, *Anayurt Oteli* (The Motherland Hotel). The former examines the struggles of a wealthy landlord in the southeast, unable to come to terms with changes in rural life. Here a severe drought is substituted for the socioeconomic forces that might have caused these changes had the film been made a decade earlier. Kavur's film is set in a small town near İzmir where an obsessive and lonely hotel-owner's life falls apart when an attractive female guest breaks a promise to make a return visit. The film breaks new ground for Turkish cinema, exploring psychological and emotive issues with a previously unknown depth. Another important late Eighties film was *Kırk Metre Kare Almanya'da* (Forty Square Metres in Germany), directed by **Tevfik Başer** in 1987, looking at the experience of Turkish migrant workers through the eyes of a village woman brought to Hamburg and confined in a dismal flat while her husband goes off to work.

Films made towards the end of the decade indicated that Turkish directors once again felt secure enough to question openly the way their society functions, and to refer directly to political conditions within Turkey. **Tunç Başaran**'s *Uçurtmayı Vurmasınlar* (Don't Let Them Shoot the Kite; 1989), about the relationship that develops in jail between a sensitive inmate and the 5-year-old son of a woman doing time for drug dealing, touches on an area of Turkish life that, earlier in the decade, would have been out of bounds to film-makers. *Blackout Nights* (1990), by **Yusuf Kürçenli**, went even further. Based on an autobiographical novel by the poet Rifat İlgaz, arrested as a suspected communist at the end of World War II, it questioned the need for censorship and attacked political oppression.

The 1990s

While the rest of the world was celebrating the hundredth anniversary of film in 1995, Turkey's industry remained in crisis. Multinational production companies dominated cinema screens so that independent Turkish operators, whose films were still plagued with technical difficulties, most noticeably their poor sound quality, found it hard to find outlets for their productions. A general lack of interest on the part of the Ministry of Culture, who withdrew funding for the subtitling of Turkish films to be shown abroad, compounded the problems.

Despite the difficulties, there were a few notable productions in an otherwise uneventful decade. In 1990, Ömer Kavur managed to release his acclaimed movie *Gizli Yüz* (The Secret Face), based on a story by writer Orhan Pamuk about a nightclub photographer and his pursuit of a beautiful woman who disappears with a watchmaker. In 1994, **Erden Kıral**'s *Mavi Sürgün* (The Blue Exile) gained worldwide attention and was nominated (unsuccessfully) for an Academy Award for Best Foreign Film. Beautifully photographed and acted, it tells of aristocrat Cevat Şakir's 1925 exile to Turkey's then-remote southwestern coast. By the end of his journey, he has come to terms with his past and started a new life based on self-understanding and his role in his adopted home.

One encouraging trend has been the emergence of **women directors**, most notably **Tomris Giritlioğlu**, whose films have received both national and international recognition. Her first, *Yaz Yağmuru* (A Passing Summer Rain), released in 1994, concerns a writer who is overwhelmed by images inspired by a young woman he sees in his garden one day; *80 Adım* (The Eightieth Step), winner of the best movie award at the İstanbul Film Festival in 1996, is about a committed left-wing political activist released from jail in 1980 as the country reels from the September 12 military coup, and deals with his personal conflicts in a changing society. Another female director, **Biket İlhan**, explores İstanbul's underworld in a thriller made in 1995, *Sokaktaki Adam* (The Man in the Street), about a ship's steward who becomes involved in smuggling and then falls for a famous prostitute.

One of the most highly acclaimed works of the decade was *İstanbul Kanatlarımın Altında* (İstanbul Beneath My Wings), made in 1995 by **Mustafa Altıoklar**. Set in seventeenth-century İstanbul during the reign of tyrant Murat IV, four close friends are tussling with the theories of flight while Murat and his janissary guards rampage around the city closing down its more riotous drinking establishments by lynching everyone they discover on the premises. Murat eventually catches up with the four heroes, whose number includes the travel chronicler Evliya Çelebi, and is advised of their appropriate fate by reactionary forces in his divan council. The film, based on a true story, disguises its contemporary political overtones with tongue-in-cheek dialogue and farcical comedy, but its plea for enlightenment in the face of fundamentalist zeal is a timely message in modern Turkey. A joint Turkish–Italian venture, the film's success led to a number of other co-productions, including the acclaimed *Hamam*, made in 1998 by Celhan Özpetek, in which its Italian star inherits a run-down Turkish bath in İstanbul. Through his efforts to restore it, he discovers his own sexuality, making this one of the few Turkish films dealing with gay relationships to have gone on general release.

After the success of *İstanbul Kanatlarımın Altında*, Turkey's filmgoers decided to give the domestic industry another chance in 1996. Financial constraints forced a group of the country's best-known directors to collaborate on two releases made up of five short made-for-TV films, *Aşık Üzerine Söylenmiş Her Şey* (Everything Untold about Love) and *Yerçekimli Aşıklar* (Loves with Gravity). These anthologies are snapshots of contemporary Turkish society, covering domestic themes with little overtly political content.

A minor boom in film production then followed, fuelled by the massive domestic success of *Eskiya* (The Bandit), made in 1996 and directed by **Yavuz Tuğrul**. Telling the tale of a former outlaw released from prison to embark on a search for his lost past, the script touched on a number of social issues while never losing its story-telling drive. As the "bandit" wanders through a modern İstanbul of petty criminals and mafia dons, his outdated rural codes seem more and more at odds with the world he encounters.

Into the new millennium

The late 1990s and the early years of the new century saw a gradual unwinding of the country's tight censorship laws, with both ethnic Turkish and ethnic Kurdish directors at the forefront of pushing out the boundaries of the permissible. *İşıklar Sönmesin* (The Lights Must Not Go Out), directed by **Reis Çelik** in 1996, was the first action film to deal directly with the war between ethnic Kurdish separatists and the army in the southeast, a subject returned to with increasing skill during subsequent years. **Kâzım Öz**'s 2001 *Fotograf* (Photograph), shot on a minuscule budget, achieved a breakthrough with its use of the Kurdish language. Also in 2001, **Handan İpekçi**'s *Büyük Adam, Küçük Aşk* (*Hejar* in Kurdish, or Great Man, Small Passion) pitted itself against the censors by throwing together the only-Kurdish-speaking child of two activists killed in a police raid and an only-Turkish-speaking former judge. Their relationship, replete with total misunderstandings and a thankfully unsentimental ending, unsettled the authorities enough for it to be temporarily banned from screening at the 2002 İstanbul Film Festival.

Portrayals of other sensitive political and social problems have also become more widespread in the last decade. **Mustafa Altıoklar**'s 1997 *Ağır Roman* (Heavy Novel), the first widely released Turkish film to display police torture, was followed by Tomris Giritlioğlu's *Salkım Hanım'ın Taneleri* (Lady Salkım's Jewels), winner of the 1999 Antalya "Golden Orange" Film Festival, which explores the punitive "wealth tax" imposed on the country's non-Muslim minorities during the 1940s. It follows the rise to fame and fortune of an unscrupulous Muslim who exploits the ruination of his Armenian ex-bosses. Also broaching a taboo subject is director **Tayfun Pirselimoğlu**'s *Hiçbiryerde* (In Nowhere Land, 2002), which takes a look at Turkey's "disappeared" – the thousands of people who vanished in mysterious circumstances during the political conflicts of the 1970s, 1980s and 1990s. Cinematically flawed, it is largely saved by the performance of one of Turkey's most talented actresses, Zuhal Ölçay.

At the same time, Turkish cinema also turned to less directly political if no less powerful films, with **Nuri Bilgi Ceylan** producing a trilogy of lyrical and photographically stunning movies. Following the same group of characters from an Anatolian backwater, this trio began with *Kasaba* (Small Town, 1998), followed by *Mayıs Sıkıntısı* (Clouds in May, 1999), and culminating in the 2003 Cannes Grand Jury Prize winner, *Uzak* (Distant, 2002). At this point, city and countryside fully collide, with job-seeking villager Yusuf (Mehmet Emin Toprak) arriving in a wintry Istanbul. Ceylan uses amateur actors like Toprak – who died soon after filming *Uzak* – and even his own grandfather in his movies, with excellent results.

Also pursuing a more personal and sociological approach is **Fatih Akın**, whose German birthplace and upbringing had both Turkey and Germany claiming his

2004 Golden Bear winner, *Duvar Karşısı* (Head On) as their own. This high-octane tale of two star-crossed Turkish–German lovers caused scandal in Turkey, as well as praise, with a clash of cultures underscoring some electrifying performances. Demonstrating that such cultural interaction can also produce great music, Akın's 2005 documentary *Crossing the Bridge: The Sound of Istanbul* has won many recent plaudits – whilst also being a great starting-point for anyone heading for Turkey's greatest city.

Updated by John Gorvett

Books

Thère are numerous books about every aspect of Turkey in English, many published or reissued since the mid-1990s. Three publishers specifically or partly dedicated to Turkology, and worth contacting directly for information on their latest offerings, are: I.B. Tauris (⊛www.ibtauris.co.uk), Saqi Books (⊛www.saqibooks.com) and The Eothen Press (⊛www.btinternet.com/~theeothenpress). Books with Turkish publishers are rarely available outside Turkey.

One particularly reliable retail source for Turk-related literature in the UK, whether in person or by mail order, is Daunt Books, 83 Marylebone High St, London W1M 4DE (☎020/7224 2295, ⊛www.dauntbooks.co.uk). Note that "o/p" means out of print.

Retail websites such as ⊛www.abe.com/.co.uk or ⊛www.bookfinder.com are excellent venues for hard-to-find or out-of-print items; almost every book in this bibliography can be found secondhand or on a print-on-demand/special-order basis through these sources.

History

The classics

Herodotus *The Histories*. A fifth-century BC native of what is now Bodrum, Herodotus is revered as the father of both systematic history and anthropology, providing descriptions of the Persian Wars and the assorted tribes and nations who inhabited Anatolia in his time.

Strabo *Geography*. A native of the Pontus, Strabo travelled widely across the Mediterranean; our best document of Roman Anatolia.

Xenophon *Anabasis, or The March Up-Country* (order through ⊛www.Indypublishing.com). The Athenian leader of the Ten Thousand, mercenaries for the Persian king Cyrus the Younger, led the long retreat from the Cunaxa battlefield in Mesopotamia to the Black Sea. An ancient travel classic still mined for titbits of ethnology, archeology and geography.

Ancient history and archeology

Ekrem Akurgal *Ancient Civilisations and Ruins of Turkey* (Türk Tarih Kurumu Basımevi, Ankara/US edition o/p). Excellent detailed survey of Anatolian sites from prehistoric times to the end of the Roman Empire. Includes site plans and interesting graphic reconstructions of monuments, as well as a few dated photos.

O.R. Gurney *The Hittites*. Non-specialist's history of the first great Anatolian civilization.

Ian Hodder *On the Surface: Çatalhöyük 1993–1995*. Neolithic Çatal Höyük is the earliest known proper city in the world, rumoured to contain the secrets of the origins of Western civilization. This volume relates the first two years of a 25-year project to excavate what's arguably the world's most important archeological site.

Seton Lloyd *Ancient Turkey – A Traveller's History of Anatolia*. Written by a former head of the British Archeological Institute in Ankara, this is indispensable on the ancient civilizations. Without sacrificing detail and convincing research, it's written in an accessible, compelling style, avoiding the dull, encyclopedic approach of most writing on the subject.

🏃 **J.G. MacQueen** *The Hittites and Their Contemporaries in Asia Minor*. Well-illustrated general history; more accessible than Gurney's tome.

Otto F.A. Meinardus *St John of Patmos and the Seven Churches of the Apocalypse* (Lycabettus Press, Athens/ Caratzas, New York). The Seven Churches were all in western Anato-

lia, and this volume, though mostly ecclesiastical history, is also a practical handbook to the sites. The same author's *St Paul in Ephesus and the Cities of Galatia and Cyprus* (Lycabettus Press, Athens; o/p) contains copious material on Christianity in Ephesus.

David Traill *Schliemann of Troy: Treasure and Deceit*. The man versus the myth of his self-publicity: not strictly ancient history, but if you're intending to visit the ruins of ancient Troy, this volume, portraying the crumbling edifice of Schliemann's reputation as an archeologist, will certainly help to bring the old walls to life.

Byzantine and early medieval history

Anna Comnena *The Alexiad*. The daughter of Emperor Alexius Komnenos I, perhaps the first female historian, wrote a history of the First Crusade from the Byzantine point of view. Accounts of military campaigns predominate, and it's all a bit dry, but holds its own for historical interest.

🏃 **Cyril Mango** *Byzantium: The Empire of the New Rome*. A single volume that makes a good, accessible introduction to Byzantium, taking in daily life, economic policy and taxation, scholarship and universities, cosmology and superstition, among other topics. The newer *Oxford History of Byzantium*, also edited by Mango, will also be of interest.

🏃 **John Julius Norwich** *Byzantium: The Early Centuries*, *The Apogee* and *The Decline*. An astonishingly detailed trilogy, well informed and above all the most readable account of a fascinating period of world history up to 1453 (a single-volume abridged version is also available). His edition of *Liuprand of Cremona* proves a colourful account of an early Lombard embassy to the already declining Byzantine Empire. Liuprand didn't care much for the Byzantines and goes to great lengths to explain why. After reading this account, the

Fourth Crusade – diverted by Venice to sack Constantinople instead of Jerusalem – begins to be more understandable.

Procopius *The Secret History*. Often raunchy account of the murkier side of the reigns of Justinian and his sluttish empress, Theodora, from no less an authority than the imperial general Belisarius's official war historian. Besides a demolition job on the grisly royal couple, Procopius's employer Belisarius, one of the greatest Byzantine generals, is also portrayed (like Justinian) as spinelessly uxorious.

Michael Psellus *Fourteen Byzantine Rulers*. Covers the turbulent period between 976 and 1078, when the scholarly author was adviser to several of the emperors of whom he writes.

Jonathan Riley-Smith *What Were the Crusades?* A slim, readable discourse on the nature of the Crusades, including recently unearthed material throwing new light on the whole movement.

🏃 **Steven Runciman** *Byzantine Style and Civilisation* (o/p). Eleven centuries of Byzantine art in one small paperback, and still fascinating. Facts are presented in interesting contexts, theories are well argued. His *The Fall of Constantinople, 1453* remains the classic study of the event, while his *The Great Church in Captivity*, a history of Orthodoxy under the Ottomans, continues the saga in a readable if partisan manner.

Speros Vryonis *The Decline of Medieval Hellenism in Asia Minor and the Process of Islamization from the Eleventh through the Fifteenth Century* (o/p). Heavy, footnoted going, but the definitive study of how the Byzantine Empire culturally became the Ottoman Empire.

Ottoman history

Jason Goodwin *Lords of the Horizons*. "Popular" history of the Ottoman Empire in the tradition of Noel Barber's long-vanished *Lords of the Golden Horn* – ie a breathless, sensational romp through the era for *Daily Mail* readers.

Halil İnalcık *The Ottoman Empire: The Classical Age, 1300–1600*. As the title says; the standard work, not superseded since its first 1973 appearance.

Patrick Balfour Kinross *The Ottoman Centuries*. Readable, balanced summary of Ottoman history from the fourteenth to the twentieth century.

M. Fuad Köprülü *The Origins of the Ottoman Empire*. Translated by Gary Leiser, early twentieth-century classic covers much the same ground as İnalcık's work.

I. Metin Kunt and Christine Woodhead *Süleyman the Magnificent and His Age*. Concise summary of the reign of the greatest Ottoman sultan, and of the cultural renaissance over which he presided.

Philip Mansel *Constantinople: City of the World's Desire, 1453–1924*. Readable, nostalgic, faintly anti-Republican popular history, focusing on the imperial capital and organized topically as well as chronologically. Obscure factoids and scandals are all here, to wit: Boğaziçi University began life as a hotbed of Bulgarian nationalism; Russian floozies have previously (1920–22) held Turkish men in thrall; coffee consumption was periodically a capital crime until the eighteenth century.

Philip Mansel *Sultans in Splendour – the Last Years of the Ottoman World*. The illustrations make this book: a collection of rare photos depicting unbelievable characters from the end of the Ottoman Empire. It's also well written, and contains much information not available elsewhere.

Alan Palmer *The Decline and Fall of the Ottoman Empire*. Particularly good for the manoeuvres and machinations of the European powers vis-à-vis Turkey in the mid-nineteenth century; spotty on the periods before and after.

Nigel Steel and Peter Hart *Defeat at Gallipoli*. Uses contemporary accounts to give a vivid impression of the siege.

Andrew Wheatcroft *The Ottomans*. Not an event-focused, chronological history but an analysis of trends in Ottoman life, and its stereotypical perceptions by the West – usefully demonstrated by period art, cartoons and photos.

Alfred C. Wood *A History of the Levant Company* (o/p). Comprehensive account of the foundation and activities of the Levant Trading Company, which controlled British commerce with the Ottoman Empire between the sixteenth and early nineteenth centuries. To be found in major reference libraries.

Modern history

Feroz Ahmad *The Making of Modern Turkey*. Not the most orthodox of histories but lively, partisan and replete with wonderful anecdotes and quotes you'll find nowhere else.

Mehmet Ali Birand *Shirts of Steel: An Anatomy of the Turkish Armed Forces*. Based on interviews by one of Turkey's top journalists, this gives a good idea of the officer corps' world view and their justifications for the numerous military interventions.

Marjorie Housepian Dobkin *Smyrna 1922: The Destruction of a City*. Partisan (ie rabidly anti-Turkish) but harrowingly graphic account of the sack of İzmir, when approximately 150,000 of the 400,000 Armenians and Greeks trapped in the city met their deaths. Most original insights are how the US coddled Republican Turkey by massaging press coverage of the incident, in hopes of postwar oil concessions in Mosul (*plus ça change . . .*), and helping to conceal the cause of the great fire so as to facilitate (ultimately unsuccessful) insurance claims against a British company. The only people who emerge honourably are American Consul George Horton, Dr Esther Lovejoy and the ordinary seamen who, against orders, fished survivors out of Izmir harbour.

Michael Hickey *Gallipoli*. Currently the best single-volume history of the campaign.

Cağlar Keyder *State and Class in Turkey: A Study in Capitalist Development* (o/p). Intertwined with the Marxist and academic rhetoric is a very useful economic history of the Republic.

Faik Okte *The Tragedy of the Turkish Capital Tax* (o/p). Short, remorseful monograph on the discriminatory World War II tax, written by the İstanbul director of finance who was responsible for its implementation.

Hugh Poulton *Top Hat, the Grey Wolves and the Crescent: Turkish Nationalism and the Turkish Republic*. After some brief operative definitions, Poulton does an excellent, thorough dissection of the "holy trinity" – secularism, ethnically based nationalism and Islam – which jostle for position in Turkey, and also summarizes the fortunes of antecedents such as Pan-Ottomanism. Plenty of asides on the fates of minorities (mostly the Kurds), but marred by numerous typos, and despite the 1997 publication date, stops short of the crucial political-Islam period.

Barry Rubin *Istanbul Intrigues*. Unputdownable account of Allied/Axis activities in neutral Turkey during World War II, and their attempts to drag it into the conflict. Surprising revelations about the extent of Turkish aid for Britain, the US and the Greek resistance, and a wealth of detailed anecdote.

Richard Tapper (ed) *Islam in Modern Turkey: Religion, Politics and Literature in a Secular State*. Short collection of essays by various specialists on the resurgence of religion in Turkish life.

Erik J. Zürcher *Turkey, A Modern History*. If you have time for only one volume covering the post-1800 period, make it this one; it's well written and breathes some revisionist fresh air over sacred cows and received truths. Also with an opinionated, annotated bibliography.

General multi-era histories

Roderic Davison and C.H. Dodd *Turkey, a Short History*. Non-chronological text which touches on everything up to 1997, particularly good for late Ottoman and early Republican events.

Geoffrey L. Lewis *Turkey* (o/p). Hard to find, but a much more witty and readable choice than Davison and Dodd – a little uneven, though, and coverage ceases at 1974.

Richard Stoneman *A Traveller's History of Turkey*. An easy-reading volume of this small series, and at less than 200 pages inevitably superficial, but it does touch on all salient points from Paleolithic times to 1992.

Biographies: Atatürk and others

Saime Göksu and Edward Timms *Romantic Communist: The Life and Works of Nazım Hikmet*. Long-overdue English-language biography of Turkey's most controversial modern poet. Banned and imprisoned for seventeen years at home, Hikmet spent much of his life in the Soviet bloc and died in Moscow. Though as yet little known outside Turkey, he once rubbed shoulders with such leftist luminaries as Pablo Neruda, Jean-Paul Sartre and Paul Robeson.

🏃 **Patrick Balfour Kinross** *Atatürk, the Rebirth of a Nation*. Long considered the definitive English biography – as opposed to hagiography – of the father of the Republic and still preferred by some to the newer Mango text (see below).

🏃 **Andrew Mango** *Atatürk*. Despite massive press acclama-tion, does not supersede Kinross's more readable tome as the best biography of the man, but merely complements it. Thorough and authoritative, but also steeped in military and conspiratorial minutiae. Sympathetic to its subject, and the Turkish national project as a whole; the compulsory post-1922 exchange of populations rates hardly a mention and the vicissitudes of the Armenians are also glossed over.

Michael Strachan *Sir Thomas Roe 1581–1644: A Life*. Biography of an influential Elizabethan statesman who spent several years as English ambassador to the Ottoman court, and head of the Levant Company. Fascinating insight into the perilous life and intrigues of Europeans in Constantinople.

Minorities and religion

🏃 **Taner Akçam** *From Empire to Republic: Turkish Nationalism and the Armenian Genocide*. Brilliant study by a Turkish academic resident in the US, which shows how the ethnic cleansing of the Armenian population from 1895 to 1923, and the subsequent suppression of any memory of these events, was both crucial to incipient Turkish nationalism – and remains at the root of the Republic's modern problems. Perhaps the most astounding of many findings – and Akçam has diligently mined Turkish official archives – is that Atatürk and other higher-ups freely admitted from 1923 onwards that hundreds of thousands of Armenians had been done away with for reasons of state, and that Turkey should expect some punishment for this; the silence and cover-up only began in earnest during the 1930s.

Alexis Alexandris *The Greek Minority of İstanbul and Greek Turkish Relations 1918–1974* (Centre for Asia Minor Studies, Athens). Effectively illustrates how the treatment of this community, whose rights were guaranteed by the Treaty of Lausanne, has functioned as a gauge of general relations between Greece and Turkey during the period in question.

🏃 **Peter Balakian** *The Burning Tigris: A History of the Armenian Genocide*. As partisan as one would expect from an Armenian-American, it is, nonetheless, a compelling and thorough analysis of the background to, and execution of, the massacres of the Armenians on Ottoman soil during the late nineteenth and early twentieth centuries. It is particularly strong on evidence from American and European missionaries operating in the region, and contains some harrowing period photographs.

Esther Benbassa and Aron Rodrigue *The Jews of the Balkans: The Judeo-Spanish Community, 15th to 20th Centuries* (o/p). Dense but brief overview of the Sephardic community in the European core of the Ottoman Empire, decimated this century by assorted nationalisms, the Nazis and emigration to Palestine.

🏃 **William Dalrymple** *From the Holy Mountain: A Journey in the Shadow of Byzantium*. A witty retracing of a classic sixth-century monkish journey through the monasteries of the Near East. Section II is devoted to Turkey, and like Kelsey (see below) he takes a suitably dim view of the sorry history and current poor treatment of Assyrian Christians and Armenian monuments in eastern Turkey.

John Freely *The Lost Messiah: In Search of the Mystical Rabbi Sabbatai Sevi*. Story of the millennial, seventeenth-century movement in İzmir and Salonica that emerged from Kabbalistic ferment and gave rise to the Dönme, a crypto-Judaic sect disproportionately prominent in modern Turkish history.

John Guest *Survival among the Kurds: A History of the Yezidis*. A very expensive hardback, but the last word on this little-known heterodox sect scattered astride Turkey's eastern borders.

F.W. Hasluck *Christianity and Islam under the Sultans* (usually o/p). Invaluable if you can find it; ample material on the history of shrines and festivals, their veneration and attendance by different sects at the turn of the last century, plus Christian and pagan contributions to Bektaşi and Alevî rites. There's a more easily available if cheaply produced reprint online from Isis Press in İstanbul. Great for dipping into, though a bit repetitive as it was edited posthumously by his widow.

🏃 **David McDowall** *The Kurds: A Nation Denied*. About one-third of this book is devoted to the Kurds of Turkey, though they are now distributed over the territory of several modern states – few of whose governments get high marks here for their treatment of Kurds, up to 1992. Consult also McDowall's more recent *A Modern History of the Kurds*.

Yaşar Nuri Öztürk *The Eye of the Heart: An Introduction to Sufism and the Tariqats of Anatolia and the Balkans* (Redhouse Press, İstanbul). A frustratingly brief description of the tenets of mystical Islam and the main dervish orders in Turkey; lavishly illustrated, easily available in the country.

🏃 **Jonathan Rugman and Roger Hutchings** *Atatürk's Children: Turkey and the Kurds*. Excellent, even-handed exploration of the topic by (in part) the *Guardian*'s former Turkey correspondent.

Stanford J. Shaw *The Jews of the Ottoman Empire and the Turkish Republic* (o/p). The story of the one Turkish minority which has usually managed to stay on the good side of those in power; pricey in hardback, try for a secondhand paperback copy.

🏃 **Christopher Walker** *Armenia: The Survival of a Nation*. A far-reaching if partisan history, with extended discussion on Armenian relations with the Turks – particularly the 1895–96 and 1915 massacres. His more recent *Visions of Ararat* is an edited collection of literary excerpts, mostly views of the Armenians by outsiders over the centuries.

Views of contemporary Turkey

Tim Kelsey *Dervish: The Invention of Modern Turkey* (o/p). The troubled soul of the 1990s country, sought amongst minority communities, faith healers, the bulging prisons, the brothels and the transsexual underground, plus the mystics of the title; bleak and pitiless analysis of Republican Turkish angst, with little optimism for Turkey's future.

Stephen Kinzer *Crescent and Star*. Engaging, entertaining account of modern Turkey from the veteran correspondent and former bureau chief for the *New York Times* based in İstanbul. Whether *rakı* drinking and *nargile* toking with ordinary Turks, interviewing leading political figures, swimming across the Bosphorus or broadcasting the blues on his own show on Turkish radio, Kinzer has a gift for bringing the country to life.

Andrew Mango *The Turks Today*. Current to 2004, this overview by a longstanding observer of the country usefully concentrates on the period from the demise of Atatürk to 2004. By no means a rose-tinted view, but he gives the country an easy "pass" in too many areas, and chapter 10 on Kurdish issues is highly disposable.

Chris Morris *The New Turkey Today*. Even more up to date than Mango's book, Morris (BBC correspondent in Turkey for four years) writes in a very readable manner on the usual topics, from political Islam to the Greeks and Armenians, and from the Kurdish question to Turkey's EU accession quest. An ideal introduction to contemporary Turkey.

Nicole and Hugh Pope *Turkey Unveiled: Atatürk and After* (UK); published also as *Turkey Unveiled: A History of Modern Turkey* (US). A series of interlinked essays, arranged both topically and chronologically, by two foreign correspondents who, after two-plus decades in harness, understand Turkey better than most outsiders. Particularly good grasp of Kurdish- and Europe-related issues, and wonderful anecdotal detail on events and personalities. Despite their affection for and optimism about the country, the authors include unflinching description of its many shortcomings.

Travel

Neal Ascherson *Black Sea*. Subtitled "The Birthplace of Civilisation and Barbarism", this excellent historical, ethnological and ecological meditation explores these supposed antitheses around Turkey's northerly sea; only two chapters specifically on the Pontus and Bosphorus, but still highly recommended.

John Ash *A Byzantine Journey*. Historically inclined reflections of a poet as he takes in all the major, and some of the minor, Byzantine sites in Anatolia; better than it sounds, and recommended.

Frederick G. Burnaby *On Horseback through Asia Minor*. Victorian officer's thousand-mile ride through snowy northeast Anatolia to spy on the Russians in the run-up to the 1877 war. Prophetically observant (especially in light of the Chechen wars) and gruesomely, if inadvertently humorous (sample conversational opener: "Are people ever impaled here?"). Anti-Armenian, condescendingly Turkophilic, plus Russophobic appendices.

Laurence Kelly (ed) *Istanbul: A Traveller's Companion*. Well-selected historical writing concerning various aspects of the city, and fascinating eyewitness accounts of historical events such as the Crusaders' sack of Constantinople.

Mary Wortley Montagu *Letters*, and the newer *Turkish Embassy Letters*. Impressions of an eccentric but perceptive traveller, resident in İstanbul during 1716–18, whose disregard for convention and popular prejudice gave her the edge over contemporary historians.

Michael Pereira *East of Trebizond* (o/p). Travels between the Black Sea and northeast Anatolia during the late 1960s, interspersed with readable history of the area. Common in secondhand travel bookshops and on websites.

Dux Schneider *Bolkar: Travels with a Donkey in the Taurus Mountains*. Entertaining, often insightful account of a trek through the Bolkar range in the early 1970s by one of the first foreign travel writers to specialize in Turkey,

long before mass tourism and/or adventure tourism had made inroads into the back country. Available most easily online through Amazon or the publisher Alibris.

Brian Sewell *South from Ephesus: An Escape from the Tyranny of Western Art*. Pre-touristic southwest-coastal Turkey and its ruins during the 1970s and 1980s, when vile hotels, domineering guides, baulky transport and amorous, bisexually inclined villagers were a constant hazard (or attraction, depending on one's point of view). As erudite and curmudgeonly as you'd expect from the controversial art critic of London's *Evening Standard*.

Freya Stark *Ionia – a Quest*, *Alexander's Path*, *Lycian Shore* and *Riding to the Tigris*. Some of the most evocative travel writing available on Turkey, if now inevitably dated.

Memoirs

Shirin Devrim *A Turkish Tapestry: The Shakirs of Istanbul*. Turbulent chronicle of a vastly eccentric, dysfunctional and talented aristocratic Ottoman family whose exploits, if anything, became even more colourful after 1923. Divorces, affairs, suicide attempts, art exhibits, travels and residence across four continents – and lurking always in the background, the notorious Şakir Paşa murder case of 1914. The author, who is niece and granddaughter of the respective protagonists, gets as close to the truth as anyone is likely to.

Aziz Nesin *İstanbul Boy* (o/p). An autobiography set in the same era and milieu as Orga's first work (see below), and strong on local colour (eg spectacular "Howling" dervish ceremonies), but not such a good read.

İrfan Orga *Portrait of a Turkish Family*. Heartbreaking story following the Orga family from an idyllic existence in late Ottoman İstanbul

through grim survival in the early Republican era. His *The Caravan Moves On: Three Weeks among Turkish Nomads* is also excellent. Set in the late 1950s, it's a fine snapshot of the Menderes era – and a suitably unsentimental portrayal of a *yörük* community in the Toros, who while comprising just 0.5 percent of the Turkish population have had plenty of uninformed, rose-tinted rubbish written about them.

Orhan Pamuk *İstanbul: Memories of a City*. A thoughtful and sometimes moving memoir by Turkey's most famous novelist (translated by Maureen Freely), reflecting on the author's troubled relationship with himself, his parents, and the city he was born and raised in. Although Pamuk has chosen to remain in İstanbul, the book's overriding theme is melancholy and decline from imperial greatness – reinforced by the copious black-and-white illustrations by Turkey's leading photographer, Ara Güler.

Mary Seacole *The Wonderful Adventures of Mrs Seacole in Many Lands*. This alternative Florence Nightingale was a black Jamaican who, unlike her paler-skinned compatriot, ministered to Crimean War casualties in İstanbul at her own expense. Seacole's bankruptcy touched the British public to such an extent that *Punch* magazine helped raise funds for her, as did proceeds from London concerts (including a sell-out at the Albert Hall). Subsequent history has not done Seacole justice, but her autobiography continues to figure amongst top feminist texts – and has remained in print almost without interruption.

Daniel de Souza *Under a Crescent Moon*. Turkish society seen from the bottom looking up: an excellent volume of prison vignettes by a jailed foreigner, and in its compassion the antithesis of *Midnight Express*. Compellingly written and spiced with interesting prejudices.

Architecture, arts and crafts

Architecture and monuments

Godfrey Goodwin *A History of Ottoman Architecture*. Definitive guide to Ottoman architecture, covering the whole of Turkey and providing a sound historical and ethno-geographical context for any Ottoman construction you care to name. Goodwin's *Sinan: Ottoman Architecture and Its Values Today* provides fascinating insights into the architect, his life and influences, made eminently readable by the author's passion for his subject. **Spiro Kostoff** *Caves of God – Cappadocia and Its Churches* (o/p). Dry rendering of a fascinating subject, but there's still no rival, and it is thorough. **Richard Krautheimer** *Early Christian and Byzantine Architecture*. An excellent survey from the Pelican "History of Art" series.

Raymond Lifchez (ed) *The Dervish Lodge: Architecture, Art and Sufism in Ottoman Turkey* (o/p). Lavishly illustrated essays by specialist scholars on all aspects of the Sufi orders in Turkey. Though nineteenth-century İstanbul is disproportionately represented, as are the Mevlevî and Bektaşi orders, and the core of the book is the relation between *tekke* layout and function, there's ample material on rural *zaviyes* of the *ahis*, Nakşibendi practice, tomb veneration and pictorial calligraphy. Among pieces on poetry, the symbolism of costumes and gravestones, ritual food and even continuing Sufi influence on contemporary Turkish culture, only a piece on music disappoints.

Cyril Mango *Byzantine Architecture*. A complete survey of the most significant Byzantine structures, around a quarter of which fall within modern Turkey. Well worth paying the slight premium for the Electa Editrice reissue. **T.A. Sinclair** *Eastern Turkey: An Archaeological and Architectural Survey* (4 vols). The standard reference, with copious plans and covering just about every monument east of Cappadocia, but prohibitively priced. Specialist or university libraries usually have copies. **Metin Sözen** *The Evolution of Turkish Art and Architecture* (Haşet Kitabevi, İstanbul). Lavishly illustrated, erudite survey of major Turkish monuments by period, followed by detailed discussion of the fine arts.

David Talbot Rice *Islamic Art*. Covers an enormous timescale and geographical area, giving useful perspectives on Ottoman and Selçuk art forms alongside those of Persia and

Muslim Spain. His *Art of the Byzantine Era*, a chronologically ordered and lavishly illustrated but still affordable study in the same "World of Art" series, is unlikely to be ever superseded even four decades after first publication. For specialists *The Church of Hagia Sophia in Trebizond* (o/p) remains the last word, from the Talbot–Rice-headed team that restored the frescoes in this landmark church.

Coffee-table illustrateds

Diana Barillari and Ezio Godoli *Istanbul 1900: Art Nouveau Architecture and Interiors*. Superbly researched and illustrated account of İstanbul's rich but neglected legacy of Art-Nouveau architecture, in particular works of Italian architect and longtime resident Raimondo D'Aronco. A nice corrective to the axiom that the city consists only of palaces, concrete towerblocks and crumbled wood terraces.

John Freely and Augusto Romano Burelli *Sinan: Architect of Süleyman the Magnificent and the Ottoman Golden Age* (o/p). Photographs by Ara Güler complement this reverential catalogue of the great sixteenth-century genius's work.

Chris Hellier and Francesco Venturi *Splendours of the Bosphorus: Houses and Palaces of İstanbul*. Not the usual coffee-table fare – inviting photographs of interiors you'd never otherwise see are supported by intelligent text that puts the shoreline *yalıs* and opulent palaces into their social and artistic context.

Stephane Yerasimos, Ara Güler and Samih Rifat *Living in Turkey* (Overseas, and by Dünya in Turkey). Covers some of the same ground as Hellier and Venturi, but with less of a focus on nobility and more on the *nouveau riche*. Landscapes and interiors to drool over, in photos by Güler and Rifat; a bit prettified but still alluring as an ideal.

Fine arts

Metin And *Turkish Miniature Painting – the Ottoman Period* (Dost Yayınları, İstanbul). Attractive, interesting account of the most important Ottoman art form. Loads of colour plates, mostly excellent production.

Jean Jenkins and Poul Rovsing Olsen *Music and Musical Instruments in the World of Islam* (o/p). Interesting introduction, not too technical but usefully illustrated with photos and line drawings.

Carpets

Alastair Hull *Kilims: The Complete Guide*. Comprehensive and thoroughly illustrated survey of Turkish kilims. His *Living with Kilims* is an excellent manual on how to use and care for (as opposed to museumize) kilims in interior-decorative situations. **James Opie** *Tribal Rugs*. Contains examples of Turcoman and Kurdish rugs as part of a general Central Asian survey.

Orient Stars. Despite the silly title, the ultimate rug book; 250 colour plates, with excellent representation of classical Turkish carpets.

Kurt Zipper and Claudia Fritzsche *Oriental Rugs: Turkish*. Volume 4 of the series entitled "Oriental Rugs". Extensive discussion of weaving techniques, symbols and rug categories, and the weavers themselves, along with a regional survey of distinctive patterns.

Specialist guidebooks

🏃 **George E. Bean** *Turkey's Southern Shore, Turkey Beyond the Maeander, Lycian Turkey, Aegean Turkey* (all o/p). A series of scholarly guides to the archeological sites of Turkey written from the original research of Professor Bean, much of which has never been superseded; thus expect some or all to come back into print soon.

Everett Blake and Anna Edmonds *Biblical Sites in Turkey* (Redhouse Press, İstanbul). If it's mentioned in the Bible (New Testament, that is), it appears here too, with description of sites. Their *Turkey's Religious Sites* (Damko, İstanbul) is more current, better produced and includes Jewish and Muslim sites.

Sevan and Müjde Nişanyan *Alistair Sawday's Special Places to Stay in Turkey.* Expensive English co-publication of the couple's classic, still in print (in English and Turkish) *Türkiye'nin Küçük Oteller* (*Small Hotels of Turkey*), which opened the floodgates to the boutique hotel business in the country back in the mid-1990s.

🏃 **Jane Taylor** *Imperial Istanbul.* Excellent, stone-by-stone guide, complete with site plans, of the major Ottoman monuments in Bursa and Edirne as well as the old capital.

Sally Taylor *A Traveller's Guide to the Woody Plants of Turkey* (Redhouse Press, İstanbul; o/p). Coverage of all native trees and shrubs of Turkey, with keying sections and an especially useful glossary of Turkish species names.

Acculturation

Arın Bayraktaroğlu *Culture Shock: Turkey.* A useful volume, especially on a prolonged stay or business trip, which helps make the Turks less inscrutable by explaining some of their more bizarre customs.

Turkish Culture for Americans (o/p). Side-splitting, problem/solution examples of cultural misunderstandings Americans may experience living in Turkey. Not likely that any book would achieve such comedic heights unintentionally, but this one does. A staple of Turkish secondhand bookstores; to be sought after and cherished.

Hiking/mountaineering

Haldun Aydıngün *Aladağlar: An Introduction* (Redhouse Press, İstanbul; o/p). Details approaches and scrambling routes in this compact karst range near Niğde.

🏃 **Kate Clow and Terry Richardson** *The Lycian Way.* Hour-by-hour, west-to-east route guide for Turkey's first officially marked long-distance trail (see p.458); supplied with folding map.

🏃 **Kate Clow and Terry Richardson** *St Paul Trail.* Guide to Turkey's second long-distance, waymarked trail (see p.608), loosely following in the footsteps of St Paul from Perge to Antioch in Pisidia, taking in some wonderful mountain and lakeland scenery en route. Detailed route description, GPS data, map and photographs included.

Marc Dubin and Enver Lucas *Trekking in Turkey* (o/p). Long and short treks – many still followable as written – in every Turkish mountain range, plus a largely obsolete section on the Turquoise Coast; worth trying to get a copy secondhand, as the maps are still among the best available.

Karl Smith *The Mountains of Turkey.*

Marginally more up-to-date than *Trekking in Turkey*, but hiking accounts – fleshed out with general tourism – are often spotty or secondhand, and the maps are poor.

Ömer Tözel *The Aladağ: Climbs and Treks in Turkey's Crimson Mountains*. More technical and much less hike-orientated than the Aydıngün volume, but also much easier to find.

Turkish fiction in translation

Sait Faik *A Dot on the Map* (o/p). A large collection of short stories, translated by various scholars, from the acknowledged Turkish master of the genre; most are set in and around İstanbul and the Sea of Marmara during the early Republican years.

Yaşar Kemal The best-known Turkish novelist in the West, thanks to English translations by his wife Thilda of virtually every one of his titles. Oldest are the epics, somewhat turgid and folksy, set in inner Anatolia: *Mehmed My Hawk*, its sequel *They Burn the Thistles* (o/p), and *The Lords of Akchasaz: Murder in the Ironsmith's Market*. The trilogy *The Wind from the Plain, Iron Earth, Copper Sky* and *The Undying Grass* is strong on human observations and detail rather than plot. Better are some later novels, mostly set in and around İstanbul, including *The Sea-Crossed Fishermen* (o/p), a psychological drama set against the background of an İstanbul sea-fishing village, contrasting an old man's struggle to save the dolphins in the Sea of Marmara with the fortunes of a desperate hoodlum at bay in the city; and *The Birds Have Also Gone* (o/p), a symbolic, gentle story about bird-catchers near İstanbul. In a more recent work, *Salman the Solitary*, Kemal returns to his native Çukurova with a tale of a displaced Kurdish family from the Van area.

Orhan Pamuk The Turkish writer with the largest overseas (and domestic) audience, Pamuk's enduring concerns are Turkey's often corrosive encounter with the West, including its colonization by all forms of media (especially old films and comics), and the irrepressibility of its Islamic heritage. His first work, *The White Castle*, was an excellent historical meditation in which a seventeenth-century Italian scholar is enslaved in the service of an Ottoman astronomer. His 1994-translated *The Black Book*, a mystery set in modern İstanbul, was more convoluted and surreal, and did well in Turkey. But Pamuk's 1998 *The New Life* was, with nearly three quarters of a million copies sold, the most successful Turkish novel ever and had foreign critics falling over themselves hailing the heir-apparent of Calvino and Borges. Many readers will disagree: despite some fine set-piece satires of provincial Turkish life, the narrator is unappealing and the tale slight. His subsequent *My Name is Red*, a late sixteenth-century Ottoman-set murder whodunnit, is again marred by poor characterization and clunky translation. *Snow*, Pamuk's newest (2004), most controversial and political novel, is arguably his best. Set in the bleak, lonely northeastern outpost of Kars, it examines once-taboo topics such as political Islam and Kurdish nationalism. The book caused a real stir amongst the secular establishment, and one provincial mayor ordered any of Pamuk's novels in municipal ownership (ie libraries) to be burned. Apparently none were to be found; Pamuk's urbane, cerebral style evidently was of little interest to pragmatic, rural Turks.

Elif Shafak *The Flea Palace*. An engaging account, in the mould of Armistead Maupin, of the interwoven, tragicomic lives of the residents of a once-grand İstanbul apartment block. The author, of Turkish origin but born in Strasbourg, raised in Spain and currently residing in the US, is also a regular columnist for the *Turkish Daily News*. Her concerns include the role of different minorities still resident in Turkey.

Latife Tekin *Berji Kristin: Tales from the Garbage Hills*. The hard underbelly

of Turkish life, in this surreal allegory set in a shantytown founded on an İstanbul rubbish dump (one of which exploded in 1993 from accumulated methane). By the same author, and similar in tone, is *Dear Shameless Death* which, among other themes, examines how rural families cope with the move to the big city.

Foreign literature set in Turkey

Louis de Bernières *Birds Without Wings*. This repeats, with mixed results, the formula of his blockbuster *Captain Corelli's Mandolin*, applied to Asia Minor of the 1910s and 1920s. Most of the action takes place in "Eskibahçe", a fictionalized version of Kaya Köyü near Fethiye, though the Gallipoli set-pieces are perhaps the best bits. Take it as an epic entertainment, and not gospel – his grip on history, Turkish language and ethnography can be shaky, and the book is often virulently anti-Greek (as in the ridiculous assertion that only two mosques remain in Greece).

Maureen Freely *The Life of the Party*. Salacious, desperate cavortings of Bosphorus University faculty and their families during the 1960s, including a thinly disguised amalgam of the author's father John Freely and others. An excellent read.

Pierre Loti *Aziyade*. For what's essentially romantic twaddle set in nine-

teenth-century Ottoman İstanbul, this is surprisingly racy, with good insights into Ottoman life and Western attitudes to the Orient. Current reissue is expensive; look for used o/p editions.

Rose Macaulay *The Towers of Trebizond*. Classic send-up of Low and High Church conflict, British ethnocentricity and proselytizing naivety, with generous slices of Turkey in the 1950s.

Edouard Roditi *The Delights of Turkey* (o/p). Twenty short stories, by turns touching or bawdy, set in rural Turkey and İstanbul, by a Sephardic Jew of Turkish descent long resident in Paris and America.

Barry Unsworth *The Rage of the Vulture*. Set in the twilight of the Ottoman Empire, with the paranoid sultan Abdülhamid during the last year of his reign observed by a troubled British officer-with-a-past stationed in İstanbul.

Poetry

Coleman Barks (trans) *Like This*; *Open Secret*, with John Moyne; and *We are Three*. Three of various volumes of Rumi poetry, in lively if not necessarily literal translations.

Yunus Emre *The City of the Heart: Verses of Wisdom and Love*. Along with Rumi, the most highly regarded Turk-

ish medieval Sufi poet; translated by Süha Faiz.

Talat S. Halman *Living Poets of Turkey* (Dost Yayınları, İstanbul). A wide selection of modern Turkish poetry, with an introduction giving the socio-political context. Halman also edited *Yunus Emre and His Mystical Poetry* (o/p), the works of the medieval Islamic folk poet, with explanatory essays.

🏃 **Nazım Hikmet** *Poems of Nazım Hikmet*. The newest (2002), most easily available, and reasonably priced anthology by the internationally renowned Turkish communist poet who died in exile in 1963. *A Sad State of Freedom* (o/p) is a collection of gentle, moving poems also worth keeping an eye peeled for.

Geoffrey L. Lewis (trans) *The Book of Dede Korkut*. The Turkish national epic, set in the age of the Oğuz Turks: by turns racy, formulaic, elegant and redundant.

Language

Language

Language

I t's worth learning as much Turkish as you can; if you travel far from the tourist centres you may well need it, and Turks always appreciate foreigners who show enough interest and courtesy to learn at least basic greetings. The main advantages of the language from the learner's point of view are that it's phonetically spelt and (98 percent of the time) grammatically regular. The disadvantages are that the vocabulary is unrelated to any language you're likely to have encountered (unless you're conversant in Arabic or Persian), and the grammar, relying heavily on suffixes, gets more alien the further you delve into it. Concepts like vowel harmony further complicate matters; trying to grasp at least the basics, though, is well worth the effort.

Phrasebooks and dictionaries

For a straightforward **phrasebook**, look no further than *Turkish: A Rough Guide Phrasebook* (Rough Guides), with useful two-way glossaries and a brief and simple grammar section. If you want to **learn** more, Geoffrey L. Lewis's *Teach Yourself Turkish* (Hodder, UK; NTC Publishing Group, US) still probably has a slight edge over Yusuf Mardin's *Colloquial Turkish* (Routledge) – or buy both, since they complement each other well. Alternatively, there's Geoffrey Lewis's *Turkish Grammar* (Oxford UP), a one-volume solution. If you're serious about learning Turkish after you arrive in the country, the best series published in Turkey is a set of three textbooks and tapes, *Türkçe Öğreniyoruz* (Engin Yayınevi), available in good bookshops in İstanbul and Ankara.

Among widely available Turkish **dictionaries**, the best are probably the Langenscheidt/Lilliput miniature or coat-pocket sizes, or the *Concise Oxford Turkish Dictionary* (distributed in Turkey by ABC Kitabevi), a hardback suitable for serious students. In Turkey, locally produced Redhouse dictionaries are the best value, though their fine print can be hard to read for some age groups. The affordable twelve-centimetre *Mini Sözlük* has the same number of entries as the twenty-centimetre desk edition and is adequate for most demands; the definitive, two-tome version even gives Ottoman Turkish script and etymologies for each word, but it costs the earth and isn't exactly portable.

Pronunciation

Pronunciation in Turkish is worth mastering, since once you've got it the phonetic spelling helps you progress fast. The following letters differ significantly from English pronunciation.

Aa short a similar to that in far.
Ee as in bet.
Iı unstressed vowel similar to the vestigial sound between the b and l

of probable.
İi as in ski.
Oo as in note.
Öö like ur in burn.

The circumflex

The **circumflex** (^), found only over the letters a, u and i in loan words from Arabic or Persian, has two uses. It usually lengthens the vowel it crowns, eg Mevlâna sounds like 'Mevlaana', Alevî is pronounced 'Alevee', but when used after the consonants g, k or l the affected vowel sounds like it's preceded by a faint y or h, and distinguishes words that are otherwise homonyms: eg *kar* (snow) versus *kâr* (profit). Although its meticulous use in the modern language is dwindling, news of the circumflex's demise has been greatly exaggerated in some sources, and you still commonly see it in media as diverse as THY publicity and newspaper headlines – while its use in historical or religious texts remains universal.

Uu as in blue.
Üü like ew in few.
Cc like j in jelly.
Çç like ch in chat.
Gg hard g as in get.
Ğğ generally silent, but either lengthens the preceding vowel or, when between two vowels approximates a y sound.
Hh as in hen, never silent.
Jj like the s in pleasure.
Şş like sh in shape.
Vv soft, somewhere between v and w.

Vowel harmony and loan words

Turkish generally tries to adhere to the principle of **vowel harmony**, whereby words contain either the so-called "back" vowels a, ı, o and u, or the "front" vowels e, i, ö and ü, but rarely mix the two types. Back and front vowels are further subdivided into "unrounded" (a and ı, e and i) and "rounded" (o and u, ö and ü), and again rounded and unrounded vowels tend to keep exclusive company, though there are further nuances to this. A small number of native Turkish words (eg *anne*, mother; *kardeş*, brother) violate the rules of vowel harmony, as do compound words, eg *bugün*, "today", formed from *bu* (this) and *gün* (day).

The main exceptions to vowel harmony, however, are foreign **loan words** from Arabic or Persian, and despite Atatürk's best efforts to substitute Turkish or French expressions (the latter again failing to follow vowel harmony), they still make up a good third of the modern Turkish vocabulary. Most words beginning with f, h, l, m, n, r, v and z are derived from Arabic and Persian.

Words and phrases

Basics

Mr; follows first name	**Bey**
Miss; precedes first name	**Bayan**
Mrs (literally lady), polite Ottoman title; follows first name	**Hanım**
Half-humorous honorific title bestowed on any tradesman; means "master craftsman"; follows first name	**Usta**
Honorific of someone who has made the pilgrimage to Mecca	**Hacı**
Good morning	**Günaydın**
Good afternoon	**İyi günler**
Good evening	**İyi akşamlar**
Good night	**İyi geceler**
Hello	**Merhaba**
Goodbye	**Allahaısmarladık**
Yes	**Evet**
No	**Hayır**

No (there isn't any)	Yok	I beg your pardon, sorry	Affedersiniz
Please	Lütfen	Excuse me (in a crowd)	Pardon
Thank you	Teşekkür ederim/ Mersi/Sağol	I'm sightseeing	Geziyorum or Dolaşıyorum
You're welcome, that's OK	Bir şey değil	I'm English/Scottish Irish/ American/ Australian	İngilizim/İskoçyalım/ İrlandalıyım/ Amerikalı/ Avustralyalım
How are you?	Nasılsınız? Nasılsın? Ne haber?		
I'm fine (thank you)	(Sağol) İyiyim/İyilik sağlık	I live in . . .	. . . 'de/da oturuyorum
Do you speak English?	İngilizce biliyormusunuz?	Today	Bugün
		Tomorrow	Yarın
I don't understand (Turkish)	Anlamadı*m/Türkçe anlamıyorum	The day after tomorrow	Öbür gün/Ertesi gün
I don't know	Bilmiyorum	Yesterday	Dün

△ Studying the Turkish alphabet

Now	Şimdi		Cheap/expensive	Ucuz/Pahalı
Later	Sonra		Early/late	Erken/Geç
Wait a minute!	Bir dakika bekle!		Hot/cold	Sıcak/Soğuk
In the morning	Sabahleyin		Near/far	Yakın/Uzak
In the afternoon	Oğle'den sonra		Vacant/occupied	Boş/Dolu
In the evening	Akşamleyin		Quickly/slowly	Hızlı/Yavaş
Here/there/over there	Bur(a)da/Şur(a)da/ Or(a)da		With/without (milk)	(Süt)lü/(Süt)süz
			With/without (meat)	(Et)li/(Et)siz
Good/bad	İyi/Kötü, Fena		Enough	Yeter
Big/small	Büyük/Küçük			

Driving

Left	Sol		No entry	Araç giremez
Right	Sağ		No through road	Çıkmaz sokak
Straight ahead	Doğru, direk		Abrupt verge	Düşük banket
Turn left/right	Sola dön/Sağ'ta dön		Slow down	Yavaşla
Parking/No parking	Park yapılır/Park yapılmaz		Road closed	Yol kapalı
			Crossroads	Dörtyol
Your car will be towed	Aracınız çekilir		Pedestrian crossing	Yaya geçidi
One-way street	Tek yön			

Some common signs

Entrance/exit	Giriş/Çıkış		No smoking	Sigara içilmez
Free/paid entrance	Giriş ücretsiz/ Ücretlidir		Don't tread on the grass	Çimenlere basmayınız
Gentlemen	Baylar		Stop, halt	Dur
Ladies	Bayanlar		Military Area	Askeri bölge
WC	WC/Tuvalet/Umumî		Entry Forbidden	Girmek yasaktır
Open/closed	Açık/Kapalı		No entry without a ticket	Biletsiz girmek yasaktır
Arrivals/departures	Varış/Kalkış		No entry without a woman	Damsız girilmez
Pull/push	Çekiniz/İtiniz			
Out of order	Arızalı		Please take off your shoes	Lütfen ayakkabılarınızı çıkartınız
Drinking water	İçilebilir su			
To let/for hire	Kiralık			
Foreign exchange	Kambiyo		No entry on foot	Yaya giremez
Beware	Dikkat			
First aid	İlk yardım			

Accommodation

Hotel	Hotel/otel		Do you have a double room for one/two/ three nights?	Bir/iki/üç gecelik çift yataklı odanızvar mı?
Pension, inn	Pansiyon			
Campsite	Kamping			
Tent	Çadır		For one/two weeks	Bir/iki haftalık
Is there a hotel nearby?	Bir yakında otel var mı?		With an extra bed	İlave yataklı
			With a double bed	Fransiz yataklı
Do you have a room?	Boş odanız var mı?		With a shower	Duşlu
Single/double/triple	Tek/çift/üç kişilik		Hot water	Sıcak su

Cold water	Soğuk su	Can we camp here?	Burda kamp
Can I see it?	Bakabilirmiyim?		edebilirmiyiz?
I have a booking	Reservasyonum var		

Questions and directions

Where is the . . . ?	...nerede?	How far is it to . . . ?	...'a/e ne kadar uzak?
When?	Ne zaman?	Can you give me a lift to...?	Beni . . . 'a/e götürebilirmisiniz?
What/What is it?	Ne/Ne dir?	What time does it open?	Kaçta açılıcak?
How much (does it cost?	Ne kadar/Kaça?		
How many?	Kaç tane?	What time does it close?	Kaçta kapanacak?
Why?	Niye?	What's it called in Turkish?	Türkcesi ne dir? or, Turkçe nasıl söylersiniz?
What time is it?	(polite) Saatınız var mı? (informal) Saat kaç?		
How do I get to . . . ?	...'a/e nasıl giderim?		

Travelling

Aeroplane	Uçak	Can I book a seat?	Reservasyon yapabılırmıyım?
Bus	Otobus	When is the next bus /train/ferry?	Bir sonraki otobus/ tren/vapur kaçta kalkıyor?
Train	Tren		
Car	Araba		
Taxi	Taksi	Where does it leave from?	Nereden kalkıyor?
Bicycle	Bisiklet	Do I have to change?	Aktarma var mı?
Ferry	Feribot, vapur	Where does it leave from?	Nereden kalkıyor?
Catamaran, sea bus	Deniz otobüsü		
Hitchhiking	Otostop	What platform does it leave from?	Hangi perondan kalkıyor?
On foot	Yaya		
Bus station	Otogar	How many kilometres is it?	Kaç kilometredir?
Railway station	Gar, tren ıstasyonu		
Ferry terminal/jetty	İskele	How long does it take?	Ne kadar sürer?
Harbour	Liman	Which bus goes to...?	Hangi otobus... 'a gider?
A ticket to...	... 'a bir bilet		
One-way	Gidiş, sadece	Which road leads to...?	Hangi yol ... 'a çıkar?
Return	Gidiş-dönüş	Can I get out at a convenient place?	Müsait bir yerde inebilirmiyim?
What time does it leave?	Kaçta kalkıyor?		

Days of the week, months and seasons

Sunday	Pazar	March	Mart
Monday	Pazartesi	April	Nisan
Tuesday	Salı*	May	Mayıs
Wednesday	Çarşamba	June	Haziran
Thursday	Perşembe	July	Temmuz
Friday	Cuma	August	Ağustos
Saturday	Cumartesi	September	Eylül
January	Ocak	October	Ekim
February	Subat	November	Kasım

December	Aralı*k		Autumn	Sonbahar
Spring	İlkbahar		Winter	Kış
Summer	Yaz			

Numbers

1	Bir		70	Yetmiş
2	İki		80	Seksen
3	Üç		90	Doksan
4	Dört		100	Yüz
5	Beş		140	Yüz kırk
6	Altı		200	İki yüz
7	Yedi		700	Yedi yüz
8	Sekiz		1000	Bin
9	Dokuz		100,000	Yüz bin
10	On		500,000	Beşyüz bin
11	On bir		1,000,000	Bir milyon
12	On iki		Compounded numbers tend to be run together	
13	On üç		in spelling: 50,784	Ellibinyediyüzseksendört
20	Yirmi			
30	Otuz		The most important ordinals, as in class of	
40	Kırk		train, restaurant, etc, are:	
50	Elli		First	Birinci
60	Altmış		Second	İkinci
			Third	Üçüncü

Time conventions

(At) 3 o'clock	Saat üç(ta)		It's 8.10	Sekizi on geçiyor
2 hours (duration)	İki saat		It's 10.45	On bire çeyrek var
Half hour (duration)	Yarım saat		At 8.10	Sekizi on geçe
5.30	Beş büçük		At 10.45	On bire çeyrek kala

Food and drink

Basics

Bal	Honey		Nane	Mint
Bulgur	Cracked wheat		Pilav, pirinç	Rice
Buz	Ice		Şeker	Sugar
Dereotu	Dill		Sirke	Vinegar
Ekmek	Bread		Su	Water
Çavdar	Rye		Süt	Milk
Kepekli	Wholegrain		Tereyağı	Butter
Mısır	Corn		Tuz	Salt
Karabiber	Black pepper		Yağ	Oil
Kekik	Oregano		Yoğurt	Yoghurt
Makarna	Pasta (noodles)		Yumurta	Eggs

Useful words

Bakarmısınız!	Polite way of getting waiter's attention	Hesap	Bill, check
Bardak	Glass	Kaşık	Spoon
Başka bir ...	Another ...	Peçete	Napkin
Bıçak	Knife	Servis ücreti	Service charge
Çatal	Fork	Garsoniye	"Waiter's" charge
		Tabak	Plate

Cooking terms

Acı	Hot, spicy	Kıymalı	With minced meat
Buğlama	Steamed	Peynirli, kaşarlı	With cheese
Çevirme	Spit-roasted	Pilaki	Vinaigrette, marinated
Etli	Containing meat	Pişmemiş	Raw
Etli mi?	Does it contain meat?	Sıcak/soğuk	Hot/cold
Etsiz yemek var mı?	Do you have any meatless food?	Soslu, salçalı	In red sauce
		Sucuklu	With sausage
Ezme	Paste; any mashed or crushed dip	Tava, sahanda	Deep-fried, fried
		Yoğurtlu	In yoghurt sauce
Fırında(n)	Baked	Yumurtalı	With egg (eg *pide*)
Haşlama	Meat stew without oil, sometimes with vegetables	Zeytinyağlı	Vegetables cooked in their own juices, spices and olive oil (*zeytin yağı*), then allowed to steep and chill
İyi pişmiş	Well-cooked		
Izgarada(n), ızgarası	Grilled		
Kızartma	Fried then chilled		

Soup (*Çorba*)

Düğün	"Wedding": egg and lemon	Tarhana	Yoghurt, soured grain and spice
Ezo gelin	Rice and vegetable broth	Tavuk	Chicken
		Yayla	Similar to *tarhana*, with *mint*
İşkembe	Tripe		
Mercimek	Lentil	Yoğurt	Yoghurt, rice and celery greens
Paça	Trotters		

Appetizers (*Meze or Zeytinyağlı*)

Amerikan salatası	Mayonnaise and vegetable salad	Cacık	Yoghurt, grated cucumber and herb dip
Antep or acılı ezmesi	Hot chilli mash with garlic, parsley, lettuce, onion	Cinter	Chanterelle mushrooms
Barbunya	Red kidney beans, marinated	Çoban salatası	Chopped tomato, cucumber, parsley, pepper and onion salad
Beyin salatası	Lamb-brains salad		
Börülce	Black-eyed peas, in the pod	Deniz börülce	Wild asparagus (approximately)

Deniz otu	Rock samphire
Haydarı	Dense garlic dip
İçli köfte	Bulgur, nuts, vegetables and meat in a spicy crust
İmam bayıldı	Cold baked aubergine, onion and tomato
Mantar sote	Sauteed mushrooms
Mücver	Courgette frittata
Pancar	Beets, marinated
Patlıcan ezmesi	Aubergine pâté
Piyaz	White haricots, onions and parsley vinaigrette
Rus salatası	"Russian" salad
	– potatoes, peas, gherkins in mayonnaise
Semizotu	Purslane, usually mixed into yoghurt
Sigara böreği	Cheese-filled pastry "cigarettes"
Tarama	Pink fish-roe
Tere	Rocket greens
Turşu	Pickled vegetables
Yaprak dolması or yılancı dolması	Stuffed vine-leaves
Yeşil salata	Green salad
Zeytin	Olives

Meat (*Et*) and poultry (*Beyaz et*)

Adana kebap	Spicy Arab-style kebab
Beyti	Minced kebab wrapped in pitta
Bıldırcın	Quail
Billur, koç yumurtası	Testicle
Böbrek	Kidney
Bonfile	Small steak
Ciğer	Liver
Çöp kebap	Literally, "rubbish kebab" – tiny chunks of offal or lamb
Dana eti	Veal
Dil	Tongue
Döner kebap	Fatty lamb from a rotisseried cone of meat slabs
İnegöl köfte	Mince rissoles impregnated with cheese
İskender or Bursa kebap	Döner drenched in yoghurt and sauce
Kaburga	Spare ribs
Kağıt kebap	Meat and vegetables
	baked in wax paper
Kanat	Chicken wing
Karışık ızgara	Mixed grill
Kiremit kebap	Meat served on a hot ceramic tray (*kiremit* = tile)
Köfte	Meatballs
Koyun	Mutton
Kuzu	Lamb
Keçi	Goat
Orman kebap	Roast lamb refried with vegetables
Pastırma	Cured meat
Piliç	Roasting chicken
Pirzola	Chop, cutlet
Saray kebap	Rissoles baked with vegetables
Sığır	Beef
Şiş kebap	Shish kebab
Tandır kebap	Side of tender, boneless lamb baked in out door oven
Tavuk	Boiling chicken
Yürek	Heart

Fish (*Balık*) and seafood

Ahtapod	Octopus
Akya	Amberjack
Alabalık	Trout
Barbunya, tekir	Red mullet, small and
	large respectively
Çineköp	Baby *lüfer*, not very esteemed
Çipura	Gilt-head bream

Fangri	Red porgy
Hamsi	Anchovy (Black Sea)
İsparoz	Annular bream
İstakoz	Aegean lobster
İstavrit	Horse mackerel
Kalamar	Squid
Kalkan	Turbot
Karagöz	Two-banded bream
Karides	Prawns
Kefal	Grey mullet (Aegean)
Kılıç	Swordfish
Kolyoz	Club mackerel
Küpes	Bogue
Levrek	Bass; usually farmed
Lüfer	Bluefish (autumn, İstanbul)

Melanurya	Saddled bream
Mendik	Type of bream
Mercan	Pandora or red bream; wild
Mezgit	Whitebait
Midye	Mussel
Orfoz	Giant grouper
Palamut, torik	Small/large bonito respectively
Sarıgoz	Black bream
Sardalya	Sardine
Sinagrit	Dentex
Skaros	Parrotfish
Uskumru	Atlantic mackerel
Yengeç	Crab

Vegetables (*Sebze*)

Acı biber	Hot chillis
Bakla	Broad beans
Bamya	Okra, lady's finger
Bezelye	Peas
Domates	Tomato
Enginar	Artichoke
Hardal	Mustard greens
Havuç	Carrot
Ispanak	Spinach
Kabak	Courgette, zucchini
Karnabahar	Cauliflower
Kuru fasulye	White haricots
Kuşkonmaz	Asparagus
Lahana	Cabbage (usually stuffed)

Mantar	Mushrooms
Marul	Lettuce
Maydanoz	Parsley
Nohut	Chickpeas
Patates	Potato
Patlıcan	Aubergine, eggplant
Roka, tere	Rocket greens
Salatalık	Cucumber
Sarımsak, sarmısak	Garlic
Sivri biber	Skinny peppers, hot or mild
Soğan	Onion
Taze fasulye	French beans
Turp	Radish

Snacks

Badem	Almonds
Börek	Rich layered pastry with varied fillings
Çerez	Bar nibbles, usually nuts
Cezer(i)ye	Carrot, honey and nut bar
Çiğ börek	"Inflated" hollow turnovers
Dürüm	Pitta-like dough roll used to wrap meat for takeaway

Fındık	Hazelnuts
Gözleme	Village crêpe with various toppings or fillings
Kestane	Chestnuts
Kokoreç	Mixed innard roulade
Kuru üzüm	Raisins
Lahmacun	Round Arabic "pizza"
Leblebi	Roasted chickpeas
Midye dolması	Mussels stuffed with rice, allspice and pine nuts

Pestil	Sheet-pressed dried fruit	Şam fıstık	Pistachios
Pide	Elongated Turkish "pizza"	Simit	Bread rings studded with sesame seeds
Poğaça	Soft round biscuit served with *börek*	Su börek	"Water börek" – runny cheese between layers of filo
		Yer fıstığı	Peanuts

Typical dishes

Civil	Variant of *muhlama*, served on Çoruh side of Kaçkar	Mıhlama, muhlama	Fondue-like Hemşin dish of cheese, butter and corn flour
Güveç	Meat and vegetable clay-pot casserole	Otlu peynir	Herb-flavoured cheese found especially in eastern Anotolia
İç pilav	Spicy rice		
Karnıyarık	Aubergine and meat dish, firmer than *mussaka*	Saç kavurma	"Wok"-fried medley
		Sebze turlu	Vegetable stew
Lahana sarma	Black-Sea version of dolma, with baby cabbage leaves	Şakşuka	Aubergine, tomato and other vegetable fry-up
Laz böreği	Meat-filled crêpes, topped with yoghurt	Tas kebap	Meat and vegetable stew especially in eastern Anatolia
Mantı	Mince-stuffed "ravioli" topped with yoghurt and chilli oil	Tatar böreği	Similar to *mantı* but served with cheese and mint
Menemen	Stir-fried omelette with tomatoes and peppers	Türlü sebze	Alias of *tas kebap*

Cheese (*Peynir*)

Beyaz	White; like Greek feta	Kaşar	Kasseri, variably aged
Çerkez	Like Edam	Tulum	Dry, crumbly, parmesan-like cheese made in a goatskin
Dil	Like mozzarella or string cheese		

Fruit (*Meyve*)

Ahududu	Raspberry	Karpuz	Watermelon
Armut	Pear	Kavun	Persian melon
Ayva	Quince	Kayısı	Apricot
Böğürtlen	Blackberry	Kiraz	Sweet cherry
Çilek	Strawberry	Limon	Lemon
Dut	Mulberry	Mandalin	Tangerine
Elma	Apple	Muz	Banana
Erik	Plum	Nar	Pomegranate
Hurma	Persimmon or date	Papaz/hoca eriği	Green plum
İncir	Figs	Portakal	Orange

| Şeftali | Peach (June) | Vişne | Sour cherry |
| Üzüm | Grape | Yarma | Bursa peach (August) |

Sweets (*Tatlı*)

Acı badem	Giant almond biscuit	Komposto	Stewed fruit
Aşure	Pulse, wheat, fruit and nut "soup"	Krem karamel	Crème caramel
Baklava	Layered honey-and-nut pie	Kurabiye	Almond-nut biscuit dusted with powdered sugar
Dondurma	Ice cream	Lokum	Turkish delight
Kaymak	Clotted cream	Muhallebi	Rice flour and rosewater pudding
Fırın sütlaç	Baked rice pudding		
İrmik helvası	Semolina and nut *helva*	Mustafakemalpaşa	Syrup-soaked dumpling
Kabak tatlısı	Baked orange-fleshed squash topped with nuts and *kaymak*	Pasta	Any pastry or cake
		Süpangile	Ultra-rich chocolate pudding, with sponge or a biscuit embedded
Kadayıf	"Shredded wheat" in syrup		
Kadın göbeği	Doughnut in syrup	Sütlaç	Rice pudding
Kaymak	Clotted cream	Tahin helvası	Sesame-paste *helva*
Kazandibi	Browned residue of *tavukgöğsü*	Tavukgöğsü	Chicken fibre, milk and semolina taffy
Keşkül	Vanilla-almond custard	Zerde	Saffron-laced jelly

Drinks

Ada çayı	Sage tea
Ayran	Drinking yoghurt
Bira	Beer
Boza	Fermented millet drink
Çay	Tea
Kahve	Coffee
Maden suyu	Mineral water (fizzy)
Memba suyu	Spring water (non-fizzy)
Meyva suyu	Fruit juice
Papatya çayı	Camomile tea
Rakı	Aniseed-flavoured spirit distilled from grape pressings
Sahlep	Orchid-root-powder drink
Şarap	Wine
Şıra	Grape must, lightly fermented

Common toasts

The closest equivalents to "Cheers" are:

Şeref'e, şerefiniz'e' To honour, to our honour

Neşe'ye To joy

The following are more formal:

Sağlığınız'a' To your health

Mutluluğ'a To happiness

Cam cam'a değil, can can'a Not glass to glass, but soul to soul

Last but not least, to a good cook one says:

Eliniz'e sağlık Literally, "health to your hands"

L

LANGUAGE | Food and drink

A glossary of recurrent terms

Many of the Turkish terms below will change their form according to their grammatical declension (eg *ada*, island, but *Eşek Adası*, Donkey Island); the genitive suffix is appended in brackets, or the form written separately when appropriate.

General medieval and modern Turkish terms

Ada(sı) Island.

Ağa A minor rank of nobility in the Ottoman Empire, and still a term of respect applied to a local worthy; follows the name (eg Ismail Ağa).

Ahi Medieval Turkish apprentice craftsmen's guild and religious brotherhood, predecessor of the more conventional dervish orders.

Arabesk Popular, derivative form of Turkish "art" music, which used to plague travellers on long bus-rides and at nightspots, but is now less ubiquitous.

Ayazma Sacred spring.

Bahçe(si) Garden.

Bekçi Caretaker or warden at an archeological site or monument.

Belediye(si) Municipality – both the corporation and the actual town hall, for a community of over 2000 inhabitants.

Bey Another minor Ottoman title like ağa, still in use; follows the first name.

Cami(i) Mosque.

Çarşaf A bedsheet – or the full-length, baggy dress-with-hood worn by religious Turkish women.

Çarşı(sı) Bazaar, market.

Çay(ı) 1) Tea, the national drink; 2) a stream or small river.

Çeşme(si) Street-corner fountain.

Çıkmaz(ı) Dead-end alley.

Dağ(ı) Mount.

Dağlar(ı) Mountains.

Dolmuş Literally "filled" – the shared-taxi system operating in larger Turkish towns; some confusing, though decreasing, overlap with "minibus", since not all of the latter are dolmuşes, and vice versa.

Entel Short for *entelektüel* – the arty, trendy set which patronizes Western-style pubs and bars in the larger cities and resorts.

Eski Old (frequent modifier of place names).

Ezan The Muslim call to prayer; these days often taped or at the very least transmitted up to an elevated loudspeaker.

Ferace Similar to a *çarşaf*, but less all-enveloping.

Gazi Warrior for the (Islamic) faith; also a common epithet of Atatürk.

Gazino Open-air nightclub, usually adorned with coloured lights and featuring live or taped *arabesk* or taverna music.

Gecekondu Literally "founded-by-night" – a reference to the Ottoman law whereby houses begun in darkness which had acquired a roof and four walls by dawn were inviolable. The continuance of the tradition is responsible for the huge *gecekondu* shantytowns around all large Turkish cities.

Gişe Ticket window or booth.

Göl(ü) Lake.

Hacı Honorific of someone who has made the pilgrimage to Mecca; precedes the name, though rarely used conversationally as a term of address.

Hamam(ı) Turkish bath.

Hamsi The Black Sea anchovy; by extension, nickname for any native of this area.

Han(ı) Traditionally a tradesmen's hall, or an urban inn; now can also mean an office block.

Harabe Ruin; *harabeler* in the plural, abbreviated "Hb" on old maps.

Harem The women's quarters in Ottoman residences.

Hastane(si) Hospital.

Hicrî The Muslim dating system, beginning with Mohammed's flight to Medina in 622 AD, and based on the thirteen-month lunar calendar; approximately six centuries behind the *Miladî* calendar. Abbreviated "H." on monuments and inscriptions.

Hisar Same as *kale*.

Hittite First great civilization (c.1800–1200 BC) to emerge in Anatolia.

Hoca Teacher in charge of religious instruction for children.

Ilıca Hot spring.

Irmak River, eg Yeşilırmak (Green River).

İl(i) Province, the largest administrative division in Turkey, subdivided into *ilçe*s (counties or districts).

İmam Usually just the prayer leader at a mosque, though it can mean a more important spiritual authority.

İmam Hatip Okulları Religious secondary schools, established in the 1980s as an alternative to secular state schools, ostensibly to train youths for mosque preaching and teach basic Arabic and the Koran.

İskele(si) Jetty, dock.

Janissary One of the sultan's praetorian guard, levied exclusively from the Christian communities of the Balkans between the fifteenth and eighteenth centuries; *yeniceri* in Turkish. Famous for their devotion to the Bektaşi order, outlandish headgear and marching music.

Kaaba Shrine at Mecca containing a sacred black stone.

Kaplıca Developed hot springs, spa.

Kervansaray(ı) Strategically located "hotel", often Selçuk, for pack animals and men on Anatolian trade routes; some overlap with *han*.

Kilim Flat-weave rug without a pile.

Kilise(si) Church.

Konak Large private residence, also the main government building of a province or city; genitive form *konağı*.

Konut Same as *Tatil köyü* (see below).

Lokanta Restaurant; rendition of the Italian *locanda*.

Mağara(sı) Cave.

Mahalle(si) District or neighbourhood of a larger municipality, village or postal area.

Meydan(ı) Public square or plaza.

Meyhane Tavern where alcohol and *meze*-type (see below) food are served together.

Meze Small plate of often vegetable-based appetizers, typically fried, pureed and/or marinated; from the Arabic *maza*.

Miladî The Christian year-numbering system; abbreviated "M." on inscriptions and monuments.

Muezzin Man who pronounces call to prayer (*ezan*) from the minaret of a mosque.

Muhtar Village headman.

Muhtarlık The office of the *muhtar*, both in the abstract and concrete sense; also designates the status of any community of under 2000.

Namaz The Muslim rite of prayer, performed five times daily.

Nehir (Nehri) River.

Otogar Bus station.

Ova(sı) Plain, plateau.

Ören Alternative term for *harabe*, "ruin"; common village name.

Pansiyon Typical budget-to-mid-priced accommodation in Turkish resorts.

Ramadan The Muslim month of fasting and prayer; spelt *Ramazan* in Turkish.

Saz Long-necked, fretted stringed instrument central to Turkish folk ballads and Alevî/Bektaşi devotional music.

Selçuk The first centralized, Muslim Turkish state based in Anatolia, lasting from the eleventh to the thirteenth centuries.

Sema A dervish ceremony; thus *semahane*, a hall where such ceremonies are conducted.

Şehzade Prince, heir apparent.

Şeyh Head of a Sufi order.

Sufi Dervish – more properly an adherent of one of the heterodox mystical branches of Islam. In Turkey the most important sects were (and to some extent still are) the Bektaşi, Mevlevî, Helveti, Nakşibendi, Cerrahi and Kadiri orders.

Sultan valide The Sultan's mother.

Tatil köyü or **site(si)** Holiday development, either for Turkish civil servants or a private co-operative – not geared for foreign tourists.

Tuğra Monogram or seal of a sultan.

Ulema The corps of Islamic scholars and authorities in Ottoman times.

Vakıf Islamic religious trust or foundation, responsible for social welfare and upkeep of religious buildings.

Vezir Vizier, the principal Ottoman minister of state, responsible for the day-to-day running of the empire.

Vilayet(ı) Formal word for province; also a common term for the provincial headquarters building itself.

Yalı Ornate wooden residence along the Bosphorus.

Yayla(sı) Pastoral mountain-hamlet occupied only in summer; in the Black Sea region, may have rustic accommodation ranging from simple to luxurious.

Yeni New (common component of Turkish place names).

Architectural/artistic terms

Acropolis Ancient fortified hilltop.

Agora Marketplace and meeting area of an ancient Lycian, Greek or Roman city.

Apse Curved or polygonal recess at the altar end of a church.

Arasta Marketplace built into the foundations of a mosque, a portion of whose revenues goes to the upkeep of the latter.

Bedesten(ı) Covered market hall for valuable goods, often lockable.

Bouleuterion Council hall of a Hellenistic or Roman city.

Camekân Changing rooms in a hamam.

Capital The top, often ornamented, of a column.

Cavea The seating curve of an ancient theatre.

Deesis or **Deisis** Portrayal of Christ between the Virgin and John the Baptist.

Diazoma A horizontal walkway dividing the two blocs of seats in an ancient theatre.

Exedra Semicircular niche.

Eyvan Domed side-chamber of an Ottoman religious building; also applies to three-sided alcoves in secular mansions.

Göbek taşı Literally "navel stone" – the hot central platform of a hamam.

Halvet Semi-private corner rooms in a hamam.

Hararet The hottest room of a hamam.

İmaret(ı) Soup kitchen and hostel for dervishes and wayfarers, usually attached to a *medrese*.

Kale(si) Castle, fort.

Kapı(sı) Gate, door.

Katholikon Central shrine of a monastery.

Kemer Series of vaults, or an aqueduct.

Khatchkar An ornate relief-carving centred around stylised crosses, on the walls of Armenian churches; also a free-standing cruciform gravestone so carved.

Köşk(ü) Kiosk, pavilion, gazebo, folly.

Kubbe Dome, cupola – as in *Kubbeli Kilise* (the Domed Church).

Kule(si) Tower, turret.

Kurna Hewn stone basin in a hamam.

Külliye(si) Building complex – term for a mosque and dependent buildings taken as a whole.

Kümbet Vault, dome; by analogy the cylindrical "hatted" Selçuk tombs of central Anatolia.

Mabet Temple, at archeological sites; genitive *mabedi*.

Medrese(si) Islamic theological academy.

Mescit Small mosque with no *mimber*; Islamic equivalent of a chapel; genitive *mescidi*.

Mezar(ı) Grave, tomb; thus *mezarlık*, cemetery.

Mihrab Niche in a mosque indicating the direction of Mecca, and prayer.

Mimber Pulpit in a mosque, from where the *imam* delivers homilies; often beautifully carved in wood or stone.

Minare(si) Turkish for "minaret", the tower from which the call to prayer is delivered.

Naos The inner sanctum of an ancient temple.

Narthex Vestibule or entrance hall of a church; also exonarthex, the outer vestibule when there is more than one.

Nave The principal lengthwise aisle of a church.

Necropolis Place of burial in an ancient Greek or Roman city.

Nymphaeum Ornate, multistoreyed facade, often with statue niches, surrounding a public fountain in an ancient city.

Pendentive Curved, triangular surface, by means of which a dome can be supported over a square ground-plan.

Pier A mass of supportive masonry.

Porphyry A hard red or purple rock containing mineral crystals.

Revetment Facing of stone, marble or tile on a wall.

Saray(ı) Palace.

Sebil Public drinking fountain, either free-standing or built into the wall of an Ottoman structure.

Selamlık Area where men receive guests in any sort of dwelling.

Serender Wooden, enclosed corn-crib on stilts, particular to the Black Sea; sometimes spelt *serander*.

Son cemaat yeri Literally "Place of the last congregation" – a mosque porch where latecomers pray.

Stoa Colonnaded walkway in ancient Greek marketplace.

Synthronon Semicircular seating for clergy, usually in the apse of a Byzantine church.

Şadırvan Ritual ablutions fountain of a mosque.

Şerefe Balcony of a minaret.

Tabhane Hospice for travelling dervishes or *ahi*s, often housed in an *eyvan*.

Tapınak Alternative term for "temple" at archeological sites; genitive *tapınağı*.

Tekke(si) Gathering place of a Sufi order.

Tersane(si) Shipyard, dry dock.

Transept The "wings" of a church, extending north and south perpendicular to the nave.

Tuff Soft, carvable rock formed from volcanic ash.

Türbe(si) Freestanding, usually domed, tomb.

Tympanum The surface, often adorned, enclosed by the top of an arch; found in churches or more ancient ruins.

Verd antique Type of green marble.

Voussoir Stripes of wedge-shaped blocks at the edge of an arch.

Zaviye Mosque built specifically as a hospice for dervishes, usually along a T-plan.

Zhamatoun Chapter (council) hall of an Armenian church.

Acronyms and abbreviations

AK *Adalet ve Kalkınma Partisi* or Justice and Development Party; Islamist movement headed by Recep Tayyip Erdoğan, which currently dominates parliament with a two-thirds majority.

ANAP *Anavatan Partisi* or Motherland Party: centre-right party founded by the late president Turgut Özal; currently without parliamentary representation.

AŞ Initials of *Anonim Şirket*, Turkish equivalent of "Ltd" or "Inc".

Bul Standard abbreviation for *bulvar(ı)* (boulevard).

Cad Standard abbreviation for *cadde(si)* (avenue).

CHP *Cumhuriyetçi Halk Partisi* or Republican People's Party (RPP) – founded by Atatürk, disbanded in 1980, revived in 1992, headed now by Deniz Baykal; the minority party in parliament at present.

DSP *Demokratik Sol Partisi* or Democratic Left Party; now out of parliament.

DYP *Doğru Yol Partisi* or True Path Party; now out of parliament.

FP *Fazilet Partisis* or Virtue Party, formed instantly as a successor entity when Islamist RP (see below) was banned; also subsequently banned, but in part gave rise to *AK Partisi* (see above).

KDV Acronym of the Turkish VAT.

MHP *Milliyet Hareket Partisi* or National Action Party; originally quasi-fascist group later rebranded – and headed – by Devlet Bahçeli; now out of parliament.

PKK *Partia Karkaris Kurdistan* or Kurdish Workers' Party, actually an armed guerilla movement, formed in 1978 and still present in the southeast.

PTT *Post Telefon ve Telegraf*, the joint postal, telegraph and (formerly) phone service in Turkey, and by extension its offices.

RP *Refah Partisi or Welfare Party*; Islamist party compulsorily disbanded in 1998.

SHP *Sosyal Demokratik Halkçı Partisi* or Social Democratic Party: centre-left party, absorbed into the CHP in 1994.

Sok Abbreviation for *sokak (sokağı)* or street.

THY *Türk Hava Yolları*, Turkish Airways.

TIR (pronounced "turr" locally) Transport International Routière – large, slow trucks, your greatest road hazard.

TDİ *Türk Denizcilik İşletmesi* or Turkish Maritime Enterprises; TML (Turkish Maritime Lines) in English.

TRT Acronym of *Türk Radyo ve Televizyon*, the Turkish public-broadcasting corporation.

TT *Türk Telekom* – entity hived off from the PTT, subsequently privatized and providing exclusively telecommunications services.

YTL Standard symbol for the "new" Turkish lira.

Travel
store

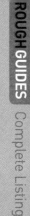

ROUGH GUIDES Complete Listing

For more information go to www.roughguides.com

ROUGH GUIDES

Rough Guides To A World Of Music

'stick to the reliable Rough Guide series'
The Guardian (UK)

Turkey is a land where Europe meets Asia, and where the music and culture is shaped by influences from virtually every direction. In the cities, discos and record stores blast the latest pop hits from the likes of Ebru Gündes , while evocative bellydance music is ready to captivate the innocent passer-by. If you turn the corner, you might find a trendy saz club, religious music or run into a Rom (Gypsy) neighbourhood and its famous all-night musical taverns. This album provides an insight into the vast array of music within Turkey, encompassing some of the country's most talented and celebrated artists.

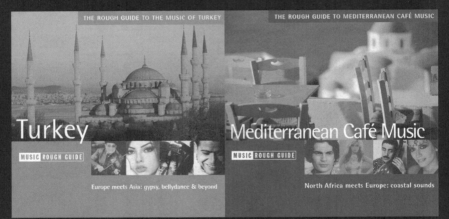

THE ROUGH GUIDE TO THE MUSIC OF TURKEY

Turkey

MUSIC ROUGH GUIDE

Europe meets Asia: gypsy, bellydance & beyond

THE ROUGH GUIDE TO MEDITERRANEAN CAFÉ MUSIC

Mediterranean Café Music

MUSIC ROUGH GUIDE

North Africa meets Europe: coastal sounds

Over the years, an intricate web of musical links has formed across the Mediterranean, despite various political borders, linguistic differences and religions. The ancient links forged by the travelling sailors and merchants that plied the Mediterranean, the conquests of the Romans, Moors and colonialists, and the influences of the modern media, have created musical connections that resonate throughout the region. *The Rough Guide To Mediterranean Café Music* explores these influences as reflected in the varied café cultures these countries share. Including the music of Turkey, this album presents some of the Mediterranean's most exhilarating coastal sounds.

Hear sound samples at WWW.WORLDMUSIC.NET

Rough Guides Radio

Now you can visit www.worldmusic.net/radio to tune into the exciting Rough Guide Radio Show, with a new show each month presenting new releases, interviews, features and competitions.

Available from book and record shops worldwide or you can order direct from **World Music Network, 6 Abbeville Mews, 88 Clapham Park Road, London SW4 7BX UK** T 020 7498 5252 F 020 7498 5353 E post@worldmusic.net W www.worldmusic.net

THE ROUGH GUIDE TO

weste

The story • The songs • The solo years

THE ROUGH GUIDE TO

The **Beatles**

Chris Ingham

THE BOOK
THE MOVIE
THE TRUTH

THE ROUGH GUIDE to

THE **DA VINCI CODE**

TOTALLY UNAUTHORISED

Michael Haag and Veronica Haag

THE ROUGH GUIDE to

Unex

Phenome

The filth • the fury • the fa

The songs • the singers • the stories • the soul

ROUGH GUIDE to

Punk

THE ROUGH GUIDE to

Soul and R&B

THE ROUGH GUIDE to

The **Rolling Stones**

Sean Egan

THE ROUG

Bl

Avoid Guilt Trips

Buy fair trade coffee + bananas ✓

Save energy - use low energy bulbs ✓

- don't leave tv on standby ✓

Offset carbon emissions from flight to Madrid ✓

Send goat to Africa ✓

Join Tourism Concern today ✓

Slowly, the world is changing.
Together we can, and will, make a difference.

Tourism Concern is the only UK registered charity fighting exploitation in one of the largest industries on earth: people forced from their homes in order that holiday resorts can be built, sweatshop labour conditions in hotels and destruction of the environment are just some of the issues that we tackle.

Sending people on a guilt trip is not something we do. We know as well as anyone that holidays are precious. But you can help us to ensure that tourism always benefits the local communities involved.

Call 020 7133 3330
or visit **tourismconcern.org.uk** to find out how.

A year's membership of Tourism Concern costs just £20 (£12 unwaged)
- that's 38 pence a week, less than the cost of a pint of milk, organic of course.

TourismConcern

Fighting Exploitation in Tourism

Small print and
Index

A Rough Guide to Rough Guides

Published in 1982, the first Rough Guide – to Greece – was a student scheme that became a publishing phenomenon. Mark Ellingham, a recent graduate in English from Bristol University, had been travelling in Greece the previous summer and couldn't find the right guidebook. With a small group of friends he wrote his own guide, combining a highly contemporary, journalistic style with a thoroughly practical approach to travellers' needs.

The immediate success of the book spawned a series that rapidly covered dozens of destinations. And, in addition to impecunious backpackers, Rough Guides soon acquired a much broader and older readership that relished the guides' wit and inquisitiveness as much as their enthusiastic, critical approach and value-for-money ethos.

These days, Rough Guides include recommendations from shoestring to luxury and cover more than 200 destinations around the globe, including almost every country in the Americas and Europe, more than half of Africa and most of Asia and Australasia. Our ever-growing team of authors and photographers is spread all over the world, particularly in Europe, the USA and Australia.

In the early 1990s, Rough Guides branched out of travel, with the publication of Rough Guides to World Music, Classical Music and the Internet. All three have become benchmark titles in their fields, spearheading the publication of a wide range of books under the Rough Guide name.

Including the travel series, Rough Guides now number more than 350 titles, covering: phrasebooks, waterproof maps, music guides from Opera to Heavy Metal, reference works as diverse as Conspiracy Theories and Shakespeare, and popular culture books from iPods to Poker. Rough Guides also produce a series of more than 120 World Music CDs in partnership with World Music Network.

Visit www.roughguides.com to see our latest publications.

Rough Guide travel images are available for commercial licensing at www.roughguidespictures.com

Rough Guide credits

Text editor: Ann-Marie Shaw and Amanda Tomlin
Layout: Diana Jarvis and Dan May
Cartography: Ed Wright
Picture editor: Sarah Smithies
Production: Aimee Hampson
Proofreader: Diane Margolis
Cover design: Chloë Roberts

....

Editorial: **London** Kate Berens, Claire Saunders, Geoff Howard, Ruth Blackmore, Polly Thomas, Richard Lim, Alison Murchie, Karoline Densley, Andy Turner, Keith Drew, Edward Aves, Nikki Birrell, Helen Marsden, Alice Park, Sarah Eno, David Paul, Lucy White, Ruth Tidball, Jo Kirby, Joe Staines, Duncan Clark, Peter Buckley, Matthew Milton, Tracy Hopkins; **New York** Andrew Rosenberg, Steven Horak, AnneLise Sorensen, Amy Hegarty, April Isaacs, Sean Mahoney, Ella Steim
Design & Pictures: **London** Simon Bracken, Dan May, Diana Jarvis, Mark Thomas, Jj Luck, Harriet Mills, Chloë Roberts; **Delhi** Madhulita Mohapatra, Umesh Aggarwal, Ajay Verma, Jessica Subramanian, Ankur Guha, Pradeep Thapliyal, Sachin Tanwar, Anita Singh

Production: Katherine Owers, Aimee Hampson
Cartography: **London** Maxine Repath, Ed Wright, Katie Lloyd-Jones; **Delhi** Jai Prakash Mishra, Rajesh Chhibber, Ashutosh Bharti, Rajesh Mishra, Animesh Pathak, Jasbir Sandhu, Karobi Gogoi, Amod Singh, Alakananda Bhattacharya
Online: **New York** Jennifer Gold, Kristin Mingrone, Cree Lawson; **Delhi** Manik Chauhan, Narender Kumar, Shekhar Jha, Rakesh Kumar, Chhandita Chakravarty, Amit Kumar, Amit Verma, Rahul Kumar
Marketing & Publicity: **London** Richard Trillo, Niki Hanmer, Louise Maher, Jess Carter; Anna Paynton, Nikki Causer, Libby Jellie; **New York** Geoff Colquitt, Megan Kennedy, Katy Ball; **Delhi** Reem Khokhar
Custom publishing and foreign rights: Philippa Hopkins
Manager India: Punita Singh
Series editor: Mark Ellingham
Reference Director: Andrew Lockett
PA to Publishing Director: Megan McIntyre
Publishing Director: Martin Dunford

Publishing information

This sixth edition published January 2007 by
Rough Guides Ltd,
80 Strand, London WC2R 0RL
345 Hudson St, 4th Floor,
New York, NY 10014, USA
14 Local Shopping Centre, Panchsheel Park,
New Delhi 110017, India
Distributed by the Penguin Group
Penguin Books Ltd,
80 Strand, London WC2R 0RL
Penguin Putnam, Inc.
375 Hudson Street, NY 10014, USA
Penguin Group (Australia)
250 Camberwell Road, Camberwell,
Victoria 3124, Australia
Penguin Books Canada Ltd,
10 Alcorn Avenue, Toronto, Ontario,
Canada M4V 1E4
Penguin Group (NZ)
67 Apollo Drive, Mairangi Bay, Auckland
1310, New Zealand
Cover concept by Peter Dyer.

Typeset in Bembo and Helvetica to an original design by Henry Iles.

Printed and bound in China

© Rosie Ayliffe, Marc Dubin, John Gawthrop and Terry Richardson 2007

No part of this book may be reproduced in any form without permission from the publisher except for the quotation of brief passages in reviews.

1108pp includes index

A catalogue record for this book is available from the British Library

ISBN 978-1-84353-606-2

The publishers and authors have done their best to ensure the accuracy and currency of all the information in **The Rough Guide to Turkey**, however, they can accept no responsibility for any loss, injury, or inconvenience sustained by any traveller as a result of information or advice contained in the guide.

3   5   7   9   8   6   4   2

Help us update

We've gone to a lot of effort to ensure that the sixth edition of **The Rough Guide to Turkey** is accurate and up to date. However, things change – places get "discovered", opening hours are notoriously fickle, restaurants and rooms raise prices or lower standards. If you feel we've got it wrong or left something out, we'd like to know, and if you can remember the address, the price, the time, the phone number, so much the better. We'll credit all contributions, and send a copy of the next edition (or any other Rough Guide if you prefer) for the best letters. Everyone who writes

to us and isn't already a subscriber will receive a copy of our full-colour thrice-yearly newsletter. Please mark letters: "**Rough Guide Turkey Update**" and send to: Rough Guides, 80 Strand, London WC2R 0RL, or Rough Guides, 4th Floor, 345 Hudson St, New York, NY 10014. Or send an email to **mail@roughguides.com**
Have your questions answered and tell others about your trip at
www.roughguides.atinfopop.com

Acknowledgements

Marc Dubin would like to thank: Hasbi Akal at the Turkish Embassy, London for arranging press accreditation; Bob Stubbs at Tapestry Holidays for travel facilities; Nikiforos Metaxas and Vassiliki Papayeoryiou in İstanbul for their usual hospitality; Erol and Pauline Şalvarlı at Bezirgan; Muzaffer Otlu and Anne Louise Thomson at Patara; İlknur and Münir İdrisoğlu in Dalyan; Phil and Allison Buckley, Tevfik Serin and everyone else at Bougainville in Kaş; Melahat in Tlos; Alison Grundy for the lowdown on Göcek, and Clare Baker for the same in Dalyan; and the Zdravets for coming along.

Joe Fullman: Many thanks to everyone in Turkey who took the time to talk to me and help me with my research, particularly Armagan in Canakkale; Alemdar in Foça; Zeynep in Alacati; Nilgun in Selçuk; Esra in Bodrum; and Tosun in Yalikavak. Biggest thanks of all to Nicola for keeping me company, reading the drafts and learning enough Turkish to understand what seni seviyorum means.

Sarah Gear would like to thank: Iffet Özgönül for her warm welcome to Turkey, and the fabulous Melek, James and Alistair Burton for looking after me so well in Ankara. Also, Rachel Beardmore for the lowdown on Ankara's nightspots, and Saadet Kart for her company in Erzurum. An enormous thank you also goes to Ali Gunes and his family, and to Suzan Taşkiran, Gülsüm and the Aktemur clan for showing me around Kars so expertly. Finally, thanks to Aslihan Köken and her lovely family for brightening my stay in Eskişehir.

Terry Richardson would like to thank; Lem, for her companionship on the road and fresh insights into a familiar country; Kate in Antalya for continued sound advice; Atıl of Middle Earth Travel for his assistance in Cappadocia; once again İsmail, Zehra, Berdan, Bager and all the Hakkari clan for taking care of him in Van; Esat and Behice for cheering him up in Antalya; Hakan for his help in İstanbul; Birsen and extended family in Eğirdir; İbrahim for background information on Eğirdir; Suha for his great kindness in Cappadocia; Professor Trevor Watkins and his wife Twin for good company in southeastern Turkey and new ways of looking at well-known sites; Erkan of Talisman travel in İstanbul for keeping driving when he should really have been in hospital; Nalan at the press office in Antalya for press accreditation; the headman of Ulu Pamir village for hospitality; Marc Dubin for keeping me on the right track on Basics and Contexts; Annie and Amanda for their patient editing and finally to almost everyone encountered on travels from İstanbul to Hakkari and back again for reminding me why Turkey is such a great country.

Paul Sentobe: My thanks go out to all the wonderful, helpful, charming and caring local people I met along the way. As always, it's the people of Turkey that shine through in my memory. In particular I would like to thank: Bülent and Köksal; Kaili Kidner from Kapadokya Balloons for an uplifting breakfast; photographer Mark Liefooghe; Thai flyer; Evren & Nilay, Alex and Michelle and Linda for beers and laughs, Mustafa Teksoy, Jen and Dean Mitchell, Cido in Ikizdere, Leon and Semra from Yediburunlar Lighthouse; fellow Rough Guider Terry; and Kâmile Ozcan for everything. Finally, however, I wish to send my heartfelt condolences to Meral, Ali and the rest of the Karataş family – it was a real pleasure to have known your father, Şaban.

The editors would like to thank Dan May for his careful typesetting; Sarah Smithies for inspired, tireless picture research; Diane Margolis for eagle-eyed proofreading; Ed Wright for expert cartography; and Claire Saunders for her invaluable support and advice.

Readers' letters

Thanks to all the readers who have taken the time to write in with comments and suggestions (and apologies if we've inadvertently omitted or misspelt anyone's name):

Sergul Aktan; Dr St Allman; Phil Andre; Elena Artolachipi; P. Baldwin; Stella Bell; Jim Berry; İlker Evrim Binbaş; Steve Bade; Federico Botana; Randall Bratu; P. Burger; John Burn; Rev H.F. Capener; Brenda Chadderton; Gillian Clark; Sophie Clark; Charles & Anne Clayton; Chris Collet; Dominique Collon; Chris Coote; Kathleen Dallison; Claire Dannebaum; Alan Dawson; Theresa Day; C.Deane; Frank Denys; Alan Fenn; Tadd Fernee; Andrew Flashberg;

Oliver Frankel; Peter Gibbons; Jennifer Gold; Anthony Goldie; Sean Gostage; Ed Gramlich; Briony Grimson; Michael Hanna; Holly Hardy; Jude Harrison; Benjamin Hekermans; Kevin Heyne; Alan Hickey; Michele Hoffman; Kenneth Holder; Ian Howells; Melis Iler; Paul Irving; Lisa Johnson; Mr & Mrs R F Jones; Louise Kreifels; Sophia Lambert; Sara Langdon; Chris Leavy; Victoria Lee; Anne Lofquist; Dennis McQuail; Karen Mann; Kevin Marren; Nadine Miller; Alick Miskin; Ghislaine Morris; Shirley Morris; Malfrid Norum; David Paine; Michael Poulson-Ellis; Patrick Reinquin; Chris Ryan; Dave Ryan; Deborah Senior; Tamara Shie; Michael Snyder; Matt Somerville; Geoff Stebens; Claudia Steiner; Ray & Joyce Stephenson; Zvi Teff; Dan Thomas; Dave Tootell; Carol Tovee; Sheila Trenholm; Guillermo Vega; Andrea Vercoe; Florence Vuillet; Jeffrey Walter; Randall Wirth; Mark Wright.

Photo credits

ROUGH GUIDES

SMALL PRINT

Selected images from our guidebooks are available for licensing from:

ROUGH**GUIDES**PICTURES.COM

Index

Map entries are in colour.

INDEX

V

W

X

Y

Z

Map symbols

maps are listed in the full index using coloured text

-----	International boundary
----	Chapter boundary
▬▬▬	Motorway
═══	Major road
═══	Minor road
▬▬▬	Pedestrianized road
────	Unpaved road
⊞⊞⊞⊞	Steps
------	Path
▬•▬•▬	Railway
------	Tramway
────	Metro line
– – –	Ferry route
────	Waterway
▪▪▪▪	Wall
✈	Airport
✦	Point of interest
⋀⋀	Mountain range
▲	Mountain peak
⌐⌐⌐⌐	Cliffs
∴	Ruins
◠	Cave
⋀⋀	Spa
⋇	Waterfall
⚲	Lighthouse
⊐	Pass

⚲	Skiing
♜	Castle
☦	Church (regional maps)
♨	Monastery
✡	Synagogue
☪	Mosque
⊙	Statue
⚠	Campsite
◉	Accommodation
■	Restaurant/café
♟	Museum
ⓘ	Tourist office
⊠	Post office
@	Internet access
⊞	Hospital
⊛	Swimming pool
★	Bus stop
Ⓜ	Metro stop
🅿	Parking
■—■	Gate
▬	Building
⊞	Church
⬭	Stadium
▨	Park
▨	Beach
⟨Y⟩	Muslim cemetery